# WORLD RUGBY
## YEARBOOK 2015

WITHDRAWN

Edited by
Karen Bond, Rob Clark and John Griffiths

**VSP**

Vision Sports Publishing
19-23 High Street
Kingston upon Thames
Surrey, KT1 1LL

# www.visionsp.co.uk

Published by Vision Sports Publishing in 2014

All pictures by Getty Images unless otherwise stated.
Kit designs by David Moor

Typeset by Palimpsest Book Production Limited, Falkirk, Stirlingshire

Printed and bound in the UK by Ashford Colour Press Ltd

MIX
Paper from
responsible sources
FSC® C011748

The World Rugby Yearbook is an independent publication supported by World Rugby but the views throughout, expressed by the different authors, do not necessarily reflect the policies and opinions of World Rugby.

World Rugby
Huguenot House
35-38 St Stephen's Green
Dublin 2, Ireland

t +353-1-240-9200
f +353-1-240-9201

# www.worldrugby.org

# Contents

## ELITE COMPETITIONS

## REFEREES

## THE BACK ROW

## WORLD RUGBY™

# A landmark year for rugby

### A message from Bernard Lapasset, Chairman of World Rugby

**W**elcome to the ninth edition of the World Rugby Yearbook. It has been yet another fantastic year with participation breaking six million for the first time, an incredible Women's Rugby World Cup in France and an emotional return to the Olympic stage among the highlights.

In August, Women's Rugby World Cup 2014 captured hearts and minds as a hugely-competitive tournament showcased the game at its breathtaking best to sold-out stadia in Paris and new audiences around the world through a record broadcast platform.

A compelling tournament with a superb final underscored just why women's rugby is the fastest-growing form of the game and it was superb to see the world's finest female players getting the global coverage that they deserved as they competed for the greatest prize in the sport.

For me, the event was significant because media and fans alike were talking about the quality of the rugby and the great advertisement it was for the game, rather than differentiating between men's and women's rugby, which is a very encouraging sign as we continue to grow the sport. There are now more than 1.5 million women and girls playing rugby worldwide and we are working hard to capitalise on the success of France 2014 to attract, engage and inspire new participants and fans as we build towards our Olympic Games return in 2016.

Before that momentous day in Rio de Janeiro, the eyes of the rugby world will turn to England for RWC 2015 and what looks set to be a very special celebration of our sport and the host nation.

Our showcase event continues to go from strength to strength and while Australia 2003 was the first truly modern Rugby World Cup, France 2007 the box-office hit that elevated the event among the world's finest and New Zealand 2011 united a nation, I have no doubt that England 2015 will be a record-breaker that has rugby and fans at heart. It will be too big to miss.

From the 13 iconic venues to the host cities, fanzones and training bases, every detail has been geared towards ensuring that the 20 teams have all they need to realise their potential on the greatest stage, while from the stadium to the armchair, the fan experience will be innovative, engaging and inclusive.

Rugby World Cup is about bringing people together and, at the time of writing, ticket sales are tracking at record levels with supporter tour sales 30 per cent up on New Zealand, ensuring that all the teams will be well supported, while we are confident the event will be broadcast to more households in more nations than ever before.

Our belief is that it will be the most competitive tournament to date. We have been working closely with tier two unions on an annual competition schedule that suits their performance needs, while a balanced RWC 2015 match schedule will give the likes of Fiji, Tonga, Samoa, Japan, USA and Canada the best-possible preparation periods.

None of this is possible without teamwork and dedication and I am delighted to say that the strong partnership between World Rugby, the England Rugby 2015 organising body and the RFU has been built upon a shared vision of making the tournament accessible to all, welcoming the world to rugby and growing participation.

Of course, Rugby World Cup 2015 is much more than a 48-match festival, it is the very lifeblood that sustains the growth and development of rugby worldwide. Thanks to the phenomenal commercial success of the event through a family of broadcasters and Worldwide Partners who share our passion for the sport, World Rugby has been able to invest record sums in the game.

From 2013–16 World Rugby will be injecting a record £180 million across our 119 national member unions in development, high performance, tournaments and player welfare so that more men, women and children can participate at community level, while building a stronger, competitive, sustainable and more attractive game at international level.

If 2014 is anything to go by then we are on track to experience a very special Rugby World Cup. The average winning margins at New Zealand 2011 were the smallest in RWC history and world-class training facilities will ensure that every need is catered for in the pursuit of peak performance.

We are also counting down to Rio 2016 when Sevens will make its debut. We do not get a second chance to make a first impression and we have been working hard to ensure that Sevens is great for the Games, great for Rio and great for rugby.

Preparation accelerated in 2014 with the beginning of the global qualification process, our Youth Olympic Games debut and a record-breaking Glasgow 2014 Commonwealth Games. Men's qualification began with the opening round of the 2014–15 HSBC Sevens World Series, kicking off a nine-round race for the all-important top four places. A further seven places will be determined by regional qualifiers and a final play-off, while Brazil automatically qualify.

The women's process mirrors the men's and kicks off in Dubai in December and promises to be hugely competitive, with the IRB Women's Sevens World Series expanded to six rounds to include Canada for the first time. The Women's Series is going from strength to strength and the qualification dynamic means that fans are set for a treat as the best teams go all out to realise their Olympic dream.

History was made in August as Sevens made its Youth Olympic Games debut in Nanjing, China. The event, rugby's first in an Olympic context for 90 years, was a very special, emotional and historic occasion for the global rugby family and the players. The competition was exciting and played in the shared values of the Youth Olympics and rugby – the future is certainly a bright one.

Off the field, the IRB continues to invest record sums in sustainable growth so that more men, women and children can enjoy the sport in all its forms. Our Get Into Rugby programme, active in more than 90 nations, has already given the opportunity for 370,000 children worldwide to 'Try, Play and Stay' in rugby around the world.

Sustainable growth is achieved through robust strategies to support players, coaches, match officials, volunteers and parents at all levels and to that end player welfare remains our number one priority. In 2014 we increased our focus on concussion education strategies, including the roll out of public guidance materials featuring a new video involving some of the sport's biggest stars. It will take time to change culture, but we are all committed to ensuring that everyone in the game recognises the dangers and implements best-practice.

Finally, I'm delighted to say that the IRB is now known as World Rugby. The rebrand reflects our mission to build a stronger connection with fans, players and new audiences worldwide. From players and fans to administrators, World Rugby is inclusive and we hope that you will join us in celebrating the sport and furthering growth as we continue to inspire and engage new audiences around the world.

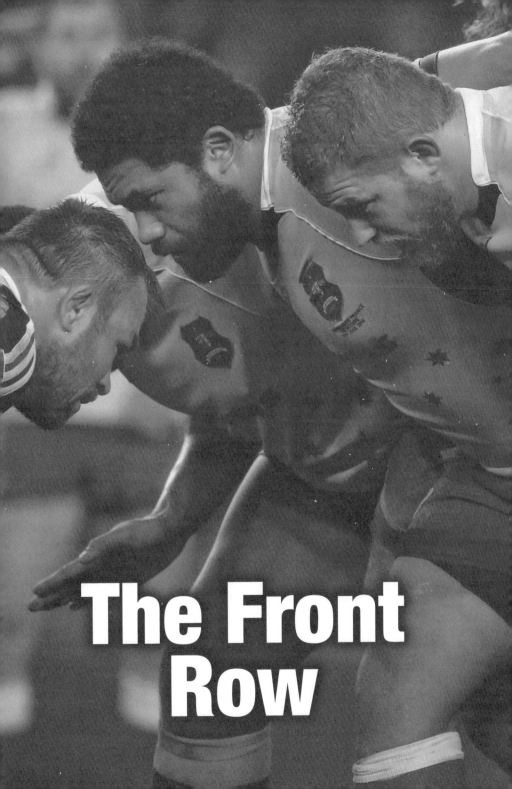

# The Front Row

# McCaw & All Blacks looking ahead not back

## By Iain Spragg

**W**hen the All Blacks beat France in the Rugby World Cup 2011 final, edging Les Bleus 8–7 in a dramatic encounter in Auckland, the whole of New Zealand almost audibly breathed a collective sigh of relief. After 24 years of waiting since their triumph at the inaugural World Cup, the All Blacks were finally world champions again.

Victory was the crowning moment in the already iconic and record-breaking career of New Zealand captain Richie McCaw, following in the footsteps of David Kirk in 1987 as he lifted the coveted Webb Ellis Cup to return the All Blacks to the undisputed pinnacle of the game.

It was also a cathartic result for a country desperate for World Cup success, but despite the euphoria that followed their victory over the French, McCaw insists he and the All Blacks will not allow themselves to be distracted by memories of their famous triumph at Eden Park once RWC 2015 gets underway.

"As a player you move on pretty quick from a World Cup final whatever the emotions after the final whistle. The sense of pride at what we were able to achieve remains, but you have to remember Test rugby is all about moving forward.

"The final is in the past and as the next tournament gets nearer the teams hoping to be champions in 2015 have forgotten what happened four years earlier and are only focused on the future. We're under no illusions that we can rest on our laurels.

"When the dust had settled after beating France, we spoke about maintaining our momentum going into the 2012 season and going out and playing like world champions. I think so far we've been able to do that on most occasions, keeping our performance levels as high as we can and

**Will All Blacks captain Richie McCaw hold aloft the Webb Ellis Cup again in 2015?**

looking to improve. It's key that we keep doing that.

"I have watched highlights of the final against France and it made me realise just how tense the match was, how much it was on a knife edge. As a player out on the pitch you focus on your own job and sometimes you're not fully aware how dramatic a Test match has been."

New Zealand have successfully preserved their status as the world's number one side since their day of destiny in Auckland, staying top of the World Rankings and remaining the dominant team in the global game.

A record-equalling run of 17 Test victories between 2013 and 2014, which was finally brought to an end after a 12–12 draw with the Wallabies in Sydney in The Rugby Championship in August, underlined the team's potency and McCaw believes the All Blacks are an even more resilient side today than they were back in 2011.

"Although the atmosphere of a World Cup final is impossible to replicate, whenever we've been in tight situations in a Test since then you do feel that if you can handle the tension of the final, you can handle anything really. It's given us a mental toughness."

The All Blacks were red hot favourites to emerge victorious on home soil in 2011. The expectation in a nation obsessed with rugby was intense and the sense of anticipation reached fever pitch as the All Blacks negotiated their way through to the final to face the French.

Eden Park was a cauldron of noise as New Zealand weathered France's stirring second-half comeback and McCaw admits the team's ability to cope with the weight of expectation throughout the tournament was central to their eventual success.

New Zealand will be bidding to become the first nation to successfully defend their Rugby World Cup crown.

"As the host nation, we went into the tournament under big pressure but personally I think there's only as much pressure as you want to experience. It's a privilege to play in a World Cup but to play in a World Cup at home is even more special and only a few players get that chance in their careers. There's always pressure when you pull on the All Blacks jersey and rather than worrying about the expectation, I focused on the positives, the chance for family and friends to share the experience.

"The atmosphere was amazing, to have so many people fascinated by the tournament and talking about it, but to an extent I was living in a bubble for six or seven weeks because I had a job to do and I couldn't afford to get swept away by the emotion. Everyone in the squad was aware what was going on out there but we also had to make sure we kept ourselves detached."

The 2011 All Blacks became only the third team to win the World Cup on home soil after the New Zealand side of 1987 and the Springboks in South Africa eight years later. England, Wales, Australia and France have all failed to lift the trophy when they have staged the tournament and although the hosts have reached the final in six of the previous seven tournaments, home advantage has not always proved a blessing.

New Zealand may have bucked the trend in 2011 but McCaw believes the relentless and unforgiving nature of a prolonged World Cup campaign is one of its greatest attractions.

"I can assure you that people make too much of home advantage. The history of the World Cup shows us that the host nation has come up short more times than becoming champions and once you get past the group stages and into the knockout phase, anything can happen. The venue becomes irrelevant at that stage and if you're not on your mettle, your tournament can be over very quickly. Three winner-takes-all knockout games in succession can make a bit of a mockery of form or world rankings."

As captain, McCaw joined an exclusive and star-studded list of World Cup winning skippers alongside Kirk, Nick Farr-Jones, Francois Pienaar, John Eales, Martin Johnson and John Smit. The image of the Crusaders flanker brandishing the Webb Ellis Cup is now an unforgettable part of All Black history and was the culmination of a decade of service as the leader of the team.

He first captained the All Blacks against Wales at the Millennium Stadium in 2004 in the absence of Tana Umaga. When Umaga announced his retirement from Test rugby the following year after leading the All Blacks to series victory over the British & Irish Lions, Graham Henry had no hesitation in handing the armband to the then 25-year-old McCaw.

He has been in the job ever since, already making him the most capped skipper in the history of the game. No-one has won more internationals at the helm and he is expected to reach the milestone of a century of Tests as New Zealand captain on their November tour. It is a phenomenal story of longevity and consistent success, but despite his wealth of experience McCaw insists he is still far from the finished article in terms of leadership.

"I don't pretend to know it all myself and the contribution of the senior players in 2011 was a massive factor in our

**McCaw is the most-capped All Black and captain in the history of the game.**

success. To lead the All Blacks to the title was incredible but captaincy is certainly not just a one-man job.

"It was hugely important to have so many experienced players, natural leaders, in the side and my role was to make sure we worked together to come up with the right answers in difficult situations in different match scenarios.

"When you have players in the team with such a huge amount of knowledge of the game, it is the skipper's job to tap into that and ensure the team is pulling in the same direction. You get that right and you've got a powerful group that can drive a team to where you want to go."

Rugby World Cup history, however, suggests the All Blacks could struggle to retain their crown in England in 2015. No team has ever successfully defended the title and only Australia in 2003 and England in 2007 have got as far as the final four years after they became world champions.

The All Blacks' own attempt to win successive tournaments after their 1987 triumph was derailed by the old enemy Australia in Dublin in 1991 at the semi-final stage and it was scant consolation for Alex Wyllie's team that they went on to win the third place play-off against Scotland at Cardiff Arms Park.

**"The 2011 final is in the past."**

The challenge of rewriting the record books is nonetheless one which McCaw welcomes while remaining wary of the side becoming preoccupied with the prospect of making history.

"No side has ever won back-to-back World Cups but we will not go into the tournament in 2015 trying to defend the title because I think that's a negative mindset. We will go in and try to win the competition.

"Being defending champions means nothing because the All Blacks will be back at the same point as every other team in the tournament, hoping to peak at the right time of the four-year cycle. All the other teams will have exactly the same desire as us to become world champions, which is why we have to make sure we are in the best condition we can be in and have the attitude to go in there and win it. There can be no excuses and no thoughts of what we have achieved in the past."

The 2015 tournament will be the fourth to be staged in Europe since England were hosts for the first time in 1991. New Zealand have not enjoyed the best fortune in the northern hemisphere while on World Cup duty, missing out on an appearance in the final each time they have ventured to Europe.

In contrast both of the Wallabies' World Cup triumphs have come north of the equator while South Africa became champions for a second time after their victory over England in Paris in 2007. It is perhaps a surprising anomaly but despite the All Blacks' previous disappointments, McCaw insists New Zealand, who begin their campaign against Argentina at Wembley Stadium, are relishing the prospect of playing in England.

"A World Cup in the UK is hugely exciting. I love going to play Test matches in the UK at the end of each year and with 80,000-odd people in the stadiums, it is always a fantastic atmosphere to play in. The tournament in New Zealand in 2011 was special because it was small and compact but to play in the stadiums in the UK in 2015 I think will be a great experience.

"There's a big rugby following in the UK and Europe so I've no doubt there will be millions of people getting into the tournament. I'm looking forward to the six or seven weeks of what will be an incredible competition."

As befits their number one ranking and status as defending champions, New Zealand will begin Rugby World Cup 2015 as favourites. The southern hemisphere challenge to the reigning champions will as ever be spearheaded by Australia and South Africa while Europe's hopes will rest squarely on the shoulders of the Six Nations sides.

It is a familiar dynamic which has produced some epic encounters over the years since 1987, not least the most recent final when France came so close to ending their Rugby World Cup drought, but McCaw is convinced the tournament has a much more far-reaching role to play in terms of the global rugby family.

"The World Cup isn't just about which teams reach the final and which country lifts the trophy. It's a chance for the lower-ranked countries to play the top nations, to gain more exposure to that level of rugby and to improve. It's vital to the health of the international game that these teams are given this kind of opportunity.

"At the moment you can say that the top eight teams are all capable of beating each other on their day but I'd like to see a dynamic in the future when we are talking about the top 10 teams on more of a par and then that leading 12. The World Cup is an important part of that process."

The seven previous Rugby World Cup finals have to date been exclusively contested by France, England, New Zealand, South Africa and Australia. At least one southern hemisphere side has featured on each occasion while the only time there was no European representation was when South Africa emerged emotional 15–12 winners over the All Blacks in 1995 after extra-time in Johannesburg.

Whether membership of the 'final' club grows or not in 2015 remains to be seen, but McCaw believes recent results are evidence that the World Cup is becoming increasingly competitive as the second tier nations close the gap on the game's traditional heavyweights.

"I think we're getting there. A few years ago shocks at Test level were relatively rare but look at the 2011 World Cup and the result that immediately springs to mind is Tonga's victory over France in the group stages in Wellington.

"France still reached the final but these kind of results are increasingly possible now. The more top level exposure teams like Tonga get, the more upsets we will see.

"For a side like the All Blacks to go and play one of the Pacific Island teams knowing we could lose if we're not at it is great for the game. Increased competition is exciting for players and spectators and reflects well on a sport which is continually looking to grow and develop."

# Too big to miss

## By Dominic Rumbles

**W**e now know the identity of all 20 nations who will grace the Rugby World Cup 2015 stage after Uruguay overcame Russia 36–27 in the 203rd and final match of the global qualification process on 11 October. Los Teros join Canada, Georgia, Romania, USA, Japan, Fiji and Namibia as the eight nations to have emerged from this process – which began in Mexico City back in March 2012 – to join the 12 teams who qualified directly after New Zealand 2011.

The biggest-ever qualification process for a Rugby World Cup has been full of twists and turns with the 83 nations involved having experienced a mix of emotions, from sheer elation at securing a place at England 2015 to utter devastation when their dream came to an end.

So, the waiting is almost over. In September 2015, the world's leading players from these 20 nations and fans from all corners of the world will arrive in England for what promises to be a very special and record-breaking six-week global festival of rugby.

And while players and fans are ticking off the days on their calendars, the foundations are in place to deliver a Rugby World Cup 2015 that has those players and fans at its heart, while furthering the development and growth of a sport that now boasts 6.6 million participants in 119 nations worldwide.

At the time of writing, England 2015 is on course to not only be the biggest event ever hosted in the United Kingdom, but it is also shaping up to be the biggest and best Rugby World Cup to date. A bold claim some may say, but all the indicators are that England 2015 will be the best attended, most viewed, most connected and most engaged tournament to date, positioning the sport's showpiece among the truly great major sporting events. It really will be too big to miss.

If the proof is in the pudding and England 2015's pudding is ticket sales, then fans around the world really do love this event. The public ticket general sale closed on 29 September and matches the length and breadth of the country were oversubscribed, which means that every single one of the 48 matches will go to a ballot in at least one of the four price categories, some across all categories.

This overwhelming interest underscores the prestige of the Rugby World Cup among not just rugby fans, but major eventers too. It is also an

**The Olympic Stadium will host five matches at RWC 2015, including the Bronze final.**

endorsement of the affordable and accessible ticketing strategy set by tournament organisers England Rugby 2015. With more than 160,000 tickets sold through the official supporter tours programme and sales tracking to topple the figure of 184,000 achieved for France 2007, and official hospitality sales set to be the biggest ever for an event in the UK, it would be fair to say that England 2015 will reach the 2.3 million attendance target and can rightly call itself the best attended and most popular tournament to date.

But the fan experience is not confined to securing a ticket for one of the 48 mouth-watering matches at Rugby World Cup 2015. No detail has been left to chance in order to ensure that player and fan experience is maximised. From the venues to host cities, ticketing to travel programmes and training bases to team preparation, the stage is set for a truly global and unprecedented celebration of rugby.

The 13 match venues selected stretch from Exeter in the south west to Newcastle in the north east and feature some of the most iconic venues in sport, including Manchester City Stadium, Wembley Stadium and the Olympic Stadium. Rugby though remains at the heart of the tournament with mouth-watering fixtures also pencilled in for Gloucester, Exeter and Cardiff.

More than 75 per cent of the population will live within 30 minutes' drive of a Rugby World Cup 2015 venue or training base, presenting a fantastic opportunity to experience and engage with the tournament, while the enthusiasm from the host cities and venues, broadcasters and commercial partners and a nationwide festival of rugby will give everyone the chance to get involved.

On the field, no stone has been left unturned to ensure that the teams have everything they need to perform to their peak potential at Rugby World Cup 2015. With performance at heart, 41 venues from the University of Exeter in the south to Newcastle Royal Grammar School in the north were selected to extend the reach of the showcase tournament, while delivering the stage for the world's best teams to shine on.

**Sandy Park, Exeter, in the south-west of England.**

However, it does not just end with the training bases or the hotels or the match venues. The International Rugby Board has also moved to ensure that England 2015 will deliver the fairest match schedule to date, meaning that the so called 'smaller' nations have every opportunity to be truly competitive against the top teams, with a hope that we will see a new team make the quarter-finals.

Rugby World Cup 2011 in New Zealand delivered the most competitive tournament to date, with average winning margins for matches in the pool stages between the tier one and tier two teams the narrowest ever at 28 points, while the volume of 'blowouts' also dropped. However, with tighter turnaround time and less strength in depth across their squads, tier two and three team performances dropped off, prompting the IRB to act to address the issue.

True to its word, the governing body has moved to ensure that the likes of Canada, Fiji, Georgia, Samoa, Tonga and USA have the same preparation time as their opponents for the big matches, creating hope of adding some more memorable upsets to the Rugby World Cup story and perhaps the likes of Samoa, Japan or Canada reaching the quarter-finals.

The match schedule alone will not deliver quarter-final glory and that is why the IRB continues to invest heavily in tournaments, Test schedules and high performance programmes to ensure that the Pacific Island nations, Georgia, Romania *et al* can perform to their peak and demonstrate the true depth, competitiveness and global spread of rugby.

With Rugby World Cup continuing to provide the financial engine to grow the sport around the world, the IRB announced, in 2013, an unprecedented global funding programme of £180 million between 2013 and 2016 in high performance, competitions, education, training, player welfare and anti-doping to ensure that these unions have the perfect platform to springboard onto the 2015 stage and beyond towards 2019.

All the indications are good. Japan achieved their highest ever position of 10th in the World Rankings in June 2014 with victories over Italy and Samoa in a record run of 10 matches unbeaten, which all bodes well for Rugby World Cup 2019 when they become the first Asian side to host the tournament. Samoa, Tonga and Canada have also produced impressive performances, while Georgia, who face Ireland at the Aviva Stadium in November, have shown improvement over the last four years.

Off the field, England 2015 will provide the financial platform for the governing body to continue to invest unprecedented sums in the growth and development of rugby. The tournament is on track to be the most commercially successful with the top tier Worldwide Partners locked down in record time and with record value, underscoring the strength of the Rugby World Cup brand in the global sporting marketplace.

**Rugby World Cup 2015 will fund the development of the game all over the world.**

Fan engagement and social and digital media innovation will also be at the heart of Rugby World Cup 2015, meaning that from the stadium to the armchair, fans new and old will be able to engage, participate and enjoy all that the tournament has to offer, on and off the field.

The tournament's IMPACT Beyond programme, launched at the two years to go marker, will ensure that Rugby World Cup 2015 will not just leave a lasting legacy of interest and participation, but will also deliver the building blocks to ensure that participation can be sustained and retained.

The work is already advanced and the RFU 'Posts in the Parks' programme and twinning of counties with emerging European rugby nations will boost participation. Underpinning it all will be the Get Into Rugby mass

participation programme that will see more than one million children across 40 European nations engaged in tag rugby programmes.

And as we continue to count down until hosts England face Fiji in the opening match on 18 September at Twickenham, RWC 2015 is on track to be an exceptional tournament that will be good for rugby and good for England. It will leave a legacy of superb facilities, provide a wonderful experience for teams and fans and will further rugby as a major global sport with a must-see pinnacle event. It really will be too big to miss!

**Demand for tickets for the 48 matches at Rugby World Cup 2015 has been huge.**

For further information and to receive news and updates on RWC 2015, visit ***www.rugbyworldcup.com*** and Join the Front Row.

## Too Big To Miss – Rugby World Cup 2015 in numbers

- **Excitement building throughout host cities, venues and across the global rugby family**
- **Hospitality package sales for RWC 2015 already exceed total volume sold for RWC 2011**
- **Six official Worldwide Partners with programme locked down in record time and with record value**
- **Thirteen match venues**
- **Forty-one team bases across England and Wales will provide world-class training facilities**
- **Eighty-three nations participated in the largest Rugby World Cup qualification process**
- **200+ broadcast territories to screen more than 20,000 hours of coverage**
- **20,000 applications for 6,000 places in 'The Pack', the official tournament volunteer programme**
- **160,000 tickets sold through official supporter tour programme, 30 per cent more than the New Zealand 2011 total**
- **400,000 overseas fans anticipated to visit England and Wales during the tournament**
- **2.3 million tickets available**
- **£330 million being invested by the IRB in development of global rugby from 2009–16 owing to commercial success of Rugby World Cup**

The Webb Ellis Cup has travelled the world in the build-up to Rugby World Cup 2015, with the Trophy Tour visiting countries such as Fiji and Madagascar.

**RUGBY**
**WORLD CUP**
**2015**

For six wonderful weeks in September and October 2015, the eyes of the sporting world will be focused on England (and Wales) for the eighth Rugby World Cup.

Twenty nations will take part in the showpiece event, from defending champions New Zealand to Uruguay, the final side to confirm their place by winning the Repechage to end a 12-year absence from the Rugby World Cup stage.

The four pools have thrown up some mouth-watering matches, including two-time champions Australia against 2003 winners and hosts England, 2011 runners-up France against Ireland and Italy and Los Pumas against New Zealand.

## THE POOLS

| Pool A | Pool B | Pool C | Pool D |
|---|---|---|---|
| Australia | South Africa | New Zealand | France |
| England | Samoa | Argentina | Ireland |
| Wales | Scotland | Tonga | Italy |
| Fiji | Japan | Georgia | Canada |
| Uruguay | USA | Namibia | Romania |

# Rugby World Cup 2015 fixtures

| DATE | TIME (UK) | POOL | MATCH DETAILS | LOCATION | STADIUM |
|---|---|---|---|---|---|
| Fri 18 Sep | 20:00 | A | England v Fiji | London | Twickenham |
| Sat 19 Sep | 12:00 | C | Tonga v Georgia | Gloucester | Kingsholm |
| Sat 19 Sep | 14:30 | D | Ireland v Canada | Cardiff | Millennium Stadium |
| Sat 19 Sep | 16:45 | B | South Africa v Japan | Brighton | Brighton Community Stadium |
| Sat 19 Sep | 20:00 | D | France v Italy | London | Twickenham |
| Sun 20 Sep | 12:00 | B | Samoa v USA | Brighton | Brighton Community Stadium |
| Sun 20 Sep | 14:30 | A | Wales v Uruguay | Cardiff | Millennium Stadium |
| Sun 20 Seap | 16:45 | C | New Zealand v Argentina | London | Wembley Stadium |
| Wed 23 Sep | 14:30 | B | Scotland v Japan | Gloucester | Kingsholm |
| Wed 23 Sep | 16:45 | A | Australia v Fiji | Cardiff | Millennium Stadium |
| Wed 23 Sep | 20:00 | D | France v Romania | London | Olympic Stadium |
| Thu 24 Sep | 20:00 | C | New Zealand v Namibia | London | Olympic Stadium |
| Fri 25 Sep | 16:45 | C | Argentina v Georgia | Gloucester | Kingsholm |
| Sat 26 Sep | 14:30 | D | Italy v Canada | Leeds | Elland Road |
| Sat 26 Sep | 16:45 | B | South Africa v Samoa | Birmingham | Villa Park |
| Sat 26 Sep | 20:00 | A | England v Wales | London | Twickenham |
| Sun 27 Sep | 12:00 | A | Australia v Uruguay | Birmingham | Villa Park |
| Sun 27 Sep | 14:30 | B | Scotland v USA | Leeds | Elland Road |
| Sun 27 Sep | 16:45 | D | Ireland v Romania | London | Wembley Stadium |
| Tue 29 Sep | 16:45 | C | Tonga v Namibia | Exeter | Sandy Park |
| Thu 1 Oct | 16:45 | A | Wales v Fiji | Cardiff | Millennium Stadium |
| Thu 1 Oct | 20:00 | D | France v Canada | Milton Keynes | Stadium MK |
| Fri 2 Oct | 20:00 | C | New Zealand v Georgia | Cardiff | Millennium Stadium |
| Sat 3 Oct | 14:30 | B | Samoa v Japan | Milton Keynes | Stadium MK |
| Sat 3 Oct | 16:45 | B | South Africa v Scotland | Newcastle | St James' Park |
| Sat 3 Oct | 20:00 | A | England v Australia | London | Twickenham |
| Sun 4 Oct | 14:30 | C | Argentina v Tonga | Leicester | Leicester City Stadium |
| Sun 4 Oct | 16:45 | D | Ireland v Italy | London | Olympic Stadium |
| Tue 6 Oct | 16:45 | D | Canada v Romania | Leicester | Leicester City Stadium |
| Tue 6 Oct | 20:00 | A | Fiji v Uruguay | Milton Keynes | Stadium MK |
| Wed 7 Oct | 16:45 | B | South Africa v USA | London | Olympic Stadium |
| Wed 7 Oct | 20:00 | C | Namibia v Georgia | Exeter | Sandy Park |
| Fri 9 Oct | 20:00 | C | New Zealand v Tonga | Newcastle | St James' Park |
| Sat 10 Oct | 14:30 | B | Samoa v Scotland | Newcastle | St James' Park |
| Sat 10 Oct | 16:45 | A | Australia v Wales | London | Twickenham |
| Sat 10 Oct | 20:00 | A | England v Uruguay | Manchester | Manchester City Stadium |
| Sun 11 Oct | 12:00 | C | Argentina v Namibia | Leicester | Leicester City Stadium |
| Sun 11 Oct | 14:30 | D | Italy v Romania | Exeter | Sandy Park |
| Sun 11 Oct | 16:45 | D | France v Ireland | Cardiff | Millennium Stadium |
| Sun 11 Oct | 20:00 | B | USA v Japan | Gloucester | Kingsholm |
| Sat 17 Oct | 16:00 | | QF1: W Pool B v RU Pool A | London | Twickenham |
| Sat 17 Oct | 20:00 | | QF2: W Pool C v RU Pool D | Cardiff | Millennium Stadium |
| Sun 18 Oct | 13:00 | | QF3: W Pool D v RU Pool C | Cardiff | Millennium Stadium |
| Sun 18 Oct | 16:00 | | QF4: W Pool A v RU Pool B | London | Twickenham |
| Sat 24 Oct | 16:00 | | SF1: W QF1 v W QF2 | London | Twickenham |
| Sun 25 Oct | 16:00 | | SF2: W QF3 v W QF4 | London | Twickenham |
| Fri 30 Oct | 20:00 | | Bronze Final | London | Olympic Stadium |
| Sat 31 Oct | 16:00 | | Final | London | Twickenham |

# Pacific Islands thrive on the Rugby World Cup stage

## By Pat Lam

I was lucky enough to play in three Rugby World Cups with Manu Samoa during my career and it was a truly amazing experience each time. Opportunities for Samoa to measure ourselves against the top tier teams remain limited and a World Cup is a rare time when we can test ourselves against the game's big guns on a global stage.

I made my Test debut as a 23-year-old in the famous 16–13 win over Wales in Cardiff at Rugby World Cup 1991. It was a hell of a way to start my international career and the biggest upset of the tournament. We were desperate to show the world what Samoan rugby was all about and I think we achieved that in '91.

It was a result that worked wonders for the profile of Manu Samoa, both at home and further afield. We were flooded by invitations to play tier one countries after that; we subsequently broke into the top eight in the rankings and although we lost to Scotland in the quarter-final, Samoan rugby was on a massive high.

We backed it up in 1995 in South Africa by reaching the last eight again after wins over Italy and Argentina in the pool stages. People had expectations of the team by then but I thought we dealt with the pressure well and there was no disgrace in going out to the Springboks at Ellis Park in the quarters.

In 1999 we came up against Wales in Cardiff again. We were the underdogs but we won the game 38–31 and became the first team ever to beat Wales in a Test match at the new Millennium Stadium.

**Western Samoa shocked the world by beating Wales at Rugby World Cup 1991.**

It was a huge privilege to skipper the team in Cardiff and although we lost to Scotland in the quarter-final play-off game at Murrayfield – my last ever Test – the World Cup in 1999 was another great advert for Manu Samoa and our brand of rugby.

It is disappointing Samoa has not made it to the quarter-finals since 1995 but I think you have to be realistic. We don't have the resources of the major teams and the World Cup has become more and more competitive with every staging of the tournament.

The World Cup in 1991 inevitably brings back memories of our captain Peter Fatialofa and it was a very sad day for everyone who knew Peter when we heard he had died in late 2013. He was only 54 and he will be sorely missed.

It's impossible to exaggerate how central Peter was to what we achieved in '91. His job description might have been captain but he was much more than that to everyone in the squad. It was Peter who did the player recruitment before the tournament and he was the heart and soul of the side during the competition. He brought people together, he could relate to young and old alike and he always had an enormous smile on his face. He put Samoan rugby on the map but he did it with real modesty and a sense of humour.

I'm cautiously optimistic about Samoa's chances at Rugby World Cup 2015. I genuinely believe Stephen Betham and his team are capable of doing something special in England.

South Africa will be the favourites to win the pool but Samoa are certainly capable of beating Scotland, Japan and the USA to go through as runners-up. We beat the Scots in Durban in 2013, we've won three of the last four games against Japan, all of which were in Tokyo, and Samoa has never lost to the Americans. It won't be a formality but Samoa will not fear anyone and will have a great chance of getting into the knockout stage.

The greatest challenge facing Samoan rugby remains the infrastructure and logistical issues. The number of Samoans playing in Super Rugby, the Top 14, the PRO12 or the Premiership in England underlines that the talent is undoubtedly there but the big issue is bringing it all together for a Test match. It has always been our Achilles heel.

Our players are working in a professional environment with their clubs but that level of organisation isn't always mirrored when they report for international duty. That is, to a degree, because of the financial situation of the Union but we must keep striving to make our logistical, medical and support set-ups as professional as we possibly can.

It's a source of great pride but at the same time an organisational nightmare that Samoans play their club rugby all over the world. The logistical problem of getting these players in the same place at the same time is constant and, with no central contracts, it is the clubs who are in control.

I remember when I was involved with Manu Samoa for the game against Wales in Cardiff in 2012. We had a squad of 30 players from 30 different clubs and we had just six training sessions to work with them before the Test match. We won the game 26–19 but it

**Tonga fans enjoying the Rugby World Cup party as their team memorably beat France in 2011.**

wasn't an ideal build-up. The players were not complete strangers to each other but I cannot imagine New Zealand or England playing a Test with that lack of preparation.

It's a tough situation. The team thrives on the challenge but as the top tier nations become more and more professional, it becomes harder for the Pacific Island teams to bridge the gap.

The other big issue for Samoa – as well as Tonga and Fiji – is the fixture list. The annual IRB Pacific Nations Cup is a good competition but all three sides need more regular matches against the tier one nations to take the next step forward.

Argentina have become significantly stronger since they joined The Rugby Championship, which is a good example of the impact regular exposure to a higher standard of rugby can have on a group of players. Logistically and financially I think it would be impossible for Samoa to commit to a global tournament but there is no doubt the Pumas have benefited enormously since they began playing the All Blacks, Springboks and Wallabies on a regular basis.

The PNC does have its critics but I believe any chance to assemble the players and work with them over a prolonged period of time is one that Samoa, Fiji or Tonga must take. Samoa won the Pacific Islands Conference in the new-look competition in 2014 and I'm sure that success will give them confidence as they prepare for the World Cup.

Those preparations received a massive boost when it was announced that New Zealand will play in Apia in July 2015. It will be the first time the All Blacks have faced Samoa in Samoa and the whole country is hugely excited about the match. To have the world's number one team come to Apia will be one of the greatest days in the history of our rugby and every Samoan player, wherever they are in the world, will be desperate to be involved.

I hope it will also encourage other top teams to play in Samoa, Tonga and Fiji in the future. Not only would such games generate much-needed revenue for the Unions, it would present us with the opportunity to tackle higher ranked sides with home advantage. We invariably have to travel for the big matches and I think there'd be some interesting results if teams from the Six Nations or The Rugby Championship travelled to the Pacific Islands.

A World Cup tends to bring out the best in Samoa, Fiji and Tonga. It's a time when they are actually able to get all the best players together and have the luxury of being in camp together for a few weeks before the start of the tournament. That's why all three teams have claimed famous scalps over the years, beating teams higher than them in the rankings.

Tonga made the headlines in 2011 when they beat the French in Wellington. It was an incredible performance which showed the potential of the Ikale Tahi when they come together and although they've pulled the short straw and will be in the same pool as the All Blacks again in 2015, I would expect them to give Argentina a real test in the pool stages. If they can beat the Pumas, they'd be in a great position to go through.

Fiji's best performance in the World Cup was in 2007 when they beat Wales in Nantes and they then pushed the Springboks close in the quarter-finals. Fiji have the toughest draw of the three Pacific Islands in 2015 with England, Australia and Wales all in the same pool but they're a dangerous side to underestimate and I wouldn't rule out them causing an upset.

There's certainly a camaraderie between the three teams when we're not playing each other. It's a sense of the three sides representing Polynesia on the world stage and if Samoa is not able to reach the quarter-finals in 2015, I hope our brothers from Fiji or Tonga can qualify.

# A Rugby World Cup celebration

**W**ith less than a year to go until Rugby World Cup 2015 kicks off in England, we take a stroll down memory lane to remember some of the iconic moments in the tournament's proud history.

The statue outside Eden Park commemorating Michael Jones' famous moment.

## 1987

### A piece of history

A bronze sculpture depicting the moment Michael Jones scored the first-ever try by a player at a Rugby World Cup is proudly on display in front of Eden Park, the venue where what is now one of the world's biggest sporting events came to life on 22 May, 1987.

Eden Park may have changed beyond all recognition since then due to its redevelopment for RWC 2011, but the sight of Jones diving over the Italian line to cap off a move instigated by Buck Shelford, Alan Whetton and Grant Fox in a match that New Zealand went on win 70–6 lives long in the memory. As debuts go, it was the stuff made of dreams.

"It was just a fantastic season in my life really, in many ways just to be selected for the All Blacks was a dream come true in the first instance and then to be playing in New Zealand, in front of our home crowds and in front of our own people and it was the inaugural World Cup," recalled Jones.

"Just all those circumstances lining up, and then to be able to score the first try in that first game, there was a lot of firsts, so just to be part of that, to be playing with all these great players who were at the top of their games at that time, it was definitely a dream come true and it seems quite surreal now looking back.

"But it is something I will always treasure and really look back on with a huge amount of fondness and really cherish that privilege that I had to be part of the first All Black World Cup winning team."

Jones went on to score one of New Zealand's three tries in the 29–9 win over France in the inaugural final and appeared in his second tournament at RWC 1991. He later went to two World Cups with Samoa, as assistant coach in 2003 and coach four years later.

## Blanco's touch of magic

You'd struggle to find too many rugby lovers who list the Concord Oval, on the outskirts of Sydney, as one of their favourite grounds. But the 20,000 capacity venue did stage one of the best matches in Rugby World Cup history when France beat co-hosts Australia 30–24 in the 1987 semi-final.

Given the names on show that day ... Michael Lynagh, David Campese, Philippe Sella and

Serge Blanco scores France's winner in the corner.

eventual match-winner Serge Blanco to name but a few, it was perhaps no great surprise that the crowd – RWC 2003-winning captain Martin Johnson included – were treated to pure rugby theatre.

A feast of attacking rugby from start to finish, the game was riveting. Australia, while never safe, appeared to have done just enough until a Didier Camberabero penalty tied the scores at 24–24. Extra-time loomed. Except no one had told the French. Australia conceded possession attempting to run the ball out of their half and Les Bleus spread the ball wide to Blanco, who, despite carrying an injury, managed to just about outpace the cover defence and squeeze over in the corner to score the try that sent France through to the final.

Sadly, France couldn't recapture the same vein of form in the final, where New Zealand won 29–9, but the Rugby World Cup flame had been lit by some brilliant players and an exceptional match.

# 1991

## "Thank goodness we weren't playing all of Samoa"

Western Samoa had been disappointed not to receive an invitation to the first Rugby World Cup, but with qualifying matches introduced for the second tournament, they made sure of their place by winning the Oceania/Asia region, pipping Japan (who also qualified) to first place, and leaving Tonga out in the cold.

The Samoans then launched themselves onto the world stage in spectacular fashion, beating hosts Wales 16–13 at the national stadium, Cardiff Arms Park. Boasting a number of players who would become household names – such as captain Peter Fatialofa, Junior Paramore, Pat Lam, Brian Lima, Stephen Bachop and Frank Bunce, the last two of whom later won All Blacks caps as well – the

**Western Samoa in action against Wales in 1991.**

Samoans played a form of the game which was beautiful and brutal in equal measure.

Mixing fabulously entertaining running rugby with huge 'hits' in defence, the Samoans quickly became a massive favourite of all bar the Welsh, especially Tony Clement, Richie Collins and Phil May who felt the full force of their opponent's physicality and were forced off the field of play. The end result gave rise to one of the most famous quips in rugby history when Welsh fans muttered "Thank goodness we weren't playing all of Samoa."

It was some introduction to World Cup rugby, but Western Samoa proved it was no fluke by running eventual winners Australia close and then overwhelming Argentina 35–12 to book a place in the knockout stages at Wales' expense. In truth, Western Samoa were well-beaten in the quarter-finals by Scotland, 28–6, but their Cardiff heroics had ensured Pacific Islands' rugby was well and truly on the map.

## From ecstasy to agony

Gordon Hamilton's 30-metre gallop to the line in the 73rd minute of Ireland's quarter-final against Australia is one of the iconic images of Rugby World Cup history. Sadly for Ireland, the flanker's maiden Test try did not prove to be a match-winning one.

Up until then, Australia had led for virtually the whole match but precision kicking from fly-half Ralph Keyes had kept Ireland within striking distance. Trailing 15–12, Ireland decided to

The celebrations after Hamilton's incredible try.

chance their arm and run the ball out of their own half from first phase possession off a scrum. Rob Saunders' dive pass found Keyes who shifted the ball onto David Curtis who then found Jim Staples joining the line at pace from full-back.

Staples got a beautifully weighted grubber kick away while taking contact and Jack Clarke, after outmuscling the slipping and sliding David Campese, scooped up the loose ball. With Marty Roebuck hanging grimly onto one of his legs, the stationary Clarke popped the ball up to Hamilton, who was anything but, and the Ulsterman – legs pumping like never before – just about had enough gas left in the tank to make it to the line despite a brave cover tackle from Bob Egerton. Cue delirium: "… the noise was phenomenal, you couldn't hear a thing. The crowd had gone ballistic, they just couldn't believe it," Egerton later recalled.

The sure-footed Keyes landed the conversion from close to the left touchline, but within the space of a few minutes the ecstatic Lansdowne Road crowd had been reduced to a hushed silence. Australia regrouped and worked their way to a promising position up field and from an attacking lineout they forced a scrum. Instead of opting for the conservative option of a drop goal which would have levelled the scores, the Wallaby backline executed a well-worked loop around move to find the hat-trick seeking Campese in the far corner. Campese was unable to force his way over but still managed to offload the ball inside to Michael Lynagh who dotted down to break Irish hearts.

# 1995

*Jonah Lomu takes the direct route to the try-line.*

## Jonah Lomu bulldozes England

Fate has a funny habit of changing the course of sporting events – and the Rugby World Cup is no different. Had it not been for Eric Rush's untimely injury, the force of nature that was Jonah Lomu would probably never have been unleashed in South Africa in 1995.

"Everybody talks about Lomu and what a great World Cup he had but he was lucky to be there," recalled former All Blacks captain Sean Fitzpatrick. "He had played terribly the year before when he made his debut against the French, they had made a mockery of him playing on the wing and he wasn't fit enough. We didn't know about his condition back then. But I remember Rushy injuring his hamstring on the Friday before the final trial in Hamilton and that meant he was out. Jonah was dragged off a plane as he was just about to fly out to Japan for a Sevens tournament and came down to Hamilton and scored five tries in the trial."

The rest, as they say, is history.
In their first match New Zealand ran riot against Ireland with Lomu scoring
two of their five tries in the 43–19 win. He scored another in the 48–30
quarter-final win over Scotland, but it was in the semi-final against England
that we saw him in all his glory.

Lomu ran riot, crossing the line four times as England defenders bounced
off him. Using his immense power and startling pace – despite standing 6ft
5in and weighing around 18-and-a-half stone, he could run 100 metres in
around 11 seconds – Lomu destroyed English dreams of a second
consecutive final with a performance which will live long in the memories
of all who saw it ... or felt it. By the time of the final though, South Africa
had done their homework on Lomu and effectively man-marked him out
of the match.

## The Rainbow Nation unites

The Rugby World Cup has
produced some incredible
matches and unbelievable
performances, from teams
and individuals. Yet one of
the most iconic moments in
its history took place
without a whistle being
blown. The sight of Nelson
Mandela, South Africa's
first black president,
turning up at Ellis Park on
the day of the final wearing
a Springboks jersey
symbolised the rebirth of a
nation once racially divided.

Instead of 63,000 fans in
the stadium backing the
team, they had the support
of 42 million South
Africans, as Francois
Pienaar pointed out shortly

**Nelson Mandela and Francois Pienaar prove the power of sport in 1995.**

after receiving the trophy from Mandela, a moment that has since been
immortalised in the Hollywood blockbuster *Invictus*.

South Africa fed off the emotion and produced a display full of guts and
passion to beat favourites New Zealand 15–12 after extra-time. "Madiba
came into the dressing room before the final against the All Blacks and his
presence was incredible. He spoke with all the players individually and it
meant so much to everyone for him to be among us before the kick-off," said
fly-half Joel Stransky, who had kicked the match-winning drop goal.

## The reluctant drop goal king

An injury to first-choice fly-half Henry Honiball had afforded Jannie de Beer his big chance and he proceeded to produce one of the most remarkable kicking displays of all time in the RWC 1999 quarter-final against England. De Beer kicked a world record five drop goals, all in the second half, as well as five penalties and the conversions of both South African tries as the defending champions beat England 44–21.

*Jannie de Beer drop-kicks England out of the Rugby World Cup 1999.*

"For the opener, I kicked up field and Matt Perry kicked back. Percy Montgomery received it and created a ruck. I got the ball and had no support, so I thought go for it and it went over. Percy then just flung the ball straight to me for the second and, in the same scenario, I hit it again," de Beer said.

"When those went over, we decided we'd give this more of a go and work for it, so the remaining three were planned and aimed for. If it wasn't for the fact that that first kick went over I probably would have given drop goals a miss."

De Beer kicked a further six penalties and one drop goal in the semi-final against Australia, but the South African defence of their crown was to end there after the Wallabies claimed a 27–21 extra-time victory. It was to prove to be the last of de Beer's 13 caps, but the quarter-final had already given him a place in Rugby World Cup history which may never be surpassed.

## C'est magnifique!

Few believed that France, the northern hemisphere's last representatives, would make much of an impression on the All Blacks in the Twickenham semi-final, particularly given that they had finished with the wooden spoon after an unimpressive Five Nations Championship earlier that year.

**France stun New Zealand to reach the 1999 final.**
And the match looked to be going exactly the way it had been predicted when Jonah Lomu bulldozed his way to two tries to give the All Blacks a comfortable 24–10 lead shortly after half-time.

Then came a revival of the kind which only France can ever conceive, let alone affect. Christophe Lamaison, who had only started the game following the withdrawal through injury of Thomas Castaignède, had already scored a try, which he converted, and a penalty in the first half. Now he scored two penalties and two drop goals in quick succession to restore French belief.

Emboldened by Lamaison's defiance, France started to attack and tries from Christophe Dominici, Richard Dourthe and Philippe Bernat-Salles turned the game on its head. From 24–10 down, France scored 33 unanswered points, a virtual impossibility against the All Blacks, and were now leading 43–24. A late Jeff Wilson try was no more than a consolation, and France were through to their first final since 1987.

# 2003

## Georgia join the party

Having come within a whisker of qualifying for RWC 1999 only to narrowly miss out to Tonga, Georgia were determined to go all the way and book their place at the next tournament in Australia. Despite taking a heavy beating (63–14) from Ireland in the first match of their qualifying group at Lansdowne Road, Georgia bounced back to pip Russia 17–13 in Tbilisi to qualify for RWC 2003. Levan Tsabadze scored their only try of the game and solid kicking from winger Malkhaz Urjukashvili accounted for the rest of their points as they recovered from a 13–6 half-time deficit to the delight of the 50,000 capacity crowd at the Avchala Stadium.

"To get to the World Cup finals is a memory that will stay with the history of the country forever," Georgia Rugby Union General Secretary Michael Burdzgla said at the time. "This is the first time we have ever achieved such a feat and we are very proud of our players."

In Australia, Georgia would do well to emulate their Sevens counterparts – the country's first national team to reach a World Cup in any sport – who won two pool matches at RWC Sevens in Argentina two years earlier, given they had been drawn alongside eventual champions England, South Africa, Samoa and Uruguay. And so it proved. England and Samoa were too powerful, as were South

**The whole world had Georgia on its mind during the 2003 tournament.**

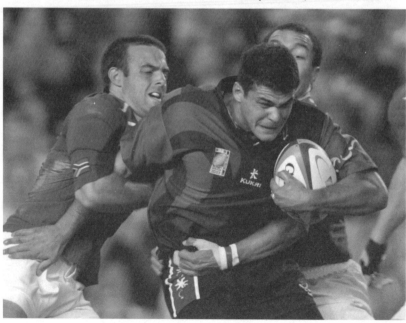

Africa, but Georgia's battling display against the Springboks, which saw them score their first tournament try through David Dadunashvili, earned them a standing ovation from the locals at the final whistle and the players responded as if they had won the World Cup. Disappointingly, Georgia's debut appearance on the ultimate stage ended with a 24–12 defeat to Uruguay, but it was the start of their Rugby World Cup story which very nearly included a shock victory over Ireland four years later.

## Jonny Wilkinson

'Is this all you've got?' sneered *The Australian* newspaper over a photo of Jonny Wilkinson landing yet another three points for England. The local press was in no doubt that if you stopped Wilkinson, you stopped England at Rugby World Cup 2003. They were right up to a point, not that Wilkinson, the archetypal team man, would ever agree.

Nevertheless the history books show that he kicked all of England's points in the 24–7 semi-final victory over France before supplying the killer blow, 26 seconds before the end of extra-time in a thrilling final against Australia in Sydney, with his snap drop goal off the 'wrong' foot winning a first Rugby World Cup for England and turning him into the most reluctant of global superstars.

"Everyone remembers where they were at the moment Jonny went for that kick, and so do I," flanker Neil Back recalls. "I was on one knee and I'd just cleared out the ruck. The phase after Matt Dawson had made his break, I found myself at nine and I looked back at Jonny and thought 'this doesn't feel right,

**Jonny Wilkinson watches as his drop goal flies towards the posts to give England a first taste of Rugby World Cup success.**

we need to give it to [Wilkinson].' We then made sure we had the best people in the best positions. We had our best passer, Dawson, give it to our best kicker, Wilkinson. Then, they just did their job."

# 2007

## Los Pumas the talk of Paris

The revelation of RWC 2007 was undoubtedly Argentina. Los Pumas had been knocking at the door to the top table for some years but while exceedingly difficult to beat at home, their away form had often left a lot to be desired.

They had almost broken through to the knockout stages in 2003, denied by a single point loss to Ireland, but in 2007 they were to become the first country outside the Tri Nations or Six Nations to reach a RWC semi-final.

Argentina boasted their usual powerful forwards, but this time could complement them with a world-class half-back pairing of their feisty and quick-witted captain Agustín Pichot at scrum-half and the sumptuous talents of Juan Martín Hernández at fly-half.

Their fairytale Rugby World Cup started and finished with victories over France, Los Pumas stunning the host nation 17–12 in the opening match in Paris. "We have a lot of hunger to write history, to make history," declared Pichot in the wake of the victory. "We're not the best tactical players

**Argentina were a revelation in 2007.**

or the best technically, but our best resources are the passion and pride when we put on the jersey."

Wins over Georgia (33–3) and Namibia (63–3) followed and a 30–15 victory over Ireland not only put them through but gave them top spot into the bargain, leading to a winnable quarter-final against Scotland. The Pumas duly won, 19–13, holding off a late Scottish rally for a very worthy place in the final four. South Africa may have tamed the Pumas in a one-sided semi-final, but third place was theirs after they proved the opening day win over Les Bleus was no fluke with a 34–10 win in the Bronze final.

## The flying Eagle

Sometimes in sport there are moments which are destined to pass into folklore even if, in the wider scheme of things, they had no bearing on the ultimate destination of the major prizes.

Such a moment took place on 30 September, 2007 in a Rugby World Cup match between South Africa and the USA. Tries from Schalk Burger, Francois Steyn and Bryan Habana, all converted by Percy Montgomery, had given the Springboks a comfortable 24–3 lead as the game neared half-time.

South Africa were attacking again as the clock ticked down but at a breakdown deep inside the Eagles' 22 scrum-half Fourie du Preez's floated pass was picked off by the USA openside Todd Clever. A powerful run out of defence saw Clever take play up field and link up with the supporting Alec Parker. The second row found his captain Mike Hercus and the fly-half immediately

**Even Bryan Habana couldn't stop Takudzwa Ngwenya from making it to the line.**

passed the ball wide to flying winger Takudzwa Ngwenya.

Although Ngwenya had space, he was still inside his own half when he received the ball and opposite number Habana looked to be lining him up. Ngwenya made a little shimmy as if to cut inside, then blasted off down the line, backing his pace to beat the cover. Habana, himself one of the world's quickest wings, was left for dead. South Africa went on to win RWC 2007, and Habana was the top try scorer, but it was Ngwenya who won the International Rugby Players' Association Try of the Year award.

# 2011

## The long wait is over

As RWC 2011 approached, it seemed unbelievable that it was getting on for a quarter of a century since New Zealand had won a competition which they had played a large part in instigating. For many of the intervening years, the All Blacks had been the best team – they had claimed 10 of the 16 Tri Nations titles since that championship had begun in 1996, they had extended their record of never having lost to any country other than South Africa, Australia, France and England while most other nations were routinely put to the sword, and on several occasions had put together long winning streaks.

The All Blacks celebrate as the final whistle goes in the RWC 2011 final.

And yet both their big southern hemisphere rivals had lifted the Webb Ellis Cup twice, while the All Blacks seemed to have almost mastered the art of peaking between tournaments rather than for them. But RWC 2011 was played on their home turf and from the start they looked determined to put the record straight, sailing through the pool stages with four comfortable victories to set up a quarter-final with Argentina.

Los Pumas were dispatched 33–10, followed by Australia, 20–6 in the semi-final. A final against France, who they had already beaten 37–17 in the pool stages almost exactly a month earlier, looked a formality. It turned out to be anything but, as the French were a team transformed and fought all the way before New Zealand sneaked home 8–7 to claim a long overdue second Rugby World Cup.

"It's such a small trophy but what it means is huge," captain Richie McCaw said, while holding the Webb Ellis Cup aloft to the cheers of an Auckland crowd estimated to be 240,000 strong at the All Blacks' victory parade a day later.

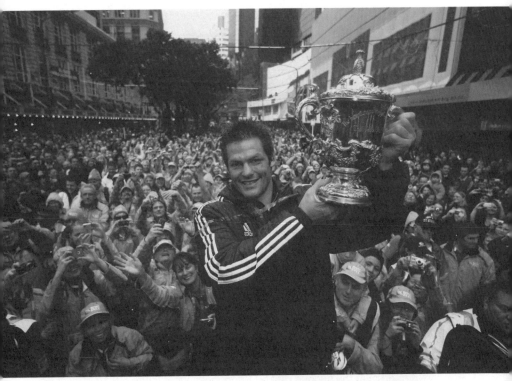

The whole of New Zealand celebrated the Rugby World Cup 2011 win.

## It's all in the numbers

Rugby World Cup 2011 was a massive success, official figures showing that 133,200 overseas visitors had come to watch, a huge increase on the forecast 95,000. And with a reported 1.35 million fans attending the 48 matches, it was the largest sporting event ever hosted by New Zealand.

In stark contrast to RWC 1987, when no matches were seen live in the northern hemisphere, the 2011 edition – which saw Russia make their debut – was broadcast in 207 countries and the cumulative television audience has been estimated at 3.9 billion.

On the playing front, the time the ball was in play in 2011 had increased by 33 per cent since 1995, there were also more passes per match in the same period with 263 compared to 179 and the amount of rucks and mauls almost doubled. The number of scrums and lineouts were reduced though, and average kicks per match went down from 75 to 41.

It tells the tale of a phenomenal success story on every level and of a Rugby World Cup which continues to grow and capture the imagination of fans all over the world with England 2015 expected to be the latest record-breaking chapter.

# World Rankings

## By Karen Bond

**N**ew Zealand are closing in on their fifth anniversary as the number one side in the World Rankings, a position they have occupied since 16 November 2009 and for a remarkable 83.94 per cent of the time since the International Rugby Board introduced the rankings in October 2003. This is the second time that the All Blacks have sat atop the rankings for more than three years, in stark contrast to the longest timeframes enjoyed by South Africa and England – the only other nations to hold the position – of less than nine months.

They may be a common sight at the top of the rankings, but the All Blacks' cushion has decreased significantly over the last two years. After the inaugural Rugby Championship in 2012, they sat 7.43 rating points above Australia. Following their 27–25 loss to South Africa on 4 October, that advantage over the second ranked Springboks was down to 2.19, a decrease of three points from this time last year. It would have shrunk even further had Colin Slade's conversion with the final kick of the match not snatched a 29-28 win for the All Blacks over Australia in the final Bledisloe Cup match of 2014. Instead the world champions headed off to the USA and Europe for a busy November schedule with their chances of reaching that anniversary strengthened.

That loss in Johannesburg was only New Zealand's second since Richie McCaw held aloft the Webb Ellis Cup in 2011 and stopped the All Blacks' unbeaten run at 22 matches, the 12–12 draw with Australia in the opening Rugby Championship match in August having prevented them from setting a new record of 18 consecutive Test victories by a major nation.

New Zealand, South Africa and USA are the only nations to have remained stationary for the last 12 months, although seven others have now returned to their positions after movement up or down. They are England (3), Australia (4), Wales (6), Argentina (10), Kenya (31), the Cook Islands (46) and Malaysia (71).

While Los Pumas climbed back to 10th after recording their first ever victory in The Rugby Championship, they had slipped to their lowest ever position in the rankings of 12th after two defeats by Ireland on home soil in June. Argentina's gain meant that Japan slipped one place, having reached

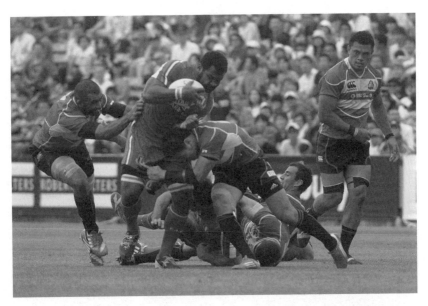

**Japan's victory over Italy in June saw them rise to a new high of 10th in the rankings.**

their highest ever position of 10th after victory over Italy in June extended the Brave Blossoms' unbeaten run to 10 matches. This sequence, which includes wins over Samoa, Canada and USA, means Japan are the biggest climbers in the top 20 over the last year, having risen four places. By contrast, France, Samoa, Tonga, Italy and Canada have all fallen two places in this period.

Italy's fall to 14th means they are one of 12 nations currently occupying their lowest position since the rankings were introduced, the others being Canada (17), Chile (28), Denmark (74), Pakistan (82), Slovenia (84), Bahamas (94), Norway (97), Indonesia, American Samoa and UAE (99) and Greece (102). This compares to eight nations who have risen to their highest ranking in Zimbabwe (27), Senegal (42), the Philippines (52), Mexico (61), Botswana (72), Cameroon (76), Mauritius (91) and Uzbekistan (96).

In total, 45 nations have seen their ranking improve over the last 12 months, while 47 ended this period lower than they began it. The World Rankings welcomed two new nations in Indonesia and Uzbekistan after they became Full Member Unions of the International Rugby Board, taking the number to 102. They both entered with a rating of 30.00, but Uzbekistan have improved that after beating the higher ranked India 23–17 in the Asian 5 Nations Division III West in June.

The last 12 months has seen some significant climbs and falls by unions. The honour of being the biggest climber over this period belongs to Austria, who have rocketed 17 places to 76th after winning four of their six European Nations Cup Division 2C matches. Three of these victories came against higher ranked opponents in Bulgaria (58–14), Slovenia (20–8) and Denmark

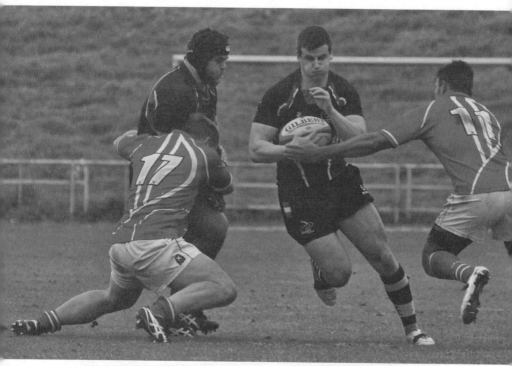

Austria climbed more places (17) than any other nation in the 12 months to October 2014.

(29–27). The most recent win, against Denmark in October, lifted Austria into the top 80 nations for the first time since April 2012. It also condemned their visitors to Vienna to a 10-place drop across the last 12 months, making them one of three teams to suffer falls into double figures.

Austria, though, are not the only nation to shoot up the rankings, with the Czech Republic and Mexico both enjoying climbs of 13 places. The Czech Republic now sit 39th after victories over the higher ranked Sweden (17–11) and Moldova (37–19) in the European Nations Cup. Those two matches were the only ones that the Czechs won in the competition spanning two years, so they were actually relegated to Division 2A for the European Nations Cup 2016.

Mexico, meanwhile, have won all four of their matches in 2014. They began by overwhelming Bermuda – a side who began the calendar year 21 places above them – 56–9 in Huixquilucan de Degollado in April and then beat the Bahamas, Jamaica and the Turks & Caicos Islands in the NACRA Caribbean Championship to top the North Zone Cup league. That earned them the right to face Bermuda in a play-off, but their opponents forfeited the match and handed their place in the North Zone Championship league for next year to Mexico.

While they did not reach double figures of positions climbed in the last 12 months, Malta (eight places to 41st), Caribbean champions Guyana (seven places to 54th), Cayman Islands (seven places to 55th), Luxembourg (seven places to 85th) and Mauritius (seven places to 91st) all enjoyed rises worthy of mention.

On the other side of the coin, two nations have seen their ranking plummet by more than 10 places. Bermuda suffered heavy defeats by the lower ranked Mexico and Cayman Islands in 2014 and as a result have the unwanted marker as the biggest fallers of the last 12 months, dropping 12 places to 66th. Sweden fared little better with an 11-place fall to 44th after failing to win a match in the second half of the European Nations Cup 2014 Division 1B competition. Three of these losses – to eventual champions Germany, Ukraine and Moldova – were by margins of more than 15 points, meaning the maximum losses possible were suffered in the rankings.

Sri Lanka and Bulgaria narrowly avoided falls into double figures, dropping nine and eight places respectively. Sri Lanka won only one match in the last 12 months, 26–25 against Poland on home soil in Colombo last November, but it was defeats by Hong Kong, Korea and particularly the lower ranked Philippines in the Asian 5 Nations in April and May which proved costly. It was only by a point, 26–25, but given 17 places had separated Sri Lanka and the Philippines before kick-off the hosts dropped six places in one swoop.

Bulgaria fared even worse with four heavy defeats, the smallest margin being 26 points against Slovenia. The most recent of these defeats, 59–12 by the lower ranked Bosnia & Herzegovina in early October, was not the best of starts to Bulgaria's life in Division 2D of the European Nations Cup 2016 after their relegation was confirmed five months earlier.

There is, though, still plenty of opportunities for movements throughout the length of the World Rankings before we welcome in 2015, with some 24 nations involved in the traditional November internationals across Europe as well as in North America, South America and Asia. The European Nations Cup 2016 will also continue with 13 matches across its seven divisions.

The World Rankings are published every Monday on ***www.worldrugby.org***. They are calculated using a points exchange system in which teams take points off each other based on the match result. Whatever one team gains, the other team loses. The exchanges are determined by the match result, the relative strength of the team and the margin of victory. There is also an allowance for home advantage.

One hundred and two of World Rugby's Member Unions have a rating, typically between 0 and 100 with the top side in the world usually having a rating above 90 – New Zealand's was 92.60 at the time of writing. Any match that is not a full international between two countries or a Test against the British & Irish Lions does not count towards the rankings. Likewise, neither does a match against a country that is not a World Rugby Full Member Union.

For more details visit ***www.worldrugby.org***.

# WORLD RANKINGS 07/10/13 – 13/10/14

| POSITION | MEMBER UNION | RATING | MOVEMENT | HIGHEST EVER | LOWEST EVER |
|---|---|---|---|---|---|
| 1 | New Zealand | 92.60 | | 1 | 2 |
| 2 | South Africa | 90.41 | | 1 | 6 |
| 3 | England | 85.68 | | 1 | 8 |
| 4 | Australia | 85.07 | | 2 | 5 |
| 5 | Ireland | 83.44 | Up 3 | 3 | 9 |
| 6 | Wales | 80.70 | | 4 | 10 |
| 7 | France | 80.01 | Down 2 | 2 | 8 |
| 8 | Scotland | 77.75 | Up 1 | 6 | 12 |
| 9 | Samoa | 76.35 | Down 2 | 7 | 13 |
| 10 | Argentina | 75.97 | | 3 | 12 |
| 11 | Japan | 75.63 | Up 4 | 10 | 20 |
| 12 | Fiji | 74.58 | Up 1 | 9 | 16 |
| 13 | Tonga | 72.83 | Down 2 | 9 | 20 |
| 14 | Italy | 70.92 | Down 2 | 8 | 14 |
| 15 | Georgia | 70.46 | Up 1 | 13 | 23 |
| 16 | Romania | 68.42 | Up 1 | 13 | 19 |
| 17 | Canada | 67.77 | Down 3 | 11 | 17 |
| 18 | USA | 67.30 | | 14 | 20 |
| 19 | Uruguay | 63.58 | Up 2 | 14 | 23 |
| 20 | Russia | 62.29 | Down 1 | 16 | 26 |
| 21 | Spain | 60.65 | Down 1 | 18 | 32 |
| 22 | Namibia | 58.39 | Up 1 | 19 | 29 |
| 23 | Portugal | 57.73 | Down 1 | 16 | 27 |
| 24 | Hong Kong | 57.63 | Up 5 | 22 | 39 |
| 25 | Korea | 57.22 | Down 1 | 20 | 33 |
| 26 | Germany | 57.19 | Up 1 | 24 | 37 |
| 27 | Zimbabwe | 55.83 | Up 5 | 27 | 35 |
| 28 | Chile | 54.54 | Down 2 | 23 | 28 |
| 29 | Moldova | 54.10 | Up 1 | 25 | 53 |
| 30 | Belgium | 53.90 | Down 5 | 21 | 55 |
| 31 | Kenya | 53.25 | | 31 | 53 |
| 32 | Netherlands | 53.16 | Up 3 | 28 | 48 |
| 33 | Ukraine | 52.37 | Up 4 | 24 | 40 |
| 34 | Morocco | 51.18 | Up 2 | 19 | 36 |
| 35 | Poland | 51.06 | Down 7 | 25 | 42 |
| 36 | Brazil | 50.63 | Down 2 | 27 | 37 |
| 37 | Paraguay | 50.42 | Up 1 | 29 | 42 |
| 38 | Tunisia | 49.89 | Up 4 | 27 | 44 |
| 39 | Czech Republic | 49.49 | Up 13 | 24 | 53 |
| 40 | Kazakhstan | 48.91 | Up 3 | 25 | 50 |
| 41 | Malta | 48.85 | Up 8 | 39 | 67 |
| 42 | Senegal | 48.69 | Up 5 | 42 | 83 |
| 43 | Madagascar | 47.69 | Up 1 | 35 | 56 |
| 44 | Sweden | 47.40 | Down 11 | 32 | 58 |
| 45 | Switzerland | 47.27 | Down 4 | 34 | 67 |
| 46 | Cook Islands | 47.11 | | 48 | 59 |
| 47 | Ivory Coast | 47.08 | Down 7 | 38 | 48 |
| 48 | Sri Lanka | 46.95 | Down 9 | 38 | 64 |
| 49 | Croatia | 46.35 | Up 4 | 34 | 56 |
| 50 | Lithuania | 43.20 | Down 5 | 35 | 73 |
| 51 | Israel | 45.75 | Down 3 | 46 | 94 |
| 52 | Philippines | 45.57 | Up 5 | 52 | 72 |
| 53 | Trinidad & Tobago | 45.50 | Down 3 | 42 | 60 |
| 54 | Guyana | 45.49 | Up 7 | 53 | 79 |

# WORLD RANKINGS 07/10/13 – 13/10/14

| POSITION | MEMBER UNION | RATING | MOVEMENT | HIGHEST EVER | LOWEST EVER |
|---|---|---|---|---|---|
| 55 | Cayman Islands | 45.41 | Up 7 | 57 | 74 |
| 56 | Papua New Guinea | 45.27 | Down 1 | 46 | 63 |
| 57 | Uganda | 44.68 | Down 6 | 31 | 69 |
| 58 | Colombia | 44.63 | Up 2 | 53 | 86 |
| 59 | Singapore | 44.54 | Down 3 | 42 | 67 |
| 60 | Thailand | 43.37 | Down 1 | 52 | 74 |
| 61 | Mexico | 43.20 | Up 13 | 61 | 76 |
| 62 | Chinese Taipei | 42.62 | Down 4 | 32 | 63 |
| 63 | Andorra | 42.54 | Up 4 | 52 | 74 |
| 64 | Latvia | 41.89 | Up 1 | 35 | 75 |
| 65 | Venezuela | 41.65 | Down 2 | 42 | 71 |
| 66 | Bermuda | 41.59 | Down 12 | 47 | 68 |
| 67 | China | 41.47 | Down 1 | 38 | 70 |
| 68 | Hungary | 41.02 | Up 2 | 61 | 89 |
| 69 | Niue Islands | 40.45 | Down 1 | 60 | 72 |
| 70 | Solomon Islands | 40.35 | Down 1 | 67 | 77 |
| 71 | Malaysia | 40.20 | | 56 | 83 |
| 72 | Botswana | 39.64 | Up 5 | 72 | 89 |
| 73 | India | 39.07 | Up 2 | 65 | 93 |
| 74 | Denmark | 39.01 | Down 10 | 36 | 74 |
| 75 | Peru | 38.84 | Down 3 | 51 | 79 |
| 76 | Austria | 38.61 | Up 17 | 63 | 93 |
| 76 | Cameroon | 38.33 | Up 2 | 76 | 85 |
| 78 | Barbados | 38.26 | Down 5 | 59 | 81 |
| 79 | Nigeria | 38.05 | Up 1 | 73 | 92 |
| 80 | Jamaica | 36.99 | Up 1 | 76 | 90 |
| 81 | St Vincent & The Grenadines | 36.84 | Up 3 | 71 | 85 |
| 82 | Pakistan | 36.74 | Down 4 | 71 | 81 |
| 83 | Serbia | 36.54 | Down 7 | 56 | 84 |
| 84 | Slovenia | 36.49 | Down 2 | 42 | 84 |
| 85 | Luxembourg | 35.94 | Up 7 | 67 | 95 |
| 86 | Tahiti | 35.37 | Up 4 | 85 | 91 |
| 87 | Monaco | 35.17 | Up 4 | 76 | 93 |
| 88 | Guam | 34.95 | Down 1 | 70 | 90 |
| 89 | Zambia | 34.77 | Down 6 | 60 | 89 |
| 90 | Bosnia & Herzegovina | 34.66 | Down 4 | 85 | 95 |
| 91 | Mauritius | 33.86 | Up 6 | 91 | 101 |
| 92 | Vanuatu | 33.45 | Up 1 | 89 | 95 |
| 93 | Bulgaria | 33.31 | Down 8 | 75 | 94 |
| 94 | Bahamas | 32.99 | Down 6 | 84 | 94 |
| 95 | Swaziland | 32.04 | Down 7 | 80 | 96 |
| 96 | Uzbekistan | 31.94 | * Down 1 | 96 | 97 |
| 97 | Norway | 31.14 | Down 2 | 78 | 95 |
| 98 | Finland | 30.97 | Up 2 | 93 | 102 |
| 99 | Indonesia | 30.00 | * Down 1 | 97 | 99 |
| 99 | American Samoa | 30.00 | Down 2 | 96 | 99 |
| 99 | UAE | 30.00 | Down 2 | 96 | 99 |
| 102 | Greece | 28.55 | Down 2 | 96 | 102 |

* Indonesia and Uzbekistan entered the World Rankings at 30.00 in November and May respectively so climb is based on their entry points of 97th and 96th.

# The Numbers Game

**932**

**Days between the first RWC 2015 qualifier in Mexico and the last one in Uruguay**

**17**

Unions who submitted tender documents to host a round of the HSBC Sevens World Series from 2015–16

**50**

**50 Tries scored in The Rugby Championship (12 matches)**

**2,322**

Tries scored across the HSBC Sevens World Series 2013–14

**311**

**The number of players to graduate from the IRB Junior World Championship to the Test arena by the conclusion of The Rugby Championship**

# 83

Nations to have taken part in the RWC 2015 qualification process

# 825

**Tries scored across the IRB Women's Sevens World Series 2013–14**

# 9,876

Number of points scored in the RWC 2015 qualification process

# 20

Years to have passed between England's first and second Women's Rugby World Cup triumphs

# 1

First titles won in 2014 by Japan (IRB Junior World Rugby Trophy), Argentina Pampas XV (IRB Pacific Rugby Cup), Argentina Jaguars (IRB Tbilisi Cup) and Emerging Ireland (IRB Nations Cup)

# 61

**Tries scored in the Six Nations (15 matches)**

# 1,786

Number of days since New Zealand returned to the IRB World Rankings top spot (up to end of The Rugby Championship)

# 20

The run of New Zealand consecutive victories on the Women's Rugby World Cup stage before they lost 17–14 to Ireland in France

**IRB Awards**

The last November internationals before Rugby World Cup 2015 will provide the climax in the race to succeed New Zealand's Kieran Read as IRB Player of the Year, just one of the IRB Awards still to be presented in 2014. The Player, Coach and Team of the Year awards will, along with the IRPA Try of the Year, bring the curtain down on another busy year of international rugby as sides build towards England 2015.

Read became the third All Black to win the coveted award, following in the footsteps of the only multiple winners, Dan Carter and Richie McCaw. The number 8 was in sublime form in 2013 and beat South Africa second row Eben Etzebeth, Wales and British & Irish Lions full-back Leigh Halfpenny, Italy captain Sergio Parisse and fellow All Black Ben Smith to the accolade.

For the fourth year in a row New Zealand were named Team of the Year, this time after becoming the first team in the professional era to win all 14 Tests they played in the calendar year. The Coach of the Year accolade also remained in New Zealand hands with Steve Hansen collecting that for a third successive year.

The winners were selected by an independent panel of judges, chaired by Australia's RWC winner John Eales and made up of former internationals with more than 500 caps between them. The panel of Will Greenwood, Gavin Hastings, Raphaël Ibanez, Francois Pienaar, Agustín Pichot, Scott Quinnell, Tana Umaga, Paul Wallace and Eales deliberated on every major Test played.

A clean sweep of the major awards was completed when Beauden Barrett's try against France was named IRPA Try of the Year for 2013, a turnover deep in the All Blacks' 22 beginning an attack which would end under the French posts. Barrett is the first New Zealander to receive this award, won in the past by the likes of Bryan Habana and Jaque Fourie.

While seven of the IRB Awards for 2014 are still to be presented at the time of writing, some have already seen their achievements recognised, including Sevens stars Samisoni Viriviri of Fiji and Australia's Emilee Cherry and Canada wing Magali Harvey.

Harvey was a standout player as Canada reached a first Women's Rugby World Cup final in August, scoring arguably the try of the tournament in the semi-final win over France. Canada lost 21–9 to England in the title decider, but Harvey was a popular choice as the IRB Women's Player of the Year.

Viriviri had, in the words of his coach Ben Ryan, a "breathtaking season", scoring 52 tries on the HSBC Sevens World Series to become the first Fijian to be named IRB Sevens Player of the Year in association with HSBC. Cherry was equally important to Australia's impressive season on the IRB Women's Sevens World Series, which saw them win two events and reach the final in two others to finish as runners-up to New Zealand.

Handré Pollard led South Africa to his second IRB Junior World Championship final in three years in June, but unlike in 2012 he ended up on the losing side, 21–20 to England at Eden Park. Eight days later the new IRB Junior Player of the Year made his Test debut for the Springboks against Scotland in Port Elizabeth.

The IRB Referee Award for Distinguished Service was also presented during JWC 2014 to New Zealand's Bob Francis, while the IRB Development Award, Spirit of Rugby Award and the Vernon Pugh Award for Distinguished Service will all be presented in November.

The 2013 event in Dublin saw the IRB recognise the achievements of four individuals who have changed the face of rugby in their countries with the presentation of prestigious awards. The recipients were Ange Guimera (IRB Special Development Award), Yoshiharu Yamaguchi (Spirit of Rugby), Robin Timmins (IRB Development Award) and Ian McIntosh (Vernon Pugh Award for Distinguished Service).

A number of inductions to the IRB Hall of Fame also took place in 2013 and 2014 under the theme of the 'British & Irish Lions and Australia', including Mark Ella, David Campese and Gavin Hastings. The IRB also announced in July that it will integrate inductees from the International Rugby Hall of Fame into its own property with 11 New Zealanders – including Sir John Kirwan and Sir Colin Meads – the first of 37 greats who will be presented with the IRB Hall of Fame cap and pin across events to mark their inductions in 2014 and 2015.

**IRB AWARD WINNERS 2014**
**IRB Women's Player of the Year:** Magali Harvey (Canada)
**IRB Sevens Player of the Year in association with HSBC:**
Samisoni Viriviri (Fiji)
**IRB Women's Sevens Player of the Year:** Emilee Cherry (Australia)
**IRB Junior Player of the Year:** Handré Pollard (South Africa)
**IRB Referee Award for Distinguished Service:** Bob Francis (New Zealand)

For more information on the IRB Awards and IRB Hall of Fame, visit
***www.worldrugby.org***

# Roll of Honour

**Women's Rugby World Cup:** England

**RBS Six Nations:** Ireland

**The Rugby Championship:** New Zealand

**RBS Women's Six Nations:** France

**IRB Nations Cup:** Emerging Ireland

**IRB Tbilisi Cup:** Argentina Jaguars

**IRB Pacific Rugby Cup:** Argentina Pampas

**IRB Americas Rugby Championship:** Argentina Jaguars

**IRB Junior World Championship:** England

**IRB Junior World Rugby Trophy:** Japan

**HSBC Sevens World Series:** New Zealand

**IRB Women's Sevens World Series:** New Zealand

**Aviva Premiership:** Northampton Saints

**Top 14:** Toulon

**RaboDirect PRO12:** Leinster

**Heineken Cup:** Toulon

**Amlin Challenge Cup:** Northampton Saints

**Super Rugby:** NSW Waratahs

# International Tournaments

# THE ROAD TO RUGBY WORLD CUP 2015

*By Karen Bond*

**W**hen Uruguay emerged victorious from the Repechage to claim the 20th and final place at Rugby World Cup 2015 they brought the curtain down on a qualifying process which had involved 83 nations and 203 matches. The road to England 2015 began in Mexico City on 24 March, 2012 when the hosts faced Jamaica and reached its conclusion 932 days later in the Uruguayan capital Montevideo.

Uruguay had fallen at this final hurdle for both the 2007 and 2011 tournaments and were desperate to avoid a hat-trick of heartbreaks. Uruguay returned home from Krasnoyarsk after a 22–21 defeat by Russia and were trailing by nine on aggregate until, inspired by their vocal supporters, they scored three tries in 18 second-half minutes through Joaquín Prada, Alejo Corral and Agustín Ormaechea to swing the qualifier in their favour. Russia battled bravely to the end, but it was the Uruguayan players and fans left celebrating a 36–27 win come the final whistle at the Estadio Charrúa.

"We qualified for the Rugby World Cup because we wanted it more, we deserve it for all the hard work we put in the last four years and because on the day we managed to understand what was required to win," insisted Uruguay coach Pablo Lemoine, whose side join Australia, hosts England, Wales and Fiji in Pool A at RWC 2015. "This is a huge day in our rugby history and one that we must enjoy knowing that from now on the hard work will be with a clear goal, to enjoy the World Cup."

Uruguay had reached the Repechage final after a strong finish saw them to a 28–3 victory over Hong Kong in Montevideo at the beginning of August. Russia's margin of victory was smaller at 23–15, although only after a great solo try by Tafadzwa Chitokwindo at the death in Krasnoyarsk.

*(One direct place – Africa 1 – and one Repechage place)*

Namibia achieved their goal of qualifying for a fifth successive Rugby World Cup by winning the Africa Cup Division 1A in early July, but they certainly did it the hard way after losing their opening match 29–22 to Kenya in Madagascar. That defeat put Namibia in the last chance saloon and meant they had to beat Zimbabwe and their hosts to keep alive their dream of qualification. Namibia achieved the first part, albeit only after scoring 14 unanswered second-half points for a 24–20 victory, but Kenya were in the driving seat with two wins from two after beating Madagascar 34–0.

It was still mathematically possible for Zimbabwe and Namibia to secure the coveted Africa 1 spot, although the latter would need to beat Madagascar with a bonus point and hope Zimbabwe beat Kenya with neither side getting a bonus point. In that scenario all three teams would finish level on 10 points and it would come down to points differential to determine who would qualify directly, enter the Repechage or miss out completely.

The first part went according to Namibia's hopes with Zimbabwe winning 28–10, which meant that the Welwitschias had to beat Madagascar by 53 points or more if they were to return home with their mission accomplished. With Kenya and Zimbabwe looking on from the stands in Antananarivo, Namibia had reached that target by half-time with a 63–10 advantage. Playing with ambition, width and pace, Namibia had stretched that to 89–10 by the final whistle to confirm their place alongside defending champions New Zealand, Argentina, Tonga and Georgia in Pool C at England 2015. Zimbabwe's hopes were also still alive after they finished second to enter the Repechage.

## AMERICAS (NACRA/CONSUR)

*(Two direct places – Americas 1 and 2 – and one Repechage place)*

Canada had already claimed the Americas 1 berth in August 2013 with victory over their neighbours USA, which left the Eagles needing to beat Uruguay over two legs to qualify as Americas 2 and join South Africa, Samoa, Scotland and the then unknown Asia 1 qualifier in Pool B.

The first leg in Montevideo ended in stalemate after a try by Ormaechea – whose father Diego captained and coached Uruguay on the Rugby World Cup stage – seven minutes from time earned Los Teros a deserved 27–27 draw. It could have been even better had Felipe Berchesi's conversion attempt not drifted agonisingly wide.

A week later the teams met again at the Fifth Third Bank Stadium in Atlanta and an upset seemed on the cards as Uruguay led 13–3 at half-time. The Eagles regrouped and scored 29 unanswered points – including tries from brothers Andrew and Shalom Suniula – to emerge victorious, 59–40 on aggregate, and send Uruguay to the Repechage.

## ASIA (ARFU)

*(One direct place – Asia 1 – and one Repechage place)*

Japan were overwhelming favourites to take the Asia 1 place alongside South Africa, Samoa, Scotland and USA in Pool B at England 2015, the RWC 2019 hosts having won all 24 of their previous Asian 5 Nations matches with a bonus point. The battle to finish as runners-up and earn a place in the Repechage was, though, expected to be fiercely contested by Hong Kong and Korea.

Japan kicked off their campaign against a Philippines side that had conceded 16 tries against Hong Kong the previous weekend and duly ran out 99–10 winners over their hosts. A week later the Brave Blossoms, with coach Eddie Jones back at the helm having recovered from the stroke he suffered the previous October, posted their third highest score in history in beating Sri Lanka 132–10 in Nagoya.

That same weekend Hong Kong made the most of home advantage to beat Korea 39–6, scoring five tries in a performance built around a strong defensive effort to secure at least a place in the Repechage.

Japan warmed up for that title decider with a 62–5 victory in Korea and then ensured that the final act of the National Stadium – the centre-piece of the 1964 Olympic Games which is being demolished to make way for a modern stadium for RWC 2019 and the 2020 Olympics – was a positive one with a 49–8 defeat of Hong Kong. The visitors made life difficult for Japan, but try bursts in the final 10 minutes of each half ensured the Brave Blossoms maintained their ever-present record at a Rugby World Cup, leaving Hong Kong to face Uruguay in the Repechage.

## EUROPE (RUGBY EUROPE)

*(Two direct places – Europe 1 and 2 – and one Repechage place)*

Thirty-one nations were involved in the European qualification process, making it the biggest of the five regions, but it was no surprise when Georgia and Romania emerged as the two direct qualifiers for England 2015.

The two sides had gone through the first phase of the European Nations Cup 2014 unbeaten – overcoming Belgium, Portugal, Russia and Spain and drawing their encounter in Bucharest – and began 2014 in the same vein to set up a winner-takes-all finale in Tbilisi on 15 March. That match would not only determine the ENC 2014 champions but also who would earn the right to face defending champions New Zealand at RWC 2015.

Georgia and Romania had already confirmed their places at the showpiece event after overcoming Russia and Spain respectively three weeks earlier, but both were desperate to qualify as Europe 1 and join the All Blacks, Argentina, Tonga and the African qualifier in Pool C.

With a crowd approaching 30,000 at the Mikheil Meskhi Stadium, Georgia emerged the 22–9 victors thanks to a titanic performance from their pack and the reliable boot of Merab Kvirikashvili to earn their date with New Zealand at the Millennium Stadium on 2 October 2015. "It's going to be huge for the Georgian team to play against the world champions and a team with the history and quality of New Zealand," admitted captain Irakli Machkaneli. "It will be wonderful for the development of rugby in Georgia."

Romania will have their own share of big occasions to look forward to as they will open their campaign against France at the Olympic Stadium and then face Ireland, Italy and Canada in Pool D.

Russia finished third in Division 1A to keep alive their own hopes of qualification, although they would have to beat Germany if they were to take Europe's place in the Repechage. They duly beat Germany 31–20 in Hamburg in late May, but not without an almighty scare with late tries by Yury Kushnarev and Evgeny Matveev sparing Russia's blushes.

## OCEANIA (FORU)

*(One direct place – Oceania 1)*

It was no surprise that Fiji claimed the Oceania 1 berth at RWC 2015 – and the honour of facing hosts England in the first match at Twickenham on 18 September – after a 108–6 victory over the Cook Islands on 28 June in Lautoka.

The Flying Fijians, in their one and only match in the qualification process, did trail 6–5 as the half hour mark approached at Churchill Park but four tries in 10 minutes turned that into a 29–6 advantage for the home side. Twelve more tries followed after the break with Nemani Nadolo completing his hat-trick and Metuisela Talebula, Adriu Delai, Nikola Matawalu and Timosi Nagusa finishing the match with two apiece.

The emphatic victory meant Fiji took their place alongside England, two-time winners Australia, Wales and the then unknown Repechage winner in Pool A at RWC 2015 with matches to look forward to at Twickenham, the Millennium Stadium and Stadium MK.

# RUGBY WORLD CUP
# RECORDS 1987–2011

## (FINAL STAGES ONLY)

## OVERALL RECORDS

### MOST MATCHES WON IN FINAL STAGES

| | |
|---|---|
| 37 | New Zealand |
| 33 | Australia |
| 30 | France |
| 29 | England |

### MOST OVERALL PENALTIES IN FINAL STAGES

| | | | |
|---|---|---|---|
| 58 | JP Wilkinson | England | 1999–2011 |
| 36 | AG Hastings | Scotland | 1987–95 |
| 35 | G Quesada | Argentina | 1999–2003 |
| 33 | MP Lynagh | Australia | 1987–95 |
| 33 | AP Mehrtens | New Zealand | 1995–99 |

### MOST OVERALL POINTS IN FINAL STAGES

| | | | |
|---|---|---|---|
| 277 | JP Wilkinson | England | 1999–2011 |
| 227 | AG Hastings | Scotland | 1987–95 |
| 195 | MP Lynagh | Australia | 1987–95 |
| 170 | GJ Fox | New Zealand | 1987–91 |
| 163 | AP Mehrtens | New Zealand | 1995–99 |

### MOST OVERALL DROP GOALS IN FINAL STAGES

| | | | |
|---|---|---|---|
| 14 | JP Wilkinson | England | 1999–2011 |
| 6 | JH de Beer | South Africa | 1999 |
| 5 | CR Andrew | England | 1987–95 |
| 5 | GL Rees | Canada | 1987–99 |
| 4 | JM Hernández | Argentina | 2003–07 |

### MOST OVERALL TRIES IN FINAL STAGES

| | | | |
|---|---|---|---|
| 15 | JT Lomu | New Zealand | 1995–99 |
| 13 | DC Howlett | New Zealand | 2003–07 |
| 11 | R Underwood | England | 1987–95 |
| 11 | JT Rokocoko | New Zealand | 2003–07 |
| 11 | CE Latham | Australia | 1999–2007 |
| 11 | V Clerc | France | 2007–11 |

### MOST MATCH APPEARANCES IN FINAL STAGES

| | | | |
|---|---|---|---|
| 22 | J Leonard | England | 1991–2003 |
| 20 | GM Gregan | Australia | 1995–2007 |
| 19 | MJ Catt | England | 1995–2007 |
| 19 | JP Wilkinson | England | 1999–2011 |
| 18 | MO Johnson | England | 1995–2003 |
| 18 | BP Lima | Samoa | 1991–2007 |
| 18 | R Ibañez | France | 1999–2007 |
| 18 | ME Ledesma | Argentina | 1999–2011 |
| 18 | LW Moody | England | 2003–11 |

### MOST OVERALL CONVERSIONS IN FINAL STAGES

| | | | |
|---|---|---|---|
| 39 | AG Hastings | Scotland | 1987–95 |
| 37 | GJ Fox | New Zealand | 1987–91 |
| 36 | MP Lynagh | Australia | 1987–95 |
| 35 | DW Carter | New Zealand | 2003–11 |
| 28 | JP Wilkinson | England | 1999–2011 |
| 27 | PJ Grayson | England | 1999–2003 |
| 27 | SM Jones | Wales | 1999–2011 |

## MOST POINTS IN ONE COMPETITION

| | | | |
|---|---|---|---|
| **126** | GJ Fox | New Zealand | 1987 |
| **113** | JP Wilkinson | England | 2003 |
| **112** | T Lacroix | France | 1995 |
| **105** | PC Montgomery | South Africa | 2007 |
| **104** | AG Hastings | Scotland | 1995 |
| **103** | F Michalak | France | 2003 |
| **102** | G Quesada | Argentina | 1999 |
| **101** | M Burke | Australia | 1999 |

## MOST PENALTY GOALS IN ONE COMPETITION

| | | | |
|---|---|---|---|
| **31** | G Quesada | Argentina | 1999 |
| **26** | T Lacroix | France | 1995 |
| **23** | JP Wilkinson | England | 2003 |
| **21** | GJ Fox | New Zealand | 1987 |
| **21** | EJ Flatley | Australia | 2003 |
| **20** | CR Andrew | England | 1995 |

## MOST TRIES IN ONE COMPETITION

| | | | |
|---|---|---|---|
| **8** | JT Lomu | New Zealand | 1999 |
| **8** | BG Habana | South Africa | 2007 |
| **7** | MCG Ellis | New Zealand | 1995 |
| **7** | JT Lomu | New Zealand | 1995 |
| **7** | DC Howlett | New Zealand | 2003 |
| **7** | JM Muliaina | New Zealand | 2003 |
| **7** | DA Mitchell | Australia | 2007 |

## MOST DROP GOALS IN ONE COMPETITION

| | | | |
|---|---|---|---|
| **8** | JP Wilkinson | England | 2003 |
| **6** | JH de Beer | South Africa | 1999 |
| **5** | JP Wilkinson | England | 2007 |
| **4** | JM Hernández | Argentina | 2007 |

## MOST CONVERSIONS IN ONE COMPETITION

| | | | |
|---|---|---|---|
| **30** | GJ Fox | New Zealand | 1987 |
| **22** | PC Montgomery | South Africa | 2007 |
| **20** | SD Culhane | New Zealand | 1995 |
| **20** | MP Lynagh | Australia | 1987 |
| **20** | LR MacDonald | New Zealand | 2003 |
| **20** | NJ Evans | New Zealand | 2007 |

RUGBY WORLD CUP TOURNAMENTS

# MATCH RECORDS

## MOST POINTS IN A MATCH
### BY A TEAM

| 145 | New Zealand v Japan | 1995 |
|---|---|---|
| 142 | Australia v Namibia | 2003 |
| 111 | England v Uruguay | 2003 |
| 108 | New Zealand v Portugal | 2007 |
| 101 | New Zealand v Italy | 1999 |
| 101 | England v Tonga | 1999 |

### BY A PLAYER

| 45 | SD Culhane | New Zealand v Japan | 1995 |
|---|---|---|---|
| 44 | AG Hastings | Scotland v Ivory Coast | 1995 |
| 42 | MS Rogers | Australia v Namibia | 2003 |
| 36 | TE Brown | New Zealand v Italy | 1999 |
| 36 | PJ Grayson | England v Tonga | 1999 |
| 34 | JH de Beer | South Africa v England | 1999 |
| 33 | NJ Evans | New Zealand v Portugal | 2007 |
| 32 | JP Wilkinson | England v Italy | 1999 |

## MOST CONVERSIONS IN A MATCH
### BY A TEAM

| 20 | New Zealand v Japan | 1995 |
|---|---|---|
| 16 | Australia v Namibia | 2003 |
| 14 | New Zealand v Portugal | 2007 |
| 13 | New Zealand v Tonga | 2003 |
| 13 | England v Uruguay | 2003 |

### BY A PLAYER

| 20 | SD Culhane | New Zealand v Japan | 1995 |
|---|---|---|---|
| 16 | MS Rogers | Australia v Namibia | 2003 |
| 14 | NJ Evans | New Zealand v Portugal | 2007 |
| 12 | PJ Grayson | England v Tonga | 1999 |
| 12 | LR MacDonald | New Zealand v Tonga | 2003 |

## MOST TRIES IN A MATCH
### BY A TEAM

| 22 | Australia v Namibia | 2003 |
|---|---|---|
| 21 | New Zealand v Japan | 1995 |
| 17 | England v Uruguay | 2003 |
| 16 | New Zealand v Portugal | 2007 |
| 14 | New Zealand v Italy | 1999 |

### BY A PLAYER

| 6 | MCG Ellis | New Zealand v Japan | 1995 |
|---|---|---|---|
| 5 | CE Latham | Australia v Namibia | 2003 |
| 5 | OJ Lewsey | England v Uruguay | 2003 |
| 4 | IC Evans | Wales v Canada | 1987 |
| 4 | CI Green | New Zealand v Fiji | 1987 |
| 4 | JA Gallagher | New Zealand v Fiji | 1987 |
| 4 | BF Robinson | Ireland v Zimbabwe | 1991 |
| 4 | AG Hastings | Scotland v Ivory Coast | 1995 |
| 4 | CM Williams | South Africa v Western Samoa | 1995 |
| 4 | JT Lomu | New Zealand v England | 1995 |
| 4 | KGM Wood | Ireland v United States | 1999 |
| 4 | JM Muliaina | New Zealand v Canada | 2003 |
| 4 | BG Habana | South Africa v Samoa | 2007 |
| 4 | V Goneva | Fiji v Namibia | 2011 |
| 4 | ZR Guildford | New Zealand v Canada | 2011 |

## MOST PENALTY GOALS IN A MATCH
### BY A TEAM

| 8 | Australia v South Africa | 1999 |
|---|---|---|
| 8 | Argentina v Samoa | 1999 |
| 8 | Scotland v Tonga | 1995 |
| 8 | France v Ireland | 1995 |

### BY A PLAYER

| 8 | M Burke | Australia v South Africa | 1999 |
|---|---|---|---|
| 8 | G Quesada | Argentina v Samoa | 1999 |
| 8 | AG Hastings | Scotland v Tonga | 1995 |
| 8 | T Lacroix | France v Ireland | 1995 |

## MOST DROP GOALS IN A MATCH
### BY A TEAM

| 5 | South Africa v England | 1999 |
|---|---|---|
| 3 | Fiji v Romania | 1991 |
| 3 | England v France | 2003 |
| 3 | Argentina v Ireland | 2007 |
| 3 | Namibia v Fiji | 2011 |

### BY A PLAYER

| 5 | JH de Beer | South Africa v England | 1999 |
|---|---|---|---|
| 3 | JP Wilkinson | England v France | 2003 |
| 3 | JM Hernández | Argentina v Ireland | 2007 |
| 3 | TAW Kotze | Namibia v Fiji | 2011 |

All Blacks captain David Kirk lifts the Webb Ellis Cup after New Zealand win the inaugural tournament in 1987.

AFP/Getty Images

# FIRST TOURNAMENT: 1987
# IN AUSTRALIA & NEW ZEALAND

## POOL 1

| Australia | 19 | England | 6 |
| USA | 21 | Japan | 18 |
| England | 60 | Japan | 7 |
| Australia | 47 | USA | 12 |
| England | 34 | USA | 6 |
| Australia | 42 | Japan | 23 |

| | P | W | D | L | F | A | Pts |
|---|---|---|---|---|---|---|---|
| Australia | 3 | 3 | 0 | 0 | 108 | 41 | 6 |
| England | 3 | 2 | 0 | 1 | 100 | 32 | 4 |
| USA | 3 | 1 | 0 | 2 | 39 | 99 | 2 |
| Japan | 3 | 0 | 0 | 3 | 48 | 123 | 0 |

## POOL 3

| New Zealand | 70 | Italy | 6 |
| Fiji | 28 | Argentina | 9 |
| New Zealand | 74 | Fiji | 13 |
| Argentina | 25 | Italy | 16 |
| Italy | 18 | Fiji | 15 |
| New Zealand | 46 | Argentina | 15 |

| | P | W | D | L | F | A | Pts |
|---|---|---|---|---|---|---|---|
| New Zealand | 3 | 3 | 0 | 0 | 190 | 34 | 6 |
| Fiji | 3 | 1 | 0 | 2 | 56 | 101 | 2 |
| Argentina | 3 | 1 | 0 | 2 | 49 | 90 | 2 |
| Italy | 3 | 1 | 0 | 2 | 40 | 110 | 2 |

## POOL 2

| Canada | 37 | Tonga | 4 |
| Wales | 13 | Ireland | 6 |
| Wales | 29 | Tonga | 16 |
| Ireland | 46 | Canada | 19 |
| Wales | 40 | Canada | 9 |
| Ireland | 32 | Tonga | 9 |

| | P | W | D | L | F | A | Pts |
|---|---|---|---|---|---|---|---|
| Wales | 3 | 3 | 0 | 0 | 82 | 31 | 6 |
| Ireland | 3 | 2 | 0 | 1 | 84 | 41 | 4 |
| Canada | 3 | 1 | 0 | 2 | 65 | 90 | 2 |
| Tonga | 3 | 0 | 0 | 3 | 29 | 98 | 0 |

## POOL 4

| Romania | 21 | Zimbabwe | 20 |
| France | 20 | Scotland | 20 |
| France | 55 | Romania | 12 |
| Scotland | 60 | Zimbabwe | 21 |
| France | 70 | Zimbabwe | 12 |
| Scotland | 55 | Romania | 28 |

| | P | W | D | L | F | A | Pts |
|---|---|---|---|---|---|---|---|
| France | 3 | 2 | 1 | 0 | 145 | 44 | 5 |
| Scotland | 3 | 2 | 1 | 0 | 135 | 69 | 5 |
| Romania | 3 | 1 | 0 | 2 | 61 | 130 | 2 |
| Zimbabwe | 3 | 0 | 0 | 3 | 53 | 151 | 0 |

## QUARTER-FINALS

| New Zealand | 30 | Scotland | 3 |
| France | 31 | Fiji | 16 |
| Australia | 33 | Ireland | 15 |
| Wales | 16 | England | 3 |

## SEMI-FINALS

| France | 30 | Australia | 24 |
| New Zealand | 49 | Wales | 6 |

## THIRD PLACE MATCH

| Wales | 22 | Australia | 21 |

### First Rugby World Cup Final, Eden Park, Auckland, 20 June 1987

# NEW ZEALAND 29 (1G 2T 4PG 1DG)
# FRANCE 9 (1G 1PG)

**NEW ZEALAND:** JA Gallagher; JJ Kirwan, JT Stanley, WT Taylor, CI Green; GJ Fox, DE Kirk (*captain*); SC McDowell, SBT Fitzpatrick, JA Drake, MJ Pierce, GW Whetton, AJ Whetton, MN Jones, WT Shelford **SCORERS:** *Tries:* Jones, Kirk, Kirwan *Conversion:* Fox *Penalty Goals:* Fox (4) *Drop Goal:* Fox

**FRANCE:** S Blanco; D Camberabero, P Sella, D Charvet, P Lagisquet; F Mesnel, P Berbizier; P Ondarts, D Dubroca (*captain*), J-P Garuet, A Lorieux, J Condom, E Champ, D Erbani, L Rodriguez

**SCORERS:** *Try:* Berbizier *Conversion:* Camberabero *Penalty Goal:* Camberabero

**REFEREE:** KVJ Fitzgerald (Australia)

# SECOND TOURNAMENT: 1991
# IN BRITAIN, IRELAND & FRANCE

## POOL 1

| New Zealand | 18 | England | 12 |
| Italy | 30 | USA | 9 |
| New Zealand | 46 | USA | 6 |
| England | 36 | Italy | 6 |
| England | 37 | USA | 9 |
| New Zealand | 31 | Italy | 21 |

| | P | W | D | L | F | A | Pts |
|---|---|---|---|---|---|---|---|
| New Zealand | 3 | 3 | 0 | 0 | 95 | 39 | 9 |
| England | 3 | 2 | 0 | 1 | 85 | 33 | 7 |
| Italy | 3 | 1 | 0 | 2 | 57 | 76 | 5 |
| USA | 3 | 0 | 0 | 3 | 24 | 113 | 3 |

## POOL 2

| Scotland | 47 | Japan | 9 |
| Ireland | 55 | Zimbabwe | 11 |
| Ireland | 32 | Japan | 16 |
| Scotland | 51 | Zimbabwe | 12 |
| Scotland | 24 | Ireland | 15 |
| Japan | 52 | Zimbabwe | 8 |

| | P | W | D | L | F | A | Pts |
|---|---|---|---|---|---|---|---|
| Scotland | 3 | 3 | 0 | 0 | 122 | 36 | 9 |
| Ireland | 3 | 2 | 0 | 1 | 102 | 51 | 7 |
| Japan | 3 | 1 | 0 | 2 | 77 | 87 | 5 |
| Zimbabwe | 3 | 0 | 0 | 3 | 31 | 158 | 3 |

## POOL 3

| Australia | 32 | Argentina | 19 |
| Western Samoa | 16 | Wales | 13 |
| Australia | 9 | Western Samoa | 3 |
| Wales | 16 | Argentina | 7 |
| Australia | 38 | Wales | 3 |
| Western Samoa | 35 | Argentina | 12 |

| | P | W | D | L | F | A | Pts |
|---|---|---|---|---|---|---|---|
| Australia | 3 | 3 | 0 | 0 | 79 | 25 | 9 |
| Western Samoa | 3 | 2 | 0 | 1 | 54 | 34 | 7 |
| Wales | 3 | 1 | 0 | 2 | 32 | 61 | 5 |
| Argentina | 3 | 0 | 0 | 3 | 38 | 83 | 3 |

## POOL 4

| France | 30 | Romania | 3 |
| Canada | 13 | Fiji | 3 |
| France | 33 | Fiji | 9 |
| Canada | 19 | Romania | 11 |
| Romania | 17 | Fiji | 15 |
| France | 19 | Canada | 13 |

| | P | W | D | L | F | A | Pts |
|---|---|---|---|---|---|---|---|
| France | 3 | 3 | 0 | 0 | 82 | 25 | 9 |
| Canada | 3 | 2 | 0 | 1 | 45 | 33 | 7 |
| Romania | 3 | 1 | 0 | 2 | 31 | 64 | 5 |
| Fiji | 3 | 0 | 0 | 3 | 27 | 63 | 3 |

## QUARTER-FINALS

| England | 19 | France | 10 |
| Scotland | 28 | Western Samoa | 6 |
| Australia | 19 | Ireland | 18 |
| New Zealand | 29 | Canada | 13 |

## SEMI-FINALS

| England | 9 | Scotland | 6 |
| Australia | 16 | New Zealand | 6 |

## THIRD PLACE MATCH

| New Zealand | 13 | Scotland | 6 |

Second Rugby World Cup Final, Twickenham, London, 2 November 1991

# AUSTRALIA 12 (1G 2PG) ENGLAND 6 (2PG)

**AUSTRALIA:** MC Roebuck; DI Campese, JS Little, TJ Horan, RH Egerton; MP Lynagh, NC Farr-Jones (*captain*); AJ Daly, PN Kearns, EJA McKenzie, RJ McCall, JA Eales, SP Poidevin, V Ofahengaue, T Coker

**SCORERS** *Try:* Daly *Conversion:* Lynagh *Penalty Goals:* Lynagh (2)

**ENGLAND:** JM Webb; SJ Halliday, WDC Carling (*captain*), JC Guscott, R Underwood; CR Andrew, RJ Hill; J Leonard, BC Moore, JA Probyn, PJ Ackford, WA Dooley, MG Skinner, PJ Winterbottom, MC Teague

**SCORER:** *Penalty Goals:* Webb (2)

**REFEREE:** WD Bevan (Wales)

# THIRD TOURNAMENT: 1995
# IN SOUTH AFRICA

**INTERNATIONAL TOURNAMENTS**

## POOL A

| | | | |
|---|---|---|---|
| South Africa | 27 | Australia | 18 |
| Canada | 34 | Romania | 3 |
| South Africa | 21 | Romania | 8 |
| Australia | 27 | Canada | 11 |
| Australia | 42 | Romania | 3 |
| South Africa | 20 | Canada | 0 |

| | P | W | D | L | F | A | Pts |
|---|---|---|---|---|---|---|---|
| South Africa | 3 | 3 | 0 | 0 | 68 | 26 | 9 |
| Australia | 3 | 2 | 0 | 1 | 87 | 41 | 7 |
| Canada | 3 | 1 | 0 | 2 | 45 | 50 | 5 |
| Romania | 3 | 0 | 0 | 3 | 14 | 97 | 3 |

## POOL B

| | | | |
|---|---|---|---|
| Western Samoa | 42 | Italy | 18 |
| England | 24 | Argentina | 18 |
| Western Samoa | 32 | Argentina | 26 |
| England | 27 | Italy | 20 |
| Italy | 31 | Argentina | 25 |
| England | 44 | Western Samoa | 22 |

| | P | W | D | L | F | A | Pts |
|---|---|---|---|---|---|---|---|
| England | 3 | 3 | 0 | 0 | 95 | 60 | 9 |
| Western Samoa | 3 | 2 | 0 | 1 | 96 | 88 | 7 |
| Italy | 3 | 1 | 0 | 2 | 69 | 94 | 5 |
| Argentina | 3 | 0 | 0 | 3 | 69 | 87 | 3 |

## POOL C

| | | | |
|---|---|---|---|
| Wales | 57 | Japan | 10 |
| New Zealand | 43 | Ireland | 19 |
| Ireland | 50 | Japan | 28 |
| New Zealand | 34 | Wales | 9 |
| New Zealand | 145 | Japan | 17 |
| Ireland | 24 | Wales | 23 |

| | P | W | D | L | F | A | Pts |
|---|---|---|---|---|---|---|---|
| New Zealand | 3 | 3 | 0 | 0 | 222 | 45 | 9 |
| Ireland | 3 | 2 | 0 | 1 | 93 | 94 | 7 |
| Wales | 3 | 1 | 0 | 2 | 89 | 68 | 5 |
| Japan | 3 | 0 | 0 | 3 | 55 | 252 | 3 |

## POOL D

| | | | |
|---|---|---|---|
| Scotland | 89 | Ivory Coast | 0 |
| France | 38 | Tonga | 10 |
| France | 54 | Ivory Coast | 18 |
| Scotland | 41 | Tonga | 5 |
| Tonga | 29 | Ivory Coast | 11 |
| France | 22 | Scotland | 19 |

| | P | W | D | L | F | A | Pts |
|---|---|---|---|---|---|---|---|
| France | 3 | 3 | 0 | 0 | 114 | 47 | 9 |
| Scotland | 3 | 2 | 0 | 1 | 149 | 27 | 7 |
| Tonga | 3 | 1 | 0 | 2 | 44 | 90 | 5 |
| Ivory Coast | 3 | 0 | 0 | 3 | 29 | 172 | 3 |

## QUARTER-FINALS

| | | | |
|---|---|---|---|
| France | 36 | Ireland | 12 |
| South Africa | 42 | Western Samoa | 14 |
| England | 25 | Australia | 22 |
| New Zealand | 48 | Scotland | 30 |

## SEMI-FINALS

| | | | |
|---|---|---|---|
| South Africa | 19 | France | 15 |
| New Zealand | 45 | England | 29 |

## THIRD PLACE MATCH

| | | | |
|---|---|---|---|
| France | 19 | England | 9 |

# SOUTH AFRICA 15 (3PG 2DG)
# NEW ZEALAND 12 (3PG 1DG) *

**SOUTH AFRICA:** AJ Joubert; JT Small, JC Mulder, HP Le Roux, CM Williams; JT Stransky, JH van der Westhuizen; JP du Randt, CLC Rossouw, IS Swart, JJ Wiese, JJ Strydom, JF Pienaar (*captain*), RJ Kruger, MG Andrews

**SUBSTITUTIONS:** GL Pagel for Swart (68 mins); RAW Straeuli for Andrews (90 mins); B Venter for Small (97 mins)

**SCORER:** *Penalty Goals:* Stransky (3) *Drop Goals:* Stransky (2)

**NEW ZEALAND:** GM Osborne; JW Wilson, FE Bunce, WK Little, JT Lomu; AP Mehrtens, GTM Bachop; CW Dowd, SBT Fitzpatrick (*captain*), OM Brown, ID Jones, RM Brooke, MR Brewer, JA Kronfeld, ZV Brooke

**SUBSTITUTIONS:** JW Joseph for Brewer (40 mins); MCG Ellis for Wilson (55 mins); RW Loe for Dowd (83 mins); AD Strachan for Bachop (temp 66 to 71 mins)

**SCORER:** *Penalty Goals:* Mehrtens (3) *Drop Goal:* Mehrtens

**REFEREE:** EF Morrison (England)

*\* after extra time: 9–9 after normal time*

Getty Images

Joel Stransky evades the attempted block of All Black Andrew Mehrtens to kick the winning drop goal in the 1995 final.

RUGBY WORLD CUP TOURNAMENTS

# FOURTH TOURNAMENT: 1999
# IN BRITAIN, IRELAND & FRANCE

## POOL A

| Spain | 15 | Uruguay | 27 |
|---|---|---|---|
| South Africa | 46 | Scotland | 29 |
| Scotland | 43 | Uruguay | 12 |
| South Africa | 47 | Spain | 3 |
| South Africa | 39 | Uruguay | 3 |
| Scotland | 48 | Spain | 0 |

| | P | W | D | L | F | A | Pts |
|---|---|---|---|---|---|---|---|
| South Africa | 3 | 3 | 0 | 0 | 132 | 35 | 9 |
| Scotland | 3 | 2 | 0 | 1 | 120 | 58 | 7 |
| Uruguay | 3 | 1 | 0 | 2 | 42 | 97 | 5 |
| Spain | 3 | 0 | 0 | 3 | 18 | 122 | 3 |

## POOL B

| England | 67 | Italy | 7 |
|---|---|---|---|
| New Zealand | 45 | Tonga | 9 |
| England | 16 | New Zealand | 30 |
| Italy | 25 | Tonga | 28 |
| New Zealand | 101 | Italy | 3 |
| England | 101 | Tonga | 10 |

| | P | W | D | L | F | A | Pts |
|---|---|---|---|---|---|---|---|
| New Zealand | 3 | 3 | 0 | 0 | 176 | 28 | 9 |
| England | 3 | 2 | 0 | 1 | 184 | 47 | 7 |
| Tonga | 3 | 1 | 0 | 2 | 47 | 171 | 5 |
| Italy | 3 | 0 | 0 | 3 | 35 | 196 | 3 |

## POOL C

| Fiji | 67 | Namibia | 18 |
|---|---|---|---|
| France | 33 | Canada | 20 |
| France | 47 | Namibia | 13 |
| Fiji | 38 | Canada | 22 |
| Canada | 72 | Namibia | 11 |
| France | 28 | Fiji | 19 |

| | P | W | D | L | F | A | Pts |
|---|---|---|---|---|---|---|---|
| France | 3 | 3 | 0 | 0 | 108 | 52 | 9 |
| Fiji | 3 | 2 | 0 | 1 | 124 | 68 | 7 |
| Canada | 3 | 1 | 0 | 2 | 114 | 82 | 5 |
| Namibia | 3 | 0 | 0 | 3 | 42 | 186 | 3 |

## POOL D

| Wales | 23 | Argentina | 18 |
|---|---|---|---|
| Samoa | 43 | Japan | 9 |
| Wales | 64 | Japan | 15 |
| Argentina | 32 | Samoa | 16 |
| Wales | 31 | Samoa | 38 |
| Argentina | 33 | Japan | 12 |

| | P | W | D | L | F | A | Pts |
|---|---|---|---|---|---|---|---|
| Wales | 3 | 2 | 0 | 1 | 118 | 71 | 7 |
| Samoa | 3 | 2 | 0 | 1 | 97 | 72 | 7 |
| Argentina | 3 | 2 | 0 | 1 | 83 | 51 | 7 |
| Japan | 3 | 0 | 0 | 3 | 36 | 140 | 3 |

## POOL E

| Ireland | 53 | United States | 8 |
|---|---|---|---|
| Australia | 57 | Romania | 9 |
| United States | 25 | Romania | 27 |
| Ireland | 3 | Australia | 23 |
| Australia | 55 | United States | 19 |
| Ireland | 44 | Romania | 14 |

| | P | W | D | L | F | A | Pts |
|---|---|---|---|---|---|---|---|
| Australia | 3 | 3 | 0 | 0 | 135 | 31 | 9 |
| Ireland | 3 | 2 | 0 | 1 | 100 | 45 | 7 |
| Romania | 3 | 1 | 0 | 2 | 50 | 126 | 5 |
| United States | 3 | 0 | 0 | 3 | 52 | 135 | 3 |

## PLAY-OFFS FOR QUARTER-FINAL PLACES

| England | 45 | Fiji | 24 |
|---|---|---|---|
| Scotland | 35 | Samoa | 20 |
| Ireland | 24 | Argentina | 28 |

## QUARTER-FINALS

| Wales | 9 | Australia | 24 |
|---|---|---|---|
| South Africa | 44 | England | 21 |
| France | 47 | Argentina | 26 |
| Scotland | 18 | New Zealand | 30 |

## SEMI-FINALS

| South Africa | 21 | Australia | 27 |
|---|---|---|---|
| New Zealand | 31 | France | 43 |

## THIRD PLACE MATCH

| South Africa | 22 | New Zealand | 18 |
|---|---|---|---|

*INTERNATIONAL TOURNAMENTS*

### Fourth Rugby World Cup Final, Millennium Stadium, Cardiff, 6 November 1999

## AUSTRALIA 35 (2G 7PG) FRANCE 12 (4PG)

**AUSTRALIA:** M Burke; BN Tune, DJ Herbert, TJ Horan, JW Roff; SJ Larkham, GM Gregan; RLL Harry, MA Foley, AT Blades, DT Giffin, JA Eales (*captain*), MJ Cockbain, DJ Wilson, RST Kefu

**SUBSTITUTIONS:** JS Little for Herbert (46 mins); ODA Finegan for Cockbain (52 mins); MR Connors for Wilson (73 mins); DJ Crowley for Harry (75 mins); JA Paul for Foley (85 mins); CJ Whitaker for Gregan (86 mins); NP Grey for Horan (86 mins)

**SCORERS:** *Tries:* Tune, Finegan *Conversions:* Burke (2) *Penalty Goals:* Burke (7)

**FRANCE:** X Garbajosa; P Bernat Salles, R Dourthe, E Ntamack, C Dominici; C Lamaison, F Galthié; C Soulette, R Ibañez (*captain*), F Tournaire, A Benazzi, F Pelous, M Lièvremont, O Magne, C Juillet

**SUBSTITUTIONS:** O Brouzet for Juillet (HT); P de Villiers for Soulette (47 mins); A Costes for Magne (temp 19 to 22 mins) and for Lièvremont (67 mins); U Mola for Garbajosa (67 mins); S Glas for Dourthe (temp 49 to 55 mins and from 74 mins); S Castaignède for Galthié (76 mins); M Dal Maso for Ibañez (79 mins)

**SCORER:** *Penalty Goals:* Lamaison (4)

**REFEREE:** AJ Watson (South Africa)

Getty Images

John Eales leads by example with a charging run for Australia during the World Cup final against France in Cardiff.

# FIFTH TOURNAMENT: 2003
# IN AUSTRALIA

## POOL A

| | | | |
|---|---|---|---|
| Australia | 24 | Argentina | 8 |
| Ireland | 45 | Romania | 17 |
| Argentina | 67 | Namibia | 14 |
| Australia | 90 | Romania | 8 |
| Ireland | 64 | Namibia | 7 |
| Argentina | 50 | Romania | 3 |
| Australia | 142 | Namibia | 0 |
| Ireland | 16 | Argentina | 15 |
| Romania | 37 | Namibia | 7 |
| Australia | 17 | Ireland | 16 |

| | P | W | D | L | F | A | Pts |
|---|---|---|---|---|---|---|---|
| Australia | 4 | 4 | 0 | 0 | 273 | 32 | 18 |
| Ireland | 4 | 3 | 0 | 1 | 141 | 56 | 15 |
| Argentina | 4 | 2 | 0 | 2 | 140 | 57 | 11 |
| Romania | 4 | 1 | 0 | 3 | 65 | 192 | 5 |
| Namibia | 4 | 0 | 0 | 4 | 28 | 310 | 0 |

## POOL C

| | | | |
|---|---|---|---|
| South Africa | 72 | Uruguay | 6 |
| England | 84 | Georgia | 6 |
| Samoa | 60 | Uruguay | 13 |
| England | 25 | South Africa | 6 |
| Samoa | 46 | Georgia | 9 |
| South Africa | 46 | Georgia | 19 |
| England | 35 | Samoa | 22 |
| Uruguay | 24 | Georgia | 12 |
| South Africa | 60 | Samoa | 10 |
| England | 111 | Uruguay | 13 |

| | P | W | D | L | F | A | Pts |
|---|---|---|---|---|---|---|---|
| England | 4 | 4 | 0 | 0 | 255 | 47 | 19 |
| South Africa | 4 | 3 | 0 | 1 | 184 | 60 | 15 |
| Samoa | 4 | 2 | 0 | 2 | 138 | 117 | 10 |
| Uruguay | 4 | 1 | 0 | 3 | 56 | 255 | 4 |
| Georgia | 4 | 0 | 0 | 4 | 46 | 200 | 0 |

## POOL B

| | | | |
|---|---|---|---|
| France | 61 | Fiji | 18 |
| Scotland | 32 | Japan | 11 |
| Fiji | 19 | United States | 18 |
| France | 51 | Japan | 29 |
| Scotland | 39 | United States | 15 |
| Fiji | 41 | Japan | 13 |
| France | 51 | Scotland | 9 |
| United States | 39 | Japan | 26 |
| France | 41 | United States | 14 |
| Scotland | 22 | Fiji | 20 |

| | P | W | D | L | F | A | Pts |
|---|---|---|---|---|---|---|---|
| France | 4 | 4 | 0 | 0 | 204 | 70 | 20 |
| Scotland | 4 | 3 | 0 | 1 | 102 | 97 | 14 |
| Fiji | 4 | 2 | 0 | 2 | 98 | 114 | 10 |
| United States | 4 | 1 | 0 | 3 | 86 | 125 | 6 |
| Japan | 4 | 0 | 0 | 4 | 79 | 163 | 0 |

## POOL D

| | | | |
|---|---|---|---|
| New Zealand | 70 | Italy | 7 |
| Wales | 41 | Canada | 10 |
| Italy | 36 | Tonga | 12 |
| New Zealand | 68 | Canada | 6 |
| Wales | 27 | Tonga | 20 |
| Italy | 19 | Canada | 14 |
| New Zealand | 91 | Tonga | 7 |
| Wales | 27 | Italy | 15 |
| Canada | 24 | Tonga | 7 |
| New Zealand | 53 | Wales | 37 |

| | P | W | D | L | F | A | Pts |
|---|---|---|---|---|---|---|---|
| New Zealand | 4 | 4 | 0 | 0 | 282 | 57 | 20 |
| Wales | 4 | 3 | 0 | 1 | 132 | 98 | 14 |
| Italy | 4 | 2 | 0 | 2 | 77 | 123 | 8 |
| Canada | 4 | 1 | 0 | 3 | 54 | 135 | 5 |
| Tonga | 4 | 0 | 0 | 4 | 46 | 178 | 1 |

## QUARTER-FINALS

| | | | |
|---|---|---|---|
| New Zealand | 29 | South Africa | 9 |
| Australia | 33 | Scotland | 16 |
| France | 43 | Ireland | 21 |
| England | 28 | Wales | 17 |

## SEMI-FINALS

| | | | |
|---|---|---|---|
| Australia | 22 | New Zealand | 10 |
| England | 24 | France | 7 |

## THIRD PLACE MATCH

| | | | |
|---|---|---|---|
| New Zealand | 40 | France | 13 |

# ENGLAND 20 (1T 4PG 1DG)
# AUSTRALIA 17 (1T 4PG) *

**ENGLAND:** JT Robinson; OJ Lewsey, WJH Greenwood, MJ Tindall, BC Cohen; JP Wilkinson, MJS Dawson; TJ Woodman, SG Thompson, PJ Vickery, MO Johnson (*captain*), BJ Kay, RA Hill, NA Back, LBN Dallaglio

**SUBSTITUTIONS:** MJ Catt for Tindall (78 mins); J Leonard for Vickery (80 mins); IR Balshaw for Lewsey (85 mins); LW Moody for Hill (93 mins)

**SCORERS:** *Try:* Robinson *Penalty Goals:* Wilkinson (4) *Drop Goal:* Wilkinson

**AUSTRALIA:** MS Rogers; WJ Sailor, SA Mortlock, EJ Flatley, L Tuqiri; SJ Larkham, GM Gregan (*captain*); WK Young, BJ Cannon, AKE Baxter, JB Harrison, NC Sharpe, GB Smith, DJ Lyons, PR Waugh

**SUBSTITUTIONS:** DT Giffin for Sharpe (48 mins); JA Paul for Cannon (56 mins); MJ Cockbain for Lyons (56 mins); JW Roff for Sailor (70 mins); MJ Dunning for Young (92 mins); MJ Giteau for Larkham (temp 18 to 30 mins; 55 to 63 mins; 85 to 93 mins)

**SCORERS:** *Try*: Tuqiri *Penalty Goals*: Flatley (4)

**REFEREE:** AJ Watson (South Africa)

*\* after extra time: 14–14 after normal time*

Getty Images

England captain Martin Johnson explodes with joy at the final whistle of the thrilling final against host nation Australia.

RUGBY WORLD CUP TOURNAMENTS

# SIXTH TOURNAMENT: 2007
# IN FRANCE, WALES & SCOTLAND

## POOL A

| | | | |
|---|---|---|---|
| England | 28 | USA | 10 |
| South Africa | 59 | Samoa | 7 |
| USA | 15 | Tonga | 25 |
| England | 0 | South Africa | 36 |
| Samoa | 15 | Tonga | 19 |
| South Africa | 30 | Tonga | 25 |
| England | 44 | Samoa | 22 |
| Samoa | 25 | USA | 21 |
| England | 36 | Tonga | 20 |
| South Africa | 64 | USA | 15 |

| | P | W | D | L | F | A | Pts |
|---|---|---|---|---|---|---|---|
| South Africa | 4 | 4 | 0 | 0 | 189 | 47 | 19 |
| England | 4 | 3 | 0 | 1 | 108 | 88 | 14 |
| Tonga | 4 | 2 | 0 | 2 | 89 | 96 | 9 |
| Samoa | 4 | 1 | 0 | 3 | 69 | 143 | 5 |
| USA | 4 | 0 | 0 | 4 | 61 | 142 | 1 |

## POOL C

| | | | |
|---|---|---|---|
| New Zealand | 76 | Italy | 14 |
| Scotland | 56 | Portugal | 10 |
| Italy | 24 | Romania | 18 |
| New Zealand | 108 | Portugal | 13 |
| Scotland | 42 | Romania | 0 |
| Italy | 31 | Portugal | 5 |
| Scotland | 0 | New Zealand | 40 |
| Romania | 14 | Portugal | 10 |
| New Zealand | 85 | Romania | 8 |
| Scotland | 18 | Italy | 16 |

| | P | W | D | L | F | A | Pts |
|---|---|---|---|---|---|---|---|
| New Zealand | 4 | 4 | 0 | 0 | 309 | 35 | 20 |
| Scotland | 4 | 3 | 0 | 1 | 116 | 66 | 14 |
| Italy | 4 | 2 | 0 | 2 | 85 | 117 | 9 |
| Romania | 4 | 1 | 0 | 3 | 40 | 161 | 5 |
| Portugal | 4 | 0 | 0 | 4 | 38 | 209 | 1 |

## POOL B

| | | | |
|---|---|---|---|
| Australia | 91 | Japan | 3 |
| Wales | 42 | Canada | 17 |
| Japan | 31 | Fiji | 35 |
| Wales | 20 | Australia | 32 |
| Fiji | 29 | Canada | 16 |
| Wales | 72 | Japan | 18 |
| Australia | 55 | Fiji | 12 |
| Canada | 12 | Japan | 12 |
| Australia | 37 | Canada | 6 |
| Wales | 34 | Fiji | 38 |

| | P | W | D | L | F | A | Pts |
|---|---|---|---|---|---|---|---|
| Australia | 4 | 4 | 0 | 0 | 215 | 41 | 20 |
| Fiji | 4 | 3 | 0 | 1 | 114 | 136 | 15 |
| Wales | 4 | 2 | 0 | 2 | 168 | 105 | 12 |
| Japan | 4 | 0 | 1 | 3 | 64 | 210 | 3 |
| Canada | 4 | 0 | 1 | 3 | 51 | 120 | 2 |

## POOL D

| | | | |
|---|---|---|---|
| France | 12 | Argentina | 17 |
| Ireland | 32 | Namibia | 17 |
| Argentina | 33 | Georgia | 3 |
| Ireland | 14 | Georgia | 10 |
| France | 87 | Namibia | 10 |
| France | 25 | Ireland | 3 |
| Argentina | 63 | Namibia | 3 |
| Georgia | 30 | Namibia | 0 |
| France | 64 | Georgia | 7 |
| Ireland | 15 | Argentina | 30 |

| | P | W | D | L | F | A | Pts |
|---|---|---|---|---|---|---|---|
| Argentina | 4 | 4 | 0 | 0 | 143 | 33 | 18 |
| France | 4 | 3 | 0 | 1 | 188 | 37 | 15 |
| Ireland | 4 | 2 | 0 | 2 | 64 | 82 | 9 |
| Georgia | 4 | 1 | 0 | 3 | 50 | 111 | 5 |
| Namibia | 4 | 0 | 0 | 4 | 30 | 212 | 0 |

## QUARTER-FINALS

| | | | |
|---|---|---|---|
| Australia | 10 | England | 12 |
| New Zealand | 18 | France | 20 |
| South Africa | 37 | Fiji | 20 |
| Argentina | 19 | Scotland | 13 |

## SEMI-FINALS

| | | | |
|---|---|---|---|
| France | 9 | England | 14 |
| South Africa | 37 | Argentina | 13 |

## BRONZE FINAL

| | | | |
|---|---|---|---|
| France | 10 | Argentina | 34 |

# SOUTH AFRICA 15 (5PG) ENGLAND 6 (2PG)

**SOUTH AFRICA:** PC Montgomery; J-PR Pietersen, J Fourie, FPL Steyn, BG Habana; AD James, PF du Preez; JP du Randt, JW Smit (*captain*), CJ van der Linde, JP Botha, V Matfield, JH Smith, SWP Burger, DJ Rossouw

**SUBSTITUTIONS:** JL van Heerden for Rossouw (72 mins); BW du Plessis for Smit (temp 71 to 76 mins)

**SCORERS:** *Penalty Goals*: Montgomery (4), Steyn

**ENGLAND:** JT Robinson; PH Sackey, MJM Tait, MJ Catt, MJ Cueto; JP Wilkinson, ACT Gomarsall; AJ Sheridan, MP Regan, PJ Vickery (*captain*), SD Shaw, BJ Kay, ME Corry, LW Moody, NJ Easter

**SUBSTITUTIONS:** MJH Stevens for Vickery (40 mins); DJ Hipkiss for Robinson (46 mins); TGAL Flood for Catt (50 mins); GS Chuter for Regan (62 mins); JPR Worsley for Moody (62 mins); LBN Dallaglio for Easter (64 mins); PC Richards for Worsley (70 mins)

**SCORER:** *Penalty Goals*: Wilkinson (2)

**REFEREE:** AC Rolland (Ireland)

AFP/Getty Images

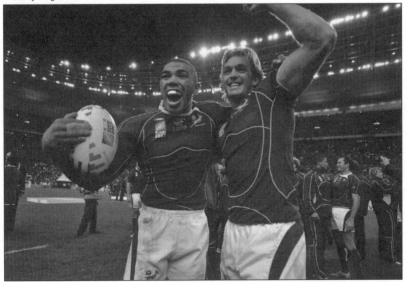

It's time to celebrate for Bryan Habana and Percy Montgomery after South Africa win the World Cup for the second time.

RUGBY WORLD CUP TOURNAMENTS

# SEVENTH TOURNAMENT: 2011
# IN NEW ZEALAND

## POOL A

| New Zealand | 41 | Tonga | 10 |
|---|---|---|---|
| France | 47 | Japan | 21 |
| Tonga | 20 | Canada | 25 |
| New Zealand | 83 | Japan | 7 |
| France | 46 | Canada | 19 |
| Tonga | 31 | Japan | 18 |
| New Zealand | 37 | France | 17 |
| Canada | 23 | Japan | 23 |
| France | 14 | Tonga | 19 |
| New Zealand | 79 | Canada | 15 |

| | P | W | D | L | F | A | Pts |
|---|---|---|---|---|---|---|---|
| New Zealand | 4 | 4 | 0 | 0 | 240 | 49 | 20 |
| France | 4 | 2 | 0 | 2 | 124 | 96 | 11 |
| Tonga | 4 | 2 | 0 | 2 | 80 | 98 | 9 |
| Canada | 4 | 1 | 1 | 2 | 82 | 168 | 6 |
| Japan | 4 | 0 | 1 | 3 | 69 | 184 | 1 |

## POOL C

| Australia | 32 | Italy | 6 |
|---|---|---|---|
| Ireland | 22 | USA | 10 |
| Russia | 6 | USA | 13 |
| Australia | 6 | Ireland | 15 |
| Italy | 53 | Russia | 17 |
| Australia | 67 | USA | 5 |
| Ireland | 62 | Russia | 12 |
| Italy | 27 | USA | 10 |
| Australia | 68 | Russia | 22 |
| Ireland | 36 | Italy | 6 |

| | P | W | D | L | F | A | Pts |
|---|---|---|---|---|---|---|---|
| Ireland | 4 | 4 | 0 | 0 | 135 | 34 | 17 |
| Australia | 4 | 3 | 0 | 1 | 173 | 48 | 15 |
| Italy | 4 | 2 | 0 | 2 | 92 | 95 | 10 |
| USA | 4 | 1 | 0 | 3 | 38 | 122 | 4 |
| Russia | 4 | 0 | 0 | 4 | 57 | 196 | 1 |

## POOL B

| Scotland | 34 | Romania | 24 |
|---|---|---|---|
| Argentina | 9 | England | 13 |
| Scotland | 15 | Georgia | 6 |
| Argentina | 43 | Romania | 8 |
| England | 41 | Georgia | 10 |
| England | 67 | Romania | 3 |
| Argentina | 13 | Scotland | 12 |
| Georgia | 25 | Romania | 9 |
| England | 16 | Scotland | 12 |
| Argentina | 25 | Georgia | 7 |

| | P | W | D | L | F | A | Pts |
|---|---|---|---|---|---|---|---|
| England | 4 | 4 | 0 | 0 | 137 | 34 | 18 |
| Argentina | 4 | 3 | 0 | 1 | 90 | 40 | 14 |
| Scotland | 4 | 2 | 0 | 2 | 73 | 59 | 11 |
| Georgia | 4 | 1 | 0 | 3 | 48 | 90 | 4 |
| Romania | 4 | 0 | 0 | 4 | 44 | 169 | 0 |

## POOL D

| Fiji | 49 | Namibia | 25 |
|---|---|---|---|
| South Africa | 17 | Wales | 16 |
| Samoa | 49 | Namibia | 12 |
| South Africa | 49 | Fiji | 3 |
| Wales | 17 | Samoa | 10 |
| South Africa | 87 | Namibia | 0 |
| Fiji | 7 | Samoa | 27 |
| Wales | 81 | Namibia | 7 |
| South Africa | 13 | Samoa | 5 |
| Wales | 66 | Fiji | 0 |

| | P | W | D | L | F | A | Pts |
|---|---|---|---|---|---|---|---|
| South Africa | 4 | 4 | 0 | 0 | 166 | 24 | 18 |
| Wales | 4 | 3 | 0 | 1 | 180 | 34 | 15 |
| Samoa | 4 | 2 | 0 | 2 | 91 | 49 | 10 |
| Fiji | 4 | 1 | 0 | 3 | 59 | 167 | 5 |
| Namibia | 4 | 0 | 0 | 4 | 44 | 266 | 0 |

## QUARTER-FINALS

| Ireland | 10 | Wales | 22 |
|---|---|---|---|
| England | 12 | France | 19 |
| South Africa | 9 | Australia | 11 |
| New Zealand | 33 | Argentina | 10 |

## SEMI-FINALS

| Wales | 8 | France | 9 |
|---|---|---|---|
| Australia | 6 | New Zealand | 20 |

## BRONZE FINAL

| Australia | 21 | Wales | 18 |
|---|---|---|---|

*INTERNATIONAL TOURNAMENTS*

# NEW ZEALAND 8 (1T 1PG) FRANCE 7 (1G)

**NEW ZEALAND:** IJA Dagg; CS Jane, CG Smith, MA Nonu, RD Kahui; AW Cruden, PAT Weepu; TD Woodcock, KF Mealamu, OT Franks, BC Thorn, SL Whitelock, J Kaino, RH McCaw (*captain*), KJ Read

**SUBSTITUTIONS:** SR Donald for Cruden (33 mins); AJ Williams for Whitelock (48 mins); AK Hore for Mealamu (48 mins); AM Ellis for Weepu (49 mins); S Williams for Nonu (75 mins)

**SCORERS:** *Try*: Woodcock *Penalty Goal*: Donald

**FRANCE:** M Médard; V Clerc, A Rougerie, M Mermoz, A Palisson; M Parra, D Yachvili; J-B Poux, W Servat, N Mas, P Papé, L Nallet, T Dusautoir (*captain*), J Bonnaire, I Harinordoquy

**SUBSTITUTIONS:** F Trinh-Duc for Parra (temp 11 to 17 mins and 22 mins); D Traille for Clerc (45 mins); D Szarzewski for Servat (64 mins); F Barcella for Poux (64 mins); J Pierre for Papé (69 mins); J-M Doussain for Yachvili (75 mins)

**SCORERS:** *Try*: Dusautoir *Conversion:* Trinh-Duc

**REFEREE:** C Joubert (South Africa)

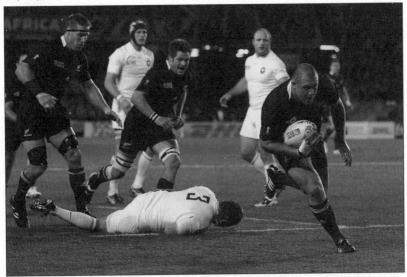

New Zealand prop Tony Woodcock charges over for their only try in the 8–7 victory over France in the RWC 2011 final.

RUGBY WORLD CUP TOURNAMENTS

Coach Joe Schmidt and captain Paul O'Connell arrive back in Dublin with the Six Nations trophy.

Getty Images

# O'DRISCOLL'S FAIRYTALE FAREWELL

## By Iain Spragg

Getty Images

Brian O'Driscoll has a reflective moment with the Six Nations trophy after his 133rd and final Test for Ireland.

There are some sporting scripts seemingly destined to become reality. The storyline may sound implausible but against the odds it unfolds on the pitch before our eyes, a rollercoaster ride of emotion and excitement which transfixes everyone.

The final chapter in the incredible and iconic international career of Brian O'Driscoll was one such moment. Ireland faced France in Paris to decide the fate of the Six Nations and for the Leinster legend it would be his last ever 80 minutes of Test rugby, his record-breaking 133rd and final game for his country and 141st Test appearance in total.

The plot demanded an Irish victory, an emotional and euphoric end to O'Driscoll's 15 years of national service but Ireland had won just once in 41 years in Paris. They had not overcome Les Bleus at any ground since 2009 and O'Driscoll himself had experienced victory just once in seven previous visits to the French capital.

The scene was set for a sporting fairytale and O'Driscoll and Ireland duly delivered after an epic tussle at the Stade de France, beating the French 22–20 to claim the Championship for only the 12th time and ensure their talismanic centre said farewell to the Test arena in the most remarkable style.

"It's exactly as I would have wanted," O'Driscoll said in Paris, a decade and a half after making his Test debut as a 20-year-old against the Wallabies in Brisbane. "Not many people get to finish their career on their own terms, certainly not with high emotions like today. I'm extremely lucky and thankful to have been a part of a great, great team.

"It's been a fantastic Six Nations for us. I've enjoyed every second and it feels great to be a two-time Six Nations winner. We have had so many second places down through the years. It's great to finish on a high in my last game in this magnificent jersey. There were a few tears earlier on when Joe [Schmidt] gave his team talk. It was quite emotional."

The 2014 Six Nations, the 120th instalment of the Championship, may have been O'Driscoll's 14th and final campaign but for new head coach Joe Schmidt it was his first and after the team's desperately disappointing performance in the tournament in 2013, Irish hopes were tempered with inevitable realism.

They began their challenge against Scotland in Dublin and it could not have been a more gentle opener as Ireland easily overpowered their visitors to the Aviva Stadium with tries from the recalled Andrew Trimble, Jamie Heaslip and Rob Kearney to record a 28–6 victory.

The return of Paul O'Connell and Gordon D'Arcy to the starting XV for the clash with Wales in Dublin six days later strengthened Schmidt's hand and Ireland were irresistible against the defending champions as they ran out impressive 26–3 winners.

A first try of Chris Henry's Test career in the 31st minute after a catch and drive at the lineout saw the home side establish a 13–0 half-time lead while replacement Paddy Jackson danced over in the dying minutes of the match. Johnny Sexton kicked 14 points and Ireland were two from two.

Round three took Schmidt and his unbeaten team to London to tackle England. With three victories in their last five trips to Twickenham, the stadium had lost some of the fear factor it once held for the men in green and with O'Driscoll declared fit for duty after a stomach problem, Ireland hoped to complete the third instalment of a possible Grand Slam. England's own dreams of a clean sweep had been dashed on the opening weekend when they were beaten 26–24 at the death by the French in Paris, but knew a victory over the visitors would revive their title aspirations.

It was to be an abrasive and tense encounter at Twickenham. An Owen Farrell penalty gave the home side an early advantage which England took into the dressing room at half-time but Ireland responded soon after the restart when Rob Kearney charged onto Heaslip's short pass and scythed through the England midfield to score under the posts. Sexton added the conversion and a 49th-minute penalty and it was suddenly 10–3 to the visitors.

Farrell was on target with a second penalty in the 53rd minute but what transpired to be the decisive moment of the match came three minutes later. Full-back Mike Brown (who was subsequently voted the Player of the Tournament) made the initial, searing break through Irish lines and scrum-half Danny Care was in support to take the crucial pass, outpacing the cover for the try. Farrell converted and England were 13–10 up.

Although there was still a full 24 minutes to play at Twickenham, there were no further points scored. A potential Irish Grand Slam had evaporated and Stuart Lancaster's England side were firmly back in the hunt for the title.

"It was very physical out there," captain O'Connell said after the game. "We mauled well when we chose to maul and we had control of the game at the start of the second half but couldn't retain it. We were well on top but we let them off the hook with a few silly errors, both defensively and how we tried to get out of our half. We put ourselves under pressure a few times and their belief went up."

The Italians in Dublin were Ireland's penultimate opponents in what was to be O'Driscoll's last international on home soil. It was also the match in which he would surpass George Gregan's record of 139 Test appearances and the Irish produced a fittingly dominant display to mark the occasion.

The floodgates opened as early as the sixth minute when Sexton danced through after a deft pass from O'Driscoll for the first of his two tries and although the Azzurri briefly levelled matters midway through the half with a score from wing Leonardo Sarto, the rest of the game was one-way traffic as Trimble, Cian Healy, Sean Cronin, Fergus McFadden and Jack McGrath all went over the line. The final score was 46–7 to Ireland and a dramatic final weekend of the Championship beckoned.

England's 29–18 triumph over Wales at Twickenham and France's narrow 19–17 success against Scotland at Murrayfield meant three teams could still win the title. An Irish victory in Paris would install Schmidt's team in pole position but a deluge of English points against the Italians in Rome could yet see Lancaster's team become champions. The good news was Ireland were scheduled to take to the field at the Stade de France hours after England had finished in Rome and would know exactly what was required of them before kick-off.

Schmidt made just one change to his starting XV for Paris, recalling flanker Peter O'Mahony in place of Iain Henderson, but more significant was the news from the Stadio Olimpico that England had beaten Italy 52–11. It was an impressive result, the highest score of the Championship featuring seven tries, but it was not enough to overhaul Ireland's superior points difference. Schmidt's side now realised a win, even by a solitary point, would be enough to take the title.

France began the brighter of the two protagonists in Paris and were rewarded with two penalties from scrum-half Maxime Machenaud but the visitors replied with the first try of the match after 20 minutes when Henry's audacious flick from the back of the hand after an attacking ruck found Sexton and the fly-half cut back across the defence to score.

Ireland's second try was created by Conor Murray's break and perfectly-timed pass to Trimble five minutes later. The French hit back on the half hour mark through full-back Brice Dulin and at half-time it was 13–12 to Philippe Saint-André's side.

It was inevitable that O'Driscoll would make his mark on proceedings at some stage in Paris and he did so as Ireland scored their third try shortly after the restart when Trimble opened up the defence and found O'Driscoll in support on his outside shoulder. The veteran sprinted towards the line but there was to be no 48th international try as he was hauled down a metre short. Ireland however recycled the ball quickly and Sexton was able to dart over untouched.

The conversion and a penalty made it 22–13 to the visitors but it quickly became 22–20 when hooker Dimitri Szarzewski muscled his way over for a converted try despite replays suggesting he had knocked on in the process of touching down.

It was a two-point game. Ireland had 18 minutes to survive the French onslaught but their resistance was almost broken in the 79th minute when Damien Chouly went over but the try was dramatically disallowed when the TMO correctly ruled that Vincent Debaty's scoring pass was forward.

Ireland held firm for the remaining few seconds at the Stade de France and when the final whistle sounded, they were Six Nations champions for a second time. England also finished on eight points but were runners-up due to their inferior points difference while Italy collected the wooden spoon for the 10th time since their admittance to the Championship in 2000.

All eyes, however, were on O'Driscoll in Paris after the final whistle. His glorious career had climaxed just as the script demanded and the great man could contemplate retirement safe in the knowledge he had left an indelible mark on both Irish and world rugby.

"The fairytale continued right to the end for the magic man and I'm just delighted for him," Schmidt said. "He's a man I respect hugely. He's a player I really enjoy coaching. His work ethic is massive. We've shown incredible discipline right through the tournament and I think it was a credit to the players today that they maintained their discipline right to the finish."

Ireland's hard-fought 22–20 victory over France in Paris saw them win the Six Nations Championship.

RBS SIX NATIONS

# RBS SIX NATIONS 2014
# FINAL TABLE

| | P | W | D | L | For | Against | Pts |
|---|---|---|---|---|---|---|---|
| Ireland | 5 | 4 | 0 | 1 | 132 | 49 | 8 |
| England | 5 | 4 | 0 | 1 | 138 | 65 | 8 |
| Wales | 5 | 3 | 0 | 2 | 122 | 79 | 6 |
| France | 5 | 3 | 0 | 2 | 101 | 100 | 6 |
| Scotland | 5 | 1 | 0 | 4 | 47 | 138 | 2 |
| Italy | 5 | 0 | 0 | 5 | 63 | 172 | 0 |

Points: Win 2; Draw 1; Defeat 0. Champions determined on superior points difference.

*There were 603 points scored at an average of 40.2 a match. The Championship record (803 points at an average of 53.5 a match) was set in 2000. Johnny Sexton was the leading individual points scorer with 66, 23 points shy of the Championship record Jonny Wilkinson set in 2001. Mike Brown and Sexton were the Championship's leading try-scorers with four each, four short of the all-time record shared between England's Cyril Lowe (1914) and Scotland's Ian Smith (1925).*

Getty Images

France full-back Brice Dulin tries to find a way through the Welsh midfield in their Six Nations match in Cardiff.

## 1 February, Millennium Stadium, Cardiff

# WALES 23 (2G 3PG) ITALY 15 (1G 1T 1PG)

**WALES**: L Halfpenny; A Cuthbert, S Williams, J Roberts, G North; R Priestland, M Phillips; P James, R Hibbard, A Jones, L Charteris, AW Jones (captain), D Lydiate, J Tipuric, T Faletau

**SUBSTITUTIONS**: A Coombs for Charteris (57 mins); R Jones & S Warburton for A Jones & Lydiate (64 mins); K Owens & R Webb for Hibbard & Phillips (67 mins); R Bevington for James (78 mins)

**SCORERS**: *Tries:* Cuthbert, Williams *Conversions:* Halfpenny (2) *Penalty Goals:* Halfpenny (3)

**ITALY**: L McLean; A Esposito, M Campagnaro, A Sgarbi, L Sarto; T Allan, E Gori; M Rizzo, L Ghiraldini, M Castrogiovanni, Q Geldenhuys, M Bortolami, A Zanni, M Bergamasco, S Parisse (captain)

**SUBSTITUTIONS**: A de Marchi for Rizzo (55 mins); D Giazzon & F Minto for Ghiraldini & M Bergamasco (57 mins); T Botes for Gori (65 mins); L Cittadini & J Furno for Castrogiovanni & Bortolami (68 mins); Bergamasco for Zanni (72 mins); T Iannone for Sarto (76 mins)

**SCORERS**: *Tries:* Campagnaro (2) *Conversion:* Allan *Penalty Goal:* Allan

**REFEREE**: J Lacey (Ireland)

## 1 February, Stade de France, Paris

# FRANCE 26 (1G 2T 3PG) ENGLAND 24 (1G 1T 3PG 1DG)

**FRANCE**: B Dulin; Y Huget, M Bastareaud, W Fofana, M Médard; J Plisson, J-M Doussain; T Domingo, B Kayser, N Mas, A Flanquart, P Papé (captain), Y Nyanga, B le Roux, L Picamoles

**SUBSTITUTIONS**: A Burban for le Roux (41 mins); D Szarzewski & Y Maestri for Kayser & Flanquart (43 mins); Y Forestier & R Slimani for Domingo & Mas (48 mins); M Machenaud for Doussain (57 mins); D Chouly for Picamoles (65 mins); G Fickou for Bastareaud (74 mins)

**SCORERS**: *Tries:* Huget (2), Fickou *Conversion:* Machenaud *Penalty Goals:* Doussain (2), Machenaud

**ENGLAND**: M Brown; J Nowell, L Burrell, B Twelvetrees, J May; O Farrell, D Care; J Marler, D Hartley, D Cole, J Launchbury, C Lawes, T Wood, C Robshaw (captain), B Vunipola

**SUBSTITUTIONS**: A Goode for May (7 mins); M Vunipola for Marler (51 mins); T Youngs for Hartley (58 mins); L Dickson for Care (61 mins); B Barritt & B Morgan for Nowell & B Vunipola (65 mins); D Attwood for Lawes (67 mins)

**SCORERS**: *Tries:* Brown, Burrell *Conversion:* Farrell *Penalty Goals:* Farrell (2), Goode *Drop Goal:* Care

**REFEREE**: N Owens (Wales)

## 2 February, Aviva Stadium, Dublin

# IRELAND 28 (2G 1T 3PG) SCOTLAND 6 (2PG)

**IRELAND**: R Kearney; A Trimble, B O'Driscoll, L Marshall, D Kearney; J Sexton, C Murray; C Healy, R Best, M Ross, D Toner, D Tuohy, P O'Mahony, C Henry, J Heaslip (captain)

**SUBSTITUTIONS**: M Moore for Ross (62 mins); J McGrath for Healy (63 mins); S Cronin & T O'Donnell for Best & O'Mahony (65 mins); I Boss, P Jackson & F McFadden for Murray, Sexton & O'Driscoll (72 mins); I Henderson for Toner (73 mins)

**SCORERS**: *Tries:* Trimble, Heaslip, R Kearney *Conversions:* Sexton (2) *Penalty Goals:* Sexton (3)

**SCOTLAND**: S Hogg; S Maitland, A Dunbar, D Taylor, S Lamont; D Weir, G Laidlaw; R Grant, R Ford, M Low, T Swinson, J Hamilton, R Wilson, K Brown (captain), D Denton

**SUBSTITUTIONS**: M Evans for Maitland (31 mins); A Dickinson for Grant (52 mins); R Gray & J Beattie for Hamilton & Brown (56 mins); M Scott for Taylor (64 mins); G Cross for Low (65 mins); P MacArthur for Ford (67 mins); C Cusiter for Laidlaw (73 mins)

**SCORERS**: *Penalty Goals:* Laidlaw (2)

**REFEREE**: C Joubert (South Africa)

## 8 February, Aviva Stadium, Dublin

# IRELAND 26 (2G 4PG) WALES 3 (1PG)

**IRELAND**: R Kearney; A Trimble, B O'Driscoll, G D'Arcy, D Kearney; J Sexton, C Murray; C Healy, R Best, M Ross, D Toner, P O'Connell (captain), P O'Mahony, C Henry, J Heaslip

**SUBSTITUTIONS**: D Tuohy & M Moore for O'Connell & Ross (54 mins); F McFadden for Trimble (61 mins); T O'Donnell for Tuohy (64 mins); J McGrath for Healy (68 mins); S Cronin for Best (73 mins); P Jackson for Sexton (74 mins); I Boss for Murray (79 mins)

**SCORERS**: *Tries:* Henry, Jackson *Conversions:* Sexton, Jackson *Penalty Goals:* Sexton (4)

**WALES**: L Halfpenny; A Cuthbert, S Williams, J Roberts, G North; R Priestland, M Phillips; G Jenkins, R Hibbard, A Jones, A Coombs, AW Jones, D Lydiate, S Warburton (captain), T Faletau

**SUBSTITUTIONS**: L Williams for S Williams (17 mins); K Owens & R Jones for Hibbard & A Jones (61 mins); P James, J Ball & J Tipuric for Jenkins, Coombs & Lydiate (71 mins)

**YELLOW CARD**: Phillips (79 mins)

**SCORERS**: *Penalty Goal:* Halfpenny

**REFEREE**: W Barnes (England)

## 8 February, Murrayfield, Edinburgh

# SCOTLAND 0 ENGLAND 20 (2G 1PG 1DG)

**SCOTLAND**: S Hogg; T Seymour, A Dunbar, M Scott, S Lamont; D Weir, G Laidlaw (captain); R Grant, R Ford, M Low, T Swinson, J Hamilton, R Wilson, C Fusaro, D Denton

**SUBSTITUTIONS**: S Lawson & A Dickinson for Ford & Grant (43 mins); J Beattie for Denton (53 mins); C Cusiter & M Evans for Laidlaw & Seymour (65 mins); G Cross & J Gray for Low & Hamilton (69 mins); D Taylor for Scott (72 mins)

**YELLOW CARD**: Dunbar (51 mins)

**ENGLAND**: M Brown; J Nowell, L Burrell, B Twelvetrees, J May; O Farrell, D Care; J Marler, D Hartley, D Cole, J Launchbury, C Lawes, T Wood, C Robshaw (captain), B Vunipola

**SUBSTITUTIONS**: D Attwood for Launchbury (63 mins); M Vunipola for Marler (65 mins); T Youngs & B Morgan for Hartley & B Vunipola (70 mins); L Dickson, B Barritt & A Goode for Care, Burrell & May (74 mins); H Thomas for Cole (76 mins)

**SCORERS**: *Tries:* Burrell, Brown *Conversions:* Farrell (2) *Penalty Goal:* Farrell *Drop Goal:* Care

**REFEREE**: J Garces (France)

## 9 February, Stade de France, Paris

# FRANCE 30 (3G 3PG) ITALY 10 (1G 1PG)

**FRANCE**: B Dulin; Y Huget, M Bastareaud, W Fofana, H Bonneval; J Plisson, J-M Doussain; T Domingo, D Szarzewski, N Mas, Y Maestri, P Papé (captain), Y Nyanga, B le Roux, L Picamoles

**SUBSTITUTIONS**: R Slimani & Y Forestier for Mas & Domingo (49 mins); D Chouly & B Kayser for Picamoles & Szarzewski (58 mins); M Machenaud for Doussain (61 mins); S Vahaamahina & F Trinh-Duc for Papé & Plisson (67 mins); G Fickou for Bastareaud (73 mins); Mas for Nyanga (75 mins); Nyanga for le Roux (76 mins)

**SCORERS**: *Tries:* Picamoles, Fofana, Bonneval *Conversions:* Doussain (3) *Penalty Goals:* Doussain (3)

**YELLOW CARD**: Vahaamahina (70 mins)

**RED CARD**: Slimani (71 mins)

**ITALY**: L McLean; T Ianonne, M Campagnaro, G Garcia, L Sarto; T Allan, E Gori; A de Marchi, L Ghiraldini, M Castrogiovanni, Q Geldenhuys, J Furno, F Minto, M Bergamasco, S Parisse (captain)

**SUBSTITUTIONS**: A Zanni for Minto (51 mins); D Giazzon, M Rizzo & L Cittadini for Ghiraldini, de Marchi & Castrogiovanni (59 mins); T Botes & L Orquera for Gori & Allan (64 mins); M Bortolami for Geldenhuys (71 mins); de Marchi for Bergamasco (75 mins)

**SCORERS**: *Try:* Iannone *Conversion:* Orquera *Penalty Goal:* Allan

**YELLOW CARD**: Rizzo (71 mins)

**REFEREE**: J Peyper (South Africa)

### 21 February, Millennium Stadium, Cardiff

## WALES 27 (1G 1T 5PG) FRANCE 6 (2PG)

**WALES**: L Halfpenny; A Cuthbert, A North, J Roberts, L Williams; R Priestland, R Webb; G Jenkins, R Hibbard, A Jones, L Charteris, J Ball, D Lydiate, S Warburton (captain), T Faletau

**SUBSTITUTIONS**: K Owens for Hibbard (56 mins); J Hook, D Biggar, P James, R Jones, A Coombs & J Tipuric for Halfpenny, Priestland, Jenkins, A Jones, Ball & Lydiate (70 mins)

**SCORERS**: *Tries*: North, Warburton *Conversion*: Halfpenny *Penalty Goals*: Halfpenny (5)

**YELLOW CARD**: Jenkins (50 mins)

**FRANCE**: B Dulin; Y Huget, M Bastareaud, W Fofana, H Bonneval; J Plisson, J-M Doussain; T Domingo, D Szarzewski, N Mas, Y Maestri, P Papé (captain), Y Nyanga, Lauret, L Picamoles

**SUBSTITUTIONS**: M Machenaud for Doussain (41 mins); V Debaty for Nyanga (50 mins); D Chouly for Debaty (62 mins); R Talès, B Mach, Y Forestier & S Vahaamahina for Plisson, Szarzewski, Domingo & Maestri (63 mins); G Fickou for Bastareaud (70 mins)

**SCORERS**: *Penalty Goals*: Doussain, Plisson

**YELLOW CARDS**: Mas (50 mins), Picamoles (62 mins)

**REFEREE**: A Rolland (Ireland)

### 22 February, Stadio Olimpico, Rome

## ITALY 20 (2G 2PG) SCOTLAND 21 (1G 1T 2PG 1DG)

**ITALY**: L McLean; A Esposito, M Campagnaro, G Garcia, L Sarto; T Allan, E Gori; A de Marchi, L Ghiraldini, M Castrogiovanni, Q Geldenhuys, J Furno, A Zanni, R Barbieri, S Parisse (captain)

**SUBSTITUTIONS**: D Giazzon for Ghiraldini (55 mins); M Aguero & L Cittadini for de Marchi & Castrogiovanni (57 mins); P Derbyshire for Barbieri (58 mins); T Botes for Gori (63 mins); L Orquera for Allan (68 mins); M Bortolami for Zanni (73 mins)

**SCORERS**: *Tries*: Allan, Furno *Conversions*: Allan, Orquera *Penalty Goals*: Allan (2)

**SCOTLAND**: S Hogg; T Seymour, A Dunbar, M Scott, S Lamont; D Weir, G Laidlaw (captain); R Grant, S Lawson, M Low, R Gray, J Hamilton, R Wilson, C Fusaro, J Beattie

**SUBSTITUTIONS**: G Cross for Low (38 mins); D Denton for Fusaro (52 mins); M Evans for Seymour (55 mins); A Dickinson for Grant (58 mins); C Cusiter for Laidlaw (63 mins); D Taylor for Dunbar (72 mins)

**SCORERS**: *Tries*: Dunbar (2) *Conversion*: Weir *Penalty Goals*: Laidlaw (2) *Drop Goal*: Weir

**REFEREE**: S Walsh (Australia)

# ENGLAND 13 (1G 2PG) IRELAND 10 (1G 1PG)

**ENGLAND:** M Brown; J Nowell, L Burrell, B Twelvetrees, J May; O Farrell, D Care; J Marler, D Hartley, D Wilson, J Launchbury, C Lawes, T Wood, C Robshaw (captain), B Vunipola

**SUBSTITUTIONS:** B Morgan for B Vunipola (36 mins); M Vunipola for Marler (64 mins); H Thomas & D Attwood for Wilson & Wood (70 mins); T Youngs for Hartley (75 mins)

**SCORERS:** *Try:* Care *Conversion:* Farrell *Penalty Goals:* Farrell (2)

**IRELAND:** R Kearney; A Trimble, B O'Driscoll, G D'Arcy, D Kearney; J Sexton, C Murray; C Healy, R Best, M Ross, D Toner, P O'Connell (captain), P O'Mahony, C Henry, J Heaslip

**SUBSTITUTIONS:** M Moore for Ross (62 mins); F McFadden for Trimble (66 mins); I Henderson for O'Mahony (70 mins); J McGrath for Healy (72 mins); S Cronin & J Murphy for Best & Henry (74 mins); I Boss & P Jackson for Murray & O'Driscoll (80 mins)

**SCORERS:** *Try:* R Kearney *Conversion:* Sexton *Penalty Goal:* Sexton

**REFEREE:** C Joubert (South Africa)

# IRELAND 46 (4G 3T 1PG) ITALY 7 (1G)

**IRELAND:** R Kearney; A Trimble, B O'Driscoll, G D'Arcy, D Kearney; J Sexton, C Murray; C Healy, R Best, M Ross, D Toner, P O'Connell (captain), I Henderson, C Henry, J Heaslip

**SUBSTITUTIONS:** E Reddan for Murray (17 mins); J McGrath for Healy (53 mins); R Ruddock for Henderson (53 mins); S Cronin for Best (54 mins); M Moore for Ross (56 mins); F McFadden for O'Driscoll (61 mins); P Jackson for Sexton (63 mins); J Murphy for Henry (73 mins)

**SCORERS:** *Tries:* Sexton (2), Trimble, Healy, Cronin, McFadden, McGrath *Conversions:* Sexton (2), Jackson (2) *Penalty Goal:* Sexton

**ITALY:** L McLean; A Esposito, M Campagnaro, G Garcia, L Sarto; L Orquera, T Tebaldi; A de Marchi, L Ghiraldini, M Castrogiovanni, Q Geldenhuys, M Bortolami (captain), J Furno, P Derbyshire, R Barbieri

**SUBSTITUTIONS:** L Cittadini for Castrogiovanni (7 mins); M Rizzo & M Vosawai for de Marchi & Derbyshire (56 mins); A Masi, T Allan & A Pavanello for Garcia, Orquera & Bortolami (63 mins); E Gori & D Giazzon for Tebaldi & Ghiraldini (70 mins)

**SCORERS:** *Try:* Sarto *Conversion:* Orquera

**REFEREE:** N Owens (Wales)

## 8 March, Murrayfield, Edinburgh

# SCOTLAND 17 (2G 1PG) FRANCE 19 (1G 4PG)

**SCOTLAND**: S Hogg; T Seymour, A Dunbar, M Scott, S Lamont; D Weir, G Laidlaw; R Grant, S Lawson, G Cross, R Gray, J Hamilton, J Beattie, K Brown (captain), D Denton

**SUBSTITUTIONS**: R Wilson for Beattie (17 mins); M Evans for Lamont (29 mins); R Ford for Lawson (51 mins); T Swinson for Hamilton (68 mins)

**SCORERS**: *Tries:* Hogg, Seymour *Conversions:* Laidlaw (2) *Penalty Goals:* Weir

**FRANCE**: B Dulin; Y Huget, M Bastareaud, M Mermoz, M Médard; J Plisson, M Machenaud; T Domingo, B Mach, N Mas, Y Maestri, P Papé (captain), S Vahaamahina, A Lapandry, D Chouly

**SUBSTITUTIONS**: R Talès for Plisson (46 mins); G Guirado for Mach (47 mins); A Flanquart & R Slimani for Maestri & Mas (59 mins); A Claassen for Vahaamahina (66 mins); G Fickou & V Debaty for Bastereaud & Domingo (68 mins); J-M Doussain for Machenaud (74 mins)

**SCORERS**: *Try:* Huget *Conversion:* Machenaud *Penalty Goals:* Machenaud (3), Doussain

**REFEREE**: C Pollock (New Zealand)

## 9 March, Twickenham, London

# ENGLAND 29 (2G 5PG) WALES 18 (6PG)

**ENGLAND**: M Brown; J Nowell, L Burrell, B Twelvetrees, J May; O Farrell, D Care; J Marler, D Hartley, D Wilson, J Launchbury, C Lawes, T Wood, C Robshaw (captain), B Morgan

**SUBSTITUTIONS**: M Vunipola for Marler (64 mins); T Youngs for Hartley (69 mins); D Attwood & H Thomas for Launchbury & Wilson (73 mins); A Goode, L Dickson, G Ford & T Johnson for Brown, Care, Farrell & Wood (79 mins)

**SCORERS**: *Tries:* Care, Burrell *Conversions:* Farrell (2) *Penalty Goals:* Farrell (5)

**WALES**: L Halfpenny; A Cuthbert, J Davies, J Roberts, G North; R Priestland, R Webb; G Jenkins, R Hibbard, A Jones, J Ball, AW Jones, D Lydiate, S Warburton (captain), T Faletau

**SUBSTITUTIONS**: M Phillips for Webb (52 mins); K Owens for Hibbard (55 mins); D Biggar for Priestland (62 mins); P James for Jenkins (64 mins); R Jones for A Jones (67 mins); A Coombs for Ball (73 mins); L Williams & J Tipuric for Halfpenny & Lydiate (76 mins)

**SCORERS**: *Penalty Goals:* Halfpenny (6)

**YELLOW CARD**: Jenkins (53 mins)

**REFEREE**: R Poite (France)

## 15 March, Stadio Olimpico, Rome

# ITALY 11 (1T 2PG) ENGLAND 52 (7G 1PG)

**ITALY**: L McLean; A Esposito, M Campagnaro, G Garcia, L Sarto; L Orquera, T Tebaldi; M Aguero, L Ghiraldini, L Cittadini, Q Geldenhuys, M Bortolami, J Furno, R Barbieri, S Parisse (captain)

**SUBSTITUTIONS**: T Allan for Orquera (44 mins); M Rizzo & A de Marchi for Aguero & Cittadini (47 mins); P Derbyshire for Furno (56 mins); G Biagi for Derbyshire (61 mins); Cittadini for Rizzo (68 mins); A Masi for Garcia (73 mins)

**SCORERS**: *Try:* Sarto *Penalty Goals:* Orquera

**YELLOW CARD**: Bortolami (51 mins)

**ENGLAND**: M Brown; J Nowell, L Burrell, B Twelvetrees, J May; O Farrell, D Care; M Vunipola, D Hartley, D Wilson, J Launchbury, C Lawes, T Wood, C Robshaw (captain), B Morgan

**SUBSTITUTIONS**: T Youngs & M Tuilagi for Hartley & Burrell (54 mins); L Dickson & T Johnson for Care & Wood (67 mins); G Ford, H Thomas & D Attwood for Twelvetrees, Wilson & Launchbury (71 mins); M Mullan for Vunipola (76 mins)

**SCORERS**: *Tries:* Brown (2), Farrell, Nowell, M Vunipola, Tuilagi, Robshaw *Conversions:* Farrell (7) *Penalty Goal:* Farrell

**REFEREE**: P Gauzere (France)

## 15 March, Millennium Stadium, Cardiff

# WALES 51 (5G 2T 2PG) SCOTLAND 3 (1PG)

**WALES**: L Williams; A Cuthbert, J Davies, J Roberts, G North; D Biggar, M Phillips; G Jenkins, K Owens, R Jones, L Charteris, AW Jones, D Lydiate, S Warburton (captain), T Faletau

**SUBSTITUTIONS**: J Tipuric & R Williams for Lydiate & Phillips (55 mins); P James, R Hibbard & A Jones for Jenkins, Owens & R Jones (58 mins); J Ball, J Hook & R Priestland for Charteris, Williams & Biggar (63 mins)

**SCORERS**: *Tries:* North (2), Roberts (2), L Williams, Faletau, R Williams *Conversions:* Biggar (4), Hook *Penalty Goals:* Biggar (2)

**SCOTLAND**: S Hogg; D Fife, A Dunbar, M Scott, M Evans; D Weir, G Laidlaw; R Grant, S Lawson, G Cross, R Gray, J Hamilton, R Wilson, K Brown (captain), D Denton

**SUBSTITUTIONS**: A Strokosch for Brown (9 mins); A Dickinson & R Ford for Grant & Lawson (46 mins); T Swinson for Hamilton (55 mins); C Cusiter for Laidlaw (62 mins); D Taylor for Fife (67 mins)

**SCORERS**: *Penalty Goal:* Laidlaw

**RED CARD**: Hogg (22 mins)

**REFEREE**: J Garces (France)

15 March, Stade de France, Paris

# FRANCE 20 (2G 2PG) IRELAND 22 (2G 1T 1PG)

**FRANCE**: B Dulin; Y Huget, M Bastareaud, G Fickou, M Médard; R Talès, M Machenaud; T Domingo, D Szarzewski, N Mas, Y Maestri, P Papé (captain), L Picamoles, A Lapandry, D Chouly

**SUBSTITUTIONS**: R Slimani for Mas (36 mins); V Debaty for Domingo (41 mins); A Flanquart for Maestri (53 mins); J-M Doussain & S Vahaamahina for Machenaud & Picamoles (66 mins); G Guirado for Szarzewski (68 mins); M Mermoz & W Lauret for Fickou & Lapandry (75 mins)

**SCORERS**: *Tries:* Dulin, Szarzewski *Conversions:* Machenaud (2) *Penalty Goals:* Machenaud (2)

**IRELAND**: R Kearney; A Trimble, B O'Driscoll, G D'Arcy, D Kearney; J Sexton, C Murray; C Healy, R Best, M Ross, D Toner, P O'Connell (captain), P O'Mahony, C Henry, J Heaslip

**SUBSTITUTIONS**: E Reddan, M Moore & I Henderson for Murray, Ross & O'Mahony (63 mins); F McFadden for D'Arcy (66 mins); I Madigan for Sexton (68 mins); J McGrath & S Cronin for Healy & Best (70 mins)

**SCORERS**: *Tries:* Sexton (2), Trimble *Conversions:* Sexton (2) *Penalty Goal:* Sexton

**REFEREE**: S Walsh (Australia)

Getty Images

Duncan Weir kicks the winning drop goal for Scotland in Rome despite the Italian players' attempts to charge him down.

**RBS SIX NATIONS**

## PREVIOUS WINNERS:

| | | |
|---|---|---|
| 1883 England | 1884 England | 1885 Not completed |
| 1886 England & Scotland | 1887 Scotland | 1888 Not completed |
| 1889 Not completed | 1890 England & Scotland | 1891 Scotland |
| 1892 England | 1893 Wales | 1894 Ireland |
| 1895 Scotland | 1896 Ireland | 1897 Not completed |
| 1898 Not completed | 1899 Ireland | 1900 Wales |
| 1901 Scotland | 1902 Wales | 1903 Scotland |
| 1904 Scotland | 1905 Wales | 1906 Ireland & Wales |
| 1907 Scotland | 1908 Wales | 1909 Wales |
| 1910 England | 1911 Wales | 1912 England & Ireland |
| 1913 England | 1914 England | 1920 England & Scotland & Wales |
| 1921 England | 1922 Wales | 1923 England |
| 1924 England | 1925 Scotland | 1926 Scotland & Ireland |
| 1927 Scotland & Ireland | 1928 England | 1929 Scotland |
| 1930 England | 1931 Wales | 1932 England & Ireland & Wales |
| 1933 Scotland | 1934 England | 1935 Ireland |
| 1936 Wales | 1937 England | 1938 Scotland |
| 1939 England & Ireland & Wales | 1947 England & Wales | 1948 Ireland |
| 1949 Ireland | 1950 Wales | 1951 Ireland |
| 1952 Wales | 1953 England | 1954 England & Wales & France |
| 1955 Wales & France | 1956 Wales | 1957 England |
| 1958 England | 1959 France | 1960 England & France |
| 1961 France | 1962 France | 1963 England |
| 1964 Scotland & Wales | 1965 Wales | 1966 Wales |
| 1967 France | 1968 France | 1969 Wales |
| 1970 Wales & France | 1971 Wales | 1972 Not completed |
| 1973 Five Nations tie | 1974 Ireland | 1975 Wales |
| 1976 Wales | 1977 France | 1978 Wales |
| 1979 Wales | 1980 England | 1981 France |
| 1982 Ireland | 1983 Ireland & France | 1984 Scotland |
| 1985 Ireland | 1986 Scotland & France | 1987 France |
| 1988 Wales & France | 1989 France | 1990 Scotland |
| 1991 England | 1992 England | 1993 France |
| 1994 Wales | 1995 England | 1996 England |
| 1997 France | 1998 France | 1999 Scotland |
| 2000 England | 2001 England | 2002 France |
| 2003 England | 2004 France | 2005 Wales |
| 2006 France | 2007 France | 2008 Wales |
| 2009 Ireland | 2010 France | 2011 England |
| 2012 Wales | 2013 Wales | 2014 Ireland |

*England and Wales have both won the title outright 26 times; France 17; Scotland 14; Ireland 12; Italy 0.*

## TRIPLE CROWN WINNERS:

**England** (24 times) 1883, 1884, 1892, 1913, 1914, 1921, 1923, 1924, 1928, 1934, 1937, 1954, 1957, 1960, 1980, 1991, 1992, 1995, 1996, 1997, 1998, 2002, 2003, 2014

**Wales** (20 times) 1893, 1900, 1902, 1905, 1908, 1909, 1911, 1950, 1952, 1965, 1969, 1971, 1976, 1977, 1978, 1979, 1988, 2005, 2008, 2012

**Scotland** (10 times) 1891, 1895, 1901, 1903, 1907, 1925, 1933, 1938, 1984, 1990

**Ireland** (10 times) 1894, 1899, 1948, 1949, 1982, 1985, 2004, 2006, 2007, 2009

## GRAND SLAM WINNERS:

**England** (12 times) 1913, 1914, 1921, 1923, 1924, 1928, 1957, 1980, 1991, 1992, 1995, 2003

**Wales** (11 times) 1908, 1909, 1911, 1950, 1952, 1971, 1976, 1978, 2005, 2008, 2012

**France** (Nine times) 1968, 1977, 1981, 1987, 1997, 1998, 2002, 2004, 2010

**Scotland** (Three times) 1925, 1984, 1990

**Ireland** (Twice) 1948, 2009

# THE SIX NATIONS CHAMPIONSHIP 2000–2014:

## COMPOSITE TABLE

| | P | W | D | L | Pts |
|---|---|---|---|---|---|
| England | 75 | 51 | 1 | 23 | 103 |
| France | 75 | 50 | 2 | 23 | 102 |
| Ireland | 75 | 49 | 2 | 24 | 100 |
| Wales | 75 | 40 | 2 | 33 | 82 |
| Scotland | 75 | 19 | 2 | 54 | 40 |
| Italy | 75 | 11 | 1 | 63 | 23 |

# INTERNATIONAL CHAMPIONSHIP RECORDS

| RECORD | DETAIL | | SET |
|---|---|---|---|
| Most team points in season | 229 by England | in five matches | 2001 |
| Most team tries in season | 29 by England | in five matches | 2001 |
| Highest team score | 80 by England | 80–23 v Italy | 2001 |
| Biggest team win | 57 by England | 80–23 v Italy | 2001 |
| Most team tries in match | 12 by Scotland | v Wales | 1887 |
| Most appearances | 65 for Ireland | BG O'Driscoll | 2000–2014 |
| Most points in matches | 557 for Ireland | RJR O'Gara | 2000–2013 |
| Most points in season | 89 for England | JP Wilkinson | 2001 |
| Most points in match | 35 for England | JP Wilkinson | v Italy, 2001 |
| Most tries in matches | 26 for Ireland | BG O'Driscoll | 2000–2014 |
| Most tries in season | 8 for England | CN Lowe | 1914 |
| | 8 for Scotland | IS Smith | 1925 |
| Most tries in match | 5 for Scotland | GC Lindsay | v Wales, 1887 |
| Most cons in matches | 89 for England | JP Wilkinson | 1998–2011 |
| Most cons in season | 24 for England | JP Wilkinson | 2001 |
| Most cons in match | 9 for England | JP Wilkinson | v Italy, 2001 |
| Most pens in matches | 109 for Ireland | RJR O'Gara | 2000–2013 |
| Most pens in season | 19 for Wales | SL Halfpenny | 2013 |
| Most pens in match | 7 for England | SD Hodgkinson | v Wales, 1991 |
| | 7 for England | CR Andrew | v Scotland, 1995 |
| | 7 for England | JP Wilkinson | v France, 1999 |
| | 7 for Wales | NR Jenkins | v Italy, 2000 |
| | 7 for France | G Merceron | v Italy, 2002 |
| | 7 for Scotland | CD Paterson | v Wales, 2007 |
| | 7 for Wales | SL Halfpenny | v Scotland, 2013 |
| Most drops in matches | 11 for England | JP Wilkinson | 1998–2011 |
| Most drops in season | 5 for France | G Camberabero | 1967 |
| | 5 for Italy | D Dominguez | 2000 |
| | 5 for Wales | NR Jenkins | 2001 |
| | 5 for England | JP Wilkinson | 2003 |
| | 5 for Scotland | DA Parks | 2010 |
| Most drops in match | 3 for France | P Albaladejo | v Ireland, 1960 |
| | 3 for France | J-P Lescarboura | v England, 1985 |
| | 3 for Italy | D Dominguez | v Scotland, 2000 |
| | 3 for Wales | NR Jenkins | v Scotland, 2001 |

INTERNATIONAL
RUGBY BOARD

In partnership with

WORLD
ANTI-DOPING
AGENCY
play true

Felipe Contepomi, Argentina
IRB Anti-Doping Ambassador

Be super NATURAL.
Join us in the fight
against doping –

Keep Rugby Clean!

# KEEP RUGBY CLEAN
## IRB ANTI-DOPING

# THE RUGBY CHAMPIONSHIP

# ALL BLACKS ON TOP AGAIN AS ARGENTINA CREATE HISTORY

*By Greg Thomas*

The All Blacks celebrate after beating Argentina to win The Rugby Championship with a round to spare.

The name on the trophy remained the same, with New Zealand securing a third successive Rugby Championship title. Somewhat concerning for South Africa, Australia and Argentina was that statistically it was the All Blacks' worst showing to date and yet the world champions were still confirmed as winners with a round to spare.

The All Blacks drew their opener 12–12 with Australia to miss out on a record 18th consecutive Test victory, and also lost their first match since the expanded Championship began in 2012, 27–25 to South Africa in Johannesburg. That match was by far the best of the 2014 edition and it took every ounce of energy by the Springboks to end the All Blacks' 22-Test unbeaten run.

Remarkably, with both teams seemingly out on their feet and the benches empty, it took a 55-metre penalty by Pat Lambie to win it. Both sides scored three tries in a fast-flowing, entertaining game with the emerging talent of Handré Pollard, who scored two tries, coming to the fore for South Africa.

"It was a great game of rugby and could have gone either way, but my heart tells me the Boks deserved it today," admitted All Blacks coach Steve Hansen. "After giving the Boks a 24–13 head-start, I thought we came home OK, we were pretty good I reckon. I will reiterate that the right team won, but having said that we're still bloody proud and would have been happy had we snuck it."

This was the last full Rugby Championship before Rugby World Cup 2015 in England, as next year's edition will see the teams only face each other once. It highlighted the strength of the New Zealand squad in terms of depth and their ability to cover injuries. Out wide Israel Dagg, Ben Smith, Julian Savea, Cory Jane, Malakai Fekitoa, Ma'a Nonu and Conrad Smith provided numerous attacking options, while at fly-half Beauden Barrett, Aaron Cruden and Colin Slade directed operations across the field.

Then there is the back row that provides the unwavering impetus for the side. The inspirational leader Richie McCaw, IRB Player of the Year 2013 Kieran Read, Jerome Kaino, Liam Messam, Sam Cane and Steven Luatua all had game time and provided the perfect link between the tight-five and the backline.

One nagging doubt for some supporters is the age of the squad, with several key figures the wrong side of 30. Others will argue that they only get better with age and in the case of McCaw it is hard to argue otherwise.

What is not in question is the pace at which New Zealand played and the ruthlessness they exhibited in counter-attack and in pouncing on opposition mistakes, something that has become a trademark of the modern All Blacks. In six matches they scored 18 tries, with destructive winger Savea crossing four times. Next best was South Africa with 13.

South Africa, like most teams, have struggled to beat the All Blacks in recent years but took great solace from that victory in Johannesburg.

However, defeats away from home in rounds three and four, to Australia in Perth (24–23) and the All Blacks in Wellington (14–10), ultimately cost them a chance of winning the title.

Coach Heyneke Meyer did experiment with his squad, but found it hard to balance the introduction of new talent like Pollard, the 20-year-old who had been named IRB Junior Player of the Year in June, and sticking with the tried and tested but ageing warriors Victor Matfield, Bryan Habana, Jean de Villiers, Schalk Burger, Juan Smith, Morné Steyn and Bakkies Botha. Like several of their All Black counterparts they are on the wrong side of 30 and it will be interesting to see if Meyer keeps faith with his warriors for another year.

The Springboks opened their campaign with matches against Argentina, but struggled to dominate the Pumas, who are clearly emerging from a rebuilding phase. They edged them 13–6 at Loftus Versfeld and 33–31 in Salta, before losing to Australia and question marks started to appear over their form. Indeed the Pumas were unlucky to lose in Salta after leading for much of the match.

To keep their title hopes alive, the Springboks had to win in Wellington. Captain de Villiers played his 100th Test on a day the visitors clearly showed intent to slow the game down and put the All Blacks off their game plan. Read was a standout for the All Blacks, making a host of dangerous offloads and he produced the play of the day when leaping to collect a cross-kick and then offloading to a charging McCaw for New Zealand's only try. There was a downside to the win, though, with Nonu suffering a broken arm to end his Championship.

Australia again had to settle for third, just as they had done in 2013. The campaign had started so promisingly in Sydney where they should have beaten the All Blacks but failed to take several opportunities, a trait that would resurface later in the Championship. A lengthy injury list and a camp that appeared far from united at times on the road struggled for most of the campaign, which yielded the draw with New Zealand and wins at home against South Africa and Argentina, but three straight defeats on the road.

Although a slight improvement on their 2013 campaign, it was a disappointing tournament as Australian fans had high hopes following the NSW Waratahs' Super Rugby success. The early draw against the defending champions appeared to inject new confidence, but that was quickly shattered a week later when the All Blacks put the Wallabies to the sword 51–20 at Eden Park. Perhaps surprisingly coach Ewen McKenzie had chosen Kurtley Beale at fly-half and Brumbies centre Matt Toomua for the two Tests against the All Blacks, thereby breaking up the very successful and potent attacking 10–12–13–15 axis of Bernard

Foley, Beale, Adam Ashley-Cooper and Israel Folau that had served the Waratahs so well.

It was a short-lived selection and Foley started the third match against the Springboks in Perth, one which saw Habana reach the milestone of 100 Tests. Foley's more assured poise and kicking reaped rewards and he slotted the late conversion to give Australia a 24–23 victory. It was a reminder of his kicking heroics for the Waratahs in the Super Rugby final against the Crusaders and the No.10 jersey was his for the rest of the Championship.

Full-back Folau continued to impress but after the Wallabies held off the brave Pumas on the Gold Coast, the campaign ended with disappointing losses in Cape Town and Mendoza. In both matches the Wallabies held handy leads and went in ahead at half-time, but each time they faltered after the break and worryingly failed to capitalise on these good starts, wasting several scoring opportunities.

In Cape Town, the Wallabies looked set to increase their 10–5 half-time advantage but were unlucky to have a try disallowed. Brave defence then kept South Africa at bay until the 70th minute before they were overrun. It could have had something to do with the 260 tackles the side made during the match or the growing number of injuries, or both. Either way, it cost the Wallabies and a drop goal and three tries in the last 10 minutes won the match for the Springboks.

The 21–17 victory for Argentina in Mendoza was just reward for a Pumas side that had come very close to beating the Springboks and acquitted themselves well against the All Blacks. It was also the first ever victory for the Pumas in The Rugby Championship, at the 18th time of asking. Trailing 14–0, the Pumas made the most of a yellow card to Wallaby scrum-half Nick Phipps early in the second half with tries from Leonardo Senatore and Juan Imhoff.

After pushing the Springboks so close it had looked as though two bonus points from those matches and another against Australia on the Gold Coast would be meagre reward for a spirited campaign. The final whistle understandably sparked jubilant celebrations and helped to cushion the fact that the Pumas had again finished bottom of the standings.

However, with a blend of developing new talent and experience the Pumas were highly competitive in all their matches. A powerful scrum, competent lineout and an appetite to play more expansive rugby than in the past revealed the Pumas could be a serious proposition at RWC 2015. Their heaviest defeat was the credible 34–13 loss to the All Blacks in La Plata that saw their visitors wrap up the title.

The experienced centres Marcelo Bosch and Juan Martín Hernández are a formidable pairing that served exciting full-back Joaquín Tuculet and young wing Manual Montero with plenty of ball out wide. Nicolás Sánchez has developed into a quality Test fly-half – he was top point scorer in the Championship – and coach Daniel Hourcade utilised his two scum-halves, Martín Landajo and Tomás Cubelli, to perfection.

The experience provided up front by the likes of Juan Martín Fernández Lobbe, Juan Manuel Leguizamón, Marcos Ayerza and captain Agustín Creevy was instrumental in driving the Pumas forward and competing at the breakdown. New blood, that had Pumas fans excited, included second row Tomas Lavanini and prop Ramiro Herrera.

Hourcade declared his delight at the victory and indicated his team was definitely heading in the right direction a year out from the World Cup. "I'm full of emotion," he said. "We gave a huge effort and this win will give us huge encouragement. This isn't just the end of the tournament, it's the start of something. We have a lot of areas to improve on and many details to work on, but this showed that we're on the right track and that's important."

Argentina's players can't hide their joy at winning a first match in The Rugby Championship at the 18th attempt.

**THE RUGBY CHAMPIONSHIP**

# THE RUGBY CHAMPIONSHIP 2014 FINAL STANDINGS

|  | P | W | D | L | F | A | BP | PTS |
|---|---|---|---|---|---|---|---|---|
| New Zealand | 6 | 4 | 1 | 1 | 164 | 91 | 4 | 22 |
| South Africa | 6 | 4 | 0 | 2 | 134 | 110 | 3 | 19 |
| Australia | 6 | 2 | 1 | 3 | 115 | 160 | 1 | 11 |
| Argentina | 6 | 1 | 0 | 5 | 105 | 157 | 3 | 7 |

Getty Images

South Africa ended New Zealand's long unbeaten run but the All Blacks still claimed The Rugby Championship title.

## 16 August, ANZ Stadium, Sydney

# AUSTRALIA 12 (4PG) NEW ZEALAND 12 (4PG)

**AUSTRALIA**: I Folau; P McCabe, A Ashley-Cooper, M Toomua, R Horne; K Beale, N White; J Slipper, N Charles, S Kepu, S Carter, R Simmons, S Fardy, M Hooper (captain), W Palu

**SUBSTITUTIONS**: S Higginbotham for Fardy (66 mins); N Phipps for White (66 mins); B Foley for Beale (70 mins); P Cowan for Slipper (70 mins); W Skelton for Palu (70 mins); B Alexander for Kepu (78 mins)

**SCORERS**: *Penalty Goals*: Beale (4)

**NEW ZEALAND**: B Smith; C Jane, M Fekitoa, M Nonu, J Savea; A Cruden, A Smith; W Crockett, D Coles, O Franks, B Retallick, S Whitelock, J Kaino, R McCaw (captain), K Read

**SUBSTITUTIONS**: B Franks for Kaino (39 mins); Kaino for Crockett (48 mins); K Mealamu for Coles (52 mins); R Crotty for Nonu (57 mins); B Barrett for Cruden (63 mins); S Cane for Kaino (69 mins); J Moody for O Franks (70 mins)

**SCORERS**: *Penalty Goals*: Cruden (4)

**YELLOW CARDS**: Crockett (39 mins); Barrett (69 mins)

**REFEREE**: J Peyper (South Africa)

## 16 August, Loftus Versfeld, Pretoria

# SOUTH AFRICA 13 (1G 2PG) ARGENTINA 6 (2PG)

**SOUTH AFRICA**: W le Roux; C Hendricks, D de Allende, J de Villiers (captain), B Habana; H Pollard, R Pienaar; T Mtawarira, B du Plessis, J du Plessis, B Botha, L de Jager, F Louw, M Coetzee, D Vermeulen

**SUBSTITUTIONS**: E Etzebeth for B Botha (41 mins); M Steyn for Pollard (45 mins); A Strauss for B du Plessis (55 mins); F Malherbe for J du Plessis (66 mins); T Nyakane for Mtawarira (79 mins)

**SCORERS**: *Try*: Pienaar *Conversion*: Pollard *Penalty Goals*: Pollard, Steyn

**ARGENTINA**: J Tuculet; H Agulla, M Bosch, S González Iglesias, M Montero; N Sánchez, M Landajo; M Ayerza, A Creevy (captain), R Herrera, M Galarza, T Lavanini, P Matera, JM Fernández Lobbe, JM Leguizamón

**SUBSTITUTIONS**: T Cubelli for Landajo (41 mins); L Senatore for Matera (57 mins); L González Amorosino for Agulla (60 mins); N Tetaz Chaparro for Herrera (60 mins); J de la Fuente for Sánchez (63 mins); M Alemanno for Lavanini (76 mins); L Noguera Paz for Ayerza (79 mins)

**SCORERS**: *Penalty Goals*: Sánchez (2)

**REFEREE**: J Lacey (Ireland)

THE RUGBY CHAMPIONSHIP

**23 August, Eden Park, Auckland**

# NEW ZEALAND 51 (6G 3PG) AUSTRALIA 20 (2G 2PG)

**NEW ZEALAND**: B Smith; C Jane, C Smith, R Crotty, J Savea; A Cruden, A Smith; W Crockett, D Coles, O Franks, B Retallick, S Whitelock, L Messam, R McCaw (captain), K Read

**SUBSTITUTIONS**: M Fekitoa for Crotty (41 mins); B Barrett for Jane (46 mins); B Franks for Crockett (60 mins); C Faumuina for O Franks (60 mins); S Luatua for Messam (64 mins); K Mealamu for Coles (67 mins); S Cane for Retallick (71 mins); TJ Perenara for Cruden (78 mins)

**SCORERS**: *Tries*: Penalty try, Savea, Read, McCaw (2), Luatua *Conversions*: Cruden (5), Barrett *Penalty Goals*: Cruden (3)

**YELLOW CARDS**: McCaw (13 mins); B Franks (78 mins)

**AUSTRALIA**: I Folau; P McCabe, A Ashley-Cooper, M Toomua, R Horne; K Beale, N White; J Slipper, N Charles, S Kepu, S Carter, R Simmons, S Fardy, M Hooper (captain), W Palu

**SUBSTITUTIONS**: J Hanson for Charles (32 mins); N Phipps for White (52 mins); B Foley for Toomua (57 mins); S Higginbotham for Palu (57 mins), W Skelton for Fardy (65 mins), B Alexander for Kepu (65 mins), T Kuridrani for McCabe (66 mins)

**SCORERS**: *Tries*: Folau, Hooper *Conversions*: Beale (2) *Penalty Goals*: Beale (2)

**YELLOW CARD**: Simmons (23 mins)

**REFEREE**: R Poite (France)

Getty Images

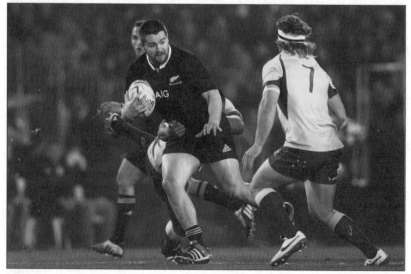

New Zealand's Dane Coles makes ground during the All Blacks' 51–20 win over Australia in The Rugby Championship.

## 23 August, Estadio Padre Ernesto Martearena, Salta

# ARGENTINA 31 (2G 1T 3PG 1DG) SOUTH AFRICA 33 (3G 4PG)

**ARGENTINA**: J Tuculet; L González Amorosino, M Bosch, JM Hernández, M Montero; N Sánchez, M Landajo; M Ayerza, A Creevy (captain), R Herrrera, M Galarza, T Lavanini, P Matera, JM Fernández Lobbe, JM Leguizamón

**SUBSTITUTIONS**: T Cubelli for Landajo (34 mins); L Senatore for Matera (36 mins); N Tetaz Chaparro for Herrera (67 mins); M Alemanno for Lavanini (70 mins); J de la Fuente for Sánchez (77 mins); B Postiglioni for Ayerza (77 mins); H Agulla for Montero (77 mins); M Cortese for Creevy (79 mins)

**SCORERS**: *Tries*: Montero, Cubelli, Tuculet *Conversions*: Sánchez (2) *Penalty Goals*: Sánchez (2), Bosch *Drop Goal*: Hernández

**SOUTH AFRICA**: W le Roux; C Hendricks, D de Allende, J de Villiers (captain), B Habana; H Pollard, R Pienaar; G Steenkamp, B du Plessis, J du Plessis, E Etzebeth, L de Jager, F Louw, J Smith, D Vermeulen

**SUBSTITUTIONS**: T Mtawarira for Steenkamp (46 mins); F Malherbe for J du Plessis (46 mins); M Coetzee for Smith (52 mins); A Strauss for B du Plessis (52 mins); M Steyn for Pollard (56 mins); F Hougaard for Pienaar (60 mins); B Botha for Etzebeth (71 mins); J du Plessis for Malherbe (78 mins)

**SCORERS**: *Tries*: Habana, Hendricks, Coetzee *Conversions*: Pollard, Steyn (2) *Penalty Goals*: Pollard (3), Steyn

**REFEREE**: S Walsh (Australia)

## 6 September, McLean Park, Napier

# NEW ZEALAND 28 (1G 3T 2PG) ARGENTINA 9 (3PG)

**NEW ZEALAND**: I Dagg; B Smith, C Smith, M Nonu, J Savea; B Barrett, A Smith; W Crockett, D Coles, O Franks, B Retallick, S Whitelock, L Messam, R McCaw (captain), K Read

**SUBSTITUTIONS**: J Thrush for Whitelock (28 mins); S Cane for Messam (44 mins); C Slade for Barrett (56 mins); J Moody for Crockett (59 mins), K Mealamu for Coles (65 mins); B Franks for O Franks (65 mins); TJ Perenara for A Smith (74 mins)

**SCORERS**: *Tries*: Savea (2), Messam, A Smith *Conversion*: Slade *Penalty Goals*: Barrett, Slade

**ARGENTINA**: J Tuculet; H Agulla, M Bosch, JM Hernández, L González Amorosino; N Sánchez, M Landajo; M Ayerza, A Creevy (captain), R Herrrera, M Galarza, T Lavanini, JM Leguizamón, JM Fernández Lobbe, L Senatore

**SUBSTITUTIONS**: T Cubelli for Landajo (54 mins); L Noguera Paz for Ayerza (65 mins); N Tetaz Chaparro for Herrera (65 mins); R Báez for Senatore (66 mins); JJ Imhoff for Agulla (66 mins); M Cortese for Creevy (74 mins); M Alemanno for Galarza (74 mins); S González Iglesias for Sánchez (74 mins)

**SCORERS**: *Penalty Goals*: Sánchez (3)

**REFEREE**: P Gauzere (France)

## 6 September, Patersons Stadium, Perth

# AUSTRALIA 24 (1G 1T 4PG) SOUTH AFRICA 23 (1T 6PG)

**AUSTRALIA**: I Folau; A Ashley-Cooper, T Kuridrani, M Toomua, R Horne; B Foley, N Phipps; J Slipper, J Hanson, S Kepu, S Carter, R Simmons, S Fardy, M Hooper (captain), W Palu

**SUBSTITUTIONS**: P Cowan for Slipper (53 mins); J Horwill for Carter (60 mins); S Higginbotham for Palu (60 mins); B Alexander for Kepu (67 mins); M Hodgson for Fardy (71 mins); K Beale for Toomua (73 mins)

**SCORERS**: *Tries*: Folau, Horne *Conversion*: Foley *Penalty Goals*: Foley (4)

**SOUTH AFRICA**: W le Roux; C Hendricks, J Serfontein, J de Villiers (captain), B Habana; M Steyn, R Pienaar; T Mtawarira, A Strauss, J du Plessis, E Etzebeth, V Matfield, F Louw, M Coetzee, D Vermeulen

**SUBSTITUTIONS**: B du Plessis for Strauss (61 mins); M van der Merwe for du Plessis (67 mins); T Nyakane for Mtawarira (69 mins); P Lambie for Louw (69 mins); L de Jager for Etzebeth (73 mins)

**SCORERS**: *Try*: Hendricks *Penalty Goals*: Steyn (6)

**YELLOW CARD**: Habana (66 mins)

**REFEREE**: G Clancy (Ireland)

## 13 September, Westpac Stadium, Wellington

# NEW ZEALAND 14 (1T 3PG) SOUTH AFRICA 10 (1G 1DG)

**NEW ZEALAND**: I Dagg; B Smith, C Smith, M Nonu, J Savea; A Cruden, A Smith; W Crockett, D Coles, O Franks, B Retallick, J Thrush, S Luatua, R McCaw (captain), K Read

**SUBSTITUTIONS**: C Jane for Nonu (41 mins); S Cane for Luatua (50 mins); J Moody for Crockett (59 mins); B Barrett for Cruden (59 mins); B Franks for O Franks (59 mins); K Mealamu for D Coles (72 mins); P Tuipulotu for Thrush (78 mins)

**SCORERS**: *Try*: McCaw *Penalty Goals*: Cruden (2), Barrett

**SOUTH AFRICA**: W le Roux; C Hendricks, J Serfontein, J de Villiers (captain), B Habana; H Pollard, R Pienaar; T Mtawarira, A Strauss, J du Plessis, E Etzebeth, V Matfield, F Louw, M Coetzee, D Vermeulen

**SUBSTITUTIONS**: F Hougaard for Pienaar (36 mins); W Whiteley for Louw (47 mins); B du Plessis for Strauss (55 mins); T Nyakane for Mtawarira (67 mins); P Lambie for le Roux (72 mins); de Jager for Etzebeth (72 mins); M van der Merwe for J du Plessis (78 mins)

**SCORERS**: *Try*: Hendricks *Conversion*: Pollard *Drop Goal*: Pollard

**REFEREE**: J Garces (France)

# AUSTRALIA 32 (1G 2T 5PG) ARGENTINA 25 (2G 1T 2PG)

**AUSTRALIA**: I Folau; P Betham, T Kuridrani, M Toomua, R Horne; B Foley, N Phipps; J Slipper, T Polota-Nau, S Kepu, S Carter, R Simmons, S Fardy, M Hooper (captain), B McCalman

**SUBSTITUTIONS**: J Hanson for Polota-Nau (41 mins); P Cowan for Slipper (50 mins); S Higginbotham for Fardy (50 mins); K Beale for Toomua (53 mins); B Alexander for Kepu (59 mins); J Horwill for Carter (62 mins); M Hodgson for McCalman (70 mins); N White for Betham (72 mins)

**SCORERS**: *Tries*: Hooper (2), Betham *Conversion*: Foley *Penalty Goals*: Foley (5)

**ARGENTINA**: J Tuculet; JJ Imhoff, M Bosch, JM Hernández, M Montero; N Sánchez, M Landajo; M Ayerza, A Creevy (captain), R Herrrera, M Galarza, M Alemanno, JM Leguizamón, JM Fernández Lobbe, L Senatore

**SUBSTITUTIONS**: B Macome for Senatore (temp 34–41 mins); R Báez for Leguizam for Leguizamón (50 mins); J de la Fuente for Hernández (50 mins); B Postiglioni for Ayerza (temp 50-59 mins & 68 mins); T Cubelli for Landajo (56 mins); N Tetaz Chaparro for Herrera (59 mins); Macome for Galarza (65 mins); M Cortese for Creevy (72 mins); L González Amorosino for Montero (79 mins)

**SCORERS**: *Tries*: Montero, Bosch, Tuculet *Conversions*: Sánchez (2) *Penalty Goals*: Sánchez (2)

**REFEREE**: G Jackson (New Zealand)

# SOUTH AFRICA 28 (1G 3T 1PG 1DG) AUSTRALIA 10 (1G 1PG)

**SOUTH AFRICA**: W le Roux; C Hendricks, J Serfontein, J de Villiers (captain), B Habana; H Pollard, F Hougaard; T Mtawarira, A Strauss, J du Plessis, E Etzebeth, V Matfield, M Coetzee, O Mohoje, D Vermeulen

**SUBSTITUTIONS**: J-P Pietersen for Habana (temp 27-37 mins & 41 mins); S Burger for Mohoje (54 mins); B du Plessis for Strauss (58 mins); P Lambie for Pollard (58 mins); B Botha for Vermeulen (61 mins); M van der Merwe for J du Plessis (65 mins); T Nyakane for Mtawarira (70 mins); C Reinach for Hougaard (77 mins)

**SCORERS**: *Tries*: Coetzee, de Villiers (2), Lambie *Conversion*: Lambie *Penalty Goal*: Pollard *Drop Goal*: Lambie

**AUSTRALIA**: I Folau; A Ashley-Cooper, T Kuridrani, M Toomua, J Tomane; B Foley, N Phipps; J Slipper, S Faingaa, S Kepu, S Carter, R Simmons, S Fardy, M Hooper (captain), B McCalman

**SUBSTITUTIONS**: J Horwill for Simmons (41 mins); K Beale for Toomua (54 mins); S Higginbotham for McCalman (59 mins); J Hanson for Faingaa (62 mins); B Robinson for Slipper (66 mins); R Horne for Tomane (67 mins); B Alexander for Kepu (70 mins)

**SCORERS**: *Try*: Ashley-Cooper *Conversion*: Foley *Penalty Goal*: Foley

**REFEREE**: N Owens (Wales)

## 27 September, Estadio Ciudad de La Plata, La Plata

# ARGENTINA 13 (1G 2PG) NEW ZEALAND 34 (4G 2PG)

**ARGENTINA**: J Tuculet; JJ Imhoff, M Bosch, JM Hernández, M Montero; N Sánchez, T Cubelli; M Ayerza, A Creevy (captain), R Herrrera, M Galarza, T Lavinini, B Macome, JM Fernández Lobbe, L Senatore

**SUBSTITUTIONS**: N Tetaz Chaparro for Herrera (54 mins); M Landajo for Cubelli (54 mins); S González Iglesias for Hernández (59 mins); R Báez for Senatore (60 mins); M Alemanno for Galarza (61 mins); L Noguera Paz for Ayerza (64 mins); H Agulla for Bosch (66 mins); M Cortese for Creevy (71 mins)

**SCORERS**: *Try*: Agulla *Conversion*: González Iglesias *Penalty Goals*: Sánchez (2)

**NEW ZEALAND**: I Dagg; B Smith, C Smith, M Fekitoa, J Savea; B Barrett, A Smith; W Crockett, K Mealamu, O Franks, B Retallick, S Whitelock, J Kaino, R McCaw (captain), K Read

**SUBSTITUTIONS**: J Moody for Crockett (temp 1-11 mins & 54 mins); J Thrush for Retallick (54 mins); S Cane for McCaw (66 mins); T Perenara for B Smith (66 mins); B Franks for O Franks (70 mins); N Harris for Mealamu (73 mins); C Slade for C Smith (73 mins)

**SCORERS**: *Tries*: B Smith, Dagg, Savea, Perenara *Conversions*: Barrett (4) *Penalty Goals*: Barrett (2)

**REFEREE**: C Joubert (South Africa)

## 4 October, Ellis Park, Johannesburg

# SOUTH AFRICA 27 (3G 2PG) NEW ZEALAND 25 (2G 1T 2PG)

**SOUTH AFRICA**: W le Roux; C Hendricks, J Serfontein, J de Villiers (captain), B Habana; H Pollard, F Hougaard; T Mtawarira, B du Plessis, J du Plessis, E Etzebeth, V Matfield, M Coetzee, O Mohoje, D Vermeulen

**SUBSTITUTIONS**: S Burger for Mohoje (50 mins); A Strauss for B du Plessis (53 mins); JP Pietersen for Hendricks (58 mins); P Lambie for Pollard (63 mins); M van der Merwe for J du Plessis (63 mins); B Botha for Etzebeth (63 mins); C Reinach for Hougaard (68 mins); T Nyakane for Mtawarira (72 mins)

**SCORERS**: *Tries*: Hougaard, Pollard (2) *Conversions*: Pollard (3) *Penalty Goals*: Pollard, Lambie

**NEW ZEALAND**: I Dagg; B Smith, C Smith, M Fekitoa, J Savea; B Barrett, A Smith; J Moody, K Mealamu, O Franks, J Thrush, S Whitelock, J Kaino, R McCaw (captain), K Read

**SUBSTITUTIONS**: B Franks for Moody (41 mins); L Messam for Thrush (49 mins); D Coles for Mealamu (49 mins); C Faumuina for O Franks (58 mins); S Luatua for Kaino (61 mins); T Kerr-Barlow for A Smith (67 mins); R Crotty for C Smith (74 mins); C Slade for Kerr-Barlow (75 mins)

**SCORERS**: *Tries*: Fekitoa, B Smith, Coles *Conversions*: Barrett (2) *Penalty Goals*: Barrett (2)

**REFEREE**: W Barnes (England)

# ARGENTINA 21 (1G 1T 3PG) AUSTRALIA 17 (2G 1PG)

**ARGENTINA**: J Tuculet; JJ Imhoff, H Agulla, JM Hernández, L González Amorosino; N Sánchez, M Landajo; M Ayerza, A Creevy (captain), N Tetaz Chaparro, M Galarza, T Lavanini, R Báez, B Macome, L Senatore

**SUBSTITUTIONS**: J Ortega Desio for Macome (15 mins); T Cubelli for Landajo (59 mins); R Herrera for Tetaz Chaparro (64 mins); B Postiglioni for Ayerza (67 mins); M Bosch for Agulla (70 mins); M Alemanno for Galarza (75 mins); J de la Fuente for Tuculet (75 mins)

**SCORERS**: *Tries*: Senatore, Imhoff *Conversion*: Sánchez *Penalty Goals*: Sánchez (3)

**AUSTRALIA**: I Folau; A Ashley-Cooper, T Kuridrani, M Toomua, J Tomane; B Foley, N Phipps; J Slipper, S Faingaa, S Kepu, S Carter, J Horwill, S Fardy, M Hooper (captain), S Higginbotham

**SUBSTITUTIONS**: R Horne for Toomua (30 mins); B Robinson for Slipper (60 mins); B Alexander for Kepu (60 mins); J Schatz for Higginbotham (60 mins); N White for Phipps (64 mins); W Skelton for Horwill (67 mins); J Mann-Rea for Faingaa (71 mins)

**SCORERS**: *Tries*: Kuridrani, Higginbotham *Conversions*: Foley (2) *Penalty Goal*: Foley

**YELLOW CARDS**: Phipps (43 mins); Hooper (74 mins)

**REFEREE**: N Owens (Wales)

APF/Getty Images

Springboks Handré Pollard (right) and Teboho Mohoje combine to stop Malakai Fekitoa in his tracks in Johannesburg.

# RUGBY CHAMPIONSHIP (FORMERLY TRI NATIONS) RECORDS 1996–2014

## PREVIOUS WINNERS

| | | | |
|---|---|---|---|
| 1996 New Zealand | 1997 New Zealand | 1998 South Africa | 1999 New Zealand |
| 2000 Australia | 2001 Australia | 2002 New Zealand | 2003 New Zealand |
| 2004 South Africa | 2005 New Zealand | 2006 New Zealand | 2007 New Zealand |
| 2008 New Zealand | 2009 South Africa | 2010 New Zealand | 2011 Australia |
| 2012 New Zealand | 2013 New Zealand | 2014 New Zealand | |

## GRAND SLAM WINNERS

**New Zealand** (Six times) 1996, 1997, 2003, 2010, 2012 and 2013
**South Africa** (Once) 1998

| TEAM RECORD | DETAIL | | SET |
|---|---|---|---|
| **Most team points in season** | 203 by S Africa | in six matches | 2013 |
| **Most team tries in season** | 24 by N Zealand | in six matches | 2013 |
| **Highest team score** | 73 by S Africa | 73–13 v Argentina (h) | 2013 |
| **Biggest team win** | 60 by S Africa | 73–13 v Argentina (h) | 2013 |
| **Most team tries in match** | 9 by S Africa | v Argentina (h) | 2013 |

| INDIVIDUAL RECORD | DETAIL | | SET |
|---|---|---|---|
| **Most appearances** | 55 for N Zealand | RH McCaw | 2002 to 2014 |
| **Most points in matches** | 531 for N Zealand | DW Carter | 2003 to 2013 |
| **Most points in season** | 99 for N Zealand | DW Carter | 2006 |
| **Most points in match** | 31 for S Africa | M Steyn | v N Zealand (h) 2009 |
| **Most tries in matches** | 18 for S Africa | BG Habana | 2005 to 2014 |
| **Most tries in season** | 8 for N Zealand | BR Smith | 2013 |
| **Most tries in match** | 4 for S Africa | JL Nokwe | v Australia (h) 2008 |
| **Most cons in matches** | 72 for N Zealand | DW Carter | 2003 to 2013 |
| **Most cons in season** | 17 for S Africa | M Steyn | 2013 |
| **Most cons in match** | 8 for S Africa | M Steyn | v Argentina (h) 2013 |
| **Most pens in matches** | 115 for N Zealand | DW Carter | 2003 to 2013 |
| **Most pens in season** | 23 for S Africa | M Steyn | 2009 |
| **Most pens in match** | 9 for N Zealand | AP Mehrtens | v Australia (h) 1999 |
| **Most drops in matches** | 4 for S Africa | AS Pretorius | 2002 to 2006 |
| | 4 for S Africa | M Steyn | 2009 to 2014 |
| | 4 for N Zealand | DW Carter | 2003 to 2013 |
| **Most drops in season** | 3 for S Africa | M Steyn | 2009 |
| **Most drops in match** | 2 for S Africa | JH de Beer | v N Zealand (h) 1997 |
| | 2 for S Africa | FPL Steyn | v Australia (h) 2007 |

From 1996 to 2005 inclusive, each nation played four matches in a season. The nations have played six matches since, except in 2007 and 2011 (Rugby World Cup years) when they reverted to four.

# SAMOA AND JAPAN SHARE HONOURS

**The 2014 edition** of the IRB Pacific Nations Cup saw the return of Samoa after a one-year sabbatical and a new-look competition with Canada and USA joining for the first time. The six teams were split into two conferences, one based in the Pacific Islands and the other in North America.

Samoa were the highest placed of the six teams in the IRB World Rankings in ninth with the USA Eagles the lowest in 18th but for every team the tournament presented an opportunity to play competitive Test matches with Rugby World Cup 2015 just over a year away.

The Samoans opened their campaign against Tonga in a hot and steamy Apia on 7 June and the 18–18 draw was a fair reflection of the Apia Park encounter, which saw the Ikale Tahi outscore their more experienced opponents two tries to one. A great solo try from Otulea Katoa was all Samoa had to show for a first half in which they enjoyed 65 per cent possession, but the introduction of Kahn Fotuali'i at the break resulted in a more coherent performance. Samoa hit the front for the first time with 15 minutes to go but were unable to hold on for victory, their ill-discipline presenting Fangatapu 'Apikotoa with a long-range penalty to tie the scores with which he made no mistake.

A week later Tonga found Fiji too hot to handle in Lautoka, slipping to a 45–17 defeat with centre Nemani Nadolo contributing 20 points for the hosts. Fiji's new coach John McKee saw room for improvement, but his side would top the Pacific conference ahead of their meeting with Samoa a week later in Suva.

That would be a fast, furious and bruising encounter as Samoa capitalised on Fijian ill-discipline in the first half to win 18–13, their first triumph at the venue since 1998. Fiji scored the only tries of the match, but six penalties from Tusi Pisi gave Samoa victory and top spot. The loss for Fiji was not ideal, coming a week before their Rugby World Cup 2015 qualifier with the Cook Islands, but they made light work of that, winning 108–6 to take their place in Pool A alongside hosts England, Australia, Wales and the Repechage winner.

Japan, meanwhile, came out on top in the high-scoring North American conference after extending their record run of consecutive Test victories to nine by overcoming hosts Canada and USA. They did it the hard way in round one, recovering from 25–9 down at half-time to Canada to roar back with tries from Yoshikazu Fujita, Yu Tamura and Hendrik Tui to triumph 34–25.

The Brave Blossoms then headed to Los Angeles to face USA and another high-scoring affair. Both sides scored four tries – Blaine Scully notching a hat-trick for the Eagles – but it was Japan who ultimately emerged with a 37–29 victory to guarantee top spot in the conference. Japan then returned home to beat Italy to enter the top 10 of the IRB World Rankings for the first time.

That left just the small matter of the battle of North America in Sacramento. The Eagles had lost seven in a row against their neighbours and looked in danger of extending that run when Canada scored 21 unanswered points to lead 28–18 at half-time. That lead grew to 17 points within minutes of the restart, but the hosts were not finished and tries from Scully and debutant Brett Thompson gave the USA a narrow 38–35 victory.

## IRB PACIFIC NATIONS CUP 2014 RESULTS

| | | |
|---|---|---|
| 07/06/2014 | Samoa 18–18 Tonga | Apia Park, Apia |
| 07/06/2014 | Canada 25–34 Japan | Swanguard Stadium, Burnaby |
| 14/06/2014 | Fiji 45–17 Tonga | Churchill Park, Lautoka |
| 14/06/2014 | USA 29–37 Japan | Stub Hub Center, Los Angeles |
| 21/06/2014 | Fiji 13–18 Samoa | ANZ Stadium, Suva |
| 21/06/2014 | USA 38–35 Canada | Cal Expo Facility, Sacramento |

## IRB PACIFIC NATIONS CUP 2014 FINAL STANDINGS
### PACIFIC ISLANDS CONFERENCE

| | P | W | D | L | PF | PA | BP | PTS |
|---|---|---|---|---|---|---|---|---|
| Samoa | 2 | 1 | 1 | 0 | 36 | 31 | 0 | 6 |
| Fiji | 2 | 1 | 0 | 1 | 58 | 35 | 2 | 6 |
| Tonga | 2 | 0 | 1 | 1 | 35 | 63 | 0 | 2 |

### NORTH AMERICAN CONFERENCE

| | P | W | D | L | PF | PA | BP | PTS |
|---|---|---|---|---|---|---|---|---|
| Japan | 2 | 2 | 0 | 0 | 71 | 54 | 1 | 9 |
| USA | 2 | 1 | 0 | 1 | 67 | 72 | 2 | 6 |
| Canada | 2 | 0 | 0 | 2 | 60 | 72 | 2 | 2 |

# IRISH TOO STRONG ON NATIONS CUP DEBUT

## By Jon Newcombe

**Tournament newcomers Emerging** Ireland ended Romania's recent hold on the IRB Nations Cup with a 31–10 win over the host nation in a largely one-sided decider in Bucharest. Though not as ruthless as they had been in their two previous victories, against Russia and Uruguay, the Irish still had too much attacking firepower for a Romanian side bidding for a hat-trick of Nations Cup titles.

"We had to dig deep in all of the matches so it's great that we managed to get three wins out of three," admitted flanker Robin Copeland, who was named player of the tournament after a series of outstanding displays.

In truth, Emerging Ireland's march to the Nations Cup title was something of a procession. They got the tournament off to an electrifying start – in more ways than one – with an opening day rout of Russia that was cut short four minutes into the second half by a severe thunderstorm. By the time referee Ian Davies called a halt to proceedings in the interests of player safety, Emerging Ireland had built up an impressive 66–0 lead after running in 10 unanswered tries past their shell-shocked opponents. Winger Andrew Conway bagged a first-half hat-trick of tries, while Copeland marked his debut outing in Irish colours with a well-deserved score. Tournament rules decreed that the result stood and the Irish were awarded five match points.

With Romania already through to Rugby World Cup 2015 and Russia and Uruguay both in with a shout of joining them, results at the ninth edition of the Nations Cup took on extra significance. So it was to everyone's relief that the storm clouds had passed by in time for the second match to take place between Romania and Uruguay. A rather uneventful match, won 34–16 by the Oaks, was only really notable for the goal-kicking exploits of centre Florin Vlaicu, who missed only one of his seven attempts at goal to become the tournament's joint all-time leading points scorer.

**102**

In round two, Emerging Ireland maintained their perfect record with another bonus-point win, 51–3 against Uruguay, and were a couple of minutes away from clinching the Nations Cup with a round to spare until Romania snatched victory from the jaws of defeat in the second match of the day to keep their title hopes alive. Trailing Russia 18–6 with 10 minutes to go, Lynn Howells' out-of-sorts side looked down and out, but their increasing dominance up front eventually told and the award of two penalty tries, both converted by Vlaicu to take him past Luciano Orquera's Nations Cup milestone of 119 points, saw them sneak home, 20–18.

Russia and Uruguay's final-day wooden spoon decider attracted as much attention as the title showdown between Emerging Ireland and Romania, given its standing as a potential precursor to a RWC 2015 Repechage meeting. Los Teros winger Franco Lamanna scored the only try of a tight match, which went to uncontested scrums in the second half and ended in a 13–6 victory to Uruguay.

Two tries in the space of three first-half minutes proved decisive in the tournament finale, dynamic captain Dominic Ryan and winger Craig Gilroy, with his fourth of the tournament, helping Emerging Ireland into a 17–3 half-time lead. Copeland put the result beyond any doubt with a try almost immediately after the restart, with the only other scores being a penalty try and conversion for either side.

## IRB NATIONS CUP 2014 RESULTS

| | | |
|---|---|---|
| 13/06/14 | Emerging Ireland 66–0 Russia | Stadionul National Arcul de Triumf, Bucharest |
| 13/06/14 | Romania 34–16 Uruguay | Stadionul National Arcul de Triumf, Bucharest |
| 18/06/14 | Emerging Ireland 51–3 Uruguay | Stadionul National Arcul de Triumf, Bucharest |
| 18/06/14 | Romania 20–18 Russia | Stadionul National Arcul de Triumf, Bucharest |
| 22/06/14 | Russia 6–13 Uruguay | Stadionul National Arcul de Triumf, Bucharest |
| 22/06/14 | Romania 10–31 Emerging Ireland | Stadionul National Arcul de Triumf, Bucharest |

## FINAL STANDINGS

| | P | W | D | L | F | A | BP | PTS |
|---|---|---|---|---|---|---|---|---|
| Emerging Ireland | 3 | 3 | 0 | 0 | 148 | 13 | 3 | 15 |
| Romania | 3 | 2 | 0 | 1 | 64 | 65 | 0 | 8 |
| Uruguay | 3 | 1 | 0 | 2 | 32 | 91 | 0 | 4 |
| Russia | 3 | 0 | 0 | 3 | 24 | 99 | 2 | 2 |

# JAGUARS SHINE IN TBILISI CUP

## By Jon Newcombe

**A**rgentina Jaguars won the IRB Tbilisi Cup 2014 after a clean sweep of wins in the Georgian capital. The Jaguars finished five points clear of their hosts, who were made to pay for an ill-disciplined showing against the South Americans in round two, with Emerging Italy and Spain in third and fourth place respectively.

After earlier wins over Emerging Italy and Georgia, Argentina Jaguars wrapped up the title in style with a five-try, 41–7 victory over Spain, who finished their debut tournament without a point to their name.

"We're really happy to win the trophy, it has been a good tournament for us and a great experience for our players, especially the younger ones," said Jaguars head coach Bernardo Urdaneta. "My players now need to grow from this and use it as a platform to push for senior honours."

Goal-kicking centre Juan Pablo Socino improved his chances of a Pumas call-up with a couple of superb displays before being rested for the Spain match. Socino, who joins English Premiership side Newcastle for the 2014–15 season, kicked 15 points against Emerging Italy and a further 21 in the win over Georgia.

Against Emerging Italy, who won the corresponding fixture in the IRB Nations Cup the year before, the Jaguars had to come from behind to join Georgia (23–13 over Spain) as winners on the opening day. Trailing 13–9 at half-time, the South Americans upped the tempo after the break to score six tries, Sebastián Poet's fantastic individual try being the pick of the bunch in a 45–20 win.

Urdaneta's side made it two wins from two in an ill-tempered affair with Georgia that saw four yellow and two red cards issued by referee Luke Pearce. Again the Jaguars found themselves behind on the score-board early on, but a flawless display of goal-kicking from Socino, who finished the match with a perfect seven from seven record, and a moment of individual brilliance two minutes from time from winger Ramiro

Moyano settled the match in the Jaguars' favour, 26–16. A dominant Emerging Italy beat Spain 37–0 in the second fixture of the midweek round of matches.

One first-half try and three more after the break, including two penalty tries, saw Georgia beat Emerging Italy 34–10 in the final round to claim second place. "The boys are pleased with themselves and know that we could have won the tournament if we had performed a little bit better in the midweek game against Argentina," admitted Lelos coach Milton Haig.

For once, the Jaguars led from start to finish as they powered to victory over Spain in the final match of the second edition of the Tbilisi Cup. Fly-half Poet, a more than capable replacement for Socino, enjoyed another fine match and his unerring accuracy from the kicking tee saw him convert all five of his side's tries, the last of which he scored himself, in addition to two penalties. Argentina Jaguars join inaugural champions South Africa President's XV on the Tbilisi Cup winners' roster.

## IRB TBILISI CUP 2014 RESULTS

| | | |
|---|---|---|
| 14/06/14 | Georgia 23–13 Spain | Avchala Stadium, Tbilisi |
| 14/06/14 | Emerging Italy 20–45 Argentina Jaguars | Avchala Stadium, Tbilisi |
| 18/06/14 | Georgia 16–26 Argentina Jaguars | Avchala Stadium, Tbilisi |
| 18/06/14 | Emerging Italy 37–0 Spain | Avchala Stadium, Tbilisi |
| 22/06/14 | Georgia 34–10 Emerging Italy | Avchala Stadium, Tbilisi |
| 22/06/14 | Argentina Jaguars 41–7 Spain | Avchala Stadium, Tbilisi |

## FINAL STANDINGS

| | P | W | D | L | F | A | BP | PTS |
|---|---|---|---|---|---|---|---|---|
| Argentina Jaguars | 3 | 3 | 0 | 0 | 112 | 43 | 2 | 14 |
| Georgia | 3 | 2 | 0 | 1 | 73 | 49 | 0 | 8 |
| Emerging Italy | 3 | 1 | 0 | 2 | 67 | 79 | 1 | 5 |
| Spain | 3 | 0 | 0 | 3 | 20 | 101 | 0 | 0 |

JUNIOR WORLD© CHAMPIONSHIP

NEW ZEALAND 2014

# ENGLAND RETAIN TITLE AS POLLARD MAKES METEORIC RISE

## By *Karen Bond*

AFP/Getty Images

England joined New Zealand as the only teams to have successfully defended the Junior World Championship title.

**S**outh Africa captain Handré Pollard went through a whirlwind of emotions in little more than a week as he endured the pain of losing the IRB Junior World Championship 2014 final to England by a single point in New Zealand and was then named IRB Junior Player of the Year. He flew home the following day and was called into the full Springbok squad for their final June international against Scotland in Port Elizabeth, duly making his Test debut just eight days after his heartbreak at Eden Park.

That Pollard, a JWC winner with South Africa on home soil in 2012, would make the step up was no surprise, with Springboks coach Heyneke Meyer a long-time fan of the fly-half, but his meteoric rise was the quickest any player has graduated from the Under 20 tournament to the Test stage. He retained his place for The Rugby Championship and started five of the six matches, scoring two tries in the dramatic win over New Zealand on the final weekend.

"Playing in the Junior World Cup for three years meant a lot to me, I really developed as a player," Pollard told *Total Rugby* before The Rugby Championship. "It's such a great breeding ground for young talent and young guys coming through. If you look at the list of guys who have played there and then gone on to play senior rugby for their countries, it's such an amazing list of players and it's just such a great honour to be part of it."

Pollard had been one of the standout players at the seventh edition of the tournament, leading South Africa's challenge with a great maturity and inspiring others to follow his example, setting up or scoring pivotal scores to turn a match in his side's favour. A prime example was the opening try in the title decider against defending champions England – 20 minutes had passed without a score until Pollard spotted a gap in the defence and put in a perfectly weighted chip for Jesse Kriel to race onto and touch down.

It was England, though, who went in with a one-point lead at half-time after Nathan Earle's try in the corner made it 11–10 in his side's favour. The two sides traded penalties early in the second half before England stretched their advantage when Joel Conlon dropped on the ball after a strong drive. Pollard gathered his troops under the posts and they hit back with some slick hands down the left wing resulting in a second try for Kriel. A break by his twin brother Dan nearly created another try minutes later as the galvanised Junior Springboks kept England pinned in their own half for much of the final quarter. They were unable to find the winning score, though, so it was England celebrating at the final whistle in Auckland.

"It is pretty special, I am struggling to put it into words at the moment. It is a really, really special moment," admitted captain Maro Itoje. "Fair play to South Africa, they brought their game, I am so glad we brought ours."

Pollard, meanwhile, summed up South Africa's campaign with a simple phrase: "One hell of a ride". It was hard to describe it as anything else after the Junior Springboks beat their hosts New Zealand not once but twice to reach the title decider. "I think the way we got here was amazing and something the guys are going to remember for the rest of their lives, beating New Zealand in New Zealand twice is not something that happens every day," admitted Pollard.

The first meeting, in the pool stages, had been impressive enough, with South Africa's forward pack laying the foundations for Pollard and the Kriel twins to shine and guide their side to a 33–24 victory despite a hat-trick by New Zealand wing Tevita Li. That win guaranteed South Africa a place in the semi-finals, where the southern hemisphere rivals would meet again after New Zealand claimed the best runner-up spot thanks to a better point differential than Australia.

It was a much-improved performance from the hosts in that semi-final, a seesaw encounter which looked to be heading for sudden-death extra-time with the sides locked at 25–25 until two minutes from time. Then South Africa got up a head of steam through a driving maul and hooker Corniel Els dotted down to end New Zealand's dream of winning the title on home soil.

"This was a proper Test match, it could have gone either way," insisted a relieved South Africa coach Dawie Theron afterwards. "I am just so proud of these guys, to hang in there, to work through it … they just never gave up and took the fight to their opponents."

If this semi-final had been a titanic battle, then the other was the total opposite with England's power, running lines and line speed in defence blowing Ireland away in the first half. The defending champions led 34–3 at the break, but the spirited Irish refused to buckle in their first JWC semi-final and, despite having lost captain Jack O'Donoghue to a head knock, battled bravely to go down 42–17. It was still a tournament to remember for the Irish, who had bounced back well from an opening loss to France to collect bonus-point victories over Wales and Fiji. Those secured them top spot in Pool B after the Welsh beat Six Nations Grand Slam winners France 13–3 on day three.

New Zealand, who would have missed out on the semi-finals had France won, had to settle for third place after failing to reach the final for a second successive year, wing Li and fly-half Richard Mo'unga both touching down twice in a 45–23 victory over Ireland at Eden Park. The Baby Blacks had dominated the formative years of the competition, not losing a match in winning four titles in a row from 2008 to 2011, and had hoped that the rare opportunity to play at home would inspire them to more title success. Two defeats by South Africa ended that dream, but third was at least one place higher than they had finished in France a year earlier.

There were also wins on the final day for Australia, Wales and

Argentina over France, Samoa and Scotland respectively. Australia certainly did it the hard way in an enthralling fifth place play-off at Eden Park, recovering from 17–0 down after only 14 minutes to beat the French 34–27 thanks to braces from captain Sean McMahon and wing Andrew Kellaway. The double for Kellaway set a new record for the most tries in a single tournament and also tied the overall record of 10 held by All Black Zac Guildford and Ireland flyer Andrew Conway.

Wales finished seventh after a 20–3 victory over Samoa at QBE Stadium in North Harbour, which also saw Argentina finish strongly with a 41–21 win over Scotland in the ninth place play-off.

The highlight of Italy's return to the Junior World Championship was unquestionably their 29–26 victory over Argentina in the pool stages. Coached by Italian legend Alessandro Troncon, the Azzurrini would still find themselves in the 11th place play-off on the final day. With Italy already confirmed as JWC 2015 hosts they couldn't be relegated to the IRB Junior World Rugby Trophy again even if they lost to Fiji, but they wanted to earn that place through their efforts on the pitch. They duly did, winning 22–17 and so while Fiji will travel to Portugal hoping to secure an immediate return, their place in Italy will be taken by JWRT 2014 winners Japan.

The tournament may not have yielded the desired result for the host nation, but like previous editions it will have left a legacy behind with the teams having all played their part in visiting local schools and clubs to interact with the children. There were also positives on the field, from a new semi-finalist in Ireland, to the performances of Samoa against both South Africa and New Zealand as they gave their more-fancied opponents a real workout. As New Zealand commentator Scotty Stevenson said after the final: "I think the tournament itself has showcased those future stars that we talk about and if you missed any of the action I think you missed out majorly."

# IRB JUNIOR WORLD CHAMPIONSHIP 2014 RESULTS

## POOL A

Round One: **Argentina** 17–36 **Australia**, **England** 63–3 **Italy**. Round Two: **Argentina** 26–29 **Italy**, **England** 38–24 **Australia**. Round Three: **Australia** 29–3 **Italy**, **England** 17–16 **Argentina**.

## POOL B

Round One: **Wales** 48–19 **Fiji**, **France** 19–13 **Ireland**. Round Two: **France** 37–5 **Fiji**, **Wales** 21–35 **Ireland**. Round Three: **Ireland** 38–0 **Fiji**, **Wales** 13–3 **France**.

## POOL C

Round One: **South Africa** 61–5 **Scotland**, **New Zealand** 48–12 **Samoa**. Round Two: **Scotland** 18–27 **Samoa**, **New Zealand** 24–33 **South Africa**. Round Three: **Samoa** 8–21 **South Africa**, **New Zealand** 54–7 **Scotland**.

# POOL TABLES

## POOL A

|  | P | W | D | L | F | A | BP | PTS |
|---|---|---|---|---|---|---|---|---|
| England | 3 | 3 | 0 | 0 | 118 | 43 | 2 | 14 |
| Australia | 3 | 2 | 0 | 1 | 89 | 58 | 2 | 10 |
| Italy | 3 | 1 | 0 | 2 | 35 | 118 | 0 | 4 |
| Argentina | 3 | 0 | 0 | 3 | 59 | 82 | 2 | 2 |

## POOL B

|  | P | W | D | L | F | A | BP | PTS |
|---|---|---|---|---|---|---|---|---|
| Ireland | 3 | 2 | 0 | 1 | 86 | 40 | 3 | 11 |
| Wales | 3 | 2 | 0 | 1 | 82 | 57 | 1 | 9 |
| France | 3 | 2 | 0 | 1 | 59 | 31 | 1 | 9 |
| Fiji | 3 | 0 | 0 | 3 | 24 | 123 | 0 | 0 |

## POOL C

|  | P | W | D | L | F | A | BP | PTS |
|---|---|---|---|---|---|---|---|---|
| South Africa | 3 | 3 | 0 | 0 | 115 | 37 | 2 | 14 |
| New Zealand | 3 | 2 | 0 | 1 | 126 | 52 | 2 | 10 |
| Samoa | 3 | 1 | 0 | 2 | 47 | 87 | 0 | 4 |
| Scotland | 3 | 0 | 0 | 3 | 30 | 142 | 0 | 0 |

**PLAY-OFFS FIRST PHASE**

| | |
|---|---|
| Ninth place semi-finals | **Argentina** 38–12 Fiji |
| | **Italy** 18–21 **Scotland** |
| Fifth place semi-finals | **Australia** 53–16 Samoa |
| | Wales 18–19 **France** |
| Semi-finals | **England** 42–15 Ireland |
| | **South Africa** 32–25 **New Zealand** |

## PLAY-OFFS SECOND PHASE

| | |
|---|---|
| 11th place play-off | Fiji 17–22 **Italy** |
| Ninth place play-off | **Argentina** 41–21 Scotland |
| Seventh place play-off | **Wales** 20–3 Samoa |
| Fifth place play-off | France 27–34 **Australia** |

## THIRD PLACE PLAY-OFF

### 20 June 2014, Eden Park, Auckland

# IRELAND 23 (2G 3PG) NEW ZEALAND 45 (5G 2T)

**IRELAND:** C Kelleher; C Gaffney, G Ringrose, H Brewer, A Wootton; R Byrne, N McCarthy; P Dooley, D Donnellan, O Heffernan, D Moloney, R Molony, P Timmins (captain), R Moloney, F Taggart

**SUBSTITUTIONS:** S Gardiner for D Moloney (41 mins); D Goggin for Wootton (53 mins); R Burke for Heffernan (55 mins); M Abbott for Donnellan (61 mins); R Foley for McCarthy (65 mins); C McKeon for Byrne (67 mins); J Murphy for R Moloney (33 mins); D Coulson for Dooley (74 mins)

**SCORERS:** *Try*: Penalty try, Heffernan *Conversions*: Byrne (2) *Penalty Goals*: Byrne (3)

**YELLOW CARD:** Kelleher (60 mins)

**NEW ZEALAND:** D McKenzie; V Tavae-Aso, A Lienert-Brown (captain), TJ Faiane, T Li; R Mo'unga, M Drummond; A Moli, H Faiva, T Koloamatangi, J Tucker, G Cridge, T Sanders, L Boshier, M Peni

**SUBSTITUTIONS:** K Harris for Sanders (25 mins); T Cadwallader for Koloamatangi (41 mins); K Finau for Faiane (44 mins); D Kaetau Havili for Lienert-Brown (48 mins); J O'Reilly for Faiva (61 mins); T Callander for Cridge (71 mins); S Mellow for Moli (73 mins); J Renton for Drummond (74 mins)

**SCORERS:** *Tries*: Li (2), Mo'unga (2), Tucker, Drummond, Boshier *Conversions*: McKenzie (5)

**YELLOW CARDS:** Tucker (27 mins); Callander (74 mins)

**REFEREE:** A Ruiz (France)

## 20 June 2014, Eden Park, Auckland

# ENGLAND 21 (1G 1T 3PG) SOUTH AFRICA 20 (2G 2PG)

**ENGLAND:** A Morris; H Packman, N Tompkins, H Sloan, N Earle; B Burns, H Taylor; D Hobbs-Awoyemi, T Woolstencroft, P Hill, M Itoje (captain), C Ewels, R Moriarty, G Jones, J Chisholm

**SUBSTITUTIONS:** J Conlon for Jones (temp 14–22 mins; 41 mins); J Walker for Woolstencroft (62 mins); A Lundberg for Hobbs-Awoyemi (70 mins)

**SCORERS:** *Tries*: Earle, Conlon *Conversion*: Burns *Penalty Goals*: Burns (2), Morris

**SOUTH AFRICA:** W Gelant; D Kriel, J Kriel, A Esterhuizen, S Petersen; H Pollard (captain), JP Smith; T du Toit, C Els, D van der Westhuizen, JD Schickerling, N van Rensburg, J Vermeulen, C Brink, A Davis

**SUBSTITUTIONS:** W Louw for Van der Westhuizen (47 mins); JL du Preez for Vermeulen (47 mins); J Dweba for Els (49 mins); D van der Merwe for Esterhuizen (53 mins); P Schoeman for du Toit (63 mins)

**SCORERS:** *Tries*: J Kriel (2) *Conversions*: Pollard (2) *Penalty Goals*: Pollard (2)

**REFEREE:** B O'Keefe (New Zealand)

# FINAL STANDINGS

| | |
|---|---|
| 1. England | 7. Wales |
| 2. South Africa | 8. Samoa |
| 3. New Zealand | 9. Argentina |
| 4. Ireland | 10. Scotland |
| 5. Australia | 11. Italy |
| 6. France | 12. Fiji |

### TOP POINTS SCORERS

| Name | Pts |
|---|---|
| Patricio Fernández (Argentina) | 73 |
| Handré Pollard (South Africa) | 65 |
| Andrew Kellaway (Australia) | 50 |
| Jake McIntyre (Australia) | 47 |
| Billy Burns (England) | 42 |
| Angus O'Brien (Wales) | 40 |
| Ross Byrne (Ireland) | 38 |
| Tevita Li (New Zealand) | 35 |
| Filippo Buscema (Italy) | 32 |
| Nathan Earle (England) | 30 |
| Richard Mo'unga (New Zealand) | 29 |

### TOP TRY SCORERS

| Name | Tries |
|---|---|
| Andrew Kellaway (Australia) | 10 |
| Tevita Li (New Zealand) | 7 |
| Nathan Earle (England) | 6 |
| James Benjamin (Wales) | 5 |
| Jesse Kriel (South Africa) | 5 |
| Gus Jones (England) | 4 |
| Nathanial Apa (Samoa) | 3 |
| Lloyd Greef (South Africa) | 3 |
| Brad Lacey (Australia) | 3 |
| Sergeal Petersen (South Africa) | 3 |
| Garry Ringrose (Ireland) | 3 |

# FOURTH TIME LUCKY FOR JAPAN

**J**apan had fallen at the final hurdle three times in the last four editions of the IRB Junior World Rugby Trophy, but they made no mistake in the 2014 title decider, running out 35–10 winners over Tonga in Hong Kong to secure their return to the IRB Junior World Championship.

The class of 2014 has been labelled 'Generation 2019' in Japan and is expected to form the nucleus of the senior team when the country becomes the first Asian side to host the Rugby World Cup that year. Two players from this title-winning side who could certainly be wearing the Brave Blossoms' jersey by then are Genki Okoshi and captain Rikiya Matsuda, the half-back pairing who superbly orchestrated Japan's four-try victory over first-time finalists Tonga in April.

"This is a very important victory for our country. This is the next generation of players, the future of Japan rugby and I'm very proud of the boys," admitted coach Keisuke Sawaki afterwards. "As a nation we must now put more focus on this squad as we look ahead to the 2019 Rugby World Cup which will be hosted in Japan."

While tries from hooker Shunta Nakamura, wing Shuhei Narita and number 8 Sota Oketani – in addition to a first-half penalty try – were enough to spark the Japanese celebrations, they had certainly not had it all their own way in the eight-team tournament played at the Hong Kong Football Club in April.

In fact, the third seeds had got off to the worst possible start with a 33–28 loss to former champions Uruguay that left Sawaki fuming, his only consolation being the two losing bonus points Japan secured. Japan had battled back from 33–14 down but ultimately came up just short against a Uruguay side that were "definitely hungrier than us", according to Sawaki.

Japan then found themselves 14–0 down against a never-say-die Namibia who had upset 2013 runners-up Canada on day one. Japan fought back to win 34–28, a victory which meant they had to beat Canada to top Pool B and deny Uruguay, the only unbeaten side in the pool stages after two wins and an 18–18 draw with Canada, a place in the final. Six tries later and a 37–12 win had been secured, with Sawaki proclaiming "this is the way we are supposed to play".

The Pool A decider, meanwhile, between Tonga and 2012 champions USA went right down to the wire. Tonga scored two tries in each half for a 28–22 victory and a priceless bonus point that meant both teams finished on 10 points. The Pacific Islanders finished top on the head-to-head result, leaving the Junior All-Americans crestfallen as they had wrongly believed their better points differential would see them into the final and had slowed play in the final stages once the losing bonus point was secured.

USA put that heartbreak behind them to edge the 'battle of the Americas' with Uruguay 26–25 to finish third. Uruguay ended with 12 players in a match marred by foul play, but were unlucky to finish on the wrong side of the result after battling back from 20–3 down to tie the scores before Ben Cima kicked the Americans ahead again.

Georgia finished strongly with a convincing 46–17 win over Namibia to finish fifth with fly-half Revaz Jinchvelashvili kicking 26 of their points. By contrast, the seventh place play-off was a much tighter affair as 14-man Canada recovered from a 21–7 half-time deficit to beat hosts and tournament debutants Hong Kong 33–30.

## IRB JUNIOR WORLD RUGBY TROPHY 2014 RESULTS

### POOL A

Round One: **Tonga** 10–34 **Georgia**, **USA** 37–0 **Hong Kong**. Round Two: **USA** 13–12 **Georgia**, **Tonga** 39–16 **Hong Kong**. Round Three: **Georgia** 21–8 **Hong Kong**, **USA** 22–28 **Tonga**.

### POOL B

Round One: **Japan** 28–33 **Uruguay**, **Canada** 25–37 **Namibia**. Round Two: **Japan** 34–28 **Namibia**, **Canada** 18–18 **Uruguay**. Round Three: **Uruguay** 16–13 **Namibia**, **Canada** 12–37 **Japan**.

## PLAY-OFFS

| | |
|---|---|
| Seventh place play-off | **Hong Kong** 30–33 **Canada** |
| Fifth place play-off | **Georgia** 46–17 **Namibia** |
| Third place play-off | **USA** 26–25 **Uruguay** |
| Final | **Tonga** 10–35 **Japan** |

## FINAL STANDINGS

| | |
|---|---|
| 1. Japan | 5. Georgia |
| 2. Tonga | 6. Namibia |
| 3. USA | 7. Canada |
| 4. Uruguay | 8. Hong Kong |

# FIVE IN A ROW FOR JAGUARS

## By Jon Newcombe

**A**rgentina Jaguars continued their dominance of the IRB Americas Rugby Championship in 2014 by claiming the title for a fifth time with three straight wins over USA Select, Uruguay and hosts Canada A.

Five of the Pumas' Rugby Championship squad as well as a number of IRB Junior World Championship graduates joined some of the country's best young talent in Langford, British Columbia, as the Jaguars set about defending the title they had made their own since the tournament was launched in 2009 to assist with player development in the region's tier two nations.

The Jaguars had the title in the bag with a round to spare after consecutive bonus-point wins over USA Select and local rivals Uruguay meant they couldn't be caught at the top of the table. Canada A and the aspiring Eagles had, at that stage, only managed a regulation four-point match win apiece.

Winger Dan Isaack starred with a hat-trick as the Jaguars began with a convincing 41–14 victory over USA Select. After a fairly even first half, the defending champions stepped up a gear to score 20 unanswered points in the second half.

The other match on day one between Canada A and Uruguay was a hotly contested clash that saw the South Americans reduced to 14 men in the second half when Nicolás Freitas was red-carded with only a converted try separating the sides. Canada A used their one-man advantage to score a second try through captain Kyle Gilmour and seal a 20–6 win.

Day two featured back-to-back 'derby' matches – one an all-South American affair and one all-North American encounter. Winger Franco Sábato got the Jaguars off to a flying start with a try after just 25 seconds but they lost their way thereafter and it took two late tries to kill off Uruguay's hopes. "We were not able to play the style we want to play. Uruguay was very good at spoiling and the ball was slippery," Jaguars captain Rodrigo Báez said after his side's 31–9 victory.

Countless errors made for a scrappy encounter between hosts Canada A and USA Select, one which neither side would have taken much satisfaction from. USA Select were on top throughout though and winger Tim Stanfill scored the match's only tries with a touchdown either side of the interval in the 16–3 win.

Stanfill crossed for another brace as USA Select signed off with a 30–5 win over Uruguay. Diego Magno had the honour of scoring Uruguay's only try of the tournament when he crossed the USA line four minutes from time. "For us, the ARC is an important step before the World Cup but it is also an opportunity to see young players that will be the core of our national team from 2016 onwards," said Los Teros assistant coach Emiliano Caffera.

Centre Joaquín Paz scored twice for the Jaguars against Canada A as they concluded another successful Americas Rugby Championship with a routine victory. Paz's first try and eight points from the boot of Patricio Fernández to three penalties from Gordon McRorie in reply made for a 13–9 half-time scoreline. The Jaguars, helped by two Canadians being dispatched to the sin-bin, added four more tries after the break to pull away and win 39–9.

"We brought a strong team with guys that played in recent Tests and some others that played in the IRB Junior World Championship and with whom we have to work with the future in mind. We are happy with how everybody developed throughout the tournament," said Jaguars coach Bernardo Urdaneta.

## IRB AMERICAS RUGBY CHAMPIONSHIP 2014 RESULTS

| 11/10/2014 | USA Select 14–41 Argentina Jaguars | Westhills Stadium |
|---|---|---|
| 11/10/2014 | Canada A 20–6 Uruguay | Westhills Stadium |
| 15/10/2014 | Uruguay 9–31 Argentina Jaguars | Westhills Stadium |
| 15/10/2014 | Canada A 3–16 USA Select | Westhills Stadium |
| 19/10/2014 | Uruguay 5–30 USA Select | Westhills Stadium |
| 19/10/2014 | Canada A 9–39 Argentina Jaguars | Westhills Stadium |

# DREAM DEBUT FOR ARGENTINA PAMPAS

### By Karen Bond

Patricio Fernández makes a break for Argentina Pampas XV in the Pacific Rugby Cup 2014 final.

The **IRB Pacific** Rugby Cup took on a new look in 2014 with the Argentina Pampas XV joining the fray for the first time and duly leaving their mark on the competition, claiming the title with an unbeaten record after overcoming the Queensland Reds A team 36–21 in the final in Sydney in March.

The majority of the Pampas XV squad had previously cut their teeth on the IRB Junior World Championship stage and the Pacific Rugby Cup provided an opportunity for the young Argentinians to test themselves against up-and-coming players in Australia as well as the A teams of Samoa, Fiji, Tonga and Japan, over a month-long period.

Funded by the International Rugby Board through its strategic initiative programme, the Pacific Rugby Cup 2014 was the ninth staging of the competition and the first to be held solely in Australia with 16 matches taking place across 10 venues in five cities, from Perth to Sydney.

The nine teams were split into two pools with five-time defending champions the Fiji Warriors and Junior Japan joining the development sides of the Western Force and Queensland Reds in Pool A. The other pool featured Samoa A, Tonga A, the Pampas XV, Gen Blue and ACT A, the development sides of the NSW Waratahs and Brumbies respectively.

The teams in each pool would play each other once, with Fiji Warriors and Junior Japan facing New South Wales Under 20s and Queensland Under 20s respectively to provide them with a fourth match in the competition. The pool winners would then meet in the final at TG Milner Oval in Sydney on 23 March with the two runners-up playing in the third place play-off as a curtain raiser.

When the revamped competition got underway in late February, it was the Australian development sides that made the better start, with the Argentina Pampas XV the only ones to deny them a clean sweep of victories in the opening round of matches after edging ACT A 32–23 in Canberra. Samoa A and the Fiji Warriors came close, losing by three points to Gen Blue and Reds A in their opening matches, while Junior Japan suffered a heavy 61–6 loss to the Western Force A in Perth. The Japanese actually scored first with Genki Okoshi's penalty but their hosts responded with nine tries scored by seven different players in the sweltering Perth conditions.

Fortunes improved for some of the touring sides in the next round of matches with Samoa A, Tonga A and Fiji Warriors all picking up their first victories, leaving only Junior Japan to suffer another heavy loss. The Pampas XV also kept up their impressive start to the Pacific Rugby Cup by overcoming Gen Blue 31–16 and then Samoa A 38–24.

While the Pampas XV were clear front-runners in Pool B, the battle to secure top spot in the other pool was still very much all to play for going into the final round of matches. Fiji Warriors certainly finished with a flourish by beating Junior Japan 99–13 thanks to hat-tricks from Nemani Rinakama and Savenaca Rawaca and a four-try haul from Vilitati Sokietai.

The Fijians would finish level on 11 points with Reds A at the top of Pool A – one clear of the Western Force A side – but missed out on the final as a result of losing the earlier meeting between the two teams. There was some consolation for the Warriors in that they had secured one more match, against Tonga A in the third place play-off. The Tongans had lost their final match 47–20 to the Pampas XV, but still finished second – albeit 10 points behind their conquerors.

Watching their defeat in the stands was national coach Mana 'Otai, who was able to find positives for the future. "The match was a very good opportunity for us to measure our players against good quality opposition. We showed in patches some very good rugby and how good we can be. I learned a lot about how the young players cope with such pressure and it was perfect for me to be here to watch them today. We are learning and improving every year and this year we have performed much better."

His side were not alone in learning lessons from every match in the Pacific Rugby Cup, though, with Pampas XV captain Martín Landajo, one of a handful of players already capped by Los Pumas, relishing the new challenges the competition provided for him and his teammates. "The tournament has been wonderful but different for us. It is perhaps a bit less physical than rugby at home or in the Vodacom Cup in South Africa where we have been playing, but here the rugby is much quicker. So now we have experience in all of these styles and it is good for our development."

The third place play-off between Fiji Warriors and Tonga A was a typical match between two Pacific Island sides with the out-going champions outscoring their rivals eight tries to three to win an entertaining match 54–21. Seven players crossed for tries in the Warriors' victory with only Senivalati Ramuwai touching down twice.

With the sun beating down in Sydney, the Pampas XV raced out of the blocks in the final, taking control with tries by Manuel Montero, Landajo and full-back Román Miralles in the opening 25 minutes. Shaken by the early pace, the Reds A team gradually worked their way back into the match to cut the deficit to 17–11 at half-time. The Australians hit the front within two minutes of the restart after wing Veresa Mataitini's try, but the Pampas XV regained their composure and added three more tries – including second scores for Montero and Landajo – in the last quarter, to run out 36–21 winners and claim the title in their debut season.

"The goal was to come in search of the right competition and to develop our team and develop it at a higher level," explained the victorious coach Martín Gaitan, who had had Pumas coach Daniel Hourcade alongside him in Australia. "The Pacific Rugby Cup is an interesting competition as you have Australian teams that play with a lot of speed and momentum. Then you have teams from the Pacific Islands that always pose a physical challenge. The more competition we have like this the better it is to develop our players."

A sentiment echoed by Reds A coach Peter Wilkins: "The Pacific Rugby Cup has been invaluable. To provide games of such a standard against various international opponents is a great initiative. It provides a quality competition to help players push for Super Rugby selection while also providing younger prospects with the opportunity to play at a higher level."

**IRB PACIFIC RUGBY CUP 2014 RESULTS**

| | | |
|---|---|---|
| 21/02/2014 | Western Force A 29–23 Reds A | McGillivray Oval, Perth |
| 23/02/2014 | Gen Blue 23–17 ACT A | Allianz Stadium, Sydney |
| 28/02/2014 | Gen Blue 17–14 Samoa A | TG Milner Oval, Sydney |
| 01/03/2014 | Western Force A 61–6 Junior Japan | nib Stadium, Perth |
| 02/03/2014 | ACT A 23–32 Argentina Pampas XV | Royal Military College, Canberra |
| 02/03/2014 | Reds A 22–19 Fiji Warriors | Ballymore, Brisbane |
| 04/03/2014 | Samoa A 27–18 Tonga A | TG Milner Oval, Sydney |
| 07/03/2014 | Reds A 81–7 Junior Japan | Suncorp Stadium, Brisbane |
| 07/03/2014 | Gen Blue 16–31 Argentina Pampas XV | David Phillips Field, Sydney |
| 09/03/2014 | ACT A 20–29 Tonga A | Royal Military College, Canberra |
| 10/03/2014 | Western Force A 24–36 Fiji Warriors | Ballymore, Brisbane |
| 11/03/2014 | Argentina Pampas XV 38–24 Samoa A | Royal Military College, Canberra |
| 13/03/2014 | Gen Blue 21–29 Tonga A | TG Milner Oval, Sydney |
| 14/03/2014 | Queensland U20 40–26 Junior Japan | Ballymore, Brisbane |
| 14/03/2014 | NSW U20 26–49 Fiji Warriors | Ballymore, Brisbane |
| 15/03/2014 | ACT A 18–17 Samoa A | GIO Stadium, Canberra |
| 18/03/2014 | Junior Japan 13–99 Fiji Warriors | Bond University, Robina |
| 19/03/2014 | Argentina Pampas XV 47–20 Tonga A | Royal Military College, Canberra |
| 23/03/2014 | Fiji Warriors 54–21 Tonga A | TG Milner Oval, Sydney |
| 23/03/2014 | Reds A 21–36 Argentina Pampas XV· | TG Milner Oval, Sydney |

# IRB PACIFIC RUGBY CUP 2014 FINAL STANDINGS

## POOL A

| | P | W | D | L | PF | PA | BP | PTS |
|---|---|---|---|---|---|---|---|---|
| Reds A | 3 | 2 | 0 | 1 | 126 | 55 | 3 | 11 |
| Fiji Warriors | 3 | 2 | 0 | 1 | 154 | 56 | 3 | 11 |
| Force A | 3 | 2 | 0 | 1 | 114 | 65 | 2 | 10 |
| Junior Japan | 3 | 0 | 0 | 3 | 26 | 241 | 0 | 0 |

## POOL B

| | P | W | D | L | PF | PA | BP | PTS |
|---|---|---|---|---|---|---|---|---|
| Pampas XV | 4 | 4 | 0 | 0 | 148 | 83 | 3 | 19 |
| Tonga A | 4 | 2 | 0 | 2 | 96 | 115 | 1 | 9 |
| Gen Blue | 4 | 2 | 0 | 2 | 77 | 91 | 0 | 8 |
| Samoa A | 4 | 1 | 0 | 3 | 82 | 91 | 3 | 7 |
| ACT A | 4 | 1 | 0 | 3 | 78 | 101 | 1 | 5 |

## ASIAN 5 NATIONS

# PERFECT FINISH FOR JAPAN WITH SEVENTH TITLE

### By Karen Bond

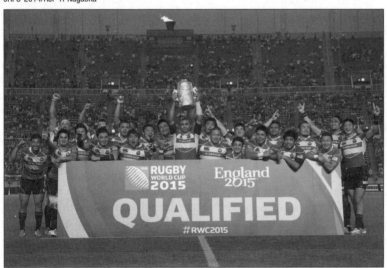

JRFU 2014/RJP H Nagaoka

Japan won the Asian 5 Nations title for a seventh successive year to qualify for Rugby World Cup 2015.

**J**apan have a proud record in the Asian 5 Nations, having won all 24 of their matches in the competition with a bonus point, and they were not about to spoil that perfect return in 2014, particularly not when the champions qualified for Rugby World Cup 2015 and would take their place alongside South Africa, Samoa, Scotland and USA in Pool B.

With Eddie Jones back at the helm after recovering from the stroke he suffered the previous October, the Brave Blossoms did not disappoint, extending their record to 28 bonus-point victories after scoring 342 points and conceding just 33 in seeing off the challenge of Sri Lanka, the Philippines, Korea and Hong Kong to lift the distinctive trophy for the seventh time in a row.

Few would have been brave enough to bet against Japan maintaining their mantle as the only Asian side to grace the Rugby World Cup stage, but it was fitting that the race to secure the Asia 1 qualification berth for England 2015 went down to the final match, between the Brave Blossoms and Hong Kong at the National Stadium in Tokyo.

A crowd of 16,370 were in attendance for the match, the final event to be held in the stadium that was the centrepiece of the 1964 Olympic Games before it is demolished to make way for a modern stadium for RWC 2019 and the 2020 Olympics.

Japan did not have things all their own way against Hong Kong, but try bursts in the final 10 minutes of each half ensured they ran out 49–8 winners to confirm their RWC 2015 place. Yoshikazu Fujita scored three of Japan's eight tries in the victory to finish as the tournament's top try scorer with seven, while full-back Ayumu Goromaru took the point-scoring honours with 92 in four matches.

"It was a tough old game but we have achieved our first goal of qualifying for the World Cup," Jones said afterwards. "Hong Kong competed very hard at the breakdown and it was difficult to get any flow to our game, but what a beautiful ending to one of the most important grounds in Japan."

Captain Michael Leitch knew that despite the dual mission being accomplished, there was plenty of room for improvement. "We will definitely need to step up a level by the time we get to the World Cup," was his simple analysis of Japan's sixth successive Test victory.

Hong Kong's runners-up spot earned them a place in the Repechage against Uruguay in August, but their bid was ended when a strong finish by the Uruguayans saw them prevail 28–3.

The Top 5 was played over five consecutive weekends, beginning in late April. Japan sat out the opening round so it was left to Korea and Hong Kong to make impressive starts to the competition by beating Sri Lanka and the Philippines respectively. It was an emotional day in Incheon with a minute's silence held before kick-off in memory of the victims of the Sewol Ferry disaster 10 days earlier and Korea ensured it was a difficult return to the top tier for Sri Lanka with a 59–3 win.

Hong Kong were even more dominant later that day, scoring 16 tries in a 108–0 victory over the Philippines, with flanker Matt Lamming claiming a hat-trick.

Things didn't get any easier for the Volcanoes with Japan next up, a **123** side that had beaten them 121–0 last year. The Brave Blossoms had the edge in size and strength, running out 99–10 winners over their hosts. It was Hong Kong who topped the table after two rounds following a 41–10 defeat of Sri Lanka though coach Leigh Jones demanded his side raise their "performance levels in a number of areas" for their key match with Korea a week later.

Both sides knew that victory at Hong Kong Football Club would secure at worst a place in the Repechage and it was the hosts who came out on top 39–6, scoring five tries in a performance built around a strong defensive effort. Captain Nick Hewson, though, was quick to point out his side weren't finished just yet. "Our dream is alive. We have booked the Repechage spot for Asia but that is not enough. For certain we'll have a crack at Japan in our final game."

The size of the task was evident when Japan recorded their third highest score and third-biggest winning margin in beating Sri Lanka 132–10 in Nagoya, scoring 20 tries – 16 of them converted by Goromaru for a new Japanese record. Jones was delighted by the win, insisting "we aim to be the greatest-ever Japan team so we should be breaking records."

Hong Kong sat out round four as Japan drew level with them on 18 points at the top of the table following a 62–5 win over Korea in Incheon, wing Akihito Yamada scoring four of their nine tries. There was finally cause for the Philippines to smile after picking up their first victory, 26–25 over Sri Lanka, to ensure they would not finish bottom of the standings.

The Asian 5 Nations will be restructured in 2015 with only Japan, Hong Kong and Korea remaining in the top tier and set to play each other home and away. This means that the Philippines and Sri Lanka will drop down to Division I where they will be joined by Singapore and Kazakhstan, who secured their places by beating UAE and Chinese Taipei respectively.

There were only two matches in Division I this year with a hat-trick by wing Luke McCabe helping Singapore to a 30–13 win over UAE at 7he Sevens in Dubai in April. A month later braces from Daulet Akymbekov and Ivan Olkhovskiy saw Kazakhstan defeat Chinese Taipei 37–8 on neutral soil in Hong Kong.

Qatar, one of the teams on the rise in Asian rugby, reached the final of Division II on home soil after overcoming Thailand 24–11 at Al Arabi Stadium, the venue for the Asian Games back in 2006. Qatar's unbeaten record in the Asian 5 Nations ended in the title decider when Malaysia ran out 31–22 winners, having earlier proved too strong for Iran.

The next two tiers were rebranded Division III East and West in 2014. China emerged as East champions, proving too strong for Guam in the final, 41–10. Indonesia finished third, edging their hosts Laos

11–10. The West honours were claimed by Lebanon following a 20–19 victory over Uzbekistan, with India beating traditional sporting rivals Pakistan 25–7 in the third place play-off.

Mongolia, meanwhile, were crowned Division IV champions after beating their hosts Brunei 38–13 and Cambodia 49–5 in the round robin competition in June.

# ASIAN 5 NATIONS 2014 RESULTS

### TOP 5

Korea 59–3 Sri Lanka, Hong Kong 108–0 Philippines, Philippines 10–99 Japan, Sri Lanka 10–41 Hong Kong, Japan 132–10 Sri Lanka, Hong Kong 39–6 Korea, Korea 5–62 Japan, Sri Lanka 25–26 Philippines, Philippines 22–52 Korea, Japan 49–8 Hong Kong

### DIVISION I

UAE 13–30 Singapore, Kazakhstan 37–8 Chinese Taipei

### DIVISION II

Malaysia 43–22 Iran, Thailand 11–24 Qatar, Iran 26–23 Thailand, Malaysia 31–22 Qatar

### DIVISION III EAST

Guam 48–10 Laos, Indonesia 6–10 China, Laos 10–11 Indonesia, Guam 10–41 China

### DIVISION III WEST

India 17–23 Uzbekistan, Lebanon 17–3 Pakistan, India 25–7 Pakistan, Lebanon 20–19 Uzbekistan

### DIVISION IV

Brunei 13–38 Mongolia, Cambodia 5–49 Mongolia, Brunei 20–25 Cambodia

# TOP 5 STANDINGS

|  | P | W | D | L | F | A | BP | PTS |
|---|---|---|---|---|---|---|---|---|
| Japan | 4 | 4 | 0 | 0 | 342 | 33 | 4 | 24 |
| Hong Kong | 4 | 3 | 0 | 1 | 196 | 65 | 0 | 15 |
| Korea | 4 | 2 | 0 | 2 | 122 | 126 | 0 | 10 |
| Philippines | 4 | 1 | 0 | 3 | 58 | 284 | 0 | 5 |
| Sri Lanka | 4 | 0 | 0 | 4 | 48 | 258 | 1 | 1 |

# International Sevens Tournaments

# NEW ZEALAND SHOW THEIR CLASS WHEN IT MATTERS MOST

## By Mike Friday

IRB/Martin Seras Lima

CHAMPIONS 2013/2014

DJ Forbes lifts the trophy as the All Blacks Sevens celebrate a 12th Sevens World Series title in 15 seasons.

It was a new season, and a new beginning too, for so many countries, with no fewer than 10 changes to coaching set-ups across the 15 core teams. Of the previous season's top six, only New Zealand retained the same head coach in Sir Gordon Tietjens, and that only added to the uncertainty of who should be feared and who shouldn't, and what styles of play would stay, change or evolve.

The Series also had a refinement with the bottom core team relegated, unlike the previous year when Scotland, Spain and Portugal all survived the qualifier play-off and effectively re-booked their places. This time, **127** the qualifier for that 15th core team would take place in Hong Kong, alongside the Series round.

Proceedings opened on the Gold Coast where we got first sight of the teams. While there were new faces in the coaches' chairs, there was a familiarity in the players on show and the pool stages went according to plan. South Africa, under new coach Neil Powell, had suffered travel problems, only arriving the night before the tournament. His side, though, was nevertheless involved in an epic semi-final with Australia, Jesse Parahi scoring the winner about eight minutes into golden point extra-time.

We saw New Zealand clinically find their way to the final and while Australia took early control to go 12–0 up, inevitably that semi-final caught up with them and the powerful Kiwis came through 40–19. England had also impressed under new coach Simon Amor, finishing third with an impressive 47–0 win over South Africa after earlier beating Ben Ryan's Fiji in a delicious quarter-final.

With all the changes, the next six weeks were vitally important to regroup and refocus for 'Sevens in the Desert' in Dubai, the rugby purists' tournament of the circuit. We saw changes in a number of squads, but the most notable was the recall of Fiji's Pio Tuwai who had been out of favour the last few years. There was no doubt that the star on day two was that man Tuwai, ably assisted by newly installed captain Osea Kolinisau, Benito Masilevu and the effervescent speedster Samisoni Viriviri, who came to the forefront as we witnessed a perfect display of Sevens in the semi-final to destroy a very experienced New Zealand side 44–0.

Eight different players scored tries in New Zealand's largest defeat under Gordon's tenure. It was simply breath-taking to watch. In the other semi-final South Africa beat England 26–12, but they were unable to contain the fluent Fijians in what was an evenly-contested final. Fiji won that 29–17, while New Zealand showed their character by beating England 17–14 to finish third.

Barely had the players drawn breath when we all moved straight on to Port Elizabeth and the Nelson Mandela Bay Stadium amid high emotion with the passing of Madiba that week. The tournament went ahead as a celebration of his life and the occasion and atmosphere as the nation unified once again under the banner of rugby was breath-taking to see. Madiba Magic was evident on day two, which historically has been a happy hunting ground for New Zealand. This time we saw the ice cool control of coach Powell as he and his team embraced the feelings of the nation.

Portugal and France had forced their way into their first Cup quarter-finals with England and Australia falling short and we also saw a number of fine individual tries – including one moment of magic from Spaniard Ignacio Martin against USA – but the 'big guns' again made it through. The semi-finals saw South Africa dispose of Argentina 31–0 with New Zealand edging past Samoa, who had earlier outplayed Fiji, 19–5.

The final was the one that everyone wanted and it didn't disappoint. New Zealand took the lead, but Madiba Magic inspired South Africa, and in particular their talisman Kyle Brown, to come back from 14–0 down to win 17–14, cheered by 30,000 fans who sounded like 130,000.

As 2014 fell upon us a change of schedule meant we next headed to Las Vegas – the trickiest of the pitches on the circuit with its narrow dimensions – and there we saw the emergence of Canada, who broke through to make their first Cup quarter-final, and then semi-final, of the season. Fiji also came up short, failing to make the Cup with a very uncharacteristic display, while Samoa continued their form on a pitch well suited to their style and powered into the semi-final with a good win over Australia. There they met South Africa and lost a highly competitive game 14–0. In the other half New Zealand were once again going about their business, beating England 24–7 to meet Canada, who had edged past France.

It was a major breakthrough for Canada to reach this Cup semi-final with Phil Mack at the centre of everything, aided by the physical John Moonlight and Connor Braid to assert their power game. The experienced New Zealanders coped, though, and with their own power through Bryce Heem, Scott Curry and IRB Sevens Player of the Year Tim Mikkelson they overcame the brave Canadians.

That win set up a repeat of the Port Elizabeth final and on the narrower pitch this was always going to be a bruising affair. Its intensity didn't let us down, with South Africa defending their title with a 14–7 win, courtesy of tries from Branco du Preez and the impact substitute Werner Kok. In fact, South Africa only conceded two tries in the entire tournament. Canada went on to finish third, their highest-ever placing, and Geraint John was clearly building a resilient, effective squad which was growing in confidence.

After a week's break it was on to Wellington and day one was full of key match-ups, with Fiji beating New Zealand and England doing the same to South Africa. Even so, all four progressed to the Cup quarters, while Canada continued their rise, this time winning their pool, and Australia also returned to winning ways to top theirs. This made for a fascinating day two, South Africa creeping past the technically astute Australians to set up a semi-final with Fiji, while New Zealand looked ominous with a powerful 24–0 victory against Canada to earn a date with England.

New Zealand asserted their power and physicality with a team who all stood over six foot and with the power and pace to match, winning 31–0. It was a clear statement of intent about the change of shape and size of athlete that Gordon wanted, which left his reliable "petit general" Tomasi Cama settling for a substitute's role. South Africa again showed their defensive prowess to shut Fiji out in the other semi, winning 10–0 with Cecil Afrika scoring his 100th Series try in a result that set up another NZ-SA final. The match was another fierce affair but this time the powerhouse New Zealanders shut out South Africa clinically to win 21–0 playing perfect knockout Sevens. Like the Boks in Vegas they had conceded just 12 points, all in the opening game against Fiji, while amassing 185.

A month later and another change in the Series schedule meant we travelled to Tokyo. The core teams at the bottom of the Series standings now knew they had to step up, with the threat of relegation looming. USA rose to that challenge, clawing their way into a first Cup quarter-final of the season after Zack Test scored a decisive try in a win over Samoa and two more in a draw against Fiji, who also progressed. USA lost narrowly to South Africa, while neighbours Canada continued their consistency by making the Cup quarter-finals, only to be edged out by England.

Fiji blew Kenya away in their quarter-final and New Zealand eased past Australia into the semi-finals but were beaten in a scintillating game by Fiji who in the final would play South Africa, victors over England. For the Blitzboks it was a fifth consecutive final and, though South Africa would travel to Hong Kong top of the Series, they would lose an enthralling final 33–26 after another moment of Fijian magic by Pio Tuwai, who put Waisea Nacuqu in for a decisive try.

Tension was building as we moved to Hong Kong, where the qualifier winner would also be guaranteed a core team place in 2014–15. Japan were the pre–tournament favourite and plotted their way through to the final, led by the playmaking skills of Lomano Lemeki. There they met a passionate Italian team coached by former England campaigner Andy Vilk, and the Brave Blossoms came out on top to earn their place in the Series for next year.

In the main draw, USA and Canada both backed up their previous week's Cup quarters, while South Africa lost their captain and talisman Brown on day one and never recovered, losing to England in the quarter-final. This opened the door for New Zealand and they took full advantage, powering their way into the final past a spirited Australian team 19–7. In the other semi England put on a tactical master-class to out-think Fiji and set up a first title shot since 2006, back when coach Amor had been the captain. As ever, England were the crowd favourites, but New Zealand had other ideas and, inspired by captain DJ Forbes, who literally ran his blood to water, they won 26–7 to return to the top of the standings with two rounds to play.

The first of those European climax events was in Glasgow in early May and it was clear that Canada were now consistently pushing the so-called 'bigger teams', topping their pool again. A revitalised Scotland team, boasting Nick De Luca and Richie Vernon, also topped their pool and progressed to the semi-finals after beating South Africa in the last eight amid remarkable scenes. There they would lose 10–7 to Canada, who themselves were to play in a first World Series Cup final. The other side of the draw was tense, Fiji squeezing past England and New Zealand overcoming Australia. The semi-final did not disappoint. Yet again the breakdown skills of Forbes, together with the physical size, technical accuracy and power of the squad, meant they had too much for Fiji, and that theme continued into the final, New Zealand emphatically beating a tired Canada 54–7. More importantly, New Zealand had taken control of the Series when it mattered most.

And so there was much expectation and excitement as we headed to Twickenham for the Series finale and 70,000 'monsters' on day one. England toppled New Zealand to finish top of their pool but the Kiwis progressed with them, in doing so guaranteeing a 12th Series title in 15 years, an outstanding achievement. South Africa maintained their high standards, with Fiji looking to finish strongly, while Australia were desperate to provide an appropriate send-off for their departing mentor Mick O'Connor, an immensely popular and technically astute coach who was stepping down at the end of the Series.

So on to day two and with the Series decided we would see who wanted the last say and the final silverware of the season. The quarter-finals were all tightly contested apart from one as New Zealand brushed South Africa aside 32–5, as if to underline their supremacy when it mattered most. One cannot help but feel, though, that losing Kyle Brown in Hong Kong proved South Africa's undoing in this relentless Series. Australia beat England in the first semi-final and New Zealand also kept up their charge and the rest happened in a blur: to say the final was end-to-end would be an understatement. The exciting Cameron Clark caused problems for the New Zealand defence and the physical foot-ballers Con Foley and Jesse Parahi matched them up front, but as so often the collective inner belief and culture came to New Zealand's rescue, Ben Lam and Scott Curry running their hearts out alongside the guile of Gillies Kaka. After finding themselves 21–0 down, the Kiwis put together a five-minute burst which yielded four unanswered tries either side of half-time and, while the Australian boys fought hard until the final whistle, New Zealand won an amazing game 52–33.

Without doubt it was a marvellous season, New Zealand and South Africa going toe to toe until the end. Fiji will not be content with third, but did have two Cup wins under new coach Ben Ryan, and England improved significantly under Simon Amor, who still awaits a first Cup win as coach. We also saw notable advances, with Canada and Australia becoming real contenders, while others slipped off the pace in Kenya, Samoa and France. The 2014–15 Series will no doubt bring added spice, with direct Olympic qualification for four teams. Will any nations dip into their 'marquee' Test players to complement the Sevens stars? It all makes for an intriguing HSBC Sevens World Series 2014–15, by the end of which four teams will have booked their place at Rio 2016.

# HSBC SEVENS WORLD SERIES 2013–14 RESULTS

## AUSTRALIA: 12–13 OCTOBER

New Zealand (22), Australia (19), England (17), South Africa (15), Fiji (13), Kenya (12), Samoa (10), Wales (10), France (8), Canada (7), Argentina (5), Scotland (5), USA (3), Portugal (2), Spain (1), Tonga (1)

## DUBAI: 29–30 NOVEMBER

Fiji (22), South Africa (19), New Zealand (17), England (15), Argentina (13), Wales (12), Scotland (10), Kenya (10), Australia (8), Portugal (7), Canada (5), Samoa (5), France (3), Spain (2), USA (1), Russia (1)

## SOUTH AFRICA: 7–8 DECEMBER

South Africa (22), New Zealand (19), Samoa (17), Argentina (15), Fiji (13), France (12), Kenya (10), Portugal (10), England (8), Australia (7), Wales (5), USA (5), Scotland (3), Canada (2), Spain (1), Zimbabwe (1)

## USA: 24–26 JANUARY

South Africa (22), New Zealand (19), Canada (17), Samoa (15), England (13), Australia (12), France (10), Argentina (10), Fiji (8), Kenya (7), Wales (5), Scotland (5), USA (3), Spain (2), Portugal (1), Uruguay (1)

## NEW ZEALAND: 7–8 FEBRUARY

New Zealand (22), South Africa (19), Fiji (17), England (15), Australia (13), Canada (12), Samoa (10), Argentina (10), Kenya (8), Scotland (7), Wales (5), France (5), USA (3), Spain (2), Tonga (1), Portugal (1)

**132**

SEVENS

## JAPAN: 22–23 MARCH

Fiji (22), South Africa (19), England (17), New Zealand (15), Australia (13), USA (12), Kenya (10), Canada (10), Wales (8), Scotland (7), France (5), Japan (5), Argentina (3), Samoa (2), Spain (1), Portugal (1)

## HONG KONG: 28–30 MARCH

New Zealand (22), England (19), Fiji (17), Australia (15), South Africa (13), Wales (12), Canada (10), USA (10), Scotland (8), France (7), Argentina (5), Samoa (5), Kenya (3), Portugal (2), Sri Lanka (1), Spain (1)

## SCOTLAND: 3–4 MAY

New Zealand (22), Canada (19), Fiji (17), Scotland (15), England (13), Kenya (12), Australia (10), South Africa (10), France (8), Argentina (7), Samoa (5), Spain (5), Wales (3), Japan (2), Portugal (1), USA (1)

## ENGLAND: 10–11 MAY

New Zealand (22), Australia (19), England (17), Fiji (15), South Africa (13), Kenya (12), Samoa (10), France (10), Canada (8), Argentina (7), Wales (5), Spain (5), USA (3), Japan (2), Portugal (1), Scotland (1)

# FINAL STANDINGS

| | |
|---|---|
| New Zealand – 180 | Scotland – 61 |
| South Africa – 152 | USA – 41 |
| Fiji – 144 | Portugal – 26 |
| England – 134 | Spain – 20 |
| Australia – 116 | Japan – 9 |
| Canada – 90 | Tonga – 2 |
| Kenya – 84 | Russia – 1 |
| Samoa – 79 | Sri Lanka – 1 |
| Argentina – 75 | Uruguay – 1 |
| France – 68 | Zimbabwe – 1 |
| Wales – 65 | |

## PREVIOUS WINNERS

| | | |
|---|---|---|
| 1999–2000 – New Zealand | 2004–2005 – New Zealand | 2007–2008 – New Zealand |
| 2000–2001 – New Zealand | 2005–2006 – Fiji | 2008–2009 – South Africa |
| 2001–2002 – New Zealand | 2006–2007 – New Zealand | 2009–2010 – Samoa |
| 2002–2003 – New Zealand | 2010–2011 – New Zealand | 2012–2013 – New Zealand |
| 2003–2004 – New Zealand | 2011–2012 – New Zealand | 2013–2014 – New Zealand |

# NEW ZEALAND PUSHED ALL THE WAY IN TITLE DEFENCE

## By Sue Day

IRB/Martin Seras Lima

Australia's Rachel Crothers scored a hat-trick in the Dubai final which set the tone for the Women's Series.

**D**ifferent year, same result, but a very different story. On the face of it very little changed between the inaugural IRB Women's Sevens World Series and the 2013–14 vintage. There was just one more tournament this time around – São Paulo proving an excellent and entertaining additional venue – and the same team, New Zealand, came out on top.

But dig a little deeper and the story is somewhat different. Last year New Zealand were runaway winners, taking the Series by a clear 14 points from a distant England. This year, with one round to play in

Amsterdam, just two points separated the top two teams, Australia and New Zealand. The Series could have gone either way up until the final games of the final tournament, illustrating the emerging and exhilarating depth in Women's Sevens.

In the end favourites and world champions New Zealand came out on top, winning the Amsterdam final by a comfortable 29–12, but all season they were pushed very hard by a fast-improving, young Australian team. The improvements made by Australia illustrate the transformational effect of the increase in funding that Women's Sevens has enjoyed over the course of the last 18 months. Last season the Wallaroos, a team of players holding down full and part-time jobs in all corners of Australia, finished in fifth place, a full 28 points behind New Zealand. This year, all contracted rugby players and centralised in Narrabeen on Sydney's northern beaches, they were so close to Series victory that their celebrated neighbours could feel them breathing down the necks of their famous black jerseys every step of the way. Of the eight core teams England were the only non-contracted one, meaning that far fewer of the world's best players now have to fit their training in at the margins of the day, exhausted from work or studies, and far more of them can spend their time honing their skills, both individually and in their squads.

This is indeed an exciting moment in Women's Sevens. And the newly emerging southern hemisphere rivalry at the heart of it could hardly have been announced in more spectacular style than in the 2013–14 Series opener in Dubai at the end of November.

In a portent of the domination to follow throughout the season, New Zealand and Australia cruised unbeaten to the final. New Zealand then surged to a five tries to one lead with a minute of the second half gone. Rarely has any New Zealand side ever given up such a position of dominance. Rarely, though, has any side come up against a squad with the belief and determination that Sharni Williams and her team bring. The Dubai crowd, and indeed the whole of the rugby world, watched in disbelief as Australia scored 28 unanswered points – the cool-headed Cobie-Jane Morgan crucially slotting every single conversion – to win 35–27 and claim their first Cup silverware. A breath-taking start to the Series and a breath-taking start to the career of 19-year-old Rachel Crothers who announced herself to the world with a hat-trick and a demonstration of the kind of power finishing that New Zealand's Portia Woodman and Kayla McAlister had made their own the previous season.

Among the teams trailing in the wake of the top two, most notable were the performances of Russia – the European champions claimed third place, ahead of both England and Canada and in the process equalled their best ever Series finish – and Fiji, who claimed their best result by winning the Bowl final.

The Series then moved on to Atlanta – a new home after Houston hosted the round the previous year – where normal service was resumed. New Zealand were the form team throughout the tournament and ran out 36–0 winners against Canada in the final, with Sarah Goss instrumental in their dominance. It seemed to be a game too far for Jen Kish's Canada who had put in such an impressive display to defeat Dubai champions Australia in the semis. Ashley Steacy, Ghislaine Landry and Kish herself had shone for the Canadians throughout, but were unable to leave their mark on the final.

It was no surprise to see the names Woodman and McAlister towards the top of the try-scoring charts in Atlanta but significantly – and ominously for the competition – they were joined there by their 18-year-old compatriot Gayle Broughton. Broughton has a classic, unreadable step off both feet and an electric turn of pace. Playing in the same position as IRB Women's Sevens Player of the Year McAlister her opportunities were limited but she took them in spectacular fashion. There was no perceptible difference in the speed, accuracy and effectiveness of New Zealand's play when McAlister made way for Broughton which says it all about the youngster's talent. The try that she scored in the final, with the game already won and with a huge smile on her face, was world-class.

And so onto São Paulo and the first time that tournaments had been played on consecutive weekends, with a meagre four rest days between kick-off in Brazil and the Atlanta final. Team pool recovery sessions and ice baths are always a little more bearable in the 30 degrees of somewhere like São Paulo – Atlanta had record-breaking snowfall during the previous week's tournament – and, perhaps consequently, all of the teams made the transition impressively. It was an eventful tournament for Canada who managed to record two disappointing losses and still finish up in third place: having suffered a surprising loss to Spain in the pool (beaten 28–26 after seemingly coasting at 17–5 up just before half-time), they then regained their concentration to beat the same opposition, easily, in the Cup quarter-final. Then in the semi-final, having been steamrollered by New Zealand by 36 clear points in the previous week's final, they fought their way to a 17–5 lead against the women in black with 30 seconds to play. And yet somehow New Zealand found a way to turn it around. The star players from the previous week came to the fore: Broughton crossing the whitewash with 20 seconds to play and Goss scoring the winning try a full two and a half minutes into added time. It was stirring stuff from New Zealand but Canada will know that it was their own naivety and poor decisions at key moments that lost it for them. Such lessons are hard to take but also ones that will never be forgotten.

It was pure belief that got New Zealand to the final, but in the end that was not enough. They came up against an Australian team rejuvenated after a disappointing Atlanta and inspired by the outstanding Emilee Cherry. Australia won 24–12 and Cherry – who was later named IRB Women's Sevens Player of the Year in Amsterdam – gave a master-class in the all-round game. She ran, with wonderful changes of pace and direction; she passed, with accuracy and exquisite timing; she kicked, cleverly; and demonstrating that modern-day backs have to be able to match the forwards in the darker arts, she stole ball in contact that George Smith himself would have been proud of. On this occasion New Zealand had no answer.

At tournament number four, however, in China, they did, beating Australia 26–12 in the final. No surprises in the identity of the finalists but the real story of the tournament was elsewhere. This was Fiji's second chance in the 2013–14 Series to mix it with the world's best Sevens teams and if they had done well in Dubai by winning the Bowl, here they well and truly announced themselves on the world stage, beating three of Europe's four core teams – Russia, England and Ireland – on their way to fourth place. They will have more opportunities to play against the best next season and surely it is only a matter of time before we see the women emulating their male counterparts and running away with a title.

And so New Zealand won the Series from Australia – three tournaments to two, 96 points to 92. Very, very tight. Canada will be disappointed with their third place but on 80 points they were a full 20 points ahead of the next closest challenger, England. Those three, of course, will be very strong again next year.

Next season should be interesting. In Amsterdam, two sleeping giants awoke from their slumber. England finished fourth in the end but beat Canada along the way and ran New Zealand mighty close in the semis. USA played, without doubt, their best rugby of the Series, beating Russia 27–12 and taking the Plate final. In 2013–14 England had less time together than any other team. Put that right next season and they will be a force to be reckoned with. In 2013–14 the USA, more than any other team, blooded inexperienced athletes from other sports. Jessica Javelet, assimilated from field hockey, looks to be the fastest player on the circuit – think Carlin Isles but with far, far more minutes on the pitch – and if she and those others continue to develop as they have so far, the US will have a team to be reckoned with too.

For now, it is New Zealand and Australia who deserve the accolades but with the investment, development and innovation that is going on around the world it will get harder and harder for those teams to dominate. Exciting times indeed for Women's Sevens.

# IRB WOMEN'S SEVENS WORLD SERIES 2013–14 RESULTS

## DUBAI: 28–29 NOVEMBER

Australia (20), New Zealand (18), Russia (16), Canada (14), England (12), Spain (10), USA (8), Brazil (6), Fiji (4), France (3), Ireland (2), Tunisia (1)

## USA: 15–16 FEBRUARY

New Zealand (20), Canada (18), Australia (16), Russia (14), USA (12), Spain (10), England (8), Japan (6), Netherlands (4), China (3), Brazil (2), Ireland (1)

## BRAZIL: 21–22 FEBRUARY

Australia (20), New Zealand (18), Canada (16), England (14), Spain (12), Russia (10), Japan (8), Netherlands (6), USA (4), Brazil (3), Ireland (2), Argentina (1)

## CHINA: 5–6 APRIL

New Zealand (20), Australia (18), Canada (16), Fiji (14), England (12), France (10), Spain (8), Russia (6), Ireland (4), China (3), USA (2), Brazil (1)

## NETHERLANDS: 16–17 MAY

New Zealand (20), Australia (18), Canada (16), England (14), USA (12), Russia (10), France (8), Brazil (6), Netherlands (4), South Africa (3), Ireland (2), Spain (1)

# FINAL STANDINGS

| | |
|---|---|
| New Zealand – 96 | Fiji – 18 |
| Australia – 92 | Japan – 14 |
| Canada – 80 | Netherlands – 14 |
| England – 60 | Ireland – 11 |
| Russia – 56 | China – 6 |
| Spain – 41 | South Africa – 3 |
| USA – 38 | Argentina – 1 |
| France – 21 | Tunisia – 1 |
| Brazil – 18 | |

# SEVENS AROUND THE WORLD

## By Seb Lauzier

The **2014–15 season** is the most important in the history of Rugby Sevens, bringing with it qualification for the 2016 Olympic Games in Brazil.

While the top four-ranked sides will qualify from both the men's and women's World Series for Rio 2016, 12 more teams will book their places from men's and women's regional events, to be played between June and December 2015.

With that in mind, the regional competitions staged in 2014 carry huge significance as teams benefit not only from confidence and new faces, but also from government backing and, in many cases, increasing investment.

### ASIA (AFRU)

While Japan's men claimed the two biggest prizes on offer in 2014, winning core team status on the HSBC Sevens World Series and also the gold medal at the Asian Games Rugby Sevens event, it was their great rivals Hong Kong who claimed the region's Sevens Series crown.

In the first round they beat surprise finalists Korea 40–0 and then saw off the Japanese 24–7 in Kuala Lumpur before completing a clean sweep with a 36–19 win over the Koreans in the final round in Beijing in October to reclaim the title they last won back in 2012.

China beat their hosts Hong Kong 38–7 in the final of the first Asian Sevens Series women's event in August. However, this was only the beginning as the continent's leading women's Sevens side then secured core team status on the World Series and claimed gold at the Asian Games before rounding off a successful season by clinching the second Asian Sevens Series title and the regional crown for 2014, although a last-minute try by Mifuyu Koide gave Japan a confidence-boosting 24–19 win over Asia's leading women's Sevens side in the Beijing final.

### EUROPE (RUGBY EUROPE)

After an indifferent 2013–14 World Series season, France's men struck gold in Rugby Europe's Sevens Grand Prix, coming back to beat Spain 22–17 in the final at the fourth round in Bucharest. It was the second title of the summer for Frédéric Pomarel's side after victory on home soil in Lyon in the opening tournament, and breathed new life into their World Series challenge for 2014–15.

England claimed the other two tournament titles, in Moscow and Manchester, but France's aggregate score from the four rounds was enough to secure the overall crown.

Russia, meanwhile, underlined their rapid advance in women's Sevens by claiming the overall European Grand Prix title for the second year running. Pavel Baronovsky's team finished runners-up to England in Moscow and to France in Brive, but their greater overall consistency allowed them to prevail and underline that they will be key contenders in the World Series battles ahead. There was also joy for the French team as they secured core team status on the World Series in 2014–15 despite losing to Fiji in an enthralling final in the qualifying tournament in Hong Kong in September.

## OCEANIA (FORU)

After two days and 56 matches of frenetic action in early October, Fiji's men and New Zealand's women were crowned Oceania Sevens champions in Noosa, Australia.

A week before the start of the new HSBC Sevens World Series 2014–15, Fiji beat the All Blacks Sevens – playing in their first Oceania Sevens – 21–5 in the final, while a revitalised Samoa were too strong for a tired looking Australia 33–7 in the third place play-off.

The women's competition came down to the expected final between New Zealand and Australia, who between them had won all five rounds of the IRB Women's Sevens World Series in 2013–14. Australia entered the tournament as defending champions, but had no answer to the reigning World Cup and World Series champions, who triumphed 31–10 to take the regional bragging rights back to New Zealand.

Fiji finished third – ahead of Samoa, Papua New Guinea, the Cook Islands and Tonga – as they continue to prepare for joining the World Series as a core team in 2014–15. They will certainly be a team no one should underestimate, as shown in their run to the Cup semi-finals at the China round of the Series in 2014.

## SOUTH AMERICA (CONSUR)

Argentina's men and Brazil's women both retained their South American Sevens titles in 2014, emerging victorious at the ODESUR Games in Santiago, Chile.

For the first time, South America's premier multi-sport event doubled as the CONSUR (Confederación Sudamericana de Rugby) Sevens Championships and as well as vying for the title of regional champions, the competing nations were also playing for places at the 2015 Pan-American Games in Toronto, Canada.

Argentina won all six of their round robin pool matches in the men's competition, before beating closest challengers Uruguay 29–5 to land the gold medal. Uruguay also sealed their place at the Pan-Am Games, while Chile beat Rio 2016 hosts Brazil 31–7 to claim bronze.

In the women's competition, nine-time regional champions Brazil started as the overwhelming favourites and lived up to that billing with six impressive pool wins before seeing off an improving Argentina 40–0 in the final. Uruguay edged Colombia 5–0 to win the bronze medal.

**SEVENS**

## AFRICA (CAR)

One week before Dubai hosts both the men's and women's World Series events, Harare will stage the African Sevens on 29–30 November. Kenya are the reigning African men's champions, while South Africa are the region's women's champions.

Indeed, 2014 proved a significant year for South African Sevens.

The country's men became the first team in history to deny New Zealand Commonwealth Games gold. In beating the All Blacks Sevens 17–12 at Glasgow 2014 in late July, the Blitzboks ended New Zealand's 16-year stranglehold on the event.

Meanwhile their female counterparts then beat the Netherlands to gain core team status on the IRB Women's Sevens World Series, thereby boosting their chances of Olympic qualification.

## NORTH AMERICA & CARIBBEAN (NACRA)

The men's and women's NACRA (North America & Caribbean Rugby Association) Sevens Championships for 2014 will take place in Mexico City on 3–4 December. Those involved will be hoping to follow in the footsteps of the 2013 champions – Trinidad & Tobago's men and Canada's women. Trinidad & Tobago beat Barbados 14–5 in the men's final in 2013, while Canada proved too strong for Mexico, winning the women's title decider 51–0.

# Women's Rugby

# PREPARATION AND DESIRE KEY TO ENGLAND SUCCESS

*By Maggie Alphonsi*

Captain Katy Mclean lifts the trophy after England beat Canada in the Women's Rugby World Cup 2014 final.

I t's hard to put into words how I felt when the final whistle blew to signify England had won the Women's Rugby World Cup 2014. It was incredible and a weight off my shoulders. I'd got to the final before and seen New Zealand celebrate so I'd always wondered what it felt like. I was overwhelmed by the whole experience. All you think about is finding your teammates and hugging them. For some of us it was eight years of hard work finally paying off. It was a special moment that only a few people can say they have really experienced.

I had knee surgery a couple of years before the World Cup and having that injury and wanting to get back is what spurred me on personally. As a team, losing the 2010 final on home soil was a huge motivation. Not many of that team retired because while we'd won the Six Nations, we still weren't classed as the best team in the world so that was the biggest thing that spurred us on.

There were a few things I feel were key to our success in France. The biggest was probably the fact we learnt from the last World Cup final about things we needed to change, both on and off the pitch in terms of our structure and preparation across the four-year cycle. In 2014 we were prepared for every scenario.

In the four years between World Cups we played against the top teams more regularly. We played New Zealand several times, both home and away, we played at Twickenham and on TV. We exposed ourselves to playing in front of a big crowd and with big expectation levels, so that wasn't new to us any more. In 2010 it was probably still a novelty for us to play New Zealand. We also had more time together, lots more camps and training time compared to previous World Cups which all helped us to understand each other better. We used every minute of those days to make sure we were a better squad.

When we arrived in France for the World Cup the atmosphere in the squad was buzzing. We were the fittest and smartest we have ever been, we were so well prepared and we weren't going to let anything stop us. When you're at a World Cup you can end up being in your own little bubble because you won't necessarily see a lot of the other teams outside of match days. Our psychologist had done a lot of work in creating a bit of culture and atmosphere and our meeting room had pictures of us accompanied by positive words. It really helped to see those good memories up on the walls every day.

Our first match was against Samoa. We hadn't played them for a long time but had seen them play against New Zealand in June. It was a very challenging game for us at the start of the tournament, but also the kind of game that we needed. We were tested physically and, like in every game, we learnt things that we needed to learn.

We hadn't played Spain in a long time either because they aren't in the Six Nations anymore, so we didn't really know what to expect of them either, but we knew they were fit, strong and committed from seeing them play on the Sevens circuit. It was a good challenge for us and we improved from the Samoa game.

Canada we knew were going to be a very physical and challenging team and that proved to be the case. It took us onto another level. We had played and beaten them twice in November and they pushed us to the very end. A draw was probably a fair reflection of the match. It was a physical game, they dominated the first half and we probably started to take control in the second. It probably wasn't our best game, it was a bit of a wake-up call really that we needed to do more.

We finished top of our pool but whatever tournament you play in, when you reach the knockout stages you wipe the slate clean and start again. Ireland had beaten New Zealand which meant they were obviously a very good side. We knew we needed to take it to another level. If you ask anyone who played in that game they will say it was the best we played in the entire tournament. We put 40 points on Ireland, which was the most ever.

That Canada game really pushed us, we knew we couldn't sit on our laurels, we knew we'd have to work for it and we definitely did that against Ireland. In any tournament you have to be good in all five games but peak at the right time. In 2010, we won all our games but by the time we got to the semi-final we'd possibly given all that we could and come the final we possibly didn't have enough left. Come this World Cup we were very smart in how we rotated players – we had 26 players who could all play and that's what won us the World Cup.

The build-up to the final was really good in terms of our work. We knew what to expect and what jobs we needed to do. Training was well structured, it was specific and had a purpose. That week was very much based on lots of players taking more ownership so that our leadership group came forward and had more responsibility for managing the team. Our psychologist was very important again, we did a lot of work on going through how we'd react if a certain situation happened. Everyone knew they could do a good job irrespective of whether they'd played in a final before or not.

I don't know whether the fact so many of us had played in a final before gave us an advantage over first-time finalists Canada. Canada had, after all, been in a World Cup final in Sevens. I watched them miss out to New Zealand in Moscow, so a few of their players had experienced playing in a final and going close. I guess the benefit for us was that we had more players who'd experienced a World Cup final and the disappointment of missing out. We'd also been more exposed to that level of pressure, the Six Nations is a very big tournament that allows us to experience playing in front of 15,000 people in a match you know you have to win otherwise you don't win the title.

Without doubt the World Cup gave women's rugby some huge exposure. 2010 was essentially the start of women's rugby being in the spotlight. The final was watched by 14,000 people at The Stoop, there were lots of TV viewers, and the newspapers acknowledged that women played rugby and played it well. The hardest thing was to maintain that continuity over the next four years.

What 2014 did was bring more exposure to the women's game. The French did a great job as hosts, the media coverage was excellent and the tournament was followed by a lot of people, not just your typical women's rugby supporters but the top men's professionals too. To see people like Jonny Wilkinson and Johnny Sexton following women's rugby or coming to watch the event was pretty cool. I think Jamie Roberts presented the shirts to the Welsh players and we had a big campaign before we went to the World Cup with people like Prince Harry and Prime Minister David Cameron showing their support for us. Social media has improved so much over the last four years which has helped raise the profile even further.

When we won the World Cup we were on the front pages of newspapers. What was even more pleasing was people were watching the World Cup and forgetting they were watching a specific gender, but just a great game of rugby. It was another step forward that women's rugby was being acknowledged for the quality of the players on show.

It's important we carry that momentum forward and it's nice that people now know the players' names. There has been a huge rush of interest in the women's game; we see more young girls wanting to get involved in the sport because they have role models to aspire to, not just in England but right across the world.

I think the good thing about women's rugby is that it is so much more competitive and there are more and more teams capable of winning the Women's Rugby World Cup. A lot of games could have gone either way which made it so exciting for the spectators. England might not have got to the final and New Zealand didn't get there for the first time in years. When England don't win a Six Nations it almost brings more attention to the tournament because it is unexpected. So at a World Cup when New Zealand get knocked out people are curious to see who is going to win it.

Ireland's win over New Zealand, who were going for a fifth title in a row, was reward for the incredible hard work they have put in over the last four years. They have always been so close to taking other teams on, but they did everything they could to become a better squad. Canada are the same, they have invested a lot in their programme. They had a few Tests against us and in New Zealand, exposing their players to a higher level of Test rugby and that can only improve them.

Now that Sevens is in the Olympics we're going to see the athleticism and standards of players go up and up, and that will filter back to the Fifteens. Going into the next World Cup, in 2017, the level of competitiveness is going to increase even further. The likes of USA are not far away from developing into a really good outfit. Samoa, Wales, Kazakhstan and Spain will only improve so it is going to be exciting to see.

I decided to retire after the tournament because I've always wanted to be a World Cup winner and now I've finally achieved that I'm happy to step away and see other girls experience what I've been fortunate to experience. All I ever wanted to do was to just play rugby. People's perception of the women's game is that we're not physical enough, not aggressive enough like the men, when actually watching myself and other women play now all those stereotypical views have been dispelled. Hopefully I've helped push the boundaries of what women can do.

# WOMEN'S RUGBY WORLD CUP 2014 RESULTS

## POOL A

Round One: **Canada** 31–5 **Spain**, **England** 65–3 **Samoa**. Round Two: **England** 45–5 **Spain**, **Canada** 42–7 **Samoa**. Round Three: **Spain** 41–5 **Samoa**, **England** 13–13 **Canada**.

## POOL B

Round One: **New Zealand** 79–5 **Kazakhstan**, **USA** 17–23 **Ireland**. Round Two: **USA** 47–7 **Kazakhstan**, **New Zealand** 14–17 **Ireland**. Round Three: **Ireland** 40–5 **Kazakhstan**, **New Zealand** 34–3 **USA**.

## POOL C

Round One: **Australia** 26–3 **South Africa**, **France** 26–0 **Wales**. Round 2: **Australia** 25–3 **Wales**, **France** 55–3 **South Africa**. Round Three: **Wales** 35–3 **South Africa**, **Australia** 3–17 **France**.

# POOL TABLES

### POOL A

|          | P | W | D | L | F   | A   | BP | PTS |
|----------|---|---|---|---|-----|-----|----|-----|
| England  | 3 | 2 | 1 | 0 | 123 | 21  | 2  | 12  |
| Canada   | 3 | 2 | 1 | 0 | 86  | 25  | 2  | 12  |
| Spain    | 3 | 1 | 0 | 2 | 51  | 81  | 1  | 5   |
| Samoa    | 3 | 0 | 0 | 3 | 15  | 148 | 0  | 0   |

### POOL B

|             | P | W | D | L | F   | A   | BP | PTS |
|-------------|---|---|---|---|-----|-----|----|-----|
| Ireland     | 3 | 3 | 0 | 0 | 80  | 36  | 2  | 13  |
| New Zealand | 3 | 2 | 0 | 1 | 127 | 25  | 3  | 11  |
| USA         | 3 | 1 | 0 | 2 | 67  | 64  | 2  | 6   |
| Kazakhstan  | 3 | 0 | 0 | 3 | 17  | 166 | 0  | 0   |

### POOL C

|              | P | W | D | L | F  | A   | BP | PTS |
|--------------|---|---|---|---|----|-----|----|-----|
| France       | 3 | 3 | 0 | 0 | 98 | 6   | 2  | 14  |
| Australia    | 3 | 2 | 0 | 1 | 54 | 23  | 0  | 8   |
| Wales        | 3 | 1 | 0 | 2 | 38 | 54  | 1  | 5   |
| South Africa | 3 | 0 | 0 | 3 | 9  | 116 | 0  | 0   |

WOMEN'S RUGBY WORLD CUP

# PLAY-OFFS FIRST PHASE

| | |
|---|---|
| Ninth place semi-finals | South Africa 25–24 **Samoa** |
| | **Spain** 18–5 Kazakhstan |
| Fifth place semi-finals | Australia 20–23 **USA** |
| | **New Zealand** 63–7 Wales |
| Semi-finals | Ireland 7–40 **England** |
| | France 16–18 **Canada** |

# PLAY-OFFS SECOND PHASE

| | |
|---|---|
| 11th place play-off | **Samoa** 31–0 Kazakhstan |
| Ninth place play-off | South Africa 0–36 **Spain** |
| Seventh place play-off | **Australia** 30–3 Wales |
| Fifth place play-off | USA 5–55 **New Zealand** |

# THIRD PLACE PLAY-OFF

## 17 August 2014, Stade Jean Bouin, Paris

# IRELAND 18 (1G 1T 2PG) FRANCE 25 (1G 3T 1PG)

**IRELAND:** N Briggs; A Baxter, G Davitt, J Murphy, A Miller; N Stapleton, T Rosser; F Coghlan (captain), G Bourke, A Egan, S Spence, ML Reilly, S Fleming, C Molloy, P Fitzpatrick

**SUBSTITUTIONS:** L Guest for Fleming (52 mins); KA Craddock for Egan (58 mins); L Muldoon for Stapleton (68 mins)

**SCORERS:** *Tries*: Briggs, Davitt *Conversion*: Briggs *Penalty Goals*: Briggs (2)

**FRANCE:** J Tremoulière; S Izar, E Poublan, M Mayans, E Guiglion; S Agricole, J Troncy; L Arricastre, G Mignot (captain), C Chobet, S Rabier, A Koita, K Djossouvi, L Grand, S N'Diaye

**SUBSTITUTIONS:** C Le Duff for Agricole (29 mins); M Andre & E Portaries for Djossouvi & Chobet (64 mins); C Ladagnous for Izar (67 mins); L Salles for Mignot (68 mins); Y Rivoalen for Troncy (76 mins)

**SCORERS:** *Tries*: Mignot, Tremoulière, Guiglion (2) *Conversion*: Agricole *Penalty Goal*: Tremoulière

**REFEREE:** S Trumbull (Canada)

WOMEN'S RUGBY

## 17 August 2014, Stade Jean Bouin, Paris

## ENGLAND 21 (1G 1T 3PG) CANADA 9 (3PG)

**ENGLAND**: D Waterman; K Merchant, E Scarratt, R Burford, K Wilson; K Mclean (captain), N Hunt; R Clark, V Fleetwood, S Hemming, T Taylor, J McGilchrist, M Packer, M Alphonsi, S Hunter

**SUBSTITUTIONS:** C Allan for Waterman (temp 47–52 mins); R Essex for Hemming (54 mins); L Keates for McGilchrist (54 mins); E Croker for Fleetwood (58 mins); A Matthews for Packer (65 mins); C Allan for Merchant (70 mins); LT Mason & C Large for Hunt & Burford (78 mins)

**SCORERS:** *Tries*: Waterman, Scarratt *Conversion*: Scarratt *Penalty Goals*: Scarratt (3)

**CANADA:** J Zussman; M Harvey, M Marchak, A Burk, J Dovanne; E Belchos, E Alarie; M-P Pinault-Reid, K Donaldson, H Leith, L Blackwood, M Samson, J Murphy, K Paquin, K Russell (captain)

**SUBSTITUTIONS:** K Mack for Samson (41 mins); L Russell for Donaldson (46 mins); B Waters for Dovanne (60 mins); O DeMerchant for Leith (70 mins); MJ Kirby & J Sugawara for Pinault-Reid & Zussman (76 mins)

**SCORERS:** *Penalty Goals*: Harvey (3)

**REFEREE:** A Perrett (Australia)

## FINAL STANDINGS

| | |
|---|---|
| 1 England | 7 Australia |
| 2 Canada | 8 Wales |
| 3 France | 9 Spain |
| 4 Ireland | 10 South Africa |
| 5 New Zealand | 11 Samoa |
| 6 USA | 12 Kazakhstan |

### TOP POINT SCORERS

| Name | Pts |
|---|---|
| Emily Scarratt (England) | 70 |
| Magali Harvey (Canada) | 61 |
| Kelly Brazier (New Zealand) | 45 |
| Niamh Briggs (Ireland) | 40 |
| Ashleigh Hewson (Australia) | 39 |
| Bella Milo (Samoa) | 35 |
| Patricia Garcia (Spain) | 33 |
| Shakira Baker (New Zealand) | 30 |
| Selica Winiata (New Zealand) | 30 |
| Honey Hireme (New Zealand) | 25 |

### TOP TRY SCORERS

| Name | Tries |
|---|---|
| Shakira Baker (New Zealand) | 6 |
| Selica Winiata (New Zealand) | 6 |
| Honey Hireme (New Zealand) | 5 |
| Tricia Brown (Australia) | 4 |
| Sioned Harries (Wales) | 4 |
| Magali Harvey (Canada) | 4 |
| Huriana Manuel (New Zealand) | 4 |
| Marlie Packer (England) | 4 |
| Kay Wilson (England) | 4 |

WOMEN'S RUGBY WORLD CUP

# A HUGE APPETITE FOR WOMEN'S RUGBY

*By Ali Donnelly*

France's power stunned England in the opening match of the Women's Six Nations, as they went on to win a Grand Slam.

**2**014 will surely be seen as a watershed 12 months for the women's game with growing numbers, the improvement in standards and the huge exposure generated by the World Cup all combining to highlight that women's rugby is on the rise – and how.

While the showpiece tournament in Paris rightly took centre stage and dominated the headlines, the enormous activity around the globe at the highest level of the game showcased perfectly the huge appetite there now is for women's rugby.

From France winning the Six Nations to China winning the Asian Sevens Series to Kenya regaining the Elgon Cup, there was a feast of action to get your teeth into over the past year.

The first real focus of the year was the Women's Six Nations, with Ireland out to defend their crown and four of the sides involved looking to lay down markers for the World Cup.

It was France, the Women's Rugby World Cup 2014 hosts, who raced out of the blocks on the opening weekend in February with a superb 18–6 win over England. In truth it was a shock result as England were back to full strength after a disappointing 2013 campaign. France, though, were led strongly by Gaëlle Mignot, the hooker crashing over for two second-half tries, both coming from driving mauls which England had huge difficulty defending all night.

Italy, out to prove a point having missed out on World Cup qualification, travelled to Wales and caused another upset after a try in the final minute from flanker Ilaria Arrighetti secured a 12–11 win at the Talbot Athletic Ground. Ireland had ensured there would not be a sweep of upsets by kicking off the Championship with a 59–0 rout of Scotland, running in 11 tries to make the best possible start to their title defence.

The second round went more to form, with Ireland edging Wales, France defeating Italy and England overcoming Scotland with ease. A fortnight later the biggest crowd of the Championship – 15,000 – saw England put paid to Ireland's unbeaten start with a 17–10 win at Twickenham. There were also wins for France, whose pack were hugely impressive in a 27–0 defeat of Wales, and Italy, as they overwhelmed Scotland 45–5.

In round four, France added to Scottish woes with another emphatic win (69–0), while Ireland and England kept their losses to just the one by recording comfortable wins over Italy and Wales respectively.

It meant the title would be decided on the final day, with Ireland needing to beat Les Bleues to stop them from winning their first title in almost a decade. It was a tight clash and France were clinging on at the end after Ireland staged a second-half resurgence, but an early try from Marion Lièvre and others from Shannon Izar and Elodie Portaries were enough to see them home 19–15 in Pau to secure a first title in nine years.

The Six Nations threw up plenty of interesting thoughts ahead of WRWC 2014 with France clearly the team having gained the most. The French pack had laid the foundations for what could be a brilliant year, while for England there was disappointment in their inability to win back the Six Nations title with which they have become synonymous in recent years. England did, though, show glimpses of real strength as they sought to rediscover the momentum they had lost from focusing on Sevens the year before. And that was to pay off in spectacular fashion at the World Cup.

For Ireland, repeating the heroics of 2013 was always a tough ask but there was plenty they could be positive about going into the rest of the year. Italy's best-ever finish of fourth was a deserved outcome for a team that is growing in strength and confidence year on year and they are no longer the tournament's also-rans.

Wales were left frustrated at a couple of narrow losses, but with a World Cup on the horizon had plenty to focus the minds, while the

Scots were the most disappointed of the lot with a fourth wooden spoon in a row. Scotland have now lost their last 22 Six Nations matches and the concession of 256 points – while scoring just five – in 2014 means there remains much work to do to catch up with the sides around them who are now surging ahead.

Away from the senior team spotlight, Canada, France, England, Scotland and USA all played at Under 20 level. At the start of the year, France and England played each other twice, with the French youngsters coming out on top on both occasions. Both wins were similar in style and the scores were almost identical with France winning 27–0 and 28–0. The global Under 20s calendar remains sparse, however, with just three more games at this level in 2014. One featured Scotland, who took on the full Belgium team and lost, while Canada comprehensively defeated neighbours USA in back-to-back games in August.

That month also saw another huge advance for women's rugby take place in China where Sevens made its debut at the Youth Olympic Games in Nanjing. The women's tournament ran alongside the men's as rugby returned to the Olympic Games family for the first time since the 1924 Games.

The women's competition featured six teams in Australia, Canada, Tunisia, Spain, USA and hosts China. Australia began as favourites for the tournament, having won the only previous Under 18 Sevens tournament of any significance – last year's Australian 'Youth Olympic Festival' in Sydney, which included China and several Pacific nations. The squad for Nanjing included two gold medalists from Sydney in co-captains Brooke Anderson and Tiana Penitani.

It was that Sydney tournament which introduced the Australian Rugby Union to the amazing talent that is Penitani and she then burst into the consciousness of everyone else at the start of the IRB Women's Sevens World Series shortly thereafter. The world had seen little of her for a year due to an enforced 13-month break following a knee injury sustained at Rugby World Cup Sevens 2013 in Moscow. This tournament marked her return to international rugby and it was no quiet return. The 18-year-old was not only given the task of co-captaining the Australian team but, as one of the biggest names at the entire Games, carried the Australian flag at the opening ceremony.

It was no surprise, then, that Australia reached the final where they faced Canada, the country who were into their third major international women's rugby final in 10 days after WRWC 2014 and the FISU World University Rugby Sevens in Brazil. Australia won the day with a 38–10 victory and the future appears very bright for the Wallaroos and their representative sides.

The Asian 4 Nations Championship was the other major competition of the year with Kazakhstan confirming their position as the leading Test nation in the region with overall victory over Hong Kong, Japan and Singapore. The Kazakhs completed their clean sweep with a 49–17 defeat of Japan, which followed a 68–0 midweek win over Singapore and a somewhat tighter 13–10 win over Hong Kong, who surprised many by finishing as runners-up.

"I'm pretty happy and we are getting closer to where we want to be, but as a coach you always want more from the players," admitted Hong Kong coach Chris Garvey. "Today was the closest that we have been to getting where I want this group to be. Credit to the girls, two of whom got hat-tricks and showed a couple of individual moments of brilliance, but the team effort has allowed those individuals to shine."

With the Sevens World Series ongoing throughout the year – in a bigger and busier format than the inaugural season – there was also time for a raft of other international competitions this year.

In July, Kenya regained the Women's Elgon Cup, beating Uganda home and away in the two-legged tournament.

Amid a host of World Cup warm-up games, the other high point of the year saw New Zealand stage a rare tournament as they welcomed Australia, Canada and Samoa. The Black Ferns had no problem going unbeaten through the series, their most significant game being against Samoa, who they hosted for the first time as a curtain-raiser to the opening Test of the All Blacks' series against England. The world champions won that 90–12 with Selica Winiata scoring five of her side's 14 tries at Eden Park.

In the Sevens form of the game, the ARFU Asian Women's Sevens Series kicked off just a week after the WRWC 2014 final and, having finished as runners-up in the Asian XV Championship in May, Hong Kong's newly-created professional women's squad reached their first Sevens final since 2003. They fell at the final hurdle on home soil, losing 38–7 to China. A real point of note amid Hong Kong's professionalism was their appointment of Black Ferns legend Anna Richards as head coach. She was understandably pretty happy with the silver medal. "This is a work in progress so it is onward and upwards for this team," she said afterwards.

Hong Kong then took their place alongside 11 nations at the Women's Sevens World Series qualifier in September, from which four teams secured core status on the 2014–15 circuit. They came up short with Fiji, France, China and South Africa securing the coveted spots and this quartet will each bring something different to the Series in a year when teams will be bidding to secure qualification for Rugby Sevens' debut at the Rio 2016 Olympic Games.

It has certainly been a year to remember, but the challenge now is to better it in 2015.

|  |  |  |
|---|---|---|
| 19/10/2013 | Namibia 31–10 Botswana | Hage Geingob Stadium, Windhoek |
| 02/11/2013 | France 29–17 Canada | Pontarlier |
| 05/11/2013 | France 6–11 Canada | Amnéville |
| 09/11/2013 | England 40–20 France | Twickenham |
| 13/11/2013 | England 32–3 Canada | Twickenham Stoop |
| 16/11/2013 | Switzerland 42–0 Czech Republic | Nyon |
| 31/01/2014 | Ireland 59–0 Scotland | Ashbourne RFC, Ashbourne |
| 01/02/2014 | France 18–6 England | Stade des Alpes, Grenoble |
| 02/02/2014 | Wales 11–12 Italy | Talbot Athletic Ground, Port Talbot |
| 07/02/2014 | Ireland 16–6 Wales | Ashbourne RFC, Ashbourne |
| 08/02/2014 | France 29–0 Italy | Stade Ernest-Argeles, Toulouse |
| 09/02/2014 | Scotland 0–63 England | Rubislaw Playing Fields, Aberdeen |
| 22/02/2014 | England 17–10 Ireland | Twickenham |
| 23/02/2014 | Wales 0–27 France | Talbot Athletic Ground, Port Talbot |
| 23/02/2014 | Italy 45–5 Scotland | Stadio Parco Urbano, Milan |
| 07/03/2014 | England 35–3 Wales | Twickenham Stoop, Twickenham |
| 08/03/2014 | Switzerland 80–0 Finland | Unterägeri |
| 08/03/2014 | Ireland 39–0 Italy | Aviva Stadium, Dublin |
| 09/03/2014 | Scotland 0–69 France | Hawthornden, Bonnyrigg |
| 14/03/2014 | France 19–15 Ireland | Stade du Hameau, Pau |
| 16/03/2014 | Wales 25–0 Scotland | Talbot Athletic Ground, Port Talbot |
| 16/03/2014 | Italy 0–24 England | Stadio Guilio e Silvio Pagani, Rovato |
| 15/04/2014 | Canada 51–7 USA | Shawnigan Lake School, Shawnigan Lake |
| 19/04/2014 | Canada 14–10 USA | Westhills Stadium, Langford |
| 18/05/2014 | Japan 37–5 Singapore | Aberdeen Sports Ground, Hong Kong |
| 18/05/2014 | Hong Kong 10–13 Kazakhstan | Aberdeen Sports Ground, Hong Kong |
| 21/05/2014 | Kazakhstan 68–0 Singapore | Aberdeen Sports Ground, Hong Kong |
| 21/05/2014 | Hong Kong 15–14 Japan | Aberdeen Sports Ground, Hong Kong |
| 24/05/2014 | Hong Kong 53–5 Singapore | Aberdeen Sports Ground, Hong Kong |
| 24/05/2014 | Kazakhstan 49–17 Japan | Aberdeen Sports Ground, Hong Kong |
| 01/06/2014 | New Zealand 38–3 Australia | Rotorua International Stadium, Rotorua |
| 06/06/2014 | Australia 0–22 Canada | The Domain, Tauranga |
| 07/06/2014 | New Zealand 90–12 Samoa | Eden Park, Auckland |
| 10/06/2014 | New Zealand 16–8 Canada | The Domain, Tauranga |
| 14/06/2014 | New Zealand 33–21 Canada | Rugby Park, Whakatane |
| 28/06/2014 | Wales 7–10 USA | Cross Keys RFC |
| 29/06/2014 | Czech Republic 3–32 Switzerland | RC Slavia Prague, Prague |
| 01/07/2014 | Spain 3–37 France | Campo de Pepe Rojo, Valladolid |
| 04/07/2014 | France 46–8 South Africa | FFR HQ, Marcoussis |
| 12/07/2014 | Uganda 15–33 Kenya | Kyadondo RFC, Kampala |
| 19/07/2014 | Kenya 39–10 Uganda | RFUEA Grounds, Nairobi |
| 01/08/2014 | New Zealand 79–5 Kazakhstan | FFR HQ, Marcoussis |
| 01/08/2014 | Canada 31–5 Spain | FFR HQ, Marcoussis |
| 01/08/2014 | Australia 26–3 South Africa | FFR HQ, Marcoussis |
| 01/08/2014 | USA 17–23 Ireland | FFR HQ, Marcoussis |
| 01/08/2014 | England 65–3 Samoa | FFR HQ, Marcoussis |
| 01/08/2014 | France 26–0 Wales | FFR HQ, Marcoussis |
| 05/08/2014 | USA 47–7 Kazakhstan | FFR HQ, Marcoussis |
| 05/08/2014 | Australia 25–3 Wales | FFR HQ, Marcoussis |
| 05/08/2014 | England 45–5 Spain | FFR HQ, Marcoussis |
| 05/08/2014 | Canada 42–7 Samoa | FFR HQ, Marcoussis |
| 05/08/2014 | New Zealand 14–17 Ireland | FFR HQ, Marcoussis |
| 05/08/2014 | France 55–3 South Africa | FFR HQ, Marcoussis |
| 09/08/2014 | Ireland 40–5 Kazakhstan | FFR HQ, Marcoussis |
| 09/08/2014 | Spain 41–5 Samoa | FFR HQ, Marcoussis |
| 09/08/2014 | England 13–13 Canada | FFR HQ, Marcoussis |
| 09/08/2014 | Wales 35–3 South Africa | FFR HQ, Marcoussis |
| 09/08/2014 | New Zealand 34–3 USA | FFR HQ, Marcoussis |
| 09/08/2014 | Australia 3–17 France | FFR HQ, Marcoussis |
| 13/08/2014 | South Africa 25–24 Samoa | FFR HQ, Marcoussis |
| 13/08/2014 | New Zealand 63–7 Wales | Stade Jean Bouin, Paris |
| 13/08/2014 | Spain 18–5 Kazakhstan | FFR HQ, Marcoussis |
| 13/08/2014 | Ireland 7–40 England | Stade Jean Bouin, Paris |
| 13/08/2014 | Australia 20–23 USA | FFR HQ, Marcoussis |
| 13/08/2014 | France 16–18 Canada | Stade Jean Bouin, Paris |
| 17/08/2014 | Samoa 31–0 Kazakhstan | FFR HQ, Marcoussis |
| 17/08/2014 | South Africa 0–36 Spain | FFR HQ, Marcoussis |
| 17/08/2014 | USA 5–55 New Zealand | Stade Jean Bouin, Paris |
| 17/08/2014 | Australia 30–3 Wales | FFR HQ, Marcoussis |
| 17/08/2014 | Ireland 18–25 France | Stade Jean Bouin, Paris |
| 17/08/2014 | England 21–9 Canada | Stade Jean Bouin, Paris |

# International Records and Statistics

# INTERNATIONAL RECORDS

## RESULTS OF INTERNATIONAL MATCHES

### UP TO 13 OCTOBER 2014

Cap matches involving senior executive council member unions only. Years for International Championship matches are for the second half of the season: eg 1972 means season 1971–72. Years for matches against touring teams from the southern hemisphere refer to the actual year of the match.

Points-scoring was first introduced in 1886, when an International Board was formed by Scotland, Ireland and Wales. Points values varied among the countries until 1890, when England agreed to join the Board, and uniform values were adopted.

| Northern hemisphere seasons | Try | Conversion | Penalty goal | Drop goal | Goal from mark |
|---|---|---|---|---|---|
| 1890–91 | 1 | 2 | 2 | 3 | 3 |
| 1891–92 to 1892–93 | 2 | 3 | 3 | 4 | 4 |
| 1893–94 to 1904–05 | 3 | 2 | 3 | 4 | 4 |
| 1905–06 to 1947–48 | 3 | 2 | 3 | 4 | 3 |
| 1948–49 to 1970–71 | 3 | 2 | 3 | 3 | 3 |
| 1971–72 to 1991–92 | 4 | 2 | 3 | 3 | 3* |
| 1992–93 onwards | 5 | 2 | 3 | 3 | – |

*The goal from mark ceased to exist when the free-kick clause was introduced, 1977–78.

WC indicates a fixture played during a Rugby World Cup. LC indicates a fixture played in the Latin Cup. TN indicates a fixture played in the Tri Nations. RC indicates a fixture played in The Rugby Championship. QT indicates a fixture in the Quadrangular Tournament.

# ENGLAND v SCOTLAND

**Played 132 England won 72, Scotland won 42, Drawn 18**
**Highest scores England** 43–3 in 2001 and 43–22 in 2005, Scotland 33–6 in 1986
**Biggest wins England** 43–3 in 2001, Scotland 33–6 in 1986

| | |
|---|---|
| 1871 Raeburn Place (Edinburgh) **Scotland** 1G 1T to 1T | 1911 Twickenham **England** 13–8 |
| | 1912 Inverleith **Scotland** 8–3 |
| 1872 The Oval (London) **England** 1G 1DG 2T to 1DG | 1913 Twickenham **England** 3–0 |
| | 1914 Inverleith **England** 16–15 |
| 1873 Glasgow **Drawn** no score | 1920 Twickenham **England** 13–4 |
| 1874 The Oval **England** 1DG to 1T | 1921 Inverleith **England** 18–0 |
| 1875 Raeburn Place **Drawn** no score | 1922 Twickenham **England** 11–5 |
| 1876 The Oval **England** 1G 1T to 0 | 1923 Inverleith **England** 8–6 |
| 1877 Raeburn Place **Scotland** 1 DG to 0 | 1924 Twickenham **England** 19–0 |
| 1878 The Oval **Drawn** no score | 1925 Murrayfield **Scotland** 14–11 |
| 1879 Raeburn Place **Drawn** Scotland 1DG England 1G | 1926 Twickenham **Scotland** 17–9 |
| | 1927 Murrayfield **Scotland** 21–13 |
| 1880 Manchester **England** 2G 3T to 1G | 1928 Twickenham **England** 6–0 |
| 1881 Raeburn Place **Drawn** Scotland 1G 1T England 1DG 1T | 1929 Murrayfield **Scotland** 12–6 |
| | 1930 Twickenham **Drawn** 0–0 |
| 1882 Manchester **Scotland** 2T to 0 | 1931 Murrayfield **Scotland** 28–19 |
| 1883 Raeburn Place **England** 2T to 1T | 1932 Twickenham **England** 16–3 |
| 1884 Blackheath (London) **England** 1G to 1T | 1933 Murrayfield **Scotland** 3–0 |
| 1885 No Match | 1934 Twickenham **England** 6–3 |
| 1886 Raeburn Place **Drawn** no score | 1935 Murrayfield **Scotland** 10–7 |
| 1887 Manchester **Drawn** 1T each | 1936 Twickenham **England** 9–8 |
| 1888 No Match | 1937 Murrayfield **England** 6–3 |
| 1889 No Match | 1938 Twickenham **Scotland** 21–16 |
| 1890 Raeburn Place **England** 1G 1T to 0 | 1939 Murrayfield **England** 9–6 |
| 1891 Richmond (London) **Scotland** 9–3 | 1947 Twickenham **England** 24–5 |
| 1892 Raeburn Place **England** 5–0 | 1948 Murrayfield **Scotland** 6–3 |
| 1893 Leeds **Scotland** 8–0 | 1949 Twickenham **England** 19–3 |
| 1894 Raeburn Place **Scotland** 6–0 | 1950 Murrayfield **Scotland** 13–11 |
| 1895 Richmond **Scotland** 6–3 | 1951 Twickenham **England** 5–3 |
| 1896 Glasgow **Scotland** 11–0 | 1952 Murrayfield **England** 19–3 |
| 1897 Manchester **England** 12–3 | 1953 Twickenham **England** 26–8 |
| 1898 Powderhall (Edinburgh) **Drawn** 3–3 | 1954 Murrayfield **England** 13–3 |
| 1899 Blackheath **Scotland** 5–0 | 1955 Twickenham **England** 9–6 |
| 1900 Inverleith (Edinburgh) **Drawn** 0–0 | 1956 Murrayfield **England** 11–6 |
| 1901 Blackheath **Scotland** 18–3 | 1957 Twickenham **England** 16–3 |
| 1902 Inverleith **England** 6–3 | 1958 Murrayfield **Drawn** 3–3 |
| 1903 Richmond **Scotland** 10–6 | 1959 Twickenham **Drawn** 3–3 |
| 1904 Inverleith **Scotland** 6–3 | 1960 Murrayfield **England** 21–12 |
| 1905 Richmond **Scotland** 8–0 | 1961 Twickenham **England** 6–0 |
| 1906 Inverleith **England** 9–3 | 1962 Murrayfield **Drawn** 3–3 |
| 1907 Blackheath **Scotland** 8–3 | 1963 Twickenham **England** 10–8 |
| 1908 Inverleith **Scotland** 16–10 | 1964 Murrayfield **Scotland** 15–6 |
| 1909 Richmond **Scotland** 18–8 | 1965 Twickenham **Drawn** 3–3 |
| 1910 Inverleith **England** 14–5 | 1966 Murrayfield **Scotland** 6–3 |

| | | | |
|---|---|---|---|
| 1967 | Twickenham **England** 27–14 | 1991 | Twickenham **England** 21–12 |
| 1968 | Murrayfield **England** 8–6 | 1991 | Murrayfield WC **England** 9–6 |
| 1969 | Twickenham **England** 8–3 | 1992 | Murrayfield **England** 25–7 |
| 1970 | Murrayfield **Scotland** 14–5 | 1993 | Twickenham **England** 26–12 |
| 1971 | Twickenham **Scotland** 16–15 | 1994 | Murrayfield **England** 15–14 |
| 1971 | Murrayfield **Scotland** 26–6 | 1995 | Twickenham **England** 24–12 |
| | Special centenary match – | 1996 | Murrayfield **England** 18–9 |
| | non-championship | 1997 | Twickenham **England** 41–13 |
| 1972 | Murrayfield **Scotland** 23–9 | 1998 | Murrayfield **England** 34–20 |
| 1973 | Twickenham **England** 20–13 | 1999 | Twickenham **England** 24–21 |
| 1974 | Murrayfield **Scotland** 16–14 | 2000 | Murrayfield **Scotland** 19–13 |
| 1975 | Twickenham **England** 7–6 | 2001 | Twickenham **England** 43–3 |
| 1976 | Murrayfield **Scotland** 22–12 | 2002 | Murrayfield **England** 29–3 |
| 1977 | Twickenham **England** 26–6 | 2003 | Twickenham **England** 40–9 |
| 1978 | Murrayfield **England** 15–0 | 2004 | Murrayfield **England** 35–13 |
| 1979 | Twickenham **Drawn** 7–7 | 2005 | Twickenham **England** 43–22 |
| 1980 | Murrayfield **England** 30–18 | 2006 | Murrayfield **Scotland** 18–12 |
| 1981 | Twickenham **England** 23–17 | 2007 | Twickenham **England** 42–20 |
| 1982 | Murrayfield **Drawn** 9–9 | 2008 | Murrayfield **Scotland** 15–9 |
| 1983 | Twickenham **Scotland** 22–12 | 2009 | Twickenham **England** 26–12 |
| 1984 | Murrayfield **Scotland** 18–6 | 2010 | Murrayfield **Drawn** 15–15 |
| 1985 | Twickenham **England** 10–7 | 2011 | Twickenham **England** 22–16 |
| 1986 | Murrayfield **Scotland** 33–6 | 2011 | Auckland WC **England** 16–12 |
| 1987 | Twickenham **England** 21–12 | 2012 | Murrayfield **England** 13–6 |
| 1988 | Murrayfield **England** 9–6 | 2013 | Twickenham **England** 38–18 |
| 1989 | Twickenham **Drawn** 12–12 | 2014 | Murrayfield **England** 20–0 |
| 1990 | Murrayfield **Scotland** 13–7 | | |

# ENGLAND v IRELAND

**Played 128 England won 74, Ireland won 46, Drawn 8**
**Highest scores** England 50–18 in 2000, Ireland 43–13 in 2007
**Biggest wins** England 46–6 in 1997, Ireland 43–13 in 2007

| | | | |
|---|---|---|---|
| 1875 | The Oval (London) **England** 1G 1DG 1T to 0 | 1890 | Blackheath (London) **England** 3T to 0 |
| | | 1891 | Dublin **England** 9–0 |
| 1876 | Dublin **England** 1G 1T to 0 | 1892 | Manchester **England** 7–0 |
| 1877 | The Oval **England** 2G 2T to 0 | 1893 | Dublin **England** 4–0 |
| 1878 | Dublin **England** 2G 1T to 0 | 1894 | Blackheath **Ireland** 7–5 |
| 1879 | The Oval **England** 2G 1DG 2T to 0 | 1895 | Dublin **England** 6–3 |
| 1880 | Dublin **England** 1G 1T to 1T | 1896 | Leeds **Ireland** 10–4 |
| 1881 | Manchester **England** 2G 2T to 0 | 1897 | Dublin **Ireland** 13–9 |
| 1882 | Dublin **Drawn** 2T each | 1898 | Richmond (London) **Ireland** 9–6 |
| 1883 | Manchester **England** 1G 3T to 1T | 1899 | Dublin **Ireland** 6–0 |
| 1884 | Dublin **England** 1G to 0 | 1900 | Richmond **England** 15–4 |
| 1885 | Manchester **England** 2T to 1T | 1901 | Dublin **Ireland** 10–6 |
| 1886 | Dublin **England** 1T to 0 | 1902 | Leicester **England** 6–3 |
| 1887 | Dublin **Ireland** 2G to 0 | 1903 | Dublin **Ireland** 6–0 |
| 1888 | No Match | 1904 | Blackheath **England** 19–0 |
| 1889 | No Match | 1905 | Cork **Ireland** 17–3 |

| | | |
|---|---|---|
| 1906 | Leicester | **Ireland** 16–6 |
| 1907 | Dublin | **Ireland** 17–9 |
| 1908 | Richmond | **England** 13–3 |
| 1909 | Dublin | **England** 11–5 |
| 1910 | Twickenham | **Drawn** 0–0 |
| 1911 | Dublin | **Ireland** 3–0 |
| 1912 | Twickenham | **England** 15–0 |
| 1913 | Dublin | **England** 15–4 |
| 1914 | Twickenham | **England** 17–12 |
| 1920 | Dublin | **England** 14–11 |
| 1921 | Twickenham | **England** 15–0 |
| 1922 | Dublin | **England** 12–3 |
| 1923 | Leicester | **England** 23–5 |
| 1924 | Belfast | **England** 14–3 |
| 1925 | Twickenham | **Drawn** 6–6 |
| 1926 | Dublin | **Ireland** 19–15 |
| 1927 | Twickenham | **England** 8–6 |
| 1928 | Dublin | **England** 7–6 |
| 1929 | Twickenham | **Ireland** 6–5 |
| 1930 | Dublin | **Ireland** 4–3 |
| 1931 | Twickenham | **Ireland** 6–5 |
| 1932 | Dublin | **England** 11–8 |
| 1933 | Twickenham | **England** 17–6 |
| 1934 | Dublin | **England** 13–3 |
| 1935 | Twickenham | **England** 14–3 |
| 1936 | Dublin | **Ireland** 6–3 |
| 1937 | Twickenham | **England** 9–8 |
| 1938 | Dublin | **England** 36–14 |
| 1939 | Twickenham | **Ireland** 5–0 |
| 1947 | Dublin | **Ireland** 22–0 |
| 1948 | Twickenham | **Ireland** 11–10 |
| 1949 | Dublin | **Ireland** 14–5 |
| 1950 | Twickenham | **England** 3–0 |
| 1951 | Dublin | **Ireland** 3–0 |
| 1952 | Twickenham | **England** 3–0 |
| 1953 | Dublin | **Drawn** 9–9 |
| 1954 | Twickenham | **England** 14–3 |
| 1955 | Dublin | **Drawn** 6–6 |
| 1956 | Twickenham | **England** 20–0 |
| 1957 | Dublin | **England** 6–0 |
| 1958 | Twickenham | **England** 6–0 |
| 1959 | Dublin | **England** 3–0 |
| 1960 | Twickenham | **England** 8–5 |
| 1961 | Dublin | **Ireland** 11–8 |
| 1962 | Twickenham | **England** 16–0 |
| 1963 | Dublin | **Drawn** 0–0 |
| 1964 | Twickenham | **Ireland** 18–5 |
| 1965 | Dublin | **Ireland** 5–0 |
| 1966 | Twickenham | **Drawn** 6–6 |
| 1967 | Dublin | **England** 8–3 |
| 1968 | Twickenham | **Drawn** 9–9 |

| | | |
|---|---|---|
| 1969 | Dublin | **Ireland** 17–15 |
| 1970 | Twickenham | **England** 9–3 |
| 1971 | Dublin | **England** 9–6 |
| 1972 | Twickenham | **Ireland** 16–12 |
| 1973 | Dublin | **Ireland** 18–9 |
| 1974 | Twickenham | **Ireland** 26–21 |
| 1975 | Dublin | **Ireland** 12–9 |
| 1976 | Twickenham | **Ireland** 13–12 |
| 1977 | Dublin | **England** 4–0 |
| 1978 | Twickenham | **England** 15–9 |
| 1979 | Dublin | **Ireland** 12–7 |
| 1980 | Twickenham | **England** 24–9 |
| 1981 | Dublin | **England** 10–6 |
| 1982 | Twickenham | **Ireland** 16–15 |
| 1983 | Dublin | **Ireland** 25–15 |
| 1984 | Twickenham | **England** 12–9 |
| 1985 | Dublin | **Ireland** 13–10 |
| 1986 | Twickenham | **England** 25–20 |
| 1987 | Dublin | **Ireland** 17–0 |
| 1988 | Twickenham | **England** 35–3 |
| 1988 | Dublin | **England** 21–10 |
| | | Non-championship match |
| 1989 | Dublin | **England** 16–3 |
| 1990 | Twickenham | **England** 23–0 |
| 1991 | Dublin | **England** 16–7 |
| 1992 | Twickenham | **England** 38–9 |
| 1993 | Dublin | **Ireland** 17–3 |
| 1994 | Twickenham | **Ireland** 13–12 |
| 1995 | Dublin | **England** 20–8 |
| 1996 | Twickenham | **England** 28–15 |
| 1997 | Dublin | **England** 46–6 |
| 1998 | Twickenham | **England** 35–17 |
| 1999 | Dublin | **England** 27–15 |
| 2000 | Twickenham | **England** 50–18 |
| 2001 | Dublin | **Ireland** 20–14 |
| 2002 | Twickenham | **England** 45–11 |
| 2003 | Dublin | **England** 42–6 |
| 2004 | Twickenham | **Ireland** 19–13 |
| 2005 | Dublin | **Ireland** 19–13 |
| 2006 | Twickenham | **Ireland** 28–24 |
| 2007 | Dublin | **Ireland** 43–13 |
| 2008 | Twickenham | **England** 33–10 |
| 2009 | Dublin | **Ireland** 14–13 |
| 2010 | Twickenham | **Ireland** 20–16 |
| 2011 | Dublin | **Ireland** 24–8 |
| 2011 | Dublin | **England** 20–9 |
| | | Non-championship match |
| 2012 | Twickenham | **England** 30–9 |
| 2013 | Dublin | **England** 12–6 |
| 2014 | Twickenham | **England** 13–10 |

INTERNATIONAL RESULTS

# ENGLAND v WALES

**Played 125 England won 57 Wales won 56, Drawn 12**
**Highest scores** England 62–5 in 2007, Wales 34–21 in 1967
**Biggest wins** England 62–5 in 2007, Wales 30–3 in 2013

| | |
|---|---|
| 1881 | Blackheath (London) **England** 7G 1DG 6T to 0 |
| 1882 | No Match |
| 1883 | Swansea **England** 2G 4T to 0 |
| 1884 | Leeds **England** 1G 2T to 1G |
| 1885 | Swansea **England** 1G 4T to 1G 1T |
| 1886 | Blackheath **England** 1GM 2T to 1G |
| 1887 | Llanelli **Drawn** no score |
| 1888 | No Match |
| 1889 | No Match |
| 1890 | Dewsbury **Wales** 1T to 0 |
| 1891 | Newport **England** 7–3 |
| 1892 | Blackheath **England** 17–0 |
| 1893 | Cardiff **Wales** 12–11 |
| 1894 | Birkenhead **England** 24–3 |
| 1895 | Swansea **England** 14–6 |
| 1896 | Blackheath **England** 25–0 |
| 1897 | Newport **Wales** 11–0 |
| 1898 | Blackheath **England** 14–7 |
| 1899 | Swansea **Wales** 26–3 |
| 1900 | Gloucester **Wales** 13–3 |
| 1901 | Cardiff **Wales** 13–0 |
| 1902 | Blackheath **Wales** 9–8 |
| 1903 | Swansea **Wales** 21–5 |
| 1904 | Leicester **Drawn** 14–14 |
| 1905 | Cardiff **Wales** 25–0 |
| 1906 | Richmond (London) **Wales** 16–3 |
| 1907 | Swansea **Wales** 22–0 |
| 1908 | Bristol **Wales** 28–18 |
| 1909 | Cardiff **Wales** 8–0 |
| 1910 | Twickenham **England** 11–6 |
| 1911 | Swansea **Wales** 15–11 |
| 1912 | Twickenham **England** 8–0 |
| 1913 | Cardiff **England** 12–0 |
| 1914 | Twickenham **England** 10–9 |
| 1920 | Swansea **Wales** 19–5 |
| 1921 | Twickenham **England** 18–3 |
| 1922 | Cardiff **Wales** 28–6 |
| 1923 | Twickenham **England** 7–3 |
| 1924 | Swansea **England** 17–9 |
| 1925 | Twickenham **England** 12–6 |
| 1926 | Cardiff **Drawn** 3–3 |
| 1927 | Twickenham **England** 11–9 |
| 1928 | Swansea **England** 10–8 |
| 1929 | Twickenham **England** 8–3 |
| 1930 | Cardiff **England** 11–3 |
| 1931 | Twickenham **Drawn** 11–11 |
| 1932 | Swansea **Wales** 12–5 |
| 1933 | Twickenham **Wales** 7–3 |
| 1934 | Cardiff **England** 9–0 |
| 1935 | Twickenham **Drawn** 3–3 |
| 1936 | Swansea **Drawn** 0–0 |
| 1937 | Twickenham **England** 4–3 |
| 1938 | Cardiff **Wales** 14–8 |
| 1939 | Twickenham **England** 3–0 |
| 1947 | Cardiff **England** 9–6 |
| 1948 | Twickenham **Drawn** 3–3 |
| 1949 | Cardiff **Wales** 9–3 |
| 1950 | Twickenham **Wales** 11–5 |
| 1951 | Swansea **Wales** 23–5 |
| 1952 | Twickenham **Wales** 8–6 |
| 1953 | Cardiff **England** 8–3 |
| 1954 | Twickenham **England** 9–6 |
| 1955 | Cardiff **Wales** 3–0 |
| 1956 | Twickenham **Wales** 8–3 |
| 1957 | Cardiff **England** 3–0 |
| 1958 | Twickenham **Drawn** 3–3 |
| 1959 | Cardiff **Wales** 5–0 |
| 1960 | Twickenham **England** 14–6 |
| 1961 | Cardiff **Wales** 6–3 |
| 1962 | Twickenham **Drawn** 0–0 |
| 1963 | Cardiff **England** 13–6 |
| 1964 | Twickenham **Drawn** 6–6 |
| 1965 | Cardiff **Wales** 14–3 |
| 1966 | Twickenham **Wales** 11–6 |
| 1967 | Cardiff **Wales** 34–21 |
| 1968 | Twickenham **Drawn** 11–11 |
| 1969 | Cardiff **Wales** 30–9 |
| 1970 | Twickenham **Wales** 17–13 |
| 1971 | Cardiff **Wales** 22–6 |
| 1972 | Twickenham **Wales** 12–3 |
| 1973 | Cardiff **Wales** 25–9 |
| 1974 | Twickenham **England** 16–12 |
| 1975 | Cardiff **Wales** 20–4 |
| 1976 | Twickenham **Wales** 21–9 |
| 1977 | Cardiff **Wales** 14–9 |
| 1978 | Twickenham **Wales** 9–6 |
| 1979 | Cardiff **Wales** 27–3 |

*INTERNATIONAL RECORDS*

| | | | | | |
|---|---|---|---|---|---|
| 1980 | Twickenham **England** 9–8 | | 2002 | Twickenham **England** 50–10 |
| 1981 | Cardiff **Wales** 21–19 | | 2003 | Cardiff **England** 26–9 |
| 1982 | Twickenham **England** 17–7 | | 2003 | Cardiff **England** 43–9 |
| 1983 | Cardiff **Drawn** 13–13 | | | Non-championship match |
| 1984 | Twickenham **Wales** 24–15 | | 2003 | Brisbane WC **England** 28–17 |
| 1985 | Cardiff **Wales** 24–15 | | 2004 | Twickenham **England** 31–21 |
| 1986 | Twickenham **England** 21–18 | | 2005 | Cardiff **Wales** 11–9 |
| 1987 | Cardiff **Wales** 19–12 | | 2006 | Twickenham **England** 47–13 |
| 1987 | Brisbane WC **Wales** 16–3 | | 2007 | Cardiff **Wales** 27–18 |
| 1988 | Twickenham **Wales** 11–3 | | 2007 | Twickenham **England** 62–5 |
| 1989 | Cardiff **Wales** 12–9 | | | Non-championship match |
| 1990 | Twickenham **England** 34–6 | | 2008 | Twickenham **Wales** 26–19 |
| 1991 | Cardiff **England** 25–6 | | 2009 | Cardiff **Wales** 23–15 |
| 1992 | Twickenham **England** 24–0 | | 2010 | Twickenham **England** 30–17 |
| 1993 | Cardiff **Wales** 10–9 | | 2011 | Cardiff **England** 26–19 |
| 1994 | Twickenham **England** 15–8 | | 2011 | Twickenham **England** 23–19 |
| 1995 | Cardiff **England** 23–9 | | | Non-championship match |
| 1996 | Twickenham **England** 21–15 | | 2011 | Cardiff **Wales** 19–9 |
| 1997 | Cardiff **England** 34–13 | | | Non-championship match |
| 1998 | Twickenham **England** 60–26 | | 2012 | Twickenham **Wales** 19–12 |
| 1999 | Wembley **Wales** 32–31 | | 2013 | Cardiff **Wales** 30–3 |
| 2000 | Twickenham **England** 46–12 | | 2014 | Twickenham **England** 29–18 |
| 2001 | Cardiff **England** 44–15 | | | |

## ENGLAND v FRANCE

**Played 98 England won 53, France won 38, Drawn 7**
**Highest scores** England 48–19 in 2001, France 37–12 in 1972
**Biggest wins** England 37–0 in 1911, France 37–12 in 1972 and 31–6 in 2006

| | | | | |
|---|---|---|---|---|
| 1906 | Paris **England** 35–8 | | 1931 | Paris **France** 14–13 |
| 1907 | Richmond (London) **England** 41–13 | | 1947 | Twickenham **England** 6–3 |
| 1908 | Paris **England** 19–0 | | 1948 | Paris **France** 15–0 |
| 1909 | Leicester **England** 22–0 | | 1949 | Twickenham **England** 8–3 |
| 1910 | Paris **England** 11–3 | | 1950 | Paris **France** 6–3 |
| 1911 | Twickenham **England** 37–0 | | 1951 | Twickenham **France** 11–3 |
| 1912 | Paris **England** 18–8 | | 1952 | Paris **England** 6–3 |
| 1913 | Twickenham **England** 20–0 | | 1953 | Twickenham **England** 11–0 |
| 1914 | Paris **England** 39–13 | | 1954 | Paris **France** 11–3 |
| 1920 | Twickenham **England** 8–3 | | 1955 | Twickenham **France** 16–9 |
| 1921 | Paris **England** 10–6 | | 1956 | Paris **France** 14–9 |
| 1922 | Twickenham **Drawn** 11–11 | | 1957 | Twickenham **England** 9–5 |
| 1923 | Paris **England** 12–3 | | 1958 | Paris **England** 14–0 |
| 1924 | Twickenham **England** 19–7 | | 1959 | Twickenham **Drawn** 3–3 |
| 1925 | Paris **England** 13–11 | | 1960 | Paris **Drawn** 3–3 |
| 1926 | Twickenham **England** 11–0 | | 1961 | Twickenham **Drawn** 5–5 |
| 1927 | Paris **France** 3–0 | | 1962 | Paris **France** 13–0 |
| 1928 | Twickenham **England** 18–8 | | 1963 | Twickenham **England** 6–5 |
| 1929 | Paris **England** 16–6 | | 1964 | Paris **England** 6–3 |
| 1930 | Twickenham **England** 11–5 | | 1965 | Twickenham **England** 9–6 |

**INTERNATIONAL RESULTS**

| | | | | |
|---|---|---|---|---|
| 1966 | Paris **France** 13–0 | | 1995 | Pretoria WC **France 19–9** |
| 1967 | Twickenham **France** 16–12 | | 1996 | Paris **France** 15–12 |
| 1968 | Paris **France** 14–9 | | 1997 | Twickenham **France** 23–20 |
| 1969 | Twickenham **England** 22–8 | | 1998 | Paris **France** 24–17 |
| 1970 | Paris **France** 35–13 | | 1999 | Twickenham **England** 21–10 |
| 1971 | Twickenham **Drawn** 14–14 | | 2000 | Paris **England** 15–9 |
| 1972 | Paris **France** 37–12 | | 2001 | Twickenham **England** 48–19 |
| 1973 | Twickenham **England** 14–6 | | 2002 | Paris **France** 20–15 |
| 1974 | Paris **Drawn** 12–12 | | 2003 | Twickenham **England** 25–17 |
| 1975 | Twickenham **France** 27–20 | | 2003 | Marseilles **France** 17–16 |
| 1976 | Paris **France** 30–9 | | | Non-championship match |
| 1977 | Twickenham **France** 4–3 | | 2003 | Twickenham **England** 45–14 |
| 1978 | Paris **France** 15–6 | | | Non-championship match |
| 1979 | Twickenham **England** 7–6 | | 2003 | Sydney WC **England** 24–7 |
| 1980 | Paris **England** 17–13 | | 2004 | Paris **France** 24–21 |
| 1981 | Twickenham **France** 16–12 | | 2005 | Twickenham **France** 18–17 |
| 1982 | Paris **England** 27–15 | | 2006 | Paris **France** 31–6 |
| 1983 | Twickenham **France** 19–15 | | 2007 | Twickenham **England** 26–18 |
| 1984 | Paris **France** 32–18 | | 2007 | Twickenham **France** 21–15 |
| 1985 | Twickenham **Drawn** 9–9 | | | Non-championship match |
| 1986 | Paris **France** 29–10 | | 2007 | Marseilles **France** 22–9 |
| 1987 | Twickenham **France** 19–15 | | | Non-championship match |
| 1988 | Paris **France** 10–9 | | 2007 | Paris WC **England** 14–9 |
| 1989 | Twickenham **England** 11–0 | | 2008 | Paris **England** 24–13 |
| 1990 | Paris **England** 26–7 | | 2009 | Twickenham **England** 34–10 |
| 1991 | Twickenham **England** 21–19 | | 2010 | Paris **France** 12–10 |
| 1991 | Paris WC **England** 19–10 | | 2011 | Twickenham **England** 17–9 |
| 1992 | Paris **England** 31–13 | | 2011 | Auckland WC **France** 19–12 |
| 1993 | Twickenham **England** 16–15 | | 2012 | Paris **England** 24–22 |
| 1994 | Paris **England** 18–14 | | 2013 | Twickenham **England** 23–13 |
| 1995 | Twickenham **England** 31–10 | | 2014 | Paris **France** 26–24 |

## ENGLAND v SOUTH AFRICA

**Played 36 England won 12, South Africa won 22, Drawn 2**
**Highest scores** England 53–3 in 2002, South Africa 58–10 in 2007
**Biggest wins** England 53–3 in 2002, South Africa 58–10 in 2007

| | | | | |
|---|---|---|---|---|
| 1906 | Crystal Palace (London) **Drawn** 3–3 | | 1994 | 1 Pretoria **England** 32–15 |
| 1913 | Twickenham **South Africa** 9–3 | | | 2 Cape Town **South Africa** 27–9 |
| 1932 | Twickenham **South Africa** 7–0 | | | Series drawn 1–1 |
| 1952 | Twickenham **South Africa** 8–3 | | 1995 | Twickenham **South Africa** 24–14 |
| 1961 | Twickenham **South Africa** 5–0 | | 1997 | Twickenham **South Africa** 29–11 |
| 1969 | Twickenham **England** 11–8 | | 1998 | Cape Town **South Africa** 18–0 |
| 1972 | Johannesburg **England** 18–9 | | 1998 | Twickenham **England** 13–7 |
| 1984 | 1 Port Elizabeth **South Africa** 33–15 | | 1999 | Paris WC **South Africa** 44–21 |
| | 2 Johannesburg **South Africa** 35–9 | | 2000 | 1 Pretoria **South Africa** 18–13 |
| | South Africa won series 2–0 | | | 2 Bloemfontein **England** 27–22 |
| 1992 | Twickenham **England** 33–16 | | | Series drawn 1–1 |

| 2000 | Twickenham **England** 25–17 |
| 2001 | Twickenham **England** 29–9 |
| 2002 | Twickenham **England** 53–3 |
| 2003 | Perth WC **England** 25–6 |
| 2004 | Twickenham **England** 32–16 |
| 2006 | 1 Twickenham **England** 23–21 |
| | 2 Twickenham **South Africa** 25–14 |
| | Series drawn 1–1 |
| 2007 | 1 Bloemfontein **South Africa** 58–10 |
| | 2 Pretoria **South Africa** 55–22 |
| | South Africa won series 2–0 |

| 2007 | Paris WC **South Africa** 36–0 |
| 2007 | Paris WC **South Africa** 15–6 |
| 2008 | Twickenham **South Africa** 42–6 |
| 2010 | Twickenham **South Africa** 21–11 |
| 2012 | 1 Durban **South Africa** 22–17 |
| | 2 Johannesburg **South Africa** 36–27 |
| | 3 Port Elizabeth **Drawn** 14–14 |
| | South Africa won series 2–0, with 1 |
| | draw |
| 2012 | Twickenham **South Africa** 16–15 |

# ENGLAND v NEW ZEALAND

**Played 39 England won 7, New Zealand won 31, Drawn 1**
**Highest scores** England 38–21 in 2012, New Zealand 64–22 in 1998
**Biggest wins** England 38–21 in 2012, New Zealand 64–22 in 1998

| 1905 | Crystal Palace (London) **New Zealand** 15–0 |
| 1925 | Twickenham **New Zealand** 17–11 |
| 1936 | Twickenham **England** 13–0 |
| 1954 | Twickenham **New Zealand** 5–0 |
| 1963 | 1 Auckland **New Zealand** 21–11 |
| | 2 Christchurch **New Zealand** 9–6 |
| | New Zealand won series 2–0 |
| 1964 | Twickenham **New Zealand** 14–0 |
| 1967 | Twickenham **New Zealand** 23–11 |
| 1973 | Twickenham **New Zealand** 9–0 |
| 1973 | Auckland **England** 16–10 |
| 1978 | Twickenham **New Zealand** 16–6 |
| 1979 | Twickenham **New Zealand** 10–9 |
| 1983 | Twickenham **England** 15–9 |
| 1985 | 1 Christchurch **New Zealand** 18–13 |
| | 2 Wellington **New Zealand** 42–15 |
| | New Zealand won series 2–0 |
| 1991 | Twickenham WC **New Zealand** 18–12 |
| 1993 | Twickenham **England** 15–9 |
| 1995 | Cape Town WC **New Zealand 45–29** |
| 1997 | 1 Manchester **New Zealand** 25–8 |
| | 2 Twickenham **Drawn** 26–26 |
| | New Zealand won series 1–0, with 1 draw |

| 1998 | 1 Dunedin **New Zealand** 64–22 |
| | 2 Auckland **New Zealand** 40–10 |
| | New Zealand won series 2–0 |
| 1999 | Twickenham WC **New Zealand** 30–16 |
| 2002 | Twickenham **England** 31–28 |
| 2003 | Wellington **England** 15–13 |
| 2004 | 1 Dunedin **New Zealand** 36–3 |
| | 2 Auckland **New Zealand** 36–12 |
| | New Zealand won series 2–0 |
| 2005 | Twickenham **New Zealand** 23–19 |
| 2006 | Twickenham **New Zealand** 41–20 |
| 2008 | 1 Auckland **New Zealand** 37–20 |
| | 2 Christchurch **New Zealand** 44–12 |
| | New Zealand won series 2–0 |
| 2008 | Twickenham **New Zealand** 32–6 |
| 2009 | Twickenham **New Zealand** 19–6 |
| 2010 | Twickenham **New Zealand** 26–16 |
| 2012 | Twickenham **England** 38–21 |
| 2013 | Twickenham **New Zealand** 30–22 |
| 2014 | 1 Auckland **New Zealand** 20–15 |
| | 2 Dunedin **New Zealand** 28–27 |
| | 3 Hamilton **New Zealand** 36–13 |
| | New Zealand won series 3–0 |

# ENGLAND v AUSTRALIA

**Played 42 England won 17, Australia won 24, Drawn 1**
**Highest scores** England 35–18 in 2010, Australia 76–0 in 1998
**Biggest wins** England 20–3 in 1973, 23–6 in 1976 and 35–18 in 2010, Australia 76–0 in 1998

| | |
|---|---|
| 1909 Blackheath (London) **Australia** 9–3 | 1998 Brisbane **Australia** 76–0 |
| 1928 Twickenham **England** 18–11 | 1998 Twickenham **Australia** 12–11 |
| 1948 Twickenham **Australia** 11–0 | 1999 Sydney **Australia** 22–15 |
| 1958 Twickenham **England** 9–6 | 2000 Twickenham **England** 22–19 |
| 1963 Sydney **Australia** 18–9 | 2001 Twickenham **England** 21–15 |
| 1967 Twickenham **Australia** 23–11 | 2002 Twickenham **England** 32–31 |
| 1973 Twickenham **England** 20–3 | 2003 Melbourne **England** 25–14 |
| 1975 1 Sydney **Australia** 16–9 | 2003 Sydney WC **England** 20–17 (aet) |
| 2 Brisbane **Australia** 30–21 | 2004 Brisbane **Australia** 51–15 |
| Australia won series 2–0 | 2004 Twickenham **Australia** 21–19 |
| 1976 Twickenham **England** 23–6 | 2005 Twickenham **England** 26–16 |
| 1982 Twickenham **England** 15–11 | 2006 1 Sydney **Australia** 34–3 |
| 1984 Twickenham **Australia** 19–3 | 2 Melbourne **Australia** 43–18 |
| 1987 Sydney WC **Australia** 19–6 | Australia won series 2–0 |
| 1988 1 Brisbane **Australia** 22–16 | 2007 Marseilles WC **England** 12–10 |
| 2 Sydney **Australia** 28–8 | 2008 Twickenham **Australia** 28–14 |
| Australia won series 2–0 | 2009 Twickenham **Australia** 18–9 |
| 1988 Twickenham **England** 28–19 | 2010 1 Perth **Australia** 27–17 |
| 1991 Sydney **Australia** 40–15 | 2 Sydney **England** 21–20 |
| 1991 Twickenham WC **Australia** 12–6 | Series drawn 1–1 |
| 1995 Cape Town WC **England** 25–22 | 2010 Twickenham **England** 35–18 |
| 1997 Sydney **Australia** 25–6 | 2012 Twickenham **Australia** 20–14 |
| 1997 Twickenham **Drawn** 15–15 | 2013 Twickenham **England** 20–13 |

## ENGLAND v NEW ZEALAND NATIVES

**Played 1 England won 1**
**Highest score** England 7–0 in 1889, NZ Natives 0–7 in 1889
**Biggest win** England 7–0 in 1889, NZ Natives no win

1889 Blackheath **England** 1G 4T to 0

## ENGLAND v RFU PRESIDENT'S XV

**Played 1 President's XV won 1**
**Highest score** England 11–28 in 1971, RFU President's XV 28–11 in 1971
**Biggest win** RFU President's XV 28–11 in 1971

1971 Twickenham **President's XV** 28–11

# ENGLAND v ARGENTINA

**Played 19 England won 14, Argentina won 4, Drawn 1**
**Highest scores** England 51–0 in 1990 and 51–26 in 2013, Argentina 33–13 in 1997
**Biggest wins** England 51–0 in 1990, Argentina 33–13 in 1997

| | | | | |
|---|---|---|---|---|
| 1981 | 1 Buenos Aires **Drawn** 19–19 | | 2000 | Twickenham **England** 19–0 |
| | 2 Buenos Aires **England** 12–6 | | 2002 | Buenos Aires **England** 26–18 |
| | England won series 1–0, with 1 draw | | 2006 | Twickenham **Argentina** 25–18 |
| 1990 | 1 Buenos Aires **England** 25–12 | | 2009 | 1 Manchester **England** 37–15 |
| | 2 Buenos Aires **Argentina** 15–13 | | | 2 Salta **Argentina** 24–22 |
| | Series drawn 1–1 | | | Series drawn 1–1 |
| 1990 | Twickenham **England** 51–0 | | 2009 | Twickenham **England** 16–9 |
| 1995 | Durban WC **England** 24–18 | | 2011 | Dunedin WC **England** 13–9 |
| 1996 | Twickenham **England** 20–18 | | 2013 | 1 Salta **England** 32–3 |
| 1997 | 1 Buenos Aires **England** 46–20 | | | 2 Buenos Aires **England** 51–26 |
| | 2 Buenos Aires **Argentina** 33–13 | | | England won series 2–0 |
| | Series drawn 1–1 | | 2013 | Twickenham **England** 31–12 |

# ENGLAND v ROMANIA

**Played 5 England won 5**
**Highest scores** England 134–0 in 2001, Romania 15–22 in 1985
**Biggest win** England 134–0 in 2001, Romania no win

| | | | | |
|---|---|---|---|---|
| 1985 | Twickenham **England** 22–15 | | 2001 | Twickenham **England** 134–0 |
| 1989 | Bucharest **England** 58–3 | | 2011 | Dunedin WC **England** 67–3 |
| 1994 | Twickenham **England** 54–3 | | | |

# ENGLAND v JAPAN

**Played 1 England won 1**
**Highest score** England 60–7 in 1987, Japan 7–60 in 1987
**Biggest win** England 60–7 in 1987, Japan no win

| | | |
|---|---|---|
| 1987 | Sydney WC **England** 60–7 |

# ENGLAND v UNITED STATES

**Played 5 England won 5**
**Highest scores** England 106–8 in 1999, United States 19–48 in 2001
**Biggest win** England 106–8 in 1999, United States no win

| | | | | |
|---|---|---|---|---|
| 1987 | Sydney WC **England** 34–6 | | 2001 | San Francisco **England** 48–19 |
| 1991 | Twickenham WC **England** 37–9 | | 2007 | Lens WC **England** 28–10 |
| 1999 | Twickenham **England** 106–8 | | | |

# ENGLAND v FIJI

**Played 5 England won 5**
**Highest scores** England 58–23 in 1989, Fiji 24–45 in 1999
**Biggest win** England 54–12 in 2012, Fiji no win

| | | | | |
|---|---|---|---|---|
| 1988 | Suva **England** 25–12 | | 1999 | Twickenham WC **England** 45–24 |
| 1989 | Twickenham **England** 58–23 | | 2012 | Twickenham **England** 54–12 |
| 1991 | Suva **England** 28–12 | | | |

# ENGLAND v ITALY

**Played 20 England won 20**
**Highest scores** England 80–23 in 2001, Italy 23–80 in 2001
**Biggest win** England 67–7 in 1999, Italy no win

| | | | | |
|---|---|---|---|---|
| 1991 | Twickenham WC **England** 36–6 | | 2005 | Twickenham **England** 39–7 |
| 1995 | Durban WC **England** 27–20 | | 2006 | Rome **England** 31–16 |
| 1996 | Twickenham **England** 54–21 | | 2007 | Twickenham **England** 20–7 |
| 1998 | Huddersfield **England** 23–15 | | 2008 | Rome **England** 23–19 |
| 1999 | Twickenham WC **England** 67–7 | | 2009 | Twickenham **England** 36–11 |
| 2000 | Rome **England** 59–12 | | 2010 | Rome **England** 17–12 |
| 2001 | Twickenham **England** 80–23 | | 2011 | Twickenham **England** 59–13 |
| 2002 | Rome **England** 45–9 | | 2012 | Rome **England** 19–15 |
| 2003 | Twickenham **England** 40–5 | | 2013 | Twickenham **England** 18–11 |
| 2004 | Rome **England** 50–9 | | 2014 | Rome **England** 52–11 |

# ENGLAND v CANADA

**Played 6 England won 6**
**Highest scores** England 70–0 in 2004, Canada 20–59 in 2001
**Biggest win** England 70–0 in 2004, Canada no win

| | | | | |
|---|---|---|---|---|
| 1992 | Wembley **England** 26–13 | | 2 | Burnaby **England** 59–20 |
| 1994 | Twickenham **England** 60–19 | | | England won series 2–0 |
| 1999 | Twickenham **England** 36–11 | | 2004 | Twickenham **England** 70–0 |
| 2001 | 1 Markham **England** 22–10 | | | |

# ENGLAND v SAMOA

**Played 6 England won 6**
**Highest scores** England 44–22 in 1995 and 44–22 in 2007, Samoa 22–44 in 1995, 22–35 in 2003 and 22–44 in 2007
**Biggest win** England 40–3 in 2005, Samoa no win

| | | | | |
|---|---|---|---|---|
| 1995 | Durban WC **England** 44–22 | | 2005 | Twickenham **England** 40–3 |
| 1995 | Twickenham **England** 27–9 | | 2007 | Nantes WC **England** 44–22 |
| 2003 | Melbourne WC **England** 35–22 | | 2010 | Twickenham **England** 26–13 |

# ENGLAND v THE NETHERLANDS

**Played 1 England won 1**
**Highest scores** England 110–0 in 1998, The Netherlands 0–110 in 1998
**Biggest win** England 110–0 in 1998, The Netherlands no win

| | |
|---|---|
| 1998 Huddersfield **England** 110–0 | |

# ENGLAND v TONGA

**Played 2 England won 2**
**Highest scores** England 101–10 in 1999, Tonga 20–36 in 2007
**Biggest win** England 101–10 in 1999, Tonga no win

| | |
|---|---|
| 1999 Twickenham WC **England** 101–10 | 2007 Paris WC **England** 36–20 |

# ENGLAND v GEORGIA

**Played 2 England won 2**
**Highest scores** England 84–6 in 2003, Georgia 10–41 in 2011
**Biggest win** England 84–6 in 2003, Georgia no win

| | |
|---|---|
| 2003 Perth WC **England** 84–6 | 2011 Dunedin WC **England** 41–10 |

# ENGLAND v URUGUAY

**Played 1 England won 1**
**Highest scores** England 111–13 in 2003, Uruguay 13–111 in 2003
**Biggest win** England 111–13 in 2003, Uruguay no win

| | |
|---|---|
| 2003 Brisbane WC **England** 111–13 | |

# ENGLAND v PACIFIC ISLANDS

**Played 1 England won 1**
**Highest scores** England 39–13 in 2008, Pacific Islands 13–39 in 2008
**Biggest win** England 39–13 in 2008, Pacific Islands no win

| | |
|---|---|
| 2008 Twickenham **England** 39–13 | |

INTERNATIONAL RESULTS

# SCOTLAND v IRELAND

**Played 129 Scotland won 65, Ireland won 58, Drawn 5, Abandoned 1**
**Highest scores** Scotland 38–10 in 1997, Ireland 44–22 in 2000
**Biggest wins** Scotland 38–10 in 1997, Ireland 36–6 in 2003

| | | | | |
|---|---|---|---|---|
| 1877 | Belfast **Scotland** 4G 2DG 2T to 0 | | 1922 | Inverleith **Scotland** 6–3 |
| 1878 | No Match | | 1923 | Dublin **Scotland** 13–3 |
| 1879 | Belfast **Scotland** 1G 1DG 1T to 0 | | 1924 | Inverleith **Scotland** 13–8 |
| 1880 | Glasgow **Scotland** 1G 2DG 2T to 0 | | 1925 | Dublin **Scotland** 14–8 |
| 1881 | Belfast **Ireland** 1DG to 1T | | 1926 | Murrayfield **Ireland** 3–0 |
| 1882 | Glasgow **Scotland** 2T to 0 | | 1927 | Dublin **Ireland** 6–0 |
| 1883 | Belfast **Scotland** 1G 1T to 0 | | 1928 | Murrayfield **Ireland** 13–5 |
| 1884 | Raeburn Place (Edinburgh) **Scotland** | | 1929 | Dublin **Scotland** 16–7 |
| | 2G 2T to 1T | | 1930 | Murrayfield **Ireland** 14–11 |
| 1885 | Belfast **Abandoned** Ireland 0 Scotland | | 1931 | Dublin **Ireland** 8–5 |
| | 1T | | 1932 | Murrayfield **Ireland** 20–8 |
| 1885 | Raeburn Place **Scotland** 1G 2T to 0 | | 1933 | Dublin **Scotland** 8–6 |
| 1886 | Raeburn Place **Scotland** 3G 1DG 2T | | 1934 | Murrayfield **Scotland** 16–9 |
| | to 0 | | 1935 | Dublin **Ireland** 12–5 |
| 1887 | Belfast **Scotland** 1G 1GM 2T to 0 | | 1936 | Murrayfield **Ireland** 10–4 |
| 1888 | Raeburn Place **Scotland** 1G to 0 | | 1937 | Dublin **Ireland** 11–4 |
| 1889 | Belfast **Scotland** 1DG to 0 | | 1938 | Murrayfield **Scotland** 23–14 |
| 1890 | Raeburn Place **Scotland** 1DG 1T to 0 | | 1939 | Dublin **Ireland** 12–3 |
| 1891 | Belfast **Scotland** 14–0 | | 1947 | Murrayfield **Ireland** 3–0 |
| 1892 | Raeburn Place **Scotland** 2–0 | | 1948 | Dublin **Ireland** 6–0 |
| 1893 | Belfast **Drawn** 0–0 | | 1949 | Murrayfield **Ireland** 13–3 |
| 1894 | Dublin **Ireland** 5–0 | | 1950 | Dublin **Ireland** 21–0 |
| 1895 | Raeburn Place **Scotland** 6–0 | | 1951 | Murrayfield **Ireland** 6–5 |
| 1896 | Dublin **Drawn** 0–0 | | 1952 | Dublin **Ireland** 12–8 |
| 1897 | Powderhall (Edinburgh) **Scotland** 8–3 | | 1953 | Murrayfield **Ireland** 26–8 |
| 1898 | Belfast **Scotland** 8–0 | | 1954 | Belfast **Ireland** 6–0 |
| 1899 | Inverleith (Edinburgh) **Ireland** 9–3 | | 1955 | Murrayfield **Scotland** 12–3 |
| 1900 | Dublin **Drawn** 0–0 | | 1956 | Dublin **Ireland** 14–10 |
| 1901 | Inverleith **Scotland** 9–5 | | 1957 | Murrayfield **Ireland** 5–3 |
| 1902 | Belfast **Ireland** 5–0 | | 1958 | Dublin **Ireland** 12–6 |
| 1903 | Inverleith **Scotland** 3–0 | | 1959 | Murrayfield **Ireland** 8–3 |
| 1904 | Dublin **Scotland** 19–3 | | 1960 | Dublin **Scotland** 6–5 |
| 1905 | Inverleith **Ireland** 11–5 | | 1961 | Murrayfield **Scotland** 16–8 |
| 1906 | Dublin **Scotland** 13–6 | | 1962 | Dublin **Scotland** 20–6 |
| 1907 | Inverleith **Scotland** 15–3 | | 1963 | Murrayfield **Scotland** 3–0 |
| 1908 | Dublin **Ireland** 16–11 | | 1964 | Dublin **Scotland** 6–3 |
| 1909 | Inverleith **Scotland** 9–3 | | 1965 | Murrayfield **Ireland** 16–6 |
| 1910 | Belfast **Scotland** 14–0 | | 1966 | Dublin **Scotland** 11–3 |
| 1911 | Inverleith **Ireland** 16–10 | | 1967 | Murrayfield **Ireland** 5–3 |
| 1912 | Dublin **Ireland** 10–8 | | 1968 | Dublin **Ireland** 14–6 |
| 1913 | Inverleith **Scotland** 29–14 | | 1969 | Murrayfield **Ireland** 16–0 |
| 1914 | Dublin **Ireland** 6–0 | | 1970 | Dublin **Ireland** 16–11 |
| 1920 | Inverleith **Scotland** 19–0 | | 1971 | Murrayfield **Ireland** 17–5 |
| 1921 | Dublin **Ireland** 9–8 | | 1972 | No Match |

| 1973 | Murrayfield **Scotland** 19–14 | 1997 | Murrayfield **Scotland** 38–10 |
|------|-------------------------------|------|-------------------------------|
| 1974 | Dublin **Ireland** 9–6 | 1998 | Dublin **Scotland** 17–16 |
| 1975 | Murrayfield **Scotland** 20–13 | 1999 | Murrayfield **Scotland** 30–13 |
| 1976 | Dublin **Scotland** 15–6 | 2000 | Dublin **Ireland** 44–22 |
| 1977 | Murrayfield **Scotland** 21–18 | 2001 | Murrayfield **Scotland** 32–10 |
| 1978 | Dublin **Ireland** 12–9 | 2002 | Dublin **Ireland** 43–22 |
| 1979 | Murrayfield **Drawn** 11–11 | 2003 | Murrayfield **Ireland** 36–6 |
| 1980 | Dublin **Ireland** 22–15 | 2003 | Murrayfield **Ireland** 29–10 |
| 1981 | Murrayfield **Scotland** 10–9 | | Non-championship match |
| 1982 | Dublin **Ireland** 21–12 | 2004 | Dublin **Ireland** 37–16 |
| 1983 | Murrayfield **Ireland** 15–13 | 2005 | Murrayfield **Ireland** 40–13 |
| 1984 | Dublin **Scotland** 32–9 | 2006 | Dublin **Ireland** 15–9 |
| 1985 | Murrayfield **Ireland** 18–15 | 2007 | Murrayfield **Ireland** 19–18 |
| 1986 | Dublin **Scotland** 10–9 | 2007 | Murrayfield **Scotland** 31–21 |
| 1987 | Murrayfield **Scotland** 16–12 | | Non-championship match |
| 1988 | Dublin **Ireland** 22–18 | 2008 | Dublin **Ireland** 34–13 |
| 1989 | Murrayfield **Scotland** 37–21 | 2009 | Murrayfield **Ireland** 22–15 |
| 1990 | Dublin **Scotland** 13–10 | 2010 | Dublin **Scotland** 23–20 |
| 1991 | Murrayfield **Scotland** 28–25 | 2011 | Murrayfield **Ireland** 21–18 |
| 1991 | Murrayfield WC **Scotland** 24–15 | 2011 | Murrayfield **Scotland** 10–6 |
| 1992 | Dublin **Scotland** 18–10 | | Non-championship match |
| 1993 | Murrayfield **Scotland** 15–3 | 2012 | Dublin **Ireland** 32–14 |
| 1994 | Dublin **Drawn** 6–6 | 2013 | Murrayfield **Scotland** 12–8 |
| 1995 | Murrayfield **Scotland** 26–13 | 2014 | Dublin **Ireland** 28–6 |
| 1996 | Dublin **Scotland** 16–10 | | |

# SCOTLAND v WALES

**Played** 119 Scotland won 48, Wales won 68, Drawn 3
**Highest scores** Scotland 35–10 in 1924, Wales 51–3 in 2014
**Biggest wins** Scotland 35–10 in 1924, Wales 51–3 in 2014

| 1883 | Raeburn Place (Edinburgh) **Scotland** 3G to 1G | 1899 | Inverleith (Edinburgh) **Scotland** 21–10 |
|------|-------------------------------------------------|------|--------------------------------------------|
| | | 1900 | Swansea **Wales** 12–3 |
| 1884 | Newport **Scotland** 1DG 1T to 0 | 1901 | Inverleith **Scotland** 18–8 |
| 1885 | Glasgow **Drawn** no score | 1902 | Cardiff **Wales** 14–5 |
| 1886 | Cardiff **Scotland** 2G 1T to 0 | 1903 | Inverleith **Scotland** 6–0 |
| 1887 | Raeburn Place **Scotland** 4G 8T to 0 | 1904 | Swansea **Wales** 21–3 |
| 1888 | Newport **Wales** 1T to 0 | 1905 | Inverleith **Wales** 6–3 |
| 1889 | Raeburn Place **Scotland** 2T to 0 | 1906 | Cardiff **Wales** 9–3 |
| 1890 | Cardiff **Scotland** 1G 2T to 1T | 1907 | Inverleith **Scotland** 6–3 |
| 1891 | Raeburn Place **Scotland** 15–0 | 1908 | Swansea **Wales** 6–5 |
| 1892 | Swansea **Scotland** 7–2 | 1909 | Inverleith **Wales** 5–3 |
| 1893 | Raeburn Place **Wales** 9–0 | 1910 | Cardiff **Wales** 14–0 |
| 1894 | Newport **Wales** 7–0 | 1911 | Inverleith **Wales** 32–10 |
| 1895 | Raeburn Place **Scotland** 5–4 | 1912 | Swansea **Wales** 21–6 |
| 1896 | Cardiff **Wales** 6–0 | 1913 | Inverleith **Wales** 8–0 |
| 1897 | No Match | 1914 | Cardiff **Wales** 24–5 |
| 1898 | No Match | 1920 | Inverleith **Scotland** 9–5 |

**170**

| | | |
|---|---|---|
| 1921 | Swansea **Scotland** 14–8 | |
| 1922 | Inverleith **Drawn** 9–9 | |
| 1923 | Cardiff **Scotland** 11–8 | |
| 1924 | Inverleith **Scotland** 35–10 | |
| 1925 | Swansea **Scotland** 24–14 | |
| 1926 | Murrayfield **Scotland** 8–5 | |
| 1927 | Cardiff **Scotland** 5–0 | |
| 1928 | Murrayfield **Wales** 13–0 | |
| 1929 | Swansea **Wales** 14–7 | |
| 1930 | Murrayfield **Scotland** 12–9 | |
| 1931 | Cardiff **Wales** 13–8 | |
| 1932 | Murrayfield **Wales** 6–0 | |
| 1933 | Swansea **Scotland** 11–3 | |
| 1934 | Murrayfield **Wales** 13–6 | |
| 1935 | Cardiff **Wales** 10–6 | |
| 1936 | Murrayfield **Wales** 13–3 | |
| 1937 | Swansea **Scotland** 13–6 | |
| 1938 | Murrayfield **Scotland** 8–6 | |
| 1939 | Cardiff **Wales** 11–3 | |
| 1947 | Murrayfield **Wales** 22–8 | |
| 1948 | Cardiff **Wales** 14–0 | |
| 1949 | Murrayfield **Scotland** 6–5 | |
| 1950 | Swansea **Wales** 12–0 | |
| 1951 | Murrayfield **Scotland** 19–0 | |
| 1952 | Cardiff **Wales** 11–0 | |
| 1953 | Murrayfield **Wales** 12–0 | |
| 1954 | Swansea **Wales** 15–3 | |
| 1955 | Murrayfield **Scotland** 14–8 | |
| 1956 | Cardiff **Wales** 9–3 | |
| 1957 | Murrayfield **Scotland** 9–6 | |
| 1958 | Cardiff **Wales** 8–3 | |
| 1959 | Murrayfield **Scotland** 6–5 | |
| 1960 | Cardiff **Wales** 8–0 | |
| 1961 | Murrayfield **Scotland** 3–0 | |
| 1962 | Cardiff **Scotland** 8–3 | |
| 1963 | Murrayfield **Wales** 6–0 | |
| 1964 | Cardiff **Wales** 11–3 | |
| 1965 | Murrayfield **Wales** 14–12 | |
| 1966 | Cardiff **Wales** 8–3 | |
| 1967 | Murrayfield **Scotland** 11–5 | |
| 1968 | Cardiff **Wales** 5–0 | |
| 1969 | Murrayfield **Wales** 17–3 | |
| 1970 | Cardiff **Wales** 18–9 | |
| 1971 | Murrayfield **Wales** 19–18 | |
| 1972 | Cardiff **Wales** 35–12 | |

| | | |
|---|---|---|
| 1973 | Murrayfield **Scotland** 10–9 | |
| 1974 | Cardiff **Wales** 6–0 | |
| 1975 | Murrayfield **Scotland** 12–10 | |
| 1976 | Cardiff **Wales** 28–6 | |
| 1977 | Murrayfield **Wales** 18–9 | |
| 1978 | Cardiff **Wales** 22–14 | |
| 1979 | Murrayfield **Wales** 19–13 | |
| 1980 | Cardiff **Wales** 17–6 | |
| 1981 | Murrayfield **Scotland** 15–6 | |
| 1982 | Cardiff **Scotland** 34–18 | |
| 1983 | Murrayfield **Wales** 19–15 | |
| 1984 | Cardiff **Scotland** 15–9 | |
| 1985 | Murrayfield **Wales** 25–21 | |
| 1986 | Cardiff **Wales** 22–15 | |
| 1987 | Murrayfield **Scotland** 21–15 | |
| 1988 | Cardiff **Wales** 25–20 | |
| 1989 | Murrayfield **Scotland** 23–7 | |
| 1990 | Cardiff **Scotland** 13–9 | |
| 1991 | Murrayfield **Scotland** 32–12 | |
| 1992 | Cardiff **Wales** 15–12 | |
| 1993 | Murrayfield **Scotland** 20–0 | |
| 1994 | Cardiff **Wales** 29–6 | |
| 1995 | Murrayfield **Scotland** 26–13 | |
| 1996 | Cardiff **Scotland** 16–14 | |
| 1997 | Murrayfield **Wales** 34–19 | |
| 1998 | Wembley **Wales** 19–13 | |
| 1999 | Murrayfield **Scotland** 33–20 | |
| 2000 | Cardiff **Wales** 26–18 | |
| 2001 | Murrayfield **Drawn** 28–28 | |
| 2002 | Cardiff **Scotland** 27–22 | |
| 2003 | Murrayfield **Scotland** 30–22 | |
| 2003 | Cardiff **Wales** 23–9 | |
| | Non-championship match | |
| 2004 | Cardiff **Wales** 23–10 | |
| 2005 | Murrayfield **Wales** 46–22 | |
| 2006 | Cardiff **Wales** 28–18 | |
| 2007 | Murrayfield **Scotland** 21–9 | |
| 2008 | Cardiff **Wales** 30–15 | |
| 2009 | Murrayfield **Wales** 26–13 | |
| 2010 | Cardiff **Wales** 31–24 | |
| 2011 | Murrayfield **Wales** 24–6 | |
| 2012 | Cardiff **Wales** 27–13 | |
| 2013 | Murrayfield **Wales** 28–18 | |
| 2014 | Cardiff **Wales** 51–3 | |

# SCOTLAND v FRANCE

**171**

Played 87 Scotland won 34, France won 50, Drawn 3
**Highest scores** Scotland 36–22 in 1999, France 51–16 in 1998 and 51–9 in 2003
**Biggest wins** Scotland 31–3 in 1912, France 51–9 in 2003

| | | | | |
|---|---|---|---|---|
| 1910 | Inverleith (Edinburgh) **Scotland** 27–0 | | 1974 | Murrayfield **Scotland** 19–6 |
| 1911 | Paris **France** 16–15 | | 1975 | Paris **France** 10–9 |
| 1912 | Inverleith **Scotland** 31–3 | | 1976 | Murrayfield **France** 13–6 |
| 1913 | Paris **Scotland** 21–3 | | 1977 | Paris **France** 23–3 |
| 1914 | No Match | | 1978 | Murrayfield **France** 19–16 |
| 1920 | Paris **Scotland** 5–0 | | 1979 | Paris **France** 21–17 |
| 1921 | Inverleith **France** 3–0 | | 1980 | Murrayfield **Scotland** 22–14 |
| 1922 | Paris **Drawn** 3–3 | | 1981 | Paris **France** 16–9 |
| 1923 | Inverleith **Scotland** 16–3 | | 1982 | Murrayfield **Scotland** 16–7 |
| 1924 | Paris **France** 12–10 | | 1983 | Paris **France** 19–15 |
| 1925 | Inverleith **Scotland** 25–4 | | 1984 | Murrayfield **Scotland** 21–12 |
| 1926 | Paris **Scotland** 20–6 | | 1985 | Paris **France** 11–3 |
| 1927 | Murrayfield **Scotland** 23–6 | | 1986 | Murrayfield **Scotland** 18–17 |
| 1928 | Paris **Scotland** 15–6 | | 1987 | Paris **France** 28–22 |
| 1929 | Murrayfield **Scotland** 6–3 | | 1987 | Christchurch WC **Drawn** 20–20 |
| 1930 | Paris **France** 7–3 | | 1988 | Murrayfield **Scotland** 23–12 |
| 1931 | Murrayfield **Scotland** 6–4 | | 1989 | Paris **France** 19–3 |
| 1947 | Paris **France** 8–3 | | 1990 | Murrayfield **Scotland** 21–0 |
| 1948 | Murrayfield **Scotland** 9–8 | | 1991 | Paris **France** 15–9 |
| 1949 | Paris **Scotland** 8–0 | | 1992 | Murrayfield **Scotland** 10–6 |
| 1950 | Murrayfield **Scotland** 8–5 | | 1993 | Paris **France** 11–3 |
| 1951 | Paris **France** 14–12 | | 1994 | Murrayfield **France** 20–12 |
| 1952 | Murrayfield **France** 13–11 | | 1995 | Paris **Scotland** 23–21 |
| 1953 | Paris **France** 11–5 | | 1995 | Pretoria WC **France** 22–19 |
| 1954 | Murrayfield **France** 3–0 | | 1996 | Murrayfield **Scotland** 19–14 |
| 1955 | Paris **France** 15–0 | | 1997 | Paris **France** 47–20 |
| 1956 | Murrayfield **Scotland** 12–0 | | 1998 | Murrayfield **France** 51–16 |
| 1957 | Paris **Scotland** 6–0 | | 1999 | Paris **Scotland** 36–22 |
| 1958 | Murrayfield **Scotland** 11–9 | | 2000 | Murrayfield **France** 28–16 |
| 1959 | Paris **France** 9–0 | | 2001 | Paris **France** 16–6 |
| 1960 | Murrayfield **France** 13–11 | | 2002 | Murrayfield **France** 22–10 |
| 1961 | Paris **France** 11–0 | | 2003 | Paris **France** 38–3 |
| 1962 | Murrayfield **France** 11–3 | | 2003 | Sydney WC **France** 51–9 |
| 1963 | Paris **Scotland** 11–6 | | 2004 | Murrayfield **France** 31–0 |
| 1964 | Murrayfield **Scotland** 10–0 | | 2005 | Paris **France** 16–9 |
| 1965 | Paris **France** 16–8 | | 2006 | Murrayfield **Scotland** 20–16 |
| 1966 | Murrayfield **Drawn** 3–3 | | 2007 | Paris **France** 46–19 |
| 1967 | Paris **Scotland** 9–8 | | 2008 | Murrayfield **France** 27–6 |
| 1968 | Murrayfield **France** 8–6 | | 2009 | Paris **France** 22–13 |
| 1969 | Paris **Scotland** 6–3 | | 2010 | Murrayfield **France** 18–9 |
| 1970 | Murrayfield **France** 11–9 | | 2011 | Paris **France** 34–21 |
| 1971 | Paris **France** 13–8 | | 2012 | Murrayfield **France** 23–17 |
| 1972 | Murrayfield **Scotland** 20–9 | | 2013 | Paris **France** 23–16 |
| 1973 | Paris **France** 16–13 | | 2014 | Paris **France** 19–17 |

**INTERNATIONAL RESULTS**

**SCOTLAND v SOUTH AFRICA**

Played 25 Scotland won 5, South Africa won 20, Drawn 0
**Highest scores** Scotland 29–46 in 1999, South Africa 68–10 in 1997
**Biggest wins** Scotland 21–6 in 2002, South Africa 68–10 in 1997

| | | | |
|---|---|---|---|
| 1906 | Glasgow **Scotland** 6–0 | | 28–19 |
| 1912 | Inverleith **South Africa** 16–0 | | South Africa won series 2–0 |
| 1932 | Murrayfield **South Africa** 6–3 | 2004 | Murrayfield **South Africa** 45–10 |
| 1951 | Murrayfield **South Africa** 44–0 | 2006 | 1 Durban **South Africa** 36–16 |
| 1960 | Port Elizabeth **South Africa** 18–10 | | 2 Port Elizabeth **South Africa** |
| 1961 | Murrayfield **South Africa** 12–5 | | 29–15 |
| 1965 | Murrayfield **Scotland** 8–5 | | South Africa won series 2–0 |
| 1969 | Murrayfield **Scotland** 6–3 | 2007 | Murrayfield **South Africa** 27–3 |
| 1994 | Murrayfield **South Africa** 34–10 | 2008 | Murrayfield **South Africa** 14–10 |
| 1997 | Murrayfield **South Africa** 68–10 | 2010 | Murrayfield **Scotland** 21–17 |
| 1998 | Murrayfield **South Africa** 35–10 | 2012 | Murrayfield **South Africa** 21–10 |
| 1999 | Murrayfield WC **South Africa** 46–29 | 2013 | Nelspruit QT **South Africa** 30–17 |
| 2002 | Murrayfield **Scotland** 21–6 | 2013 | Murrayfield **South Africa** 28–0 |
| 2003 | 1 Durban **South Africa** 29–25 | 2014 | Port Elizabeth **South Africa** 55–6 |
| | 2 Johannesburg **South Africa** | | |

**SCOTLAND v NEW ZEALAND**

Played 29 Scotland won 0, New Zealand won 27, Drawn 2
**Highest scores** Scotland 31–62 in 1996, New Zealand 69–20 in 2000
**Biggest wins** Scotland no win, New Zealand 69–20 in 2000

| | | | |
|---|---|---|---|
| 1905 | Inverleith (Edinburgh) **New Zealand** | | New Zealand won series 2–0 |
| | 12–7 | 1991 | Cardiff WC **New Zealand** 13–6 |
| 1935 | Murrayfield **New Zealand** 18–8 | 1993 | Murrayfield **New Zealand** 51–15 |
| 1954 | Murrayfield **New Zealand** 3–0 | 1995 | Pretoria WC **New Zealand** 48–30 |
| 1964 | Murrayfield **Drawn** 0–0 | 1996 | 1 Dunedin **New Zealand** 62–31 |
| 1967 | Murrayfield **New Zealand** 14–3 | | 2 Auckland **New Zealand** 36–12 |
| 1972 | Murrayfield **New Zealand** 14–9 | | New Zealand won series 2–0 |
| 1975 | Auckland **New Zealand** 24–0 | 1999 | Murrayfield WC **New Zealand** 30–18 |
| 1978 | Murrayfield **New Zealand** 18–9 | 2000 | 1 Dunedin **New Zealand** 69–20 |
| 1979 | Murrayfield **New Zealand** 20–6 | | 2 Auckland **New Zealand** 48–14 |
| 1981 | 1 Dunedin **New Zealand** 11–4 | | New Zealand won series 2–0 |
| | 2 Auckland **New Zealand** 40–15 | 2001 | Murrayfield **New Zealand** 37–6 |
| | New Zealand won series 2–0 | 2005 | Murrayfield **New Zealand** 29–10 |
| 1983 | Murrayfield **Drawn** 25–25 | 2007 | Murrayfield WC **New Zealand** 40–0 |
| 1987 | Christchurch WC **New Zealand** 30–3 | 2008 | Murrayfield **New Zealand** 32–6 |
| 1990 | 1 Dunedin **New Zealand** 31–16 | 2010 | Murrayfield **New Zealand** 49–3 |
| | 2 Auckland **New Zealand** 21–18 | 2012 | Murrayfield **New Zealand** 51–22 |

## SCOTLAND v AUSTRALIA

173

Played 28 Scotland won 9, Australia won 19, Drawn 0
**Highest scores** Scotland 24–15 in 1981, Australia 45–3 in 1998
**Biggest wins** Scotland 24–15 in 1981, Australia 45–3 in 1998

| | | | | |
|---|---|---|---|---|
| 1927 | Murrayfield **Scotland** 10–8 | | 1997 | Murrayfield **Australia** 37–8 |
| 1947 | Murrayfield **Australia** 16–7 | | 1998 | 1 Sydney **Australia** 45–3 |
| 1958 | Murrayfield **Scotland** 12–8 | | | 2 Brisbane **Australia** 33–11 |
| 1966 | Murrayfield **Scotland** 11–5 | | | Australia won series 2–0 |
| 1968 | Murrayfield **Scotland** 9–3 | | 2000 | Murrayfield **Australia** 30–9 |
| 1970 | Sydney **Australia** 23–3 | | 2003 | Brisbane WC **Australia** 33–16 |
| 1975 | Murrayfield **Scotland** 10–3 | | 2004 | 1 Melbourne **Australia** 35–15 |
| 1981 | Murrayfield **Scotland** 24–15 | | | 2 Sydney **Australia** 34–13 |
| 1982 | 1 Brisbane **Scotland** 12–7 | | | Australia won series 2–0 |
| | 2 Sydney **Australia** 33–9 | | 2004 | 1 Murrayfield **Australia** 31–14 |
| | Series drawn 1–1 | | | 2 Glasgow **Australia** 31–17 |
| 1984 | Murrayfield **Australia** 37–12 | | | Australia won series 2–0 |
| 1988 | Murrayfield **Australia** 32–13 | | 2006 | Murrayfield **Australia** 44–15 |
| 1992 | 1 Sydney **Australia** 27–12 | | 2009 | Murrayfield **Scotland** 9–8 |
| | 2 Brisbane **Australia** 37–13 | | 2012 | Newcastle (Aus) **Scotland** 9–6 |
| | Australia won series 2–0 | | 2013 | Murrayfield **Australia** 21–15 |
| 1996 | Murrayfield **Australia** 29–19 | | | |

## SCOTLAND v SRU PRESIDENT'S XV

Played 1 Scotland won 1
**Highest scores** Scotland 27–16 in 1972, SRU President's XV 16–27 in 1973
**Biggest win** Scotland 27–16 in 1973, SRU President's XV no win

| | |
|---|---|
| 1973 | Murrayfield **Scotland** 27–16 |

## SCOTLAND v ROMANIA

Played 13 Scotland won 11 Romania won 2, Drawn 0
**Highest scores** Scotland 60–19 in 1999, Romania 28–55 in 1987 and 28–22 in 1984
**Biggest wins** Scotland 48–6 in 2006 and 42–0 in 2007, Romania 28–22 in 1984 and 18–12 in 1991

| | | | | |
|---|---|---|---|---|
| 1981 | Murrayfield **Scotland** 12–6 | | 1999 | Glasgow **Scotland** 60–19 |
| 1984 | Bucharest **Romania** 28–22 | | 2002 | Murrayfield **Scotland** 37–10 |
| 1986 | Bucharest **Scotland** 33–18 | | 2005 | Bucharest **Scotland** 39–19 |
| 1987 | Dunedin WC **Scotland** 55–28 | | 2006 | Murrayfield **Scotland** 48–6 |
| 1989 | Murrayfield **Scotland** 32–0 | | 2007 | Murrayfield WC **Scotland** 42–0 |
| 1991 | Bucharest **Romania** 18–12 | | 2011 | Invercargill WC **Scotland** 34–24 |
| 1995 | Murrayfield **Scotland** 49–16 | | | |

INTERNATIONAL RESULTS

# SCOTLAND v ZIMBABWE

**Played 2 Scotland won 2**
**Highest scores** Scotland 60–21 in 1987, Zimbabwe 21–60 in 1987
**Biggest win** Scotland 60–21 in 1987 and 51–12 in 1991, Zimbabwe no win

| | | | | |
|---|---|---|---|---|
| 1987 | Wellington WC **Scotland** 60–21 | | 1991 | Murrayfield WC **Scotland** 51–12 |

# SCOTLAND v FIJI

**Played 6 Scotland won 5, Fiji won 1**
**Highest scores** Scotland 38–17 in 1989, Fiji 51–26 in 1998
**Biggest win** Scotland 38–17 in 1989, Fiji 51–26 in 1998

| | | | |
|---|---|---|---|
| 1989 | Murrayfield **Scotland** 38–17 | 2003 | Sydney WC **Scotland** 22–20 |
| 1998 | Suva **Fiji** 51–26 | 2009 | Murrayfield **Scotland** 23–10 |
| 2002 | Murrayfield **Scotland** 36–22 | 2012 | Lautoka **Scotland** 37–25 |

# SCOTLAND v ARGENTINA

**Played 14 Scotland won 5, Argentina won 9, Drawn 0**
**Highest scores** Scotland 49–3 in 1990, Argentina 31–22 in 1999
**Biggest wins** Scotland 49–3 in 1990, Argentina 31–22 in 1999 and 25–16 in 2001

| | | | |
|---|---|---|---|
| 1990 | Murrayfield **Scotland** 49–3 | | 2 Buenos Aires **Scotland** 26–14 |
| 1994 | 1 Buenos Aires **Argentina** 16–15 | | Series drawn 1–1 |
| | 2 Buenos Aires **Argentina** 19–17 | 2009 | Murrayfield **Argentina** 9–6 |
| | Argentina won series 2–0 | 2010 | 1 Tucumán **Scotland** 24–16 |
| 1999 | Murrayfield **Argentina** 31–22 | | 2 Mar del Plata **Scotland** 13–9 |
| 2001 | Murrayfield **Argentina** 25–16 | | Scotland won series 2–0 |
| 2005 | Murrayfield **Argentina** 23–19 | 2011 | Wellington WC **Argentina** 13–12 |
| 2007 | Paris WC **Argentina** 19–13 | 2014 | Córdoba **Scotland** 21–19 |
| 2008 | 1 Rosario **Argentina** 21–15 | | |

# SCOTLAND v JAPAN

**Played 4 Scotland won 4**
**Highest scores** Scotland 100–8 in 2004, Japan 17–42 in 2013
**Biggest win** Scotland 100–8 in 2004, Japan no win

| | | | |
|---|---|---|---|
| 1991 | Murrayfield WC **Scotland** 47–9 | 2004 | Perth **Scotland** 100–8 |
| 2003 | Townsville WC **Scotland** 32–11 | 2013 | Murrayfield **Scotland** won 42–17 |

# SCOTLAND v SAMOA

**Played 9 Scotland won 7, Samoa won 1, Drawn 1**
**Highest scores** Scotland 38–3 in 2004, Samoa 27–17 in 2013
**Biggest win** Scotland 38–3 in 2004, Samoa 27–17 in 2013

| | | | |
|---|---|---|---|
| 1991 | Murrayfield WC **Scotland** 28–6 | 2005 | Murrayfield **Scotland** 18–11 |
| 1995 | Murrayfield **Drawn** 15–15 | 2010 | Aberdeen **Scotland** 19–16 |
| 1999 | Murrayfield WC **Scotland** 35–20 | 2012 | Apia **Scotland** 17–16 |
| 2000 | Murrayfield **Scotland** 31–8 | 2013 | Durban QT **Samoa** 27–17 |
| 2004 | Wellington (NZ) **Scotland** 38–3 | | |

# SCOTLAND v CANADA

**Played 4 Scotland won 3, Canada won 1**
**Highest scores** Scotland 41–0 in 2008, Canada 26–23 in 2002
**Biggest win** Scotland 41–0 in 2008, Canada 26–23 in 2002

| | | | |
|---|---|---|---|
| 1995 | Murrayfield **Scotland** 22–6 | 2008 | Aberdeen **Scotland** 41–0 |
| 2002 | Vancouver **Canada** 26–23 | 2014 | Toronto **Scotland** 19–17 |

# SCOTLAND v IVORY COAST

**Played 1 Scotland won 1**
**Highest scores** Scotland 89–0 in 1995, Ivory Coast 0–89 in 1995
**Biggest win** Scotland 89–0 in 1995, Ivory Coast no win

| | |
|---|---|
| 1995 | Rustenburg WC **Scotland** 89–0 |

# SCOTLAND v TONGA

**Played 3 Scotland won 2, Tonga won 1**
**Highest scores** Scotland 43–20 in 2001, Tonga 21–15 in 2012
**Biggest win** Scotland 41–5 in 1995, Tonga 21–15 in 2012

| | | | |
|---|---|---|---|
| 1995 | Pretoria WC **Scotland** 41–5 | 2012 | Aberdeen **Tonga** 21–15 |
| 2001 | Murrayfield **Scotland** 43–20 | | |

# SCOTLAND v ITALY

**Played 22 Scotland won 15, Italy won 7**
**Highest scores** Scotland 47–15 in 2003, Italy 37–17 in 2007
**Biggest wins** Scotland 47–15 in 2003, Italy 37–17 in 2007

| | | | |
|---|---|---|---|
| 1996 | Murrayfield **Scotland** 29–22 | 2002 | Rome **Scotland** 29–12 |
| 1998 | Treviso **Italy** 25–21 | 2003 | Murrayfield **Scotland** 33–25 |
| 1999 | Murrayfield **Scotland** 30–12 | 2003 | Murrayfield **Scotland** 47–15 |
| 2000 | Rome **Italy** 34–20 | | Non-championship match |
| 2001 | Murrayfield **Scotland** 23–19 | 2004 | Rome **Italy** 20–14 |

| 2005 | Murrayfield **Scotland** 18–10 | 2011 | Murrayfield **Scotland** 21–8 |
|---|---|---|---|
| 2006 | Rome **Scotland** 13–10 | 2011 | Murrayfield **Scotland** 23–12 |
| 2007 | Murrayfield **Italy** 37–17 | | Non-championship match |
| 2007 | Saint Etienne WC **Scotland** 18–16 | 2012 | Rome **Italy** 13–6 |
| 2008 | Rome **Italy** 23–20 | 2013 | Murrayfield **Scotland** 34–10 |
| 2009 | Murrayfield **Scotland** 26–6 | 2013 | Pretoria QT **Scotland** 30–29 |
| 2010 | Rome **Italy** 16–12 | 2014 | Rome **Scotland** 21–20 |

# SCOTLAND v URUGUAY

**Played 1 Scotland won 1**
**Highest scores** Scotland 43–12 in 1999, Uruguay 12–43 in 1999
**Biggest win** Scotland 43–12 in 1999, Uruguay no win

| 1999 | Murrayfield WC **Scotland** 43–12 |
|---|---|

# SCOTLAND v SPAIN

**Played 1 Scotland won 1**
**Highest scores** Scotland 48–0 in 1999, Spain 0–48 in 1999
**Biggest win** Scotland 48–0 in 1999, Spain no win

| 1999 | Murrayfield WC **Scotland** 48–0 |
|---|---|

# SCOTLAND v UNITED STATES

**Played 4 Scotland won 4**
**Highest scores** Scotland 65–23 in 2002, United States 23–65 in 2002
**Biggest win** Scotland 53–6 in 2000, United States no win

| 2000 | Murrayfield **Scotland** 53–6 | 2003 | Brisbane WC **Scotland** 39–15 |
|---|---|---|---|
| 2002 | San Francisco **Scotland** 65–23 | 2014 | Houston **Scotland** 24–6 |

# SCOTLAND v PACIFIC ISLANDS

**Played 1 Scotland won 1**
**Highest scores** Scotland 34–22 in 2006, Pacific Islands 22–34 in 2006
**Biggest win** Scotland 34–22 in 2006, Pacific Islands no win

| 2006 | Murrayfield **Scotland** 34–22 |
|---|---|

# SCOTLAND v PORTUGAL

**Played 1 Scotland won 1**
**Highest scores** Scotland 56–10 in 2007, Portugal 10–56 in 2007
**Biggest win** Scotland 56–10 in 2007, Portugal no win

| 2007 | Saint Etienne WC **Scotland** 56–10 |
|---|---|

## SCOTLAND v GEORGIA

Played 1 Scotland won 1
**Highest scores** Scotland 15–6 in 2011, Georgia 6–15 in 2011
**Biggest win** Scotland 15–6 in 2011, Georgia no win

| | | |
|---|---|---|
| 2011 | Invercargill WC **Scotland** 15–6 | |

## IRELAND v WALES

Played 120 Ireland won 49, Wales won 65, Drawn 6
**Highest scores** Ireland 54–10 in 2002, Wales 34–9 in 1976
**Biggest wins** Ireland 54–10 in 2002, Wales 29–0 in 1907

| | | | | |
|---|---|---|---|---|
| 1882 | Dublin **Wales** 2G 2T to 0 | | 1922 | Swansea **Wales** 11–5 |
| 1883 | No Match | | 1923 | Dublin **Ireland** 5–4 |
| 1884 | Cardiff **Wales** 1DG 2T to 0 | | 1924 | Cardiff **Ireland** 13–10 |
| 1885 | No Match | | 1925 | Belfast **Ireland** 19–3 |
| 1886 | No Match | | 1926 | Swansea **Wales** 11–8 |
| 1887 | Birkenhead **Wales** 1DG 1T to 3T | | 1927 | Dublin **Ireland** 19–9 |
| 1888 | Dublin **Ireland** 1G 1DG 1T to 0 | | 1928 | Cardiff **Ireland** 13–10 |
| 1889 | Swansea **Ireland** 2T to 0 | | 1929 | Belfast **Drawn** 5–5 |
| 1890 | Dublin **Drawn** 1G each | | 1930 | Swansea **Wales** 12–7 |
| 1891 | Llanelli **Wales** 6–4 | | 1931 | Belfast **Wales** 15–3 |
| 1892 | Dublin **Ireland** 9–0 | | 1932 | Cardiff **Ireland** 12–10 |
| 1893 | Llanelli **Wales** 2–0 | | 1933 | Belfast **Ireland** 10–5 |
| 1894 | Belfast **Ireland** 3–0 | | 1934 | Swansea **Wales** 13–0 |
| 1895 | Cardiff **Wales** 5–3 | | 1935 | Belfast **Ireland** 9–3 |
| 1896 | Dublin **Ireland** 8–4 | | 1936 | Cardiff **Wales** 3–0 |
| 1897 | No Match | | 1937 | Belfast **Ireland** 5–3 |
| 1898 | Limerick **Wales** 11–3 | | 1938 | Swansea **Wales** 11–5 |
| 1899 | Cardiff **Ireland** 3–0 | | 1939 | Belfast **Wales** 7–0 |
| 1900 | Belfast **Wales** 3–0 | | 1947 | Swansea **Wales** 6–0 |
| 1901 | Swansea **Wales** 10–9 | | 1948 | Belfast **Ireland** 6–3 |
| 1902 | Dublin **Wales** 15–0 | | 1949 | Swansea **Ireland** 5–0 |
| 1903 | Cardiff **Wales** 18–0 | | 1950 | Belfast **Wales** 6–3 |
| 1904 | Belfast **Ireland** 14–12 | | 1951 | Cardiff **Drawn** 3–3 |
| 1905 | Swansea **Wales** 10–3 | | 1952 | Dublin **Wales** 14–3 |
| 1906 | Belfast **Ireland** 11–6 | | 1953 | Swansea **Wales** 5–3 |
| 1907 | Cardiff **Wales** 29–0 | | 1954 | Dublin **Wales** 12–9 |
| 1908 | Belfast **Wales** 11–5 | | 1955 | Cardiff **Wales** 21–3 |
| 1909 | Swansea **Wales** 18–5 | | 1956 | Dublin **Ireland** 11–3 |
| 1910 | Dublin **Wales** 19–3 | | 1957 | Cardiff **Wales** 6–5 |
| 1911 | Cardiff **Wales** 16–0 | | 1958 | Dublin **Wales** 9–6 |
| 1912 | Belfast **Ireland** 12–5 | | 1959 | Cardiff **Wales** 8–6 |
| 1913 | Swansea **Wales** 16–13 | | 1960 | Dublin **Wales** 10–9 |
| 1914 | Belfast **Wales** 11–3 | | 1961 | Cardiff **Wales** 9–0 |
| 1920 | Cardiff **Wales** 28–4 | | 1962 | Dublin **Drawn** 3–3 |
| 1921 | Belfast **Wales** 6–0 | | 1963 | Cardiff **Ireland** 14–6 |

| | | | | | |
|---|---|---|---|---|---|
| 1964 | Dublin **Wales** 15–6 | | 1991 | Cardiff **Drawn** 21–21 | |
| 1965 | Cardiff **Wales** 14–8 | | 1992 | Dublin **Wales** 16–15 | |
| 1966 | Dublin **Ireland** 9–6 | | 1993 | Cardiff **Ireland** 19–14 | |
| 1967 | Cardiff **Ireland** 3–0 | | 1994 | Dublin **Wales** 17–15 | |
| 1968 | Dublin **Ireland** 9–6 | | 1995 | Cardiff **Ireland** 16–12 | |
| 1969 | Cardiff **Wales** 24–11 | | 1995 | Johannesburg WC **Ireland** 24–23 | |
| 1970 | Dublin **Ireland** 14–0 | | 1996 | Dublin **Ireland** 30–17 | |
| 1971 | Cardiff **Wales** 23–9 | | 1997 | Cardiff **Ireland** 26–25 | |
| 1972 | No Match | | 1998 | Dublin **Wales** 30–21 | |
| 1973 | Cardiff **Wales** 16–12 | | 1999 | Wembley **Ireland** 29–23 | |
| 1974 | Dublin **Drawn** 9–9 | | 2000 | Dublin **Wales** 23–19 | |
| 1975 | Cardiff **Wales** 32–4 | | 2001 | Cardiff **Ireland** 36–6 | |
| 1976 | Dublin **Wales** 34–9 | | 2002 | Dublin **Ireland** 54–10 | |
| 1977 | Cardiff **Wales** 25–9 | | 2003 | Cardiff **Ireland** 25–24 | |
| 1978 | Dublin **Wales** 20–16 | | 2003 | Dublin **Ireland** 35–12 | |
| 1979 | Cardiff **Wales** 24–21 | | 2004 | Dublin **Ireland** 36–15 | |
| 1980 | Dublin **Ireland** 21–7 | | 2005 | Cardiff **Wales** 32–20 | |
| 1981 | Cardiff **Wales** 9–8 | | 2006 | Dublin **Ireland** 31–5 | |
| 1982 | Dublin **Ireland** 20–12 | | 2007 | Cardiff **Ireland** 19–9 | |
| 1983 | Cardiff **Wales** 23–9 | | 2008 | Dublin **Wales** 16–12 | |
| 1984 | Dublin **Wales** 18–9 | | 2009 | Cardiff **Ireland** 17–15 | |
| 1985 | Cardiff **Ireland** 21–9 | | 2010 | Dublin **Ireland** 27–12 | |
| 1986 | Dublin **Wales** 19–12 | | 2011 | Cardiff **Wales** 19–13 | |
| 1987 | Cardiff **Ireland** 15–11 | | 2011 | Wellington WC **Wales** 22–10 | |
| 1987 | Wellington WC **Wales** 13–6 | | 2012 | Dublin **Wales** 23–21 | |
| 1988 | Dublin **Wales** 12–9 | | 2013 | Cardiff **Ireland** 30–22 | |
| 1989 | Cardiff **Ireland** 19–13 | | 2014 | Dublin **Ireland** 26–3 | |
| 1990 | Dublin **Ireland** 14–8 | | | | |

# IRELAND v FRANCE

**Played 92 Ireland won 30, France won 55, Drawn 7**
**Highest scores** Ireland 31–43 in 2006, France 45–10 in 1996
**Biggest wins** Ireland 24–0 in 1913, France 44–5 in 2002

| | | | | | |
|---|---|---|---|---|---|
| 1909 | Dublin **Ireland** 19–8 | | 1930 | Belfast **France** 5–0 | |
| 1910 | Paris **Ireland** 8–3 | | 1931 | Paris **France** 3–0 | |
| 1911 | Cork **Ireland** 25–5 | | 1947 | Dublin **France** 12–8 | |
| 1912 | Paris **Ireland** 11–6 | | 1948 | Paris **Ireland** 13–6 | |
| 1913 | Cork **Ireland** 24–0 | | 1949 | Dublin **France** 16–9 | |
| 1914 | Paris **Ireland** 8–6 | | 1950 | Paris **Drawn** 3–3 | |
| 1920 | Dublin **France** 15–7 | | 1951 | Dublin **Ireland** 9–8 | |
| 1921 | Paris **France** 20–10 | | 1952 | Paris **Ireland** 11–8 | |
| 1922 | Dublin **Ireland** 8–3 | | 1953 | Belfast **Ireland** 16–3 | |
| 1923 | Paris **France** 14–8 | | 1954 | Paris **France** 8–0 | |
| 1924 | Dublin **Ireland** 6–0 | | 1955 | Dublin **France** 5–3 | |
| 1925 | Paris **Ireland** 9–3 | | 1956 | Paris **France** 14–8 | |
| 1926 | Belfast **Ireland** 11–0 | | 1957 | Dublin **Ireland** 11–6 | |
| 1927 | Paris **Ireland** 8–3 | | 1958 | Paris **France** 11–6 | |
| 1928 | Belfast **Ireland** 12–8 | | 1959 | Dublin **Ireland** 9–5 | |
| 1929 | Paris **Ireland** 6–0 | | 1960 | Paris **France** 23–6 | |

| 1961 | Dublin **France** 15–3 |
| 1962 | Paris **France** 11–0 |
| 1963 | Dublin **France** 24–5 |
| 1964 | Paris **France** 27–6 |
| 1965 | Dublin **Drawn** 3–3 |
| 1966 | Paris **France** 11–6 |
| 1967 | Dublin **France** 11–6 |
| 1968 | Paris **France** 16–6 |
| 1969 | Dublin **Ireland** 17–9 |
| 1970 | Paris **France** 8–0 |
| 1971 | Dublin **Drawn** 9–9 |
| 1972 | Paris **Ireland** 14–9 |
| 1972 | Dublin **Ireland** 24–14 |
|      | Non-championship match |
| 1973 | Dublin **Ireland** 6–4 |
| 1974 | Paris **France** 9–6 |
| 1975 | Dublin **Ireland** 25–6 |
| 1976 | Paris **France** 26–3 |
| 1977 | Dublin **France** 15–6 |
| 1978 | Paris **France** 10–9 |
| 1979 | Dublin **Drawn** 9–9 |
| 1980 | Paris **France** 19–18 |
| 1981 | Dublin **France** 19–13 |
| 1982 | Paris **France** 22–9 |
| 1983 | Dublin **Ireland** 22–16 |
| 1984 | Paris **France** 25–12 |
| 1985 | Dublin **Drawn** 15–15 |
| 1986 | Paris **France** 29–9 |
| 1987 | Dublin **France** 19–13 |
| 1988 | Paris **France** 25–6 |
| 1989 | Dublin **France** 26–21 |
| 1990 | Paris **France** 31–12 |

| 1991 | Dublin **France** 21–13 |
| 1992 | Paris **France** 44–12 |
| 1993 | Dublin **France** 21–6 |
| 1994 | Paris **France** 35–15 |
| 1995 | Dublin **France** 25–7 |
| 1995 | Durban WC **France** 36–12 |
| 1996 | Paris **France** 45–10 |
| 1997 | Dublin **France** 32–15 |
| 1998 | Paris **France** 18–16 |
| 1999 | Dublin **France** 10–9 |
| 2000 | Paris **Ireland** 27–25 |
| 2001 | Dublin **Ireland** 22–15 |
| 2002 | Paris **France** 44–5 |
| 2003 | Dublin **Ireland** 15–12 |
| 2003 | Melbourne WC **France** 43–21 |
| 2004 | Paris **France** 35–17 |
| 2005 | Dublin **France** 26–19 |
| 2006 | Paris **France** 43–31 |
| 2007 | Dublin **France** 20–17 |
| 2007 | Paris WC **France** 25–3 |
| 2008 | Paris **France** 26–21 |
| 2009 | Dublin **Ireland** 30–21 |
| 2010 | Paris **France** 33–10 |
| 2011 | Dublin **France** 25–22 |
| 2011 | Bordeaux **France** 19–12 |
|      | Non-championship match |
| 2011 | Dublin **France** 26–22 |
|      | Non-championship match |
| 2012 | Paris **Drawn** 17–17 |
| 2013 | Dublin **Drawn** 13–13 |
| 2014 | Paris **Ireland** 22–20 |

## IRELAND v SOUTH AFRICA

**Played 21 Ireland won 4, South Africa won 16, Drawn 1**
**Highest scores** Ireland 32–15 in 2006, South Africa 38–0 in 1912
**Biggest wins** Ireland 32–15 in 2006, South Africa 38–0 in 1912

| 1906 | Belfast **South Africa** 15–12 |
| 1912 | Dublin **South Africa** 38–0 |
| 1931 | Dublin **South Africa** 8–3 |
| 1951 | Dublin **South Africa** 17–5 |
| 1960 | Dublin **South Africa** 8–3 |
| 1961 | Cape Town **South Africa** 24–8 |
| 1965 | Dublin **Ireland** 9–6 |
| 1970 | Dublin **Drawn** 8–8 |
| 1981 | 1 Cape Town **South Africa** 23–15 |
|      | 2 Durban **South Africa** 12–10 |
|      | South Africa won series 2–0 |
| 1998 | 1 Bloemfontein **South Africa** 37–13 |

| | 2 Pretoria **South Africa** 33–0 |
| | South Africa won series 2–0 |
| 1998 | Dublin **South Africa** 27–13 |
| 2000 | Dublin **South Africa** 28–18 |
| 2004 | 1 Bloemfontein **South Africa** 31–17 |
|      | 2 Cape Town **South Africa** 26–17 |
|      | South Africa won series 2–0 |
| 2004 | Dublin **Ireland** 17–12 |
| 2006 | Dublin **Ireland** 32–15 |
| 2009 | Dublin **Ireland** 15–10 |
| 2010 | Dublin **South Africa** 23–21 |
| 2012 | Dublin **South Africa** 16–12 |

**INTERNATIONAL RESULTS**

# IRELAND v NEW ZEALAND

Played 28 Ireland won 0, New Zealand won 27, Drawn 1
**Highest scores** Ireland 29–40 in 2001, New Zealand 66–28 in 2010
**Biggest win** Ireland no win, New Zealand 60–0 in 2012

| | | | |
|---|---|---|---|
| 1905 | Dublin **New Zealand** 15–0 | 2002 | 1 Dunedin **New Zealand** 15–6 |
| 1924 | Dublin **New Zealand** 6–0 | | 2 Auckland **New Zealand** 40–8 |
| 1935 | Dublin **New Zealand** 17–9 | | New Zealand won series 2–0 |
| 1954 | Dublin **New Zealand** 14–3 | 2005 | Dublin **New Zealand** 45–7 |
| 1963 | Dublin **New Zealand** 6–5 | 2006 | 1 Hamilton **New Zealand** 34–23 |
| 1973 | Dublin **Drawn** 10–10 | | 2 Auckland **New Zealand** 27–17 |
| 1974 | Dublin **New Zealand** 15–6 | | New Zealand won series 2–0 |
| 1976 | Wellington **New Zealand** 11–3 | 2008 | Wellington **New Zealand** 21–11 |
| 1978 | Dublin **New Zealand** 10–6 | 2008 | Dublin **New Zealand** 22–3 |
| 1989 | Dublin **New Zealand** 23–6 | 2010 | New Plymouth **New Zealand** 66–28 |
| 1992 | 1 Dunedin **New Zealand** 24–21 | 2010 | Dublin **New Zealand** 38–18 |
| | 2 Wellington **New Zealand** 59–6 | 2012 | 1 Auckland **New Zealand** 42–10 |
| | New Zealand won series 2–0 | | 2 Christchurch **New Zealand** 22–19 |
| 1995 | Johannesburg WC **New Zealand** 43–19 | | 3 Hamilton **New Zealand** 60–0 |
| | | | New Zealand won series 3–0 |
| 1997 | Dublin **New Zealand** 63–15 | 2013 | Dublin **New Zealand** 24–22 |
| 2001 | Dublin **New Zealand** 40–29 | | |

# IRELAND v AUSTRALIA

Played 31 Ireland won 9, Australia won 21, Drawn 1
**Highest scores** Ireland 27–12 in 1979, Australia 46–10 in 1999
**Biggest wins** Ireland 27–12 in 1979 and 21–6 in 2006, Australia 46–10 in 1999

| | | | |
|---|---|---|---|
| 1927 | Dublin **Australia** 5–3 | | Australia won series 2–0 |
| 1947 | Dublin **Australia** 16–3 | 1996 | Dublin **Australia** 22–12 |
| 1958 | Dublin **Ireland** 9–6 | 1999 | 1 Brisbane **Australia** 46–10 |
| 1967 | Dublin **Ireland** 15–8 | | 2 Perth **Australia** 32–26 |
| 1967 | Sydney **Ireland** 11–5 | | Australia won series 2–0 |
| 1968 | Dublin **Ireland** 10–3 | 1999 | Dublin WC **Australia** 23–3 |
| 1976 | Dublin **Australia** 20–10 | 2002 | Dublin **Ireland** 18–9 |
| 1979 | 1 Brisbane **Ireland** 27–12 | 2003 | Perth **Australia** 45–16 |
| | 2 Sydney **Ireland** 9–3 | 2003 | Melbourne WC **Australia** 17–16 |
| | Ireland won series 2–0 | 2005 | Dublin **Australia** 30–14 |
| 1981 | Dublin **Australia** 16–12 | 2006 | Perth **Australia** 37–15 |
| 1984 | Dublin **Australia** 16–9 | 2006 | Dublin **Ireland** 21–6 |
| 1987 | Sydney WC **Australia** 33–15 | 2008 | Melbourne **Australia** 18–12 |
| 1991 | Dublin WC **Australia** 19–18 | 2009 | Dublin **Drawn** 20–20 |
| 1992 | Dublin **Australia** 42–17 | 2010 | Brisbane **Australia** 22–15 |
| 1994 | 1 Brisbane **Australia** 33–13 | 2011 | Auckland WC **Ireland** 15–6 |
| | 2 Sydney **Australia** 32–18 | 2013 | Dublin **Australia** 32–15 |

## IRELAND v NEW ZEALAND NATIVES

Played 1 New Zealand Natives won 1
**Highest scores** Ireland 4–13 in 1888, Zew Zealand Natives 13–4 in 1888
**Biggest win** Ireland no win, New Zealand Natives 13–4 in 1888

| | | |
|---|---|---|
| 1888 | Dublin **New Zealand Natives** 4G 1T to 1G 1T | |

## IRELAND v IRU PRESIDENT'S XV

Played 1 Drawn 1
**Highest scores** Ireland 18–18 in 1974, IRFU President's XV 18–18 in 1974

| | | |
|---|---|---|
| 1974 | Dublin **Drawn** 18–18 | |

## IRELAND v ROMANIA

Played 8 Ireland won 8
**Highest scores** Ireland 60–0 in 1986, Romania 35–53 in 1998
**Biggest win** Ireland 60–0 in 1986, Romania no win

| 1986 | Dublin **Ireland** 60–0 | 2001 | Bucharest **Ireland** 37–3 |
|---|---|---|---|
| 1993 | Dublin **Ireland** 25–3 | 2002 | Limerick **Ireland** 39–8 |
| 1998 | Dublin **Ireland** 53–35 | 2003 | Gosford WC **Ireland** 45–17 |
| 1999 | Dublin WC **Ireland** 44–14 | 2005 | Dublin **Ireland** 43–12 |

## IRELAND v CANADA

Played 6 Ireland won 5 Drawn 1
**Highest scores** Ireland 55–0 in 2008, Canada 27–27 in 2000
**Biggest win** Ireland 55–0 in 2008, Canada no win

| 1987 | Dunedin WC **Ireland** 46–19 | 2008 | Limerick **Ireland** 55–0 |
|---|---|---|---|
| 1997 | Dublin **Ireland** 33–11 | 2009 | Vancouver **Ireland** 25–6 |
| 2000 | Markham **Drawn** 27–27 | 2013 | Toronto **Ireland** 40–14 |

## IRELAND v TONGA

Played 2 Ireland won 2
**Highest scores** Ireland 40–19 in 2003, Tonga 19–40 in 2003
**Biggest win** Ireland 32–9 in 1987, Tonga no win

| 1987 | Brisbane WC **Ireland** 32–9 | 2003 | Nuku'alofa **Ireland** 40–19 |
|---|---|---|---|

# IRELAND v SAMOA

**Played 6 Ireland won 5, Samoa won 1, Drawn 0**
**Highest scores** Ireland 49–22 in 1988, Samoa 40–25 in 1996
**Biggest wins** Ireland 40–9 in 2013, Samoa 40–25 in 1996

| | | | | |
|---|---|---|---|---|
| 1988 | Dublin **Ireland** 49–22 | | 2003 | Apia **Ireland** 40–14 |
| 1996 | Dublin **Samoa** 40–25 | | 2010 | Dublin **Ireland** 20–10 |
| 2001 | Dublin **Ireland** 35–8 | | 2013 | Dublin **Ireland** 40–9 |

# IRELAND v ITALY

**Played 23 Ireland won 19, Italy won 4, Drawn 0**
**Highest scores** Ireland 61–6 in 2003, Italy 37–29 in 1997 and 37–22 in 1997
**Biggest wins** Ireland 61–6 in 2003, Italy 37–22 in 1997

| | | | | |
|---|---|---|---|---|
| 1988 | Dublin **Ireland** 31–15 | | 2006 | Dublin **Ireland** 26–16 |
| 1995 | Treviso **Italy** 22–12 | | 2007 | Rome **Ireland** 51–24 |
| 1997 | Dublin **Italy** 37–29 | | 2007 | Belfast **Ireland** 23–20 |
| 1997 | Bologna **Italy** 37–22 | | | Non-championship match |
| 1999 | Dublin **Ireland** 39–30 | | 2008 | Dublin **Ireland** 16–11 |
| 2000 | Dublin **Ireland** 60–13 | | 2009 | Rome **Ireland** 38–9 |
| 2001 | Rome **Ireland** 41–22 | | 2010 | Dublin **Ireland** 29–11 |
| 2002 | Dublin **Ireland** 32–17 | | 2011 | Rome **Ireland** 13–11 |
| 2003 | Rome **Ireland** 37–13 | | 2011 | Dunedin WC **Ireland** 36–6 |
| 2003 | Limerick **Ireland** 61–6 | | 2012 | Dublin **Ireland** 42–10 |
| | Non-championship match | | 2013 | Rome **Italy** 22–15 |
| 2004 | Dublin **Ireland** 19–3 | | 2014 | Dublin **Ireland** 46–7 |
| 2005 | Rome **Ireland** 28–17 | | | |

# IRELAND v ARGENTINA

**Played 15 Ireland won 10 Argentina won 5**
**Highest scores** Ireland 46–24 in 2012, Argentina 34–23 in 2000
**Biggest win** Ireland 46–24 in 2012, Argentina 16–0 in 2007

| | | | | |
|---|---|---|---|---|
| 1990 | Dublin **Ireland** 20–18 | | | Argentina won series 2–0 |
| 1999 | Dublin **Ireland** 32–24 | | 2007 | Paris WC **Argentina** 30–15 |
| 1999 | Lens WC **Argentina** 28–24 | | 2008 | Dublin **Ireland** 17–3 |
| 2000 | Buenos Aires **Argentina** 34–23 | | 2010 | Dublin **Ireland** 29–9 |
| 2002 | Dublin **Ireland** 16–7 | | 2012 | Dublin **Ireland** 46–24 |
| 2003 | Adelaide WC **Ireland** 16–15 | | 2014 | 1 Resistencia **Ireland** 29–17 |
| 2004 | Dublin **Ireland** 21–19 | | | 2 Tucumán **Ireland** 23–17 |
| 2007 | 1 Santa Fé **Argentina** 22–20 | | | Ireland won series 2–0 |
| | 2 Buenos Aires **Argentina** 16–0 | | | |

# IRELAND v NAMIBIA

**Played 4 Ireland won 2, Namibia won 2**
**Highest scores** Ireland 64–7 in 2003, Namibia 26–15 in 1991
**Biggest win** Ireland 64–7 in 2003, Namibia 26–15 in 1991

| | | | |
|---|---|---|---|
| 1991 | 1 Windhoek **Namibia** 15–6 | 2003 | Sydney WC **Ireland** 64–7 |
| | 2 Windhoek **Namibia** 26–15 | 2007 | Bordeaux WC **Ireland** 32–17 |
| | Namibia won series 2–0 | | |

# IRELAND v ZIMBABWE

**Played 1 Ireland won 1**
**Highest scores** Ireland 55–11 in 1991, Zimbabwe 11–55 in 1991
**Biggest win** Ireland 55–11 in 1991, Zimbabwe no win

| | |
|---|---|
| 1991 | Dublin WC **Ireland** 55–11 |

# IRELAND v JAPAN

**Played 5 Ireland won 5**
**Highest scores** Ireland 78–9 in 2000, Japan 28–50 in 1995
**Biggest win** Ireland 78–9 in 2000, Japan no win

| | | | |
|---|---|---|---|
| 1991 | Dublin WC **Ireland** 32–16 | 2005 | 1 Osaka **Ireland** 44–12 |
| 1995 | Bloemfontein WC **Ireland** 50–28 | | 2 Tokyo **Ireland** 47–18 |
| 2000 | Dublin **Ireland** 78–9 | | Ireland won series 2–0 |

# IRELAND v UNITED STATES

**Played 8 Ireland won 8**
**Highest scores** Ireland 83–3 in 2000, United States 18–25 in 1996
**Biggest win** Ireland 83–3 in 2000, United States no win

| | | | |
|---|---|---|---|
| 1994 | Dublin **Ireland** 26–15 | 2004 | Dublin **Ireland** 55–6 |
| 1996 | Atlanta **Ireland** 25–18 | 2009 | Santa Clara **Ireland** 27–10 |
| 1999 | Dublin WC **Ireland** 53–8 | 2011 | New Plymouth WC **Ireland** 22–10 |
| 2000 | Manchester (NH) **Ireland** 83–3 | 2013 | Houston **Ireland** 15–12 |

# IRELAND v FIJI

**Played 3 Ireland won 3**
**Highest scores** Ireland 64–17 in 2002, Fiji 17–64 in 2002
**Biggest win** Ireland 64–17 in 2002, Fiji no win

| | | | |
|---|---|---|---|
| 1995 | Dublin **Ireland** 44–8 | 2009 | Dublin **Ireland** 41–6 |
| 2002 | Dublin **Ireland** 64–17 | | |

# IRELAND v GEORGIA

**Played 3 Ireland won 3**
**Highest scores** Ireland 70–0 in 1998, Georgia 14–63 in 2002
**Biggest win** Ireland 70–0 in 1998, Georgia no win

| | | | |
|---|---|---|---|
| 1998 | Dublin **Ireland** 70–0 | 2007 | Bordeaux WC **Ireland** 14–10 |
| 2002 | Dublin **Ireland** 63–14 | | |

# IRELAND v RUSSIA

**Played 2 Ireland won 2**
**Highest scores** Ireland 62–12 in 2011, Russia 12–62 in 2011
**Biggest win** Ireland 62–12 in 2011, Russia no win

| | | | |
|---|---|---|---|
| 2002 | Krasnoyarsk **Ireland** 35–3 | 2011 | Rotorua WC **Ireland** 62–12 |

# IRELAND v PACIFIC ISLANDS

**Played 1 Ireland won 1**
**Highest scores** Ireland 61–17 in 2006, Pacific Islands 17–61 in 2006
**Biggest win** Ireland 61–17 in 2006, Pacific Islands no win

| | |
|---|---|
| 2006 | Dublin **Ireland** 61–17 |

# WALES v FRANCE

**Played 92 Wales won 46, France won 43, Drawn 3**
**Highest scores** Wales 49–14 in 1910, France 51–0 in 1998
**Biggest wins** Wales 47–5 in 1909, France 51–0 in 1998

| | | | | |
|---|---|---|---|---|
| 1908 | Cardiff **Wales** 36–4 | | 1931 | Swansea **Wales** 35–3 |
| 1909 | Paris **Wales** 47–5 | | 1947 | Paris **Wales** 3–0 |
| 1910 | Swansea **Wales** 49–14 | | 1948 | Swansea **France** 11–3 |
| 1911 | Paris **Wales** 15–0 | | 1949 | Paris **France** 5–3 |
| 1912 | Newport **Wales** 14–8 | | 1950 | Cardiff **Wales** 21–0 |
| 1913 | Paris **Wales** 11–8 | | 1951 | Paris **France** 8–3 |
| 1914 | Swansea **Wales** 31–0 | | 1952 | Swansea **Wales** 9–5 |
| 1920 | Paris **Wales** 6–5 | | 1953 | Paris **Wales** 6–3 |
| 1921 | Cardiff **Wales** 12–4 | | 1954 | Cardiff **Wales** 19–13 |
| 1922 | Paris **Wales** 11–3 | | 1955 | Paris **Wales** 16–11 |
| 1923 | Swansea **Wales** 16–8 | | 1956 | Cardiff **Wales** 5–3 |
| 1924 | Paris **Wales** 10–6 | | 1957 | Paris **Wales** 19–13 |
| 1925 | Cardiff **Wales** 11–5 | | 1958 | Cardiff **France** 16–6 |
| 1926 | Paris **Wales** 7–5 | | 1959 | Paris **France** 11–3 |
| 1927 | Swansea **Wales** 25–7 | | 1960 | Cardiff **France** 16–8 |
| 1928 | Paris **France** 8–3 | | 1961 | Paris **France** 8–6 |
| 1929 | Cardiff **Wales** 8–3 | | 1962 | Cardiff **Wales** 3–0 |
| 1930 | Paris **Wales** 11–0 | | 1963 | Paris **France** 5–3 |

| 1964 | Cardiff **Drawn** 11–11 | | 1992 | Cardiff **France** 12–9 |
|------|------------------------|---|------|-------------------------|
| 1965 | Paris **France** 22–13 | | 1993 | Paris **France** 26–10 |
| 1966 | Cardiff **Wales** 9–8 | | 1994 | Cardiff **Wales** 24–15 |
| 1967 | Paris **France** 20–14 | | 1995 | Paris **France** 21–9 |
| 1968 | Cardiff **France** 14–9 | | 1996 | Cardiff **Wales** 16–15 |
| 1969 | Paris **Drawn** 8–8 | | 1996 | Cardiff **France** 40–33 |
| 1970 | Cardiff **Wales** 11–6 | | | Non-championship match |
| 1971 | Paris **Wales** 9–5 | | 1997 | Paris **France** 27–22 |
| 1972 | Cardiff **Wales** 20–6 | | 1998 | Wembley **France** 51–0 |
| 1973 | Paris **France** 12–3 | | 1999 | Paris **Wales** 34–33 |
| 1974 | Cardiff **Drawn** 16–16 | | 1999 | Cardiff **Wales** 34–23 |
| 1975 | Paris **Wales** 25–10 | | | Non-championship match |
| 1976 | Cardiff **Wales** 19–13 | | 2000 | Cardiff **France** 36–3 |
| 1977 | Paris **France** 16–9 | | 2001 | Paris **Wales** 43–35 |
| 1978 | Cardiff **Wales** 16–7 | | 2002 | Cardiff **France** 37–33 |
| 1979 | Paris **France** 14–13 | | 2003 | Paris **France** 33–5 |
| 1980 | Cardiff **Wales** 18–9 | | 2004 | Cardiff **France** 29–22 |
| 1981 | Paris **France** 19–15 | | 2005 | Paris **Wales** 24–18 |
| 1982 | Cardiff **Wales** 22–12 | | 2006 | Cardiff **France** 21–16 |
| 1983 | Paris **France** 16–9 | | 2007 | Paris **France** 32–21 |
| 1984 | Cardiff **France** 21–16 | | 2007 | Cardiff **France** 34–7 |
| 1985 | Paris **France** 14–3 | | | Non-championship match |
| 1986 | Cardiff **France** 23–15 | | 2008 | Cardiff **Wales** 29–12 |
| 1987 | Paris **France** 16–9 | | 2009 | Paris **France** 21–16 |
| 1988 | Cardiff **France** 10–9 | | 2010 | Cardiff **France** 26–20 |
| 1989 | Paris **France** 31–12 | | 2011 | Paris **France** 28–9 |
| 1990 | Cardiff **France** 29–19 | | 2011 | Auckland WC **France** 9–8 |
| 1991 | Paris **France** 36–3 | | 2012 | Cardiff **Wales** 16–9 |
| 1991 | Cardiff **France** 22–9 | | 2013 | Paris **Wales** 16–6 |
| | Non-championship match | | 2014 | Cardiff **Wales** 27–6 |

## WALES v SOUTH AFRICA

**Played 29 Wales won 1, South Africa won 27, Drawn 1**
**Highest scores** Wales 36–38 in 2004, South Africa 96–13 in 1998
**Biggest win** Wales 29–19 in 1999, South Africa 96–13 in 1998

| 1906 | Swansea **South Africa** 11–0 | | | South Africa won series 2–0 |
|------|------------------------------|---|------|-----------------------------|
| 1912 | Cardiff **South Africa** 3–0 | | 2004 | Pretoria **South Africa** 53–18 |
| 1931 | Swansea **South Africa** 8–3 | | 2004 | Cardiff **South Africa** 38–36 |
| 1951 | Cardiff **South Africa** 6–3 | | 2005 | Cardiff **South Africa** 33–16 |
| 1960 | Cardiff **South Africa** 3–0 | | 2007 | Cardiff **South Africa** 34–12 |
| 1964 | Durban **South Africa** 24–3 | | 2008 | 1 Bloemfontein **South Africa** 43–17 |
| 1970 | Cardiff **Drawn** 6–6 | | | 2 Pretoria **South Africa** 37–21 |
| 1994 | Cardiff **South Africa** 20–12 | | | South Africa won series 2–0 |
| 1995 | Johannesburg **South Africa** 40–11 | | 2008 | Cardiff **South Africa** 20–15 |
| 1996 | Cardiff **South Africa** 37–20 | | 2010 | Cardiff **South Africa** 34–31 |
| 1998 | Pretoria **South Africa** 96–13 | | 2010 | Cardiff **South Africa** 29–25 |
| 1998 | Wembley **South Africa** 28–20 | | 2011 | Wellington WC **South Africa** 17–16 |
| 1999 | Cardiff **Wales** 29–19 | | 2013 | Cardiff **South Africa** 24–15 |
| 2000 | Cardiff **South Africa** 23–13 | | 2014 | 1 Durban **South Africa** 38–16 |
| 2002 | 1 Bloemfontein **South Africa** 34–19 | | | 2 Nelspruit **South Africa** 31–30 |
| | 2 Cape Town **South Africa** 19–8 | | | South Africa won series 2–0 |

INTERNATIONAL RESULTS

# WALES v NEW ZEALAND

**Played 29 Wales won 3, New Zealand won 26, Drawn 0**
**Highest scores** Wales 37–53 in 2003, New Zealand 55–3 in 2003
**Biggest wins** Wales 13–8 in 1953, New Zealand 55–3 in 2003

| | | | | |
|---|---|---|---|---|
| 1905 | Cardiff **Wales** 3–0 | | 1989 | Cardiff **New Zealand** 34–9 |
| 1924 | Swansea **New Zealand** 19–0 | | 1995 | Johannesburg WC **New Zealand 34–9** |
| 1935 | Cardiff **Wales** 13–12 | | 1997 | Wembley **New Zealand** 42–7 |
| 1953 | Cardiff **Wales** 13–8 | | 2002 | Cardiff **New Zealand** 43–17 |
| 1963 | Cardiff **New Zealand** 6–0 | | 2003 | Hamilton **New Zealand** 55–3 |
| 1967 | Cardiff **New Zealand** 13–6 | | 2003 | Sydney WC **New Zealand** 53–37 |
| 1969 | 1 Christchurch **New Zealand** 19–0 | | 2004 | Cardiff **New Zealand** 26–25 |
| | 2 Auckland **New Zealand** 33–12 | | 2005 | Cardiff **New Zealand** 41–3 |
| | New Zealand won series 2–0 | | 2006 | Cardiff **New Zealand** 45–10 |
| 1972 | Cardiff **New Zealand** 19–16 | | 2008 | Cardiff **New Zealand** 29–9 |
| 1978 | Cardiff **New Zealand** 13–12 | | 2009 | Cardiff **New Zealand** 19–12 |
| 1980 | Cardiff **New Zealand** 23–3 | | 2010 | 1 Dunedin **New Zealand** 42–9 |
| 1987 | Brisbane WC **New Zealand** 49–6 | | | 2 Hamilton **New Zealand** 29–10 |
| 1988 | 1 Christchurch **New Zealand** 52–3 | | | New Zealand won series 2–0 |
| | 2 Auckland **New Zealand** 54–9 | | 2010 | Cardiff **New Zealand** 37–25 |
| | New Zealand won series 2–0 | | 2012 | Cardiff **New Zealand** 33–10 |

# WALES v AUSTRALIA

**Played 37 Wales won 10, Australia won 26, Drawn 1**
**Highest scores** Wales 29–29 in 2006, Australia 63–6 in 1991
**Biggest wins** Wales 28–3 in 1975, Australia 63–6 in 1991

| | | | | |
|---|---|---|---|---|
| 1908 | Cardiff **Wales** 9–6 | | 1999 | Cardiff WC **Australia** 24–9 |
| 1927 | Cardiff **Australia** 18–8 | | 2001 | Cardiff **Australia** 21–13 |
| 1947 | Cardiff **Wales** 6–0 | | 2003 | Sydney **Australia** 30–10 |
| 1958 | Cardiff **Wales** 9–3 | | 2005 | Cardiff **Wales** 24–22 |
| 1966 | Cardiff **Australia** 14–11 | | 2006 | Cardiff **Drawn** 29–29 |
| 1969 | Sydney **Wales** 19–16 | | 2007 | 1 Sydney **Australia** 29–23 |
| 1973 | Cardiff **Wales** 24–0 | | | 2 Brisbane **Australia** 31–0 |
| 1975 | Cardiff **Wales** 28–3 | | | Australia won series 2–0 |
| 1978 | 1 Brisbane **Australia** 18–8 | | 2007 | Cardiff WC **Australia** 32–20 |
| | 2 Sydney **Australia** 19–17 | | 2008 | Cardiff **Wales** 21–18 |
| | Australia won series 2–0 | | 2009 | Cardiff **Australia** 33–12 |
| 1981 | Cardiff **Wales** 18–13 | | 2010 | Cardiff **Australia** 25–16 |
| 1984 | Cardiff **Australia** 28–9 | | 2011 | Auckland WC **Australia** 21–18 |
| 1987 | Rotorua WC **Wales** 22–21 | | 2011 | Cardiff **Australia** 24–18 |
| 1991 | Brisbane **Australia** 63–6 | | 2012 | 1 Brisbane **Australia** 27–19 |
| 1991 | Cardiff WC **Australia** 38–3 | | | 2 Melbourne **Australia** 25–23 |
| 1992 | Cardiff **Australia** 23–6 | | | 3 Sydney **Australia** 20–19 |
| 1996 | 1 Brisbane **Australia** 56–25 | | | Australia won series 3–0 |
| | 2 Sydney **Australia** 42–3 | | 2012 | Cardiff **Australia** 14–12 |
| | Australia won series 2–0 | | 2013 | Cardiff **Australia** 30–26 |
| 1996 | Cardiff **Australia** 28–19 | | | |

## WALES v NEW ZEALAND NATIVES

**Played 1 Wales won 1**
**Highest scores** Wales 5–0 in 1888, New Zealand Natives 0–5 in 1888
**Biggest win** Wales 5–0 in 1888, New Zealand Natives no win

| | | |
|---|---|---|
| 1888 | Swansea **Wales** 1G 2T to 0 | |

## WALES v NEW ZEALAND ARMY

**Played 1 New Zealand Army won 1**
**Highest scores** Wales 3–6 in 1919, New Zealand Army 6–3 in 1919
**Biggest win** Wales no win, New Zealand Army 6–3 in 1919

| | | |
|---|---|---|
| 1919 | Swansea **New Zealand Army** 6–3 | |

## WALES v ROMANIA

**Played 8 Wales won 6, Romania won 2**
**Highest scores** Wales 81–9 in 2001, Romania 24–6 in 1983
**Biggest wins** Wales 81–9 in 2001, Romania 24–6 in 1983

| 1983 | Bucharest **Romania** 24–6 | 2001 | Cardiff **Wales** 81–9 |
|---|---|---|---|
| 1988 | Cardiff **Romania** 15–9 | 2002 | Wrexham **Wales** 40–3 |
| 1994 | Bucharest **Wales** 16–9 | 2003 | Wrexham **Wales** 54–8 |
| 1997 | Wrexham **Wales** 70–21 | 2004 | Cardiff **Wales** 66–7 |

## WALES v FIJI

**Played 9 Wales won 7, Fiji won 1, Drawn 1**
**Highest scores** Wales 66–0 in 2011, Fiji 38–34 in 2007
**Biggest win** Wales 66–0 in 2011, Fiji 38–34 in 2007

| 1985 | Cardiff **Wales** 40–3 | 2005 | Cardiff **Wales** 11–10 |
|---|---|---|---|
| 1986 | Suva **Wales** 22–15 | 2007 | Nantes WC **Fiji** 38–34 |
| 1994 | Suva **Wales** 23–8 | 2010 | Cardiff **Drawn** 16–16 |
| 1995 | Cardiff **Wales** 19–15 | 2011 | Hamilton WC **Wales** 66–0 |
| 2002 | Cardiff **Wales** 58–14 | | |

## WALES v TONGA

**Played 7 Wales won 7**
**Highest scores** Wales 51–7 in 2001, Tonga 20–27 in 2003
**Biggest win** Wales 51–7 in 2001, Tonga no win

| 1986 | Nuku'Alofa **Wales** 15–7 | 2001 | Cardiff **Wales** 51–7 |
|---|---|---|---|
| 1987 | Palmerston North WC **Wales** 29–16 | 2003 | Canberra WC **Wales** 27–20 |
| 1994 | Nuku'Alofa **Wales** 18–9 | 2013 | Cardiff **Wales** 17–7 |
| 1997 | Swansea **Wales** 46–12 | | |

# WALES v SAMOA

**Played 9 Wales won 5, Samoa won 4, Drawn 0**
**Highest scores** Wales 50–6 in 2000, Samoa 38–31 in 1999
**Biggest wins** Wales 50–6 in 2000, Samoa 34–9 in 1994

| | | | | |
|---|---|---|---|---|
| 1986 | Apia **Wales** 32–14 | | 2000 | Cardiff **Wales** 50–6 |
| 1988 | Cardiff **Wales** 28–6 | | 2009 | Cardiff **Wales** 17–13 |
| 1991 | Cardiff WC **Samoa** 16–13 | | 2011 | Hamilton WC **Wales** 17–10 |
| 1994 | Moamoa **Samoa** 34–9 | | 2012 | Cardiff **Samoa** 26–19 |
| 1999 | Cardiff WC **Samoa** 38–31 | | | |

# WALES v CANADA

**Played 12 Wales won 11, Canada won 1, Drawn 0**
**Highest scores** Wales 61–26 in 2006, Canada 26–24 in 1993 and 26–61 in 2006
**Biggest wins** Wales 60–3 in 2005, Canada 26–24 in 1993

| | | | | |
|---|---|---|---|---|
| 1987 | Invercargill WC **Wales** 40–9 | | 2003 | Melbourne WC **Wales** 41–10 |
| 1993 | Cardiff **Canada** 26–24 | | 2005 | Toronto **Wales** 60–3 |
| 1994 | Toronto **Wales** 33–15 | | 2006 | Cardiff **Wales** 61–26 |
| 1997 | Toronto **Wales** 28–25 | | 2007 | Nantes WC **Wales** 42–17 |
| 1999 | Cardiff **Wales** 33–19 | | 2008 | Cardiff **Wales** 34–13 |
| 2002 | Cardiff **Wales** 32–21 | | 2009 | Toronto **Wales** 32–23 |

# WALES v UNITED STATES

**Played 7 Wales won 7**
**Highest scores** Wales 77–3 in 2005, United States 23–28 in 1997
**Biggest win** Wales 77–3 in 2005, United States no win

| | | | | |
|---|---|---|---|---|
| 1987 | Cardiff **Wales** 46–0 | | | Wales won series 2–0 |
| 1997 | Cardiff **Wales** 34–14 | | 2000 | Cardiff **Wales** 42–11 |
| 1997 | 1 Wilmington **Wales** 30–20 | | 2005 | Hartford **Wales** 77–3 |
| | 2 San Francisco **Wales** 28–23 | | 2009 | Chicago **Wales** 48–15 |

# WALES v NAMIBIA

**Played 4 Wales won 4**
**Highest scores** Wales 81–7 in 2011, Namibia 30–34 in 1990
**Biggest win** Wales 81–7 in 2011, Namibia no win

| | | | | |
|---|---|---|---|---|
| 1990 | 1 Windhoek **Wales** 18–9 | | 1993 | Windhoek **Wales** 38–23 |
| | 2 Windhoek **Wales** 34–30 | | 2011 | New Plymouth WC **Wales** 81–7 |
| | Wales won series 2–0 | | | |

# WALES v BARBARIANS

**Played 4 Wales won 2, Barbarians won 2**
**Highest scores** Wales 31–10 in 1996, Barbarians 31–24 in 1990 and 31–28 in 2011
**Biggest wins** Wales 31–10 in 1996, Barbarians 31–24 in 1990

| | | | |
|---|---|---|---|
| 1990 | Cardiff **Barbarians** 31–24 | 2011 | Cardiff **Barbarians** 31–28 |
| 1996 | Cardiff **Wales** 31–10 | 2012 | Cardiff **Wales** 30–21 |

# WALES v ARGENTINA

**Played 15 Wales won 10, Argentina won 5**
**Highest scores** Wales 44–50 in 2004, Argentina 50–44 in 2004
**Biggest wins** Wales won 40–6 in 2013, Argentina 45–27 in 2006

| | | | |
|---|---|---|---|
| 1991 | Cardiff WC **Wales** 16–7 | | Series drawn 1–1 |
| 1998 | Llanelli **Wales** 43–30 | 2006 | 1 Puerto Madryn **Argentina** 27–25 |
| 1999 | 1 Buenos Aires **Wales** 36–26 | | 2 Buenos Aires **Argentina** 45–27 |
| | 2 Buenos Aires **Wales** 23–16 | | Argentina won series 2–0 |
| | Wales won series 2–0 | 2007 | Cardiff **Wales** 27–20 |
| 1999 | Cardiff WC **Wales** 23–18 | 2009 | Cardiff **Wales** 33–16 |
| 2001 | Cardiff **Argentina** 30–16 | 2011 | Cardiff **Wales** 28–13 |
| 2004 | 1 Tucumán **Argentina** 50–44 | 2012 | Cardiff **Argentina** 26–12 |
| | 2 Buenos Aires **Wales** 35–20 | 2013 | Cardiff **Wales** 40–6 |

# WALES v ZIMBABWE

**Played 3 Wales won 3**
**Highest scores** Wales 49–11 in 1998, Zimbabwe 14–35 in 1993
**Biggest win** Wales 49–11 in 1998, Zimbabwe no win

| | | | |
|---|---|---|---|
| 1993 | 1 Bulawayo **Wales** 35–14 | | Wales won series 2–0 |
| | 2 Harare **Wales** 42–13 | 1998 | Harare **Wales** 49–11 |

# WALES v JAPAN

**Played 9 Wales won 8, Japan won 1**
**Highest scores** Wales 98–0 in 2004, Japan 30–53 in 2001
**Biggest win** Wales 98–0 in 2004, Japan 23–8 in 2013

| | | | |
|---|---|---|---|
| 1993 | Cardiff **Wales** 55–5 | 2004 | Cardiff **Wales** 98–0 |
| 1995 | Bloemfontein WC **Wales 57–10** | 2007 | Cardiff WC **Wales** 72–18 |
| 1999 | Cardiff WC **Wales** 64–15 | 2013 | 1 Osaka **Wales** 22–18 |
| 2001 | 1 Osaka **Wales** 64–10 | | 2 Tokyo **Japan** 23–8 |
| | 2 Tokyo **Wales** 53–30 | | Series drawn 1–1 |
| | Wales won series 2–0 | | |

# WALES v PORTUGAL

**Played 1 Wales won 1**
**Highest scores** Wales 102–11 in 1994, Portugal 11–102 in 1994
**Biggest win** Wales 102–11 in 1994, Portugal no win

| | | |
|---|---|---|
| 1994 | Lisbon | **Wales** 102–11 |

# WALES v SPAIN

**Played 1 Wales won 1**
**Highest scores** Wales 54–0 in 1994, Spain 0–54 in 1994
**Bigegst win** Wales 54–0 in 1994, Spain no win

| | | |
|---|---|---|
| 1994 | Madrid | **Wales** 54–0 |

# WALES v ITALY

**Played 21 Wales won 18, Italy won 2, Drawn 1**
**Highest scores** Wales 60–21 in 1999, Italy 30–22 in 2003
**Biggest win** Wales 60–21 in 1999 and 47–8 in 2008, Italy 30–22 in 2003

| | | | | | |
|---|---|---|---|---|---|
| 1994 | Cardiff | **Wales** 29–19 | 2005 | Rome | **Wales** 38–8 |
| 1996 | Cardiff | **Wales** 31–26 | 2006 | Cardiff | **Drawn** 18–18 |
| 1996 | Rome | **Wales** 31–22 | 2007 | Rome | **Italy** 23–20 |
| 1998 | Llanelli | **Wales** 23–20 | 2008 | Cardiff | **Wales** 47–8 |
| 1999 | Treviso | **Wales** 60–21 | 2009 | Rome | **Wales** 20–15 |
| 2000 | Cardiff | **Wales** 47–16 | 2010 | Cardiff | **Wales** 33–10 |
| 2001 | Rome | **Wales** 33–23 | 2011 | Rome | **Wales** 24–16 |
| 2002 | Cardiff | **Wales** 44–20 | 2012 | Cardiff | **Wales** 24–3 |
| 2003 | Rome | **Italy** 30–22 | 2013 | Rome | **Wales** 26–9 |
| 2003 | Canberra WC | **Wales** 27–15 | 2014 | Cardiff | **Wales** 23–15 |
| 2004 | Cardiff | **Wales** 44–10 | | | |

# WALES v PACIFIC ISLANDS

**Played 1 Wales won 1**
**Highest scores** Wales 38–20 in 2006, Pacific Islands 20–38 in 2006
**Biggest win** Wales 38–20 in 2006, Pacific Islands no win

| | | |
|---|---|---|
| 2006 | Cardiff | **Wales** 38–20 |

# BRITISH/IRISH ISLES v SOUTH AFRICA

**Played 46 British/Irish won 17, South Africa won 23, Drawn 6**
**Highest scores:** British/Irish 28–9 in 1974 and 2009, South Africa 35–16 in 1997
**Biggest wins:** British/Irish 28–9 in 1974 and 2009, South Africa 34–14 in 1962

1891 1 Port Elizabeth **British/Irish** 4–0
2 Kimberley **British/Irish** 3–0
3 Cape Town **British/Irish** 4–0
British/Irish won series 3–0

1896 1 Port Elizabeth **British/Irish** 8–0
2 Johannesburg **British/Irish** 17–8
3 Kimberley **British/Irish** 9–3
4 Cape Town **South Africa** 5–0
British/Irish won series 3–1

1903 1 Johannesburg **Drawn** 10–10
2 Kimberley **Drawn** 0–0
3 Cape Town **South Africa** 8–0
South Africa won series 1–0 with two drawn

1910 1 Johannesburg **South Africa** 14–10
2 Port Elizabeth **British/Irish** 8–3
3 Cape Town **South Africa** 21–5
South Africa won series 2–1

1924 1 Durban **South Africa** 7–3
2 Johannesburg **South Africa** 17–0
3 Port Elizabeth **Drawn** 3–3
4 Cape Town **South Africa** 16–9
South Africa won series 3–0, with 1 draw

1938 1 Johannesburg **South Africa** 26–12
2 Port Elizabeth **South Africa** 19–3
3 Cape Town **British/Irish** 21–16
South Africa won series 2–1

1955 1 Johannesburg **British/Irish** 23–22
2 Cape Town **South Africa** 25–9
3 Pretoria **British/Irish** 9–6
4 Port Elizabeth **South Africa** 22–8
Series drawn 2–2

1962 1 Johannesburg **Drawn** 3–3
2 Durban **South Africa** 3–0
3 Cape Town **South Africa** 8–3
4 Bloemfontein **South Africa** 34–14
South Africa won series 3–0, with 1 draw

1968 1 Pretoria **South Africa** 25–20
2 Port Elizabeth **Drawn** 6–6
3 Cape Town **South Africa** 11–6
4 Johannesburg **South Africa** 19–6
South Africa won series 3–0, with 1 draw

1974 1 Cape Town **British/Irish** 12–3
2 Pretoria **British/Irish** 28–9
3 Port Elizabeth **British/Irish** 26–9
4 Johannesburg **Drawn** 13–13
British/Irish won series 3–0, with 1 draw

1980 1 Cape Town **South Africa** 26–22
2 Bloemfontein **South Africa** 26–19
3 Port Elizabeth **South Africa** 12–10
4 Pretoria **British/Irish** 17–13
South Africa won series 3–1

1997 1 Cape Town **British/Irish** 25–16
2 Durban **British/Irish** 18–15
3 Johannesburg **South Africa** 35–16
British/Irish won series 2–1

2009 1 Durban **South Africa** 26–21
2 Pretoria **South Africa** 28–25
3 Johannesburg **British/Irish** 28–9
South Africa won series 2–1

# BRITISH/IRISH ISLES v NEW ZEALAND

**Played 35 British/Irish won 6, New Zealand won 27, Drawn 2**
**Highest scores:** British/Irish 20–7 in 1993, New Zealand 48–18 in 2005
**Biggest wins:** British/Irish 20–7 in 1993, New Zealand 38–6 in 1983

1904 Wellington **New Zealand** 9–3

1930 1 Dunedin **British/Irish** 6–3
2 Christchurch **New Zealand** 13–10
3 Auckland **New Zealand** 15–10
4 Wellington **New Zealand** 22–8
New Zealand won series 3–1

1950 1 Dunedin **Drawn** 9–9
2 Christchurch **New Zealand** 8–0

INTERNATIONAL RESULTS

3 Wellington **New Zealand** 6–3
4 Auckland **New Zealand** 11–8
New Zealand won series 3–0, with 1 draw

1959 1 Dunedin **New Zealand** 18–17
2 Wellington **New Zealand** 11–8
3 Christchurch **New Zealand** 22–8
4 Auckland **British/Irish** 9–6
New Zealand won series 3–1

1966 1 Dunedin **New Zealand** 20–3
2 Wellington **New Zealand** 16–12
3 Christchurch **New Zealand** 19–6
4 Auckland **New Zealand** 24–11
New Zealand won series 4–0

1971 1 Dunedin **British/Irish** 9–3
2 Christchurch **New Zealand** 22–12
3 Wellington **British/Irish** 13–3
4 Auckland **Drawn** 14–14
British/Irish won series 2–1, with 1 draw

1977 1 Wellington **New Zealand** 16–12
2 Christchurch **British/Irish** 13–9
3 Dunedin **New Zealand** 19–7
4 Auckland **New Zealand** 10–9
New Zealand won series 3–1

1983 1 Christchurch **New Zealand** 16–12
2 Wellington **New Zealand** 9–0
3 Dunedin **New Zealand** 15–8
4 Auckland **New Zealand** 38–6
New Zealand won series 4–0

1993 1 Christchurch **New Zealand** 20–18
2 Wellington **British/Irish** 20–7
3 Auckland **New Zealand** 30–13
New Zealand won series 2–1

2005 1 Christchurch **New Zealand** 21–3
2 Wellington **New Zealand** 48–18
3 Auckland **New Zealand** 38–19
New Zealand won series 3–0

## ANGLO–WELSH v NEW ZEALAND

**Played 3 New Zealand won 2, Drawn 1**
**Highest scores** Anglo Welsh 5–32 in 1908, New Zealand 32–5 in 1908
**Biggest win** Anglo Welsh no win, New Zealand 29–0 in 1908

1908 1 Dunedin **New Zealand** 32–5
2 Wellington **Drawn** 3–3
3 Auckland **New Zealand** 29–0

New Zealand won series 2–0, with 1 draw

## BRITISH/IRISH ISLES v AUSTRALIA

**Played 23 British/Irish won 17, Australia won 6, Drawn 0**
**Highest scores:** British/Irish 41–16 in 2013, Australia 35–14 in 2001
**Biggest wins:** British/Irish 31–0 in 1966, Australia 35–14 in 2001

1899 1 Sydney **Australia** 13–3
2 Brisbane **British/Irish** 11–0
3 Sydney **British/Irish** 11–10
4 Sydney **British/Irish** 13–0
British/Irish won series 3–1

1904 1 Sydney **British/Irish** 17–0
2 Brisbane **British/Irish** 17–3
3 Sydney **British/Irish** 16–0
British/Irish won series 3–0

1930 Sydney **Australia** 6–5

1950 1 Brisbane **British/Irish** 19–6

2 Sydney **British/Irish** 24–3
British/Irish won series 2–0

1959 1 Brisbane **British/Irish** 17–6
2 Sydney **British/Irish** 24–3
British/Irish won series 2–0

1966 1 Sydney **British/Irish** 11–8
2 Brisbane **British/Irish** 31–0
British/Irish won series 2–0

1989 1 Sydney **Australia** 30–12
2 Brisbane **British/Irish** 19–12
3 Sydney **British/Irish** 19–18

| | | | |
|---|---|---|---|
| | British/Irish won series 2–1 | 2013 | 1 Brisbane **British/Irish** 23–21 |
| 2001 | 1 Brisbane **British/Irish** 29–13 | | 2 Melbourne **Australia** 16–15 |
| | 2 Melbourne **Australia** 35–14 | | 3 Sydney **British/Irish** 41–16 |
| | 3 Sydney **Australia** 29–23 | | British/Irish won series 2–1 |
| | Australia won series 2–1 | | |

# BRITISH/IRISH ISLES v ARGENTINA

Played 1 British/Irish won 0, Argentina won 0, Drawn 1
**Highest scores:** British/Irish 25–25 in 2005, Argentina 25–25 in 2005
**Biggest wins:** British/Irish no win to date, Argentina no win to date

2005   Cardiff **Drawn** 25–25

# FRANCE v SOUTH AFRICA

Played 39 France won 11, South Africa won 22, Drawn 6
**Highest scores** France 36–26 in 2006, South Africa 52–10 in 1997
**Biggest wins** France 30–10 in 2002, South Africa 52–10 in 1997

| | | | |
|---|---|---|---|
| 1913 | Bordeaux **South Africa** 38–5 | 1992 | 1 Lyons **South Africa** 20–15 |
| 1952 | Paris **South Africa** 25–3 | | 2 Paris **France** 29–16 |
| 1958 | 1 Cape Town **Drawn** 3–3 | | Series drawn 1–1 |
| | 2 Johannesburg **France** 9–5 | 1993 | 1 Durban **Drawn** 20–20 |
| | France won series 1–0, with 1 draw | | 2 Johannesburg **France** 18–17 |
| 1961 | Paris **Drawn** 0–0 | | France won series 1–0, with 1 draw |
| 1964 | Springs (SA) **France** 8–6 | 1995 | Durban WC **South Africa** 19–15 |
| 1967 | 1 Durban **South Africa** 26–3 | 1996 | 1 Bordeaux **South Africa** 22–12 |
| | 2 Bloemfontein **South Africa** 16–3 | | 2 Paris **South Africa** 13–12 |
| | 3 Johannesburg **France** 19–14 | | South Africa won series 2–0 |
| | 4 Cape Town **Drawn** 6–6 | 1997 | 1 Lyons **South Africa** 36–32 |
| | South Africa won series 2–1, with 1 draw | | 2 Paris **South Africa** 52–10 |
| 1968 | 1 Bordeaux **South Africa** 12–9 | | South Africa won series 2–0 |
| | 2 Paris **South Africa** 16–11 | 2001 | 1 Johannesburg **France** 32–23 |
| | South Africa won series 2–0 | | 2 Durban **South Africa** 20–15 |
| 1971 | 1 Bloemfontein **South Africa** 22–9 | | Series drawn 1–1 |
| | 2 Durban **Drawn** 8–8 | 2001 | Paris **France** 20–10 |
| | South Africa won series 1–0, with 1 draw | 2002 | Marseilles **France** 30–10 |
| 1974 | 1 Toulouse **South Africa** 13–4 | 2005 | 1 Durban **Drawn** 30–30 |
| | 2 Paris **South Africa** 10–8 | | 2 Port Elizabeth **South Africa** 27–13 |
| | South Africa won series 2–0 | | South Africa won series 1–0, with 1 draw |
| 1975 | 1 Bloemfontein **South Africa** 38–25 | 2005 | Paris **France** 26–20 |
| | 2 Pretoria **South Africa** 33–18 | 2006 | Cape Town **France** 36–26 |
| | South Africa won series 2–0 | 2009 | Toulouse **France** 20–13 |
| 1980 | Pretoria **South Africa** 37–15 | 2010 | Cape Town **South Africa** 42–17 |
| | | 2013 | Paris **South Africa** 19–10 |

# FRANCE v NEW ZEALAND

**Played 55 France won 12, New Zealand won 42, Drawn 1**
**Highest scores** France 43–31 in 1999, New Zealand 61–10 in 2007
**Biggest wins** France 22–8 in 1994, New Zealand 61–10 in 2007

| | | | | |
|---|---|---|---|---|
| 1906 | Paris **New Zealand** 38–8 | | | New Zealand won series 2–0 |
| 1925 | Toulouse **New Zealand** 30–6 | | 1994 | 1 Christchurch **France** 22–8 |
| 1954 | Paris **France** 3–0 | | | 2 Auckland **France** 23–20 |
| 1961 | 1 Auckland **New Zealand** 13–6 | | | France won series 2–0 |
| | 2 Wellington **New Zealand** 5–3 | | 1995 | 1 Toulouse **France** 22–15 |
| | 3 Christchurch **New Zealand** 32–3 | | | 2 Paris **New Zealand** 37–12 |
| | New Zealand won series 3–0 | | | Series drawn 1–1 |
| 1964 | Paris **New Zealand** 12–3 | | 1999 | Wellington **New Zealand** 54–7 |
| 1967 | Paris **New Zealand** 21–15 | | 1999 | Twickenham WC **France** 43–31 |
| 1968 | 1 Christchurch **New Zealand** 12–9 | | 2000 | 1 Paris **New Zealand** 39–26 |
| | 2 Wellington **New Zealand** 9–3 | | | 2 Marseilles **France** 42–33 |
| | 3 Auckland **New Zealand** 19–12 | | | Series drawn 1–1 |
| | New Zealand won series 3–0 | | 2001 | Wellington **New Zealand** 37–12 |
| 1973 | Paris **France** 13–6 | | 2002 | Paris **Drawn** 20–20 |
| 1977 | 1 Toulouse **France** 18–13 | | 2003 | Christchurch **New Zealand** 31–23 |
| | 2 Paris **New Zealand** 15–3 | | 2003 | Sydney WC **New Zealand** 40–13 |
| | Series drawn 1–1 | | 2004 | Paris **New Zealand** 45–6 |
| 1979 | 1 Christchurch **New Zealand** 23–9 | | 2006 | 1 Lyons **New Zealand** 47–3 |
| | 2 Auckland **France** 24–19 | | | 2 Paris **New Zealand** 23–11 |
| | Series drawn 1–1 | | | New Zealand won series 2–0 |
| 1981 | 1 Toulouse **New Zealand** 13–9 | | 2007 | 1 Auckland **New Zealand** 42–11 |
| | 2 Paris **New Zealand** 18–6 | | | 2 Wellington **New Zealand** 61–10 |
| | New Zealand won series 2–0 | | | New Zealand won series 2–0 |
| 1984 | 1 Christchurch **New Zealand** 10–9 | | 2007 | Cardiff WC **France** 20–18 |
| | 2 Auckland **New Zealand** 31–18 | | 2009 | 1 Dunedin **France** 27–22 |
| | New Zealand won series 2–0 | | | 2 Wellington **New Zealand** 14–10 |
| 1986 | Christchurch **New Zealand** 18–9 | | | Series drawn 1–1 |
| 1986 | 1 Toulouse **New Zealand** 19–7 | | 2009 | Marseilles **New Zealand** 39–12 |
| | 2 Nantes **France** 16–3 | | 2011 | Auckland WC **New Zealand** 37–17 |
| | Series drawn 1–1 | | 2011 | Auckland WC **New Zealand** 8–7 |
| 1987 | Auckland WC **New Zealand** 29–9 | | 2013 | 1 Auckland **New Zealand** 23–13 |
| 1989 | 1 Christchurch **New Zealand** 25–17 | | | 2 Christchurch **New Zealand** 30–0 |
| | 2 Auckland **New Zealand** 34–20 | | | 3 New Plymouth **New Zealand** 24–9 |
| | New Zealand won series 2–0 | | | New Zealand won series 3–0 |
| 1990 | 1 Nantes **New Zealand** 24–3 | | 2013 | Paris **New Zealand** 26–19 |
| | 2 Paris **New Zealand** 30–12 | | | |

# FRANCE v AUSTRALIA

**Played 45 France won 17, Australia won 26, Drawn 2**
**Highest scores** France 34–6 in 1976, Australia 59–16 in 2010
**Biggest wins** France 34–6 in 1976, Australia 59–16 in 2010

| | |
|---|---|
| 1928 Paris **Australia** 11–8 | Australia won series 2–1 |
| 1948 Paris **France** 13–6 | 1993 1 Bordeaux **France** 16–13 |
| 1958 Paris **France** 19–0 | 2 Paris **Australia** 24–3 |
| 1961 Sydney **France** 15–8 | Series drawn 1–1 |
| 1967 Paris **France** 20–14 | 1997 1 Sydney **Australia** 29–15 |
| 1968 Sydney **Australia** 11–10 | 2 Brisbane **Australia** 26–19 |
| 1971 1 Toulouse **Australia** 13–11 | Australia won series 2–0 |
| 2 Paris **France** 18–9 | 1998 Paris **Australia** 32–21 |
| Series drawn 1–1 | 1999 Cardiff WC **Australia** 35–12 |
| 1972 1 Sydney **Drawn** 14–14 | 2000 Paris **Australia** 18–13 |
| 2 Brisbane **France** 16–15 | 2001 Marseilles **France** 14–13 |
| France won series 1–0, with 1 draw | 2002 1 Melbourne **Australia** 29–17 |
| 1976 1 Bordeaux **France** 18–15 | 2 Sydney **Australia** 31–25 |
| 2 Paris **France** 34–6 | Australia won series 2–0 |
| France won series 2–0 | 2004 Paris **France** 27–14 |
| 1981 1 Brisbane **Australia** 17–15 | 2005 Brisbane **Australia** 37–31 |
| 2 Sydney **Australia** 24–14 | 2005 Marseilles **France** 26–16 |
| Australia won series 2–0 | 2008 1 Sydney **Australia** 34–13 |
| 1983 1 Clermont–Ferrand **Drawn** 15–15 | 2 Brisbane **Australia** 40–10 |
| 2 Paris **France** 15–6 | Australia won series 2–0 |
| France won series 1–0, with 1 draw | 2008 Paris **Australia** 18–13 |
| 1986 Sydney **Australia** 27–14 | 2009 Sydney **Australia** 22–6 |
| 1987 Sydney WC **France** 30–24 | 2010 Paris **Australia** 59–16 |
| 1989 1 Strasbourg **Australia** 32–15 | 2012 Paris **France** 33–6 |
| 2 Lille **France** 25–19 | 2014 1 Brisbane **Australia** 50–23 |
| Series drawn 1–1 | 2 Melbourne **Australia** 6–0 |
| 1990 1 Sydney **Australia** 21–9 | 3 Sydney **Australia** 39–13 |
| 2 Brisbane **Australia** 48–31 | Australia won series 3–0 |
| 3 Sydney **France** 28–19 | |

# FRANCE v UNITED STATES

**Played 7 France won 6, United States won 1, Drawn 0**
**Highest scores** France 41–9 in 1991 and 41–14 in 2003, United States 31–39 in 2004
**Biggest wins** France 41–9 in 1991, United States 17–3 in 1924

| | |
|---|---|
| 1920 Paris **France** 14–5 | *Abandoned after 43 mins |
| 1924 Paris **United States** 17–3 | France won series 2–0 |
| 1976 Chicago **France** 33–14 | 2003 Wollongong WC **France** 41–14 |
| 1991 1 Denver **France** 41–9 | 2004 Hartford **France** 39–31 |
| 2 Colorado Springs **France** 10–3* | |

# FRANCE v ROMANIA

**Played 49 France won 39, Romania won 8, Drawn 2**
**Highest scores** France 67–20 in 2000, Romania 21–33 in 1991
**Biggest wins** France 59–3 in 1924, Romania 15–0 in 1980

| | | | | |
|---|---|---|---|---|
| 1924 | Paris **France** 59–3 | | 1981 | Narbonne **France** 17–9 |
| 1938 | Bucharest **France** 11–8 | | 1982 | Bucharest **Romania** 13–9 |
| 1957 | Bucharest **France** 18–15 | | 1983 | Toulouse **France** 26–15 |
| 1957 | Bordeaux **France** 39–0 | | 1984 | Bucharest **France** 18–3 |
| 1960 | Bucharest **Romania** 11–5 | | 1986 | Lille **France** 25–13 |
| 1961 | Bayonne **Drawn** 5–5 | | 1986 | Bucharest **France** 20–3 |
| 1962 | Bucharest **Romania** 3–0 | | 1987 | Wellington WC **France** 55–12 |
| 1963 | Toulouse **Drawn** 6–6 | | 1987 | Agen **France** 49–3 |
| 1964 | Bucharest **France** 9–6 | | 1988 | Bucharest **France** 16–12 |
| 1965 | Lyons **France** 8–3 | | 1990 | Auch **Romania** 12–6 |
| 1966 | Bucharest **France** 9–3 | | 1991 | Bucharest **France** 33–21 |
| 1967 | Nantes **France** 11–3 | | 1991 | Béziers WC **France** 30–3 |
| 1968 | Bucharest **Romania** 15–14 | | 1992 | Le Havre **France** 25–6 |
| 1969 | Tarbes **France** 14–9 | | 1993 | Bucharest **France** 37–20 |
| 1970 | Bucharest **France** 14–3 | | 1993 | Brive **France** 51–0 |
| 1971 | Béziers **France** 31–12 | | 1995 | Bucharest **France** 24–15 |
| 1972 | Constanza **France** 15–6 | | 1995 | Tucumán LC **France** 52–8 |
| 1973 | Valence **France** 7–6 | | 1996 | Aurillac **France** 64–12 |
| 1974 | Bucharest **Romania** 15–10 | | 1997 | Bucharest **France** 51–20 |
| 1975 | Bordeaux **France** 36–12 | | 1997 | Lourdes LC **France** 39–3 |
| 1976 | Bucharest **Romania** 15–12 | | 1999 | Castres **France** 62–8 |
| 1977 | Clermont–Ferrand **France** 9–6 | | 2000 | Bucharest **France** 67–20 |
| 1978 | Bucharest **France** 9–6 | | 2003 | Lens **France** 56–8 |
| 1979 | Montauban **France** 30–12 | | 2006 | Bucharest **France** 62–14 |
| 1980 | Bucharest **Romania** 15–0 | | | |

# FRANCE v NEW ZEALAND MAORI

**Played 1 New Zealand Maori won 1**
**Highest scores** France 3–12 in 1926, New Zealand Maori 12–3 in 1926
**Biggest win** France no win, New Zealand Maori 12–3 in 1926

| | | |
|---|---|---|
| 1926 | Paris **New Zealand Maori** 12–3 |

# FRANCE v GERMANY

**Played 15 France won 13, Germany won 2, Drawn 0**
**Highest scores** France 38–17 in 1933, Germany 17–16 in 1927 and 17–38 in 1933
**Biggest wins** France 34–0 in 1931, Germany 3–0 in 1938

| | | | |
|---|---|---|---|
| 1927 | Paris **France** 30–5 | 1934 | Hanover **France** 13–9 |
| 1927 | Frankfurt **Germany** 17–16 | 1935 | Paris **France** 18–3 |
| 1928 | Hanover **France** 14–3 | 1936 | 1 Berlin **France** 19–14 |
| 1929 | Paris **France** 24–0 | | 2 Hanover **France** 6–3 |
| 1930 | Berlin **France** 31–0 | | France won series 2–0 |
| 1931 | Paris **France** 34–0 | 1937 | Paris **France** 27–6 |
| 1932 | Frankfurt **France** 20–4 | 1938 | Frankfurt **Germany** 3–0 |
| 1933 | Paris **France** 38–17 | 1938 | Bucharest **France** 8–5 |

# FRANCE v ITALY

**Played 35 France won 32, Italy won 3, Drawn 0**
**Highest scores** France 60–13 in 1967, Italy 40–32 in 1997
**Biggest wins** France 60–13 in 1967, Italy 40–32 in 1997

| | | | |
|---|---|---|---|
| 1937 | Paris **France** 43–5 | 1997 | Grenoble **Italy** 40–32 |
| 1952 | Milan **France** 17–8 | 1997 | Auch LC **France 30–19** |
| 1953 | Lyons **France** 22–8 | 2000 | Paris **France** 42–31 |
| 1954 | Rome **France** 39–12 | 2001 | Rome **France** 30–19 |
| 1955 | Grenoble **France** 24–0 | 2002 | Paris **France** 33–12 |
| 1956 | Padua **France** 16–3 | 2003 | Rome **France** 53–27 |
| 1957 | Agen **France** 38–6 | 2004 | Paris **France** 25–0 |
| 1958 | Naples **France** 11–3 | 2005 | Rome **France** 56–13 |
| 1959 | Nantes **France** 22–0 | 2006 | Paris **France** 37–12 |
| 1960 | Treviso **France** 26–0 | 2007 | Rome **France** 39–3 |
| 1961 | Chambéry **France** 17–0 | 2008 | Paris **France** 25–13 |
| 1962 | Brescia **France** 6–3 | 2009 | Rome **France** 50–8 |
| 1963 | Grenoble **France** 14–12 | 2010 | Paris **France** 46–20 |
| 1964 | Parma **France** 12–3 | 2011 | Rome **Italy** 22–21 |
| 1965 | Pau **France** 21–0 | 2012 | Paris **France** 30–12 |
| 1966 | Naples **France** 21–0 | 2013 | Rome **Italy** 23–18 |
| 1967 | Toulon **France** 60–13 | 2014 | Paris **France** 30–10 |
| 1995 | Buenos Aires LC **France 34–22** | | |

# FRANCE v BRITISH XVs

**Played 5 France won 2, British XVs won 3, Drawn 0**
**Highest scores** France 27–29 in 1989, British XV 36–3 in 1940
**Biggest wins** France 21–9 in 1945, British XV 36–3 in 1940

| | | | |
|---|---|---|---|
| 1940 | Paris **British XV** 36–3 | 1946 | Paris **France** 10–0 |
| 1945 | Paris **France** 21–9 | 1989 | Paris **British XV** 29–27 |
| 1945 | Richmond **British XV** 27–6 | | |

**198**

# FRANCE v WALES XVs

**Played** 2 France won 1, Wales XV won 1
**Highest scores** France 12–0 in 1946, Wales XV 8–0 in 1945
**Biggest win** France 12–0 in 1946, Wales XV 8–0 in 1945

| | |
|---|---|
| 1945 Swansea **Wales XV** 8–0 | 1946 Paris **France** 12–0 |

# FRANCE v IRELAND XVs

**Played** 1 France won 1
**Highest scores** France 4–3 in 1946, Ireland XV 3–4 in 1946
**Biggest win** France 4–3 in 1946, Ireland XV no win

1946 Dublin **France** 4–3

# FRANCE v NEW ZEALAND ARMY

**Played** 1 New Zealand Army won 1
**Highest scores** France 9–14 in 1946, New Zealand Army 14–9 in 1946
**Biggest win** France no win, New Zealand Army 14–9 in 1946

1946 Paris **New Zealand Army** 14–9

# FRANCE v ARGENTINA

**Played** 47 France won 34, Argentina won 12, Drawn 1
**Highest scores** France 49–10 in 2012, Argentina 41–13 in 2010
**Biggest wins** France 49–10 in 2012, Argentina 41–13 in 2010

| | |
|---|---|
| 1949 1 Buenos Aires **France** 5–0 | France won series 1–0, with 1 draw |
| 2 Buenos Aires **France** 12–3 | 1982 1 Toulouse **France** 25–12 |
| France won series 2–0 | 2 Paris **France** 13–6 |
| 1954 1 Buenos Aires **France** 22–8 | France won series 2–0 |
| 2 Buenos Aires **France** 30–3 | 1985 1 Buenos Aires **Argentina** 24–16 |
| France won series 2–0 | 2 Buenos Aires **France** 23–15 |
| 1960 1 Buenos Aires **France** 37–3 | Series drawn 1–1 |
| 2 Buenos Aires **France** 12–3 | 1986 1 Buenos Aires **Argentina** 15–13 |
| 3 Buenos Aires **France** 29–6 | 2 Buenos Aires **France** 22–9 |
| France won series 3–0 | Series drawn 1–1 |
| 1974 1 Buenos Aires **France** 20–15 | 1988 1 Buenos Aires **France** 18–15 |
| 2 Buenos Aires **France** 31–27 | 2 Buenos Aires **Argentina** 18–6 |
| France won series 2–0 | Series drawn 1–1 |
| 1975 1 Lyons **France** 29–6 | 1988 1 Nantes **France** 29–9 |
| 2 Paris **France** 36–21 | 2 Lille **France** 28–18 |
| France won series 2–0 | France won series 2–0 |
| 1977 1 Buenos Aires **France** 26–3 | 1992 1 Buenos Aires **France** 27–12 |
| 2 Buenos Aires **Drawn** 18–18 | 2 Buenos Aires **France** 33–9 |

INTERNATIONAL RECORDS

|      | France won series 2–0 |
| 1992 | Nantes **Argentina** 24–20 |
| 1995 | Buenos Aires LC **France** 47–12 |
| 1996 | 1 Buenos Aires **France** 34–27 |
|      | 2 Buenos Aires **France** 34–15 |
|      | France won series 2–0 |
| 1997 | Tarbes LC **France** 32–27 |
| 1998 | 1 Buenos Aires **France** 35–18 |
|      | 2 Buenos Aires **France** 37–12 |
|      | France won series 2–0 |
| 1998 | Nantes **France** 34–14 |
| 1999 | Dublin WC **France** 47–26 |
| 2002 | Buenos Aires **Argentina** 28–27 |
| 2003 | 1 Buenos Aires **Argentina** 10–6 |

|      | 2 Buenos Aires **Argentina** 33–32 |
|      | Argentina won series 2–0 |
| 2004 | Marseilles **Argentina** 24–14 |
| 2006 | Paris **France** 27–26 |
| 2007 | Paris WC **Argentina** 17–12 |
| 2007 | Paris WC **Argentina** 34–10 |
| 2008 | Marseilles **France** 12–6 |
| 2010 | Buenos Aires **Argentina** 41–13 |
| 2010 | Montpellier **France** 15–9 |
| 2012 | 1 Cordoba **Argentina** 23–20 |
|      | 2 Tucuman **France** 49–10 |
|      | Series drawn 1–1 |
| 2012 | Lille **France** 39–22 |

# FRANCE v CZECHOSLOVAKIA

**Played 2 France won 2**
**Highest scores** France 28–3 in 1956, Czechoslovakia 6–19 in 1968
**Biggest win** France 28–3 in 1956, Czechoslovakia no win

| 1956 | Toulouse **France** 28–3 | 1968 | Prague **France** 19–6 |

# FRANCE v FIJI

**Played 8 France won 8**
**Highest scores** France 77–10 in 2001, Fiji 19–28 in 1999
**Biggest win** France 77–10 in 2001, Fiji no win

| 1964 | Paris **France** 21–3 | 1999 | Toulouse WC **France** 28–19 |
| 1987 | Auckland WC **France** 31–16 | 2001 | Saint Etienne **France** 77–10 |
| 1991 | Grenoble WC **France** 33–9 | 2003 | Brisbane WC **France** 61–18 |
| 1998 | Suva **France** 34–9 | 2010 | Nantes **France** 34–12 |

# FRANCE v JAPAN

**Played 3 France won 3**
**Highest scores** France 51–29 in 2003, Japan 29–51 in 2003
**Biggest win** France 51–29 in 2003, Japan no win

| 1973 | Bordeaux **France** 30–18 | 2011 | Albany WC **France** 47–21 |
| 2003 | Townsville WC **France** 51–29 |

# FRANCE v ZIMBABWE

**Played 1 France won 1**
**Highest scores** France 70–12 in 1987, Zimbabwe 12–70 in 1987
**Biggest win** France 70–12 in 1987, Zimbabwe no win

| | | |
|---|---|---|
| 1987 | Auckland WC **France** 70–12 | |

# FRANCE v CANADA

**Played 8 France won 7, Canada won 1, Drawn 0**
**Highest scores** France 50–6 in 2005, Canada 20–33 in 1999
**Biggest wins** France 50–6 in 2005, Canada 18–16 in 1994

| | | | | |
|---|---|---|---|---|
| 1991 | Agen WC **France** 19–13 | | 2002 | Paris **France** 35–3 |
| 1994 | Nepean **Canada** 18–16 | | 2004 | Toronto **France** 47–13 |
| 1994 | Besançon **France** 28–9 | | 2005 | Nantes **France** 50–6 |
| 1999 | Béziers WC **France** 33–20 | | 2011 | Napier WC **France** 46–19 |

# FRANCE v TONGA

**Played 5 France won 3, Tonga won 2**
**Highest scores** France 43–8 in 2005, Tonga 20–16 in 1999
**Biggest win** France 43–8 in 2005, Tonga 19–14 in 2011

| | | | | |
|---|---|---|---|---|
| 1995 | Pretoria WC **France** 38–10 | | 2011 | Wellington WC **Tonga** 19–14 |
| 1999 | Nuku'alofa **Tonga** 20–16 | | 2013 | Le Havre **France** 38–18 |
| 2005 | Toulouse **France** 43–8 | | | |

# FRANCE v IVORY COAST

**Played 1 France won 1**
**Highest scores** France 54–18 in 1995, Ivory Coast 18–54 in 1995
**Biggest win** France 54–18 in 1995, Ivory Coast no win

| | | |
|---|---|---|
| 1995 | Rustenburg WC **France** 54–18 | |

# FRANCE v SAMOA

**Played 3 France won 3**
**Highest scores** France 43–5 in 2009, Samoa 22–39 in 1999
**Biggest win** France 43–5 in 2009, Samoa no win

| | | | | |
|---|---|---|---|---|
| 1999 | Apia **France** 39–22 | | 2012 | Paris **France** 22–14 |
| 2009 | Paris **France** 43–5 | | | |

# FRANCE v NAMIBIA

**Played 2 France won 2**
**Highest scores** France 87–10 in 2007, Namibia 13–47 in 1999
**Biggest win** France 87–10 in 2007, Namibia no win

| 1999 Bordeaux WC **France** 47–13 | 2007 Toulouse WC **France** 87–10 |
|---|---|

# FRANCE v GEORGIA

**Played 1 France won 1**
**Highest scores** France 64–7 in 2007, Georgia 7–64 in 2007
**Biggest win** France 64–7 in 2007, Georgia no win

| 2007 Marseilles WC **France** 64–7 |
|---|

# FRANCE v PACIFIC ISLANDS

**Played 1 Wales won 1**
**Highest scores** France 42–17 in 2008, Pacific Islands 17–42 in 2008
**Biggest win** France 42–17 in 2008, Pacific Islands no win

| 2008 Sochaux **France** 42–17 |
|---|

# SOUTH AFRICA v NEW ZEALAND

**Played 89 New Zealand won 51, South Africa won 35, Drawn 3**
**Highest scores** New Zealand 55–35 in 1997, South Africa 46–40 in 2000
**Biggest wins** New Zealand 52–16 in 2003, South Africa 17–0 in 1928

| | |
|---|---|
| 1921 1 Dunedin **New Zealand** 13–5 | South Africa won series 4–0 |
| 2 Auckland **South Africa** 9–5 | 1956 1 Dunedin **New Zealand** 10–6 |
| 3 Wellington **Drawn** 0–0 | 2 Wellington **South Africa** 8–3 |
| Series drawn 1–1, with 1 draw | 3 Christchurch **New Zealand** 17–10 |
| 1928 1 Durban **South Africa** 17–0 | 4 Auckland **New Zealand** 11–5 |
| 2 Johannesburg **New Zealand** 7–6 | New Zealand won series 3–1 |
| 3 Port Elizabeth **South Africa** 11–6 | 1960 1 Johannesburg **South Africa** 13–0 |
| 4 Cape Town **New Zealand** 13–5 | 2 Cape Town **New Zealand** 11–3 |
| Series drawn 2–2 | 3 Bloemfontein **Drawn** 11–11 |
| 1937 1 Wellington **New Zealand** 13–7 | 4 Port Elizabeth **South Africa** 8–3 |
| 2 Christchurch **South Africa** 13–6 | South Africa won series 2–1, with 1 |
| 3 Auckland **South Africa** 17–6 | draw |
| South Africa won series 2–1 | 1965 1 Wellington **New Zealand** 6–3 |
| 1949 1 Cape Town **South Africa** 15–11 | 2 Dunedin **New Zealand** 13–0 |
| 2 Johannesburg **South Africa** 12–6 | 3 Christchurch **South Africa** 19–16 |
| 3 Durban **South Africa** 9–3 | 4 Auckland **New Zealand** 20–3 |
| 4 Port Elizabeth **South Africa** 11–8 | New Zealand won series 3–1 |

| | |
|---|---|
| 1970 | 1 Pretoria **South Africa** 17–6 |
| | 2 Cape Town **New Zealand** 9–8 |
| | 3 Port Elizabeth **South Africa** 14–3 |
| | 4 Johannesburg **South Africa** 20–17 |
| | South Africa won series 3–1 |
| 1976 | 1 Durban **South Africa** 16–7 |
| | 2 Bloemfontein **New Zealand** 15–9 |
| | 3 Cape Town **South Africa** 15–10 |
| | 4 Johannesburg **South Africa** 15–14 |
| | South Africa won series 3–1 |
| 1981 | 1 Christchurch **New Zealand** 14–9 |
| | 2 Wellington **South Africa** 24–12 |
| | 3 Auckland **New Zealand** 25–22 |
| | New Zealand won series 2–1 |
| 1992 | Johannesburg **New Zealand** 27–24 |
| 1994 | 1 Dunedin **New Zealand** 22–14 |
| | 2 Wellington **New Zealand** 13–9 |
| | 3 Auckland **Drawn** 18–18 |
| | New Zealand won series 2–0, with |
| | 1 draw |
| 1995 | Johannesburg WC **South Africa** 15–12 |
| | (aet) |
| 1996 | Christchurch TN **New Zealand** 15–11 |
| 1996 | Cape Town TN **New Zealand** 29–18 |
| 1996 | 1 Durban **New Zealand** 23–19 |
| | 2 Pretoria **New Zealand** 33–26 |
| | 3 Johannesburg **South Africa** 32–22 |
| | New Zealand won series 2–1 |
| 1997 | Johannesburg TN **New Zealand** 35–32 |
| 1997 | Auckland TN **New Zealand** 55–35 |
| 1998 | Wellington TN **South Africa** 13–3 |
| 1998 | Durban TN **South Africa** 24–23 |
| 1999 | Dunedin TN **New Zealand** 28–0 |
| 1999 | Pretoria TN **New Zealand** 34–18 |
| 1999 | Cardiff WC **South Africa** 22–18 |

| | |
|---|---|
| 2000 | Christchurch TN **New Zealand** 25–12 |
| 2000 | Johannesburg TN **South Africa** 46–40 |
| 2001 | Cape Town TN **New Zealand** 12–3 |
| 2001 | Auckland TN **New Zealand** 26–15 |
| 2002 | Wellington TN **New Zealand** 41–20 |
| 2002 | Durban TN **New Zealand** 30–23 |
| 2003 | Pretoria TN **New Zealand** 52–16 |
| 2003 | Dunedin TN **New Zealand** 19–11 |
| 2003 | Melbourne WC **New Zealand** 29–9 |
| 2004 | Christchurch TN **New Zealand** 23–21 |
| 2004 | Johannesburg TN **South Africa** 40–26 |
| 2005 | Cape Town TN **South Africa** 22–16 |
| 2005 | Dunedin TN **New Zealand** 31–27 |
| 2006 | Wellington TN **New Zealand** 35–17 |
| 2006 | Pretoria TN **New Zealand** 45–26 |
| 2006 | Rustenburg TN **South Africa** 21–20 |
| 2007 | Durban TN **New Zealand** 26–21 |
| 2007 | Christchurch TN **New Zealand** 33–6 |
| 2008 | Wellington TN **New Zealand** 19–8 |
| 2008 | Dunedin TN **South Africa** 30–28 |
| 2008 | Cape Town TN **New Zealand** 19–0 |
| 2009 | Bloemfontein TN **South Africa** 28–19 |
| 2009 | Durban TN **South Africa** 31–19 |
| 2009 | Hamilton TN **South Africa** 32–29 |
| 2010 | Auckland TN **New Zealand** 32–12 |
| 2010 | Wellington TN **New Zealand** 31–17 |
| 2010 | Soweto TN **New Zealand** 29–22 |
| 2011 | Wellington TN **New Zealand** 40–7 |
| 2011 | Port Elizabeth TN **South Africa** 18–5 |
| 2012 | Dunedin RC **New Zealand** 21–11 |
| 2012 | Soweto RC **New Zealand** 32–16 |
| 2013 | Auckland RC **New Zealand** 29–13 |
| 2013 | Johannesburg RC **New Zealand** 38–27 |
| 2014 | Wellington RC **New Zealand** 14–10 |
| 2014 | Johannesburg RC **South Africa** 27–25 |

# SOUTH AFRICA v AUSTRALIA

**Played 80 South Africa won 45, Australia won 34, Drawn 1**
**Highest scores** South Africa 61–22 in 1997, Australia 49–0 in 2006
**Biggest wins** South Africa 53–8 in 2008, Australia 49–0 in 2006

| | |
|---|---|
| 1933 | 1 Cape Town **South Africa** 17–3 |
| | 2 Durban **Australia** 21–6 |
| | 3 Johannesburg **South Africa** 12–3 |
| | 4 Port Elizabeth **South Africa** 11–0 |
| | 5 Bloemfontein **Australia** 15–4 |
| | South Africa won series 3–2 |
| 1937 | 1 Sydney **South Africa** 9–5 |
| | 2 Sydney **South Africa** 26–17 |

| | |
|---|---|
| | South Africa won series 2–0 |
| 1953 | 1 Johannesburg **South Africa** 25–3 |
| | 2 Cape Town **Australia** 18–14 |
| | 3 Durban **South Africa** 18–8 |
| | 4 Port Elizabeth **South Africa** 22–9 |
| | South Africa won series 3–1 |
| 1956 | 1 Sydney **South Africa** 9–0 |
| | 2 Brisbane **South Africa** 9–0 |

| | | | |
|---|---|---|---|
| | South Africa won series 2–0 | 2000 | Sydney TN **Australia** 26–6 |
| 1961 | 1 Johannesburg **South Africa** 28–3 | 2000 | Durban TN **Australia** 19–18 |
| | 2 Port Elizabeth **South Africa** 23–11 | 2001 | Pretoria TN **South Africa** 20–15 |
| | South Africa won series 2–0 | 2001 | Perth TN **Drawn** 14–14 |
| 1963 | 1 Pretoria **South Africa** 14–3 | 2002 | Brisbane TN **Australia** 38–27 |
| | 2 Cape Town **Australia** 9–5 | 2002 | Johannesburg TN **South Africa** 33–31 |
| | 3 Johannesburg **Australia** 11–9 | 2003 | Cape Town TN **South Africa** 26–22 |
| | 4 Port Elizabeth **South Africa** 22–6 | 2003 | Brisbane TN **Australia** 29–9 |
| | Series drawn 2–2 | 2004 | Perth TN **Australia** 30–26 |
| 1965 | 1 Sydney **Australia** 18–11 | 2004 | Durban TN **South Africa** 23–19 |
| | 2 Brisbane **Australia** 12–8 | 2005 | Sydney **Australia** 30–12 |
| | Australia won series 2–0 | 2005 | Johannesburg **South Africa** 33–20 |
| 1969 | 1 Johannesburg **South Africa** 30–11 | 2005 | Pretoria TN **South Africa** 22–16 |
| | 2 Durban **South Africa** 16–9 | 2005 | Perth TN **South Africa** 22–19 |
| | 3 Cape Town **South Africa** 11–3 | 2006 | Brisbane TN **Australia** 49–0 |
| | 4 Bloemfontein **South Africa** 19–8 | 2006 | Sydney TN **Australia** 20–18 |
| | South Africa won series 4–0 | 2006 | Johannesburg TN **South Africa** 24–16 |
| 1971 | 1 Sydney **South Africa** 19–11 | 2007 | Cape Town TN **South Africa** 22–19 |
| | 2 Brisbane **South Africa** 14–6 | 2007 | Sydney TN **Australia** 25–17 |
| | 3 Sydney **South Africa** 18–6 | 2008 | Perth TN **Australia** 16–9 |
| | South Africa won series 3–0 | 2008 | Durban TN **Australia** 27–15 |
| 1992 | Cape Town **Australia** 26–3 | 2008 | Johannesburg TN **South Africa** 53–8 |
| 1993 | 1 Sydney **South Africa** 19–12 | 2009 | Cape Town TN **South Africa** 29–17 |
| | 2 Brisbane **Australia** 28–20 | 2009 | Perth TN **South Africa** 32–25 |
| | 3 Sydney **Australia** 19–12 | 2009 | Brisbane TN **Australia** 21–6 |
| | Australia won series 2–1 | 2010 | Brisbane TN **Australia** 30–13 |
| 1995 | Cape Town WC **South Africa** 27–18 | 2010 | Pretoria TN **South Africa** 44–31 |
| 1996 | Sydney TN **Australia** 21–16 | 2010 | Bloemfontein TN **Australia** 41–39 |
| 1996 | Bloemfontein TN **South Africa** 25–19 | 2011 | Sydney TN **Australia** 39–20 |
| 1997 | Brisbane TN **Australia** 32–20 | 2011 | Durban TN **Australia** 14–9 |
| 1997 | Pretoria TN **South Africa** 61–22 | 2011 | Wellington WC **Australia** 11–9 |
| 1998 | Perth TN **South Africa** 14–13 | 2012 | Perth RC **Australia** 26–19 |
| 1998 | Johannesburg TN **South Africa** 29–15 | 2012 | Pretoria RC **South Africa** 31–8 |
| 1999 | Brisbane TN **Australia** 32–6 | 2013 | Brisbane RC **South Africa** 38–12 |
| 1999 | Cape Town TN **South Africa** 10–9 | 2013 | Cape Town RC **South Africa** 28–8 |
| 1999 | Twickenham WC **Australia** 27–21 | 2014 | Perth RC **Australia** 24–23 |
| 2000 | Melbourne **Australia** 44–23 | 2014 | Cape Town RC **South Africa** 28–10 |

## SOUTH AFRICA v WORLD XVs

**Played 3 South Africa won 3**
**Highest scores** South Africa 45–24 in 1977, World XV 24–45 in 1977
**Biggest win** South Africa 45–24 in 1977, World XV no win

| | | | |
|---|---|---|---|
| 1977 | Pretoria **South Africa** 45–24 | | 2 Johannesburg **South Africa** 22–16 |
| 1989 | 1 Cape Town **South Africa** 20–19 | | South Africa won series 2–0 |

# SOUTH AFRICA v SOUTH AMERICA

**Played 8 South Africa won 7, South America won 1, Drawn 0**
**Highest scores** South Africa 50–18 in 1982, South America 21–12 in 1982
**Biggest wins** South Africa 50–18 in 1982, South America 21–12 in 1982

| | |
|---|---|
| 1980 1 Johannesburg **South Africa** 24–9 | 1982 1 Pretoria **South Africa** 50–18 |
| 2 Durban **South Africa** 18–9 | 2 Bloemfontein **South America** 21–12 |
| South Africa won series 2–0 | Series drawn 1–1 |
| 1980 1 Montevideo **South Africa** 22–13 | 1984 1 Pretoria **South Africa** 32–15 |
| 2 Santiago **South Africa** 30–16 | 2 Cape Town **South Africa** 22–13 |
| South Africa won series 2–0 | South Africa won series 2–0 |

# SOUTH AFRICA v UNITED STATES

**Played 3 South Africa won 3**
**Highest scores** South Africa 64–10 in 2007, United States 20–43 in 2001
**Biggest win** South Africa 64–10 in 2007, United States no win

| | |
|---|---|
| 1981 Glenville **South Africa** 38–7 | 2007 Montpellier WC **South Africa** 64–10 |
| 2001 Houston **South Africa** 43–20 | |

# SOUTH AFRICA v NEW ZEALAND CAVALIERS

**Played 4 South Africa won 3, New Zealand Cavaliers won 1, Drawn 0**
**Highest scores** South Africa 33–18 in 1986, New Zealand Cavaliers 19–18 in 1986
**Biggest wins** South Africa 33–18 in 1986, New Zealand Cavaliers 19–18 in 1986

| | |
|---|---|
| 1986 1 Cape Town **South Africa** 21–15 | 3 Pretoria **South Africa** 33–18 |
| 2 Durban **New Zealand Cavaliers** | 4 Johannesburg **South Africa** 24–10 |
| 19–18 | South Africa won series 3–1 |

# SOUTH AFRICA v ARGENTINA

**Played 19 South Africa won 18, Drawn 1**
**Highest scores** South Africa 73–13 in 2013, Argentina 33–37 in 2000
**Biggest wins** South Africa 73–13 in 2013, Argentina no win

| | |
|---|---|
| 1993 1 Buenos Aires **South Africa** 29–26 | 2003 Port Elizabeth **South Africa** 26–25 |
| 2 Buenos Aires **South Africa** 52–23 | 2004 Buenos Aires **South Africa** 39–7 |
| South Africa won series 2–0 | 2005 Buenos Aires **South Africa** 34–23 |
| 1994 1 Port Elizabeth **South Africa** 42–22 | 2007 Paris WC **South Africa** 37–13 |
| 2 Johannesburg **South Africa** 46–26 | 2008 Johannesburg **South Africa** 63–9 |
| South Africa won series 2–0 | 2012 Cape Town RC **South Africa** 27–6 |
| 1996 1 Buenos Aires **South Africa** 46–15 | 2012 Mendoza RC **Drawn** 16–16 |
| 2 Buenos Aires **South Africa** 44–21 | 2013 Soweto RC **South Africa** 73–13 |
| South Africa win series 2–0 | 2013 Mendoza RC **South Africa** 22–17 |
| 2000 Buenos Aires **South Africa** 37–33 | 2014 Pretoria RC **South Africa** 13–6 |
| 2002 Springs **South Africa** 49–29 | 2014 Salta RC **South Africa** 33–31 |

# SOUTH AFRICA v SAMOA

Played 8 South Africa won 8
Highest scores South Africa 60–8 in 1995, 60–18 in 2002 and 60–10 in 2003, Samoa 23–56 in 2013
Biggest win South Africa 60–8 in 1995 and 59–7 in 2007, Samoa no win

| | | | | |
|---|---|---|---|---|
| 1995 | Johannesburg **South Africa** 60–8 | | 2007 | Johannesburg **South Africa** 35–8 |
| 1995 | Johannesburg WC **South Africa** 42–14 | | 2007 | Paris WC **South Africa** 59–7 |
| 2002 | Pretoria **South Africa** 60–18 | | 2011 | Albany WC **South Africa** 13–5 |
| 2003 | Brisbane WC **South Africa** 60–10 | | 2013 | Pretoria QT **South Africa** 56–23 |

# SOUTH AFRICA v ROMANIA

Played 1 South Africa won 1
Highest score South Africa 21–8 in 1995, Romania 8–21 in 1995
Biggest win South Africa 21–8 in 1995, Romania no win

| | |
|---|---|
| 1995 | Cape Town WC **South Africa** 21–8 |

# SOUTH AFRICA v CANADA

Played 2 South Africa won 2
Highest scores South Africa 51–18 in 2000, Canada 18–51 in 2000
Biggest win South Africa 51–18 in 2000, Canada no win

| | | | | |
|---|---|---|---|---|
| 1995 | Port Elizabeth WC **South Africa** 20–0 | | 2000 | East London **South Africa** 51–18 |

# SOUTH AFRICA v ITALY

Played 11 South Africa won 11
Highest scores South Africa 101–0 in 1999, Italy 31–62 in 1997
Biggest win South Africa 101–0 in 1999, Italy no win

| | | | | |
|---|---|---|---|---|
| 1995 | Rome **South Africa** 40–21 | | 2008 | Cape Town **South Africa** 26–0 |
| 1997 | Bologna **South Africa** 62–31 | | 2009 | Udine **South Africa** 32–10 |
| 1999 | 1 Port Elizabeth **South Africa** 74–3 | | 2010 | 1 Witbank **South Africa** 29–13 |
| | 2 Durban **South Africa** 101–0 | | | 2 East London **South Africa** 55–11 |
| | South Africa won series 2–0 | | | South Africa won series 2–0 |
| 2001 | Port Elizabeth **South Africa** 60–14 | | 2013 | Durban QT **South Africa** 44–10 |
| 2001 | Genoa **South Africa** 54–26 | | | |

# SOUTH AFRICA v FIJI

**Played 3 South Africa won 3**
**Highest scores** South Africa 49–3 in 2011, Fiji 20–37 in 2007
**Biggest win** South Africa 49–3 in 2011, Fiji no win

| | | | |
|---|---|---|---|
| 1996 | Pretoria **South Africa** 43–18 | 2011 | Wellington WC **South Africa** 49–3 |
| 2007 | Marseilles WC **South Africa** 37–20 | | |

# SOUTH AFRICA v TONGA

**Played 2 South Africa won 2**
**Higest scores** South Africa 74–10 in 1997, Tonga 25–30 in 2007
**Biggest win** South Africa 74–10 in 1997, Tonga no win

| | | | |
|---|---|---|---|
| 1997 | Cape Town **South Africa** 74–10 | 2007 | Lens WC **South Africa** 30–25 |

# SOUTH AFRICA v SPAIN

**Played 1 South Africa won 1**
**Highest scores** South Africa 47–3 in 1999, Spain 3–47 in 1999
**Biggest win** South Africa 47–3 in 1999, Spain no win

| | |
|---|---|
| 1999 | Murrayfield WC **South Africa** 47–3 |

# SOUTH AFRICA v URUGUAY

**Played 3 South Africa won 3**
**Highest scores** South Africa 134–3 in 2005, Uruguay 6–72 in 2003
**Biggest win** South Africa 134–3 in 2005, Uruguay no win

| | | | |
|---|---|---|---|
| 1999 | Glasgow WC **South Africa** 39–3 | | Perth WC **South Africa** 72–6 |
| 2003 | Glasgow WC **South Africa** 39–3 | 2005 | East London **South Africa** 134–3 |

# SOUTH AFRICA v GEORGIA

**Played 1 South Africa won 1**
**Highest scores** South Africa 46–19 in 2003, Georgia 19–46 in 2003
**Biggest win** South Africa 46–19 in 2003, Georgia no win

| | |
|---|---|
| 2003 | Sydney WC **South Africa** 46–19 |

# SOUTH AFRICA v PACIFIC ISLANDS

Played 1 South Africa won 1
Highest scores South Africa 38–24 in 2004, Pacific Islands 24–38 in 2004
Biggest win South Africa 38–24 in 2004, Pacific Islands no win

| | | |
|---|---|---|
| 2004 | Gosford (Aus) **South Africa** 38–24 | |

# SOUTH AFRICA v NAMIBIA

Played 2 South Africa won 2
Highest scores South Africa 105–13 in 2007, Namibia 13–105 in 2007
Biggest win South Africa 105–13 in 2007, Namibia no win

| 2007 | Cape Town **South Africa** 105–13 | 2011 | Albany WC **South Africa** 87–0 |
|---|---|---|---|

# NEW ZEALAND v AUSTRALIA

Played 151 New Zealand won 103, Australia won 41, Drawn 7
Highest scores New Zealand 50–21 in 2003, Australia 35–39 in 2000
Biggest wins New Zealand 43–6 in 1996, Australia 28–7 in 1999

| | | | | |
|---|---|---|---|---|
| 1903 | Sydney **New Zealand** 22–3 | | 3 Sydney **New Zealand** 21–13 | |
| 1905 | Dunedin **New Zealand** 14–3 | | New Zealand won series 2–1 | |
| 1907 | 1 Sydney **New Zealand** 26–6 | 1934 | 1 Sydney **Australia** 25–11 | |
| | 2 Brisbane **New Zealand** 14–5 | | 2 Sydney **Drawn** 3–3 | |
| | 3 Sydney **Drawn** 5–5 | | Australia won series 1–0, with 1 | |
| | New Zealand won series 2–0, with 1 | | draw | |
| | draw | 1936 | 1 Wellington **New Zealand** 11–6 | |
| 1910 | 1 Sydney **New Zealand** 6–0 | | 2 Dunedin **New Zealand** 38–13 | |
| | 2 Sydney **Australia** 11–0 | | New Zealand won series 2–0 | |
| | 3 Sydney **New Zealand** 28–13 | 1938 | 1 Sydney **New Zealand** 24–9 | |
| | New Zealand won series 2–1 | | 2 Brisbane **New Zealand** 20–14 | |
| 1913 | 1 Wellington **New Zealand** 30–5 | | 3 Sydney **New Zealand** 14–6 | |
| | 2 Dunedin **New Zealand** 25–13 | | New Zealand won series 3–0 | |
| | 3 Christchurch **Australia** 16–5 | 1946 | 1 Dunedin **New Zealand** 31–8 | |
| | New Zealand won series 2–1 | | 2 Auckland **New Zealand** 14–10 | |
| 1914 | 1 Sydney **New Zealand** 5–0 | | New Zealand won series 2–0 | |
| | 2 Brisbane **New Zealand** 17–0 | 1947 | 1 Brisbane **New Zealand** 13–5 | |
| | 3 Sydney **New Zealand** 22–7 | | 2 Sydney **New Zealand** 27–14 | |
| | New Zealand won series 3–0 | | New Zealand won series 2–0 | |
| 1929 | 1 Sydney **Australia** 9–8 | 1949 | 1 Wellington **Australia** 11–6 | |
| | 2 Brisbane **Australia** 17–9 | | 2 Auckland **Australia** 16–9 | |
| | 3 Sydney **Australia** 15–13 | | Australia won series 2–0 | |
| | Australia won series 3–0 | 1951 | 1 Sydney **New Zealand** 8–0 | |
| 1931 | Auckland **New Zealand** 20–13 | | 2 Sydney **New Zealand** 17–11 | |
| 1932 | 1 Sydney **Australia** 22–17 | | 3 Brisbane **New Zealand** 16–6 | |
| | 2 Brisbane **New Zealand** 21–3 | | New Zealand won series 3–0 | |

| 1952 | 1 Christchurch **Australia** 14–9 |
| | 2 Wellington **New Zealand** 15–8 |
| | Series drawn 1–1 |
| 1955 | 1 Wellington **New Zealand** 16–8 |
| | 2 Dunedin **New Zealand** 8–0 |
| | 3 Auckland **Australia** 8–3 |
| | New Zealand won series 2–1 |
| 1957 | 1 Sydney **New Zealand** 25–11 |
| | 2 Brisbane **New Zealand** 22–9 |
| | New Zealand won series 2–0 |
| 1958 | 1 Wellington **New Zealand** 25–3 |
| | 2 Christchurch **Australia** 6–3 |
| | 3 Auckland **New Zealand** 17–8 |
| | New Zealand won series 2–1 |
| 1962 | 1 Brisbane **New Zealand** 20–6 |
| | 2 Sydney **New Zealand** 14–5 |
| | New Zealand won series 2–0 |
| 1962 | 1 Wellington **Drawn** 9–9 |
| | 2 Dunedin **New Zealand** 3–0 |
| | 3 Auckland **New Zealand** 16–8 |
| | New Zealand won series 2–0, with |
| | 1 draw |
| 1964 | 1 Dunedin **New Zealand** 14–9 |
| | 2 Christchurch **New Zealand** 18–3 |
| | 3 Wellington **Australia** 20–5 |
| | New Zealand won series 2–1 |
| 1967 | Wellington **New Zealand** 29–9 |
| 1968 | 1 Sydney **New Zealand** 27–11 |
| | 2 Brisbane **New Zealand** 19–18 |
| | New Zealand won series 2–0 |
| 1972 | 1 Wellington **New Zealand** 29–6 |
| | 2 Christchurch **New Zealand** 30–17 |
| | 3 Auckland **New Zealand** 38–3 |
| | New Zealand won series 3–0 |
| 1974 | 1 Sydney **New Zealand** 11–6 |
| | 2 Brisbane **Drawn** 16–16 |
| | 3 Sydney **New Zealand** 16–6 |
| | New Zealand won series 2–0, with 1 |
| | draw |
| 1978 | 1 Wellington **New Zealand** 13–12 |
| | 2 Christchurch **New Zealand** 22–6 |
| | 3 Auckland **Australia** 30–16 |
| | New Zealand won series 2–1 |
| 1979 | Sydney **Australia** 12–6 |
| 1980 | 1 Sydney **Australia** 13–9 |
| | 2 Brisbane **New Zealand** 12–9 |
| | 3 Sydney **Australia** 26–10 |
| | Australia won series 2–1 |
| 1982 | 1 Christchurch **New Zealand** 23–16 |
| | 2 Wellington **Australia** 19–16 |

| | 3 Auckland **New Zealand** 33–18 |
| | New Zealand won series 2–1 |
| 1983 | Sydney **New Zealand** 18–8 |
| 1984 | 1 Sydney **Australia** 16–9 |
| | 2 Brisbane **New Zealand** 19–15 |
| | 3 Sydney **New Zealand** 25–24 |
| | New Zealand won series 2–1 |
| 1985 | Auckland **New Zealand** 10–9 |
| 1986 | 1 Wellington **Australia** 13–12 |
| | 2 Dunedin **New Zealand** 13–12 |
| | 3 Auckland **Australia** 22–9 |
| | Australia won series 2–1 |
| 1987 | Sydney **New Zealand** 30–16 |
| 1988 | 1 Sydney **New Zealand** 32–7 |
| | 2 Brisbane **Drawn** 19–19 |
| | 3 Sydney **New Zealand** 30–9 |
| | New Zealand won series 2–0, with |
| | 1 draw |
| 1989 | Auckland **New Zealand** 24–12 |
| 1990 | 1 Christchurch **New Zealand** 21–6 |
| | 2 Auckland **New Zealand** 27–17 |
| | 3 Wellington **Australia** 21–9 |
| | New Zealand won series 2–1 |
| 1991 | 1 Sydney **Australia** 21–12 |
| | 2 Auckland **New Zealand** 6–3 |
| 1991 | Dublin WC **Australia** 16–6 |
| 1992 | 1 Sydney **Australia** 16–15 |
| | 2 Brisbane **Australia** 19–17 |
| | 3 Sydney **New Zealand** 26–23 |
| | Australia won series 2–1 |
| 1993 | Dunedin **New Zealand** 25–10 |
| 1994 | Sydney **Australia** 20–16 |
| 1995 | Auckland **New Zealand** 28–16 |
| 1995 | Sydney **New Zealand** 34–23 |
| 1996 | Wellington TN **New Zealand** 43–6 |
| 1996 | Brisbane TN **New Zealand** 32–25 |
| | New Zealand won series 2–0 |
| 1997 | Christchurch **New Zealand** 30–13 |
| 1997 | Melbourne TN **New Zealand** 33–18 |
| 1997 | Dunedin TN **New Zealand** 36–24 |
| | New Zealand won series 3–0 |
| 1998 | Melbourne TN **Australia** 24–16 |
| 1998 | Christchurch TN **Australia** 27–23 |
| 1998 | Sydney Australia 19–14 |
| | Australia won series 3–0 |
| 1999 | Auckland TN **New Zealand** 34–15 |
| 1999 | Sydney TN **Australia** 28–7 |
| | Series drawn 1–1 |
| 2000 | Sydney TN **New Zealand** 39–35 |
| 2000 | Wellington TN **Australia** 24–23 |

| | | |
|---|---|---|
| | Series drawn 1–1 | |
| 2001 | Dunedin TN **Australia** 23–15 | |
| 2001 | Sydney TN **Australia** 29–26 | |
| | Australia won series 2–0 | |
| 2002 | Christchurch TN **New Zealand** 12–6 | |
| 2002 | Sydney TN **Australia** 16–14 | |
| | Series drawn 1–1 | |
| 2003 | Sydney TN **New Zealand** 50–21 | |
| 2003 | Auckland TN **New Zealand** 21–17 | |
| | New Zealand won series 2–0 | |
| 2003 | Sydney WC **Australia** 22–10 | |
| 2004 | Wellington TN **New Zealand** 16–7 | |
| 2004 | Sydney TN **Australia** 23–18 | |
| | Series drawn 1–1 | |
| 2005 | Sydney TN **New Zealand** 30–13 | |
| 2005 | Auckland TN **New Zealand** 34–24 | |
| | New Zealand won series 2–0 | |
| 2006 | Christchurch TN **New Zealand** 32–12 | |
| 2006 | Brisbane TN **New Zealand** 13–9 | |
| 2006 | Auckland TN **New Zealand** 34–27 | |
| | New Zealand won series 3–0 | |
| 2007 | Melbourne TN **Australia** 20–15 | |
| 2007 | Auckland TN **New Zealand** 26–12 | |
| | Series drawn 1–1 | |
| 2008 | Sydney TN **Australia** 34–19 | |
| 2008 | Auckland TN **New Zealand** 39–10 | |
| 2008 | Brisbane TN **New Zealand** 28–24 | |

| | | |
|---|---|---|
| 2008 | Hong Kong **New Zealand** 19–14 | |
| | New Zealand won series 3–1 | |
| 2009 | Auckland TN **New Zealand** 22–16 | |
| 2009 | Sydney TN **New Zealand** 19–18 | |
| 2009 | Wellington TN **New Zealand** 33–6 | |
| 2009 | Tokyo **New Zealand** 32–19 | |
| | New Zealand won series 4–0 | |
| 2010 | Melbourne TN **New Zealand** 49–28 | |
| 2010 | Christchurch TN **New Zealand** 20–10 | |
| 2010 | Sydney TN **New Zealand** 23–22 | |
| 2010 | Hong Kong **Australia** 26–24 | |
| | New Zealand won series 3–1 | |
| 2011 | Auckland TN **New Zealand** 30–14 | |
| 2011 | Brisbane TN **Australia** 25–20 | |
| 2011 | Auckland WC **New Zealand** 20–6 | |
| 2012 | Sydney RC **New Zealand** 27–19 | |
| 2012 | Auckland RC **New Zealand** 22–0 | |
| 2012 | Brisbane **Drawn** 18–18 | |
| | New Zealand won series 2–0, with 1 draw | |
| 2013 | Sydney RC **New Zealand** 47–29 | |
| 2013 | Wellington RC **New Zealand** 27–16 | |
| 2013 | Dunedin **New Zealand** 41–33 | |
| | New Zealand won series 3–0 | |
| 2014 | Sydney RC **Drawn** 12–12 | |
| 2014 | Auckland RC **New Zealand** 51–20 | |

## NEW ZEALAND v UNITED STATES

**Played 2 New Zealand won 2**
**Highest scores** New Zealand 51–3 in 1913, United States 6–46 in 1991
**Biggest win** New Zealand 51–3 in 1913, United States no win

| | |
|---|---|
| 1913 Berkeley **New Zealand** 51–3 | 1991 Gloucester WC **New Zealand** 46–6 |

## NEW ZEALAND v ROMANIA

**Played 2 New Zealand won 2**
**Highest score** New Zealand 85–8 in 2007, Romania 8–85 in 2007
**Biggest win** New Zealand 85–8 in 2007, Romania no win

| | |
|---|---|
| 1981 Bucharest **New Zealand** 14–6 | 2007 Toulouse WC **New Zealand** 85–8 |

# NEW ZEALAND v ARGENTINA

**Played 20 New Zealand won 19, Drawn 1**
**Highest scores** New Zealand 93–8 in 1997, Argentina 21–21 in 1985
**Biggest win** New Zealand 93–8 in 1997, Argentina no win

| | | | |
|---|---|---|---|
| 1985 | 1 Buenos Aires **New Zealand** 33–20 | | New Zealand won series 2–0 |
| | 2 Buenos Aires **Drawn** 21–21 | 2001 | Christchurch **New Zealand** 67–19 |
| | New Zealand won series 1–0, with 1 draw | 2001 | Buenos Aires **New Zealand** 24–20 |
| 1987 | Wellington WC **New Zealand** 46–15 | 2004 | Hamilton **New Zealand** 41–7 |
| 1989 | 1 Dunedin **New Zealand** 60–9 | 2006 | Buenos Aires **New Zealand** 25–19 |
| | 2 Wellington **New Zealand** 49–12 | 2011 | Auckland WC **New Zealand** 33–10 |
| | New Zealand won series 2–0 | 2012 | Wellington RC **New Zealand** 21–5 |
| 1991 | 1 Buenos Aires **New Zealand** 28–14 | 2012 | La Plata RC **New Zealand** 54–15 |
| | 2 Buenos Aires **New Zealand** 36–6 | 2013 | Hamilton RC **New Zealand** 28–13 |
| | New Zealand won series 2–0 | 2013 | La Plata RC **New Zealand** 33–15 |
| 1997 | 1 Wellington **New Zealand** 93–8 | 2014 | Napier RC **New Zealand** 28–9 |
| | 2 Hamilton **New Zealand** 62–10 | 2014 | La Plata RC **New Zealand** 34–13 |

# NEW ZEALAND v ITALY

**Played 12 New Zealand won 12**
**Highest scores** New Zealand 101–3 in 1999, Italy 21–31 in 1991
**Biggest win** New Zealand 101–3 in 1999, Italy no win

| | | | |
|---|---|---|---|
| 1987 | Auckland WC **New Zealand** 70–6 | 2003 | Melbourne WC **New Zealand** 70–7 |
| 1991 | Leicester WC **New Zealand** 31–21 | 2004 | Rome **New Zealand** 59–10 |
| 1995 | Bologna **New Zealand** 70–6 | 2007 | Marseilles WC **New Zealand** 76–14 |
| 1999 | Huddersfield WC **New Zealand** 101–3 | 2009 | Christchurch **New Zealand** 27–6 |
| 2000 | Genoa **New Zealand** 56–19 | 2009 | Milan **New Zealand** 20–6 |
| 2002 | Hamilton **New Zealand** 64–10 | 2012 | Rome **New Zealand** 42–10 |

# NEW ZEALAND v FIJI

**Played 5 New Zealand won 5**
**Highest scores** New Zealand 91–0 in 2005, Fiji 18–68 in 2002
**Biggest win** New Zealand 91–0 in 2005, Fiji no win

| | | | |
|---|---|---|---|
| 1987 | Christchurch WC **New Zealand** 74–13 | 2005 | Albany **New Zealand** 91–0 |
| 1997 | Albany **New Zealand** 71–5 | 2011 | Dunedin **New Zealand** 60–14 |
| 2002 | Wellington **New Zealand** 68–18 | | |

# NEW ZEALAND v CANADA

**Played 5 New Zealand won 5**
**Highest scores** New Zealand 79–15 in 2011, Canada 15–79 in 2011
**Biggest win** New Zealand 73–7 in 1995, Canada no win

| | | | |
|---|---|---|---|
| 1991 | Lille WC **New Zealand** 29–13 | 2007 | Hamilton **New Zealand** 64–13 |
| 1995 | Auckland **New Zealand** 73–7 | 2011 | Wellington WC **New Zealand** 79–15 |
| 2003 | Melbourne WC **New Zealand** 68–6 | | |

# NEW ZEALAND v WORLD XVs

**Played 3 New Zealand won 2, World XV won 1, Drawn 0**
**Highest scores** New Zealand 54–26 in 1992, World XV 28–14 in 1992
**Biggest wins** New Zealand 54–26 in 1992, World XV 28–14 in 1992

| | |
|---|---|
| 1992   1 Christchurch **World XV** 28–14 | 3 Auckland **New Zealand** 26–15 |
| 2 Wellington **New Zealand** 54–26 | New Zealand won series 2–1 |

# NEW ZEALAND v SAMOA

**Played 5 New Zealand won 5**
**Highest scores** New Zealand 101–14 in 2008, Samoa 14–101 in 2008
**Biggest win** New Zealand 101–14 in 2008, Samoa no win

| | |
|---|---|
| 1993   Auckland **New Zealand** 35–13 | 2001   Albany **New Zealand** 50–6 |
| 1996   Napier **New Zealand** 51–10 | 2008   New Plymouth **New Zealand** 101–14 |
| 1999   Albany **New Zealand** 71–13 | |

# NEW ZEALAND v JAPAN

**Played 3 New Zealand won 3**
**Highest scores** New Zealand 145–17 in 1995, Japan 17–145 in 1995
**Biggest win** New Zealand 145–17 in 1995, Japan no win

| | |
|---|---|
| 1995   Bloemfontein WC **New Zealand** | 2011   Hamilton WC **New Zealand** 83–7 |
| 145–17 | 2013   Tokyo **New Zealand** 54–6 |

# NEW ZEALAND v TONGA

**Played 4 New Zealand won 4**
**Highest scores** New Zealand 102–0 in 2000, Tonga 10–41 in 2011
**Biggest win** New Zealand 102–0 in 2000, Tonga no win

| | |
|---|---|
| 1999   Bristol WC **New Zealand** 45–9 | 2003   Brisbane WC **New Zealand** 91–7 |
| 2000   Albany **New Zealand** 102–0 | 2011   Auckland WC **New Zealand** 41–10 |

# NEW ZEALAND v PACIFIC ISLANDS

**Played 1 New Zealand won 1**
**Highest scores** New Zealand 41–26 in 2004, Pacific Islands 26–41 in 2004
**Biggest win** New Zealand 41–26 in 2004, Pacific Islands no win

| |
|---|
| 2004   Albany **New Zealand 41–26** |

INTERNATIONAL RESULTS

# NEW ZEALAND v PORTUGAL

**Played 1 New Zealand won 1**
**Highest scores** New Zealand 108–13 in 2007, Portugal 13–108 in 2007
**Biggest win** New Zealand 108–13 in 2007, Portugal no win

| | | |
|---|---|---|
| 2007 | Lyons WC **New Zealand** 108–13 | |

# AUSTRALIA v UNITED STATES

**Played 7 Australia won 7**
**Highest scores** Australia 67–9 in 1990 and 67–5 in 2011, United States 19–55 in 1999
**Biggest win** Australia 67–5 in 2011, United States no win

| 1912 | Berkeley **Australia** 12–8 | 1990 | Brisbane **Australia** 67–9 |
|---|---|---|---|
| 1976 | Los Angeles **Australia** 24–12 | 1999 | Limerick WC **Australia** 55–19 |
| 1983 | Sydney **Australia** 49–3 | 2011 | Wellington WC **Australia** 67–5 |
| 1987 | Brisbane WC **Australia** 47–12 | | |

# AUSTRALIA v NEW ZEALAND XVs

**Played 24 Australia won 6, New Zealand XVs won 18, Drawn 0**
**Highest scores** Australia 26–20 in 1926, New Zealand XV 38–11 in 1923 and 38–8 in 1924
**Biggest win** Australia 17–0 in 1921, New Zealand XV 38–8 in 1924

| 1920 | 1 Sydney **New Zealand XV** 26–15 | | New Zealand XV won series 2–1 |
|---|---|---|---|
| | 2 Sydney **New Zealand XV** 14–6 | 1925 | 1 Sydney **New Zealand XV** 26–3 |
| | 3 Sydney **New Zealand XV** 24–13 | | 2 Sydney **New Zealand XV** 4–0 |
| | New Zealand XV won series 3–0 | | 3 Sydney **New Zealand XV** 11–3 |
| 1921 | Christchurch **Australia** 17–0 | | New Zealand XV won series 3–0 |
| 1922 | 1 Sydney **New Zealand XV** 26–19 | 1925 | Auckland **New Zealand XV** 36–10 |
| | 2 Sydney **Australia** 14–8 | 1926 | 1 Sydney **Australia** 26–20 |
| | 3 Sydney **Australia** 8–6 | | 2 Sydney **New Zealand XV** 11–6 |
| | Australia won series 2–1 | | 3 Sydney **New Zealand XV** 14–0 |
| 1923 | 1 Dunedin **New Zealand XV** 19–9 | | 4 Sydney **New Zealand XV** 28–21 |
| | 2 Christchurch **New Zealand XV** 34–6 | | New Zealand XV won series 3–1 |
| | 3 Wellington **New Zealand XV** 38–11 | 1928 | 1 Wellington **New Zealand XV** 15–12 |
| | New Zealand XV won series 3–0 | | 2 Dunedin **New Zealand XV** 16–14 |
| 1924 | 1 Sydney **Australia** 20–16 | | 3 Christchurch **Australia** 11–8 |
| | 2 Sydney **New Zealand XV** 21–5 | | New Zealand XV won series 2–1 |
| | 3 Sydney **New Zealand XV** 38–8 | | |

# AUSTRALIA v SOUTH AFRICA XVs

**Played 3 South Africa XVs won 3**
**Highest scores** Australia 11–16 in 1921, South Africa XV 28–9 in 1921
**Biggest win** Australia no win, South Africa XV 28–9 in 1921

| | | |
|---|---|---|
| 1921 | 1 Sydney **South Africa XV** 25–10 | 3 Sydney **South Africa XV** 28–9 |
| | 2 Sydney **South Africa XV** 16–11 | South Africa XV won series 3–0 |

# AUSTRALIA v NEW ZEALAND MAORIS

**Played 16 Australia won 8, New Zealand Maoris won 6, Drawn 2**
**Highest scores** Australia 31–6 in 1936, New Zealand Maoris 25–22 in 1922
**Biggest wins** Australia 31–6 in 1936, New Zealand Maoris 20–0 in 1946

| | | | | |
|---|---|---|---|---|
| 1922 | 1 Sydney **New Zealand Maoris** 25–22 | 1946 | Hamilton **New Zealand Maoris** 20–0 |
| | 2 Sydney **Australia** 28–13 | 1949 | 1 Sydney **New Zealand Maoris** 12–3 |
| | 3 Sydney **New Zealand Maoris** 23–22 | | 2 Brisbane **Drawn** 8–8 |
| | New Zealand Maoris won series 2–1 | | 3 Sydney **Australia** 18–3 |
| 1923 | 1 Sydney **Australia** 27–23 | | Series drawn 1–1, with 1 draw |
| | 2 Sydney **Australia** 21–16 | 1958 | 1 Brisbane **Australia** 15–14 |
| | 3 Sydney **Australia** 14–12 | | 2 Sydney **Drawn** 3–3 |
| | Australia won series 3–0 | | 3 Melbourne **New Zealand Maoris** |
| 1928 | Wellington **New Zealand Maoris** 9–8 | | 13–6 |
| 1931 | Palmerston North **Australia** 14–3 | | Series drawn 1–1, with 1 draw |
| 1936 | Palmerston North **Australia** 31–6 | | |

# AUSTRALIA v FIJI

**Played 19 Australia won 16, Fiji won 2, Drawn 1**
**Highest scores** Australia 66–20 in 1998, Fiji 28–52 in 1985
**Biggest wins** Australia 49–0 in 2007, Fiji 17–15 in 1952 and 18–16 in 1954

| | | | | |
|---|---|---|---|---|
| 1952 | 1 Sydney **Australia** 15–9 | | 3 Sydney **Australia** 27–17 |
| | 2 Sydney **Fiji** 17–15 | | Australia won series 3–0 |
| | Series drawn 1–1 | 1980 | Suva **Australia** 22–9 |
| 1954 | 1 Brisbane **Australia** 22–19 | 1984 | Suva **Australia** 16–3 |
| | 2 Sydney **Fiji** 18–16 | 1985 | 1 Brisbane **Australia** 52–28 |
| | Series drawn 1–1 | | 2 Sydney **Australia** 31–9 |
| 1961 | 1 Brisbane **Australia** 24–6 | | Australia won series 2–0 |
| | 2 Sydney **Australia** 20–14 | 1998 | Sydney **Australia** 66–20 |
| | 3 Melbourne **Drawn** 3–3 | 2007 | Perth **Australia** 49–0 |
| | Australia won series 2–0, with 1 draw | 2007 | Montpellier WC **Australia** 55–12 |
| 1972 | Suva **Australia** 21–19 | 2010 | Canberra **Australia** 49–3 |
| 1976 | 1 Sydney **Australia** 22–6 | | |
| | 2 Brisbane **Australia** 21–9 | | |

# AUSTRALIA v TONGA

**Played 4 Australia won 3, Tonga won 1, Drawn 0**
**Highest scores** Australia 74–0 in 1998, Tonga 16–11 in 1973
**Biggest wins** Australia 74–0 in 1998, Tonga 16–11 in 1973

| | |
|---|---|
| 1973 1 Sydney **Australia** 30–12 | 1993 Brisbane **Australia** 52–14 |
| 2 Brisbane **Tonga** 16–11 | 1998 Canberra **Australia** 74–0 |
| Series drawn 1–1 | |

# AUSTRALIA v JAPAN

**Played 4 Australia won 4**
**Highest scores** Australia 91–3 in 2007, Japan 25–50 in 1973
**Biggest win** Australia 91–3 in 2007, Japan no win

| | |
|---|---|
| 1975 1 Sydney **Australia** 37–7 | 1987 Sydney WC **Australia** 42–23 |
| 2 Brisbane **Australia** 50–25 | 2007 Lyons WC **Australia** 91–3 |
| Australia won series 2–0 | |

# AUSTRALIA v ARGENTINA

**Played 23 Australia won 17, Argentina won 5, Drawn 1**
**Highest scores** Australia 54–17 in 2013, Argentina 27–19 in 1987
**Biggest wins** Australia 53–6 in 2000, Argentina 18–3 in 1983

| | |
|---|---|
| 1979 1 Buenos Aires **Argentina** 24–13 | Australia won series 2–0 |
| 2 Buenos Aires **Australia** 17–12 | 1997 1 Buenos Aires **Australia** 23–15 |
| Series drawn 1–1 | 2 Buenos Aires **Argentina** 18–16 |
| 1983 1 Brisbane **Argentina** 18–3 | Series drawn 1–1 |
| 2 Sydney **Australia** 29–13 | 2000 1 Brisbane **Australia** 53–6 |
| Series drawn 1–1 | 2 Canberra **Australia** 32–25 |
| 1986 1 Brisbane **Australia** 39–19 | Australia won series 2–0 |
| 2 Sydney **Australia** 26–0 | 2002 Buenos Aires **Australia** 17–6 |
| Australia won series 2–0 | 2003 Sydney WC **Australia** 24–8 |
| 1987 1 Buenos Aires **Drawn** 19–19 | 2012 Robina RC **Australia** 23–19 |
| 2 Buenos Aires **Argentina** 27–19 | 2012 Rosario RC **Australia** 25–19 |
| Argentina won series 1–0, with 1 draw | 2013 Perth RC **Australia** 14–13 |
| 1991 Llanelli WC **Australia** 32–19 | 2013 Rosario RC **Australia** 54–17 |
| 1995 1 Brisbane **Australia** 53–7 | 2014 Robina RC **Australia** 32–25 |
| 2 Sydney **Australia** 30–13 | 2014 Mendoza RC **Argentina** 21–17 |

# AUSTRALIA v SAMOA

**Played 5 Australia won 4, Samoa won 1**
**Highest scores** Australia 74–7 in 2005, Samoa 32–23 in 2011
**Biggest win** Australia 73–3 in 1994, Samoa 32–23 in 2011

| | | | |
|---|---|---|---|
| 1991 | Pontypool WC **Australia** 9–3 | 2005 | Sydney **Australia** 74–7 |
| 1994 | Sydney **Australia** 73–3 | 2011 | Sydney **Samoa** 32–23 |
| 1998 | Brisbane **Australia** 25–13 | | |

# AUSTRALIA v ITALY

**Played 16 Australia won 16**
**Highest scores** Australia 69–21 in 2005, Italy 21–69 in 2005
**Biggest win** Australia 55–6 in 1988, Italy no win

| | | | |
|---|---|---|---|
| 1983 | Rovigo **Australia** 29–7 | 2006 | Rome **Australia** 25–18 |
| 1986 | Brisbane **Australia** 39–18 | 2008 | Padua **Australia** 30–20 |
| 1988 | Rome **Australia** 55–6 | 2009 | 1 Canberra **Australia** 31–8 |
| 1994 | 1 Brisbane **Australia** 23–20 | | 2 Melbourne **Australia** 34–12 |
| | 2 Melbourne **Australia** 20–7 | | Australia won series 2–0 |
| | Australia won series 2–0 | 2010 | Florence **Australia** 32–14 |
| 1996 | Padua **Australia** 40–18 | 2011 | Albany WC **Australia** 32–6 |
| 2002 | Genoa **Australia** 34–3 | 2012 | Florence **Australia** 22–19 |
| 2005 | Melbourne **Australia** 69–21 | 2013 | Turin **Australia** 50–20 |

# AUSTRALIA v CANADA

**Played 6 Australia won 6**
**Highest scores** Australia 74–9 in 1996, Canada 16–43 in 1993
**Biggest win** Australia 74–9 in 1996, Canada no win

| | | | |
|---|---|---|---|
| 1985 | 1 Sydney **Australia** 59–3 | 1995 | Port Elizabeth WC **Australia** 27–11 |
| | 2 Brisbane **Australia** 43–15 | 1996 | Brisbane **Australia** 74–9 |
| | Australia won series 2–0 | 2007 | Bordeaux WC **Australia** 37–6 |
| 1993 | Calgary **Australia** 43–16 | | |

# AUSTRALIA v KOREA

**Played 1 Australia won 1**
**Highest scores** Australia 65–18 in 1987, Korea 18–65 in 1987
**Biggest win** Australia 65–18 in 1987, Korea no win

| | |
|---|---|
| 1987 | Brisbane **Australia** 65–18 |

# AUSTRALIA v ROMANIA

**Played 3 Australia won 3**
**Highest scores** Australia 90–8 in 2003, Romania 9–57 in 1999
**Biggest win** Australia 90–8 in 2003, Romania no win

| | | | | |
|---|---|---|---|---|
| 1995 | Stellenbosch WC **Australia** 42–3 | | 2003 | Brisbane WC **Australia** 90–8 |
| 1999 | Belfast WC **Australia** 57–9 | | | |

# AUSTRALIA v SPAIN

**Played 1 Australia won 1**
**Highest scores** Australia 92–10 in 2001, Spain 10–92 in 2001
**Biggest win** Australia 92–10 in 2001, Spain no win

| | |
|---|---|
| 2001 | Madrid **Australia** 92–10 |

# AUSTRALIA v NAMIBIA

**Played 1 Australia won 1**
**Highest scores** Australia 142–0 in 2003, Namibia 0–142 in 2003
**Biggest win** Australia 142–0 in 2003, Namibia no win

| | |
|---|---|
| 2003 | Adelaide WC **Australia** 142–0 |

# AUSTRALIA v PACIFIC ISLANDS

**Played 1 Australia won 1**
**Highest scores** Australia 29–14 in 2004, Pacific Islands 14–29 in 2004
**Biggest win** Australia 29–14 in 2004, Pacific Islands no win

| | |
|---|---|
| 2004 | Adelaide **Australia** 29–14 |

# AUSTRALIA v RUSSIA

**Played 1 Australia won 1**
**Highest scores** Australia 68–22 in 2011, Russia 22–68 in 2011
**Biggest win** Australia 68–22 in 2011, Russia no win

| | |
|---|---|
| 2011 | Nelson WC **Australia** 68–22 |

*The match and career records cover official Test matches played up to 13 October 2014.*

## MATCH RECORDS

### MOST CONSECUTIVE TEST WINS

| | |
|---|---|
| **18 by Lithuania** | 2006 *Hun, Nor, Bul* 2007 *Aus, Hun, Bul* 2008 *Lat, Aus, Hun, Nor, And, Swi* 2009 *Ser, Arm, Isr, Hol, And* 2010 *Ser* |
| **17 by N Zealand** | 1965 *SA* 4, 1966 *BI* 1,2,3,4, 1967 *A, E, W, F, S,* 1968 *A* 1,2, *F* 1,2,3, 1969 *W* 1,2 |
| **17 by S Africa** | 1997 *A* 2, *It, F* 1,2, *E, S,* 1998 *I* 1,2, *W* 1, *E* 1, *A* 1, *NZ* 1,2, *A* 2, *W* 2, *S, I* 3 |
| **17 by N Zealand** | 2013 *F* 1,2,3, *A* 1,2, *Arg* 1, *SA* 1, *Arg* 2, *SA* 2, *A* 3, *J, F* 4, *E, I,* 2014 *E* 1,2,3 |

\* Cyprus have won 23 consecutive Tests since 2008 but are not an IRB Member Union.

### MOST CONSECUTIVE TESTS WITHOUT DEFEAT

| Matches | Wins | Draws | Period |
|---|---|---|---|
| **23 by N Zealand** | 22 | 1 | 1987 to 1990 |
| **22 by N Zealand** | 21 | 1 | 2013 to 2014 |
| **20 by N Zealand** | 19 | 1 | 2011 to 2012 |
| **18 by Lithuania** | 18 | 0 | 2006 to 2010 |
| **17 by N Zealand** | 15 | 2 | 1961 to 1964 |
| **17 by N Zealand** | 17 | 0 | 1965 to 1969 |
| **17 by S Africa** | 17 | 0 | 1997 to 1998 |

### MOST POINTS IN A MATCH

#### BY A TEAM

| Pts | Opponents | Venue | Year |
|---|---|---|---|
| **164 by Hong Kong** | Singapore | Kuala Lumpur | 1994 |
| **155 by Japan** | Chinese Taipei | Tokyo | 2002 |
| **152 by Argentina** | Paraguay | Mendoza | 2002 |
| **147 by Argentina** | Venezuela | Santiago | 2004 |
| **145 by N Zealand** | Japan | Bloemfontein | 1995 |
| **144 by Argentina** | Paraguay | Montevideo | 2003 |
| **142 by Australia** | Namibia | Adelaide | 2003 |
| **135 by Korea** | Malaysia | Hong Kong | 1992 |

#### BY A PLAYER

| Pts | Player | Opponents | Venue | Year |
|---|---|---|---|---|
| **60 for Japan** | T Kurihara | Chinese Taipei | Tainan | 2002 |
| **50 for Argentina** | E Morgan | Paraguay | San Pablo | 1973 |
| **50 for H Kong** | A Billington | Singapore | Kuala Lumpur | 1994 |
| **45 for N Zealand** | S D Culhane | Japan | Bloemfontein | 1995 |
| **45 for Argentina** | J-M Nuñez-Piossek | Paraguay | Montevideo | 2003 |
| **44 for Scotland** | A G Hastings | Ivory Coast | Rustenburg | 1995 |
| **44 for England** | C C Hodgson | Romania | Twickenham | 2001 |
| **42 for Australia** | M S Rogers | Namibia | Adelaide | 2003 |
| **41 for Sweden** | J Hagstrom | Luxembourg | Cessange | 2001 |
| **40 for Argentina** | G M Jorge | Brazil | Sao Paulo | 1993 |
| **40 for Japan** | D Ohata | Chinese Taipei | Tokyo | 2002 |
| **40 for Scotland** | C D Paterson | Japan | Perth | 2004 |

INTERNATIONAL RESULTS

## MOST TRIES IN A MATCH
### BY THE TEAM

| Tries | Opponents | Venue | Year |
|---|---|---|---|
| 26 by Hong Kong | Singapore | Kuala Lumpur | 1994 |
| 25 by Fiji | Solomon Is | Port Moresby | 1969 |
| 24 by Argentina | Paraguay | Mendoza | 2002 |
| 24 by Argentina | Paraguay | Montevideo | 2003 |
| 23 by Japan | Chinese Taipei | Tokyo | 2002 |
| 23 by Argentina | Venezuela | Santiago | 2004 |
| 22 by Australia | Namibia | Adelaide | 2003 |
| 21 by Fiji | Niue Island | Apia | 1983 |
| 21 by N Zealand | Japan | Bloemfontein | 1995 |
| 21 by S Africa | Uruguay | East London | 2005 |

### BY A PLAYER

| Tries | Player | Opponents | Venue | Year |
|---|---|---|---|---|
| 11 for Argentina | U O'Farrell | Brazil | Buenos Aires | 1951 |
| 10 for H Kong | A Billington | Singapore | Kuala Lumpur | 1994 |
| 9 for Argentina | J-M Nuñez-Piossek | Paraguay | Montevideo | 2003 |
| 8 for Argentina | G M Jorge | Brazil | Sao Paulo | 1993 |
| 8 for Japan | D Ohata | Chinese Taipei | Tokyo | 2002 |
| 6 for Argentina | E Morgan | Paraguay | San Pablo | 1973 |
| 6 for Fiji | T Makutu | Papua New Guinea | Suva | 1979 |
| 6 for Argentina | G M Jorge | Brazil | Montevideo | 1989 |
| 6 for Namibia | G Mans | Portugal | Windhoek | 1990 |
| 6 for N Zealand | M C G Ellis | Japan | Bloemfontein | 1995 |
| 6 for Japan | T Kurihara | Chinese Taipei | Tainan | 2002 |
| 6 for S Africa | T Chavhanga | Uruguay | East London | 2005 |
| 6 for Japan | D Ohata | Hong Kong | Tokyo | 2005 |
| 6 for Japan | Y Fujita | UAE | Fukuoka | 2012 |
| 6 for Argentina | F Barrea | Brazil | Santiago | 2012 |

## MOST CONVERSIONS IN A MATCH
### BY THE TEAM

| Cons | Opponents | Venue | Year |
|---|---|---|---|
| 20 by N Zealand | Japan | Bloemfontein | 1995 |
| 20 by Japan | Chinese Taipei | Tokyo | 2002 |
| 19 by Fiji | Solomon Islands | Port Moresby | 1969 |
| 18 by Fiji | Niue Island | Apia | 1983 |
| 17 by Hong Kong | Singapore | Kuala Lumpur | 1994 |
| 17 by Japan | Chinese Taipei | Singapore | 1998 |
| 17 by Tonga | Korea | Nuku'alofa | 2003 |
| 16 by Argentina | Paraguay | Mendoza | 2002 |
| 16 by Australia | Namibia | Adelaide | 2003 |
| 16 by Argentina | Venezuela | Santiago | 2004 |
| 16 by Japan | Sri Lanka | Nagoya | 2014 |

### BY A PLAYER

| Cons | Player | Opponents | Venue | Year |
|---|---|---|---|---|
| 20 for New Zealand | S D Culhane | Japan | Bloemfontein | 1995 |
| 18 for Fiji | S Koroduadua | Niue Island | Apia | 1983 |
| 17 for Hong Kong | J McKee | Singapore | Kuala Lumpur | 1994 |
| 17 for Tonga | P Hola | Korea | Nuku'alofa | 2003 |
| 16 for Argentina | J-L Cilley | Paraguay | Mendoza | 2002 |
| 16 for Australia | M S Rogers | Namibia | Adelaide | 2003 |
| 16 for Japan | A Goromaru | Sri Lanka | Nagoya | 2014 |
| 15 for England | P J Grayson | Netherlands | Huddersfield | 1998 |
| 15 for Japan | T Kurihara | Chinese Taipei | Tainan | 2002 |
| 14 for England | C C Hodgson | Romania | Twickenham | 2001 |
| 14 for Wales | G L Henson | Japan | Cardiff | 2004 |
| 14 for New Zealand | N J Evans | Portugal | Lyon | 2007 |
| 14 for Japan | A Goromaru | Philippines | Fukuoka | 2013 |

INTERNATIONAL RECORDS

## MOST PENALTIES IN A MATCH
### BY THE TEAM

| Penalties | Opponents | Venue | Year |
|---|---|---|---|
| 9 by Japan | Tonga | Tokyo | 1999 |
| 9 by N Zealand | Australia | Auckland | 1999 |
| 9 by Wales | France | Cardiff | 1999 |
| 9 by Portugal | Georgia | Lisbon | 2000 |
| 9 by N Zealand | France | Paris | 2000 |
| 8 by many countries | | | |

### BY A PLAYER

| Penalties | Player | Opponents | Venue | Year |
|---|---|---|---|---|
| 9 for Japan | K Hirose | Tonga | Tokyo | 1999 |
| 9 for N Zealand | A P Mehrtens | Australia | Auckland | 1999 |
| 9 for Wales | N R Jenkins | France | Cardiff | 1999 |
| 9 for Portugal | T Teixeira | Georgia | Lisbon | 2000 |
| 9 for N Zealand | A P Mehrtens | France | Paris | 2000 |
| 8 by many players | | | | |

## MOST DROP GOALS IN A MATCH
### BY THE TEAM

| Drops | Opponents | Venue | Year |
|---|---|---|---|
| 5 by South Africa | England | Paris | 1999 |
| 4 by Romania | W Germany | Bucharest | 1967 |
| 4 by Uruguay | Chile | Montevideo | 2002 |
| 4 by South Africa | England | Twickenham | 2006 |
| 3 by several nations | | | |

### BY A PLAYER

| Drops | Player | Opponents | Venue | Year |
|---|---|---|---|---|
| 5 for S Africa | J H de Beer | England | Paris | 1999 |
| 4 for Uruguay | J Menchaca | Chile | Montevideo | 2002 |
| 4 for S Africa | A S Pretorius | England | Twickenham | 2006 |
| 3 for several nations | | | | |

INTERNATIONAL RESULTS

# CAREER RECORDS

## MOST TEST APPEARANCES

| Tests | Player | Career Span |
|---|---|---|
| 141 (8) | B G O'Driscoll (Ireland/Lions) | 1999 to 2014 |
| 139 | G M Gregan (Australia) | 1994 to 2007 |
| 133 | R H McCaw (N Zealand) | 2001 to 2014 |
| 130 (2) | R J R O'Gara (Ireland/Lions) | 2000 to 2013 |
| 119 (5) | J Leonard (England/Lions) | 1990 to 2004 |
| 119 | K F Mealamu (N Zealand) | 2002 to 2014 |
| 118 | F Pelous (France) | 1995 to 2007 |
| 117 | V Matfield (S Africa) | 2001 to 2014 |
| 116 | N C Sharpe (Australia) | 2002 to 2012 |
| 112 (5) | G D Jenkins (Wales/Lions) | 2002 to 2014 |
| 111 | P Sella (France) | 1982 to 1995 |
| 111 | J W Smit (S Africa) | 2000 to 2011 |
| 111 | G B Smith (Australia) | 2000 to 2013 |
| 110 (6) | S M Jones (Wales/Lions) | 1998 to 2011 |
| 110 | T D Woodcock (N Zealand) | 2002 to 2014 |
| 109 | C D Paterson (Scotland) | 1999 to 2011 |
| 107 (2) | J J Hayes (Ireland/Lions) | 2000 to 2011 |
| 107 | M Bortolami (Italy) | 2001 to 2014 |
| 105 | M-L Castrogiovanni (Italy) | 2002 to 2014 |
| 105 | S Parisse (Italy) | 2002 to 2014 |

*The figures include Test appearances for the British/Irish Lions which are shown in brackets. Thus 141 (8) for Brian O'Driscoll (Ireland/Lions) indicates 133 caps for Ireland and eight Tests for the Lions.*

## MOST TESTS AS CAPTAIN

| Tests | Captain | Span as captain |
|---|---|---|
| 96* | R H McCaw (N Zealand) | 2004 to 2014 |
| 84 (1) | B G O'Driscoll (Ireland/Lions) | 2002 to 2012 |
| 83 | J W Smit (S Africa) | 2003 to 2011 |
| 59 | W D C Carling (England) | 1988 to 1996 |
| 59 | G M Gregan (Australia) | 2001 to 2007 |
| 57 | S Parisse (Italy) | 2008 to 2014 |
| 55 | J A Eales (Australia) | 1996 to 2001 |
| 51 | S B T Fitzpatrick (N Zealand) | 1992 to 1997 |

\* McCaw's figure includes the world record of 84 Test wins as captain.

*The figures include Test captaincies of the British/Irish Lions which are shown in brackets. Thus 84 (1) for Brian O'Driscoll (Ireland/Lions) indicates 83 captaincies for Ireland and one in Tests for the Lions.*

## MOST CONSECUTIVE TESTS

| Tests | Player | Career Span |
|---|---|---|
| 63 | S B T Fitzpatrick (N Zealand) | 1986 to 1995 |
| 62 | J W C Roff (Australia) | 1996 to 2001 |
| 58 | A Zanni (Italy) | 2008 to 2014 |
| 53 | G O Edwards (Wales) | 1967 to 1978 |
| 52 | W J McBride (Ireland) | 1964 to 1975 |
| 51 | C M Cullen (N Zealand) | 1996 to 2000 |

## MOST POINTS IN TESTS

| Points | Player | Tests | Career Span |
|---|---|---|---|
| 1442 | D W Carter (N Zealand) | 100 | 2003 to 2013 |
| 1246 (67) | J P Wilkinson (England/Lions) | 97 (6) | 1998 to 2011 |
| 1090 (41) | N R Jenkins (Wales/Lions) | 91 (4) | 1991 to 2002 |
| 1083 (0) | R J R O'Gara (Ireland/Lions) | 130 (2) | 2000 to 2013 |
| 1010 (27) | D Dominguez (Italy/Argentina) | 76 (2) | 1989 to 2003 |
| 970 (53) | S M Jones (Wales/Lions) | 110 (6) | 1998 to 2011 |
| 967 | A P Mehrtens (N Zealand) | 70 | 1995 to 2004 |
| 911 | M P Lynagh (Australia) | 72 | 1984 to 1995 |
| 893 | P C Montgomery (S Africa) | 102 | 1997 to 2008 |
| 878 | M C Burke (Australia) | 81 | 1993 to 2004 |
| 809 | C D Paterson (Scotland) | 109 | 1999 to 2011 |
| 733 (66) | A G Hastings (Scotland/Lions) | 67 (6) | 1986 to 1995 |
| 688 | M Steyn (S Africa) | 59 | 2009 to 2014 |
| 684 | M J Giteau (Australia) | 92 | 2002 to 2011 |
| 670 | N J Little (Fiji) | 71 | 1996 to 2011 |

The figures include Test appearances for the British/Irish Lions or second nation (shown in brackets). Thus 1246 (67) for Jonny Wilkinson (England/Lions) indicates 1179 points for England and 67 in Tests for the Lions.

## MOST TRIES IN TESTS

| Tries | Player | Tests | Career Span |
|---|---|---|---|
| 69 | D Ohata (Japan) | 58 | 1996 to 2006 |
| 64 | D I Campese (Australia) | 101 | 1982 to 1996 |
| 60 (2) | S M Williams (Wales/Lions) | 91 (4) | 2000 to 2011 |
| 56 | B G Habana (South Africa) | 103 | 2004 to 2014 |
| 55 | H Onozawa (Japan) | 81 | 2001 to 2013 |
| 50 (1) | R Underwood (England/Lions) | 91 (6) | 1984 to 1996 |
| 49 | D C Howlett (N Zealand) | 62 | 2000 to 2007 |
| 47 (1) | B G O'Driscoll (Ireland/Lions) | 141 (8) | 1999 to 2014 |
| 46 | C M Cullen (N Zealand) | 58 | 1996 to 2002 |
| 46 | J T Rokocoko (N Zealand) | 68 | 2003 to 2010 |
| 44 | J W Wilson (N Zealand) | 60 | 1993 to 2001 |
| 41 (1) | Gareth Thomas (Wales/Lions) | 103 (3) | 1995 to 2007 |
| 40 | C E Latham (Australia) | 78 | 1998 to 2007 |

The figures include Test appearances for the British/Irish Lions which are shown in brackets. Thus 60 (2) for Shane Williams (Wales/Lions) indicates 58 tries for Wales and two in Tests for the Lions.

Getty Images

New Zealand's Richie McCaw has led his country in more Tests than anyone else.

## MOST CONVERSIONS IN TESTS

| Cons | Player | Tests | Career Span |
|---|---|---|---|
| 257 | D W Carter (N Zealand) | 100 | 2003 to 2013 |
| 176 (0) | R J R O'Gara (Ireland/Lions) | 130 (2) | 2000 to 2013 |
| 169 | A P Mehrtens (N Zealand) | 70 | 1995 to 2004 |
| 169 (7) | J P Wilkinson (England/Lions) | 97 (6) | 1998 to 2011 |
| 160 (7) | S M Jones (Wales/Lions) | 110 (6) | 1998 to 2011 |
| 153 | P C Montgomery (S Africa) | 102 | 1997 to 2008 |
| 140 | M P Lynagh (Australia) | 72 | 1984 to 1995 |
| 133 (6) | D Dominguez (Italy/Argentina) | 76 (2) | 1989 to 2003 |
| 131 (1) | N R Jenkins (Wales/Lions)) | 91 (4) | 1991 to 2002 |
| 128 | A Goromaru (Japan) | 41 | 2005 to 2014 |
| 118 | G J Fox (N Zealand) | 46 | 1985 to 1993 |

*The figures include Test appearances for the British/Irish Lions or a second nation which are shown in brackets. Thus 169 (7) for Jonny Wilkinson (England/Lions) indicates 162 conversions for England and seven in Tests for the Lions.*

## MOST PENALTY GOALS IN TESTS

| Penalties | Player | Tests | Career Span |
|---|---|---|---|
| 255 (16) | J P Wilkinson (England/Lions) | 97 (6) | 1998 to 2011 |
| 255 | D W Carter (N Zealand) | 100 | 2003 to 2013 |
| 248 (13) | N R Jenkins (Wales/Lions) | 91 (4) | 1991 to 2002 |
| 214 (5) | D Dominguez (Italy/Argentina) | 76 (2) | 1989 to 2003 |
| 202 (0) | R J R O'Gara (Ireland/Lions) | 130 (2) | 2000 to 2013 |
| 198 (12) | S M Jones (Wales/Lions) | 110 (6) | 1998 to 2011 |
| 188 | A P Mehrtens (N Zealand) | 70 | 1995 to 2004 |
| 177 | M P Lynagh (Australia) | 72 | 1984 to 1995 |
| 174 | M C Burke (Australia) | 81 | 1993 to 2004 |
| 170 | C D Paterson (Scotland) | 109 | 1999 to 2011 |
| 160 (20) | A G Hastings (Scotland/Lions) | 67 (6) | 1986 to 1995 |

*The figures include Test appearances for the British/Irish Lions or a second nation which are shown in brackets. Thus 255 (16) for Jonny Wilkinson (England/Lions) indicates 239 penalties for England and 16 in Tests for the Lions.*

## MOST DROP GOALS IN TESTS

| Drops | Player | Tests | Career Span |
|---|---|---|---|
| 36 (0) | J P Wilkinson (England/Lions) | 97 (6) | 1998 to 2011 |
| 28 (2) | H Porta (Argentina/Jaguars) | 68 (8) | 1971 to 1999 |
| 23 (2) | C R Andrew (England/Lions) | 76 (5) | 1985 to 1997 |
| 19 (0) | D Dominguez (Italy/Argentina) | 76 (2) | 1989 to 2003 |
| 18 | H E Botha (S Africa) | 28 | 1980 to 1992 |
| 17 | S Bettarello (Italy) | 55 | 1979 to 1988 |
| 17 | D A Parks (Scotland) | 67 | 2004 to 2012 |
| 15 | J-P Lescarboura (France) | 28 | 1982 to 1990 |
| 15 (0) | R J R O'Gara (Ireland/Lions) | 130 (2) | 2000 to 2013 |

*The figures include Test appearances for the British/Irish Lions, South American Jaguars or a second nation shown in brackets. Thus 28 (2) for Hugo Porta (Argentina/Jaguars) indicates 26 dropped goals for Argentina and two in Tests (against South Africa in the 1980s) for the South American Jaguars.*

# The Countries

Argentina competed strongly in every match in The Rugby Championship 2014, even against the All Blacks.

Getty Images

# ARGENTINA

## ARGENTINA'S 2013–14 TEST RECORD

| OPPONENTS | DATE | VENUE | RESULT |
| --- | --- | --- | --- |
| England | 9 Nov | A | Lost 31–12 |
| Wales | 16 Nov | A | Lost 40–6 |
| Italy | 23 Nov | A | Won 19–14 |
| Uruguay | 17 May | A | Won 65–9 |
| Chile | 25 May | A | Won 73–12 |
| Ireland | 7 Jun | H | Lost 17–29 |
| Ireland | 14 Jun | H | Lost 17–23 |
| Scotland | 20 Jun | H | Lost 19–21 |
| South Africa | 16 Aug | A | Lost 13–6 |
| South Africa | 23 Aug | H | Lost 31–33 |
| New Zealand | 6 Sep | A | Lost 28–9 |
| Australia | 13 Sep | A | Lost 32–25 |
| New Zealand | 27 Sep | H | Lost 13–34 |
| Australia | 4 Oct | H | Won 21–17 |

# HISTORIC WIN GIVES ARGENTINA RENEWED CONFIDENCE

## By Frankie Deges

Captain Agustín Creevy and his teammates celebrate in Mendoza after Argentina's first ever victory in The Rugby Championship.

**W**hen **Los Pumas** created history by beating Australia in their final match of the 2014 Rugby Championship in Mendoza, they did so with a match day squad featuring no fewer than 18 players who, at some point in their careers, had been part of the Pampas XV, a team created to give local players a higher standard of competition.

That so many players have been able to step up to the Test arena speaks volumes for both the individual ability of players and the standards imposed by the Unión Argentina de Rugby High Performance Academy. The joyous 21–17 win against the Wallabies was living proof of the well-nurtured talent and the hunger of players, coaches and officials at the UAR. Los Pumas may have failed to win in 17 previous attempts since joining The Rugby Championship in 2012, but they were facing the top three teams in the world. Some of those defeats were heavy, but in 2014 Argentina could have won or drawn three matches before that historic victory and got close enough to earn three losing bonus points.

With a new plan of how to play against New Zealand, South Africa and Australia and a renewed confidence, Los Pumas managed to halt a down-trend in results which had seen them slip to their lowest ever position of 12th in the IRB World Rankings. The victory over the Wallabies lifted Argentina back to 10th and they will hope to improve that further when they face Scotland, Italy and France in November.

Turn the clock back 12 months and a 54–17 loss to Australia in The Rugby Championship was to prove the final act for Santiago Phelan as he resigned with two months remaining in his contract. Daniel Hourcade was duly offered the job upon returning to Buenos Aires after guiding the Argentina Jaguars to another IRB Americas Rugby Championship title in Canada. With a CV that included coaching Argentina at Under 21 and Sevens levels, the Pampas XV and Jaguars, as well as a stint as Portugal assistant coach when they qualified and played at Rugby World Cup 2007, he embraced the opportunity.

His first tour was understandably not an easy one. Taking charge of a squad that had already been named, with the captain injured and so little time to prepare, he adjusted his ideas to work with the players he had for matches in England, Wales and Italy.

England at Twickenham were strong in the set-pieces and scored four tries, the game all but over by half-time with the home side holding an 18-point advantage. A week after that 31–12 loss, Argentina travelled to the Millennium Stadium and failed to take their opportunities in the first half, in complete contrast to Wales who turned each and every one of theirs into points. Tries either side of half-time and the efficient boot of Leigh Halfpenny were counteracted by two Nicolás Sánchez penalties in a 40–6 defeat.

Call it divine intervention or inspiration, but Argentina visited Pope Francis at the Vatican 48 hours before their season finale against Italy. Although he did not attend the match, the team shaded most of the exchanges with Italy under a Roman downpour. A try by Juan Imhoff, the speedy and elusive wing, and 14 points from the boot of Sánchez gave Los Pumas a 19–14 win and renewed hope for 2014.

Over the summer months in Argentina, Hourcade and his staff worked hard, made some tough but necessary decisions and returned with a new game plan. Those who had played under him over the years knew he enjoyed open rugby, with lots of phases, offloads and quick ball. Taking that approach into the Test arena was going to be the challenge.

A testing ground was the Pampas XV's two-month trip to Australia

ARGENTINA

where they played a couple of friendlies against the Western Force and Waratahs, and won the new-look IRB Pacific Rugby Cup. In search of competition to fill the gap between domestic and international rugby, it was the fifth season the Pampas XV had travelled overseas, having previously played in South Africa's Vodacom Cup. "We learnt a lot, were able to test some of our ideas and see what we could expect from our players," admitted Hourcade, who joined the team for some of the tour. Report cards for every player were positive and the hatched plan was beginning to take shape.

The next challenge came when Ireland arrived to face a team based on the Pampas XV. Lacking Test experience, they found the going tough and despite a wonderful score by winger Manuel Montero and a late Tomás de la Vega try to give the score some respectability, Ireland were deserving 29–17 winners, their first win in Argentina. A week later in Tucumán, two second-half tries after Argentina had led 10–9 at the break saw them clinch the series.

The June window finished with another loss, 21–19 against Scotland in Córdoba, with a late Duncan Weir penalty settling affairs. Argentina were not winning, but they were developing their game and the way they wanted to play.

When The Rugby Championship came around in August, Hourcade overlooked a handful of players that had been integral to the Pumas in previous years and even selected a new captain in hooker Agustín Creevy. "I was very proud of being captain, but if the new coach prefers another captain I am OK; I still retain my on-field responsibilities," said Juan Martín Fernández Lobbe, one of Argentina's best players in the tournament who missed the only win after the birth of his son.

The opening match saw South Africa welcome Los Pumas in a hailstorm. After the Springboks had scored a first-minute try, Argentina were the stronger team all round for the remaining 78 minutes, finishing the game with two attacking scrums that didn't produce the points to earn a draw. The 13–6 loss was still significantly better than the 73–13 defeat in this fixture in 2013.

A week later in the extreme heat of northern Argentina, Los Pumas played their best rugby of the Hourcade era, scoring three tries against a Springbok side that looked lost. But with strength coming from the bench, Heyneke Meyer's team managed to turn around a 15-point deficit in the dying minutes to win 33–31.

A trip to New Zealand and Australia followed and both games were played in the rain. In Napier, Los Pumas were denied a try that, while it might not have changed the final outcome, could have affected the game. On the Gold Coast a week later, Australia dominated for 60 minutes and only a strong defence kept the score close. Rising from the ashes, two tries and a penalty brought Argentina within a converted try of a draw. A five-metre scrum gave them an opportunity ... but it wasn't to be.

Returning home, the focus was on recovery as in the previous two years tiredness had seen Argentina drop their standards in the final two matches. With the All Blacks needing a bonus-point win to secure their third consecutive title, Los Pumas were unable to contain the Richie McCaw-led tide, only managing a late consolation try in a 34–13 defeat.

So to Mendoza and an early 14–0 deficit against Australia. But hungry and confident, the players refused to let that unsettle them and continued to attack with the ball in hand. Continuity and a clear idea of what, and where, they wanted to do things enabled them not only to turn the game around, but to record that elusive first victory.

"We have identified the way we want to play and now it is about giving our players experience to take on to the Rugby World Cup," said a buoyant yet reflective Hourcade. "Planning for England 2015 started almost from the moment I took the job and we have mapped everything out to ensure that we can aim for big things."

The production line continues to produce quality players, although Los Pumitas had a disappointing IRB Junior World Championship in New Zealand and finished ninth. Despite this, a couple of players could find their way into the Pumas sooner rather than later. The Jaguars, Argentina's second string, claimed the two trophies they competed for in the Americas Rugby Championship and the IRB Tbilisi Cup in June. These teams, along with the Pampas XV, will provide the nucleus of future national teams, and of the Super Rugby franchise which will operate from 2016.

In the Sevens form of the game, with the legendary Santiago Gómez Cora installed as coach, Argentina's clear goal is the 2016 Olympic Games in Rio. For this, the team endured a 2013–14 season devoid of good results, but used as part of a building block. They finished ninth overall in the HSBC Sevens World Series and know that unless they secure a top four position in 2014–15, their road to Rio will have to be through the South America regional tournament where they continue to dominate. Argentina's women's Sevens team continue to develop, but remain behind Brazil in South America.

Big goals and dreams are looming large on Argentina's rugby horizon. Rugby World Cup 2015 will come first and the team should be very competitive by then. Then in 2016 the inclusion of an Argentine team in Super Rugby can only help players to develop, while the qualification process for Rio 2016 is already underway. Los Pumas are moving in the right direction and will be hoping that all their hard work over the last year will pay off in the months ahead.

ARGENTINA

# ARGENTINA INTERNATIONAL STATISTICS

## MATCH RECORDS UP TO 13 OCTOBER 2014

### WINNING MARGIN

| Date | Opponent | Result | Winning Margin |
|------|----------|--------|---------------|
| 01/05/2002 | Paraguay | 152–0 | 152 |
| 27/04/2003 | Paraguay | 144–0 | 144 |
| 01/05/2004 | Venezuela | 147–7 | 140 |
| 02/10/1993 | Brazil | 114–3 | 111 |
| 23/05/2012 | Brazil | 111 – 0 | 111 |

### MOST POINTS IN A MATCH
### BY THE TEAM

| Date | Opponent | Result | Points |
|------|----------|--------|--------|
| 01/05/2002 | Paraguay | 152–0 | 152 |
| 01/05/2004 | Venezuela | 147–7 | 147 |
| 27/04/2003 | Paraguay | 144–0 | 144 |
| 02/10/1993 | Brazil | 114–3 | 114 |
| 23/05/2012 | Brazil | 111–0 | 111 |

### BY A PLAYER

| Date | Player | Opponent | Points |
|------|--------|----------|--------|
| 14/10/1973 | Eduardo Morgan | Paraguay | 50 |
| 27/04/2003 | José María Nuñez Piossek | Paraguay | 45 |
| 02/10/1993 | Gustavo Jorge | Brazil | 40 |
| 24/10/1977 | Martin Sansot | Brazil | 36 |
| 13/09/1951 | Uriel O'Farrell | Brazil | 33 |

### MOST DROP GOALS IN A MATCH
### BY THE TEAM

| Date | Opponent | Result | DGs |
|------|----------|--------|-----|
| 27/10/1979 | Australia | 24–13 | 3 |
| 02/11/1985 | New Zealand | 21–21 | 3 |
| 26/05/2001 | Canada | 20–6 | 3 |
| 21/09/1975 | Uruguay | 30–15 | 3 |
| 07/08/1971 | SA Gazelles | 12–0 | 3 |
| 30/09/2007 | Ireland | 30–15 | 3 |

### BY A PLAYER

| Date | Player | Opponent | DGs |
|------|--------|----------|-----|
| 27/10/1979 | Hugo Porta | Australia | 3 |
| 02/11/1985 | Hugo Porta | New Zealand | 3 |
| 07/08/1971 | Tomas Harris-Smith | SA Gazelles | 3 |
| 26/05/2001 | Juan Fernández Miranda | Canada | 3 |
| 30/09/2007 | Juan Martín Hernández | Ireland | 3 |

### MOST CONVERSIONS IN A MATCH
### BY THE TEAM

| Date | Opponent | Result | Cons |
|------|----------|--------|------|
| 01/05/2002 | Paraguay | 152–0 | 16 |
| 01/05/2004 | Venezuela | 147–7 | 16 |
| 09/10/1979 | Brazil | 109–3 | 15 |
| | 13 on 3 occasions | | |

### BY A PLAYER

| Date | Player | Opponent | Cons |
|------|--------|----------|------|
| 01/05/2002 | Jose Cilley | Paraguay | 16 |
| 21/09/1985 | Hugo Porta | Paraguay | 13 |
| 14/10/1973 | Eduardo Morgan | Paraguay | 13 |
| 25/09/1975 | Eduardo de Forteza | Paraguay | 11 |

### MOST PENALTIES IN A MATCH
### BY THE TEAM

| Date | Opponent | Result | Pens |
|------|----------|--------|------|
| 10/10/1999 | Samoa | 32–16 | 8 |
| 10/03/1995 | Canada | 29–26 | 8 |
| 17/06/2006 | Wales | 45–27 | 8 |
| 22/06/2013 | Georgia | 29–18 | 8 |

### BY A PLAYER

| Date | Player | Opponent | Pens |
|------|--------|----------|------|
| 10/10/1999 | Gonzalo Quesada | Samoa | 8 |
| 10/03/1995 | Santiago Meson | Canada | 8 |
| 17/06/2006 | Federico Todeschini | Wales | 8 |
| 22/06/2013 | Martin Bustos Moyano | Georgia | 8 |

### MOST TRIES IN A MATCH
### BY THE TEAM

| Date | Opponent | Result | Tries |
|------|----------|--------|-------|
| 01/05/2002 | Paraguay | 152–0 | 24 |
| 27/04/2003 | Paraguay | 144–0 | 24 |
| 01/05/2004 | Venezuela | 147–7 | 23 |
| 08/10/1989 | Brazil | 103–0 | 20 |

### BY A PLAYER

| Date | Player | Opponent | Tries |
|------|--------|----------|-------|
| 13/09/1951 | Uriel O'Farrell | Brazil | 11 |
| 27/04/2003 | José María Nuñez Piossek | Paraguay | 9 |
| 02/10/1993 | Gustavo Jorge | Brazil | 8 |
| 08/10/1989 | Gustavo Jorge | Brazil | 6 |
| 14/10/1973 | Eduardo Morgan | Paraguay | 6 |

| MOST CAPPED PLAYERS | |
|---|---|
| Name | Caps |
| Felipe Contepomi | 87 |
| Lisandro Arbizu | 86 |
| Rolando Martin | 86 |
| Mario Ledesma | 84 |
| Pedro Sporleder | 78 |

| LEADING PENALTY SCORERS | |
|---|---|
| Name | Penalties |
| Felipe Contepomi | 139 |
| Gonzalo Quesada | 103 |
| Hugo Porta | 101 |
| Santiago Meson | 63 |
| Federico Todeschini | 54 |

| LEADING TRY SCORERS | |
|---|---|
| Name | Tries |
| José María Nuñez Piossek | 29 |
| Diego Cuesta Silva | 28 |
| Gustavo Jorge | 24 |
| Facundo Soler | 18 |
| Rolando Martin | 18 |

| LEADING DROP GOAL SCORERS | |
|---|---|
| Name | DGs |
| Hugo Porta | 26 |
| Lisandro Arbizu | 11 |
| Gonzalo Quesada | 7 |
| Juan Martin Hernandez | 7 |
| Tomas Harris-Smith | 6 |

| LEADING CONVERSIONS SCORERS | |
|---|---|
| Name | Conversions |
| Hugo Porta | 84 |
| Felipe Contepomi | 74 |
| Gonzalo Quesada | 68 |
| Santiago Meson | 68 |
| Juan Fernández Miranda | 41 |

| LEADING POINTS SCORERS | |
|---|---|
| Name | Points |
| Felipe Contepomi | 651 |
| Hugo Porta | 590 |
| Gonzalo Quesada | 486 |
| Santiago Meson | 370 |
| Federico Todeschini | 256 |

# ARGENTINA INTERNATIONAL PLAYERS
## UP TO 13 OCTOBER 2014

**A Abadie** 2007 *CHL*, 2009 *E, W, S*
**A Abella** 1969 *Ur, CHL*
**C Abud** 1975 *Par, Bra, CHL*
**H Achaval** 1948 *OCC*
**J Aguilar** 1983 *CHL, Ur*
**A Aguirre** 1997 *Par, CHL*
**ME Aguirre** 1990 *E, S*, 1991 *Sa*
**B Agulla** 2010 *Ur, CHL*, 2011 *CHL, Ur*, 2012 *It, F*, 2013 *E, E, Geo*
**H Agulla** 2005 *Sa*, 2006 *Ur, E, It*, 2007 *It, F, Nm, I, S, SA, F*, 2008 *S, It, SA, F, It, I*, 2009 *E, E, E, W, S*, 2010 *Ur, CHL, S, S, F, I*, 2011 *W, E, R, S, Geo, NZ*, 2012 *SA, SA, NZ, A, NZ, A, W, F*, 2013 *SA, SA, NZ, A, NZ, A, E, W, It*, 2014 *SA, SA, NZ, NZ, A*
**A Ahualli De Chazal** 2014 *Ur, CHL, I, S*
**L Ahualli De Chazal** 2012 *Ur, CHL*, 2014 *Ur, CHL*
**P Albacete** 2003 *Par, Ur, F, SA, Ur, C, A, R*, 2004 *W, W, NZ, F, I*, 2005 *It, It*, 2006 *E, It, F*, 2007 *W, F, Geo, Nm, I, S, SA, F*, 2008 *SA, F, It, I*, 2009 *E, E, E, W, S*, 2010 *S, S, F, F, I*, 2011 *W, E, R, S, Geo, NZ*, 2012 *SA, SA, NZ, A, NZ, A*, 2013 *SA, NZ, A, E, W*
**DL Albanese** 1995 *Ur, C, E, F*, 1996 *Ur, F, SA, E*, 1997 *NZ, Ur, R, It, F, A, A*, 1998 *F, F, R, US, C, It, F, W*, 1999 *W, W, S, I, W, Sa, J, I, F*, 2000 *I, A, A, SA*, 2001 *NZ, It, W, S, NZ*, 2002 *F, E, SA, A, It, I*, 2003 *F, F, SA, US, C, A, Nm, I*
**F Albarracin** 2007 *CHL*
**M Albina** 2001 *Ur, US*, 2003 *Par, Ur, Fj*, 2004 *CHL, Ven, W, W*, 2005 *J*

**C Aldao** 1961 *CHL, Bra, Ur*
**MI Alemanno** 2014 *Ur, CHL, I, I, S, SA, SA, NZ, A, NZ, A*
**P Alexenicer** 1997 *Par, CHL*
**H Alfonso** 1936 *BI, CHL*
**G Allen** 1977 *Par*
**JG Allen** 1981 *C*, 1985 *F, F, Ur, NZ, NZ*, 1986 *F, F, A, A*, 1987 *Ur, Fj, It, NZ, Sp, A, A*, 1988 *F, F, F, F*, 1989 *Bra, CHL, Par, Ur, US*
**L Allen** 1951 *Ur, Bra, CHL*
**M Allen** 1990 *C, E, S*, 1991 *NZ, CHL*
**F Allogio** 2011 *CHL, Ur*
**A Allub** 1997 *Par, It, F, A, A*, 1998 *F, F, US, C, J, It, F, W*, 1999 *W, W, S, I, W, Sa, J, I, F*, 2000 *I, A, A, SA, E*, 2001 *NZ, It, F, A, A*, 2004 *F, I*, 2006 *W, W, NZ, CHL, Ur*, 2007 *I, It, W, F, Geo, Nm, I, S, SA, F*, 2008 *SA, F, It, I*, 2009 *E*
**M Alonso** 1973 *R, R, S*, 1977 *F, F*
**A Altberg** 1972 *SAG, SAG*, 1973 *R, R, Par*
**J Altube** 1998 *Par, CHL, Ur*
**C Alvarez** 1958 *Ur, Per, CHL*, 1959 *JSB, JSB*, 1960 *F*
**GM Alvarez** 1975 *Ur, Par, Bra, CHL*, 1976 *NZ*, 1977 *Bra, Ur, Par, CHL*
**S Alvarez** 2013 *Ur, CHL, Bra*
**R Álvarez Kairelis** 1998 *Par, CHL, Ur*, 2001 *Ur, US, C, W, S, NZ*, 2002 *F, E, SA, A, It, I*, 2003 *F, SA, Fj, Ur, C, Nm, I*, 2004 *F, I*, 2006 *W, W, NZ, CHL, Ur*, 2007 *I, It, W, F, Geo, Nm, I, S, SA, F*, 2008 *SA, F, It, I*, 2009 *E*
**G Alvarez** 2004 *Ur, Ven*
**S Ambrosio** 2012 *Ur, Bra*
**F Amelong** 2007 *CHL*
**A Amuchastegui** 2002 *Ur, Par, CHL*

**GP Angaut** 1987 *NZ, Ur, CHL*, 1990 *S*, 1991 *NZ, Sa*
**JJ Angelillo** 1987 *Ur, CHL, A*, 1988 *F, F, F*, 1989 *It, Bra, CHL, Par, Ur, US*, 1990 *C, US, E, E*, 1994 *US, S, S, US*, 1995 *Par, CHL, R, F*
**W Aniz** 1960 *F*
**R Annichini** 1983 *CHL, Ur*, 1985 *F, CHL, Par*
**A Anthony** 1965 *OCC, CHL*, 1967 *Ur, CHL*, 1968 *W, W*, 1969 *S, S, Ur, CHL*, 1970 *I, I*, 1971 *SAG, SAG, OCC*, 1972 *SAG, SAG*, 1974 *F, F*
**F Aranguren** 2007 *CHL*, 2011 *CHL, Ur*
**G Araoz** 2012 *Bra, CHL*
**L Arbizu** 1990 *I, S*, 1991 *NZ, NZ, CHL, A, W, Sa*, 1992 *F, F, Sp, Sp, R, F*, 1993 *J, J, Bra, CHL, Par, Ur, SA, SA*, 1995 *Ur, A, A, E, Sa, It, Par, CHL, Ur, R, It, F*, 1996 *Ur, US, Ur, C, SA, SA, E*, 1997 *E, E, NZ, NZ, R, It, F, A, A*, 1998 *F, F, R, US, C, It, F, W*, 1999 *W, W, S, I, W, Sa, J, I, F*, 2000 *A, A, SA, E*, 2001 *NZ, It, W, S, NZ*, 2002 *F, A, It, I*, 2003 *F, F, US, C*, 2005 *It, It*
**F Argerich** 1979 *Ur*
**G Aristide** 1997 *E*
**J Arocena Messones** 2005 *Sa*
**E Arriaga** 1936 *CHL, CHL*
**S Artese** 2004 *SA*
**G Ascarate** 2007 *CHL*, 2010 *CHL*, 2012 *It, F*, 2013 *E, E, Geo, W, It*, 2014 *Ur, CHL, I, I*
**M Avellaneda** 1948 *OCC, OCC*, 1951 *Bra, CHL*
**M Avramovic** 2005 *J, Sa*, 2006 *CHL, Ur, E, It*, 2007 *I*, 2008 *It, SA, I*, 2009 *E*
**M Ayerra** 1927 *GBR*
**MI Ayerza** 2004 *SA*, 2005 *J, It, Sa*, 2006 *W, W, CHL, Ur, E, It, F*, 2007 *I, I, Geo, F*, 2008 *S, S, SA, F, It, I*, 2009 *E, E, E, W, S*, 2010 *S, S, F, It, F, I*, 2011 *Geo, NZ*, 2012 *SA, SA, NZ, W, F, I*, 2013 *SA, NZ, A, NZ, A, E, W, It*, 2014 *SA, SA, NZ, A, NZ, A*
**N Azorin** 2012 *Ur, Bra*
**M Azpiroz** 1956 *OCC*, 1958 *Ur, Per, CHL*, 1959 *JSB, JSB*

**J Bach** 1975 *Par, Bra, CHL*
**A Badano** 1977 *Bra, Ur, Par, CHL*
**J Baeck** 1983 *Par*
**M Baeck** 1985 *Ur, CHL, Par*, 1990 *US, E, E*
**DR Baetti Sabah** 1980 *WXV, Fj, Fj*, 1981 *E, E, C*, 1983 *WXV*, 1987 *Ur, Par, CHL*, 1988 *F, F*, 1989 *It, NZ, NZ*
**R Baez** 2010 *CHL*, 2011 *CHL, Ur*, 2012 *F, F*, 2013 *E, Geo*, 2014 *Ur, I, I, S, NZ, A, NZ, A*
**L Balfour** 1977 *Bra, Ur, Par, CHL*
**T Baravalle** 2011 *Ur*
**C Barrea** 1996 *Ur, C, SA*
**F Barrea** 2012 *Ur, Bra, CHL, F*
**O Bartolucci** 1996 *US, C, SA*, 1998 *CHL, Ur*, 1999 *W, W, S, I, W, Sa*, 2000 *I, A, A, SA, E*, 2001 *US, C*, 2003 *Par, Ur*
**E Basile** 1983 *CHL, Ur*
**JL Basile** 2011 *CHL, Ur*
**L Bavio** 1954 *F*
**R Bazan** 1951 *Ur, Bra, CHL*, 1956 *OCC*
**D Beccar Varela** 1975 *F, F*, 1976 *W, NZ*, 1977 *F, F*
**M Beccar Varela** 1965 *Rho, OCC, OCC*
**G Begino** 2007 *CHL*
**J Benzi** 1965 *Rho*, 1969 *S, Ur, CHL*
**E Bergamaschi** 2001 *US*
**O Bernacchi** 1954 *F*, 1956 *OCC, OCC*, 1958 *Ur, Per, CHL*
**G Bernardi** 1997 *CHL*
**O Bernat** 1932 *JSB*
**MM Berro** 1964 *Ur, Bra, CHL*
**MJS Bertranou** 1989 *It, NZ, NZ, CHL, Par*, 1990 *C, US, C, E, E, I, E, S*, 1993 *SA*
**E Bianchetti** 1959 *JSB, JSB*
**G Blacksley** 1971 *SAG*
**T Blades** 1938 *CHL*
**G Bocca** 1998 *J, Par*
**C Bofelli** 1997 *Ur*, 1998 *Par*, 2004 *CHL, Ur, Ven*
**A Bordoy** 2012 *F, F*
**L Borges** 2003 *Par, CHL, Ur*, 2004 *CHL, Ur, Ven, W, W, NZ, F, I, SA*, 2005 *SA, S*, 2006 *W, W, CHL, Ur*, 2007 *W, F, Geo, I, S, SA*, 2008 *S, It*, 2009 *E, W, S*, 2010 *Ur, S, I*
**T Borghi** 2013 *Ur, CHL, Bra*
**C Bori** 1975 *F*

**F Bosch** 2004 *CHL, SA*, 2005 *J, Sa*
**MT Bosch** 2007 *It*, 2008 *It*, 2010 *F, I*, 2011 *W, E, R, S, Geo, NZ*, 2012 *SA, SA, NZ, A, NZ, A, F, I*, 2013 *SA, SA, NZ, NZ, A, E, W*, 2014 *SA, SA, NZ, A, NZ, A*
**MA Bosch** 1991 *A, Sa*, 1992 *F, F*
**N Bossicovich** 1995 *Ur, C*
**CA Bottarini** 1973 *Par, Ur, Bra, I*, 1974 *F*, 1975 *F, F*, 1979 *Ur, CHL, Bra*, 1983 *CHL, Par, Ur*
**R Botting** 1927 *GBR, GBR, GBR*
**S Bottini** 2011 *CHL, Ur*
**L Bouza** 1932 *Sp*
**M Bouza** 1966 *SAG, SAG*, 1967 *Ur, CHL*
**P Bouza** 1996 *Ur, F, F, E*, 1997 *E, NZ, NZ, Ur, R*, 1998 *Ur, 2002 Ur, Par, CHL*, 2003 *Par, CHL, Ur, US, Ur, Nm, R*, 2004 *CHL, Ur, Ven, W, NZ, SA*, 2005 *J, It, It, SA, S, It*, 2006 *CHL, Ur*, 2007 *I, I*
**A Bovet** 1910 *GBR*
**N Bozzo** 1975 *Bra*
**JG Braceras** 1971 *Bra, Par*, 1976 *W, NZ*, 1977 *F*
**W Braddon** 1927 *GBR*
**EN Branca** 1976 *W, NZ, NZ*, 1977 *F, F*, 1980 *Fj*, 1981 *E, E, C*, 1983 *WXV, A, A*, 1985 *F, F, Ur, CHL, Par, NZ, NZ*, 1986 *F, F, A, A*, 1987 *Ur, Fj, It, NZ, Sp, A, A*, 1988 *F, F, F, F*, 1989 *Bra, Par, Ur*, 1990 *E, E*
**M Brandi** 1997 *Par, CHL*, 1998 *Par, CHL, Ur*
**J Bridger** 1932 *JSB*
**J Brolese** 1998 *CHL, Ur*
**E Brouchou** 1975 *Ur, Par, Bra, CHL*
**R Bruno** 2010 *Ur, CHL*, 2012 *Bra, CHL, F*
**F Buabse** 1991 *Ur, Bra, Par*, 1992 *Sp*
**PM Buabse** 1989 *NZ, US*, 1991 *Sa*, 1993 *Bra*, 1995 *Ur, C, A*
**E Buckley** 1938 *CHL*
**R Bullrich** 1991 *Ur, Bra*, 1992 *R*, 1993 *Bra, CHL, SA*, 1994 *SA, SA*
**S Bunader** 1989 *US*, 1990 *C*
**K Bush** 1938 *CHL*
**E Bustamante** 1927 *GBR, GBR, GBR, GBR*
**F Bustillo** 1977 *F, F, Bra, Ur, Par, CHL*
**G Bustos** 2003 *Par, Ur*, 2004 *CHL, Ven*
**MA Bustos** 2012 *I*, 2013 *E, E, Geo, E, W, It*
**MJ Bustos Moyano** 2013 *E, E, Geo*

**CJ Cáceres** 2010 *Ur, CHL*
**E Caffarone** 1949 *F, F*, 1951 *Bra, CHL*, 1952 *I, I*, 1954 *F, F*
**M Caldwell** 1956 *OCC*
**GO Camacho** 2009 *E, E*, 2010 *It, F*, 2011 *W, E, R, S, NZ*, 2012 *SA, SA, NZ, A, NZ, A, W, F, I*, 2013 *SA, SA, NZ*
**GF Camardon** 1990 *E*, 1991 *NZ, CHL, A, W, Sa*, 1992 *F, F, Sp, R, F*, 1993 *J, Par, Ur, SA, SA*, 1995 *A*, 1996 *Ur, US, Ur, C, SA, E*, 1999 *W, W, Sa, J, I, F*, 2001 *US, C, NZ, It, W, S, NZ*, 2002 *F, E, SA, It, I*
**PJ Camerlinckx** 1989 *Bra, Par, Ur*, 1990 *C, US*, 1994 *S*, 1995 *CHL*, 1996 *Ur, F, F, US, Ur, C, SA, SA, E*, 1997 *E, E, NZ, NZ, Ur, R, It, F, A, A*, 1998 *R, US, C, F, W*, 1999 *W*
**A Cameron** 1936 *BI, CHL, CHL*, 1938 *CHL*
**R Cameron** 1927 *GBR, GBR*
**J Caminotti** 1987 *Ur, Par, CHL*
**M Campo** 1978 *E, It*, 1979 *NZ, NZ, A, A*, 1980 *WXV, Fj*, 1981 *E, E, C*, 1982 *F, F, Sp*, 1983 *WXV, A, A*, 1987 *Ur, Fj, NZ*
**AT Campos** 2007 *CHL*, 2008 *S, It, F, It*, 2009 *E, W, S*, 2010 *Ur, S, F, CHL, Ur*
**A Canalda** 1999 *S, I, F*, 2000 *A*, 2001 *Ur, US, C*
**R Cano** 1997 *Par*
**J Capalbo** 1975 *Bra*, 1977 *Bra, Ur, CHL*
**AE Capelletti** 1977 *F, F*, 1978 *E, It*, 1979 *NZ, NZ, A, A*, 1980 *WXV, Fj, Fj*, 1981 *E, E*
**J Cappiello** 2013 *Ur, CHL, Bra*
**R Carballo** 2006 *W, CHL, Ur*, 2008 *SA, It, I*, 2010 *S, F*
**N Carbone** 1969 *Ur, CHL*, 1971 *SAG*, 1973 *I, S*
**PF Cardinali** 2001 *US*, 2002 *Ur, Par*, 2004 *W*, 2007 *I*
**M Carizza** 2004 *SA*, 2005 *J, SA, S, It*, 2006 *W, CHL, Ur*, 2007 *It*, 2008 *E, I, E, S, F, It, F*, 2011 *W, E, R, S, NZ*, 2012 *SA, SA, NZ, A, NZ, A, W, F, I*, 2013 *SA, NZ, A, A, W, F, I*, 2014 *I, I, S*
**J Carlos Galvalisi** 1983 *Par, Ur*
**MA Carluccio** 1973 *R, R, Ur, Bra, I*, 1975 *F, F*, 1976 *NZ*, 1977 *F, F*

**233**

R Espagnol 1971 *SAG*

AM Etchegaray 1964 *Ur, Bra, CHL*, 1965 *Rho, JSB, CHL*, 1967 *Ur, CHL*, 1968 *W, W*, 1969 *S, S*, 1971 *SAG, OCC, OCC*, 1972 *SAG, SAG*, 1973 *Par, Bra, I*, 1974 *F, F*, 1976 *W, NZ, NZ*

R Etchegoyen 1991 *Ur, Par, Bra*

C Ezcurra 1958 *Ur, Per, CHL*

E Ezcurra 1990 *I, E, S*

F Ezcurra 2014 *Ur, CHL*

JA Farias Cabello 2010 *F, I*, 2011 *W, E, S, Geo, NZ*, 2012 *It, F, F, SA, SA, NZ, A, NZ, A, W, F, I*, 2013 *E, E, SA, SA, NZ, A, NZ, A, E, W, It*

R Fariello 1973 *Par, Ur, CHL, S*

M Farina 1968 *W, W*, 1969 *S, S*

D Farrell 1951 *Ur*

P Felisari 1956 *OCC*

JJ Fernandez 1971 *SAG, CHL, Bra, Par, Ur*, 1972 *SAG, SAG*, 1973 *R, R, Par, Ur, CHL, I, S*, 1974 *F, F*, 1975 *F*, 1976 *W, NZ, NZ*, 1977 *F, F*

S Fernandez 2008 *It, I*, 2009 *E, E, E, W, S*, 2010 *S, S, F, It, F*, 2011 *W, E, R, S, Geo, NZ*, 2012 *SA, SA, NZ, A, NZ, A, I*, 2013 *NZ, A, NZ, A, E, W*

Pablo Fernandez Bravo 1993 *SA, SA*

E Fernandez del Casal 1951 *Ur, Bra, CHL*, 1952 *I, I*, 1956 *OCC, OCC*

PF Fernandez 2013 *CHL, Bra*

CI Fernandez Lobbe 1996 *US*, 1997 *E, E*, 1998 *F, F, R, US, Ur, C, J, It, F*, 1999 *W, W, S, I, W, Sa, J, I, F*, 2000 *I, A, A, SA, E*, 2001 *NZ, It, W, S, NZ*, 2002 *F, E, SA, A, It, I*, 2003 *F, F, SA, US, C, A, Nm, I*, 2004 *W, W, NZ*, 2005 *SA, S, It*, 2006 *W, W, NZ, E, F*, 2007 *It, W, F, Nm, I, S, SA*, 2008 *S, S*

JM Fernandez Lobbe 2004 *Ur, Ven*, 2005 *S, It, Sa*, 2006 *W, W, NZ, E, It, F*, 2007 *I, I, It, W, F, Geo, Nm, I, S, SA, F*, 2008 *S, S, SA, F, It, I*, 2009 *E, E, E, W, S*, 2010 *S, S, F, It, F, I*, 2011 *W, E, R, S*, 2012 *SA, SA, NZ, A, NZ, A, W, F, I*, 2013 *NZ, A, NZ, A*, 2014 *SA, SA, NZ, A, NZ*

JC Fernández Miranda 1997 *Ur, R, It*, 1998 *Ur, It*, 2000 *I*, 2001 *US, C*, 2002 *Ur, Par, CHL, It, I*, 2003 *Par, CHL, Ur, Fj, US, Nm, R*, 2004 *W, NZ, SA*, 2005 *J, Sa*, 2006 *CHL, Ur*, 2007 *It*

N Fernandez Miranda 1994 *US, S, S, US*, 1995 *CHL, Ur*, 1996 *F, SA, SA, E*, 1997 *E, E, NZ, NZ, Ur, R*, 1998 *R, US, C, It*, 1999 *I, F*, 2002 *Ur, CHL, It*, 2003 *CHL, Ur, F, F, SA, US, Ur, Nm, R*, 2004 *W, NZ, SA*, 2005 *J, It, It*, 2006 *W, It*, 2007 *W, Geo, Nm, F*

N Ferrari 1992 *Sp, Sp*

G Fessia 2007 *I*, 2009 *E*, 2010 *S, S, F, It, F, I*, 2011 *R, S, Geo*, 2012 *It*

JG Figallo 2010 *F, It, I*, 2011 *W, E, R, S, Geo, NZ*, 2012 *SA, SA, NZ, A, NZ, A, W, F*, 2013 *SA, SA, NZ, A, NZ*

A Figuerola 2008 *It, I*, 2009 *E, W, S*, 2010 *S, S*

R Follett 1948 *OCC, OCC*, 1952 *I, I*, 1954 *F*

G Foster 1971 *CHL, Bra, Par, Ur*

R Foster 1965 *Rho, JSB, OCC, OCC, CHL*, 1966 *SAG, SAG*, 1970 *I, I*, 1971 *SAG, SAG, OCC*, 1972 *SAG, SAG*

P Franchi 1987 *Ur, Par, CHL*

JL Francombe 1932 *JSB, JSB*, 1936 *BI*

J Freixas 2003 *CHL, Ur*

R Frigerio 1948 *OCC, OCC*, 1954 *F*

J Frigoli 1936 *BI, CHL, CHL*

C Fruttero 2012 *Ur, Bra, CHL*, 2013 *Ur, CHL, Bra*

P Fuselli 1998 *J, Par*

E Gahan 1954 *F, F*

M Gaitan 1998 *Ur*, 2002 *Par, CHL*, 2003 *Fj, US, Nm, R*, 2004 *W*, 2007 *It, W*

MT Galarza 2010 *S, F, It, F, I*, 2011 *W, E, R, Geo*, 2013 *E, E, Geo, SA, SA, NZ, A, NZ, E, It*, 2014 *SA, SA, NZ, A, NZ, A*

AM Galindo 2004 *Ur, Ven*, 2008 *S, It, SA, F*, 2009 *E*, 2010 *Ur, It, F*, 2012 *SA, SA*

R Gallo 1964 *Bra*

P Gambarini 2006 *W, CHL, Ur*, 2007 *I, It, CHL*, 2008 *S*

E Garbarino 1992 *Sp, Sp*

FL Garcia 1994 *SA*, 1995 *A, A, Par, CHL*, 1996 *Ur, F, F*, 1997 *NZ*, 1998 *R, Ur, J*

J Garcia 1998 *Par, Ur*, 2000 *A*

PT Garcia 1948 *OCC*

SE Garcia Botta 2013 *CHL, Bra*

E Garcia Hamilton 1993 *Bra*

P Garcia Hamilton 1998 *CHL*

HM Garcia Simon 1990 *I*, 1992 *F*

M Garcia Veiga 2012 *Ur, Bra, CHL*, 2013 *E, E, Geo*

G Garcia-Orsetti 1992 *R, F*

PA Garreton 1987 *Sp, Ur, CHL, A, A*, 1988 *F, F, F, F*, 1989 *It, NZ, Bra, CHL, Ur, US*, 1990 *C, E, E, I, E, S*, 1991 *NZ, NZ, CHL, A, W, Sa*, 1992 *F, F*, 1993 *J, J*

P Garzon 1990 *C*, 1991 *Par, Bra*

G Gasso 1983 *CHL, Par*

JM Gauweloose 1975 *F, F*, 1976 *W, NZ, NZ*, 1977 *F, F*, 1981 *C*

E Gavina 1956 *OCC, OCC*, 1958 *Ur, Per, CHL*, 1959 *JSB, JSB*, 1960 *F, F*, 1961 *CHL, Bra, Ur*

OST Gebbie 1910 *GBR*

FA Genoud 2004 *CHL, Ur, Ven*, 2005 *J, It*

J Genoud 1952 *I, I*, 1956 *OCC, OCC*

M Gerosa 1987 *Ur, CHL*

D Giannantonio 1996 *Ur*, 1997 *Par, Ur, It, A, A*, 1998 *F, F*, 2000 *A*, 2002 *E*

MC Giargia 1973 *Par, Ur, Bra*, 1975 *Par, CHL*

T Gilardon 2013 *Ur, CHL, Bra*

R Giles 1948 *OCC*, 1949 *F, F*, 1951 *Ur*, 1952 *I, I*

C Giuliano 1959 *JSB, JSB*, 1960 *F*

L Glastra 1948 *OCC, OCC*, 1952 *I, I*

M Glastra 1979 *Ur, CHL*, 1981 *C*

FE Gomez 1985 *Ur*, 1987 *Ur, Fj, It, NZ*, 1989 *NZ*, 1990 *C, E, E*

JF Gomez 2006 *It*, 2008 *S, S, It*, 2012 *W*

N Gomez 1997 *Par, CHL*

PM Gomez Cora 2004 *NZ, SA*, 2005 *Sa*, 2006 *E*

F Gómez Kodela 2011 *CHL, Ur*, 2012 *It, F, F, I*, 2013 *E, E, Geo*

D Gonzalez 1987 *Par*, 1988 *F, F*

T Gonzalez 1975 *Ur, CHL*

LP Gonzalez Amorosino 2007 *CHL*, 2009 *E, E*, 2010 *S, S, F, It, F, I*, 2011 *R, S, Geo, NZ*, 2012 *SA, SA, NZ, A, NZ, A, F, I*, 2013 *SA, NZ, A, NZ, A, E, W, It*, 2014 *CHL, I, I, S, SA, SA, NZ, A, A*

S Gonzalez Bonorino 2001 *Ur, US, C*, 2002 *Par, CHL*, 2003 *F, SA*, 2007 *I, I, It, W, F, Geo*, 2008 *S, S*

E Gonzalez del Solar 1960 *F*, 1961 *CHL, Bra, Ur*

N Gonzalez del Solar 1964 *Ur, Bra, CHL*, 1965 *Rho, JSB, OCC, OCC, CHL*

S Gonzalez Iglesias 2011 *CHL*, 2014 *Ur, I, I, S, SA, NZ, NZ*

AO Gosio 2011 *Geo*, 2012 *It, F*

H Goti 1961 *CHL, Bra, Ur*, 1964 *Ur, Bra, CHL*, 1965 *Rho*, 1966 *SAG*

LM Gradin 1965 *OCC, OCC, CHL*, 1966 *SAG, SAG*, 1969 *CHL*, 1970 *I, I*, 1973 *R, R, Par, Ur, CHL, S*

P Grande 1998 *Par, CHL, Ur*

RD Grau 1993 *J, Bra, CHL*, 1995 *Par, CHL*, 1996 *F, F, US, Ur, C, SA, SA, E*, 1997 *E, E, NZ, NZ, A, A*, 1998 *F, It, F*, 1999 *W, W, S, I, W, F*, 2000 *A, SA, E*, 2001 *NZ, W, S, NZ*, 2002 *F, E, SA, A, It*, 2003 *F, SA, US, Ur, C, A, I*

L Gravano 1997 *CHL*, 1998 *CHL, Ur*

LH Gribell 1910 *GBR*

B Grigolon 1948 *OCC*, 1954 *F, F*

V Grimoldi 1927 *GBR, GBR*

J Grondona 1990 *C*

R Grosse 1952 *I, I*, 1954 *F, F*

P Guarrochena 1977 *Par*

A Guastella 1956 *OCC*, 1959 *JSB, JSB*, 1960 *F*

J Guidi 1958 *Ur, Per, CHL*, 1959 *JSB*, 1960 *F*, 1961 *CHL, Bra, Ur*

MR Guidone 2011 *CHL, Ur*, 2013 *Ur, Bra, E, E, Geo*

E Guinazu 2003 *Par, CHL, Ur*, 2004 *CHL, Ur, Ven, W, W, SA*, 2005 *J, It*, 2007 *I, It, F*, 2009 *E*, 2012 *It, F, F, SA, SA, NZ, A, NZ, A, W, F, I*, 2013 *SA, NZ, A, NZ, A, E, W, It*

JA Guzman 2007 *CHL*, 2010 *Ur, CHL*

SN Guzmán 2010 *S, I*, 2012 *Ur, Bra, CHL, It*

D Halle 1989 *Bra, CHL, Ur, US*, 1990 *US*

R Handley 1966 *SAG, SAG*, 1968 *W, W*, 1969 *S, S, Ur, CHL*, 1970 *I, I*, 1971 *SAG, SAG*, 1972 *SAG, SAG*

G Hardie 1948 *OCC*
TA Harris-Smith 1969 *S, S,* 1971 *SAG, OCC, OCC,* 1973 *Par, Ur*
O Hasan Jalil 1995 *Ur,* 1996 *Ur, C, SA, SA,* 1997 *E, E, NZ, R, It, F, A,* 1998 *F, F, R, US, C, It, F, W,* 1999 *W, W, S, W, Sa, J, I,* 2000 *SA, E,* 2001 *NZ, It, W, S, NZ,* 2002 *F, E, SA, A, It, I,* 2003 *US, C, A, R,* 2004 *W, W, NZ, F, I,* 2005 *It, It, SA, S, It,* 2006 *NZ, E, F,* 2007 *It, Geo, Nm, I, S, SA, F*
WM Hayman 1910 *GBR*
BH Heatlie 1910 *GBR*
P Henn 2004 *CHL, Ur, Ven,* 2005 *J, It,* 2007 *It,* 2012 *F,* 2013 *E, E*
F Henrys 1910 *GBR*
F Heriot 1910 *GBR*
JM Hernández 2003 *Par, Ur, F, F, SA, C, A, Nm, R,* 2004 *F, I, SA,* 2005 *SA, S, It,* 2006 *W, W, NZ, E, It, F,* 2007 *F, Geo, I, SA, F,* 2008 *It, F, NZ,* 2009 *E, E,* 2012 *SA, NZ, A, NZ, A, W, I,* 2013 *SA, NZ, A, NZ, A,* 2014 *SA, NZ, A, NZ, A*
M Hernandez 1927 *GBR, GBR, GBR*
L Herrera 1991 *Ur, Par*
R Herrera 2014 *I, I, SA, SA, NZ, A, NZ, A*
FA Higgs 2004 *Ur, Ven,* 2005 *J*
D Hine 1938 *CHL*
C Hirsch 1960 *F*
C Hirsch 1960 *F*
E Hirsch 1954 *F,* 1956 *OCC*
R Hogg 1958 *Ur, Per, CHL,* 1959 *JSB, JSB,* 1961 *CHL, Bra, Ur*
S Hogg 1956 *OCC, OCC,* 1958 *Ur, Per, CHL,* 1959 *JSB, JSB*
E Holmberg 1948 *OCC*
B Holmes 1949 *F, F*
E Holmgren 1958 *Ur, Per, CHL,* 1959 *JSB, JSB,* 1960 *F, F*
G Holmgren 1985 *NZ, NZ*
E Horan 1956 *OCC*
L Hughes 1936 *CHL*
M Hughes 1954 *F, F*
M Hughes 1949 *F, F*
CA Huntley Robertson 1932 *JSB, JSB*

A Iachetti 1977 *Bra,* 1987 *CHL*
A Iachetti 1975 *Ur, Par,* 1977 *Ur, Par, CHL,* 1978 *E, It,* 1979 *NZ, NZ, A, A,* 1980 *WXV, Fj, Fj,* 1981 *E, E,* 1982 *F, F, Sp,* 1987 *Ur, Par, A, A,* 1988 *F, F, F, F,* 1989 *It, NZ,* 1990 *C, E, E*
ME Iachetti 1979 *NZ, NZ, A, A*
M Iglesias 1973 *R,* 1974 *F, F*
S Iglesias Valdez 2013 *Ur, CHL, E, W,* 2014 *Ur, CHL, I, S*
G Illia 1965 *Rho*
JL Imhoff 1967 *Ur, CHL*
JJ Imhoff 2010 *CHL,* 2011 *W, E, R, Geo, NZ,* 2012 *A, NZ, A, W, F, I,* 2013 *SA, A, NZ, A, E, It,* 2014 *NZ, A, NZ, A*
P Imhoff 2013 *Ur, CHL, Bra*
V Inchausti 1936 *BI, CHL, CHL*
F Insua 1971 *CHL, Bra, Par, Ur,* 1972 *SAG, SAG,* 1973 *R, R, Bra, CHL, I, S,* 1974 *F, F,* 1976 *W, NZ, NZ,* 1977 *F, F*
R Iraneta 1974 *F,* 1976 *W, NZ*
FJ Irarrazabal 1991 *Sa,* 1992 *Sp, Sp*
S Irazoqui 1993 *J, CHL, Par, Ur,* 1995 *E, Sa, Par*
A Irigoyen 1997 *Par*
DJ Isaack 2013 *Ur, CHL*

C Jacobi 1979 *CHL, Par*
AG Jacobs 1927 *GBR, GBR*
AGW Jones 1948 *OCC*
GM Jorge 1989 *Bra, CHL, Par, Ur,* 1990 *I, E,* 1992 *F, F, Sp, Sp, R, F,* 1993 *J, J, Bra, CHL, Ur, SA, SA,* 1994 *US, S, S, US*
E Jurado 1995 *A, A, E, Sa, It, Par, CHL, Ur, R, It, F,* 1996 *SA, E,* 1997 *E, E, NZ, NZ, Ur, R, It, F, A, A,* 1998 *F, Ur, C, It,* 1999 *W*

E Karplus 1959 *JSB, JSB,* 1960 *F, F, F*
A Ker 1936 *CHL,* 1938 *CHL*
E Kossler 1960 *F, F, F*

EH Laborde 1991 *A, W, Sa*
G Laborde 1979 *CHL, Bra*

J Lacarra 1989 *Par, Ur*
R Lagarde 1956 *OCC*
A Lalanne 2008 *SA,* 2009 *E, E, W, S,* 2010 *S, I,* 2011 *R, Geo, NZ*
M Lamas 1998 *Par, CHL*
FJ Lamy 2013 *Ur, CHL, Bra*
M Landajo 2010 *Ur, CHL,* 2012 *Ur, Bra, CHL, It, F, SA, SA, NZ, A, NZ, A, W, F, I,* 2013 *E, SA, SA, NZ, A, NZ, A, E, W, It,* 2014 *CHL, I, I, S, SA, SA, NZ, A, NZ, A*
TR Landajo 1977 *F, Bra, Ur, CHL,* 1978 *E,* 1979 *A, A,* 1980 *WXV, Fj, Fj,* 1981 *E, E*
M Lanfranco 1991 *Ur, Par, Bra*
AR Lanusse 1932 *JSB*
M Lanusse 1951 *Ur, Bra, CHL*
J Lanza 1985 *F, Ur, Par, NZ, NZ,* 1986 *F, F, A, A,* 1987 *Ur, Fj, It, NZ*
P Lanza 1983 *CHL, Par, Ur,* 1985 *F, F, Ur, CHL, Par, NZ, NZ,* 1986 *F, F, A, A,* 1987 *It, NZ*
J Lasalle 1964 *Ur*
TE Lavanini 2013 *Ur, Bra, SA, W, It,* 2014 *Ur, CHL, I, I, S, SA, SA, NZ, NZ, A*
J Lavayen 1961 *CHL, Bra, Ur*
CG Lazcano Miranda 1998 *CHL,* 2004 *CHL, Ur, Ven,* 2005 *J*
RA le Fort 1990 *I, E,* 1991 *NZ, NZ, CHL, A, W,* 1992 *R, F,* 1993 *J, SA, SA,* 1995 *Ur, It*
F Lecot 2003 *Par, Ur,* 2005 *J,* 2007 *CHL*
P Ledesma 2008 *It, SA*
ME Ledesma Arocena 1996 *Ur, C,* 1997 *NZ, NZ, Ur, R, It, F, A, A,* 1998 *F, F, Ur, C, J, Ur, F, W,* 1999 *W, W, Sa, J, I, F,* 2000 *SA,* 2001 *It, W, NZ,* 2002 *F, E, SA, A, It, I,* 2003 *F, SA, Fj, US, C, A, Nm, R,* 2004 *W, NZ, F, I,* 2005 *It, It, SA, S, It,* 2006 *W, W, NZ, CHL, Ur, E, It, F,* 2007 *W, F, Geo, I, S, SA,* 2008 *SA, F, It, I,* 2009 *E, E, W,* 2010 *S, S, F, It, F, I,* 2011 *W, E, R, S, Geo, NZ*
J Legora 1996 *F, F, US, Ur,* 1997 *CHL,* 1998 *Par*
JM Leguizamon 2005 *J, It, It, SA, S, It,* 2006 *W, NZ, CHL, Ur, E, It, F,* 2007 *I, I, It, W, F, Geo, Nm, S, SA, F,* 2008 *S, S, It, SA, I,* 2009 *E, E,* 2010 *S, S, F,* 2011 *W, E, R, S, Geo, NZ,* 2012 *NZ, A, NZ, A, W, F, I,* 2013 *SA, NZ, A,* 2014 *SA, SA, NZ, A*
GP Leiros 1973 *Bra, I*
C Lennon 1958 *Ur, Per*
TC Leonardi 2009 *E, W, S,* 2012 *It, F, SA, SA, NZ, A, NZ, A, W, I,* 2013 *E, E, Geo*
FJ Leonelli Morey 2001 *Ur,* 2004 *Ur, Ven,* 2005 *J, It, SA, S, It,* 2006 *W, W,* 2007 *I, I, It,* 2008 *F, I,* 2009 *E*
M Lerga 1995 *Par, CHL, Ur*
Lesianado 1948 *OCC*
I Lewis 1932 *JSB*
GA Llanes 1990 *I, E, S,* 1991 *NZ, NZ, CHL, A, W,* 1992 *F, F, Sp, R, F,* 1993 *Bra, CHL, SA, SA,* 1994 *US, S, S, SA, SA,* 1995 *A, A, E, Sa, It, R, It, F,* 1996 *SA, SA, E,* 1997 *E, E, NZ, NZ, R, It, F,* 1998 *F,* 2000 *A*
MA Lobato 2010 *Ur, CHL*
N Lobo 2012 *F, I,* 2013 *SA, NZ, A, NZ, A, E, W, It*
L Lobrauco 1996 *US,* 1997 *CHL,* 1998 *J, CHL, Ur*
MH Loffreda 1978 *E,* 1979 *NZ, NZ, A, A,* 1980 *WXV, Fj, Fj,* 1981 *E, E, C,* 1982 *F, F, Sp,* 1983 *WXV, A, A,* 1985 *Ur, CHL, Par,* 1987 *Par, CHL, A, A,* 1988 *F, F, F, F,* 1989 *It, NZ, Bra, CHL, Par, US,* 1990 *C, US, E, E,* 1994 *US, S, S, US, SA, SA*
G Logan 1936 *BI*
GM Longo Elía 1999 *W, W, S, I, W, Sa, I, F,* 2000 *I, A, A, SA, E,* 2001 *US, NZ, It, W, S, NZ,* 2002 *F, E, SA, A, It, I,* 2003 *F, F, SA, Fj, C, A, I,* 2004 *W, W, NZ, F, I,* 2005 *It, It, SA,* 2006 *W, W, NZ, E, It, F,* 2007 *W, Nm, I, S, SA, F*
L Lopez Fleming 2004 *Ur, Ven, W,* 2005 *Sa*
A Lopresti 1997 *Par, CHL*
J Loures 1954 *F*
R Loyola 1964 *Ur, CHL,* 1965 *Rho, JSB, OCC, OCC, CHL,* 1966 *SAG, SAG,* 1968 *W, W,* 1969 *S, S,* 1970 *I, I,* 1971 *CHL, Bra, Par, Ur*
E Lozada 2006 *E, It,* 2007 *I, I, Geo, F,* 2008 *S, It, SA, F, It, I,* 2009 *E, E, E,* 2010 *It,* 2012 *F, F,* 2013 *E, E, Geo*
F Lucioni 1927 *GBR*
R Lucke 1975 *Ur, Par, Bra, CHL,* 1981 *C*

**FD Luna** 2011 *Ur*
**J Luna** 1995 *Par, CHL, Ur, R, It, F,* 1997 *Par, CHL*

**P Macadam** 1949 *F, F*
**AM Macome** 1990 *I, E,* 1995 *Ur, C*
**B Macome** 2012 *Ur, Bra, CHL, It, F, F,* 2013 *E, E, Geo, SA, NZ, NZ, A, E, It,* 2014 *I, A, NZ, A*
**B Madero** 2011 *CHL, Ur,* 2013 *E, Geo*
**RM Madero** 1978 *E, It,* 1979 *NZ, NZ, A, A,* 1980 *WXV, Fj, Fj, 1981 E, E, C,* 1982 *F, F, Sp,* 1983 *WXV, A, A,* 1985 *F, NZ,* 1986 *A, A,* 1987 *Ur, It, NZ, Sp, Ur, Par, CHL, A, A,* 1988 *F, F, F,* 1989 *It, NZ, NZ,* 1990 *E, E*
**L Maguire** 2014 *CHL*
**M Maineri** 2011 *CHL, Ur*
**L Makin** 1927 *GBR*
**A Mamanna** 1991 *Par,* 1997 *Par*
**G Manso** 2013 *CHL, Bra*
**J Manuel Belgrano** 1956 *OCC*
**R Marguery** 1991 *Ur, Bra,* 1993 *CHL, Par*
**R Martin** 1938 *CHL*
**RA Martin** 1994 *US, S, S, US, SA, SA,* 1995 *Ur, C, A, A, E, Sa, It, CHL, Ur, R, It, F,* 1996 *Ur, F, F, Ur, C, SA, SA, E,* 1997 *E, E, NZ, NZ, It, F, A, A,* 1998 *F, F, R, US, Ur, J, Par, CHL, Ur, It, W,* 1999 *W, W, S, I, W, Sa, J, I, F,* 2000 *I, A, A, SA, E,* 2001 *Ur, US, C, NZ, It, W, S, NZ,* 2002 *Ur, Par, CHL, F, E, SA, A, It, I,* 2003 *Par, CHL, Ur, F, SA, Ur, C, A, R, I*
**F Martin Aramburu** 2004 *CHL, Ven, W, NZ, F, I,* 2005 *It, SA, S, It,* 2006 *NZ,* 2007 *Geo, F,* 2008 *S, SA, F, It, I,* 2009 *E, S*
**J Martin Copella** 1989 *CHL, Par*
**C Martinez** 1969 *Ur, CHL,* 1970 *I, I*
**E Martinez** 1971 *CHL, Bra, Ur*
**O Martinez Basante** 1954 *F*
**M Martinez Mosquera** 1971 *CHL*
**RC Mastai** 1975 *F,* 1976 *W, NZ, NZ,* 1977 *F, F, Bra, Ur, Par, CHL,* 1980 *WXV*
**R Matarazzo** 1971 *SAG, SAG, Par, Ur,* 1972 *SAG, SAG,* 1973 *R, R, Par, Ur, CHL, I, S,* 1974 *F, F*
**PN Matera** 2013 *CHL, Bra, SA, SA, NZ, A, NZ, A, E, W, It,* 2014 *SA, SA*
**H Maurer** 1932 *JSB, JSB*
**L Maurette** 1948 *OCC, OCC*
**C Mazzini** 1977 *F, F*
**CJ McCarthy** 1910 *GBR*
**G McCormick** 1964 *Bra, CHL,* 1965 *Rho, OCC, OCC, CHL,* 1966 *SAG, SAG*
**M McCormick** 1927 *GBR*
**A Memoli** 1979 *Ur, Par, Bra*
**FJ Mendez** 1991 *Ur, Par, Bra,* 1992 *Sp, Sp*
**FE Méndez** 1990 *I, E,* 1991 *NZ, NZ, CHL, A, W,* 1992 *F, F, Sp, Sp, R, F,* 1994 *S, US, SA, SA,* 1995 *Ur, C, A, A, E, Sa, It, Par, CHL, Ur, R, It, F,* 1996 *SA, SA,* 1997 *E,* 1998 *F, F, R, US, Ur, C, It, F, W,* 1999 *W, W,* 2000 *I, A, A, SA, E,* 2001 *NZ, It, W, S, NZ,* 2002 *Ur, CHL, F, E, SA, A,* 2003 *F, F, SA, Fj, Ur, Nm, I,* 2004 *CHL, Ur, W, W, NZ, SA*
**H Mendez** 1967 *Ur, CHL*
**L Mendez** 1958 *Ur, Per, CHL,* 1959 *JSB*
**S Mendez** 2013 *Ur, CHL, Bra*
**CI Mendy** 1987 *Ur, Par, CHL, A, A,* 1988 *F, F, F, F,* 1989 *It, NZ, NZ, US,* 1990 *C,* 1991 *Ur, Bra*
**FJ Merello** 2007 *CHL,* 2010 *Ur, CHL*
**I Merlo** 1993 *Bra, CHL*
**P Merlo** 1985 *CHL, Par*
**SE Meson** 1987 *Par,* 1989 *Bra, Par, Ur, US,* 1990 *US, C, S, 1991 NZ, NZ, CHL, SA,* 1992 *F, F, Sp, R, F,* 1993 *J, Bra, Par, Ur, SA, SA,* 1994 *US, S, S, US,* 1995 *Ur, C, A, A,* 1996 *US, C,* 1997 *CHL*
**I Mieres** 2007 *CHL,* 2010 *Ur, CHL,* 2012 *It, F*
**BH Miguens** 1983 *WXV, A, A,* 1985 *F, F, NZ, NZ,* 1986 *F, F, A, A,* 1987 *Sp*
**E Miguens** 1975 *Ur, Par, CHL*
**H Miguens** 1969 *S, S, Ur, CHL,* 1970 *I, I,* 1971 *OCC,* 1972 *SAG, SAG,* 1973 *R, R, Par, Ur, Bra, CHL, I, S,* 1975 *F*
**J Miguens** 1982 *F,* 1985 *F, F,* 1986 *F, F, A, A*
**GE Milano** 1982 *F, F, Sp,* 1983 *WXV, A, A,* 1985 *F, Ur, CHL,*

*Par, NZ, NZ,* 1986 *F, F, A, A,* 1987 *Ur, Fj, Sp, Ur, CHL, A, A,* 1988 *F, F, F,* 1989 *It, NZ, NZ*
**A Mimesi** 1998 *J, Par, CHL*
**B Minguez** 1975 *Par, Bra, CHL,* 1979 *Ur, CHL, Par,* 1983 *WXV, A, A,* 1985 *Ur, CHL*
**R Miralles** 2011 *CHL,* 2012 *CHL, F*
**B Mitchelstein** 1936 *BI*
**E Mitchelstein** 1956 *OCC,* 1960 *F, F*
**C Mold** 1910 *GBR*
**LE Molina** 1985 *CHL,* 1987 *Ur, Fj, It, NZ,* 1989 *NZ, NZ, Bra, CHL, Par,* 1990 *C, E,* 1991 *W*
**M Molina** 1998 *Par, CHL, Ur*
**M Montero** 2012 *Ur, Bra, CHL, It, F, F, I,* 2013 *E, E,* 2014 *Ur, I, I, S, SA, SA, A, NZ*
**G Montes de Oca** 1961 *CHL, Bra, Ur*
**JS Montoya** 2014 *Ur, CHL, I, S*
**E Montpelat** 1948 *OCC, OCC*
**G Morales Oliver** 2001 *Ur, US, C*
**C Morea** 1951 *Ur, Bra, CHL*
**FR Morel** 1979 *A, A,* 1980 *WXV, Fj, Fj,* 1981 *E, E, C,* 1982 *F,* 1985 *F, F, Ur, Par, NZ, NZ,* 1986 *F, F, A,* 1987 *Ur, Fj*
**D Morgan** 1967 *CHL,* 1970 *I, I,* 1971 *SAG, SAG, OCC, OCC,* 1972 *SAG, SAG*
**E Morgan** 1969 *S, S,* 1972 *SAG, SAG,* 1973 *R, R, Par, Ur, Bra, CHL, I, S,* 1975 *F, F*
**G Morgan** 1977 *Bra, Ur, Par, CHL,* 1979 *Ur, Par, Bra*
**M Morgan** 1971 *SAG, OCC, OCC*
**JS Morganti** 1951 *Ur, Bra, CHL*
**M Moroni** 2014 *S*
**J Mostany** 1987 *Ur, Fj, NZ*
**R Moyano** 2011 *CHL, Ur,* 2012 *Ur, Bra,* 2014 *Ur, CHL*
**E Muliero** 1997 *CHL*
**S Muller** 1927 *GBR*
**R Muniz** 1975 *Par, Bra, CHL*

**M Nannini** 2002 *Ur, Par, CHL,* 2003 *Par, CHL*
**A Navajas** 1932 *JSB, JSB*
**E Naveyra** 1998 *CHL*
**G Nazassi** 1997 *CHL*
**ML Negri** 1979 *CHL, Bra*
**E Neri** 1960 *F, F,* 1961 *CHL, Bra, Ur,* 1964 *Ur, Bra, CHL,* 1965 *Rho, JSB, OCC,* 1966 *SAG, SAG*
**CM Neyra** 1975 *F, F,* 1976 *W, NZ, NZ,* 1983 *WXV*
**A Nicholson** 1979 *Ur, Par, Bra*
**HM Nicola** 1971 *SAG, OCC, OCC, CHL, Bra, Par, Ur,* 1975 *F, F,* 1978 *E, It,* 1979 *NZ, NZ*
**L Noguera Paz** 2014 *Ur, CHL, I, I, S, SA, NZ, NZ*
**EP Noriega** 1991 *Par,* 1992 *Sp, Sp, R, F,* 1993 *J, J, CHL, Par, Ur, SA, SA,* 1994 *US, S, S, US, SA, SA,* 1995 *Ur, C, A, A, E, Sa, It*
**JM Nuñez Piossek** 2001 *Ur, NZ,* 2002 *Ur, Par, CHL, A,* 2003 *Par, Ur, F, SA, Ur, C, A, R, I,* 2004 *CHL, Ur, W, W,* 2005 *It, It,* 2006 *W, W, NZ, E, F,* 2008 *S, SA*

**R Ochoa** 1956 *OCC*
**M Odriozola** 1961 *CHL, Ur*
**J O'Farrell** 1948 *OCC,* 1951 *Ur, Bra,* 1956 *OCC*
**U O'Farrell** 1951 *Ur, Bra, CHL*
**C Ohanian** 1998 *Par, Ur*
**C Olivera** 1958 *Ur, Per, CHL,* 1959 *JSB, JSB*
**R Olivieri** 1960 *F, F,* 1961 *CHL, Bra, Ur*
**J Orengo** 1996 *Ur,* 1997 *Ur, R, It,* 1998 *F, F, R, US, C, F, W,* 1999 *W,* 2000 *A, SA, E,* 2001 *Ur, US, C, NZ, W, S, NZ,* 2002 *F, E, SA, A, It, I,* 2003 *F, SA, Ur, C, A, I,* 2004 *W, W*
**JP Orlandi** 2008 *F, It, I,* 2009 *E, E,* 2012 *SA, NZ, A, NZ, A,* 2013 *SA, NZ, NZ, A, E*
**M Orlando** 2012 *Ur, Bra, CHL,* 2013 *E, E, Geo,* 2014 *Ur, I, S*
**J Ortega Desio** 2012 *Ur, Bra, CHL,* 2014 *Ur, CHL, I, I, S, A*
**C Orti** 1949 *F, F*
**L Ortiz** 2003 *Par, CHL, Ur*
**A Orzabal** 1974 *F, F*
**L Ostiglia** 1999 *W, W, S, I, W, J, F,* 2001 *NZ, It, W, S,* 2002 *E, SA,* 2003 *Par, CHL, Ur, F, SA, Nm, I,* 2004 *W, W, NZ, F, I, SA,* 2007 *F, Nm, I, S, SA*
**B Otaño** 1960 *F, F, F,* 1961 *CHL, Bra, Ur,* 1964 *Ur, Bra, CHL,*

1965 *Rho, JSB, OCC, OCC, CHL,* 1966 *SAG, SAG,* 1968 *W, W,* 1969 *S, S, Ur, CHL,* 1970 *I, I,* 1971 *SAG, OCC, OCC*
**J Otaola** 1970 *I,* 1971 *CHL, Bra, Par, Ur,* 1974 *F, F*

**M Pacheco** 1938 *CHL*
**RL Pacheco** 2010 *Ur, CHL*
**A Palma** 1949 *F, F,* 1952 *I, I,* 1954 *F, F*
**D Palma** 2012 *Ur, CHL*
**JMC Palma** 1982 *F, Sp,* 1983 *WXV, A, A*
**R Palma** 1985 *CHL, Par*
**M Palou** 1996 *US, Ur*
**F Panessi** 2013 *Ur, CHL*
**M Parra** 1975 *Ur, Bra, CHL*
**A Pasalagua** 1927 *GBR, GBR*
**M Pascual** 1965 *Rho, JSB, OCC, OCC, CHL,* 1966 *SAG, SAG,* 1967 *Ur, CHL,* 1968 *W, W,* 1969 *S, S, Ur, CHL,* 1970 *I, I,* 1971 *SAG, SAG, OCC, OCC*
**HR Pascuali** 1936 *BI*
**H Pasman** 1936 *CHL*
**R Passaglia** 1977 *Bra, Ur, CHL,* 1978 *E, It*
**G Paz** 1979 *Ur, CHL, Par, Bra,* 1983 *CHL, Par, Ur*
**J Paz** 2013 *Ur, CHL, Bra*
**JJ Paz** 1991 *Ur, Bra*
**S Peretti** 1993 *Bra, Par, SA*
**L Pereyra** 2010 *Ur, CHL*
**N Perez** 1968 *W*
**RN Perez** 1992 *F, F, Sp, R, F,* 1993 *Bra, Par, Ur, SA,* 1995 *Ur, R, It, F,* 1996 *US, Ur, C, SA, SA,* 1998 *Ur,* 1999 *I*
**J Perez Cobo** 1979 *NZ, NZ,* 1980 *Fj,* 1981 *E, E, C*
**M Peri Brusa** 1998 *CHL*
**R Pesce** 1958 *Ur, Per, CHL*
**TA Petersen** 1978 *E, It,* 1979 *NZ, NZ, A, A,* 1980 *Fj, Fj,* 1981 *E, E, C,* 1982 *F,* 1983 *WXV, A, A,* 1985 *F, F, Ur, CHL, Par, NZ, NZ,* 1986 *F, F, A*
**AD Petrilli** 2004 *SA,* 2005 *J*
**J Petrone** 1949 *F, F*
**R Petti** 1995 *Par, CHL*
**M Pfister** 1994 *SA, SA,* 1996 *F,* 1998 *R, Ur, J*
**S Phelan** 1997 *Ur, CHL, R, It,* 1998 *F, F, R, US, C, It,* 1999 *S, I, W, Sa, J, I, F,* 2000 *I, A, SA, E,* 2001 *NZ, It, W, S, NZ,* 2002 *Ur, Par, CHL, F, E, SA, A, It, I,* 2003 *CHL, Ur, F, SA, Fj, C, A, R*
**A Phillips** 1948 *OCC,* 1949 *F, F*
**JP Piccardo** 1981 *E,* 1983 *CHL, Par, Ur*
**A Pichot** 1995 *A, R, It, F,* 1996 *Ur, F, F,* 1997 *It, F, A, A,* 1998 *F, F, R, It, F, W,* 1999 *W, W, S, I, W, Sa, J, I, F,* 2000 *I, A, A, SA, E,* 2001 *Ur, US, C, NZ, It, W, S, NZ,* 2002 *F, E, SA, A, It, I,* 2003 *Ur, C, A, R, I,* 2004 *F, I, SA,* 2005 *It, SA, S, It,* 2006 *W, W, NZ, CHL, Ur, E, F,* 2007 *W, F, Nm, I, S, SA, F*
**G Pimentel** 1971 *Bra*
**R Pineo** 1954 *F*
**E Pittinari** 1991 *Ur, Par, Bra*
**SA Poet** 2013 *Ur, CHL, Bra*
**E Poggi** 1965 *JSB, OCC, OCC, CHL,* 1966 *SAG,* 1967 *Ur,* 1969 *Ur*
**C Pollano** 1927 *GBR*
**L Ponce** 2014 *Ur, CHL*
**S Ponce** 2007 *CHL*
**R Pont Lezica** 1951 *Ur, Bra, CHL*
**H Porta** 1971 *CHL, Bra, Par, Ur,* 1972 *SAG, SAG,* 1973 *R, R, Ur, Bra, CHL, I, S,* 1974 *F, F,* 1975 *F, F,* 1976 *W, NZ, NZ,* 1977 *F, F,* 1978 *E, It,* 1979 *NZ, NZ, A, A,* 1980 *WXV, Fj, Fj,* 1981 *E, E, C,* 1982 *F, F, Sp,* 1983 *A, A,* 1985 *F, F, Ur, CHL, Par, NZ, NZ,* 1986 *F, F, A,* 1987 *Fj, It, NZ, Sp, A, A,* 1990 *I, E, S*
**O Portillo** 1995 *Par, CHL,* 1997 *Par, CHL*
**J Posse** 1977 *Par*
**S Posse** 1991 *Par,* 1993 *Bra, CHL, Ur*
**B Postiglioni** 2012 *Ur, Bra, CHL, It, F, F, W,* 2013 *Geo,* 2014 *Ur, CHL, I, I, S, SA, A, A*
**C Promansio** 1995 *C,* 1996 *Ur, F, F, E,* 1997 *E, E, NZ, Ur,* 1998 *R, J*
**U Propato** 1956 *OCC*
**L Proto** 2010 *Ur, CHL*
**A Puccio** 1979 *CHL, Par, Bra*

**M Puigdeval** 1964 *Ur, Bra*
**J Pulido** 1960 *F*

**JC Queirolo** 1964 *Ur, Bra, CHL*
**G Quesada** 1996 *US, Ur, C, SA, E,* 1997 *E, E, NZ, NZ,* 1998 *F, R, US, C, It,* 1999 *W, S, I, W, Sa, J, I, F,* 2000 *I, SA, E,* 2001 *NZ, It, NZ,* 2002 *F, E, SA,* 2003 *F, SA, Ur, C, Nm, R, I*
**E Quetglas** 1965 *CHL*

**R Raimundez** 1959 *JSB, JSB*
**C Ramallo** 1979 *Ur, CHL, Par*
**S Ratcliff** 1936 *CHL*
**F Rave** 1997 *Par*
**M Reggiardo** 1996 *Ur, F, F, E,* 1997 *E, E, NZ, NZ, R, F, A, A,* 1998 *F, F, R, US, Ur, C, It, W,* 1999 *W, W, S, I, W, Sa, J, I, F,* 2000 *I, SA,* 2001 *NZ, It, W, S, NZ,* 2002 *F, E, SA, A, It, I,* 2003 *F, SA, Fj, US, Ur, A, Nm, I*
**A Reid** 1910 *GBR*
**C Reyes** 1927 *GBR, GBR, GBR*
**R Ricci** 1987 *Sp*
**A Riganti** 1927 *GBR, GBR, GBR*
**MA Righentini** 1989 *NZ*
**J Rios** 1960 *F, F*
**G Rivero** 1996 *Ur, US, Ur*
**G Roan** 2010 *Ur, CHL,* 2013 *E, E, Geo*
**T Roan** 2007 *CHL*
**F Robson** 1927 *GBR*
**M Roby** 1992 *Sp,* 1993 *J*
**A Rocca** 1989 *US,* 1990 *C, US, C, E,* 1991 *Ur, Bra*
**S Rocchia** 2013 *Ur, CHL, Bra*
**O Rocha** 1974 *F, F*
**D Rodriguez** 1998 *J, Par, CHL, Ur*
**D Rodriguez** 2002 *Ur, Par, CHL*
**EE Rodriguez** 1979 *NZ, NZ, A, A,* 1980 *WXV, Fj, Fj,* 1981 *E, E, C,* 1983 *WXV, A, A*
**F Rodriguez** 2007 *CHL*
**M Rodriguez** 2009 *E, W, S,* 2010 *S, S, F, It, F, I,* 2011 *W, E, R, S, Geo, NZ,* 2012 *SA, SA, NZ, NZ*
**A Rodriguez Jurado** 1965 *JSB, OCC, OCC, CHL,* 1966 *SAG, SAG,* 1968 *W, W,* 1969 *S, CHL,* 1970 *I,* 1971 *SAG,* 1973 *R, Par, Bra, CHL, I, S,* 1974 *F, F,* 1975 *F, F*
**A Rodriguez Jurado** 1927 *GBR, GBR, GBR, GBR,* 1932 *JSB, JSB,* 1936 *CHL, CHL*
**M Rodriguez Jurado** 1971 *SAG, OCC, CHL, Bra, Par, Ur*
**J Rojas** 2012 *Ur, Bra, CHL,* 2013 *It,* 2014 *CHL*
**L Roldan** 2001 *Ur, C*
**AS Romagnoli** 2004 *CHL, Ur, Ven*
**R Roncero** 1998 *J,* 2002 *Ur, Par, CHL,* 2003 *Fj, US, Nm, R,* 2004 *W, NZ, F, I,* 2005 *It, SA, S, It,* 2006 *W, W, NZ,* 2007 *W, F, Nm, I, S, SA, F,* 2008 *It, SA, F, It, I,* 2009 *E, E, W, S,* 2010 *S, S, F, It, F, I,* 2011 *W, E, R, S, NZ,* 2012 *It, SA, SA, NZ, A, NZ, A*
**S Rondinelli** 2005 *Sa*
**T Rosati** 2011 *CHL, Ur*
**S Rosatti** 1977 *Par, CHL*
**M Rospide** 2003 *Par, CHL, Ur*
**F Rossi** 1991 *Ur, Par, Bra,* 1998 *F*
**D Rotondo** 1997 *Par, CHL*
**MA Ruiz** 1997 *NZ, CHL, R, It, F, A, A,* 1998 *F, F, R, US, Ur, C, J, It, F, W,* 1999 *W, Sa, J, F,* 2002 *Ur, Par, CHL*

**I Saenz Lancuba** 2012 *Ur, Bra,* 2013 *Ur, CHL, Bra*
**JE Saffery** 1910 *GBR*
**CMS Sainz Trapaga** 1979 *Ur, Par, Bra*
**A Salinas** 1954 *F,* 1956 *OCC,* 1958 *Ur, CHL,* 1960 *F, F*
**S Salvat** 1987 *Ur, Fj, It,* 1988 *F,* 1989 *It, NZ,* 1990 *C, US, C, E, E,* 1991 *Ur, Par, Bra,* 1992 *Sp, F,* 1993 *Bra, CHL, Par, CHL, Ur, R, It, F*
**T Salzman** 1936 *BI, CHL, CHL*
**M Sambucetti** 2001 *Ur, US, C,* 2002 *Ur, CHL,* 2003 *Par, CHL, Fj,* 2005 *It, Sa,* 2009 *W*
**HA San Martin** 2009 *W, S*
**FN Sanchez** 2010 *Ur, CHL,* 2011 *R,* 2012 *SA, A, W, F, I,* 2013 *SA, SA, NZ, A, NZ, A, E, W, It,* 2014 *CHL, I, I, S, SA, SA, NZ, A, NZ, A*

E Verardo 1958 *CHL*, 1959 *JSB, JSB*, 1964 *Ur, Bra, CHL*, 1967 *Ur, CHL*
N Vergallo 2005 *Sa*, 2006 *CHL, Ur*, 2007 *I, I, CHL*, 2008 *S, S, It, SA, F, It, I*, 2009 *E*, 2010 *F, It, F, I*, 2011 *W, E, R, S, Geo, NZ*, 2012 *SA, SA, NZ, A, NZ, W, I*, 2013 *E, E*
AV Vernet Basualdo 2004 *SA*, 2005 *J*, 2006 *It*, 2007 *I, Geo, Nm, I, F*, 2008 *SA, It*, 2009 *E, E, S*
G Veron 1997 *Par*
M Viazzo 2010 *Ur, CHL*
J Vibart 1960 *F*
H Vidou 1987 *Par*, 1990 *C, US, E, E*, 1991 *NZ*
H Vidou 1960 *F*, 1961 *Bra*
C Viel Temperley 1993 *Bra, CHL, Par, Ur*, 1994 *US, S, S, US, SA, SA*, 1995 *Ur, C, A, A, E, Sa, It, Par, Ur, R, It, F*, 1996 *SA*, 1997 *E, NZ*
E Vila 1975 *Ur, Par, CHL*
M Villaluenga 2013 *CHL, Bra*
JJ Villar 2001 *Ur, US, C*, 2002 *Par, CHL*
D Villen 1998 *J, Par*
M Viola 1993 *Bra*
J Virasoro 1973 *R, R, Ur, Bra, CHL, S*
JL Visca 1985 *Par*

J Walther 1971 *OCC*
M Walther 1967 *Ur, CHL*, 1968 *W, W*, 1969 *S, S, Ur, CHL*, 1970 *I, I*, 1971 *SAG, OCC, OCC*, 1973 *Bra, CHL*, 1974 *F, F*
WA Watson 1910 *GBR*
W Weiss 2011 *Ur*
F Werner 1996 *US*, 1997 *Ur*
Wessek 1960 *F*
R Wilkins 1936 *CHL, CHL*
J Wittman 1971 *SAG, SAG, OCC, OCC, Ur*, 1972 *SAG, SAG*, 1973 *R*

L Yanez 1965 *Rho, JSB, OCC, OCC, CHL*, 1966 *SAG, SAG*, 1968 *W, W*, 1969 *S, S, Ur, CHL*, 1970 *I, I*, 1971 *SAG, OCC, OCC, Ur*
EP Yanguela 1956 *OCC*
M Yanguela 1987 *It*
B Yustini 1954 *F*, 1956 *OCC*

R Zanero 1990 *C*
E Zapiola 1998 *Par*
A Zappa 1927 *GBR*

Leonardo Senatore scores for Los Pumas as they beat Australia in Mendoza to record their first win in The Rugby Championship.

With the teams due to meet at RWC 2015, Australia will be desperate to get one over on England this November.

# AUSTRALIA

## AUSTRALIA'S 2013–14 TEST RECORD

| OPPONENTS | DATE | VENUE | RESULT |
|---|---|---|---|
| New Zealand | 19 Oct | A | Lost 41–33 |
| England | 2 Nov | A | Lost 20–13 |
| Italy | 9 Nov | A | Won 50–20 |
| Ireland | 16 Nov | A | Won 32–15 |
| Scotland | 23 Nov | A | Won 21–15 |
| Wales | 30 Nov | A | Won 30–26 |
| France | 7 Jun | H | Won 50–23 |
| France | 14 Jun | H | Won 6–0 |
| France | 21 Jun | H | Won 39–13 |
| New Zealand | 16 Aug | H | Drew 12–12 |
| New Zealand | 23 Aug | A | Lost 51–20 |
| South Africa | 6 Sep | H | Won 24–23 |
| Argentina | 13 Sep | H | Won 32–25 |
| South Africa | 27 Sep | A | Lost 28–10 |
| Argentina | 4 Oct | A | Lost 21–17 |
| New Zealand | 18 Oct | H | Lost 28–29 |

# AUSTRALIA'S FORTUNES FLUCTUATE

## By Iain Spragg

Getty Images

Australia's results in The Rugby Championship were mixed but they did end New Zealand's 17-Test winning run.

**The definition of** a successful season can be as subjective as it is elusive. Results alone do not always paint a complete picture and that was the case when Ewen McKenzie announced his resignation as Australia coach after the last-gasp 29–28 loss to New Zealand in the final Bledisloe Cup match of 2014.

There were indisputable highlights in the 16 Tests the Wallabies had played in the last 12 months under McKenzie. The All Blacks were held to a draw in Sydney to bring the old enemy's 17-match winning run to an abrupt end, there was a series whitewash of France, a first victory over the Springboks since 2012 and seven Test victories on the bounce, the Wallabies' longest successful sequence in international rugby since 2000 when they were world champions.

Conversely there were also significant low points. The campaign began with defeat by England at Twickenham and included an historic loss to

Argentina in Mendoza, Australia's first-ever reverse against the South Americans in The Rugby Championship and a first defeat to the Pumas since 1997. The side's 51–20 annihilation by New Zealand in Auckland was as comprehensive as it was chastening, while they also spurned the chance to claim South Africa's scalp in Cape Town and then to beat the All Blacks in Brisbane in what was Adam Ashley-Cooper's 100th Test.

Despite the Jekyll and Hyde nature of both results and performances, John Eales, the man who captained the Wallabies to victory over France in the Rugby World Cup final in 1999, believes the current Australian team will be in good shape to challenge for the trophy again at the 2015 instalment of the tournament.

"There was undeniably good and bad on show from the Wallabies through the year, but I've no doubt making the World Cup final in England in 2015 will be the minimum target for the coach and the players," Eales said. "Like any of the top-ranked teams, Australia have very high expectations and will have set their sights on winning the tournament.

"I thought there were plenty of positives to take from the trip to Europe. It was frustrating they weren't able to complete the Grand Slam for the first time since the Andrew Slack team of 1984 after they came unstuck against England at Twickenham, but it was still a very successful tour with four wins from five.

"The Wallabies have had trouble in Dublin in recent years but they beat Ireland comfortably and followed up with results against Scotland and then Wales in Cardiff. That consistency at the end of a long season was a major plus point.

"Australia thumped France 50–23 in the first of their three Tests back home and showed enterprise and a willingness to run with the ball and create space. It was dour in the 6–0 win in the second Test a week later because neither the French nor the Australians played with any daring or enterprise in that game, but the Wallabies signed off with a 39–13 victory in the last match and Ewen would have been satisfied with the performances overall.

"The displays in The Rugby Championship were a mixed bag. They made a great start against the All Blacks but finished poorly with back-to-back defeats on the road against South Africa and Argentina. It was impressive the way the team recovered from their heavy defeat against New Zealand at Eden Park to edge out the Springboks in Perth two weeks later and it's worth remembering Australia were unbeaten at home all year.

"Some people were surprised by the defeat in Argentina, but I felt it was the year the Pumas really emerged as a force in the Championship. Argentina pushed South Africa close twice and it was probably only a matter of time before they got their first win in the tournament."

AUSTRALIA

The European tour was not without incident off the pitch and in the wake of the team's 32–15 victory in Dublin, McKenzie suspended six players for one match for a breach of team discipline after they were involved in a late-night drinking session. The story briefly threatened to distract from the Wallabies' results on the pitch but blew over when a team shorn of the culprits triumphed at Murrayfield.

"Players will celebrate after matches," Eales said. "But only they know whether they stepped over a line because each dressing room has its own rules and culture. It's difficult to judge from the outside but I was pleased with the reaction in terms of getting a result against Scotland that weekend."

Australia started the November tour with a change of captaincy when McKenzie decided to relieve James Horwill of the armband and promote Brumbies number 8 Ben Mowen into the role. Mowen led the side for five Tests but when he confirmed he was quitting Super Rugby at the end of the 2014 campaign to ply his trade in Europe (subsequently signing for Top 14 side Montpellier), the Wallabies needed a new captain.

The coach turned to veteran hooker Stephen Moore but his reign was cut cruelly short when he suffered an anterior knee ligament injury after only two minutes of his first game in charge against the French. McKenzie once again was in need of a replacement leader and it was 22-year-old Waratahs flanker Michael Hooper who got the job, the third player to skipper the Wallabies in the season.

"It was a shame to lose Ben from the Test team, but it's a fully professional game these days and it is every player's prerogative to play wherever they choose in the world," Eales said. "Everyone is aware of the ARU's policy of only picking home-based players for the Wallabies and although that means we sometimes lose players, you have to be philosophical about it.

"Some worry about rich clubs targeting more Wallaby players but it's not exclusively an Australian issue. There's an element of sadness when you see players like Matt Giteau collecting the Top 14 Player of the Year award after a great season with Toulon because he's still only 32 and I think he left Australia too early, but the Wallabies will survive losing one or two players.

"Michael has started really well as captain. You've got to remember he's one of the youngest guys in the team but he came in and has shown a great willingness and capacity to learn. He'll be better for the experience and the Wallabies a stronger side going forward."

The 2013–14 campaign was McKenzie's first full year at the helm following his appointment as the successor to Robbie Deans. His side's record of two victories and a draw in six outings in the 2014 Rugby

Championship was a marginal improvement on the Wallabies' return in the tournament a year earlier and his overall record of nine wins in 16 Tests significantly superior to what Australia had achieved in recent years.

"Ewen came in at a difficult time for the Australian team in 2013," said Eales. "They'd just lost the series to the Lions and the side wasn't in a particularly good place.

"A lot of players really progressed under his coaching regime. Aside from what I've already said about his captaincy, Hooper was excellent. Openside is a tough position but I felt he really added something to the Wallaby pack at seven and showed resilience in every game. I was impressed by James Slipper at prop. His game has developed enormously in the last year and his work-rate and consistency were high throughout. Tevita Kuridrani came into the team in 2013 and made a real impact. His all-round game was excellent and he looks like a great find.

"The unexpected resignation of Ewen meant a new coach was required for the Spring tour leading into Rugby World Cup 2015. Fortunately for the Wallabies Michael Cheika was coming off a successful Super Rugby tournament with the Waratahs and was available and very keen to take on the challenging job."

Australia have their annual foray to Europe at the end of 2014 and a truncated Rugby Championship in 2015 to fine-tune their preparations for the World Cup. The 1991 and 1999 champions will face hosts England, Wales, Fiji and Uruguay in the initial stage of the tournament and it was not long after the draw was made that this was dubbed the 'Pool of Death'.

They kick off their tournament against the Fijians at the Millennium Stadium on 23 September and Eales, a veteran of three separate World Cup campaigns, concedes the Wallabies face a stern challenge as they bid to become the first country to lift the Webb Ellis Cup for a third time.

"There's no doubt they've got the toughest group," he said. "Any one of those top four teams are capable of beating each other and Michael has to make sure it's not the Wallabies who are on the wrong end of the results.

"It's been pretty even between England and Australia in recent years, so that's a tough one to call. The Wallabies have beaten Wales nine times on the bounce but most of them have only been by six points or so and while it's true to say Australia are Wales' bogey side, it would be wrong to get complacent. Warren Gatland is a bright coach who gets the best out of his players.

"I'd have to throw Fiji into the mix as well. The Pacific Islands teams usually have a rough ride when it comes to preparation and the availability of their best players. It will be different at the World Cup, Fiji will have had time together and assembled their strongest possible squad, and they'll definitely be capable of causing an upset."

AUSTRALIA

# AUSTRALIA INTERNATIONAL STATISTICS
## MATCH RECORDS UP TO 13 OCTOBER 2014

### MOST CONSECUTIVE TEST WINS

**10** 1991 Arg, WS, W, I, NZ, E, 1992 S 1,2, NZ 1,2
**10** 1998 NZ 3, Fj, Tg, Sm, F, E 2, 1999 I 1,2, E, SA 1
**10** 1999 NZ 2, R, I 3, US, W, SA 3, F, 2000 Arg 1,2,SA 1

### MOST CONSECUTIVE TESTS WITHOUT DEFEAT

| Matches | Wins | Draws | Period |
|---|---|---|---|
| 10 | 10 | 0 | 1991 to 1992 |
| 10 | 10 | 0 | 1998 to 1999 |
| 10 | 10 | 0 | 1999 to 2000 |

### MOST POINTS IN A MATCH
### BY THE TEAM

| Pts | Opponents | Venue | Year |
|---|---|---|---|
| 142 | Namibia | Adelaide | 2003 |
| 92 | Spain | Madrid | 2001 |
| 91 | Japan | Lyons | 2007 |
| 90 | Romania | Brisbane | 2003 |
| 76 | England | Brisbane | 1998 |
| 74 | Canada | Brisbane | 1996 |
| 74 | Tonga | Canberra | 1998 |
| 74 | W Samoa | Sydney | 2005 |
| 73 | W Samoa | Sydney | 1994 |
| 69 | Italy | Melbourne | 2005 |
| 68 | Russia | Nelson | 2011 |
| 67 | United States | Brisbane | 1990 |
| 67 | United States | Wellington | 2011 |

### MOST POINTS IN A MATCH
### BY A PLAYER

| Pts | Player | Opponents | Venue | Year |
|---|---|---|---|---|
| 42 | MS Rogers | Namibia | Adelaide | 2003 |
| 39 | MC Burke | Canada | Brisbane | 1996 |
| 30 | EJ Flatley | Romania | Brisbane | 2003 |
| 29 | SA Mortlock | South Africa | Melbourne | 2000 |
| 29 | JD O'Connor | France | Paris | 2010 |
| 28 | MP Lynagh | Argentina | Brisbane | 1995 |
| 27 | MJ Giteau | Fiji | Montpellier | 2007 |
| 25 | MC Burke | Scotland | Sydney | 1998 |
| 25 | MC Burke | France | Cardiff | 1999 |
| 25 | MC Burke | British/Irish Lions | Melbourne | 2001 |
| 25 | EJ Flatley* | Ireland | Perth | 2003 |
| 25 | CE Latham | Namibia | Adelaide | 2003 |
| 24 | MP Lynagh | United States | Brisbane | 1990 |
| 24 | MP Lynagh | France | Brisbane | 1990 |
| 24 | MC Burke | New Zealand | Melbourne | 1998 |
| 24 | MC Burke | South Africa | Twickenham | 1999 |

\* includes a penalty try

### MOST TRIES IN A MATCH
### BY THE TEAM

| Tries | Opponents | Venue | Year |
|---|---|---|---|
| 22 | Namibia | Adelaide | 2003 |
| 13 | South Korea | Brisbane | 1987 |
| 13 | Spain | Madrid | 2001 |
| 13 | Romania | Brisbane | 2003 |
| 13 | Japan | Lyons | 2007 |
| 12 | United States | Brisbane | 1990 |
| 12 | Wales | Brisbane | 1991 |
| 12 | Tonga | Canberra | 1998 |
| 12 | Samoa | Sydney | 2005 |
| 11 | Western Samoa | Sydney | 1994 |
| 11 | England | Brisbane | 1998 |
| 11 | Italy | Melbourne | 2005 |
| 11 | United States | Wellington | 2011 |

### BY A PLAYER

| Tries | Player | Opponents | Venue | Year |
|---|---|---|---|---|
| 5 | CE Latham | Namibia | Adelaide | 2003 |
| 4 | G Cornelsen | New Zealand | Auckland | 1978 |
| 4 | DI Campese | United States | Sydney | 1983 |
| 4 | JS Little | Tonga | Canberra | 1998 |
| 4 | CE Latham | Argentina | Brisbane | 2000 |
| 4 | LD Tuqiri | Italy | Melbourne | 2005 |

## MOST CONVERSIONS IN A MATCH
### BY THE TEAM

| Cons | Opponents | Venue | Year |
|------|-----------|-------|------|
| 16 | Namibia | Adelaide | 2003 |
| 12 | Spain | Madrid | 2001 |
| 11 | Romania | Brisbane | 2003 |
| 10 | Japan | Lyons | 2007 |
| 9 | Canada | Brisbane | 1996 |
| 9 | Fiji | Parramatta | 1998 |
| 9 | Russia | Nelson | 2011 |
| 8 | Italy | Rome | 1988 |
| 8 | United States | Brisbane | 1990 |
| 7 | Canada | Sydney | 1985 |
| 7 | Tonga | Canberra | 1998 |
| 7 | Samoa | Sydney | 2005 |
| 7 | Italy | Melbourne | 2005 |
| 7 | Fiji | Canberra | 2010 |

### BY A PLAYER

| Cons | Player | Opponents | Venue | Year |
|------|--------|-----------|-------|------|
| 16 | MS Rogers | Namibia | Adelaide | 2003 |
| 11 | EJ Flatley | Romania | Brisbane | 2003 |
| 10 | MC Burke | Spain | Madrid | 2001 |
| 9 | MC Burke | Canada | Brisbane | 1996 |
| 9 | JA Eales | Fiji | Parramatta | 1998 |
| 9 | JD O'Connor | Russia | Nelson | 2011 |
| 8 | MP Lynagh | Italy | Rome | 1988 |
| 8 | MP Lynagh | United States | Brisbane | 1990 |
| 7 | MP Lynagh | Canada | Sydney | 1985 |
| 7 | SA Mortlock | Japan | Lyons | 2007 |

## MOST DROP GOALS IN A MATCH
### BY THE TEAM

| Drops | Opponents | Venue | Year |
|-------|-----------|-------|------|
| 3 | England | Twickenham | 1967 |
| 3 | Ireland | Dublin | 1984 |
| 3 | Fiji | Brisbane | 1985 |

### BY A PLAYER

| Drops | Player | Opponents | Venue | Year |
|-------|--------|-----------|-------|------|
| 3 | PF Hawthorne | England | Twickenham | 1967 |
| 2 | MG Ella | Ireland | Dublin | 1984 |
| 2 | DJ Knox | Fiji | Brisbane | 1985 |

## MOST PENALTIES IN A MATCH
### BY THE TEAM

| Penalties | Opponents | Venue | Year |
|-----------|-----------|-------|------|
| 8 | South Africa | Twickenham | 1999 |
| 7 | New Zealand | Sydney | 1999 |
| 7 | France | Cardiff | 1999 |
| 7 | Wales | Cardiff | 2001 |
| 7 | England | Twickenham | 2008 |
| 6 | New Zealand | Sydney | 1984 |
| 6 | France | Sydney | 1986 |
| 6 | England | Brisbane | 1988 |
| 6 | Argentina | Buenos Aires | 1997 |
| 6 | Ireland | Perth | 1999 |
| 6 | France | Paris | 2000 |
| 6 | British/Irish Lions | Melbourne | 2001 |
| 6 | New Zealand | Sydney | 2004 |
| 6 | Italy | Padua | 2008 |
| 6 | New Zealand | Sydney | 2009 |
| 6 | South Africa | Brisbane | 2010 |
| 6 | Italy | Florence | 2010 |
| 6 | Wales | Melbourne | 2012 |
| 6 | Argentina | Rosario | 2012 |
| 6 | New Zealand | Brisbane | 2012 |

### BY A PLAYER

| Pens | Player | Opponents | Venue | Year |
|------|--------|-----------|-------|------|
| 8 | MC Burke | South Africa | Twickenham | 1999 |
| 7 | MC Burke | New Zealand | Sydney | 1999 |
| 7 | MC Burke | France | Cardiff | 1999 |
| 7 | MC Burke | Wales | Cardiff | 2001 |
| 6 | MP Lynagh | France | Sydney | 1986 |
| 6 | MP Lynagh | England | Brisbane | 1988 |
| 6 | DJ Knox | Argentina | Buenos Aires | 1997 |
| 6 | MC Burke | France | Paris | 2000 |
| 6 | MC Burke | British/Irish Lions | Melbourne | 2001 |
| 6 | MJ Giteau | England | Twickenham | 2008 |
| 6 | MJ Giteau | New Zealand | Sydney | 2009 |
| 6 | BS Barnes | Italy | Florence | 2010 |
| 6 | MJ Harris | Argentina | Rosario | 2012 |

**AUSTRALIA**

# CAREER RECORDS

## MOST CAPPED PLAYERS

| Caps | Player | Career Span |
|---|---|---|
| 139 | GM Gregan | 1994 to 2007 |
| 116 | NC Sharpe | 2002 to 2012 |
| 111 | GB Smith | 2000 to 2013 |
| 102 | SJ Larkham | 1996 to 2007 |
| 101 | DI Campese | 1982 to 1996 |
| 99 | AP Ashley-Cooper | 2005 to 2014 |
| 92 | MJ Giteau | 2002 to 2011 |
| 92 | ST Moore | 2005 to 2014 |
| 86 | JA Eales | 1991 to 2001 |
| 86 | JWC Roff | 1995 to 2004 |
| 81 | MC Burke | 1993 to 2004 |
| 80 | TJ Horan | 1989 to 2000 |
| 80 | SA Mortlock | 2000 to 2009 |
| 79 | DJ Wilson | 1992 to 2000 |
| 79 | PR Waugh | 2000 to 2009 |
| 78 | CE Latham | 1998 to 2007 |
| 75 | JS Little | 1989 to 2000 |
| 75 | RD Elsom | 2005 to 2011 |
| 72 | MP Lynagh | 1984 to 1995 |
| 72 | JA Paul | 1998 to 2006 |

## MOST CONSECUTIVE TESTS

| Tests | Player | Span |
|---|---|---|
| 62 | JWC Roff | 1996 to 2001 |
| 46 | PN Kearns | 1989 to 1995 |
| 44 | GB Smith | 2003 to 2006 |
| 42 | DI Campese | 1990 to 1995 |
| 37 | PG Johnson | 1959 to 1968 |
| 35 | JA Slipper | 2012 to 2014 |

## MOST TESTS AS CAPTAIN

| Tests | Captain | Span |
|---|---|---|
| 59 | GM Gregan | 2001 to 2007 |
| 55 | JA Eales | 1996 to 2001 |
| 36 | NC Farr Jones | 1988 to 1992 |
| 29 | SA Mortlock | 2006 to 2009 |
| 24 | RD Elsom | 2009 to 2011 |
| 19 | AG Slack | 1984 to 1987 |
| 16 | JE Thornett | 1962 to 1967 |
| 16 | GV Davis | 1969 to 1972 |
| 16 | JE Horwill | 2011 to 2013 |

## MOST POINTS IN TESTS

| Points | Player | Tests | Career |
|---|---|---|---|
| 911 | MP Lynagh | 72 | 1984 to 1995 |
| 878 | MC Burke | 81 | 1993 to 2004 |
| 684 | MJ Giteau | 92 | 2002 to 2011 |
| 489 | SA Mortlock | 80 | 2000 to 2009 |
| 315 | DI Campese | 101 | 1982 to 1996 |
| 260 | PE McLean | 30 | 1974 to 1982 |
| 249* | JW Roff | 86 | 1995 to 2004 |
| 223 | JD O'Connor | 44 | 2008 to 2013 |
| 200 | CE Latham | 78 | 1998 to 2007 |
| 200 | BS Barnes | 51 | 2007 to 2013 |
| 187* | EJ Flatley | 38 | 1997 to 2005 |
| 173 | JA Eales | 86 | 1991 to 2001 |

\* Roff and Flatley's totals include a penalty try

## MOST TRIES IN TESTS

| Tries | Player | Tests | Career |
|---|---|---|---|
| 64 | DI Campese | 101 | 1982 to 1996 |
| 40 | CE Latham | 78 | 1998 to 2007 |
| 31* | JW Roff | 86 | 1995 to 2004 |
| 30 | TJ Horan | 80 | 1989 to 2000 |
| 30 | LD Tuqiri | 67 | 2003 to 2008 |
| 30 | DA Mitchell | 63 | 2005 to 2012 |
| 29 | MC Burke | 81 | 1993 to 2004 |
| 29 | SA Mortlock | 80 | 2000 to 2009 |
| 29 | MJ Giteau | 92 | 2002 to 2011 |
| 28 | AP Ashley-Cooper | 99 | 2005 to 2014 |
| 25 | SJ Larkham | 102 | 1996 to 2007 |
| 24 | BN Tune | 47 | 1996 to 2006 |
| 21 | JS Little | 75 | 1989 to 2000 |

\* Roff's total includes a penalty try

## MOST CONVERSIONS IN TESTS

| Cons | Player | Tests | Career |
|---|---|---|---|
| 140 | MP Lynagh | 72 | 1984 to 1995 |
| 104 | MC Burke | 81 | 1993 to 2004 |
| 103 | MJ Giteau | 92 | 2002 to 2011 |
| 61 | SA Mortlock | 80 | 2000 to 2009 |
| 39 | JD O'Connor | 44 | 2008 to 2013 |
| 31 | JA Eales | 86 | 1991 to 2001 |
| 30 | EJ Flatley | 38 | 1997 to 2005 |
| 27 | PE McLean | 30 | 1974 to 1982 |
| 27 | MS Rogers | 45 | 2002 to 2006 |
| 20 | JW Roff | 86 | 1995 to 2004 |
| 19 | DJ Knox | 13 | 1985 to 1997 |
| 19 | QS Cooper | 50 | 2008 to 2013 |

## MOST PENALTY GOALS IN TESTS

| Penalties | Player | Tests | Career |
|---|---|---|---|
| 177 | MP Lynagh | 72 | 1984 to 1995 |
| 174 | MC Burke | 81 | 1993 to 2004 |
| 107 | MJ Giteau | 92 | 2002 to 2011 |
| 74 | SA Mortlock | 80 | 2000 to 2009 |
| 62 | PE McLean | 30 | 1974 to 1982 |
| 34 | JA Eales | 86 | 1991 to 2001 |
| 34 | EJ Flatley | 38 | 1997 to 2005 |
| 34 | BS Barnes | 51 | 2007 to 2013 |
| 31 | CP Leali'ifano | 13 | 2013 to 2013 |
| 25 | JD O'Connor | 44 | 2008 to 2013 |
| 23 | MC Roebuck | 23 | 1991 to 1993 |

## MOST DROP GOALS IN TESTS

| Drops | Player | Tests | Career |
|---|---|---|---|
| 9 | PF Hawthorne | 21 | 1962 to 1967 |
| 9 | MP Lynagh | 72 | 1984 to 1995 |
| 8 | MG Ella | 25 | 1980 to 1984 |
| 8 | BS Barnes | 51 | 2007 to 2013 |
| 4 | PE McLean | 30 | 1974 to 1982 |
| 4 | MJ Giteau | 92 | 2002 to 2011 |

# RUGBY CHAMPIONSHIP (FORMERLY TRI NATIONS) RECORDS

AUSTRALIA

| RECORD | DETAIL | HOLDER | SET |
|---|---|---|---|
| Most points in season | 162 | in six matches | 2010 |
| Most tries in season | 17 | in six matches | 2010 |
| Highest score | 54 | 54–17 v Argentina (a) | 2013 |
| Biggest win | 49 | 49–0 v S Africa (h) | 2006 |
| Highest score conceded | 61 | 22–61 v S Africa (a) | 1997 |
| Biggest defeat | 45 | 8–53 v S Africa (a) | 2008 |
| Most appearances | 48 | GM Gregan | 1996 to 2007 |
| Most points in matches | 271 | MC Burke | 1996 to 2004 |
| Most points in season | 72 | MJ Giteau | 2009 |
| Most points in match | 24 | MC Burke | v N Zealand (h) 1998 |
| Most tries in matches | 10 | AP Ashley-Cooper | 2005 to 2014 |
| Most tries in season | 5 | I Folau | 2013 |
| Most tries in match | 3 | I Folau | v Argentina (a) 2013 |
| Most cons in matches | 36 | MJ Giteau | 2003 to 2010 |
| Most cons in season | 12 | SA Mortlock | 2006 |
| Most cons in match | 5 | SA Mortlock | v S Africa (h) 2006 |
| Most pens in matches | 65 | MC Burke | 1996 to 2004 |
| Most pens in season | 18 | CP Leali'ifano | 2013 |
| Most pens in match | 7 | MC Burke | v N Zealand (h) 1999 |

# MISCELLANEOUS RECORDS

| RECORD | HOLDER | DETAIL |
|--------|--------|--------|
| Longest Test Career | GM Cooke | 1932–1948 |
| Youngest Test Cap | BW Ford | 18 yrs 90 days in 1957 |
| Oldest Test Cap | AR Miller | 38 yrs 113 days in 1967 |

## CAREER RECORDS OF AUSTRALIAN INTERNATIONAL PLAYERS

## UP TO 13 OCTOBER 2014

| PLAYER<br>BACKS: | DEBUT | CAPS | T | C | P | D | PTS |
|------------------|-------|------|---|---|---|---|-----|
| AP Ashley-Cooper | 2005 v SA | 99 | 28 | 0 | 0 | 0 | 140 |
| BS Barnes | 2007 v J | 51 | 8 | 17 | 34 | 8 | 200 |
| KJ Beale | 2009 v W | 47 | 11 | 2 | 18 | 0 | 113 |
| PJJ Betham | 2013 v NZ | 2 | 1 | 0 | 0 | 0 | 5 |
| QS Cooper | 2008 v It | 50 | 7 | 19 | 15 | 2 | 124 |
| NM Cummins | 2012 v Arg | 15 | 6 | 0 | 0 | 0 | 30 |
| AS Faingaa | 2010 v NZ | 23 | 2 | 0 | 0 | 0 | 10 |
| C Feauai-Sautia | 2013 v SA | 2 | 2 | 0 | 0 | 0 | 10 |
| I Folau | 2013 v BI | 24 | 15 | 0 | 0 | 0 | 75 |
| BT Foley | 2013 v Arg | 13 | 1 | 17 | 15 | 0 | 84 |
| SW Genia | 2009 v NZ | 55 | 8 | 0 | 0 | 0 | 40 |
| MJ Harris | 2012 v S | 10 | 1 | 1 | 16 | 0 | 55 |
| RG Horne | 2010 v Fj | 22 | 4 | 0 | 0 | 0 | 20 |
| DAN Ioane | 2007 v W | 35 | 11 | 0 | 0 | 0 | 55 |
| RTRN Kuridrani | 2013 v NZ | 16 | 3 | 0 | 0 | 0 | 15 |
| CP Leali'ifano | 2013 v BI | 13 | 1 | 13 | 31 | 0 | 124 |
| PJ McCabe | 2010 v It | 24 | 5 | 0 | 0 | 0 | 25 |
| JD Mogg | 2013 v BI | 3 | 0 | 0 | 0 | 0 | 0 |
| LJ Morahan | 2012 v S | 1 | 0 | 0 | 0 | 0 | 0 |
| JD O'Connor | 2008 v It | 44 | 14 | 39 | 25 | 0 | 223 |
| NJ Phipps | 2011 v Sm | 23 | 1 | 0 | 0 | 0 | 5 |
| JM Tomane | 2012 v S | 11 | 3 | 0 | 0 | 0 | 15 |
| MP Toomua | 2013 v NZ | 19 | 3 | 0 | 0 | 0 | 15 |
| NW White | 2013 v NZ | 17 | 0 | 0 | 1 | 0 | 3 |

| | | | | | | | |
|---|---|---|---|---|---|---|---|
| BE Alexander | 2008 v F | 68 | 4 | 0 | 0 | 0 | 20 |
| STG Carter | 2014 v F | 7 | 0 | 0 | 0 | 0 | 0 |
| NL Charles | 2014 v F | 4 | 0 | 0 | 0 | 0 | 0 |
| PJM Cowan | 2009 v It | 10 | 0 | 0 | 0 | 0 | 0 |
| DA Dennis | 2012 v S | 18 | 0 | 0 | 0 | 0 | 0 |
| KP Douglas | 2012 v Arg | 14 | 0 | 0 | 0 | 0 | 0 |
| SM Faingaa | 2010 v Fj | 31 | 0 | 0 | 0 | 0 | 0 |
| SM Fardy | 2013 v NZ | 19 | 0 | 0 | 0 | 0 | 0 |
| LB Gill | 2012 v NZ | 15 | 0 | 0 | 0 | 0 | 0 |
| JE Hanson | 2012 v NZ | 5 | 0 | 0 | 0 | 0 | 0 |
| S Higginbotham | 2010 v F | 30 | 3 | 0 | 0 | 0 | 15 |
| MJ Hodgson | 2010 v Fj | 8 | 0 | 0 | 0 | 0 | 0 |
| MK Hooper | 2012 v S | 37 | 7 | 0 | 0 | 0 | 35 |
| JE Horwill | 2007 v Fj | 55 | 6 | 0 | 0 | 0 | 30 |
| LM Jones | 2014 v F | 1 | 0 | 0 | 0 | 0 | 0 |
| SM Kepu | 2008 v It | 47 | 0 | 0 | 0 | 0 | 0 |
| BJ McCalman | 2010 v SA | 34 | 2 | 0 | 0 | 0 | 10 |
| JW Mann-Rea | 2014 v Arg | 1 | 0 | 0 | 0 | 0 | 0 |
| ST Moore | 2005 v Sm | 92 | 5 | 0 | 0 | 0 | 25 |
| BSC Mowen | 2013 v BI | 15 | 1 | 0 | 0 | 0 | 5 |
| DP Palmer | 2012 v S | 1 | 0 | 0 | 0 | 0 | 0 |
| WL Palu | 2006 v E | 54 | 1 | 0 | 0 | 0 | 5 |
| DW Pocock | 2008 v NZ | 46 | 4 | 0 | 0 | 0 | 20 |
| SUT Polota-Nau | 2005 v E | 50 | 2 | 0 | 0 | 0 | 10 |
| BA Robinson | 2006 v SA | 68 | 3 | 0 | 0 | 0 | 15 |
| PJ Ryan | 2012 v F | 3 | 0 | 0 | 0 | 0 | 0 |
| JW Schatz | 2014 v Arg | 1 | 0 | 0 | 0 | 0 | 0 |
| RA Simmons | 2010 v SA | 45 | 0 | 0 | 0 | 0 | 0 |
| ST Sio | 2013 v NZ | 5 | 0 | 0 | 0 | 0 | 0 |
| WRJ Skelton | 2014 v F | 4 | 1 | 0 | 0 | 0 | 5 |
| JA Slipper | 2010 v E | 58 | 0 | 0 | 0 | 0 | 0 |
| S Timani | 2011 v Sm | 18 | 0 | 0 | 0 | 0 | 0 |
| LS Weeks | 2014 v F | 2 | 0 | 0 | 0 | 0 | 0 |

**AUSTRALIA** (side margin)

# AUSTRALIAN INTERNATIONAL PLAYERS
## UP TO 13 OCTOBER 2014

Entries in square brackets denote matches played in RWC Finals.

**Abrahams, A M F** (NSW) 1967 NZ, 1968 NZ 1, 1969 W

**Adams, N J** (NSW) 1955 NZ 1

**Adamson, R W** (NSW) 1912 US

**Alexander, B E** (ACT) 2008 F 1(R), 2(R), It, F 3, 2009 It 1(R), 2, F(R), NZ 1(R), SA 1(R), NZ 2(t&R), SA 2, 3, NZ 3, 4, E, I, S, W, 2010 Fj, NZ 4, W, E 3, It, F, 2011 Sm, SA 1, NZ 1, SA 2, NZ 2, [It, I, US, SA, NZ, W(R)], W(R), 2012 S(R), W1(R), 2(R), 3(R), NZ2, SA1, Arg1, SA2, Arg2, E, It, W4, 2013 BI1, 2, 3, NZ1, 2, SA1(R), Arg1, SA2, Arg2, NZ3, E, It, S(R), W(R), 2014 NZ1(R), 2(R), SA1(R), Arg1(R), SA2(R), Arg2(R)

**Allan, T** (NSW) 1946 NZ 1, M, NZ 2, 1947 NZ 2, S, I, W, 1948 E, F, 1949 M 1, 2, 3, NZ 1, 2

**Anderson, R P** (NSW) 1925 NZ 1

Anlezark, E A (NSW) 1905 NZ
Armstrong, A R (NSW) 1923 NZ 1, 2
Ashley-Cooper, A P (ACT, NSW) 2005 SA4(R), 2007 W1, 2, Fj, SA1(R), NZ1, SA2, NZ2, [J, Fj, C, E], 2008 F1(R), 2, SA1, NZ1, 2, SA3, NZ3, 4, It, E, F3, 2009 It1(R), 2(t&R), F, NZ1, SA1, NZ2, SA2, 3, NZ3, 4, E, I, S, W, 2010 Fj, E2(R), I, SA1, NZ1, 2, SA2, 3, NZ3, 4, W, E3, It, F, 2011 Sm, SA1, NZ1, SA2, NZ2, [It, I, US, Ru, SA, NZ, W], W, 2012 W1, 2, 3, NZ1, 2, SA1, Arg1, SA2, NZ3, F, E, It, W4, 2013 BI 1, 2, 3, NZ1, 2, SA1, Arg1, SA2, Arg2, NZ3, E, It, I, W, 2014 F1, 2, 3, NZ1, 2, SA1, 2, Arg2
Austin, L R (NSW) 1963 E

Baker, R L (NSW) 1904 BI 1, 2
Baker, W H (NSW) 1914 NZ 1, 2, 3
Ballesty, J P (NSW) 1968 NZ 1, 2, F, I, S, 1969 W, SA 2, 3, 4,
Bannon, D P (NSW) 1946 M
Bardsley, E J (NSW) 1928 NZ 1, 3, M (R)
Barker, H S (NSW) 1952 Fj 1, 2, NZ 1, 2, 1953 SA 4, 1954 Fj 1, 2
Barnes, B S (Q, NSW) 2007 [J(R), W, Fj, E], 2008 I, F1, 2, SA1, NZ1, 2, SA2, NZ4(R), It, 2009 It1, 2, F, NZ1, SA1, NZ2, SA3, NZ3, 2010 E1, SA1(R), NZ1, SA3(R), NZ3(t&R), 4(R), W(R), E3(R), It, F, 2011 [US(R), Ru, SA(R), NZ(t&R), W], W, 2012 S, W1, 2, 3, NZ1, 2, SA1, Arg1, SA2, F(R), E, It, W4, 2013 BI 1
Barnett, J T (NSW) 1907 NZ 1, 2, 3, 1908 W, 1909 E
Barry, M J (Q) 1971 SA 3
Bartholomeusz, M A (ACT) 2002 It (R)
Barton, R F D (NSW) 1899 BI 3
Batch, P G (Q) 1975 S, W, 1976 E, Fj 1, 2, 3, F 1, 2, 1978 W 1, 2, NZ 1, 2, 3, 1979 Arg 2
Batterham, R P (NSW) 1967 NZ, 1970 S
Battishall, B R (NSW) 1973 E
Baxter, A J (NSW) 1949 M 1, 2, 3, NZ 1, 2, 1951 NZ 1, 2, 1952 NZ 1, 2
Baxter, A K E (NSW) 2003 NZ 2(R), [Arg, R, I(R), S(R), NZ(R), E], 2004 S1, 2, E1, PI, NZ1, SA1, NZ2, SA2, S3, F, S4, E2, 2005 It, F1, SA1, 2, 3(R), NZ1, SA4, NZ2, F2, E, I(R), W(R), 2006 E1(R), 2(R), I1(R), NZ1(R), SA1(R), NZ3(R), SA3(R), W, It, I2, S(R), 2007 Fj, SA1(R), NZ1(R), SA2(R), NZ2(R), [J, W(R), C, E(R)], 2008 I(R), F1, 2, SA1, NZ1, 2, SA2(R), 3(R), NZ3, 4, E, F3, W, 2009 It1, F, NZ1, SA1, NZ2
Baxter, T J (Q) 1958 NZ 3
Beale, K J (NSW, MR) 2009 W(R), 2010 Fj, E1(R), I(R), NZ1(R), 2, SA2, 3, NZ3, 4, W, E3, It, F, 2011 Sm(R), SA1, NZ1, SA2, NZ2, [It, I, US, SA, W], 2012 W3, NZ1, 2(R), SA1, Arg1(t&R), SA2, Arg2, NZ3, F, E, It, W4, 2013 BI 1(R), 2, 3, 2014 F1(R), 2(R), 3(R), NZ1, 2, SA1(R), Arg1(R), SA2(R)
Beith, B McN (NSW) 1914 NZ 3, 1920 NZ 1, 2, 3
Bell, K R (Q) 1968 S
Bell, M D (NSW) 1996 C
Bennett, W G (Q) 1931 M, 1933 SA 1, 2, 3,
Bermingham, J V (Q) 1934 NZ 1, 2, 1937 SA 1
Berne, J E (NSW) 1975 S
Besomo, K S (NSW) 1979 I 2
Betham, P J J (NSW) 2013 NZ3, 2014 Arg1
Betts, T N (Q) 1951 NZ2, 1954 Fj 2
Biilmann, R R (NSW) 1933 SA 2, 3, 4
Birt, R S W (Q) 1914 NZ2
Black, J W (NSW) 1985 C1, 2, NZ, Fj1
Blackwood, J G (NSW) 1922 M 1, NZ 1, 2, 3, 1923 M 1, NZ 1, 2, 3, 1924 NZ 1, 2, 3, 1925 NZ 1, 4, 1926 NZ 1, 2, 3, 1927 I, W, S, 1928 E, F
Blades, A T (NSW) 1996 S, I, W 3, 1997 NZ 1(R), E 1(R), SA 1(R), NZ 3, SA 2, Arg 1, 2, E 2, S, 1998 E 1, S 1, 2, NZ 1, SA 1, NZ 2, SA 2, NZ 3, Fj, WS, F, E 2, 1999 I 1(R), SA 2, NZ 2, [R, I 3, W, SA 3, F]
Blades, C D (NSW) 1997 E 1
Blake, R C (Q) 2006 E1, 2, NZ2, SA2, NZ3, SA3, W
Blair, M R (NSW) 1928 F, 1931 M, NZ
Bland, G V (NSW) 1928 NZ 3, M, 1932 NZ 1, 2, 3, 1933 SA 1, 2, 4, 5
Blomley, J (NSW) 1949 M 1, 2, 3, NZ 1, 2, 1950 BI 1, 2
Boland, S B (Q) 1899 BI 3, 4, 1903 NZ
Bond, G S G (ACT) 2001 SA 2(R), Sp (R), E (R), F, W
Bond, J H (NSW) 1920 NZ 1, 2, 3, 1921 NZ
Bondfield, C (NSW) 1925 NZ 2
Bonis, E T (Q) 1929 NZ 1, 2, 3, 1930 BI, 1931 M, NZ, 1932 NZ 1, 2, 3, 1933 SA 1, 2, 3, 4, 5, 1934 NZ 1, 2, 1936 NZ 1, 2, M, 1937 SA 1, 1938 NZ 1

Bonner, J E (NSW) 1922 NZ 1, 2, 3, 1923 M 1, 2, 3, 1924 NZ 1, 2
Bosler, J M (NSW) 1953 SA 1
Bouffler, R G (NSW) 1899 BI 3
Bourke, T K (Q) 1947 NZ 2
Bowden, R (NSW) 1926 NZ 4
Bowen, S (NSW) 1993 SA 1, 2, 3, 1995 [R], NZ 1, 2, 1996 C, NZ 1, SA 2
Bowers, A J A (NSW) 1923 M 2(R), 3, NZ, 3, 1925 NZ 1, 4, 1926 NZ 1, 1927 I
Bowman, T M (NSW) 1998 E 1, S 1, 2, NZ 1, SA 1, NZ 2, SA 2, NZ 3, Fj, WS, F, E 2, 1999 I 1, 2, SA 2, [US]
Boyce, E S (NSW) 1962 NZ 1, 2, 1964 NZ 1, 2, 3, 1965 SA 1, 2, 1966 W, S, 1967 E, I 1, F, I 2
Boyce, J S (NSW) 1962 NZ 3, 4, 5, 1963 E, SA 1, 2, 3, 4, 1964 NZ 1, 3, 1965 SA 1, 2
Boyd, A (NSW) 1899 BI 3
Boyd, A F McC (Q) 1958 M 1
Brass, J E (NSW) 1966 BI 2, W, S, 1967 E, I 1, F, I 2, NZ, 1968 NZ 1, F, I, S
Breckenridge, J W (NSW) 1925 NZ 2(R), 3, 1927 I, W, S, 1928 E, F, 1929 NZ 1, 2, 3, 1930 BI
Brial, M C (NSW) 1993 F 1(R), 2, 1996 W 1(R), 2, C, NZ 1, SA 1, NZ 2, SA 2, It, I, W 3, 1997 NZ 2
Bridle, O L (V) 1931 M, 1932 NZ 1, 2, 3, 1933 SA 3, 4, 5, 1934 NZ 1, 2, 1936 NZ 1, 2, M
Broad, E G (Q) 1949 M 1
Brockhoff, J D (NSW) 1949 M 2, 3, NZ 1, 2, 1950 BI 1, 2, 1951 NZ 2, 3
Brown, B R (Q) 1972 NZ 1, 3
Brown, J V (NSW) 1956 SA 1, 2, 1957 NZ 1, 2, 1958 W, I, E, S, F
Brown, R C (NSW) 1975 E 1, 2
Brown, R N (WF) 2008 NZ3(R), 4, It, E, W, 2009 It1, F, NZ1, SA1, NZ2, SA2, S(R), 2010 Fj, E1, 2, I, SA1, NZ1, 2, SA2, 3(R), NZ3(R), E3(R)
Brown, S W (NSW) 1953 SA 2, 3, 4
Bryant, H (NSW) 1925 NZ 1, 3, 4
Buchan, A J (NSW) 1946 NZ 1, 2, 1947 NZ 1, 2, S, I, W, 1948 E, F, 1949 M 3
Buchanan, P N (NSW) 1923 M 2(R), 3
Bull, D (NSW) 1928 M
Buntine, H (NSW) 1923 NZ 1(R), 1924 NZ 2
Burdon, A (NSW) 1903 NZ, 1904 BI 1, 2, 1905 NZ
Burge, A B (NSW) 1907 NZ 3, 1908 W
Burge, P H (NSW) 1907 NZ 1, 2, 3
Burge, R (NSW) 1907 NZ 1, 2, 3(R), M (R)
Burgess, L (NSW) 2008 I, F1, 2, SA1, NZ1, 2, 4, It, E, F3, W, 2009 It1, 2, F, NZ1, SA1, NZ2, SA3, NZ3(R), S(R), W(R), 2010 Fj, E1, I, NZ1(R), SA3(R), NZ3(R), 4(R), W(R), E3(R), It, F(R), 2011 NZ2(R), [It(R), US(R), Ru, W(R)]
Burke, B T (NSW) 1988 S (R)
Burke, C T (NSW) 1946 NZ 2, 1947 NZ 1, 2, S, I, W, 1948 E, F, 1949 M 2, 3, NZ 1, 2, 1950 BI 1, 2, 1951 NZ 1, 2, 3, 1953 SA 2, 3, 4, 1954 Fj 1, 1955 NZ 1, 2, 3, 1956 SA 1, 2,
Burke, M C (NSW) 1993 SA 3(R), F 1, 1994 I 1, 2, It 1, 2, 1995 [C, R, E], NZ 1, 2, 1996 W 1, 2, C, NZ 1, SA 1, NZ 2, It, S, I, W 3, 1997 E 1, NZ 2, 1998 E 1, S 1, 2, NZ 1, SA 1, NZ 2, SA 2, NZ 3, 1999 I 2(R), E (R), SA 1, NZ 1, SA 2, NZ 2, [R, I 3, US, W, SA 3, F], 2000 F, S, E, 2001 BI 1(R), 2, 3, SA 1, NZ 1, SA 2, NZ 2, Sp, E, F, W, 2002 F 1, 2, NZ 1, SA 1, NZ 2, SA 2, Arg, I, E, It, 2003 SA 1, NZ 1, SA 2(R), NZ 2(R), [Arg, R, Nm(R), I], 2004 S1(R), PI(R), SA1(R), NZ2(t&R), SA2(R)
Burke, M P (NSW) 1984 E F, 1985 C 1, 2, NZ, Fj 1, 2, 1986 It (R), F, Arg 1, 2, NZ 1, 2, 3, 1987 SK, [US, J, I, F, W], NZ, Arg 1, 2
Burnet, D R (NSW) 1972 F 1, 2, NZ 1, 2, 3, Fj
Butler, O F (NSW) 1969 SA 1, 2, 1970 S, 1971 SA 2, 3, F 1, 2

Calcraft, W J (NSW) 1985 C 1, 1986 It, Arg 2
Caldwell, B C (NSW) 1928 NZ 3
Cameron, A S (NSW) 1951 NZ 1, 2, 3, 1952 Fj 1, 2, NZ 1, 2, 1953 SA 1, 2, 3, 4, 1954 Fj 1, 2, 1955 NZ 1, 2, 3, 1956 SA 1, 2, 1957 NZ 1, 1958 I
Campbell, A M (ACT) 2005 F1(R), 2006 It(R), I2(R), S
Campbell, J D (NSW) 1910 NZ 1, 2, 3
Campbell, W A (NSW) 1984 Fj, 1986 It, F, Arg 1, 2, NZ 1, 2, 3, 1987 SK, [E, US, J (R), I, F], NZ, 1988 E, 1989 BI 1, 2, 3, NZ, 1990 NZ 2, 3
Campese, D I (ACT, NSW) 1982 NZ 1, 2, 3, 1983 US, Arg 1, 2, NZ, It, F 1, 2, 1984 Fj, NZ 1, 2, 3, E, I, W, S, 1985 Fj 1, 2,

1986 It, F, Arg 1, 2, NZ 1, 2, 3, 1987 [E, US, J, I, F, W], NZ, 1988 E 1, 2, NZ 1, 2, 3, E, S, It, 1989 BI 1, 2, 3, NZ, F 1, 2, 1990 F 2, 3, US, NZ 1, 2, 3, 1991 W, E, NZ 1, 2, [Arg, WS, W, I, NZ, E], 1992 S 1, 2, NZ 1, 2, 3, SA, I, W, 1993 Tg, NZ, SA 1, 2, 3, C, F 1, 2, 1994 I 1, 2, It 1, 2, WS, NZ, 1995 Arg 1, 2, [SA, C, E], NZ 2(R), 1996 W 1, 2, C, NZ 1, SA 1, NZ 2, SA 2, It, W 3

**Canniffe, W D** (Q) 1907 NZ 2

**Cannon, B J** (NSW, WF) 2001 BI 2(R), NZ 1(R), Sp (R), F (R), W (R), 2002 F 1(R), 2, SA 1(t), 2(R), I (t), It (R), 2003 I (R), W (R), E (R), SA 1, NZ 1, SA 2, NZ 2, [Arg, R, I, S, NZ, E], 2004 S1, 2, E1, PI, NZ1, 2, SA2, S3(R), 4(R), 2005 NZ1(R), SA4, NZ2, F2, E, I, W, 2006 W(R), It

**Caputo, M E** (ACT) 1996 W 1, 2, 1997 F 1, 2, NZ 1

**Carberry, C M** (NSW, Q) 1973 Tg 2, E, 1976 I, US, Fj 1, 2, 3, 1981 F 1, 2, I, W, S, 1982 E

**Cardy, A M** (NSW) 1966 BI 1, 2, W, S, 1967 E, I 1, F, 1968 NZ 1, 2

**Carew, P J** (Q) 1899 BI 1, 2, 3, 4

**Carmichael, P** (Q) 1904 BI 2, 1907 NZ 1, 1908 W, 1909 E

**Carozza, P V** (Q) 1990 F 1, 2, 3, NZ 2, 3, 1992 S 1, 2, NZ 1, 2, 3, SA, I, W, 1993 Tg, NZ

**Carpenter, M G** (V) 1938 NZ 1, 2,

**Carr, E T A** (NSW) 1913 NZ 1, 2, 3, 1914 NZ 1, 2, 3

**Carr, E W** (NSW) 1921 SA 1, 2, 3, NZ (R)

**Carroll, D B** (NSW) 1908 W, 1912 US

**Carroll, J C** (NSW) 1953 SA 1

**Carroll, J H** (NSW) 1958 M 2, 3, NZ 1, 2, 3, 1959 BI 1, 2

**Carson, J** (NSW) 1899 BI 1

**Carson, P J** (NSW) 1979 NZ, 1980 NZ 3

**Carter, D G** (NSW) 1988 E 1, 2, NZ 1, 1989 F 1, 2

**Carter, S T G** (ACT) 2014 F1, NZ1, 2, SA1, Arg1, SA2, Arg2

**Casey, T V** (NSW) 1963 SA 2, 3, 4, 1964 NZ 1, 2, 3

**Catchpole, K W** (NSW) 1961 Fj 1, 2, 3, SA 1, 2, F, 1962 NZ 1, 2, 4, 1963 SA 2, 3, 4, 1964 NZ 1, 2, 3, 1965 SA 1, 2, 1966 BI 1, 2, W, S, 1967 E, I 1, F, I 2, NZ, 1968 NZ 1

**Cawsey, R M** (NSW) 1949 M 1, NZ 1, 2

**Cerutti, W H** (NSW) 1928 NZ 1, 2, 3, M, 1929 NZ 1, 2, 3, 1930 BI, 1931 M, NZ, 1932 NZ 1, 2, 3, 1933 SA 1, 2, 3, 4, 5, 1936 M, 1937 SA 1, 2

**Challoner, R L** (NSW) 1899 BI 2

**Chambers, R** (NSW) 1920 NZ 1, 3

**Chapman, G A** (NSW) 1962 NZ 3, 4, 5

**Charles, N L** (WF) 2014 F2(R), 3(R), NZ1, 2

**Chisholm, M D** (ACT) 2004 S3(R), 2005 Sm, It, F1, SA1, 2, 3(R), NZ1(R), 2, F2, E(t&R), I(R), W(R), 2006 E1(R), 2, I1, NZ1, SA1(R), NZ2(R), SA2(R), NZ3(t&R), SA3(R), W(R), It, I2, S(t&R), 2007 W1, 2(R), Fj, SA1(R), NZ1(R), 2(R), [W(R), Fj, C], 2008 NZ4, It, E, F3(R), W, 2009 SA2, 3, NZ3, 4, E, I, S, W(R), 2010 E1(R), 2(R), I, SA3, NZ3, 4, W, E3, It(R), F(R)

**Clark, J G** (Q) 1931 M, NZ, 1932 NZ 1, 2, 1933 SA 1

**Clarken, J C** (NSW) 1905 NZ, 1910 NZ 1, 2, 3

**Cleary, M A** (NSW) 1961 Fj 1, 2, 3, SA 1, 2, F

**Clements, P** (NSW) 1982 NZ 3

**Clifford, M** (NSW) 1938 NZ 3

**Cobb, W G** (NSW) 1899 BI 3, 4

**Cockbain, M J** (Q) 1997 F 2(R), NZ 1, SA 1, 2, 1998 E 1, S 1, 2, NZ 1, SA 1, NZ 2, SA 2, NZ 3, Fj, Tg (R), WS, F, E 2, 1999 I 1, 2, E, SA 1, NZ 1, SA 2, NZ 2, [US (t&R), W, SA 3, F], 2000 Arg 1, 2, SA 2(t&R), 3(t&R), F, S, E (R), 2001 BI 1(R), 2(R), 3(R), SA 1(R), NZ 1(R), SA 2(R), Sp (R), E (R), F (t+R), W, 2002 F 1(R), 2(R), NZ 1(R), SA 1(R), NZ 2(R), SA 2(R), Arg, I, E, It, 2003 [Arg(R), R(R), Nm(R), I(R), S(R), NZ(R), E(R)]

**Cocks, M R** (NSW, Q) 1972 F 1, 2, NZ 2, 3, Fj, 1973 Tg 1, 2, W, E, 1975 J 1

**Codey, D** (NSW Country, Q) 1983 Arg 1, 1984 E, W, S, 1985 C 2, NZ, 1986 F, Arg 1, 1987 [US, J, F (R), W], NZ

**Cody, E W** (NSW) 1913 NZ 1, 2, 3

**Coker, T** (Q, ACT) 1987 [E, US, F, W], 1991 NZ 2, [Arg, WS, NZ, E], 1992 NZ 1, 2, 3, W (R), 1993 Tg, NZ, 1995 Arg 2, NZ 1(R), 1997 F 1(R), 2, NZ 1, E 1, NZ 2(R), SA 1(R), NZ 3, SA 2, Arg 1, 2

**Colbert, R** (NSW) 1952 Fj 2, NZ 1, 2, 1953 SA 2, 3, 4

**Cole, J W** (NSW) 1968 NZ 1, 2, F, I, S, 1969 W, SA 1, 2, 3, 4, 1970 S, 1971 SA 1, 2, 3, F 1, 2, 1972 NZ 1, 2, 3, 1973 Tg 1, 2, 1974 NZ 1, 2, 3

**Collins, P K** (NSW) 1937 SA 2, 1938 NZ 2, 3

**Colton, A J** (Q) 1899 BI 1, 3

**Colton, T** (Q) 1904 BI 1, 2

**Comrie-Thomson, I R** (NSW) 1926 NZ 4, 1928 NZ 1, 2, 3 M

**Connor, D M** (Q) 1958 W, I, E, S, F, M 2, 3, NZ 1, 2, 3, 1959 BI 1, 2

**Connors, M R** (Q) 1999 SA 1(R), NZ 1(R), SA 2(R), NZ 2, [R (R), I 3, US, W (R), SA 3(R), F(R)], 2000 Arg 1(R), 2(R), SA 1, NZ 1, SA 2, NZ 2(t&R), SA 3, F (R), S (R), E (R)

**Constable, R** (Q) 1994 I 2(t & R)

**Cook, M T** (Q) 1986 F, 1987 SK, [J], 1988 E 1, 2, NZ 1, 2, 3, E, S, It

**Cooke, B P** (Q) 1979 I 1

**Cooke, G M** (Q) 1932 NZ 1, 2, 3, 1933 SA 1, 2, 3, 1946 NZ 2, 1947 NZ 2, S, I, W, 1948 E, F

**Coolican, J E** (NSW) 1982 NZ 1, 1983 It, F 1, 2

**Cooney, R C** (NSW) 1922 M 2

**Cooper, Q S** (Q) 2008 It(R), F3(R), W(R), 2009 It1(R), 2, SA2(R), 3(R), E, I, S, W, 2010 Fj, E1, 2, I, SA1, 2, 3, NZ3, 4, W, E3, It, F, 2011 SA1, NZ1, SA2, NZ2, [It, I, US, Ru, SA, NZ, W], 2012 NZ2, SA1, Arg1, 2013 NZ1(R), 2(R), SA1, Arg1, SA2, Arg2, NZ3, E, It, I, S, W

**Cordingley, S J** (A, Grenoble) 2000 Arg 1(R), SA 1(R), F, S, E, 2006 E2, I1(R), NZ1(R), SA1(R), NZ2(R), SA2(R), 2007 Fj(R), [Fj(R), C], 2008 I(R), F1(R), 2(t&R), SA1(R), 2, 3, NZ3, F3(R)

**Corfe, A C** (Q) 1899 BI 2

**Cornelsen, G** (NSW) 1974 NZ 2, 3, 1975 J 2, S, W, 1976 E, F 1, 2, 1978 W 1, 2, NZ, 1979 I 1, 2, NZ, Arg 1, 2, 1980 NZ 1, 2, 3, 1981 I, W, S, 1982 E

**Cornes, J R** (Q) 1972 Fj

**Cornforth, R G W** (NSW) 1947 NZ 1, 1950 BI 2

**Cornish, P** (ACT) 1990 F 2, 3, NZ 1

**Costello, P P S** (Q) 1950 BI 2

**Cottrell, N V** (Q) 1949 M 1, 2, 3, NZ 1, 2, 1950 BI 1, 2, 1951 NZ 1, 2, 3, 1952 Fj 1, 2, NZ 1, 2

**Cowan, P J M** (WF) 2009 It2, SA3(R), NZ3(R), 2010 Fj(R), 2011 SA1(R), 2014 F1(R), 2(R), NZ1(R), SA1(R), Arg1(R)

**Cowper, D L** (V) 1931 NZ, 1932 NZ 1, 2, 3, 1933 SA 1, 2, 3, 4, 5

**Cox, B P** (NSW) 1952 Fj 1, 2, NZ 1, 2, 1954 Fj 2, 1955 NZ 1, 1956 SA 2, 1957 NZ 1, 2

**Cox, M H** (NSW) 1981 W, S

**Cox, P A** (NSW) 1979 Arg 1, 2, 1980 Fj, NZ 1, 2, 1981 W (R), S, 1982 S 1, 2, NZ 1, 2, 3, 1984 Fj, NZ 1, 2, 3

**Craig, R R** (NSW) 1908 W

**Crakanthorp, J S** (NSW) 1923 NZ 3

**Cremin, J F** (NSW) 1946 NZ 1, 2, 1947 NZ 1

**Crittle, C P** (NSW) 1962 NZ 4, 5, 1963 SA 2, 3, 4, 1964 NZ 1, 2, 3, 1965 SA 1, 2, 1966 BI 1, 2, S, 1967 E, I

**Croft, B H D** (NSW) 1928 M

**Croft, D N** (Q) 2002 Arg (t&R), I (R), E (t&R), It (R), 2003 [Nm]

**Cross, J R** (NSW) 1955 NZ 1, 2, 3

**Cross, K A** (NSW) 1949 M 1, NZ 1, 2, 1950 BI 1, 2, 1951 NZ 2, 3, 1952 NZ 1, 1953 SA 1, 2, 3, 4, 1954 Fj 1, 2, 1955 NZ 3, 1956 SA 1, 2, 1957 NZ 1, 2

**Cross, R P** (WF) 2008 F1(R), 2(R), SA1(R), NZ1, 2(R), SA2(R), 3(R), NZ3, 4, E, W, 2009 It2, F(R), NZ2(R), SA2, NZ4, E(R), S NZ3, 4, E, W, 2009 It2, F(R), NZ2(R), SA2, NZ4, E(R), S

**Crossman, O C** (NSW) 1923 M 1(R), 2, 3, 1924, NZ 1, 2, 3, 1925 NZ 1, 3, 4, 1926 NZ 1, 2, 3, 4, 1929 NZ 2, 1930 BI

**Crowe, P J** (NSW) 1976 F 2, 1978 W 1, 2, 1979 I 2, NZ, Arg 1

**Crowley, D J** (Q) 1989 BI 1, 2, 3, 1991 [WS], 1992 I, W, 1993 C (R), 1995 Arg 1, 2, [SA, E], NZ 1, 1996 W 2(R), C, NZ 1, SA 1, 2, I, W 3, 1998 E 1, S 1(R), 2(R), NZ 1(R), SA 1, NZ 2, SA 2, NZ 3, Tg, WS, 1999 I 1, 2(R), E (R), SA 1, NZ 1(R), [R (R), I 3(t&R), US, F(R)]

**Cummins, N M** (WF) 2012 Arg2, NZ3, F, E, It, W4, 2013 SA1, Arg1, E, It, I, W, 2014 F1, 2, 3

**Curley, T G P** (NSW) 1957 NZ 1, 2, 1958 W, I, E, S, F, M 1, NZ 1, 2, 3

**Curran, D J** (NSW) 1980 NZ 3, 1981 F 1, 2, W, 1983 Arg 1

**Currie, E W** (Q) 1899 BI 2

**Cutler, S A G** (NSW) 1982 NZ 2(R), 1984 NZ 1, 2, 3, E, I, W, S, 1985 C 1, 2, NZ, Fj 1, 2, 1986 It, F, NZ 1, 2, 3, 1987 SK, [E, J, I, F, W], NZ, Arg 1, 2, 1988 E 1, 2, NZ 1, 2, 3, E, S, It, 1989 BI 1, 2, 3, NZ, 1991 [WS]

**Daley, B P** (Q) 2010 E1, 2, I

**Daly, A J** (NSW) 1989 NZ, F 1, 2, 1990 F 1, 2, 3, US, NZ 1, 2, 3, 1991 W, NZ 1, 2, [Arg, W, I, NZ, E], 1992 S 1, 2, NZ 1, 2, 3, SA, 1993 Tg, NZ, SA 1, 2, 3, C, F 1, 2, 1994 I 1, 2, It 1, 2, WS, NZ, 1995 [C, R]

**D'Arcy, A M** (Q) 1980 Fj, NZ 3, 1981 F 1, 2, I, W, S, 1982 E, S 1, 2

**Darveniza, P** (NSW) 1969 W, SA 2, 3, 4

**Darwin, B J** (ACT) 2001 BI 1(R), SA 1(R), NZ 1(R), SA 2(R), NZ 2(t&R), Sp, E, F, W, 2002 NZ 1(R), SA 1(R), NZ 2(R), SA 2, Arg (R), I (R), E (R), It (R), 2003 I (R), W (t&R), E (R), SA 1(R), NZ 1(R), [Arg(R), R(R), Nm, I, S, NZ]

Francis, E (Q) 1914 NZ 1, 2
Frawley, D (Q, NSW) 1986 Arg 2(R), 1987 Arg 1, 2, 1988 E 1, 2, NZ 1, 2, 3, S, It
Freedman, J E (NSW) 1962 NZ 3, 4, 5, 1963 SA 1
Freeman, E (NSW) 1946 NZ 1(R), M
Freier, A L (NSW) 2002 Arg (R), I, E (R), It, 2003 SA 1(R), NZ 1(t), 2005 NZ2(R), 2006 E2, 2007 W1(R), 2(R), Fj, SA1(R), NZ1(R), SA2, NZ2(R), [J(R), W(R), Fj(R), C, E(R)], 2008 I(R), F1(R), 2(R), NZ3(R), W(t&R)
Freney, M E (Q) 1972 NZ 1, 2, 3, 1973 Tg 1, W, E (R)
Friend, W S (NSW) 1920 NZ 3, 1921 SA 1, 2, 3, 1922 NZ 1, 2, 3, 1923 M 1, 2, 3
Furness, D C (NSW) 1946 M
Futter, F C (NSW) 1904 BI 3

Gardner, J M (Q) 1987 Arg 2, 1988 E 1, NZ 1, E
Gardner, W C (NSW) 1950 BI 1
Garner, R L (NSW) 1949 NZ 1, 2
Gavin, K A (NSW) 1909 E
Gavin, T B (NSW) 1988 NZ 2, 3, S, It (R), 1989 NZ (R), F 1, 2, 1990 F 1, 2, 3, US, NZ 1, 2, 3, 1991 W, E, NZ 1, 1992 S 1, 2, SA, I, W, 1993 Tg, NZ, SA 1, 2, 3, C, F 1, 2, 1994 I 1, 2, It 1, 2, WS, NZ, 1995 Arg 1, 2, [SA, C, R, E], NZ 1, 2, 1996 NZ 2(R), SA 2, W 3
Gelling, A M (NSW) 1972 NZ 1, Fj
Genia, S W (Q) 2009 NZ1(R), SA1(R), NZ2(R), SA2(R), 3, NZ3, 4, E, I, S, W, 2010 E2, SA1, NZ1, 2, SA2, 3, NZ3, 4, W, E3, F, 2011 Sm(R), SA1, NZ1, SA2, NZ2, [It, I, US, SA, NZ, W], W, 2012 S, W1, 2, 3, NZ1, 2, SA1, 2013 BI 1, 2, 3, NZ1, 2, SA1, 2(R), Arg2, NZ3, E, It, I, S, W
George, H W (NSW) 1910 NZ 1, 2, 3, 1912 US, 1913 NZ 1, 3, 1914 NZ 1, 3
George, W G (NSW) 1923 M 1, 3, NZ 1, 2, 1924 NZ 3, 1925 NZ 2, 3, 1926 NZ 4, 1928 NZ 1, 2, 3, M
Gerrard, M A (ACT, MR) 2005 It(R), SA1(R), NZ1, 2, E, I, W, 2006 E1, 2, I1, NZ1, SA2, SA2, NZ3(t), SA3(R), I2, S, 2007 W1, 2(R), SA2, NZ2, [J(R)], 2011 Sm
Gibbons, E de C (NSW) 1936 NZ 1, 2, M
Gibbs, P R (V) 1966 S
Giffin, D T (ACT) 1996 W 3, 1997 F 1, 2, 1999 I 1, 2, E, SA 1, NZ 1, SA 2, NZ 2, [R, I 3, US (R), W, SA 3, F], 2000 Arg 1, 2, SA 1, NZ 1, SA 2, NZ 2, SA 3, F, S, E, 2001 BI 1, 2, SA 1, NZ 2, Sp, E, F, W, 2002 Arg (R), I, E (R), It (R), 2003 I, W, E, SA 1, NZ 1, SA 2, NZ 2, [Arg, Nm(R)], I, NZ(t&R), E(R)]
Gilbert, H (NSW) 1910 NZ 1, 2, 3
Gill, L B (Q) 2012 NZ2(R), SA1(R), Arg1(R), SA2(R), Arg2(R), NZ3(R), F(R), E(t&R), 2013 BI 1(R), 2(R), NZ1(R), 2(R), SA1(R), It(R), I(R)
Girvan, B (ACT) 1988 E
Giteau, M J (ACT, WF) 2002 E (R), It (R), 2003 SA 2(R), NZ 2(R), [Arg(R), R(R), Nm, I(R), S(R), E(t)], 2004 S1, E1, PI, NZ1, SA1, NZ2, SA2, S3, F, S4, E2, 2005 Sm, It, F1, SA1, 2, 3, NZ1, SA4, F2, E(t&R), 2006 NZ1(R), SA1, SA2, W, NZ3, SA3, W, It, I2, S, 2007 W1, 2, SA1, NZ1, SA2, NZ2, [J, W, Fj, E], 2008 I, F1, 2, SA1, NZ1, 2, SA2, 3, It(R), E, F3, W, 2009 It1, F, NZ1, SA1, NZ2, SA2, 3, NZ3, 4, E, I, S, W, 2010 Fj, E2, I, SA1, NZ1, 2, SA2, NZ3, 4, W, E3, F(R), 2011 Sm
Gordon, G C (NSW) 1929 NZ 1
Gordon, K M (NSW) 1950 BI 1, 2
Gould, R G (Q) 1980 NZ 1, 2, 3, 1981 I, W, S, 1982 S 2, NZ 1, 2, 3, 1983 US, Arg 1, F 1, 2, 1984 NZ 1, 2, 3, E, I, W, S, 1985 NZ, 1986 It, 1987 SK, [E]
Gourley, S R (NSW) 1988 S, It, 1989 BI 1, 2, 3
Graham, C S (Q) 1899 BI 2
Graham, R (NSW) 1973 Tg 1, 2, W, E, 1974 NZ 2, 3, 1975 E 2, J 1, 2, S, W, 1976 I, US, Fj 1, 2, 3, F 1, 2
Gralton, A S I (Q) 1899 BI 1, 4, 1903 NZ
Grant, J C (NSW) 1988 E 1, NZ 2, 3, E
Graves, R H (NSW) 1907 NZ 1(R)
Greatorex, E N (NSW) 1923 M 3, NZ 3, 1924 NZ 1, 2, 3, 1925 NZ 1, 1928 E, F
Gregan, G M (ACT) 1994 It 1, 2, WS, NZ, 1995 Arg 1, 2, [SA, C (R), R, E], 1996 W 1, C (t), SA 1, NZ 2, SA 2, It, I, W 3, 1997 F 1, 2, NZ 1, E 1, NZ 2, SA 1, NZ 3, SA 2, Arg 1, 2, E 2, S, 1998 E 1, S, I, 2, NZ 1, SA 1, NZ 2, SA 2, NZ 2, Fj, WS, F, E 2, 1999 I 1, 2, E, SA 1, NZ 1, SA 2, NZ 2, [R, I 3, W, SA 3, F], 2000 Arg 1, 2, SA 1, NZ 1, SA 2, NZ 2, Sp, E, F, W, 2002 F 1, 2, NZ 1, SA 1, NZ 2, SA 2, Arg, I, E, It, 2003 I, W, E, SA 1, NZ 1, SA 2, NZ 2, [Arg, R, I, S, NZ, E], 2004 S1, 2, E1, PI, SA1,

NZ2, SA2, S3, F, S4, E2, 2005 It, F1, SA1, 2, 3, NZ1, SA4, NZ2, F2, E, I, W, 2006 E1, 2(R), I1, NZ1, SA1, NZ2, SA2, NZ3, SA3, 2007 W1(R), 2(R), Fj, SA1, NZ1, SA2, NZ2, [J, W, Fj, C(R), E]
Gregory, S C (Q) 1968 NZ 3, F, I, S, 1969 SA 1, 3, 1971 SA 1, 3, F 1, 2, 1972 F 1, 2, 1973 Tg 1, 2, W, E
Grey, G O (NSW) 1972 F 2(R), NZ 1, 2, 3, Fj (R)
Grey, N P (NSW) 1998 S 2(R), SA 2(R), Fj(R), Tg(R), F, E 2, 1999 I 1(R), 2(R), E, SA 1, NZ 1, SA 2, NZ 2(t&R), [R(R), I 3(R), US, SA 3(R), F(R)], 2000 S(R), E(R), 2001 BI 1, 2, 3, SA 1, NZ 1, SA 2, NZ 2, Sp, E, F, 2003 I(R), W(R), E, [Nm, NZ(t)]
Griffin, T S (NSW) 1907 NZ 1, 3, 1908 W, 1910 NZ 1, 2, 1912 US
Grigg, P C (Q) 1980 NZ 3, 1982 S2, NZ1, 2, 3, 1983 Arg2, NZ, 1984 Fj, W, S, 1985 C1, 2, NZ, Fj1, 2, 1986 Arg1, 2, NZ1, 2, 1987 SK, [E, J, I, F, W]
Grimmond, D N (NSW) 1964 NZ 2
Gudsell, K E (NSW) 1951 NZ 1, 2, 3
Guerassimoff, J (Q) 1963 SA2, 3, 4, 1964 NZ1, 2, 3, 1965 SA2, 1966 BI1, 2, 1967 E, I, F
Gunther, W J (NSW) 1957 NZ2

Hall, D (Q) 1980 Fj, NZ 1, 2, 3, 1981 F 1, 2, 1982 S1, 2, NZ1, 2, 1983 US, Arg1, 2, NZ, It
Hamalainen, H A (Q) 1929 NZ 1, 2, 3
Hamilton, B G (NSW) 1946 M
Hammand, C A (NSW) 1908 W, 1909 E
Hammon, J D C (V) 1937 SA 2
Handy, C B (Q) 1978 NZ 3, 1979 NZ, Arg1, 2, 1980 NZ1, 2
Hanley, R G (Q) 1983 US (R), It (R), 1985 Fj2(R)
Hanson, J E (Q) 2012 NZ3(R), 2014 NZ2(R), SA1, Arg1(R), SA2(R)
Hardcastle, P A (NSW) 1946 NZ 1, M, NZ 2, 1947 NZ 1, 1949 M 3
Hardcastle, W R (NSW) 1899 BI 4, 1903 NZ
Harding, M A (NSW) 1983 It
Hardman, S P (Q) 2002 F 2(R), 2006 SA1(R), 2007 SA2(t&R), [C(R)]
Hardy, M D (ACT) 1997 F 1(t), 2(R), NZ 1(R), 3(R), Arg 1(R), 2(R), 1998 Tg, WS
Harris, M J (Q) 2012 S, W2(R), SA1(R), 2(R), Arg2, NZ3, F, W4(R), 2013 S, W(R)
Harrison, J B (ACT, NSW) 2001 BI 3, NZ1, SA2, Sp, E, F, W (R), 2002 F1, 2, NZ1, SA1, NZ2, SA2, Arg, I (R), E, It, 2003 [R(R), Nm, S, NZ, E], 2004 S1, 2, E1, PI, NZ1, SA1, NZ2, SA2, S3, F, S4, E2
Harry, R L L (NSW) 1996 W1, 2, NZ 1, SA 1(t), It, S, 1997 F 1, 2, NZ1, 2, SA1, NZ3, SA2, Arg1, 2, E2, S, 1998 Arg1, 2, NZ1, Fj, 1999 SA2, NZ2, [R, I3, W, SA3, F], 2000 Arg1, 2, SA1, NZ1, SA2, NZ2, SA3
Hartill, M N (NSW) 1986 NZ1, 2, 3, 1987 SK, [J], Arg1, 1988 NZ1, 2, E, It, 1989 BI 1(R), 2, 3, F1, 2, 1995 Arg1(R), 2(R), [C], NZ1, 2
Harvey, P B (Q) 1949 M1, 2
Harvey, R M (NSW) 1958 F, M3
Hatherell, W I (Q) 1952 Fj 1, 2
Hauser, R G (Q) 1975 J 1(R), 2, W (R), 1976 E, I, US, Fj1, 2, 3, F1, 2, 1978 W1, 2, 1979 I1, 2
Hawker, M J (NSW) 1980 Fj, NZ 1, 2, 3, 1981 F1, 2, I, W, 1982 E, S1, 2, NZ1, 2, 3, 1983 US, Arg1, 2, NZ, It, F1, 2, 1984 NZ1, 2, 3, 1987 NZ
Hawthorne, P F (NSW) 1962 NZ3, 4, 5, 1963 E, SA1, 2, 3, 4, 1964 NZ1, 2, 3, 1965 SA1, 2, 1966 BI1, 2, W, 1967 E, I1, F, I2, NZ
Hayes, E S (Q) 1934 NZ1, 2, 1938 NZ 1, 2, 3
Heath, A (NSW) 1996 C, SA 1, NZ 2, SA 2, It, 1997 NZ 2, SA 1, E 2(R)
Heenan, D P (Q, ACT) 2003 W, 2006 E1
Heinrich, E L (NSW) 1961 Fj 1, 2, 3, SA 2, F, 1962 NZ 1, 2, 3, 1963 E, SA 1
Heinrich, V (NSW) 1954 Fj 1, 2
Heming, R J (NSW) 1961 Fj 2, 3, SA 1, 2, F, 1962 NZ 2, 3, 4, 5, 1963 SA 2, 3, 4, 1964 NZ 1, 2, 3, 1965 SA 1, 2, 1966 BI 1, 2, W, 1967 F
Hemingway, W H (NSW) 1928 NZ 2, 3, 1931 M, NZ, 1932 NZ 3
Henderson, N J (ACT) 2004 PI(R), 2005 Sm(R), 2006 It(R)
Henjak, M T (ACT) 2004 E1(R), NZ1(R), 2005 Sm(R), I(R)
Henry, A R (Q) 1899 BI 2
Herbert, A G (Q) 1987 SK (R), [F (R)], 1990 F 1(R), US, NZ 2, 3, 1991 [WS], 1992 NZ 3(R), 1993 NZ (R), SA 2(R)
Herbert, D J (Q) 1994 I 2, It 1, 2, WS (R), 1995 Arg 1, 2, [SA, R], 1996 C, SA 2, It, S, I, 1997 NZ 1, 1998 E 1, S 1, 2, NZ 1, SA 1, NZ 2, SA 2, Fj, Tg, WS, F, E 2, 1999 I 1, 2, E, SA 1, NZ 1, SA 2, NZ 2, [R, I 3, W, SA 3, F], 2000 Arg 1, 2, SA 1, NZ 1, SA

Lamb, J S (NSW) 1928 NZ 1, 2, M
Lambie, J K (NSW) 1974 NZ 1, 2, 3, 1975 W
Lane, R E (NSW) 1921 SA 1
Lane, T A (Q) 1985 C 1, 2, NZ
Lang, C W P (V) 1938 NZ 2, 3
Langford, J F (ACT) 1997 NZ 3, SA 2, E 2, S
Larkham, S J (ACT) 1996 W 2(R), 1997 F 1, 2, NZ 1, 2(R), SA 1,
   NZ 3, SA 2, Arg 1, 2, E 2, S, 1998 E 1, S 1, 2, NZ 1, SA 1,
   NZ 2, SA 2, NZ 3, Fj, Tg (t), WS, F, E 2, 1999 [I 3, US, W, SA
   3, F], 2000 Arg 1, 2, SA 1, NZ 1, SA 2, NZ 2, SA 3, 2001 BI
   1, 2, NZ 1, SA 2, NZ 2, Sp, E, F, W, 2002 F 1, 2, NZ 1, SA
   1, NZ 2, SA 2, Arg, I, E, 2003 SA 1(R), NZ 1, SA 2, NZ 2,
   [Arg, R, I, S, NZ, E], 2004S1, 2, E1, PI, NZ1, SA1, NZ2, SA2,
   S3, F, S4, 2005 Sm(R), It, F1, SA1, 2, 3, 2006 E1, 2, I1, NZ1,
   SA1, NZ2, SA2, NZ3, SA3, W, I2, S, 2007 W2, SA1,
   NZ1, SA2, NZ2, [J]
Larkin, E R (NSW) 1903 NZ
Larkin, K K (Q) 1958 M 2, 3
Latham, C E (Q) 1998 F, E 2, 1999 I 1, 2, E, [US], 2000 Arg 1, 2,
   SA 1, NZ 1, SA 2, NZ 2, SA 3, F, S, E, 2001 BI 1, 2(R), SA
   1(R), NZ 1(R), SA 2, NZ 2, Sp, E, F, W (R), 2002 F 1, 2, NZ
   1, SA 1, NZ 2, SA 2, 2003 I, W, E, NZ 1(R), SA 2, NZ 2, [Nm],
   2004 S1(R), 2(R), E1(R), PI(t&R), SA1, NZ2, SA2, S3, F,
   S4, E2, 2005 Sm, F1, SA2, 3, F2, E, I, W, 2006 E1, 2, I1, NZ1,
   SA1, NZ2, SA2, NZ3, SA3, W, It, I2, S, 2007 NZ2(R), [J, W,
   Fj, C, E]
Latimer, N B (NSW) 1957 NZ 2
Lawton, R (Q) 1988 E 1, NZ 2(R), 3, S
Lawton, T (NSW, Q) 1920 NZ 1, 2, 1925 NZ 4, 1927 I, W, S, 1928
   E, F, 1929 NZ 1, 2, 3, 1930 BI, 1932 NZ 1, 2
Lawton, T A (Q) 1983 F 1(R), 2, 1984 Fj, NZ 1, 2, 3, E, I, W, S,
   1985 C 1, 2, NZ, Fj 1, 1986 It, F, Arg 1, 2, NZ 1, 2, 3, 1987
   SK, [E, US, I, F, W], NZ, Arg 1, 2, 1988 E 1, 2, NZ 1, 2, 3, E,
   S, It, 1989 BI 1, 2, 3
Laycock, W M B (NSW) 1925 NZ 2, 3, 4, 1926 NZ 2
Leali'ifano, C P (ACT) 2013 BI 1, 2, 3, NZ1, 2, SA1, Arg1, SA2,
   Arg2, It(R), I(R), S, W
Leeds, A J (NSW) 1986 NZ 3, 1987 [US, W], NZ, Arg 1, 2, 1988
   E 1, 2, NZ 1, 2, 3, E, S, It
Lenehan, J K (NSW) 1958 W, E, S, F, M 1, 2, 3, 1959 BI 1, 2,
   1961 SA 1, 2, F, 1962 NZ 2, 3, 4, 5, 1965 SA 1, 2, 1966 W,
   S, 1967 E, I 1, F, I 2
L'Estrange, R D (Q) 1971 F 1, 2, 1972 NZ 1, 2, 3, 1973 Tg 1, 2,
   W, E, 1974 NZ 1, 2, 3, 1975 S, W, 1976 I, US
Lewis, L S (Q) 1934 NZ 1, 2, 1936 NZ 2, 1938 NZ 1
Lidbury, S (NSW) 1987 Arg 1, 1988 E 2
Lillicrap, C P (Q) 1985 Fj 2, 1987 [US, I, F, W], 1989 BI 1, 1991
   [WS]
Lindsay, R T G (Q) 1932 NZ 3
Lisle, R J (NSW) 1961 Fj 1, 2, 3, SA 1
Little, J S (Q, NSW) 1989 F 1, 2, 1990 F 1, 2, 3, US, 1991 W, E,
   NZ 1, 2, [Arg, W, I, NZ, E], 1992 NZ 1, 2, 3, SA, I, W, 1993
   Tg, NZ, SA 1, 2, 3, C, F 1, 2, 1994 WS, NZ, 1995 Arg 1, 2,
   [SA, C, E], NZ 1, 2, 1996 It (R), I, W 3, 1997 F 1, 2, NZ 1,
   2, SA 1, NZ 3, SA 2, 1998 E 1(R), S 2(R), NZ 2, SA 2(R), NZ
   3, Fj, Tg, WS, F, E 2, 1999 I 1(R), 2, NZ 2, [R, I 3(t&R),
   US, W (R), SA 3(t&R) F (R)], 2000 Arg 1(R), 2(R), SA 1(R), NZ
   1, SA 2, NZ 2, SA 3
Livermore, A E (Q) 1946 NZ 1, M
Loane, M E (Q) 1973 Tg 1, 2, 1974 NZ 1, 1975 E 1, 2, J 1, 1976
   E, I, Fj 1, 2, 3, F 1, 2, 1978 W 1, 2, 1979 I 1, 2, NZ, Arg 1,
   2, 1981 F 1, 2, I, W, S, 1982 E, S 1, 2
Logan, D L (NSW) 1958 M 1
Loudon, D B (NSW) 1921 NZ, 1922 M 1, 2, 3
Loudon, R B (NSW) 1923 NZ 1(R), 2, 3, 1928 NZ 1, 2, 3, M, 1929
   NZ 2, 1933 SA 2, 3, 4, 5, 1934 NZ 2
Love, E W (NSW) 1932 NZ 1, 2, 3
Lowth, D R (NSW) 1958 NZ 1
Lucas, B C (Q) 1905 NZ
Lucas, P W (NSW) 1982 NZ 1, 2, 3
Lutge, D (NSW) 1903 NZ, 1904 BI 1, 2, 3
Lynagh, M P (Q) 1984 Fj, E, I, W, S, 1985 C 1, 2, NZ, 1986 It, F,
   Arg 1, 2, NZ 1, 2, 3, 1987 [E, US, J, I, F, W], Arg 1, 2, 1988
   E 1, 2, NZ 1, 3(R), E, S, It, 1989 BI 1, 2, 3, NZ, F 1, 2, 1990
   F 1, 2, 3, US, NZ 1, 2, 3, 1991 W, E, NZ 1, 2, [Arg, WS, W,
   I, NZ, E], 1992 S 1, 2, NZ 1, 2, 3, SA, I, 1993 Tg, C, F 1, 2,
   1994 I 1, 2, It 1, 1995 Arg 1, 2, [SA, C, E]
Lyons, D J (NSW) 2000 Arg 1(t&R), 2(R), 2001 BI 1(R), SA 1(R),
   2002 F 1(R), 2, NZ 1(R), SA 1(R), NZ 2(R), SA 2(t+R), 2003 I,
   W, E, SA 1, [Arg, R, Nm, I, S, NZ, E], 2004 S1, 2, E1, PI, NZ1,

SA1, NZ2, SA2, S3(R), F(R), S4, E2, 2005 Sm, It, F1, SA1, 2,
NZ1, SA4, 2006 S, 2007 Fj, SA2(R), [C]

McArthur, M (NSW) 1909 E
McBain, M I (Q) 1983 It, F 1, 1985 Fj 2, 1986 It (R), 1987 [J], 1988
   E 2(R), 1989 BI 1(R)
MacBride, J W T (NSW) 1946 NZ 1, M, NZ 2, 1947 NZ 1, 2, S, I,
   W, 1948 E, F
McCabe, A J M (NSW) 1909 E
McCabe, P J (ACT) 2010 It(R), 2011 Sm, SA1, NZ1, SA2, NZ2, [It,
   I, US(R), SA, NZ], 2012 W1, 2, 3, Arg1, SA2, Arg2, NZ3, F,
   2013 BI 1(R), 2014 F1(R), 2(R), NZ1, 2
McCall, R J (Q) 1989 F 1, 2, 1990 F 1, 2, 3, US, NZ 1, 2, 3, 1991
   W, E, NZ 1, 2, [Arg, W, I, NZ, E], 1992 S 1, 2, NZ 1, 2, 3, SA,
   I, W, 1993 Tg, NZ, SA 1, 2, 3, C, F 1, 2, 1994 It 2, 1995 NZ
   1, 2, [SA, R, E]
McCalman, B J (WF) 2010 SA1(R), 2(R), 3, NZ3, 4, W, E3, It, F,
   2011 Sm, SA1, NZ1, 2(R), [It(R), I, US, Ru, SA(R), NZ(R), W],
   W, 2013 BI 3(R), SA1(t&R), Arg1(R), SA2(R), Arg2(R), NZ3,
   E(R), S(R), 2014 F1(R), 2, 3(R), Arg1, SA2
McCarthy, F J C (Q) 1950 BI 1
McCowan, R H (Q) 1899 BI 1, 2, 4
McCue, P A (NSW) 1907 NZ 1, 3, 1908 W, 1909 E
McDermott, L C (Q) 1962 NZ 1, 2
McDonald, B S (NSW) 1969 SA 4, 1970 S
McDonald, J C (Q) 1938 NZ 2, 3
Macdougall, D G (NSW) 1961 Fj 1, SA 1
Macdougall, S G (NSW, ACT) 1971 SA 3, 1973 E, 1974 NZ 1, 2,
   3, 1975 E 1, 2, 1976 E
McGhie, G H (Q) 1929 NZ 2, 3, 1930 BI
McGill, A N (NSW) 1968 NZ 1, 2, F, 1969 W, SA 1, 2, 3, 4, 1970
   S, 1971 SA 1, 2, 3, F 1, 2, 1972 F 1, 2, NZ 1, 2, 3, 1973 Tg
   1, 2
McIntyre, A J (Q) 1982 NZ 1, 2, 3, 1983 F 1, 2, 1984 Fj, NZ 1, 2,
   3, E, I, W, S, 1985 C 1, 2, NZ, Fj 1, 2, 1986 It, F, Arg 1, 2,
   1987 [E, US, I, F, W], NZ, Arg 2, 1988 E 1, 2, NZ 1, 2, 3, E,
   S, It, 1989 NZ
McIsaac, T P (WF) 2006 E1, I1, NZ1, 2(R), SA2, 3(R), W, I2
McKay, G R (NSW) 1920 NZ 2, 1921 SA 2, 3, 1922 M 1, 2, 3
MacKay, L J (NSW) 2005 NZ2(R)
McKenzie, E J A (NSW, ACT) 1990 F 1, 2, 3, US, NZ 1, 2, 3, 1991
   W, E, NZ 1, 2, [Arg, W, I, NZ, E], 1992 S 1, 2, NZ 1, 2, 3, SA,
   I, W, 1993 Tg, NZ, SA 1, 2, 3, C, F 1, 2, 1994 I 1, 2, It 1, 2,
   WS, NZ, 1995 Arg 1, 2, [SA, C (R), R, E], NZ 2, 1996 W 1,
   2, 1997 F 1, 2, NZ 1
McKid, W A (NSW) 1976 E, Fj 1, 1978 NZ 2, 3, 1979 I 1, 2
McKinnon, A (Q) 1904 BI 2
McKivat, C H (NSW) 1907 NZ 1, 3, 1908 W, 1909 E
McLaren, S D (NSW) 1926 NZ 4
McLaughlin, R E M (NSW) 1936 NZ 1, 2
McLean, A D (Q) 1933 SA 1, 2, 3, 4, 5, 1934 NZ 1, 2, 1936 NZ
   1, 2, M
McLean, J D (Q) 1904 BI 2, 3, 1905 NZ
McLean, J J (Q) 1971 SA 2, 3, F 1, 2, 1972 F 1, 2, NZ 1, 2, 3,
   Fj, 1973 W, E, 1974 NZ 1
McLean, P E (Q) 1974 NZ 1, 2, 3, 1975 J 1, 2, S, W, 1976 E, I,
   Fj 1, 2, 3, F 1, 2, 1978 W 1, 2, NZ 2, 1979 I 1, 2, NZ, Arg 1,
   2, 1980 Fj, 1981 F 1, 2, I, W, S, 1982 E, S 1, 2
McLean, P W (Q) 1978 NZ 1, 2, 3, 1979 I 1, 2, NZ, Arg 1, 2, 1980
   Fj, NZ 3, 1981 I, W, S, 1982 E, S 1, 2
McLean, R A (NSW) 1971 SA 1, 2, 3, F 1, 2
McLean, W M (Q) 1946 NZ 1, M, NZ 2, 1947 NZ 1, 2
McMahon, M J (Q) 1913 NZ 1
McMaster, R E (Q) 1946 NZ 1, M, NZ 2, 1947 NZ 1, 2, I, W
McMeniman, H J (Q, WF) 2005 Sm(R), It(R), F2(R), E, I, W, 2007
   SA2(R), NZ2(R), [J(R), Fj(R), C, E(t&R)], 2008 F2(R), SA1(t&R),
   NZ2(R), SA3, NZ3(R), It, E, F3, W, 2013 NZ1
MacMillan, D J (Q) 1950 BI 1, 2
McMullen, K V (NSW) 1962 NZ 3, 5, 1963 E, SA 1
McShane, J M S (NSW) 1937 SA 1, 2
Ma'afu, R S L (ACT, WF) 2010 Fj, E1, 2, I, SA1, NZ1, SA2, 3,
   NZ3, 2011 NZ2(R), [Ru(R), W], W
Mackay, G (NSW) 1926 NZ 4
Mackney, W A R (NSW) 1933 SA 1, 5, 1934 NZ 1, 2
Magrath, H (NSW) 1961 Fj 1, SA 2, F
Maguire, D J (Q) 1989 BI 1, 2, 3
Malcolm, S J (NSW) 1927 S, 1928 E, F, NZ 1, 2, M, 1929 NZ 1,
   2, 3, 1930 BI, 1931 NZ, 1932 NZ 1, 2, 3, 1933 SA 4, 5, 1934
   NZ 1, 2
Malone, J H (NSW) 1936 NZ 1, 2, M, 1937 SA 2

Malouf, B P (NSW) 1982 NZ 1
Mandible, E F (NSW) 1907 NZ 2, 3, 1908 W
Manning, J (NSW) 1904 BI 2
Manning, R C S (Q) 1967 NZ
Mann-Rea, J W (ACT) 2014 Arg2(R)
Mansfield, B W (NSW) 1975 J 2
Manu, D T (NSW) 1995 [R (t)], NZ 1, 2, 1996 W 1, 2(R), SA 1, NZ 2, It, S, I, 1997 F 1, NZ 1(t), E 1, NZ 2, SA 1
Marks, H (NSW) 1899 BI 1, 2
Marks, R J P (Q) 1962 NZ 4, 5, 1963 E, SA 2, 3, 4, 1964 NZ 1, 2, 3, 1965 SA 1, 2, 1966 W, S, 1967 E, I 1, F, I 2
Marrott, R (NSW) 1920 NZ 1, 3
Marrott, W J (NSW) 1922 NZ 2, 3, 1923 M 1, 2, 3, NZ 1, 2
Marshall, J S (NSW) 1949 M 1
Martin, G J (Q) 1989 BI 1, 2, 3, NZ, F 1, 2, 1990 F 1, 3(R), NZ 1
Martin, M C (NSW) 1980 Fj, NZ 1, 2, 1981 F 1, 2, W (R)
Massey-Westropp, M (NSW) 1914 NZ 3
Mathers, M J (NSW) 1980 Fj, NZ 2(R)
Maund, J W (NSW) 1903 NZ
Mayne, A V (NSW) 1920 NZ 1, 2, 3, 1922 M 1
Meadows, J E C (V, Q) 1974 NZ 1, 1975 S, W, 1976 I, US, Fj 1, 3, F 1, 2, 1978 NZ 1, 2, 3, 1979 I 1, 2, 1981 I, S, 1982 E, NZ 2, 3, 1983 US, Arg 2, NZ
Meadows, R W (NSW) 1958 M 1, 2, 3, NZ 1, 2, 3
Meagher, F W (NSW) 1923 NZ 3, 1924 NZ 3, 1925 NZ 4, 1926 NZ 1, 2, 3, 1927 I, W
Meibusch, J H (Q) 1904 BI 3
Meibusch, L S (Q) 1912 US
Melrose, T C (NSW) 1978 NZ 3, 1979 I 1, 2, NZ, Arg 1, 2
Merrick, S (NSW) 1995 NZ 1, 2
Messenger, H H (NSW) 1907 NZ 2, 3
Middleton, S A (NSW) 1909 E, 1910 NZ 1, 2, 3
Miller, A R (NSW) 1952 Fj 1, 2, NZ 1, 2, 1953 SA 1, 2, 3, 4, 1954 Fj 1, 2, 1955 NZ 1, 2, 3, 1956 SA 1, 2, 1957 NZ 1, 2, 1958 W, E, S, F, M 1, 2, 3, 1959 BI 1, 2, 1961 Fj 1, 2, 3, SA 2, F, 1962 NZ 1, 2, 1966 BI 1, 2, W, S, 1967 I 1, F, NZ
Miller, J M (NSW) 1962 NZ 1, 1963 E, SA 1, 1966 W S, 1967 E
Miller, J S (Q) 1986 NZ 2, 3, 1987 SK, [US, I, F], NZ, Arg 1, 2, 1988 E 1, 2, NZ 2, 3, E, S, It, 1989 BI 1, 2, 3, NZ, 1990 F 1, 3, 1991 W, [WS, W, I]
Miller, S W J (NSW) 1899 BI 3
Mingey, N (NSW) 1920 NZ 3, 1921 SA 1, 2, 3, 1923 M 1, NZ 1, 2
Mitchell, D A (Q, WF, NSW) 2005 SA1(R), 2(R), 3(R), NZ1, SA4, NZ2, F2(R), E, I, W, 2007 F 1, 2, Fj, SA1, 2(R), 2(R), SA 2(R), Fj, C, E(R)], 2008 SA1(R), NZ2(R), SA2, 3(R), NZ4, E, F3, W, 2009 It1, F, NZ1, SA1, NZ2, SA2(R), 3, NZ3, E, I, S, W, 2010 Fjt(8R), E1, 2, I, SA1, NZ1, 2, SA2, 3, W, NZ3, It, F, 2011 [I(R), US, Ru], 2012 NZ2, 3(R), E(R), It, W4
Mogg, J D (ACT) 2013 BI 3(R), NZ1, 2
Monaghan, L E (NSW) 1973 E, 1974 NZ 1, 2, 3, 1975 E 1, 2, S, W, 1976 E, I, US, F 1, 1978 W 1, 2, NZ 1, 1979 I 1, 2
Monti, C I A (Q) 1938 NZ 2
Moon, B J (Q) 1978 NZ 2, 3, 1979 I 1, 2, NZ, Arg 1, 2, 1980 Fj, NZ 1, 2, 3, 1981 F 1, 2, I, W, S, 1982 E, S 1, 2, 1983 US, Arg 1, 2, NZ, It, F 1, 2, 1984 Fj, NZ 1, 2, 3, E, 1986 It, F, Arg 1, 2
Mooney, T P (Q) 1954 Fj 1, 2
Moore, R C (ACT, NSW) 1999 [US], 2001 BI 2, 3, SA 1, NZ 1, SA 2, NZ 2, Sp (R), E (R), F (R), W(R), 2002 F 1(R), 2(R), SA 2(R)
Moore, S T (Q, ACT) 2005 Sm(R), It(R), F1(R), SA2(R), 3(R), F2(t&R), 2006 It(t), I2(R), S, 2007 W1, 2, Fj(R), SA1, NZ1, 2, [J, W, Fj, E], 2008 I, F1, 2, SA1, NZ1, 2, SA2, 3(R), NZ3, 4, It, E3, W, 2009 It1, F, NZ1, SA1, NZ2, SA2, 3(R), NZ3(R), 4, E, I, S, W, 2010 SA1(R), NZ1, SA2(t), 3, NZ3, 4, E3, F, 2011 Sm, SA1, NZ1, SA2, NZ2, [It, US(R), Ru, SA, NZ] , W(R), 2012 S, W1(R), 2(R), 3(R), NZ1(R), 2, F(R), E(R), It, W4(R), 2013 BI 1, 2, 3, NZ1, 2, SA1, Arg1, Arg2, NZ3, E, It, I, S, W, 2014 F1
Morahan, L J (Q) 2012 S
Moran, H M (NSW) 1908 W
Morgan, G (Q) 1992 NZ 1(R), 3(R), W, 1993 Tg, NZ, 1, 2, 3, C, F 1, 2, 1994 I 1, 2, It 1, WS, NZ, 1996 W 1, 2, C, NZ 1, SA 1, NZ 2, 1997 E 1, NZ 2
Morrissey, C V (NSW) 1925 NZ 2, 3, 4, 1926 NZ 2, 3
Morrissey, W (NSW) 1914 NZ 2
Mortlock, S A (ACT) 2000 Arg 1, 2, SA 1, NZ 1, SA 2, NZ 2, SA 3, F, S, E, 2002 F 1, 2, SA 1, NZ 2, SA 2, Arg, I, E, It, 2003 [R(R), Nm, S, NZ, E], 2004 S2, E1, PI, NZ1, SA1, NZ2, SA2, S3, F, S4, 2005 Sm, It, F1, SA2, 3(R), NZ1, 2006 E1, 2,

I1, NZ1, SA1, NZ2, SA2, NZ3, SA3, It, I2, S, 2007 W1, 2, Fj(R), SA1, NZ1, SA2, NZ2, [J, W, E], 2008 I, F1, 2, SA1, NZ2, SA2, 3, NZ3, 4, It, E, F3, W, 2009 It1, F, NZ1, SA1
Morton, A R (NSW) 1957 NZ 1, 2, 1958 F, M 1, 2, 3, NZ 1, 2, 3, 1959 BI 1, 2
Mossop, R P (NSW) 1949 NZ 1, 2, 1950 BI 1, 2, 1951 NZ 1
Moutray, I E (NSW) 1963 SA 2
Mowen, B S C (ACT) 2013 BI 1, 2, 3, NZ1, 2, SA1, Arg1, SA2, Arg2, NZ3, E, It, I, S, W
Mulligan, P J (NSW) 1925 NZ 1(R)
Mumm, D W (NSW) 2008 I(t&R), F1(R), 2, SA2(R), 3(R), NZ4, It, E(R), F3, W(R), 2009 It1, 2, F, NZ1(t), SA1(R), NZ2(R), 4(R), E(R), S(R), W, 2010 Fj, E1, 2, I, SA1, NZ1, 2, SA2, 3(R), NZ3(R), 4(R), W(R), E3(R)
Munsie, A (NSW) 1928 NZ 2
Murdoch, A N (NSW) 1993 F 1, 1996 W 1
Murphy, P J (Q) 1910 NZ 1, 2, 3, 1913 NZ 1, 2, 3, 1914 NZ 1, 2, 3
Murphy, W (Q) 1912 US

Nasser, B P (Q) 1989 F 1, 2, 1990 F 1, 2, 3, US, NZ 2, 1991 [WS]
Newman, E W (NSW) 1922 NZ 1
Nicholson, F C (Q) 1904 BI 3
Nicholson, F V (Q) 1903 NZ, 1904 BI 1
Niuqila, A S (NSW) 1988 S, It, 1989 BI 1
Noriega, E P (ACT, NSW) 1998 F, E 2, 1999 I 1, 2, E, SA 1, NZ 1, SA 2(R), NZ 2(R), 2002 F 1, 2, SA 1, NZ 2, Arg, I, E, It, 2003 I, W, E, SA 1, NZ 1, SA 2
Norton-Knight, S H (NSW) 2007 W1, Fj(R)
Nothling, O E (NSW) 1921 SA 1, 2, 3, NZ, 1922 M 1, 2, 3, NZ 1, 2, 3, 1923 M 1, 2, 3, NZ 1, 2, 3
Nucifora, D V (Q) 1991 [Arg (R)], 1993 C (R)

O'Brien, F W H (NSW) 1937 SA 2, 1938 NZ 3
O'Connor, J A (NSW) 1928 NZ 1, 2, 3, M
O'Connor, J D (WF, MR) 2008 It( R), 2009 It1, 2, F(R), NZ1(R), SA1(R), NZ2, SA2, SA3, 4, I(R), S(R), W(R), 2010 E1, 2, I, SA1, NZ1, 2, SA2, 3, W, E3, F, 2011 SA1, NZ1, SA2, [It(R), I, Ru, SA, NZ, W], W, 2013 BI 1, 2, 3, NZ1, 2, SA1, Arg1
O'Connor, M (ACT) 1994 I 1
O'Connor, M D (ACT, Q) 1979 Arg 1, 2, 1980 Fj, NZ 1, 2, 3, 1981 F 1, 2, I, 1982 E, S 1, 2
O'Donnell, C (NSW) 1913 NZ 1, 2
O'Donnell, I C (NSW) 1899 BI 3, 4
O'Donnell, J B (NSW) 1928 NZ 1, 3, M
O'Donnell, J M (NSW) 1899 BI 4
O'Gorman, J F (NSW) 1961 Fj 1, SA 1, 2, F, 1962 NZ 2, 1963 E, SA 1, 2, 3, 4, 1965 SA 1, 2, 1966 W, S, 1967 E, I 1, F, I 2
O'Neill, D J (Q) 1964 NZ 1, 2
O'Neill, J M (Q) 1952 NZ 1, 2, 1956 SA 1, 2
Ofahengaue, V (NSW) 1990 NZ 1, 2, 3, 1991 W, E, NZ 1, 2, [Arg, W, I, NZ, E], 1992 S 1, 2, SA, I, W, 1994 WS, NZ, 1995 Arg 1, 2(R), [SA, C, E], NZ 1, 2, 1997 Arg 1(t + R), 2(R), E 2, S, 1998 E 1(R), S 1(R), 2(R), NZ 1(R), SA 1(R), NZ 2(R), SA 2(R), NZ 3(R), Fj, WS, F (R)
Ormiston, I W L (NSW) 1920 NZ 1, 2, 3
Osborne, D H (V) 1975 E 1, 2, J 1
Outterside, R (NSW) 1959 BI 1, 2
Oxenham, A McE (Q) 1904 BI 2, 1907 NZ 2
Oxlade, A M (Q) 1904 BI 2, 3, 1905 NZ, 1907 NZ 2
Oxlade, B D (Q) 1938 NZ 1, 2, 3

Palfreyman, J R L (NSW) 1929 NZ 1, 1930 BI, 1931 NZ, 1932 NZ 3
Palmer, D P (ACT) 2012 S
Palu, W L (NSW) 2006 E2(t&R), I1(R), SA2, NZ3, SA3, W, It, I2, S(R), 2007 W1, 2, SA1, NZ1, [J, W, Fj, E], 2008 I, F1, SA1, NZ1, 2, SA2, 3, NZ3, It(R), E(R), F3, 2009 NZ1, SA1, NZ3(t&R), 4, E, I, S, W, 2011 [I(R), US], 2012 W1, 2, 3, NZ3, F, E, It, W4, 2013 BI 1, 2, 3, 2014 F1, 3, NZ1, 2, SA1
Panoho, G M (Q) 1998 SA 2(R), NZ 3(R), Fj (R), Tg, WS (R), 1999 I 2, E, SA 1(R), NZ 1, 2000 Arg 1(R), 2(R), SA 1(R), NZ 1(R), SA 2(R), 3(R), F (R), S(R), E (R), 2001 BI 1, 2003 SA 2(R), NZ 2
Papworth, B (NSW) 1985 Fj 1, 2, 1986 It, Arg 1, 2, NZ 1, 2, 3, 1987 [E, US, J (R), I, F], NZ, Arg 1, 2
Parker, A J (Q) 1983 Arg 1(R), 2, NZ
Parkinson, C E (Q) 1907 NZ 2
Pashley, J J (NSW) 1954 Fj 1, 2, 1958 M 1, 2, 3

Paul, J A (ACT) 1998 S 1(R), NZ 1(R), SA 1(t), Fj (R), Tg, 1999 I 1, 2, E, SA 1, NZ 1, [R (R), I 3(R), W (t), F (R)], 2000 Arg 1(R), 2(R), SA 1(R), NZ 1(R), SA 2(R), NZ 2(R), SA 3(R), F (R), S (R), E (R), 2001 BI 1, 2002 F 1, NZ 1, SA 1, NZ 2, SA 2, Arg, E, 2003 I, W, E, SA 2(t&R), NZ2(R), [Arg(R), R(R), Nm, I(R), S(R)), NZ(R), E(R)], 2004 S1(R), 2(R), E1(R), PI(R), NZ1(t&R), SA1, NZ2(R), SA2(R), S3, F, S4, E2, 2005 Sm, It, F1, SA1, 2, 3, NZ1, 2006 E1(R), 2(R), I1(R), NZ1(R), SA1, NZ2, SA2(R), NZ3, SA3
Pauling, T P (NSW) 1936 NZ 1, 1937 SA 1
Payne, S J (NSW) 1996 W 2, C, NZ 1, S, 1997 F 1(t), NZ 2(R), Arg 2(t)
Pearse, G K (NSW) 1975 W (R), 1976 I, US, Fj 1, 2, 3, 1978 NZ 1, 2, 3
Penman, A P (NSW) 1905 NZ
Perrin, P D (Q) 1962 NZ 1
Perrin, T D (NSW) 1931 M, NZ
Phelps, R (NSW) 1955 NZ 2, 3, 1956 SA 1, 2, 1957 NZ 1, 2, 1958 W, I, E, S, F, M 1, NZ 1, 2, 3, 1961 Fj 1, 2, 3, SA 1, 2, F, 1962 NZ 1, 2
Phipps, J A (NSW) 1953 SA 1, 2, 3, 4, 1954 Fj 1, 2, 1955 NZ 1, 2, 3, 1956 SA 1, 2
Phipps, N J (MR, NSW) 2011 Sm, SA1(R), [Ru(R)], 2012 SA1(R), Arg1, SA2, Arg2, NZ3, F, E, It(R), W4, 2013 BI 1(R), 3(R), 2014 F1(R), 2(R), 3(R), NZ1(R), 2(R), SA1, Arg1, SA2, Arg2
Phipps, W J (NSW) 1928 NZ 2
Piggott, H R (NSW) 1922 M 3(R)
Pilecki, S J (Q) 1978 W 1, 2, NZ 1, 2, 1979 I 1, 2, NZ, Arg 1, 2, 1980 Fj, NZ 1, 2, 1982 S 1, 2, 1983 US, Arg 1, 2, NZ
Pini, M (Q) 1994 I 1, It 2, WS, NZ, 1995 Arg 1, 2, [SA, R (t)]
Piper, B J C (NSW) 1946 NZ 1, M, NZ 2, 1947 NZ 1, S, I, W, 1948 E, F, 1949 M, 1, 2, 3
Pocock, D W (WF, ACT) 2008 NZ4(R), It(R), 2009 It1(R), 2, F(R), NZ1(R), SA1(R), NZ2(R), SA2(R), 3, NZ3, 4, E(R), I, W, 2010 Fj, E1, 2, I, SA1, NZ1, 2, SA2, 3, NZ3, 4, W, E3, It, F, 2011 SA1, NZ1, SA2, NZ2, [It, Ru, SA, NZ, W], W, 2012 S, W1, 2, 3, NZ1, W4
Poidevin, S P (NSW) 1980 Fj, NZ 1, 2, 3, 1981 F 1, 2, I, W, S, 1982 E, NZ 1, 2, 3, 1983 US, Arg 1, 2, NZ, It, F 1, 2, 1984 Fj, NZ 1, 2, 3, E, I, W, S, 1985 C 1, 2, NZ, Fj 1, 2, 1986 It, F, Arg 1, 2, NZ 1, 2, 3, 1987 SK, [E, J, I, F, W], Arg 1, 1988 NZ 1, 2, 3, 1989 NZ, 1991 E, NZ 1, 2, [Arg, W, I, NZ, E]
Polota-Nau, S U T (NSW) 2005 E(R), I(R), 2006 S(R), 2008 SA1(R), NZ1(R), 2(R), SA2(R), 3, It(R), 6(R) 2009 It1(R), 2, F(R), SA1(R), NZ2(t&R), SA2(R), 3, NZ3, 4(R), E(R), I(R), S(R), W(R), 2010 It(R), F(R), 2011 [It(R), I, US, SA(R), NZ(R), W], W, 2012 W1, 2, 3, NZ1, SA1, Arg1, SA2, Arg2, NZ3, F, E, W4, 2013 I(R), W(R), 2014 F1(R), 2, 3, Arg1
Pope, A M (Q) 1968 NZ 2(R)
Potter, R T (Q) 1961 Fj 2
Potts, J M (NSW) 1957 NZ 1, 2, 1958 W, I, 1959 BI 1
Prentice, C W (NSW) 1914 NZ 3
Prentice, W S (NSW) 1908 W, 1909 E, 1910 NZ 1, 2, 3, 1912 US
Price, R A (NSW) 1974 NZ 1, 2, 3, 1975 E 1, 2, J 1, 2, 1976 US
Primmer, C J (Q) 1951 NZ 1, 3
Proctor, I J (NSW) 1967 NZ
Prosser, R B (NSW) 1967 E, I 1, 2, NZ, 1968 NZ 1, 2, F, I, S, 1969 W, SA 1, 2, 3, 4, 1971 SA 1, 2, 3, F 1, 2, 1972 F 1, 2, NZ 1, 2, 3, Fj
Pugh, G H (NSW) 1912 US
Purcell, M P (Q) 1966 W, S, 1967 I 2
Purkis, E M (NSW) 1958 S, M 1
Pym, J E (NSW) 1923 M 1

Rainbow, A E (NSW) 1925 NZ 1
Ramalli, C (NSW) 1938 NZ 2, 3
Ramsay, K M (NSW) 1936 M, 1937 SA 1, 1938 NZ 1, 3
Rankin, R (NSW) 1936 NZ 1, 2, M, 1937 SA 1, 2, 1938 NZ 1, 2
Rathbone, C (ACT) 2004 S1, 2(R), E1, PI, NZ1, SA1, NZ2, SA2, S3, F, S4, 2005 Sm, NZ1(R), SA4, NZ2, 2006 E1(R), 2(R), I1(R), SA1(R), NZ2(R), SA2(R), NZ3, SA3, W, It, I2
Rathie, D S (Q) 1972 F 1, 2
Raymond, R L (NSW) 1920 NZ 1, 2, 1921 SA 2, 3, NZ, 1922 M 1, 2, 3, NZ 1, 2, 3, 1923 M 1, 2
Redwood, C (Q) 1903 NZ, 1904 BI 1, 2, 3
Reid, E J (NSW) 1925 NZ 2, 3, 4
Reid, T W (NSW) 1961 Fj 1, 2, 3, SA 1, 1962 NZ 1
Reilly, N P (Q) 1968 NZ 1, 2, F, I, S, 1969 W, SA 1, 2, 3, 4
Reynolds, L J (NSW) 1910 NZ 2(R), 3
Reynolds, R J (NSW) 1984 Fj, NZ 1, 2, 3, 1985 Fj 1, 2, 1986 Arg 1, 2, NZ 1, 1987 [J]

Richards, E W (Q) 1904 BI 1, 3, 1905 NZ, 1907 NZ 1(R), 2
Richards, G (NSW) 1978 NZ 2(R), 3, 1981 F 1
Richards, T J (Q) 1908 W, 1909 E, 1912 US
Richards, V S (NSW) 1936 NZ 1, 2(R), M, 1937 SA 1, 1938 NZ 1
Richardson, G C (Q) 1971 SA 1, 2, 3, 1972 NZ 2, 3, Fj, 1973 Tg 1, 2, W
Rigney, W A (NSW) 1925 NZ 2, 4, 1926 NZ 4
Riley, S A (NSW) 1903 NZ
Ritchie, E V (NSW) 1924 NZ 1, 3, 1925 NZ 2, 3
Roberts, B T (NSW) 1956 SA 2
Roberts, H F (Q) 1961 Fj 1, 3, SA 2, F
Robertson, I J (NSW) 1975 J 1, 2
Robinson, B A (NSW) 2006 SA3, I2(R), S, 2007 W1(R), 2, Fj(R), 2008 I, F1, 2, SA1, NZ1, 2, SA2, 3, NZ3, 4, E, W, 2009 It1, F, NZ1, SA1, NZ2, SA2, 3, NZ3, 4, E, I, S, W, 2010 SA1, NZ1, 2, SA2, 3, NZ3, 4, It, W4, 2013 BI 1, 2, 3, SA2(t&R), NZ3(R), E(R), It(R), I(R), W(R), 2014 SA2(R), Arg2(R)
Robinson, B J (ACT) 1996 It (R), S (R), I (R), 1997 F 1, 2, NZ 1, E 1, NZ 2, SA 1(R), NZ 3(R), SA 2(R), Arg 1, 2, E 2, S, 1998 Tg
Robinson, B S (Q) 2011 Sm(R)
Roche, C (Q) 1982 S 1, 2, NZ 1, 2, 3, 1983 US, Arg 1, 2, NZ, It, F 1, 2, 1984 Fj, NZ 1, 2, 3, I
Rodriguez, E E (NSW) 1984 Fj, NZ 1, 2, 3, E, I, W, S, 1985 C 1, 2, NZ, Fj 1, 1986 It, F, Arg 1, 2, NZ 1, 2, 3, 1987 SK, [E, J, W (R)], NZ, Arg 1, 2
Roe, J A (Q) 2003 [Nm(R)], 2004 E1(R), SA1(R), NZ2(R), SA2(t&R), S3, F, 2005 Sm(R), It(R), F1(R), SA1(R), 3, NZ1, SA4(t&R), NZ2(R), F2(R), E, I, W
Roebuck, M C (NSW) 1991 W, E, NZ 1, 2, [Arg, WS, W, I, NZ, E], 1992 S 1, 2, NZ 2, 3, SA, I, W, 1993 Tg, SA 1, 2, 3, C, F 2
Roff, J W (ACT) 1995 [C, R], NZ 1, 2, 1996 W 1, 2, NZ 1, SA 1, NZ 2, SA 2(R), S, I, W 3, 1997 F 1, 2, NZ 1, E 1, NZ 2, SA 1, NZ 3, SA 2, Arg 1, 2, E 2, S, 1998 E 1, S 1, 2, NZ 1, SA 1, NZ 2, SA 2, NZ 3, W, SA, F E 2, 1999 I 1, 2, E, SA 1, NZ 1, SA 2, NZ 2(R), [R (R), I 3, US (R), W, SA 3, F], 2000 Arg 1, 2, SA 1, NZ 1, SA 2, NZ 2, SA 3, F, S, E, 2001 BI 1, 2, 3, SA 1, NZ 1, SA 2, NZ 2, Sp, E, F, W, 2003 I, W, E, SA 1, [Arg, R, I, S(R), NZ(t&R), E(R)], 2004 S1, 2, E1, PI
Rogers, M S (NSW) 2002 F 1(R), 2(R), NZ 1(R), SA 1(R), NZ 2(R), SA 2(t&R), Arg, 2003 E (R), SA 1, NZ 1, SA 2, NZ 2, [Arg, R, Nm, I, S, NZ, E], 2004S3(R), F(R), S4(R), E2(R), 2005 Sm(R), It, F1(R), SA1, 4, NZ2, F2, E, I1, NZ1, SA1(R), NZ2(R), SA2(R), NZ3(R), W, It, I2(R), S(R)
Rose, H A (NSW) 1967 I 2, NZ, 1968 NZ 1, 2, F, I, S, 1969 W, SA 1, 2, 3, 4, 1970 S
Rosenblum, M E (NSW) 1928 NZ 1, 2, 3, M
Rosenblum, R G (NSW) 1969 SA 1, 3, 1970 S
Rosewell, J S H (NSW) 1907 NZ 1, 3
Ross, A W (NSW) 1925 NZ 1, 2, 3, 1926 NZ 1, 2, 3, 1927 I, W, S, 1928 E, F, 1929 NZ 1, 1930 BI, 1931 M, NZ, 1932 NZ 2, 3, 1933 SA 5, 1934 NZ 1, 2
Ross, W S (Q) 1979 I 1, 2, Arg 2, 1980 Fj, NZ 1, 2, 3, 1982 S 1, 2, 1983 US, Arg 1, 2, NZ
Rothwell, P R (NSW) 1951 NZ 1, 2, 3, 1952 Fj 1
Row, F L (NSW) 1899 BI 1, 3, 4
Row, N E (NSW) 1907 NZ 1, 3, 1909 E, 1910 NZ 1, 2, 3
Rowles, P G (NSW) 1972 Fj, 1973 E
Roxburgh, J R (NSW) 1968 NZ 1, 2, F, 1969 W, SA 1, 2, 3, 4, 1970 S
Ruebner, G (NSW) 1966 BI 1, 2
Russell, C J (NSW) 1907 NZ 1, 2, 3, 1908 W, 1909 E
Ryan, J R (NSW) 1975 J 2, 1976 I, US, Fj 1, 2, 3
Ryan, K J (Q) 1958 E, M 1, NZ 1, 2, 3
Ryan, P F (NSW) 1963 E, SA 1, 1966 BI 1, 2
Ryan, P J (NSW) 2012 F(R), 2013 I(R), 2014 F1(R)
Rylance, M H (NSW) 1926 NZ 4(R)

Sailor, W J (Q) 2002 F 1, 2, Arg (R), I, E, It, 2003 I, W, E, SA 1, NZ 1, SA 2, NZ 2, [Arg, R, I, S, NZ, E], 2004 S1, 2, NZ1(R), 2(R), SA2(R), S3(R), F(R), S4(R), E2, 2005 Sm, It, F1, SA1, 2, 3, F2, I(R), W(R)
Samo, U R (ACT, Q) 2004 S1, 2, E1, PI, NZ1, S4(R), 2011 SA2(R), NZ2, [It, I, US(R), Ru, SA, NZ, W(t&R)], W(R), 2012 NZ1(R), 2(R), SA1, Arg1, SA2, Arg2, F(R)
Sampson, J H (NSW) 1899 BI 4
Sayle, J L (NSW) 1967 NZ

1962 NZ 2, 3, 4, 5, 1963 E, SA 1, 2, 3, 4, 1964 NZ 1, 2, 3, 1965 SA 1, 2, 1966 BI 1, 2, 1967 F
**Thornett, R N** (NSW) 1961 Fj 1, 2, 3, SA 1, 2, F, 1962 NZ 1, 2, 3, 4, 5
**Thorpe, A C** (NSW) 1929 NZ 1(R)
**Timani, S** (NSW) 2011 Sm, 2012 S, W3, NZ1, 2, SA1, Arg2, NZ3, E, It, 2013 Arg1(R), SA2(R), Arg2(R), NZ3(R), E, It, I(R), S(R)
**Timbury, F R V** (Q) 1910 NZ 1, 2,
**Tindall, E N** (NSW) 1973 Tg 2
**Toby, A E** (NSW) 1925 NZ 1, 4
**Tolhurst, H A** (NSW) 1931 M, NZ
**Tomane, J M** (ACT) 2012 S, 2013 BI 2, 3, SA2, Arg2, It(R), I(R), S, W, 2014 SA2, Arg2
**Tombs, R C** (NSW) 1992 S 1, 2, 1994 I 2, It 1, 1996 NZ 2
**Tonkin, A E J** (NSW) 1947 S, I, W, 1948 E, F, 1950 BI 2
**Toomua, M P** (ACT) 2013 NZ1, 2, SA1(R), Arg1(R), SA2(R), Arg2(R), NZ3, E, It, I, 2014 F1, 2, 3, NZ1, 2, SA1, Arg1, SA2, Arg2
**Tooth, R M** (NSW) 1951 NZ 1, 2, 3, 1954 Fj 1, 2, 1955 NZ 1, 2, 3, 1957 NZ 1, 2
**Towers, C H T** (NSW) 1926 NZ 1, 3(R), 4, 1927 I, 1928 E, F, NZ 1, 2, 3, M, 1929 NZ 1, 3, 1930 BI, 1931 M, NZ, 1934 NZ 1, 2, 1937 SA 1, 2
**Trivett, R K** (Q) 1966 BI 1, 2
**Tune, B N** (Q) 1996 W 2, C, NZ 1, SA 1, NZ 2, SA 2, 1997 F 1, 2, NZ 1, E 1, NZ 2, SA 1, NZ 3, SA 2, Arg, 1, 2, E 2, S, 1998 E 1, S 1, 2, NZ 1, SA 1, 2, NZ 3, 1999 I 1, E, SA 1, NZ 1, SA 2, NZ 2, [R, I 3, W, SA 3, F], 2000 SA 2(R), NZ 2(t&R), SA 3(R), 2001 F (R), W, 2002 NZ 1, SA 1, NZ 2, SA 2, Arg, 2006 NZ1(R)
**Tuqiri, L D** (NSW) 2003 I (R), W (R), E (R), SA 1(R), NZ 1, SA 2, NZ 2, [Arg(R), R(R), Nm, I(R), S, NZ, E], 2004 S1, 2, E1, PI, NZ1, SA1, NZ2, SA2, S3, F, S4, E2, 2005 It, F1, SA1, 2, 3, NZ1, SA4, NZ2, F2, E, I, W, 2006 E1, 2, I1, NZ1, SA1, NZ2, SA2, NZ3, W, It, I2, S, 2007 Fj, SA1, NZ1, [J, W, Fj, C, E], 2008 I, F1, SA1, NZ1, 2, SA2, 3, NZ3, W(R)
**Turinui, M P** (NSW) 2003 I, W, E, 2003 [Nm(R)], 2004 S1(R), 2, E2, 2005 Sm, It(R), F1(R), SA1, 2(t&R), 3, NZ1, SA4, NZ2, F2, E, I, W
**Turnbull, A** (V) 1961 Fj 3
**Turnbull, R** (NSW) 1968 I
**Turner, L D** (NSW) 2008 F2, It, 2009 It1, 2, F, NZ1, SA1, NZ2, SA2, 3, NZ3, 2010 NZ3, It, F(R), 2011 W
**Tuynman, S N** (NSW) 1983 F 1, 2, 1984 E, I, W, S, 1985 C 1, 2, NZ, Fj 1, 2, 1986 It, F, Arg 1, 2, NZ 1, 2, 3, 1987 SK, [E, US, J, I, W], NZ, Arg 1(R), 2, 1988 E, It, 1989 BI 1, 2, 3, NZ, 1990 NZ 1
**Tweedale, E** (NSW) 1946 NZ 1, 2, 1947 NZ 2, S, I, 1948 E, F, 1949 M 1, 2, 3

**Valentine, J J** (Q, WF) 2006 E1(R), W(R), I2(R), S(R), 2009 It2(R), F(R)
**Vaughan, D** (NSW) 1983 US, Arg 1, It, F 1, 2
**Vaughan, G N** (V) 1958 E, S, F, M 1, 2, 3
**Verge, A** (NSW) 1904 BI 1, 2
**Vickerman, D J** (ACT, NSW) 2002 F 2(R), Arg, E, It, 2003 I (R), W (R), E (R), SA 1, NZ 1, SA 2, NZ 2, [Arg(R), R, I(R), S(R)], 2004 S1(t&R), 2(R), E1(R), PI(R), NZ1(R), SA1(R), NZ2(R), SA2(R), S3, F, S4, E2, 2005 SA2(R), 3, NZ1, SA4, 2006 E1, 2, I1, NZ1, SA1, NZ2, SA2, NZ2, [J, W, Fj, E], 2008 NZ1(R), 2(t&R), SA2, 2011 Sm(R), NZ1(R), 2, [It, I, US(R), SA, NZ]
**Vuna, K C** (MR) 2012 W1, 2

**Walden, R J** (NSW) 1934 NZ 2, 1936 NZ 1, 2, M
**Walker, A K** (NSW) 1947 NZ 1, 1948 E, F, 1950 BI 1, 2
**Walker, A M** (ACT) 2000 NZ 1(R), 2001 BI 1, 2, 3, SA 1, NZ 1, 2(R)
**Walker, A S B** (NSW) 1912 US, 1920 NZ 1, 2, 1921 SA 1, 2, 3, NZ, 1922 M 1, 3, NZ 1, 2, 3, 1923 M 2, 3, 1924 NZ 1, 2
**Walker, L F** (NSW) 1988 NZ 2, 3, S, It, 1989 BI 1, 2, 3, NZ
**Walker, L R** (NSW) 1982 NZ 2, 3
**Wallace, A C** (NSW) 1921 NZ, 1926 NZ 3, 4, 1927 I, W, S, 1928 E, F
**Wallace, T M** (NSW) 1994 It 1(R), 2
**Wallach, C** (NSW) 1913 NZ 1, 3, 1914 NZ 1, 2, 3
**Walsh, J J** (NSW) 1953 SA 1, 2, 3, 4
**Walsh, P B** (NSW) 1904 BI 1, 2, 3
**Walsham, K P** (NSW) 1962 NZ 3, 1963 E
**Ward, P G** (NSW) 1899 BI 1, 2, 3, 4
**Ward, T** (Q) 1899 BI 2

**Watson, G W** (Q) 1907 NZ 1
**Watson, W T** (NSW) 1912 US, 1913 NZ 1, 2, 3, 1914 NZ 1, 1920 NZ 1, 2, 3
**Waugh, P R** (NSW) 2000 E (R), 2001 NZ 1(R), SA 2(R), NZ 2(R), Sp (R), E (R), F, W, 2003 I (R), W, E, SA 1, NZ 1, SA 2, NZ2, [Arg, R, I, S, NZ, E], 2004 S1(R), 2, E1, PI, NZ1, SA1, NZ2, SA2, S3, F, S4, E2, 2005 SA1(R), 2(R), 3, NZ1(R), SA4, NZ2, F2, E, I, W, 2006 E1(R), 2(R), I1(R), NZ1(R), SA1(R), NZ2(R), SA2(R), NZ3, SA3, W, I2, S(R), 2007 W1, 2(R), Fj, SA1(R), NZ1(R), SA2(R), NZ2(R) , [WF(R), Fj, C(R), E(R)], 2008 I(R), F1(R), 2, SA1(R), NZ1(R), 2, SA2(t&R), 3, NZ4(R), It, W, 2009 It2(R), F(R)
**Waugh, W W** (NSW, ACT) 1993 SA 1, 1995 [C], NZ 1, 2, 1996 S, I, 1997 Arg 1, 2
**Weatherstone, L J** (ACT) 1975 E 1, 2, J 1, 2, S (R), 1976 E, I
**Webb, W** (NSW) 1899 BI 3, 4
**Welborn J P** (NSW) 1996 SA 2, It, 1998 Tg, 1999 E, SA 1, NZ 1
**Wells, B G** (NSW) 1958 M 1
**Weeks, L S** (MR) 2014 F2(R), 3(R)
**Westfield, R E** (NSW) 1928 NZ 1, 2, 3, M, 1929 NZ 2, 3
**Whitaker, C J** (NSW) 1998 SA 2(R), Fj (R), Tg, 1999 NZ 2(R), [R (R), US, F (R)], 2000 S (R), 2001 Sp (R), W (R), 2002 Arg (R), It (R), 2003 I (R), W (R), SA 2(R), [Arg(R), Nm, S(R)], 2004 PI(R), NZ1, 2005 Sm, It(R), F1(R), SA1(R), 2(R), NZ1(t&R), SA4(R), NZ2(R), F2(R), E(R), W(R)
**White, C J B** (NSW) 1899 BI 1, 1903 NZ, 1904 BI 1
**White, J M** (NSW) 1904 BI 3
**White, J P L** (NSW) 1958 NZ 1, 2, 3, 1961 Fj 1, 2, 3, SA 1, 2, F, 1962 NZ 1, 2, 3, 4, 5, 1963 E, SA 1, 2, 3, 4, 1964 NZ 1, 2, 3, 1965 SA 1, 2
**White, M C** (Q) 1931 M, NZ 1932 NZ 1, 2, 1933 SA 1, 2, 3, 4, 5
**White, N W** (ACT) 2013 NZ1(R), 2(R), SA1(R), Arg1, SA2, Arg2(R), E(R), It(R), I(R), S(R), 2014 F1, 2, 3, NZ1, 2, Arg1(R), 2(R)
**White, S W** (NSW) 1956 SA 1, 2, 1958 I, E, S, M 2, 3
**White, W G S** (Q) 1933 SA 1, 2, 3, 4, 5, 1934 NZ 1, 2, 1936 NZ 1, 2, M
**White, W J** (NSW) 1928 NZ 1, M, 1932 NZ 1
**Wickham, S M** (NSW) 1903 NZ, 1904 BI 1, 2, 3, 1905 NZ
**Williams, D** (Q) 1913 NZ 3, 1914 NZ 1, 2, 3
**Williams, I M** (NSW) 1987 Arg 1, 2, 1988 E 1, 2, NZ 1, 2, 3, 1989 BI 2, 3, NZ 1, F 1, 2, 1990 F 1, 2, 3, US, NZ 1
**Williams, J L** (NSW) 1963 SA 1, 3, 4
**Williams, R W** (ACT) 1999 I 1(t&R), 2(t&R), E (R), [US], 2000 Arg 1, 2, SA 1, NZ 1, SA 2, NZ 2, SA 3, F (R), S (R), E
**Williams, S A** (NSW) 1980 Fj, NZ 1, 2, 1981 F 1, 2, 1982 E, NZ 1, 2, 3, 1983 US, Arg 1(R), 2, NZ, It, F 1, 2, 1984 NZ 1, 2, 3, E, I, W, S, 1985 C 1, 2, NZ, Fj 1, 2
**Wilson, B J** (NSW) 1949 NZ 1, 2
**Wilson, C R** (Q) 1957 NZ 1, 1958 NZ 1, 2, 3
**Wilson, D J** (Q) 1992 S 1, 2, NZ 1, 2, 3, SA, I, W, 1993 Tg, NZ, SA 1, 2, 3, C, F 1, 2, 1994 I 1, 2, It 1, 2, WS, NZ, 1995 Arg 1, 2, [SA, R, E], 1996 W 1, 2, C, NZ 1, SA 1, NZ 2, SA 2, It, S, I, W 3, 1997 F 1, 2, NZ 1, E 1(t + R), NZ 2(R), SA 1, NZ 3, SA 2, E 2(R), S, 1998 E 1, S 1, 2, NZ 1, SA 1, NZ 2, SA 2, NZ 3, Fj, WS, F, E 2, 1999 I 1, 2, E, SA 1, NZ 1, SA 2, NZ 2, [R, I 3, W, SA 3, F], 2000 Arg 1, 2, SA 1, NZ 1, SA 2, NZ 2, SA 3
**Wilson, V W** (Q) 1937 SA 1, 2, 1938 NZ 1, 2, 3
**Windon, C J** (NSW) 1946 NZ 1, 2, 1947 NZ 1, S, I, W, 1948 E, F, 1949 M 1, 2, 3, NZ 1, 2, 1951 NZ 1, 2, 3, 1952 Fj 1, 2, NZ 1, 2
**Windon, K S** (NSW) 1937 SA 1, 2, 1946 M
**Windsor, J C** (Q) 1947 NZ 2
**Winning, K C** (Q) 1951 NZ 1
**Wogan, L W** (NSW) 1913 NZ 1, 2, 3, 1914 NZ 1, 2, 3, 1920 NZ 1, 2, 3, 1921 NZ 1, 2, 3, NZ, 1922 M 3, NZ 1, 2, 3, 1923 M 1, 2, 1924 NZ 1, 2, 3
**Wood, F** (NSW) 1907 NZ 1, 2, 3, 1910 NZ 1, 2, 3, 1913 NZ 1, 2, 3, 1914 NZ 1, 2, 3
**Wood, R N** (Q) 1972 Fj
**Woods, H F** (NSW) 1925 NZ 4, 1926 NZ 1, 2, 3, 1927 I, W, S, 1928 E
**Wright, K J** (NSW) 1975 E 1, 2, J 1, 1976 US, F 1, 2, 1978 NZ 1, 2, 3
**Wyld, G** (NSW) 1920 NZ 2

**Yanz, K** (NSW) 1958 F
**Young, W K** (ACT, NSW) 2000 F, S, E, 2002 F 1, 2, NZ 1, SA 1, NZ 2, SA 2, Arg, E, It, 2003 I, W, E, SA 1, NZ 1, SA 2, NZ 2, [Arg, R, I, S, NZ, E], 2004 S1, 2, E1, PI, NZ1, SA1, NZ2, SA2, S3, F, S4, E2, 2005 Sm, It, F1, SA1, 2, 3, NZ1, SA4, NZ2

# RUGBY
## WORLD CUP
### 2015

## FOR TICKET INFORMATION ON
## RUGBY WORLD CUP 2015

# JOIN THE FRONT ROW

## WWW.RUGBYWORLDCUP.COM/FRONTROW

### England
### 2015™

#RWC2015    f rugbyworldcup    🐦 @rugbyworldcup    ▶ rugbyworldcup

# CANADA

## CANADA'S 2013–14 TEST RECORD

| OPPONENTS | DATE | VENUE | RESULT |
|-----------|------|-------|--------|
| Georgia | 9 Nov | A | Lost 19–15 |
| Romania | 16 Nov | A | Lost 21–20 |
| Portugal | 23 Nov | A | Won 52–8 |
| Japan | 7 Jun | H | Lost 25–34 |
| Scotland | 14 Jun | H | Lost 17–19 |
| USA | 21 Jun | A | Lost 38–35 |

# CLOSE BUT NOT CLOSE ENOUGH FOR CANADA

## By Ian Gilbert

Judy Teasdale

Canada's run of seven successive victories over their neighbours the USA came to an end in the Pacific Nations Cup.

**C**anada's Test season was a tale of agonising near-misses, the most significant being when they came within a whisker of toppling Scotland. That two-point defeat seemed to sum things up for Canada, who would have been celebrating a stellar year but for a handful of points.

The bare statistics make miserable reading – won one, lost five – but delve a little deeper and the Canadians have plenty of grounds for optimism before Rugby World Cup 2015. The five reverses were by a total of only 19 points, and defeat by Scotland – the highest-ranked opponents Canada met – offered a fair measure of the team's ability.

Fly-half Harry Jones slotted a penalty to put Canada ahead 17–16 and on the brink of their first win over the Scots since 2002. But the 10 minutes left were enough for Greig Laidlaw to kick the penalty that would break Canadian hearts.

Aside from the disappointment of running a Six Nations side so close, the match was a useful lesson for coach Kieran Crowley as to what will be required at the World Cup if Canada are to progress beyond the pool stages for only the second time. To repeat their feat of 1991 when they reached the quarter-finals they would probably need to beat either Ireland or France, something they have achieved against the latter – in 1994, a Canadian side with players such as Gareth Rees and Al Charron in their ranks were victorious against a side captained by Philippe Saint-André and featuring Philippe Sella and Abdelatif Benazzi – but never against the former.

They will also face Italy and Romania, another side that Canada ran agonisingly close, in Bucharest, in November. Certainly, the Canadians are undaunted by higher-ranked opponents.

"On our day I think we can beat teams like Italy," insisted Crowley. "Against Scotland and New Zealand Maori, we were right in those games – we can pressure against them but we need an 80-minute effort. If you look at our record over the past eight or nine games like that, we could easily have won eight of them."

Canada began the 2013–14 season on a high, with Rugby World Cup 2015 qualification already secured after winning both the home and away legs against the USA in August.

First up were the Maori All Blacks in November – a non-Test match in so far as they are a national representative side but who nonetheless fielded All Blacks such as Zac Guildford. The wing weighed in with two tries as the Maori were ultimately convincing 40–15 winners, but Canada initially kept with them by scoring the first try and keeping them pegged back for much of the first half.

From there it was on to Europe for Canada and valuable Test exposure against sides near them in the IRB World Rankings in Georgia, Romania and Portugal.

In the first match, Canada lost 19–15 to Georgia in an ill-tempered affair in Tbilisi that saw a player from each side sent off. The Canadians led 12–9 at half-time in front of a crowd of 12,000, but after the break Georgia scored the only try of the game to set up their victory.

The Canadians endured another desperately close game with a 21–20 loss to Romania despite the tourists outscoring their hosts by two tries to none. They were left to rue a late chance when Ciaran Hearn's pass to Phil Mack went loose with the line begging.

In the final game of a challenging tour, things clicked for Canada as they overran Portugal 52–8 in Lisbon, Hearn and James Pritchard each crossing for two tries. With Pritchard also assuming kicking duties, he finished the game with a personal tally of 27 points.

Canada thus ended the tour on a high note before the next call to international duty, in June for home matches against Japan, Scotland and USA.

Unfortunately Canada's habit of failing to close out the game reappeared against Japan in their IRB Pacific Nations Cup encounter in Vancouver. The Canadians led 25–9 at half-time against opponents ranked several places higher, only to allow them back into the game to score 25 unanswered points in the second half to win 34–25. The sides each scored three tries, but full-back Ayumu Goromaru's kicking proved crucial to Japan with three penalties more than Canada.

Next came Scotland and another defeat, albeit a marked improvement on the 41–0 reverse when the sides last met in 2008.

While those matches were frustrating, the reverse against neighbour and most regular adversary the USA was especially galling. Canada have enjoyed something of a monopoly on the fixture in recent years, winning seven on the trot, and in four of those encounters they had won by at least two scores.

But their ascendancy in the fixture came to an abrupt end in Sacramento as the Eagles broke their hoodoo with a 38–35 win – their first victory in the fixture since 2009.

Once again Canada squandered a dominant position: they led by 17 points in the second half, but allowed USA to claw their way back into the Pacific Nations Cup match as wing Brett Thompson scored the winning try, converted by full-back Chris Wyles.

"It was a disappointing summer for us," admitted Crowley. "We led Japan by 16 points; against Scotland we were unfortunate, we couldn't finish that off; and we were poor against the US."

The World Cup will be a tough challenge, but it's not one Crowley is shirking from.

"They are all tough groups aren't they?" said the pragmatic New Zealander. "We've got to target three games to get out of it. It's going to be a massive challenge – three of them are Six Nations teams, and Romania, a lot of their players play in Europe and particularly France. So it's a challenge, but if you look at world rankings there's not a lot between them – Italy, Romania and we are in there as well."

The absence of a professional club tournament in Canada means several of the better players are based overseas, such as DTH van der Merwe (Glasgow Warriors) and Tyler Ardron (Ospreys). Canada's huge geographical area adds another obstacle to national training with Toronto well over 4,000km from Vancouver.

However, the lead-up to RWC 2015 will feature an extended period when the players are in camp, which will hopefully help them hone the big-match nous required to close out tight encounters like the ones they had this year.

# CANADA INTERNATIONAL STATISTICS

## MATCH RECORDS UP TO 13 OCTOBER 2014

### WINNING MARGIN

| Date | Opponent | Result | Winning Margin |
|------|----------|--------|----------------|
| 24/06/2006 | Barbados | 69–3 | 66 |
| 14/10/1999 | Namibia | 72–11 | 61 |
| 12/08/2006 | USA | 56–7 | 49 |
| 06/07/1996 | Hong Kong | 57–9 | 48 |

### MOST POINTS IN A MATCH
#### BY THE TEAM

| Date | Opponent | Result | Points |
|------|----------|--------|--------|
| 14/10/1999 | Namibia | 72–11 | 72 |
| 24/06/2006 | Barbados | 69–3 | 69 |
| 15/07/2000 | Japan | 62–18 | 62 |
| 13/11/2010 | Spain | 60–22 | 60 |
| 06/07/1996 | Hong Kong | 57–9 | 57 |

#### BY A PLAYER

| Date | Player | Opponent | Points |
|------|--------|----------|--------|
| 12/08/2006 | James Pritchard | USA | 36 |
| 24/06/2006 | James Pritchard | Barbados | 29 |
| 14/10/1999 | Gareth Rees | Namibia | 27 |
| 23/11/2013 | James Pritchard | Portugal | 27 |
| 13/07/1996 | Bobby Ross | Japan | 26 |

### MOST TRIES IN A MATCH
#### BY THE TEAM

| Date | Opponent | Result | Tries |
|------|----------|--------|-------|
| 24/06/2006 | Barbados | 69–3 | 11 |
| 14/10/1999 | Namibia | 72–11 | 9 |
| 11/05/1991 | Japan | 49–26 | 8 |
| 15/07/2000 | Japan | 62–18 | 8 |
| 13/11/2010 | Spain | 60–22 | 8 |

#### BY A PLAYER

| Date | Player | Opponent | Tries |
|------|--------|----------|-------|
| 15/07/2000 | Kyle Nichols | Japan | 4 |
| 24/06/2006 | James Pritchard | Barbados | 3 |
| 12/08/2006 | James Pritchard | USA | 3 |
| 10/05/1987 | Steve Gray | USA | 3 |

### MOST CONVERSIONS IN A MATCH
#### BY THE TEAM

| Date | Opponent | Result | Cons |
|------|----------|--------|------|
| 14/10/1999 | Namibia | 72–11 | 9 |
| 15/07/2000 | Japan | 62–18 | 8 |
| 7 on 4 occasions | | | |

#### BY A PLAYER

| Date | Player | Opponent | Cons |
|------|--------|----------|------|
| 14/10/1999 | Gareth Rees | Namibia | 9 |
| 15/07/2000 | Jared Barker | Japan | 8 |
| 7 on 4 occasions | | | |

### MOST PENALTIES IN A MATCH
#### BY THE TEAM

| Date | Opponent | Result | Pens |
|------|----------|--------|------|
| 25/05/1991 | Scotland | 24–19 | 8 |
| 22/08/1998 | Argentina | 28–54 | 7 |
| 6 on 6 occasions | | | |

#### BY A PLAYER

| Date | Player | Opponent | Pens |
|------|--------|----------|------|
| 25/05/1991 | Mark Wyatt | Scotland | 8 |
| 22/08/1998 | Gareth Rees | Argentina | 7 |
| 6 on 5 occasions | | | |

### MOST DROP GOALS IN A MATCH
#### BY THE TEAM

| Date | Opponent | Result | DGs |
|------|----------|--------|-----|
| 08/11/1986 | USA | 27–16 | 2 |
| 04/07/2001 | Fiji | 23–52 | 2 |
| 08/06/1980 | USA | 16–0 | 2 |
| 24/05/1997 | Hong Kong | 35–27 | 2 |
| 18/09/2011 | France | 19–46 | 2 |

#### BY A PLAYER

| Date | Player | Opponent | DGs |
|------|--------|----------|-----|
| 04/07/2001 | Bobby Ross | Fiji | 2 |
| 24/05/1997 | Bobby Ross | Hong Kong | 2 |
| 18/09/2011 | Ander Monro | France | 2 |

CANADA

## MOST CAPPED PLAYERS

| Name | Caps |
|---|---|
| Al Charron | 76 |
| Winston Stanley | 66 |
| Scott Stewart | 64 |
| Rod Snow | 62 |

## LEADING PENALTY SCORERS

| Name | Penalties |
|---|---|
| Gareth Rees | 110 |
| James Pritchard | 99 |
| Bobby Ross | 84 |
| Mark Wyatt | 64 |
| Jared Barker | 55 |

## LEADING TRY SCORERS

| Name | Tries |
|---|---|
| Winston Stanley | 24 |
| James Pritchard | 18 |
| DTH van der Merwe | 14 |
| Morgan Williams | 13 |
| Aaron Carpenter | 11 |

## LEADING DROP GOAL SCORERS

| Name | DGs |
|---|---|
| Bobby Ross | 10 |
| Gareth Rees | 9 |
| Mark Wyatt | 5 |

## LEADING CONVERSIONS SCORERS

| Name | Conversions |
|---|---|
| James Pritchard | 101 |
| Bobby Ross | 52 |
| Gareth Rees | 51 |
| Jared Barker | 24 |
| Mark Wyatt | 24 |

## LEADING POINTS SCORERS

| Name | Points |
|---|---|
| James Pritchard | 589 |
| Gareth Rees | 491 |
| Bobby Ross | 421 |
| Mark Wyatt | 263 |
| Jared Barker | 226 |

# CANADA INTERNATIONAL PLAYERS
## UP TO 13 OCTOBER 2014

**AD Abrams** 2003 *US, NZ, Tg,* 2004 *US, J, EngA, US, F, It, E,* 2005 *US, J, W, EngA, US, Ar, F, R,* 2006 *S, E, US, It*

**MJ Alder** 1976 *Bb*

**P Aldous** 1971 *W*

**TJ Ardron** 2012 *US, It, Geo, Sa, Rus,* 2013 *US, Fj, Tg, I, J, US, Geo, R,* 2014 *J, S, US*

**AS Arthurs** 1988 *US*

**M Ashton** 1971 *W*

**F Asselin** 1999 *Fj,* 2000 *Tg, US, SA,* 2001 *Ur, Ar, Fj,* 2002 *S, US, US, Ur, Ur, CHL, W, F*

**O Atkinson** 2005 *J, Ar,* 2006 *E, US, It*

**S Ault** 2006 *W, It,* 2008 *US, Pt,* 2009 *Geo, US, US*

**JC Bain** 1932 *J*

**RG Banks** 1999 *J, Fj, Sa, US, Tg, W, E, F, Nm,* 2000 *US, SA, I, J, It,* 2001 *US, Ur, Ar, E, Fj, J,* 2002 *S, US, US, Ur, CHL, Ur, CHL, W, F,* 2003 *EngA, US, M, M, Ur, NZ, It*

**S Barber** 1973 *W,* 1976 *Bb*

**M Barbieri** 2006 *E, US*

**B Barker** 1966 *BI,* 1971 *W*

**J Barker** 2000 *Tg, J, It,* 2002 *S, US, US, Ur, CHL, Ur, CHL, W,* 2003 *US, NZ, It,* 2004 *US, J, F, It*

**R Barkwill** 2012 *Sa, Rus,* 2013 *US, Fj, Tg, I, J, US, US, Geo, Pt,* 2014 *J, S, US*

**T Bauer** 1977 *US, E,* 1978 *US, F,* 1979 *US*

**DR Baugh** 1998 *J, HK, US, HK, J, Ur, Ar,* 1999 *J, Fj, Sa, US, Tg, W, E, F, Fj, Nm,* 2000 *US, SA, I, It,* 2001 *E, E,* 2002 *S, US, Ur, CHL*

**BG Beukeboom** 2012 *US, Geo, Sa,* 2013 *US, Tg, J, Geo, R, Pt*

**A Bianco** 1966 *BI*

**AJ Bibby** 1979 *US, F,* 1980 *W, US, NZ,* 1981 *US, Ar*

**R Bice** 1996 *US, A,* 1997 *US, J, HK, US, W, I,* 1998 *US, US, HK, J, Ur, US, Ar,* 1999 *J, Fj, Sa, US, Tg, W, F*

**P Bickerton** 2004 *US, J*

**D Biddle** 2006 *S, E, Bar,* 2007 *W, Fj, A*

**JM Billingsley** 1974 *Tg,* 1977 *US,* 1978 *F,* 1979 *US,* 1980 *W,* 1983 *US, It, It,* 1984 *US*

**WG Bjarneson** 1962 *Bb*

**TJH Blackwell** 1973 *W*

**N Blevins** 2009 *J, J,* 2010 *Bel, Sp, Geo, Pt,* 2012 *Sa, Rus,* 2013 *US, Fj, Tg, J, US, Geo, R, Pt,* 2014 *J, S*

**B Bonenberg** 1983 *US, It, It*

**J Boone** 1932 *J, J*

**T Bourne** 1967 *E*

**CJ Braid** 2010 *Bel, Geo,* 2012 *Sa, Rus,* 2013 *US, Fj, I, J, Pt,* 2014 *J, S, US*

**R Breen** 1986 *US,* 1987 *W,* 1990 *US,* 1991 *J, S, US, R,* 1993 *E, US*

**R Breen** 1983 *E,* 1987 *US*

**R Brewer** 1967 *E*

**STT Brown** 1989 *I, US*

**N Browne** 1973 *W,* 1974 *Tg*

**S Bryan** 1996 *Ur, US, Ar,* 1997 *HK, J, US, W,* 1998 *HK, J, US, Ar,* 1999 *Fj, Sa, US, Tg, W, E, F, Fj, Nm*

**M Burak** 2004 *US, J, EngA, US, F, It, E,* 2005 *EngA, US, Ar,*

A, SA, US, 1996 US, HK, J, A, HK, J, 1997 US, J, HK, HK, US, W, I, 1998 J, HK, US, US, HK, J, Ur, US, Ar, 1999 J, Fj, Sa, US, Tg, F, Nm
**W Granleese** 1962 W23
**G Grant** 1977 E, E, 1978 US, 1979 US, F, 1980 W
**I Grant** 1983 US, It, It, E
**PR Grantham** 1962 Bb, W23, 1966 BI
**SD Gray** 1984 US, 1987 US, W, US, 1989 I, 1990 Ar, US, Ar, 1991 J, S, Fj, F, NZ, 1992 US, E, 1993 E, E, US, A, W, 1994 US, F, W, E, F, 1995 S, Ar, Fj, NZ, R, A, SA, US, 1996 US, US, HK, J, A, HK, J, US, Ar, 1997 US, J, HK, J, US
**GR Greig** 1973 W
**JR Grieg** 1977 US, E, 1978 US, 1979 US, F, 1980 W, US, NZ, 1981 Ar
**J Grout** 1995 Ur
**MR Gudgeon** 2010 Bel, 2011 Rus
**G Gudmundseth** 1973 W

**N Hadley** 1987 US, 1989 I, US, 1990 Ar, 1991 S, US, Fj, R, F, NZ, 1992 US, E, 1993 E, 1994 E, F
**J Haley** 1996 Ur
**J Hall** 1996 US, US, 1997 HK, 1998 J, HK, J, US, Ar
**GRO Hamilton** 2010 Ur, 2011 Rus, US, US, Tg, F, J, NZ, 2012 US, Sa, Rus, 2013 US, Fj, Tg, I, J, US
**WT Handson** 1985 A, A, US, 1986 J, US, 1987 US, Tg, I, W
**J Hassler** 2012 US, Geo, Sa, Rus, 2013 Geo, R, 2014 J, S, US
**JP Hawthorn** 1982 J, J, E, 1983 US, It, It
**A Healy** 1996 HK, J, HK, J, Ur, US, Ar, 1997 US, HK, HK, I, 1998 HK, J, Ur, 1999 J
**AR Heaman** 1988 US
**C Hearn** 2008 I, W, S, 2009 I, W, Geo, US, US, J, J, 2010 Ur, Bel, Sp, Geo, Pt, 2011 US, US, Tg, F, 2012 US, It, Geo, Sa, Rus, 2013 US, Fj, Tg, I, J, US, US, R, Pt, 2014 J, S, US
**B Henderson** 2005 J, F, R
**S Hendry** 1996 Ur, US, Ar
**G Henrikson** 1971 W
**L Hillier** 1973 W
**RE Hindson** 1973 W, 1974 Tg, 1976 Bb, 1977 US, E, E, 1978 US, F, 1979 US, F, 1980 W, US, NZ, 1981 US, Ar, 1982 J, J, E, US, 1983 US, It, It, 1984 US, 1985 A, A, US, 1986 J, 1987 US, I, W, 1990 Ar
**G Hirayama** 1977 E, E, 1978 US, 1979 US, F, 1980 W, US, NZ, 1981 US, 1982 J, E, US
**NS Hirayama** 2008 Pt, S, 2009 J, J, Rus, 2010 Bel, 2011 US, F, NZ, 2013 Tg, I, US, US, 2014 US
**M Holmes** 1987 US
**TN Hotson** 2008 US, Pt, I, W, S, 2009 I, W, Geo, US, US, J, J, Rus, 2010 Ur, Sp, Geo, Pt, 2011 Rus, US, US, Tg, F, J, NZ, 2012 US, It, Geo, Sa, Rus, 2013 US, Fj, Tg, I, US, US, Geo, R, Pt, 2014 J, S, US
**P Howlett** 1974 Tg
**BM Hunnings** 1932 J, J
**E Hunt** 1966 BI, 1967 E
**S Hunter** 2005 R
**J Hutchinson** 1993 E, A, W, 1995 S, Ar, Fj, A, SA, US, 1996 US, US, HK, J, A, HK, J, Ur, US, Ar, 1997 US, J, HK, HK, J, US, W, I, 1998 J, HK, US, US, HK, J, US, Ar, 1999 J, Fj, Sa, US, Tg, W, E, F, Fj, Nm, 2000 US, Sa, Fj, J
**I Hyde-Lay** 1986 J, 1987 US, 1988 US

**J Ilnicki** 2013 Geo, Pt, 2014 J, S, US
**M Irvine** 2000 Tg, SA, I, Sa, Fj, J, 2001 US, Ar

**DC Jackart** 1991 J, S, US, Fj, R, F, 1992 US, E, 1993 E, E, US, A, W, 1994 US, F, W, E, F, 1995 S, Ar, Fj
**RO Jackson** 1970 Fj, 1971 W
**J Jackson** 2003 Ur, US, Ar, W, It, Tg, 2004 EngA, US, It, E, 2005 W, US, Ar, R, 2006 S, 2007 US, NZ, J, 2008 I, W, S, 2009 J, 2010 Sp, Geo
**MB James** 1994 US, F, W, E, F, 1995 S, Ur, Ar, Fj, NZ, R, A, US, 1996 US, US, HK, J, A, HK, J, 1997 J, US, W, I, 1998 US, Ur, US, Ar, 1999 Sa, W, E, F, Fj, Nm, 2000 It, 2002 S, US, US, Ur, CHL, W, F, 2003 M, M, Ur, US, Ar, W, Tg, 2005 F, 2006 US, 2007 Pt, W, Fj, J, A

**G Jennings** 1981 Ar, 1983 US, It, It, E
**O Johnson** 1970 Fj
**G Johnston** 1978 F
**RR Johnstone** 2001 Ur, Fj, J, 2002 CHL, Ur, CHL, 2003 EngA
**CWB Jones** 1987 US
**C Jones** 1983 E
**EL Jones** 1982 J, 1983 US
**H Jones** 2012 Rus, 2013 US, Fj, I, US, US, Geo, R, Pt, 2014 J, S, US

**TK Kariya** 1967 E, 1970 Fj, 1971 W
**A Kennedy** 1985 A, A
**I Kennedy** 1993 A, W
**ED Kettleson** 1985 US
**B Keys** 2008 US, Pt, I, W, S, 2009 Geo, US, J
**MMG King** 2002 US, Ur, 2003 M, US, Ar, NZ, 2005 US, J, W, EngA, US, Ar
**A Kingham** 1974 Tg
**A Kleeberger** 2005 F, R, 2006 S, E, US, Bar, It, 2007 US, NZ, Pt, J, 2008 US, Pt, I, W, S, 2009 I, W, Geo, US, US, J, J, Rus, 2010 Ur, Bel, Sp, Geo, Pt, 2011 US, US, Tg, F, J, NZ, 2013 R, Pt, 2014 J
**ERP Knaggs** 2000 Tg, US, SA, I, Sa, Fj, J, 2001 US, Ur, Ar, E, E, Fj, J, 2002 S, 2003 EngA, Ur, Ar, NZ
**JD Knauer** 1992 E, 1993 E, E, US, W
**MJ Kokan** 1984 US, 1985 US
**P Kyle** 1984 US
**JA Kyne** 2010 Bel, 2011 J

**A La Carte** 2004 US, J
**M Langley** 2004 EngA, 2005 Ar
**MJ Lawson** 2002 US, Ur, CHL, Ur, CHL, F, 2003 EngA, US, M, M, Ur, US, Ar, W, It, Tg, 2004 F, It, E, 2005 US, J, F, R, 2006 Bar, US, W
**P le Blanc** 1994 F, 1995 Ur, Fj, NZ
**CE le Fevre** 1976 Bb
**J Lecky** 1962 Bb, W23
**JL Lecky** 1982 J, US, 1983 US, It, It, 1984 US, 1985 A, US, 1986 J, US, 1987 I, W, US, 1991 J, S, Fj, R
**GB Legh** 1973 W, 1974 Tg, 1976 Bb
**LSF Leroy** 1932 J
**J Lorenz** 1966 BI, 1970 Fj, 1971 W
**DC Lougheed** 1990 Ar, 1991 J, US, 1992 US, E, 1993 E, E, US, 1994 F, W, E, F, 1995 Fj, NZ, R, A, SA, 1996 A, HK, 1997 J, W, I, 1998 US, Ar, 1999 US, Tg, W, E, F, Fj, Nm, 2003 W, It
**J Loveday** 1993 E, E, US, A, 1996 HK, J, 1998 J, Ur, 1999 Sa, US
**B Luke** 2004 US, J
**M Luke** 1974 Tg, 1976 Bb, 1977 US, E, E, 1978 US, F, 1979 US, F, 1980 W, US, NZ, 1981 US, 1982 J, US
**S Lytton** 1995 Ur, Ar, US, 1996 US, HK, J, J, US, Ar

**GDT MacDonald** 1998 HK
**G MacDonald** 1970 Fj
**P Mack** 2009 I, W, Geo, US, US, J, J, Rus, 2012 Rus, 2013 US, Fj, Tg, I, US, US, Geo, R, Pt, 2014 J, S, US
**I MacKay** 1993 A, W
**JL Mackenzie** 2010 Bel, Sp, 2011 US, 2013 Geo, Pt
**PW Mackenzie** 2008 Pt, I, 2010 Ur, Sp, Geo, Pt, 2011 Rus, US, US, Tg, F, J, NZ, 2012 US, It, Geo, Sa, 2013 US, US, Geo, R
**GI MacKinnon** 1985 US, 1986 J, 1988 US, 1989 I, US, 1990 Ar, Ar, 1991 J, S, Fj, R, F, NZ, 1992 US, E, 1993 E, 1994 US, F, W, E, F, 1995 S, Ur, Ar, Fj, NZ, A, SA
**S MacKinnon** 1992 US, 1995 Ur, Ar, Fj
**C MacLachlan** 1981 Ar, 1982 J, E
**P Maclean** 1983 US, It, It, E
**I Macmillan** 1981 Ar, 1982 J, J, E, US
**M MacSween** 2009 Rus
**B Major** 2001 Fj, J
**D Major** 1999 E, Fj, Nm, 2000 Tg, SA, I, Fj, 2001 Ur, E, E
**A Marshall** 1997 J, 1998 Ur
**JA Marshall** 2008 S, 2010 Ur, Bel, Sp, Geo, Pt, 2011 US, US, Tg, F, J, NZ, 2012 US, It, Geo, Sa, Rus, 2013 US, Fj, Tg, I, J, US, US, 2014 J, S, US

**RGA Snow** 1995 *Ar, NZ, R, A, SA, US,* 1996 *HK, J, A, HK, J,* 1997 *US, HK, J, W, I,* 1998 *US, US, US, Ar,* 1999 *J, Fj, Sa, US, W, E, F, Fj, Nm,* 2000 *I, J, It,* 2001 *US, Ar, E, E, Fj, J,* 2002 *S, US, US, Ur, CHL, Ur, CHL, W, F,* 2003 *Ur, US, Ar, W, NZ, It, Tg,* 2006 *US, Bar, US,* 2007 *Pt, W, Fj, J, A*

**D Spicer** 2004 *E,* 2005 *R,* 2006 *S, E, US, Bar, US, W,* 2007 *US, NZ, Pt, W, Fj, J,* 2008 *US,* 2009 *I, W*

**DA Speirs** 1988 *US,* 1989 *I, US,* 1991 *Fj, NZ*

**WE Spofford** 1981 *Ar*

**W Stanley** 1994 *US, F,* 1995 *S, Ur, Ar, R, A, SA, US,* 1996 *US, US, A, HK, J,* 1997 *US, J, HK, HK, US, W, I,* 1998 *US, US, HK, Ur, US, Ar,* 1999 *J, Fj, Sa, US, Tg, W, E, F, Fj, Nm,* 2000 *Tg, US, SA, I, Sa, Fj, J, It,* 2001 *E, E,* 2002 *S, US, US, Ur, CHL, Ur, CHL, W, F,* 2003 *EngA, US, M, M, Ur, US, Ar, W, It, Tg*

**AI Stanton** 1971 *W,* 1973 *W,* 1974 *Tg*

**E Stapleton** 1978 *US, F*

**D Steen** 1966 *BI*

**SM Stephen** 2005 *EngA, US,* 2006 *S, E, Bar, US, W,* 2007 *US, NZ, Pt, W, Fj, A,* 2008 *I, W, S,* 2009 *I, W,* 2010 *Sp, Geo, Pt*

**C Stewart** 1991 *S, US, Fj, R, F, NZ,* 1994 *E, F,* 1995 *S, Fj, NZ, R, A, SA*

**R Stewart** 2005 *R*

**DS Stewart** 1989 *US,* 1990 *Ar,* 1991 *US, Fj, R, F, NZ,* 1992 *E,* 1993 *E, E, US, A, W,* 1994 *US, F, W, E, F,* 1995 *S, Fj, NZ, R, A, SA, US,* 1996 *US, US, A, HK, J, Ur, US, Ar,* 1997 *US, J, HK, HK, J, US, W, I,* 1998 *US, J, Ur, Ar,* 1999 *Sa, US, Tg, W, E, F, Fj, Nm,* 2000 *US, SA, I, Sa, Fj, It,* 2001 *US, Ar, E, E*

**B Stoikos** 2001 *Ur*

**G Stover** 1962 *Bb*

**R Strang** 1983 *E*

**C Strubin** 2004 *EngA, E*

**IC Stuart** 1984 *US,* 1985 *A, A,* 1986 *J,* 1987 *US, Tg, I, W, US,* 1988 *US,* 1989 *US,* 1990 *Ar, US, Ar,* 1992 *E,* 1993 *A, W,* 1994 *US, F, W, E*

**JD Stubbs** 1962 *Bb, W23*

**FJ Sturrock** 1971 *W*

**CW Suter** 1932 *J*

**KF Svoboda** 1985 *A, A, US,* 1986 *J, US,* 1987 *W,* 1990 *Ar, US, Ar,* 1991 *J, US, R, F,* 1992 *US, E,* 1993 *E, E, US,* 1994 *F, W, F,* 1995 *Fj, A, US*

**P Szabo** 1989 *I, US,* 1990 *Ar, US, Ar,* 1991 *NZ,* 1993 *US, A, W*

**JN Tait** 1997 *US, J, HK, HK, J, US, W, I,* 1998 *US, Ur, Ar,* 1999 *J, Fj, Sa, US, Tg, W, E, F, Fj, Nm,* 2000 *Tg, US, SA, I, Sa, Fj, J, It,* 2001 *US, Ar, E, E,* 2002 *US, W, F*

**L Tait** 2005 *US, J, W, EngA,* 2006 *S, E, US, Bar, US, W, It,* 2007 *US, NZ, Pt, W, Fj, A,* 2009 *I, W,* 2010 *Ur*

**WG Taylor** 1978 *F,* 1979 *US, F,* 1980 *W, US, NZ,* 1981 *US, Ar,* 1983 *US, It*

**J Thiel** 1998 *HK, J, Ur,* 1999 *J, Fj, Sa, US, Tg, W, E, F, Fj, Nm,* 2000 *SA, I, Sa, Fj, J,* 2001 *US, Ar, E, E,* 2002 *S, US, US, Ur, CHL, Ur, CHL, W, F,* 2003 *Ur, US, Ar, W, It,* 2004 *F,* 2007 *Pt, W, Fj, J, A,* 2008 *I, W*

**S Thompson** 2001 *Fj, J,* 2004 *US*

**W Thomson** 1970 *Fj*

**AA Tiedemann** 2009 *W, Geo, US, US,* 2010 *Ur, Bel, Geo, Pt,* 2011 *Rus, US, NZ,* 2012 *US, It, Geo, Sa, Rus,* 2013 *US, Fj, I, J, US, US, Geo, R, Pt,* 2014 *J, S, US*

**K Tkachuk** 2000 *Tg, US, SA, Sa, Fj, It,* 2001 *Fj, J,* 2002 *CHL, Ur, CHL, W, F,* 2003 *EngA, US, M, M, Ur, US, Ar, W, NZ, It, Tg,* 2004 *EngA, US, F, It, E,* 2005 *US, J, W, Ar, F, R,* 2006 *US, W, It,* 2007 *US, NZ,* 2008 *US, Pt, I, W, S,* 2009 *I, W, Geo, US, US, J, J, Rus,* 2010 *Sp, Geo*

**H Toews** 1998 *J, HK, HK, Ur,* 1999 *Tg,* 2000 *US, Sa, J, It,* 2001 *Fj, J*

**R Toews** 1993 *W,* 1994 *US, F, W, E,* 1995 *S, Ur, Ar, Fj,* 1996 *US, HK, J, A,* 1997 *HK, US, I*

**J Tomlinson** 1996 *A,* 2001 *Ur*

**CA Trainor** 2011 *Rus, Tg, F, J, NZ,* 2012 *It, Geo,* 2013 *Geo, R, Pt*

**N Trenkel** 2007 *A*

**DM Tucker** 1985 *A, A, US,* 1986 *US,* 1987 *US, W*

**A Tyler** 2005 *Ar*

**A Tynan** 1995 *Ur, Ar, NZ, US,* 1997 *J*

**CJ Tynan** 1987 *US,* 1988 *US,* 1990 *Ar, US, Ar,* 1991 *J, US,* *Fj, F, NZ,* 1992 *US,* 1993 *E, E, US, W,* 1996 *US, J,* 1997 *HK, J,* 1998 *US*

**LD Underwood** 2013 *US, Fj, Tg, I, J, Geo*

**DN Ure** 1962 *Bb, W23*

**PC Vaesen** 1985 *US,* 1986 *J,* 1987 *US, Tg, US*

**D van Camp** 2005 *J, R,* 2006 *It,* 2007 *US, NZ,* 2008 *Pt, W, 2009 I, Geo*

**R van den Brink** 1986 *US,* 1987 *Tg,* 1988 *US,* 1991 *J, US, R, F, NZ*

**D Van Der Merwe** 2006 *Bar, It,* 2007 *Pt, W, Fj, J, A,* 2009 *I, W, Geo, US, US,* 2010 *Ur, Sp, Geo,* 2011 *US, US, Tg, F, J, NZ,* 2012 *US, It, Geo,* 2013 *US, US,* 2014 *J, S, US*

**D Van Eeuwen** 1978 *F,* 1979 *US*

**A van Staveren** 2000 *Tg, Sa, Fj,* 2002 *US, US, Ur, CHL, Ur, CHL, F, J,* 2003 *EngA, US, M, M, Ur, US, W, NZ, Tg*

**J Verstraten** 2000 *US, SA, Fj, J*

**J Vivian** 1983 *E,* 1984 *US*

**FG Walsh** 2008 *I, W, S,* 2009 *US*

**KC Walt** 1976 *Bb,* 1977 *US, E, E,* 1978 *US, F*

**JM Ward** 1962 *W23*

**M Webb** 2004 *US, J, US, F, It,* 2005 *US, J, W, EngA, US, Ar, F,* 2006 *US, W, It,* 2007 *J, A,* 2008 *US*

**M Weingart** 2004 *J,* 2005 *J, EngA, US, F, R,* 2007 *Pt*

**GJM Wessels** 1962 *W23*

**WR Wharton** 1932 *J, J*

**ST White** 2009 *J, J, Rus,* 2010 *Ur, Bel, Sp, Geo, Pt,* 2011 *Rus, US, F, J, NZ,* 2012 *US, It, Geo, Sa,* 2013 *US, Fj, Tg, I, J, US, US*

**K Whitley** 1995 *S*

**C Whittaker** 1993 *US, A,* 1995 *Ur,* 1996 *A,* 1997 *J,* 1998 *J, HK, US, US, US, Ar,* 1999 *J, Fj, US*

**LW Whitty** 1967 *E*

**DW Whyte** 1974 *Tg,* 1977 *US, E, E*

**RR Wickland** 1966 *BI,* 1967 *E*

**JP Wiley** 1977 *US, E, E,* 1978 *US, F,* 1979 *US,* 1980 *W, US, NZ,* 1981 *US*

**K Wilke** 1971 *W,* 1973 *W,* 1976 *Bb,* 1978 *US*

**K Wilkinson** 1976 *Bb,* 1978 *F,* 1979 *F*

**BN Williams** 1962 *W23*

**J Williams** 2001 *US, Ur, Ar, Fj, J*

**M Williams** 1992 *E,* 1993 *A, W*

**MH Williams** 1978 *US, F,* 1980 *US,* 1982 *J*

**M Williams** 1999 *Tg, W, E, F, Fj, Nm,* 2000 *Tg, SA, I, Sa, Fj, J, It,* 2001 *E, E, Fj, J,* 2002 *S, US, US, Ur, CHL, W, F,* 2003 *EngA, US, M, M, Ur, US, Ar, W, It, Tg,* 2004 *EngA, US, F,* 2005 *W, Ar, F, R,* 2006 *E, US, Bar, US, W, It,* 2007 *US, NZ, W, Fj, J, A,* 2008 *Pt, W, S*

**A Wilson** 2008 *US*

**EA Wilson** 2012 *Sa, Rus*

**PG Wilson** 1932 *J, J*

**RS Wilson** 1962 *Bb*

**K Wirachowski** 1992 *E,* 1993 *US,* 1996 *US, HK, Ur, US, Ar,* 1997 *US, HK,* 2000 *It,* 2001 *Ur, E, Fj, J,* 2002 *S, CHL,* 2003 *EngA, US, M*

**T Wish** 2004 *US, J*

**K Witkowski** 2005 *EngA, Ar,* 2006 *E*

**N Witkowski** 1998 *US, J,* 2000 *Tg, US, SA, I, Sa, Fj, J, It,* 2001 *US, E, E,* 2002 *S, US, US, Ur, CHL, Ur, CHL, W, F,* 2003 *EngA, US, M, M, Ur, Ar, W, NZ, Tg,* 2005 *EngA, US,* 2006 *E*

**AH Woller** 1967 *E*

**S Wood** 1977 *E*

**TA Woods** 1984 *US,* 1986 *J, US,* 1987 *US, Tg, I, W,* 1988 *US,* 1989 *I, US,* 1990 *Ar, US,* 1991 *S, F, NZ,* 1996 *US, US,* 1997 *US, J*

**DP Wooldridge** 2009 *I, Geo, J, J, Rus,* 2010 *Ur,* 2012 *Geo, Sa, Rus,* 2013 *Tg, I, US, US*

**MA Wyatt** 1982 *J, J, E, US,* 1983 *US, It, It, E,* 1985 *A, A, US,* 1986 *J, US,* 1987 *Tg, I, W,* 1988 *US,* 1989 *I, US,* 1990 *Ar, US, Ar,* 1991 *J, S, US, R, F, NZ*

**H Wyndham** 1973 *W*

**JJ Yeganegi** 1996 *US,* 1998 *J*

**C Yukes** 2001 *Ur, Fj, J,* 2002 *S, US, Ur, Ur,* 2003 *EngA, US, M, M, US, Ar, W, NZ, It, Tg,* 2004 *US, J, EngA, US, F, It, E,* 2005 *W, EngA, US,* 2006 *Bar, US,* 2007 *US, NZ, Pt, W, Fj, J, A*

# ENGLAND

## ENGLAND'S 2013–14 TEST RECORD

| OPPONENTS | DATE | VENUE | RESULT |
|-----------|------|-------|--------|
| Australia | 2 Nov | H | Won 20–13 |
| Argentina | 9 Nov | H | Won 31–12 |
| New Zealand | 16 Nov | H | Lost 22–30 |
| France | 1 Feb | A | Lost 26–24 |
| Scotland | 8 Feb | A | Won 20–0 |
| Ireland | 22 Feb | H | Won 13–10 |
| Wales | 9 Mar | H | Won 29–18 |
| Italy | 15 Mar | A | Won 52–11 |
| New Zealand | 7 Jun | A | Lost 20–15 |
| New Zealand | 14 Jun | A | Lost 28–27 |
| New Zealand | 21 Jun | A | Lost 36–13 |

# ENGLAND UNDERLINE WORLD CUP CREDENTIALS

## By *Lawrence Dallaglio*

England captain Chris Robshaw will be hoping to repeat England's victory over Australia at Rugby World Cup 2015.

**W**atching England over the course of the season, I certainly got a strong sense that Stuart Lancaster's side is one on the way up. They have not yet individually or collectively reached their full potential, for me there is perhaps 20 or 30 per cent more to come, but England continued to make progress and found a way to win matches they would have lost a year ago.

It's important to put Lancaster's reign as head coach into context. He took over in the wake of a poor World Cup in New Zealand on and off the pitch in 2011 and he's had significant success in instilling a work ethic back into the squad, rediscovering the team's moral compass and, just as importantly, reconnecting with the England supporters. England were not in a great place culturally in 2011 but Lancaster has reminded the players what it means to represent their country.

That has begun to translate into results and although there were disappointments during the season, I firmly believe you cannot be successful on the pitch until you have created the right environment off it. The players and coaches appear fiercely united and have a shared vision for the team.

Since he took charge, Lancaster has steered the team to victory over every major nation except South Africa and in the process the players have been gaining more and more invaluable international experience.

I wasn't surprised when the RFU announced in October they were extending his contract until 2020. It was a ringing endorsement of the job he and the other coaches have done so far and a show of faith in how the RFU believe he will mould the team going forward.

Some questioned the RFU's decision to add caveats to the new deal and include a review of England's performance after the World Cup in 2015 but that to me is only logical. The RFU have publicly backed their man but they are entitled to re-evaluate after the World Cup if they think it's necessary.

I think there are parallels here with Clive Woodward's career as England coach. We had a poor World Cup in 1999 and it was not a certainty that Clive would continue as coach until conversations were had in private and the RFU decided to renew his contract and with hindsight it was, of course, absolutely the right decision. The point is that it would not be unprecedented if Lancaster had to sit down with the RFU and convince them he was still the right man for the job.

England began the season with the autumn internationals and although they weren't able to beat the All Blacks at Twickenham as they had the previous year, they did win against the Wallabies and Argentina.

With England and Australia in the same pool at the World Cup, that was a significant psychological boost. As it did in my day, claiming the scalp of one of the southern hemisphere sides really resonates in the dressing room. It breeds massive confidence but it also sows the seeds of doubt in the minds of the opposition and I'm sure England's 20–13 win over Australia won't be forgotten when the two teams meet again in early October 2015.

The Six Nations was extremely encouraging but also deeply frustrating. The wins over Ireland and Wales at Twickenham revealed a maturing England side, a team learning to get the job done when they're not at their fluent best, but it was also obvious from Lancaster that they were hugely frustrated not to win the title. It was the defeat to France in Paris that did the damage, the one that got away.

I was particularly impressed with the Ireland result. The Irish team was overflowing with old heads and far, far more experienced than England but they held their nerve and ground out the win. It wasn't quite a coming of age but it was close.

England scored 14 tries in the Championship, which is their best haul since 2009 and a sign they are growing as an attacking force. England certainly look more potent out wide than they have for a few years and they will need that threat if they are to realistically challenge the 'big three' at the World Cup.

There's no doubt in my mind that Lancaster and England have been helped in their bid to play a more expansive game by the quality of the Aviva Premiership. The rugby is less attritional these days and teams are showing more guile and more intelligence. That more subtle approach is definitely benefiting England in attack and giving the team more of a cutting edge.

England went to New Zealand in the summer and although the tour ended in a series whitewash against the All Blacks, they went very close in the first and second Tests before coming unstuck in the third in Hamilton.

They could and probably should have won one of the first two games and that is the challenge facing England now, finding the knack to win the biggest of matches rather than suffering narrow, albeit fairly heroic defeats. It's the fractions that separate good teams from great teams and a message I'm sure Lancaster will be trying to hammer home.

Personally I would like to see England touring New Zealand on a far more regular basis. If they are the world's number one team and we have aspirations to dethrone them, we should be going to New Zealand more often rather than waiting for the All Blacks' annual, one-off visits to Twickenham. There remains a certain mystique about playing the All Blacks but that would be dispelled quickly if, like the other teams in The Rugby Championship, we faced them more frequently.

The positives that emerged over the season were many. The first choice England pack is getting stronger by the match and the back row of Tom Wood, Chris Robshaw and Billy Vunipola is one I like both individually and collectively. The young second rows, Joe Launchbury and Courtney Lawes, developed at an extraordinary rate. Out wide I felt England had more competition for places and more leadership in the key position of fly-half and in the midfield than they did 12 or 24 months earlier.

That competition for places will be key. No player would ever admit it publicly but if you feel your place is assured, there is always the danger of complacency, however subconscious. Coaches also love competition because they never know when the next injury is around the corner and with a viable replacement kicking his heels on the bench, they can use it to extract even better performances from the man in possession of the shirt.

England were not particularly lucky during the year in terms of front row injuries with Dan Cole and Alex Corbisiero both sidelined and with the World Cup looming, that could be a worry. The replacement props, players like David Wilson, have never let England down but Lancaster will want as many of his frontline scrummagers available as possible.

There were questions about England's fitness and I do think the players have room for improvement there. It is a prerequisite of being the best team in the world that you're the fittest and that's a part of England's journey that is yet to be completed.

The video analysis shows the ball is in play for significantly longer in a Test between the southern hemisphere sides than it is in an international in Europe and that is reflected in the fitness levels of the Springbok, All Black and Australia squads. They get through more work.

England have time to surpass them in terms of fitness but each and every one of the current squad needs to take a long, hard look in the mirror in the morning and be honest with themselves about the work they're putting in. Am I really working hard enough, am I dedicated enough?

To win a World Cup it isn't good enough to merely be the best player in England in your position. You have to aspire to be the best in the world and for this England squad, that means being better and stronger and fitter than their opposite numbers in New Zealand or South Africa. We were the fittest team at the World Cup in 2003 and although it wasn't the only reason for our success, I don't believe we would have become champions if that wasn't true.

I remain upbeat though about the team's chances in 2015. Lancaster's side are at a different stage of the development curve than the team of 2003 were heading into the tournament but I genuinely believe they are capable of winning it. They have enough time to apply the finishing touches and when the World Cup arrives, most of the first choice starting XV will have reached the golden 30-cap plus mark. You cannot win the tournament with an inexperienced side.

The All Blacks will be clear favourites, with the Springboks as the second ranked side in the world not far behind, but no-one relishes playing the host nation and virtually all of England's games, however many that will be, are at Twickenham. The Twickenham crowd can be a formidable beast and if England can harness the power inside the stadium rather than succumbing to the nerves that come with being the home side, it will be a massive factor as the tournament unfolds.

*Lawrence Dallaglio is an England Rugby 2015 Ambassador.*

# ENGLAND INTERNATIONAL STATISTICS

## MATCH RECORDS UP TO 13 OCTOBER 2014

### MOST CONSECUTIVE TESTS WITHOUT DEFEAT

| Matches | Wins | Draws | Period |
|---|---|---|---|
| 14 | 14 | 0 | 2002 to 2003 |
| 12 | 10 | 2 | 1882 to 1887 |
| 11 | 10 | 1 | 1922 to 1924 |
| 11 | 11 | 0 | 2000 to 2001 |

### MOST CONSECUTIVE TEST WINS

| | |
|---|---|
| 14 | 2002 W, It, Arg, NZ, A, SA, 2003 F1, W1, It, S, I, NZ, A, W2 |
| 11 | 2000 SA 2, A, Arg, SA3, 2001 W, It, S, F, C1, 2, US |
| 10 | 1882 W, 1883 I, S, 1884 W, I, S, 1885 W, I, 1886 W, I |
| 10 | 1994 R, C, 1995 I, F, W, S, Arg, It, WS, A |
| 10 | 2003 F, Gg, SA, Sm, U, W, F, A, 2004 It, S |

### MOST POINTS IN A MATCH
#### BY THE TEAM

| Pts | Opponents | Venue | Year |
|---|---|---|---|
| 134 | Romania | Twickenham | 2001 |
| 111 | Uruguay | Brisbane | 2003 |
| 110 | Netherlands | Huddersfield | 1998 |
| 106 | USA | Twickenham | 1999 |
| 101 | Tonga | Twickenham | 1999 |
| 84 | Georgia | Perth | 2003 |
| 80 | Italy | Twickenham | 2001 |

#### BY A PLAYER

| Pts | Player | Opponents | Venue | Year |
|---|---|---|---|---|
| 44 | C Hodgson | Romania | Twickenham | 2001 |
| 36 | PJ Grayson | Tonga | Twickenham | 1999 |
| 35 | JP Wilkinson | Italy | Twickenham | 2001 |
| 32 | JP Wilkinson | Italy | Twickenham | 1999 |
| 30 | CR Andrew | Canada | Twickenham | 1994 |
| 30 | PJ Grayson | Netherlands | Huddersfield | 1998 |
| 30 | JP Wilkinson | Wales | Twickenham | 2002 |
| 29 | DJH Walder | Canada | Burnaby | 2001 |
| 27 | CR Andrew | South Africa | Pretoria | 1994 |
| 27 | JP Wilkinson | South Africa | Bloemfontein | 2000 |
| 27 | CC Hodgson | South Africa | Twickenham | 2004 |
| 27 | JP Wilkinson | Scotland | Twickenham | 2007 |
| 26 | JP Wilkinson | United States | Twickenham | 1999 |

### MOST TRIES IN A MATCH
#### BY THE TEAM

| Tries | Opponents | Venue | Year |
|---|---|---|---|
| 20 | Romania | Twickenham | 2001 |
| 17 | Uruguay | Brisbane | 2003 |
| 16 | Netherlands | Huddersfield | 1998 |
| 16 | United States | Twickenham | 1999 |
| 13 | Wales | Blackheath | 1881 |
| 13 | Tonga | Twickenham | 1999 |
| 12 | Georgia | Perth | 2003 |
| 12 | Canada | Twickenham | 2004 |
| 10 | Japan | Sydney | 1987 |
| 10 | Fiji | Twickenham | 1989 |
| 10 | Italy | Twickenham | 2001 |
| 10 | Romania | Dunedin | 2011 |

#### BY A PLAYER

| Tries | Player | Opponents | Venue | Year |
|---|---|---|---|---|
| 5 | D Lambert | France | Richmond | 1907 |
| 5 | R Underwood | Fiji | Twickenham | 1989 |
| 5 | OJ Lewsey | Uruguay | Brisbane | 2003 |
| 4 | GW Burton | Wales | Blackheath | 1881 |
| 4 | A Hudson | France | Paris | 1906 |
| 4 | RW Poulton | France | Paris | 1914 |
| 4 | C Oti | Romania | Bucharest | 1989 |
| 4 | JC Guscott | Netherlands | Huddersfield | 1998 |
| 4 | NA Back | Netherlands | Huddersfield | 1998 |
| 4 | JC Guscott | United States | Twickenham | 1999 |
| 4 | J Robinson | Romania | Twickenham | 2001 |
| 4 | N Easter | Wales | Twickenham | 2007 |
| 4 | CJ Ashton | Italy | Twickenham | 2011 |

## MOST CONVERSIONS IN A MATCH
### BY THE TEAM

| Cons | Opponents | Venue | Year |
|---|---|---|---|
| 15 | Netherlands | Huddersfield | 1998 |
| 14 | Romania | Twickenham | 2001 |
| 13 | United States | Twickenham | 1999 |
| 13 | Uruguay | Brisbane | 2003 |
| 12 | Tonga | Twickenham | 1999 |
| 9 | Italy | Twickenham | 2001 |
| 9 | Georgia | Perth | 2003 |
| 8 | Romania | Bucharest | 1989 |
| 8 | Italy | Twickenham | 2011 |

### BY A PLAYER

| Cons | Player | Opponents | Venue | Year |
|---|---|---|---|---|
| 15 | PJ Grayson | Netherlands | Huddersfield | 1998 |
| 14 | C Hodgson | Romania | Twickenham | 2001 |
| 13 | JP Wilkinson | United States | Twickenham | 1999 |
| 12 | PJ Grayson | Tonga | Twickenham | 1999 |
| 11 | PJ Grayson | Uruguay | Brisbane | 2003 |
| 9 | JP Wilkinson | Italy | Twickenham | 2001 |
| 8 | SD Hodgkinson | Romania | Bucharest | 1989 |
| 7 | JM Webb | Japan | Sydney | 1987 |
| 7 | SD Hodgkinson | Argentina | Twickenham | 1990 |
| 7 | PJ Grayson | Wales | Twickenham | 1998 |
| 7 | JP Wilkinson | Wales | Twickenham | 2007 |
| 7 | OA Farrell | Italy | Rome | 2014 |

## MOST DROP GOALS IN A MATCH
### BY THE TEAM

| Drops | Opponents | Venue | Year |
|---|---|---|---|
| 3 | France | Sydney | 2003 |
| 2 | Ireland | Twickenham | 1970 |
| 2 | France | Paris | 1978 |
| 2 | France | Paris | 1980 |
| 2 | Romania | Twickenham | 1985 |
| 2 | Fiji | Suva | 1991 |
| 2 | Argentina | Durban | 1995 |
| 2 | France | Paris | 1996 |
| 2 | Australia | Twickenham | 2001 |
| 2 | Wales | Cardiff | 2003 |
| 2 | Ireland | Dublin | 2003 |
| 2 | South Africa | Perth | 2003 |
| 2 | Samoa | Nantes | 2007 |
| 2 | Tonga | Paris | 2007 |
| 2 | Wales | Twickenham | 2011 |
| 2 | Argentina | Manchester | 2009 |

### BY A PLAYER

| Drops | Player | Opponents | Venue | Year |
|---|---|---|---|---|
| 3 | JP Wilkinson | France | Sydney | 2003 |
| 2 | R Hiller | Ireland | Twickenham | 1970 |
| 2 | AGB Old | France | Paris | 1978 |
| 2 | JP Horton | France | Paris | 1980 |
| 2 | CR Andrew | Romania | Twickenham | 1985 |
| 2 | CR Andrew | Fiji | Suva | 1991 |
| 2 | CR Andrew | Argentina | Durban | 1995 |
| 2 | PJ Grayson | France | Paris | 1996 |
| 2 | JP Wilkinson | Australia | Twickenham | 2001 |
| 2 | JP Wilkinson | Wales | Cardiff | 2003 |
| 2 | JP Wilkinson | Ireland | Dublin | 2003 |
| 2 | JP Wilkinson | South Africa | Perth | 2003 |
| 2 | JP Wilkinson | Samoa | Nantes | 2007 |
| 2 | JP Wilkinson | Tonga | Paris | 2007 |
| 2 | AJ Goode | Argentina | Manchester | 2009 |
| 2 | JP Wilkinson | Wales | Twickenham | 2011 |

## MOST PENALTIES IN A MATCH
### BY THE TEAM

| Penalties | Opponents | Venue | Year |
|---|---|---|---|
| 8 | South Africa | Bloemfontein | 2000 |
| 7 | Wales | Cardiff | 1991 |
| 7 | Scotland | Twickenham | 1995 |
| 7 | France | Twickenham | 1999 |
| 7 | Fiji | Twickenham | 1999 |
| 7 | South Africa | Paris | 1999 |
| 7 | South Africa | Twickenham | 2001 |
| 7 | Australia | Twickenham | 2010 |

### BY A PLAYER

| Pens | Player | Opponents | Venue | Year |
|---|---|---|---|---|
| 8 | JP Wilkinson | South Africa | Bloemfontein | 2000 |
| 7 | SD Hodgkinson | Wales | Cardiff | 1991 |
| 7 | CR Andrew | Scotland | Twickenham | 1995 |
| 7 | JP Wilkinson | France | Twickenham | 1999 |
| 7 | JP Wilkinson | Fiji | Twickenham | 1999 |
| 7 | JP Wilkinson | South Africa | Twickenham | 2001 |
| 7 | TGAL Flood | Australia | Twickenham | 2010 |

ENGLAND

# CAREER RECORDS

## MOST CAPPED PLAYERS

| Caps | Player | Career Span |
|------|--------|-------------|
| 114 | J Leonard | 1990 to 2004 |
| 91 | JP Wilkinson | 1998 to 2011 |
| 85 | R Underwood | 1984 to 1996 |
| 85 | LBN Dallaglio | 1995 to 2007 |
| 84 | MO Johnson | 1993 to 2003 |
| 78 | JPR Worsley | 1999 to 2011 |
| 77 | MJS Dawson | 1995 to 2006 |
| 75 | MJ Catt | 1994 to 2007 |
| 75 | MJ Tindall | 2000 to 2011 |
| 73 | PJ Vickery | 1998 to 2009 |
| 73 | SG Thompson | 2002 to 2011 |
| 72 | WDC Carling | 1988 to 1997 |
| 71 | CR Andrew | 1985 to 1997 |
| 71 | RA Hill | 1997 to 2004 |
| 71 | LW Moody | 2001 to 2011 |
| 71 | SD Shaw | 1996 to 2011 |
| 69 | DJ Grewcock | 1997 to 2007 |
| 66 | NA Back | 1994 to 2003 |
| 65 | JC Guscott | 1989 to 1999 |

## MOST CONSECUTIVE TESTS

| Tests | Player | Span |
|-------|--------|------|
| 44 | WDC Carling | 1989 to 1995 |
| 40 | J Leonard | 1990 to 1995 |
| 36 | JV Pullin | 1968 to 1975 |
| 33 | WB Beaumont | 1975 to 1982 |
| 30 | R Underwood | 1992 to 1996 |

## MOST TESTS AS CAPTAIN

| Tests | Captain | Span |
|-------|---------|------|
| 59 | WDC Carling | 1988 to 1996 |
| 39 | MO Johnson | 1998 to 2003 |
| 27 | CDC Robshaw | 2012 to 2014 |
| 22 | LBN Dallaglio | 1997 to 2004 |
| 21 | WB Beaumont | 1978 to 1982 |
| 21 | SW Borthwick | 2008 to 2010 |
| 17 | ME Corry | 2005 to 2007 |
| 15 | PJ Vickery | 2002 to 2008 |
| 13 | WW Wakefield | 1924 to 1926 |
| 13 | NM Hall | 1949 to 1955 |
| 13 | E Evans | 1956 to 1958 |
| 13 | REG Jeeps | 1960 to 1962 |
| 13 | JV Pullin | 1972 to 1975 |

## MOST POINTS IN TESTS

| Points | Player | Tests | Career |
|--------|--------|-------|--------|
| 1179 | JP Wilkinson | 91 | 1998 to 2011 |
| 400 | PJ Grayson | 32 | 1995 to 2004 |
| 396 | CR Andrew | 71 | 1985 to 1997 |
| 301 | TGAL Flood | 60 | 2006 to 2013 |
| 296 | JM Webb | 33 | 1987 to 1993 |
| 271 | OA Farrell | 25 | 2012 to 2014 |
| 269 | CC Hodgson | 38 | 2001 to 2012 |
| 240 | WH Hare | 25 | 1974 to 1984 |
| 210 | R Underwood | 85 | 1984 to 1996 |

## MOST TRIES IN TESTS

| Tries | Player | Tests | Career |
|-------|--------|-------|--------|
| 49 | R Underwood | 85 | 1984 to 1996 |
| 31 | WJH Greenwood | 55 | 1997 to 2004 |
| 31 | BC Cohen | 57 | 2000 to 2006 |
| 30 | JC Guscott | 65 | 1989 to 1999 |
| 28 | JT Robinson | 51 | 2001 to 2007 |
| 24 | DD Luger | 38 | 1998 to 2003 |
| 22 | OJ Lewsey | 55 | 1998 to 2007 |
| 20 | MJ Cueto | 55 | 2004 to 2011 |
| 19 | CJ Ashton | 39 | 2010 to 2014 |
| 18 | CN Lowe | 25 | 1913 to 1923 |
| 17 | LBN Dallaglio | 85 | 1995 to 2007 |

## MOST CONVERSIONS IN TESTS

| Cons | Player | Tests | Career |
|------|--------|-------|--------|
| 162 | JP Wilkinson | 91 | 1998 to 2011 |
| 78 | PJ Grayson | 32 | 1995 to 2004 |
| 44 | CC Hodgson | 38 | 2001 to 2012 |
| 41 | JM Webb | 33 | 1987 to 1993 |
| 40 | TGAL Flood | 60 | 2006 to 2013 |
| 35 | SD Hodgkinson | 14 | 1989 to 1991 |
| 33 | CR Andrew | 71 | 1985 to 1997 |
| 33 | OA Farrell | 25 | 2012 to 2014 |
| 17 | L Stokes | 12 | 1875 to 1881 |

THE COUNTRIES

## MOST PENALTY GOALS IN TESTS

| Penalties | Player | Tests | Career |
|---|---|---|---|
| 239 | JP Wilkinson | 91 | 1998 to 2011 |
| 86 | CR Andrew | 71 | 1985 to 1997 |
| 72 | PJ Grayson | 32 | 1995 to 2004 |
| 67 | WH Hare | 25 | 1974 to 1984 |
| 66 | JM Webb | 33 | 1987 to 1993 |
| 66 | TGAL Flood | 60 | 2006 to 2013 |
| 64 | OA Farrell | 25 | 2012 to 2014 |
| 44 | CC Hodgson | 38 | 2001 to 2012 |
| 43 | SD Hodgkinson | 14 | 1989 to 1991 |

## MOST DROP GOALS IN TESTS

| Drops | Player | Tests | Career |
|---|---|---|---|
| 36 | JP Wilkinson | 91 | 1998 to 2011 |
| 21 | CR Andrew | 71 | 1985 to 1997 |
| 6 | PJ Grayson | 32 | 1995 to 2004 |
| 4 | JP Horton | 13 | 1978 to 1984 |
| 4 | L Cusworth | 12 | 1979 to 1988 |
| 4 | AJ Goode | 17 | 2005 to 2009 |

Getty Images

Rugby World Cup 2003 winner Jason Leonard remains the only England player to have won more than 100 caps.

ENGLAND

# INTERNATIONAL CHAMPIONSHIP RECORDS

| RECORD | DETAIL | | SET |
|---|---|---|---|
| Most points in season | 229 | in five matches | 2001 |
| Most tries in season | 29 | in five matches | 2001 |
| Highest score | 80 | 80–23 v Italy | 2001 |
| Biggest win | 57 | 80–23 v Italy | 2001 |
| Highest score conceded | 43 | 13–43 v Ireland | 2007 |
| Biggest defeat | 30 | 13–43 v Ireland | 2007 |
| Most appearances | 54 | J Leonard | 1991–2004 |
| Most points in matches | 546 | JP Wilkinson | 1998–2011 |
| Most points in season | 89 | JP Wilkinson | 2001 |
| Most points in match | 35 | JP Wilkinson | v Italy, 2001 |
| Most tries in matches | 18 | CN Lowe | 1913–1923 |
|  | 18 | R Underwood | 1984–1996 |
| Most tries in season | 8 | CN Lowe | 1914 |
| Most tries in match | 4 | RW Poulton | v France, 1914 |
|  | 4 | CJ Ashton | v Italy, 2011 |
| Most cons in matches | 89 | JP Wilkinson | 1998–2011 |
| Most cons in season | 24 | JP Wilkinson | 2001 |
| Most cons in match | 9 | JP Wilkinson | v Italy, 2001 |
| Most pens in matches | 105 | JP Wilkinson | 1998–2011 |
| Most pens in season | 18 | SD Hodgkinson | 1991 |
|  | 18 | JP Wilkinson | 2000 |
| Most pens in match | 7 | SD Hodgkinson | v Wales, 1991 |
|  | 7 | CR Andrew | v Scotland, 1995 |
|  | 7 | JP Wilkinson | v France, 1999 |
| Most drops in matches | 11 | JP Wilkinson | 1998–2011 |
| Most drops in season | 5 | JP Wilkinson | 2003 |
| Most drops in match | 2 | R Hiller | v Ireland, 1970 |
|  | 2 | AGB Old | v France, 1978 |
|  | 2 | JP Horton | v France, 1980 |
|  | 2 | PJ Grayson | v France, 1996 |
|  | 2 | JP Wilkinson | v Wales, 2003 |
|  | 2 | JP Wilkinson | v Ireland, 2003 |

## THE COUNTRIES

# MISCELLANEOUS RECORDS

| RECORD | HOLDER | DETAIL |
|---|---|---|
| Longest Test Career | SD Shaw | 1996 to 2011 |
| Youngest Test Cap | HCC Laird | 18 yrs 134 days in 1927 |
| Oldest Test Cap | F Gilbert | 38 yrs 362 days in 1923 |

## UP TO 13 OCTOBER 2014

| PLAYER<br>BACKS : | DEBUT | CAPS | T | C | P | D | PTS |
|---|---|---|---|---|---|---|---|
| CJ Ashton | 2010 v F | 39 | 19 | 0 | 0 | 0 | 95 |
| BM Barritt | 2012 v S | 18 | 1 | 0 | 0 | 0 | 5 |
| MN Brown | 2007 v SA | 29 | 5 | 0 | 0 | 0 | 25 |
| FS Burns | 2012 v NZ | 5 | 1 | 8 | 12 | 0 | 57 |
| LD Burrell | 2014 v F | 7 | 3 | 0 | 0 | 0 | 15 |
| DS Care | 2008 v NZ | 48 | 7 | 0 | 0 | 3 | 44 |
| DJ Cipriani | 2008 v W | 9 | 1 | 7 | 11 | 0 | 52 |
| LAW Dickson | 2012 v S | 18 | 0 | 0 | 0 | 0 | 0 |
| KO Eastmond | 2013 v Arg | 4 | 1 | 0 | 0 | 0 | 5 |
| OA Farrell | 2012 v S | 25 | 2 | 33 | 64 | 1 | 271 |
| TGAL Flood | 2006 v Arg | 60 | 4 | 40 | 66 | 1 | 301 |
| BJ Foden | 2009 v It | 34 | 7 | 0 | 0 | 0 | 35 |
| GT Ford | 2014 v W | 2 | 0 | 0 | 0 | 0 | 0 |
| DA Goode | 2012 v SA | 16 | 0 | 0 | 1 | 0 | 3 |
| JJ May | 2013 v Arg | 7 | 0 | 0 | 0 | 0 | 0 |
| JT Nowell | 2014 v F | 5 | 1 | 0 | 0 | 0 | 5 |
| CJ Pennell | 2014 v NZ | 1 | 0 | 0 | 0 | 0 | 0 |
| D Strettle | 2007 v I | 14 | 2 | 0 | 0 | 0 | 10 |
| JA Tomkins | 2013 v A | 3 | 0 | 0 | 0 | 0 | 0 |
| EM Tuilagi | 2011 v W | 25 | 11 | 0 | 0 | 0 | 55 |
| WWF Twelvetrees | 2013 v S | 14 | 3 | 0 | 0 | 0 | 15 |
| C Wade | 2013 v Arg | 1 | 0 | 0 | 0 | 0 | 0 |
| M Yarde | 2013 v Arg | 5 | 4 | 0 | 0 | 0 | 20 |
| BR Youngs | 2010 v S | 38 | 6 | 0 | 0 | 0 | 30 |

ENGLAND

## FORWARDS :

| | | | | | | | |
|---|---|---|---|---|---|---|---|
| DMJ Attwood | 2010 v NZ | 12 | 0 | 0 | 0 | 0 | 0 |
| K Brookes | 2014 v NZ | 2 | 0 | 0 | 0 | 0 | 0 |
| DR Cole | 2010 v W | 45 | 1 | 0 | 0 | 0 | 5 |
| AR Corbisiero | 2011 v It | 19 | 0 | 0 | 0 | 0 | 0 |
| TR Croft | 2008 v F | 38 | 4 | 0 | 0 | 0 | 20 |
| JA Gray | 2014 v NZ | 1 | 0 | 0 | 0 | 0 | 0 |
| DM Hartley | 2008 v PI | 57 | 1 | 0 | 0 | 0 | 5 |
| JAW Haskell | 2007 v W | 51 | 4 | 0 | 0 | 0 | 20 |
| TA Johnson | 2012 v SA | 8 | 1 | 0 | 0 | 0 | 5 |
| MB Kvesic | 2013 v Arg | 2 | 0 | 0 | 0 | 0 | 0 |
| JO Launchbury | 2012 v Fj | 22 | 2 | 0 | 0 | 0 | 10 |
| CL Lawes | 2009 v A | 32 | 0 | 0 | 0 | 0 | 0 |
| JWG Marler | 2012 v SA | 22 | 0 | 0 | 0 | 0 | 0 |
| BJ Morgan | 2012 v S | 23 | 2 | 0 | 0 | 0 | 10 |
| MJ Mullan | 2010 v It | 5 | 0 | 0 | 0 | 0 | 0 |
| GMW Parling | 2012 v S | 21 | 1 | 0 | 0 | 0 | 5 |
| CDC Robshaw | 2009 v Arg | 28 | 2 | 0 | 0 | 0 | 10 |
| HM Thomas | 2013 v Arg | 7 | 0 | 0 | 0 | 0 | 0 |
| MWIN Vunipola | 2012 v Fj | 15 | 1 | 0 | 0 | 0 | 5 |
| VML Vunipola | 2013 v Arg | 10 | 1 | 0 | 0 | 0 | 5 |
| RW Webber | 2012 v It | 8 | 1 | 0 | 0 | 0 | 5 |
| DG Wilson | 2009 v Arg | 37 | 0 | 0 | 0 | 0 | 0 |
| TA Wood | 2011 v W | 30 | 0 | 0 | 0 | 0 | 0 |
| TN Youngs | 2012 v Fj | 17 | 0 | 0 | 0 | 0 | 0 |

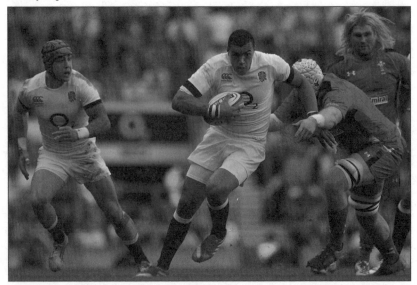

England's Luther Burrell makes a break during the Six Nations match against Wales at Twickenham in March.

Note: Years given for International Championship matches are for second half of season; eg 1972 means season 1971–72. Years for all other matches refer to the actual year of the match. Entries in square brackets denote matches played in RWC Finals.

**Aarvold, C D** (Cambridge U, W Hartlepool, Headingley, Blackheath) 1928 A, W, I, F, S, 1929 W, I, F, 1931 W, S, F, 1932 SA, W, I, S, 1933 W

**Abbott, S R** (Wasps, Harlequins) 2003 W2, F3, [Sm, U, W(R)], 2004 NZ1(t&R), 2, 2006 I, A2(R)

**Abendanon, N A** (Bath) 2007 SA2(R), F2

**Ackford, P J** (Harlequins) 1988 A, 1989 S, I, F, W, R, Fj, 1990 I, F, W, S, Arg 3, 1991 W, S, I, F, A, [NZ, It, F, S, A]

**Adams, A A** (London Hospital) 1910 F

**Adams, F R** (Richmond) 1875 I, S, 1876 S, 1877 I, 1878 S, 1879 S, I

**Adebayo, A A** (Bath) 1996, It, 1997 Arg 1, 2, A 2, NZ 1, 1998 S

**Adey, G J** (Leicester) 1976 I, F

**Adkins, S J** (Coventry) 1950 I, F, S, 1953 W, I, F, S

**Agar, A E** (Harlequins) 1952 SA, W, S, I, F, 1953 W, I

**Alcock, A** (Guy's Hospital) 1906 SA

**Alderson, F H R** (Hartlepool R) 1891 W, I, S, 1892 W, S, 1893 W

**Alexander, H** (Richmond) 1900 I, S, 1901 W, I, S, 1902 W, I

**Alexander, W** (Northern) 1927 F

**Allen, A O** (Gloucester) 2006 NZ, Arg

**Allison, D F** (Coventry) 1956 W, I, S, F, 1957 W, 1958 W, S

**Allport, A** (Blackheath) 1892 W, 1893 I, 1894 W, I, S

**Anderson, S** (Rockcliff) 1899 I

**Anderson, W F** (Orrell) 1973 NZ 1

**Anderton, C** (Manchester FW) 1889 M

**Andrew, C R** (Cambridge U, Nottingham, Wasps, Toulouse, Newcastle) 1985 R, F, S, I, W, 1986 W, S, I, F, 1987 I, F, W, [J (R), US], 1988 S, I 1, 2, A 1, 2, Fj, A, 1989 S, I, F, Fj, 1990 I, F, W, S, Arg 3, 1991 W, S, I, F, Fj, A, [NZ, It, US, F, S, A], 1992 S, I, F, W, C, SA, 1993 F, W, NZ, 1994 S, I, F, W, SA 1, 2, R, C, 1995 I, F, W, S, [Arg, It, A, NZ, F], 1997 W (R)

**Appleford, G N** (London Irish) 2002 Arg

**Archer, G S** (Bristol, Army, Newcastle) 1996 S, I, 1997 A 2, NZ 1, SA, NZ 2, 1998 F, W, S, I, A 1, H, It, 1999 Tg, Fj, 2000 I, F, W, It, S

**Archer, H** (Bridgwater A) 1909 W, F, I

**Armitage, D A** (London Irish) 2008 PI, A, SA, NZ3, 2009 It, W, I, F, S, Arg 1, 2, 2010 W, It, I, S, A2(R), NZ(R), A3(R), Sm(R), 2011 W2, 3(t&R), I2(R), [Arg, Gg, R(R), S]

**Armitage, S E** (London Irish) 2009 It, Arg 1, 2, 2010 W(R), It(R)

**Armstrong, R** (Northern) 1925 W

**Arthur, T G** (Wasps) 1966 W, I

**Ashby, R C** (Wasps) 1966 I, F, 1967 A

**Ashcroft, A** (Waterloo) 1956 W, I, S, F, 1957 W, I, F, S, 1958 W, A, I, F, S, 1959 I, F, S

**Ashcroft, A H** (Birkenhead Park) 1909 A

**Ashford, W** (Richmond) 1897 W, I, 1898 S, W

**Ashton, C J** (Northampton, Saracens) 2010 F, A1, 2, NZ, A3, Sm, SA, 2011 W1, It, F, S, I1, 2, [Arg, Gg, R, S, F], 2012 S, It, W, F, I, SA 1, 2, 3, A, SA4, NZ, 2013 S, I, F, It, W, A, Arg3, NZ, 2014 NZ2(R), 3

**Ashworth, A** (Oldham) 1892 I

**Askew, J G** (Cambridge U) 1930 W, I, F

**Aslett, A R** (Richmond) 1926 W, I, F, S, 1929 S, F

**Assinder, E W** (O Edwardians) 1909 A, W

**Aston, R L** (Blackheath) 1890 S, I

**Attwood, D M J** (Gloucester, Bath) 2010 NZ(R), Sm(R), 2013 Arg1, 2, A(R), 2014 F(R), S(R), I(R), W(R), It(R), NZ1R), 3(t&R)

**Auty, J R** (Headingley) 1935 S

**Back, N A** (Leicester) 1994 S, I, 1995 [Arg (t), It, WS], 1997 NZ 1(R), SA, NZ 2, 1998 F, W, S, I, H, It, A 2, SA 2, 1999 S, I, F, W, A, US, C, [It, NZ, Fj, SA], 2000 I, F, W, It, S, SA 1, 2, A, Arg, SA 3, 2001 W, It, S, F, I, A, R, SA, 2002 S, I, F, W, It, NZ (t + R), A, SA, 2003 F 1, W 1, S, I, NZ, A, F 3, [Gg, SA, Sm, W, F, A]

**Bailey, M D** (Cambridge U, Wasps) 1984 SA 1, 2, 1987 [US], 1989 Fj, 1990 I, F, S (R)

**Bainbridge, S** (Gosforth, Fylde) 1982 F, W, 1983 F, W, S, I, NZ, 1984 S, I, F, W, 1985 NZ 1, 2, 1987 F, W, S, [J, US]

**Baker, D G S** (OMTs) 1955 W, I, F, S

**Baker, E M** (Moseley) 1895 W, I, S, 1896 W, I, S, 1897 W

**Baker, H C** (Clifton) 1887 W

**Balshaw, I R** (Bath, Leeds, Gloucester) 2000 I (R), F (R), It (R), S (R), A (R), Arg, SA 3(R), 2001 W, It, S, F, I, 2002 S (R), I (R), 2003 F2, 3, [Sm, U, A(R)], 2004 It, S, I, 2005 It, S, 2006 A1, 2, NZ, Arg, 2007 It, SA1, 2008 W, It, F, S, I

**Banahan, M A** (Bath) 2009 Arg 1, 2, A, Arg 3, NZ, 2010 Sm, SA(R), 2011 It(R), F(R), S(R), I1, W2, 3, [Gg(R), S(R), F(R)]

**Bance, J F** (Bedford) 1954 S

**Barkley, O J** (Bath) 2001 US, 2004 It(R), I(t), W, F, NZ2(R), A1(R), 2005 W(R), F, I, It, S, A(R), Sm(R), 2006 A1, 2(R), 2007 F2, 3(R), [US, Sm, Tg], 2008 NZ1, 2(R)

**Barley, B** (Wakefield) 1984 I, F, W, A, 1988 A 1, 2, Fj

**Barnes, S** (Bristol, Bath) 1984 A, 1985 R (R), NZ 1 2, 1986 S (R), F (R), 1987 I (R), 1988 Fj, 1993 S, I

**Barr, R J** (Leicester) 1932 SA, W, I

**Barrett, E I M** (Lennox) 1903 S

**Barrington, T J M** (Bristol) 1931 W, I

**Barrington-Ward, L E** (Edinburgh U) 1910 W, I, F, S

**Barritt, B M** (Saracens) 2012 S, It, W, F, I, SA 1, 3(t&R), Fj, A, SA4, NZ, 2013 S, I, F, It, W, 2014 F(R), S(R)

**Barron, J H** (Bingley) 1896 S, 1897 W, I

**Bartlett, J T** (Waterloo) 1951 W

**Bartlett, R M** (Harlequins) 1957 W, I, F, S, 1958 I, F, S

**Barton, J** (Coventry) 1967 I, F, W, 1972 F

**Batchelor, T B** (Oxford U) 1907 F

**Bates, S M** (Wasps) 1989 R

**Bateson, A H** (Otley) 1930 W, I, F, S

**Bateson, H D** (Liverpool) 1879 I

**Batson, T** (Blackheath) 1872 S, 1874 S, 1875 I

**Batten, J M** (Cambridge U) 1874 S

**Baume, J L** (Northern) 1950 S

**Baxendell, J J N** (Sale) 1998 NZ 2, SA 1

**Baxter, J** (Birkenhead Park) 1900 W, I, S

**Bayfield, M C** (Northampton) 1991 Fj, A 1992 S, I, F, W, C, SA, 1993 F, W, S, I, 1994 S, I, SA 1, 2, R, C, 1995 I, F, W, S, [Arg, It, A, NZ, F], SA, WS, 1996 F, W

**Bazley, R C** (Waterloo) 1952 I, F, 1953 W, I, F, S, 1955 W, I, F, S

**Beal, N D** (Northampton) 1996 Arg, 1997 A 1, 1998 NZ 1, 2, SA 1, H (R), SA 2, 1999 S, F (R), A (t), C (R), [It (R), Tg (R), Fj, SA]

**Beaumont, W B** (Fylde) 1975 I, A 1(R), 2, 1976 A, W, S, I, F, 1977 S, I, F, W, 1978 F, W, S, I, NZ, 1979 S, I, F, W, NZ, 1980 I, F, W, S, 1981 W, S, I, F, Arg 1, 2, 1982 A, S

**Bedford, H** (Morley) 1889 M, 1890 S, I

**Bedford, L L** (Headingley) 1931 W, I

**Beer, I D S** (Harlequins) 1955 F, S

**Beese, M C** (Liverpool) 1972 W, I, F

**Beim, T D** (Sale) 1998 NZ 1(R), 2

Bell, D S C (Bath) 2005 It(R), S, 2009 A(R), Arg 3, NZ
Bell, F J (Northern) 1900 W
Bell, H (New Brighton) 1884 I
Bell, J L (Darlington) 1878 I
Bell, P J (Blackheath) 1968 W, I, F, S
Bell, R W (Northern) 1900 W, I, S
Bendon, G J (Wasps) 1959 W, I, F, S
Bennett, N O (St Mary's Hospital, Waterloo) 1947 W, S, F, 1948 A, W, I, S
Bennett, W N (Bedford, London Welsh) 1975 S, A1, 1976 S (R), 1979 S, I, F, W
Bennetts, B B (Penzance) 1909 A, W
Bentley, J (Sale, Newcastle) 1988 I 2, A 1, 1997 A 1, SA
Bentley, J E (Gipsies) 1871 S, 1872 S
Benton, S (Gloucester) 1998 A 1
Berridge, M J (Northampton) 1949 W, I
Berry, H (Gloucester) 1910 W, I, F, S
Berry, J (Tyldesley) 1891 W, I, S
Berry, J T W (Leicester) 1939 W, I, S
Beswick, E (Swinton) 1882 I, S
Biggs, J M (UCH) 1878 S, 1879 I
Birkett, J G G (Harlequins) 1906 S, F, SA, 1907 F, W, S, 1908 F, W, I , S, 1910 W, I, S, 1911 W, F, I , S, 1912 W, I , S, F
Birkett L (Clapham R) 1875 S, 1877 I, S
Birkett, R H (Clapham R) 1871 S, 1875 S, 1876 S, 1877 I
Bishop, C C (Blackheath) 1927 F
Black (Blackheath) 1930 W, I, F, S, 1931 W, I, S, F, 1932 S, 1933 W
Blacklock, J H (Aspatria) 1898 I, 1899 I
Blakeway, P J (Gloucester) 1980 I, F, W, S, 1981 W, S, I, F, 1982 I, F, W, 1984 I, F, W, SA 1, 1985 R, F, S, I
Blakiston, A F (Northampton) 1920 S, 1921 W, I, S, F, 1922 W, 1923 S, F, 1924 W, I, F, S, 1925 NZ, W, I, S, F
Blatherwick, T (Manchester) 1878 I
Body, J A (Gipsies) 1872 S, 1873 S
Bolton, C A (United Services) 1909 F
Bolton, R (Harlequins) 1933 W, 1936 S, 1937 S, 1938 W, I
Bolton, W N (Blackheath) 1882 I, S, 1883 W, I, S, 1884 W, I, S, 1885 I, 1887 I, S
Bonaventura, M S (Blackheath) 1931 W
Bond, A M (Sale) 1978 NZ, 1979 S, I, NZ, 1980 I, 1982 I
Bonham-Carter, E (Oxford U) 1891 S
Bonsor, F F (Bradford) 1886 W, I, S, 1887 W, S, 1889 M
Boobbyer, B (Rosslyn Park) 1950 W, I, F, S, 1951 W, F, 1952 S, I, F
Booth, L A (Headingley) 1933 W, I, S, 1934 S, 1935 W, I, F
Borthwick, S W (Bath, Saracens) 2001 F, C 1, 2(R), US, R, 2003 A(t), W 2(t), F 2, 2004 I, F(R), NZ1(R), 2, A1, C, SA, A2, 2005 W(R), It(R), S(R), A, NZ, Sm, 2006 W, It, S, F, I, 2007 W2, F3, [SA1(t&R), Sm(R), Tg], 2008 W, It, F, S, I, NZ1, 2, PI, A, SA, NZ3, 2009 It, W, I, F, S, Arg 1, 2, A, Arg 3, NZ, 2010 W, It, I, S
Botha, M J (Saracens) 2011 W2(R), 2012 S, It, W, F, I, SA 1, 2, 3(R), 4(R)
Botting, I J (Oxford U) 1950 W, I
Boughton, H J (Gloucester) 1935 W, I, S
Boyle, C W (Oxford U) 1873 S
Boyle, S B (Gloucester) 1983 W, S, I
Boylen, F (Hartlepool R) 1908 F, W, I, S
Bracken, K P P (Bristol, Saracens) 1993 NZ, 1994 S, I, C, 1995 I, F, W, S, [It, WS (t)], SA, 1996 It (R), 1997 Arg 1, 2, A 2, NZ 1, 2, 1998 F, W, 1999 S(R), I, F, A, 2000 SA 1, 2, A, 2001 It (R), S (R), F (R), C 1, 2, US, I (R), A, R (R), SA, 2002 S, I, F, W, It, 2003 W 1, It(R), I(t), NZ, A, F3, [SA, U(R), W(R), F(t&R)]
Bradby, M S (United Services) 1922 I, F
Bradley, R (W Hartlepool) 1903 W
Bradshaw, H (Bramley) 1892 S, 1893 W, I, S, 1894 W, I, S
Brain, S E (Coventry) 1984 SA 2, A (R), 1985 R, F, S, I, W, NZ 1, 2, 1986 W, S, I, F
Braithwaite, J (Leicester) 1905 NZ
Braithwaite-Exley, B (Headingley) 1949 W
Brettargh, A T (Liverpool OB) 1900 W, 1903 I, S, 1904 W, I, S, 1905 I, S
Brewer, J V (Gipsies) 1876 I
Briggs, A (Bradford) 1892 W, I, S
Brinn, A (Gloucester) 1972 W, I, S

Broadley, T (Bingley) 1893 W, S, 1894 W, I, S, 1896 S
Bromet, W E (Richmond) 1891 W, I, 1892 W, I, S, 1893 W, I, S, 1895 W, I, S, 1896 I
Brook, P W P (Harlequins) 1930 S, 1931 F, 1936 S
Brooke, T J (Richmond) 1968 F, S
Brookes, K (Newcastle) 2014 NZ2(R), 3(R)
Brooks, F G (Bedford) 1906 SA
Brooks, M J (Oxford U) 1874 S
Brophy, T J (Liverpool) 1964 I, F, S, 1965 W, I, 1966 W, I, F
Brough, J W (Silloth) 1925 NZ, W
Brougham, H (Harlequins) 1912 W, I, S, F
Brown, A A (Exeter) 1938 S
Brown A T (Gloucester) 2006 A1, 2007 SA1, 2
Brown, L G (Oxford U, Blackheath) 1911 W, F, I, S, 1913 SA, W, F, I, S, 1914 W, I, S, F, 1921 W, I, S, F, 1922 W
Brown, M N (Harlequins) 2007 SA1, 2, 2008 NZ1, 2012 S(R), W(R), I(R), SA 1, Fj(R), A(R), SA4, NZ, 2013 S, I, F, A, Arg1, 2, A, Arg3, NZ, 2014 F, S, I, W, It, NZ1, 2, 3
Brown S P (Richmond) 1998 A 1, SA 1
Brown, T W (Bristol) 1928 S, 1929 W, I, S, F, 1932 S, 1933 W, I, S
Brunton, J (N Durham) 1914 W, I, S
Brutton, E B (Cambridge U) 1886 S
Bryden, C C (Clapham R) 1876 I, 1877 S
Bryden, H A (Clapham R) 1874 S
Buckingham, R A (Leicester) 1927 F
Bucknall, A L (Richmond) 1969 SA, 1970 I, W, S, F, 1971 W, I, F, S (2[1C])
Buckton, J R D (Saracens) 1988 A (R), 1990 Arg 1, 2
Budd, A J (Blackheath) 1878 I, 1879 S, I, 1881 W, S
Budworth, R T D (Blackheath) 1890 W, 1891 W, S
Bull, A G (Northampton) 1914 W
Bullough, E (Wigan) 1892 W, I, S
Bulpitt, M P (Blackheath) 1970 S
Bulteel, A M (Manchester) 1876 I
Bunting, W L (Moseley) 1897 I, S, 1898 I, S, W, 1899 S, 1900 S, 1901 I, S
Burns, B H (Blackheath) 1871 S
Burns, F S (Gloucester, Leicester) 2012 NZ(R), 2013 Arg1, 2, 2014 NZ1, 3
Burrell, L D (Northampton) 2014 F, S, I, W, It, NZ2, 3(R)
Burton, G W (Blackheath) 1879 S, I, 1880 S, 1881 I, W, S
Burton, H C (Richmond) 1926 W
Burton, M A (Gloucester) 1972 W, I, F, S, SA, 1974 F, W, 1975 S, A 1, 2, 1976 A, W, S, I, F, 1978 F, W
Bush, J A (Clifton) 1872 S, 1873 S, 1875 S, 1876 I, S
Butcher, C J S (Harlequins) 1984 SA 1, 2, A
Butcher, W V (Streatham) 1903 S, 1904 W, I, S, 1905 W, I, S
Butler, A G (Harlequins) 1937 W, I
Butler, P E (Gloucester) 1975 A 1, 1976 F
Butterfield, J (Northampton) 1953 F, S, 1954 W, NZ, I, S, F, 1955 W, I, F, S, 1956 W, I, S, F, 1957 W, I, F, S, 1958 W, A, I, F, S, 1959 W, I, F, S
Byrne, F A (Moseley) 1897 W
Byrne, J F (Moseley) 1894 W, I, S, 1895 I, S, 1896 I, 1897 W, I, S, 1898 I, S, W, 1899 I

Cain, J J (Waterloo) 1950 W
Cairns, M I (Saracens) 2007 SA1(R)
Callard, J E B (Bath) 1993 NZ, 1994 S, I, 1995 [WS], SA
Campbell, D A (Cambridge U) 1937 W, I
Candler, P L (St Bart's Hospital) 1935 W, 1936 NZ, W, I, S, 1937 W, I, S, 1938 W, S
Cannell, L B (Oxford U, St Mary's Hospital) 1948 F, 1949 W, I, F, S, 1950 W, I, F, S, 1952 SA, W, 1953 W, I, F, 1956 I, S, F, 1957 W, I
Caplan, D W N (Headingley) 1978 S, I
Cardus, R M (Roundhay) 1979 F, W
Care, D S (Harlequins) 2008 NZ1(R), 2, PI, A, SA, NZ3, 2009 I(R), F(R), S(R), Arg 1, 2, A, Arg 3(R), NZ(R), 2010 W, It, I, S, F, A1, 2(R), NZ(R), A3(R), Sm(R), SA(R), 2011 W1(R), It(R), F(R), S(R), I1(R), W2, 3(R), 2012 SA 3, Fj, A, SA4(R), NZ(R), 2013 S(R), F(R), It, W(R), Arg3(R), 2014 F, S, I, W, It, NZ2
Carey, G M (Blackheath) 1895 W, I, S, 1896 W, I
Carleton, J (Orrell) 1979 NZ, 1980 I, F, W, S, 1981 W, S, I, F,

Arg 1, 2, 1982 A, S, I, F, W, 1983 F, W, S, I, NZ, 1984 S, I, F, W, A

**Carling, W D C** (Durham U, Harlequins) 1988 F, W, S, I 1, 2, A2, Fj, A, 1989 S, I, F, W, Fj, 1990 I, F, W, S, Arg 1, 2, 3, 1991 W, S, I, F, Fj, A, [NZ, It, US, F, S, A], 1992 S, I, F, W, C, SA, 1993 F, W, S, I, NZ, 1994 S, I, F, W, SA 1, 2, R, C, 1995 I, F, W, S, [Arg, WS, A, NZ, F], SA, WS, 1996 F, W, S, I, It, Arg, 1997 S, I, F, W

**Carpenter, A D** (Gloucester) 1932 SA

**Carr, R S L** (Manchester) 1939 W, I, S

**Cartwright, V H** (Nottingham) 1903 W, I, S, 1904 W, S, 1905 W, I, S, NZ, 1906 W, I, S, F, SA

**Catcheside, H C** (Percy Park) 1924 W, I, F, S, 1926 W, I, 1927 I, S

**Catt, M J** (Bath, London Irish) 1994 W (R), C (R), 1995 I, F, W, S, [Arg, It, WS, A, NZ, F], SA, WS, 1996 F, W, S, I, It, Arg, 1997 W, Arg 1, A 1, 2, NZ 1, SA, 1998 F, W (R), I, A 2(R), SA 2, 1999 S, F, W, A, C (R), [Tg (R), Fj, SA (R)], 2000 I, F, W, It, S, SA 1, 2, A, Arg, 2001 W, It, S, F, I, A, R (R), SA, 2003 [Sm(R), U, W(R), F, A(R)], 2004 W(R), F(R), NZ1, A1, 2006 A1, 2, 2007 F1, W1, F2, [US, SA1, A, F, SA2]

**Cattell, R H B** (Blackheath) 1895 W, I, S, 1896 W, I, S, 1900 W

**Cave, J W** (Richmond) 1889 M

**Cave, W T C** (Blackheath) 1905 W

**Challis, R** (Bristol) 1957 I, F, S

**Chambers, E L** (Bedford) 1908 F, 1910 W, I

**Chantrill, B S** (Bristol) 1924 W, I, F, S

**Chapman, C E** (Cambridge U) 1884 W

**Chapman D E** (Richmond) 1998 A 1(R)

**Chapman, F E** (Hartlepool) 1910 W, I, F, S, 1912 W, 1914 W, I

**Cheesman, W I** (OMTs) 1913 SA, W, F, I

**Cheston, E C** (Richmond) 1873 S, 1874 S, 1875 I, S, 1876 S

**Chilcott, G J** (Bath) 1984 A, 1986 I, F, 1987 F (R), W, [J, US, W (R)], 1988 I 2(R), Fj, 1989 I (R), F, W, R

**Christophers, P D** (Bristol) 2002 Arg, SA, 2003 W 1 (R)

**Christopherson, P** (Blackheath) 1891 W, S

**Chuter, G S** (Leicester) 2006 A1(R), 2, NZ, Arg, SA1, 2(R), 2007 S, It, I, F1, W1, 2(R), [US(R), SA1(R), Sm, Tg, A(R), F(R), SA2(R)], 2008 S(R), I(R), 2009 Arg 2(R), 2010 A1(R), 2(R)

**Cipriani, D J** (Wasps, Sale) 2008 W(R), It(R), I, PI, A, SA, NZ3(R), 2014 NZ1(R), 3(R)

**Clark, C W H** (Liverpool) 1876 I

**Clarke, A R** (Coventry) 1935 W, I, S, 1936 NZ, W, I

**Clarke, B B** (Bath, Richmond) 1992 SA, 1993 F, W, S, I, NZ, 1994 S, F, W, SA 1, 2, R, C, 1995 I, F, W, S, [Arg, It, A, NZ, F], SA, WS, 1996 F, W, S, I, Arg (R), 1997 W, Arg 1, 2, A 1(R), 1998 A 1(t), NZ 1, 2, SA 1, H, It, 1999 A (R)

**Clarke, S J S** (Cambridge U, Blackheath) 1963 W, I, F, S, NZ 1, 2, A, 1964 NZ, W, I, 1965 I, F, S

**Clayton, J H** (Liverpool) 1871 S

**Clements, J W** (O Cranleighans) 1959 I, F, S

**Cleveland, C R** (Blackheath) 1887 W, S

**Clibborn, W G** (Richmond) 1886 W, I, S, 1887 W, I, S

**Clough, F J** (Cambridge U, Orrell) 1986 I, F, 1987 [J (R), US]

**Coates, C H** (Yorkshire W) 1880 S, 1881 S, 1882 S

**Coates, V H M** (Bath) 1913 SA, W, F, I, S

**Cobby, W** (Hull) 1900 W

**Cockerham, A** (Bradford Olicana) 1900 W

**Cockerill, R** (Leicester) 1997 Arg 1(R), 2, A 2(t+R), NZ 1, SA, NZ 2, 1998 W, S, I, A 1, NZ 1, 2, SA 1, H, It, A 2, SA 2, 1999 S, I, F, W, A, C (R), [It, NZ, Tg (R), Fj (R)]

**Codling, A J** (Harlequins) 2002 Arg

**Cohen, B C** (Northampton) 2000 I, F, W, It, S, SA 2, Arg, SA 3, 2001 W, It, S, F, R, 2002 S, I, F, W, It, NZ, A, SA, 2003 F 1, W 1, S, I, NZ, A, F2, 3, [Gg, SA, Sm, W, F, A], 2004 It, S, I, W, F, NZ1, 2, A1, C(R), A2(R), 2005 F(R), A, NZ, 2006 W, It, S, F, I, NZ 1, 2, A1, C(R), A2(R), 2005 F(R), A, NZ, 2006 W, It, S, F, I, Arg

**Coley, E** (Northampton) 1929 F, 1932 W

**Collins, P J** (Camborne) 1952 S, I, F

**Collins, W E** (O Cheltonians) 1874 S, 1875 I, S, 1876 I, S

**Considine, S G U** (Bath) 1925 F

**Conway, G S** (Cambridge U, Rugby, Manchester) 1920 F, I, S, 1921 F, 1922 W, I, F, S, 1923 W, I, S, F, 1924 W, I, F, S, 1925 NZ, 1927 W

**Cook, J G** (Bedford) 1937 S

**Cook, P W** (Richmond) 1965 I, F

**Cooke, D A** (Harlequins) 1976 W, S, I, F

**Cooke, D H** (Harlequins) 1981 W, S, I, F, 1984 I, 1985 R, F, S, I, W, NZ 1, 2

**Cooke, P** (Richmond) 1939 W, I

**Coop, T** (Leigh) 1892 S

**Cooper, J G** (Moseley) 1909 A, W

**Cooper, M J** (Moseley) 1973 F, S, NZ 2(R), 1975 F, W, 1976 A, W, 1977 S, I, F, W

**Coopper, S F** (Blackheath) 1900 W, 1902 W, I, 1905 W, I, S, 1907 W

**Corbett, L J** (Bristol) 1921 F, 1923 W, I, 1924 W, I, F, S, 1925 NZ, W, I, S, F, 1927 W, I, S, F

**Corbisiero, A R** (London Irish, Northampton) 2011 It, F(R), S, I1, W2, 3, [Gg(R), R, S(R), F(R)], 2012 S, It, W, F, I, SA 2(t&R) 4, NZ, 2013 Arg3(R)

**Corless, B J** (Coventry, Moseley) 1976 A, I (R), 1977 S, I, F, W, 1978 F, W, S, I

**Corry, M E** (Bristol, Leicester) 1997 Arg 1, 2, 1998 H, It, SA 2(t), 1999 F(R), A, C (t), [It (R), NZ (t+R), SA (R)], 2000 I (R), F (R), W (R), It (R), S (R), Arg (R), SA 3(t), 2001 W (R), It (R), F (t), C 1, I, 2002 F (t+R), W (R), 2003 W 2, F 2, 3, [U], 2004 A1(R), C, SA, A2, 2005 F, I, It, S, A, NZ, Sm, 2006 W, It, S, F, I, NZ, Arg, SA1, 2, 2007 S, It, I, F1, W1, 2, F2(R), 3, [US(R), SA1, Sm, Tg, A, F, SA2]

**Cotton, F E** (Loughborough Colls, Coventry, Sale) 1971 S (2[1C]), P, 1973 W, I, F, S, NZ 2, A, 1974 S, I, 1975 I, F, W, 1976 A, W, S, I, F, 1977 S, I, F, W, 1978 S, I, 1979 NZ, 1980 I, F, W, S, 1981 W

**Coulman, M J** (Moseley) 1967 A, I, F, S, W, 1968 W, I, F, S

**Coulson, T J** (Coventry) 1927 W, 1928 A, W

**Court, E D** (Blackheath) 1885 W

**Coverdale, H** (Blackheath) 1910 F, 1912 I, F, 1920 W

**Cove-Smith, R** (OMTs) 1921 S, F, 1922 I, F, S, 1923 W, I, S, F, 1924 W, I, S, F, 1925 NZ, W, I, S, F, 1927 W, I, S, F, 1928 A, W, I, F, S, 1929 W, I

**Cowling, R J** (Leicester) 1977 S, I, F, W, 1978 F, NZ, 1979 S, I

**Cowman, A R** (Loughborough Colls, Coventry) 1971 S (2[1C]), P, 1973 W, I

**Cox, N S** (Sunderland) 1901 S

**Crane, J S** (Leicester) 2008 SA(R), 2009 Arg 1(R), A

**Cranmer, P** (Richmond, Moseley) 1934 W, I, S, 1935 W, I, S, 1936 NZ, W, I, S, 1937 W, I, S, 1938 W, I, S

**Creed, R N** (Coventry) 1971 P

**Cridlan, A G** (Blackheath) 1935 W, I, S

**Croft, T R** (Leicester) 2008 F(R), S, I, NZ2(R), PI, A, SA(R), NZ3(R), 2009 It(R), W(R), I(R), F, S, A, Arg 3, NZ(R), 2010 A1, 2, NZ, A3, Sm(R), SA, 2011 S(R), I1(R), W2, I2, [Arg, Gg(R), R, S, F], 2012 S, It, W, F, I, 2013 It(R), W

**Crompton, C A** (Blackheath) 1871 S

**Crompton, D E** (Bristol) 2007 SA1(R)

**Crosse, C W** (Oxford U) 1874 S, 1875 I

**Cueto, M J** (Sale) 2004 C, SA, A2, 2005 W, F, I, It, S, A, NZ, Sm, 2006 W, It, S, F, I, SA1, 2, 2007 W1, F3, [US, Sm, Tg, SA2], 2009 It, W, I, F, S, Arg 1, 2, A, Arg 3, NZ, 2010 W, It, I, S, F, A1, 2, NZ, A3, Sm, SA, 2011 W1, It, F, S, I1, W2, 3, I2, [R, F]

**Cumberlege, B S** (Blackheath) 1920 W, I, S, 1921 W, I, S, F, 1922 W

**Cumming, D C** (Blackheath) 1925 S, F

**Cunliffe, F L** (RMA) 1874 S

**Currey, F I** (Marlborough N) 1872 S

**Currie, J D** (Oxford U, Harlequins, Bristol) 1956 W, I, S, F, 1957 W, I, F, S, 1958 W, A, I, F, S, 1959 W, I, F, S, 1960 W, I, F, S, 1961 SA, 1962 W, I, F

**Cusani, D A** (Orrell) 1987 I

**Cusworth, L** (Leicester) 1979 NZ, 1982 F, W, 1983 W, NZ, 1984 S, I, F, W, 1988 F, W

**D'Aguilar, F B G** (Royal Engineers) 1872 S

**Dallaglio, L B N** (Wasps) 1995 SA (R), WS, 1996 F, W, S, I, It, Arg, 1997 S, I, F, A 1, 2, NZ 1, SA, NZ 2, 1998 F, W, S, I,

A 2, SA 2, 1999 S, I, F, W, US, C, [It, NZ, Tg, Fj, SA], 2000 I, F, W, It, S, SA 1, 2, A, Arg, SA 3, 2001 W, It, S, F, 2002 It (R), NZ, A (t), SA(R), 2003 F 1 (R), W 1, It, S, I, NZ, A, [Gg, SA, Sm, U, W, F, A], 2004 It, S, I, W, F, NZ1, 2, A1, 2006 W(t&R), It(R), S(R), F(R), 2007 W2(R), F2, 3(R), [US, Tg(R), A(R), F(R), SA2(R)]

**Dalton, T J** (Coventry) 1969 S(R)
**Danby, T** (Harlequins) 1949 W
**Daniell, J** (Richmond) 1899 W, 1900 I, S, 1902 I, S, 1904 I, S 1(R), 3(R)
**Darby, A J L** (Birkenhead Park) 1899 I
**Davenport, A** (Ravenscourt Park) 1871 S
**Davey, J** (Redruth) 1908 S, 1909 W
**Davey, R F** (Teignmouth) 1931 W
**Davidson, Jas** (Aspatria) 1897 S, 1898 S, W, 1899 I, S
**Davidson, Jos** (Aspatria) 1899 W, S
**Davies, G H** (Cambridge U, Coventry, Wasps) 1981 S, I, F, Arg 1, 2, 1982 A, S, I, 1983 F, W, S, 1984 S, SA 1, 2, 1985 R (R), NZ 1, 2, 1986 W, S, I, F
**Davies, P H** (Sale) 1927 I
**Davies, V G** (Harlequins) 1922 W, 1925 NZ
**Davies, W J A** (United Services, RN) 1913 SA, W, F, I, S, 1914 I, S, F, 1920 F, I, S, 1921 W, I, S, F, 1922 I, F, S, 1923 W, I, S, F
**Davies, W P C** (Harlequins) 1953 S, 1954 NZ, I, 1955 W, I, F, S, 1956 W, 1957 F, S, 1958 W
**Davis, A M** (Torquay Ath, Harlequins) 1963 W, I, S, NZ 1, 2, 1964 NZ, W, I, F, S, 1966 W, I, 1967 A, 1969 SA, 1970 I, W, S
**Dawe, R G R** (Bath) 1987 I, F, W, [US], 1995 [WS]
**Dawson, E F** (RIEC) 1878 I
**Dawson, M J S** (Northampton, Wasps) 1995 WS, 1996 F, W, S, I, 1997 A 1, SA, NZ 2(R), 1998 W (R), S, I, NZ 1, 2, SA 1, H, It, A 2, SA 2, 1999 S, F(R), W, A(R), US, C, [It, NZ, Tg, Fj, SA], 2000 I, F, W, It, S, A (R), Arg, SA 3, 2001 W, It, S, F, I, 2002 W (R), It (R), NZ, A, SA, 2003 It, S, I, A(R), F3(R), [Gg, Sm, W, F, A], 2004It(R), S(R), I, W, F, NZ1, 2(R), A1(R), 2005 W, F(R), I(R), It(R), S(R), A, NZ, 2006 W(R), It(R), S(t&R), F, I(R)
**Day, H L V** (Leicester) 1920 W, 1922 W, F, 1926 S
**Deacon, L P** (Leicester) 2005 Sm, 2006 A1, 2(R), 2007 S, It, I, F1(R), W1(R), 2009 Arg 1, 2, A, Arg 3, NZ(R), 2010 W(R), It(R), I(R), S, F, 2011 W1, It, F, S, I1, W3, I2, [Arg, R, S, F]
**Dean, G J** (Harlequins) 1931 I
**Dee, J M** (Hartlepool R) 1962 S, 1963 NZ 1
**Devitt, Sir T G** (Blackheath) 1926 I, F, 1928 A, W
**Dewhurst, J H** (Richmond) 1887 W, I, S, 1890 W
**De Glanville, P R** (Bath) 1992 SA (R), 1993 W (R), NZ, 1994 S, I, F, W, SA 1, 2, C (R), 1995 [Arg (R), It, WS], SA (R), 1996 W (R), I (R), It, 1997 S, I, F, W, Arg 1, 2, A 1, 2, NZ 1, 2, 1998 W (R), S (R), I (R), A 2, SA 2, 1999 A (R), US, [It, NZ, Fj (R), SA]
**De Winton, R F C** (Marlborough N) 1893 W
**Dibble, R** (Bridgwater A) 1906 S, F, SA, 1908 F, W, I, S, 1909 A, W, F, I, S, 1910 S, 1911 W, F, S, 1912 W, I, S
**Dicks, J** (Northampton) 1934 W, I, S, 1935 W, I, S, 1936 S, 1937 I
**Dickson, L A W** (Northampton) 2012 S(R), It(R), W, F, I, SA 1(R), 2(R), 2013 Arg1, 2, A, Arg3, NZ, 2014 F(R), S(R), W(R), It(R), NZ1(R), 3(R)
**Dillon, E W** (Blackheath) 1904 W, I, S, 1905 W
**Dingle, A J** (Hartlepool R) 1913 I, 1914 S, F
**Diprose, A J** (Saracens) 1997 Arg 1, 2, A 2, NZ 1, 1998 W (R), S (R), I, A 1, NZ 2, SA 1
**Dixon, P J** (Harlequins, Gosforth) 1971 P, 1972 W, I, F, S, 1973 I, F, S, 1974 S, I, F, W, 1975 I, 1976 F, 1977 S, I, F, W, 1978 F, S, I, NZ
**Dobbs, G E B** (Plymouth Albion) 1906 W, I
**Doble, S A** (Moseley) 1972 SA, 1973 NZ 1, W
**Dobson, D D** (Newton Abbot) 1902 W, I, S, 1903 W, I, S
**Dobson, T H** (Bradford) 1895 S
**Dodge, P W** (Leicester) 1978 W, S, I, NZ, 1979 S, I, F, W, 1980 W, S, 1981 W, S, I, F, Arg 1, 2, 1982 A, S, F, W, 1983 F, W, S, I, NZ, 1985 R, F, S, I, W, NZ 1, 2
**Donnelly, M P** (Oxford U) 1947 I
**Dooley, W A** (Preston Grasshoppers, Fylde) 1985 R, F, S, I, W, NZ 2(R), 1986 W, S, I, F, 1987 F, W, [A, US, W], 1988 F, W, S, I 1, 2, A 1, 2, Fj, A, 1989 S, I, F, W, R, Fj, 1990 I, F, W,

S, Arg 1, 2, 3, 1991 W, S, I, F, [NZ, US, F, S, A], 1992 S, I, F, W, C, SA, 1993 W, S, I
**Doran-Jones, P P L** (Gloucester, Northampton) 2009 Arg 3(R), 2011 S(R), I1(R), 2012 SA 1(R), 2013 Arg1(R), 2(R)
**Dovey, B A** (Rosslyn Park) 1963 W, I
**Down, P J** (Bristol) 1909 A
**Dowson, A O** (Moseley) 1899 S
**Dowson, P D A** (Northampton) 2012 S, It, W(R), F(R), I(R), SA 1(R), 3(R)
**Drake-Lee, N J** (Cambridge U, Leicester) 1963 W, I, F, S, 1964 NZ, W, I, 1965 W
**Duckett, H** (Bradford) 1893 I, S
**Duckham, D J** (Coventry) 1969 I, F, S, W, SA, 1970 I, W, S, F, 1971 W, I, F, S (2[1C]), P, 1972 W, I, F, S, 1973 NZ 1, W, I, F, S, NZ 2, A, 1974 S, I, F, W, 1975 I, F, W, 1976 A, W, S
**Dudgeon, H W** (Richmond) 1897 S, 1898 I, S, W, 1899 W, I, S
**Dugdale, J M** (Ravenscourt Park) 1871 S
**Dun, A F** (Wasps) 1984 W
**Duncan, R F H** (Guy's Hospital) 1922 I, F, S
**Duncombe, N S** (Harlequins) 2002 S (R), I (R)
**Dunkley, P E** (Harlequins) 1931 I, S, 1936 NZ, W, I, S
**Duthie, J** (W Hartlepool) 1903 W
**Dyson, J W** (Huddersfield) 1890 S, 1892 S, 1893 I, S

**Easter, N J** (Harlequins) 2007 It, F1, SA1, 2, W2, F3, [SA1, Sm, Tg, A, F, SA2], 2008 It, F, S, I, PI, A, SA, NZ3, 2009 It, W, I, F, S, Arg 1, 2, 2010 W, It, I, S, F, A1, 2, NZ, A3, Sm, SA, 2011 W1, It, F, S, I1, W3, [Arg, S(t&R), F]
**Eastmond, K O** (Bath) 2013 Arg1(R), 2, 2014 NZ1, 3
**Ebdon, P J** (Wellington) 1897 W, I
**Eddison, J H** (Headingley) 1912 W, I, S, F
**Edgar, C S** (Birkenhead Park) 1901 S
**Edwards, R** (Newport) 1921 W, I, S, F, 1922 W, F, 1923 W, 1924 W, F, S, 1925 NZ
**Egerton, D W** (Bath) 1988 I 2, A 1, Fj (R), A, 1989 Fj, 1990 I, Arg 2(R)
**Elliot, C H** (Sunderland) 1886 W
**Elliot, E W** (Sunderland) 1901 W, I, S, 1904 W
**Elliot, W** (United Services, RN) 1932 I, S, 1933 W, I, S, 1934 W, I
**Elliott, A E** (St Thomas's Hospital) 1894 S
**Ellis, H A** (Leicester) 2004 SA(R), A2(R), 2005 W(R), F, I, It, S, Sm, 2006 W, It, S, F(R), I, 2007 S, It, I, F1, W1, 2008 PI(R), A(R), SA(R), NZ3(R), 2009 It, W, I, F, S
**Ellis, J** (Wakefield) 1939 S
**Ellis, S S** (Queen's House) 1880 I
**Emmott, C** (Bradford) 1892 W
**Enthoven, H J** (Richmond) 1878 I
**Erinle, A O** (Biarritz) 2009 A(R), NZ
**Estcourt, N S D** (Blackheath) 1955 S
**Evans, B J** (Leicester) 1988 A 2, Fj
**Evans, E** (Sale) 1948 A, 1950 W, 1951 I, F, S, 1952 SA, W, S, I, F, 1953 I, F, S, 1954 W, NZ, I, F, 1956 W, I, S, F, 1957 W, I, F, S, 1958 W, A, I, F, S
**Evans, G W** (Coventry) 1972 S, 1973 W (R), F, S, NZ 2, 1974 S, I, F, W
**Evans, N L** (RNEC) 1932 W, I, S, 1933 W, I
**Evanson, A M** (Richmond) 1883 W, I, S, 1884 S
**Evanson, W A D** (Richmond) 1875 S, 1877 S, 1878 S, 1879 S, I
**Evershed, F** (Blackheath) 1889 M, 1890 W, S, I, 1892 W, I, S, 1893 W, I, S
**Eyres, W C T** (Richmond) 1927 I

**Fagan, A R St L** (Richmond) 1887 I
**Fairbrother, K E** (Coventry) 1969 I, F, S, W, SA, 1970 I, W, S, F, 1971 W, I, F
**Faithfull, C K T** (Harlequins) 1924 I, 1926 F, S
**Fallas, H** (Wakefield T) 1884 I
**Farrell, A D** (Saracens) 2007 S, It, I, W2, F3, [US(R), SA1, Tg(R)]
**Farrell, O A** (Saracens) 2012 S, It, W, F, I, SA 1, 2(R), 3(R), Fj(R), A(R), SA4(t&R), NZ, 2013 S, I, F, W, A, Arg3, NZ, 2014 F, S, I, W, It, NZ2
**Fegan, J H C** (Blackheath) 1895 W, I, S
**Fernandes, C W L** (Leeds) 1881 I, W, S
**Fidler, J H** (Gloucester) 1981 Arg 1, 2, 1984 SA 1, 2
**Fidler, R J** (Gloucester) 1998 NZ 2, SA 1

ENGLAND

Horsfall, E L (Harlequins) 1949 W
Horton, A L (Blackheath) 1965 W, I, F, S, 1966 F, S, 1967 NZ
Horton, J P (Bath) 1978 W, S, I, NZ, 1980 I, F, W, S, 1981 W, 1983 S, I, 1984 SA 1, 2
Horton, N E (Moseley, Toulouse) 1969 I, F, S, W, 1971 I, F, S, 1974 I, 1975 W, 1977 S, I, F, W, 1978 F, W, 1979 S, I, F, W, 1980 I
Hosen, R W (Bristol, Northampton) 1963 NZ 1, 2, A, 1964 F, S, 1967 A, I, F, S, W
Hosking, G R d'A (Devonport Services) 1949 W, I, F, S, 1950 W
Houghton, S (Runcorn) 1892 I, 1896 W
Howard, P D (O Millhillians) 1930 W, I, F, S, 1931 W, I, S, F
Hubbard, G C (Blackheath) 1892 W, I
Hubbard, J C (Harlequins) 1930 S
Hudson, A (Gloucester) 1906 W, I, F, 1908 F, W, I, S, 1910 F
Hughes, G E (Barrow) 1896 S
Hull, P A (Bristol, RAF) 1994 SA 1, 2, R, C
Hulme, F C (Birkenhead Park) 1903 W, I, 1905 W, I
Hunt, J T (Manchester) 1882 I, S, 1884 W
Hunt, R (Manchester) 1880 I, 1881 W, S, 1882 I
Hunt, W H (Manchester) 1876 S, 1877 I, S, 1878 I
Hunter, I (Northampton) 1992 C, 1993 F, W, 1994 F, W, 1995 [WS, F]
Huntsman, R P (Headingley) 1985 NZ 1, 2
Hurst, A C B (Wasps) 1962 S
Huskisson, T F (OMTs) 1937 W, I, S, 1938 W, I, 1939 W, I, S
Hutchinson, F (Headingley) 1909 F, I, S
Hutchinson, J E (Durham City) 1906 I
Hutchinson, W C (RIE Coll) 1876 S, 1877 I
Hutchinson, W H H (Hull) 1875 I, 1876 I
Huth, H (Huddersfield) 1879 S
Hyde, J P (Northampton) 1950 F, S
Hynes, W B (United Services, RN) 1912 F

Ibbitson, E D (Headingley) 1909 W, F, I, S
Imrie, H M (Durham City) 1906 NZ, 1907 I
Inglis, R E (Blackheath) 1886 W, I, S
Irvin, S H (Devonport A) 1905 W
Isherwood, F W (Ravenscourt Park) 1872 S

Jackett, E J (Leicester, Falmouth) 1905 NZ, 1906 W, I, S, F, SA, 1907 W, I, S, 1909 W, F, I, S
Jackson, A H (Blackheath) 1878 I, 1880 I
Jackson, B S (Broughton Park) 1970 S (R), F
Jackson, P B (Coventry) 1956 W, I, F, 1957 W, I, F, S, 1958 W, A, F, S, 1959 W, I, F, S, 1961 S, 1963 W, I, F, S
Jackson, W J (Halifax) 1894 S
Jacob, F (Cambridge U) 1897 W, S, 1898 I, S, W, 1899 W, I
Jacob, H P (Blackheath) 1924 W, I, F, S, 1930 F
Jacob, P G (Blackheath) 1898 I
Jacobs, C R (Northampton) 1956 W, I, S, F, 1957 W, I, F, S, 1958 W, A, I, F, S, 1960 W, I, F, S, 1961 SA, W, I, F, S, 1963 NZ 1, 2, A, 1964 W, I, F, S
Jago, R A (Devonport A) 1906 W, I, SA, 1907 W, I
Janion, J P A G (Bedford) 1971 W, I, F, S (2[1C]), P, 1972 W, S, SA, 1973 A, 1975 A 1, 2
Jarman, J W (Bristol) 1900 W
Jeavons, N C (Moseley) 1981 S, I, F, Arg 1, 2, 1982 A, S, I, F, W, 1983 F, W, S, I
Jeeps, R E G (Northampton) 1956 W, 1957 W, I, F, S, 1958 W, A, I, F, S, 1959 I, 1960 W, I, F, S, 1961 SA, W, I, F, S, 1962 W, I, F, S
Jeffery, G L (Blackheath) 1886 W, I, S, 1887 W, I, S
Jennins, C R (Waterloo) 1967 A, I, F
Jewitt, J (Hartlepool R) 1902 W
Johns, W A (Gloucester) 1909 W, F, I, S, 1910 W, I, F
Johnson, M O (Leicester) 1993 F, NZ, 1994 S, I, F, W, R, C, 1995 I, F, W, S, [Arg, It, WS, A, NZ, F], SA, WS, 1996 F, W, S, I, It, Arg, 1997 S, I, F, W, A 2, NZ 1, 2, 1998 F, W, S, I, H, It, A 2, SA 2, 1999 S, I, F, W, A, US, C, [It, NZ, Tg, Fj, SA], 2000 SA 1, 2, A, Arg, SA 3, 2001 W, It, S, F, SA, 2002 S, I, F, It (t+R), NZ, A, SA, 2003 F 1, W 1, I, NZ, A, F 3, [Gg, SA, Sm, U(R), W, F, A]
Johnson, T A (Exeter) 2012 SA 1, 2, 3, Fj, A, 2014 W(R), It(R), NZ1(R)
Johnston, J B (Saracens) 2002 Arg, NZ (R)

Johnston, W R (Bristol) 1910 W, I, S, 1912 W, I, S, F, 1913 SA, W, F, I, S, 1914 W, I, S, F
Jones, C M (Sale) 2004 It(R), S, I(R), W, NZ1, 2005 W, 2006 A1(R), 2, SA1(R), 2, 2007 SA1, 2(R)
Jones, F P (New Brighton) 1893 S
Jones, H A (Barnstaple) 1950 W, I, F
Jorden, A M (Cambridge U, Blackheath, Bedford) 1970 F, 1973 I, F, S, 1974 F, 1975 W, S
Joseph, J B A (London Irish) 2012 SA 1(R), 2, 3, NZ(R), 2013 Arg1, 2
Jowett, D (Heckmondwike) 1889 M, 1890 S, I, 1891 W, I, S
Judd, P E (Coventry) 1962 W, I, F, S, 1963 S, NZ 1, 2, A, 1964 NZ, 1965 I, F, S, 1966 W, I, F, S, 1967 A, I, F, S, W, NZ

Kay, B J (Leicester) 2001 C 1, 2, A, R, SA (t+R), 2002 S, I, F, W, It, Arg, NZ (R), A, SA, 2003 F 1, W 1, It, S, I, NZ, A, F 3, [Gg, SA, Sm, W, F, A], 2004 It, S, I, W, F, C(R), SA(R), 2005 W, F, I, It, S, 2006 A2, NZ, Arg, SA1, 2(R), 2007 F2, [US, SA1, Sm, Tg, A, F, SA2], 2008 W(R), It(R), F(R), S(R), I(R), NZ1(R), 2(R), 2009 Arg 1(R), 2(t&R)
Kayll, H E (Sunderland) 1878 S
Keeling, J H (Guy's Hospital) 1948 A, W
Keen, B W (Newcastle U) 1968 W, I, F, S
Keeton, G H (Leicester) 1904 W, I, S
Kelly, G A (Bedford) 1947 W, I, S, 1948 W
Kelly, T S (London Devonians) 1906 W, I, S, F, SA, 1907 F, W, I, S, 1908 F, I, S
Kemble, A T (Liverpool) 1885 W, I, 1887 I
Kemp, D T (Blackheath) 1935 W
Kemp, T A (Richmond) 1937 W, I, 1939 S, 1948 A, W
Kendall, P D (Birkenhead Park) 1901 S, 1902 W, 1903 S
Kendall-Carpenter, J MacG K (Oxford U, Bath) 1949 I, F, S, 1950 W, I, F, S, 1951 I, F, S, 1952 SA, W, S, I, F, 1953 W, I, F, S, 1954 W, NZ, I, F
Kendrew, D A (Leicester) 1930 W, I, 1933 I, S, 1934 S, 1935 W, I, 1936 NZ, W, I
Kennedy, N J (London Irish) 2008 PI, NZ3, 2009 It, W, I, F(R), S(R)
Kennedy, R D (Camborne S of M) 1949 I, F, S
Kent, C P (Rosslyn Park) 1977 S, I, F, W, 1978 F (R)
Kent, T (Salford) 1891 W, I, S, 1892 W, I, S
Kershaw, C A (United Services, RN) 1920 W, F, I, S, 1921 W, I, S, F, 1922 W, I, F, S, 1923 W, I, S, F
Kewley, E (Liverpool) 1874 S, 1875 S, 1876 I, S, 1877 I, S, 1878 S
Kewney, A L (Leicester) 1906 W, I, S, F, 1909 A, W, F, I, S, 1911 W, F, I, S, 1912 I, S, 1913 SA
Key, A (O Cranleighans) 1930 I, 1933 W
Keyworth, M (Swansea) 1976 A, W, S, I
Kilner, B (Wakefield T) 1880 I
Kindersley, R S (Exeter) 1883 W, 1884 S, 1885 W
King, A D (Wasps) 1997 Arg 2(R), 1998 SA 2(R), 2000 It (R), 2001 C 2(R), 2003 W2
King, I (Harrogate) 1954 W, NZ, I
King, J A (Headingley) 1911 W, F, I, S, 1912 W, I, S, 1913 SA, W, F, I, S
King, Q E M A (Army) 1921 S
Kingston, P (Gloucester) 1975 A 1, 2, 1979 I, F, W
Kitching, A E (Blackheath) 1913 I
Kittermaster, H J (Harlequins) 1925 NZ, W, I, 1926 W, I, F, S
Knight, F (Plymouth) 1909 A
Knight, P M (Bristol) 1972 F, S, SA
Knowles, E (Millom) 1896 S, 1897 S
Knowles, T C (Birkenhead Park) 1931 S
Krige, J A (Guy's Hospital) 1920 W
Kvesic, M B (Worcester) 2013 Arg 1, 2

Labuschagne, N A (Harlequins, Guy's Hospital) 1953 W, 1955 W, I, F, S
Lagden, R O (Richmond) 1911 S
Laird, H C C (Harlequins) 1927 W, I, S, 1928 A, W, I, F, S, 1929 W, I
Lambert, D (Harlequins) 1907 F, 1908 F, W, S, 1911 W, F, I
Lampkowski, M S (Headingley) 1976 A, W, S, I
Lapage, W N (United Services, RN) 1908 F, W, I, S
Larter, P J (Northampton, RAF) 1967 A, NZ, 1968 W, I, F, S, 1969 I, F, S, W, SA, 1970 I, W, F, S, 1971 W, I, F, S (2[1C]), P, 1972 SA, 1973 NZ 1, W

**Launchbury, J O** (Wasps) 2012 Fj(R), A(R), SA4, NZ, 2013 S, I, F, It, W, Arg1, 2, A, Arg3, NZ, 2014 F, S, I, W, It, NZ1, 2, 3
**Law, A F** (Richmond) 1877 S
**Law, D E** (Birkenhead Park) 1927 I
**Lawes, C L** (Northampton) 2009 A(R), 2010 S(R), A1(R), 2, NZ, A3, Sm, SA, 2011 W3, I2, [Arg, S, F(R)], 2012 W(R), NZ(R), 2013 S(R), I(R), F, It(R), W(R), Arg1(R), 2(R), A, Arg3, NZ, 2014 F, S, I, W, It, NZ2(R), 3
**Lawrence, Hon H A** (Richmond) 1873 S, 1874 S, 1875 I, S
**Lawrie, P W** (Leicester) 1910 S, 1911 S
**Lawson, R G** (Workington) 1925 I
**Lawson, T M** (Workington) 1928 A, W
**Leadbetter, M M** (Broughton Park) 1970 F
**Leadbetter, V H** (Edinburgh Wands) 1954 S, F
**Leake, W R M** (Harlequins) 1891 W, I, S
**Leather, G** (Liverpool) 1907 I
**Lee, F H** (Marlborough N) 1876 S, 1877 I
**Lee, H** (Blackheath) 1907 F
**Le Fleming, J** (Blackheath) 1887 W
**Leonard, J** (Saracens, Harlequins) 1990 Arg 1, 2, 3, 1991 W, S, I, F, Fj, A, [NZ, It, US, F, S, A], 1992 S, I, F, W, C, SA, 1993 F, W, S, I, NZ, 1994 S, I, F, W, SA 1, 2, R, C, 1995 I, F, W, S, [Arg, It, A, NZ, F], SA, WS, 1996 F, W, S, I, It, Arg, 1997 S, I, F, W, A 2, NZ 1, SA, NZ 2, 1998 F, W, S, I, H, It, A 2 SA 2, 1999 S, I, F, W, A, C (R), [It, NZ, Fj, SA], 2000 I, F, W, It, S, SA 1, 2, A, Arg, SA 3, 2001 W, It, S, F, I, R, 2002 S (R), I (R), F (R), It (R), A, SA, 2003 F 1, S, I, NZ, W 2, F 2(t+R), 3(R), [Gg(t&R), SA(R), Sm, U, W, F(t&R), A(R)], 2004 It(R)
**Leslie-Jones, F A** (Richmond) 1895 W, I
**Lewis, A O** (Bath) 1952 SA, W, S, I, F, 1953 W, I, F, S, 1954 F
**Lewsey, O J** (Wasps) 1998 NZ 1, 2, SA 1, 2001 C 1, 2, US, 2003 It, S, I, NZ, A, F2, 3(t+R), [Gg, SA, U, F, A], 2004 It, S, I, W, F, NZ1, 2, A1, C, SA, A2, 2005 W, F, I, It, S, A, NZ, Sm, 2006 W, S, F, Arg(R), SA1, 2, 2007 S, It, I, F1, 2, 3, [US, SA1, Sm, Tg, A, F]
**Leyland, R** (Waterloo) 1935 W, I, S
**Linnett, M S** (Moseley) 1989 Fj
**Lipman, M R** (Bath) 2004 NZ2(R), A1(R), 2006 A2, 2008 It, F, S, I, PI(R), A(R), NZ3
**Livesay, R O'H** (Blackheath) 1898 W, 1899 W
**Lloyd, L D** (Leicester) 2000 SA 1(R), 2(R), 2001 C 1, 2, US
**Lloyd, R H** (Harlequins) 1967 NZ, 1968 W, I, F, S
**Locke, H M** (Birkenhead Park) 1923 S, F, 1924 W, F, S, 1925 W, I, F, 1927 W, I, S
**Lockwood, R E** (Heckmondwike) 1887 W, I, S, 1889 M, 1891 W, I, S, 1892 W, I, S, 1893 W, I, 1894 W, I
**Login, S H M** (RN Coll) 1876 I
**Lohden, F C** (Blackheath) 1893 W
**Long, A E** (Bath) 1997 A 2, 2001 US (R)
**Longland, R J** (Northampton) 1932 S, 1933 W, S, 1934 W, I, S, 1935 W, I, S, 1936 NZ, W, I, S, 1937 W, I, S, 1938 W, I, S
**Lowe, C N** (Cambridge U, Blackheath) 1913 SA, W, F, I, S, 1914 W, I, S, F, 1920 W, F, I, S, 1921 W, I, S, F, 1922 W, I, F, S, 1923 W, I, S, F
**Lowrie, F W** (Wakefield T) 1889 M, 1890 W
**Lowry, W M** (Birkenhead Park) 1920 F
**Lozowski, R A P** (Wasps) 1984 A
**Luddington, W G E** (Devonport Services) 1923 W, I, S, F, 1924 W, I, F, S, 1925 W, I, S, F, 1926 W
**Luger, D D** (Harlequins, Saracens) 1998 H, It, SA 2, 1999 S, I, F, W, A, US, C, [It, NZ, Tg, Fj, SA], 2000 SA 1, A, Arg, SA 3, 2001 W, I, A, R, SA, 2002 F (R), W, It, 2003 F 1, W 1, It, S (R), I (R), NZ(R), W 2, [Gg(R), SA(R), U, W]
**Lund, M B** (Sale) 2006 A1, 2(R), NZ(R), Arg(t&R), 2007 S, It, I, F1(R), W1(R), SA2
**Luscombe, F** (Gipsies) 1872 S, 1873 S, 1875 I, S, 1876 I, S
**Luscombe, J H** (Gipsies) 1871 S
**Luxmoore, A F C C** (Richmond) 1900 S, 1901 W
**Luya, H F** (Waterloo, Headingley) 1948 W, I, S, F, 1949 W
**Lyon, A** (Liverpool) 1871 S
**Lyon, G H d'O** (United Services, RN) 1908 S, 1909 A

**McCanlis, M A** (Gloucester) 1931 W, I
**McCarthy, N** (Gloucester) 1999 I (t), US (R), 2000 It (R)
**McFadyean, C W** (Moseley) 1966 I, F, S, 1967 A, I, F, S, W, NZ, 1968 W, I

**MacIlwaine, A H** (United Services, Hull & E Riding) 1912 W, I, S, F, 1920 I
**Mackie, O G** (Wakefield T, Cambridge U) 1897 S, 1898 I
**Mackinlay, J E H** (St George's Hospital) 1872 S, 1873 S, 1875 I
**MacLaren, W** (Manchester) 1871 S
**MacLennan, R R F** (OMTs) 1925 I, S, F
**McLeod, N F** (RIE Coll) 1879 S, I
**Madge, R J P** (Exeter) 1948 A, W, I, S
**Malir, F W S** (Otley) 1930 W, I, S
**Mallett, J A** (Bath) 1995 [WS (R)]
**Mallinder, J** (Sale) 1997 Arg 1, 2
**Mangles, R H** (Richmond) 1897 W, I
**Manley, D C** (Exeter) 1963 W, I, F, S
**Mann, W E** (United Services, Army) 1911 W, F, I
**Mantell, N D** (Rosslyn Park) 1975 A 1
**Mapletoft, M S** (Gloucester) 1997 Arg 2
**Markendale, E T** (Manchester R) 1880 I
**Marler, J W G** (Harlequins) 2012 SA 1, 2, 3, Fj, A, 2013 S, I, F, It(R), W, Arg1, 2, A(R), Arg3, NZ, 2014 F, S, I, W, NZ1, 2, 3
**Marques, R W D** (Cambridge U, Harlequins) 1956 W, I, S, F, 1957 W, I, F, S, 1958 W, A, I, F, S, 1959 W, I, F, S, 1960 W, I, F, S, 1961 SA, W
**Marquis, J C** (Birkenhead Park) 1900 I, S
**Marriott, C J B** (Blackheath) 1884 W, I, S, 1886 W, I, S, 1887 I
**Marriott, E E** (Manchester) 1876 I
**Marriott, V R** (Harlequins) 1963 NZ 1, 2, A, 1964 NZ
**Marsden, G H** (Morley) 1900 W, I, S
**Marsh, H** (RIE Coll) 1873 S
**Marsh, J** (Swinton) 1892 I
**Marshall, H** (Blackheath) 1893 W
**Marshall, M W** (Blackheath) 1873 S, 1874 S, 1875 I, S, 1876 I, S, 1877 I, S, 1878 S, I
**Marshall, R M** (Oxford U) 1938 I, S, 1939 W, I, S
**Martin, C R** (Bath) 1985 F, S, I, W
**Martin, N O** (Harlequins) 1972 F (R)
**Martindale, S A** (Kendal) 1929 F
**Massey, E J** (Leicester) 1925 W, I, S
**Mather, B-J** (Sale) 1999 W
**Mathias, J L** (Bristol) 1905 W, I, S, NZ
**Matters, J C** (RNE Coll) 1899 S
**Matthews, J R C** (Harlequins) 1949 F, S, 1950 I, F, S, 1952 SA, W, S, I, F
**Maud, P** (Blackheath) 1893 W, I
**Maxwell, A W** (New Brighton, Headingley) 1975 A 1, 1976 A, W, S, I, F, 1978 F
**Maxwell-Hyslop, J E** (Oxford U) 1922 I, F, S
**May, J J** (Gloucester) 2013 Arg 2, 2014 F, S, I, W, It, NZ1
**May, T A** (Newcastle) 2009 Arg 1, 2
**Maynard, A F** (Cambridge U) 1914 W, I, S
**Mears, L A** (Bath) 2005 Sm(R), 2006 W(R), It(R), F(R), I, A1, 2(R), NZ(R), Arg(R), SA1(R), 2, 2007 S(R), It(R), I(R), W1(R), F2(R), 3(R), [Tg(R)], 2008 W(R), It(R), F(R), S, I, NZ1, 2, PI, A, SA, NZ3, 2009 It, W, I, F, S, 2010 I(R), 2011 W2(R), 3(R), [R(R)], 2012 I(R), SA 1(R), 2(R), 3(t)
**Meikle, G W C** (Waterloo) 1934 W, I, S
**Meikle, S S C** (Waterloo) 1929 S
**Mellish, F W** (Blackheath) 1920 W, F, I, S, 1921 W, I
**Melville, N D** (Wasps) 1984 A, 1985 I, W, NZ 1, 2, 1986 W, S, I, F, 1988 F, W, S, I, I
**Merriam, L P B** (Blackheath) 1920 W, F
**Michell, A T** (Oxford U) 1875 I, S, 1876 I
**Middleton, B B** (Birkenhead Park) 1882 I, 1883 I
**Middleton, J A** (Richmond) 1922 S
**Miles, J H** (Leicester) 1903 W
**Millett, H** (Richmond) 1920 F
**Mills, F W** (Marlborough N) 1872 S, 1873 S
**Mills, S G F** (Gloucester) 1981 Arg 1, 2, 1983 W, 1984 SA 1, A
**Mills, W A** (Devonport A) 1906 W, I, S, F, SA, 1907 F, W, I, S, 1908 F, W
**Milman, D L K** (Bedford) 1937 W, 1938 W, I, S
**Milton, C H** (Camborne S of M) 1906 I
**Milton, J G** (Camborne S of M) 1904 W, I, S, 1905 S, 1907 I
**Milton, W H** (Marlborough N) 1874 S, 1875 I
**Mitchell, F** (Blackheath) 1895 W, I, S, 1896 W, I, S
**Mitchell, W G** (Richmond) 1890 W, S, I, 1891 W, I, S, 1893 S
**Mobbs, E R** (Northampton) 1909 A, W, F, I, S, 1910 I, F
**Moberley, W O** (Ravenscourt Park) 1872 S

Monye, Y C C (Harlequins) 2008 PI, A, SA, NZ3, 2009 F, S, A, Arg 3, NZ, 2010 W, It, I, S, 2012 Fj

Moody, L W (Leicester, Bath) 2001 C 1, 2, US, I (R), R, SA (R), 2002 I (R), W, It, Arg, NZ, A, SA, 2003 F 1, W 2, F 2, 3(R), [Gg(R), SA, Sm(R), U, W, F(R), A(R)], 2004 C, SA, A2, 2005 F, I, It, S, A, NZ, Sm, 2006 W, It, S, F, I, A1, NZ, Arg, SA1(R), 2(R), W2(R), 2007 [US(R), SA1(R), Sm(R), Tg, A, F, SA2], 2008 W, 2009 A, Arg 3, NZ, 2010 W, It, I, S(R), F, A1, 2, NZ, A3, SA, 2011 W2, [Gg, R, S, F]

Moore, B C (Nottingham, Harlequins) 1987 S, [A, J, W], 1988 F, W, S, I 1, 2, A 1, 2, Fj, A, 1989 S, I, F, W, R, Fj, 1990 I, F, W, S, Arg 1, 2, 1991 W, S, I, F, Fj, A, [NZ, It, F, S, A], 1992 S, I, F, W, SA, 1993 F, W, S, I, NZ, 1994 S, I, F, W, SA 1, 2, R, C, 1995 I, F, W, S, [Arg, It, WS (R), A, NZ, F]

Moore, E J (Blackheath) 1883 I, S

Moore, N J N H (Bristol) 1904 W, I, S

Moore, P B C (Blackheath) 1951 W

Moore, W K T (Leicester) 1947 W, I, 1949 F, S, 1950 I, F, S

Mordell, R J (Rosslyn Park) 1978 W

Morfitt, S (W Hartlepool) 1894 W, I, S, 1896 W, I, S

Morgan, B J (Scarlets, Gloucester) 2012 S(R), It(R), W, F, I, SA 1, 2, 4, NZ, 2013 S, Arg1, 2, A(R), Arg3(R), NZ(R), 2014 F(R), S(R), I(R), W, It, NZ1, 2, 3(R)

Morgan, J R (Hawick) 1920 W

Morgan, O C (Gloucester) 2007 S, I

Morgan, W G D (Medicals, Newcastle) 1960 W, I, F, S, 1961 SA, W, I, F, S

Morley, A J (Bristol) 1972 SA, 1973 NZ 1, W, I, 1975 S, A 1, 2

Morris, A D W (United Services, RN) 1909 A, W, F

Morris, C D (Liverpool St Helens, Orrell) 1988 A, 1989 S, I, F, W, 1992 S, I, F, W, C, SA, 1993 F, W, S, I, 1994 F, W, SA 1, 2, R, 1995 S (t), [Arg, WS, A, NZ, F]

Morris, R (Northampton) 2003 W 1, It

Morrison, P H (Cambridge U) 1890 W, S, I, 1891 I

Morse, S (Marlborough N) 1873 S, 1874 S, 1875 S

Mortimer, W (Marlborough N) 1899 W

Morton, H J S (Blackheath) 1909 I, S, 1910 W, I

Moss, F J S (Broughton Rangers) 1885 W, I, 1886 W

Mullan, M J (Worcester, Wasps) 2010 It(R), 2013 NZ(R), 2014 It(R), NZ2(R), 3(R)

Mullins, A R (Harlequins) 1989 Fj

Mycock, J (Sale) 1947 W, I, S, F, 1948 A

Myers, E (Bradford) 1920 I, S, 1921 W, I, 1922 W, I, F, S, 1923 W, I, S, F, 1924 W, I, F, S, 1925 S, F

Myers, H (Keighley) 1898 I

Myler, S J (Northampton) 2013 Arg 2(R)

Nanson, W M B (Carlisle) 1907 F, W

Narraway, L J W (Gloucester) 2008 W, It(R), S(R), NZ1, 2, 2009 W(R), I(R)

Nash, E H (Richmond) 1875 I

Neale, B A (Rosslyn Park) 1951 I, F, S

Neale, M E (Blackheath) 1912 F

Neame, S (O Cheltonians) 1879 S, I, 1880 I, S

Neary, A (Broughton Park) 1971 W, I, F, S (2[1C]), P, 1972 W, I, F, S, SA, 1973 NZ 1, W, I, F, S, NZ 2, A, 1974 S, I, F, W, 1975 I, F, W, S, A 1, 1976 A, W, S, I, F, 1977 I, 1978 F (R), 1979 S, I, F, W, NZ, 1980 I, F, W, S

Nelmes, B G (Cardiff) 1975 A 1, 2, 1978 W, S, I, NZ

Newbold, C J (Blackheath) 1904 W, I, S, 1905 W, I, S

Newman, S C (Oxford U) 1947 F, 1948 A, W

Newton, A W (Blackheath) 1907 S

Newton, P A (Blackheath) 1882 S

Newton-Thompson, J O (Oxford U) 1947 S, F

Nicholl, W (Brighouse R) 1892 W, S

Nicholas, P L (Exeter) 1902 W

Nicholson, B E (Harlequins) 1938 W, I

Nicholson, E S (Leicester) 1935 W, I, S, 1936 NZ, W

Nicholson, E T (Birkenhead Park) 1900 W, I

Nicholson, T (Rockcliff) 1893 I

Ninnes, B F (Coventry) 1971 W

Noon, J D (Newcastle) 2001 C 1, 2, US, 2003 W 2, F 2(t+R), 2005 W, F, I, It, S, A, NZ, 2006 W, It, S, F, I, 2006 A1(R), 2, NZ, Arg, SA1, 2, 2007 SA2, F2, [US, SA1], 2008 It, F, S, I, NZ1(R), 2, PI, A, SA, NZ3, 2009 It

Norman, D J (Leicester) 1932 SA, W

North, E H G (Blackheath) 1891 W, I, S

Northmore, S (Millom) 1897 I

Novak, M J (Harlequins) 1970 W, S, F

Novis, A L (Blackheath) 1929 S, F, 1930 W, I, F, 1933 I, S

Nowell, J T (Exeter) 2014 F, S, I, W, It

Oakeley, F E (United Services, RN) 1913 S, 1914 I, S, F

Oakes, R F (Hartlepool R) 1897 W, I, S, 1898 I, S, W, 1899 W, S

Oakley, L F L (Bedford) 1951 W

Obolensky, A (Oxford U) 1936 NZ, W, I, S

Ojo, T O (London Irish) 2008 NZ1, 2

Ojomoh, S O (Bath, Gloucester) 1994 I, F, SA 1(R), 2, R, 1995 S (R), [Arg, WS, A (t), F], 1996 F, 1998 NZ 1

Old, A G B (Middlesbrough, Leicester, Sheffield) 1972 W, I, F, S, SA, 1973 NZ 2, A, 1974 S, I, F, W, 1975 I, A 2, 1976 S, I, 1978 F

Oldham, W L (Coventry) 1908 S, 1909 A

Olver, C J (Northampton) 1990 Arg 3, 1991 [US], 1992 C

O'Neill, A (Teignmouth, Torquay A) 1901 W, I, S

Openshaw, W E (Manchester) 1879 I

Orwin, J (Gloucester, RAF, Bedford) 1985 R, F, S, I, W, NZ 1, 2, 1988 F, W, S, I 1, 2, A 1, 2

Osborne, R R (Manchester) 1871 S

Osborne, S H (Oxford U) 1905 S

Oti, C (Cambridge U, Nottingham, Wasps) 1988 S, I 1, 1989 S, I, F, W, R, 1990 Arg 1, 2, 1991 Fj, A, [NZ, It]

Oughtred, B (Hartlepool R) 1901 S, 1902 W, I, S, 1903 W, I

Owen, J E (Coventry) 1963 W, I, F, S, A, 1964 NZ, 1965 W, I, F, S, 1966 I, F, S, 1967 NZ

Owen-Smith, H G O (St Mary's Hospital) 1934 W, I, S, 1936 NZ, W, I, S, 1937 W, I, S

Page, J J (Bedford, Northampton) 1971 W, I, F, S, 1975 S

Paice, D J (London Irish) 2008 NZ1(R), 2(R), 2012 Fj(R), A(R), SA4(R), NZ2(R), 2013 Arg1(R), 2(R)

Pallant, J N (Notts) 1967 I, F, S

Palmer, A C (London Hospital) 1909 I, S

Palmer, F H (Richmond) 1905 W

Palmer, G V (Richmond) 1928 I, F, S

Palmer, J A (Bath) 1984 SA 1, 2, 1986 I (R)

Palmer, T P (Leeds, Wasps, Stade Français) 2001 US (R), 2006 Arg(R), SA1, 2, 2007 It(R), I(R), F1, W1, 2008 NZ1, 2, PI(R), A, SA, 2010 F(R), A1, 2, NZ, A3, Sm, SA, 2011 W1, It, F, S, I1, W2, 3(R), I2(R), [Arg(R), Gg, R, S(R), F], 2012 S, It, F(R), I(R), SA 1(R), 2(R), 3, Fj, A

Pargetter, T A (Coventry) 1962 S, 1963 F, NZ 1

Parker, G W (Gloucester) 1938 I, S

Parker, Hon S (Liverpool) 1874 S, 1875 S

Parling, G M W (Leicester) 2012 S(R), It(R), W, F, I, SA 1, 2, 3, Fj, A, SA4, 2013 S, I, F, It, W, Arg3(R), NZ(R), 2014 NZ1, 2

Parsons, E I (RAF) 1939 S

Parsons, M J (Northampton) 1968 W, I, F, S

Patterson, W M (Sale) 1961 SA, W

Pattisson, R M (Blackheath) 1883 I, S

Paul, H R (Gloucester) 2002 F(R), 2004 It(t&R), S(R), C, SA, A2

Paul, J E (RIE Coll) 1875 S

Payne, A T (Bristol) 1935 I, S

Payne, C M (Harlequins) 1964 I, F, S, 1965 I, F, S, 1966 W, I, F, S

Payne, J H (Broughton) 1882 S, 1883 W, I, S, 1884 I, 1885 W, I

Payne, T A N (Wasps) 2004 A1, 2006 A1(R), 2(R), 2007 F1, W1, 2008 It, NZ1(R), 2, SA, NZ3, 2009 Arg 1, 2, A, Arg 3, NZ, 2010 W, It, I, S, F, A1, 2

Pearce, G S (Northampton) 1979 S, I, F, W, 1981 Arg 1, 2, 1982 A, S, 1983 F, W, S, I, NZ, 1984 S, A 2, A, 1985 R, F, S, I, W, NZ 1, 2, 1986 W, S, I, F, 1987 I, F, W, S, [A, US, W], 1988 Fj, 1991 [US]

Pears, D (Harlequins) 1990 Arg 1, 2, 1992 F (R), 1994 F

Pearson, A W (Blackheath) 1875 I, S, 1876 I, S, 1877 S, 1878 S, I

Peart, T G A H (Hartlepool R) 1964 F, S

Pease, F E (Hartlepool R) 1887 I

Pennell, C J (Worcester) 2014 NZ1(R)

Penny, S H (Leicester) 1909 A

Penny, W J (United Hospitals) 1878 I, 1879 S, I

Percival, L J (Rugby) 1891 I, 1892 I, 1893 S

**Periton, H G** (Waterloo) 1925 W, 1926 W, I, F, S, 1927 W, I, S, F, 1928 A, I, F, S, 1929 W, I, S, F, 1930 W, I, F, S
**Perrott**, E S (O Cheltonians) 1875 I
**Perry, D G** (Bedford) 1963 F, S, NZ 1, 2, A 1964 NZ, W, I, 1965 W, I, F, S, 1966 W, I, F
**Perry, M B** (Bath) 1997 A 2, NZ 1, SA, NZ 2, 1998 W, S, I, A 1, NZ 1, 2, SA 1, H, It, A 2, 1999 I, F, W, A US, C, [It, NZ, Tg, Fj, SA], 2000 I, F, W, It, S, SA 1, 2, A, SA 3, 2001 W (R), F (R)
**Perry, S A** (Bristol) 2006 NZ, Arg, SA1(R), 2(R), 2007 I(R), F1(R), W1(R), SA1(R), 2(R), W2, F2, 3, [US, SA1]
**Perry, S V** (Cambridge U, Waterloo) 1947 W, I, 1948 A, W, I, S, F
**Peters, J** (Plymouth) 1906 S, F, 1907 I, S, 1908 W
**Phillips, C** (Birkenhead Park) 1880 S, 1881 I, S
**Phillips, M S** (Fylde) 1958 A, I, F, S, 1959 W, I, F, S, 1960 W, I, F, S, 1961 W, 1963 W, I, F, S, NZ 1, 2, A, 1964 NZ, W, I, F, S
**Pickering, A S** (Harrogate) 1907 I
**Pickering, R D A** (Bradford) 1967 I, F, S, W, 1968 F, S
**Pickles, R C W** (Bristol) 1922 I, F
**Pierce, R** (Liverpool) 1898 I, 1903 S
**Pilkington, W N** (Cambridge U) 1898 S
**Pillman, C H** (Blackheath) 1910 W, I, F, S, 1911 W, F, I, S, 1912 W, F, 1913 SA, W, F, I, S, 1914 W, I, S
**Pillman, R L** (Blackheath) 1914 F
**Pinch, J** (Lancaster) 1896 W, I, 1897 S
**Pinching, W W** (Guy's Hospital) 1872 S
**Pitman, I J** (Oxford U) 1922 S
**Plummer, K C** (Bristol) 1969 W, 1976 S, I, F
**Pool-Jones, R J** (Stade Francais) 1998 A 1
**Poole, F O** (Oxford U) 1895 W, I, S
**Poole, R W** (Hartlepool R) 1896 S
**Pope, E B** (Blackheath) 1931 W, S, F
**Portus, G V** (Blackheath) 1908 F, I
**Potter, S** (Leicester) 1998 A 1(t)
**Poulton, R W** (later Poulton Palmer) (Oxford U, Harlequins, Liverpool) 1909 F, I, S, 1910 W, 1911 S, 1912 W, I, S, 1913 SA, W, F, I, S, 1914 W, I, S, F
**Powell, D L** (Northampton) 1966 W, I, 1969 I, F, S, W, 1971 W, I, F, S (2[1C])
**Pratten, W E** (Blackheath) 1927 S, F
**Preece, I** (Coventry) 1948 I, S, F, 1949 F, S, 1950 W, I, F, S, 1951 W, I, F
**Preece, P S** (Coventry) 1972 SA, 1973 NZ 1, W, I, F, S, NZ 2, 1975 I, F, W, A 2, 1976 W (R)
**Preedy, M** (Gloucester) 1984 SA 1
**Prentice, F D** (Leicester) 1928 I, F, S
**Prescott, R E** (Harlequins) 1937 W, I, 1938 I, 1939 W, I, S
**Preston, N J** (Richmond) 1979 NZ, 1980 I, F
**Price, H L** (Harlequins) 1922 I, S, 1923 W, I
**Price, J** (Coventry) 1961 I
**Price, P L A** (RIE Coll) 1877 I, S, 1878 S
**Price, T W** (Cheltenham) 1948 S, F, 1949 W, I, F, S
**Probyn, J A** (Wasps, Askeans) 1988 F, W, S, I 1, 2, A 1, 2, A, 1989 S, I, R (R), 1990 I, F, W, S, Arg 1, 2, 3, 1991 W, S, I, F, Fj, A, [NZ, It, F, S, A], 1992 S, I, F, W, 1993 F, W, S, I
**Prout, D H** (Northampton) 1968 W, I
**Pullin, J V** (Bristol) 1966 W, 1968 W, I, F, S, 1969 I, F, S, W, SA, 1970 I, W, S, F, 1971 W, I, F, S (2[1C]), P, 1972 W, I, F, S, SA, 1973 NZ 1, W, I, F, S, NZ 2, A, 1974 S, I, F, W, 1975 I, W (R), S, A 1, 2, 1976 F
**Purdy, S J** (Rugby) 1962 S
**Pyke, J** (St Helens Recreation) 1892 W
**Pym, J A** (Blackheath) 1912 W, I, S, F

**Quinn, J P** (New Brighton) 1954 W, NZ, I, S, F

**Rafter, M** (Bristol) 1977 S, F, W, 1978 F, W, S, I, NZ, 1979 S, I, F, W, NZ, 1980 W(R), 1981 W, Arg 1, 2
**Ralston, C W** (Richmond) 1971 S (C), P, 1972 W, I, F, S, SA, 1973 NZ 1, W, I, F, S, NZ 2, A, 1974 S, I, F, W, 1975 I, F, W, S
**Ramsden, H E** (Bingley) 1898 S, W
**Ranson, J M** (Rosslyn Park) 1963 NZ 1, 2, A, 1964 W, I, F, S
**Raphael, J E** (OMTs) 1902 W, I, S, 1905 W, S, NZ, 1906 W, S, F
**Ravenscroft, J** (Birkenhead Park) 1881 I

**Ravenscroft, S C W** (Saracens) 1998 A 1, NZ 2(R)
**Rawlinson, W C W** (Blackheath) 1876 S
**Redfern, S P** (Leicester) 1984 I (R)
**Redman, N C** (Bath) 1984 A, 1986 S (R), 1987 I, S, [A, J, W], 1988 Fj, 1990 Arg 1, 2, 1991 Fj, [It, US], 1993 NZ, 1994 F, W, SA 1, 2, 1997 Arg 1, A 1
**Redmond, G F** (Cambridge U) 1970 F
**Redwood, B W** (Bristol) 1968 W, I
**Rees, D L** (Sale) 1997 A 2, NZ 1, SA, NZ 2, 1998 F, W, SA 2(R), 1999 S, I, F, A
**Rees, G W** (Nottingham) 1984 SA 2(R), A, 1986 I, F, 1987 F, W, S, [A, J, US, W], 1988 S (R), I 1, 2, A 1, 2, Fj, 1989 W (R), R (R), Fj (R), 1990 Arg 3(R), 1991 Fj, [US]
**Rees, T** (Wasps) 2007 S(R), It(R), I(R), F1, W1, F3, [US, SA1], 2008 W(R), NZ1, 2, PI, A, SA, NZ3(R)
**Reeve, J S R** (Harlequins) 1929 F, 1930 W, I, F, S, 1931 W, I, S
**Regan, M** (Liverpool) 1953 W, I, F, S, 1954 W, NZ, I, S, 1956 I, S, F
**Regan, M P** (Bristol, Bath, Leeds) 1995 SA, WS, 1996 F, W, S, I, It, Arg, 1997 S, I, F, W, A 1, NZ 2(R), 1998 F, 2000 SA 1(t), A(R), Arg, SA 3(t), 2001 It(R), S(R), C 2(R), R, 2003 F 1(t), It(R), W 2, [Ga(R), Sm], 2004 It(R), I(R), NZ1(R), 2, A1, 2007 SA1, 2, W2, F2, 3, [US, SA1, A, F, SA2], 2008 W, It, F
**Rendall, P A G** (Wasps, Askeans) 1984 W, SA 2, 1986 W, S, 1987 I, F, S, [A, J, W], 1988 F, W, S, I 1, 2, A 1, 2, A, 1989 S, I, F, W, R, 1990 I, F, W, S, 1991 [It (R)]
**Rew, H** (Blackheath) 1929 S, F, 1930 F, S, 1931 W, S, F, 1934 W, I, S
**Reynolds, F J** (O Cranleighans) 1937 S, 1938 I, S
**Reynolds, S** (Richmond) 1900 W, I, S, 1901 I
**Rhodes, J** (Castleford) 1896 W, I, S
**Richards, D** (Leicester) 1986 I, F, 1987 S, [A, J, US, W], 1988 F, W, S, I 1, A 1, 2, Fj, A, 1989 S, I, F, W, R, 1990 Arg 3, 1991 W, S, I, F, Fj, A, [NZ, It, US], 1992 S (R), F, W, C, 1993 NZ, 1994 W, SA 1, C, 1995 I, F, W, S, [WS, A, NZ], 1996 F (t), S, I
**Richards, E E** (Plymouth A) 1929 S, F
**Richards, J J** (Bradford) 1891 W, I, S
**Richards, P C** (Gloucester, London Irish) 2006 A1, 2, NZ(R), Arg(R), SA1, 2, 2007 [US(R), SA1(R), Tg(R), A(t), F(R), SA2(R)], 2008 NZ2(R)
**Richards, S B** (Richmond) 1965 W, I, F, S, 1967 A, I, F, S, W
**Richardson, J V** (Birkenhead Park) 1928 A, W, I, F, S
**Richardson, W R** (Manchester) 1881 I
**Rickards, C H** (Gipsies) 1873 S
**Rimmer, G** (Waterloo) 1949 W, I, 1950 W, 1951 W, I, F, 1952 SA, W, 1954 W, NZ, I, S
**Rimmer, L I** (Bath) 1961 SA, W, I, F, S
**Ripley, A G** (Rosslyn Park) 1972 W, I, F, S, SA, 1973 NZ 1, W, I, F, S, NZ 2, A, 1974 S, I, F, W, 1975 I, F, S, A 1, 2, 1976 A, W, S
**Risman, A B W** (Loughborough Coll) 1959 W, I, F, S, 1961 SA, W, I, F
**Ritson, J A S** (Northern) 1910 F, S, 1912 F, 1913 SA, W, F, I, S
**Rittson-Thomas, G C** (Oxford U) 1951 W, I, F
**Robbins, G L** (Coventry) 1986 W, S
**Robbins, P G D** (Oxford U, Moseley, Coventry) 1956 W, I, S, F, 1957 W, I, F, S, 1958 W, A, I, S, 1960 W, I, F, S, 1961 SA, W, 1962 S
**Roberts, A D** (Northern) 1911 W, F, I, S, 1912 I, S, F, 1914 I
**Roberts, E W** (RNE Coll) 1901 W, I, 1905 NZ, 1906 W, I, 1907 S
**Roberts, G D** (Harlequins) 1907 S, 1908 F, W
**Roberts, J** (Sale) 1960 W, I, F, S, 1961 SA, W, I, F, S, 1962 W, I, F, S, 1963 W, I, F, S, 1964 NZ
**Roberts, R S** (Coventry) 1932 I
**Roberts, S** (Swinton) 1887 W, I
**Roberts, V G** (Penryn, Harlequins) 1947 F, 1949 W, I, F, S, 1950 I, F, S, 1951 W, I, F, S, 1956 W, I, S, F
**Robertshaw, A R** (Bradford) 1886 W, I, S, 1887 W, S
**Robinson, A** (Blackheath) 1889 M, 1890 W, S, I
**Robinson, E T** (Coventry) 1954 S, 1961 I, F, S
**Robinson, G C** (Percy Park) 1897 I, S, 1898 I, 1899 W, 1900 I, S, 1901 I, S
**Robinson, J** (Sale) 2001 It (R), S (R), F (R), I, A, R, SA, 2002 S, I, F, It, NZ, A, SA, 2003 F 1, W 1, S, I, NZ, A, F 3, [Gg, SA, Sm, U(R), W, F, A], 2004 It, S, I, W, F, C, SA, A2, 2005 W, F, I, 2007 S, It, F1, W1, SA1, W2, F3, [US, SA1, A, F, SA2]

Robinson, J J (Headingley) 1893 S, 1902 W, I, S
Robinson, R A (Bath) 1988 A 2, Fj, A, 1989 S, I, F, W, 1995 SA
Robshaw, C D C (Harlequins) 2009 Arg 2, 2012 S, It, W, F, I, SA 1, 2, Fj, A, SA4, NZ, 2013 S, I, F, It, W, A, Arg3, NZ, 2014 F, S, I, W, It, NZ1, 2, 3
Robson, A (Northern) 1924 W, I, F, S, 1926 W
Robson, M (Oxford U) 1930 W, I, F, S
Rodber, T A K (Army, Northampton) 1992 S, I, 1993 NZ, 1994 I, F, W, SA 1, 2, R, C, 1995 I, F, W, S, [Arg, It, WS (R), A, NZ, F], SA, WS, 1996 W, S (R), I (t), It, Arg, 1997 S, I, F, W, A 1, 1998 H (R), It (R), A 2, SA 2, 1999 S, I, F, W, A, US (R), [NZ (R), Fj (R)]
Rogers, D P (Bedford) 1961 I, F, S, 1962 W, I, F, 1963 W, I, F, S, NZ 1, 2, A, 1964 NZ, W, I, F, S, 1965 W, I, F, S, 1966 W, I, F, S, 1967 A, S, W, NZ, 1969 I, F, S, W
Rogers, J H (Moseley) 1890 W, S, I, 1891 S
Rogers, W L Y (Blackheath) 1905 W, I
Rollitt, D M (Bristol) 1967 I, F, S, W, 1969 I, F, S, W, 1975 S, A 1, 2
Roncoroni, A D S (West Herts, Richmond) 1933 W, I, S
Rose, W M H (Cambridge U, Coventry, Harlequins) 1981 I, F, 1982 A, S, I, 1987 I, F, W, S, [A]
Rossborough, P A (Coventry) 1971 W, 1973 NZ 2, A, 1974 S, I, 1975 I, F
Rosser, D W A (Wasps) 1965 W, I, F, S, 1966 W
Rotherham, Alan (Richmond) 1883 W, S, 1884 W, S, 1885 W, I, 1886 W, I, S, 1887 W, I, S
Rotherham, Arthur (Richmond) 1898 S, W, 1899 W, I, S
Roughley, D (Liverpool) 1973 A, 1974 S, I
Rowell, R E (Leicester) 1964 W, 1965 W
Rowley, A J (Coventry) 1932 SA
Rowley, H C (Manchester) 1879 S, I, 1880 I, S, 1881 I, W, S, 1882 I, S
Rowntree, G C (Leicester) 1995 S (t), [It, WS], WS, 1996 F, W, S, I, It, Arg, 1997 S, I, F, W, A 1, 1998 A 1, NZ 1, 2, SA 1, H (R), It (R), 1999 US, C, [It (R), Tg, Fj (R)], 2001 C 1, 2, US, I(R), A, SA, 2002 S, I, F, W, It, 2003 F 1(R), W 1, It, S, I, NZ, F 2, 2004 C, SA, A2, 2005 W, F, I, It, 2006 A1, 2
Royds, P M R (Blackheath) 1898 S, W, 1899 W
Royle, A V (Broughton R) 1889 M
Rudd, E L (Liverpool) 1965 W, I, S, 1966 W, I, S
Russell, R F (Leicester) 1905 NZ
Rutherford, D (Percy Park, Gloucester) 1960 W, I, F, S, 1961 SA, 1965 W, I, F, S, 1966 W, I, F, S, 1967 NZ
Ryalls, H J (New Brighton) 1885 W, I
Ryan, D (Wasps, Newcastle) 1990 Arg 1, 2, 1992 C, 1998 S
Ryan, P H (Richmond) 1955 W, I

Sackey, P H (Wasps) 2006 NZ, Arg, 2007 F2, 3(R), [SA1, Sm, Tg, A, F, SA2], 2008 W, It, F, S, I, PI, A, SA, NZ3, 2009 It, W, I
Sadler, E H (Army) 1933 I, S
Sagar, J W (Cambridge U) 1901 W, I
Salmon, J L B (Harlequins) 1985 NZ 1, 2, 1986 W, S, 1987 I, F, W, S, [A, J, US, W]
Sample, C H (Cambridge U) 1884 I, 1885 I, 1886 S
Sampson, P C (Wasps) 1998 SA 1, 2001 C 1, 2
Sanders, D L (Harlequins) 1954 W, NZ, I, S, F, 1956 W, I, S, F
Sanders, F W (Plymouth A) 1923 I, S, F
Sanderson, A (Sale) 2001 R (R), 2002 Arg, 2003 It(t + R), W 2(R), F 2
Sanderson, P H (Sale, Harlequins, Worcester) 1998 NZ 1, 2, SA 1, 2001 C 1(R), 2(R), US(t+R), 2005 A, NZ, Sm, 2006 A1, 2, NZ, Arg, SA1, 2, 2007 SA1(R)
Sandford, J R P (Marlborough N) 1906 I
Sangwin, R D (Hull and E Riding) 1964 NZ, W
Sargent, G A F (Gloucester) 1981 I (R)
Savage, K F (Northampton) 1966 W, I, F, S, 1967 A, I, F, S, W, NZ, 1968 W, F, S
Sawyer, C M (Broughton) 1880 S, 1881 I
Saxby, L E (Gloucester) 1932 SA, W
Scarbrough, D G R (Leeds, Saracens) 2003 W 2, 2007 SA2
Schofield, D F (Sale) 2007 SA1, 2(R)
Schofield, J W (Manchester) 1880 I
Scholfield, J A (Preston Grasshoppers) 1911 W
Schwarz, R O (Richmond) 1899 S, 1901 W, I
Scorfield, E S (Percy Park) 1910 F

Scott, C T (Blackheath) 1900 W, I, 1901 W, I
Scott, E K (St Mary's Hospital, Redruth) 1947 W, 1948 A, W, I, S
Scott, F S (Bristol) 1907 W
Scott, H (Manchester) 1955 F
Scott, J P (Rosslyn Park, Cardiff) 1978 F, W, S, I, NZ, 1979 S (R), I, F, W, NZ, 1980 I, F, W, S, 1981 W, S, I, F, Arg 1, 2, 1982 I, F, W, 1983 F, W, S, I, NZ, 1984 S, I, F, W, SA 1, 2
Scott, J S M (Oxford U) 1958 F
Scott, M T (Cambridge U) 1887 I, 1890 S, I
Scott, W M (Cambridge U) 1889 M
Seddon, R L (Broughton R) 1887 W, I, S
Sellar, K A (United Services, RN) 1927 W, I, S, 1928 A, W, I, F
Sever, H S (Sale) 1936 NZ, W, I, S, 1937 W, I, S, 1938 W, I, S
Shackleton, I R (Cambridge U) 1969 SA, 1970 I, W, S
Sharp, R A W (Oxford U, Wasps, Redruth) 1960 W, I, F, S, 1961 I, F, 1962 W, I, F, 1963 W, I, F, S, 1967 A
Sharples, C D J (Gloucester) 2011 W2(R), 2012 F, Fj, A
Shaw, C H (Moseley) 1906 S, SA, 1907 F, W, I, S
Shaw, F (Cleckheaton) 1898 I
Shaw, J F (RNE Coll) 1898 S, W
Shaw, S D (Bristol, Wasps) 1996 It, Arg, 1997 S, I, F, W, A 1, SA (R), 2000 I, F, W, It, S, SA 1(R), 2(R), 2001 C 1(R), 2, US, I, 2003 It (R), W 2, F 2(R), 3(R), 2004 It(t&R), S(R), NZ1, 2, A1, 2005 Sm(R), 2006 W(R), It(R), S(R), F(R), I, 2007 W2, F2, 3, [US, SA1, Sm, A, F, SA2], 2008 W, It, F, S, I, A(R), SA(R), 2009 F, S, NZ, 2010 W, It, I, F, A1, 2(R), 3(R), SA(R), 2011 W1(R), It(R), F(R), S(R), I1(R), W2, I2(R), [Gg, R(R), F(R)]
Sheasby, C M A (Wasps) 1996 It, Arg, 1997 W (R), Arg 1(R), 2(R), SA (R), NZ 2(t)
Sheppard, A (Bristol) 1981 W (R), 1985 W
Sheridan, A J (Sale) 2004 C(R), 2005 A, NZ, Sm, 2006 W, It, S, F(R), I, NZ, SA1, 2007 W2, F2, [US, SA1, Sm, Tg, A, F, SA2], 2008 W, F, S, I, NZ1, PI, A, 2009 It, W, I, F, S, 2010 NZ, A3, Sm, SA, 2011 W1, F, I2, [Arg]
Sherrard, C W (Blackheath) 1871 S, 1872 S
Sherriff, G A (Saracens) 1966 S, 1967 A, NZ
Shewring, H E (Bristol) 1905 I, NZ, 1906 W, S, F, SA, 1907 F, W, I, S
Shooter, J H (Morley) 1899 I, S, 1900 I, S
Shuttleworth, D W (Headingley) 1951 S, 1953 S
Sibree, H J H (Harlequins) 1908 F, 1909 I, S
Silk, N (Harlequins) 1965 W, I, F, S
Simms, K G (Cambridge U, Liverpool, Wasps) 1985 R, F, S, I, W, 1986 I, F, 1987 I, F, W, [A, J, W], 1988 F, W
Simpson, C P (Harlequins) 1965 W
Simpson, J P M (Wasps) 2011 [Gg(R)]
Simpson, P D (Bath) 1983 NZ, 1984 S, 1987 I
Simpson, T (Rockcliff) 1902 S, 1903 W, I, S, 1904 I, S, 1905 I, S, 1906 S, SA, 1909 F
Simpson-Daniel, J D (Gloucester) 2002 NZ, A, 2003 W 1(t + R), It, W 2, 2004 I(R), NZ1, 2005 Sm, 2006 It(R), 2007 SA1(R)
Sims, D (Gloucester) 1998 NZ 1(R), 2, SA 1
Skinner, M G (Harlequins) 1988 F, W, S, I 1, 2, 1989 Fj, 1990 I, F, W, S, Arg 1, 2, 1991 Fj (R), [US, F, S, A], 1992 S, I, F, W
Skirving, B D (Saracens) 2007 SA2
Sladen, G M (United Services, RN) 1929 W, I, S
Sleightholme, J M (Bath) 1996 F, W, S, I, It, Arg, 1997 S, I, F, W, Arg 1, 2
Slemen, M A C (Liverpool) 1976 I, F, 1977 S, I, F, W, 1978 F, W, S, I, NZ, 1979 S, I, F, W, NZ, 1980 I, F, W, S, 1981 W, W, S, I, F, 1982 A, S, I, F, W, 1983 F, 1984 S
Slocock, L A N (Liverpool) 1907 F, W, I, S, 1908 F, W, I, S
Slow, C F (Leicester) 1934 S
Small, H D (Oxford U) 1950 W, I, F, S
Smallwood, A M (Leicester) 1920 F, I, 1921 W, I, S, F, 1922 I, S, 1923 W, I, S, F, 1925 I, S
Smart, C E (Newport) 1979 F, W, NZ, 1981 S, I, F, Arg 1, 2, 1982 A, S, I, F, W, 1983 F, W, S, I
Smart, S E J (Gloucester) 1913 SA, W, F, I, S, 1914 W, I, S, F, 1920 W, I, S
Smeddle, R W (Cambridge U) 1929 W, I, S, 1931 F
Smith, C C (Gloucester) 1901 W
Smith, D F (Richmond) 1910 W, I
Smith, J V (Cambridge U, Rosslyn Park) 1950 W, I, F, S
Smith, K (Roundhay) 1974 F, W, 1975 W, S
Smith, M J K (Oxford U) 1956 W

Travers, B H (Harlequins) 1947 W, I, 1948 A, W, 1949 F, S
Treadwell, W T (Wasps) 1966 I, F, S
Trick, D M (Bath) 1983 I, 1984 SA 1
Tristram, H B (Oxford U) 1883 S, 1884 W, S, 1885 W, 1887 S
Troop, C L (Aldershot S) 1933 I, S
Tucker, J S (Bristol) 1922 W, 1925 NZ, W, I, S, F, 1926 W, I, F,
S, 1927 W, I, S, F, 1928 A, W, I, F, S, 1929 W, I, F, 1930 W,
I, F, S, 1931 W
Tucker, W E (Blackheath) 1894 W, I, 1895 W, I, S
Tucker, W E (Blackheath) 1926 I, 1930 W, I
Tuilagi, E M (Leicester) 2011 W2, I2, [Arg, Gg, R, S, F], 2012
W, F, I, SA 1, 2, 3, Fj, A, SA4, NZ, 2013 I(R), F, It, W, 2014
It(R), NZ1, 2, 3
Turner, D P (Richmond) 1871 S, 1872 S, 1873 S, 1874 S, 1875
I, S
Turner, E B (St George's Hospital) 1876 I, 1877 I, 1878 I
Turner, G R (St George's Hospital) 1876 S
Turner, H J C (Manchester) 1871 S
Turner, M F (Blackheath) 1948 S, F
Turner, S C (Sale) 2007 W1(R), SA1, 2(R)
Turner-Hall, J (Harlequins) 2012 S(R), It(R)
Turquand-Young, D (Richmond) 1928 A, W, 1929 I, S, F
Twelvetrees, W W F (Gloucester) 2013 S, I, It(R), W(R), Arg1, A,
Arg3, NZ, 2014 F, S, I, W, It, NZ2
Twynam, H T (Richmond) 1879 I, 1880 I, 1881 W, 1882 I, 1883
I, 1884 W, I, S

Ubogu, V E (Bath) 1992 C, SA, 1993 NZ, 1994 S, I, F, W, SA 1,
2, R, C, 1995 I, F, W, S, [Arg, WS, A, NZ, F], SA, 1999 F
(R), W (R), A (R)
Underwood, A M (Exeter) 1962 W, I, F, S, 1964 I
Underwood, R (Leicester, RAF) 1984 I, F, W, A, 1985 R, F, S, I,
W, 1986 W, I, F, 1987 I, F, W, S, [A, J, W], 1988 F, W, S, I 1,
2, A 1, 2, Fj, A, 1989 S, I, F, W, R, Fj, 1990 I, F, W, S, Arg 3,
1991 W, S, I, F, Fj, A, [NZ, It, US, F, S, A], 1992 S, I, F, W,
SA, 1993 F, W, S, I, NZ, 1994 S, I, F, W, SA 1, 2, R, C, 1995
I, F, W, S, [Arg, It, WS, A, NZ, F], SA, WS, 1996 F, W, S, I
Underwood, T (Leicester, Newcastle) 1992 C, SA, 1993 S, I, NZ,
1994 S, I, W, SA 1, 2, R, C, 1995 I, F, W, S, [Arg, It, A, NZ],
1996 Arg, 1997 S, I, F, W, 1998 A 2, SA 2
Unwin, E J (Rosslyn Park, Army) 1937 S, 1938 W, I, S
Unwin, G T (Blackheath) 1898 S
Uren, H (Waterloo) 1948 I, S, F, 1950 I
Uttley, R M (Gosforth) 1973 I, F, S, NZ 2 A, 1974 I, F, W, 1975
F, W, S, A 1, 2, 1977 S, I, F, W, 1978 NZ 1979 S, 1980 I, F,
W, S

Vainikolo, L P I (Gloucester) 2008 W(R), It, F, S, I
Valentine J (Swinton) 1890 W, 1896 W, I, S
Vanderspar, C H R (Richmond) 1873 S
Van Gisbergen, M C (Wasps) 2005 A(t)
Van Ryneveld, C B (Oxford U) 1949 W, I, F, S
Varley, H (Liversedge) 1892 S
Varndell, T W (Leicester) 2005 Sm(R), 2006 A1, 2, 2008 NZ2
Vassall, H (Blackheath) 1881 W, S, 1882 I, S, 1883 W
Vassall, H H (Blackheath) 1908 I
Vaughan, D B (Headingley) 1948 A, W, I, S, 1949 I, F, S, 1950 W
Vaughan-Jones, A (Army) 1932 I, S, 1933 W
Verelst, C L (Liverpool) 1876 I, 1878 I
Vernon, G F (Blackheath) 1878 S, I, 1880 I, S, 1881 I
Vesty, S B (Leicester) 2009 Arg 1(R), 2(R)
Vickery, G (Aberavon) 1905 I
Vickery, P J (Gloucester, Wasps) 1998 W, A 1, NZ 1, 2, SA 1,
1999 US, C, [It, NZ, Tg, SA], 2000 I, F, W, S, A, Arg (R), SA
3(R), 2001 W, It, S, A, SA, 2002 I, F, Arg, NZ, A, SA, 2003
NZ(R), A, [Gg, SA, Sm(R), U, W], 2004 It, S, I, W, F,
2005 W(R), F, A, NZ, 2006 SA1(R), 2, 2007 S, It, I, W2,
F2(R), 3, [US, Tg(R), A, F, SA2], 2008 W, F, S, I, PI(R), A,
SA, NZ3, 2009 It, W, I, F, S
Vivyan, E J (Devonport A) 1901 W, 1904 W, I, S
Voyce, A T (Gloucester) 1920 I, S, 1921 W, I, S, F, 1922 W, I,
F, S, 1923 W, I, S, F, 1924 W, I, F, S, 1925 NZ, W, I, S, F,
1926 W, I, F, S
Voyce, T M D (Bath, Wasps) 2001 US (R), 2004 NZ2, A1, 2005
Sm, 2006 W(R), It, F(R), I, A1
Vunipola, M W I N (Saracens) 2012 Fj(R), A(R), SA4(R), NZ2(R), 2013
S(R), I(R), F(R), It, W(R), A, 2014 F(R), S(R), I(R), W(R), It

Vunipola, V M L (Wasps, Saracens) 2013 Arg1(R), 2(R), A, Arg3,
NZ, 2014 F, S, I, NZ2(R), 3
Vyvyan, H D (Saracens) 2004 C(R)

Wackett, J A S (Rosslyn Park) 1959 W, I
Wade, C (Wasps) 2013 Arg 1
Wade, C G (Richmond) 1883 W, I, S, 1884 W, S, 1885 W, 1886
W, I
Wade, M R (Cambridge U) 1962 W, I, F
Wakefield, W W (Harlequins) 1920 W, F, I, S, 1921 W, I, S, F,
1922 W, I, F, S, 1923 W, I, S, F, 1924 W, I, F, S, 1925 NZ,
W, I, S, F, 1926 W, I, F, S, 1927 S, F
Walder, D J H (Newcastle) 2001 C 1, 2, US, 2003 W 2(R)
Waldrom, T R (Leicester) 2012 SA 2(R), 3, Fj, A, 2013 I(R)
Walker, G A (Blackheath) 1939 W, I
Walker, H W (Coventry) 1947 W, I, S, F, 1948 A, W, I, S, F
Walker, R (Manchester) 1874 S, 1875 I, 1876 S, 1879 S, 1880 S
Wallens, J N S (Waterloo) 1927 F
Walshe, N P J (Bath) 2006 A1(R), 2(R)
Walton, E J (Castleford) 1901 W, I, 1902 I, S
Walton, W (Castleford) 1894 S
Ward, H (Bradford) 1895 W
Ward, J A G (Leicester) 1913 W, F, S, 1914 W, I, S
Ward, J I (Richmond) 1881 I, 1882 I
Ward, J W (Castleford) 1896 W, I, S
Wardlow, C S (Northampton) 1969 SA (R), 1971 W, I, F, S (2[1C])
Warfield, P J (Rosslyn Park, Durham U) 1973 NZ 1, W, I, 1975
I, F, S
Warr, A L (Oxford U) 1934 W, I
Waters, F H H (Wasps) 2001 US, 2004 NZ2(R), A1(R)
Watkins, J A (Gloucester) 1972 SA, 1973 NZ 1, W, NZ 2, A,
1975 F, W
Watkins, J K (United Services, RN) 1939 W, I, S
Watson, F B (United Services, RN) 1908 S, 1909 S
Watson, J H D (Blackheath) 1914 W, S, F
Watt, D E J (Bristol) 1967 I, F, S, W
Webb, C S H (Devonport Services, RN) 1932 SA, W, I, S, 1933
W, I, S, 1935 S, 1936 NZ, W, I, S
Webb, J M (Bristol, Bath) 1987 [A (R), J, US, W], 1988 F, W, S,
I 1, 2, A 1, 2, 1989 S, I, F, W, 1991 Fj, A, [NZ, It, F, S,
A], 1992 S, I, F, W, C, SA, 1993 F, W, S, I
Webb, J W G (Northampton) 1926 F, S, 1929 S
Webb, R E (Coventry) 1967 S, W, NZ, 1968 I, F, S, 1969 I, F, S,
W, 1972 I, F
Webb, St L H (Bedford) 1959 W, I, F, S
Webber, R W (Wasps, Bath) 2012 It(R), W(R), F(R), 2013 Arg1,
2, 2014 NZ1, 2, 3(R)
Webster, J G (Moseley) 1972 W, I, SA, 1973 NZ 1, W, NZ 2,
1974 S, W, 1975 I, F, W
Wedge, T G (St Ives) 1907 F, 1909 W
Weighill, R H G (RAF, Harlequins) 1947 S, F, 1948 S, F
Wells, C M (Cambridge U, Harlequins) 1893 S, 1894 W, S, 1896
S, 1897 W, S
West, B R (Loughborough Colls, Northampton) 1968 W, I, F, S,
1969 SA, 1970 I, W, S
West, D E (Leicester) 1998 F (R), S (R), 2000 Arg (R), 2001 W,
It, S, F (t), C 1, 2, US, I (R), A, SA, 2002 F (R), W (R), It (R),
2003 W 2(R), F 2, 3(t+R ), [U, F(R)]
West, R (Gloucester) 1995 [WS]
Weston, H T F (Northampton) 1901 S
Weston, L E (W of Scotland) 1972 F, S
Weston, M P (Richmond, Durham City) 1960 W, I, F, S, 1961
SA, W, I, F, S, 1962 W, I, F, 1963 W, I, F, S, NZ 1, 2, A,
1964 NZ, W, I, F, S, 1965 F, S, 1966 S, 1968 F, S
Weston, W H (Northampton) 1933 I, S, 1934 I, S, 1935 W, I, S,
1936 NZ, W, S, 1937 W, I, S, 1938 W, I, S
Wheatley, A A (Coventry) 1937 W, I, S, 1938 W, S
Wheatley, H F (Coventry) 1936 I, 1937 S, 1938 W, S, 1939 W, I, S
Wheeler, P J (Leicester) 1975 F, W, 1976 A, W, S, I, 1977 S, I,
F, W, 1978 F, W, S, I, NZ, 1979 S, I, F, W, NZ, 1980 I, F, W,
S, 1981 W, S, I, F, 1982 A, S, I, F, W, 1983 F, S, I, NZ, 1984
S, I, F, W
White, C (Gosforth) 1983 NZ, 1984 S, I, F
White, D F (Northampton) 1947 W, I, S, 1948 I, F, 1951 S, 1952
SA, W, S, I, F, 1953 W, I, S
White, J M (Saracens, Bristol, Leicester) 2000 SA 1, 2, Arg, SA
3, 2001 F, C 1, 2, US, I, R (R), 2002 S, W, It, 2003 F 1(R),

**297**
**ENGLAND**

W 2, F 2, 3, [Sm, U(R)], 2004 W(R), F(R), NZ1, 2, A1, C, SA, A2, 2005 W, 2006 W(R), It(R), S, F, I, A1, 2, NZ, Arg, SA1, 2, 2007 S(R), It(R), I(R), F1, W1, 2009 It(R), W(R), I(t&R), F(t&R), S(R), Arg 1(R), 2

**White-Cooper, W R S** (Harlequins) 2001 C 2, US
**Whiteley, E C P** (O Alleynians) 1931 S, F
**Whiteley, W** (Bramley) 1896 W
**Whitely, H** (Northern) 1929 W
**Wightman, B J** (Moseley, Coventry) 1959 W, 1963 W, I, NZ 2, A
**Wigglesworth, H J** (Thornes) 1884 I
**Wigglesworth, R E P** (Sale, Saracens) 2008 It(R), F, S, I, NZ1, 2011 W2(R), 3, I2, [Arg, R(R), S(R), F(R)], 2013 Arg1(R), 2(R)
**Wilkins, D T** (United Services, RN, Roundhay) 1951 W, I, F, S, 1952 SA, W, S, I, F, 1953 W, I, F, S
**Wilkinson, E** (Bradford) 1886 W, I, S, 1887 W, S
**Wilkinson, H** (Halifax) 1929 W, I, S, 1930 F
**Wilkinson, H J** (Halifax) 1889 M
**Wilkinson, J P** (Newcastle, Toulon) 1998 I (R), A 1, NZ 1, 1999 S, I, F, W, A, US, C, [It, NZ, Fj, SA (R)], 2000 I, F, W, It, S, SA 2, A, Arg, SA 3, 2001 W, It, S, F, I, A, SA, 2002 S, I, F, W, It, NZ, A, SA, 2003 F 1, W 1, It, S, I, NZ, A, F 3, [Gg, SA, Sm, W, F, A], 2007 S, It, I, SA1, 2, W2, F2(R), F3, [Sm, Tg, A, F, SA2], 2008 W, It, F, S, I(R), 2009 A, Arg 3, NZ, 2010 W, It, I, S, F(R), A1(R), 2(R), 2011 W1(R), It(R), F(R), S(R), I1(R), W2, I2, [Arg, R, S, F]
**Wilkinson, P** (Law Club) 1872 S
**Wilkinson, R M** (Bedford) 1975 A 2, 1976 A, W, S, I, F
**Willcocks, T H** (Plymouth Albion) 1902 W
**Willcox, J G** (Oxford U, Harlequins) 1961 I, F, S, 1962 W, I, F, S, 1963 W, I, F, S, 1964 NZ, W, I, F, S
**William-Powlett, P B R W** (United Services, RN) 1922 S
**Williams, C G** (Gloucester, RAF) 1976 F
**Williams, C S** (Manchester) 1910 F
**Williams, J E** (O Millhillians, Sale) 1954 F, 1955 W, I, F, S, 1956 I, S, F, 1965 W
**Williams, J M** (Penzance-Newlyn) 1951 I, S
**Williams, P N** (Orrell) 1987 S, [A, J, W]
**Williams, S G** (Devonport A) 1902 W, I, S, 1903 I, S, 1907 I, S
**Williams, S H** (Newport) 1911 W, F, I, S
**Williamson, R H** (Oxford U) 1908 W, I, S, 1909 A, F
**Wilson, A J** (Camborne S of M) 1909 I
**Wilson, C E** (Blackheath) 1898 I
**Wilson, C P** (Cambridge U, Marlborough N) 1881 W
**Wilson, D G** (Newcastle, Bath) 2009 Arg 1, 2(R), A, NZ(R), 2010 W, It(R), I(R), S(R), F(R), A1(R), 2(t&R), NZ(R), A3(R), Sm, SA(R), 2011 W1(R), It(R), W2(R), [R(R)], 2012 Fj(R), SA4(R), NZ(R), 2013 S(R), I(R), It(R), W(R), Arg1, 2, A(R), Arg3, NZ(R), 2014 I, W, It, NZ1, 2, 3
**Wilson, D S** (Met Police, Harlequins) 1953 F, 1954 W, NZ, I, S, F, 1955 F, S
**Wilson, G S** (Tyldesley) 1929 W, I
**Wilson, K J** (Gloucester) 1963 F
**Wilson, R P** (Liverpool OB) 1891 W, I, S
**Wilson, W C** (Richmond) 1907 I, S
**Winn, C E** (Rosslyn Park) 1952 SA, W, S, I, F, 1954 W, S, F
**Winterbottom, P J** (Headingley, Harlequins) 1982 A, S, I, F, W, 1983 W, S, I, NZ, 1984 S, F, W, SA 1, 2, 1986 W, S, I, F, 1987 I, F, W, [A, J, US, W], 1988 F, W, S, 1989 R, Fj, 1990 I, F, W, S, Arg 1, 2, 3, 1991 W, S, I, F, A, [NZ, It, F, S, A], 1992 S, I, F, W, C, SA, 1993 F, W, S, I
**Winters, R A** (Bristol) 2007 SA1(R), 2
**Wintle, T C** (Northampton) 1966 S, 1969 I, F, S, W
**Wodehouse, N A** (United Services, RN) 1910 F, 1911 W, F, I, S, 1912 W, I, S, F, 1913 SA, W, F, I, S
**Wood, A** (Halifax) 1884 I
**Wood, A E** (Gloucester, Cheltenham) 1908 F, W, I

**Wood, G W** (Leicester) 1914 W
**Wood, M B** (Wasps) 2001 C 2(R), US (R)
**Wood, R** (Liversedge) 1894 I
**Wood, R D** (Liverpool OB) 1901 I, 1903 W, I
**Wood, T A** (Northampton) 2011 W1, It, F, S, I1, W2(R), 3, [Gg, R(R)], 2012 Fj(R), A(R), SA4, NZ, 2013 S, I, F, It, W, Arg1, 2, A, Arg3, NZ, 2014 F, S, I, W, It, NZ2, 3
**Woodgate, E E** (Paignton) 1952 W
**Woodhead, E** (Huddersfield) 1880 I
**Woodman, T J** (Gloucester) 1999 US (R), 2000 I (R), It (R), 2001 W (R), It (R), 2002 NZ, 2003 S (R), I(t + R), A, F 3, [Gg, SA, W(R), F, A], 2004 It, S, I, W, F, NZ1, 2
**Woodruff, C G** (Harlequins) 1951 W, I, F, S
**Woods, S M J** (Cambridge U, Wellington) 1890 W, S, I, 1891 W, I, S, 1892 I, S, 1893 W, I, 1895 W, I, S
**Woods, T** (Bridgwater) 1908 S
**Woods, T** (United Services, RN, Pontypool) 1920 S, 1921 W, I, S, F
**Woodward, C R** (Leicester) 1980 I (R), F, W, S, 1981 W, S, I, F, Arg 1, 2, 1982 A, S, I, F, W, 1983 I, NZ, 1984 S, I, F, W
**Woodward, J E** (Wasps) 1952 SA, W, S, 1953 W, I, F, S, 1954 W, NZ, I, S, F, 1955 W, I, 1956 S
**Wooldridge, C S** (Oxford U, Blackheath) 1883 W, I, S, 1884 W, I, S, 1885 I
**Wordsworth, A J** (Cambridge U) 1975 A 1(R)
**Worsley, J P R** (Wasps) 1999 [Tg, Fj], 2000 It (R), S (R), SA 1(R), 2(R), 2001 It (R), F(R), C 1, 2, US, A, R, SA, 2002 S, I, F, W (t+R), Arg, 2003 W 1(R), It, S(R), I(t), NZ(R), A(R), W 2, [SA(t), Sm, U], 2004 It, I, W(R), F, NZ1(R), 2, A1, SA, A2, 2005 W, F, I, S, 2006 W, It, S, F, I, A1(R), 2, SA1, 2, 2007 S, I, F1, W1, 2, F2, 3(R), [US, Sm, A(R), F(R), SA2(R)], 2008 NZ1(R), 2(R), 2009 It(R), W, I, F, S, Arg 3(R), NZ, 2010 I(R), S, F, 2011 W1(R)
**Worsley, M A** (London Irish, Harlequins) 2003 It(R), 2004 A1(R), 2005 S(R)
**Worton, J R B** (Harlequins, Army) 1926 W, 1927 W
**Wrench, D F B** (Harlequins) 1964 F, S
**Wright, C C G** (Cambridge U, Blackheath) 1909 I, S
**Wright, F T** (Edinburgh Acady, Manchester) 1881 S
**Wright, I D** (Northampton) 1971 W, I, F, S (R)
**Wright, J C** (Met Police) 1934 W
**Wright, J F** (Bradford) 1890 W
**Wright, T P** (Blackheath) 1960 W, I, F, S, 1961 SA, W, I, F, S, 1962 W, I, F, S
**Wright, W H G** (Plymouth) 1920 W, F
**Wyatt, D M** (Bedford) 1976 S (R)

**Yarde, M** (London Irish) 2013 Arg 2, A, 2014 NZ1, 2, 3
**Yarranton, P G** (RAF, Wasps) 1954 W, NZ, I, 1955 F, S
**Yates, K P** (Bath, Saracens) 1997 Arg 1, 2, 2007 SA1, 2
**Yiend, W** (Hartlepool R, Gloucester) 1889 M, 1892 W, I, S, 1893 I, S
**Young, A T** (Cambridge U, Blackheath, Army) 1924 W, I, F, S, 1925 NZ, F, 1926 I, F, S, 1927 I, S, F, 1928 A, W, I, F, S, 1929 I
**Young, J R C** (Oxford U, Harlequins) 1958 I, 1960 W, I, F, S, 1961 SA, W, I, F
**Young, M** (Gosforth) 1977 S, I, F, W, 1978 F, W, S, I, NZ, 1979 S, I, F, W, S, Arg 1, 2, 3, 1991 W, S, I, F, A, [NZ, It, F, S, A], 1992 S, I, F, W, C, SA, 1993 F, W, S, I
**Young, P D** (Dublin Wands) 1954 W, NZ, I, S, F, 1955 W, I, F, S
**Youngs, N G** (Leicester) 1983 I, NZ, 1984 S, I, F, W
**Youngs, B R** (Leicester) 2010 S(R), A1(R), 2, NZ, A3, Sm, SA, 2011 W1, It, F, S, I1, [Arg(R), Gg, R, S, F], 2012 S, It, W(R), F(R), I(R), SA 1, 2, Fj(R), A(R), SA4, NZ, 2013 S, I, F, It(R), W, A(R), NZ(R), 2014 NZ1, 2(R), 3
**Youngs, T N** (Leicester) 2012 Fj, A, SA4, NZ, 2013 S, I, F(R), It, W, A, Arg3(R), NZ(R), 2014 F(R), S(R), I(R), W(R), It(R)

# FIJI

## FIJI'S 2013–14 TEST RECORD

| OPPONENTS | DATE | VENUE | RESULT |
|---|---|---|---|
| Portugal | 9 Nov | A | Won 36–13 |
| Italy | 16 Nov | A | Lost 37–31 |
| Romania | 23 Nov | A | Won 26–7 |
| Italy | 7 Jun | H | Won 25–14 |
| Tonga | 14 Jun | H | Won 45–17 |
| Samoa | 21 Jun | H | Lost 13–18 |
| Cook Islands | 28 Jun | H | Won 108–6 |

# FIJI SEAL WORLD CUP QUALIFICATION

### By Iain Spragg

Fiji experienced an up and down 12 months but a massive win over the Cook Islands saw them qualify for RWC 2015.

**Fijian rugby may** have experienced some testing times off the pitch in 2013–14, but they achieved their main target for the season with qualification secured for Rugby World Cup 2015 in England, their fifth consecutive appearance and seventh overall.

Qualification came courtesy of a resounding 108–6 defeat of the Cook Islands at Churchill Park in Lautoka on 28 June, confirming Fiji's place in Pool A alongside hosts England, Wales, Australia and Repechage winners Uruguay.

It was a fitting climax to a season which had seen the Fiji Rugby Union (FRU) celebrate their centenary and also have their funding temporarily suspended by the International Rugby Board pending key reporting, administration and governance reforms. The IRB and Federation of Oceania Rugby Unions continued to work closely with the FRU and less than six months later the suspension was lifted.

The season had begun for Fiji with the annual foray to Europe in November and although Portugal were dispatched 36–13 in the tour opener in Lisbon, Italy proved sterner opposition seven days later and despite late tries from Timoci Nagusa and Napolioni Nalaga, the game finished in a 37–31 defeat for Inoke Male's team. The tour continued with a 26–7 win over Romania in Bucharest and after a Fiji XV was beaten 43–19 by the Barbarians at the Twickenham Stoop – in a match to commemorate the Union's centenary – the focus inevitably turned to the defence of their IRB Pacific Nations Cup crown the following summer.

Preparations, however, did not run smoothly. In January the IRB announced the suspension of financial support and 16 days later the FRU dispensed with the services of Male and four other coaches as part of a restructuring process. In May, New Zealand-born John McKee, a former technical advisor to Tonga and a specialist coach with the Pacific Islanders side, was unveiled as the new Fiji head coach.

McKee's reign began encouragingly with a 25–14 win over Italy in Suva in early June – Fiji's first win over a tier one country since their triumph over Wales at RWC 2007 – and a week later he steered the team to a comfortable 45–17 success against Tonga in their IRB Pacific Nations Cup opener in Lautoka, courtesy of 20 points from Crusaders star Nemani Nadolo.

In what was a remodelled tournament in 2014 featuring two separate conferences with Fiji, Tonga and Samoa in the Pacific Islands Conference and Japan, the USA and Canada in the North American Conference, McKee's side remained in contention after beating Tonga but hope turned to disappointment against Samoa a week later, losing 18–13 to their perennial rivals in Suva.

The big prize remained RWC 2015 qualification, with the Cook Islands standing in Fiji's way. It was ultimately to be a one-sided affair, but as the half hour mark approached it was the visitors who led 6–5.

It was as close as the Cook Islands were to get as Fiji then embarked on a 17-try blitz. Nadolo scored a hat-trick while there were also braces for full-back Metuisela Talebula and replacements Adriu Delai, Nikola Matawalu and Nagusa as Fiji confirmed their qualification in emphatic style.

"We knew the Cook Islands would come at us in the forwards in the first 20 minutes," said captain Akapusi Qera. "We expected that and we managed to compensate and come out with the win. It's a big thing for a rugby player growing up to qualify for the World Cup and that's what motivated us in the second half."

Beyond the senior side, Fiji teams enjoyed mixed fortunes with the Sevens side finishing third in the HSBC Sevens World Series after the

FIJI

country's second string – the Fiji Warriors – surrendered their IRB Pacific Rugby Cup title.

The highlights of the Sevens campaign came with victory in Dubai in November, which included a stunning 44–0 destruction of New Zealand in the semi-finals, and Tokyo in March. Samisoni Viriviri finished as the Series' top try-scorer with 52 and in May the Montpellier-bound player was named IRB Sevens Player of the Year, the first time a Fijian had received the accolade since its inauguration a decade earlier.

There was more good news in July when coach Ben Ryan announced the Union would be providing 15 central contracts to players for the 2014–15 Series, the first time Fiji have been able to offer its stars full-time deals.

Fiji's women also made waves on the IRB Women's Sevens World Series after beating England and Russia to reach a first Cup semi-final in China in April. Under the guidance of former men's coach Iliesa Tanivula they then confirmed their place as a core team on the 2014–15 Series by winning the qualifier in Hong Kong in September, beating France in an enthralling final.

The Warriors had meanwhile been unable to register a sixth successive triumph in what was a new-look Pacific Rugby Cup, the tournament taking place solely in Australia and featuring development sides from four Super Rugby franchises alongside Junior Japan, the Argentina Pampas XV and the Samoa and Tonga A teams.

The Warriors had won the competition in its various guises every year since 2009 but a 22–19 loss to Queensland Reds A in their tournament opener in March effectively put paid to their hopes of another successful title defence. They recovered to beat Western Force A (36–24) and Junior Japan (99–13), before accounting for Tonga A 54–21 in the third place play-off in Sydney where the Pampas XV succeeded them as champions by beating Reds A in the final.

Worse was to follow at the IRB Junior World Championship in New Zealand in June where the Fiji Under 20s struggled to impose themselves, losing all five matches to be relegated to the second tier IRB Junior World Rugby Trophy in 2015.

On the domestic front, the FRU also launched the IRB's Get Into Rugby as part of its restructured development programme. More than 2,200 children – 37 per cent of them girls – have participated in the programme and the Union has partnered with the Fiji Sports Council to ensure the curriculum is delivered to remote parts of the country by FSC development officers as well as the FRU development team.

## MATCH RECORDS UP TO 13 OCTOBER 2014

### WINNING MARGIN

| Date | Opponent | Result | Winning Margin |
|---|---|---|---|
| 10/09/1983 | Niue Island | 120–4 | 116 |
| 28/06/2014 | Cook Islands | 108–6 | 102 |
| 21/08/1969 | Solomon Islands | 113–13 | 100 |
| 08/09/1983 | Solomon Islands | 86–0 | 86 |
| 30/08/1979 | Papua New Guinea | 86–0 | 86 |

### MOST POINTS IN A MATCH
### BY THE TEAM

| Date | Opponent | Result | Points |
|---|---|---|---|
| 10/09/1983 | Niue Island | 120–4 | 120 |
| 21/08/1969 | Solomon Islands | 113–13 | 113 |
| 28/06/2014 | Cook Islands | 108–6 | 108 |
| 23/08/1969 | Papua New Guinea | 88–3 | 88 |

### BY A PLAYER

| Date | Player | Opponent | Points |
|---|---|---|---|
| 10/09/1983 | Severo Koroduadua | Niue Island | 36 |
| 21/08/1969 | Semesa Sikivou | Solomon Islands | 27 |
| 28/08/1999 | Nicky Little | Italy | 25 |
| 30/08/1979 | Tevita Makutu | Papua New Guinea | 24 |
| 29/09/1996 | Nicky Little | Hong Kong | 24 |

### MOST TRIES IN A MATCH
### BY THE TEAM

| Date | Opponent | Result | Tries |
|---|---|---|---|
| 21/08/1969 | Solomon Islands | 113–13 | 25 |
| 10/09/1983 | Niue Island | 120–4 | 21 |
| 23/08/1969 | Papua New Guinea | 88–3 | 20 |
| 18/08/1969 | Papua New Guinea | 79–0 | 19 |
| 30/08/1979 | Papua New Guinea | 86–0 | 18 |

### BY A PLAYER

| Date | Player | Opponent | Tries |
|---|---|---|---|
| 30/08/1979 | Tevita Makutu | Papua New Guinea | 6 |
| 18/08/1969 | George Sailosi | Papua New Guinea | 5 |

### MOST CONVERSIONS IN A MATCH
### BY THE TEAM

| Date | Opponent | Result | Cons |
|---|---|---|---|
| 21/08/1969 | Solomon Islands | 113–13 | 19 |
| 10/09/1983 | Niue Island | 120–4 | 18 |
| 23/08/1969 | Papua New Guinea | 88–3 | 14 |
| 18/08/1969 | Papua New Guinea | 79–0 | 11 |

### BY A PLAYER

| Date | Player | Opponent | Cons |
|---|---|---|---|
| 10/09/1983 | Severo Koroduadua | Niue Island | 18 |
| 21/08/1969 | Semesa Sikivou | Solomon Islands | 12 |
| 07/10/1989 | Severo Koroduadua | Belgium | 10 |

### MOST PENALTIES IN A MATCH
### BY THE TEAM

| Date | Opponent | Result | Pens |
|---|---|---|---|
| 08/07/2001 | Samoa | 28–17 | 7 |
| | 6 on 4 occasions | | |

### BY A PLAYER

| Date | Player | Opponent | Pens |
|---|---|---|---|
| 08/07/2001 | Nicky Little | Samoa | 7 |
| 26/05/2000 | Nicky Little | Tonga | 6 |
| 25/05/2001 | Nicky Little | Tonga | 6 |
| 05/10/1996 | Nicky Little | Hong Kong | 6 |
| 08/07/1967 | Inoke Tabualevu | Tonga | 6 |

### MOST DROP GOALS IN A MATCH
### BY THE TEAM

| Date | Opponent | Result | DGs |
|---|---|---|---|
| 02/07/1994 | Samoa | 20–13 | 3 |
| 12/10/1991 | Romania | 15–17 | 3 |

### BY A PLAYER

| Date | Player | Opponent | Pens |
|---|---|---|---|
| 02/07/1994 | Opeti Turuva | Samoa | 3 |
| 12/10/1991 | Tomasi Rabaka | Romania | 2 |

## MOST CAPPED PLAYERS

| Name | Caps |
|---|---|
| Nicky Little | 71 |
| Jacob Rauluni | 50 |
| Joeli Veitayaki | 49 |
| Sisa Koyamaibole | 48 |
| Seremaia Baikeinuku | 48 |

## LEADING TRY SCORERS

| Name | Tries |
|---|---|
| Senivalati Laulau | 18 |
| Norman Ligairi | 16 |
| Viliame Satala | 16 |
| Fero Lasagavibau | 16 |

## LEADING CONVERSIONS SCORERS

| Name | Cons |
|---|---|
| Nicky Little | 117 |
| Severo Koroduadua | 56 |
| Seremaia Baikeinuku | 51 |
| Waisale Serevi | 40 |

## LEADING PENALTY SCORERS

| Name | Pens |
|---|---|
| Nicky Little | 140 |
| Seremaia Baikeinuku | 49 |
| Severo Koroduadua | 47 |
| Waisale Serevi | 27 |

## LEADING DROP GOAL SCORERS

| Name | DGs |
|---|---|
| Opeti Turuva | 5 |
| Severo Koroduadua | 5 |
| Waisale Serevi | 3 |

## LEADING POINTS SCORERS

| Name | Points |
|---|---|
| Nicky Little | 670 |
| Seremaia Baikeinuku | 277 |
| Severo Koroduadua | 268 |
| Waisale Serevi | 221 |
| Taniela Rawaqa | 103 |

# FIJI INTERNATIONAL PLAYERS
## UP TO 13 OCTOBER 2014

**A Apimeleki** 1924 *Sa, Tg, Tg, Sa,* 1926 *Tg, Tg*
**S Aria** 1986 *W,* 1988 *Tg, Sa, E, Tg,* 1991 *C, F,* 1993 *Sa, Tg,* 1994 *J*
**LE Atalifo** 2014 *Coo*

**S Baikeinuku** 2000 *J, US, C, It,* 2001 *Tg, Sa, Tg,* 2002 *W, I, S,* 2004 *Tg, Sa,* 2005 *M, NZ, Tg, Sa, Tg, Sa, W, It,* 2006 *Tg, It, Sa, J,* 2007 *J, C, A, W, SA,* 2009 *Sa, J, S, I,* 2010 *F, W, It,* 2011 *J, NZ, Tg, Nm, SA, Sa, W,* 2013 *US, Tg, Pt, It, R*
**J Bale** 2004 *Tg, Sa,* 2005 *M, NZ, Tg, Sa, Tg, Sa, W, It,* 2006 *Tg, It, Sa, J*
**P Bale** 1995 *C, Sa, Tg, W, I*
**S Baleca** 1951 *M,* 1952 *A, A,* 1954 *A, A*
**DV Baleinadogo** 2001 *Tg, Sa, Tg, Sa, C, Sa,* 2002 *Sa, Tg,* 2007 *Sa, J*
**K Baleisawani** 2004 *Tg, Sa*
**N Baleiverata** 1988 *Tg, Sa, E,* 1990 *J*
**D Baleiwai** 1990 *J, HK,* 1991 *Tg, C, F, R*
**J Balewai** 1926 *Tg, Tg,* 1928 *Tg, Tg, Sa,* 1932 *Tg, Tg, Tg*
**S Banuve** 1990 *Tg*
**S Baravilala** 1934 *Tg, Tg,* 1947 *Tg, Tg,* 1948 *M, M*
**M Bari** 1995 *Tg, W, I,* 1996 *Sa, Tg, HK, HK, M,* 1997 *NZ, Coo, Sa,* 1998 *S, US, A, Tg,* 1999 *Ur, F*
**G Barley** 1964 *W, F,* 1970 *M, C*
**I Basiyalo** 1994 *J*
**S Basiyalo** 1976 *I*
**A Batibasaga** 1967 *Tg,* 1968 *Tg, Tg,* 1969 *W, PNG, SI, PNG*
**I Batibasaga** 1974 *M*
**I Batibasaga** 1970 *C,* 1972 *Tg, Tg, Tg, A,* 1973 *Tg, E,* 1974 *M, M,* 1976 *I,* 1977 *Tg, Tg,* 1979 *M*
**A Batikaciwa** 1932 *Tg, Tg,* 1934 *Tg, Tg, Tg*
**E Batimala** 1994 *J, M, W, Sa, Tg,* 1995 *C, Sa, Tg,* 1996 *HK,* 1998 *S*

**J Bibi** 1928 *Tg, Tg, Tg, Sa*
**TM Biumaiwai** 1954 *A, A, M, M*
**PTQ Biu** 1999 *Sp, Ur,* 2000 *J, Tg, Sa,* 2001 *It, F,* 2002 *Sa, Tg, Sa, NZ, Tg,* 2003 *CHL*
**M Black** 1996 *SA, Sa, Tg, HK*
**S Bobo** 2004 *Tg, Sa,* 2005 *M, NZ, Tg, W, Pt,* 2007 *W, SA,* 2010 *A,* 2013 *J, US, Tg,* 2014 *Tg, Sa*
**R Bogisa** 1994 *J, W,* 1995 *C, W*
**K Bogiwalu** 1924 *Sa, Tg, Tg, Tg, Sa,* 1926 *Tg, Tg*
**A Boko** 2009 *S, I, R*
**A Bola** 1934 *Tg*
**D Bola** 1983 *Sa, Niu, Tg,* 1984 *A, Sa, NZ*
**E Bola** 1939 *M*
**IC Bolakoro** 2009 *Sa,* 2011 *Sa*
**K Bola** 2009 *R,* 2010 *Tg, Sa,* 2012 *J, Sa, Tg, E, Geo*
**FV Bolavucu** 2009 *Tg, J*
**E Bolawaqatabu** 1963 *Sa, Tg, Sa, Tg,* 1969 *W, PNG, SI, PNG,* 1970 *M, M,* 1972 *Tg, Tg, Tg, A,* 1973 *M, M*
**P Bolea** 2001 *Sa*
**A Bose** 1932 *Tg, Tg,* 1934 *Tg, Tg, Tg*
**E Bose** 1998 *Sa*
**K Bose** 1958 *Tg, Tg,* 1959 *Tg,* 1961 *A, A, A*
**V Bose** 1980 *A*
**Botia** 2013 *Pt*
**I Buadromo** 1970 *C*
**VT Buatava** 2007 *Sa, J, A,* 2010 *A,* 2011 *Tg, Sa, J, NZ, Tg, Tg, Nm, SA, Sa, W*
**T Bucaonadi** 1983 *Tg, Sa*
**S Bueta** 1986 *Tg*
**V Bueta** 1982 *Sa, Sa, E*
**V Buli** 1963 *Sa, Tg, Sa, Tg*
**A Burogolevu** 1954 *A, A*
**A Buto** 2012 *J, Sa, S*

M Kunavore 2005 *Sa, Pt, It*, 2006 *It, J*, 2007 *C, A*
W Kunavula 1951 *M*
A Kunawave 1957 *M, M*, 1958 *Tg, Tg, Tg*, 1959 *Tg*
M Kurisaru 1968 *Tg, Tg, Tg*, 1969 *PNG, SI, PNG*, 1970 *M, C,* 1972 *Tg, Tg, Tg*, 1973 *M, Tg, E*, 1976 *A*
A Kuruisaqila 1957 *M*, 1959 *Tg*
R Kuruisiga 1926 *Tg, Tg, Tg*

M Labaibure 1948 *M, M*, 1952 *A*, 1954 *A, M, M, M*
E Labalaba 1979 *E, F, PNG, Sa, Tg*, 1980 *M*, 1981 *Tg, Tg, Tg*
P Lagilagi 1939 *M*
S Lala Ragata 1999 *Ur*, 2000 *J, Tg, Sa, US*
A Laqeretabua 1924 *Sa, Tg, Tg, Tg, Sa*, 1926 *Tg, Tg, Tg*, 1928 *Tg, Tg, Tg, Sa*, 1932 *Tg, Tg, Tg*, 1934 *Tg, Tg, Tg*, 1938 *M, M*
F Lasagavibau 1997 *NZ, Tg, Coo, Sa*, 1998 *S, F, US, Sa, Tg*, 1999 *C, US, Tg, Sa, M, Sp, Nm, C, F*, 2001 *It, F*, 2002 *W, I, S*
T Latianara 2002 *Sa, Tg*
T Latianara 1976 *I*
R Latilevu 1970 *C*, 1972 *Tg, Tg*, 1973 *E*, 1974 *NZ*, 1976 *A, A*
S Laulau 1980 *A, It, M, NZ, Ar, Ar*, 1981 *Sa, Sa, Tg, Tg, Tg*, 1982 *Sa, Sa, Sa, Tg*, 1983 *Tg, Sa, SI, Niu, Tg, Sa*, 1984 *A, Sa, Tg, Tg, NZ*, 1985 *Sa, Tg, A, A, I, W*
K Leawere 2002 *S*, 2003 *Tg, Tg, Ar, CHL, F, J*, 2004 *Tg, Sa,* 2005 *W, Pt, It*, 2007 *Sa, A, Tg, J, C, W, SA*, 2008 *Sa, M, J, Tg*, 2009 *Tg, Sa, J*
S Leawere 2003 *Tg, Ar, CHL*, 2006 *Tg, J*
I Ledua 2009 *Tg, Sa, J, S, I, R*
P Lese 1951 *M*
J Levula 1951 *M*, 1952 *A, A*, 1954 *A, A, M, M, M*, 1957 *M, M*, 1958 *Tg, Tg, Tg*, 1959 *Tg*, 1961 *A, A, A*
RWG Lewaravu 2007 *Sa, J, A, J, A, SA*, 2008 *Sa, M*, 2009 *S, I*, 2010 *F, It*, 2011 *Tg, Tg, Nm, SA, W*, 2013 *J, C, Tg, Pt, It, R*, 2014 *It, Sa*
I Leweniqila 1984 *Tg*
NAS Ligairi 2000 *Tg, Sa, US, C, It*, 2001 *Sa, Tg, Sa, C, Sa*, 2002 *Sa, Tg, Sa, NZ, Tg, W, I, S*, 2003 *Ar, CHL, F, I, S*, 2004 *Tg, Sa*, 2005 *M, NZ, Tg, Sa, Sa, W, It*, 2006 *Tg, It, Sa, J*, 2007 *Tg, J, C, A, W, SA*, 2009 *I, R*, 2010 *F, It*
S Ligamamada 1970 *C*, 1977 *Tg*
V Lilidamu 1986 *Tg, Tg*, 1988 *Tg*
L Little 1995 *C, Sa, Tg, W, I*, 1996 *SA, M*, 1997 *Tg, Coo, Sa,* 1998 *S*, 1999 *US, Tg, Sp*
N Little 1996 *SA, Sa, Tg, HK, HK, M*, 1997 *NZ, Tg, Coo, Sa,* 1998 *S, F, US, Sa*, 1999 *C, US, J, Tg, Sa, Sp, It, Nm, C, F, E*, 2000 *J, Tg, Sa, US, C, It*, 2001 *Tg, Sa, Sa, C, Sa, It, F*, 2002 *Sa, Tg, Sa, NZ, W, I*, 2003 *Tg, Tg, Ar, CHL, F, US, J, S*, 2005 *M, NZ, Tg, Sa, Tg, Sa, It*, 2007 *J, C, W,* 2009 *S, I*, 2011 *Tg, Sa, Tg, SA, Sa, W*
Livai 1926 *Tg*
V Loba 1939 *M*
D Lobendhan 1973 *M, Tg*, 1976 *A*
IM Male 1998 *A*, 1999 *Ur, E*, 2000 *J, Tg, Sa, US, C, It*, 2001 *Tg, Sa, Tg, Sa, C, Sa*
J Lotawa 2004 *Tg, Sa*, 2006 *Tg, J*
T Lovo 1989 *S, E*, 1990 *HK*, 1991 *Tg, C, F*, 1993 *S, Sa, Tg*
GV Lovobalavu 2007 *J, A, Tg, A, SA*, 2009 *S, I, R*, 2010 *F, W, It*, 2011 *Tg, Nm, SA, Sa, W*
E Lovodua 1958 *Tg, Tg, Tg*, 1961 *A, A, A*, 1963 *Sa, Tg, Sa, Tg*, 1964 *M*
S Lovokuru 1986 *W, Sa, Tg*, 1987 *NZ*
I Lutumailagi 1979 *F, PNG*, 1980 *It, NZ, M, Ar, Ar*, 1982 *Tg*
JB Lutumailagi 2013 *J, C*
WS Luveniyali 2007 *Tg, A*, 2008 *Sa, M, J, Tg*, 2009 *Sa, J*, 2010 *A*, 2011 *Sa, J, Tg, Tg, Nm, SA, Sa*, 2013 *Pt*

GDC Ma'afu 2010 *A, J, Tg, Sa, W, It*, 2011 *Sa, NZ, Tg, Tg, Nm, SA, Sa, W*, 2013 *J, C, US, Tg, Pt, It, R*, 2014 *It, Tg, Sa, Coo*
V Maimuri 2003 *Ar, F, US, J, S*
I Makutu 1976 *A, A, A*
RPN Makutu 2011 *Tg, Sa, J*, 2012 *E*
T Makutu 1979 *PNG, Sa, Tg*, 1980 *NZ, M, NZ, Ar, Ar*, 1981 *Sa, Sa, Tg, Tg, Tg*, 1982 *Sa, Sa*
K Malai 1988 *Tg, Sa, Tg*
E Malele 1973 *Tg*, 1976 *I*
D Manaseitava 1981 *Sa*, 1983 *Niu, Sa*, 1985 *Sa, Tg*

DT Manu 2009 *S*, 2010 *A, F, W, It*, 2011 *Tg, Sa, NZ, Tg, Nm, SA, Sa*, 2012 *E*
A Mara 1928 *Tg, Tg, Tg, Sa*
RT Rawaqa 2007 *Sa, J, A*, 2008 *Sa, M, J, Tg*, 2009 *Tg, Sa, J,* 2010 *A, Tg, Sa, W*, 2011 *Sa, J, NZ*
W Masirewa 1995 *Sa, W, I*, 1998 *A*
M Masitabua 1974 *M*
MS Matadigo 2006 *Tg*, 2009 *Tg*, 2011 *Sa, NZ, Tg, SA, W*, 2013 *US, It, R*
E Matalau 1976 *A, A*
S Matalulu 1994 *M, W, Sa*
RDT Tonawai 2007 *Tg*, 2010 *Tg, Sa*
J Matanatabu 1993 *Sa, Tg*
A Matanibuka 1932 *Tg, Tg, Tg*, 1934 *Tg, Tg, Tg*
A Matanibukaca 2005 *M, NZ, Tg, Tg*
S Matasarasara 1928 *Tg, Tg*
JL Matavesi 2009 *S, I, R*, 2010 *F, W*, 2012 *E*
S Matavesi 2013 *C, R*
NL Matawalu 2010 *J, Tg, Sa*, 2012 *J, S, Tg, E, Geo*, 2013 *J, US, Tg, Pt, It*, 2014 *It, Tg, Sa, Coo*
L Matea 1924 *Sa, Tg, Tg, Tg, Sa*
W Mateiwai 1993 *Sa, Tg, Tg*
N Matirawa 1984 *Tg*, 1989 *Tg, Tg, E*
JTF Matson 1999 *M, Ur*
J McLennan 1994 *M, W, Sa, Tg*, 1995 *C*, 1996 *HK*
T Mitchell 1986 *Tg, Tg*, 1987 *It, F, Sa, Tg*, 1988 *Tg, Sa, E, Tg, Tg*
V Mocelutu 1974 *NZ, M, M*
M Mocetadra 2012 *Tg*
S Morrell 2009 *J*
I Mow 2002 *Sa, Tg, Sa, Tg*, 2003 *Tg*
A Mucunabita 1994 *J, J*
J Mucunabitu 1957 *M, M*, 1959 *Tg*, 1964 *M, W, F*, 1968 *NZ, Tg, Tg*
K Murimurivalu 2011 *Tg, Tg, Tg, Nm, SA, Sa*
I Musanamasi 1982 *Sa, Sa, E*, 1983 *SI*
K Musunamasi 1977 *Tg, Tg, Tg, BI*, 1979 *M, E, PNG, Sa*

L Nabaro 1976 *I*
N Nabaro 1957 *M, M*, 1959 *Tg*, 1961 *A, A, A*, 1964 *M*
M Nabati 1985 *A, A, W*
O Nabavu 1926 *Tg, Tg*
K Nabili 1926 *Tg*, 1928 *Tg, Tg, Tg, Sa*
K Nabili 1985 *Tg*
I Nabobo 1976 *I*
G Naborisi 1992 *Tg*
G Naborisi 1954 *A*
I Nabou 1961 *A, A, A*
M Nabuta 1967 *Tg, Tg*, 1968 *NZ, Tg, Tg, Tg*, 1969 *PNG, SI, PNG*
S Nacaka 1981 *Tg*, 1982 *Sa, Tg, S*
F Naceba 1924 *Sa, Tg, Tg, Tg, Sa*
I Nacewa 2003 *S*
S Nacolai 1968 *NZ, Tg, Tg*, 1969 *W, SI, PNG*
V Nadaku 1934 *Tg, Tg*, 1938 *M, M, M*
A Nadolo 1987 *It, F, Sa, Tg*, 1988 *E, Tg, Tg*, 1989 *Tg, Tg, 1991 Sa, Tg, Tg, R*, 1992 *Sa, Tg*, 1993 *S, Sa, Tg, Tg*, 1995 *C, Sa, Tg, I*
J Nadolo 2000 *Tg, Sa, US, C, It*
A Nadredre 1964 *F, C*, 1968 *Tg*
M Nadridri 2004 *Sa*, 2005 *Sa, Tg*
N Nadruku 1988 *Tg, Sa, E, Tg, Tg*, 1989 *Tg, Bel, S, E*, 1990 *J, HK*, 1991 *C, R*
S Nadruku 1981 *Sa, Sa, Tg, Tg*, 1982 *Sa, Sa, Tg, S, E,* 1983 *SI, Tg*, 1984 *Sa, Tg, NZ*
A Naevo 1996 *HK, HK, M*, 1997 *NZ, Tg, Sa*, 1998 *S, F, US, Sa, Tg*, 1999 *J, Tg, Sa, M, Sp, It, Nm, C*, 2001 *Tg, Sa, Tg, Sa, C, Sa*, 2002 *W, I, S*, 2003 *Tg, Tg, F, US, S*
I Nagatalevu 1939 *M*
A Nagi 2001 *It, F*, 2004 *Tg, Sa*, 2005 *W, Pt, It*, 2006 *Tg, It, Sa, J*
A Nagicu 1996 *HK*
N Ngusa 2012 *Geo*, 2013 *R*, 2014 *It, Tg, Sa*
T Nagusa 2008 *Sa, M, J*, 2009 *Tg, I, R*, 2010 *A, J*, 2011 *Tg, J, NZ*, 2013 *US, Pt, It, R*, 2014 *It, Tg, Coo*
Naibuka 1968 *Tg*
T Naidole 1954 *M*, 1957 *M, M*, 1958 *Tg, Tg, Tg*, 1959 *Tg*

L Raitilava 1968 *NZ*, 1969 *W, PNG, SI, PNG*, 1972 *Tg, Tg, Tg, A*, 1976 *A, A*
S Raiwalui 1997 *NZ, Tg, Coo, Sa*, 1998 *S, F, US, A, Sa, Tg*, 1999 *C, US, J, Tg, Sa, M, Sp, It, Nm, C, F, E*, 2000 *J, Tg, Sa, US, C, It*, 2001 *Sa, C, Sa*, 2002 *Sa, Tg, Sa, NZ, Tg, W, I, S*, 2006 *Tg, It, Sa, J*
E Rakai 1983 *SI, Tg, Sa*, 1984 *A, Sa, Tg*, 1985 *Sa, Tg, A, A, I, W*, 1986 *W, Sa, Tg*, 1987 *NZ, F*
K Rakoroi 1983 *Tg, SI, Niu, Tg*, 1984 *A, Sa, Tg*, 1985 *A, A, I, W*, 1986 *W, Tg, Sa, Tg*, 1987 *Ar, NZ, It, F, Sa, Tg*
S Ralagi 1951 *M*, 1952 *A, A*, 1954 *A, A*
S Ralawa 1934 *Tg, Tg, Tg*, 1938 *M, M, M*, 1939 *M*
J Ralulu 2008 *Sa, Tg*, 2010 *J, Tg, Sa*, 2012 *S, Tg, Geo*, 2014 *It, Tg, Sa, Coo*
TD Ralumu 1979 *E, F*
T Ranavue 1947 *Tg, Tg*, 1952 *A, A*, 1954 *A, A, M, M, M*
NS Kenatale 2008 *J, Tg*, 2009 *Tg, Sa, J*, 2010 *F, W, It*, 2011 *Tg, Sa, NZ, Tg, Nm, SA, Sa, W*, 2012 *Sa, S*, 2013 *J, C, US, Tg, Pt, It*, 2014 *It, Tg, Coo*
S Rarasea 1961 *A*
V Rarawa 2010 *It*
L Rasala 1994 *J, J*
M Rasari 1988 *Tg, Sa, E, Tg*, 1989 *Bel, S, E*, 1990 *Sa*, 1991 *Sa, Tg*
I Rasila 1992 *Sa, M*, 1998 *S, F, A*, 1999 *C, US, Sp, Ur, E*, 2000 *J, Tg, Sa, US, C, It*, 2001 *Tg, Sa, Tg, Sa, C, Sa, It*, 2002 *Sa, Tg, Sa, NZ, S*, 2003 *Tg, Tg, Ar, CHL, J, S*
P Rasiosateki 1963 *Sa, Tg*, 1964 *M, W, F, C*
S Rasolea 1984 *Tg, NZ*, 1985 *Sa, Tg, A*
S Rasua 1961 *A, A, A*
J Ratu 1980 *NZ, Ar, Ar*, 1981 *Sa, Tg, Tg, Tg*, 1982 *Sa, Tg, S, E*
Q Ratu 1976 *I*, 1977 *Tg, Tg, Tg, BI*
R Ratu 2009 *Sa, J*, 2010 *A, J, Tg, Sa, W*
S Ratu 1968 *Tg*
J Ratu 2009 *S, R*
N Ratudina 1972 *Tg, Tg*, 1973 *M, M, E*, 1974 *NZ, M, M*, 1977 *Tg, Tg, Tg, BI*, 1979 *M, F*
E Ratudradra 1980 *A, M, NZ, Ar, Ar*, 1981 *Tg, Tg, Tg*
V Ratudradra 1976 *A, A*, 1977 *Tg, BI*, 1979 *M, E*, 1980 *NZ, M*, 1981 *Sa, Sa, Sa*, 1984 *Tg*
S Ratumaiyali 1947 *Tg*
K Ratumuri 1980 *M*, 1981 *Sa*
E Ratuniata 2001 *Sa, Tg*, 2002 *Sa, Sa*
A Ratuniyarawa 2012 *E, Geo*, 2013 *J, C, US, Tg, Pt*, 2014 *It, Tg, Sa, Coo*
RARG Ratuva 2005 *M, NZ, Tg, Tg, Sa, W, It*, 2006 *Sa, J*, 2007 *Tg, J, A, W, SA*, 2008 *Sa, M, J, Tg*
I Ratuva 2012 *J, Sa, S, Tg, E, Geo*, 2013 *C, US*
N Ratuveilawa 1961 *A*, 1963 *Sa, Tg, Sa, Tg*, 1964 *C*
K Ratuvou 2005 *Sa, W, Pt, It*, 2006 *Tg, It, Sa, J*, 2007 *Tg, J, C, W, SA*, 2008 *Sa, M, J*, 2012 *Sa, S*
SD Raulini 1997 *Sa*
T Raulumi 1973 *M*
J Rauluni 1995 *C, Sa, Tg, W, I*, 1996 *SA, Sa, Tg*, 1997 *NZ, Tg*, 1998 *S, F, US, Sa, Tg*, 1999 *J, M, Ur, It, Nm, C, F, E*, 2000 *Sa, C, It*, 2001 *Sa, Tg, Sa, C, Sa*, 2002 *Sa, Tg, Sa, NZ, Tg, W, I, S*, 2003 *Tg, S*, 2005 *M, NZ, Tg, Sa, Tg*, 2006 *It, Sa, J*
MN Rauluni 1996 *M*, 1997 *Tg, Coo, Sa*, 1998 *A*, 1999 *Sp, It, C, E*, 2000 *J, Tg, US, C, It*, 2001 *Tg*, 2003 *Ar, CHL, F, US, J, S*, 2004 *Tg, Sa*, 2005 *M, NZ, Tg, Sa, Tg, Sa, W, Pt, It*, 2007 *A, Tg, J, C, A, W, SA*, 2008 *Sa, M*, 2009 *S, I*
P Rauluni 1984 *A, Sa, Tg*, 1986 *Sa, Tg*
T Rauluni 1968 *Tg*, 1972 *Tg*, 1974 *NZ, M*
V Rauluni 1990 *Sa*, 1991 *Sa, Tg, E*
V Rauluni 2007 *Sa, J, A*
V Rauluni 1992 *Sa*, 1993 *S, Tg*
J Rauto 1976 *A, A, A*, 1977 *Tg, Tg, BI*, 1979 *M, E*, 1980 *Ar, Ar*, 1981 *Sa, Tg, Tg, Tg*, 1982 *Sa, Sa, Tg, E*, 1984 *Tg, NZ*
P Ravaga 1926 *Tg, Tg*, 1928 *Tg, Tg, Tg, Sa*
J Ravai 1928 *Tg, Tg, Sa*
M Ravai 1928 *Tg, Tg*
PR Ravai 2013 *R*
E Ravi 1961 *A, A, A*
E Ravouvou 1928 *Tg, Tg, Tg, Sa*

I Ravouvou 1958 *Tg, Tg, Tg*, 1959 *Tg*
I Ravouvou 1986 *Sa, Tg*, 1987 *Sa, Tg*
J Ravouvou 1979 *PNG, Sa, Tg*, 1980 *NZ, M, NZ, Ar, Ar*
N Ravouvou 1967 *Tg, Tg, Tg*, 1968 *NZ, Tg, Tg*, 1969 *W, PNG, SI, PNG*, 1970 *M, M, C*, 1972 *A*, 1973 *M, M, Tg, E*
T Ravouvou 1948 *M*
J Ravu 1948 *M, M*, 1954 *M, M, M*
T Ravualala 1976 *I*
L Tabuarua 2013 *J, C, US*
M Ravula 1958 *Tg, Tg*
RMM Ravulo 2010 *F, W*, 2011 *Tg, Sa, NZ, Tg, Nm, Sa, W*, 2012 *J, Sa, S, E, Geo*, 2013 *J, C, US, Tg, Pt, It, R*, 2014 *It, Tg, Sa, Coo*
AQ Qiodravu 2000 *US, C, It*, 2001 *Tg, Sa, Tg, Sa, C, Sa, It, F*, 2007 *A, Tg, J, C, A, W, SA*
I Rawaqa 2002 *Sa, Tg, Sa, NZ, Tg, I*, 2003 *Ar, CHL, F, US, S*, 2004 *Tg, Sa*, 2005 *M, NZ, Tg, Sa, Tg, Sa, W, Pt, It*, 2006 *Tg, It*, 2007 *J, A, Tg, C, A, W, SA*, 2008 *Sa, M, J*, 2009 *Sa, S, I*, 2010 *W*, 2011 *J*
F Rayasi 1994 *M, W, Sa, Tg*, 1995 *C, Sa, Tg, W, I*, 1996 *SA, HK, HK*, 1997 *NZ*
E Rayawa 1961 *A*
J Rayawa 1979 *F, PNG, Sa, Tg*
P Rika 1958 *Tg, Tg*
A Rinakama 2001 *Sa, C, Sa*
A Robe 1964 *W, F, C*
S Rokini 2000 *J, Tg, Sa, US*, 2001 *Sa, Tg, Sa, C, Sa, It*, 2003 *CHL*
AV Rokobaro 2013 *Pt, R*
S Rokobaro 2004 *Tg, Sa*, 2005 *M, NZ*
N Rokobiau 2009 *I, R*
E Rokowailoa 1982 *Sa, Tg, S*, 1983 *Tg, Niu, Tg, Sa*, 1987 *Ar, NZ, It*, 1990 *J, Tg, Sa*, 1992 *M*, 1993 *S, Sa, Tg, Tg*
RMS Saulo 2012 *E, Geo*, 2013 *J, C, US, Tg, Pt, It, R*, 2014 *It, Tg, Sa, Coo*
D Rouse 1995 *C, Tg, W*, 1996 *SA, Sa, Tg, HK, HK, M*, 1997 *NZ, Tg, Coo, Sa*, 1998 *US, A, Sa, Tg*, 1999 *US, J, Tg, Sa, M, Ur, It, Nm, C, F, E*
S Rovuaka 1947 *Tg, Tg*
E Ruivadra 2002 *Tg, Tg, W, S*, 2003 *Tg, J, S*, 2005 *M, NZ, Tg, Sa, Tg, W, Pt, It*, 2006 *Tg, J*, 2010 *J, Sa*
S Sacere 1993 *Tg*
S Sadria 1991 *Sa, Tg, Tg*, 1993 *Sa, Tg*, 1994 *J, J, M*
P Sailasa 1934 *Tg*
G Sailosi 1969 *W, PNG, PNG*
K Salabogi 2005 *W, Pt, It*, 2006 *It*
W Salabogi 1951 *M*, 1952 *A, A*, 1954 *A, A*
L Saladoka 1947 *Tg*
K Salawa 2003 *Tg, Tg, Ar, CHL, F, S*
I Salusalu 2012 *Sa*, 2013 *C*
K Salusalu 1982 *Tg, S, E*, 1983 *Tg, Sa, SI, Niu, Tg, Sa*, 1987 *It, F, Sa, Tg*, 1990 *Sa*
R Samo 2005 *Tg, Tg*, 2006 *Tg, It, Sa, J*
R Samuels 1973 *M, M, Tg, E*, 1974 *NZ, M, M*
J Sanday 1987 *Ar, It*
K Sarai 1988 *Tg, Sa, Tg*
M Sarasau 1976 *I*
A Sassen 1993 *Tg*
S Satala 2005 *Tg, Sa, Tg*, 2007 *A*, 2009 *I, R*
V Satala 1999 *C, US, J, Tg, Sa, M, Sp, It, Nm, C, F, E*, 2000 *C, It*, 2001 *Tg, Sa, Tg, C, Sa, It, F*, 2002 *Tg, Sa, NZ, Tg, I, S*, 2005 *M, NZ*
RMS Naevo 2006 *Sa, J*, 2007 *J, C, W, SA*, 2008 *Sa, M, J*, 2009 *Tg, Sa*, 2010 *F, W, It*
I Saukuru 1994 *J, J, M*
J Saukuru 1954 *A, A, M, M, M*, 1957 *M, M*, 1958 *Tg, Tg, M*, 1959 *Tg*, 1963 *Sa, Tg, Sa, Tg*
WR Saukuru 2010 *Tg, Sa*
S Saumaisue 1998 *S, F, US*
M Saunaki 1984 *NZ*
S Sautu 1957 *M, M*, 1958 *Tg, Tg, Tg*
V Sauturaga 2007 *Tg, C, A, W*, 2008 *Sa, M, J*, 2009 *R*
I Savai 1984 *A, Sa, Tg, Tg, NZ*, 1985 *Sa, Tg, A*, 1987 *Ar, NZ, It, F*, 1989 *Tg, Tg, Bel, S, E*, 1990 *J, Tg, Sa, HK*, 1991 *Sa, Tg, E, C, F, R*, 1992 *Sa, Tg, M*, 1993 *Tg, Sa, J, J, M, W, Sa, Tg*, 1995 *C*

M Seavula 1988 *Sa*, 1989 *Tg, Bel*
A Secake 1957 *M*, 1958 *Tg*, 1959 *Tg*
N Senilagakali 1980 *NZ, Ar, Ar*
RHW Seniloli 2013 *R*
M Seniloli 1926 *Tg, Tg, Tg*, 1928 *Tg, Sa*
R Seniloli 1934 *Tg, Tg, Tg*
T Seniloli 1926 *Tg*, 1928 *Sa*
I Senivau 1968 *NZ*
N Serelevu 2013 *R*
W Serevi 1989 *Bel, S*, 1990 *J, Sa*, 1991 *Tg, E, C, F*, 1992 *Sa*, 1993 *S*, 1996 *SA, Tg, M*, 1998 *S, F, US, A, Sa, Tg*, 1999 *Tg, Sa, M, Sp, It, Nm, C, E*, 2001 *It, F*, 2002 *W, I, S*, 2003 *Tg, Ar, CHL, F, J*
F Seru 1990 *Tg, Sa, HK*, 1991 *Tg, E, C, F, R*, 1992 *Sa*, 1993 *Tg*
N Seru 2003 *Ar, CHL, F, US, J, S*
S Seru 1980 *M, NZ*
S Seruvakula 2002 *Sa*
SG Seruvatu 1952 *A, A*, 1954 *A, M, M, M*, 1959 *Tg*
V Seuseu 2008 *Sa, M, J, Tg*, 2009 *Tg, Sa, I, R*
S Sevu 2001 *Sa*
K Sewabu 1999 *C, US, J, Tg, Sa, M, Sp, It, Nm, C, F, E*, 2000 *US, C, It*, 2002 *Sa, NZ, Tg*, 2003 *Tg, Tg, Ar, US, J, S*
S Sikivou 1968 *Tg*, 1969 *W, PNG, SI, PNG*, 1970 *M, M*, 1973 *M*
R Silotolu 1954 *M, M, M*
M Sisiwa 1994 *J*
G Smith 1995 *W, I*, 1996 *SA, Sa, Tg, HK, HK, M*, 1997 *NZ, Tg, Coo, Sa*, 1998 *US, Sa, Tg*, 1999 *J, Tg, Sa, M, It, Nm, C, F, E*, 2000 *US, C, It*, 2001 *Tg, Sa, Tg, Sa, C, Sa*, 2002 *Sa, Tg, Sa, NZ, Tg, W, I, S*, 2003 *F, US, J, S*
J Sokovata 1963 *Sa, Tg, Tg*, 1964 *M*
S Somoca 2011 *J, NZ, Tg, Sa, W*, 2012 *J, Sa, S, Tg, E, Geo*, 2013 *J, C, US, Tg, Pt, It, R*
TN Soqeta 2007 *Sa, J, A*
A Soqosoqo 1964 *M, W, F, C*
SC Sorovaki 1995 *C, Sa, Tg, W, I*, 1996 *SA, Sa, Tg, HK, HK, M*, 1997 *NZ, Tg, Coo, Sa*, 1998 *S, F, US, A, Sa, Tg*
W Sotutu 1999 *C, US, J, Tg, M, Sp, Ur, It, Nm, C, F, E*
V Sovalevu 1992 *Sa, Tg*
J Sovau 1970 *M, M, C*, 1972 *A*, 1973 *M*, 1974 *M*, 1976 *A, A*, 1979 *PNG, Sa, Tg*
Sovu 1928 *Sa*
W Suka 1990 *HK*, 1993 *Sa, Tg*
WS Sukanaveita 2009 *Tg, J*
J Suluaqalo 1932 *Tg, Tg, Tg*
A Suluoqalo 1964 *M*
J Susu 1948 *M, M, M*, 1951 *M*, 1952 *A, A*

J Tabaiwalu 1957 *M, M*, 1958 *Tg, Tg*, 1959 *Tg*, 1961 *A, A, A*, 1963 *Sa, Sa*
S Tabua 2005 *M, NZ*
I Tabualevu 1984 *Sa, Tg*
I Tabualevu 1958 *Tg, Tg*, 1967 *Tg, Tg, Tg*
S Tabualevu 1983 *Sa*
M Tabukaci 1947 *Tg, Tg*
P Tabulutu 1986 *Tg, Sa, Tg*, 1987 *Ar, Sa, Tg*, 1988 *Tg, E, Tg, Tg*, 1990 *J, Sa*, 1991 *Sa, Tg, E, C, F, R*
S Tadulala 2009 *R*
MV Taga 1987 *NZ*, 1988 *Tg, Sa, E, Tg*, 1989 *Tg, Tg, Bel, S, E*, 1990 *J, Tg, HK*, 1991 *Sa, Tg, E, C, F*, 1992 *Sa, Tg, M*, 1993 *S, Sa, Tg, Tg*, 1996 *HK, M*, 1997 *NZ, Coo*, 1998 *S, F, A*
N Taga 1952 *A*
N Tagi 2004 *Tg, Sa*
ML Tagicakibau 2007 *Tg*, 2008 *J*, 2010 *W*, 2011 *Tg, W*
JR Railomo 2005 *NZ*, 2007 *J, C, A, W, SA*, 2008 *Sa, M, J, Tg*
MS Tagivetaua 1981 *Tg, Tg*, 1982 *Sa, Tg*, 1983 *Tg, Sa*
S Taka 2006 *Tg*, 2007 *Sa, J*, 2010 *F, W*
V Taliga 1928 *Tg, Sa*
S Tamanibeka 1924 *Sa, Tg, Tg, Sa*, 1926 *Tg*, 1928 *Tg, Tg, Tg, Sa*

M Tamanitoakula 1998 *S, F, A*
I Tabua 1990 *J, Tg*, 1995 *W*, 1998 *F, A, Sa, Tg*, 1999 *C, US, J, Tg, Sa, M, Sp, It, C, F*
S Tamanivalu 1967 *Tg, Tg, Tg*
T Tamanivalu 1995 *I*, 1996 *SA, Sa, Tg, HK, HK, M*
M Tamata 1981 *Sa, Sa, Tg, Tg, Tg*, 1982 *Tg, S, E*
N Tamaya 1981 *Sa*
B Tanivukavu 1957 *M*
I Taoba 1974 *M*, 1976 *A, A, A*, 1977 *Tg, Tg, Tg, Bl*, 1980 *A, It, NZ*, 1981 *Sa, Sa, Tg, Tg, Tg*, 1982 *Tg, S, E*
J Taqaiwai 1991 *Tg, E*
J Taqiri 1976 *A*
A Tarogi 2009 *J, I, R*
I Tasere 1974 *NZ, M, M*
E Tatawaqa 1981 *Tg, Tg, Tg*, 1982 *Sa, Sa, Sa, Tg, S*
P Tatukivei 1958 *Tg*
E Tauga 1994 *F*
I Taukei 1924 *Sa, Tg, Tg, Tg, Sa*, 1926 *Tg*
I Tawake 1986 *W*, 1987 *Sa, Tg*, 1988 *Tg, Tg*, 1990 *J*, 1991 *Tg, E, C, F, R*, 1992 *Sa, Tg, M*, 1993 *S, Sa, Tg*, 1994 *J, J, M, W, Sa, Tg*, 1995 *C, Sa, Tg, W, I*, 1996 *SA, Sa, Tg, HK, M*, 1997 *NZ, Coo, Sa*, 1998 *S, F, US, A*, 1999 *C, US, Tg, Sp, Ur, E*
S Tawake 1992 *Sa, M*, 1998 *Sa, Tg*, 1999 *C, US, J, M, It, Nm, C, F, E*, 2002 *Sa, NZ, Tg, W, I, S*, 2003 *CHL*
S Tawase 1961 *A, A*
E Teleni 1982 *Sa, Sa, S, E*, 1983 *Tg, Sa, Niu, Tg, Sa*, 1984 *A, Sa, Tg*, 1985 *A, A, I, W*, 1986 *W*, 1988 *Tg, Tg, Bel, S, E*
L Temani 1924 *Sa, Tg, Tg, Tg, Sa*
DD Thomas 2007 *Tg*, 2008 *M, Tg*
I Tikoduadua 1982 *S, E*, 1983 *Sa*
T Matawalu 2005 *Pt*, 2007 *Sa, J*
E Tikoidraubuta 1992 *Tg*
A Tikoirotuma 2013 *Pt, It, R*, 2014 *It, Sa, Coo*
P Bosco 1968 *Tg, Tg*, 1970 *M, M*, 1972 *Tg, Tg, Tg, A*, 1973 *M, M, Tg, E*, 1977 *Tg, Tg, Tg, Bl*, 1979 *M, E*
I Tikomaimakogai 1999 *US, J, Tg, Sa, M, Ur, It, Nm, E*, 2000 *J, Tg*
K Tilalati 2000 *J, Tg*
A Toga 1963 *Tg, Sa, Tg*
S Toga 1964 *W, C*, 1967 *Tg, Tg*, 1968 *NZ, Tg*, 1969 *W, PNG, SI, PNG*, 1970 *C*
A Tokairavua 1967 *W*, 1970 *M, C*, 1972 *Tg, Tg, Tg, A*, 1973 *M, Tg*, 1977 *Tg, Tg*
J Toloi 1994 *M, W, Sa, Tg*
S Tolotu 1964 *F*
J Tora 2005 *Tg, Sa, Tg, Sa, Pt*, 2006 *Tg, J*
P Tora 1986 *Sa, Tg*
P Tove 1951 *M*
TD Tuapati 2010 *A, J, Tg, Sa, F, W, It*, 2011 *Tg, Sa, Tg, SA, Sa*, 2012 *Sa, S, Tg, Geo*, 2013 *J, C, US, Tg*, 2014 *It, Tg, Sa*
T Tubananitu 1980 *A, It, NZ*, 1981 *Sa, Sa, Tg, Tg, Tg*, 1982 *Sa, Sa, Sa, Tg, S*, 1983 *Niu, Tg, Sa*, 1984 *Tg, NZ*, 1985 *A*
W Tubu 1967 *Tg*
P Tubui 1981 *Sa, Sa*
S Tubuna 1932 *Tg, Tg, Tg*
N Tubutubu 1924 *Sa, Tg, Tg, Tg, Sa*
E Tudia 1973 *Tg*
P Tuidraki 1994 *J, J, M, W, Sa, Tg*
P Tuidraki 1932 *Tg, Tg, Tg*
J Tuikabe 1999 *US, Sa, Ur*, 2000 *J, Tg, Sa, US, C, It*, 2001 *Tg, Sa, Tg, Sa, C, Sa, It, F*
A Tuilevu 1996 *SA, Sa, Tg, HK*, 1997 *Tg, Coo, Sa*, 1998 *S, F, A, Sa*, 2003 *Tg, Tg, Ar, F, US, J, S*, 2004 *Tg*
J Tuilevu 2008 *Tg*
W Tuinagiagia 1968 *Tg*, 1976 *I*
E Tuisese 2001 *F*
I Tuisese 1969 *W, SI*, 1970 *M, M, C*, 1972 *Tg, Tg, Tg*, 1973 *E*, 1974 *NZ, M, M*, 1976 *A, A*, 1977 *Tg, Tg, Bl*
I Tuisese 2000 *J, Sa*
S Tuisese 1958 *Tg*, 1963 *Sa, Tg, Sa, Tg*, 1964 *M, W, F*
W Tuisese 1947 *Tg*, 1948 *M, M, M*
A Tuitavua 1938 *M, M, M*, 1939 *M, M*, 1947 *Tg*, 1948 *M, M, M*, 1952 *A, A*, 1954 *A, A, M, M, M*
E Tuivunivono 1993 *Tg*

# FRANCE

## FRANCE'S 2013–14 TEST RECORD

| OPPONENTS | DATE | VENUE | RESULT |
|-----------|------|-------|--------|
| New Zealand | 9 Nov | H | Lost 19–26 |
| Tonga | 16 Nov | H | Won 38–18 |
| South Africa | 23 Nov | H | Lost 10–19 |
| England | 1 Feb | H | Won 26–24 |
| Italy | 9 Feb | H | Won 30–10 |
| Wales | 21 Feb | A | Lost 27–6 |
| Scotland | 8 Mar | A | Won 19–17 |
| Ireland | 15 Mar | H | Lost 20–22 |
| Australia | 7 Jun | A | Lost 50–23 |
| Australia | 14 Jun | A | Lost 6–0 |
| Australia | 21 Jun | A | Lost 39–13 |

# SAINT-ANDRÉ CRITICAL OF FRENCH FOREIGN LEGION

## By Iain Spragg

France's inconsistent season included a narrow defeat by Ireland in the Six Nations in March.

**C**onsistency is a priceless but frequently elusive commodity in Test rugby and for a second season in succession it frustratingly proved beyond the collective reach of France as Philippe Saint-André's struggling side slumped to seven defeats in their 11 international engagements.

There was some solace for Les Bleus as they avoided the ignominy of claiming the wooden spoon as they had in the 2013 Six Nations, and there was a 38–18 victory over Tonga in November to avenge their infamous loss to the Pacific Islanders at Rugby World Cup 2011, but positives were ultimately in short supply.

The nadir of what was a turbulent campaign, however, came in Brisbane in June when France were crushed 50–23 by the Wallabies. France eventually succumbed to a series whitewash in Australia, suffering another heavy defeat in the third and final Test in Sydney, and as a result Les Bleus slid to seventh in the IRB World Rankings.

# 2013–14 IN PICTURES

**story makers:** England ended a long wait for econd Women's Rugby World Cup title while sts France reached the semi-finals and Ireland used a huge upset by beating four-time ampions New Zealand in the pool stages.

**Sevens gold:** South Africa ended New Zealand's hold on the Commonwealth Games' gold medal before a record crowd of 171,000 across two days in Glasgow, while Australia's women and France's men created history (right) by winning the first Rugby Sevens Olympic gold medals at the Youth Olympic Games in Nanjing.

**Time to celebrate:** Australia's Emilee Cherry (top) was named IRB Women's Sevens Player of the Year in 2014 but New Zealand edged them in the title race. The All Blacks Sevens won a 12th Sevens World Series title in 15 years, while Japan secured the coveted core team place on the 2014–15 HSBC Sevens World Series.

**Sheer delight:** England retained their IRB Junior World Championship title in New Zealand after a 21-20 win over South Africa in the final.

**Meteoric rise:** IRB Junior Player of the Year 2014 Handré Pollard made his Test debut eight days after guiding South Africa to the JWC 2014 final in New Zealand.

**Champions:** Ireland and New Zealand celebrate after winning the RBS Six Nations and The Rugby Championship in 2014.

**Worth the wait:** Argentina's players celebrate after recording a first win in The Rugby Championship, 21-17 over Australia in Mendoza.

**ying high:** Jonny Wilkinson lifts the Heineken Cup for Toulon, while Adam Ashley-Cooper dives
er for a try as the Waratahs win a first Super Rugby title.

**On tour:** The RWC 2015 Trophy Tour has included stops in Japan, Madagascar and Australia in 2014.

**Mission accomplished:** (below) Uruguay celebrate after becoming the 20th and final qualifier for RWC 2015.

It was a thoroughly dejected Saint-André who faced the media after the climax of the Australia tour and, not for the first time during his tenure as head coach, he insisted a major factor in the national team's struggles was the continuing influx of foreign players into the Top 14.

"Seven or eight years ago there were 70 per cent foreigners in the [English] Premiership," he said. "Now there are 70 per cent English. With us, it's the other way round. Suddenly the pool to choose from becomes scarce. There are not currently 10 wingers on our list of those available to play for France."

That there were only three Frenchmen in the Toulon XV which had beaten Saracens in the Heineken Cup final just a month earlier, or that a mere 13 of the 30 players who started the Top 14 final held French passports, certainly lent weight to the argument, but with a meagre 11 victories in his 29 games in charge, Saint-André knew his record – as much as the French game's domestic resources – was in the spotlight.

Ironically, Les Bleus began their year with what was a thoroughly encouraging performance against the All Blacks at the Stade de France, albeit one that ended in defeat. The New Zealanders arrived in Paris on an 11-Test winning streak but the home side were undaunted and when full-back Brice Dulin went over in the 68th minute to bring the French within seven points at 26–19 hope sprang eternal of a famous victory. Sadly there was no further scoring, but French supporters were content with their team's display if not the result.

Saint-André made five changes for the Tonga clash in Le Havre, handing a debut to Perpignan wing Sofiane Guitoune, and with the scars of losing to the Tongans in the pool stages of RWC 2011 still relatively fresh, it was paramount that the side registered a win.

They did so with ease at the Stade Océane. Guitoune justified his selection with a try after only five minutes, and further scores from number 8 Damien Chouly, Dulin and replacement hooker Benjamin Kayser, supplemented by 18 points from the combined boots of Morgan Parra and Frédéric Michalak, saw France canter to a cathartic 38–18 triumph.

South Africa were the final opponents of 2013. Les Bleus had claimed the scalp of the Springboks on their previous four visits to France, but JP Pietersen scored for the visitors in the first minute in Paris and it was an early lead that the South Africans would not relinquish. A try from Yoann Huget before half-time kept France in touch, but 2013 was to end with a 19–10 defeat for Saint-André's embattled side.

The loss of captain Thierry Dusautoir ahead of the Six Nations campaign with a bicep injury was not the news the coach was hoping for and with England first up in Paris, the pressure was steadily growing on Saint-André.

**FRANCE**

He named uncapped Stade Français fly-half Jules Plisson in his XV to face the English, but it was another French youngster, 19-year-old Toulouse centre Gaël Fickou, who was to make the pivotal contribution in a pulsating clash at the Stade de France.

France stormed into the lead in Paris with a first-half double from Huget. England fought back with two tries of their own and with six minutes on the clock and the visitors protecting a 24–19 lead, Saint-André introduced Fickou to the fray. Two minutes later he produced the moment of magic his side yearned for, taking Dimitri Szarzewski's pass, artfully dummying the English defence and gliding over for the winning try. Maxime Machenaud added the extras and France were ahead by two.

"We must remember we have won the game and this is a very good start for 2014," Saint-André said after his team's dramatic 26–24 win. "This is not a revolution, more an evolution. There's a lot of work to do still. But what we'll have to remember is the victory, the smiles on the players' faces after the game."

Eight days later France comfortably despatched Italy 30–10 in Paris, courtesy of second-half tries from Louis Picamoles, Wesley Fofana and Hugo Bonneval to maintain the momentum, but almost as soon as tentative talk of a Grand Slam began, reality struck when they faced defending champions Wales in Cardiff.

Les Bleus were never truly in the match at the Millennium Stadium after George North scored for the hosts in the fifth minute and although Jean-Marc Doussain and Plisson were both successful with first-half penalties, indiscipline and yellow cards for Nicolas Mas and Picamoles after the break dashed French hopes of a fight-back and they were well beaten, 27–6.

Saint-André made seven changes to the side to play Scotland a fortnight later, including dropping Picamoles for dissent to referee Alain Rolland after he was sent to the sin-bin.

The new-look French side did not produce the coherent performance the coach was looking for, but they did get the result in Edinburgh. The visitors leaked two early tries to the Scots but a stunning interception try from inside his own 22 by Huget redressed the balance and it was Doussain who clinched a 19–17 victory in the 78th minute at Murrayfield with a seemingly nerveless penalty.

The result meant France could still claim the title if they could overcome Ireland in Paris and England were ambushed by the Italians on the final day. Ireland, however, were also title contenders and significantly quicker out of the blocks at the Stade de France, with tries from Johnny Sexton (2) and Andrew Trimble in the opening 45 minutes. The home side replied with a score from Dulin before the break and when

Szarzewski crashed over in the 62nd minute, the score was 22–20 to the visitors.

But Doussain missed a late penalty opportunity while Chouly had a last-minute try disallowed for a forward pass and the Six Nations title was Ireland's.

The timing of the Top 14 final coupled with Saint-André's desire to afford some of his leading players a summer of rest and recuperation saw France head Down Under to face Australia with a depleted 31-man squad, including three uncapped players, and they were to pay a heavy price for their lack of firepower.

The first Test in Brisbane was catastrophic as the Wallabies ruthlessly dismantled the French defence, running in seven tries in the first 70 minutes to storm into a 50–9 lead. There were some crumbs of comfort for the visitors with a late Parra try and then a penalty try to give the final 50–23 scoreline some gloss but the stark reality was Les Bleus had conceded a half-century of points for only the second time in the 86-year history of the fixture.

"Some players showed their limits," Saint-André admitted after the match. "At this level, you pay for every mistake. I am not the first coach of a team to let in 50 points in the southern hemisphere, but this one gives me a headache."

The return of captain Dusautoir was one of 10 changes for the second Test in Melbourne a week later and if the first clash between the two sides had brought a deluge of points, the rematch was one of the lowest scoring internationals in recent memory.

Remarkably there were no points whatsoever in the first half, but it was the Wallabies who drew first blood after the break with penalties from Bernard Foley on 52 minutes and another from Nic White 12 minutes later. France threatened through Dulin and Mathieu Bastareaud late on, but Australia held firm to emerge 6–0 winners.

Sadly, Saint-André's troops reverted to type for the third Test in Sydney and the home side were on the board as early as the second minute with a Foley penalty. By the time hooker Guilhem Guirado scored Les Bleus' only try of a one-sided contest in the 65th minute, Australia had already helped themselves to four of their own. French misery was completed when Nick Phipps scored a fifth try seven minutes from time and Les Bleus were soundly beaten 39–13.

It was a chastening conclusion to another up-and-down year for France and although the supporters' finger of blame was pointed variously at the onerous domestic fixture list, Saint-André's coaching regime and the perceived paucity of home-grown players in the Top 14, the consensus was that Les Bleus have a mountain to climb as Rugby World Cup 2015 looms.

# FRANCE INTERNATIONAL STATISTICS

## MATCH RECORDS UP TO 13 OCTOBER 2014

### MOST CONSECUTIVE TEST WINS

| | |
|---|---|
| 10 | 1931 E,G, 1932 G, 1933 G, 1934 G, 1935 G, 1936 G1,2, 1937 G,It |
| 8 | 1998 E, S, I, W, Arg 1,2, Fj, Arg 3 |
| 8 | 2001 SA3, A, Fj 2002 It, W, E, S, I |
| 8 | 2004 I, It, W, S, E, US, C, A |

### MOST CONSECUTIVE TESTS WITHOUT DEFEAT

| Matches | Wins | Draws | Period |
|---|---|---|---|
| 10 | 10 | 0 | 1931 to 1938 |
| 10 | 8 | 2 | 1958 to 1959 |
| 10 | 9 | 1 | 1986 to 1987 |

### MOST POINTS IN A MATCH
#### BY THE TEAM

| Pts | Opponents | Venue | Year |
|---|---|---|---|
| 87 | Namibia | Toulouse | 2007 |
| 77 | Fiji | Saint Etienne | 2001 |
| 70 | Zimbabwe | Auckland | 1987 |
| 67 | Romania | Bucharest | 2000 |
| 64 | Romania | Aurillac | 1996 |
| 64 | Georgia | Marseilles | 2007 |
| 62 | Romania | Castres | 1999 |
| 62 | Romania | Bucharest | 2006 |
| 61 | Fiji | Brisbane | 2003 |
| 60 | Italy | Toulon | 1967 |

#### BY A PLAYER

| Pts | Player | Opponents | Venue | Year |
|---|---|---|---|---|
| 30 | D Camberabero | Zimbabwe | Auckland | 1987 |
| 28 | C Lamaison | New Zealand | Twickenham | 1999 |
| 28 | F Michalak | Scotland | Sydney | 2003 |
| 27 | G Camberabero | Italy | Toulon | 1967 |
| 27 | C Lamaison | New Zealand | Marseilles | 2000 |
| 27 | G Merceron | South Africa | Johannesburg | 2001 |
| 27 | J-B Elissalde | Namibia | Toulouse | 2007 |
| 26 | T Lacroix | Ireland | Durban | 1995 |
| 26 | F Michalak | Fiji | Brisbane | 2003 |
| 25 | J-P Romeu | United States | Chicago | 1976 |
| 25 | P Berot | Romania | Agen | 1987 |
| 25 | T Lacroix | Tonga | Pretoria | 1995 |

### MOST TRIES IN A MATCH
#### BY THE TEAM

| Tries | Opponents | Venue | Year |
|---|---|---|---|
| 13 | Romania | Paris | 1924 |
| 13 | Zimbabwe | Auckland | 1987 |
| 13 | Namibia | Toulouse | 2007 |
| 12 | Fiji | Saint Etienne | 2001 |
| 11 | Italy | Toulon | 1967 |
| 10 | Romania | Aurillac | 1996 |
| 10 | Romania | Bucharest | 2000 |

#### BY A PLAYER

| Tries | Player | Opponents | Venue | Year |
|---|---|---|---|---|
| 4 | A Jauréguy | Romania | Paris | 1924 |
| 4 | M Celhay | Italy | Paris | 1937 |

### MOST CONVERSIONS IN A MATCH
#### BY THE TEAM

| Cons | Opponents | Venue | Year |
|---|---|---|---|
| 11 | Namibia | Toulouse | 2007 |
| 9 | Italy | Toulon | 1967 |
| 9 | Zimbabwe | Auckland | 1987 |
| 8 | Romania | Wellington | 1987 |
| 8 | Romania | Lens | 2003 |

#### BY A PLAYER

| Cons | Player | Opponents | Venue | Year |
|---|---|---|---|---|
| 11 | J-B Elissalde | Namibia | Toulouse | 2007 |
| 9 | G Camberabero | Italy | Toulon | 1967 |
| 9 | D Camberabero | Zimbabwe | Auckland | 1987 |
| 8 | G Laporte | Romania | Wellington | 1987 |

## MOST PENALTIES IN A MATCH
### BY THE TEAM

| Penalties | Opponents | Venue | Year |
|---|---|---|---|
| 8 | Ireland | Durban | 1995 |
| 7 | Wales | Paris | 2001 |
| 7 | Italy | Paris | 2002 |
| 6 | Argentina | Buenos Aires | 1977 |
| 6 | Scotland | Paris | 1997 |
| 6 | Italy | Auch | 1997 |
| 6 | Ireland | Paris | 2000 |
| 6 | South Africa | Johannesburg | 2001 |
| 6 | Argentina | Buenos Aires | 2003 |
| 6 | Fiji | Brisbane | 2003 |
| 6 | England | Twickenham | 2005 |
| 6 | Wales | Paris | 2007 |
| 6 | England | Twickenham | 2007 |
| 6 | Ireland | Dublin | 2011 |

### BY A PLAYER

| Pens | Player | Opponents | Venue | Year |
|---|---|---|---|---|
| 8 | T Lacroix | Ireland | Durban | 1995 |
| 7 | G Merceron | Italy | Paris | 2002 |
| 6 | J-M Aguirre | Argentina | Buenos Aires | 1977 |
| 6 | C Lamaison | Scotland | Paris | 1997 |
| 6 | C Lamaison | Italy | Auch | 1997 |
| 6 | G Merceron | Ireland | Paris | 2000 |
| 6 | G Merceron | South Africa | Johannesburg | 2001 |
| 6 | F Michalak | Fiji | Brisbane | 2003 |
| 6 | D Yachvili | England | Twickenham | 2005 |

## MOST DROP GOALS IN A MATCH
### BY THE TEAM

| Drops | Opponents | Venue | Year |
|---|---|---|---|
| 3 | Ireland | Paris | 1960 |
| 3 | England | Twickenham | 1985 |
| 3 | New Zealand | Christchurch | 1986 |
| 3 | Australia | Sydney | 1990 |
| 3 | Scotland | Paris | 1991 |
| 3 | New Zealand | Christchurch | 1994 |

### BY A PLAYER

| Drops | Player | Opponents | Venue | Year |
|---|---|---|---|---|
| 3 | P Albaladejo | Ireland | Paris | 1960 |
| 3 | J-P Lescarboura | England | Twickenham | 1985 |
| 3 | J-P Lescarboura | New Zealand | Christchurch | 1986 |
| 3 | D Camberabero | Australia | Sydney | 1990 |

# CAREER RECORDS

## MOST CAPPED PLAYERS

| Caps | Player | Career Span |
|---|---|---|
| 118 | F Pelous | 1995 to 2007 |
| 111 | P Sella | 1982 to 1995 |
| 98 | R Ibañez | 1996 to 2007 |
| 93 | S Blanco | 1980 to 1991 |
| 89 | O Magne | 1997 to 2007 |
| 86 | D Traille | 2001 to 2011 |
| 84 | S Marconnet | 1998 to 2011 |
| 82 | I Harinordoquy | 2002 to 2012 |
| 79 | D Szarzewski | 2004 to 2014 |
| 78 | A Benazzi | 1990 to 2001 |
| 76 | A Rougerie | 2001 to 2012 |
| 75 | J Bonnaire | 2004 to 2012 |
| 74 | L Nallet | 2000 to 2012 |
| 73 | Y Jauzion | 2001 to 2011 |
| 73 | N Mas | 2003 to 2014 |

## MOST CONSECUTIVE TESTS

| Tests | Player | Span |
|---|---|---|
| 46 | R Bertranne | 1973 to 1979 |
| 45 | P Sella | 1982 to 1987 |
| 44 | M Crauste | 1960 to 1966 |
| 42 | M Parra | 2009 to 2013 |
| 35 | B Dauga | 1964 to 1968 |

## MOST TESTS AS CAPTAIN

| Tests | Captain | Span |
|---|---|---|
| 43 | T Dusautoir | 2009 to 2014 |
| 42 | F Pelous | 1997 to 2006 |
| 41 | R Ibanez | 1998 to 2007 |
| 34 | J-P Rives | 1978 to 1984 |
| 34 | P Saint-André | 1994 to 1997 |
| 25 | D Dubroca | 1986 to 1988 |
| 25 | F Galthié | 1999 to 2003 |
| 24 | G Basquet | 1948 to 1952 |
| 22 | M Crauste | 1961 to 1966 |

FRANCE

## MOST POINTS IN TESTS

| Points | Player | Tests | Career |
|---|---|---|---|
| 380 | C Lamaison | 37 | 1996 to 2001 |
| 377 | F Michalak | 71 | 2001 to 2014 |
| 373 | D Yachvili | 61 | 2002 to 2012 |
| 367 | T Lacroix | 43 | 1989 to 1997 |
| 354 | D Camberabero | 36 | 1982 to 1993 |
| 325 | M Parra | 56 | 2008 to 2014 |
| 267 | G Merceron | 32 | 1999 to 2003 |
| 265 | J-P Romeu | 34 | 1972 to 1977 |
| 247 | T Castaignède | 54 | 1995 to 2007 |
| 233 | S Blanco | 93 | 1980 to 1991 |
| 214 | J-B Elissalde | 35 | 2000 to 2008 |
| 200 | J-P Lescarboura | 28 | 1982 to 1990 |

## MOST CONVERSIONS IN TESTS

| Cons | Player | Tests | Career |
|---|---|---|---|
| 59 | C Lamaison | 37 | 1996 to 2001 |
| 54 | F Michalak | 71 | 2001 to 2014 |
| 51 | D Yachvili | 61 | 2002 to 2012 |
| 48 | D Camberabero | 36 | 1982 to 1993 |
| 45 | M Vannier | 43 | 1953 to 1961 |
| 42 | T Castaignède | 54 | 1995 to 2007 |
| 41 | M Parra | 56 | 2008 to 2014 |
| 40 | J-B Elissalde | 35 | 2000 to 2008 |
| 36 | R Dourthe | 31 | 1995 to 2001 |
| 36 | G Merceron | 32 | 1999 to 2003 |
| 32 | T Lacroix | 43 | 1989 to 1997 |
| 29 | P Villepreux | 34 | 1967 to 1972 |

## MOST TRIES IN TESTS

| Tries | Player | Tests | Career |
|---|---|---|---|
| 38 | S Blanco | 93 | 1980 to 1991 |
| 34 | V Clerc | 67 | 2002 to 2013 |
| 33* | P Saint-André | 69 | 1990 to 1997 |
| 30 | P Sella | 111 | 1982 to 1995 |
| 26 | E Ntamack | 46 | 1994 to 2000 |
| 26 | P Bernat Salles | 41 | 1992 to 2001 |
| 25 | C Dominici | 67 | 1998 to 2007 |
| 23 | C Darrouy | 40 | 1957 to 1967 |
| 23 | A Rougerie | 76 | 2001 to 2012 |

* Saint-André's total includes a penalty try against Romania in 1992

## MOST PENALTY GOALS IN TESTS

| Penalties | Player | Tests | Career |
|---|---|---|---|
| 89 | T Lacroix | 43 | 1989 to 1997 |
| 85 | D Yachvili | 61 | 2002 to 2012 |
| 78 | C Lamaison | 37 | 1996 to 2001 |
| 75 | M Parra | 56 | 2008 to 2014 |
| 64 | F Michalak | 71 | 2001 to 2014 |
| 59 | D Camberabero | 36 | 1982 to 1993 |
| 57 | G Merceron | 32 | 1999 to 2003 |
| 56 | J-P Romeu | 34 | 1972 to 1977 |
| 38 | J-B Elissalde | 35 | 2000 to 2008 |
| 33 | P Villepreux | 34 | 1967 to 1972 |
| 33 | P Bérot | 19 | 1986 to 1989 |

## MOST DROP GOALS IN TESTS

| Drops | Player | Tests | Career |
|---|---|---|---|
| 15 | J-P Lescarboura | 28 | 1982 to 1990 |
| 12 | P Albaladejo | 30 | 1954 to 1964 |
| 11 | G Camberabero | 14 | 1961 to 1968 |
| 11 | D Camberabero | 36 | 1982 to 1993 |
| 9 | J-P Romeu | 34 | 1972 to 1977 |
| 9 | F Michalak | 71 | 2001 to 2014 |

| RECORD | DETAIL | HOLDER | SET |
|---|---|---|---|
| Most points in season | 156 | in five matches | 2002 |
| Most tries in season | 18 | in four matches | 1998 |
| | 18 | in five matches | 2006 |
| Highest score | 56 | 56–13 v Italy | 2005 |
| Biggest win | 51 | 51–0 v Wales | 1998 |
| Highest score conceded | 49 | 14–49 v Wales | 1910 |
| Biggest defeat | 37 | 0–37 v England | 1911 |
| Most appearances | 50 | P Sella | 1983–1995 |
| Most points in matches | 217 | D Yachvili | 2003–2012 |
| Most points in season | 80 | G Merceron | 2002 |
| Most points in match | 24 | S Viars | v Ireland, 1992 |
| | 24 | C Lamaison | v Scotland, 1997 |
| | 24 | J-B Elissalde | v Wales, 2004 |
| Most tries in matches | 14 | S Blanco | 1981–1991 |
| | 14 | P Sella | 1983–1995 |
| Most tries in season | 5 | P Estève | 1983 |
| | 5 | E Bonneval | 1987 |
| | 5 | E Ntamack | 1999 |
| | 5 | P Bernat Salles | 2001 |
| | 5 | V Clerc | 2008 |
| Most tries in match | 3 | M Crauste | v England, 1962 |
| | 3 | C Darrouy | v Ireland, 1963 |
| | 3 | E Bonneval | v Scotland, 1987 |
| | 3 | D Venditti | v Ireland, 1997 |
| | 3 | E Ntamack | v Wales, 1999 |
| | 3 | V Clerc | v Ireland, 2008 |
| Most cons in matches | 30 | D Yachvili | 2003–2012 |
| Most cons in season | 11 | M Parra | 2010 |
| Most cons in match | 6 | D Yachvili | v Italy, 2003 |
| Most pens in matches | 49 | D Yachvili | 2003–2012 |
| Most pens in season | 18 | G Merceron | 2002 |
| Most pens in match | 7 | G Merceron | v Italy, 2002 |
| Most drops in matches | 9 | J-P Lescarboura | 1982–1988 |
| Most drops in season | 5 | G Camberabero | 1967 |
| Most drops in match | 3 | P Albaladejo | v Ireland, 1960 |
| | 3 | J-P Lescarboura | v England, 1985 |

FRANCE

# MISCELLANEOUS RECORDS

| RECORD | HOLDER | DETAIL |
|---|---|---|
| Longest Test Career | F Haget | 1974 to 1987 |
| | C Califano | 1994 to 2007 |
| | S Marconnet | 1998 to 2011 |
| | F Michalak | 2001 to 2014 |
| Youngest Test Cap | C Dourthe | 18 yrs 7 days in 1966 |
| Oldest Test Cap | A Roques | 37 yrs 329 days in 1963 |

## CAREER RECORDS OF FRANCE INTERNATIONAL PLAYERS

## UP TO 13 OCTOBER 2014

| PLAYER BACKS : | DEBUT | CAPS | T | C | P | D | PTS |
|---|---|---|---|---|---|---|---|
| M Bastareaud | 2009 v W | 25 | 2 | 0 | 0 | 0 | 10 |
| H Bonneval | 2014 v It | 4 | 1 | 0 | 0 | 0 | 5 |
| V Clerc | 2002 v SA | 67 | 34 | 0 | 0 | 0 | 170 |
| J-M Doussain | 2011 v NZ | 10 | 0 | 3 | 10 | 0 | 36 |
| B Dulin | 2012 v Arg | 18 | 3 | 0 | 1 | 0 | 18 |
| G Fickou | 2013 v S | 9 | 1 | 0 | 0 | 0 | 5 |
| W Fofana | 2012 v It | 27 | 9 | 0 | 0 | 0 | 45 |
| F Fritz | 2005 v SA | 34 | 3 | 0 | 0 | 3 | 24 |
| S Guitoune | 2013 v Tg | 2 | 1 | 0 | 0 | 0 | 5 |
| Y Huget | 2010 v Arg | 30 | 6 | 0 | 0 | 0 | 30 |
| R Lamerat | 2014 v A | 3 | 0 | 0 | 0 | 0 | 0 |
| F Le Bourhis | 2014 v A | 1 | 0 | 0 | 0 | 0 | 0 |
| M Machenaud | 2012 v Arg | 18 | 1 | 7 | 8 | 0 | 43 |
| M Médard | 2008 v Arg | 40 | 11 | 0 | 0 | 1 | 58 |
| M Mermoz | 2008 v A | 27 | 2 | 0 | 0 | 0 | 10 |
| F Michalak | 2001 v SA | 71 | 10 | 54 | 64 | 9 | 377 |
| M Parra | 2008 v S | 56 | 3 | 41 | 75 | 1 | 325 |
| J Pélissié | 2013 v Tg | 1 | 0 | 0 | 0 | 0 | 0 |
| J Plisson | 2014 v E | 4 | 0 | 0 | 1 | 0 | 3 |
| R Tales | 2013 v NZ | 10 | 0 | 0 | 0 | 0 | 0 |
| F Trinh-Duc | 2008 v S | 49 | 9 | 2 | 1 | 6 | 70 |

## FORWARDS :

| | | | | | | | |
|---|---|---|---|---|---|---|---|
| A Burban | 2014 v E | 3 | 0 | 0 | 0 | 0 | 0 |
| D Chouly | 2007 v NZ | 21 | 1 | 0 | 0 | 0 | 5 |
| A D Claassen | 2013 v E | 6 | 0 | 0 | 0 | 0 | 0 |
| V Debaty | 2006 v R | 25 | 0 | 0 | 0 | 0 | 0 |
| T Domingo | 2009 v W | 36 | 1 | 0 | 0 | 0 | 5 |
| L Ducalcon | 2010 v S | 17 | 0 | 0 | 0 | 0 | 0 |
| T Dusautoir | 2006 v R | 67 | 6 | 0 | 0 | 0 | 30 |
| A Flanquart | 2013 v NZ | 8 | 0 | 0 | 0 | 0 | 0 |
| Y Forestier | 2012 v A | 11 | 0 | 0 | 0 | 0 | 0 |
| G Guirado | 2008 v It | 23 | 1 | 0 | 0 | 0 | 5 |
| B Kayser | 2008 v A | 24 | 1 | 0 | 0 | 0 | 5 |
| A Lapandry | 2009 v Sm | 10 | 2 | 0 | 0 | 0 | 10 |
| W Lauret | 2010 v SA | 7 | 0 | 0 | 0 | 0 | 0 |
| B Le Roux | 2013 v NZ | 8 | 0 | 0 | 0 | 0 | 0 |
| B Mach | 2014 v W | 3 | 0 | 0 | 0 | 0 | 0 |
| Y Maestri | 2012 v It | 28 | 0 | 0 | 0 | 0 | 0 |
| N Mas | 2003 v NZ | 73 | 0 | 0 | 0 | 0 | 0 |
| A Menini | 2014 v A | 2 | 0 | 0 | 0 | 0 | 0 |
| Y Nyanga | 2004 v US | 39 | 5 | 0 | 0 | 0 | 25 |
| F Ouedraogo | 2007 v NZ | 36 | 1 | 0 | 0 | 0 | 5 |
| P Papé | 2004 v I | 54 | 3 | 0 | 0 | 0 | 15 |
| L Picamoles | 2008 v I | 44 | 6 | 0 | 0 | 0 | 30 |
| C Samson | 2012 v Arg | 5 | 0 | 0 | 0 | 0 | 0 |
| R Slimani | 2013 v NZ | 10 | 0 | 0 | 0 | 0 | 0 |
| J Suta | 2012 v A | 5 | 0 | 0 | 0 | 0 | 0 |
| D Szarzewski | 2004 v C | 79 | 7 | 0 | 0 | 0 | 35 |
| C-E Tolofua | 2012 v Arg | 4 | 0 | 0 | 0 | 0 | 0 |
| S Vahaamahina | 2012 v A | 14 | 0 | 0 | 0 | 0 | 0 |

FRANCE

# FRENCH INTERNATIONAL PLAYERS

## UP TO 13 OCTOBER 2014

Note: Years given for International Championship matches are for second half of season; eg 1972 means season 1971–72. Years for all other matches refer to the actual year of the match. Entries in square brackets denote matches played in RWC Finals.

**THE COUNTRIES**

**Abadie, A** (Pau) 1964 I

**Abadie, A** (Graulhet) 1965 R, 1967 SA 1, 3, 4, NZ, 1968 S, I

**Abadie, L** (Tarbes) 1963 R

**Accoceberry, G** (Bègles) 1994 NZ 1, 2, C 2, 1995 W, E, S, I, R 1, [Iv, S], It, 1996 I, W 1, R, Arg 1, W 2(R), SA 2, 1997 S, It 1

**Aguerre, R** (Biarritz O) 1979 S

**Aguilar, D** (Pau) 1937 G

**Aguirre, J-M** (Bagnères) 1971 A 2, 1972 S, 1973 W, I, J, R, 1974 I, W, Arg 2, R, SA 1, 1976 W (R), E, US, A 2, R, 1977 W, E, S, I, Arg 1, 2, NZ 1, 2, R, 1978 E, S, I, W, R, 1979 I, W, E, S, NZ 1, 2, R, 1980 W, I

**Ainciart, E** (Bayonne) 1933 G, 1934 G, 1935 G, 1937 G, It, 1938 G 1

**Albaladéjo, P** (Dax) 1954 E, It, 1960 W, I, It, R, 1961 S, SA, E, W, I, NZ 1, 2, A, 1962 S, E, W, I, 1963 S, I, E, W, It, 1964 S, NZ, W, It, I, SA, Fj

**Albouy, A** (Castres) 2002 It (R)

**Alvarez, A-J** (Tyrosse) 1945 B2, 1946 B, I, K, W, 1947 S, I, W, E, 1948 I, A, S, W, E, 1949 I, E, W, 1951 S, E, W

**Amand, H** (SF) 1906 NZ

**Ambert, A** (Toulouse) 1930 S, I, E, G, W

**Amestoy, J-B** (Mont-de-Marsan) 1964 NZ, E

**André, G** (RCF) 1913 SA, E, W, I, 1914 I, W, E

**Andreu, M** (Castres) 2010 W(R), It, E, SA(R), Arg2, A(R), 2013 NZ3

**Andrieu, M** (Nîmes) 1986 Arg 2, NZ 1, R 2, NZ 2, 1987 [R, Z], R, 1988 E, S, I, W, Arg 1, 2, 3, 4, R, 1989 I, W, E, S, NZ 2, B, A 2, 1990 W, E, I (R)

**Anduran, J** (SCUF) 1910 W

**Aqua, J-L** (Toulon) 1999 R, Tg, NZ 1(R)

**Araou, R** (Narbonne) 1924 R

**Arcalis, R** (Brive) 1950 S, I, 1951 I, E, W

**Arias, J** (SF) 2009 A(R), 2010 Fj

**Arino, M** (Agen) 1962 R

**Aristouy, P** (Pau) 1948 S, 1949 Arg 2, 1950 S, I, E, W

**Arlettaz, P** (Perpignan) 1995 R 2

**Armary, L** (Lourdes) 1987 [R], R, 1988 S, I, W, Arg 3, 4, R, 1989 W, S, A 1, 2, 1990 W, E, S, I, A 1, 2, 3, NZ 1, 1991 W 2, 1992 S, I, R, Arg 1, 2, SA 1, 2, Arg, , 1993 E, S, I, W, SA 1, 2, R 2, A 1, 2, 1994 I, W, NZ 1(t), 2(t), 1995 I, R 1 [Tg, I, SA]

**Arnal, J-M** (RCF) 1914 I, W

**Arnaudet, M** (Lourdes) 1964 I, 1967 It, W

**Arotca, R** (Bayonne) 1938 R

**Arrieta, J** (SF) 1953 E, W

**Arthapignet, P** (see Harislur-Arthapignet)

**Artiguste, E** (Castres) 1999 WS

**Astre, R** (Béziers) 1971 R, 1972 I 1, 1973 E (R), 1975 E, S, I, SA 1, 2, Arg 2, 1976 A 2, R

**Attoub, D** (Castres, SF) 2006 R, 2012 W, Arg 1, 2

**Aucagne, D** (Pau) 1997 W (R), S, It 1, R 1(R), A 1, R 2(R), SA 2(R), 1998 S (R), W (R), Arg 2(R), Fj (R), Arg 3, A, 1999 W 1(R), S (R)

**Audebert, A** (Montferrand) 2000 R, 2002 W (R)

**Aué, J-M** (Castres) 1998 W (R)

**Augé, J** (Dax) 1929 S, W

**Augras-Fabre, L** (Agen) 1931 I, S, W

**August, B** (Biarritz) 2007 W1(R)

**Auradou, D** (SF) 1999 E (R), S (R), WS (R), Tg, NZ 1, W 2(R), [Arg (R)], 2000 A (R), NZ 1, 2, 2001 S, I, It, W, E (R), SA 1, 2, NZ (R), SA 3, A, Fj, 2002 It, E, I (R), C (R), 2003 S (R), It (R), W (R), Arg, 1, 2, NZ (R), R (R), E 2(R), 3, [J(R), US, NZ] , 2004 I(R), It(R), S(R), E(R)

**Averous, J-L** (La Voulte) 1975 S, I, SA 1, 2, 1976 I, W, E, US, A 1, 2, R, 1977 W, E, S, I, Arg 1, R, 1978 E, S, I, 1979 NZ 1, 2, 1980 E, S, 1981 A 2

**Avril, D** (Biarritz) 2005 A1

**Azam, O** (Montferrand, Gloucester) 1995 R 2, Arg (R), 2000 A (R), NZ 2(R), 2001 SA 2(R), NZ, 2002 E (R), I (R), Arg (R), A 1

**Azarete, J-L** (Dax, St Jean-de-Luz) 1969 W, R, 1970 S, I, W, R, 1971 S, I, E, SA 1, 2, A 1, 1972 E, W, I 2, A 1, R, 1973 NZ, W, I, R, 1974 I, R, SA 1, 2, 1975 W

**Baby, B** (Toulouse, Clermont-Auvergne) 2005 I, SA2(R), A1, 2008 Arg, R, A3, 2009 I(R), S, W

**Bacqué, N** (Pau) 1997 R 2

**Bader, E** (Primevères) 1926 M, 1927 I, S

**Badin, C** (Chalon) 1973 W, I, 1975 Arg 1

**Baillette, M** (Perpignan) 1925 I, NZ, S, 1926 W, M, 1927 I, W, G 2, 1929 G, 1930 S, I, E, G, 1931 I, S, E, 1932 G

**Baladie, G** (Agen) 1945 B 1, 2, W, 1946 B, I, K

**Ballarin, J** (Tarbes) 1924 E, 1925 NZ, S

**Baquey, J** (Toulouse) 1921 I

**Barbazanges, A** (Roanne) 1932 G, 1933 G

**Barcella, F** (Auch, Biarritz) 2008 It, W, Arg, 2009 S, W, It, NZ1, 2, A, SA, NZ3, 2010 Arg1, 2011 I3(R), [J, C(t&R)], NZ1(R), Tg(R), E(R), W(R), NZ2(R)]

**Barrau, M** (Beaumont, Toulouse) 1971 S, E, W, 1972 E, W, A 1, 2, 1973 S, NZ, E, I, J, R, 1974 I, S

**Barrau, M** (Agen) 2004 US, C(R), NZ(R)

**Barrère, P** (Toulon) 1929 G, 1931 W

**Barrière, R** (Béziers) 1960 R

**Barthe, F** (SBUC) 1925 W, E

**Barthe, J** (Lourdes) 1954 Arg 1, 2, 1955 S, 1956 I, W, It, E, Cz, 1957 S, I, E, W, R 1, 2, 1958 S, E, A, W, It, I, SA 1, 2, 1959 S, E, It, W

**Basauri, R** (Albi) 1954 Arg 1

**Bascou, P** (Bayonne) 1914 E

**Basquet, G** (Agen) 1945 W, 1946 B, I, K, W, 1947 S, I, W, E, 1948 I, A, S, W, E, 1949 S, I, E, W, Arg 1, 1950 S, I, E, W, 1951 S, I, E, W, 1952 S, I, SA, W, E, It

**Bastareaud, M** (SF, Toulon) 2009 W, E, It(R), NZ1, 2010 S, I, W, It(R), E, 2013 It(R), W, E, I(t&R), S, NZ2(R), 3(t&R), Tg(t&R), SA(R), 2014 E, It, W, S, I, A2, 3

**Bastiat, J-P** (Dax) 1969 R, 1970 S, I, W, 1971 S, I, SA 2, 1972 S, A 1, 1973 E, 1974 Arg 1, 2, SA 2, 1975 W, Arg 1, 2, R, 1976 S, I, W, E, A 1, 2, R, 1977 W, E, S, I, 1978 E, S, I, W

**Baudry, N** (Montferrand) 1949 S, I, W, Arg 1, 2

**Baulon, R** (Vienne, Bayonne) 1954 S, NZ, W, E, It, 1955 I, E, W, It, 1956 S, I, W, It, E, Cz, 1957 S, I, It

**Baux, J-P** (Lannemezan) 1968 NZ 1, 2, SA 1, 2

**Bavozet, J** (Lyon) 1911 S, E, W

**Bayard, J** (Toulouse) 1923 S, W, E, 1924 W, R, US

**Bayardon, J** (Chalon) 1964 S, NZ, E

Beaurin-Gressier, C (SF) 1907 E, 1908 E
Beauxis, L (SF, Toulouse) 2007 It(R), I(R), W1(R), E1(R), S, W2, [Nm(R), I(R), Gg, NZ, E, Arg 2(R)], 2009 I, S, A, 2012 It(R), S(R), I(R), E, W
Bégu, J (Dax) 1982 Arg 2(R), 1984 E, S
Béguerie, C (Agen) 1979 NZ 1
Béguet, L (RCF) 1922 I, 1923 S, W, E, I, 1924 S, I, E, R, US
Béhotéguy, A (Bayonne, Cognac) 1923 E, 1924 S, I, E, W, R, US, 1926 E, 1927 E, G 1, 2, 1928 A, I, E, G, W, 1929 S, W, E
Béhotéguy, H (RCF, Cognac) 1923 W, 1928 A, I, E, G, W
Bélascain, C (Bayonne) 1977 R, 1978 E, S, I, W, R, 1979 I, W, E, S, 1982 W, E, S, I, 1983 E, S, I, W
Belletante, G (Nantes) 1951 I, E, W
Belot, F (Toulouse) 2000 I (R)
Ben Arous, E (Racing Métro) 2013 NZ3(R)
Benazzi, A (Agen) 1990 A 1, 2, 3, NZ 1, 2, 1991 E, US 1(R), 2, [R, Fj, C], 1992 SA 1(R), 2, Arg, 1993 E, S, I, W, A 1, 2, 1994 I, W, E, S, C 1, NZ 1, 2, C 2, 1995 W, E, S, I, [Tg, Iv, S, I, SA, E], NZ 1, 2, 1996 E, S, I, W 1, Arg 1, 2, W 2, SA 1, 2, 1997 I, W, E, S, R 1, A 1, 2, It 2, R 2(R), Arg, SA 1, 2, 1999 R, WS, W 2, [C, Nm (R), Fj, Arg, NZ 2, A], 2000 W, E, I, It (R), R, 2001 S (R), I (t&R), E
Bénésis, R (Narbonne) 1969 R, 1970 S, I, W, E, R, 1971 S, I, E, W, A 2, R, 1972 S, I 1, E, W, I 2, A 1, R, 1973 NZ, E, W, I, J, R, 1974 I, W, E, S
Benetière, J (Roanne) 1954 It, Arg 1
Benetton, P (Agen) 1989 B, 1990 NZ 2, 1991 US 2, 1992 Arg 1, 2(R), SA 1(R), 2, Arg, 1993 E, S, I, W, SA 1, 2, R 2, A 1, 2, 1994 I, W, E, S, C 1, NZ 1, 2, C 2, 1995 W, E, S, I, [Tg, Iv (R), S], It, R 2(R), Arg, NZ 1, 2, 1996 Arg 1, 2, W 2, SA 1, 2, 1997 I, It 1, 2(R), R 2, Arg, SA 1, 2 1998 E, S (R), I (R), W (R), Arg 1(R), 2(R), Fj (R), 1999 I, W 1, S (R)
Benezech, L (RCF) 1994 E, S, C 1, NZ 1, 2, C 2, 1995 W, E, [Iv, S, E], Arg, NZ 1, 2
Berbizier, P (Lourdes, Agen) 1981 S, I, W, E, NZ 1, 2, 1982 I, R, 1983 S, I, 1984 S (R), NZ 1, 2, 1985 Arg 1, 2, 1986 S, I, W, E, R 1, Arg 1, A, NZ 1, R 2, NZ 2, 3, 1987 W, E, S, I, [S, R, Fj, A, NZ], R, 1988 E, S, I, W, Arg 1, 2, 1989 I, W, E, S, NZ 1, 2, B, A 1, 1990 W, E, 1991 S, I, W 1, E
Berejnoï, J-C (Tulle) 1963 R, 1964 S, W, It, I, SA, Fj, R, 1965 S, I, E, W, It, R, 1966 S, I, E, W, It, R, 1967 S, A, E, It, W, I, R
Bergès, B (Toulouse) 1926 I
Berges-Cau, R (Lourdes) 1976 E (R)
Bergese, F (Bayonne) 1936 G 2, 1937 G, It, 1938 G 1, R, G 2
Bergougnan, Y (Toulouse) 1945 B 1, W, 1946 B, I, K, W, 1947 S, I, W, E, 1948 S, W, E, 1949 S, E, Arg 1, 2
Bernard, R (Bergerac) 1951 S, I, E, W
Bernat-Salles, P (Pau, Bègles-Bordeaux, Biarritz) 1992 Arg, 1993 R 1, SA 1, 2, R 2, A 1, 2, 1994 I, 1995 E, S, 1996 E (R), 1997 R 1, A 1, 2, 1998 E, S, I, W, Arg 1, 2, Fj, Arg 3(R), A 1999 I, W 1, R, Tg, [Nm, Fj, Arg, NZ 2, A], 2000 I, It, NZ 1(R), 2, 2001 S, I, It, W, E
Bernon, J (Lourdes) 1922 I, 1923 S
Bérot, J-L (Toulouse) 1968 NZ 3, A, 1969 S, I, 1970 E, R, 1971 S, I, E, W, SA 1, 2, A 1, 2, R, 1972 S, I 1, E, W, A 1, 1974 I
Bérot, P (Agen) 1986 R 2, NZ 2, 3, 1987 W, E, S, I, R, 1988 E, S, I, Arg 1, 2, 3, 4, R, 1989 S, NZ 1, 2
Bertrand, P (Bourg) 1951 I, E, W, 1953 S, I, E, W, It
Bertranne, R (Bagnères) 1971 E, W, SA 2, A 1, 2, 1972 S, I 1, 1973 NZ, E, J, R, 1974 I, W, E, S, Arg 1, 2, R, SA 1, 2, 1975 W, E, S, I, SA 1, 2, Arg 1, 2, 1976 S, I, W, E, US, A 1, 2, R, 1977 W, E, S, I, Arg 1, 2, NZ 1, 2, R, 1978 E, S, I, W, R, 1979 I, W, E, S, R, 1980 W, E, S, I, SA, R, 1981 S, I, W, E, R, NZ 1, 2
Berty, D (Toulouse) 1990 NZ 2, 1992 R (R), 1993 R 2, 1995 NZ 1(R), 1996 W 2(R), SA 1
Besset, E (Grenoble) 1924 S
Besset, L (SCUF) 1914 W, E
Besson, M (CASG) 1924 I, 1925 I, E, 1926 S, W, 1927 I
Besson, P (Brive) 1963 S, I, E, 1965 R, 1968 SA 1
Betsen, S (Biarritz) 1997 It 1(R), 2000 W (R), E (R), A (R), NZ 1(R), 2(R), 2001 S (R), I (R), It (R), W (R), SA 3(R), A, Fj, 2002 It, W, E, S, I, Arg, A 1, 2, SA, NZ, C, 2003 E 1, S, I, It, W, R, E 2, [Fj, J, S, I, E], 2004 I, It, W, S, E, A, Arg, NZ,

2005 E, W, I, It, 2006 SA, NZ2(R), Arg(R), 2007 It, I, W1, E1, S, E2, W2, [Arg 1, I, Gg, NZ, E]
Bianchi, J (Toulon) 1986 Arg 1
Bichindaritz, J (Biarritz O) 1954 It, Arg 1, 2
Bidabé, P (Biarritz) 2004 C, 2006 R
Bidart, L (La Rochelle) 1953 W
Biémouret, P (Agen) 1969 E, W, 1970 I, W, E, 1971 W, SA 1, 2, A 1, 1972 E, W, I 2, A 2, R, 1973 S, NZ, E, W, I
Biénès, R (Cognac) 1950 S, I, E, W, 1951 S, I, E, W, 1952 S, I, SA, W, E, It, 1953 S, I, E, 1954 S, I, NZ, W, E, Arg 1, 2, 1956 S, I, W, It, E
Bigot, C (Quillan) 1930 S, E, 1931 I, S
Bilbao, L (St Jean-de-Luz) 1978 I, 1979 I
Billac, E (Bayonne) 1920 S, E, W, I, US, 1921 S, W, 1922 W, 1923 E
Billière, M (Toulouse) 1968 NZ 3
Bioussa, A (Toulouse) 1924 W, US, 1925 I, NZ, S, E, 1926 S, I, E, 1928 E, G, W, 1929 I, S, W, E, 1930 S, I, E, G, W
Bioussa, C (Toulouse) 1913 W, I, 1914 I
Biraben, M (Dax) 1920 W, I, US, 1921 S, W, E, I, 1922 S, E, I
Blain, A (Carcassonne) 1934 G
Blanco, S (Biarritz O) 1980 SA, R, 1981 S, W, E, A 1, 2, R, NZ 1, 2, 1982 W, E, S, I, R, Arg 1, 2, 1983 E, S, I, W, 1984 I, W, E, S, NZ 1, 2, R, 1985 E, S, I, W, Arg 1, 2, 1986 S, I, W, E, R 1, Arg 2, A, NZ 1, R 2, NZ 2, 3, 1987 W, E, S, I, [S, R, Fj, A, NZ], R, 1988 E, S, I, W, Arg 1, 2, 3, 4, R, 1989 I, W, E, S, NZ 1, 2, B, A 1, 1990 E, S, I, R, A 1, 2, 3, NZ 1, 2, 1991 S, I, W, I, E, R, US 1, 2, W 2, [R, Fj, C, E]
Blond, J (SF) 1935 G, 1936 G 2, 1937 G, 1938 G 1, R, G 2
Blond, X (RCF) 1990 A 3, 1991 S, I, W 1, E, 1994 NZ 2(R)
Boffelli, V (Aurillac) 1971 A 2, R, 1972 S, I 1, 1973 J, R, 1974 I, W, E, S, Arg 1, 2, R, SA 1, 2, 1975 W, S, I
Bonal, J-M (Toulouse) 1968 E, W, Cz, NZ 2, 3, SA 1, 2, R, 1969 S, I, E, R, 1970 W, E
Bonamy, R (SB) 1928 A, I
Bondouy, P (Narbonne, Toulouse) 1997 S (R), It 1, A 2(R), R 2, 2000 R (R)
Bonetti, S (Biarritz) 2001 It, W, NZ (R)
Boniface, A (Mont-de-Marsan) 1954 I, NZ, W, E, It, Arg 1, 2, 1955 S, I, 1956 S, I, W, It, Cz, 1957 S, I, W, R 2, 1958 S, E, 1959 E, 1961 NZ 1, 3, A, R, 1962 E, W, I, It, R, 1963 S, I, E, W, It, R, 1964 S, NZ, E, W, It, 1965 W, It, R, 1966 S, I, E, W
Boniface, G (Mont-de-Marsan) 1960 W, I, It, R, Arg 1, 2, 3, 1961 S, SA, E, W, It, I, NZ 1, 2, 3, R, 1962 R, 1963 S, I, E, W, It, R, 1964 S, 1965 S, I, E, W, 1966 S, I, E, W
Bonnaire, J (Bourgoin, Clermont-Auvergne) 2004 S(t&R), A(R), NZ(R), 2005 S, E, W, I, It, SA1, 2, A1, C, Tg, SA3, 2006 S, I, It(R), E(R), W, R, SA(R), NZ1, 2, Arg, 2007 It, I(R), W1, E1, S, E2, 3(R), [Arg1(R), Nm, I, Gg, NZ, E], 2008 S(R), I, E, It(R), W, 2009 E(R), It, SA(R), Sm, NZ3, 2010 S(R), I(R), W, It, E, SA, Arg1, 2, A(R), 2011 S, I1, E(R), It, W, I2(R), 3, [J(R), C, NZ1, Tg, E, W, NZ2], 2012 It, S(R), I, E, W
Bonnes, E (Narbonne) 1924 W, R, US
Bonneval, E (Toulouse) 1984 NZ 2(R), 1985 W, Arg 1, 1986 W, E, R 1, Arg 1, 2, A, R 2, NZ 2, 3, 1987 W, E, S, I, [Z], 1988 E
Bonneval, H (SF) 2014 It, W, A, 3
Bonnus, F (Toulon) 1950 S, I, E, W
Bonnus, M (Toulon) 1937 It, 1938 G 1, R, G 2, 1940 B
Bontemps, D (La Rochelle) 1968 SA 2
Borchard, G (RCF) 1908 E, 1909 E, W, I, 1911 I
Borde, F (RCF) 1920 I, US, 1921 S, W, E, 1922 S, W, 1923 S, I, 1924 E, 1925 I, 1926 E
Bordenave, L (Toulon) 1948 A, S, W, E, 1949 S
Bory, D (Montferrand) 2000 I, It, A, NZ 1, 2001 S, I, SA 1, 2, 3, A, Fj, 2002 It, E, S, C, 2003 [US, NZ]
Boubée, J (Tarbes) 1921 S, E, I, 1922 E, W, 1923 E, I, 1925 NZ, S
Boudreaux, R (SCUF) 1910 W, S
Bouet, D (Dax) 1989 NZ 1, 2, B, A 2, 1990 A 3
Bouguyon, G (Grenoble) 1961 SA, E, W, It, I, NZ 1, 2, 3, A
Bouic, G (Agen) 1996 SA 1
Bouilhou, J (Toulouse) 2001 NZ, 2003 Arg 1
Boujet, C (Grenoble) 1968 NZ 2, A (R), SA 1
Bouquet, J (Bourgoin, Vienne) 1954 S, 1955 E, 1956 S, I, W, It, E, Cz, 1957 S, E, W, R 2, 1958 S, E, 1959 S, It, W, I, 1960 S, E, W, I, R, 1961 S, SA, E, W, It, R, 1962 S, E, W, I

1, 2, 1955 S, I, E, W, It, 1956 S, I, W, It, E, Cz 1957 S, I,
E, W, R 2, 1958 S, E, A, W, It, 1959 S, E, 1960 S, E, W, I,
R, Arg 1, 2, 3, 1961 S, SA, E, W, It, I, NZ 1, 2, 3, A, R
**Celhay, M** (Bayonne) 1935 G, 1936 G 1, 1937 G, It, 1938 G 1,
1940 B
**Cermeno, F** (Perpignan) 2000 R
**Cessieux, N** (Lyon) 1906 NZ
**Cester, E** (TOEC, Valence) 1966 S, I, E, 1967 W, 1968 S, I, E,
W, Cz, NZ 1, 3, A, SA 1, 2, R, 1969 S, I, E, W, 1970 S, I,
W, E, 1971 A 1, 1972 R, 1973 S, NZ, W, I, J, R, 1974 I,
W, E, S
**Chabal, S** (Bourgoin, Sale, Racing-Metro) 2000 S, 2001 SA 1, 2,
NZ (R), Fj (R), 2002 Arg (R), A 2, SA (R), NZ (t), C (R), 2003
E 1(R), S (R), I (R), Arg 2, NZ (R), E 2(R), 3, [J(R), US, NZ],
2005 S, E, A2(R), Tg, 2007 It, I, E1, NZ1, 2, E2(R), W2,
[Arg1(R), Nm, I, NZ(R), E(R), Arg 2(R)], 2008 A1, 2, Arg(R),
Pl(R), A3, 2009 I, S(R), W, E, It, NZ1(R), 2, SA(R), Sm, NZ3,
2010 W(R), It(R), E(R), Fj(R), Arg2, A, 2011 S(R), I1(R), E, It
**Chaban-Delmas, J** (CASG) 1945 B 2
**Chabowski, H** (Nice, Bourgoin) 1985 Arg 2, 1986 R 2, NZ 2,
1989 B (R)
**Chadebech, P** (Brive) 1982 R, Arg 1, 2, 1986 S, I
**Champ, E** (Toulon) 1985 Arg 1, 2, 1986 I, W, E, R 1, Arg 1, 2,
A, NZ 1, R 2, NZ 2, 3, 1987 W, E, S, I, [S, R, Fj, A, NZ],
R, 1988 E, S, Arg 1, 3, 4, R, 1989 W, S, A 1, 2, 1990 W,
E, NZ 1, 1991 R, US 1, [R, Fj, C, E]
**Chapuy, L** (SF) 1926 S
**Charpentier, G** (SF) 1911 E, 1912 W, E
**Charton, P** (Montferrand) 1940 B
**Charvet, D** (Toulouse) 1986 W, E, R 1, Arg 1, A, NZ 1, 3, 1987
W, E, S, I, [S, R, Z, Fj, A, NZ], R, 1989 E (R), 1990 W, E,
1991 S, I
**Chassagne, J** (Montferrand) 1938 G 1
**Chatau, A** (Bayonne) 1913 SA
**Chaud, E** (Toulon) 1932 G, 1934 G, 1935 G
**Chazalet, A** (Bourgoin) 1999 Tg
**Chenevay, C** (Grenoble) 1968 SA 1
**Chevallier, B** (Montferrand) 1952 S, I, SA, W, E, It, 1953 E, W,
It, 1954 S, I, NZ, W, Arg 1, 1955 S, I, E, W, It, 1956 S, I,
W, It, E, Cz, 1957 S
**Chiberry, J** (Chambéry) 1955 It
**Chilo, A** (SF) 1920 S, W, 1925 I, NZ
**Cholley, G** (Castres) 1975 E, S, I, SA 1, 2, Arg 1, 2, R, 1976
S, I, W, E, A 1, 2, R, 1977 W, E, S, I, Arg 1, 2, NZ 1, 2, R,
1978 E, S, I, W, R, 1979 I, S
**Chouly, D** (Brive, Perpignan, Clermont-Auvergne) 2007 NZ1(R),
2, 2009 NZ2(R), A(R), 2012 A(R), Arg3(R), Sm(R), 2013 It(R),
W(R), NZ3, 4, Tg, SA, 2014 E(R), It(R), W(R), S, I, A1, 2, 3
**Choy J** (Narbonne) 1930 S, I, E, G, W, 1931 I, 1933 G, 1934
G, 1935 G, 1936 G 2
**Cigagna, A** (Toulouse) 1995 [E]
**Cimarosti, J** (Castres) 1976 US (R)
**Cistacq, J-C** (Agen) 2000 R (R)
**Claassen, A D** (Castres) 2013 E(R), I(R), S, NZ3, 4(R), 2014 S(R)
**Clady, A** (Lezignan) 1929 G, 1931 I, S, E, G
**Clarac, H** (St Girons) 1938 G 1
**Claudel, R** (Lyon) 1932 G, 1934 G
**Clauzel, F** (Béziers) 1924 E, W, 1925 W
**Clavé, J** (Agen) 1936 G 2, 1938 R, G 2
**Claverie, H** (Lourdes) 1954 NZ, W
**Cléda, T** (Pau) 1998 E (R), S(R), I (R), W (R), Arg 1(R), Fj (R),
Arg 3(R), 1999 I (R), S
**Clément, G** (RCF) 1931 W
**Clément, J** (RCF) 1921 S, W, E, 1922 S, E, W, I, 1923 S, W, I
**Clemente, M** (Oloron) 1978 R, 1980 S, I
**Clerc, V** (Toulouse) 2002 SA, NZ, C, 2003 E 1, S, I, It (R), W
(R), Arg 2, NZ, 2004 I, It, W, 2005 SA2, Tg, 2006 SA, 2007
I, W1, E1, S, E2, W2, [Nm, I, Gg(R), NZ, E, Arg 2(R)], 2008
S, I, E, It(t), W, 2009 NZ1, 2, A(R), SA, Sm, NZ3, 2010 E(R),
I, SA, Arg(t), 2011 S(R), I1(R), E, It, W, I2, 3(R), [J, C, NZ1,
Tg, E, W, NZ2], 2012 It, S, I, E, A, Arg3, Sm, 2013 E, I, S
**Cluchague, L** (Biarritz O) 1924 S, 1925 E
**Coderc, J** (Chalon) 1932 G, 1933 G, 1934 G, 1935 G, 1936 G
1
**Codorniou, D** (Narbonne) 1979 NZ 1, 2, R, 1980 W, E, S, I,
1981 S, W, E, A 2, 1983 E, S, I, W, A 1, 2, R, 1984 I, W,
E, S, NZ 1, 2, R, 1985 E, S, I, W, Arg 1, 2

**Coeurveille, C** (Agen) 1992 Arg 1(R), 2
**Cognet, L** (Montferrand) 1932 G, 1936 G 1, 2, 1937 G, It
**Collazo, P** (Bègles) 2000 R
**Colombier, J** (St Junien) 1952 SA, W, E
**Colomine, G** (Narbonne) 1979 NZ 1
**Comba, F** (SF) 1998 Arg 1, 2, Fj, Arg 3, 1999 I, W 1, E, S, 2000
A, NZ 1, 2, 2001 S, I
**Combe, J** (SF) 1910 S, E, I, 1911 S
**Combes, G** (Fumel) 1945 B 2
**Communeau, M** (SF) 1906 NZ, E, 1907 E, 1908 E, W, 1909 E,
W, I, 1910 S, E, I, 1911 S, E, I, 1912 I, S, W, E, 1913 SA,
E, W
**Condom, J** (Boucau, Biarritz O) 1982 R, 1983 E, S, I, W, A 1,
2, R, 1984 I, W, E, S, NZ 1, 2, R, 1985 E, S, I, W, Arg 1,
2, 1986 S, I, W, E, R 1, Arg 1, 2, NZ 1, R 2, NZ 2, 3, 1987
W, E, S, I, [S, R, Z, A, NZ], R, 1988 E, S, W, Arg 1, 2, 3,
4, R, 1989 I, W, E, S, NZ 1, 2, A 1, 1990 I, R, A 2, 3(R)
**Conilh de Beyssac, J-J** (SBUC) 1912 I, S, 1914 I, W, E
**Constant, G** (Perpignan) 1920 W
**Correia, P** (Albi) 2008 A2
**Coscolla, G** (Béziers) 1921 S, W
**Costantino, J** (Montferrand) 1973 R
**Costes, A** (Montferrand) 1994 C 2, 1995 R 1, [Iv], 1997 It 1,
1999 WS, Tg (R), NZ 1, [Nm (R), Fj (R), Arg (R), NZ 2(R),
A (t&R)], 2000 S (R), I
**Costes, F** (Montferrand) 1979 E, S, NZ 1, 2, R, 1980 W, I
**Couffignal, H** (Colomiers) 1993 R 1
**Coulon, E** (Grenoble) 1928 S
**Courtiols, M** (Bègles) 1991 R, US 1, W 2
**Coux, J-F** (Bourgoin) 2007 NZ1, 2
**Couzinet, D** (Biarritz) 2004 US, C(R), 2008 A1(R)
**Crabos, R** (RCF) 1920 S, E, W, I, US, 1921 S, W, E, I, 1922 S,
E, W, I, 1923 S, I, 1924 S, I
**Crampagne, J** (Bègles) 1967 SA 4
**Crancée, R** (Lourdes) 1960 Arg 3, 1961 S
**Crauste, M** (RCF, Lourdes) 1957 R 1, 2, 1958 S, E, A, W, It, I,
1959 E, It, W, I, 1960 S, E, W, I, It, R, Arg 1, 3, 1961 S,
SA, E, W, It, I, NZ 1, 2, 3, A, R, 1962 S, E, W, I, It, R, 1963
S, I, E, W, It, R, 1964 S, NZ, E, W, It, I, SA, Fj, R, 1965 S,
I, E, W, It, R, 1966 S, I, E, W
**Cremaschi, M** (Lourdes) 1980 R, 1981 R, NZ 1, 2, 1982 W, S,
1983 A 1, 2, R, 1984 I, W
**Crenca, J-J** (Agen) 1996 SA 2(R), 1999 R, Tg, WS (R), NZ 1(R),
2001 SA 1, 2, NZ (R), SA 3, A, Fj, 2002 It, W, E, S, I, Arg,
A 2, SA, NZ, C, 2003 E 1, S, I, It, W, R, E 2, [Fj, J(t&R), S,
I, E, NZ(R)], 2004 I(R), It(R), W(R), S(R), E(R)
**Crichton, W H** (Le Havre) 1906 NZ, E
**Cristina, J** (Montferrand) 1979 R
**Cussac, P** (Biarritz O) 1934 G
**Cutzach, A** (Quillan) 1929 G

**Daguerre, F** (Biarritz O) 1936 G 1
**Daguerre, J** (CASG) 1933 G
**Dal Maso, M** (Mont-de-Marsan, Agen, Colomiers) 1988 R (R),
1990 NZ 2, 1996 SA 1(R), 2, 1997 I, W, E, S, It 1, R 1(R),
A 1, 2, It 2, Arg, NZ 1, 2, 1998 W (R), Arg 1(t), Fj (R), 1999
R (R), WS (R), Tg, NZ 1(R), W 2(R), [Nm (R), Fj (R), Arg (R),
A (R)], 2000 W, E, S, I, It
**Danion, J** (Toulon) 1924 I
**Danos, P** (Toulon, Béziers) 1954 Arg 1, 2, 1957 R 2, 1958 S,
E, W, It, I, SA 1, 2, 1959 S, E, It, W, I, 1960 S, E
**Dantiacq, D** (Pau) 1997 R 1
**Darbos, P** (Dax) 1969 R
**Darracq, R** (Dax) 1957 It
**Darrieussecq, A** (Biarritz O) 1973 E
**Darrieussecq, J** (Mont-de-Marsan) 1953 It
**Darrouy, C** (Mont-de-Marsan) 1957 I, E, W, It, R 1, 1959 E,
1961 R, 1963 S, I, E, W, It, 1964 NZ, E, W, It, I, SA, Fj, R,
1965 S, I, E, It, W, R, 1966 S, I, E, W, It, R, 1967 S, A, E, It,
W, I, SA 1, 2, 4
**Daudé, J** (Bourgoin) 2000 S
**Daudignon, G** (SF) 1928 S
**Dauga, B** (Mont-de-Marsan) 1964 S, NZ, E, W, It, I, SA, Fj, R,
1965 S, I, E, W, It, R, 1966 S, I, E, W, It, R, 1967 S, A, E,
It, W, I, SA 1, 2, 3, 4, NZ, R, 1968 S, I, NZ 1, 2, 3, A, SA
1, 2, R, 1969 S, I, E, R, 1970 S, I, W, E, R, 1971 S, I, E,
W, SA 1, 2, A 1, 2, R, 1972 S, I 1, W

**Dauger, J** (Bayonne) 1945 B 1, 2, 1953 S
**Daulouède, P** (Tyrosse) 1937 G, It, 1938 G 1, 1940 B
**David, Y** (Bourgoin, Toulouse) 2008 It, 2009 SA, Sm(R), NZ3(R)
**Debaty, V** (Perpignan, Clermont-Auvergne) 2006 R(R), 2012 It,
S(R), I(R), E(R), W(R), Arg 1(R), 2, A(R), Arg3(R), Sm(R), 2013
It(R), W(R), E(R), I(R), S(R), NZ1(R), 2(R), 4(R), Tg(R), 2014
W(t), S(R), I(R), A1(R), 3(R)
**De Besombes, S** (Perpignan) 1998 Arg 1(R), Fj (R)
**Decamps, P** (RCF) 1911 S
**Dedet, J** (SF) 1910 S, E, I, 1911 W, I, 1912 S, 1913 E, I
**Dedeyn, P** (RCF) 1906 NZ
**Dedieu, P** (Béziers) 1963 E, It, 1964 W, It, I, SA, Fj, R, 1965
S, I, E, W
**De Gregorio, J** (Grenoble) 1960 S, E, W, I, It, R, Arg 1, 2, 1961
S, SA, E, W, It, I, 1962 S, E, W, 1963 S, W, 1964 NZ,
E
**Dehez, J-L** (Agen) 1967 SA 2, 1969 R
**De Jouvencel, E** (SF) 1909 W, I
**De Laborderie, M** (RCF) 1921 I, 1922 I, 1925 W, E
**Delage, C** (Agen) 1983 S, I
**De Malherbe, H** (CASG) 1932 G, 1933 G
**De Malmann, R** (RCF) 1908 E, W, 1909 E, W, I, 1910 E, I
**De Muizon, J J** (SF) 1910 I
**Delaigue, G** (Toulon) 1973 J, R
**Delaigue, Y** (Toulon, Toulouse, Castres) 1994 S, NZ 2(R), C 2,
1995 I, R 1, [Tg, Iv], It, R 2(R), 1997 It 1, 2003 Arg 1, 2,
2005 S, E, W, I, It, A2(R), Tg, SA3(R)
**Delmotte, G** (Toulon) 1999 R, Tg
**Delque, A** (Toulouse) 1937 It, 1938 G 1, R, G 2
**De Rougemont, M** (Toulon) 1995 E (t), R 1(t), [Iv], NZ 1, 2, 1996
I (R), Arg 1, 2, W 2, SA 1, 1997 E (R), S (R), It 1
**Desbrosse, C** (Toulouse) 1999 [Nm (R)], 2000 I
**Descamps, P** (SB) 1927 G 2
**Desclaux, F** (RCF) 1949 Arg 1, 2, 1953 It
**Desclaux, J** (Perpignan) 1934 G, 1935 G, 1936 G 1, 2, 1937
G, It, 1938 G 1, R, G 2, 1945 B 1
**Deslandes, C** (RCF) 1990 A 1, NZ 2, 1991 W 1, 1992 R, Arg
1, 2
**Desnoyer, L** (Brive) 1974 R
**Destarac, L** (Tarbes) 1926 S, I, E, W, M, 1927 W, E, G 1, 2
**Desvouges, R** (SF) 1914 W
**Detrez, P-E** (Nîmes) 1983 A 2(R), 1986 Arg 1(R), 2, A (R), NZ1
**Devergie, T** (Nîmes) 1988 R, 1989 NZ 1, 2, B, A 2, 1990 W, E,
S, I, R, A 1, 2, 3, 1991 US 2, W 2, 1992 R (R), Arg 2(R)
**De Villiers, P** (SF) 1999 W 2, [Arg (R), NZ 2(R), A (R)], 2000 W
(R), E (R), S (R), I (R), It (R), NZ 1(R), 2, 2001 S, I, It, W, E,
SA 1, 2, NZ (R), SA 3, A, Fj, 2002 It, W, E, I, SA, NZ, C,
2003 Arg 1, 2, NZ (R), 2004 I, It, W, S, E, US, C, NZ, 2005
S, I(R), It(R), SA1(R), 2, A1(R), 2, C, Tg(R), SA3, 2006 S, I,
It, E, W, SA, NZ1, 2, Arg, 2007 It, I, E1, S, W2, [Arg1, Nm,
I, NZ, E]
**Deygas, M** (Vienne) 1937 It
**Deylaud, C** (Toulouse) 1992 R, Arg 1, 2, SA 1, 1994 C 1, NZ
1, 2, 1995 W, E, S, [Iv (R), S, I, SA], It, Arg
**Diarra, I** (Montauban) 2008 It
**Dintrans, P** (Tarbes) 1979 NZ 1, 2, R, 1980 E, S, I, SA, R, 1981
S, I, W, E, A 1, 2, R, NZ 1, 2, 1982 W, E, S, I, R, Arg 1, 2,
1983 E, W, A 1, 2, R, 1984 I, W, E, S, NZ 1, 2, R, 1985 E,
S, I, W, Arg 1, 2, 1987 [R], 1988 Arg 1, 2, 3, 1989 W, E,
S, 1990 R
**Dispagne, S** (Toulouse) 1996 I (R), W 1
**Dizabo, P** (Tyrosse) 1948 A, S, E, 1949 S, I, E, W, Arg 2, 1950
S, I, 1960 Arg 1, 2, 3
**Domec, A** (Carcassonne) 1929 W
**Domec, H** (Lourdes) 1953 W, It, 1954 S, I, NZ, W, E, It, 1955
S, I, E, W, 1956 I, W, It, 1958 E, A, W, It, I
**Domenech, A** (Vichy, Brive) 1954 W, E, It, 1955 S, I, E, W, 1956
S, I, W, It, E, Cz, 1957 S, I, E, W, It, R 1, 2, 1958 S, E, It,
1959 It, 1960 S, E, W, I, It, R, Arg 1, 2, 3, 1961 S, SA, E,
W, It, I, NZ 1, 2, 3, A, R, 1962 S, E, W, I, It, R, 1963 W, It
**Domercq, J** (Bayonne) 1912 I, S
**Domingo, T** (Clermont-Auvergne) 2009 W(R), E(R), It(R), NZ2(R),
Sm, 2010 S, I, W, It, E, SA, Arg2, A, 2011 S, I1, E, W, 2012
Arg 2(R), A(R), Arg3(R), Sm, 2013 E, I, S, NZ1, 2, 3, SA(R),
2014 E, It, W, S, I, A1, 2(R), 3(R)
**Dominici, C** (SF) 1998 E, S, Arg 1, 2, 1999 E, S, WS, NZ 1, W
2, [C, Fj, Arg, NZ 2, A], 2000 W, E, S, R, 2001 I (R), It, W,

E, SA 1, 2, NZ, Fj, 2003 Arg 1, R, E 2, 3, [Fj, J, S, I, E],
2004 I, It, W, S, E, A(R), NZ(R), 2005 S, E, W, I, It, 2006
S, I, It, E, W, NZ1, 2(R), Arg, 2007 It, I, W1, E1, S(R), E3,
W2(R), [Arg 1, Gg, NZ(R), E(R), Arg 2]
**Dorot, J** (RCF) 1935 G
**Dospital, P** (Bayonne) 1977 R, 1980 I, 1981 S, I, W, E, 1982 I,
R, Arg 1, 2, 1983 E, S, I, W, 1984 E, S, NZ 1, 2, R, 1985
E, S, I, W, Arg 1
**Dourthe, C** (Dax) 1966 R, 1967 S, A, E, W, I, SA 1, 2, 3, NZ,
1968 W, NZ 3, SA 1, 2, 1969 W, 1971 SA 2(R), R, 1972 I
1, 2, A, 1, 2, R, 1973 S, NZ, E, 1974 I, Arg 1, 2, SA 1, 2,
1975 W, E, S
**Dourthe, M** (Dax) 2000 NZ 2(t)
**Dourthe, R** (Dax, SF, Béziers) 1995 R 2, Arg, NZ 1 2, 1996 E,
R, 1996 Arg 1, 2, W 2, SA 1, 2, 1997 W, A 1, 1999 I, W
1, 2, [C, Nm, Fj, Arg, NZ 2, A], 2000 W, E, It, R, A, NZ 1,
2, 2001 S, I
**Doussain, J-M** (Toulouse) 2011 [NZ2(R)], 2013 NZ1(R), 3, 4(R),
SA(R), 2014 E, It, W, S(R), I(R)
**Doussau, E** (Angoulême) 1938 R
**Droitecourt, M** (Montferrand) 1972 R, 1973 NZ (R), E, 1974 E,
S, Arg 1, SA 2, 1975 SA 1, 2, Arg 1, 2, R, 1976 S, I, W, A
1, 1977 Arg 2
**Dubertrand, A** (Montferrand) 1971 A 1, 2, R, 1972 I 2, 1974 I,
W, E, SA 2, 1975 Arg 1, 2, R, 1976 S, US
**Dubois, D** (Bègles) 1971 S
**Dubroca, D** (Agen) 1979 NZ 2, 1981 NZ 2(R), 1982 E, S, 1984
W, E, S, 1985 Arg 2, 1986 S, I, W, E, R 1, Arg 2, A, NZ 1,
R 2, NZ 2, 3, 1987 W, E, S, I, [S, Z, Fj, A, NZ], R, 1988 E,
S, I, W
**Ducalcon, L** (Castres, Racing Métro) 2010 S(R), Fj, Arg2(R),
2011 S(R), It(R), W(R), I2, [C, NZ1, Tg], 2013 It(R), W(R),
E(R), S(R), NZ1, 2(R), 3(R)
**Duché, A** (Limoges) 1929 G
**Duclos, A** (Lourdes) 1931 S
**Ducousso, J** (Tarbes) 1925 S, W, E
**Dufau, G** (RCF) 1948 I, A, 1949 I, W, 1950 S, E, W, 1951 S, I,
E, W, 1952 SA, W, 1953 S, I, E, W, 1954 S, I, NZ, W, E,
It, 1955 S, I, E, W, It, 1956 S, I, W, It, 1957 S, I, E, W, It,
R 1
**Dufau, J** (Biarritz) 1912 I, S, W, E
**Duffaut, Y** (Agen) 1954 Arg 1, 2
**Duffour, R** (Tarbes) 1911 W
**Dufourcq, J** (SBUC) 1906 NZ, E, 1907 E, 1908 W
**Duhard, Y** (Bagnères) 1980 E
**Duhau, J** (SF) 1928 I, 1930 I, G, 1931 I, S, W, 1933 G
**Dulaurens, C** (Toulouse) 1926 I, 1928 S, 1929 W
**Dulin, B** (Agen, Castres) 2012 Arg 1, 2, A, Arg3, Sm, 2013
NZ2(R), 3, 4, Tg, SA, 2014 E, It, W, S, I, A1(R), 2, 3
**Duluc, A** (Béziers) 1934 G
**Du Manoir, Y le P** (RCF) 1925 I, NZ, S, W, E, 1926 S, 1927 I, S
S, 1927 E, G 1, 2, 1928 A, G, W, 1929 I
**Dupont, C** (Lourdes) 1923 S, W, I, 1924 S, I, W, R, US, 1925
S, 1927 E, G 1, 2, 1928 A, G, W, 1929 I
**Dupont, J-L** (Agen) 1983 S
**Dupont, L** (RCF) 1934 G, 1935 G, 1936 G 1, 2, 1938 R, G 2
**Dupouy, A** (SB) 1924 W, R
**Duprat, B** (Bayonne) 1966 E, W, It, R, 1967 S, A, E, SA 2, 3,
1968 S, I, 1972 E, W, I 2, A 1
**Dupré, P** (RCF) 1909 W
**Dupuy, J** (Leicester, SF) 2009 NZ1, 2, A(R), SA, Sm(R), NZ3,
2012 S(R), I(R)
**Dupuy, J-V** (Tarbes) 1956 S, I, W, It, E, Cz, 1957 S, I, E, W, It,
R 2, 1958 S, E, SA 1, 2, 1959 S, E, It, W, I, 1960 W, I, It,
Arg 1, 3, 1961 S, SA, E, NZ 2, R, 1962 S, E, W, I, It, 1963
W, It, R, 1964 S
**Durand, N** (Perpignan) 2007 NZ1, 2
**Dusautoir, T** (Biarritz, Toulouse) 2006 R, SA, NZ1, 2007 E3,
W2(R), [Nm, I, NZ, E, Arg 2], 2008 S, I, E, W, Arg, PI, A3,
2009 I, S, W, E, It, NZ1, 2, A, SA, Sm, NZ3, 2010 S, I, W,
It, E, SA, Arg1, 2, A, 2011 S, I1, E, It, W, I2, [J, NZ1, Tg,
E, W, NZ2], 2012 It, S, I, E, W, 2013 It, W, E, I, S, NZ1, 2,
A, W2, 2014 A2, 3
**Du Souich, C J** (see Judas du Souich)
**Dutin, B** (Mont-de-Marsan) 1968 NZ 2, A, SA 2, R
**Dutour, F X** (Toulouse) 1911 E, I, 1912 S, W, E, 1913 S
**Dutrain, H** (Toulouse) 1945 W, 1946 B, I, 1947 S, I, E, W,
Arg 1

Dutrey, J (Lourdes) 1940 B
Duval, R (SF) 1908 E, W, 1909 E, 1911 E, W, I

Echavé, L (Agen) 1961 S
Elhorga, P (Agen) 2001 NZ, 2002 A 1, 2, 2003 Arg 2, NZ (R), R, [Fj(R), US, I(R), NZ], 2004 I(R), It(R), S, E, 2005 S, E, 2006 NZ2, Arg, 2008 A1
Elissalde, E (Bayonne) 1936 G 2, 1940 B
Elissalde, J-B (La Rochelle, Toulouse) 2000 S (R), R (R), 2003 It (R), W (R), 2004 I, It, W, A, Arg, 2005 SA1, 2(R), A1, 2, SA3, 2006 S, I, It, W(R), NZ1(R), 2, 2007 E2(R), 3, W2(R), [Arg 1(R), Nm, I, Gg(R), NZ, E, Arg 2], 2008 S, I, W, Arg, PI
Elissalde, J-P (La Rochelle) 1980 SA, R, 1981 A 1, 2, R
Empereur-Buisson, H (Béziers) 1931 E, G
Erbani, D (Agen) 1981 A 1, 2, NZ 1, 2, 1982 Arg 1, 2, 1983 S (R), I, W, A 1, 2, R, 1984 W, E, R, 1985 E, W (R), Arg 2, 1986 S, I, W, E, R 1, Arg 2, NZ 1, 2(R), 3, 1987 W, E, S, I, [S, R, Fj, A, NZ], 1988 E, S, 1989 I (R), W, E, S, NZ 1 A 2, 1990 W, E
Escaffre, P (Narbonne) 1933 G, 1934 G
Escommier, M (Montelimar) 1955 It
Esponda, J-M (RCF) 1967 SA 1, 2, R, 1968 NZ 1, 2, SA 2, R, 1969 S, I (R), E
Estebanez, F (Brive, Racing Metro) 2010 Fj, Arg2(R), A(R), 2011 W(R), I3, [J, NZ1(R), Tg(R)]
Estève, A (Béziers) 1971 SA 1, 1972 I 1, E, W, I 2, A 2, R, 1973 S, NZ, E, I, 1974 I, W, E, S, R, SA 1, 2, 1975 W, E
Estève, P (Narbonne, Lavelanet) 1982 R, Arg 1, 2, 1983 E, S, I, W, A 1, 2, R, 1984 I, W, E, S, NZ 1, 2, R, 1985 E, S, I, W, 1986 S, I, 1987 [S, Z]
Etcheberry, J (Rochefort, Cognac) 1923 W, I, 1924 S, I, E, W, R, US, 1926 S, I, E, M, 1927 I, S, W, G 2
Etchenique, J-M (Biarritz O) 1974 R, SA 1, 1975 E, Arg 2
Etchepare, A (Bayonne) 1922 I
Etcheverry, M (Pau) 1971 S, I
Eutrope, A (SCUF) 1913 I

Fabre, E (Toulouse) 1937 It, 1938 G 1, 2
Fabre, J (Toulouse) 1963 S, I, E, W, It, 1964 S, NZ, E
Fabre, L (Lezignan) 1930 G
Fabre, M (Béziers) 1981 A 1, R, NZ 1, 2, 1982 I, R
Failliot, P (RCF) 1911 S, W, I, 1912 I, S, E, 1913 E, W
Fall, B (Bayonne, Racing Métro) 2009 Sm, 2010 S, 2012 Arg 2, 2013 It, W, E
Fargues, G (Dax) 1923 I
Fauré, F (Tarbes) 1914 I, W, E
Faure, L (Sale) 2008 S, I, E, A1, PI, A3, 2009 I, E
Fauvel, J-P (Tulle) 1980 R
Favre, M (Lyon) 1913 E, W
Ferrand, L (Chalon) 1940 B
Ferrien, R (Tarbes) 1950 S, I, E, W
Fickou, G (Toulouse) 2013 S(R), NZ4(R), Tg, 2014 E(R), It(R), W(R), S(R), I, A1
Finat, R (CASG) 1932 G, 1933 G
Fite, R (Brive) 1963 W, It
Flanquart, A (SF) 2013 NZ1(R), 3, 2014 E, S(R), I(R), A1(R), 2, 3
Floch, A (Clermont-Auvergne) 2008 E(R), It, W
Fofana, W (Clermont-Auvergne) 2012 It, S, I, E, W, Arg 1, 2(R), A, Arg3, Sm, 2013 It, W, E, I, S, NZ1, 2, 3, 4, Tg, SA, 2014 E, It, W, A1, 2, 3
Forest, M (Bourgoin) 2007 NZ1(R), 2(R)
Forestier, J (SCUF) 1912 W
Forestier, Y (Castres) 2012 A, Arg3, Sm(R), 2013 It, W, NZ4, Tg, SA, 2014 E(R), It(R), W(R)
Forgues (Bayonne) 1911 S, E, W, 1912 I, W, E, 1913 S, SA, W, 1914 I, E
Fort, J (Agen) 1967 It, W, I, SA 1, 2, 3, 4
Fourcade, G (BEC) 1909 E, W
Foures, H (Toulouse) 1951 S, I, E, W
Fournet, F (Montferrand) 1950 W
Fouroux, J (La Voulte) 1972 I 2, R, 1974 W, E, Arg 1, 2, R, SA 1, 2, 1975 W, Arg 1, R, 1976 S, I, W, E, US, A 1, 1977 W, E, S, I, Arg 1, 2, NZ 1, 2, R
Francquenelle, A (Vaugirard) 1911 S, 1913 W, I
Fritz, F (Toulouse) 2005 SA1, A2, SA3, 2006 S, I, It, E, W, SA,

NZ1, 2, Arg, 2007 It, 2009 I, E(R), It, NZ2(R), A, 2010 Arg1, 2012 W, Arg 1, 2, A, Arg3, Sm, 2013 It, W(R), E(R), I, NZ1, 2, 3, 4, SA **327**
Froment, R (Castres) 2004 US(R)
Furcade, R (Perpignan) 1952 S

Gabernet, S (Toulouse) 1980 E, S, 1981 S, I, W, E, A 1, 2, R, NZ 1, 2, 1982 I, 1983 A 2, R
Gachassin, J (Lourdes) 1961 S, I, 1963 R, 1964 S, NZ, E, W, It, I, SA, Fj, R, 1965 S, I, E, W, It, R, 1966 S, I, E, W, 1967 S, A, It, W, I, NZ, 1968 I, E, 1969 S, I
Galasso, A (Toulon, Montferrand) 2000 R (R), 2001 E (R)
Galau, H (Toulouse) 1924 S, I, E, W, US
Galia, J (Quillan) 1927 E, G 1, 2, 1928 S, A, I, E, W, 1929 I, E, G, 1930 S, I, E, G, W, 1931 S, W, E, G
Gallart, P (Béziers) 1990 R, A 1, 2(R), 3, 1992 S, I, R, Arg 1, 2, SA 1, 2, Arg 1994 I, W, E, 1995 I (t), R 1, [Tg]
Gallion, J (Toulon) 1978 E, S, I, W, 1979 I, W, E, S, NZ 2, R, 1980 W, E, S, I, 1983 A 1, 2, R, 1984 I, W, E, S, R, 1985 E, S, I, W, 1986 Arg 2
Galthié, F (Colomiers, SF) 1991 R, US 1, [R, Fj, C, E], 1992 W, E, S, R, Arg, 1994 I, W, E, 1995 [SA, E], 1996 W 1(R), 1997 I, It 2, SA 1, 2, 1998 W (R), Fj (R), 1999 R, WS (R), Tg, NZ 1(R), [Fj (R), Arg, NZ 2, A], 2000 W, E, A, NZ 1, 2, 2001 S, It, W, E, SA 1, 2, NZ, SA 3, A, Fj, 2002 E, S, I, SA, NZ, C, 2003 E 1, S, Arg 1, 2, NZ, R, E 2, [Fj, J, S, E]
Galy, J (Perpignan) 1953 W
Garbajosa, X (Toulouse) 1998 I, W, Arg 2(R), Fj, 1999 W 1(R), E, S, WS, NZ 1, W 2, [C, Nm (R), Fj (R), Arg, NZ 2, A], 2000 A, NZ 1, 2, 2001 S, I, E, 2002 It (R), W, SA (R), C (R), 2003 E 1, S, I, It, W, E 3
Garuet-Lempirou, J-P (Lourdes) 1983 A 1, 2, R, 1984 I, NZ 1, 2, R, 1985 E, S, I, W, Arg 1, 1986 S, I, W, E, R 1, Arg 1, NZ 1 R 2, NZ 2, 3, 1987 W, E, S, I, [S, R, Fj, A, NZ], 1988 E, S, Arg 1, 2, R, 1989 E (R), S, NZ 1, 2, 1990 W, E
Gasc, J (Graulhet) 1977 NZ 2
Gasparotto, G (Montferrand) 1976 A 2, R
Gauby, G (Perpignan) 1956 Cz
Gaudermen, P (RCF) 1906 E
Gayraud, W (Toulouse) 1920 I
Gelez, F (Agen) 2001 SA 3, 2002 I (R), A 1, SA, NZ, C (R), 2003 S, I
Geneste, R (BEC) 1945 B 1, 1949 Arg 2
Genet, J-P (RCF) 1992 S, I, R
Gensane, R (Béziers) 1962 S, E, W, I, It, R, 1963 S
Gérald, G (RCF) 1927 E, G 2, 1928 S, 1929 I, S, W, E, G, 1930 S, I, E, G, W, 1931 I, S, E, G
Gérard, D (Bègles) 1999 Tg
Gérintes, G (CASG) 1924 R, 1925 I, 1926 W
Geschwind, P (RCF) 1936 G 1, 2
Giacardy, M (SBUC) 1907 E
Gimbert, P (Bègles) 1991 R, US 1, 1992 W, E
Giordani, P (Dax) 1999 E, S
Glas, S (Bourgoin) 1996 S (t), I (R), W 1, R, Arg 2(R), W 2, SA 1, 2, 1997 I, W, It, S, It 2(R), R 2, Arg, SA 1, 2, 1998 E, S, I, W, Arg 1, 2, Fj, Arg 3, A, 1999 W 2, [C, Nm, Arg (R), NZ 2(R), A (t&R)], 2000 I, 2001 E, SA 1, 2, NZ
Gomès, A (SF) 1998 Arg 1, 2, Fj, Arg 3, A, 1999 I (R)
Gommes, J (RCF) 1909 I
Gonnet, C-A (Albi) 1921 E, I, 1922 E, W, 1924 S, E, 1926 S, I, E, W, M, 1927 I, S, W, E, G 1
Gonzalez, J-M (Bayonne) 1992 Arg 1, 2, SA 1, 2, Arg, 1993 R 1, SA 1, 2, R 2, A 1, 2, 1994 I, W, E, S, C 1, NZ 1, 2, C 2, 1995 W, E, S, I, R 1, [Tg, S, I, SA, E], It, Arg, 1996 E, S, I, W 1
Got, R (Perpignan) 1920 I, US, 1921 S, W, 1922 S, E, W, I, 1924 I, E, W, R, US
Gourdon, J-F (RCF, Bagnères) 1974 S, Arg 1, 2, R, SA 1, 2, 1975 W, E, I, S, R, 1976 S, I, W, E, 1978 E, S, 1979 W, E, S, R, 1980 I
Gourragne, J-F (Béziers) 1990 NZ 2, 1991 W 1
Goutta, B (Perpignan) 2004 C
Goyard, A (Lyon U) 1936 G 1, 2, 1937 G, It, 1938 G 1, R, G 2
Graciet, R (SBUC) 1926 I, W, 1927 S, G 1, 1929 E, 1930 W
Grandclaude, J-P (Perpignan) 2005 E(R), W(R), 2007 NZ1

**329**

FRANCE

**Lubrano, A** (Béziers) 1972 A 2, 1973 S
**Lux, J-P** (Tyrosse, Dax) 1967 E, It, W, I, SA 1, 2, 4, R, 1968 I, E, Cz, NZ 3, A, SA 1, 2, 1969 S, I, E, 1970 S, I, W, E, R, 1971 S, I, E, W, A 1, 2, 1972 S, I 1, E, W, I 2, A 1, 2, R, 1973 S, NZ, E, 1974 I, W, E, S, Arg 1, 2, 1975 W

**Macabiau, A** (Perpignan) 1994 S, C 1
**Mach, B** (Castres) 2014 W(R), S, A2(R)
**Machenaud, M** (Agen, Racing Métro) 2012 Arg 2, A, Arg3, Sm(R), 2013 It, W, E(R), S(R), NZ1, 2, 3(R), 2014 E(R), It(R), W(R), S, I, A1, 3
**Maclos, P** (SF) 1906 E, 1907 E
**Maestri, Y** (Toulouse) 2012 It(R), S, I, E, W, Arg 1, 2, 3, Sm, 2013 It, W, E, I, S, NZ1, 2, 3, 4, Tg, SA, 2014 E(R), It, W, S, I, A1, 2, 3
**Magne, O** (Dax, Brive, Montferrand, Clermont-Auvergne, London Irish) 1997 W (R), E, S, R 1(R), A 1, 2, It 2(R), R 2, Arg (R), 1998 E, S, I, W, Arg 1, 2, Fj, Arg 3, A, 1999 I, R, WS, NZ 1, W 2, [C, Nm, Fj, Arg, NZ 2, A], 2000 W, E, S, It, R, A, NZ 1, 2, 2001 S, I, It, W, E, SA 1, 2, NZ, SA 3, A, Fj, 2002 It, E, S, I, Arg, A 1, 2(R), SA, NZ, C, 2003 E 1, S, I, It, W, R, E 2, 3(R), [Fj, J, S, I, E, NZ(R)], 2004 I, It, W(R), S, E, A, Arg, NZ, 2005 SA1, 2(R), A1, 2006 I, It, E, W(R), 2007 NZ1, 2
**Magnanou, C** (RCF) 1923 E, 1925 W, E, 1926 S, 1929 S, W, 1930 S, I, E, W
**Magnol, L** (Toulouse) 1928 S, 1929 S, W, E
**Magois, H** (La Rochelle) 1968 SA 1, 2, R
**Majérus, R** (SF) 1928 W, 1929 I, S, 1930 S, I, E, G, W
**Malbet, J-C** (Agen) 1967 SA 2, 4
**Maleig, A** (Oloron) 1979 W, E, NZ 2, 1980 W, E, SA, R
**Mallier, L** (Brive) 1999 R, W 2(R), [C (R)], 2000 I (R), It
**Malquier, Y** (Narbonne) 1979 S
**Malzieu, J** (Clermont-Auvergne) 2008 S, It, W, Arg, PI, A3, 2009 I, S(R), W, E, It(R), 2010 I(R), W, It(R), E(R), Arg1, 2012 It, S, I, E
**Manterola, T** (Lourdes) 1955 It, 1957 R 1
**Mantoulan, C** (Pau) 1959 I
**Marcet, J** (Albi) 1925 I, NZ, S, W, E, 1926 I, E
**Marchal, J-F** (Castres) 1979 S, R, 1980 W, S, I
**Marconnet, S** (SF, Biarritz) 1998 Arg 3, A, 1999 I (R), W 1(R), E, S (R), R, Tg, 2000 A, NZ 1, 2, 2001 S, I, It (R), W (R), E, 2002 S (R), Arg (R), A 1, 2, SA (R), C (R), 2003 E1(R), S, I, It, W, Arg 1(t+R), 2, NZ, R, E 2, 3(t+R), [S, US(R), I, E, NZ], 2004 I, It, W, S, E, A, Arg, NZ, 2005 S, E, W, I, It, SA1, 2, A1(R), 2(R), C, Tg, SA3(R), 2006 S, I(R), It(R), E, W, R, SA, NZ1, 2(R), Arg(R), 2007 It(R), I, W1(R), 2009 W, E, It, NZ1, A, SA(R), Sm, NZ3, 2010 I(R), 2011 I1(R), E(R), It, I2
**Marchand, R** (Poitiers) 1920 S, W
**Marfaing, M** (Toulouse) 1992 R, Arg 1
**Marlu, J** (Montferrand, Biarritz) 1998 Fj (R), 2002 S (R), I (R), 2005 E
**Marocco, P** (Montferrand) 1968 S, I, W, E, R 1, Arg 1, 2, A, 1988 Arg 4, 1989 I, 1990 E (R), NZ 1(R), 1991 S, I, W 1, E, US 2, [R, Fj, C, E]
**Marot, A** (Brive) 1969 R, 1970 S, I, W, 1971 SA 1, 1972 I 2, 1976 A 1
**Marquesuzaa, A** (RCF) 1958 It, SA 1, 2, 1959 S, E, It, W, 1960 S, E, Arg 1
**Marracq, H** (Pau) 1961 R
**Marsh, T** (Montferrand) 2001 SA 3, A, Fj, 2002 It, W, E, S, I, Arg, A 1, 2, 2003 [Fj, J, S, I, E, NZ], 2004 C, A, Arg, NZ
**Martin, C** (Lyon) 1909 I, 1910 W, S
**Martin, H** (SBUC) 1907 E, 1908 W
**Martin, J-L** (Béziers) 1971 A 2, R, 1972 S, I 1
**Martin, L** (Pau) 1948 I, A, S, W, E, 1950 S
**Martin, R** (SF, Bayonne) 2002 E (t+R), S (R), I (R), 2005 SA1(t&R), 2, A1, 2, C, SA3, 2006 S, I(t&R), R, SA(R), NZ1(R), 2, Arg, 2007 E2, W2, [Arg 1, Gg(R), Arg 2(R)], 2009 NZ2(R), A(R)
**Martine, R** (Lourdes) 1952 S, I, It, 1953 It, 1954 S, I, NZ, W, E, It, Arg 2, 1955 S, I, W, 1958 A, W, It, I, SA 1, 2, 1960 S, E, Arg 3, 1961 S, It
**Martinez, A** (Narbonne) 2002 A 1, 2004 C
**Martinez, G** (Toulouse) 1982 W, E, S, Arg 1, 2, 1983 E, W
**Marty, D** (Perpignan) 2005 It, C, Tg, 2006 I, It(R), R(R), NZ1(R), Arg(R), 2007 I, W1, E1, S, E2, [Nm, I, Gg, NZ, E, Arg 2],

2008 S, I, E, 2009 SA(R), Sm, NZ3, 2010 S(R), I(R), W(R), It, E(R), SA, Fj, 2011 W, I2, [J(R), C, E(R)]
**Mas, F** (Béziers) 1962 R, 1963 S, I, E, W
**Mas, N** (Perpignan, Montpellier) 2003 NZ, 2005 E, W, I, It, 2007 W1, NZ1, 2(R), E2(R), 3(R), W2, [Nm(R), Gg(R), Arg 2], 2008 S(R), I, E, It, W, Arg(R), PI, A3, 2009 I(R), S, NZ1(R), 2, A(R), SA, Sm(R), NZ3(R), 2010 S, I, W, It, E, SA, Arg1, 2, A, 2011 S, I1, E, It, W, I3, [J, E, W, NZ2], 2012 It, S, I, E, A, Arg3, Sm, 2013 It, W, E, I, S, NZ2, 3, 4, Tg, SA, 2014 E, It, W, S, I, A1, 2(R)
**Maso, J** (Perpignan, Narbonne) 1966 It, R, 1967 S, R, 1968 S, W, Cz, NZ 1, 2, 3, A, R, 1969 S, I, W, 1971 SA 1, 2, R, 1972 E, W, A 2, 1973 W, I, J, R
**Massare, J** (PUC) 1945 B 1, 2, W, 1946 B, I, W
**Massé, A** (SBUC) 1908 W, 1909 E, W, 1910 W, S, E, I
**Masse, H** (Grenoble) 1937 G
**Matheu-Cambas, J** (Agen) 1945 W, 1946 B, I, K, W, 1947 S, I, W, E, 1948 I, A, S, W, E, 1949 S, I, E, W, Arg 1, 2, 1950 E, W, 1951 S, I
**Matiu, L** (Biarritz) 2000 W, E
**Mauduy, G** (Périgueux) 1957 It, R 1, 2, 1958 S, E, 1961 W, It
**Mauran, J** (Castres) 1952 SA, W, E, It, 1953 I, E
**Mauriat, P** (Lyon) 1907 E, 1908 E, W, 1909 W, I, 1910 W, S, E, I, 1911 S, E, W, I, 1912 I, S, 1913 S, SA, W, I
**Maurin, G** (ASF) 1906 E
**Maury, A** (Toulouse) 1925 I, NZ, S, W, E, 1926 S, I, E
**Mayssonnié, A** (Toulouse) 1908 E, W, 1910 W
**Mazars, L** (Narbonne, Bayonne) 2007 NZ2, 2010 Arg1
**Mazas, L** (Colomiers, Biarritz) 1992 Arg, 1996 SA 1
**Médard, M** (Toulouse) 2008 Arg, PI, A3, 2009 I, S, W, E, It, NZ1, 2, A, SA(R), Sm, NZ3, 2010 Fj, 2011 S, I1, It, W, I2(R), 3, [J, C(R), NZ1, Tg, E, W, NZ2], 2012 It, S, 2013 I, S, NZ1, 2, 4, Tg, 2014 E, S, I, A2
**Mela, A** (Albi) 2008 S(R), I, It(R), W(R)
**Melville, E** (Toulon) 1990 I (R), A 1, 2, 3, NZ 1, 1991 US 2
**Menini, A** (Biarritz) 2014 A2, 3
**Menrath, R** (SCUF) 1910 W
**Menthiller, Y** (Romans) 1964 W, It, SA, R, 1965 E
**Merceron, G** (Montferrand) 1999 R (R), Tg, 2000 S, I, R, 2001 S (R), W, E, SA 1, 2, NZ (R), Fj, 2002 It, W, E, S, I, Arg, A 2, C, 2003 E 1, It (R), W (R), NZ (t+R), R (R), E 3, [Fj(R), J(R), S(R), US, E(R), NZ]
**Meret, F** (Tarbes) 1940 B
**Mericq, S** (Agen) 1959 I, 1960 S, E, W, 1961 I
**Merle, O** (Grenoble, Montferrand) 1993 SA 1, 2, R 2, A 1, 2, 1994 I, W, E, S, C 1, NZ 1, 2, C 2, 1995 W, I, R 1, [Tg, S, I, SA, E], It, R 2, Arg, NZ 1, 2, 1996 E, S, R, Arg 1, 2, W 2, SA 2, 1997 I, W, E, S, It 1, R 1, A 1, 2, It 2, R 2, SA 1(R), 2
**Mermoz, M** (Toulouse, Perpignan, Toulon) 2008 A2, 2009 S(R), NZ2, A, SA, 2010 SA, Arg1(R), 2011 S, I2, [C, NZ1, Tg, E, W, NZ2], 2012 It(R), E(R), Arg 1(R), 2, A, Arg3, Sm, 2013 It, W, NZ1(R), 2014 S, I(R)
**Merquey, J** (Toulon) 1950 S, I, E, W
**Mesnel, F** (RCF) 1986 NZ 2(R), 3, 1987 W, E, S, I, [S, Z, Fj, A, NZ], R, 1988 E, Arg 1, 2, 3, 4, R, 1989 I, W, E, S, NZ 1, A 1, 2, 1990 E, S, I, A 2, 3, NZ 1, 2, 1991 S, I, W 1, E, R, US 1, 2, W 2, [R, Fj, C, E], 1992 W, E, S, I, SA 1, 2, 1993 E (R), W, 1995 I, R 1, [Iv, E]
**Mesny, P** (RCF, Grenoble) 1979 NZ 1, 2, 1980 SA, R, 1981 I, W (R), A 1, 2, R, NZ 1, 2, 1982 I, Arg 1, 2
**Meyer, G-S** (Périgueux) 1960 S, E, It, R, Arg 2
**Meynard, J** (Cognac) 1954 Arg 1, 1956 Cz
**Mias, L** (Mazamet) 1951 S, I, E, W, 1952 I, SA, W, E, It, 1953 S, I, W, It, 1954 S, I, NZ, W, 1957 R 2, 1958 S, E, A, W, I, SA 1, 2, 1959 S, It, W, I
**Michalak, F** (Toulouse, Natal Sharks, Toulon) 2001 SA 3(R), A, Fj (R), 2002 It A 1, 2, 2003 It, W, Arg 2(R), NZ, R, E 2, [Fj, J, S, I, E, NZ(R)], 2004 I, W, S, E, A, Arg, NZ, 2005 S(R), E(R), W(R), I(R), It(R), SA1, 2, A1, 2, C, Tg(R), SA3, 2006 S, I, It, E, W, 2007 E2(R), 3, [Arg1(t&R), Nm, I, NZ(R), E(R), Arg 2], 2009 It(R), 2010 S(R), I(R), W(R), 2012 Arg 1(R), 2, A, Arg3, Sm, 2013 It, W, E(R), I, S, NZ1(R), 2, Tg(R), SA(R), 2014 A1, 2(R), 3(R)
**Mignardi, A** (Agen) 2007 NZ1, 2
**Mignoni, P** (Béziers, Clermont-Auvergne)) 1997 R 2(R), Arg (t), 1999 R (R), WS, NZ 1, W 2(R), [C, Nm], 2002 W, E

(R), I (R), Arg, A 2(R), 2005 S, It(R), C(R), 2006 R, 2007 It, I, W1, E1(R), S, E2, 3(R), W2, [Arg 1, Gg, Arg 2(R)]
**Milhères, C** (Biarritz) 2001 E
**Milliand, P** (Grenoble) 1936 G 2, 1937 G, It
**Millo-Chluski, R** (Toulouse) 2005 SA1, 2008 Arg, PI, A3(R), 2009 I(R), S, W(R), NZ1, 2, A, SA, Sm(R), NZ3, 2010 SA, Fj, A(R), 2011 I2, [C]
**Milloud, O** (Bourgoin) 2000 R (R), 2001 NZ, 2002 W (R), E (R), 2003 It (R), W (R), Arg 1, R (R), E 2(t+R), 3, [J, S(R), US, I(R), E(R)], 2004 US, C(R), A, Arg, NZ(R), 2005 S(R), E(R), W(R), SA1, 2(R), A1, 2, C(R), Tg, SA3, 2006 S(R), I, It, E(R), W(R), NZ1(R), 2, Arg, 2007 It, I(R), W1, E1, S, E2, 3, [Arg 1, I, Gg, NZ, E]
**Minjat, R** (Lyon) 1945 B 1
**Miorin, H** (Toulouse) 1996 R, SA 1, 1997 I, W, E, S, It 1, 2000 It (R), R (R)
**Mir, J-H** (Lourdes) 1967 R, 1968 I
**Mir, J-P** (Lourdes) 1967 A
**Modin, R** (Brive) 1987 [Z]
**Moga, A-M-A** (Bègles) 1945 B 1, 2, W, 1946 B, I, K, W, 1947 S, I, W, E, 1948 I, A, S, W, E, 1949 S, I, E, W, Arg 1, 2
**Mola, U** (Dax, Castres) 1997 S (R), 1999 R (R), WS, Tg (R), NZ 1, W 2, [C, Nm, Fj, Arg (R), NZ 2(R), A (R)]
**Momméjat, B** (Cahors, Albi) 1958 It, I, SA 1, 2, 1959 S, E, It, W, I, 1960 S, E, I, R, 1962 S, E, W, I, It, R, 1963 S, I, W
**Moncla, F** (RCF, Pau) 1956 Cz, 1957 I, E, W, It, R 1, 1958 SA 1, 2, 1959 S, E, It, W, I, 1960 S, E, W, I, It, R, Arg 1, 2, 3, 1961 S, SA, E, W, It, I, NZ 1, 2, 3
**Moni, C** (Nice, SF) 1996 R, 2000 A, NZ 1, 2, 2001 S, I, It, W
**Monié, R** (Perpignan) 1956 Cz, 1957 E
**Monier, R** (SBUC) 1911 I, 1912 S
**Monniot, M** (RCF) 1912 W, E
**Montade, A** (Perpignan) 1925 I, NZ, S, W, 1926 W
**Montanella, F** (Auch) 2007 NZ1(R)
**Montlaur, P** (Agen) 1992 E (R), 1994 S (R)
**Moraïtis, B** (Toulon) 1969 E, W
**Morel, A** (Grenoble) 1954 Arg 2
**Morère, J** (Toulouse) 1927 E, G 1, 1928 S, A
**Moscato, V** (Bègles) 1991 R, US 1, 1992 W, E
**Mougeot, C** (Bègles) 1992 W, E, Arg
**Mouniq, P** (Toulouse) 1911 S, E, W, I, 1912 I, E, 1913 S, SA, E
**Moure, H** (SCUF) 1908 E
**Moureu, P** (Béziers) 1920 I, US, 1921 W, E, I, 1922 S, W, I, 1923 S, W, E, I, 1924 S, I, E, W, 1925 E
**Mournet, A** (Bagnères) 1981 A 1(R)
**Mouronval, F** (SF) 1909 I
**Muhr, A H** (RCF) 1906 NZ, E, 1907 E
**Murillo, G** (Dijon) 1954 It, Arg 1

**Nallet, L** (Bourgoin, Castres, Racing-Métro) 2000 R, 2001 E, SA 1(R), 2(R), NZ, SA3(R), A (R), Fj (R), 2003 NZ, 2005 A2(R), C, Tg(R), SA3, 2006 I(R), It(R), E(R), W(R), R, SA(R), NZ1(R), 2, Arg, 2007 It, I, W1, E1, S, E3(R), [Nm, I(R), Gg, Arg 2], 2008 S, I, E, It, W, A1, 2, Arg, PI, A3, 2009 I, S, W, E, It, SA, NZ3(R), 2010 S, I, W, It, E, SA, Arg1, 2, 2011 S, I1, E, It, W, I2(R), 3, [J, NZ1, Tg, E, W, NZ2] 2012 It(R), S, I, I(R), E(R)
**Namur, R** (Toulon) 1931 E, G
**Noble, J-C** (La Voulte) 1968 E, W, Cz, NZ 3, A, R
**Noirot, B** (Racing Metro) 2010 Fj(R)
**Normand, A** (Toulouse) 1957 R 1
**Novès, J** (Toulouse) 1977 NZ 1, 2, R, 1978 W, R, 1979 I, W
**Ntamack, E** (Toulouse) 1994 W, C 1, NZ 1, 2, C 2, 1995 W, I, R 1, [Tg, S, I, SA, E], It, R 2, Arg, NZ 1, 2, 1996 E, S, I, W 1, R (R), Arg 1, 2, W 2, 1997 I, 1998 Arg 3, 1999 I, W 1, E, S, WS, NZ 1, W 2(R), [C (R), Nm, Fj, Arg, NZ 2, A], 2000 W, E, S, I, It
**Ntamack F** (Colomiers) 2001 SA 3
**Nyanga, Y** (Béziers, Toulouse) 2004 US, C, 2005 S(R), E(R), W, I, It, SA1, 2, A1(R), 2, C(t&R), Tg, SA3, 2006 S, I, It, E, W, 2007 E2(R), 3, [Nm, I(R), Gg, Arg 2], 2012 A, Arg3, Sm, 2013 E, I, S(t&R), NZ1(R), 2(R), SA(R), 2014 E, It, W, A2, 3(R)

**Olibeau, O** (Perpignan) 2007 NZ1(R), 2(R)
**Olive, D** (Montferrand) 1951 I, 1952 I

**Ondarts, P** (Biarritz O) 1986 NZ 3, 1987 W, E, S, I, [S, Z, Fj, A, NZ], R, 1988 E, I, W, Arg 1, 2, 3, 4, R, 1989 I, W, E, NZ 1, 2, A 2, 1990 W, E, S, I, R (R), NZ 1, 2, 1991 S, I, W 1, E, US 2, W 2, [R, Fj, C, E]
**Orso, J-C** (Nice, Toulon) 1982 Arg 1, 2, 1983 E, S, A 1, 1984 E (R), S, NZ 1, 1985 I (R), W, 1988 I
**Othats, J** (Dax) 1960 Arg 2, 3
**Ouedraogo, F** (Montpellier) 2007 NZ2(R), 2008 S, I, E(R), It, W, A1, 2, Arg(R), PI, A3, 2009 I, S, W, NZ1, 2, A, NZ3, 2010 S, I, Fj, A, 2011 I3, [C, W(R)], 2012 Arg 1, 2, A, Arg3, Sm, 2013 It, W, NZ1, Tg, 2014 A1, 3
**Ougier, S** (Toulouse) 1992 R, Arg 1, 1993 E (R), 1997 It 1

**Paco, A** (Béziers) 1974 Arg 1, 2, R, SA 1, 2, 1975 W, E, Arg 1, 2, R, 1976 S, I, W, E, US, A 1, 2, R, 1977 W, E, S, I, NZ 1, 2, R, 1978 E, S, I, W, R, 1979 I, W, E, S, 1980 W
**Palat, J** (Perpignan) 1938 G 2
**Palisson, A** (Brive, Toulon) 2008 A1, 2, Arg(R), PI(R), A3(R), 2010 I, W, It, E, Fj(R), Arg2, A, 2011 E(R), W, I2, 3, [Tg, E, W, NZ2], 2012 W
**Palmié, M** (Béziers) 1975 SA 1, 2, Arg 1, 2, R, 1976 S, I, W, E, US, 1977 W, E, S, I, Arg 1, 2, NZ 1, 2, R, 1978 E, S, I, W, NZ2], 2012 W
**Paoli, R** (see Simonpaoli)
**Paparemborde, R** (Pau) 1975 SA 1, 2, Arg 1, 2, R, 1976 S, I, W, E, US, A 1, 2, R, 1977 W, E, S, I, Arg 1, NZ 1, 2, 1978 E, S, I, W, R, 1979 I, W, E, S, NZ 1, 2, R, 1980 W, E, S, SA, R, 1981 S, I, W, E, A 1, 2, R, NZ 1, 2, 1982 W, I, R, Arg 1, 2 1983 E, S, I, W
**Papé, P** (Bourgoin, Castres, SF) 2004 I, It, W, S, E, C, NZ(R), 2005 I(R), It(R), SA1, A1, 2006 NZ1, 2, 2007 It(R), I, S(R), NZ1, 2, 2008 E, 2009 NZ1, A, Sm, 2010 S, I, Arg1, 2011 W(R), I3, [J(R), C, NZ1, Tg, E, W, NZ2], 2012 It, S, I, E, W, Arg 1, 2, A, Arg3, Sm, 2013 It, NZ4, Tg(R), SA, 2014 E, It, W, S, I
**Pardo, L** (Hendaye) 1924 I, E
**Pardo, L** (Bayonne) 1980 SA, R, 1981 S, I, W, E, A 1, 1982 W, E, S, 1983 A 1(R), 1985 S, I, Arg 2
**Pargade, J-H** (Lyon U) 1953 It
**Pariès, L** (Biarritz O) 1968 SA 2, R, 1970 S, I, W, 1975 E, S, I
**Parra, M** (Bourgoin, Clermont-Auvergne) 2008 S(R), I(R), E, Arg(R), 2009 I(R), S(R), W, E, It, SA(R), Sm, NZ3(R), 2010 S, I, W, It, E, SA, Arg1, Fj(R), Arg2, A, 2011 S, I1, E(R), It, W, I2(R), 3, [J(R), C, NZ1, Tg, E, W, NZ2], 2012 It(R), S, I, E(R), W(R), Arg 1, 2(R), A(R), Arg3(R), Sm, 2013 It(R), W(R), E, I, S, NZ4, Tg, SA, 2014 A1(R), 2
**Pascalin, P** (Mont-de-Marsan) 1950 I, E, W, 1951 S, I, E, W
**Pascarel, J-R** (TOEC) 1912 W, E, 1913 S, SA, E, I
**Pascot, J** (Perpignan) 1922 S, E, I, 1923 S, 1926 I, 1927 G 2
**Paul, R** (Montferrand) 1940 B
**Pauthe, G** (Graulhet) 1956 E
**Pebeyre, E-J** (Fumel, Brive) 1945 W, 1946 I, K, W, 1947 S, I, W, E
**Pebeyre, M** (Vichy, Montferrand) 1970 E, R, 1971 I, SA 1, 2, A 1, 1973 W
**Péclier, A** (Bourgoin) 2004 US, C
**Pécune, J** (Tarbes) 1974 W, E, S, 1975 Arg 1, 2, R, 1976 I, W, E, US
**Pédeutour, P** (Bègles) 1980 I
**Pélissié, J** (Montpellier) 2013 Tg(R)
**Pellissier, L** (RCF) 1928 A, I, E, G, W
**Pelous, F** (Dax, Toulouse) 1995 R 2, Arg, NZ 1, 2, 1996 E, S, I, R (R), Arg 1, 2, W 2, SA 1, 2, 1997 I, W, E, S, It 1, R 1, A 1, 2, It 2, R 2, Arg, SA 1, 2, 1998 E, S, I, W, Arg 1, 2, Fj, Arg 3, A, 1999 I, W 1, E, R (R), WS, Tg (R), NZ 1, W 2, [C, Nm, Fj, Arg], 2000 W, E, S, I, It, A, NZ 1, 2, 2001 S, I, It, W, E, 2002 It (R), W (R), E (R), S, I, Arg, A 1, 2, SA, NZ, C, 2003 E 1, S, I, It, W, R, E 2, 3(R), [Fj, J, S, I, E, NZ(R)], 2004 I, It, W, S, E, US, C, A, Arg, 2005 S, E, W, I, It, A2, 2006 S, I, It, E, W, R, SA, NZ1, 2007 E2, 3, W2(R), [Arg1, Nm(R), Gg(R), NZ, E]
**Penaud, A** (Brive, Toulouse) 1992 W, E, S, I, R, Arg 1, 2, SA 1, 2, Arg, 1993 R 1, SA 1, 2, R 2, A 1, 2, 1994 I, W, E, 1995 NZ 1, S, R, Arg 1, 2, W 2, 1997 I, E, R 1, A 2, 2000 W (R), It
**Périé, M** (Toulon) 1996 E, S, I (R)
**Péron, P** (RCF) 1975 SA 1, 2

**Perrier, P** (Bayonne) 1982 W, E, S, I (R)
**Pesteil, J-P** (Béziers) 1975 SA 1, 1976 A 2, R
**Petit, C** (Lorrain) 1931 W
**Peyras, J-B** (Bayonne) 2008 A2(R)
**Peyrelade, H** (Tarbes) 1940 B
**Peyrelongue, J** (Biarritz) 2004 It, S(R), C(R), A(R), Arg(R), NZ
**Peyroutou, G** (Périgueux) 1911 S, E
**Phliponeau, J-F** (Montferrand) 1973 W, I
**Piazza, A** (Montauban) 1968 NZ 1, A
**Picamoles, L** (Montpellier, Toulouse) 2008 I(R), E, It, A1, 2(t&R),
    Arg, PI(R), A3(R), 2009 I(R), S(R), E(R), It(R), NZ1, 2, SA,
    2010 SA(R), Arg1, 2011 I3, [C, NZ1, E(R)], 2012 It, S, I(R),
    E(R), W(R), Arg 1, 2, A, Arg3, Sm, 2013 It, W, E, I, S, NZ1,
    2, 2014 E, It, W, I, A2(R), 3(R)
**Picard, T** (Montferrand) 1985 Arg 2, 1986 R 1(R), Arg 2
**Pierre, J** (Bourgoin, Clermont-Auvergne) 2007 NZ1, 2, 2010
    S(R), I(R), W, E, SA(R), Arg1(R), Fj(R), Arg2, 2011 S,
    I1, E, It, W, I2, 3(R), [J, C(R), NZ1(R), Tg(R), E(R), W(R),
    NZ2(R)], 2012 W(R)
**Pierrot, G** (Pau) 1914 I, W, E
**Pilon, J** (Périgueux) 1949 E, 1950 E
**Piqué, J** (Pau) 1961 NZ 2, 3, A, 1962 S, It, 1964 NZ, E, W, It,
    I, SA, Fj, R, 1965 S, I, E, W, It
**Piquemal, M** (Tarbes) 1927 I, S, 1929 I, G, 1930 S, I, E, G, W
**Piquiral, E** (RCF) 1924 S, I, E, W, R, US, 1925 E, 1926 S, I, E,
    W, M, 1927 I, S, W, E, G 1, 2, 1928 E
**Piteu, R** (Pau) 1921 S, W, E, I, 1922 S, E, W, I, 1923 E, 1924
    E, 1925 I, NZ, W, E, 1926 E
**Plante, A** (Perpignan) 2013 NZ1, 2
**Plantefol, A** (RCF) 1967 SA 2, 3, 4, NZ, R, 1968 E, W, Cz, NZ
    2, 1969 E, W
**Plantey, S** (RCF) 1961 A, 1962 It
**Plisson, J** (SF) 2014 E, It, W, S
**Podevin, G** (SF) 1913 W, I
**Poeydebasque, F** (Bayonne) 1914 I, W
**Poirier, A** (SCUF) 1907 E
**Poitrenaud, C** (Toulouse) 2001 SA 3, A, Fj, 2003 E 1, S, I, It,
    W, Arg 1, NZ, E 3, [J, US, E(R), NZ], 2007 E2, 3, W2(R),
    Arg(R), NZ, 2006 R, 2007 It, I, W1, E1, S, E2, 3, [Nm, I,
    Gg, Arg 2], 2009 I, S, 2010 S, I, W, It, E, SA, Arg1(R) 2011
    S(R), I1, E, 2012 I, E, W
**Pomathios, M** (Agen, Lyon U, Bourg) 1948 I, A, S, W, E, 1949
    S, I, E, W, Arg 1, 2, 1950 S, I, W, 1951 S, I, E, W, 1952
    W, E, 1953 S, I, W, 1954 S
**Pons, P** (Toulouse) 1920 S, E, W, 1921 S, W, 1922 S
**Porcu, C** (Agen) 2002 Arg (R), A 1, 2(R)
**Porical, J** (Perpignan) 2010 Arg1, Fj, Arg2(R), A
**Porra, M** (Lyon) 1931 I
**Porthault, A** (RCF) 1951 S, E, W, 1952 I, 1953 S, I, It
**Portolan, C** (Toulouse) 1986 A, 1989 I, E
**Potel, A** (Begles) 1932 G
**Poux, J-B** (Narbonne, Toulouse) 2001 Fj (R), 2002 S, I (R), Arg,
    A 1(R), 2(R), 2003 E 3, [Fj, J, US, NZ], 2007 E2, 3, W2(R),
    [Nm, I(R), Gg, NZ(R), E(R), Arg 2], 2008 E(R), It(R), W(R),
    2010 W(R), It(R), E(R), SA(R), Arg1(R), 2011 I2(R), 3, [J(R),
    C, NZ1, Tg, E, W, NZ2], 2012 It(R), S, I, E, W
**Prat, J** (Lourdes) 1945 B 1, 2, W, 1946 B, I, K, W, 1947 S,
    I, W, E, 1948 I, A, S, W, E, 1949 S, I, E, W, Arg 1, 2,
    1950 S, I, E, W, 1951 S, E, W, 1952 S, I, SA, W, E, It,
    1953 S, I, E, W, It, 1954 I, NZ, W, E, It, 1955 S, I, E,
    W, It
**Prat, M** (Lourdes) 1951 I, 1952 S, I, SA, W, E, 1953 S, I, E,
    1954 I, NZ, W, E, It, 1955 S, I, E, W, 1956 I, W, It, Cz,
    1957 S, I, W, It, R 1, 1958 A, W, I
**Prévost, A** (Albi) 1926 M, 1927 I, S, W
**Prin-Clary, J** (Cavaillon, Brive) 1945 B 1, 2, W, 1946 B, I, K,
    W, 1947 S, I, W
**Privat, T** (Béziers, Clermont-Auvergne) 2001 SA 3, A, Fj, 2002
    It, W, S (R), SA (R), 2003 [NZ], 2005 SA2, A1(R)
**Puech, L** (Toulouse) 1920 S, E, I, 1921 E, I
**Puget, M** (Toulouse) 1961 It, 1966 S, I, It, 1967 SA 1, 3, 4, NZ,
    1968 Cz, NZ 1, 2, SA 1, 2, R, 1969 E, R, 1970 W
**Puig, A** (Perpignan) 1926 S, E
**Pujol, A** (SOE Toulouse) 1906 NZ
**Pujolle, M** (Nice) 1989 B, A 1, 1990 S, I, R, A 1, 2, NZ 2
**Puricelli, J** (Bayonne) 2009 NZ1(R), A, Sm(R), NZ3(R)

**Quaglio, A** (Mazamet) 1957 R 2, 1958 S, E, A, W, I, SA 1, 2,
    1959 S, E, It, W, I
**Quilis, A** (Narbonne) 1967 SA 1, 4, NZ, 1970 R, 1971 I

**Rabadan, P** (SF) 2004 US(R), C(R)
**Ramis, R** (Perpignan) 1922 E, I, 1923 W
**Rancoule, H** (Lourdes, Toulon, Tarbes) 1955 E, W, It, 1958 A,
    W, It, I, SA 1, 1959 S, It, W, 1960 I, It, R, Arg 1, 2, 1961
    SA, E, W, It, NZ 1, 2, 1962 S, E, W, I, It
**Rapin, A** (SBUC) 1938 R
**Raymond, F** (Toulouse) 1925 S, 1927 W, 1928 I
**Raynal, F** (Perpignan) 1935 G, 1936 G 1, 2, 1937 G, It
**Raynaud, F** (Carcassonne) 1933 G
**Raynaud, M** (Narbonne) 1999 W 1, E (R)
**Razat, J-P** (Agen) 1962 R, 1963 S, I, R
**Rebujent, R** (RCF) 1963 E
**Revailler, D** (Graulhet) 1981 S, I, W, E, A 1, 2, R, NZ 1, 2, 1982
    W, S, I, R, Arg 1
**Revillon, J** (RCF) 1926 I, E, 1927 S
**Ribère, E** (Perpignan, Quillan) 1924 I, 1925, I, NZ, S, 1926 S,
    I, W, M, 1927 I, S, W, E, G 1, 2, 1928 S, A, I, E, G, W,
    1929 I, E, G, 1930 S, I, E, W, 1931 I, S, W, E, G, 1932 G,
    1933 G
**Rives, J-P** (Toulouse, RCF) 1975 E, S, I, Arg 1, 2, R, 1976 S,
    I, W, E, US, A 1, 2, R, 1977 W, E, S, I, Arg 1, 2, R, 1978
    E, S, I, W, R, 1979 I, W, E, S, NZ 1, 2, R, 1980 W, E, S, I,
    SA, 1981 S, I, W, E, A 2, 1982 W, E, S, I, R, 1983 E, S, I,
    W, A 1, 2, R, 1984 I, W, E, S
**Rochon, A** (Montferrand) 1936 G 1
**Rodrigo, M** (Mauléon) 1931 I, W
**Rodriguez, L** (Mont-de-Marsan, Montferrand, Dax) 1981 A 1,
    2, R, NZ 1, 2, 1982 W, E, S, I, R, 1983 E, S, 1984 I, NZ
    1, 2, R, 1985 E, S, I, W, 1986 Arg 1, A, R 2, NZ 2, 3, 1987
    W, E, S, I, [S, Z, Fj, A, NZ], R, 1988 E, S, I, W, Arg 1, 2,
    3, 4, R, 1989 I, E, S, NZ 1, 2, B, A 1, 1990 W, E, S, I, NZ
    1
**Rogé, L** (Béziers) 1952 It, 1953 E, W, It, 1954 S, Arg 1, 2, 1955
    S, I, 1956 W, It, E, 1957 S, 1960 S, E
**Rollet, J** (Bayonne) 1960 Arg 3, 1961 NZ 3, A, 1962 It, 1963
    I
**Romero, H** (Montauban) 1962 S, E, W, I, It, R, 1963 E
**Romeu, J-P** (Montferrand) 1972 R, 1973 S, NZ, E, W, I, R, 1974
    W, E, S, Arg 1, 2, R, SA 1, 2(R), 1975 W, SA 2, Arg 1, 2,
    R, 1976 S, I, W, E, US, 1977 W, E, S, I, Arg 1, 2, NZ 1, 2,
    R
**Roques, A** (Cahors) 1958 A, W, It, I, SA 1, 2, 1959 S, E, W, I,
    1960 S, E, W, I, It, Arg 1, 2, 3, 1961 S, SA, E, W, It, I, 1962
    S, E, W, I, It, 1963 S
**Roques, J-C** (Brive) 1966 S, I, It, R
**Rossignol, J-C** (Brive) 1972 A 2
**Rouan, J** (Narbonne) 1953 S, I
**Roucariès, G** (Perpignan) 1956 S
**Rouffia, L** (Narbonne) 1945 B 2, W, 1946 W, 1948 I
**Rougerie, A** (Montferrand, Clermont-Auvergne) 2001 SA 3, A,
    Fj (R), 2002 It, W, E, S, I, Arg, A 1, 2, 2003 E 1, S, I, It, W,
    Arg 1, 2, NZ, R, E 2, 3(R), [Fj, J, S, I, E], 2004 US, C, A,
    Arg, NZ, 2005 S, W, A2, C, Tg, SA3, 2006 I, It, E, W, NZ1,
    2, 2007 E2, W2, [Arg1, Nm(R), I(R), Gg, Arg 2], 2008 S(R),
    I, E, It, 2010 S, SA, Arg2, A, 2011 S, I1, E, It, I3, [J, C,
    NZ1, Tg, E, W, NZ2], 2012 It, S, I, E, W
**Rougerie, J** (Montferrand) 1973 J
**Rougé-Thomas, P** (Toulouse) 1989 NZ 1, 2
**Roujas, F** (Tarbes) 1910 I
**Roumat, O** (Dax) 1989 NZ 2(R), B, 1990 W, E, S, I, R, A 1, 2,
    3, NZ 1, 2, 1991 S, I, W 1, E, R, US 1, W 2, [R, Fj, C, E],
    1992 W (R), E (R), S, I, SA 1, 2, Arg, 1993 E, S, I, W, R 1,
    SA 1, 2, R 2, A 1, 2, 1994 I, W, E, C 1, NZ 1, 2, C 2, 1995
    W, E, S, [Iv, S, I, SA, E], 1996 E, S, I, W 1, Arg 1, 2
**Rousie, M** (Villeneuve) 1931 S, 1932 G, 1933 G, 1933 G
**Rousset, G** (Béziers) 1975 SA 1, 1976 US
**Rué, J-B** (Agen) 2002 SA (R), C (R), 2003 E 1(R), S (R), It (R),
    W (R), Arg 1, 2(R)
**Ruiz, A** (Tarbes) 1968 SA 2, R
**Rupert, J-J** (Tyrosse) 1963 R, 1964 S, Fj, 1965 E, W, It, 1966
    S, I, E, W, It, 1967 It, R, 1968 S

**Sadourny, J-L** (Colomiers) 1991 W 2(R), [C (R)], 1992 E (R), S,

I, Arg 1(R), 2, SA 1, 2, 1993 R 1, SA 1, 2, R 2, A 1, 2, 1994 I, W, E, S, C 1, NZ 1, 2, C 2, 1995 W, E, S, I, R 1, [Tg, S, I, SA, E], It, R 2, Arg, NZ 1, 2, 1996 E, S, I, W 1, Arg 1, 2, W 2, SA 1, 2, 1997 I, W, E, S, It 1, R 1, A 1, 2, It 2, R 2, Arg, SA 1, 2, 1998 E, S, I, W, 1999 R, Tg, NZ 1(R), 2000 NZ 2, 2001 It, W, E

**Sagot, P** (SF) 1906 NZ, 1908 E, 1909 W

**Sahuc, A** (Métro) 1945 B 1, 2

**Sahuc, F** (Toulouse) 1936 G 2

**Saint-André, P** (Montferrand, Gloucester) 1990 R, A 3, NZ 1, 2, 1991 I (R), W 1, E, US 1, 2, W 2, [R, Fj, C, E], 1992 W, E, S, I, R, Arg 1, 2, SA 1, 2, 1993 E, S, I, W, SA 1, 2, A 1, 2, 1994 I, W, E, S, C 1, NZ 1, 2, C 2, 1995 W, E, S, I, R 1, [Tg, Iv, S, I, SA, E], It, R 2, Arg, NZ 1, 2, 1996 E, S, I, W 1, R, Arg 1, 2, W 2, 1997 It 1, 2, R 2, Arg, SA 1, 2

**Saisset, O** (Béziers) 1971 R, 1972 S, I 1, A 1, 2, 1973 S, NZ, E, W, I, J, R, 1974 I, Arg 2, SA 1, 2, 1975 W

**Salas, P** (Narbonne) 1979 NZ 1, 2, R, 1980 W, E, 1981 A 1, 1982 Arg 2

**Salinié, R** (Perpignan) 1923 E

**Sallefranque, M** (Dax) 1981 A 2, 1982 W, E, S

**Salut, J** (TOEC) 1966 R, 1967 S, 1968 I, E, Cz, NZ 1, 1969 I

**Samatan, R** (Agen) 1930 S, I, E, G, W, 1931 I, S, W, E, G

**Samson, C** (Toulon, Castres) 2012 Arg 2(R), 2013 E, I, S(R), NZ2

**Sanac, A** (Perpignan) 1952 It, 1953 S, I, 1954 E, 1956 Cz, 1957 S, I, E, W, It

**Sangalli, F** (Narbonne) 1975 I, SA 1, 2, 1976 S, A 1, 2, R, 1977 W, E, S, I, Arg 1, 2, NZ 1, 2

**Sanz, H** (Narbonne) 1988 Arg 3, 4, R, 1989 A 2, 1990 S, I, R, A 1, 2, NZ 2, 1991 W 2

**Sappa, M** (Nice) 1973 J, R, 1977 R

**Sarrade, R** (Pau) 1929 I

**Sarraméa, O** (Castres) 1999 R, WS (R), Tg, NZ 1

**Saux, J-P** (Pau) 1960 W, It, Arg 1, 2, 1961 SA, E, W, It, I, NZ 1, 2, 3, A 1962 S, E, W, I, It, 1963 S, I, E, It

**Savitsky, M** (La Voulte) 1969 R

**Savy, M** (Montferrand) 1931 I, S, W, E, 1936 G 1

**Sayrou, J** (Perpignan) 1926 W, M, 1928 E, G, W, 1929 S, W, E, G

**Schuster, J** (Perpignan) 2010 Fj, A(R)

**Scohy, R** (BEC) 1931 S, W, E, G

**Sébedio, J** (Tarbes) 1913 S, E, 1914 I, 1920 S, I, US, 1922 S, E, 1923 S

**Séguier, R** (Béziers) 1973 J, R

**Seigne, L** (Agen, Merignac) 1989 B, A 1, 1990 NZ 1, 1993 E, S, I, W, R 1, A 1, 2, 1994 S, C 1, 1995 E (R), S

**Sella, P** (Agen) 1982 R, Arg 1, 2, 1983 E, S, I, W, A 1, 2, R, 1984 I, W, E, S, NZ 1, 2, R, 1985 E, S, I, W, Arg 1, 2, 1986 S, I, W, E, R 1, Arg 1, 2, A, NZ 1, R 2, NZ 2, 3, 1987 W, E, S, I, [S, R, Z (R), Fj, A, NZ], 1988 E, S, I, W, Arg 1, 2, 3, 4, R, 1989 I, W, E, S, NZ 1, 2, B, A 1, 2, 1990 W, E, S, I, A 1, 2, 1991 W 1, E, R, US 1, 2, W 2, [Fj, C, E], 1992 W, E, S, I, Arg, 1993 E, S, I, W, R 1, SA 1, 2, R 2, A 1, 2, 1994 I, W, E, S, C 1, NZ 1, 2, C 2, 1995 W, E, S, I, [Tg, S, I, SA, E]

**Semmartin, J** (SCUF) 1913 W, I

**Sénal, G** (Béziers) 1974 Arg 1, 2, R, SA 1, 2, 1975 W

**Sentilles, J** (Tarbes) 1912 W, E, 1913 S, SA

**Serin, L** (Béziers) 1928 E, 1929 W, E, G, 1930 S, I, E, G, W, 1931 I, W, E

**Serre, P** (Perpignan) 1920 S, E

**Serrière, P** (RCF) 1986 A, 1987 R, 1988 E

**Servat, W** (Toulouse) 2004 I, It, W, S, E, US, C, A, Arg, NZ 2005 S, E(R), W(R), It(R), SA1(R), 2, 2008 S, I(R), E(R), W(R), 2009 It(R), NZ1, 2, SA, NZ3, 2010 S, I, W, It, E, Arg2, A, 2011 S, I1, E, It, W, [J, C, NZ1(R), Tg, E, W, NZ2], 2012 It, S(R), I(R), E(R), W

**Servole, L** (Toulon) 1931 I, S, W, E, G, 1934 G, 1935 G

**Sicart, N** (Perpignan) 1922 I

**Sillières, J** (Tarbes) 1968 R, 1970 S, I, 1971 S, I, E, 1972 E, W

**Siman, M** (Montferrand) 1948 E, 1949 S, I, 1950 S, I, E, W

**Simon, S** (Bègles) 1991 R, US 1

**Simonpaoli, R** (SF) 1911 I, 1912 I, S

**Sitjar, M** (Agen) 1964 W, It, I, R, 1965 It, R, 1967 A, E, It, W, I, SA 1, 2

**Skrela, D** (Colomiers, SF, Toulouse) 2001 NZ, 2007 It, I, W1, E1, 2, 3(R), W2, [Arg 1, Gg(R), Arg 2], 2008 S(R), I, E(R), W, Arg, PI, A3, 2010 SA(R), Fj(R), 2011 I2(R), 3, [J(R)]

**Skrela, J-C** (Toulouse) 1971 SA 2, A 1, 2, 1972 I 1(R), E, W, I 2, A 1, 1973 W, J, R, 1974 W, E, S, Arg 1, R, 1975 W (R), E, S, I, SA 1, 2, Arg 1, 2, R, 1976 S, I, W, E, US, A 1, 2, R, 1977 W, E, S, I, Arg 1, 2, NZ 1, 2, R, 1978 E, S, I, W

**Slimani, R** (SF) 2013 NZ4(R), Tg(R), SA(R), 2014 E(R), It(R), S(R), I(R), A1(R), 2, 3

**Soler, M** (Quillan) 1929 G

**Soro, R** (Lourdes, Romans) 1945 B 1, 2, W, 1946 B, I, K, 1947 S, I, W, E, 1948 I, A, S, W, E, 1949 S, I, E, W, Arg 1, 2

**Sorondo, L-M** (Montauban) 1946 K, 1947 S, I, W, E, 1948 I

**Soulette, C** (Béziers, Toulouse) 1997 R 2, 1998 S (R), I (R), W (R), Arg 1, 2, Fj, 1999 W 2(R), [C (R), Nm (R), Arg, NZ 2, A]

**Soulié, E** (CASG) 1920 E, I, US, 1921 S, E, I, 1922 E, W, I

**Sourgens, J** (Bègles) 1926 M

**Sourgens, O** (Bourgoin) 2007 NZ2

**Souverbie, J-M** (Bègles) 2000 R

**Spanghero, C** (Narbonne) 1971 E, W, SA 1, 2, A 1, 2, R, 1972 S, E, W, I 2, A 1, 2, 1974 I, W, E, S, R, SA 1, 1975 E, S, I

**Spanghero, W** (Narbonne) 1964 SA, Fj, R, 1965 S, I, E, W, It, R, 1966 S, I, E, W, It, R, 1967 S, A, E, SA 1, 2, 3, 4, NZ, 1968 S, I, E, W, NZ 1, 2, 3, A, SA 1, 2, R, 1969 S, I, W, 1970 R, 1971 E, W, SA 1, 1972 E, I 2, A 1, 2, R, 1973 S, NZ, E, W, I

**Stener, G** (PUC) 1956 S, I, E, 1958 SA 1, 2

**Struxiano, P** (Toulouse) 1913 W, I, 1920 S, E, W, I, US

**Suta, J** (Toulon) 2012 A, Arg3(R), Sm(R), 2013 W, E(R)

**Sutra, G** (Narbonne) 1967 SA 2, 1969 W, 1970 S, I

**Swierczinski, C** (Bègles) 1969 E, 1977 Arg 2

**Szarzewski, D** (Béziers, SF, Racing Métro) 2004 C(R), 2005 I(R), A1, 2, SA3, 2006 S, E(R), W(t&R), R(R), SA, NZ1, 2(R), Arg(R), 2007 It(R), E2(R), W2, [Arg1(R), Nm, I(R), Gg(R), NZ(R), E(R)], 2008 S(R), I, E, It, W, Arg, PI, A3, 2009 I, S, W, E, It, Nz1(R), 2(R), A, SA(R), Sm, NZ3(R), 2010 S(R), I(R), W(R), It(R), E(R), SA, Arg1, 2011 I2, 3, [J(R), NZ1, Tg(R), E(R), W(R), NZ2(R)], 2012 It(R), S, I, E, W(R), Arg 1, 2, A, Arg3, Sm(R), 2013 It, W, E(R), NZ1, 2, 3(R), 4(R), Tg, SA(R), 2014 E(R), It, W, I

**Tabacco, P** (SF) 2001 SA 1, 2, NZ, SA 3, A, Fj, 2003 It (R), W (R), Arg, NZ, E 2(R), 3, [S(R), US, I(R), NZ], 2004 US, 2005 S

**Tachdjian, M** (RCF) 1991 S, I, E

**Taffary, M** (RCF) 1975 W, E, S, I

**Taillantou, J** (Pau) 1930 I, G, W

**Tales, R** (Castres) 2013 NZ2(R), 3, 4, Tg, SA, 2014 W(R), S(R), I, A2, 3

**Taofifenua, R** (Perpignan) 2012 Arg 1(R), 2013 It(R), W(R)

**Tarricq, P** (Lourdes) 1958 A, W, It, I

**Tavernier, H** (Toulouse) 1913 I

**Téchoueyres, W** (SBUC) 1994 E, S, 1995 [Iv]

**Terreau, M-M** (Bourg) 1945 W, 1946 B, I, K, W, 1947 S, I, W, E, 1948 I, A, W, E, 1949 S, Arg 1, 2, 1951 S

**Theuriet, A** (SCUF) 1909 E, W, 1910 S, 1911 W, 1913 E

**Thevenot, M** (SCUF) 1910 W, E, I

**Thierry, R** (RCF) 1920 S, E, W, US

**Thiers, P** (Montferrand) 1936 G 1, 2, 1937 G, It, 1938 G 1, 2, 1940 B, 1945 B, 1, 2

**Thiéry, B** (Bayonne, Biarritz) 2007 NZ1, 2(R), 2008 A1, 2

**Thion, J** (Perpignan, Biarritz) 2003 Arg 1, 2, NZ, R, E 2, [Fj, S, I, E], 2004 A, Arg, NZ 2005 S, E, W, I, It, A2, C, Tg, SA3, 2006 S, I, It, E, W, R(R), SA, 2007 It, I(R), W1, E1, S, E2, 3, W2, [Arg 1, I, Gg, NZ, E, Arg 2], 2008 E(R), It, W, 2009 E, It(R), 2010 Fj, Arg2(R), A, 2011 S(R), I1(R), E(R), It(R)

**Tignol, P** (Toulouse) 1953 S, I

**Tilh, H** (Nantes) 1912 W, E, 1913 S, SA, E, W

**Tillous-Borde, S** (Castres) 2008 A1(R), 2, PI(R), A3, 2009 I, S, W(R), E(R)

**Tolofua, C-E** (Toulouse) 2012 Arg 1(R), 2(R), 2014 A1(R), 3(R)

**Tolot, J-L** (Agen) 1987 [Z]

**Tomas, J** (Clermont-Auvergne, Montpellier) 2008 It(R), A3(R), 2011 W(R)

**THE COUNTRIES**

Tordo, J-F (Nice) 1991 US 1(R), 1992 W, E, S, I, R, Arg 1, 2, SA 1, Arg, 1993 E, S, I, W, R 1

Torossian, F (Pau) 1997 R 1

Torreilles, S (Perpignan) 1956 S

Tournaire, F (Narbonne, Toulouse) 1995 It, 1996 I, W 1, R, Arg 1, 2(R), W 2, SA 1, 2, 1997 I, E, S, It 1, R 1, A 1, 2, It 2, R 2, Arg, SA 1, 2, 1998 E, S, I, W, Arg 1, 2, Fj, Arg 3, A, 1999 I, W 1, E, S, R (R), WS, NZ 1, [C, Nm, Fj, Arg, NZ 2, A], 2000 W, E, S, I, It, A (R)

Tourte, R (St Girons) 1940 B

Traille, D (Pau, Biarritz) 2001 SA 3, A, Fj, 2002 It, W, E, S, I, Arg, A 1, 2, SA, NZ, C, 2003 E 1, S, I, It, W, Arg, 1, 2, NZ, R, E 2, [Fj(R), J, S(R), US, NZ], 2004 I, It, W, S, E, 2005 S, E, W, It(R), SA1(R), 2, A1(R), 2006 It, E, W, R, SA, NZ1, 2, Arg, 2007 S(R), E2, 3, W2(R), [Arg 1, Nm, I, NZ, E], 2008 S, I, E, It(R), W, A1, PI(R), A3(R), 2009 E(R), It, NZ1, 2, A, SA, Sm(R), NZ3, 2010 Fj, Arg2, A, 2011 S, I1, E(R), It(R), W, I2, [C, NZ1, 2(R)]

Trillo, J (Bègles) 1967 SA 3, 4, NZ, R, 1968 S, I, NZ 1, 2, 3, A, 1969 I, E, W, R, 1970 E, R, 1971 S, I, SA 1, 2, A 1, 2, 1972 S, A 1, 2, R, 1973 S, E

Trinh-Duc, F (Montpellier) 2008 S, I(R), E, It, W(R), A1, 2, 2009 W(R), E, It, NZ1, 2, SA, Sm, NZ3, 2010 S, I, W, It, E, SA, Arg1, 2011 S, I1, E, It, W, I2, 3(R), [J, C, NZ1(R), Tg(R), E(R), NZ2(t&R)], 2012 It, S, I, E(R), W(R), Arg 1, 2(R), A(R), Arg3(R), 2013 It(R), W(R), E, S(R), 2014 It(R)

Triviaux, R (Cognac) 1931 E, G

Tucco-Chala, M (PUC) 1940 B

Ugartemendia, J-L (St Jean-de-Luz) 1975 S, I

Vahaamahina, S (Perpignan) 2012 A(R), 2013 I(R), S, NZ1, 2(R), 3(R), 4(R), Tg, SA(R), 2014 It(R), W(R), S, I(R), A1

Vaills, G (Perpignan) 1928 A, 1929 G

Valbon, L (Brive) 2004 US, 2005 S(R), 2006 S, E(R), 2007 NZ1(R)

Vallot, C (SCUF) 1912 S

Van Heerden, A (Tarbes) 1992 E, S

Vannier, M (RCF, Chalon) 1953 W, 1954 S, I, Arg 1, 2, 1955 S, I, E, W, It, 1956 S, I, W, It, E, 1957 S, I, E, W, It, R 1, 2, 1958 S, E, A, W, It, I, 1960 S, E, W, I, It, R, Arg 1, 3, 1961 SA, E, W, It, I, NZ 1, A

Vaquer, F (Perpignan) 1921 S, W, 1922 W

Vaquerin, A (Béziers) 1971 R, 1972 S, I 1, A 1, 1973 S, 1974 W, E, S, Arg 1, 2, R, SA 1, 2, 1975 W, E, S, I, 1976 US, A 1(R), 2, R, 1977 Arg 2, 1979 W, E, 1980 S, I

Vareilles, C (SF) 1907 E, 1908 E, W, 1910 S, E

Varenne, F (RCF) 1952 S

Varvier, T (RCF) 1906 E, 1909 E, W, 1911 E, W, 1912 I

Vassal, G (Carcassonne) 1938 R, G 2

Vaysse, J (Albi) 1924 US, 1926 M

Vellat, E (Grenoble) 1927 I, E, G 1, 2, 1928 A

Venditti, D (Bourgoin, Brive) 1996 R, SA 1(R), 2, 1997 I, W, E, S, R 1, A 1, SA 2, 2000 W (R), E, S, It (R)

Vergé, L (Bègles) 1993 R 1(R)

Verger, A (SF) 1927 W, E, G 1, 1928 I, E, G, W

Verges, S-A (SF) 1906 NZ, E, 1907 E

Vermeulen, E (Brive, Montferrand, Clermont-Auvergne) 2001 SA 1(R), 2(R), 2003 NZ, 2006 NZ1, 2, Arg, 2007 W1, S(R), 2008 S, W(R)

Viard, G (Narbonne) 1969 W, 1970 S, R, 1971 S, I

Viars, S (Brive) 1992 W, E, I, R, Arg 1, 2, SA 1, 2(R), Arg, 1993 R 1, 1994 C 1(R), NZ 1(t), 1995 E (R), [Iv], 1997 R 1(R), A 1(R), 2

Vigerie, M (Agen) 1931 W

Vigier, R (Montferrand) 1956 S, W, It, E, Cz, 1957 S, E, W, It, R 1, 2, 1958 S, E, A, W, It, I, SA 1, 2, 1959 S, E, It, W, I

Vigneau, A (Bayonne) 1935 G

Vignes, C (RCF) 1957 R 1, 2, 1958 S, E

Vila, E (Tarbes) 1926 M

Vilagra, J (Vienne) 1945 B 2

Villepreux, P (Toulouse) 1967 It, I, SA 2, NZ, 1968 I, Cz, NZ 1, 2, 3, A, 1969 S, I, E, W, R, 1970 S, I, W, E, R, 1971 S, I, E, W, A 1, 2, R, 1972 S, I 1, E, W, I 2, A 1, 2

Viviès, B (Agen) 1978 E, S, I, W, 1980 SA, R, 1981 S, A 1, 1983 A 1(R)

Volot, M (SF) 1945 W, 1946 B, I, K, W

Watremez, Y (Biarritz) 2012 Arg 1

Weller, S (Grenoble) 1989 A 1, 2, 1990 A 1, NZ 1

Wolf, J-P (Béziers) 1980 SA, R, 1981 A 2, 1982 E

Yachvili, D (Biarritz) 2002 C (R), I, It, W, R (R), E 3, [US, NZ], 2004 I(R), It(R), W(R), S, E, 2005 S(R), E, W, I, It, SA1(R), 2, C, Tg, 2006 S(R), I(R), It(R), E, W, SA, NZ1, 2(R), Arg, 2007 E1, 2008 E(R), It, W(R), A1, 2(R), 2009 NZ1(R), A, 2010 It(R), SA(R), Arg1(R), Fj, Arg2(R), A(R), 2011 S(R), I1(R), E, I2, 3(R), [J, C(R), NZ1, Tg, E, W, NZ2], 2012 It, W

Yachvili, M (Tulle, Brive) 1968 E, W, Cz, NZ 3, A, R, 1969 S, I, R, 1971 E, SA 1, 2 A 1, 1972 R, 1975 SA 2

Zago, F (Montauban) 1963 I, E

Fly-half Frédéric Michalak is closing in on becoming France's leading Test points scorer.

# GEORGIA

## GEORGIA'S 2013–14 TEST RECORD

| OPPONENTS | DATE | VENUE | RESULT |
|-----------|------|-------|--------|
| Canada | 9 Nov | H | Won 19–15 |
| USA | 16 Nov | H | Lost 23–25 |
| Samoa | 23 Nov | H | Won 16–15 |
| Belgium | 1 Feb | H | Won 35–0 |
| Portugal | 8 Feb | A | Won 34–9 |
| Russia | 22 Feb | H | Won 36–10 |
| Spain | 8 Mar | A | Won 24–17 |
| Romania | 15 Mar | H | Won 22–9 |
| Spain | 14 Jun | H | Won 23–13 |

# LELOS EVOLVING AS OPPORTUNITIES GROW

## By Lúcás O'Ceallacháin

Georgia celebrate beating Romania to retain the European Nations Cup title and qualify for RWC 2015 as Europe 1.

**G**eorgia cemented their status as one of the teams most likely to cause an upset at Rugby World Cup 2015 by putting together some solid results against strong opposition in the last year, reaping the benefits of the IRB's expanded Test schedule for tier two nations to beat the higher ranked Canada and Samoa in November 2013.

The Lelos kicked off their November programme with a feisty affair against Canada which saw South African referee Lourens van der Merwe send a player off from each side late in the first half after Viktor Kolelishvili's high tackle on Liam Underwood provoked a reaction from Canadian captain Tyler Ardron.

Georgia managed to shake off the rust and ground out a narrow 19–15 victory. In front of a crowd of 12,000, the kickers had traded blows in the first half, Harry Jones kicking Canada into a 12–9 half-time lead after Underwood and Merab Kvirikashvili had traded penalties.

After the break, the Lelos pushed on to create and convert one of the few try-scoring chances in the match as Tedo Zibzibadze, an early replacement for captain Irakli Machkaneli, went over and Kvirikashvili added the conversion to put Georgia ahead. Jones cut the deficit to one with another penalty, but Kvirikashvili replied to take pressure off the Georgian defence and allow them to close out the win.

Next up was a USA Eagles side hoping to end a seven-Test losing streak. Kvirikashvili was in exceptional form again for Georgia – the man who plays for Montluçon in France's Fédérale 1 scored a try, two conversions and three penalties for a personal haul of 18 points, but despite his best efforts it was the Eagles who capitalised out wide with tries from Chris Wyles and Blaine Scully. Georgia battled back from 22–13 down with Merab Sharikadze's try and Kvirikashvili's penalty to lead going into the final minutes, only for Adam Siddall to snatch a 25–23 victory at the death.

The loss hurt the Lelos, especially in front of a home crowd, but the following week saw them pull off a surprise 16–15 victory over Samoa, who at the time sat nine places higher in the IRB World Rankings. A second try in as many weeks from centre Sharikadze, aided by the boot of Kvirikashvili, saw the Lelos record their first-ever win over the Pacific Islanders. This time it was the Georgians who snatched victory at the death thanks to Kvirikashvili's boot, ensuring that the 30,000 crowd in the Mikheil Meskhi Stadium went home happy.

Georgia's New Zealand coach Milton Haig was clearly delighted with the progress and Georgia's first victory over a top 10 team: "That game was won on solid defence and a willingness not to give up right to the last whistle and it gave us huge confidence and self-belief."

Attentions then turned to the climax of the European Nations Cup at the start of February. The Lelos duly continued their dominance of the competition with five victories in a row to secure their place at Rugby World Cup 2015 as Europe 1. They did so without losing a single match in Division 1A which spans two seasons, recording nine wins and a draw, against Romania.

First up were Belgium in Tbilisi and, despite a brave effort, the visitors were defeated 35–0 in a poor Georgian performance. More seasoned campaigners Portugal should have provided sterner opposition for the Lelos in Lisbon a week later, but Georgia were on a mission and brushed their hosts aside 34–9.

Russia arrived in Tbilisi needing a win to keep alive their hopes of direct qualification for RWC 2015, but Georgia were not in a charitable mood and ran out 36–10 winners in front of a 54,000 crowd at the Dinamo Arena with tries from David Zirakashvili, Kolelishvili, Mamuka

Gorgodze and Zibzibadze. A nervy 24–17 victory over Spain in Madrid followed to set the Lelos up for a grandstand finale at home against Romania to determine not only the title but who would qualify for RWC 2015 as Europe 1 and Europe 2.

Spurred on by the home crowd, Georgia secured yet another European Nations Cup title with a 22–9 victory over the Oaks. Over the two years of the competition, the Lelos scored 286 points and conceded 106 with the head-to-head record with Romania all that separated the two sides, the Oaks finishing three points behind Georgia in the standings.

The November internationals, RWC 2015 qualification and European success were all important in reconfirming Georgia's confidence that they can mix it with higher-ranked nations given the opportunity. Haig was also delighted with the development in his side's play. "We managed to evolve our game so that it has become a more rounded game that allows us to play different styles when needed depending on the opposition."

With 37 Georgian players currently playing in the Top 14 in France, additional international fixtures and the advent of professional domestic structures, the future is looking very bright.

"Georgia has eight pro teams in a Super League. The players are full-time but not paid the sums found in western Europe. It's because of the high performance structures we have put in place, such as the National Academy of Rugby and the continued coach and referee development, that the game and players are improving," explained Richie Dixon, the High Performance Consultant for the Georgian Rugby Union. "There's still much to do as it is a work in progress, but rugby is now very much on the up in Georgia with good progress from RWC 2011."

On the domestic front, the Armia club from Tbilisi secured the league title, but many of the clubs have been involved in providing players to the age grade national team and senior set-up, as well as the academy. The domestic system is helping Georgia to build real depth for the future.

A one-point loss to USA in the IRB Junior World Rugby Trophy in Hong Kong in April prevented Georgia from progressing to a first final, but the Junior Lelos scored four tries to secure fifth place with a 46–17 win over Namibia.

Georgia then wrapped up their season with strong performances in the IRB Tbilisi Cup, a competition that continues to go from strength to strength. The 2014 edition saw Georgia record impressive wins over Spain (23–13) and Emerging Italy (34–10), but the largely experimental side made up of less experienced players then went down 26–16 to the Argentina Jaguars.

The defeats to USA in November and Argentina Jaguars in the Tbilisi Cup will only add fuel to the flames of desire for the Lelos in the year ahead. The players, home and abroad, will be aiming for a place in the final squad for England where Georgia line up in Pool C alongside defending champions New Zealand, Argentina, Tonga and African champions Namibia.

# GEORGIA INTERNATIONAL STATISTICS

## MATCH RECORDS UP TO 13 OCTOBER 2014

### WINNING MARGIN

| Date | Opponent | Result | Winning Margin |
|------|----------|--------|----------------|
| 07/04/2007 | Czech Republic | 98–3 | 95 |
| 03/02/2002 | Netherlands | 88–0 | 88 |
| 06/02/2010 | Germany | 77–3 | 74 |
| 26/02/2005 | Ukraine | 65–0 | 65 |
| 12/06/2005 | Czech Republic | 75–10 | 65 |

### MOST CONVERSIONS IN A MATCH
#### BY THE TEAM

| Date | Opponent | Result | Cons |
|------|----------|--------|------|
| 06/02/2010 | Germany | 77–3 | 11 |
| 03/02/2002 | Netherlands | 88–0 | 9 |
| 07/04/2007 | Czech Republic | 98–3 | 9 |
| 12/06/2005 | Czech Republic | 75–10 | 7 |
| | 6 on 5 occasions | | |

#### BY A PLAYER

| Date | Player | Opponent | Cons |
|------|--------|----------|------|
| 06/02/2010 | Merab Kvirikashvili | Germany | 11 |
| 03/02/2002 | Pavle Jimsheladze | Netherlands | 9 |
| 07/04/2007 | Merab Kvirikashvili | Czech Republic | 9 |
| 12/06/2005 | Malkhaz Urjukashvili | Czech Republic | 7 |
| | 6 on 2 occasions | | |

### MOST DROP GOALS IN A MATCH
#### BY THE TEAM

| Date | Opponent | Result | DGs |
|------|----------|--------|-----|
| 20/10/1996 | Russia | 29–20 | 2 |
| 21/11/1991 | Ukraine | 19–15 | 2 |
| 15/07/1992 | Ukraine | 15–0 | 2 |
| 04/06/1994 | Switzerland | 22–21 | 2 |

#### BY A PLAYER

| Date | Player | Opponent | DGs |
|------|--------|----------|-----|
| 15/07/1992 | Davit Chavleishvili | Ukraine | 2 |

### MOST POINTS IN A MATCH
#### BY THE TEAM

| Date | Opponent | Result | Points |
|------|----------|--------|--------|
| 07/04/2007 | Czech Republic | 98–3 | 98 |
| 03/02/2002 | Netherlands | 88–0 | 88 |
| 06/02/2010 | Germany | 77–3 | 77 |
| 12/06/2005 | Czech Republic | 75–10 | 75 |
| 23/03/1995 | Bulgaria | 70–8 | 70 |

#### BY A PLAYER

| Date | Player | Opponent | Points |
|------|--------|----------|--------|
| 06/02/2010 | Merab Kvirikashvili | Germany | 32 |
| 08/02/2014 | Merab Kvirikashvili | Portugal | 24 |
| 08/03/2003 | Pavle Jimsheladze | Russia | 23 |
| 07/04/2007 | Merab Kvirikashvili | Czech Republic | 23 |
| 17/11/2012 | Merab Kvirikashvili | Japan | 22 |

### MOST TRIES IN A MATCH
#### BY THE TEAM

| Date | Opponent | Result | Tries |
|------|----------|--------|-------|
| 07/04/2007 | Czech Republic | 98–3 | 16 |
| 03/02/2002 | Netherlands | 88–0 | 14 |
| | 11 on 4 occasions | | |

#### BY A PLAYER

| Date | Player | Opponent | Tries |
|------|--------|----------|-------|
| | 3 on 6 occasions | | |

### MOST PENALTIES IN A MATCH
#### BY THE TEAM

| Date | Opponent | Result | Pens |
|------|----------|--------|------|
| 08/03/2003 | Russia | 23–17 | 6 |
| 28/09/2011 | Romania | 25–9 | 6 |
| | 5 on 5 occasions | | |

#### BY A PLAYER

| Date | Player | Opponent | Pens |
|------|--------|----------|------|
| 08/03/2003 | Pavle Jimsheladze | Russia | 6 |
| | 5 on 4 occasions | | |

GEORGIA

| MOST CAPPED PLAYERS | |
|---|---|
| Player | Caps |
| Irakli Abuseridze | 85 |
| Merab Kvirikashvili | 77 |
| Tedo Zibzibadze | 75 |
| Giorgi Chkhaidze | 74 |

| LEADING TRY SCORERS | |
|---|---|
| Player | Tries |
| Irakli Machkhaneli | 23 |
| Mamuka Gorgodze | 23 |
| Tedo Zibzibadze | 21 |
| Malkhaz Urjukashvili | 18 |

| LEADING CONVERSIONS SCORERS | |
|---|---|
| Player | Cons |
| Merab Kvirikashvili | 101 |
| Pavle Jimsheladze | 61 |
| Malkhaz Urjukashvili | 45 |
| Lasha Malaguradze | 18 |

| LEADING PENALTY SCORERS | |
|---|---|
| Player | Pens |
| Merab Kvirikashvili | 96 |
| Pavle Jimsheladze | 48 |
| Malkhaz Urjukashvili | 45 |
| Nugzar Dzagnidze | 22 |

| LEADING DROP GOAL SCORERS | |
|---|---|
| Player | DGs |
| Kakha Machitidze | 4 |
| 3 by 4 players | |

| LEADING POINTS SCORERS | |
|---|---|
| Player | Points |
| Merab Kvirikashvili | 554 |
| Pavle Jimsheladze | 320 |
| Malkhaz Urjukashvili | 318 |
| Irakli Machkhaneli | 115 |
| Mamuka Gorgodze | 115 |

# GEORGIA INTERNATIONAL PLAYERS
## UP TO 13 OCTOBER 2014

**V Abashidze** 1998 *It, Ukr, I,* 1999 *Tg, Tg,* 2000 *It, Mor, Sp,* 2001 *H, Pt, Rus, Sp, R,* 2006 *J*
**N Abdaladze** 1997 *Cro, De*
**I Abuseridze** 2000 *It, Pt, Mor, Sp, H, R,* 2001 *H, Pt, Rus, Sp, R,* 2002 *Pt, Rus, Sp, R, I, Rus,* 2003 *Pt, Rus, CZR, R, It, E, Sa, SA,* 2004 *Rus,* 2005 *Pt, Ukr, R,* 2006 *Rus, R, Pt, Ukr, J, R, Sp, Pt, Pt,* 2007 *R, Rus, CZR, Nm, ESp, ItA, Ar, I, Nm, F,* 2008 *R, Pt, Rus, Sp, S,* 2009 *Ger, Pt, Sp, R, Rus, ArJ, ItA,* 2010 *Pt, Sp, R, Rus, C, US,* 2011 *Ukr, Sp, Pt, R, Rus, S, E, R, Ar,* 2012 *Sp, R, Rus, Ukr, US, C, J, Fj,* 2013 *Sp*
**V Akhvlediani** 2007 *CZR*
**K Alania** 1993 *Lux,* 1994 *Swi,* 1996 *CZR, CZR, Rus,* 1997 *Pt, Pol, Cro, De,* 1998 *It,* 2001 *H, Pt, Sp, F, SA,* 2002 *H, Pt, Rus, Sp, R, I, Rus,* 2003 *Rus,* 2004 *Pt, Sp*
**N Andghuladze** 1997 *Pol,* 2000 *It, Pt, Mor, Sp, H, R,* 2004 *Sp, Rus, CZR, R*
**D Ashvetia** 1998 *Ukr,* 2005 *Pt,* 2006 *R,* 2007 *Sp*
**K Asieshvili** 2008 *ItA,* 2010 *S, ItA, Nm,* 2012 *Sp,* 2014 *Sp*

**G Babunashvili** 1992 *Ukr, Ukr, Lat,* 1993 *Rus, Pol, Lux,* 1996 *CZR*
**Z Bakuradze** 1989 *Z,* 1990 *Z,* 1991 *Ukr, Ukr,* 1993 *Rus, Pol*
**D Baramidze** 2000 *H*
**O Barkalaia** 2002 *I,* 2004 *Sp, Rus, CZR, R, Ur, CHL, Rus,* 2005 *Pt, Ukr, R, CZR, CHL,* 2006 *Rus, R, Pt, Ukr, J, Bb,*

*R, Sp,* 2007 *Nm, ItA, I, F,* 2008 *Pt, R, Pt, Rus, Sp, ESp, Ur, ItA, S,* 2009 *Ger, Sp, R*
**D Basilaia** 2008 *Pt, R, Pt, CZR, Rus, Sp, S,* 2009 *Ger, Sp, R, C, US, ItA,* 2011 *Nm, S, E, R,* 2012 *Sp, Pt, R, Rus,* 2013 *Bel, Pt, Rus, Sp, R,* 2014 *Bel, Pt, Rus, R, Sp*
**G Begadze** 2012 *Pt, R, Rus, Ukr, US, J,* 2013 *Bel, Pt, Rus, R, Ur, Ar, C, US, Sa,* 2014 *Bel, Pt, Rus, Sp, R, Sp*
**R Belkania** 2004 *Sp,* 2005 *CHL,* 2007 *Sp, Rus,* 2012 *Pt, R, Rus, Ukr, US, C,* 2013 *Bel, Pt, Sp, Ur, Ar*
**G Beriashvili** 1993 *Rus, Pol,* 1995 *Ger*
**G Berishvili** 2011 *Nm, E, R,* 2012 *Sp, Pt, R, Rus, US, C,* 2013 *Ur,* 2014 *Sp, Sp*
**M Besselia** 1991 *Ukr,* 1993 *Rus, Pol,* 1996 *Rus,* 1997 *Pt*
**B Bitsadze** 2012 *Ukr, US, C, Fj,* 2013 *Pt, Ur, Ar*
**D Bolgashvili** 2000 *It, Pt, H, R,* 2001 *H, Pt, Rus, Sp, R, F, SA,* 2002 *H, Pt, Rus, I,* 2003 *Pt, Rus, CZR, R, E, Sa, SA,* 2004 *Rus, Ur, CHL, Rus,* 2005 *CZR,* 2007 *Sp,* 2010 *ItA*
**J Bregvadze** 2008 *ESp, ItA,* 2009 *C, IrA,* 2010 *Sp, R, S, Nm,* 2011 *Ukr, Sp, R, Rus, Nm, S, E, R, Ar,* 2013 *R, Ar,* 2014 *Bel, Pt, Rus, Sp, R*
**G Buguianishvili** 1996 *CZR, Rus,* 1997 *Pol,* 1998 *It, Rus, I, R,* 2000 *Sp, H, R,* 2001 *H, F, SA,* 2002 *Rus*

**D Chavleishvili** 1990 *Z, Z,* 1992 *Ukr, Ukr, Lat,* 1993 *Pol, Lux*
**D Chichua** 2008 *CZR*

I **Chikava** 1993 *Pol, Lux,* 1994 *Swi,* 1995 *Bul, Mol, H,* 1996 *CZR, CZR,* 1997 *Pol,* 1998 *I*
R **Chikvaidze** 2004 *Ur, CHL*
L **Chikvinidze** 1994 *Swi,* 1995 *Bul, Mol, Ger, H,* 1996 *CZR, Rus*
L **Chilachava** 2012 *Sp, C,* 2013 *Bel, Ur, Ar, C, US, Sa,* 2014 *Bel, Pt, Rus, Sp, R*
G **Chkhaidze** 2002 *H, R, I, Rus,* 2003 *Pt, CZR, It, E, SA, Ur,* 2004 *CZR, R,* 2006 *Pt, Ukr,* 2007 *R, Rus, CZR, Nm, ESp, ItA, Ar, I, Nm, F,* 2008 *R, Pt, CZR, Rus, Sp,* 2009 *Ger, Pt, Sp, R, Rus, ArJ, ItA,* 2010 *Ger, Pt, Sp, R, Rus, C, US,* 2011 *Ukr, Sp, Pt, R, Rus, S, E, R, Ar,* 2012 *Sp, Pt, R, Rus, Ukr, US, C,* 2013 *Bel, Pt, Rus, Sp, R, Ur, Ar, C, US, Sa,* 2014 *Bel, Pt, Rus, Sp, R*
S **Chkhenkeli** 1997 *Pol*
I **Chkhikvadze** 2005 *CHL,* 2007 *Sp,* 2008 *Pt, R, Pt, CZR, Rus, ESp, Ur, ItA, S,* 2009 *Ger, Sp, Pt, ItA,* 2010 *Sp, Rus, S, ItA, Nm, C, US,* 2011 *Pt, Nm, R,* 2012 *Pt*
I **Chkonia** 2007 *ESp, ItA*

D **Dadunashvili** 2003 *It, E, SA, Ur,* 2004 *Sp, Rus, CZR, R,* 2005 *CHL,* 2007 *Sp, Rus, CZR, Nm, ItA,* 2008 *Pt, R, Pt, CZR, Rus, Sp, S,* 2009 *C, IrA, US, ItA,* 2010 *Sp, S, ItA, Nm*
L **Datunashvili** 2004 *Sp,* 2005 *Pt, Ukr, R, CZR,* 2006 *Rus, R, Pt, Ukr, J, Bb, CZR, Pt, Pt,* 2007 *R, Rus, Nm, ESp, ItA, I, Nm, F,* 2008 *Pt, Pt,* 2009 *Sp, R, Rus, C, US, ArJ,* 2010 *Ger, Pt, Sp, R, Rus, C, US,* 2011 *Ukr, Sp, Pt, R, Rus, S, E, R, Ar,* 2012 *Sp, Pt, Rus, J, Fj,* 2013 *Sp, R, Ar, C, US, Sa,* 2014 *Bel, Pt, Rus, R*
V **Didebulidze** 1991 *Ukr,* 1994 *Kaz,* 1995 *Bul, Mol,* 1996 *CZR,* 1997 *De,* 1999 *Tg,* 2000 *H,* 2001 *H, Pt, Rus, Sp, R, F, SA,* 2002 *H, Pt, Rus, Sp, R, I, Rus,* 2003 *Pt, Sp, Rus, CZR, R, It, E, Sa, SA,* 2004 *Rus,* 2005 *Pt,* 2006 *R, R,* 2007 *R, Sp, Rus, CZR, Nm, ESp, ItA, Ar, Nm, F*
E **Dzagnidze** 1992 *Ukr, Ukr, Lat,* 1993 *Rus, Pol,* 1995 *Bul, Mol, Ger, H,* 1998 *I*
N **Dzagnidze** 1989 *Z,* 1990 *Z, Z,* 1991 *Ukr,* 1992 *Ukr, Ukr, Lat,* 1993 *Rus, Pol,* 1994 *Swi,* 1995 *Ger, H*
T **Dzagnidze** 2008 *ESp*
D **Dzneladze** 1992 *Ukr, Lat,* 1993 *Lux,* 1994 *Kaz*
P **Dzotsenidze** 1995 *Ger, H,* 1997 *Pt, Pol*

G **Elizbarashvili** 2002 *Rus,* 2003 *Sp,* 2004 *CHL,* 2005 *CZR,* 2006 *Pt, Ukr, J, Bb, CZR, Pt,* 2007 *R, Sp, Rus, I, F,* 2009 *C, IrA*
O **Eloshvili** 2002 *H,* 2003 *SA,* 2006 *Bb, CZR,* 2007 *Sp, CZR, Nm, ESp, ItA, I, F*
S **Essakia** 1999 *Tg, Tg,* 2000 *It, Mor, Sp, H,* 2004 *CZR, R*

M **Gagnidze** 1991 *Ukr, Ukr*
D **Gasviani** 2004 *Sp, Rus,* 2005 *CZR, CHL,* 2006 *Ukr, J,* 2007 *Rus, CZR,* 2008 *ESp, Ur, ItA, S*
A **Ghibradze** 1992 *Ukr, Ukr, Lat,* 1994 *Swi,* 1995 *Bul, Mol, Ger,* 1996 *CZR*
D **Ghudushauri** 1989 *Z,* 1991 *Ukr, Ukr*
L **Ghvaberidze** 2004 *Pt*
R **Gigauri** 2006 *Ukr, J, Bb, CZR, Sp, Pt, Pt,* 2007 *R, Nm, ESp, ItA, Ar, Nm, F,* 2008 *Pt, R, Pt, Rus, Sp, ESp, Ur,* 2009 *C, IrA, US, ArJ, ItA,* 2010 *S, ItA, Nm,* 2011 *Nm, S, E, R,* 2012 *Sp,* 2014 *Sp*
A **Giorgadze** 1996 *CZR,* 1998 *It, Ukr, Rus, R,* 1999 *Tg, Tg,* 2000 *It, Pt, Mor, H, R,* 2001 *H, Pt, Rus, Sp, R, F, SA,* 2002 *H, Pt, Rus, Sp, R, I, Rus,* 2003 *Pt, Sp, Rus, R, It, E, Sa, SA, Ur,* 2005 *Pt, Ukr,* 2006 *Rus, R, Pt, Bb, CZR, Sp, Pt,* 2007 *R, Ar, I, Nm, F,* 2009 *Ger, Pt, Sp, ArJ,* 2010 *Ger, Pt, C, US,* 2011 *Pt, S, Ar*
I **Giorgadze** 2001 *F, SA,* 2003 *Pt, Sp, Rus, R, It, E, Sa, Ur,* 2004 *Rus,* 2005 *Pt, R, CZR,* 2006 *Rus, R, Pt, Bb, CZR, R, Sp, Pt, Pt,* 2007 *R, Sp, Rus, CZR, Ar, Nm, F,* 2008 *R,* 2009 *Ger, Pt, Sp, Rus,* 2010 *Ger, Sp, R, Rus,* 2011 *Ukr*
M **Giorgadze** 2014 *Sp*
M **Gorgodze** 2003 *Sp, Rus,* 2004 *Pt, Sp, Rus, CZR, R, Ur, CHL, Rus,* 2005 *Pt, Ukr, R, CZR, CHL,* 2006 *Rus, Pt, Bb, CZR, R, Sp, Pt, Pt,* 2007 *Ar, I, Nm,* 2008 *R, Rus, Sp,* 2009 *Ger, Pt, Sp, R, Rus, ArJ,* 2011 *R, Rus, S, E, R, Ar,* 2012 *Pt, R, Rus, J, Fj,* 2013 *Bel, Pt, Rus, Sp, R, C, US, Sa,* 2014 *Rus, Sp, R*

E **Gueguchadze** 1990 *Z, Z*
L **Gugava** 2004 *Sp, Rus, CZR, Ur, CHL, Rus,* 2005 *Pt, Ukr,* 2006 *Bb, CZR,* 2009 *C, IrA, US,* 2010 *C, US,* 2011 *Ukr, Sp, Pt, R, Rus, Nm, Ar,* 2012 *Ukr, C*
I **Guiorkhelidze** 1998 *R,* 1999 *Tg, Tg*
G **Guiunashvili** 1989 *Z,* 1990 *Z,* 1991 *Ukr, Ukr,* 1992 *Ukr, Ukr, Lat,* 1993 *Rus, Pol, Lux,* 1994 *Swi,* 1996 *Rus,* 1997 *Pt*
K **Guiunashvili** 1990 *Z, Z,* 1991 *Ukr, Ukr,* 1992 *Ukr, Ukr, Lat*
B **Gujaraidze** 2008 *ESp,* 2012 *Ukr*
S **Gujaraidze** 2003 *SA, Ur*
I **Gundishvili** 2002 *I,* 2003 *Pt, Sp, Rus, CZR,* 2008 *ESp, Ur, ItA,* 2009 *C, US*
D **Gurgenidze** 2007 *Sp, ItA*
A **Gusharashvili** 1998 *Ukr*

D **Iobidze** 1993 *Rus, Pol*
E **Iovadze** 1993 *Lux,* 1994 *Kaz,* 1995 *Bul, Mol, Ger, H,* 2001 *Sp, F, SA,* 2002 *H, Rus, Sp, R, I*
A **Issakadze** 1989 *Z*
N **Iurini** 1991 *Ukr,* 1994 *Swi,* 1995 *Ger, H,* 1996 *CZR, CZR, Rus,* 1997 *Pt, Pol, Cro, De,* 1998 *Ukr, Rus,* 2000 *It, Sp, H, R*

S **Janelidze** 1991 *Ukr, Ukr,* 1993 *Rus,* 1994 *Kaz,* 1995 *Ger,* 1997 *Pt,* 1998 *Ukr, I, R,* 1999 *Tg,* 2000 *R*
R **Japarashvili** 1992 *Ukr, Ukr, Lat,* 1993 *Pol, Lux,* 1996 *CZR,* 1997 *Pt*
L **Javelidze** 1997 *Cro,* 1998 *I,* 2001 *H, R, F, SA,* 2002 *H, R,* 2004 *R,* 2005 *Ukr,* 2007 *Sp*
G **Jgenti** 2004 *Ur,* 2005 *CHL,* 2007 *Sp, CZR, Nm, ESp, ItA,* 2009 *C, IrA, US,* 2011 *R*
D **Jghenti** 2004 *CZR, R*
D **Jhamutashvili** 2005 *CHL*
P **Jimsheladze** 1995 *Bul, Mol, H,* 1996 *CZR, CZR, Rus,* 1997 *De,* 1998 *It, Ukr, Rus, I, R,* 1999 *Tg, Tg,* 2000 *Pt, Mor, Sp, H, R,* 2001 *H, Pt, Rus, Sp, R, F, SA,* 2002 *H, Pt, Rus, Sp, I, Rus,* 2003 *Pt, Sp, Rus, CZR, R, It, E, Sa, SA, Ur,* 2004 *Sp,* 2005 *R,* 2006 *Rus, R, Pt, Ukr,* 2007 *R, Pt, Rus, CZR, R*
K **Jintcharadze** 1993 *Rus, Pol,* 2000 *It, Mor*

D **Kacharava** 2006 *Ukr, J, R, Sp, Pt,* 2007 *R, Sp, Rus, CZR, Nm, ESp, ItA, I, Nm,* 2008 *Pt, R, Pt, CZR, Rus, Sp, S,* 2009 *Ger, Pt, Sp, R, Rus, C, IrA, US, ArJ, ItA,* 2010 *Ger, Pt, Sp, R, Rus, C, US,* 2011 *Ukr, Sp, Pt, R, Rus, S, E, R, Ar,* 2012 *Sp, Pt, R, Rus, Ukr, US, C, J, Fj,* 2013 *Bel, Pt, Rus, Sp, R, Ur, Ar, C, US, Sa,* 2014 *Bel, Pt, Rus, R, Sp*
G **Kacharava** 2005 *Ukr,* 2006 *J, Bb, CZR, R,* 2007 *Sp,* 2008 *CZR*
G **Kakhiani** 1995 *Bul, Mol*
V **Kakovin** 2008 *S,* 2009 *C, IrA, US,* 2010 *S, ItA, Nm,* 2011 *Ukr, Sp, Pt, Rus, Nm, R, Ar,* 2012 *Pt, R, Rus,* 2013 *Rus, Sp, R, Ar*
G **Kalmakhelidze** 2012 *Sp, Ukr*
V **Katsadze** 1997 *Pol,* 1998 *It, Ukr, Rus, I, R,* 1999 *Tg, Tg,* 2000 *Pt, Mor, Sp, H, R,* 2001 *H, Pt, Rus, Sp, R,* 2002 *Pt, Rus, Sp, R, I, Rus,* 2003 *Pt, Sp, CZR, R, E, Sa, SA, Ur,* 2004 *Sp,* 2005 *Ukr*
A **Kavtarashvili** 1994 *Swi,* 1995 *Bul, Mol, Ger,* 1996 *CZR, Rus,* 1997 *Pt, Cro, De,* 1998 *It, Rus, I, R,* 1999 *Tg, Tg,* 2000 *It, H, R,* 2001 *H,* 2003 *SA, Ur*
G **Kavtidze** 2008 *S*
I **Kerauli** 1991 *Ukr, Ukr,* 1992 *Ukr, Ukr*
L **Khachirashvili** 2005 *Ukr*
T **Khakhaleishili** 1994 *Kaz*
B **Khamashuridze** 1989 *Z*
B **Khamashuridze** 1998 *It, Ukr, Rus, I, R,* 1999 *Tg, Tg,* 2000 *It, Pt, Sp, H, R,* 2001 *Pt, Rus, Sp, R, F, SA,* 2002 *H, Pt, Rus, Sp, R, I, Rus,* 2003 *Pt, CZR, R, It, E, Sa, SA, Ur,* 2004 *Pt, Rus, Rus,* 2005 *Pt, Ukr, CHL,* 2006 *Rus, R, Pt, R, Sp, Pt, Pt,* 2007 *Rus, CZR, ESp, Ar, Nm, F,* 2008 *Pt,* 2010 *US,* 2011 *Ukr, Sp, R, Rus, Nm*
M **Kharshiladze** 1991 *Ukr*
B **Khekhelashvili** 1999 *Tg, Tg,* 2000 *It, Pt, Mor, Sp, H, R,* 2001 *H, Pt, R, F, SA,* 2002 *H, Pt, Rus, Sp, R, I,* 2003 *Sp, Rus, CZR, R, E, Sa,* 2004 *Sp*
D **Khinchagishvili** 2003 *Sp, CZR,* 2004 *Pt, Sp, Rus,* 2006 *Bb,*

**T Odisharia** 1989 *Z*, 1994 *Kaz*

**S Papashvili** 2001 *SA*, 2004 *CZR, R*, 2006 *Bb, CZR*, 2007 *Sp*
**S Partsikanashvili** 1994 *Kaz*, 1996 *CZR, Rus*, 1997 *Pol*, 1999 *Tg, Tg*, 2000 *It, Pt, Mor*
**A Peikrishvili** 2008 *Pt, Pt*, 2009 *R*, 2010 *Pt, R, Rus*, 2011 *Sp*, 2013 *Ar*, 2014 *Pt, Sp, R*
**G Peradze** 1991 *Ukr*
**Z Peradze** 1997 *Pol*, 1998 *Rus*
**Z Petriashvili** 2009 *C*
**D Pinchukovi** 2004 *CZR*
**L Pirpilashvili** 2004 *Rus, CZR, R, Ur, CHL*, 2005 *Ukr, R, CZR*
**G Pirtskhalava** 1989 *Z*, 1995 *Ger*, 1996 *CZR, Rus*, 1997 *Pt, Pol*
**T Pkhakadze** 1989 *Z*, 1990 *Z, Z*, 1993 *Rus, Pol, Lux*, 1994 *Kaz*, 1996 *CZR*

**G Rapava-Ruskini** 1990 *Z*, 1992 *Ukr, Lat*, 1994 *Kaz*, 1996 *Rus*, 1997 *Pt, Cro, De*, 1998 *It, Ukr, Rus, R*, 1999 *Tg*
**T Ratianidze** 2000 *It*, 2001 *H, Pt, Sp, R, SA*, 2002 *Pt, Rus, Sp, R, I, Rus*, 2003 *Pt, Sp, Rus, CZR, R*
**Z Rekhviashvili** 1995 *H*, 1997 *Pt, Pol*
**G Rokhvadze** 2008 *ItA*, 2009 *C, IrA, US*, 2010 *S, ItA*, 2014 *Sp*

**S Sakandelidze** 1996 *CZR*, 1998 *Ukr*
**S Sakvarelidze** 2010 *S, ItA*
**B Samkharadze** 2004 *Pt, Sp, Rus, CZR, R, Ur, CHL*, 2005 *CZR, CHL*, 2006 *Rus, R, Pt, Ukr, Bb, CZR, R, Sp, Pt, Pt*, 2007 *R, Sp, Rus, CZR, Nm, ESp, Ar, I, Nm, F*, 2008 *Pt, R, Pt, Sp, ESp, Ur, ItA, S*, 2009 *Ger, Sp, R, ArJ, ItA*, 2010 *Ger, Pt, Sp, R, S, ItA, Nm, C*, 2011 *Ukr, Sp, Pt, Nm, E, R, Ar*, 2012 *Pt, C*
**A Sanadze** 2004 *CHL*
**P Saneblidze** 1994 *Kaz*
**G Sanikidze** 2004 *Ur, CHL*
**B Sardanashvili** 2004 *CHL*
**V Satseradze** 1989 *Z*, 1990 *Z*, 1991 *Ukr*, 1992 *Ukr, Ukr, Lat*
**E Shanidze** 1994 *Swi*
**M Sharikadze** 2012 *Sp, Pt, R, Rus, Ukr, US, J, Fj*, 2013 *Bel, Pt, Rus, Sp, R, Ur, Ar, C, US, Sa*, 2014 *Bel, Rus, Sp, R*
**B Sheklashvili** 2010 *S, ItA, Nm*, 2011 *Sp*, 2012 *Sp*
**G Shkinin** 2004 *CZR, R, CHL*, 2005 *CHL*, 2006 *Rus, R, Ukr, J, R, Sp, Pt, Pt*, 2007 *R, Sp, Rus, CZR, Nm, ESp, ItA, Ar, I, Nm*, 2008 *R, Pt, CZR, Rus, Sp, ESp, Ur, ItA, S*, 2009 *Pt*, 2012 *Sp, Pt, R*, 2013 *Sa*, 2014 *Bel, Pt*
**B Shvanguiradze** 1990 *Z, Z*, 1992 *Ukr, Ukr, Lat*, 1993 *Rus, Pol, Lux*
**G Shvelidze** 1998 *I, R*, 1999 *Tg, Tg*, 2000 *It, Pt, Sp, H, R*, 2001 *H, Pt, Sp, F, SA*, 2002 *H, Rus, I, Rus*, 2003 *Pt, Sp, Rus, CZR, R, It, E, Sa, Ur*, 2004 *Rus*, 2005 *Pt, CZR*, 2006 *Rus, R, Pt, R, Sp, Pt, Pt*, 2007 *Ar, I, Nm, F*, 2008 *Pt, R, Pt, CZR, Rus*, 2009 *Ger, Pt, Sp, R, Rus, ArJ*, 2010 *Sp, R, Rus, C, US*, 2011 *Pt, Nm, E, R, Ar*
**I Sikharulidze** 1994 *Kaz*
**T Sokhadze** 2005 *CZR*, 2006 *Rus, R, Pt, Ukr, J, Pt, Pt*, 2009 *C, IrA*
**M Sujashvili** 2004 *Pt, Rus*, 2005 *Pt, Ukr, R, CZR*, 2006 *Pt, Ukr, J, Bb, CZR*
**S Sultanishvili** 1998 *Ukr*
**S Sutiashvili** 2005 *CHL*, 2006 *Ukr*, 2007 *CZR, Nm, ESp*, 2008 *Pt, R, CZR, Rus, S*, 2010 *S, ItA, Nm, C, US*, 2011 *Ukr, Sp, Pt, R, Rus, S, E*, 2012 *Pt, R, Rus, C, J, Fj*, 2013 *Bel, Pt, Rus, Sp, R, Ur, Ar, C, US, Sa*, 2014 *Pt, Sp, Sp*
**P Svanidze** 1992 *Ukr*

**T Tavadze** 1991 *Ukr, Ukr*
**L Tavartkiladze** 2009 *ItA*, 2010 *Ger, Sp, R, Rus, S, ItA, Nm*, 2011 *Sp*

**N Tchavtchavadze** 1998 *It, Ukr*, 2004 *CZR, R, Ur, CHL*
**M Tcheishvili** 1989 *Z*, 1990 *Z, Z*, 1995 *H*
**B Tepnadze** 1995 *H*, 1996 *CZR*, 1997 *Cro*, 1998 *I, R*, 1999 *Tg*
**G Tkhilaishvili** 2012 *Ukr, US, C, J*, 2013 *C, US, Sa*, 2014 *Bel, Sp, Sp*
**A Todua** 2008 *CZR, Rus, Sp, ESp, Ur, ItA, S*, 2009 *Sp, R, C, IrA, US, ArJ, ItA*, 2010 *Ger, Pt, R, Rus, S, ItA, Nm*, 2011 *Nm, S, E, R, Ar*, 2012 *Sp, Pt, R, Rus, US, C, J, Fj*, 2013 *Bel, Ur*, 2014 *Sp*
**P Tqabladze** 1993 *Lux*, 1995 *Bul*
**L Tsabadze** 1994 *Kaz, Swi*, 1995 *Bul, Ger, H*, 1996 *CZR, Rus*, 1997 *Cro, De*, 1998 *It, Rus, I, R*, 1999 *Tg, Tg*, 2000 *Pt, Mor, Sp, R*, 2001 *H, Pt, Rus, Sp, R, F, SA*, 2002 *H, Pt, Rus, Sp, R, I, Rus*
**B Tsiklauri** 2008 *ItA*, 2012 *Pt, Ukr*, 2013 *Bel, Rus, Sp, Ur, Ar, US, Sa*, 2014 *Bel, Sp, Sp*
**G Tsiklauri** 2003 *SA, Ur*
**D Tskhvediani** 1998 *Ukr*
**V Tskitishvili** 1994 *Swi*, 1995 *Bul, Mol*
**T Turdzeladze** 1989 *Z*, 1990 *Z, Z*, 1991 *Ukr*, 1995 *Ger, H*

**K Uchava** 2002 *Sp*, 2004 *Sp*, 2008 *Pt, R, Pt, Rus, Sp, ESp, Ur, ItA, S*, 2009 *Ger, Pt, R, C, IrA*, 2010 *S, ItA, Nm*
**B Udesiani** 2001 *Sp, F*, 2002 *H*, 2004 *Pt, Sp, CZR, R, Rus*, 2005 *Pt, Ukr, R, CZR, CHL*, 2006 *Rus, R, Ukr, J, Bb, CZR, R, Sp, Pt, Pt*, 2007 *R, Rus, CZR, Ar, Nm*, 2008 *CZR, Sp, ESp, Ur, ItA, S*, 2010 *Ger, Pt, Sp, R, Rus, C, US*, 2011 *Ukr*
**B Urjukashvili** 2011 *Ukr, Sp, Pt, Rus, Nm*
**M Urjukashvili** 1997 *Cro, De*, 1998 *Ukr, Rus, R*, 1999 *Tg, Tg*, 2000 *It, Pt, Mor, Sp*, 2001 *Pt, Rus, Sp, R, F, SA*, 2002 *H, Pt, Sp, R, I, Rus*, 2003 *Pt, Sp, Rus, R, It, E, Sa, Ur*, 2004 *Pt, Rus, Ur, CHL, Rus*, 2005 *Pt, R, CZR*, 2006 *Rus, R, Pt, Ukr, J, R, Sp, Pt, Pt*, 2007 *Rus, CZR, Nm, ESp, ItA, Ar, I, Nm, F*, 2008 *Sp*, 2009 *Rus, Sp, R, Rus, Rus, ItA, Nm, C*, 2011 *Nm, S, R, Ar*
**R Urushadze** 1997 *Pol*, 2002 *R*, 2004 *Pt, Rus, Rus*, 2005 *Pt, Ukr, R, CZR, CHL*, 2006 *Rus, R, Pt, Bb, CZR, R, Sp, Pt*, 2007 *Nm, ESp, ItA, I, Nm, F*, 2008 *Pt, R, Pt, Rus, Sp, S*, 2009 *Ger, Pt, Sp, R, Rus, C, IrA, US, ArJ, ItA*

**Z Valishvili** 2004 *CHL*
**D Vartaniani** 1991 *Ukr, Ukr*, 1992 *Ukr, Ukr, Lat*, 1997 *Pol*, 2000 *Sp, H, R*
**L Vashadze** 1991 *Ukr*, 1992 *Ukr, Ukr, Lat*

**G Yachvili** 2001 *H, Pt, R*, 2003 *Pt, Sp, Rus, CZR, R, It, E, Sa, Ur*

**I Zedginidze** 1998 *I*, 2000 *It, Pt, Mor, Sp, H, R*, 2001 *H, Pt, Rus, Sp, R*, 2002 *H, Rus, Sp, I, Rus*, 2003 *Pt, Sp, Rus, CZR, R, It, Sa, SA, Ur*, 2004 *Pt, Sp, Rus, CZR, R, Rus*, 2005 *Pt, Ukr, R, CZR*, 2006 *Rus, R, Pt, Ukr, CZR, R, Sp, Pt, R, Sp, Pt*, 2007 *R, Ar, I*, 2008 *S*, 2009 *Ger, Pt, Sp, Rus, ArJ, ItA*, 2010 *Ger, Pt, Sp, R, Rus*, 2011 *Nm, E, R, Ar*
**Z Zhvania** 2013 *Sp, R, Sa*, 2014 *Bel, Pt, Rus, Sp, Sp*
**T Zibzibadze** 2000 *It, Pt, Mor, Sp*, 2001 *H, Pt, Rus, Sp, R, F, SA*, 2002 *H, Pt, Rus, Sp, R, I, Rus*, 2003 *Pt, Sp, Rus, CZR, R, It, E, Sa, Ur*, 2004 *Pt, Sp, Rus, CZR, R, Rus*, 2005 *Pt, Ukr, R, CZR*, 2009 *Ger, Pt, Sp, R, ArJ*, 2010 *Ger, Pt, Sp, R, Rus, S, ItA, Nm, C, US*, 2011 *Sp, Pt, R, C, US, Sa*, 2012 *R, Rus, C, J*, 2013 *Pt, Rus, R, Ur, C, US, Sa*, 2014 *Pt, Rus, Sp, R0*
**D Zirakashvili** 2004 *Ur, CHL, Rus*, 2005 *Ukr, R, CZR*, 2006 *Rus, R, Pt, Sp, Pt*, 2007 *R, Ar, Nm, F*, 2008 *R*, 2009 *Ger*, 2010 *Ger, Pt, Sp, Rus, C, US*, 2011 *Ukr, Pt, R, Rus, S, E, R*, 2012 *Ukr, US, C, J, Fj*, 2013 *Pt, Rus, Sp, R, Ur, Ar*, 2014 *Rus, R*

Ireland will be hoping to make the running again as they defend their Six Nations title in 2015.

# IRELAND

## IRELAND'S 2013–14 TEST RECORD

| OPPONENTS | DATE | VENUE | RESULT |
|---|---|---|---|
| Samoa | 9 Nov | H | Won 40–9 |
| Australia | 16 Nov | H | Lost 15–32 |
| New Zealand | 24 Nov | H | Lost 22–24 |
| Scotland | 2 Feb | H | Won 28–6 |
| Wales | 8 Feb | H | Won 26–3 |
| England | 22 Feb | A | Lost 13–10 |
| Italy | 8 Mar | H | Won 46–7 |
| France | 15 Mar | A | Won 22–20 |
| Argentina | 7 Jun | A | Won 29–17 |
| Argentina | 14 Jun | A | Won 23–17 |

# O'DRISCOLL GETS THE PERFECT SWANSONG

## By Ruaidhri O'Connor

AFP/Getty Images

Captain Paul O'Connell and the retiring Brian O'Driscoll hold the Six Nations trophy aloft after victory in Paris.

**I**reland's season of the long goodbye ended with renewed hope about the state of the nation. Brian O'Driscoll may no longer be wearing the green jersey, but under the stewardship of Joe Schmidt the Six Nations champions look ready for life after BOD.

The New Zealander played a major role in convincing the legendary centre to play on for one more year, his first in charge since being promoted from Leinster to the national team.

In November, Ireland came within agonising seconds of a famous first win over the All Blacks, but they bounced back to claim the Six Nations and finished off with a somewhat underwhelming first series win in Argentina in the summer.

Ryan Crotty's injury-time try and Aaron Cruden's subsequent conversion may have denied O'Driscoll and Ireland their marquee win over New Zealand after one of their greatest performances, but his final cap in Paris will go down as a day to remember. The Stade de France is the venue where O'Driscoll made his name as a fresh-faced youngster wearing an old-school baggy jersey back in 2000, scoring a hat-trick of tries in a display that catapulted him onto the world stage.

Time may have robbed O'Driscoll of his explosive pace, but he was a key contributor to the Six Nations victory as Ireland won in Paris for the first time since his breakthrough moment.

The latter years of O'Driscoll's career had been marked by success at provincial level for Leinster and a first successful Lions series win – albeit having been infamously dropped for the decisive final Test in Australia – but he felt his Ireland medal haul was a little shy.

"It's a wonderful feeling," he said in the aftermath of Ireland's 22–20 win in the French capital. "I've played a long time for Ireland and to only have won one Six Nations Championship would have been disappointing so I'm really delighted for this group of players, for how talented they are, how hard they worked. It feels great to be a two-time Six Nations winner. So many seconds along the years and so many disappointments, it is great to finish my career on a high. When I do hang this jersey up on the hook inside it will be with fond memories."

The centre would finish the season with a RaboDirect PRO12 medal to boot – although he was forced off with injury just minutes into the final win over Glasgow Warriors – but a fourth Heineken Cup evaded his grasp as Leinster came up well short in the quarter-final meeting with eventual champions Toulon.

Life after O'Driscoll has long been a scary prospect for Ireland, but the country is facing Rugby World Cup 2015 with renewed optimism and that is largely down to the former Leinster coach, whose record of five trophies in the last four seasons is getting fans excited. Schmidt has been doing his best to temper expectations but the performances since the New Zealand heartbreak underline a team growing in confidence under the steady captaincy of Paul O'Connell.

Ireland's end-of-season tour to Argentina afforded Schmidt a chance to rest some key players, who needed a break, while he blooded a host of new faces.

Over the course of the season, he fielded 48 different players, 10 of whom were new caps. Tellingly, however, the New Zealander stuck largely with the same team who went so close against the world champions on 24 November.

That the Six Nations win was achieved without injured Lions Sean O'Brien and Tommy Bowe was a feather in the team's cap which emphasises the strength in depth available in the back row and back three in particular.

However, Ireland are not so lucky in other areas with Martin Moore's emergence at tighthead prop lightening the load somewhat on Mike Ross, while O'Driscoll's retirement has opened up a vacancy at outside centre for the first time since 1999.

Along with Ross, Jonathan Sexton's fitness remains paramount to Irish success. The fly-half's move to Racing Métro removed him from the protective bubble of the Irish season and the gruelling schedule took its toll.

His inspired performance in his adopted home city of Paris, where he scored two tries against France in the Championship decider, served to underline his importance to the cause and Schmidt will be hoping his club will be less reliant on his talents this season.

Sexton will have mixed memories of the season, however. He had a kick to put the game beyond New Zealand in November, but pulled it right. Minutes later, the enormity of the error became all too apparent as he watched from the sidelines as Crotty levelled.

"When they took their shot at goal that would have put it out to eight points, the reality is that if that had gone over then it was game over," All Black captain Richie McCaw admitted.

The winning try was a sight to behold. Nigel Owens penalised Jack McGrath for going off his feet at a ruck in the Irish half with 20 seconds remaining and Aaron Smith tapped the penalty and the All Blacks went 60 metres, through 11 phases to score in the corner.

The defeat came from a half-time position of real strength after tries from Conor Murray, Rory Best and Rob Kearney gave the hosts a 22–7 cushion at the break. It was followed by second halves in London and Paris during the Six Nations that saw England storm from behind to win and France come agonisingly close to doing the same in the final match.

That won't have gone unnoticed and Schmidt will expect improvements this season.

Still, with Ireland winning their last four games of the season and improving massively from their hammering at home by Australia in November, Schmidt is looking to keep the winning habit going ahead of the return of the Wallabies, South Africa and Georgia in November.

That process began in Argentina where Ireland struggled for the same level of performance in Resistencia and Tucumán, but ran out comfortable winners over an under-strength Pumas side all the same.

"We always try and judge ourselves by performances, while results are important," full-back Rob Kearney said. "If, after winning the Six Nations, we are striving to be proper World Cup contenders then you have to judge yourself on performances. The World Cup is still a long way away, but that's what we're striving to do. We want to build a squad here that can be World Cup contenders – we've always said that on our day we can match or beat the best. But the standard is increasing right across the world. New Zealand are getting harder to beat, the English are getting strong and South Africa bashed Wales [in their first Test]. We have to keep evolving and improving because, if we don't, we'll be left behind."

That is the challenge for Schmidt as he looks ahead to his first World Cup as an international coach.

The loss of popular forward's coach John Plumtree, who returned home to New Zealand after just one successful season, and the middling displays on the tour to Argentina have taken some of the wind out of Ireland's sails, but the former Leinster supremo will be intent on wresting momentum back in November.

By then, fellow Kiwi Jared Payne will have qualified through residency and he is expected to do battle with Connacht's Robbie Henshaw for the vacant No.13 jersey, while O'Brien and Bowe will be well-rested and, fingers crossed, injury free.

As those who have been in the squad since the 2009 Grand Slam know, past glories are no marker of future success and defence coach Les Kiss – part of the previous coaching ticket who never achieved the same level of consistency from their charges after that first season win – warned that complacency would not be tolerated.

"The Six Nations success doesn't guarantee future success, we have got to refresh things, be very specific about what we refresh because people should be confident about what they've achieved but not so confident that they forget what got them there," said the Australian, who will combine his role with a new posting as director of rugby at Ulster.

"I think we're now more advanced from that. We've a really strong group of players and we're big on them driving it and Joe has made that clear. They've really stepped up to the plate in a more advanced fashion.

"There was a flow on, an afterglow that stuck on afterwards in '09. But it is about maintaining it in the longer term, renewing it and refreshing your message as much as possible around certain elements of the game that makes sense and that are logically bettering each other."

That is the challenge for players and coaches alike as they face the most important season of every four-year cycle.

O'Driscoll may have stepped aside, while Stephen Ferris's injuries have also caused him to retire prematurely, but the coach is inspiring optimism all round.

The defeats to New Zealand, Australia and England will keep Irish feet on the ground, but the side got a taste of glory in Paris and had history cruelly snatched from their grasp against the All Blacks.

That should guard against complacency, along with Schmidt's incessant drive for higher standards and more success.

# IRELAND INTERNATIONAL STATISTICS

## MATCH RECORDS UP TO 13 OCTOBER 2014

### MOST CONSECUTIVE TEST WINS

| | |
|---|---|
| 10 | 2002 R, Ru, Gg, A, Fj, Arg, 2003 S1, It1, F, W1 |
| 8 | 2003 Tg, Sm, W2, It2, S2, R, Nm, Arg |
| 8 | 2008 Arg, 2009 F, It, E, S, W ,C, US |
| 6 | 1968 S, W, A, 1969 F, E, S |
| 6 | 2004 SA, US, Arg, 2005 It, S, E |

### MOST CONSECUTIVE TESTS WITHOUT DEFEAT

| Matches | Wins | Draws | Period |
|---|---|---|---|
| 12 | 11 | 1 | 2008 to 2010 |
| 10 | 10 | 0 | 2002 to 2003 |
| 8 | 8 | 0 | 2003 |
| 7 | 6 | 1 | 1968 to 1969 |
| 6 | 6 | 0 | 2004 to 2005 |

### MOST POINTS IN A MATCH

#### BY THE TEAM

| Pts | Opponents | Venue | Year |
|---|---|---|---|
| 83 | United States | Manchester (NH) | 2000 |
| 78 | Japan | Dublin | 2000 |
| 70 | Georgia | Dublin | 1998 |
| 64 | Fiji | Dublin | 2002 |
| 64 | Namibia | Sydney | 2003 |
| 63 | Georgia | Dublin | 2002 |
| 62 | Russia | Rotorua | 2011 |
| 61 | Italy | Limerick | 2003 |
| 61 | Pacific Islands | Dublin | 2006 |
| 60 | Romania | Dublin | 1986 |
| 60 | Italy | Dublin | 2000 |

#### BY A PLAYER

| Pts | Player | Opponents | Venue | Year |
|---|---|---|---|---|
| 32 | RJR O'Gara | Samoa | Apia | 2003 |
| 30 | RJR O'Gara | Italy | Dublin | 2000 |
| 26 | DG Humphreys | Scotland | Murrayfield | 2003 |
| 26 | DG Humphreys | Italy | Limerick | 2003 |
| 26 | P Wallace | Pacific Islands | Dublin | 2006 |
| 24 | PA Burke | Italy | Dublin | 1997 |
| 24 | DG Humphreys | Argentina | Lens | 1999 |
| 23 | RP Keyes | Zimbabwe | Dublin | 1991 |
| 23 | RJR O'Gara | Japan | Dublin | 2000 |
| 22 | DG Humphreys | Wales | Dublin | 2002 |

### MOST TRIES IN A MATCH

#### BY THE TEAM

| Tries | Opponents | Venue | Year |
|---|---|---|---|
| 13 | United States | Manchester (NH) | 2000 |
| 11 | Japan | Dublin | 2000 |
| 10 | Romania | Dublin | 1986 |
| 10 | Georgia | Dublin | 1998 |
| 10 | Namibia | Sydney | 2003 |
| 9 | Fiji | Dublin | 2003 |
| 9 | Russia | Rotorua | 2011 |
| 8 | Western Samoa | Dublin | 1988 |
| 8 | Zimbabwe | Dublin | 1991 |
| 8 | Georgia | Dublin | 2002 |
| 8 | Italy | Limerick | 2003 |
| 8 | Pacific Islands | Dublin | 2006 |
| 8 | Italy | Rome | 2007 |
| 8 | Canada | Limerick | 2008 |

#### BY A PLAYER

| Tries | Player | Opponents | Venue | Year |
|---|---|---|---|---|
| 4 | BF Robinson | Zimbabwe | Dublin | 1991 |
| 4 | KGM Wood | United States | Dublin | 1999 |
| 4 | DA Hickie | Italy | Limerick | 2003 |
| 3 | R Montgomery | Wales | Birkenhead | 1887 |
| 3 | JP Quinn | France | Cork | 1913 |
| 3 | E O'D Davy | Scotland | Murrayfield | 1930 |
| 3 | SJ Byrne | Scotland | Murrayfield | 1953 |
| 3 | KD Crossan | Romania | Dublin | 1986 |
| 3 | BJ Mullin | Tonga | Brisbane | 1987 |
| 3 | MR Mostyn | Argentina | Dublin | 1999 |
| 3 | BG O'Driscoll | France | Paris | 2000 |
| 3 | MJ Mullins | United States | Manchester (NH) | 2000 |
| 3 | DA Hickie | Japan | Dublin | 2000 |
| 3 | RAJ Henderson | Italy | Rome | 2001 |
| 3 | BG O'Driscoll | Scotland | Dublin | 2002 |
| 3 | KM Maggs | Fiji | Dublin | 2002 |
| 3 | FL McFadden | Canada | Toronto | 2013 |

THE COUNTRIES

## MOST CONVERSIONS IN A MATCH
### BY THE TEAM

| Cons | Opponents | Venue | Year |
|------|-----------|-------|------|
| 10 | Georgia | Dublin | 1998 |
| 10 | Japan | Dublin | 2000 |
| 9 | United States | Manchester (NH) | 2000 |
| 7 | Romania | Dublin | 1986 |
| 7 | Georgia | Dublin | 2002 |
| 7 | Namibia | Sydney | 2003 |
| 7 | United States | Dublin | 2004 |
| 7 | Russia | Rotorua | 2011 |
| 6 | Japan | Bloemfontein | 1995 |
| 6 | Romania | Dublin | 1998 |
| 6 | United States | Dublin | 1999 |
| 6 | Italy | Dublin | 2000 |
| 6 | Italy | Limerick | 2003 |
| 6 | Japan | Tokyo | 2005 |
| 6 | Pacific Islands | Dublin | 2006 |
| 6 | Canada | Limerick | 2008 |

### BY A PLAYER

| Cons | Player | Opponents | Venue | Year |
|------|--------|-----------|-------|------|
| 10 | EP Elwood | Georgia | Dublin | 1998 |
| 10 | RJR O'Gara | Japan | Dublin | 2000 |
| 8 | RJR O'Gara | United States | Manchester (NH) | 2000 |
| 7 | MJ Kiernan | Romania | Dublin | 1986 |
| 7 | RJR O'Gara | Namibia | Sydney | 2003 |
| 7 | DG Humphreys | United States | Dublin | 2004 |
| 6 | PA Burke | Japan | Bloemfontein | 1995 |
| 6 | RJR O'Gara | Italy | Dublin | 2000 |
| 6 | DG Humphreys | Italy | Limerick | 2003 |
| 6 | DG Humphreys | Japan | Tokyo | 2005 |
| 6 | P Wallace | Pacific Islands | Dublin | 2006 |
| 6 | RJR O'Gara | Russia | Rotorua | 2011 |

## MOST PENALTIES IN A MATCH
### BY THE TEAM

| Penalties | Opponents | Venue | Year |
|-----------|-----------|-------|------|
| 8 | Italy | Dublin | 1997 |
| 7 | Argentina | Lens | 1999 |
| 6 | Scotland | Dublin | 1982 |
| 6 | Romania | Dublin | 1993 |
| 6 | United States | Atlanta | 1996 |
| 6 | Western Samoa | Dublin | 1996 |
| 6 | Italy | Dublin | 2000 |
| 6 | Wales | Dublin | 2002 |
| 6 | Australia | Dublin | 2002 |
| 6 | Samoa | Apia | 2003 |
| 6 | Japan | Osaka | 2005 |

### BY A PLAYER

| Pens | Player | Opponents | Venue | Year |
|------|--------|-----------|-------|------|
| 8 | P A Burke | Italy | Dublin | 1997 |
| 7 | D G Humphreys | Argentina | Lens | 1999 |
| 6 | S O Campbell | Scotland | Dublin | 1982 |
| 6 | E P Elwood | Romania | Dublin | 1993 |
| 6 | S J P. Mason | Western Samoa | Dublin | 1996 |
| 6 | R J R O'Gara | Italy | Dublin | 2000 |
| 6 | D G Humphreys | Wales | Dublin | 2002 |
| 6 | R J R O'Gara | Australia | Dublin | 2002 |

## MOST DROP GOALS IN A MATCH
### BY THE TEAM

| Drops | Opponents | Venue | Year |
|-------|-----------|-------|------|
| 2 | Australia | Dublin | 1967 |
| 2 | France | Dublin | 1975 |
| 2 | Australia | Sydney | 1979 |
| 2 | England | Dublin | 1981 |
| 2 | Canada | Dunedin | 1987 |
| 2 | England | Dublin | 1993 |
| 2 | Wales | Wembley | 1999 |
| 2 | New Zealand | Dublin | 2001 |
| 2 | Argentina | Dublin | 2004 |
| 2 | England | Dublin | 2005 |

### BY A PLAYER

| Drops | Player | Opponents | Venue | Year |
|-------|--------|-----------|-------|------|
| 2 | C M H Gibson | Australia | Dublin | 1967 |
| 2 | W M McCombe | France | Dublin | 1975 |
| 2 | S O Campbell | Australia | Sydney | 1979 |
| 2 | E P Elwood | England | Dublin | 1993 |
| 2 | D G Humphreys | Wales | Wembley | 1999 |
| 2 | D G Humphreys | New Zealand | Dublin | 2001 |
| 2 | R J R O'Gara | Argentina | Dublin | 2004 |
| 2 | R J R O'Gara | England | Dublin | 2005 |

# CAREER RECORDS

## MOST CAPPED PLAYERS

| Caps | Player | Career Span |
|---|---|---|
| 133 | BG O'Driscoll | 1999 to 2014 |
| 128 | RJR O'Gara | 2000 to 2013 |
| 105 | JJ Hayes | 2000 to 2011 |
| 98 | PA Stringer | 2000 to 2011 |
| 94 | DP O'Callaghan | 2003 to 2013 |
| 94 | PJ O'Connell | 2002 to 2014 |
| 92 | ME O'Kelly | 1997 to 2009 |
| 82 | GT Dempsey | 1998 to 2008 |
| 79 | GW D'Arcy | 1999 to 2014 |
| 77 | RD Best | 2005 to 2014 |
| 72 | DG Humphreys | 1996 to 2005 |
| 72 | DP Wallace | 2000 to 2011 |
| 72 | GEA Murphy | 2000 to 2011 |
| 70 | KM Maggs | 1997 to 2005 |
| 69 | CMH Gibson | 1964 to 1979 |

## MOST CONSECUTIVE TESTS

| Tests | Player | Span |
|---|---|---|
| 52 | WJ McBride | 1964 to 1975 |
| 49 | PA Orr | 1976 to 1986 |
| 43 | DG Lenihan | 1981 to 1989 |
| 39 | MI Keane | 1974 to 1981 |
| 38 | PA Stringer | 2003 to 2007 |
| 37 | GV Stephenson | 1920 to 1929 |

## MOST TESTS AS CAPTAIN

| Tests | Captain | Span |
|---|---|---|
| 83 | BG O'Driscoll | 2002 to 2012 |
| 36 | KGM Wood | 1996 to 2003 |
| 24 | TJ Kiernan | 1963 to 1973 |
| 19 | CF Fitzgerald | 1982 to 1986 |
| 17 | JF Slattery | 1979 to 1981 |
| 17 | DG Lenihan | 1986 to 1990 |

## MOST POINTS IN TESTS

| Points | Player | Tests | Career |
|---|---|---|---|
| 1083 | RJR O'Gara | 128 | 2000 to 2013 |
| 565* | DG Humphreys | 72 | 1996 to 2005 |
| 391 | JJ Sexton | 45 | 2009 to 2014 |
| 308 | MJ Kiernan | 43 | 1982 to 1991 |
| 296 | EP Elwood | 35 | 1993 to 1999 |
| 245 | BG O'Driscoll | 133 | 1999 to 2014 |
| 217 | SO Campbell | 22 | 1976 to 1984 |
| 158 | TJ Kiernan | 54 | 1960 to 1973 |
| 145 | DA Hickie | 62 | 1997 to 2007 |
| 130 | TJ Bowe | 54 | 2004 to 2013 |
| 113 | AJP Ward | 19 | 1978 to 1987 |
| * Humphreys's total includes a penalty try against Scotland in 1999 | | | |

## MOST TRIES IN TESTS

| Tries | Player | Tests | Career |
|---|---|---|---|
| 46 | BG O'Driscoll | 133 | 1999 to 2014 |
| 29 | DA Hickie | 62 | 1997 to 2007 |
| 26 | TJ Bowe | 54 | 2004 to 2013 |
| 21 | SP Horgan | 65 | 2000 to 2009 |
| 19 | GT Dempsey | 82 | 1998 to 2008 |
| 18 | GEA Murphy | 72 | 2000 to 2011 |
| 17 | BJ Mullin | 55 | 1984 to 1995 |
| 16 | RJR O'Gara | 128 | 2000 to 2013 |
| 16 | AD Trimble | 57 | 2005 to 2014 |
| 15 | KGM Wood | 58 | 1994 to 2003 |
| 15 | KM Maggs | 70 | 1997 to 2005 |
| 14 | GV Stephenson | 42 | 1920 to 1930 |

## MOST CONVERSIONS IN TESTS

| Cons | Player | Tests | Career |
|---|---|---|---|
| 176 | RJR O'Gara | 128 | 2000 to 2013 |
| 88 | DG Humphreys | 72 | 1996 to 2005 |
| 45 | JJ Sexton | 45 | 2009 to 2014 |
| 43 | EP Elwood | 35 | 1993 to 1999 |
| 40 | MJ Kiernan | 43 | 1982 to 1991 |
| 26 | TJ Kiernan | 54 | 1960 to 1973 |
| 16 | RA Lloyd | 19 | 1910 to 1920 |
| 15 | SO Campbell | 22 | 1976 to 1984 |

## MOST PENALTY GOALS IN TESTS

| Penalties | Player | Tests | Career |
|---|---|---|---|
| 202 | RJR O'Gara | 128 | 2000 to 2013 |
| 110 | DG Humphreys | 72 | 1996 to 2005 |
| 85 | JJ Sexton | 45 | 2009 to 2014 |
| 68 | EP Elwood | 35 | 1993 to 1999 |
| 62 | MJ Kiernan | 43 | 1982 to 1991 |
| 54 | SO Campbell | 22 | 1976 to 1984 |
| 31 | TJ Kiernan | 54 | 1960 to 1973 |
| 29 | AJP Ward | 19 | 1978 to 1987 |

## MOST DROP GOALS IN TESTS

| Drops | Player | Tests | Career |
|---|---|---|---|
| 15 | RJR O'Gara | 128 | 2000 to 2013 |
| 8 | DG Humphreys | 72 | 1996 to 2005 |
| 7 | RA Lloyd | 19 | 1910 to 1920 |
| 7 | SO Campbell | 22 | 1976 to 1984 |
| 6 | CMH Gibson | 69 | 1964 to 1979 |
| 6 | BJ McGann | 25 | 1969 to 1976 |
| 6 | MJ Kiernan | 43 | 1982 to 1991 |

| RECORD | DETAIL | HOLDER | SET |
|---|---|---|---|
| Most points in season | 168 | In five matches | 2000 |
| Most tries in season | 17 | In five matches | 2000 |
| | 17 | in five matches | 2004 |
| | 17 | in five matches | 2007 |
| Highest score | 60 | 60–13 v Italy | 2000 |
| Biggest win | 47 | 60–13 v Italy | 2000 |
| Highest score conceded | 50 | 18–50 v England | 2000 |
| Biggest defeat | 40 | 6–46 v England | 1997 |
| Most appearances | 66 | BG O'Driscoll | 2000–2014 |
| Most points in matches | 557 | RJR O'Gara | 2000–2013 |
| Most points in season | 82 | RJR O'Gara | 2007 |
| Most points in match | 30 | RJR O'Gara | v Italy, 2000 |
| Most tries in matches | 26 | BG O'Driscoll | 2000–2014 |
| Most tries in season | 5 | JE Arigho | 1928 |
| | 5 | BG O'Driscoll | 2000 |
| | 5 | TJ Bowe | 2012 |
| Most tries in match | 3 | R Montgomery | v Wales, 1887 |
| | 3 | JP Quinn | v France, 1913 |
| | 3 | EO'D Davy | v Scotland, 1930 |
| | 3 | SJ Byrne | v Scotland, 1953 |
| | 3 | BG O'Driscoll | v France, 2000 |
| | 3 | RA J Henderson | v Italy, 2001 |
| | 3 | BG O'Driscoll | v Scotland, 2002 |
| Most cons in matches | 81 | RJR O'Gara | 2000–2013 |
| Most cons in season | 11 | RJR O'Gara | 2000 |
| | 11 | RJR O'Gara | 2004 |
| Most cons in match | 6 | RJR O'Gara | v Italy, 2000 |
| Most pens in matches | 109 | RJR O'Gara | 2000–2013 |
| Most pens in season | 17 | RJR O'Gara | 2006 |
| Most pens in match | 6 | SO Campbell | v Scotland, 1982 |
| | 6 | RJR O'Gara | v Italy, 2000 |
| | 6 | DG Humphreys | v Wales, 2002 |
| Most drops in matches | 7 | RA Lloyd | 1910–1920 |
| Most drops in season | 2 | on several occasions | |
| Most drops in match | 2 | WM McCombe | v France, 1975 |
| | 2 | EP Elwood | v England, 1993 |
| | 2 | DG Humphreys | v Wales, 1999 |
| | 2 | RJR O'Gara | v England, 2005 |

IRELAND

# MISCELLANEOUS RECORDS

| RECORD | HOLDER | DETAIL |
|---|---|---|
| Longest Test Career | AJF O'Reilly | 1955 to 1970 |
| | CMH Gibson | 1964 to 1979 |
| | BG O'Driscoll | 1999 to 2014 |
| | GW D'Arcy | 1999 to 2014 |
| Youngest Test Cap | FS Hewitt | 17 yrs 157 days in 1924 |
| Oldest Test Cap | JJ Hayes | 37 yrs 277 days in 2011 |

## CAREER RECORDS OF IRELAND INTERNATIONAL PLAYERS

## UP TO 13 OCTOBER 2014

| PLAYER BACKS : | DEBUT | CAPS | T | C | P | D | PTS |
|---|---|---|---|---|---|---|---|
| IJ Boss | 2006 v NZ | 20 | 3 | 0 | 0 | 0 | 15 |
| TJ Bowe | 2004 v US | 54 | 26 | 0 | 0 | 0 | 130 |
| DM Cave | 2009 v C | 7 | 1 | 0 | 0 | 0 | 5 |
| GW D'Arcy | 1999 v R | 79 | 7 | 0 | 0 | 0 | 35 |
| KG Earls | 2008 v C | 39 | 12 | 0 | 0 | 0 | 60 |
| LM Fitzgerald | 2006 v PI | 27 | 2 | 0 | 0 | 0 | 10 |
| CJH Gilroy | 2012 v Arg | 5 | 2 | 0 | 0 | 0 | 10 |
| R Henshaw | 2013 v US | 3 | 0 | 0 | 0 | 0 | 0 |
| DP Jackson | 2013 v S | 9 | 1 | 9 | 11 | 0 | 56 |
| FA Jones | 2011 v S | 6 | 0 | 0 | 0 | 0 | 0 |
| D Kearney | 2013 v Sm | 7 | 2 | 0 | 0 | 0 | 10 |
| RDJ Kearney | 2007 v Arg | 55 | 10 | 1 | 0 | 0 | 52 |
| I Madigan | 2013 v F | 10 | 1 | 4 | 8 | 0 | 37 |
| KD Marmion | 2014 v Arg | 2 | 0 | 0 | 0 | 0 | 0 |
| LD Marshall | 2013 v S | 6 | 0 | 0 | 0 | 0 | 0 |
| P Marshall | 2013 v It | 3 | 0 | 0 | 0 | 0 | 0 |
| FL McFadden | 2011 v It | 28 | 9 | 0 | 0 | 0 | 45 |
| C Murray | 2011 v F | 28 | 2 | 0 | 0 | 0 | 10 |
| BG O'Driscoll | 1999 v A | 133 | 46 | 0 | 0 | 5 | 245 |
| EG Reddan | 2006 F | 55 | 2 | 0 | 0 | 0 | 10 |
| N Reid | 2014 v Arg | 1 | 0 | 0 | 0 | 0 | 0 |
| JJ Sexton | 2009 v Fj | 45 | 8 | 45 | 85 | 2 | 391 |
| AD Trimble | 2005 v A | 57 | 16 | 0 | 0 | 0 | 80 |
| SR Zebo | 2012 v NZ | 8 | 3 | 0 | 0 | 0 | 15 |

## FORWARDS :

| | | | | | | | |
|---|---|---|---|---|---|---|---|
| R Ah You | 2014 v Arg | 1 | 0 | 0 | 0 | 0 | 0 |
| S Archer | 2013 v It | 2 | 0 | 0 | 0 | 0 | 0 |
| M Bent | 2012 v SA | 2 | 0 | 0 | 0 | 0 | 0 |
| RD Best | 2005 v NZ | 77 | 8 | 0 | 0 | 0 | 40 |
| J Cronin | 2014 v Arg | 1 | 0 | 0 | 0 | 0 | 0 |
| SM Cronin | 2009 v Fj | 35 | 1 | 0 | 0 | 0 | 5 |
| RJE Diack | 2014 v Arg | 1 | 0 | 0 | 0 | 0 | 0 |
| DJ Fitzpatrick | 2012 v NZ | 7 | 0 | 0 | 0 | 0 | 0 |
| CE Healy | 2009 v A | 47 | 3 | 0 | 0 | 0 | 15 |
| JPR Heaslip | 2006 v Pl | 67 | 9 | 0 | 0 | 0 | 45 |
| WI Henderson | 2012 v SA | 12 | 0 | 0 | 0 | 0 | 0 |
| CG Henry | 2010 v A | 16 | 2 | 0 | 0 | 0 | 10 |
| RW Herring | 2014 v Arg | 1 | 0 | 0 | 0 | 0 | 0 |
| D Kilcoyne | 2012 v SA | 10 | 0 | 0 | 0 | 0 | 0 |
| MP McCarthy | 2011 v S | 15 | 0 | 0 | 0 | 0 | 0 |
| JC McGrath | 2013 v Sm | 10 | 1 | 0 | 0 | 0 | 5 |
| KR McLaughlin | 2010 v It | 8 | 0 | 0 | 0 | 0 | 0 |
| MJ Moore | 2014 v S | 5 | 0 | 0 | 0 | 0 | 0 |
| J Murphy | 2014 v E | 4 | 0 | 0 | 0 | 0 | 0 |
| SK O'Brien | 2009 v Fj | 30 | 3 | 0 | 0 | 0 | 15 |
| DP O'Callaghan | 2003 v W | 94 | 1 | 0 | 0 | •0 | 5 |
| PJ O'Connell | 2002 v W | 94 | 6 | 0 | 0 | 0 | 30 |
| T O'Donnell | 2013 v US | 4 | 1 | 0 | 0 | 0 | 5 |
| P O'Mahony | 2012 v It | 23 | 1 | 0 | 0 | 0 | 5 |
| MA Ross | 2009 v C | 41 | 0 | 0 | 0 | 0 | 0 |
| RJ Ruddock | 2010 v A | 3 | 0 | 0 | 0 | 0 | 0 |
| DC Ryan | 2008 v Arg | 28 | 0 | 0 | 0 | 0 | 0 |
| M Sherry | 2013 v US | 1 | 0 | 0 | 0 | 0 | 0 |
| CR Strauss | 2012 v SA | 4 | 1 | 0 | 0 | 0 | 5 |
| D Toner | 2010 v Sm | 17 | 0 | 0 | 0 | 0 | 0 |
| DM Tuohy | 2010 v NZ | 9 | 1 | 0 | 0 | 0 | 5 |
| DA Varley | 2010 v A | 3 | 0 | 0 | 0 | 0 | 0 |

# IRELAND INTERNATIONAL PLAYERS
## UP TO 13 OCTOBER 2014

Note: Years given for International Championship matches are for second half of season; eg 1972 means season 1971–72. Years for all other matches refer to the actual year of the match. Entries in square brackets denote matches played in RWC Finals.

**Abraham, M** (Bective Rangers) 1912 E, S, W, SA, 1914 W
**Adams, C** (Old Wesley), 1908 E, 1909 E, F, 1910 F, 1911 E, S, W, F, 1912 S, W, SA, 1913 W, F, 1914 F, E, S
**Agar, R D** (Malone) 1947 F, E, S, W, 1948 F, 1949 S, W, 1950 F, E, W
**Agnew, P J** (CIYMS) 1974 F (R), 1976 A
**Ahearne, T** (Queen's Coll, Cork) 1899 E
**Aherne, L F P** (Dolphin, Lansdowne) 1988 E 2, WS, It, 1989 F, W, E, S, NZ, 1990 E, S, F, W (R), 1992 E, S, F, A
**Ah You, R** (Connacht) 2014 Arg 1(R)
**Alexander, R** (NIFC, Police Union) 1936 E, S, W, 1937 E, S, W, 1938 E, S, 1939 E, S, W
**Allen, C E** (Derry, Liverpool) 1900 E, S, W, 1901 E, S, W, 1903 S, W, 1904 E, S, W, 1905 E, S, W, NZ, 1906 E, S, W, SA, 1907 S, W
**Allen, G G** (Derry, Liverpool) 1896 E, S, W, 1897 E, S, 1898 E, S, 1899 E, W
**Allen, T C** (NIFC) 1885 E, S 1
**Allen, W S** (Wanderers) 1875 E
**Allison, J B** (Edinburgh U) 1899 E, S, 1900 E, S, W, 1901 E, S, W, 1902 E, S, W, 1903 S
**Anderson, F E** (Queen's, Belfast, NIFC) 1953 F, E, S, W, 1954 NZ, F, E, S, W, 1955 F, E, S, W
**Anderson, H J** (Old Wesley) 1903 E, S, 1906 E, S
**Anderson, W A** (Dungannon) 1984 A, 1985 S, F, W, E, 1986 F, S, R, 1987 E, S, F, W, [W, C, Tg, A], 1988 S, F, W, E 1, 2, 1989 F, W, E, NZ, 1990 E, S
**Andrews, G** (NIFC) 1875 E, 1876 E
**Andrews, H W** (NIFC) 1888 M, 1889 S, W
**Archer, A M** (Dublin U, NIFC) 1879 S
**Archer, S** (Munster) 2013 It(R), A(R)
**Arigho, J E** (Lansdowne) 1928 F, E, W, 1929 F, E, S, W, 1930 F, E, S, W, 1931 F, E, S, W, SA
**Armstrong, W K** (NIFC) 1960 SA, 1961 E
**Arnott, D T** (Lansdowne) 1876 E
**Ash, W H** (NIFC) 1875 E, 1876 E, 1877 S
**Aston, H R** (Dublin U) 1908 E, W
**Atkins, A P** (Bective Rangers) 1924 F
**Atkinson, J M** (NIFC) 1927 F, A
**Atkinson, J R** (Dublin U) 1882 W, S

**Bagot, J C** (Dublin U, Lansdowne) 1879 S, E, 1880 E, S, 1881 S
**Bailey, A H** (UC Dublin, Lansdowne) 1934 W, 1935 E, S, W, NZ, 1936 E, S, W, 1937 E, S, W, 1938 E, S
**Bailey, N** (Northampton) 1952 E
**Bardon, M E** (Bohemians) 1934 E
**Barlow, M** (Wanderers) 1875 E
**Barnes, R J** (Dublin U, Armagh) 1933 W
**Barr, A** (Belfast Collegians) 1898 W, 1899 S, 1901 E, S
**Barry, N J** (Garryowen) 1991 Nm 2(R)
**Beamish, C E St J** (RAF, Leicester) 1933 W, S, 1934 S, W, E, S, W, NZ, 1936 E, S, W, 1938 W
**Beamish, G R** (RAF, Leicester) 1925 E, S, W, 1928 F, E, S, W, 1929 F, E, S, W, 1930 F, S, W, 1931 F, E, S, W, SA, 1932 E, S, W, 1933 E, W, S
**Beatty, W J** (NIFC, Richmond) 1910 F, 1912 F, W
**Becker, V A** (Lansdowne) 1974 F, W
**Beckett, G G P** (Dublin U) 1908 E, S, W
**Bell, J C** (Ballymena, Northampton, Dungannon) 1994 A 1, 2,

US, 1995 S, It, [NZ, W, F], Fj, 1996 US, S, F, W, E, WS, A, 1997 It 1, F, W, E, S, 1998 Gg, R, SA 3, 1999 F, W, S It (R), A 2, [US (R), A 3(R), R], 2001 R (R), 2003 Tg, Sm, It 2(R)
**Bell, R J** (NIFC) 1875 E, 1876 E
**Bell, W E** (Belfast Collegians) 1953 F, E, S, W
**Bennett, F** (Belfast Collegians) 1913 S
**Bent, G C** (Dublin U) 1882 W, E
**Bent, M** (Leinster) 2012 SA(R), Arg(R)
**Berkery, P J** (Lansdowne) 1954 W, 1955 W, 1956 S, W, 1957 F, E, S, W, 1958 A, E, S
**Bermingham, J J C** (Blackrock Coll) 1921 E, S, W, F
**Best, N A** (Ulster) 2005 NZ(R), R, 2006 NZ1, 2, A1, SA, A2, 2007 F(R), E(R), S1(R), Arg1, 2(R), S2, It2, [Nm(R), Gg(R), F(R), Arg(t&R]
**Best, R D** (Ulster) 2005 NZ(R), A(t), 2006 W(R), A1(R), SA, A2, PI(R), 2007 W, F, E, S1, It1, S2(R), It2, [Nm, Gg, Arg(R)], 2008 It, F(R), S(R), W, E, NZ1(R), A, C(R), NZ2, Arg(R), 2009 F(R), It(R), E(R), S, W(R), C, US, 2010 It(R), F(R), E, W, S, SA, Sm(R), NZ2, 2011 It, F1, S1, W, E1, F2, 3, E2(R), [US, A, It, W], 2012 W, It, F, S, E, NZ 1, 2, 3, 2013 W, E, S, F, It, Sm, A, NZ, 2014 S, W, E, It, F, Arg 1, 2
**Best, S J** (Belfast Harlequins, Ulster) 2003 Tg (R), W 2, S 2(R), 2003 [Nm(R)], 2004 W(R), US(R), 2005 J1, 2, NZ(R), R, 2006 F(R), W(R), PI(R), 2007 E(R), S1, It1(R), Arg1, 2, S2, It2(R), Nm(R), Gg(R), F(R)]
**Bishop, J P** (London Irish) 1998 SA, 1, 2, Gg, R, SA 3, 1999 F, W, E, S, It, A 1, 2, [US, A 3, Arg 2], 2000 E, Arg, C, 2002 NZ 1, 2, Fj, Arg, 2003 W 1, F
**Blackham, J C** (Queen's Coll, Cork) 1909 S, W, F, 1910 E, S, W
**Blake-Knox, S E F** (NIFC) 1976 E, S, 1977 F (R)
**Blayney, J J** (Wanderers) 1950 S
**Bond, A T W** (Derry) 1894 S, W
**Bornemann, W W** (Wanderers) 1960 E, S, W, SA
**Boss, I J** (Ulster, Leinster) 2006 NZ2(R), A1(R), SA(R), A2, PI(R), 2007 F, E(R), Arg1, S2, It2(R), [Gg(R), Arg(R)], 2010 Sm(R), 2011 S2(R), [Ru], 2013 US, C, 2014 S(R), W(R), E(R)
**Bowe, T J** (Ulster, Ospreys) 2004 US, 2005 J1, 2, NZ, A, R, 2006 It, F, 2007 Arg1, S2, 2008 S, W, E, NZ1, A, C, NZ2, Arg, 2009 F, It, E, S, W, A, SA, 2010 It, F, E, W, S, NZ1, A, Sm, NZ2, Arg, 2011 S1, W, E1, 2, [US, A, It, W], 2012 W, It, F, S, E, SA, Arg, 2013 Sm, A, NZ
**Bowen, D St J** (Cork Const) 1977 W, E, S
**Boyd, C A** (Dublin U) 1900 S, 1901 S, W
**Boyle, C V** (Dublin U) 1935 NZ, 1936 E, S, W, 1937 E, S, W, 1938 W, 1939 W
**Brabazon, H M** (Dublin U) 1884 E, 1885 S 1, 1886 E
**Bradley, M J** (Dolphin) 1920 W, F, 1922 E, S, W, F, 1923 E, S, W, F, 1925 F, S, W, 1926 F, E, S, W, 1927 F, W
**Bradley, M T** (Cork Constitution) 1984 A, 1985 S, F, W, E, 1986 F, W, E, S, R, 1987 E, S, F, W, [W, C, Tg, A], 1988 S, F, W, E 1, 1990 W, 1992 NZ 1, 2, 1993 S, F, W, E, 1994 F, W, E, S, A 1, 2, US, 1995 S, F, [NZ]
**Bradshaw, G** (Belfast Collegians) 1903 W
**Bradshaw, R M** (Wanderers) 1885 E, S 1, 2
**Brady, A M** (UC Dublin, Malone) 1966 S, 1968 E, S, W
**Brady, J A** (Wanderers) 1976 E, S
**Brady, J R** (CIYMS) 1951 S, W, 1953 F, E, S, W, 1954 W, 1956 W, 1957 F, E, S, W

Costello, R A (Garryowen) 1993 S
Costello, V C P (St Mary's Coll, London Irish) 1996 US, F, W,
E. WS (R), 1997 C, It 2(R), 1998 S (R), F, W, E, SA 1, 2,
Gg, R, SA 3, 1999 F, W (R), E, S (R), It, A 1, 2002 R (R),
A, Arg, 2003 S 1, It 1, F, E, A, It 2, S 2, [R, Arg, F], 2004
F(R), W(R), It(R), S(R)
Cotton, J (Wanderers) 1889 W
Coulter, H H (Queen's U, Belfast) 1920 E, S, W
Court, T G (Ulster) 2009 It(R), W(t), C, US(R), Fj, 2010 It(R),
F(t&R), NZ1(R), A(R), SA(R), Sm, NZ2, Arg(R), 2011 It(R),
F1(R), S1(R), W(R), E1(R), S2, F3(R), E2(R), [US, A(R), It(R)],
2012 W(R), It(R), F(R), S(t&R), E(R), 2013 S, US( R), C
Courtney, A W (UC Dublin) 1920 S, W, F, 1921 E, S, W, F
Cox, H L (Dublin U) 1875 E, 1876 E, 1877 E, S
Craig, R G (Queen's U, Belfast) 1938 S, W
Crawford, E C (Dublin U) 1885 E, S 1
Crawford, W E (Lansdowne) 1920 E, S, W, F, 1921 E, S, W, F,
1922 E, S, 1923 E, S, W, F, 1924 F, E, W, NZ, 1925 F, E,
S, W, 1926 F, E, S, W, 1927 F, E, S, W
Crean, T J (Wanderers) 1894 E, S, W, 1895 E, S, W, 1896 E,
S, W
Crichton, R Y (Dublin U) 1920 E, S, W, F, 1921 F, 1922 E, 1923
W, F, 1924 F, E, S, W, NZ, 1925 E, S
Croker, E W D (Limerick) 1878 E
Cromey, G E (Queen's U, Belfast) 1937 E, S, W, 1938 E, S, W,
1939 E, S, W
Cronin, B M (Garryowen) 1995 S, 1997 S
Cronin, J (Munster) 2014 Arg 2(R)
Cronin, S M (Connacht, Leinster) 2009 Fj(R), 2010 W(R), NZ1,
A, Sm, NZ2(R), Arg, 2011 It(R), F1(R), S1(R), W(R), E1(R),
S2, [Ru, It(R)], 2012 It(R), F(R), S(R), E(R), NZ 1(R), 3(R),
SA(t&R), Arg(R), 2013 E(R), F(R), It(R), C(R), Sm(R), A(R),
NZ(R), 2014 S(R), W(R), E(R), It(R), F(R)
Cronyn, A P (Dublin U, Lansdowne) 1875 E, 1876 E, 1880 S
Crossan, K D (Instonians) 1982 S, 1984 F, W, E, S, 1985 S, F,
W, E, 1986 E, S, R, 1987 E, S, F, W, [W, C, Tg, A], 1988
S, F, W, E 1, WS, It, 1989 W, S, NZ, 1990 E, S, F, W, Arg,
1991 E, S, Nm 2 [Z, J, S], 1992 W
Crotty, D J (Garryowen) 1996 A, 1997 It 1, F, W, 2000 C
Crowe, J F (UC Dublin) 1974 NZ
Crowe, L (Old Belvedere) 1950 E, S, W
Crowe, M P (Lansdowne) 1929 W, 1930 E, S, W, 1931 F, S, W,
SA, 1932 S, W, 1933 W, S, 1934 E
Crowe, P M (Blackrock Coll) 1935 E, 1938 E
Cullen, L F M (Blackrock Coll, Leinster, Leicester) 2002 NZ 2(R),
R (R), Ru (R), Gg (R), A (R), Fj, Arg (R), 2003 S 1(R), It (R),
F (R), W 1, Tg, Sm, It 2, 2004 US(R), 2005 J1, 2, R, 2007
Arg2, 2009 Fj, 2010 It, F, E(R), W(R), 2011 It(R), F1(R), S1(R),
W(R), E1(R), S2, F2, [Ru]
Cullen, T J (UC Dublin) 1949 F
Cullen, W J (Monkstown and Manchester) 1920 E
Culliton, M G (Wanderers) 1959 E, S, W, F, 1960 E, S, W, F,
SA, 1961 E, S, W, F, 1962 S, F, 1964 E, S, W, F
Cummins, W E A (Queen's Coll, Cork) 1879 S, 1881 E, 1882 E
Cunningham, D McC (NIFC) 1923 E, S, W, 1925 F, E, W
Cunningham, M J (UC Dublin) 1955 F, E, S, W, 1956 F, S, W
Cunningham, V J G (St Mary's Coll) 1988 E 2, It, 1990 Arg (R),
1991 Nm 1, 2, [Z, J(R)], 1992 NZ 1, 2, A, 1993 S, F, W, E,
R, 1994 F
Cunningham, W A (Lansdowne) 1920 W, 1921 E, S, W, F, 1922
E, 1923 S, W
Cuppaidge, J L (Dublin U) 1879 E, 1880 E, S
Currell, J (NIFC) 1877 S
Curtis, A B (Oxford U) 1950 F, E, S
Curtis, D M (London Irish) 1991 W, E, S, Nm 1, 2, [Z, J, S, A],
1992 W, E, S (R), F
Cuscaden, W A (Dublin U, Bray) 1876 E
Cussen, D J (Dublin U) 1921 E, S, W, F, 1922 E, 1923 E, S, W,
F, 1926 F, E, S, W, 1927 F, E

Daly, J C (London Irish) 1947 F, E, S, W, 1948 E, S, W
Daly, M J (Harlequins) 1938 E
Danaher, P P A (Lansdowne, Garryowen) 1988 S, F, W, WS, It,
1989 F, NZ (R), 1990 F, 1992 E, S, F, W, NZ 1, A, 1993 S, F, W,
E, R, 1994 F, W, E, S, A 1, 2, US, 1995 E, S, F, W
D'Arcy, G W (Lansdowne, Leinster) 1999 [R (R)], 2002 Fj (R),
2003 Tg (R), Sm (R), W 2(R), 2004 F, W, E, It, S, SA1, 2005

It, NZ, A, R, 2006 It, F, W, S, E, NZ1, 2, A1, SA, A2, PI(R),
2007 W, F, E, S1, It1, 2, [Nm, Gg, F, Arg], 2008 It, 2009
F(t&R), It(R), S, W, Fj, SA(R), 2010 It, F, E, W, S, NZ1, SA,
NZ2, Arg, 2011 It, F1, S1, W, E1, F3, E2, [US, A, It, W],
2012 W, It, F, S, E, NZ2, SA, Arg, 2013 W, E, Sm, NZ, 2014
W, E, It, F
Dargan, M J (Old Belvedere) 1952 S, W
Davidson, C T (NIFC) 1921 F
Davidson, I G (NIFC) 1899 E, 1900 S, W, 1901 E, S, W, 1902
E, S, W
Davidson, J C (Dungannon) 1969 F, E, S, W, 1973 NZ, 1976
NZ
Davidson, J W (Dungannon, London Irish, Castres) 1995 Fj,
1996 S, F, W, E, WS, A, 1997 It 1, F, W, E, S, 1998 Gg (R),
R (R), SA 3(R), 1999 F, W, E, S, It, A 1, 2(R), Arg 1, [US, A
(R), Arg 2], 2000 S (R), W (R), US, C, 2001 It (R), S
Davies, F E (Lansdowne) 1892 S, W, 1893 E, S, W
Davis, J J (Monkstown) 1898 E, S
Davis, W J N (Edinburgh U, Bessbrook) 1890 S, W, E, 1891 E,
S, W, 1892 E, S, 1895 S
Davison, W (Belfast Academy) 1887 W
Davy, E O'D (UC Dublin, Lansdowne) 1925 W, 1926 F, E, S, W,
1927 F, E, S, W, A, 1928 F, E, S, W, 1929 F, E, S, W, 1930
F, E, S, W, 1931 F, E, S, W, SA, 1932 E, S, W, 1933 E, W,
S, 1934 E
Dawson, A R (Wanderers) 1958 A, E, S, W, F, 1959 E, S, W, F,
1960 F, SA, 1961 E, S, W, F, SA, 1962 S, F, W, 1963 F, E,
S, W, NZ, 1964 E, S, F
Dawson, K (London Irish) 1997 NZ, C, 1998 S, 1999 [R, Arg
2], 2000 E, S, It, F, W, J, SA, 2001 R, S, W (R), E (R), Sm,
2002 Fj, 2003 Tg, It 2(R), S 2(R)
Dean, P M (St Mary's Coll) 1981 SA 1, 2, A, 1982 W, E, S, F,
1984 A, 1985 S, F, W, E, 1986 F, W, R, 1987 E, S, F, W,
[W, A], 1988 S, F, W, E 1, 2, WS, It, 1989 F, W, E, S
Deane, E C (Monkstown) 1909 E
Deering, M J (Bective Rangers) 1929 W
Deering, S J (Bective Rangers) 1935 E, S, W, NZ, 1936 E, S,
W, 1937 E, S
Deering, S M (Garryowen, St Mary's Coll) 1974 W, 1976 F, W,
E, S, 1977 W, E, 1978 NZ
De Lacy, H (Harlequins) 1948 E, S
Delany, M G (Bective Rangers) 1895 W
Dempsey, G T (Terenure Coll, Leinster) 1998 Gg (R). SA 3, 1999
F, E, S, It, A 2, 2000 E (R), S, It, F, W, SA, 2001 It, F, S,
W, E, NZ, 2002 W, E, S, It, F, NZ 1, 2, R, Ru, Gg, A, Arg,
2003 S 1, E (R), A, Sm, W 2(R), It 2, S 2(R), [R, Nm, Arg,
A, F], 2004 F, W, E, It, S, SA1, 2, 3, US(R), Arg, 2005 It(R),
S, E, F, W, J1, 2, NZ(R), R(R), 2006 E(R), NZ1(R), 2(t&R),
A1, SA, A2(R), PI, 2007 W, F, E, S1, It1, 2, [Nm, Gg, F],
2008 It, F, A(R), NZ2
Dennison, S P (Garryowen) 1973 F, 1975 E, S
Diack, R J E (Ulster) 2014 Arg 1
Dick, C J (Ballymena) 1961 W, F, SA, 1962 W, 1963 F, E, S,
W
Dick, J S (Queen's U, Belfast) 1962 E
Dick, J S (Queen's U, Cork) 1887 E, S, W
Dickson, J A N (Dublin U) 1920 E, W, F
Doherty, A E (Old Wesley) 1974 P (R)
Doherty, W D (Guy's Hospital) 1920 E, S, W, 1921 E, S, W, F
Donaldson, J A (Belfast Collegians) 1958 A, E, S, W
Donovan, T M (Queen's Coll, Cork) 1889 S
Dooley, J F (Galwegians) 1959 E, S, W
Doran, B R W (Lansdowne) 1900 S, W, 1901 E, S, W, 1902 E,
S, W
Doran, E F (Lansdowne) 1890 S, W
Doran, G P (Lansdowne) 1899 S, W, 1900 E, S, 1902 S, W,
1903 W, 1904 E
Douglas, A C (Instonians) 1923 F, 1924 E, S, 1927 A, 1928 S
Dowling, I (Munster) 2009 C, US
Downey, J (Munster) 2013 C
Downing, A J (Dublin U) 1882 W
Dowse, J C A (Monkstown) 1914 F, S, W
Doyle, J A P (Greystones) 1984 E, S
Doyle, J T (Bective Rangers) 1935 W
Doyle, M G (Blackrock Coll, UC Dublin, Cambridge U, Edinburgh
Wands) 1965 F, E, S, W, SA, 1966 F, E, S, W, 1967 A 1,
E, S, W, F, A 2, 1968 F, E, S, W, A

IRELAND

McFarland, B A T (Derry) 1920 S, W, F, 1922 W
McGann, B J (Lansdowne) 1969 F, E, S, W, 1970 SA, F, E, S, W, 1971 F, E, S, W, 1972 F 1, E, F 2, 1973 NZ, E, S, W, 1976 F, W, E, S, NZ
McGowan, A N (Blackrock Coll) 1994 US
McGown, T M W (NIFC) 1899 E, S, 1901 S
McGrath, D G (UC Dublin, Cork Const) 1984 S, 1987 [W, C, Tg, A]
McGrath, J C (Leinster) 2013 Sm, A(R), NZ(R), 2014 S(R), W(R), E(R), It(R), F(R), Arg 1, 2(R)
McGrath, N F (Oxford U, London Irish) 1934 W
McGrath, P J (UC Cork) 1965 E, S, W, SA, 1966 F, E, S, W, 1967 A 1, A 2
McGrath, R J M (Wanderers) 1977 W, E, F (R), 1981 SA 1, 2, A, 1982 W, E, S, F, 1983 S, F, W, E, 1984 F, W
McGrath, T (Garryowen) 1956 W, 1958 F, 1960 E, S, W, F, 1961 SA
McGuinness, C D (St Mary's Coll) 1997 NZ, C, 1998 F, W, E, SA 1, 2, Gg, R (R), SA 3, 1999 F, W, E, S
McGuire, E P (UC Galway) 1963 E, S, W, NZ, 1964 E, S, W, F 1967 S, W, F
McHale, S (Lansdowne) 1965 F, E, S, W, SA, 1966 F, E, S, W, 1967 S, W, F
McHugh, M (St Mary's Coll) 2003 Tg
McIldowie, G (Malone) 1906 SA, 1910 E, S, W
McIlrath, J A (Ballymena) 1976 A, F, NZ, 1977 W, E
McIlwaine, E H (NIFC) 1895 S, W
McIlwaine, E N (NIFC) 1875 E, 1876 E
McIlwaine, J E (NIFC) 1897 E, S, 1898 E, S, W, 1899 E, W
McIntosh, L M (Dublin U) 1884 S
MacIvor, C V (Dublin U) 1912 F, E, S, W, 1913 E, S, F
McIvor, S C (Garryowen) 1996 A, 1997 It 1, S (R)
McKay, J W (Queen's U, Belfast) 1947 F, E, S, W, A, 1948 F, E, S, W, 1949 F, E, S, W, 1950 F, E, S, W, 1951 F, E, S, W, SA, 1952 F
McKee, W D (NIFC) 1947 A, 1948 F, E, S, W, 1949 F, E, S, W, 1950 F, E, 1951 SA
McKeen, A J W (Lansdowne) 1999 [R (R)]
McKelvey, J M (Queen's U, Belfast) 1956 F, E
McKenna, P (St Mary's Coll) 2000 Arg
McKibbin, A R (Instonians, London Irish) 1977 W, E, S, 1978 S, F, W, E, NZ, 1979 F, W, E, S, 1980 E, S
McKibbin, C H (Instonians) 1976 S (R)
McKibbin, D (Instonians) 1950 F, E, S, W, 1951 F, E, S, W
McKibbin, H R (Queen's U, Belfast) 1938 W, 1939 E, S, W
McKinney, S A (Dungannon) 1972 F 1, E, F 2, 1973 W, F, 1974 F, E, S, P, NZ, 1975 E, S, 1976 A, F, W, E, S, NZ, 1977 W, E, S, 1978 S (R), F, W, E
McLaughlin, J H (Derry) 1887 E, S, 1888 W, S
McLaughlin, K R (Leinster) 2010 It, 2011 S2(R), 2012 NZ 1(R), 2, 3, 2013 C, A(R), NZ(R)
McLean, R E (Dublin U) 1881 S, 1882 W, E, S, 1883 E, S, 1884 E, S, 1885 E, S 1
Maclear, B (Cork County, Monkstown) 1905 E, S, W, NZ, 1906 E, S, W, SA, 1907 E, S, W
McLennan, A C (Wanderers) 1977 F, 1978 S, F, W, E, NZ, 1979 F, W, E, S, 1980 E, F, 1981 F, W, E, S, SA 1, 2
McLoughlin, F M (Northern) 1976 A
McLoughlin, G A J (Shannon) 1979 F, W, E, S, A 1, 2, 1980 E, 1981 SA 1, 2, 1982 W, E, S, F, 1983 S, F, W, E, 1984 F
McLoughlin, R J (UC Dublin, Blackrock Coll, Gosforth) 1962 E, S, F, 1963 E, S, W, NZ, 1964 E, S, 1965 F, E, S, W, SA, 1966 F, E, S, W, 1971 F, E, S, W, 1972 F 1, E, F 2, 1973 NZ, E, S, W, F, 1974 F, W, E, S, P, NZ, 1975 E, S, W
McMahon, L B (Blackrock Coll, UC Dublin) 1931 E, SA, 1933 E, 1934 E, 1936 E, S, W, 1937 E, S, W, 1938 E, S
McMaster, A W (Ballymena) 1972 F 1, E, F 2, 1973 NZ, E, S, W, F, 1974 F, E, S, P, 1975 F, W, 1976 A, F, W, NZ
McMordie, J (Queen's Coll, Belfast) 1886 S
McMorrow, A (Garryowen) 1951 W
McMullen, A R (Cork) 1881 E, S
McNamara, V (UC Cork) 1914 E, S, W
McNaughton, P P (Greystones) 1978 S, F, W, E, 1979 F, W, E, S, A 1, 2, 1980 E, S, F, W, 1981 F
MacNeill, H P (Dublin U, Oxford U, Blackrock Coll, London Irish) 1981 F, W, E, S, A, 1982 W, E, S, F, 1983 S, F, W, E, 1984 F, W, E, A, 1985 F, W, E, 1986 F, W, E, S, R, 1987 E, S, F, W, [W, C, Tg, A], 1988 S (R), E 1, 2

McQuilkin, K P (Bective Rangers, Lansdowne) 1996 US, S, F, 1997 F (t & R), S
MacSweeney, D A (Blackrock Coll) 1955 S
McVicker, H (Army, Richmond) 1927 E, S, W, A, 1928 F
McVicker, J (Collegians) 1924 F, E, S, W, NZ, 1925 F, E, S, W, 1926 F, E, S, W, 1927 F, E, S, W, A, 1928 W, 1930 F
McVicker, S (Queen's U, Belfast) 1922 E, S, W, F
McWeeney, J P J (St Mary's Coll) 1997 NZ
Madden, M N (Sunday's Well) 1955 E, S, W
Madigan, I (Leinster) 2013 F(R), It(R), US, C, Sm(R), A(R), NZ(R), 2014 F(R), Arg 1(R), 2(R)
Magee, A M (Louis) (Bective Rangers, London Irish) 1895 E, S, W, 1896 E, S, W, 1897 E, S, 1898 E, S, W, 1899 E, S, W, 1900 E, S, W, 1901 E, S, W, 1902 E, S, W, 1903 E, S, W, 1904 W
Magee, J T (Bective Rangers) 1895 E, S
Maggs, K M (Bristol, Bath, Ulster) 1997 NZ (R), C, It 2, 1998 S, F, W, E, SA 1, 2, Gg, R (R), SA 3, 1999 F, W, E, S, It, A 1, 2, Arg 1, [US, A 3, Arg 2], 2000 E, F, Arg, US (R), C, 2001 It (R), F (R), R, S (R), W, E, Sm, NZ, 2002 W, E, S, R, Ru, Gg, A, Fj, Arg, 2003 S 1, It 1, F, W 1, E, A, W 2, S 2, [R, Nm, Arg, A, F], 2004 F, W(R), E(R), It(R), S(R), SA1(R), 2, US, 2005 S, F, W, J1
Maginiss, R M (Dublin U) 1875 E, 1876 E
Magrath, R M (Cork Constitution) 1909 S
Maguire, J F (Cork) 1884 S
Mahoney, J (Dolphin) 1923 E
Malcomson, G L (RAF, NIFC) 1935 NZ, 1936 E, S, W, 1937 E, S, W
Malone, N G (Oxford U, Leicester) 1993 S, F, 1994 US (R)
Mannion, N P (Corinthians, Lansdowne, Wanderers) 1988 WS, It, 1989 F, W, E, S, NZ, 1990 E, S, F, W, Arg, 1991 Nm 1(R), 2, [J], 1993 S
Marmion, K D (Connacht) 2014 Arg 1(R), 2(R)
Marshall, B D E (Queen's U, Belfast) 1963 E
Marshall, L D (Ulster) 2013 S, F, It, A, 2014 S, Arg 1
Marshall, P (Ulster) 2013 It(R), US(R), C(R)
Mason, S J P (Orrell, Richmond) 1996 W, E, WS
Massey-Westropp, R H (Limerick, Monkstown) 1886 S
Matier, R N (NIFC) 1878 E, 1879 S
Matthews, P M (Ards, Wanderers) 1984 A, 1985 S, F, W, E, 1986 R, 1987 E, S, F, W, [W, Tg, A], 1988 S, F, W, E 1, 2, WS, It, 1989 F, W, E, S, NZ, 1990 E, S, 1991 F, W, E, S, Nm 1 [Z, S, A], 1992 W, E, S
Mattsson, J (Wanderers) 1948 E
Mayne, R B (Queen's U, Belfast) 1937 W, 1938 E, W, 1939 E, S, W
Mayne, R H (Belfast Academy) 1888 W, S
Mayne, T (NIFC) 1921 E, S, F
Mays, K M A (UC Dublin) 1973 NZ, E, S, W
Meares, A W D (Dublin U) 1899 S, W, 1900 E, W
Megaw, J (Richmond, Instonians) 1934 W, 1938 E
Millar, H J (Monkstown) 1904 W, 1905 E, S, W
Millar, S (Ballymena) 1958 F, 1959 E, S, W, F, 1960 E, S, W, F, SA, 1961 E, S, W, F, SA, 1962 E, S, F, 1963 F, E, S, W, 1964 F, 1968 F, E, S, W, A, 1969 F, E, S, W, 1970 SA, F, E, S, W
Millar, W H J (Queen's U, Belfast) 1951 E, S, W, 1952 S, W
Miller, A (Kingstown) 1880 E, S, 1883 E
Miller, E R P (Leicester, Tererure Coll, Leinster) 1997 It 1, F, W, E, NZ, It 2, 1998 S, W (R), Gg, R, 1999 F, W, E, S, Arg 1(R), [US (R), A 3(t&R), Arg 2(R)], 2000 US, C (R), SA, 2001 R, W, E, Sm, NZ, 2002 E, S, It (R), Fj (R), 2003 W 1(t+R), Tg, Sm, It 2, S 2, [Nm, Arg(R), A(t&R), F(R)], 2004 SA3(R), US, Arg(R), 2005 It(R), S(R), F(R), W(R), J1(R), 2
Miller, F H (Wanderers) 1886 S
Milliken, R A (Bangor) 1973 E, S, W, F, 1974 F, W, E, S, P, NZ, 1975 E, S, F, W
Millin, T J (Dublin U) 1925 W
Minch, J B (Bective Rangers) 1912 SA, 1913 E, S, 1914 E, S
Moffat, J (Belfast Academy) 1888 W, S, M, 1889 S, 1890 S, W, 1891 S
Moffatt, J E (Old Wesley) 1904 S, 1905 E, S, W
Moffett, J W (Ballymena) 1961 E, S
Molloy, M G (UC Galway, London Irish) 1966 F, E, 1967 A 1, E, S, W, F, A 2, 1968 F, E, S, W, A, 1969 F, E, S, W, 1970 F, E, S, W, 1971 F, E, S, W, 1973 F, 1976 A

**Moloney, J J** (St Mary's Coll) 1972 F 1, E, F 2, 1973 NZ, E, S, W, F, 1974 F, W, E, S, P, NZ, 1975 E, S, F, W, 1976 S, 1978 S, F, W, E, 1979 A 1, 2, 1980 S, W
**Moloney, L A** (Garryowen) 1976 W (R), S, 1978 S (R), NZ
**Molony, J U** (UC Dublin) 1950 S
**Monteith, J D E** (Queen's U, Belfast) 1947 E, S, W
**Montgomery, A** (NIFC) 1895 S
**Montgomery, F P** (Queen's U, Belfast) 1914 E, S, W
**Montgomery, R** (Cambridge U) 1887 E, S, W, 1891 E, 1892 W
**Moore, A H** (Windsor) 1876 E, 1877 S
**Moore, C M** (Dublin U) 1887 S, 1888 W, S
**Moore, D F** (Wanderers) 1883 E, S, 1884 E, W
**Moore, F W** (Wanderers) 1884 W, 1885 E, S 2, 1886 S
**Moore, H** (Queen's U, Belfast) 1910 S, 1911 W, F, 1912 F, E, S, W, SA
**Moore, M J** (Leinster) 2014 S(R), W(R), E(R), It(R), F(R)
**Moore, T A P** (Highfield) 1967 A 2, 1973 NZ, E, S, W, F, 1974 F, W, E, S, P, NZ
**Moore, W D** (Queen's Coll, Belfast) 1878 E
**Moran, F G** (Clontarf) 1936 E, 1937 E, S, W, 1938 S, W, 1939 E, S, W
**Morell, H B** (Dublin U) 1881 E, S, 1882 W, E
**Morgan, G J** (Clontarf) 1934 E, S, W, 1935 E, S, W, NZ, 1936 E, S, W, 1937 E, S, W, 1938 E, S, W, 1939 E, S, W
**Moriarty, C C H** (Monkstown) 1899 W
**Moroney, J C M** (Garryowen) 1968 W, A, 1969 F, E, S, W
**Moroney, R J M** (Lansdowne) 1984 F, W, 1985 F
**Moroney, T A** (UC Dublin) 1964 W, 1967 A 1, E
**Morphy, E McG** (Dublin U) 1908 E
**Morris, D P** (Bective Rangers) 1931 W, 1932 E, 1935 E, S, W, NZ
**Morrow, J W R** (Queen's Coll, Belfast) 1882 S, 1883 E, S, 1884 E, W, 1885 S 1, 2, 1886 E, S, 1888 S
**Morrow, R D** (Bangor) 1986 F, E, S
**Mortell, M** (Bective Rangers, Dolphin) 1953 F, E, S, W, 1954 NZ, F, E, S, W
**Morton, W A** (Dublin U) 1888 S
**Mostyn, M R** (Galwegians) 1999 A 1, Arg 1, [US, A 3, R, Arg 2]
**Moyers, L W** (Dublin U) 1884 W
**Moylett, M M F** (Shannon) 1988 E 1
**Mulcahy, W A** (UC Dublin, Bective Rangers, Bohemians) 1958 A, E, S, W, F, 1959 E, S, W, F, 1960 E, S, W, SA, 1961 E, S, W, SA, 1962 E, S, F, W, 1963 F, E, S, W, NZ, 1964 E, S, W, F, 1965 F, E, S, W, SA
**Muldoon, J** (Connacht) 2009 C, US, 2010 NZ1
**Mullan, B** (Clontarf) 1947 F, E, S, W, 1948 F, E, S, W
**Mullane, J P** (Limerick Bohemians) 1928 W, 1929 F
**Mullen, K D** (Old Belvedere) 1947 F, E, S, W, A, 1948 F, E, S, W, 1949 F, E, S, W, 1950 F, E, S, W, 1951 F, E, S, W, SA, 1952 F, S, W
**Mulligan, A A** (Wanderers) 1956 F, E, 1957 F, E, S, W, 1958 A, E, S, F, 1959 E, S, W, F, 1960 E, S, W, F, SA, 1961 W, F, SA
**Mullin, B J** (Dublin U, Oxford U, Blackrock Coll, London Irish) 1984 A, 1985 S, W, E, 1986 F, W, E, S, R, 1987 E, S, F, W, [W, C, Tg, A], 1988 S, F, W, E 1, 2, WS, It, 1989 F, W, E, S, NZ, 1990 E, S, W, Arg, 1991 F, W, E, S, Nm 1, 2, [J, S, A], 1992 W, E, S, 1994 US, 1995 E, S, F, W, It, [NZ, J, W, F]
**Mullins, M J** (Young Munster, Old Crescent) 1999 Arg 1(R), [R], 2000 E, S, It, Arg (t&R), US, C, 2001 It, R, W (R), E (R), Sm (R), NZ (R), 2003 Tg, Sm
**Murphy, B J** (Munster) 2007 Arg 1(R), 2, 2009 C, US
**Murphy, C J** (Lansdowne) 1939 E, S, W, 1947 F, E
**Murphy, G E A** (Leicester) 2000 US, C (R), J, 2001 R, S, Sm, 2002 W, E, NZ 1, 2, Fj, 2003 S 1(R), It 1, F, W 1, E, A, W 2, It 2(R), S 2, 2004 It, S, SA1, 3, US, Arg, 2005 It, S, E, F, W, NZ, A, R, 2006 It, F, W, S, NZ 1, 2, A1(R), SA(R), A2, 2007 W(t&R), F, Arg1(t&R), 2, S2, It2, [Nm(R), Arg], 2008 It, F, S, E, NZ1(R), A(R), Arg, 2009 F(R), It(R), S(R), W(R), 2010 E, W, S, NZ1(R), A(R), Arg, 2011 E2, [US, Ru(R)]
**Murphy, J** (Leinster) 2014 E(R), It(R), Arg 1, 2(R)
**Murphy, J G M W** (London Irish) 1951 SA, 1952 S, W, E, 1954 NZ, 1958 W
**Murphy, J J** (Greystones) 1981 SA 1, 1982 W (R), 1984 S
**Murphy, J N** (Greystones) 1992 A

**Murphy, K J** (Cork Constitution) 1990 E, S, F, W, Arg, 1991 F, W (R), S (R), 1992 S, F, NZ 2(R)
**Murphy, N A A** (Cork Constitution) 1958 A, E, S, W, F, 1959 E, S, W, F, 1960 E, S, W, F, SA, 1961 E, S, W, 1962 E, 1963 NZ, 1964 E, S, W, F, 1965 F, E, S, W, SA, 1966 F, E, S, W, 1967 A 1, E, S, W, F, 1969 F, E, S, W
**Murphy, N F** (Cork Constitution) 1930 E, W, 1931 F, E, S, W, SA, 1932 E, S, W, 1933 E
**Murphy-O'Connor, J** (Bective Rangers) 1954 E
**Murray, C** (Munster) 2011 F2(R), E2(R), [US, A(R), It, W], 2012 W, It, F, NZ 1, 2, 3, SA, Arg, 2013 W, E, S, F, It, Sm, A(R), NZ, 2014 S, W, E, It, F, Arg 1
**Murray, H W** (Dublin U) 1877 S, 1878 E, 1879 E
**Murray, J B** (UC Dublin) 1963 F
**Murray, P F** (Wanderers) 1927 F, 1929 F, E, S, 1930 F, E, S, W, 1931 F, E, S, W, SA, 1932 E, S, W, 1933 E, W, S
**Murtagh, C W** (Portadown) 1977 S
**Myles, J** (Dublin U) 1875 E

**Nash, L C** (Queen's Coll, Cork) 1889 S, 1890 W, E, 1891 E, S, W
**Neely, M R** (Collegians) 1947 F, E, S, W
**Neill, H J** (NIFC) 1885 E, S 1, 2, 1886 S, 1887 E, S, W, 1888 W, S
**Neill, J McF** (Instonians) 1926 F
**Nelson, J E** (Malone) 1947 A, 1948 E, S, W, 1949 F, E, S, W, 1950 F, E, S, W, 1951 F, E, W, 1954 F
**Nelson, R** (Queen's Coll, Belfast) 1882 E, S, 1883 S, 1886 S
**Nesdale, R P** (Newcastle) 1997 W, E, S, NZ (R), C, 1998 F (R), W (R), Gg, SA 3(R), 1999 It, A 2(R), [US (R), R]
**Nesdale, T J** (Garryowen) 1961 F
**Neville, W C** (Dublin U) 1879 S, E
**Nicholson, P C** (Dublin U) 1900 E, S, W
**Norton, G W** (Bective Rangers) 1949 F, E, S, W, 1950 F, E, S, W, 1951 F, E, S
**Notley, J R** (Wanderers) 1952 F, S
**Nowlan, K W** (St Mary's Coll) 1997 NZ, C, It 2

**O'Brien, B** (Derry) 1893 S, W
**O'Brien, B A P** (Shannon) 1968 F, E, S
**O'Brien, D J** (London Irish, Cardiff, Old Belvedere) 1948 E, S, W, 1949 F, E, S, W, 1950 F, E, S, W, 1951 F, E, S, W, SA, 1952 F, S, W, E
**O'Brien, K A** (Broughton Park) 1980 E, 1981 SA 1(R), 2
**O'Brien, S K** (Leinster) 2009 Fj(R), SA(R), 2010 It(R), Sm, 2011 It, F1, W, E1, F2, 3, [A, Ru, It, W], 2012 W, It, F, E, NZ 1, 2, 3, 2013 W, E, S, F, It, Sm(R), A, NZ
**O'Brien-Butler, P E** (Monkstown) 1897 S, 1898 E, S, 1899 S, W, 1900 E
**O'Callaghan, C T** (Carlow) 1910 W, F, 1911 E, S, W, F, 1912 F
**O'Callaghan, D P** (Cork Const, Munster) 2003 W 1(R), Tg (R), Sm (R), W 2(R), It2(R), [R(R), A(t&R)], 2004 F(t&R), W, It, S(t&R), SA2(R), US, 2005 It(R), S(R), W(R), NZ, A, R, 2006 It(R), F(R), W, S(R), E(R), NZ1, 2, A1, SA, A2, PI(R), 2007 W, F, E, S1, It1, 2, [Nm, Gg, F, Arg], 2008 It, F, S, W, E, NZ1, A, C, NZ2, Arg, 2009 F, It, E, S, W, A, Fj(R), SA, 2010 E, W, S, NZ1, A, Sm, NZ2, Arg, 2011 F1, S1, W, E1, F2, 3, E2, [US, A, Ru, It, W], 2012 W, It, F, S, E, NZ 1(R), 2(R), 3(R), SA(t&R), Arg(R), 2013 W(R), E(R), S, F(R)
**O'Callaghan, M P** (Sunday's Well) 1962 W, 1964 E, F
**O'Callaghan, P** (Dolphin) 1967 A 1, E, A 2, 1968 F, E, S, W, 1969 F, E, S, W, 1970 SA, F, E, S, W, 1976 F, W, E, S, NZ
**O'Connell, K D** (Sunday's Well) 1994 F, E (t)
**O'Connell, P** (Bective Rangers) 1913 W, F, 1914 F, E, S, W
**O'Connell, P J** (Young Munster, Munster) 2002 W, It (R), F (R), NZ 1, 2003 E (R), A (R), Tg, Sm, W 2, S 2, [R, Nm, Arg, A, F], 2004 F, W, E, S, SA1, 2, 3, US, Arg, 2005 It, S, E, F, W, 2006 It, F, S, E, NZ1, 2, A1, SA, A2, PI, 2007 W, F, E, S1, 2, It2, [Nm, Gg, F, Arg], 2008 S(R), W, E, NZ1, A, C, NZ2, Arg, 2009 F, It, E, S, W, A, Fj, SA, 2010 It, F, E, W, S, 2011 It, F1, S1, W, E1, F2(R), 3, E2, [US, A, It, W], 2012 W, It, F, 2013 Sm(t&R), A, NZ, 2014 W, E, It, F, Arg 1, 2
**O'Connell, W J** (Lansdowne) 1955 F
**O'Connor, H S** (Dublin U) 1957 F, E, S, W
**O'Connor, J** (Garryowen) 1895 S
**O'Connor, J H** (Bective Rangers) 1888 M, 1890 S, W, E, 1891 E, S, 1892 E, W, 1893 E, S, 1894 E, S, W, 1895 E, 1896 E, S, W

**O'Connor, J H** (Wasps) 2004 SA3, Arg, 2005 S, E, F, W, J1, NZ, A, R, 2006 W(R), E(t&R)
**O'Connor, J J** (Garryowen) 1909 F
**O'Connor, J J** (UC Cork) 1933 S, 1934 E, S, W, 1935 E, S, W, NZ, 1936 S, W, 1938 S
**O'Connor, P J** (Lansdowne) 1887 W
**O'Cuinneagain, D** (Sale, Ballymena) 1998 SA 1, 2, Gg (R), R (R), SA 3, 1999 F, W, E, S, It, A 1, 2, Arg 1, [US, A 3, R, Arg 2], 2000 E, It (R)
**Odbert, R V M** (RAF) 1928 F
**O'Donnell, R C** (St Mary's Coll) 1979 A 1, 2, 1980 S, F, W
**O'Donnell, T** (Munster) 2013 US(t&R), C, 2014 S(R), W(R)
**O'Donoghue, P J** (Bective Rangers) 1955 F, E, S, W, 1956 W, 1957 F, E, 1958 A, E, S, W
**O'Driscoll, B G** (Blackrock Coll, Leinster) 1999 A 1, 2, Arg 1, [US, A 3, R (R), Arg 2], 2000 E, S, It, F, W, J, SA, 2001 F, S, W, E, Sm, NZ, 2002 W, E, S, It, F, NZ 1, 2, R, Ru, Gg, A, Fj, Arg, 2003 S 1, It 1, F, W 1, E, W 2, It 2, S 2, [R, Nm, Arg, A, F], 2004 W, E, It, S, SA1, 2, 3, US, Arg, 2005 It, E, F, W, 2006 It, F, W, S, E, NZ1, 2, A1, SA, A2, PI, 2007 W, E, S1, It1, S2, [Nm, Gg, F, Arg], 2008 It, F, S, W, NZ1, A, C, NZ2, Arg, 2009 F, It, E, S, W, A, Fj, SA, 2010 It, F, E, W, S, NZ1, A, SA, Sm, NZ2, Arg, 2011 It, F1, S1, W, E1, F3, [US, A, It, W], 2012 NZ 1, 2, 3, 2013 W, E, S, F, It, Sm, A, NZ, 2014 S, W, E, It, F
**O'Driscoll, B J** (Manchester) 1971 F (R), E, S, W
**O'Driscoll, J B** (London Irish, Manchester) 1978 S, 1979 A 1, 2, 1980 E, S, F, W, 1981 F, W, E, S, SA 1, 2, A, 1982 W, E, S, F, 1983 S, F, W, E, 1984 F, W, E, S
**O'Driscoll, M R** (Cork Const, Munster) 2001 R (R), 2002 Fj (R), 2005 R(R), 2006 W(R), NZ1(R), 2(R), A1(R), 2007 E(R), It1, Arg1(t&R), 2, 2008 It(R), F(R), S, E(R), 2009 C, US, 2010 NZ1, A, SA, NZ2, Arg, 2011 S2(R)
**O'Flanagan, K P** (London Irish) 1947 A
**O'Flanagan, M** (Lansdowne) 1948 S
**O'Gara, R J R** (Cork Const, Munster) 2000 S, It, F, W, Arg (R), US, C (R), J, SA, 2001 It, F, S, W (R), E (R), Sm, 2002 W (R), E (R), S (R), It (R), F, NZ 1, 2, R, Ru, Gg, A, Arg, 2003 W 1(R), E (R), A (t+R), Tg, Sm, S 2, [R(R), Nm, Arg(R)], A, F], 2004 F, W, E, It, S, SA1, 2, 3, Arg, 2005 It, S, E, F, W, NZ, A, R(R), 2006 It, F, W, S, E, NZ1, A, C, NZ2, Arg, PI(R), 2007 W, F, E, S1, It1, S2(R), It2, [Nm, Gg, F, Arg], 2008 It, F, S, W, E, NZ1, A, C, NZ2, Arg, 2009 F, It, E, S, W, A, 2010 It, F, E(R), W(R), S(R), NZ1, SA(R), Sm, NZ2(R), Arg(R), 2011 It(R), F1(R), S1, W, E1(R), F2, 3(R), E2, [US(R), A(R), Ru, It, W], 2012 W(R), It(R), F(R), S(R), E(R), NZ 1(R), 2(R), 3(R), SA(R), Arg(R), 2013 E(R), S(R)
**O'Grady, D** (Sale) 1997 It 2
**O'Hanlon, B** (Dolphin) 1947 E, S, W, 1948 F, E, S, W, 1949 F, E, S, W, 1950 F
**O'Hara, P T J** (Sunday's Well, Cork Const) 1988 WS (R), 1989 F, W, E, NZ, 1990 E, S, F, W, 1991 Nm 1, [J], 1993 F, W, E, 1994 US
**O'Kelly, M E** (London Irish, St Mary's Coll, Leinster) 1997 NZ, C, It 2, 1998 S, F, W, E, SA 1, 2, Gg, R, SA 3, 1999 A 1(R), 2, Arg 1(R), [US (R), A 3, R, Arg 2], 2000 E, S, It, F, W, Arg, J, SA, 2001 It, F, S, W, E, NZ, 2002 E, S, It, F, NZ 1(R), 2, R, Ru, Gg, A, Fj, Arg, 2003 S 1, It 1, F, W 1, E, A, W 2, S 2, [R, Nm, Arg, A, F(R), W(R), E, It, S, SA1, 2, 3, Arg, 2005 It, S, E, F, W, NZ, A, 2006 It, F, W, S, E, SA(R), A2(R), PI, 2007 Arg1, 2(R), S2, It2(R), [F(R), Arg(R)], 2008 It, F, 2009 It(R)
**Olding, S** (Ulster) 2013 US
**O'Leary, A** (Cork Constitution) 1952 S, W, E
**O'Leary, T G** (Munster) 2007 Arg1(R), 2008 NZ2, Arg, 2009 F, It, E, S(R), W, A, Fj(R), SA, 2010 It, F, E, W, S, NZ1, A, 2011 It, F1, S2, F3, 2012 S(R), E(R)
**O'Loughlin, D B** (UC Cork) 1938 E, S, W, 1939 E, S, W
**O'Mahony, David** (Cork Constitution) 1995 It
**O'Mahony, D W** (UC Dublin, Moseley, Bedford) 1995 It, [F], 1997 It 2, 1998 R
**O'Mahony, P** (Munster) 2012 It(R), F(R), S, E(R), NZ 1, 2(R), 3, SA, 2013 W, E, S, F, It, US, C, Sm, A, NZ, 2014 S, W, E, It
**O'Meara, B T** (Cork Constitution) 1997 E (R), S, NZ (R), 1998 S, 1999 [US (R), R (R)], 2001 It (R), 2003 Sm (R), It 2(R)
**O'Meara, J A** (UC Cork, Dolphin) 1951 F, E, S, W, SA, 1952 F,

S, W, E, 1953 F, E, S, W, 1954 NZ, F, E, S, 1955 F, E, 1956 S, W, 1958 W
**O'Neill, H O'H** (Queen's U, Belfast, UC Cork) 1930 E, S, W, 1933 E, S, W
**O'Neill, J B** (Queen's U, Belfast) 1920 S
**O'Neill, W A** (UC Dublin, Wanderers) 1952 E, 1953 F, E, S, W, 1954 NZ
**O'Reilly, A J F** (Old Belvedere, Leicester) 1955 F, E, S, W, 1956 F, E, S, W, 1957 F, E, S, W, 1958 A, E, S, W, F, 1959 E, S, W, F, 1960 E, 1961 E, F, SA, 1963 F, S, W, 1970 E
**Orr, P A** (Old Wesley) 1976 F, W, E, S, NZ, 1977 W, E, S, F, 1978 S, F, W, E, NZ, 1979 F, W, E, S, A 1, 2, 1980 E, S, F, W, 1981 F, W, E, S, SA 1, 2, A, 1982 W, E, S, F, 1983 S, F, W, E, 1984 F, W, E, S, A, 1985 S, F, W, E, 1986 F, S, R, 1987 E, S, F, W, [W, C, A]
**O'Shea, C M P** (Lansdowne, London Irish) 1993 R, 1994 F, W, E, S, A 1, 2, US, 1995 E, S, [J, W, F], 1997 It 1, F, S (R), 1998 S, F, SA 1, 2, Gg, R, SA 3, 1999 F, W, E, S, It, A 1, Arg 1, [US, A 3, R, Arg 2], 2000 E
**O'Sullivan, A C** (Dublin U) 1882 S
**O'Sullivan, J M** (Limerick) 1884 S, 1887 S
**O'Sullivan, P J A** (Galwegians) 1957 F, E, S, W, 1959 E, S, W, F, 1960 SA, 1961 E, S, 1962 F, W, 1963 F, NZ
**O'Sullivan, W** (Queen's Coll, Cork) 1895 S
**Owens, R H** (Dublin U) 1922 E, S

**Parfrey, P** (UC Cork) 1974 NZ
**Parke, J C** (Monkstown) 1903 W, 1904 E, S, W, 1905 W, NZ, 1906 E, S, W, SA, 1907 E, S, W, 1908 E, S, W, 1909 E, S, W, F
**Parr, J S** (Wanderers) 1914 F, E, S, W
**Patterson, C S** (Instonians) 1978 NZ, 1979 F, W, E, S, A 1, 2, 1980 E, S, F, W
**Patterson, R d'A** (Wanderers) 1912 F, S, W, SA, 1913 E, S, W, F
**Payne, C T** (NIFC) 1926 E, 1927 F, E, S, A, 1928 F, E, S, W, 1929 F, E, W, 1930 F, E, S, W
**Pedlow, A C** (CIYMS) 1953 W, 1954 NZ, F, E, 1955 F, E, S, W, 1956 F, E, S, W, 1957 F, E, S, W, 1958 A, E, S, W, F, 1959 E, 1960 E, S, W, F, SA, 1961 S, 1962 W, 1963 F
**Pedlow, J** (Bessbrook) 1882 S, 1884 W
**Pedlow, R** (Bessbrook) 1891 W
**Pedlow, T B** (Queen's Coll, Belfast) 1889 S, W
**Peel, T** (Limerick) 1892 E, S, W
**Peirce, W** (Cork) 1881 E
**Phipps, G C** (Army) 1950 E, W, 1952 F, W, E
**Pike, T O** (Lansdowne) 1927 E, S, W, A, 1928 F, E, S, W
**Pike, V J** (Lansdowne) 1931 E, S, W, SA, 1932 E, S, W, 1933 E, W, S, 1934 E, S, W
**Pike, W W** (Kingstown) 1879 E, 1881 E, S, 1882 E, 1883 S
**Pinion, G** (Belfast Collegians) 1909 E, S, W, F
**Piper, O J S** (Cork Constitution) 1909 E, S, W, F, 1910 E, S, W, F
**Polden, S E** (Clontarf) 1913 W, F, 1914 F, 1920 F
**Popham, I** (Cork Constitution) 1922 S, W, F, 1923 F
**Popplewell, N J** (Greystones, Wasps, Newcastle) 1989 NZ, 1990 Arg, 1991 Nm 1, 2, [Z, S, A], 1992 W, E, S, F, NZ 1, 2, A, 1993 S, F, W, E, R, 1994 F, W, E, S, US, 1995 E, S, F, W, It, [NZ, J, W, F], 1996 US, S, F, W, E, A, 1997 It 1, F, W, E, NZ, C, 1998 S (t), F (R)
**Potterton, H N** (Wanderers) 1920 W
**Pratt, R H** (Dublin U) 1933 E, W, S, 1934 E, S
**Price, A H** (Dublin U) 1920 S, F
**Pringle, J C** (NIFC) 1902 S, W
**Purcell, N M** (Lansdowne) 1921 E, S, W, F
**Purdon, H** (NIFC) 1879 S, E, 1880 E, 1881 E, S
**Purdon, W B** (Queen's Coll, Belfast) 1906 E, S, W
**Purser, F C** (Dublin U) 1898 E, S, W

**Quinlan, A N** (Shannon, Munster) 1999 [R (R)], 2001 It, F, 2002 NZ 2(R), Ru (R), Gg (R), A (R), Fj, Arg (R), 2003 S 1(R), It 1(R), F (R), W 1, E (R), A, W 2, [R(R), Nm, Arg], 2004 SA1(R), 2(R), 2005 J1, 2(t&R), 2007 Arg2, S2(t&R), [F(R), Arg(R)], NZ2
**Quinlan, D P** (Northampton) 2005 J1(R), 2
**Quinlan, S V J** (Blackrock Coll) 1956 F, E, W, 1958 W
**Quinn, B T** (Old Belvedere) 1947 F
**Quinn, F P** (Old Belvedere) 1981 F, W, E

Spunner, H F (Wanderers) 1881 E, S, 1884 W

Stack, C R R (Dublin U) 1889 S

Stack, G H (Dublin U) 1875 E

Staples, J E (London Irish, Harlequins) 1991 W, E, S, Nm 1, 2, [Z, J, S, A], 1992 W, E, NZ 1, 2, A, 1995 F, W, It, [NZ], Fj, 1996 US, S, F, A, 1997 W, E, S

Staunton, J W (Garryowen, Wasps) 2001 Sm, 2005 J1(R), 2(R), 2006 A1(R), 2007 Arg2

Steele, H W (Ballymena) 1976 E, 1977 F, 1978 F, W, E, 1979 F, W, E, A 1, 2

Stephenson, G V (Queen's U, Belfast, London Hosp) 1920 F, 1921 E, S, W, F, 1922 E, S, W, F, 1923 E, S, W, F, 1924 F, E, S, W, NZ, 1925 F, E, S, W, 1926 F, E, S, W, 1927 F, E, S, W, A, 1928 F, E, S, W, 1929 F, E, W, 1930 F, E, S, W

Stephenson, H W V (United Services) 1922 S, W, F, 1924 F, E, S, W, NZ, 1925 F, E, S, W, 1927 A, 1928 E

Stevenson, J (Dungannon) 1888 M, 1889 S

Stevenson, J B (Instonians) 1958 A, E, S, W, F

Stevenson, R (Dungannon) 1887 E, S, W, 1888 M, 1889 S, W, 1890 S, W, E, 1891 W, 1892 W, 1893 E, S, W

Stevenson, T H (Belfast Acad) 1895 E, W, 1896 E, S, W, 1897 E, S

Stewart, A L (NIFC) 1913 W, F, 1914 F

Stewart, J W (Queen's U, Belfast, NIFC) 1922 F, 1924 S, 1928 F, E, S, W, 1929 F, E, S, W

Stoker, E W (Wanderers) 1888 W, S

Stoker, F O (Wanderers) 1886 S, 1888 W, M, 1889 S, 1891 W

Stokes, O S (Cork Bankers) 1882 E, 1884 E

Stokes, P (Garryowen) 1913 E, S, 1914 F, 1920 E, S, W, F, 1921 E, S, F, 1922 W, F

Stokes, R D (Queen's Coll, Cork) 1891 S, W

Strathdee, E (Queen's U, Belfast) 1947 E, S, W, A, 1948 W, F, 1949 E, S, W

Strauss, C R (Leinster) 2012 SA, Arg, 2013 US, C

Stringer, P A (Shannon, Munster) 2000 S, It, F, W, Arg, C, J, SA, 2001 It, F, R, S (R), W, E, Sm, NZ, 2002 W, E, S, It, F, NZ 1, 2, R, Ru, Gg, A, Arg, 2003 S 1, It 1, F, W 1, E, A, W 2, S 2, [Nm, Arg, A, F], 2004 F, W, E, It, S, SA1, 2, 3, US(R), Arg, 2005 It, S, E, F, W, J1, 2, NZ, A, R(R), 2006 It, F, W, S, E, NZ1, 2, A1, SA, A2(R), PI, 2007 W, E, S1, It1, 2, [Nm, Gg, A], 2008 It(R), S(R), E(R), NZ1(R), A, C(R), 2009 It(t&R), E(R), S, W(R), C, US, 2010 SA(R), Sm, NZ2(R), Arg, 2011 S1(R), W(R), E1(R)

Stuart, C P (Clontarf) 1912 SA

Stuart, I M B (Dublin U) 1924 E, S

Sugars, H S (Dublin U) 1905 NZ, 1906 SA, 1907 S

Sugden, M (Wanderers) 1925 F, E, S, W, 1926 F, E, S, W, 1927 E, S, W, A, 1928 F, E, S, W, 1929 F, E, S, W, 1930 F, E, S, W, 1931 F, E, S, W

Sullivan, D B (UC Dublin) 1922 E, S, W, F

Sweeney, J A (Blackrock Coll) 1907 E, S, W

Symes, G R (Monkstown) 1895 E

Synge, J S (Lansdowne) 1929 S

Taggart, T (Dublin U) 1887 W

Taylor, A S (Queen's Coll, Belfast) 1910 E, S, W, 1912 F

Taylor, D R (Queen's Coll, Belfast) 1903 E

Taylor, J (Belfast Collegians) 1914 E, S, W

Taylor, J W (NIFC) 1879 S, 1880 E, S, 1881 S, 1882 E, S, 1883 E, S, W

Tector, W R (Wanderers) 1955 F, E, S

Tedford, A (Malone) 1902 E, S, W, 1903 E, S, W, 1904 E, S, W, 1905 E, S, W, NZ, 1906 E, S, W, SA, 1907 E, S, W, 1908 E, S, W

Teehan, C (UC Cork) 1939 E, S, W

Thompson, C (Belfast Collegians) 1907 E, S, 1908 E, S, W, 1909 E, S, W, F, 1910 E, S, W, F

Thompson, J A (Queen's Coll, Belfast) 1885 S 1, 2

Thompson, J K S (Dublin U) 1921 W, 1922 E, S, F, 1923 E, S, W, F

Thompson, R G (Lansdowne) 1882 W

Thompson, R H (Instonians) 1951 SA, 1952 F, 1954 NZ, F, E, S, W, 1955 F, S, W, 1956 W

Thornhill, T (Wanderers) 1892 E, S, W, 1893 E

Thrift, H (Dublin U) 1904 W, 1905 E, S, W, NZ, 1906 E, W, SA, 1907 E, S, W, 1908 E, S, W, 1909 E, S, W, F

Tierney, D (UC Cork) 1938 S, W, 1939 E

Tierney, T A (Garryowen) 1999 A 1, 2, Arg 1, [US, A 3, R, Arg 2], 2000 E

Tillie, C R (Dublin U) 1887 E, S, 1888 W, S

Todd, A W P (Dublin U) 1913 W, F, 1914 F

Toner, D (Leinster) 2010 Sm, NZ2(R), Arg(R), 2013 S(R), It(R), US, C, Sm, A, NZ, 2014 S, W, E, It, F, Arg 1(R), 2

Topping, J A (Ballymena) 1996 WS, A, 1997 It 1, F, E, 1999 [R], 2000 US, 2003 A

Torrens, J D (Bohemians) 1938 W, 1939 E, S, W

Trimble, A D (Ulster) 2005 A, R, 2006 F(R), W, S, E, NZ1, 2, A1, SA, 2007 W, F(R), E(R), It1(R), Arg1, S2(R), It2, [Nm, F], 2008 It, F, S, W, E, 2009 Fj(R), 2010 It, E(R), NZ1, A, Sm, Arg, 2011 E1, S2, F2, 3, E2, [US(R), A(t&R), Ru, It(R), , W(R)], 2012 W, It, F, S, E, NZ 2, 3(t&R), SA, 2013 C, 2014 S, W, E, It, F, Arg 1, 2

Tucker, C C (Shannon) 1979 F, W, 1980 F (R)

Tuke, B B (Bective Rangers) 1890 E, 1891 E, S, 1892 E, 1894 E, S, W, 1895 E, S

Tuohy, D M (Ulster) 2010 NZ1(R), A(t&R), 2012 NZ 1, 2, 3, 2013 US(R), C, 2014 S, W(R)

Turley, N (Blackrock Coll) 1962 E

Tweed, D A (Ballymena) 1995 F, W, It, [J]

Tydings, J J (Young Munster) 1968 A

Tyrrell, W (Queen's U, Belfast) 1910 F, 1913 E, S, W, F, 1914 F, E, S, W

Uprichard, R J H (Harlequins, RAF) 1950 S, W

Varley, D A (Munster) 2010 A(R), Arg(R), 2014 Arg 1(R)

Waide, S L (Oxford U, NIFC) 1932 E, S, W, 1933 E, W

Waites, J (Bective Rangers) 1886 S, 1888 M, 1889 W, 1890 S, W, E, 1891 E

Waldron, O C (Oxford U, London Irish) 1966 S, W, 1968 A

Walker, S (Instonians) 1934 E, S, 1935 E, S, W, NZ, 1936 E, S, W, 1937 E, S, W, 1938 E, S, W

Walkington, D B (NIFC) 1887 E, W, 1888 W, 1890 W, 1891 E, S, W

Walkington, R B (NIFC) 1875 E, 1876 E, 1877 E, S, 1878 E, 1879 S, 1880 S, E, 1882 E, S

Wall, H (Dolphin) 1965 S, W

Wallace, D P (Garryowen, Munster) 2000 Arg, US, 2001 It, F, R (R), S (R), W, E, NZ, 2002 W, E, S, It, F, 2003 Tg (R), Sm (R), W 2(t+R), S 2, 2004 S, SA1, 2, 2005 J2, 2006 It, F, W, S, E, NZ1, 2, A1, SA, A2, 2007 W, F, E, S1, It1, [Nm, Gg, F, Arg], 2008 It, F, S, W, E, NZ1, C(R), NZ2, Arg, 2009 F, It, E, S, W, A, SA, 2010 It, F, E, W, S, NZ1, SA, NZ2, Arg, 2011 It, F1, S1, W, E1, 2

Wallace, Jas (Wanderers) 1904 E, S

Wallace, Jos (Wanderers) 1903 S, W, 1904 E, S, W, 1905 E, S, W, NZ, 1906 W

Wallace, P R (Ulster) 2006 SA(R), PI, 2007 E(R), Arg1, S2, [Nm(R)], 2008 S(R), E(R), NZ1, A, C(R), NZ2(R), 2009 F, It, E, W(R), A, Fj(R), SA, 2010 It(R), F(t&R), A, Sm, 2011 It(R), W(R), E1(R), S2, F2, [Ru], 2012 NZ 3

Wallace, P S (Blackrock Coll, Saracens) 1995 [J], Fj, 1996 US, W, E, WS, A, 1997 It 1, F, W, E, S, NZ, C, 1998 S, F, W, E, SA 1, 2, Gg, R, 1999 F, W, E, S, It (R), 1999 A 1, 2, Arg 1, [US, A 3, R, Arg 2], 2000 E, US, C (R), 2002 W (R), E (R), S (R), It (R), F (R), NZ 2(R), Ru (R), Gg (R)

Wallace, R M (Garryowen, Saracens) 1991 Nm 1(R), 1992 W, E, S, F, A, 1993 S, F, W, E, R, 1994 F, W, E, S, 1995 W, It, [NZ, J, W], Fj, 1996 US, S, F, WS, 1998 S, F, W, E

Wallace, T H (Cardiff) 1920 E, S, W

Wallis, A K (Wanderers) 1892 E, S, W, 1893 E, W

Wallis, C O'N (Old Cranleighans, Wanderers) 1935 NZ

Wallis, T G (Wanderers) 1921 F, 1922 E, S, W, F

Wallis, W A (Wanderers) 1880 S, 1881 E, S, 1882 W, 1883 S

Walmsley, G (Bective Rangers) 1894 E

Walpole, A (Dublin U) 1888 S, M

Walsh, E J (Lansdowne) 1887 E, S, W, 1892 E, S, W, 1893 E

Walsh, H D (Dublin U) 1875 E, 1876 E

Walsh, J C (UC Cork, Sunday's Well) 1960 S, SA, 1961 E, S, F, SA, 1963 E, S, W, NZ, 1964 E, S, W, F, 1965 F, S, W, SA, 1966 F, S, W, 1967 E, S, W, F, A 2

Ward, A J (Ballynahinch) 1998 F, W, E, SA 1, 2, Gg, R, SA 3, 1999 W, E, S, It (R), A 1, 2, Arg 1, [US, A 3, R, Arg 2],

2000 F (R), W (t&R), Arg (R), US (R), C, J, SA (R), 2001 It (R), F (R)

**Ward, A J P** (Garryowen, St Mary's Coll, Greystones) 1978 S, F, W, E, NZ, 1979 F, W, E, S, 1981 W, E, S, A, 1983 E (R), 1984 E, S, 1986 S, 1987 [C, Tg]

**Warren, J P** (Kingstown) 1883 E

**Warren, R G** (Lansdowne) 1884 W, 1885 E, S 1, 2, 1886 E, 1887 E, S, W, 1888 W, S, M, 1889 S, W, 1890 S, W, E

**Watson, R** (Wanderers) 1912 SA

**Wells, H G** (Bective Rangers) 1891 S, W, 1894 E, S

**Westby, A J** (Dublin U) 1876 E

**Wheeler, G H** (Queen's Coll, Belfast) 1884 S, 1885 E

**Wheeler, J R** (Queen's U, Belfast) 1922 E, S, W, F, 1924 E

**Whelan, P C** (Garryowen) 1975 E, S, 1976 NZ, 1977 W, E, S, F, 1978 S, F, W, E, NZ, 1979 F, W, E, S, 1981 F, W, E

**White, M** (Queen's Coll, Cork) 1906 E, S, W, SA, 1907 E, W

**Whitestone, A M** (Dublin U) 1877 E, 1879 S, E, 1880 E, 1883 S

**Whitten, I W** (Ulster) 2009 C, US

**Whittle, D** (Bangor) 1988 F

**Wilkinson, C R** (Malone) 1993 S

**Wilkinson, R W** (Wanderers) 1947 A

**Williamson, F W** (Dolphin) 1930 E, S, W

**Willis, J W W** (Lansdowne) 1879 E

**Wilson, F** (CIYMS) 1977 W, E, S

**Wilson, H G** (Glasgow U, Malone) 1905 E, S, W, NZ, 1906 E, S, W, SA, 1907 E, S, W, 1908 E, S, W, 1909 E, S, W, 1910 W

**Wilson, R G** (Ulster) 2005 J1

**Wilson, W H** (Bray) 1877 E, S

**Withers, H H C** (Army, Blackheath) 1931 F, E, S, W, SA

**Wolfe, E J** (Armagh) 1882 E

**Wood, G H** (Dublin U) 1913 W, 1914 F

**Wood, B G M** (Garryowen) 1954 E, S, 1956 F, E, S, W, 1957 F, E, S, W, 1958 A, E, S, W, F, 1959 E, S, W, F, 1960 E, S, W, F, SA, 1961 E, S, W, F, SA

**Wood, K G M** (Garryowen, Harlequins) 1994 A 1, 2, US, 1995 E, S, [J], 1996 A, 1997 It 1, F, 1997 NZ, It 2, 1998 S, F, W, E, SA 1, 2, R (R), SA 3, 1999 F, W, E, S, It (R), A 1, 2, Arg 1, [US, A 3, R (R), Arg 2], 2000 E, S, It, F, W, Arg, US, C, J, SA, 2001 It, F, S, W, E, NZ, 2002 F, NZ 1, 2, Ru, 2003 W 2, S 2, [R, Nm, Arg, A, F]

**Woods, D C** (Bessbrook) 1888 M, 1889 S

**Woods, N K P J** (Blackrock Coll, London Irish) 1994 A 1, 2, 1995 E, F, 1996 F, W, E, 1999 W

**Wright, R A** (Monkstown) 1912 S

**Yeates, R A** (Dublin U) 1889 S, W

**Young, B G** (Ulster) 2006 NZ2(R), A1(R), SA(R), A2, PI, 2007 Arg1, 2, S2

**Young, G** (UC Cork) 1913 E

**Young, R M** (Collegians) 1965 F, E, S, W, SA, 1966 F, E, S, W, 1967 W, F, 1968 W, A, 1969 F, E, S, W, 1970 SA, F, E, S, W, 1971 F, E, S, W

**Zebo, S R** (Munster) 2012 NZ 1, SA, Arg, 2013 W, E, US, 2014 Arg 1, 2

Getty Images

Jamie Heaslip on the charge as Ireland notched up a rare win in Paris to clinch the Six Nations Championship.

# ITALY

## ITALY'S 2013–14 TEST RECORD

| OPPONENTS | DATE | VENUE | RESULT |
|-----------|------|-------|--------|
| Australia | 9 Nov | H | Lost 20–50 |
| Fiji | 16 Nov | H | Won 37–31 |
| Argentina | 23 Nov | H | Lost 14–19 |
| Wales | 1 Feb | A | Lost 23–15 |
| France | 9 Feb | A | Lost 30–10 |
| Scotland | 22 Feb | H | Lost 20–21 |
| Ireland | 8 Mar | A | Lost 46–7 |
| England | 15 Mar | H | Lost 11–52 |
| Fiji | 7 Jun | A | Lost 25–14 |
| Samoa | 14 Jun | A | Lost 15–0 |
| Japan | 21 Jun | A | Lost 26–23 |

# A YEAR OF TRANSITION FOR ITALY

## *With Sergio Parisse*

The running and handling of Michele Campagnaro was one of the biggest pluses of the year for Italy.

**T**ake a quick look at Italy's record over the last 12 months and it is easy to see why they have dropped to their lowest ever position of 14th in the IRB World Rankings. The Azzurri have managed just one win – against Fiji in November 2013 – in 11 Tests. There were some positives to come out of the 2013–14 season in terms of young players like Michele Campagnaro, Angelo Esposito and Leonardo Sarto stepping up into the Test arena, but there were plenty of low points with a half-century of points conceded against Australia and England at home and a last-minute loss to Scotland.

"In one word, I would say the season was difficult," admitted Italy's talisman and captain Sergio Parisse. "But it was a difficult season for the whole of Italian rugby. It was a transitional year, no doubt about that. The young players coming in was definitely a positive from last year, but we paid a bit with the lack of experience."

The season had not got off to the best of starts with a 50–20 loss to Australia at the Stadio Olimpico in Turin. That said, Italy had started brightly to lead 10–0, but the Wallabies hit back with seven tries to record a convincing victory, one that left Parisse somewhat frustrated. "We started pretty well against them and were leading 10–0 after the first 10 minutes. It was an encouraging start, but the final score was a disappointing one. We changed our defensive system approaching the autumn internationals and we struggled to adapt to the new one quickly. The Wallabies had travelled to Europe after a disappointing Rugby Championship and we were confident that we were capable of putting them to the sword, or at least in making their life difficult in Turin. It wasn't to be."

Fiji provided the opposition a week later in Cremona, a special occasion for Parisse and veteran front row Martin Castrogiovanni as they became Italy's latest centurions, following in the footsteps of Alessandro Troncon, Marco Bortolami and Andrea Lo Cicero. Italy marked the day with a win, albeit closer than it could have been after a 37–17 lead became just a six-point win after two late Fijian tries in a match which saw six yellow cards, five of them for the visitors. "It was a special moment for both of us, a good goal to reach together, especially because we won our first caps together against the All Blacks in Hamilton in 2002," admitted Parisse. "We didn't close out the game when we had the chance to do that and Fiji were brave enough to fight back in the final minutes. But the result was never in question from my point of view."

The November series concluded with a 19–14 defeat to Argentina in Rome, the Pumas coming from behind to win courtesy of Nicolás Sánchez's penalty and drop goal. The difference between the two sides for Parisse was that "they took the only chance to score a try and we weren't able to the same."

The November internationals may not have gone according to plan for the Italians, but for Parisse it hadn't been a "catastrophic" series. "To win at least one game was a good goal in the end, but most of all we saw some new young and interesting players making their debut. It wasn't a successful November, but neither was it a catastrophic one."

Italy only had a couple of months to regroup before the Six Nations, which began with a trip to the Millennium Stadium to take on Wales. Conceding a try in the opening five minutes wasn't what Italy had been wanting to do but despite the 23–15 loss there was one massive positive in the "superb" performance of Campagnaro on his tournament debut, the 20-year-old centre scoring two tries in the Welsh capital to live up to his billing as a player to watch for the future.

The Azzurri travelled to France the following weekend hoping to repeat their victory of a year earlier, but three converted tries in the 12 minutes after half-time blew Italy away and Tommaso Iannone's late try was nothing more than a consolation score in a 30–10 defeat at the Stade de France.

Italy's first home match of the Championship saw Scotland visit the Stadio Olimpico in Rome, a match which – with Ireland away and England at home to come – presented their best chance of a victory. Things went according to plan in the first half with Tommaso Allan, who had represented Scotland at Under 20 level, scoring all of Italy's points for a 13–6 lead at half-time. A second half double from Alex Dunbar edged Scotland ahead, but Italy looked to have sneaked it when Josh Furno's try made it 20–18 to the hosts with seven minutes remaining. There was still time for one final act, though, as Duncan Weir kicked a drop goal at the death to give Scotland their first win over Italy in Rome since the 2006 Six Nations.

"We dominated them for most of the game and they won with a last-gasp drop goal," recalled Parisse. "We were in the right position to win that game, but credit to their fly-half for scoring the drop and to the whole Scottish team for the spirit they showed coming back into the game."

Italy finished the Six Nations with two heavy defeats, 46–7 to Ireland in Dublin and 52–11 to England in Rome, and were left propping up the table for the first time since 2010. "We played a good first half (against Ireland), but we lacked possession and while we defended pretty well, it's tough to defend for 80 minutes at international level, especially when you're facing Ireland. They play great rugby and we suffered a lot with them playing with the ball in their hands for most of the game ... Game after game we weren't playing as it was expected, things were getting worse and worse."

It wasn't only on the international stage where Italian teams were struggling in 2013–14 as their two representatives in the RaboDirect PRO12 – Benetton Treviso and Zebre – finished the season in the bottom two positions, both having won only five of their 22 matches. Not the ideal preparation then for a tour to Fiji, Samoa and Japan in June, particularly not without their injured captain Parisse and Castrogiovanni whom coach Jacques Brunel elected to rest ahead of what will be a busy year in the countdown to Rugby World Cup 2015 in England. Italy would also travel without the experienced Gonzalo Canale and

Alessandro Zanni, with Brunel handing the captaincy to second row Quentin Geldenhuys.

Italy had never lost on Fijian soil, but that record came to an abrupt end before a crowd of just over 10,000 at ANZ Stadium in Suva on 7 June. The visitors had dominated the set-pieces and were awarded a penalty try in each half after scrums collapsed, but Fiji took control in the second half and Napolioni Nalaga's try two minutes from time made certain of a 25–14 victory.

Brunel made a raft of changes for the encounter with Samoa a week later at Apia Park, but it had little impact against a side that had won four of their five previous meetings with Italy. Five penalties from the boot of Tusi Pisi were enough to hand Italy an eighth successive Test defeat and ensure they would head to Japan hoping to record a first victory in 2014.

While Italy were struggling and low on confidence after such a barren run, the Brave Blossoms were riding high after a record nine consecutive Test victories, with a youthful Samoa as well as Canada and USA among their conquests. Japan coach Eddie Jones referred to it being a "real privilege" to face Italy, but for the Azzurri it was the last opportunity to halt the losing streak and build some confidence ahead of a November series which will see them face Samoa, Argentina and South Africa.

The two sides were locked at 13–13 at half-time at the Prince Chichibu Memorial Stadium in Tokyo with a penalty try for Italy cancelling out Akihito Yamada's early score for Japan. The Brave Blossoms started the second half the brighter and the boot of Ayumu Goromaru, together with a try from Male Sa'u, gave them a 26–16 lead by the hour mark. Italy did cut the deficit to three with Robert Barbieri's try, but the tourists ran out of time to find a winning score and were left to return home disappointed and without a win from their tour.

Stopping the rot will be the target for November and then to build on that through the Six Nations as Italy prepare to face 2011 runners-up France, Ireland, Canada and Romania in Pool D at Rugby World Cup 2015. If not, the dream of reaching a first quarter-final in rugby's showpiece event may remain just that. Parisse knows that won't be easy, but hopes that a return to home soil will spark a change of fortune.

"We need to come back to the team we were in 2013 and welcome back the guys who missed the last season due to injuries," insisted Parisse. "We will play three difficult matches in November, but overall we will have seven home matches from now until Rugby World Cup 2015. To play at home on a regular basis will help us to regain our confidence, while many Italian internationals will play overseas this season and this will boost their experience ahead of the World Cup."

# ITALY INTERNATIONAL STATISTICS

## MATCH RECORDS UP TO 13 OCTOBER 2014

### WINNING MARGIN

| Date | Opponent | Result | Winning Margin |
|------|----------|--------|----------------|
| 18/05/1994 | Czech Republic | 104–8 | 96 |
| 07/10/2006 | Portugal | 83–0 | 83 |
| 17/06/1993 | Croatia | 76–11 | 65 |
| 19/06/1993 | Morocco | 70–9 | 61 |
| 02/03/1996 | Portugal | 64–3 | 61 |

### MOST POINTS IN A MATCH
#### BY THE TEAM

| Date | Opponent | Result | Points |
|------|----------|--------|--------|
| 18/05/1994 | Czech Republic | 104–8 | 104 |
| 07/10/2006 | Portugal | 83–0 | 83 |
| 17/06/1993 | Croatia | 76–11 | 76 |
| 19/06/1993 | Morocco | 70–9 | 70 |
| | 67 on 2 occasions | | |

#### BY A PLAYER

| Date | Player | Opponent | Points |
|------|--------|----------|--------|
| 10/11/2001 | Diego Dominguez | Fiji | 29 |
| 05/02/2000 | Diego Dominguez | Scotland | 29 |
| 01/07/1983 | Stefano Bettarello | Canada | 29 |
| 21/05/1994 | Diego Dominguez | Netherlands | 28 |
| 20/12/1997 | Diego Dominguez | Ireland | 27 |

### MOST TRIES IN A MATCH
#### BY THE TEAM

| Date | Opponent | Result | Tries |
|------|----------|--------|-------|
| 18/05/1994 | Czech Republic | 104–8 | 16 |
| 07/10/2006 | Portugal | 83–0 | 13 |
| 18/11/1998 | Netherlands | 67–7 | 11 |
| 17/06/1993 | Croatia | 76–11 | 11 |
| | 10 on 4 occasions | | |

#### BY A PLAYER

| Date | Player | Opponent | Tries |
|------|--------|----------|-------|
| 19/06/1993 | Ivan Francescato | Morocco | 4 |
| 10/10/1937 | Renzo Cova | Belgium | 4 |

### MOST CONVERSIONS IN A MATCH
#### BY THE TEAM

| Date | Opponent | Result | Cons |
|------|----------|--------|------|
| 18/05/1994 | Czech Republic | 104–8 | 12 |
| 19/06/1993 | Morocco | 70–9 | 10 |
| 17/06/1993 | Croatia | 76–11 | 9 |
| 07/10/2006 | Portugal | 83–0 | 9 |
| | 8 on 2 occasions | | |

#### BY A PLAYER

| Date | Player | Opponent | Cons |
|------|--------|----------|------|
| 18/05/1994 | Luigi Troiani | Czech Republic | 12 |
| 19/06/1993 | Gabriel Filizzola | Morocco | 10 |
| 17/06/1993 | Luigi Troiani | Croatia | 9 |
| | 8 on 3 occasions | | |

### MOST PENALTIES IN A MATCH
#### BY THE TEAM

| Date | Opponent | Result | Pens |
|------|----------|--------|------|
| 01/10/1994 | Romania | 24–6 | 8 |
| 27/11/2010 | Fiji | 24–16 | 8 |
| 10/11/2001 | Fiji | 66–10 | 7 |
| | 6 on 10 occasions | | |

#### BY A PLAYER

| Date | Player | Opponent | Pens |
|------|--------|----------|------|
| 01/10/1994 | Diego Dominguez | Romania | 8 |
| 27/11/2010 | Mirco Bergamasco | Fiji | 8 |
| 10/11/2001 | Diego Dominguez | Fiji | 7 |

### MOST DROP GOALS IN A MATCH
#### BY THE TEAM

| Date | Opponent | Result | DGs |
|------|----------|--------|-----|
| 07/10/1990 | Romania | 29–21 | 3 |
| 05/02/2000 | Scotland | 34–20 | 3 |
| 11/07/1973 | Transvaal | 24–28 | 3 |

#### BY A PLAYER

| Date | Player | Opponent | DGs |
|------|--------|----------|-----|
| 05/02/2000 | Diego Dominguez | Scotland | 3 |
| 11/07/1973 | Rocco Caligiuri | Transvaal | 3 |

| MOST CAPPED PLAYERS | |
|---|---|
| Player | Caps |
| Marco Bortolami | 107 |
| Sergio Parisse | 105 |
| Martin Castrogiovanni | 105 |
| Andrea Lo Cicero | 103 |
| Alessandro Troncon | 101 |

| LEADING PENALTY SCORERS | |
|---|---|
| Player | Pens |
| Diego Dominguez | 209 |
| Stefano Bettarello | 106 |
| Luigi Troiani | 57 |
| Ramiro Pez | 52 |
| Mirco Bergamasco | 49 |

| LEADING TRY SCORERS | |
|---|---|
| Player | Tries |
| Marcello Cuttitta | 25 |
| Paolo Vaccari | 22 |
| Manrico Marchetto | 21 |
| Carlo Checchinato | 21 |
| Alessandro Troncon | 19 |

| LEADING DROP GOAL SCORERS | |
|---|---|
| Player | DGs |
| Diego Dominguez | 19 |
| Stefano Bettarello | 15 |
| Ramiro Pez | 6 |

| LEADING POINTS SCORERS | |
|---|---|
| Player | Points |
| Diego Dominguez | 983 |
| Stefano Bettarello | 483 |
| Luigi Troiani | 294 |
| Ramiro Pez | 260 |
| Mirco Bergamasco | 256 |

| LEADING CONVERSIONS SCORERS | |
|---|---|
| Player | Cons |
| Diego Dominguez | 127 |
| Luigi Troiani | 57 |
| Stefano Bettarello | 46 |
| David Bortolussi | 35 |
| Ramiro Pez | 33 |

ITALY

# ITALY INTERNATIONAL PLAYERS
## UP TO 13 OCTOBER 2014

E **Abbiati** 1968 *WGe*, 1970 *R*, 1971 *Mor, F*, 1972 *Pt, Sp, Sp, Yug*, 1973 *Pt, ETv*, 1974 *Leo*
A **Agosti** 1933 *Cze*
M **Aguero** 2005 *Tg, Ar, Fj*, 2006 *Fj*, 2007 *Ur, Ar, I, Pt*, 2008 *A, Ar, PI*, 2009 *A*, 2010 *I, E, S, F, W*, 2013 *SA, S, A, Fj, Ar*, 2014 *S, E, Fj, Sa*
A **Agujari** 1967 *Pt*
E **Aio** 1974 *WGe*
G **Aiolfi** 1952 *Sp, Ger, F*, 1953 *F*, 1955 *Ger, F*
A **Alacevich** 1939 *R*
A **Albonico** 1934 *R*, 1935 *F*, 1936 *Ger, R*, 1937 *Ger, R, Bel, Ger, F*, 1938 *Ger*
N **Aldorvandi** 1994 *Sp, CZR, H*
M **Alfonsetti** 1994 *F*
T **Allan** 2013 *A, Fj, Ar*, 2014 *W, F, S, I, E, Sa, J*
E **Allevi** 1929 *Sp*, 1933 *Cze*
I **Aloisio** 1933 *Cze, Cze*, 1934 *Cat, R*, 1935 *Cat*, 1936 *Ger, R*
A **Altigeri** 1973 *Rho, WTv, Bor, NEC, Nat, Leo, FS, Tva, Cze, Yug, A*, 1974 *Pt, WGe*, 1975 *F, E, Pol, H, Sp*, 1976 *F, R, J*, 1978 *Ar, USS, Sp*, 1979 *F, Pol, R*
T **Altissimi** 1929 *Sp*
V **Ambron** 1962 *Ger, R*, 1963 *F*, 1964 *Ger, F*, 1965 *F, Cze, 1966 *F, Ger, R*, 1967 *Pt, R*, 1968 *Pt, WGe, Yug*, 1969 *Bul, Sp, Bel*, 1970 *Mad, Mad*, 1971 *Mor*, 1972 *Sp, Sp*
R **Ambrosio** 1987 *NZ, USS, Sp*, 1988 *F, R, A, I*, 1989 *R, Sp, Ar, Z, USS*
B **Ancillotti** 1978 *Sp*, 1979 *F, Pol, R*
E **Andina** 1952 *F*, 1955 *F*
C **Angelozzi** 1979 *E, Mor*, 1980 *Coo*

A **Angioli** 1960 *Ger, F*, 1961 *Ger, F*, 1962 *F, Ger, R*, 1963 *F*
A **Angrisiani** 1979 *Mor, F, Pol, USS, Mor*, 1980 *Coo*, 1984 *Tun*
S **Annibal** 1980 *Fj, Coo, Pol, Sp*, 1981 *F, WGe*, 1982 *R, E, WGe*, 1983 *F, USS, Sp, Mor, F, A*, 1984 *F*, 1985 *F, Z, Z, 1986 *Tun, F, Pt*, 1990 *F*
JM **Antoni** 2001 *Nm, SA*
C **Appiani** 1976 *Sp*, 1977 *Mor, Pol, Sp*, 1978 *USS*
S **Appiani** 1985 *R*, 1986 *Pt*, 1988 *A*, 1989 *F*
O **Arancio** 1993 *Rus*, 1994 *CZR, H, A, A, R, W, F*, 1995 *S, I, Sa, E, Ar, F, R, NZ, SA*, 1996 *W, Pt, W, A, E, S*, 1997 *I, I, 1998 *S, Ar, E*, 1999 *F, W, I, SA, E, NZ*
D **Armellin** 1965 *Cze*, 1966 *Ger*, 1968 *Pt, WGe, Yug*, 1969 *Bul, Sp, Bel, F*
A **Arrigoni** 1949 *Cze*
G **Artuso** 1977 *Pol, R*, 1978 *Sp*, 1979 *F, E, NZ, Mor*, 1980 *F, R, JAB*, 1981 *F*, 1982 *F, E, Mor*, 1983 *F, R, USS, C, C*, 1984 *USS*, 1985 *R, EngB, USS, R*, 1986 *Tun, F, Tun*, 1987 *Pt, F, R, NZ*
E **Augeri** 1962 *F, Ger, R*, 1963 *F*
A **Autore** 1961 *Ger, F*, 1962 *F*, 1964 *Ger*, 1966 *Ger*, 1968 *Pt, WGe, Yug*, 1969 *Bul, Sp, Bel, F*
L **Avigo** 1959 *F*, 1962 *F, Ger, R*, 1963 *F*, 1964 *Ger, F*, 1965 *F, Cze*, 1966 *Ger, R*
R **Aymonod** 1933 *Cze*, 1934 *Cat, R*, 1935 *F*
A **Azzali** 1981 *WGe*, 1982 *F, R, WGe*, 1983 *F, R, USS, Sp, Mor, F*, 1984 *F, Mor, R*, 1985 *R, EngB, Sp*

S **Babbo** 1996 *Pt*
A **Bacchetti** 2009 *I, S*
A **Balducci** 1929 *Sp*

F Baraldi 1973 *Cze, Yug*, 1974 *Mid, Sus, Oxo*, 1975 *E, Pol, H, Sp*, 1976 *F, R, A*, 1977 *F, Mor, Cze*
R Baraldi 1971 *R*
A Barattin 1996 *A, E*
S Barba 1985 *R, EngB*, 1986 *E, A*, 1987 *Pt, F, R, Ar, Fj*, 1988 *R, USS, A*, 1990 *F, Pol, Sp, H, R, USS*, 1991 *F, R, Nm, Nm, US, E, USS*, 1992 *Sp, F, R, R, S*, 1993 *Sp, F, Cro, Mor, Sp*
RJ Barbieri 2006 *J, Fj, Pt*, 2007 *Ur, Ar, I*, 2008 *SA*, 2010 *Ar, A, Fj*, 2011 *E, W, F, S, S, A*, 2012 *F, E, I, W, S, Ar, C, US, Tg, NZ, A*, 2013 *E, SA, S, A, Ar*, 2014 *S, I, E, Sa, J*
G Barbini 1978 *USS*
M Barbini 2002 *NZ, Sp, Ar, A*, 2003 *I, NZ*, 2004 *F, I, R, J, NZ, US*, 2005 *W, E*, 2007 *I*
N Barbini 1953 *Ger, R*, 1954 *Sp, F*, 1955 *Ger, F, Sp, Cze*, 1956 *Ger*, 1957 *Ger*, 1958 *R*, 1960 *Ger, F*
F Bargelli 1979 *E, Sp, Mor, F, Pol, USS, NZ, Mor*, 1980 *F, R, Fj, Sp*, 1981 *F, R*
S Barilari 1948 *Cze*, 1953 *Ger, R*
M Baroni 1999 *F, W, I, SA, SA*, 2000 *C*
V Barzaghi 1929 *Sp*, 1930 *Sp*, 1933 *Cze*
JL Basei 1979 *E, Sp, Mor, F, Pol, USS, NZ, Mor*, 1980 *F, R, Fj, JAB, Coo, USS*, 1981 *F, R*
A Battagion 1948 *F, Cze*
F Battaglini 1948 *F*
M Battaglini 1940 *R, Ger*, 1951 *Sp*, 1953 *F, R*
A Becca 1937 *R*, 1938 *Ger*, 1939 *R*, 1940 *Ger*
E Bellinazzo 1958 *R*, 1959 *F*, 1960 *Ger, F*, 1961 *Ger, F*, 1962 *F, Ger*, 1964 *Ger, F*, 1966 *F, Ger, R*, 1967 *F*
A Benatti 2001 *Fj, SA, Sa*, 2002 *W*, 2003 *NZ*
A Benettin 2012 *C*
C Bentivoglio 1977 *Pol*
T Benvenuti 2010 *Ar, A, Fj*, 2011 *W, F, S, J, S, A, Rus, US, I*, 2012 *F, E, I, W, S, Ar, C, US, Tg, NZ, A*, 2013 *F, S, W, E, I, A, Ar*
D Beretta 1993 *S*
A Bergamasco 1973 *Bor, Tva*, 1977 *Pol*, 1978 *USS*
M Bergamasco 1998 *H, E*, 1999 *SA, E*, 2000 *S, W, I, E, F, C*, 2001 *I, E, F, S, W, Fj, SA, SA*, 2002 *F, S, W, I, E, NZ, Sp, R, A*, 2003 *W, I, S, I, Geo, NZ, Tg, W*, 2004 *J, C, NZ*, 2005 *I, W, Ar, A, Ar, Fj*, 2006 *I, E, F, J, Fj, Pt, Rus, A, Ar, C*, 2007 *F, S, W, J, NZ, R, Pt, S*, 2008 *I, E, W, Ar, A, Ar, Pl*, 2009 *E, I, S, W, F, A, NZ, NZ, SA, Sa*, 2010 *I, E, S, F, W, SA, SA, Ar, A, Fj*, 2011 *I, E, W, F, S, S, A, US, I*, 2012 *W, S, NZ, A*
M Bergamasco 2002 *F, S, W, Ar, A*, 2003 *W, I, E, F, S, S, Geo, NZ, C*, 2004 *E, F, S, I, W*, 2005 *I, W, S, Tg, Ar, Fj*, 2006 *I, E, F, W, S, J, Fj, Pt, Rus, A, Ar, C*, 2007 *F, E, S, W, E, I, J, I, NZ, R, S*, 2008 *I, E, W, F, S, Ar, A, Ar, Pl*, 2009 *E, I, S, W, F, A, NZ, NZ, SA, Sa*, 2010 *I, E, S, F, W, SA, SA, Ar, A, Fj*, 2011 *I, E, W, F, S, S, A, US, I*, 2012 *W, S, NZ, A*
L Bernabo 1970 *Mad, Mad, R*, 1972 *Sp, Sp*
V Bernabò 2004 *US*, 2005 *Tg, Fj*, 2007 *E, S, W, I, Ur, Ar, J, I, NZ, R*, 2010 *W, SA*, 2011 *I, E, W, S*, 2013 *SA, Sa, Fj, Ar*
F Berni 1985 *R, Sp, Z, Z*, 1986 *E, A*, 1987 *R, NZ*, 1988 *A, 1989 *F*
D Bertoli 1967 *R*
V Bertolotto 1936 *Ger, R*, 1937 *Ger, R*, 1942 *R*, 1948 *F*
O Bettarello 1958 *F*, 1959 *F*, 1961 *Ger*
R Bettarello 1953 *Ger, R*
S Bettarello 1979 *Pol, E, Sp, F, NZ, Mor*, 1980 *F, R, Fj, JAB, Coo, Pol, USS, Sp*, 1981 *F, R, USS, WGe*, 1982 *F, R, E, WGe, Mor*, 1983 *F, R, USS, C, Sp, Mor, F, A*, 1984 *F, Mor, R, Tun, USS*, 1985 *F, R, EngB, Sp, Z, USS, R*, 1986 *Tun, F, Pt, E, A, Tun, USS*, 1987 *R, USS, Sp*, 1988 *USS, A*
L Bettella 1969 *Sp, Bel, F*
R Bevilacqua 1937 *Bel, Ger, F*, 1938 *Ger*, 1939 *Ger, R*, 1940 *R, Ger*, 1942 *R*
C Bezzi 2003 *W, I, E, F, S, I, NZ, W*, 2004 *US*, 2005 *Ar, A*
G Biadene 1958 *R*, 1959 *F*
Biagi 2014 *E, Fj, Sa*
G Bigi 1930 *Sp*, 1933 *Cze*
M Bimbati 1989 *Z*
M Birtig 1998 *H*, 1999 *F*
F Blessano 1975 *F, R, Pol, H, Sp*, 1976 *F, R, J*, 1977 *F, Mor, Pol, R, Cze, R, Sp*, 1978 *F, Ar, Sp*, 1979 *F, Pol, R*

L Boccaletto 1969 *Bul, Bel, F*, 1970 *Cze, Mad, Mad, R*, 1971 *F, R*, 1972 *Pt, Sp, Sp*, 1975 *E*
S Boccazzi 1985 *Z*, 1988 *USS*
R Bocchino 2010 *I, F, W, SA, A, Fj*, 2011 *J, S, A, Rus, US, I*, 2012 *Ar, US*
M Bocconelli 1967 *R*
M Bollesan 1963 *F*, 1964 *F*, 1965 *F*, 1966 *F, Ger*, 1967 *F, Pt*, 1968 *Pt, WGe, Yug*, 1969 *Bul, Sp, Bel, F*, 1970 *Cze, Mad, Mad, R*, 1971 *Mor, F, R*, 1972 *Pt, Pt, Sp, Sp, Yug*, 1973 *Pt, Rho, WTv, Bor, NEC, Nat, ETv, Leo, FS, Tva, Yug, A*, 1974 *Pt, Mid, Sus, Oxo, WGe, Leo*, 1975 *F, Sp, Cze*
A Bona 1972 *Sp, Yug*, 1973 *Rho, WTv, Bor, NEC, Nat, ETv, Leo, FS, Tva, Cze, Yug, A*, 1974 *Pt, WGe, Leo*, 1975 *F, Sp, R, Cze, E, Pol, H, Sp*, 1976 *F, R, J, A, Sp*, 1977 *F, Mor*, 1978 *Ar, USS, Sp*, 1979 *F, Sp, Mor, F, Pol, USS, NZ, Mor*, 1980 *F, R, Fj, JAB, Pol, Sp*, 1981 *F*
L Bonaiti 1979 *R*, 1980 *Pol*
G Bonati 1939 *Ger, R*
S Bonetti 1972 *Yug*, 1973 *Rho, WTv, Bor, NEC, Nat, ETv, Leo, FS, Tva, Cze, Yug, A*, 1974 *Pt, WGe, Leo*, 1975 *F, Sp, R, Cze, E, Pol, H, Sp*, 1976 *R, J, A, Sp*, 1977 *F, Mor, R, Sp*, 1978 *F, R*, 1979 *F*, 1980 *USS*
S Bonfante 1936 *Ger, R*
G Bonino 1949 *F*
M Bonomi 1988 *F, R*, 1990 *Sp, H, R, USS*, 1991 *F, R, Nm, Nm, E, NZ, USS*, 1992 *R, R*, 1993 *Cro, Mor, Sp, F, S*, 1994 *Sp, R, H, A, A, W*, 1995 *S, I, Sa, F, Ar, R, NZ*, 1996 *W*
S Bordon 1990 *R, USS*, 1991 *Nm, USS*, 1992 *F, R*, 1993 *Sp, F, Pt, Rus, F*, 1994 *R, A, A, R, W, F*, 1995 *I, E, Ar, F, Ar, NZ, SA*, 1996 *W, A, E*, 1997 *I, F*
L Borsetto 1977 *Pol*
V Borsetto 1948 *F, Cze*
M Bortolami 2001 *Nm, SA, Fj, SA, Sa*, 2002 *F, S, W, I, E, NZ, Sp, R, Ar, A*, 2003 *W, I, E, S, Geo, Tg, C*, 2004 *E, F, S, I, W, R, J, C, NZ*, 2005 *I, W, S, E, F, Ar, A, A, Tg, Ar, Fj*, 2006 *I, E, F, W, S, J, Fj, Pt, Rus, A, Ar, C*, 2007 *F, E, S, W, I, J, I, NZ, R, Pt*, 2008 *W, F, S, A, Ar, Pl*, 2009 *E, S, W, F, A, A, NZ*, 2010 *I, E, S, F, W, SA, SA*, 2011 *J, A, Rus, I*, 2012 *F, E, I, W, S, Ar, C, US*, 2013 *SA, Sa, S, A, Ar*, 2014 *W, F, S, I, E, Fj, Sa, J*
G Bortolini 1933 *Cze*, 1934 *Cat*
D Bortolussi 2006 *J, Fj, Pt, Rus, Ar, C*, 2007 *Ur, Ar, J, I, NZ, R, Pt, S*, 2008 *I, E*
L Boscaino 1967 *Pt*
L Bossi 1940 *R, Ger*
T Botes 2012 *F, E, I, W, S, Tg, NZ, A*, 2013 *F, S, W, E, I, SA, Sa, S, A, Fj, Ar*, 2014 *W, F, S*
A Bottacchiara 1991 *NZ, USS*, 1992 *Sp, F, R, R*
G Bottacin 1956 *Cze*
O Bottonelli 1929 *Sp*, 1934 *R*, 1935 *Cat, F*, 1937 *Ger*, 1939 *Ger*
L Bove 1948 *Cze*, 1949 *F, Cze*
O Bracaglia 1939 *R*
M Braga 1958 *F*
L Bricchi 1929 *Sp*, 1930 *Sp*, 1933 *Cze*
L Brighetti 1934 *Cat*
A Brunelli 1969 *Bel*, 1970 *Mad*, 1971 *F*
M Brunello 1988 *I*, 1989 *F*, 1990 *F, Sp, H, R, USS*, 1993 *Pt*
S Brusin 1957 *Ger*
KS Burton 2007 *Ur, A*, 2009 *A, NZ*, 2011 *I, E, W, F, S*, 2012 *F, E, I, W, S, Ar, C, US, Tg*, 2013 *F, S, W*
P Buso 2008 *W*
G Busson 1957 *Ger*, 1958 *R*, 1959 *F*, 1960 *Ger, F*, 1961 *Ger, F*, 1962 *F, Ger*, 1963 *F*

F Caccia-Dominioni 1935 *F*, 1937 *Ger*
C Caione 1995 *R*, 1996 *Pt*, 1997 *F, R*, 1998 *Rus, Ar, H, E*, 1999 *F, S, SA, Ur, Sp, Fj, Tg, NZ*, 2000 *Sa, Fj, C, R, NZ*, 2001 *I, E, S, Fj*
R Caligiuri 1969 *F*, 1973 *Pt, Rho, WTv, NEC, Nat, ETv, Leo, FS, Tva*, 1975 *E, Pol, H, Sp*, 1976 *F, R, J, A, Sp*, 1978 *F, Ar, USS, Sp*, 1979 *F, Pol, R*
A Caluzzi 1970 *R*, 1971 *Mor, F*, 1972 *Pt, Pt, Sp, Sp*, 1973 *Pt*, 1974 *Oxo, WGe, Leo*
P Camiscioni 1975 *E*, 1976 *R, J, A, Sp*, 1977 *F*, 1978 *F*
M Campagna 1933 *Cze*, 1934 *Cat*, 1936 *Ger, R*, 1937 *Ger, R, Bel*, 1938 *Ger*

**M Campagnaro** 2013 *Fj, Ar,* 2014 *W, F, S, I, E, Fj, J*
**GJ Canale** 2003 *S, Geo, NZ, Tg, C, W,* 2004 *S, I, W, R, J, C,* 2005 *I, Ar, Ar, A, Tg, Ar, Fj,* 2006 *I, E, F, W, S, A, Ar, C,* 2007 *F, E, S, W, J, I, R, Pt, S,* 2008 *I, E, W, F, S, A,* 2009 *E, I, S, W, F, A, NZ, NZ, Sa,* 2010 *I, E, S, F, W, SA, SA, Ar, A, Fj,* 2011 *I, E, W, F, S, J, S, A, Rus, US, I,* 2012 *F, E, I, W, S,* 2013 *F, S, W, E, I, Sa, S, Fj, Ar*
**PL Canavosio** 2005 *A, Tg, Fj,* 2006 *I, E, F, W, S, Fj, Pt, Rus, A, Ar,* 2007 *Ar, J, I, Pt,* 2008 *I, SA, Ar, A, Ar,* 2009 *S, W, F, A,* 2010 *E, S, F, W, Ar, A,* 2011 *I, E, W, S, J, Rus*
**C Cantoni** 1956 *Ger, F, Cze,* 1957 *Ger*
**L Capitani** 1989 *F, R, Sp, Ar, Z, USS*
**M Capuzzoni** 1993 *Cro,* 1995 *I*
**A Caranci** 1989 *R*
**M Carli** 1955 *Sp, Cze*
**C Carloni** 1935 *F*
**D Carpente** 2004 *R, J*
**T Carraro** 1937 *R*
**T Casagrande** 1977 *R*
**U Cassellato** 1990 *Sp,* 1992 *R, S,* 1993 *Sp, F, Pt, Cro, Mor, F, S*
**R Cassina** 1992 *R, S*
**A Castellani** 1994 *CZR,* 1995 *Ar, R,* 1996 *W, S,* 1997 *Ar, R, I,* 1998 *S, W, Rus, H, E,* 1999 *F, W, Ur, Sp, Fj, Tg, NZ*
**ML Castrogiovanni** 2002 *NZ, Sp, R, Ar, A,* 2003 *I, E, F, S, I, Geo, NZ, Tg, C, W,* 2004 *E, F, S, I, W, J,* 2005 *I, W, S, E, F, Ar, A, Ar, Fj,* 2006 *I, E, F, W, S, Pt, Rus, A, Ar, C,* 2007 *F, E, S, J, I, NZ, R, Pt, S,* 2008 *I, E, W, F, S,* 2009 *E, I, S, W, F, NZ, SA, Sa,* 2010 *I, E, S, F, W, SA, Ar, A, Fj,* 2011 *I, E, W, F, S, J, S, A, Rus, US, I,* 2012 *F, E, S, Ar, C, US, Tg, A,* 2013 *F, S, W, E, SA, Sa, S, A, Fj, Ar,* 2014 *W, F, S, I*
**L Catotti** 1979 *Pol, E*
**A Cazzini** 1933 *Cze, Cze,* 1934 *Cat, R,* 1935 *Cat, F,* 1936 *Ger, R,* 1937 *Ger, R, Bel, Ger, F,* 1939 *R,* 1942 *R*
**G Cecchetto** 1955 *F*
**A Cecchetto-Milani** 1952 *Sp, Ger, F*
**G Cecchin** 1970 *Cze, R,* 1971 *F, R,* 1972 *Pt*
**G Ceccotti** 1972 *Pt, Sp*
**L Cedaro** 2013 *S*
**A Centinari** 1930 *Sp*
**R Centinari** 1935 *F,* 1936 *Ger, R,* 1937 *Bel, F,* 1939 *Ger*
**A Cepolino** 1999 *Ur, Sp, Fj, Tg, NZ*
**L Cesani** 1929 *Sp,* 1930 *Sp,* 1935 *Cat, F*
**F Ceselin** 1989 *F, R*
**C Checchinato** 1990 *Sp,* 1991 *Nm, Nm, US, NZ, USS,* 1992 *Sp, F, R, S,* 1993 *Pt, Cro, Sp, F, Rus, F, S,* 1994 *Sp, R, CZR, A, A, R, W, F,* 1995 *Sa, F, Ar, R, NZ,* 1996 *W, E,* 1997 *I, F, Ar, R, SA, I,* 1998 *Rus, Ar, H, E,* 1999 *F, S, SA, SA, Ur, Fj, E, Tg, NZ,* 2000 *S, W, I, E, F, Sa, Fj,* 2001 *I, E, F, S, W, Nm, SA, Ur, Ar, Fj, SA, Sa,* 2002 *F, S, W, Sp, R,* 2003 *Geo, NZ, Tg, C, W,* 2004 *E, F, I*
**G Chechinato** 1973 *Cze, Yug, A,* 1974 *WGe, Leo*
**G Cherubini** 1949 *Cze,* 1951 *Sp*
**A Chillon** 2013 *S*
**D Chistolini** 2014 *Sa, J*
**T Ciccio** 1992 *R,* 1993 *Sp, F, Mor, F*
**E Cicognani** 1940 *Ger*
**R Cinelli** 1968 *Pt,* 1969 *Sp*
**G Cinti** 1973 *Rho, WTv, ETv*
**F Cioni** 1967 *Pt, R,* 1968 *Pt,* 1969 *Bul, Sp, Bel,* 1970 *Cze, Mad, Mad, R*
**L Cittadini** 2008 *I,* 2010 *SA, A,* 2011 *J, S, A, Rus,* 2012 *F, E, I, W, S, Tg, NZ, A,* 2013 *F, S, W, E, I, SA, Sa, S, A, Fj, Ar,* 2014 *W, F, S, I, E, Fj, Sa, J*
**L Clerici** 1939 *Ger*
**A Colella** 1983 *R, USS, C, C, Sp, Mor, F, A, USS,* 1984 *R, Tun, USS,* 1985 *F, R, EngB, Sp, Z, Z, USS, R,* 1986 *Tun, F, Pt, E, A, Tun, USS,* 1987 *Pt, F, A, Fj, USS, Sp,* 1988 *F, R, USS,* 1989 *R, Sp, Ar,* 1990 *Pol, R*
**O Collodo** 1977 *Pol, Cze, R, Sp,* 1978 *F,* 1986 *Pt, E, A, USS,* 1987 *Pt, F, R, NZ, Ar, Fj*
**S Colombini** 1971 *R*
**F Colombo** 1933 *Cze*
**G Colussi** 1957 *F,* 1958 *F,* 1964 *Ger, F,* 1965 *F, Cze,* 1968 *Pt*
**C Colusso** 1982 *F*
**A Comin** 1955 *Ger, F, Sp, F, Cze,* 1956 *F, Cze,* 1958 *F*

**U Conforto** 1965 *Cze,* 1966 *Ger, R,* 1967 *F, R,* 1968 *Pt, WGe, Yug,* 1969 *Bul, Sp, Bel, F,* 1970 *Cze,* 1971 *Mor, F,* 1972 *Yug,* 1973 *Pt*
**F Coppio** 1993 *F, Pt, Cro, Mor, Sp*
**L Cornella** 1999 *Sp*
**R Corvo** 1985 *F, Sp, Z*
**U Cossara** 1971 *Mor, F, R,* 1972 *Pt, Sp,* 1973 *Pt, Rho, NEC, Nat, Leo, FS, Tva, Cze,* 1975 *F, Sp, R, Cze, E, Pol, H,* 1976 *F, J, A,* 1977 *Pol*
**A Costa** 1940 *R, Ger,* 1942 *R*
**S Costanzo** 2004 *R, C, NZ, US*
**E Cottafava** 1973 *Pt*
**R Cova** 1937 *Bel, Ger, F,* 1938 *Ger,* 1939 *Ger, R,* 1942 *R*
**C Covi** 1988 *F, R, USS,* 1989 *F, R, Sp, Ar, Z, USS,* 1990 *F, Pol, R,* 1991 *F, R, Nm, Nm,* 1996 *E*
**F Crepaz** 1972 *Pt*
**M Crescenzo** 1984 *R*
**U Crespi** 1933 *Cze, Cze,* 1934 *Cat, R,* 1935 *Cat,* 1937 *Ger*
**W Cristofoletto** 1992 *R,* 1993 *Mor, Sp, F,* 1996 *Pt, A, E, S,* 1997 *I, F, F, Ar, SA, I,* 1998 *S, W, Rus, Ar, E,* 1999 *F, S, W, I, SA, SA, Sp, Fj, E, NZ,* 2000 *E, F*
**G Croci** 1990 *Sp, H, R, USS,* 1991 *F, R, Nm, US, E, NZ, USS,* 1992 *Sp, F,* 1993 *S,* 1996 *S,* 1997 *I, F, F, Ar, R, SA, I,* 1998 *S, W*
**R Crotti** 1993 *S,* 1995 *SA*
**L Cuccharelli** 1966 *R,* 1967 *R*
**G Cucchiella** 1973 *A,* 1974 *Sus,* 1979 *Sp, F, Pol, USS, NZ, Mor,* 1980 *F, R, Fj, JAB, Coo,* 1985 *USS, R,* 1986 *Tun, F, Pt, E,* 1987 *Pt, F, Fj*
**M Cuttita** 1987 *Pt, F, R, NZ, Ar, Fj, USS, Sp,* 1988 *F, R,* 1989 *Z, USS,* 1990 *Pol, R,* 1991 *F, R, Nm, US, E, NZ, USS,* 1992 *Sp, F, R, R, S,* 1993 *Sp, F, Mor, Sp, F, F,* 1994 *Sp, R, H, A, A, F,* 1995 *S, I, Sa,* 1996 *S,* 1997 *I, F, F, Ar, R, SA, I,* 1998 *S, W, Rus, Ar,* 1999 *F*
**M Cuttitta** 1990 *Pol, R, Sp, H, R, USS,* 1991 *F, Nm, Nm, US, E, NZ, USS,* 1992 *Sp, F, R, R, S,* 1993 *Sp, F, Pt, Cro, Mor, Sp, F, Rus, F, S,* 1994 *Sp, R, CZR, H, A, A, W, F,* 1995 *S, I, Sa, E, Ar, F, R, NZ, SA,* 1996 *W, Pt, W, E, S,* 1997 *I, F, F, Ar, SA, I,* 1998 *W, Rus, Ar, H, E,* 1999 *F, S, W,* 2000 *S, W, I, E*

**G Dagnini** 1949 *F*
**D Dal Maso** 2000 *Sa, Fj,* 2001 *I, E,* 2004 *J, C, NZ, US,* 2005 *I, W, S, E, F, A*
**M Dal Sie** 1993 *Pt,* 1994 *R, W, F,* 1995 *F, Ar,* 1996 *A*
**A D'Alberton** 1966 *F, Ger, R,* 1967 *F, R*
**D Daldoss** 1979 *Pol, R, E, Sp, Mor*
**C D'Alessio** 1937 *R, Bel, F,* 1938 *Ger,* 1939 *Ger*
**D Dallan** 1999 *F, S, W,* 2000 *S, W, I, E, F, C, R, NZ,* 2001 *I, E, F, W, Fj, SA, Sa,* 2002 *F, S, I, E, NZ, Sp, R,* 2003 *W, I, E, F, S, Tg, C, W,* 2004 *E, F, S, I, W, C,* 2006 *J,* 2007 *F, E, F, S*
**M Dallan** 1997 *Ar, R, I,* 1998 *Ar, H, E,* 1999 *SA, SA,* 2000 *S, Sa, C,* 2001 *F, S,* 2003 *Tg, C,* 2004 *E, F, S*
**A Danieli** 1955 *Ger, F, Sp, F, Cze*
**V D'Anna** 1993 *Rus*
**T D'Apice** 2011 *J, S, Rus,* 2012 *F, E, I, W, S, C, US*
**P Dari** 1951 *Sp,* 1952 *Sp, Ger, F,* 1953 *Ger, R,* 1954 *Sp, F*
**G De Angelis** 1934 *Cat, R,* 1935 *Cat, F,* 1937 *R*
**E De Anna** 1972 *Yug,* 1973 *Cze, A,* 1975 *F, Sp, R, Cze, E, Pol, H, Sp,* 1976 *F, R,* 1978 *Ar, USS, Sp,* 1979 *F, R, Sp, Mor, F, USS, NZ,* 1980 *F, R, Fj, JAB*
**R De Bernardo** 1980 *USS, Sp,* 1981 *F, R, USS, WGe,* 1982 *R, E,* 1983 *R, USS, C, C, Sp, Mor, F, A, USS,* 1984 *F, USS,* 1985 *R, EngB,* 1988 *I,* 1989 *Ar, Z*
**CF De Biase** 1987 *Sp,* 1988 *F, A*
**G De Carli** 1996 *W,* 1997 *R,* 1998 *S, Rus, Ar, H, E,* 1999 *F, I, SA, SA, Ur, Fj,* 2000 *S, Sa, Fj,* 2001 *I, E, W, SA, Ur, Fj, SA, Sa,* 2002 *F, S, W, I, E,* 2003 *W, I, E*
**B de Jager** 2006 *J*
**L De Joanni** 1983 *C, Mor, F, A, USS,* 1984 *R, Tun, USS,* 1985 *F, R, EngB, Sp, Z,* 1986 *A, Tun,* 1989 *F, R, Sp, Ar, Z,* 1990 *R*
**A De Marchi** 2012 *Ar, US, Tg, NZ,* 2013 *F, S, W, E, I, SA, Sa, S,* 2014 *W, F, S, I, E, Fj, Sa, J*
**A De Marchi** 2014 *Fj, J*
**R De Marchis** 1935 *F*

H De Marco 1993 *Pt*

JR de Marigny 2004 *E, F, S, I, W, US*, 2005 *I, W, S*, 2007 *F, E, S, W, I, Ur, J, I, NZ, Pt*

A de Rossi 1999 *Ur, Sp, E*, 2000 *I, E, F, Sa, C, R, NZ*, 2001 *SA, Ur, Ar*, 2002 *I, E, NZ, Sp, R*, 2003 *W, I, E, F, S, I, Geo, Tg, C, W*, 2004 *E, F, S, I, W, R*

C De Rossi 1994 *Sp, H, R*

L De Santis 1952 *Sp*

M De Stefani 1989 *Z*

C De Vecchi 1948 *F*

G Degli Antoni 1963 *F*, 1965 *F*, 1966 *F, Ger, R*, 1967 *F*

M Del Bono 1960 *Ger, F*, 1961 *Ger, F*, 1962 *F, Ger, R*, 1963 *F*, 1964 *Ger, F*

G Del Bono 1951 *Sp*

CA Del Fava 2004 *W, R, J*, 2005 *I, W, S, E, F, Tg, Ar, Fj*, 2006 *I, E, F, W, S, J, Fj, Pt*, 2007 *Ur, Ar, Pt, S*, 2008 *I, E, W, F, S, SA, Ar, A, Ar*, 2009 *I, S, W, F, A, NZ, NZ, SA, Sa*, 2010 *I, S, F, SA, Ar, A, Fj*, 2011 *I, E, F, S, S, A*

S Dellapè 2002 *F, S, I, E, NZ, Sp, Ar*, 2003 *F, S, S, Geo, Tg, C, W*, 2004 *E, F, S, I, W, C, NZ*, 2005 *I, W, S, E, F, Ar*, 2006 *I, E, W, S, J, Fj, Pt, Rus, A, Ar, C*, 2007 *F, E, S, W, I, J, NZ, R, S*, 2008 *I, E, W, SA, Ar*, 2009 *E, I, S, W, F*, 2010 *Ar, A, Fj*, 2011 *I, E, W, F*

G Delli Ficorilli 1969 *F*

PE Derbyshire 2009 *A*, 2010 *E, F, SA, SA, Ar, A, Fj*, 2011 *F, S, J, S, A, Rus, US, I*, 2013 *F, S, W, I*, 2014 *S, I, E, Fj*

A Di Bello 1930 *Sp*, 1933 *Cze, Cze*, 1934 *Cat*

A Di Bernardo 2013 *SA, Sa, S, A*

F Di Carlo 1975 *Sp, R, Cze, Sp*, 1976 *F, Sp*, 1977 *Pol, R, Pol, 1978 Ar, USS*

B Di Cola 1973 *A*

G Di Cola 1972 *Sp, Sp*, 1973 *A*

F Di Maura 1971 *Mor*

A Di Zitti 1958 *R*, 1960 *Ger*, 1961 *Ger, F*, 1962 *F, Ger, R*, 1964 *Ger, F*, 1965 *F, Cze*, 1966 *F, Ger, R*, 1967 *F, Pt, R*, 1969 *Bul, Sp, Bel*, 1972 *Pt, Sp*

R Dolfato 1985 *F*, 1986 *A*, 1987 *Pt, Fj, USS, Sp*, 1988 *F, R, USS*

D Dominguez 1991 *F, R, Nm, Nm, US, E, NZ, USS*, 1992 *Sp, F, R, S*, 1993 *Sp, F, Rus, F, S*, 1994 *R, H, R, W*, 1995 *S, I, Sa, E, Ar, SA*, 1996 *W, Pt, W, A, E, S*, 1997 *I, F, F, Ar, R, SA, I*, 1998 *S, W, Rus, Ar, H, E*, 1999 *F, S, W, I, Ur, Sp, Fj, E, Tg, NZ*, 2000 *S, W, I, E, F, SA, Sa*, 2002 *F, S, I, E, Ar*, 2003 *W, I*

D Dondana 1929 *Sp*, 1930 *Sp*

G Dora 1929 *Sp*

R D'Orazio 1969 *Bul*

M Dotti IV 1939 *R*, 1940 *R, Ger*

F Dotto 1971 *Mor, F*, 1972 *Pt, Pt, Sp*

P Dotto 1993 *Sp, Cro*, 1994 *Sp, R*

J Erasmus 2008 *F, S, SA*

A Esposito 2014 *W, S, I, E, Sa*

U Faccioli 1948 *F*

A Falancia 1975 *E, Pol*

G Faliva 1999 *SA*, 2002 *NZ, Ar, A*

G Faltiba 1993 *Pt*

G Fanton 1979 *Pol*

P Farina 1987 *F, NZ, Fj*

P Farinelli 1940 *R*, 1949 *F, Cze*, 1951 *Sp*, 1952 *Sp*

T Fattori 1936 *Ger, R*, 1937 *R, Ger, F*, 1938 *Ger*, 1939 *Ger, R*, 1940 *R, Ger*

E Fava 1948 *F, Cze*

P Favaretto 1951 *Sp*

R Favaro 1988 *F, USS, A, I*, 1989 *F, R, Sp, Ar, Z, USS*, 1990 *F, Pol, R, H, R, USS*, 1991 *F, R, Nm, Nm, US, E, NZ, USS*, 1992 *Sp, F, R*, 1993 *Sp, F, Cro, Sp, F*, 1994 *CZR, A, A, R, W, F*, 1995 *S, I, Sa*, 1996 *Pt*

S Favaro 2009 *A, NZ, NZ, SA, Sa*, 2010 *SA*, 2012 *F, I, W, S, Ar, C, US, Tg, NZ, A*, 2013 *F, S, W, E, I*

G Favretto 1948 *Cze*, 1949 *Cze*

A Fedrigo 1972 *Yug*, 1973 *Pt, Rho, WTv, Bor, NEC, Nat, ETv, Leo, FS, Cze, Yug, A*, 1974 *Pt, Mid, Sus, Oxo, WGe, Leo*, 1975 *F, Sp, R, Cze, E, Pol, H, Sp*, 1976 *F, J, A, Sp*, 1977 *F, Pol, R, Cze, R, Sp*, 1978 *F, Ar*, 1979 *Pol, R*

P Fedrigo 1973 *Pt*

I Fernandez- Rouyet 2008 *SA, Ar*, 2009 *A, NZ, NZ, SA, Sa*

P Ferracin 1975 *R, Cze, E, Pol, H, Sp*, 1976 *F*, 1977 *Mor, Pol, 1978 USS*

C Festuccia 2003 *W, I, E, F, S, S, I, Geo, NZ, Tg, C, W*, 2004 *E, F, S, I*, 2005 *F, Ar, Ar, A, Tg, Ar*, 2006 *E, F, W, S, Pt, Rus, A, Ar, C*, 2007 *F, E, S, W, I, Ur, Ar, J, NZ, R, S*, 2008 *I, E, W*, 2009 *E, I*, 2010 *A, Fj*, 2011 *F, S*, 2012 *Ar, C, US*

G Figari 1940 *R, Ger*, 1942 *R*

EG Filizzola 1993 *Pt, Mor, Sp, F, Rus, F, S*, 1994 *Sp, CZR, A*, 1995 *R, NZ*

M Finocchi 1968 *Yug*, 1969 *F*, 1970 *Cze, Mad, Mad, R*, 1971 *Mor, R*

G Fornari 1952 *Sp, Ger, F*, 1953 *F, Ger, R*, 1954 *Sp, F*, 1955 *Ger, F, Sp, F, Cze*, 1956 *Ger, F, Cze*

B Francescato 1977 *Cze, R, Sp*, 1978 *F, Sp*, 1979 *F*, 1981 *R*

I Francescato 1990 *R, USS*, 1991 *F, R, US, E, NZ, USS*, 1992 *R, S*, 1993 *Mor, F*, 1994 *Sp, H, R, W, F*, 1995 *S, I, Sa, E, Ar, F, Ar, R, NZ, SA*, 1996 *W, Pt, W, A, E, S*, 1997 *F, F, Ar, F, Ar, R, NZ, SA*

N Francescato 1972 *Yug*, 1973 *Rho, WTv, Bor, NEC, Nat, ETv, Leo*, 1974 *Pt*, 1976 *J, A, Sp*, 1977 *F, Mor, Pol, R, R, Sp*, 1978 *F, Ar, USS, Sp*, 1979 *F, R, E, Sp, Mor, F, Pol, USS, NZ*, 1980 *F, R, Fj, JAB, Coo, Pol, USS, Sp*, 1981 *F, R*, 1982 *Mor*

R Francescato 1976 *Sp*, 1978 *Ar, USS*, 1979 *Sp, F, Pol, USS, NZ, Mor*, 1980 *F, R, Fj, JAB, Coo, Pol, USS, Sp*, 1981 *F, R*, 1982 *WGe*, 1983 *F, R, USS, C, C, Sp, Mor, F, A*, 1984 *Mor, R, Tun*, 1985 *F, Sp, Z, USS*, 1986 *Tun, F*

G Franceschini 1975 *H, Sp*, 1976 *F, J*, 1977 *F, Pol, Pol, Cze, R, Sp*

A Francese 1939 *R*, 1940 *R*

J Francesio 2000 *W, I, Sa*, 2001 *Ur*

F Frati 2000 *C, NZ*, 2001 *I, S*

F Frelich 1955 *Cze*, 1957 *F, Ger*, 1958 *F, R*

M Fumei 1984 *F*

J Furno 2011 *S*, 2012 *S, Ar, C, US, Tg*, 2013 *E, I, SA, S, A, Fj, Ar*, 2014 *W, F, S, I, Fj, Sa, J*

A Fusco 1982 *E*, 1985 *R*, 1986 *Tun, F, Tun*

E Fusco 1960 *Ger, F*, 1961 *F*, 1962 *F, Ger, R*, 1963 *F*, 1964 *Ger, F*, 1965 *F*, 1966 *F*

M Fuser 2012 *C*, 2014 *J*

R Gabanella 1951 *Sp*, 1952 *Sp*

P Gabrielli 1948 *Cze*, 1949 *F, Cze*, 1951 *Sp*, 1954 *F*

F Gaetaniello 1980 *Sp*, 1982 *E*, 1984 *USS*, 1985 *R, Sp, Z, Z, USS, R*, 1986 *Pt, E, A, Tun, USS*, 1987 *Pt, F, NZ, Ar, Fj, USS, Sp*, 1988 *F*, 1990 *F, R, Sp, H*, 1991 *Nm, US, E, NZ*

F Gaetaniello 1975 *H*, 1976 *R, A, Sp*, 1977 *F, Pol, R, Pol, R, Sp*, 1978 *Sp*, 1979 *Pol, R, E, Sp, Mor, F, Pol, USS, NZ, Mor*, 1980 *Fj, JAB, Sp*, 1981 *F, R, USS, WGe*, 1982 *F, R, E, WGe, Mor*, 1983 *F, R, USS, C, C, Sp*

A Galante 2007 *Ur, Ar*

A Galeazzo 1985 *Sp*, 1987 *Pt, R, Ar, USS*

M Galletto 1972 *Pt, Sp, Yug*

E Galon 2001 *I*, 2005 *Tg, Ar, Fj*, 2006 *W, S, Rus*, 2007 *I, Ur, Ar, I, NZ, R, S*, 2008 *I, E, W, F, S*

R Ganzerla 1973 *Bor, NEC*

G Garcia 2008 *SA, Ar, A, Ar, Pl*, 2009 *E, I, S, A, NZ, NZ, SA, Sa*, 2010 *I, E, S, F, W*, 2011 *I, E, F, S, A, US, I*, 2013 *W, E, I, Sa*, 2014 *F, S, I, E, Sa, J*

M Gardin 1981 *USS, WGe*, 1982 *Mor*, 1983 *F, R*, 1984 *Mor, R, USS*, 1985 *EngB, USS, R*, 1986 *Tun, F, Pt, Tun, USS*, 1987 *F, R, NZ, Ar, Fj, USS, Sp*, 1988 *R*

JM Gardner 1992 *R, S*, 1993 *Rus, F*, 1994 *Sp, R, H, F*, 1995 *R, I, Sa, Ar*, 1996 *W*, 1997 *I, F, SA, I*, 1998 *S, W*

P Gargiullo 1973 *FS*, 1974 *Mid, Sus, Oxo*

F Gargiulo 1972 *Yug*

F Garguilo 1967 *F, Pt*, 1968 *Yug*, 1974 *Sus*

S Garozzo 2001 *Ur, Ar*, 2002 *Ar*

M Gatto 1967 *Pt, R*

G Gattoni 1933 *Cze, Cze*

Q Geldenhuys 2009 *A, A, NZ, NZ, SA, SA, Sa*, 2010 *I, E, S, F, W, SA, SA, Ar, A, Fj*, 2011 *I, E, W, F, S, J, Rus, US, I*, 2012 *F, E, I, W, S, Tg, NZ, A*, 2013 *F, S, W, E, I, A, Fj, Ar*, 2014 *W, F, S, I, E, Fj, Sa, J*

**A Gerardo** 1968 *Yug*, 1969 *Sp*, 1970 *Cze*, *Mad*, 1971 *R*, 1972 *Sp*

**F Geremia** 1980 *JAB*, *Pol*

**G Geremia** 1956 *Cze*

**E Gerosa** 1952 *Sp*, *Ger*, *F*, 1953 *F*, *Ger*, *R*, 1954 *Sp*

**M Gerosa** 1994 *CZR*, *A*, *A*, *R*, *W*, 1995 *E*, *Ar*

**C Ghezzi** 1938 *Ger*, 1939 *Ger*, *R*, 1940 *R*, *Ger*

**A Ghini** 1981 *USS*, *WGe*, 1982 *F*, *R*, *E*, *Mor*, 1983 *F*, *R*, *C*, *Mor*, *F*, *A*, *USS*, 1984 *F*, *Mor*, *R*, *USS*, 1985 *F*, *R*, *EngB*, *Z*, *Z*, *USS*, 1987 *Fj*, 1988 *R*, *USS*

**L Ghiraldini** 2006 *J*, *Fj*, 2007 *I*, *J*, *Pt*, 2008 *I*, *E*, *W*, *F*, *S*, *SA*, *Ar*, *A*, *Ar*, *Pl*, 2009 *S*, *W*, *F*, *A*, *A*, *NZ*, *NZ*, *SA*, *Sa*, 2010 *I*, *E*, *S*, *F*, *W*, *SA*, *SA*, *Ar*, 2011 *I*, *E*, *W*, *F*, *S*, *J*, *A*, *US*, *I*, 2012 *F*, *E*, *I*, *W*, *Tg*, *NZ*, *A*, 2013 *F*, *S*, *W*, *E*, *I*, *SA*, *Sa*, *S*, *A*, *Fj*, *Ar*, 2014 *W*, *F*, *S*, *I*, *E*, *Fj*, *Sa*, *J*

**S Ghizzoni** 1977 *F*, *Mor*, *Pol*, *R*, *Pol*, *Cze*, *R*, *Sp*, 1978 *F*, *Ar*, *USS*, 1979 *F*, *Pol*, *Sp*, *Mor*, *F*, *Pol*, 1980 *R*, *Fj*, *JAB*, *Coo*, *Pol*, *USS*, *Sp*, 1981 *F*, 1982 *F*, *R*, *E*, *WGe*, *Mor*, 1983 *F*, *USS*, *C*, *C*, *Sp*, *Mor*, *F*, *A*, *USS*, 1984 *F*, *Mor*, *R*, *Tun*, *USS*, 1985 *F*, *R*, *EngB*, *Z*, *Z*, *USS*, 1986 *F*, *E*, *A*, *Tun*, *USS*, 1987 *Pt*, *F*, *R*, *NZ*

**M Giacheri** 1992 *R*, 1993 *Sp*, *F*, *Pt*, *Rus*, *F*, *S*, 1994 *Sp*, *R*, *CZR*, *H*, *A*, *A*, *F*, 1995 *S*, *I*, *E*, *Ar*, *F*, *Ar*, *R*, *NZ*, *SA*, 1996 *W*, 1999 *S*, *W*, *I*, *Ur*, *Fj*, *E*, *Tg*, *NZ*, 2001 *Nm*, *SA*, *Ur*, *Ar*, *SA*, 2002 *F*, *S*, *W*, *I*, *E*, *NZ*, *A*, 2003 *E*, *F*, *S*, *I*

**G Giani** 1966 *Ger*, *R*, 1967 *F*, *Pt*, *R*

**D Giazzon** 2012 *Ar*, *US*, *Tg*, *NZ*, *A*, 2013 *F*, *S*, *W*, *E*, *I*, *SA*, *S*, *A*, *Fj*, *Ar*, 2014 *W*, *F*, *S*, *I*, *Fj*

**G Gini** 1968 *Pt*, *WGe*, *Yug*, 1969 *Bul*, *Sp*, *Bel*, *F*, 1970 *Cze*, *Mad*, *Mad*, *R*, 1971 *Mor*, *F*, 1972 *Pt*, *Pt*, 1974 *Mid*, *Oxo*

**G Giorgio** 1968 *Pt*, *WGe*

**M Giovanelli** 1989 *Z*, *USS*, 1990 *Pol*, *Sp*, *H*, *R*, *USS*, 1991 *F*, *R*, *Nm*, *E*, *NZ*, *USS*, 1992 *Sp*, *F*, *S*, 1993 *Sp*, *F*, *Pt*, *Cro*, *Mor*, *Sp*, *F*, 1994 *R*, *CZR*, *H*, *A*, *A*, 1995 *F*, *Ar*, *R*, *NZ*, *SA*, 1996 *A*, *E*, *S*, 1997 *F*, *F*, *A*, *R*, 1998 *S*, *W*, *Rus*, *Ar*, *H*, *E*, 1999 *S*, *W*, *I*, *SA*, *SA*, *Ur*, *Sp*, *Fj*, *E*, *Tg*, *NZ*, 2000 *S*

**E Giugovaz** 1965 *Cze*, 1966 *F*

**R Giuliani** 1951 *Sp*

**E Gori** 2010 *A*, *Fj*, 2011 *I*, *J*, *S*, *A*, *Rus*, *US*, *I*, 2012 *F*, *E*, *I*, *S*, *Ar*, *C*, *US*, *Tg*, *NZ*, *A*, 2013 *F*, *S*, *W*, *E*, *I*, *SA*, *Sa*, *A*, *Fj*, *Ar*, 2014 *W*, *F*, *S*, *I*, *E*

**M Gorni** 1939 *R*, 1940 *R*, *Ger*

**M Goti** 1990 *H*

**C Gower** 2009 *A*, *A*, *NZ*, *NZ*, *SA*, *Sa*, 2010 *I*, *E*, *S*, *F*, *W*, *SA*, *SA*, *Ar*

**G Grasselli** 1952 *Ger*

**G Grespan** 1989 *F*, *Sp*, *USS*, 1990 *F*, *R*, 1991 *R*, *NZ*, *USS*, 1992 *R*, *S*, 1993 *Sp*, *F*, *Cro*, *Sp*, *F*, *Rus*, 1994 *Sp*, *CZR*, *R*, *W*

**PR Griffen** 2004 *E*, *F*, *S*, *I*, *W*, *R*, *J*, *C*, *NZ*, *US*, 2005 *W*, *S*, *F*, *Ar*, *Ar*, *A*, *Tg*, *Ar*, *Fj*, 2006 *I*, *E*, *F*, *W*, *S*, *J*, *Fj*, *Rus*, *A*, *Ar*, *C*, 2007 *F*, *I*, *Ur*, *Ar*, *I*, *NZ*, *Pt*, 2009 *I*, *S*, *W*, *F*

**A Gritti** 1996 *Pt*, 2000 *S*, *W*, *I*, *E*, *F*, *Sa*, *Fj*, *C*, *R*, *NZ*, 2001 *E*, *F*, *S*, *W*

**G Guidi** 1996 *Pt*, *E*, 1997 *F*, *Ar*, *R*

**T Iannone** 2012 *Tg*, 2013 *SA*, *Sa*, *A*, *Fj*, *Ar*, 2014 *W*, *F*, *Sa*, *J*

**M Innocenti** 1981 *WGe*, 1982 *F*, *R*, *E*, *WGe*, *Mor*, 1983 *F*, *USS*, *C*, *C*, *Mor*, *F*, *A*, *USS*, 1984 *F*, *Mor*, *Tun*, *USS*, 1985 *F*, *R*, *EngB*, *Sp*, *USS*, 1986 *Tun*, *F*, *Pt*, *E*, *A*, *Tun*, *USS*, 1987 *Pt*, *F*, *R*, *NZ*, *Ar*, *Fj*, *USS*, *Sp*, 1988 *F*, *R*, *A*

**G Intoppa** 2004 *R*, *J*, *C*, *NZ*, 2005 *I*, *W*, *E*

**C Jannone** 1981 *USS*, 1982 *F*, *R*

**S Lanfranchi** 1949 *F*, *Cze*, 1953 *F*, *Ger*, *R*, 1954 *Sp*, *F*, 1955 *F*, 1956 *Ger*, *Cze*, 1957 *F*, 1958 *F*, 1959 *F*, 1960 *F*, 1961 *F*, 1962 *F*, *Ger*, *R*, 1963 *F*, 1964 *Ger*, *F*

**G Lanzi** 1998 *Ar*, *H*, *E*, 1999 *Sp*, 2000 *S*, *W*, *I*, 2001 *I*

**G Lari** 1972 *Yug*, 1973 *Yug*, *A*, 1974 *Pt*, *Mid*, *Sus*, *Oxo*, *Leo*

**E Lazzarini** 1970 *Cze*, 1971 *Mor*, *F*, *R*, 1972 *Pt*, *Pt*, *Sp*, *Sp*, 1973 *Pt*, *Rho*, *WTv*, *Bor*, *NEC*, *Leo*, *FS*, *Tva*, *Cze*, *Yug*, *A*, 1974 *Pt*, *Mid*, *Sus*, *Oxo*, *WGe*

**U Levorato** 1956 *Ger*, *F*, 1957 *F*, 1958 *F*, *R*, 1959 *F*, 1961 *Ger*, *F*, 1962 *F*, *Ger*, *R*, 1963 *F*, *Ger*, *F*, 1965 *F*

**A Lijoi** 1977 *Pol*, *R*, 1978 *Sp*, 1979 *R*, *Mor*

**G Limone** 1979 *E*, *Mor*, *USS*, *Mor*, 1980 *JAB*, *Sp*, 1981 *USS*, *WGe*, 1982 *E*, 1983 *USS*

**A Lo Cicero** 2000 *E*, *F*, *Sa*, *Fj*, *C*, *R*, *NZ*, 2001 *I*, *E*, *F*, *S*, *W*, *Fj*, *SA*, *Sa*, 2002 *F*, *S*, *W*, *Sp*, *R*, *A*, 2003 *F*, *S*, *S*, *I*, *Geo*, *Tg*, *C*, *W*, 2004 *E*, *F*, *S*, *I*, *W*, *R*, *J*, *C*, *NZ*, *US*, 2005 *I*, *W*, *S*, *E*, *F*, *Ar*, *Ar*, *C*, 2007 *F*, *E*, *S*, *W*, *Ur*, *Ar*, *J*, *NZ*, *R*, *Pt*, *S*, 2008 *I*, *E*, *W*, *F*, *S*, *Ar*, *Pl*, 2010 *Ar*, *A*, *Fj*, 2011 *I*, *E*, *W*, *F*, *S*, *J*, *S*, *A*, *US*, *I*, 2012 *F*, *E*, *W*, *S*, *Tg*, *NZ*, *A*, 2013 *F*, *S*, *W*, *E*, *I*

**C Loranzi** 1973 *Nat*, *ETv*, *Leo*, *FS*, *Tva*

**F Lorigiola** 1979 *Sp*, *F*, *Pol*, *USS*, *NZ*, *Mor*, 1980 *F*, *R*, *Fj*, *JAB*, *Pol*, *USS*, *Sp*, 1981 *F*, *R*, *USS*, 1982 *WGe*, 1983 *R*, *USS*, *C*, *Sp*, 1984 *Tun*, 1985 *Sp*, 1986 *Pt*, *E*, *A*, *Tun*, *USS*, 1987 *Pt*, *F*, *R*, *NZ*, *Ar*, 1988 *F*

**G Luchini** 1973 *Rho*, *Nat*

**L Luise** 1955 *Ger*, *F*, *Sp*, *F*, *Cze*, 1956 *Ger*, *F*, *Cze*, 1957 *Ger*, 1958 *F*

**R Luise III** 1959 *F*, 1960 *Ger*, *F*, 1961 *Ger*, *F*, 1962 *F*, *Ger*, *R*, 1965 *F*, *Cze*, 1966 *F*, 1971 *R*, 1972 *Pt*, *Sp*, *Sp*

**T Lupini** 1987 *R*, *NZ*, *Ar*, *Fj*, *USS*, *Sp*, 1988 *F*, *R*, *USS*, *A*, 1989 *R*

**O Maestri** 1935 *Cat*, *F*, 1937 *Ger*

**R Maffioli** 1933 *Cze*, *Cze*, 1934 *Cat*, *R*, 1935 *Cat*, 1936 *Ger*, *R*, 1937 *Ger*, *R*, *Bel*, *Ger*

**R Maini** 1948 *F*, *Cze*

**G Malosti** 1953 *F*, 1954 *Sp*, 1955 *F*, 1956 *F*, 1957 *F*, 1958 *F*

**G Mancini** 1952 *Ger*, *F*, 1953 *F*, *Ger*, *R*, 1954 *Sp*, *F*, 1955 *Cze*, 1956 *Ger*, *F*, *Cze*, 1957 *F*

**R Mandelli** 2004 *I*, *W*, *R*, *J*, *US*, 2007 *F*, *E*, *Ur*, *Ar*

**A Manici** 2013 *Sa*, 2014 *Sa*, *J*

**A Mannato** 2004 *US*, 2005 *Ar*, *A*

**E Manni** 1976 *J*, *A*, *Sp*, 1977 *Mor*

**L Manteri** 1996 *W*, *A*, *E*, *S*

**A Marcato** 2006 *J*, *Pt*, 2008 *I*, *E*, *W*, *F*, *S*, *SA*, *Ar*, *A*, *Ar*, *Pl*, 2009 *E*, *S*, *W*, *F*

**M Marchetto** 1972 *Yug*, 1973 *Pt*, *Cze*, *Yug*, 1974 *Pt*, *Mid*, *Sus*, *WGe*, *Leo*, 1975 *F*, *Sp*, *R*, *Cze*, *E*, *Pol*, *H*, *Sp*, 1976 *F*, *R*, *J*, *A*, *Sp*, 1977 *F*, *Mor*, *Pol*, *R*, *Cze*, *R*, *Sp*, 1978 *F*, *USS*, *Sp*, 1979 *F*, *Pol*, *R*, *E*, *Pol*, *USS*, *Mor*, 1980 *F*, *Coo*, 1981 *USS*

**A Marescalchi** 1933 *Cze*, 1935 *F*, 1937 *R*

**P Mariani** 1976 *R*, *A*, *Sp*, 1977 *F*, *Pol*, 1978 *F*, *Ar*, *USS*, *Sp*, 1979 *F*, *Pol*, *R*, *Sp*, *F*, *Pol*, *USS*, *NZ*, *Mor*, 1980 *F*, *R*, *Fj*, *JAB*

**P Marini** 1949 *F*, *Cze*, 1951 *Sp*, 1953 *F*, *Ger*, *R*, 1955 *Ger*

**L Martin** 1997 *F*, *R*, 1998 *S*, *W*, *Rus*, *H*, *E*, 1999 *F*, *S*, *W*, *I*, *SA*, *Ar*, *Ur*, *Sp*, *Fj*, *E*, 2000 *S*, *W*, *I*, *E*, *F*, *Sa*, *Fj*, *C*, *R*, *NZ*, 2001 *I*, *E*, *S*, *W*, *SA*, *Ar*, *Fj*, *SA*, *Sa*, 2002 *F*, *S*

**F Martinenghi** 1952 *Sp*, *Ger*

**R Martinez-Frugoni** 2002 *NZ*, *Sp*, *R*, 2003 *W*, *I*, *E*, *F*, *S*, *S*, *NZ*

**G Martini** 1965 *F*, 1967 *F*, 1968 *Pt*

**R Martini** 1959 *F*, 1960 *Ger*, *F*, 1961 *Ger*, *F*, 1964 *Ger*, *F*, 1965 *F*, 1968 *WGe*, *Yug*

**P Masci** 1948 *Cze*, 1949 *F*, *Cze*, 1952 *Sp*, *Ger*, *F*, 1953 *F*, 1954 *Sp*, 1955 *F*

**M Mascioletti** 1977 *Mor*, *Pol*, 1978 *Ar*, *USS*, *Sp*, 1979 *Pol*, *E*, *Sp*, *Mor*, *F*, *Pol*, *USS*, *NZ*, *Mor*, 1980 *F*, *R*, *Fj*, 1981 *WGe*, 1982 *F*, *R*, *WGe*, 1983 *F*, *R*, *USS*, *C*, *C*, *Sp*, *Mor*, *F*, *A*, *USS*, 1984 *F*, *Mor*, *Tun*, 1985 *F*, *R*, *Z*, *Z*, *USS*, *R*, 1986 *Tun*, *F*, *Pt*, *E*, *Tun*, *USS*, 1987 *NZ*, *Ar*, *Fj*, 1989 *Sp*, *Ar*, *Z*, *USS*, 1990 *Pol*

**A Masi** 1999 *Sp*, 2003 *E*, *F*, *S*, *S*, *I*, *NZ*, *Tg*, *C*, *W*, 2004 *E*, *I*, *W*, *R*, *J*, *C*, 2005 *I*, *W*, *S*, *E*, *F*, *Ar*, *Ar*, *A*, 2006 *J*, *Fj*, *Pt*, *Rus*, *I*, *J*, *S*, *J*, *NZ*, *R*, *Pt*, *S*, 2008 *I*, *E*, *W*, *F*, *S*, *SA*, *SA*, *Ar*, *A*, 2009 *I*, 2010 *I*, *E*, *S*, *F*, *SA*, *SA*, *Ar*, *A*, *Fj*, 2011 *I*, *E*, *W*, *F*, *S*, *S*, *A*, *Rus*, *I*, 2012 *F*, *E*, *I*, *W*, *S*, *Tg*, *NZ*, *A*, 2013 *F*, *S*, *W*, *E*, *I*, *SA*, *Sa*, *S*, 2014 *I*, *F*, *Fj*, *Sa*

**L Mastrodomenico** 2000 *Sa*, *C*, *NZ*, 2001 *Nm*, *Ar*

**I Matacchini** 1948 *F*, *Cze*, 1949 *F*, *Cze*, 1954 *Sp*, 1955 *Ger*, *F*, *Sp*, *F*

**L Mattarolo** 1973 *Bor*, *Nat*, *ETv*, *Leo*, *FS*, *Tva*, *Cze*

**M Mattei** 1967 *R*

**R Mattei** 1978 *F*, *USS*

**F Mazzantini** 1965 *Cze*, 1966 *F*, 1967 *F*

**M Mazzantini** 2000 *S*, 2001 *S*, *W*, 2002 *E*, *NZ*, 2003 *E*, *F*, *Geo*, *NZ*, *C*

**F Mazzariol** 1995 *F*, *Ar*, *R*, *NZ*, 1996 *Pt*, 1997 *F*, *R*, *SA*, 1998 *Ar*,

ITALY

H, 1999 F, SA, SA, Sp, E, NZ, 2000 Fj, C, 2001 Nm, SA, Ur, Ar, Fj, SA, 2002 W, NZ, Sp, 2003 S, I, NZ, C, W, 2004 R
**G Mazzi** 1998 H, 1999 SA, SA, Ur, Sp
**N Mazzucato** 1995 SA, 1996 Pt, S, 1997 I, 1999 Sp, E, Tg, NZ, 2000 F, Sa, Fj, R, 2001 Nm, SA, Ur, Ar, 2002 W, I, E, NZ, Sp, R, Ar, A, 2003 E, F, S, I, NZ, Tg, W, 2004 E, F, S, I, W, R, J
**I Mazzucchelli** 1965 F, Cze, 1966 F, Ger, R, 1967 F, 1968 Pt, WGe, 1969 Bul, F, 1971 F, 1972 Pt, Sp, 1974 WGe, 1975 F, R, Cze, Pol, 1976 F, R
**LJ McLean** 2008 SA, Ar, Pl, 2009 E, I, S, W, F, A, A, NZ, NZ, SA, Sa, 2010 I, E, S, F, W, S, J, A, Rus, US, I, 2012 F, E, I, W, US, Tg, NZ, A, 2013 F, S, W, E, I, SA, Sa, S, A, Fj, Ar, 2014 W, F, S, I, E, Fj, Sa, J
**P Menapace** 1996 Pt
**E Michelon** 1969 Bel, F, 1970 Cze, Mad, Mad, R, 1971 R
**A Miele** 1968 Yug, 1970 Mad, 1971 R, 1972 Pt, Sp
**GE Milano** 1990 USS
**F Minto** 2012 NZ, A, 2013 F, S, W, E, I, 2014 W, F
**A Mioni** 1955 Ger, F, F, 1957 R
**A Modonesi** 1929 Sp
**L Modonesi** 1966 Ger, R, 1967 F, Pt, R, 1968 Pt, WGe, 1970 Cze, Mad, Mad, R, 1971 F, 1974 Leo, 1975 F, Sp, R, Cze
**N Molari** 1957 F, 1958 R
**F Molinari** 1973 NEC
**G Molinari** 1948 F
**P Monfeli** 1970 R, 1971 Mor, F, 1972 Pt, 1976 J, A, Sp, 1977 F, R, Cze, R, Sp, 1978 F
**JF Montauriol** 2009 E, A
**G Morelli** 1981 WGe, 1982 R, E, Mor, 1983 USS, 1984 F
**G Morelli** 1976 F, 1982 F, R, Mor, 1983 R, C, Sp, A, USS, 1984 Mor, R, USS, 1985 R, EngB, Z, Z, USS, R, 1986 Tun, F, E, A, Tun, USS, 1987 F, NZ
**G Morelli** 1988 I, 1989 F, R
**A Moreno** 1999 Tg, NZ, 2002 F, S, 2008 Ar
**A Moretti** 1997 R, 1998 Rus, 1999 Ur, Sp, Tg, NZ, 2002 E, NZ, Sp, R, A, 2005 Ar
**U Moretti** 1933 Cze, 1934 R, 1935 Cat, 1937 R, Ger, F, 1942 R
**A Morimondi** 1930 Sp, 1933 Cze, 1934 Cat, 1935 Cat
**LE Morisi** 2012 E, US, 2013 SA, S, A, Fj
**A Moscardi** 1993 Pt, 1995 R, 1996 S, 1998 Ar, H, E, 1999 F, S, W, I, SA, SA, Ur, Fj, E, Tg, NZ, 2000 S, W, I, E, F, Sa, Fj, C, R, NZ, 2001 I, E, F, S, W, Nm, SA, Ur, Ar, Fj, SA, Sa, 2002 F, S, W, I, E
**A Muraro** 2000 C, R, NZ, 2001 I, E, Nm, SA, Ur, Ar, Fj, SA, Sa, 2002 F

**E Nathan** 1930 Sp
**G Navarini** 1957 Ger, 1958 R
**M Nicolosi** 1982 R
**C Nieto** 2002 E, 2005 Ar, Ar, A, Tg, Ar, Fj, 2006 I, E, F, W, J, Fj, A, Ar, C, 2007 F, S, W, I, Ar, 2008 E, F, S, SA, Ar, A, Ar, Pl, 2009 E, I, S, W, F
**A Nisti** 1929 Sp, 1930 Sp
**L Nitoglia** 2004 C, NZ, US, 2005 I, W, S, E, F, Ar, Tg, Ar, Fj, 2006 I, E, F, W, S

**F Ongaro** 2000 C, 2001 Nm, SA, Ur, Ar, 2002 Ar, A, 2003 E, F, S, I, Geo, NZ, Tg, C, W, 2004 E, F, S, I, W, R, J, C, NZ, US, 2005 I, W, S, E, F, Tg, Ar, Fj, 2006 I, E, F, W, S, J, Fj, Pt, Rus, Ar, C, 2007 F, S, W, Ar, I, NZ, S, 2008 E, F, S, W, Nm, SA, Ur, Ar, Fj, SA, Sa, 2002 F, S, W, I, E
**A Murаro** — *(see above)*

**C Orlandi** 1992 S, 1993 Sp, F, Mor, F, Rus, F, S, 1994 Sp, CZR, H, A, A, R, W, 1995 S, I, Sa, E, Ar, F, Ar, R, NZ, SA, 1996 W, Pt, W, A, E, S, 1997 I, F, F, Ar, R, SA, I, 1998 S, W, 2000 W, F
**S Orlando** 2004 E, S, W, C, NZ, US, 2005 E, F, Ar, A, 2006 J, 2007 Ur, Ar, Pt
**L Orquera** 2004 C, NZ, US, 2005 I, W, S, E, F, Ar, Tg, 2008 A, Ar, 2009 W, F, 2010 Ar, A, Fj, 2011 I, E, W, F, S, J, S, A, US, I, 2012 NZ, A, 2013 F, S, E, I, SA, Sa, Fj, A, 2014 F, S, I, E, Fj, Sa, J
**A Osti** 1981 F, R, USS, 1982 E, Mor, 1983 R, C, A, USS, 1984 R, USS, 1985 F, 1986 Tun, 1988 R

**S Pace** 1977 Mor, 1984 R, Tun
**S Pace** 2001 SA, Sa, 2005 Fj
**P Pacifici** 1969 Bul, Sp, F, 1970 Cze, Mad, Mad, R, 1971 Mor, F
**R Paciucci** 1937 R, Ger, F
**F Paganelli** 1972 Sp
**G Palazzani** 2014 Fj, Sa, J
**S Palmer** 2002 Ar, A, 2003 I, E, F, S, S, NZ, C, W, 2004 I, R
**P Paoletti** 1972 Pt, Sp, Yug, 1973 Pt, Rho, WTv, Bor, NEC, Nat, ETv, Leo, FS, Tva, 1974 Mid, Oxo, WGe, Leo, 1975 F, Sp, 1976 R
**T Paoletti** 2000 S, W, I, E, F, Sa, C, R, NZ, 2001 F, Nm, Ur, Ar, Fj, SA
**G Paolin** 1929 Sp
**S Parisse** 2002 NZ, Sp, R, Ar, A, 2003 S, I, Geo, NZ, Tg, C, W, 2004 E, F, S, 2005 I, W, S, E, F, Ar, A, Tg, Ar, Fj, 2006 I, E, F, W, S, Fj, Pt, Rus, A, Ar, C, 2007 F, E, S, W, I, J, I, NZ, R, Pt, S, 2008 I, E, W, F, S, Ar, A, Pl, 2009 E, I, S, W, F, S, J, S, A, Rus, US, I, 2012 F, E, I, W, S, Tg, NZ, A, 2013 F, S, E, I, SA, Sa, S, A, Fj, Ar, 2014 W, F, S, E
**E Parmiggiani** 1942 R, 1948 Cze
**P Paselli** 1929 Sp, 1930 Sp, 1933 Cze
**E Passarotto** 1975 Sp
**E Patrizio** 2007 Ur, 2008 F, S, SA
**R Pavan** 2008 SA
**A Pavanello** 2007 Ar, 2009 SA, Sa, 2012 E, I, Ar, C, US, Tg, NZ, A, 2013 F, S, W, E, I, SA, Sa, S, A, 2014 I
**E Pavanello** 2002 R, Ar, A, 2004 R, J, C, NZ, US, 2005 Ar, A
**P Pavesi** 1977 Pol, 1979 Mor, 1980 USS
**M Pavin** 1980 USS, 1986 F, Pt, E, A, Tun, USS, 1987 Ar
**R Pedrazzi** 2001 Nm, Ar, 2002 F, S, W, 2005 S, E, F
**P Pedroni** 1989 Z, USS, 1990 F, Pol, R, 1991 F, R, Nm, 1993 Rus, F, 1994 Sp, R, CZR, H, 1995 I, Sa, E, Ar, F, Ar, R, NZ, SA, 1996 W, W
**G Peens** 2002 W, I, E, NZ, Sp, R, Ar, A, 2003 E, F, S, S, I, 2004 I, NZ, 2005 E, F, Ar, Ar, A, 2006 Pt, A
**L Pelliccione** 1983 Sp, Mor, F
**L Pelliccione** 1977 Pol
**M Percudani** 1952 F, 1954 F, 1955 Ger, Sp, F, Cze, 1956 Cze, 1957 F, 1958 R
**F Perrini** 1955 Sp, F, Cze, 1956 Ger, F, Cze, 1957 F, 1958 F, 1959 F, 1962 R, 1963 F
**F Perrone** 1951 Sp
**AR Persico** 2000 S, W, E, F, Sa, Fj, 2001 F, S, W, Nm, SA, Ur, Ar, Fj, SA, Sa, 2002 F, S, W, I, E, NZ, Sp, R, Ar, A, 2003 W, I, E, F, S, I, Geo, C, W, 2004 E, F, S, I, W, R, J, C, NZ, 2005 I, W, S, E, F, 2006 I, E
**J Pertile** 1994 R, 1995 Ar, 1996 W, A, E, S, 1997 I, F, SA, 1998 Rus, 1999 S, W, I, SA, Sa
**S Perugini** 2000 I, F, Sa, Fj, 2001 S, W, Nm, SA, Ur, Ar, 2002 W, I, 2003 W, S, Geo, Tg, W, 2004 E, F, I, W, C, NZ, US, 2005 I, W, S, E, F, 2006 I, E, F, W, S, Pt, Rus, 2007 F, E, S, W, I, J, I, NZ, Pt, S, 2008 I, E, W, F, S, A, Ar, Pl, 2009 E, I, S, W, F, S, Rus, US, I, W, SA, SA, Ar, Fj, 2011 I, E, W, F, S, Rus, US, I
**L Perziano** 1993 Pt
**M Perziano** 2000 NZ, 2001 F, S, W, Nm, SA, Ur, Ar, Fj, SA
**V Pesce** 1988 I, 1989 R
**P Pescetto** 1956 Ger, Cze, 1957 F
**G Petralia** 1984 F
**R Pez** 2000 Sa, Fj, C, R, NZ, 2001 I, 2002 S, W, E, A, 2003 I, E, F, S, S, Geo, 2005 Ar, A, Tg, Ar, Fj, 2006 I, E, F, W, S, J, Fj, Pt, Rus, Ar, 2007 F, E, S, W, I, J, R, S
**M Phillips** 2002 F, S, W, I, E, 2003 W, I, E, F, S, S, I, NZ, W
**G Pianna** 1934 R, 1935 Cat, F, 1936 Ger, R, 1938 Ger
**A Piazza** 1990 USS
**F Piccini** 1963 F, 1964 Ger, 1966 F
**S Picone** 2004 I, W, 2005 F, 2006 E, F, S, J, Pt, Rus, Ar, C, 2008 E, W, F, S, SA, Ar, 2009 NZ, SA, Sa, 2010 I, SA, SA
**F Pietroscanti** 1987 USS, Sp, 1988 A, I, 1989 F, R, Sp, Ar, Z, USS, 1990 F, Pol, R, H, 1991 Nm, Nm, 1992 Sp, F, R, 1993 Sp, Mor, Sp, F, Rus, F
**F Pignotti** 1968 WGe, Yug, 1969 Bul, Sp, Bel
**C Pilat** 1997 I, 1998 S, W, 2000 E, Sa, 2001 I, W
**MJ Pini** 1998 H, E, 1999 F, Ur, Fj, E, Tg, NZ, 2000 S, W, I, F
**M Piovan** 1973 Pt, 1974 Pt, Mid, Sus, Oxo, 1976 A, 1977 F, Mor, R, 1979 F

R **Piovan** 1996 *Pt*, 1997 *R*, 2000 *R*, *NZ*
M **Piovene** 1995 *NZ*
E **Piras** 1971 *R*
M **Pisaneschi** 1948 *Cze*, 1949 *Cze*, 1953 *F*, *Ger*, *R*, 1954 *Sp*, *F*, 1955 *Ger*, *F*, *Sp*, *F*, *Cze*
F **Pitorri** 1948 *Cze*, 1949 *F*
M **Pitorri** 1973 *NEC*
G **Pivetta** 1979 *R*, *E*, *Mor*, 1980 *Coo*, *USS*, 1981 *R*, *USS*, *WGe*, 1982 *F*, *R*, *WGe*, *Mor*, 1983 *F*, *USS*, *C*, *Sp*, *Mor*, *F*, *USS*, 1984 *F*, *Mor*, *R*, *Tun*, 1985 *F*, *R*, *Sp*, *Z*, *Z*, 1986 *Pt*, 1987 *Sp*, 1989 *R*, *Sp*, 1990 *F*, *Pol*, *R*, *Sp*, *R*, *USS*, 1991 *F*, *R*, *Nm*, *Nm*, *US*, *E*, *NZ*, *USS*, 1992 *Sp*, *F*, *R*, *R*, 1993 *Cro*, *Mor*, *Sp*
M **Platania** 1994 *F*, 1995 *F*, *R*, 1996 *Pt*
I **Ponchia** 1955 *F*, *Sp*, *F*, *Cze*, 1956 *F*, 1957 *Ger*, 1958 *F*
E **Ponzi** 1973 *Cze*, *A*, 1974 *WGe*, 1975 *F*, *Sp*, *R*, *Cze*, *E*, *Pol*, *H*, *Sp*, 1976 *F*, *R*, *J*, *A*, *Sp*, 1977 *F*, *Mor*, *Pol*, *R*
G **Porcellato** 1989 *R*
G **Porzio** 1970 *Cze*, *Mad*, *Mad*
C **Possamai** 1970 *Cze*, *Mad*, *Mad*
W **Pozzebon** 2001 *I*, *E*, *F*, *S*, *W*, *Nm*, *SA*, *Ur*, *Ar*, *Fj*, *SA*, *Sa*, 2002 *NZ*, *Sp*, 2004 *R*, *J*, *C*, *NZ*, *US*, 2005 *W*, *E*, 2006 *C*
A **Pratichetti** 2012 *C*
C **Pratichetti** 1988 *R*, 1990 *Pol*
M **Pratichetti** 2004 *NZ*, 2007 *E*, *W*, *I*, *Ur*, *Ar*, *I*, *Pt*, 2008 *SA*, *Ar*, *Ar*, *Pl*, 2009 *E*, *I*, *S*, *W*, *F*, *A*, *NZ*, *SA*, 2010 *W*, *SA*, 2011 *J*, *Rus*
G **Preo** 1999 *I*, 2000 *I*, *E*, *Sa*, *Fj*, *R*, *NZ*
P **Presutti** 1974 *Mid*, *Sus*, *Oxo*, 1977 *Pol*, *Cze*, *R*, *Sp*, 1978 *F*
FP **Properzi-Curti** 1990 *Pol*, *Sp*, *H*, *R*, 1991 *F*, *Nm*, *Nm*, *US*, *E*, *NZ*, 1992 *Sp*, *F*, *R*, 1993 *Cro*, *Mor*, *F*, *Rus*, *F*, *S*, 1994 *Sp*, *R*, *H*, *A*, *A*, 1995 *S*, *I*, *Sa*, *E*, *Ar*, *NZ*, *SA*, 1996 *W*, *Pt*, *W*, *A*, *E*, 1997 *I*, *F*, *F*, *Ar*, *SA*, 1998 *Ar*, 1999 *S*, *W*, *I*, *SA*, *SA*, *Ur*, *E*, *Tg*, *NZ*, 2001 *F*, *S*, *W*
C **Prosperini** 1966 *R*, 1967 *F*, *R*, *R*
F **Pucciarello** 1999 *Sp*, *Fj*, *E*, 2002 *S*, *W*, *I*, *E*, *Ar*
G **Puglisi** 1971 *F*, 1972 *Yug*, 1973 *Cze*
M **Pulli** 1968 *Pt*, 1972 *Pt*, *Pt*
A **Puppo** 1972 *Pt*, *Pt*, *Sp*, *Sp*, 1973 *Pt*, *Rho*, *WTv*, *Bor*, *NEC*, *Nat*, *ETv*, *Leo*, *FS*, *Tva*, 1974 *Mid*, *Sus*, *Oxo*, *WGe*, *Leo*, 1977 *R*

I **Quaglio** 1970 *R*, 1971 *R*, 1972 *Pt*, *Sp*, 1973 *WTv*, *Bor*, *NEC*, *Nat*, *Leo*, *FS*, *Tva*, 1975 *H*, *Sp*, 1976 *F*, *R*
M **Quaglio** 1984 *Tun*, 1988 *F*, *R*
R **Quartaroli** 2009 *W*, *F*, *A*, 2012 *Ar*, *US*
JM **Queirolo** 2000 *Sa*, *Fj*, 2001 *E*, *F*, *Fj*, 2002 *NZ*, *Sp*, *A*, 2003 *Geo*
P **Quintavala** 1958 *R*

C **Raffo** 1929 *Sp*, 1930 *Sp*, 1933 *Cze*, *Cze*, 1937 *R*, *Bel*
G **Raineri** 1998 *H*, 2000 *Fj*, *R*, *NZ*, 2001 *I*, *E*, *S*, *W*, *Nm*, *SA*, *Ur*, *Ar*, 2002 *W*, *I*, *E*, *NZ*, 2003 *W*, *I*, *E*, *F*, *S*, *Geo*
G **Raisi** 1956 *Ger*, *F*, 1957 *F*, *Ger*, 1960 *Ger*, 1964 *Ger*, *F*
R **Rampazzo** 1996 *W*, 1999 *I*
M **Ravazzolo** 1993 *Cro*, *Sp*, *F*, *S*, 1994 *Sp*, *R*, *CZR*, *H*, 1995 *S*, *I*, *Sa*, *F*, *Ar*, *NZ*, 1996 *W*, *Pt*, *W*, *A*, 1997 *F*, *Ar*, *R*, *SA*
A **Re Garbagnati** 1936 *Ger*, *R*, 1937 *Ger*, *Bel*, *Ger*, *F*, 1938 *Ger*, 1939 *Ger*, *R*, 1940 *R*, *Ger*, 1942 *R*
P **Reale** 1987 *USS*, 1988 *USS*, *A*, *I*, 1989 *Z*, 1992 *S*
T **Reato** 2008 *I*, *SA*, *Ar*, *A*, *Ar*, *Pl*, 2009 *E*, *I*, *A*
G **Riccardi** 1955 *Ger*, *F*, *Sp*, *F*, *Cze*, 1956 *F*, *Cze*
G **Ricci** 1967 *Pt*, 1969 *Bul*, *Sp*, *Bel*, *F*
G **Ricciarelli** 1962 *Ger*
L **Riccioni** 1951 *Sp*, 1952 *Sp*, *Ger*, *F*, 1953 *F*, *Ger*, 1954 *F*
S **Rigo** 1992 *S*, 1993 *Sp*, *F*, *Pt*
A **Rinaldo** 1977 *Mor*, *Pol*, *R*, *Cze*
W **Rista** 1968 *Yug*, 1969 *Bul*, *Sp*, *Bel*, *F*
M **Rivaro** 2000 *S*, *W*, *I*, 2001 *E*
M **Rizzo** 2005 *A*, 2008 *SA*, 2012 *I*, *C*, *US*, *A*, 2013 *I*, *Sa*, *A*, *Fj*, *Ar*, 2014 *W*, *F*, *I*, *E*
G **Rizzoli** 1935 *F*, 1936 *Ger*, *R*
C **Robazza** 1978 *Ar*, *Sp*, 1979 *F*, *Pol*, *R*, *E*, *Sp*, *F*, *Pol*, *USS*, *NZ*, *Mor*, 1980 *F*, *R*, *Fj*, *JAB*, *Coo*, *Pol*, *Sp*, 1981 *F*, *R*, *USS*, *WGe*, 1982 *E*, *WGe*, 1983 *F*, *USS*, *C*, *Mor*, *F*, 1984 *F*, *Tun*, 1985 *F*
KP **Robertson** 2004 *R*, *J*, *C*, *NZ*, *US*, 2005 *I*, *W*, *S*, *F*, *Ar*, *Ar*, *A*, 2006 *Pt*, *Rus*, 2007 *F*, *E*, *S*, *W*, *I*, *Ur*, *Ar*, *J*, *I*, *NZ*, *R*, *S*,

2008 *I*, *E*, *F*, *S*, *SA*, *Ar*, *A*, *Ar*, *Pl*, 2009 *E*, *I*, *A*, *NZ*, *NZ*, *Sa*, 2010 *I*, *E*, *S*, *F*, *W*, *SA*
A **Rocca** 1973 *WTv*, *Bor*, *NEC*, 1977 *R*
G **Romagnoli** 1965 *F*, *Cze*, 1967 *Pt*, *R*
S **Romagnoli** 1982 *Mor*, 1984 *R*, *Tun*, *USS*, 1985 *F*, *Z*, *Z*, 1986 *Tun*, *Pt*, *A*, *Tun*, *USS*, 1987 *Pt*, *F*, *Fj*
G **Romano** 1942 *R*
L **Romano** 2012 *Ar*, *C*
P **Romano** 1942 *R*
F **Roselli** 1995 *F*, *R*, 1996 *W*, 1998 *Rus*, *Ar*, *H*, *E*, 1999 *F*, *S*, *W*, *I*, *SA*, *SA*, *Ur*, *Fj*, *Tg*
P **Rosi** 1948 *F*, *Cze*, 1949 *F*, *Cze*, 1951 *Sp*, 1952 *Ger*, *F*, 1953 *F*, *Ger*, *R*, 1954 *Sp*, *F*
G **Rossi** 1981 *USS*, *WGe*, 1982 *E*, *WGe*, *Mor*, 1983 *F*, *R*, *USS*, *C*, *C*, *Mor*, *F*, *A*, *USS*, 1984 *Mor*, 1985 *F*, *R*, *EngB*, *Sp*, *Z*, *USS*, *R*, 1986 *Tun*, *F*, *E*, *A*, *Tun*, *USS*, 1987 *R*, *NZ*, *Ar*, *USS*, *Sp*, 1988 *USS*, *A*, *I*, 1989 *F*, *R*, *Sp*, *Ar*, *Z*, *USS*, 1990 *F*, *R*, 1991 *R*
N **Rossi** 1973 *Yug*, 1974 *Pt*, *Mid*, *Sus*, *Oxo*, *WGe*, *Leo*, 1975 *Sp*, *Cze*, *E*, *H*, 1976 *J*, *A*, *Sp*, 1977 *Cze*, 1980 *USS*
Z **Rossi** 1959 *F*, 1961 *Ger*, *F*, 1962 *F*, *Ger*, *R*
E **Rossini** 1948 *F*, *Cze*, 1949 *F*, *Cze*, 1951 *Sp*, 1952 *Ger*
B **Rovelli** 1960 *Ger*, *F*, 1961 *Ger*, *F*
G **Rubini** 2009 *S*, *W*, *F*, *A*
A **Russo** 1986 *E*

D **Sacca** 2003 *I*
R **Saetti** 1957 *Ger*, 1958 *F*, *R*, 1959 *F*, 1960 *F*, 1961 *Ger*, *F*, 1964 *Ger*, *F*
R **Saetti** 1988 *USS*, *I*, 1989 *F*, *R*, *Sp*, *Ar*, *Z*, *USS*, 1990 *F*, *Sp*, *H*, *R*, *USS*, 1991 *R*, *Nm*, *Nm*, *US*, *E*, 1992 *R*
A **Sagramora** 1970 *Mad*, *Mad*, 1971 *R*
E **Saibene** 1957 *F*, *Ger*
C **Salmasco** 1965 *F*, 1967 *F*
L **Salsi** 1971 *Mor*, 1972 *Pt*, *Sp*, *Yug*, 1973 *Pt*, *Rho*, *WTv*, *Nat*, *ETv*, *Leo*, *FS*, *Tva*, *Cze*, *Yug*, *A*, 1974 *Pt*, *Oxo*, *WGe*, *Leo*, 1975 *Sp*, *R*, *Sp*, 1977 *R*, *Pol*, *Cze*, *R*, *Sp*, 1978 *F*
F **Salvadego** 1985 *Z*
R **Salvan** 1973 *Yug*, 1974 *Pt*
L **Salvati** 1987 *USS*, 1988 *USS*, *I*
R **Santofadre** 1952 *Sp*, *Ger*, *F*, 1954 *Sp*, *F*
**Sarto** 2013 *S*, *A*, 2014 *W*, *F*, *S*, *I*, *E*, *Fj*, *J*
F **Sartorato** 1956 *Ger*, *F*, 1957 *F*
M **Savi** 2004 *R*, *J*, 2005 *E*
S **Saviozzi** 1998 *Rus*, *H*, 1999 *W*, *I*, *SA*, *Ur*, *Fj*, *Tg*, *NZ*, 2000 *C*, *NZ*, 2002 *NZ*, *Sp*
F **Sbaraglini** 2009 *S*, *F*, *A*, *NZ*, 2010 *SA*
D **Scaglia** 1994 *R*, *W*, 1995 *S*, 1996 *W*, *A*, 1999 *W*
E **Scalzotto** 1974 *Mid*, *Sus*, *Oxo*
A **Scanavacca** 1999 *Ur*, 2001 *E*, 2002 *Sp*, *R*, 2004 *US*, 2006 *Ar*, *C*, 2007 *F*, *E*, *S*, *I*
R **Sciacol** 1965 *Cze*
I **Scodavolpe** 1954 *Sp*
F **Screnci** 1977 *Cze*, *R*, *Sp*, 1978 *F*, 1979 *Pol*, *R*, *E*, 1982 *F*, 1984 *Mor*
A **Selvaggio** 1973 *Rho*, *WTv*, *ETv*, *Leo*, *FS*, *Tva*
F **Semenzato** 2011 *E*, *W*, *F*, *S*, *A*, *US*, *I*, 2012 *F*, *E*, *I*, *W*
M **Sepe** 2006 *J*, *Fj*, 2010 *SA*
D **Sesenna** 1992 *R*, 1993 *Cro*, *Mor*, *F*, 1994 *R*
G **Sessa** 1930 *Sp*
G **Sessi** 1942 *R*
A **Sgarbi** 2008 *E*, *W*, 2009 *A*, *A*, *SA*, 2010 *Ar*, *A*, *Fj*, 2011 *I*, *E*, *W*, *S*, *J*, *Rus*, 2012 *F*, *I*, *W*, *Ar*, *C*, *US*, *Tg*, *NZ*, *A*, 2013 *F*, *SA*, *S*, *A*, 2014 *W*, *Fj*
E **Sgorbati** 1933 *Cze*, 1934 *Cat*, *R*, 1935 *Cat*, *F*, 1936 *Ger*, 1937 *Ger*, 1938 *Ger*, 1939 *Ger*, 1940 *R*, *Ger*, 1942 *R*
E **Sgorbati** 1968 *WGe*, *Yug*
A **Sgorlon** 1993 *Pt*, *Mor*, *Sp*, *F*, *Rus*, *F*, *S*, 1994 *CZR*, *R*, *W*, 1995 *S*, *E*, *Ar*, *F*, *Ar*, *R*, *NZ*, *SA*, 1996 *W*, *Pt*, *W*, *A*, *E*, *S*, 1997 *I*, *F*, *F*, *Ar*, *R*, *SA*, *I*, 1998 *S*, *W*, *Rus*, 1999 *F*, *S*, *W*
P **Sguario** 1958 *R*, 1959 *F*, 1960 *Ger*, *F*, 1961 *Ger*, 1962 *R*
M **Silini** 1955 *Ger*, *Sp*, *F*, *Cze*, 1956 *Cze*, 1957 *Ger*, 1958 *F*, 1959 *F*
S **Silvestri** 1954 *F*
U **Silvestri** 1949 *F*, *Cze*
U **Silvestri** 1967 *R*, *Pt*, 1968 *Pt*, *WGe*
L **Simonelli** 1956 *Ger*, *F*, *Cze*, 1958 *F*, 1960 *Ger*, *F*

# JAPAN

## JAPAN'S 2013–14 TEST RECORD

| OPPONENTS | DATE | VENUE | RESULT |
|---|---|---|---|
| New Zealand | Nov 2 | H | Lost 6–54 |
| Scotland | Nov 9 | A | Lost 42–17 |
| Russia | Nov 16 | N | Won 40–13 |
| Spain | Nov 23 | A | Won 40–7 |
| Philippines | May 3 | A | Won 99–10 |
| Sri Lanka | May 10 | H | Won 132–10 |
| Korea | May 17 | A | Won 62–5 |
| Hong Kong | May 25 | H | Won 49–8 |
| Samoa | May 30 | H | Won 33–14 |
| Canada | Jun 7 | A | Won 34–25 |
| USA | Jun 14 | A | Won 37–29 |
| Italy | Jun 21 | H | Won 26–23 |

# BRAVE BLOSSOMS BREAK INTO WORLD'S TOP 10

## By Rich Freeman

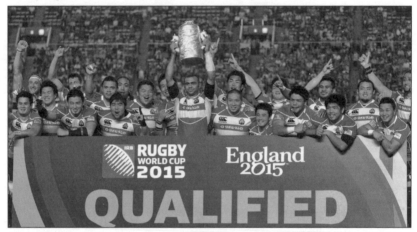

Japan celebrate after beating Hong Kong to win the Asian 5 Nations and qualify for Rugby World Cup 2015.

**Japan's international year** started on a low with head coach Eddie Jones hospitalised, but it finished with him restored to full fitness and the Brave Blossoms putting together a record-breaking 10-match winning streak.

Japan came into the 2013–14 season on the back of an historic win over Wales. And even though their first Test was against world champions New Zealand, hopes were high the side could put in a performance that showed they were ready to break into the world's top 10. However, two weeks before the All Blacks were due to arrive in Tokyo, disaster struck with Jones rushed to hospital after suffering a stroke. The Rugby World Cup 2007 winner would remain in hospital for 40 days with Scott Wisemantel taking over as interim head coach.

Quite how the off-field drama affected the team is debatable. The Brave Blossoms started well before a sold-out Prince Chichibu Memorial Rugby Stadium, taking a scrum against the head early on. But in the end the All Blacks were too strong, running in eight tries in a 54–6 win. Jones later admitted that Japan seemed to have frozen and didn't try to play their normal attacking game.

Japan's subsequent tour of Europe began in Edinburgh and although it ended in a 42–17 defeat to Scotland, two tries from Kenki Fukuoka gave glimpses of what the team had to offer. Unfortunately the Brave Blossoms' nemesis – the restarts – was to be their downfall again, most notably when they had made it an 18–17 game early in the second half. "We can take a lot of positives," Wisemantel said afterwards. "We came to attack and run the ball. But our game tempo and control at certain stages let us down."

Following a midweek loss to Gloucester, that allowed Wisemantel to see – somewhat unsuccessfully in some cases – what kind of depth the squad had, the Brave Blossoms headed to North Wales to take on Russia. Despite giving away an early intercept try, Japan were too strong for the Russians with Male Sa'u scoring two of the Brave Blossoms' five tries in a 40–13 win.

Having played three games in six days in Scotland, England and Wales, Wisemantel and his squad then headed for Madrid, where, perhaps unsurprisingly, they started slowly against Spain. But spurred on by their forwards, Toshiaki Hirose and his side finally kicked into gear in the second half, scoring four unanswered tries to secure a 40–7 victory.

A busy month ended with good news as Jones was released from hospital, vowing to return to the national side in the spring once his recovery was complete. His first game back in charge saw a Japan XV lose to the Asia Pacific Dragons, but the team's whole focus was on the Asian 5 Nations, which this year also served as the final Asian qualifying tournament for Rugby World Cup 2015. Japan's opening game was played an hour south of Manila, and it took Hendrik Tui just 35 seconds to get the scoreboard ticking over. The Philippines fought back to lead 10–7 but that was as good as it got for the Volcanoes as Japan ran in a further 14 tries.

A week later it was Sri Lanka who felt the force of Japan's attacking prowess as the Brave Blossoms crossed 20 times in a 132–10 victory, the third highest score and third biggest winning margin in Japan Test match history.

The records kept following a week later as Ayumu Goromaru kicked seven conversions and a penalty in a 62–5 win over Korea, the 17-point haul allowing Goromaru to pass Keiji Hirose as the leading points scorer in Japan Test history, and help set up a winner-takes-all clash with Hong Kong.

The game with Hong Kong was the last ever sporting event to be played at Tokyo's National Stadium, the venue of the 1964 Olympics. A new venue is set to be completed by the opening game of Rugby World Cup 2019 and the Brave Blossoms ensured it was a farewell to remember, the 49–8 victory securing a place alongside South Africa, Samoa, Scotland and USA in Pool B.

Yoshikazu Fujita grabbed a hat-trick of tries as Japan claimed their seventh straight Asian 5 Nations title with their 28th consecutive bonus-point win in the competition.

A weakened Samoa side was then dispatched 33–14 a week later as Japan posted a record seventh straight win and ensured Hitoshi Ono, who became his nation's most capped player with 82 Tests, had a night to truly remember.

The Hong Kong game had seen Wisemantel bid sayonara to the side; he was replaced by Leigh Jones, formerly head coach of Hong Kong. Former England captain Steve Borthwick also joined the coaching staff and with them on board Japan headed to North America to play Canada and the United States in the revamped IRB Pacific Nations Cup.

Canada were dispatched 34–25 in a remarkable game that had seen the hosts lead 25–9 at the break. But with the forwards providing plenty of possession, Fujita, Yu Tamura and Tui all crossed in the second half to hand Japan their first win in Canada in 28 years.

A week later, first-half tries from Fumiaki Tanaka and Akihito Yamada and a brace from Ryu Koliniasi Holani saw Jones' men down the US Eagles 37–29 to top their Pacific Nations Cup conference.

The year finished with the visit of Italy to Tokyo, and the Brave Blossoms never looked like losing, despite the 26–23 scoreline, which saw them break into the top 10 for the first time since the IRB World Rankings were introduced in October 2003. The scrum laid the foundations for the win, testament to the work put in by former France hooker Marc Dal Maso. Yamada and Sa'u both crossed the whitewash while Goromaru added four penalties and two conversions.

Jones said he hoped the result would lead to even greater things. "I want to go to the World Cup and make the quarter-finals and in the process I want us to become the most popular sporting team in Japan," he said.

On the domestic front, the arrival of former Wallaby Berrick Barnes and the occasional coaching input of Robbie Deans (who will take over as head coach next season) saw Panasonic Wild Knights to a league and cup double.

League MVP Barnes helped the Wild Knights beat Suntory Sungoliath 45–22 to claim the Top League title before they downed Toshiba Brave Lupus 30–21 in the All-Japan Championship.

# JAPAN INTERNATIONAL STATISTICS

## MATCH RECORDS UP TO 13 OCTOBER 2014

### WINNING MARGIN

| Date | Opponent | Result | Winning Margin |
|------|----------|--------|----------------|
| 06/07/2002 | Chinese Taipei | 155–3 | 152 |
| 27/10/1998 | Chinese Taipei | 134–6 | 128 |
| 10/05/2014 | Sri Lanka | 132–10 | 122 |
| 20/04/2013 | Philippines | 121–0 | 121 |
| 21/07/2002 | Chinese Taipei | 120–3 | 117 |

### MOST POINTS IN A MATCH
#### BY THE TEAM

| Date | Opponent | Result | Points |
|------|----------|--------|--------|
| 06/07/2002 | Chinese Taipei | 155–3 | 155 |
| 27/10/1998 | Chinese Taipei | 134–6 | 134 |
| 10/05/2014 | Sri Lanka | 132–10 | 132 |
| 20/04/2013 | Philippines | 121–0 | 121 |
| 21/07/2002 | Chinese Taipei | 120–3 | 120 |

#### BY A PLAYER

| Date | Player | Opponent | Points |
|------|--------|----------|--------|
| 21/07/2002 | Toru Kurihara | Chinese Taipei | 60 |
| 06/07/2002 | Daisuke Ohata | Chinese Taipei | 40 |
| 10/05/2014 | Ayumu Goromaru | Sri Lanka | 37 |
| 20/04/2013 | Ayumu Goromaru | Philippines | 36 |
| 16/06/2002 | Toru Kurihara | Korea | 35 |

### MOST TRIES IN A MATCH
#### BY THE TEAM

| Date | Opponent | Result | Tries |
|------|----------|--------|-------|
| 06/07/2002 | Chinese Taipei | 155–3 | 23 |
| 27/10/1998 | Chinese Taipei | 134–6 | 20 |
| 10/05/2014 | Sri Lanka | 132–10 | 20 |
| | 18 on 3 occasions | | |

#### BY A PLAYER

| Date | Player | Opponent | Tries |
|------|--------|----------|-------|
| 06/07/2002 | Daisuke Ohata | Chinese Taipei | 8 |
| 21/07/2002 | Toru Kurihara | Chinese Taipei | 6 |
| 08/05/2005 | Daisuke Ohata | Hong Kong | 6 |
| 05/05/2012 | Yoshikazu Fujita | United Arab Emirates | 6 |

### MOST CONVERSIONS IN A MATCH
#### BY THE TEAM

| Date | Opponent | Result | Cons |
|------|----------|--------|------|
| 06/07/2002 | Chinese Taipei | 155–3 | 20 |
| 27/10/1998 | Chinese Taipei | 134–6 | 17 |
| 10/05/2014 | Sri Lanka | 132–10 | 16 |
| 21/07/2002 | Chinese Taipei | 120–3 | 15 |
| 20/04/2013 | Philippines | 121–0 | 14 |

#### BY A PLAYER

| Date | Player | Opponent | Cons |
|------|--------|----------|------|
| 10/05/2014 | Ayumu Goromaru | Sri Lanka | 16 |
| 21/07/2002 | Toru Kurihara | Chinese Taipei | 15 |
| 20/04/2013 | Ayumu Goromaru | Philippines | 14 |
| | 12 on 3 occasions | | |

### MOST PENALTIES IN A MATCH
#### BY THE TEAM

| Date | Opponent | Result | Pens |
|------|----------|--------|------|
| 08/05/1999 | Tonga | 44–17 | 9 |
| 08/04/1990 | Tonga | 28–16 | 6 |
| 23/11/2013 | Spain | 40–7 | 6 |

#### BY A PLAYER

| Date | Player | Opponent | Pens |
|------|--------|----------|------|
| 08/05/1999 | Keiji Hirose | Tonga | 9 |
| 08/04/1990 | Takahiro Hosokawa | Tonga | 6 |
| 23/11/2013 | Ayumu Goromaru | Spain | 6 |

### MOST DROP GOALS IN A MATCH
#### BY THE TEAM

| Date | Opponent | Result | DGs |
|------|----------|--------|-----|
| 15/09/1998 | Argentina | 44–29 | 2 |

#### BY A PLAYER

| Date | Player | Opponent | DGs |
|------|--------|----------|-----|
| 15/09/1998 | Kensuke Iwabuchi | Argentina | 2 |

JAPAN

| MOST CAPPED PLAYERS | |
|---|---|
| Name | Caps |
| Hitoshi Ono | 85 |
| Hirotoki Onozawa | 81 |
| Yukio Motoki | 79 |
| Takashi Kikutani | 68 |
| Takeomi Ito | 62 |

| LEADING PENALTY SCORERS | |
|---|---|
| Name | Pens |
| Keiji Hirose | 76 |
| Ayumu Goromaru | 58 |
| Toru Kurihara | 35 |
| James Arlidge | 28 |
| Takahiro Hosokawa | 24 |

| LEADING TRY SCORERS | |
|---|---|
| Name | Tries |
| Daisuke Ohata | 69 |
| Hirotoki Onozawa | 55 |
| Takashi Kikutani | 33 |
| Terunori Masuho | 28 |
| Yoshikazu Fujita | 22 |

| LEADING DROP GOAL SCORERS | |
|---|---|
| Name | DGs |
| Kyohei Morita | 5 |

| LEADING POINTS SCORERS | |
|---|---|
| Name | Points |
| Ayumu Goromaru | 510 |
| Keiji Hirose | 413 |
| Toru Kurihara | 347 |
| Daisuke Ohata | 345 |
| James Arlidge | 286 |
| Hirotoki Onozawa | 275 |

| LEADING CONVERSIONS SCORERS | |
|---|---|
| Name | Cons |
| Ayumua Goromaru | 128 |
| James Arlidge | 78 |
| Keiji Hirose | 77 |
| Toru Kurihara | 71 |
| Ryan Nicholas | 53 |

# JAPAN INTERNATIONAL PLAYERS
## UP TO 13 OCTOBER 2014

**T Adachi** 1932 *C, C*
**M Aizawa** 1984 *Kor*, 1986 *US, C, S, E, Kor*, 1987 *A, NZ, NZ*, 1988 *OU, Kor*
**H Akama** 1973 *F*, 1975 *A, W*, 1976 *S, E, It, Kor*, 1977 *S*
**T Akatsuka** 1994 *Fj*, 1995 *Tg, NZ*, 1996 *Kor*, 2005 *Sp*, 2006 *HK, Kor*
**J Akune** 2001 *W, C*
**M Amino** 2000 *Kor, C*, 2003 *Rus, AuA, Kor, E, E, S, Fj, US*
**E Ando** 2006 *AG, Kor, Geo, Tg, Sa, JAB, Fj*, 2007 *HK, Fj, Tg, Sa, JAB, It*
**D Anglesey** 2002 *Tg, Tai, Tai*
**T Aoi** 1959 *BCo, BCo, OCC*, 1963 *BCo*
**S Aoki** 1989 *S*, 1990 *Fj*, 1991 *US, C*, 1993 *W*
**Y Aoki** 2007 *Kor, AuA, JAB*, 2008 *Kor, Kaz, HK, AuA, Tg, Fj, Sa, US, US*, 2009 *Kaz, Sin, Sa, JAB, Tg, Fj*, 2011 *Sa, Tg, US, NZ*, 2013 *PHP, HK, Kor, UAE, Tg, Fj, NZ, S*
**S Arai** 1959 *BCo, BCo*
**R Arita** 2012 *Kaz, UAE, Kor, HK, Fj, Tg, Sa*
**JA Arlidge** 2007 *Kor*, 2008 *Kor, AG, Kaz, HK, AuA, Tg, Fj, M, Sa*, 2009 *Sa, JAB, Tg, Fj, C, C*, 2010 *Kor, AG, Kaz, HK, Fj, Sa, Tg, Sa, Rus*, 2011 *Kaz, UAE, Tg, It, F, Tg, C*
**G Aruga** 2006 *HK, Kor*, 2007 *Kor, HK, AuA, Sa, JAB, Fj, C*, 2008 *Kor, HK*, 2009 *C, C*, 2011 *UAE, Fj*, 2012 *R, Geo*
**K Aruga** 1974 *NZU*, 1975 *A, A, W, W*, 1976 *S, E, It, Kor*
**T Asahara** 2013 *PHP, HK, Kor, UAE, Fj*

**R Asano** 2003 *AuA, AuA, F, Fj*, 2005 *Ar, HK, Kor, R, C, I, I, Sp*, 2006 *Kor, Geo, Tg, It, HK, Kor*, 2007 *Kor, It, W*
**M Atokawa** 1969 *HK*, 1970 *Tha, BCo*, 1971 *E, E*
**H Atou** 1976 *BCo*

**T Baba** 1932 *C*
**GTM Bachop** 1999 *C, Tg, Sa, Fj, Sp, Sa, W, Ar*
**I Basiyalo** 1997 *HK, US, US, C, HK*
**D Bickle** 1996 *HK, HK, C, US, US, C*
**M Broadhurst** 2012 *R, Geo*, 2013 *PHP, HK, Kor, UAE, Tg, Fj, W, W, C, US, NZ, S, Rus, Sp*

**KCC Chang** 1930 *BCo*, 1932 *C, C*
**T Chiba** 1930 *BCo*
**M Chida** 1980 *Kor*, 1982 *HK, C, C, Kor*, 1983 *W*, 1984 *F, F, Kor*, 1985 *US, I, I, F, F*, 1986 *US, C, S, E, Kor*, 1987 *US, E*

**H Daimon** 2004 *S, W*

**K Endo** 2004 *It*, 2006 *AG, Kor, Geo, Tg, It, JAB, Fj*, 2007 *HK, Fj, Tg, Sa, JAB, It, Fj, W, C*, 2008 *AuA, Tg, Fj, M, US, US*, 2009 *C, C*, 2010 *Kor, AG, Kaz, HK, Fj, Sa, Tg*, 2011 *Sa, Rus*, 2011 *UAE, Sa, Tg, It, F, Tg, C*
**J Enomoto** 2005 *Sp*
**R Enomoto** 1959 *BCo, BCo*

K Matsubara 1930 *BCo*
T Matsubara 1932 *C, C*
Y Matsubara 2004 *Kor, Rus, C, It,* 2005 *Sp,* 2006 *AG, Kor, Geo, Tg, It, Sa, JAB, Fj, Kor,* 2007 *Kor, Fj, Tg, Sa, JAB, It, Fj, W, C*
T Matsuda 1992 *HK,* 1993 *W,* 1994 *Fj, HK, Kor,* 1995 *Tg, R, W, I, NZ,* 1996 *HK, HK, C, US, US, C, Kor,* 1998 *US, HK, HK, US, C, Ar, Kor, Tai, HK, Kor,* 1999 *C, Fj, US, Sp, Sa, Ar,* 2001 *Kor, Tai, W,* 2003 *US, AuA, Kor, E, S, Fj, US*
J Matsumoto 1977 *S,* 1978 *F,* 1980 *H,* 1982 *C, C*
T Matsunaga 1985 *F, F*
Y Matsunobu 1963 *BCo*
H Matsuo 2003 *AuA, AuA, Kor, E, E*
K Matsuo 1986 *US, C, S, E, Kor,* 1987 *E, NZ,* 1988 *Kor,* 1990 *Tg, Kor, Sa, US,* 1991 *US, HK, S, I, Z,* 1993 *Ar,* 1994 *Fj, Fj, HK,* 1995 *Tg*
Y Matsuo 1974 *SL,* 1976 *BCo, E, It, Kor,* 1977 *S,* 1979 *HK, E, E,* 1982 *HK, C, C,* 1983 *OCC, W,* 1984 *F, F, Kor*
S Matsuoka 1963 *BCo,* 1970 *Tha*
K Matsushima 2014 *PHP, SL, Kor, Sa*
K Matsushita 2008 *US, US,* 2010 *AG, HK, Fj, Sa, Tg*
F Mau 2004 *Rus, C, It, S, R, W*
AF McCormick 1996 *HK, HK, US,* 1997 *HK, C, US, US, C, HK,* 1998 *C, US, HK, Ar, Kor, Tai, HK,* 1999 *C, Tg, Sa, Fj, US, Sp, Sa, W, Ar*
M Mikami 2013 *PHP, HK, UAE, Tg, Fj, W, W, C, US, NZ, S, Rus, Sp,* 2014 *PHP, SL, Kor, HK, Sa, C, US, It*
R Miki 1999 *Sp,* 2002 *Tg, Tai, Kor, Tai, Kor,* 2004 *S, R, W*
A Miller 2002 *Rus, Kor, Tai, Kor, Tai,* 2003 *Kor, S, F, Fj, US*
S Miln 1998 *C, US, HK, HK, US*
Y Minamikawa 1976 *BCo,* 1978 *F, Kor,* 1979 *HK, E, E,* 1980 *H, F, Kor,* 1982 *HK, C, C, Kor*
M Mishima 1930 *BCo,* 1932 *C, C*
T Miuchi 2002 *Rus, Kor, Kor, Tai, Kor,* 2003 *US, Rus, AuA, Kor, E, E, S, F, Fj, US,* 2004 *Rus, C, It, S, R, W,* 2005 *Ur, Ar, HK, Kor, R, C, I, I,* 2006 *HK, Kor,* 2007 *Kor, HK, Fj, Tg, Sa, It, Fj, W, C,* 2008 *Kor, AG, Kaz, HK, AuA, Tg, Fj, Sa*
S Miura 1963 *BCo*
K Miyai 1959 *BCo, BCo,* 1963 *BCo*
K Miyaji 1969 *HK*
K Miyajima 1959 *BCo, BCo*
H Miyaji-Yoshizawa 1930 *BCo*
T Miyake 2005 *Sp,* 2006 *Sa, JAB, Fj*
K Miyamoto 1986 *S, E,* 1987 *US, E, A,* 1988 *Kor,* 1991 *I*
K Miyata 1971 *E, E,* 1972 *HK*
M Miyauchi 1975 *W,* 1976 *It, Kor*
K Mizobe 1997 *C*
K Mizoguchi 1997 *C*
K Mizube 1997 *HK*
H Mizuno 2004 *R,* 2005 *HK, Kor, R, C, I,* 2006 *AG, Geo, Tg, It, Sa, JAB*
M Mizutani 1970 *Tha,* 1971 *E*
N Mizuyama 2008 *Tg, M, Sa, US*
Y Mochizuki 2012 *Kaz, UAE, Kor, HK, Fj, Tg, Sa*
S Mori 1974 *NZU, SL,* 1975 *A, A, W, W,* 1976 *BCo, S, E, It, Kor,* 1977 *S,* 1978 *F,* 1979 *HK, E, E, CU,* 1980 *NZU, H, F, Kor,* 1981 *AuUn*
K Morikawa 2012 *UAE*
K Morioka 1982 *Kor*
K Morita 2004 *C, It,* 2005 *Ur, Ar, Kor, R, C, I*
A Moriya 2006 *Tg, It, Sa, JAB, Fj,* 2008 *AG, Kaz*
Y Motoki 1991 *US, US, C,* 1992 *HK,* 1993 *Ar, Ar,* 1994 *Fj, Fj, Kor,* 1995 *Tg, Tg, R, W, I, NZ,* 1996 *HK, HK, C, US, US, C, Kor,* 1997 *HK, C, US, US, C, HK,* 1998 *C, US, HK, HK, US, C, Ar, Kor, HK, Kor,* 1999 *C, Tg, Sa, Fj, US, Sp, Sa, W, Ar,* 2001 *W, W, Sa, C,* 2002 *Rus, Tg, Kor, Tai, Kor, Tai, Kor,* 2003 *US, Rus, C, It, S, R, W,* 2005 *Ur, Ar, HK, Kor, R, C, I, I*
K Motoyoshi 2001 *Tai*
S Mukai 1985 *I, I, F,* 1986 *US, C, E, Kor,* 1987 *US, A, NZ, NZ*
M Mukoyama 2004 *Kor, C, It, S, R, W*
K Muraguchi 1976 *S, Kor*
D Murai 1985 *I, I, F, F,* 1987 *E*
D Murata 2014 *PHP, SL*

K Murata 1963 *BCo*
W Murata 1991 *US, S,* 1995 *Tg, NZ,* 1996 *HK, HK, C, US, US, C, Kor,* 1997 *HK, C, US, US, HK,* 1998 *HK, HK, US, C, Ar, Kor, Kor,* 1999 *US, W,* 2001 *W, W, Sa,* 2002 *Rus, Tg, Kor, Tai, Kor, Tai,* 2003 *US, AuA, E,* 2005 *Ur, Ar, Kor, I, I*
Y Murata 1971 *E, E,* 1972 *HK,* 1973 *W,* 1974 *NZU, SL*

Y Nagae 2012 *Kaz, UAE, Kor, HK, Fj, Tg, Sa, R, Geo,* 2013 *W, W, C, US, NZ, S,* 2014 *PHP, SL*
M Nagai 1988 *Kor*
Y Nagatomo 2010 *Kor, AG, Kaz,* 2012 *Kaz, UAE, Kor, HK, Fj, Sa*
Y Nagatomo 1993 *W,* 1994 *Fj, HK,* 1995 *Tg,* 1996 *US, US,* 1997 *C*
T Naito 1934 *AuUn*
M Nakabayashi 2005 *HK, Kor, R, I*
T Nakai 2005 *Ur, HK, C, I, I, Sp,* 2006 *AG, Kor, Geo, Tg, It, Fj*
T Nakamichi 1996 *HK, HK, US, US, C,* 1998 *Ar, Kor,* 1999 *C, Sa, Fj, Sp, W, Ar,* 2000 *Fj, US, Tg*
N Nakamura 1998 *C, US, HK, HK, US, C, Ar, Kor, Tai, HK, Kor,* 1999 *C, Tg, Sa, Fj, US, Sp, W, Ar,* 2000 *I*
R Nakamura 2013 *UAE,* 2014 *PHP, Kor, Sa*
S Nakamura 2009 *Kaz, Sin,* 2010 *AG, Kaz, HK, Fj*
S Nakashima 1989 *S,* 1990 *Fj, Tg, Kor, Sa, US,* 1991 *US, US, C, HK, S*
T Nakayama 1976 *BCo,* 1978 *F,* 1979 *E,* 1980 *H,* 1982 *C, C*
Y Nakayama 2008 *Kor, AG, Kaz, HK, Tg, M,* 2009 *HK, Kor, Sin, Tg, Fj*
H Namba 2000 *Fj, US, Tg, Sa, Kor, C, I,* 2001 *Tai, W, W, C,* 2002 *Rus, Tg, Kor, Tai, Kor,* 2003 *US, Rus, AuA, AuA, Kor, E, E, F*
RT Nicholas 2008 *Kor, Kaz, HK, AuA, Tg, Fj, Sa, US, US,* 2009 *HK, Kor, Sa, JAB, Tg, Fj, C, C,* 2010 *Kor, Kaz, HK, Fj, Sa, Tg, Sa, Rus,* 2011 *HK, UAE, Sa, Tg, Fj, It, US, F, Tg, C,* 2012 *Fj, Tg, Sa*
H Nishida 1994 *Fj*
S Nishigaki 1932 *C, C*
T Nishiura 2004 *W,* 2006 *HK, Kor,* 2007 *Kor, Fj, Tg, Sa, It, Fj, W, C,* 2008 *Kor, HK, AuA, Tg, Fj, Sa*
H Nishizumi 1963 *BCo*
M Niwa 1932 *C*
I Nogami 1932 *C,* 1936 *NZU*
T Nozawa 2000 *Tg, Sa, Kor, C*

M Oda 2000 *US, Tg, Sa, Kor, I*
H Ogasawara 1969 *HK,* 1970 *Tha, BCo,* 1971 *E, E,* 1973 *F,* 1974 *NZU,* 1975 *A, A, W, W,* 1976 *NZU,* 1977 *S*
K Oguchi 1997 *US, C, HK,* 1998 *Tai,* 1999 *Sa, Ar,* 2000 *Fj, Tg, Sa, Kor*
K Ohara 1998 *Kor, Tai,* 2000 *Kor, C, I*
D Ohata 1996 *Kor,* 1997 *HK, C, US,* 1998 *HK, C, Ar, Kor, HK,* 1999 *C, Tg, Sa, Fj, US, Sp, Sa, W, Ar,* 2000 *Fj, US, Kor, C, I,* 2002 *Rus, Kor, Tai, Kor, Tai, Kor,* 2003 *US, Rus, AuA, AuA, Kor, E, E, S, F, Fj, US,* 2004 *Kor, Rus, C, It,* 2005 *Ur, Ar, HK, Kor, R, C, I, I,* 2006 *AG, Kor, Geo, Tg, HK, Kor*
K Ohigashi 1973 *W, F,* 1974 *NZU, SL*
K Ohigashi 2004 *Kor, Rus, C,* 2007 *Kor, HK, AuA, JAB*
K Ohotsuka 1959 *BCo*
S Oikawa 1980 *H*
E Okabe 1963 *BCo,* 1967 *NZU*
Y Okada 1932 *C, C*
M Okidoi 1987 *A, NZ, NZ*
N Okubo 1999 *Tg, Sa, Fj, US, Sp, Sa, W, Ar,* 2000 *Fj, US, Tg, Sa, Kor, C,* 2002 *Rus, Tg, Kor, Tai, Kor, Tai,* 2003 *US, Rus, S, F, Fj, US,* 2004 *S, R, W*
T Omata 1970 *NZU, BCo, NZU*
S Onishi 2000 *Fj, US, Tg, Sa, Kor, C,* 2001 *Kor, Tai, W, C,* 2005 *Sp,* 2006 *AG, Kor, Geo, Tg, It, JAB, HK, Kor,* 2007 *HK, Tg, AuA, Sa, JAB, It, Fj, W, C,* 2008 *Kor, AG, HK, M, Sa*
H Ono 2004 *Kor, Rus, C, S,* 2005 *Ar, Kor, I,* 2006 *Kor, Geo, It, Sa, JAB, Fj, HK, Kor,* 2007 *Kor, Fj, Tg, Sa, JAB, It, Fj, W, C,* 2008 *Kor, AG, AuA, Tg, Fj, US,* 2009 *HK, Sin, Sa, JAB, Tg, C, C,* 2010 *Kor, Kaz, HK, Fj, Sa, Tg, Sa, Rus,*

HK, 1999 Sa, Fj, US, Sp, Sa, W, Ar, 2000 Fj, US, Tg, Sa, Kor, C, I, 2001 Kor, Tai, W, W, Sa, C, 2002 Kor, 2003 AuA, E, F

**J Tarrant** 2009 Kaz, HK, Kor, Sa, JAB, Tg, Fj

**H Tatekawa** 2012 Kaz, UAE, Kor, HK, Fj, Tg, Sa, R, Geo, 2013 PHP, HK, Kor, UAE, Tg, Fj, W, W, C, US, NZ, 2014 Kor, HK, Sa, C, US, It

**M Tatsukawa** 2000 Sa

**T Taufa** 2009 Kaz, Kor, Sin, Sa, JAB, Tg, Fj, C, C, 2010 Kor, AG, Kaz, HK, Fj, Sa, Tg, Sa, 2011 HK, Kaz, UAE, SL, C

**N Taumoefolau** 1985 F, F, 1986 US, C, S, E, Kor, 1987 US, E, A, NZ, 1988 Kor, 1989 S, 1990 Fj

**T Terai** 1969 HK, 1970 Tha, 1971 E, E, 1972 HK, 1973 W, F, 1974 NZU, 1975 A, W, W, 1976 S, E, It, Kor

**S Teramura** 1930 BCo

**LM Thompson** 2007 HK, Fj, Tg, Sa, JAB, It, Fj, W, C, 2008 M, Sa, US, US, 2009 Kaz, Kor, Sa, Tg, Fj, 2010 Kor, AG, Kaz, HK, Fj, Sa, Tg, Sa, Rus, 2011 HK, Kaz, SL, Sa, Tg, It, US, F, Tg, C, 2012 R, Geo, 2013 NZ, S, Rus, Sp, 2014 HK, Sa, C, US, It

**R Thompson** 1998 C, US, HK, HK, US, C

**Z Toba-Nakajima** 1930 BCo, 1932 C

**K Todd** 2000 Fj, Sa, I

**H Tominaga** 1959 BCo, BCo

**K Tomioka** 2008 US, US, 2009 Kor, Sin, Sa, JAB

**T Tomioka** 2005 I, I

**T Toshi** 1932 C, C

**H Toshima** 1980 H, F, 1982 HK, C, C, 1984 F, F, Kor

**M Toyoda** 2008 US

**N Toyoda** 1982 HK

**S Toyoda** 1974 SL

**T Toyoda** 1978 Kor

**M Toyota** 2009 Sin, Sa, Tg, Fj, 2010 Kor, AG, Kaz, HK

**K Toyoyama** 1976 BCo, 1979 E, E, 1980 H

**M Toyoyama** 2000 Fj, US, Sa, C, 2001 Kor, W, W, Sa, C, 2002 Rus, Kor, Tai, Kor, Tai, 2003 US, Rus, AuA, Kor, E, E, S, Fj, US

**H Tsuboi** 2012 Kaz, UAE

**M Tsuchida** 1985 F

**T Tsuchiya** 1956 AuUn, 1959 BCo, BCo

**E Tsuji** 1980 Kor, 1982 Kor

**T Tsuji** 2003 S, Fj, US, 2005 HK, R, C, 2006 Kor

**Y Tsujimoto** 2001 Kor

**K Tsukagoshi** 2002 Kor, 2005 Ur, Ar, HK, Kor, R, C, I, I

**S Tsukda** 2001 Kor, C, 2002 Tg, Tai, Kor, Tai, Kor, 2003 AuA, E

**T Tsuyama** 1976 BCo, Kor

**H Tui** 2012 Tg, Sa, R, Geo, 2013 PHP, HK, Kor, UAE, Tg, Fj, W, W, C, US, NZ, S, Rus, Sp, 2014 PHP, SL, HK, Sa, C, US, It

**P Tuidraki** 1997 HK, C, 1998 C, US, HK, HK, US, C, Tai, 1999 Tg, Sa, Fj, Sa, W, Ar, 2000 I, 2001 Tai, W, W

**A Tupuailai** 2009 C, C, 2010 Kor, AG, Kaz, HK, Fj, Sa, Tg, Sa, Rus, 2011 HK, Kaz, SL, It, US, F, NZ, Tg, C

**K Uchida** 2012 Kaz, UAE, 2013 UAE, Fj, 2014 PHP, SL, Kor, HK

**M Uchida** 1969 HK

**A Ueda** 1975 W, 1978 Kor, 1979 E, E

**T Ueda** 2011 HK, Kaz, UAE, SL, US, NZ

**S Ueki** 1963 BCo

**R Ueno** 2011 SL

**N Ueyama** 1973 F, 1974 NZU, SL, 1975 A, A, W, W, 1976 BCo, E, It, Kor, 1978 F, 1980 Kor

**H Ujino** 1976 BCo, 1977 S, 1978 F, Kor, 1979 HK, E, E, 1980 H, Kor, 1982 HK, Kor

**R Umei** 1958 NZ23, NZ23, NZ23

**Y Uryu** 2000 Sa, 2001 Kor

**T Usuzuki** 2011 UAE, SL, Sa, Fj, It, US, NZ

**S Vatuvei** 2010 Kor, AG, Kaz, Sa, 2011 US, NZ, Tg, C

**K Wada** 1997 HK, US, US, C, HK

**K Wada** 2010 AG, Kaz, Fj, Tg, Rus

**S Wada** 1930 BCo

**T Wada** 1975 A, 1976 S, 1979 E, E

**J Washington** 2005 Ur, Ar, HK, Kor, R, C, I

**M Washiya** 2000 Kor, C

**H Watanabe** 1990 Sa

**T Watanabe** 2002 Kor

**Y Watanabe** 1996 HK, HK, 1998 C, US, HK, HK, Ar, Kor, Tai, HK, 1999 C, Tg, US, Sp, Sa, 2000 Fj, US, I, 2003 Rus, AuA, AuA, E, S, 2004 Kor, 2005 HK, R, C, 2007 HK, Fj, Tg, Sa, JAB, A, W

**SJ Webb** 2008 AG, Kaz, HK, AuA, Tg, Fj, M, US, US, 2009 Kaz, Kor, Sa, Tg, Fj, C, C, 2010 Kor, Kaz, HK, Fj, Sa, Tg, 2011 HK, Kaz, UAE, SL, Sa, Tg, Fj, It, US, F, NZ, Tg, C

**IM Williams** 1993 W

**MC Williams** 2011 Sa, Fj, US, F, NZ, C

**C Wing** 2013 UAE, Fj, W, W, US, NZ, S

**T Yagai** 1930 BCo

**T Yajima** 1978 Kor, 1979 E

**A Yamada** 2013 Rus, Sp, 2014 SL, Kor, HK, Sa, C, US, It

**K Yamada** 1963 BCo

**K Yamaguchi** 1936 NZU

**T Yamaguchi** 2004 S, R, W

**Y Yamaguchi** 1970 Tha, BCo, 1971 E, E, 1972 HK

**E Yamamoto** 2001 Kor, W, 2002 Tg, Kor

**I Yamamoto** 1973 W

**M Yamamoto** 2002 Rus, Kor, Tai, Kor, 2003 Rus, AuA, AuA, Kor, E, E, Fj, US, 2004 Kor, Rus, C, S, R, W, 2006 Sa, JAB, Fj, 2007 HK, Fj, AuA, JAB, A

**M Yamamoto** 2004 C, S, W, 2006 HK, Kor, 2007 HK, Fj, Tg, AuA, Sa

**T Yamamoto** 1988 Kor, 1989 S, 1990 Fj

**R Yamamura** 2001 W, 2002 Tg, Tai, Tai, 2003 AuA, F, 2004 Kor, Rus, C, It, S, R, W, 2005 Ur, Ar, HK, Kor, R, C, I, I, Sp, 2006 Kor, Geo, It, Sa, JAB, Fj, HK, Kor, 2007 Kor, Tg, AuA, Sa, JAB, It, A, Fj, W, C

**R Yamanaka** 2010 AG

**T Yamaoka** 2004 It, S, R, W, 2005 Sp, 2006 AG, Kor, Geo, Tg, It, Sa, JAB, Fj

**H Yamashita** 2009 Kaz, HK, Kor, Sin, Sa, JAB, Tg, Fj, 2012 Kor, HK, Fj, Tg, Sa, R, Geo, 2013 PHP, HK, Kor, UAE, Tg, Fj, W, W, C, US, NZ, S, Rus, Sp, 2014 PHP, SL, Kor, HK, Sa, C, It

**O Yamashita** 1974 SL

**M Yasuda** 1984 F

**N Yasuda** 2000 Kor, I

**Y Yasue** 2009 HK, Kor

**R Yasui** 2013 UAE, W

**T Yasui** 1976 S, E, 1977 S, 1978 F, Kor, 1979 HK, E

**K Yasumi** 1986 C, 1987 US, NZ

**Y Yatomi** 2006 Kor, 2007 HK, Fj, Tg, AuA, Sa, JAB, A, Fj, 2009 Kaz, Kor, JAB, C

**O Yatsuhashi** 1996 US, C, 1998 US, HK, HK, US, C, Ar, Tai, Kor, 2000 Kor, C

**A Yokoi** 1969 HK, 1970 Tha, NZU, BCo, 1971 E, 1972 AuUn, AuUn, HK, 1973 W, E, F, 1974 NZU

**A Yoshida** 1995 R, W, I, NZ, 1996 C, US, C, Kor, 1997 US, HK, 1999 Sa, 2000 Fj, US, Tg, Sa, Kor, C

**H Yoshida** 2001 Sa, C, 2002 Tg, Tai, 2004 R, W, 2006 AG, Kor, Geo, Tg, Sa, JAB, Fj, HK, Kor

**H Yoshida** 2008 Kor, AG, Kaz, M, 2009 Kaz, HK, Sin

**J Yoshida** 1973 W, F

**M Yoshida** 1974 NZU, 1975 A, A, W, 1976 BCo, S, E, It, Kor, 1977 S, 1978 F, Kor

**T Yoshida** 2002 Tg, Tai, Kor, 2003 E

**T Yoshida** 2007 Kor, Fj, Tg, Sa, It, Fj, W, C, 2008 Kor, Kaz, AuA, Tg, M, Sa, US, 2009 Kor, Sa, JAB, C, C, 2010 AG, HK, Sa, 2011 US, NZ

**Y Yoshida** 1988 Kor, 1989 S, 1990 Fj, Tg, Kor, Sa, US, Kor, 1991 US, US, C, HK, S, I, Z, 1992 HK, 1993 Ar, Ar, W, 1994 Fj, Fj, HK, Kor, 1995 Tg, R, I, NZ, 1996 HK

**K Yoshinaga** 1986 Kor, 1987 US, A, NZ, 1990 Sa

**K Yoshino** 1973 W

**T Yoshino** 1985 US, I, I, F, F, 1986 Kor, 1987 NZ

**H Yuhara** 2010 Kor, AG, HK, Fj, Rus, 2011 HK, UAE, SL, NZ, 2013 PHP, Kor, Rus, Sp, 2014 PHP, SL, Sa

**Namibia were relieved to qualify for Rugby World Cup 2015 after a tough Africa Cup campaign.**

# NAMIBIA

## NAMIBIA'S 2013–14 TEST RECORD

| OPPONENTS | DATE | VENUE | RESULT |
|---|---|---|---|
| **Zimbabwe** | 8 Nov | H | Won 35–26 |
| **Kenya** | 16 Nov | H | Won 55–35 |
| **Kenya** | 28 Jun | N | Lost 29–22 |
| **Zimbabwe** | 2 Jul | N | Won 24–20 |
| **Madagascar** | 6 Jul | A | Won 89–10 |

# FROM DESPAIR TO ELATION FOR NAMIBIA

## By Ken Borland

Namibia's emphatic victory over Madagascar saw them claim the African qualifier place at RWC 2015.

**A**n emotional rollercoaster is the only way to describe Namibia's quest to qualify for Rugby World Cup 2015, one that went from the low of defeat by Kenya on day one of the Africa Cup Division 1A to the elation of an emphatic victory over hosts Madagascar on day three.

On 28 June in Antananarivo the Namibians looked set to be shedding tears of sadness after a surprise 29–22 defeat by Kenya left their hopes of securing the Africa 1 berth at England 2015 – or even a place in the Repechage – hanging by the slimmest of threads.

A week later and the tears being shed were of joy after an extraordinary 89–10 victory over Madagascar at the Mahamasina Stadium had confirmed Namibia's place at England 2015 as the Africa Cup winners, albeit only on points differential from Zimbabwe and Kenya after all three finished with 10 points.

Following that opening day loss, just their second against Kenya since

2006, results had fallen Namibia's way to keep their qualification hopes alive. The Welwitschias bounced back to beat Zimbabwe 24–20 to stay in contention, while Zimbabwe then did them a favour by beating Kenya 28–10 on the final day.

Crucially, neither Zimbabwe nor Kenya managed to pick up a bonus point in that match, which left Namibia needing to beat Madagascar by 53 points to qualify for the global showpiece. The pressure was on, but Namibia rose to the challenge to earn a place in Pool C alongside defending champions New Zealand, Argentina, Tonga and Georgia.

"We were down in the dumps up to the last day, but we just believed until the very end. We had the will to keep on fighting until our last breath, until all 15 of us had to be carried off the field if necessary," admitted flanker Tinus du Plessis afterwards. "We had a massive points difference to work on, so we just planned to take it 10 minutes at a time. It's amazing to think that we'll now be playing our first match against the All Blacks!"

The Africa Cup in Madagascar more than doubled the number of Tests that Namibia had played last season, with coach Danie Vermeulen having used matches against the Blue Bulls and Western Province in Windhoek to prepare for the Welwitschias' most important matches in four years.

A penalty after the final hooter by Theuns Kotze – one of six he kicked along with a conversion – gave Namibia a 30–28 victory over a youthful Western Province side, who had outscored their hosts by three tries to two.

The following week, Namibia were beaten 34–13 by a powerful Bulls outfit. It was a highly physical encounter in which the Bulls only pulled away in the second half, and Namibia Rugby Union chief executive Sybrand de Beer believed his team were perhaps still affected by it when they played Kenya in Madagascar seven days later.

"I think the Blue Bulls game took a lot out of the team. They were just not in the moment and we beat ourselves really. It meant World Cup qualification was no longer in our own control, we had to rely on other results," explained De Beer.

Two tries in the first 10 minutes by wing Heinrich Smit gave Namibia a great start and they led 22–19 going into the final quarter, but in trying to keep the strong-finishing Kenyans out they conceded a raft of penalties – and a fourth try and crucial bonus point, to start their campaign on a poor note.

Next up was Zimbabwe, who were trying to qualify for their first World Cup since 1991, as well as ending a six-match losing streak against the Welwitschias, and they were forced to overturn a 17–10 half-time deficit.

The Sables, boosted by the presence of former Natal Sharks and Gauteng

Lions fly-half Guy Cronje, used their dangerous backs to score the opening try, and although Namibia's dominant forwards rumbled their way to a penalty try, Zimbabwe's backs conjured another try just before half-time and a second Cronje penalty stretched their lead to 20–10.

Namibia hit back with tries from flanker Renaldo Bothma, after a great break by replacement hooker Dian Wiese, and Rohan Kitshoff to keep their World Cup hopes alive. Namibia had to defend stoutly for the last 10 minutes after PJ van Lill was sent to the sin-bin, but they did so to keep their chances of progressing alive.

The final match against Madagascar provided the chance for Namibia's attacking players to shine and it took the Welwitschias just 12 minutes to stamp their mark on proceedings with centre Johan Deysel's opening try.

Two more tries, superb long-range efforts by wing David Philander and Exeter Chiefs-bound full-back Chrysander Botha, were scored before the end of the first quarter and an outstanding display saw Namibia go into the break 63–10 up and firmly back in RWC 2015 contention.

Experienced props Johnny Redelinghuys and Jaco Engels both scored tries, while the explosive Bothma scored twice, Philander completed his brace and there was a penalty try as well. Further tries by Kotze, left wing Johan Tromp, a third by Bothma and another penalty try were the knockout blow for Zimbabwe and Kenya.

It was a moment of great joy for Namibia and a sign that they are past the difficulties which plagued rugby in the country around the time of the last World Cup.

"Rugby in Namibia was quite badly hit in 2011 when the EXCO resigned and technically we were insolvent," explained De Beer. "But the latest financial statements have been declared clean and passed without any qualifications and there is good governance and the basic foundation in place. We are now back to concentrating on rugby."

For a country with a small playing base, development is crucial and the IRB's Get Into Rugby mass participation programme is reaching tens of thousands of schoolchildren all over the vast south-west African country. The chance to witness their heroes playing on rugby's greatest stage can only inspire more to take up the game.

The inclusion of Namibia in South Africa's Vodacom Cup competition, the tier below Super Rugby, will be a massive aid in their preparations for RWC 2015 where the Welwitschias will be seeking a first ever win in the showpiece event.

Namibia have, for the last two years, played the Tri-Nations Series at home in November, the 2013 edition seeing them beat their rivals Zimbabwe (35–26) and Kenya (55–35). In 2014, though, they will head to Europe to face Canada, the French Barbarians and Portugal, with the challenge being to continue the resurgence of Namibian rugby.

# NAMIBIA INTERNATIONAL STATISTICS

## MATCH RECORDS UP TO 13 OCTOBER 2014

### Winning Margin

| Date | Opponent | Result | Winning Margin |
|---|---|---|---|
| 15/06/2002 | Madagascar | 112–0 | 112 |
| 06/07/2014 | Madagascar | 89–10 | 79 |
| 21/04/1990 | Portugal | 86–9 | 77 |
| 27/05/2006 | Kenya | 82–12 | 70 |
| 26/05/2007 | Zambia | 80–10 | 70 |

### MOST POINTS IN A MATCH
#### BY THE TEAM

| Date | Opponent | Result | Points |
|---|---|---|---|
| 15/06/2002 | Madagascar | 112–0 | 112 |
| 06/07/2014 | Madagascar | 89–10 | 89 |
| 21/04/1990 | Portugal | 86–9 | 86 |
| 31/08/2003 | Uganda | 82–13 | 82 |
| 27/05/2006 | Kenya | 82–12 | 82 |

#### BY A PLAYER

| Date | Player | Opponent | Points |
|---|---|---|---|
| 06/07/1993 | Jaco Coetzee | Kenya | 35 |
| 26/05/2007 | Justinus van der Westhuizen | Zambia | 33 |
| 27/06/2009 | Chrysander Botha | Cote D'Ivoire | 29 |
| 06/07/2014 | Theuns Kotze | Madagascar | 29 |
| 21/04/1990 | Moolman Olivier | Portugal | 26 |

### MOST TRIES IN A MATCH
#### BY THE TEAM

| Date | Opponent | Result | Tries |
|---|---|---|---|
| 15/06/2002 | Madagascar | 112–0 | 18 |
| 21/04/1990 | Portugal | 86–9 | 16 |
| 17/10/1999 | Germany | 79–13 | 13 |
| 06/07/2014 | Madagascar | 89–10 | 13 |

#### BY A PLAYER

| Date | Player | Opponent | Tries |
|---|---|---|---|
| 21/04/1990 | Gerhard Mans | Portugal | 6 |
| 15/06/2002 | Riaan van Wyk | Madagascar | 5 |
| 16/05/1992 | Eden Meyer | Zimbabwe | 4 |
| 16/08/2003 | Melrick Africa | Kenya | 4 |

### MOST CONVERSIONS IN A MATCH
#### BY THE TEAM

| Date | Opponent | Result | Cons |
|---|---|---|---|
| 06/07/2014 | Madagascar | 89–10 | 12 |
| 15/06/2002 | Madagascar | 112–0 | 11 |
| 21/04/1990 | Portugal | 86–9 | 11 |
| 31/08/2003 | Uganda | 82–13 | 11 |
| 27/05/2006 | Kenya | 82–12 | 11 |

#### BY A PLAYER

| Date | Player | Opponent | Cons |
|---|---|---|---|
| 06/07/2014 | Theuns Kotze | Madagascar | 12 |
| 21/04/1990 | Moolman Olivier | Portugal | 11 |
| 27/05/2006 | Morne Schreuder | Kenya | 11 |
| 26/05/2007 | Justinus van der Westhuizen | Zambia | 9 |

### MOST PENALTIES IN A MATCH
#### BY THE TEAM

| Date | Opponent | Result | Pens |
|---|---|---|---|
| 17/11/2012 | Spain | 37–38 | 6 |
| 5 on 6 occasions | | | |

#### BY A PLAYER

| Date | Player | Opponent | Pens |
|---|---|---|---|
| 17/11/2012 | Theuns Kotze | Spain | 6 |
| 5 on 6 occasions | | | |

### MOST DROP GOALS IN A MATCH
#### BY THE TEAM

| Date | Opponent | Result | DGs |
|---|---|---|---|
| 10/09/2011 | Fiji | 25–49 | 3 |

#### BY A PLAYER

| Date | Player | Opponent | DGs |
|---|---|---|---|
| 10/09/2011 | Theuns Kotze | Fiji | 3 |

NAMIBIA

## MOST CAPPED PLAYERS

| Name | Caps |
|---|---|
| Johnny Redelinghuys | 40 |
| Tinus Du Plessis | 38 |
| Eugene Jantjies | 38 |
| Hugo Horn | 35 |
| Herman Lindvelt | 33 |

## LEADING PENALTY SCORERS

| Name | Pens |
|---|---|
| Jaco Coetzee | 46 |
| Theuns Kotze | 32 |
| Emile Wessels | 21 |
| Morne Schreuder | 18 |
| Rudi van Vuuren | 14 |

## LEADING TRY SCORERS

| Name | Tries |
|---|---|
| Gerhard Mans | 27 |
| Eden Meyer | 21 |
| Chrysander Botha | 15 |
| Melrick Africa | 12 |

## LEADING DROP GOAL SCORERS

| Name | DGs |
|---|---|
| Theuns Kotze | 4 |
| Jaco Coetzee | 3 |
| Eugene Jantjies | 2 |

## LEADING CONVERSIONS SCORERS

| Name | Cons |
|---|---|
| Jaco Coetzee | 82 |
| Theuns Kotze | 45 |
| Morne Schreuder | 36 |
| Rudi van Vuuren | 26 |

## LEADING POINTS SCORERS

| Name | Points |
|---|---|
| Jaco Coetzee | 340 |
| Theuns Kotze | 213 |
| Morne Schreuder | 146 |
| Chrysander Botha | 142 |
| Gerhard Mans | 118 |

# NAMIBIA INTERNATIONAL PLAYERS
## UP TO 13 OCTOBER 2014

**MJ Africa** 2003 Sa, Ken, Uga, Ar, I, A, 2005 Mad, Mor, 2006 Ken, Tun, Ken, Tun, Mor, Mor, 2007 Za, Geo, R, Uga, SA, I, F, Ar, Geo

**W Alberts** 1991 Sp, Pt, It, It, Z, Z, I, I, Z, Z, Z, 1995 Z, 1996 Z, Z

**H Amakali** 2005 Mad

**CT Arries** 2013 Ken

**J Augustyn** 1991 Z, 1998 Iv, Mor, Z

**RS Bardenhorst** 2007 Geo, R

**J Barnard** 1990 Z, Pt, W, W, F, F, 1991 Sp, Pt, It, It, Z, Z, I, I, Z, Z, Z, 1992 Z, Z

**R Becker** 2012 Z, Sp, 2013 Sen, Z, Ken, 2014 Ken, Z, Mad

**D Beukes** 2000 Z, Ur, 2001 Z, Z

**E Beukes** 1990 Z, F, WGe

**J Beukes** 1994 Z, Mor, 1995 Z

**AJ Blaauw** 1996 Z, Z, 1997 Tg, 1998 Pt, Tun, Z, Iv, Mor, Z, 1999 Z, Fj, F, C, Ger, 2000 Z, Z, Ur, 2001 It, 2003 Ar, I, A, R, 2004 Mor

**ML Blom** 2010 Sp, 2011 Pt, Geo, 2012 Sen, Mad, 2013 Sen, Tun, Z, Ken, 2014 Ken, Z, Mad

**JH Bock** 2005 Mad, Mor, 2006 Ken, Tun, Ken, Tun, Mor, Mor, 2007 Za, R, SA, I, F, Ar, Geo, 2009 Pt, Tun, 2010 R, Geo, 2011 R, Pt, Geo, SA

**J Bock** 2005 Mad, Mor, 2009 Iv, Iv, 2010 R, Geo, Pt

**J Booysen** 2003 Sa, Ken, Ar, A, 2007 Uga

**M Booysen** 1993 W, AG, Z, 1994 Rus, Z, HK, 1996 Z, Z

**LW Botes** 2006 Ken, Mor, 2007 Za, Geo, R, Uga, SA, F

**CA Botha** 2008 Z, 2009 Iv, Iv, Pt, Tun, Tun, 2010 Rus, R, Geo, Pt, Sp, 2011 R, Pt, Geo, Fj, Sa, SA, W, 2012 Sen, Mad, Z, 2013 Sen, Tun, Z, Ken, 2014 Ken, Z, Mad

**HP Botha** 2000 Z, Z, Ur

**H Botha** 2012 Z, Sp

**R Botha** 2014 Ken, Z, Mad

**AC Bouwer** 2012 Sen, Mad, Sp, 2013 Sen, Tun, Ken, 2014 Ken, Z, Mad

**H Breedt** 1998 Tun, Z

**H Brink** 1992 Z, Z, 1993 W, Ken, 1994 Rus, Z, Iv, Mor, HK

**J Britz** 1996 Z

**B Buitendag** 1990 W, W, F, F, WGe, 1991 Sp, Pt, It, It, Z, Z, I, I, Z, Z, Z, 1992 Z, Z, 1993 W, AG, Ken, Z

**E Buitendag** 2010 Rus, 2013 Sen, Tun, Z, 2014 Ken, Z, Mad

**J Burger** 2004 Za, Ken, Z, Mor, 2006 Tun, Tun, Mor, Mor, 2007 Za, Geo, R, SA, I, F, Ar, Geo, 2008 Z, 2009 Iv, Iv, Pt, Tun, Tun, 2010 R, Geo, Pt, 2011 Fj, Sa, SA, W

**B Calitz** 1995 Z

**C Campbell** 2008 Z

**DJ Coetzee** 1990 Pt, W, F, F, WGe, 1991 Sp, Pt, It, It, Z, Z, I, I, Z, Z, Z, 1992 Z, Z, 1993 W, AG, Ken, Z, 1994 Z, Iv, Mor, HK, 1995 Z, Z

**JC Coetzee** 1990 W

**M Couw** 2006 Ken

**B Cronjé** 1994 Rus

HDP Dames 2011 Fj, Sa, SA, W, 2012 Sen, Mad
HDP Dames 2013 Sen, Tun
J Dames 1998 Tun, Z
D de Beer 2000 Z
S de Beer 1995 Z, 1997 Tg, 1998 Tun, Z, Iv, Mor, Z, 1999 Ger
AD de Klerk 2009 Iv, Iv
CJ De Koe 2010 Geo, Pt, Sp
DP De La Harpe 2010 Rus, R, Geo, Pt, Sp, 2011 R, Pt, Geo, Fj, Sa, SA, W, 2012 Z, Sp, 2013 Sen, Tun, Z, Ken, 2014 Ken, Z, Mad
RCA De La Harpe 2011 R, Pt, Geo, Fj, SA, W
SC De La Harpe 2010 Sp, 2012 Z, Sp, 2013 Z, Ken
H de Waal 1990 Z, Pt
N de Wet 2000 Ur
R Dedig 2004 Mor, Za, Ken, Z, Mor
CJH Derks 1990 Z, Pt, W, W, F, F, WGe, 1991 Sp, Pt, It, It, Z, Z, I, I, Z, Z, Z, 1992 Z, Z, 1993 W, AG, Z, 1994 Rus, Z, Iv, Mor, HK
J Deysel 1990 Z, Pt, W, W, 1991 Sp, Pt, It, It, Z, Z, I, I, Z, Z, Z, 1992 Z
J Deysel 2013 Ken, 2014 Ken, Z, Mad
VA Dreyer 2002 Z, 2003 Ar, I, R
J Drotsky 2006 Ken, 2008 Sen
AJ Du Plessis 2010 Pt, Sp
I du Plessis 2005 Mor, 2009 Tun
M du Plessis 2001 Z, 2005 Mor
N du Plessis 1993 Ken, 1994 Rus, 1995 Z
O Du Plessis 2008 Sen
T Du Plessis 2006 Ken, Tun, Mor, Mor, 2007 Geo, R, Uga, SA, I, F, Ar, Geo, 2008 Sen, Z, 2009 Iv, Iv, Pt, Tun, Tun, 2010 R, Geo, Pt, Sp, 2011 R, Pt, Geo, Fj, SA, W, 2012 Sen, Sp, 2013 Sen, Tun, Z, Ken, 2014 Ken, Z, Mad
P du Plooy 1992 Z, Z, 1994 Z, Mor, HK
S Du Preez 2013 Ken, 2014 Mad
S du Rand 2007 Geo, R, Uga
JA Du Toit 2007 Za, Geo, R, Uga, SA, I, F, Geo, 2008 Sen, Z, 2009 Pt, Tun, Tun, 2010 Rus, R, Geo, Pt, Sp, 2011 R, Pt, Geo, Sa, SA, W
N du Toit 2002 Tun, 2003 Sa, Ar, I, A, R
V du Toit 1990 Pt, W, W, F
JH Duvenhage 2000 Z, Z, 2001 It, Z, Z, 2002 Mad, 2003 Sa, Uga, Ar, I, R, 2007 Za, R, Uga

A Engelbrecht 2000 Z
J Engelbrecht 1990 WGe, 1994 Rus, Z, Iv, Mor, HK, 1995 Z, Z
N Engelbrecht 1996 Z
H Engels 1990 F, WGe
JB Engels 2013 Sen, Tun, Z, Ken, 2014 Ken, Z, Mad
E Erasmus 1997 Tg
G Esterhuizen 2008 Sen, Z
SF Esterhuizen 2008 Z, 2009 Iv, Iv, Pt, Tun, Tun, 2010 Rus, R, Geo, Pt, Sp, 2011 R, Pt, 2012 Sen, Mad
N Esterhuyse 2006 Ken, Tun, Mor, 2007 Za, Geo, R, Uga, SA, I, F, Ar, Geo, 2008 Z, 2009 Iv, Iv, Pt, Tun, Tun, 2010 Rus, R, Geo, Pt, Sp, 2011 R, Pt, Geo, Fj, Sa, SA, W

D Farmer 1997 Tg, 1998 Pt, Iv, Mor, Z, 1999 Z, Fj, Ger
F Fisch 1999 Z, Ger
TR Forbes 2010 Rus, 2014 Mad
HH Franken 2011 Sa, 2012 Sen, Mad
S Furter 1999 Z, Fj, F, C, Ger, 2001 It, 2002 Mad, Z, Tun, Tun, 2003 Sa, Ken, Uga, Ar, I, A, R, 2004 Mor, 2006 Ken, Tun, Ken

E Gaoab 2005 Mad, Mor
I Gaya 2004 Za, Ken
J Genis 2000 Z, Z, Ur, 2001 Z
N Genis 2006 Mor
R Gentz 2001 It
R Glundeung 2006 Ken
CJ Goosen 1991 Sp, Pt, It, It, 1993 W
D Gouws 2000 Z, Z, Ur, 2001 It, Z, Z
T Gouws 2003 Ken, Uga, 2004 Za, Ken, 2006 Ken, Tun
A Graham 2001 It, Z, Z, 2002 Mad, Tun, 2003 Ken, Uga, I, 2004 Mor
A Greeff 1997 Tg

D Grobelaar 2008 Z
DP Grobler 2001 Z, 2002 Mad, Tun, Tun, 2003 Sa, Ken, Uga, Ar, I, A, R, 2004 Mor, Za, Ken, Z, Mor, 2006 Ken, Tun, Ken, 2007 Za, Geo, R, SA, Ar
HJ Grobler 1990 Z, Pt, W, W, F, F, WGe, 1991 Sp, Pt, It, It, Z, Z, I, I, Z, Z, Z, 1992 Z, Z
T Grünewald 1990 Z
D Grunschloss 2003 A, R

F Hartung 1996 Z, Z
RJ Herridge 2009 Pt, Tun, Tun
L Holtzhausen 1997 Tg, 1998 Pt, Tun, Z, Iv, Mor, Z, 1999 Ger
F Horn 2005 Mad, Mor, 2006 Ken
H Horn 1997 Tg, 1998 Pt, Iv, Mor, Z, 1999 Z, Fj, F, C, Ger, 2001 It, 2002 Mad, Z, Tun, 2003 Sa, 2007 Za, Geo, R, Uga, SA, I, F, Ar, Geo, 2008 Sen, Z, 2009 Iv, Iv, Tun, Tun, 2010 Rus, 2011 Fj, Sa, SA, W
K Horn 1997 Tg, 1998 Pt
Q Hough 1995 Z, Z, 1998 Pt, Tun, Z, Iv, Mor, Z, 1999 Z, Fj, F, C
P Human 2012 Sen, Mad
D Husselman 1993 AG, 1994 Z, Mor, 2002 Mad, Z, Tun, 2003 Sa, Ar, I, A
JJ Husselman 2004 Za, Ken

E Isaacs 1993 Ken, 1994 Iv
P Isaacs 2000 Z, Z, Ur, 2001 Z, Z, 2003 A, 2005 Mad, Mor
E Izaacs 1998 Pt, 1999 Z, Ger, 2000 Z, Z, Ur, 2001 It, Z, Z, 2002 Mad, Z, Tun, Tun, 2003 Sa, Ken, Ar, A, R

M Jacobs 1999 Z, Fj, F, Ger
E Jansen 2006 Ken
EA Jantjies 2006 Ken, Tun, Ken, Tun, 2007 Za, Geo, R, Uga, SA, I, F, Ar, Geo, 2008 Sen, Z, 2009 Iv, Iv, Pt, Tun, Tun, 2010 Rus, R, Geo, Pt, Sp, 2011 R, Pt, Geo, Fj, Sa, SA, W, 2012 Sen, Mad, Z, Sp, 2013 Z, Ken
R Jantjies 1994 HK, 1995 Z, Z, 1996 Z, 1998 Pt, Tun, Iv, Mor, Z, 1999 Z, Fj, F, C, 2000 Z, Z
M Jeary 2003 Uga, 2004 Ken, Z, Mor
R Jeary 2000 Z, Ur
D Jeffrey 1990 F
J Jenkins 2002 Mad, Tun, 2003 Ken
AJ Jevu 2012 Sen

SM Kaizemi 2012 Sp
D Kamonga 2004 Mor, Za, Ken, Z, Mor, 2007 Uga, Geo
M Kapitako 2000 Z, Z, 2001 It, Z, Z, 2003 Uga, 2004 Za, 2006 Tun
HI Kasera 2012 Mad
M Kasirngwa 2012 Z, Sp
M Katjiuanjo 2005 Mad, Mor
M Kazombiaze 2006 Ken, Tun
U Kazombiaze 2006 Ken, Tun, Mor, Mor, 2007 Za, Uga, SA, I, F, Ar, Geo, 2008 Sen, Z, 2009 Iv, Iv, Pt, Tun, Tun, 2010 Rus, Geo, 2011 W
R Kitshoff 2010 Pt, Sp, 2011 R, Pt, Geo, Fj, Sa, SA, W, 2013 Sen, Tun, Z, Ken, 2014 Ken, Z, Mad
DPW Koen 2006 Tun
HVW Koll 2009 Pt, Tun, 2010 Rus, R, Geo, Pt, Sp, 2011 R, Pt, Geo, Fj, Sa, SA, W, 2012 Sen, Mad
A Kotze 1991 Sp, Z, Z, I, I 1993 W, AG, Z
D Kotze 1993 W, AG, Ken, Z, 1994 Rus, HK
J Kotze 1995 Z, Z, 1996 Z, Z, 2000 Z, Z, 2001 It, Z, Z, 2002 Mad, Z, Tun, Tun, 2004 Za, Ken, Z, Mor
P Kotze 2001 It
P Kotze 1996 Z
TAW Kotze 2011 Pt, Fj, Sa, SA, W, 2012 Sen, Mad, Z, Sp, 2013 Sen, Tun, Z, Ken, 2014 Ken, Z, Mad
L Kotzee 2008 Z
JL Kruger 2011 It, Z, Z
R Kruger 2003 Ken, Uga, 2005 Mad, Mor
R Kruger 2004 Mor, Za, Ken, Mor

SO Lambert 2000 Z, Ur, 2001 It, Z, Z, 2003 Ken, Uga, 2004 Mor, 2005 Mad, 2006 Ken, Tun, Ken
B Langenhoven 2007 SA, I, F, Ar, Geo, 2008 Sen, Z, 2009 Pt, Tun, Tun, 2010 Rus

NAMIBIA

**PJ Van Lill** 2006 *Ken*, 2008 *Sen*, *Z*, 2009 *Iv*, *Pt*, *Tun*, *Tun*, 2010 *Rus*, *R*, *Geo*, *Pt*, *Sp*, 2011 *R*, *Pt*, *Geo*, *Fj*, *Sa*, *SA*, 2012 *Sen*, *Mad*, *Z*, *Sp*, 2013 *Sen*, *Tun*, *Z*, *Ken*, 2014 *Ken*, *Z*, *Mad*

**RE Van Neel** 2010 *Rus*, 2011 *Sa*, 2012 *Z*

**F van Rensburg** 1995 *Z*, 1996 *Z*, *Z*, 1997 *Tg*, 1998 *Tun*, *Z*, 1999 *Z*, *Fj*, *F*, *C*, *Ger*, 2000 *Z*, 2001 *It*, *Z*, *Z*

**SJ van Rensburg** 1998 *Z*, *Iv*, *Mor*, *Z*, 1999 *Z*, *Fj*, *F*, *Ger*, 2000 *Z*, *Ur*

**SL Van Rooi** 2003 *Uga*, *A*, 2004 *Mor*, 2005 *Mor*

**A van Rooyen** 1991 *Sp*, *Pt*, *It*, *It*, *I*, 1992 *Z*, *Z*

**M van Rooyen** 1996 *Z*, 1998 *Pt*, *Tun*, *Z*, *Mor*, *Z*, 1999 *Z*, *F*, *C*

**C van Schalkwyk** 1993 *AG*, *Z*

**A Van Tonder** 1995 *Z*

**CJ van Tonder** 2002 *Tun*, 2003 *Sa*, *Ken*, *Uga*, *I*, *A*, *R*, 2004 *Mor*, *Za*, *Ken*, *Z*, *Mor*, 2006 *Ken*, *Ken*, 2007 *Za*, 2012 *Sp*

**JH Van Tonder** 2004 *Mor*, *Ken*, *Z*, *Mor*, 2006 *Ken*, *Tun*, 2007 *Uga*, *SA*, *I*, *F*, *Ar*, *Geo*, 2008 *Z*, 2009 *Iv*, *Iv*, *Pt*, *Tun*

**N van Vuuren** 1993 *AG*

**RJ van Vuuren** 1997 *Tg*, 1998 *Pt*, *Tun*, *Z*, 1999 *Z*, *Ger*, 2000 *Z*, *Z*, *Ur*, 2002 *Mad*, *Z*, 2003 *Ken*, *Uga*, *R*

**A van Wyk** 1993 *W*, *Ken*, 1994 *Iv*, *HK*

**D Van Wyk** 2011 *R*, *Pt*, *Geo*, *Fj*, *Sa*, *SA*, *W*, 2012 *Z*, *Sp*

**G van Wyk** 1999 *Z*, *Fj*, *F*, *C*, 2000 *Z*, *Z*, *Ur*, 2001 *It*

**L van Wyk** 2004 *Mor*

**M Van Wyk** 2009 *Iv*, *Iv*, *Pt*, 2010 *Rus*, *Geo*, *Pt*, 2011 *R*, *Pt*, *Geo*, 2012 *Sp*

**R van Wyk** 2004 *Za*, *Ken*, *Z*, *Mor*

**R van Wyk** 2002 *Mad*, *Z*, *Tun*, *Tun*, 2003 *Sa*, 2004 *Mor*, *Za*, *Ken*, *Z*, *Mor*

**J van Zyl** 2008 *Sen*

**WP Van Zyl** 2007 *SA*, *I*, *F*, *Ar*, *Geo*, 2008 *Z*, 2009 *Iv*, *Iv*, *Pt*, *Tun*, *Tun*, 2010 *R*, *Geo*, *Pt*, *Sp*, 2011 *Fj*, *Sa*, *SA*, *W*

**R van Zyl** 1997 *Tg*, 1998 *Tun*, *Z*, *Iv*, *Mor*, *Z*

**J Venter** 2013 *Z*, *Ken*

**M Venter** 2003 *Uga*, 2004 *Mor*, 2008 *Z*, 2009 *Iv*, *Iv*, *Pt*, *Tun*, *Tun*, 2010 *Rus*

**D Vermaak** 1998 *Z*

**JJ Vermaak** 1990 *Pt*, 1994 *Rus*, 1996 *Z*

**A Vermeulen** 2010 *Rus*

**B Vermeulen** 1995 *Z*

**D Vermeulen** 1996 *Z*, *Z*, 1997 *Tg*, 1998 *Pt*

**G Vermeulen** 1991 *Z*

**M Visser** 2007 *Za*, *Geo*, *R*, *Uga*, *SA*, *Ar*, *Geo*, 2009 *Iv*, *Iv*, *Pt*, *Tun*, *Tun*, 2010 *Rus*, *R*, *Geo*, *Pt*, *Sp*, 2011 *SA*

**CW Viviers** 2010 *Sp*, 2011 *R*, *Pt*, *Geo*

**P von Wielligh** 1991 *It*, *Z*, 1992 *Z*, 1993 *AG*, *Z*, 1994 *Iv*, *Mor*, 1995 *Z*, 1996 *Z*

**B Walters** 2009 *Pt*

**GAE Walters** 2008 *Z*, 2009 *Iv*, 2010 *R*, *Geo*, *Pt*, *Sp*

**W Wentzel** 1991 *Sp*, *Z*, *Z*

**E Wessels** 2002 *Tun*, *Tun*, 2003 *Sa*, *Ar*, *I*, *A*, *R*, 2006 *Tun*, *Mor*, *Mor*, 2007 *SA*, *I*, *F*, 2009 *Iv*, *Pt*, *Tun*, *Tun*, 2010 *Rus*

**DG Wiese** 2014 *Z*

**LP Winkler** 2008 *Z*, 2009 *Iv*, *Iv*, 2010 *Rus*, *R*, *Geo*, 2011 *R*, *Pt*, *Geo*, *Fj*, *Sa*

**RC Witbooi** 2004 *Za*, *Z*, 2005 *Mor*, 2006 *Ken*, *Tun*, *Ken*, 2007 *Za*, *Geo*, *R*, *Uga*, *I*, *F*, *Geo*, 2008 *Sen*

**J Wohler** 2005 *Mad*, *Mor*

**J Zaayman** 1997 *Tg*, 1998 *Pt*, *Tun*, *Z*, *Iv*, *Mor*, *Z*, 1999 *Z*, *Fj*, *F*, *C*, *Ger*

Getty Images

Johan Tromp of Namibia gets away from the covering defenders during his country's win over Madagascar in July.

**NAMIBIA**

Beauden Barrett celebrates scoring the try which won him the IRPA Try of the Year Award.

# NEW ZEALAND

## NEW ZEALAND'S 2013–14 TEST RECORD

| OPPONENTS | DATE | VENUE | RESULT |
|---|---|---|---|
| Australia | 19 Oct | H | Won 41–33 |
| Japan | 2 Nov | A | Won 54–6 |
| France | 9 Nov | A | Won 26–19 |
| England | 16 Nov | A | Won 30–22 |
| Ireland | 24 Nov | A | Won 24–22 |
| England | 7 Jun | H | Won 20–15 |
| England | 14 Jun | H | Won 28–27 |
| England | 21 Jun | H | Won 36–13 |
| Australia | 16 Aug | A | Drew 12–12 |
| Australia | 23 Aug | H | Won 51–20 |
| Argentina | 6 Sep | H | Won 28–9 |
| South Africa | 13 Sep | H | Won 14–10 |
| Argentina | 27 Sep | A | Won 34–13 |
| South Africa | 4 Oct | A | Lost 27–25 |
| Australia | 18 Oct | A | Won 28–27 |

# ALL BLACKS RISE TO THE CHALLENGE

*By Ian Jones*

Ben Smith scores for the All Blacks in the 34–13 victory over Argentina which secured The Rugby Championship title.

It was a busy but remarkable year for the All Blacks in which they played some sublime rugby in 13 Test outings, developed more depth to what was already a strong squad and won The Rugby Championship for a third consecutive season with a game to spare. New Zealand were certainly pushed close more than once but the incredible self-belief the current group of players possess got them through.

I thought overall the standard of Test rugby played by the All Blacks, as well as their opponents, was extremely high. Test matches are a real spectacle at the moment with teams consistently looking to play positive rugby, taking advantage of laws designed for that exact reason, and what gave New Zealand the edge was their ability to maintain their intensity for longer than the other teams and their knack for minimising the damage when they were inevitably tested.

I've no doubt Steve Hansen and the players relished the series of challenges thrown at them. The hallmark of this team has always been its appetite to improve and develop, the burning desire not to stagnate, and South Africa, England, Ireland, Australia and France all asked serious questions of the All Blacks over the course of the year.

The 27–25 defeat to the Springboks in Johannesburg aside, they repeatedly found the answers because they are constantly working on their skill set, they have a collective dedication and every time they take to the pitch they have 14 players busting a gut to create something for the 15th man.

The loss to South Africa followed the 14–10 win New Zealand posted against our greatest rivals in Wellington in September and they were two titanic clashes, which you would expect between the number one and two ranked teams in the world.

The rivalry between the All Blacks and the Springboks is massive but there was a nice moment after the Test in Wellington when Richie McCaw presented Jean de Villiers and Bryan Habana with bottles of champagne to celebrate them reaching their 100th Tests for South Africa. It is that mutual respect, a camaraderie irrespective of which team you play for or which country you represent, that makes rugby such a great sport.

There were many highlights for New Zealand during the year. The clash with Ireland in Dublin in November was a magnificent game of football which the All Blacks closed out 24–22 at the death. The level of Ireland's play was superb but New Zealand had just enough in the tank to score a winning try from Ryan Crotty with the last play. It was Test rugby at its very best.

The first 40 minutes of rugby New Zealand played in the third Test against England in Hamilton was the best half I think this team has strung together. It was incredible to watch and a good England side just couldn't cope with it.

It was also the match in which I felt Aaron Cruden truly emerged from Dan Carter's shadow. It was the defining performance of his Test career and in my eyes it was the game in which he really established himself as New Zealand's first choice 10. Carter will have something to say about that when he regains full fitness but Cruden is now the man in possession of the shirt.

Hansen and his coaching team will not have been happy with the South Africa defeat or the 12–12 draw with the Wallabies in Sydney at the start of the Championship but good teams learn from their setbacks. I've no doubt Steve will have emphasised to the boys how much it sucks to lose and urged them not to experience the same feeling again.

The draw against Australia brought the All Blacks' 17-match winning

**NEW ZEALAND**

run to an end, denying the team the chance to set a new record of 18 consecutive victories by a top tier nation. In public at least they weren't interested in talking about records but privately I'm sure they were disappointed not to have made a bit of history.

After speaking to some of the boys, I know they were embarrassed by aspects of the performance against the Australians but they took it on the chin, worked hard and responded with a massive 51–20 demolition of the Wallabies at Eden Park a week later. I've said it before, a mark of a great side is how it responds to disappointment and the display in Auckland spoke volumes. They learned from their mistakes and it was a devastating performance.

I think it also revealed something of the mentality that comes with being an All Black. New Zealand were unbeaten at Eden Park in 31 games before the Australia game, a record stretching back 20 years, and you could sense the current players were desperate not to let down the former players and previous All Blacks teams who'd come before them and established such a proud record in Auckland. They were playing for them and for the honour of New Zealand rugby.

It was, of course, another good year for Steve Hansen. What consistently impresses me about Steve's impact on the All Blacks is how the decision makers in his team play with such freedom. They're not frightened to try things, to make mistakes, and this creates an environment in which they can express themselves.

This was perfectly illustrated in the first Test against England in Auckland. It was late in the game, the score was 15–15 and New Zealand won a penalty. A lot of teams would have gone for the posts but Cruden tapped and went and Conrad Smith eventually scored the try in the corner. Cruden's confidence in the set-up, the absence of fear of making the wrong decision even at such a crucial time – as well as his quick thinking – won the match for the All Blacks. That all stems from Steve's coaching philosophy.

Steve capped 11 new players over the course of the year and his future-proofing of the team is another of the hallmarks of his regime. He rarely rushes a player into the team but when he does bring them in, they're invariably the right choice.

A case in point is Malakai Fekitoa, who came off the bench for his debut against England in Auckland and played four times in The Rugby Championship. In my opinion, he was the All Blacks rookie of the year and more than justified Steve's faith in him.

In terms of individual performances, it was a great year for Dane Coles at hooker. He really blossomed in his role as a starter in the side and put to bed concerns about Keven Mealamu's ageing legs. Julian

Savea couldn't stop scoring and nailed his spot down while Brodie Retallick was my player of the year. Richie McCaw played as well as ever and looked like he has plenty of gas left in the tank even after all these years.

New Zealand are in a good place and for me, Steve only has one or two selection issues to resolve. Aaron Smith is now the undisputed number one scrum-half but there's still a question over who to promote as number two while the All Blacks could struggle in the second row if Retallick or Sam Whitelock picked up a serious knock.

The big news was the confirmation that New Zealand Rugby had agreed to play an historic game against Samoa in Apia in July 2015. It will be the first time the All Blacks have played a Test in Samoa.

It was great news. As the world champions and the number one ranked team, I do think New Zealand have a responsibility to help spread the rugby gospel whenever and wherever possible. They played Japan in Tokyo last November and faced the USA Eagles in Chicago this year and breaking new ground, including the Apia fixture, can only be good for the game worldwide.

All the talk after the Samoa announcement focused on the positive impact the match will have on rugby on the Island nations but I think it will also be a fantastic experience for the All Blacks. Take someone like McCaw, who has made more than 130 Test match appearances but has never had the opportunity to play in Apia. What I'm trying to say is that it's not one-way traffic and New Zealand as well as Samoa will benefit. I hope it's the start of a new trend in terms of the international rugby calendar and more regular big games for the lower tier nations.

The World Cup in England in 2015 is of course looming and the All Blacks have plenty of reasons to be optimistic ahead of the tournament. No country has ever won back-to-back titles and that's a challenge I know they will embrace enthusiastically.

There'll be no talk of defending the title in England because that implies a certain negativity. The All Blacks will only focus on winning the competition rather than trying to hold onto something they achieved in the past. It's all about looking forward rather backwards.

New Zealand's results in 2013–14 showed there are teams who can and will push them. They'll go into the tournament as the favourites but they'll have to be on top of their game if they're to lift the trophy again.

**NEW ZEALAND**

# NEW ZEALAND INTERNATIONAL STATISTICS

## MATCH RECORDS UP TO 13 OCTOBER 2014

### MOST CONSECUTIVE TEST WINS

**17** 1965 SA 4, 1966 BI 1, 2, 3, 4, 1967 A, E, W, F, S, 1968 A 1,2, F 1, 2, 3, 1969 W 1, 2

**17** 2013 F 1, 2, 3, A 1, 2, Arg 1, SA 1, Arg 2, SA 2, A 3, J, F 4, E, I, 2014 E 1,2,3

**16** 2011 Tg, J, F, C, Arg, A, F, 2012 I 1, 2, 3, A1,2, Arg1, SA1, Arg2, SA2

**15** 2005 A 1, SA 2, A 2, W, I E, S, 2006 I 1, 2, Arg, A 1, SA 1, A 2, 3, SA 2

**15** 2009 A 3, 4, W,It E,F 3, 2010 I 1, W 1,2, SA 1, 2, A 1, 2, SA 3, A 3

**12** 1988 A 3, 1989 F 1, 2, Arg 1,2, A, W, I, 1990 S 1,2, A 1,2

### MOST CONSECUTIVE TESTS WITHOUT DEFEAT

| Matches | Wins | Draws | Period |
|---|---|---|---|
| 23 | 22 | 1 | 1987 to 1990 |
| 22 | 21 | 1 | 2013 to 2014 |
| 20 | 19 | 1 | 2011 to 2012 |
| 17 | 17 | 0 | 1965 to 1969 |
| 17 | 15 | 2 | 1961 to 1964 |
| 15 | 15 | 0 | 2005 to 2006 |
| 15 | 15 | 0 | 2009 to 2010 |

### MOST POINTS IN A MATCH
#### BY THE TEAM

| Pts | Opponents | Venue | Year |
|---|---|---|---|
| 145 | Japan | Bloemfontein | 1995 |
| 108 | Portugal | Lyons | 2007 |
| 102 | Tonga | Albany | 2000 |
| 101 | Italy | Huddersfield | 1999 |
| 101 | Samoa | N Plymouth | 2008 |
| 93 | Argentina | Wellington | 1997 |
| 91 | Tonga | Brisbane | 2003 |
| 91 | Fiji | Albany | 2005 |
| 85 | Romania | Toulouse | 2007 |
| 83 | Japan | Hamilton | 2011 |
| 79 | Canada | Wellington | 2011 |
| 76 | Italy | Marseilles | 2007 |
| 74 | Fiji | Christchurch | 1987 |
| 73 | Canada | Auckland | 1995 |
| 71 | Fiji | Albany | 1997 |
| 71 | Samoa | Albany | 1999 |

#### BY A PLAYER

| Pts | Player | Opponents | Venue | Year |
|---|---|---|---|---|
| 45 | SD Culhane | Japan | Bloemfontein | 1995 |
| 36 | TE Brown | Italy | Huddersfield | 1999 |
| 33 | CJ Spencer | Argentina | Wellington | 1997 |
| 33 | AP Mehrtens | Ireland | Dublin | 1997 |
| 33 | DW Carter | British/Irish | Wellington | 2005 |
| 33 | NJ Evans | Portugal | Lyons | 2007 |
| 32 | TE Brown | Tonga | Albany | 2000 |
| 30 | MCG Ellis | Japan | Bloemfontein | 1995 |
| 30 | TE Brown | Samoa | Albany | 2001 |
| 29 | AP Mehrtens | Australia | Auckland | 1999 |
| 29 | AP Mehrtens | France | Paris | 2000 |
| 29 | LR MacDonald | Tonga | Brisbane | 2003 |
| 29 | DW Carter | Canada | Hamilton | 2007 |

### MOST TRIES IN A MATCH
#### BY THE TEAM

| Tries | Opponents | Venue | Year |
|---|---|---|---|
| 21 | Japan | Bloemfontein | 1995 |
| 16 | Portugal | Lyons | 2007 |
| 15 | Tonga | Albany | 2000 |
| 15 | Fiji | Albany | 2005 |
| 15 | Samoa | N Plymouth | 2008 |
| 14 | Argentina | Wellington | 1997 |
| 14 | Italy | Huddersfield | 1999 |
| 13 | U S A | Berkeley | 1913 |
| 13 | Tonga | Brisbane | 2003 |
| 13 | Romania | Toulouse | 2007 |
| 13 | Japan | Hamilton | 2011 |
| 12 | Italy | Auckland | 1987 |
| 12 | Fiji | Christchurch | 1987 |
| 12 | Canada | Wellington | 2011 |

#### BY A PLAYER

| Tries | Player | Opponents | Venue | Year |
|---|---|---|---|---|
| 6 | MCG Ellis | Japan | Bloemfontein | 1995 |
| 5 | JW Wilson | Fiji | Albany | 1997 |
| 4 | D McGregor | England | Crystal Palace | 1905 |
| 4 | CI Green | Fiji | Christchurch | 1987 |
| 4 | JA Gallagher | Fiji | Christchurch | 1987 |
| 4 | JJ Kirwan | Wales | Christchurch | 1988 |
| 4 | JT Lomu | England | Cape Town | 1995 |
| 4 | CM Cullen | Scotland | Dunedin | 1996 |
| 4 | JW Wilson | Samoa | Albany | 1999 |
| 4 | JM Muliaina | Canada | Melbourne | 2003 |
| 4 | SW Sivivatu | Fiji | Albany | 2005 |
| 4 | ZR Guildford | Canada | Wellington | 2011 |

## MOST CONVERSIONS IN A MATCH
### BY THE TEAM

| Cons | Opponents | Venue | Year |
|---|---|---|---|
| 20 | Japan | Bloemfontein | 1995 |
| 14 | Portugal | Lyons | 2007 |
| 13 | Tonga | Brisbane | 2003 |
| 13 | Samoa | N Plymouth | 2008 |
| 12 | Tonga | Albany | 2000 |
| 11 | Italy | Huddersfield | 1999 |
| 10 | Fiji | Christchurch | 1987 |
| 10 | Argentina | Wellington | 1997 |
| 10 | Romania | Toulouse | 2007 |
| 9 | Canada | Melbourne | 2003 |
| 9 | Italy | Marseilles | 2007 |
| 9 | Ireland | N Plymouth | 2010 |
| 9 | Japan | Hamilton | 2011 |
| 8 | Italy | Auckland | 1987 |
| 8 | Wales | Auckland | 1988 |
| 8 | Fiji | Albany | 1997 |
| 8 | Italy | Hamilton | 2003 |
| 8 | Fiji | Albany | 2005 |
| 8 | Canada | Wellington | 2011 |

### BY A PLAYER

| Cons | Player | Opponents | Venue | Year |
|---|---|---|---|---|
| 20 | SD Culhane | Japan | Bloemfontein | 1995 |
| 14 | NJ Evans | Portugal | Lyons | 2007 |
| 12 | TE Brown | Tonga | Albany | 2000 |
| 12 | LR MacDonald | Tonga | Brisbane | 2003 |
| 11 | TE Brown | Italy | Huddersfield | 1999 |
| 10 | GJ Fox | Fiji | Christchurch | 1987 |
| 10 | CJ Spencer | Argentina | Wellington | 1997 |
| 9 | DW Carter | Canada | Melbourne | 2003 |
| 9 | CR Slade | Japan | Hamilton | 2011 |
| 8 | GJ Fox | Italy | Auckland | 1987 |
| 8 | GJ Fox | Wales | Auckland | 1988 |
| 8 | AP Mehrtens | Italy | Hamilton | 2002 |

## MOST DROP GOALS IN A MATCH
### BY THE TEAM

| Drops | Opponents | Venue | Year |
|---|---|---|---|
| 3 | France | Christchurch | 1986 |

### BY A PLAYER

| Drops | Player | Opponents | Venue | Year |
|---|---|---|---|---|
| 2 | OD Bruce | Ireland | Dublin | 1978 |
| 2 | FM Botica | France | Christchurch | 1986 |
| 2 | AP Mehrtens | Australia | Auckland | 1995 |

## MOST PENALTIES IN A MATCH
### BY THE TEAM

| Penalties | Opponents | Venue | Year |
|---|---|---|---|
| 9 | Australia | Auckland | 1999 |
| 9 | France | Paris | 2000 |
| 7 | Western Samoa | Auckland | 1993 |
| 7 | South Africa | Pretoria | 1999 |
| 7 | South Africa | Wellington | 2006 |
| 7 | Australia | Auckland | 2007 |
| 7 | Argentina | Auckland | 2011 |
| 6 | British/Irish Lions | Dunedin | 1959 |
| 6 | England | Christchurch | 1985 |
| 6 | Argentina | Wellington | 1987 |
| 6 | Scotland | Christchurch | 1987 |
| 6 | France | Paris | 1990 |
| 6 | South Africa | Auckland | 1994 |
| 6 | Australia | Brisbane | 1996 |
| 6 | Ireland | Dublin | 1997 |
| 6 | South Africa | Cardiff | 1999 |
| 6 | Scotland | Murrayfield | 2001 |
| 6 | South Africa | Christchurch | 2004 |
| 6 | Australia | Sydney | 2004 |
| 6 | South Africa | Dunedin | 2008 |
| 6 | Australia | Tokyo | 2009 |
| 6 | Australia | Brisbane | 2012 |

### BY A PLAYER

| Pens | Player | Opponents | Venue | Year |
|---|---|---|---|---|
| 9 | AP Mehrtens | Australia | Auckland | 1999 |
| 9 | AP Mehrtens | France | Paris | 2000 |
| 7 | GJ Fox | Western Samoa | Auckland | 1993 |
| 7 | AP Mehrtens | South Africa | Pretoria | 1999 |
| 7 | DW Carter | South Africa | Wellington | 2006 |
| 7 | DW Carter | Australia | Auckland | 2007 |
| 7 | PAT Weepu | Argentina | Auckland | 2011 |
| 6 | DB Clarke | British/Irish Lions | Dunedin | 1959 |
| 6 | KJ Crowley | England | Christchurch | 1985 |
| 6 | GJ Fox | Argentina | Wellington | 1987 |
| 6 | GJ Fox | Scotland | Christchurch | 1987 |
| 6 | GJ Fox | France | Paris | 1990 |
| 6 | SP Howarth | South Africa | Auckland | 1994 |
| 6 | AP Mehrtens | Australia | Brisbane | 1996 |
| 6 | AP Mehrtens | Ireland | Dublin | 1997 |
| 6 | AP Mehrtens | South Africa | Cardiff | 1999 |
| 6 | AP Mehrtens | Scotland | Murrayfield | 2001 |
| 6 | DW Carter | South Africa | Dunedin | 2008 |
| 6 | DW Carter | Australia | Tokyo | 2009 |
| 6 | DW Carter | Australia | Brisbane | 2012 |

NEW ZEALAND

# CAREER RECORDS

## MOST CAPPED PLAYERS

| Caps | Player | Career Span |
|---|---|---|
| 133 | RH McCaw | 2001 to 2014 |
| 119 | KF Mealamu | 2002 to 2014 |
| 110 | TD Woodcock | 2002 to 2014 |
| 100 | JM Muliaina | 2003 to 2011 |
| 100 | DW Carter | 2003 to 2014 |
| 94 | MA Nonu | 2003 to 2014 |
| 92 | SBT Fitzpatrick | 1986 to 1997 |
| 83 | AK Hore | 2002 to 2013 |
| 82 | CG Smith | 2004 to 2014 |
| 81 | JW Marshall | 1995 to 2005 |
| 79 | ID Jones | 1990 to 1999 |
| 77 | AJ Williams | 2002 to 2012 |
| 74 | JF Umaga | 1997 to 2005 |
| 71 | PAT Weepu | 2004 to 2013 |
| 70 | AP Mehrtens | 1995 to 2004 |
| 68 | JT Rokocoko | 2003 to 2010 |
| 68 | KJ Read | 2008 to 2014 |
| 67 | CR Jack | 2001 to 2007 |
| 66 | GM Somerville | 2000 to 2008 |

## MOST CONSECUTIVE TESTS

| Tests | Player | Span |
|---|---|---|
| 63 | SBT Fitzpatrick | 1986 to 1995 |
| 51 | CM Cullen | 1996 to 2000 |
| 49 | RM Brooke | 1995 to 1999 |
| 41 | JW Wilson | 1996 to 1999 |
| 40 | GW Whetton | 1986 to 1991 |

## MOST TESTS AS CAPTAIN

| Tests | Captain | Span |
|---|---|---|
| 96 | RH McCaw | 2004 to 2014 |
| 51 | SBT Fitzpatrick | 1992 to 1997 |
| 30 | WJ Whineray | 1958 to 1965 |
| 23 | RD Thorne | 2002 to 2007 |
| 22 | TC Randell | 1998 to 2002 |
| 21 | JF Umaga | 2004 to 2005 |
| 19 | GNK Mourie | 1977 to 1982 |
| 18 | BJ Lochore | 1966 to 1970 |
| 17 | AG Dalton | 1981 to 1985 |

## MOST POINTS IN TESTS

| Points | Player | Tests | Career |
|---|---|---|---|
| 1442 | DW Carter | 100 | 2003 to 2013 |
| 967 | AP Mehrtens | 70 | 1995 to 2004 |
| 645 | GJ Fox | 46 | 1985 to 1993 |
| 291 | CJ Spencer | 35 | 1997 to 2004 |
| 256 | AW Cruden | 35 | 2010 to 2014 |
| 245 | DC Howlett | 62 | 2000 to 2007 |
| 236 | CM Cullen | 58 | 1996 to 2002 |
| 234 | JW Wilson | 60 | 1993 to 2001 |
| 230 | JT Rokocoko | 68 | 2003 to 2010 |
| 207 | DB Clarke | 31 | 1956 to 1964 |
| 201 | AR Hewson | 19 | 1981 to 1984 |

## MOST TRIES IN TESTS

| Tries | Player | Tests | Career |
|---|---|---|---|
| 49 | DC Howlett | 62 | 2000 to 2007 |
| 46 | CM Cullen | 58 | 1996 to 2002 |
| 46 | JT Rokocoko | 68 | 2003 to 2010 |
| 44 | JW Wilson | 60 | 1993 to 2001 |
| 37 | JT Lomu | 63 | 1994 to 2002 |
| 37* | JF Umaga | 74 | 1997 to 2005 |
| 35 | JJ Kirwan | 63 | 1984 to 1994 |
| 34 | JM Muliaina | 100 | 2003 to 2011 |
| 29 | DW Carter | 100 | 2003 to 2013 |
| 29 | SW Sivivatu | 45 | 2005 to 2011 |
| 27 | SJ Savea | 28 | 2012 to 2014 |
| 26 | MA Nonu | 94 | 2003 to 2014 |
| 25 | CG Smith | 82 | 2004 to 2014 |
| 25* | RH McCaw | 133 | 2001 to 2014 |
| 24 | JW Marshall | 81 | 1995 to 2005 |
| 20 | FE Bunce | 55 | 1992 to 1997 |
| * Umaga and McCaw's hauls each include a penalty try | | | |

## MOST CONVERSIONS IN TESTS

| Cons | Player | Tests | Career |
|---|---|---|---|
| 257 | DW Carter | 100 | 2003 to 2013 |
| 169 | AP Mehrtens | 70 | 1995 to 2004 |
| 118 | GJ Fox | 46 | 1985 to 1993 |
| 49 | CJ Spencer | 35 | 1997 to 2004 |
| 44 | AW Cruden | 35 | 2010 to 2014 |
| 43 | TE Brown | 18 | 1999 to 2001 |
| 33 | DB Clarke | 31 | 1956 to 1964 |
| 32 | SD Culhane | 6 | 1995 to 1996 |

## MOST PENALTY GOALS IN TESTS

| Pens | Player | Tests | Career |
|---|---|---|---|
| 255 | DW Carter | 100 | 2003 to 2013 |
| 188 | AP Mehrtens | 70 | 1995 to 2004 |
| 128 | GJ Fox | 46 | 1985 to 1993 |
| 50 | AW Cruden | 35 | 2010 to 2014 |
| 43 | AR Hewson | 19 | 1981 to 1984 |
| 41 | CJ Spencer | 35 | 1997 to 2004 |
| 38 | DB Clarke | 31 | 1956 to 1964 |
| 24 | WF McCormick | 16 | 1965 to 1971 |

## MOST DROP GOALS IN TESTS

| Drops | Player | Tests | Career |
|---|---|---|---|
| 10 | AP Mehrtens | 70 | 1995 to 2004 |
| 7 | GJ Fox | 46 | 1985 to 1993 |
| 6 | DW Carter | 100 | 2003 to 2013 |
| 5 | DB Clarke | 31 | 1956 to 1964 |
| 5 | MA Herewini | 10 | 1962 to 1967 |
| 5 | OD Bruce | 14 | 1976 to 1978 |

# RUGBY CHAMPIONSHIP (FORMERLY TRI NATIONS) RECORDS

| RECORD | DETAIL | HOLDER | SET |
|---|---|---|---|
| Most points in season | 202 | in six matches | 2013 |
| Most tries in season | 24 | in six matches | 2013 |
| Highest score | 55 | 55–35 v S Africa (h) | 1997 |
| Biggest win | 39 | 54–15 v Argentina (a) | 2012 |
| Highest score conceded | 46 | 40–46 v S Africa (a) | 2000 |
| Biggest defeat | 21 | 7–28 v Australia (a) | 1999 |
| Most appearances | 55 | RH McCaw | 2002 to 2014 |
| Most points in matches | 531 | DW Carter | 2003 to 2013 |
| Most points in season | 99 | DW Carter | 2006 |
| Most points in match | 29 | AP Mehrtens | v Australia (h) 1999 |
| Most tries in matches | 16 | CM Cullen | 1996 to 2002 |
| Most tries in season | 8 | BR Smith | 2013 |
| Most tries in match | 3 | JT Rokocoko | v Australia (a) 2003 |
| | 3 | DC Howlett | v Australia (h) 2005 |
| | 3 | CS Jane | v Argentina (a) 2012 |
| | 3 | BR Smith | v Australia (a) 2013 |
| Most cons in matches | 72 | DW Carter | 2003 to 2013 |
| Most cons in season | 14 | DW Carter | 2006 |
| Most cons in match | 5 | AW Cruden | v Australia (h) 2014 |
| Most pens in matches | 115 | DW Carter | 2003 to 2013 |
| Most pens in season | 21 | DW Carter | 2006 |
| Most pens in match | 9 | AP Mehrtens | v Australia (h) 1999 |

# MISCELLANEOUS RECORDS

| RECORD | HOLDER | DETAIL |
|---|---|---|
| Longest Test Career | E Hughes/CE Meads | 1907–21/1957–71 |
| Youngest Test Cap | JT Lomu | 19 yrs 45 days in 1994 |
| Oldest Test Cap | E Hughes | 40 yrs 123 days in 1921 |

**NEW ZEALAND**

# CAREER RECORDS OF NEW ZEALAND INTERNATIONAL PLAYERS
## UP TO 13 OCTOBER 2014

| BACKS : | DEBUT: | CAPS | T | C | P | D | PTS |
|---|---|---|---|---|---|---|---|
| BJ Barrett | 2012 v I | 25 | 4 | 19 | 12 | 0 | 94 |
| DW Carter | 2003 v W | 100 | 29 | 257 | 255 | 6 | 1442 |
| RS Crotty | 2013 v A | 9 | 1 | 0 | 0 | 0 | 5 |
| AW Cruden | 2010 v I | 35 | 3 | 44 | 50 | 1 | 256 |
| IJA Dagg | 2010 v I | 43 | 13 | 1 | 1 | 0 | 70 |
| MF Fekitoa | 2014 v E | 6 | 1 | 0 | 0 | 0 | 5 |
| F Halai | 2013 v J | 1 | 1 | 0 | 0 | 0 | 5 |
| CS Jane | 2008 v A | 51 | 16 | 0 | 0 | 0 | 80 |
| TNJ Kerr-Barlow | 2012 v S | 15 | 0 | 0 | 0 | 0 | 0 |
| MA Nonu | 2003 v E | 94 | 26 | 0 | 0 | 0 | 130 |
| TTR Perenara | 2014 v E | 6 | 1 | 0 | 0 | 0 | 5 |
| ST Piutau | 2013 v F | 10 | 3 | 0 | 0 | 0 | 15 |
| F Saili | 2013 v Arg | 2 | 0 | 0 | 0 | 0 | 0 |
| SJ Savea | 2012 v I | 28 | 27 | 0 | 0 | 0 | 135 |
| CR Slade | 2010 v A | 14 | 3 | 19 | 4 | 0 | 65 |
| AL Smith | 2012 v I | 35 | 10 | 1 | 0 | 0 | 52 |
| BR Smith | 2009 v It | 35 | 16 | 0 | 0 | 0 | 80 |
| CG Smith | 2004 v It | 82 | 25 | 0 | 0 | 0 | 125 |
| TJ Taylor | 2013 v A | 3 | 0 | 1 | 4 | 0 | 14 |
| S Williams | 2010 v E | 19 | 6 | 0 | 0 | 0 | 30 |
| **FORWARDS :** | | | | | | | |
| DJ Bird | 2013 v J | 1 | 0 | 0 | 0 | 0 | 0 |
| SJ Cane | 2012 v I | 19 | 7 | 0 | 0 | 0 | 35 |
| DS Coles | 2012 v S | 23 | 1 | 0 | 0 | 0 | 5 |
| WWV Crockett | 2009 v It | 32 | 1 | 0 | 0 | 0 | 5 |
| CC Faumuina | 2012 v Arg | 22 | 0 | 0 | 0 | 0 | 0 |
| BJ Franks | 2010 v I | 37 | 2 | 0 | 0 | 0 | 10 |
| OT Franks | 2009 v It | 63 | 0 | 0 | 0 | 0 | 0 |
| N Harris | 2014 v Arg | 1 | 0 | 0 | 0 | 0 | 0 |
| AK Hore | 2002 v E | 83 | 8 | 0 | 0 | 0 | 40 |
| J Kaino | 2006 v I | 54 | 8 | 0 | 0 | 0 | 40 |
| DS Luatua | 2013 v F | 14 | 1 | 0 | 0 | 0 | 5 |
| RH McCaw | 2001 v I | 133 | 25* | 0 | 0 | 0 | 125 |
| KF Mealamu | 2002 v W | 119 | 12 | 0 | 0 | 0 | 60 |
| LJ Messam | 2008 v S | 35 | 6 | 0 | 0 | 0 | 30 |
| J Moody | 2014 v A | 5 | 0 | 0 | 0 | 0 | 0 |
| KJ Read | 2008 v S | 68 | 16 | 0 | 0 | 0 | 80 |
| BA Retallick | 2012 v I | 32 | 1 | 0 | 0 | 0 | 5 |

| L Romano | 2012 v I | 16 | 1 | 0 | 0 | 0 | 5 | **415** |
| JI Thrush | 2013 v F | 9 | 1 | 0 | 0 | 0 | 5 | |
| MB Todd | 2013 v F | 2 | 0 | 0 | 0 | 0 | 0 | |
| JL To'omaga-Allen | 2013 v J | 1 | 0 | 0 | 0 | 0 | 0 | |
| PT Tuipulotu | 2014 v E | 3 | 0 | 0 | 0 | 0 | 0 | |
| VVJ Vito | 2010 v I | 24 | 2 | 0 | 0 | 0 | 10 | |
| LC Whitelock | 2013 v J | 1 | 0 | 0 | 0 | 0 | 0 | |
| SL Whitelock | 2010 v I | 59 | 4 | 0 | 0 | 0 | 20 | |
| AJ Williams | 2002 v E | 77 | 7 | 0 | 0 | 0 | 35 | |
| TD Woodcock | 2002 v W | 110 | 9 | 0 | 0 | 0 | 45 | |

*NB McCaw's figures include a penalty try awarded against Ireland in 2008.*

# NEW ZEALAND INTERNATIONAL PLAYERS
## UP TO 13 OCTOBER 2014
Entries in square brackets denote matches played in RWC Finals.

**Abbott, H L** (Taranaki) 1906 F
**Afeaki, B T P** (North Harbour) 2013 F1(R)
**Afoa, I F** (Auckland) 2005 I, S, 2006 E(R), 2008 I1, SA2, A1(R), 2(R), SA3(R), A3(R), S, I2(t&R), W(R), E3(R), 2009 F1(R), 2(R), It1, SA2(R), A2(R), SA3(R), A3(R), 4(R), It2(R), E(R), 2010 SA3(R), A3(R), 4(R), E(R), S(R), I2(R), W3(R), 2011 Fj(R), SA1(R), 2, A2(R), [J(R), Arg(R)]
**Aitken, G G** (Wellington) 1921 SA 1, 2
**Alatini, P F** (Otago) 1999 F 1(R), [It, SA 3(R)], 2000 Tg, S 1, A 1, SA 1, A 2, SA 2, It, 2001 Sm, Arg 1, F, SA 1, A 1, SA 2, A 2
**Allen, F R** (Auckland) 1946 A 1, 2, 1947 A 1, 2, 1949 SA 1, 2
**Allen, M R** (Taranaki, Manawatu) 1993 WS (t), 1996 S 2 (t), 1997 Arg 1(R), 2(R), SA 2(R), A 3(R), E 2, W (R)
**Allen, N H** (Counties) 1980 A 3, W
**Alley, G T** (Canterbury) 1928 SA 1, 2, 3
**Anderson, A** (Canterbury) 1983 S, E, 1984 A 1, 2, 1987 [Fj]
**Anderson, B L** (Wairarapa-Bush) 1986 A 1
**Anesi, S R** (Waikato) 2005 Fj(R)
**Archer, W R** (Otago, Southland) 1955 A 1, 2, 1956 SA 1, 3
**Argus, W G** (Canterbury) 1946 A 1, 2, 1947 A 1, 2
**Arnold, D A** (Canterbury) 1963 I, W, 1964 E, F
**Arnold, K D** (Waikato) 1947 A 1, 2
**Ashby, D L** (Southland) 1958 A 2
**Asher, A A** (Auckland) 1903 A
**Ashworth, B G** (Auckland) 1978 A 1, 2
**Ashworth, J C** (Canterbury, Hawke's Bay) 1978 A 1, 2, 3, 1980 A 1, 2, 3, 1981 SA 1, 2, 3, 1982 A 1, 2, 1983 BI 1, 2, 3, 4, A, 1984 F 1, 2, A 1, 2, 3, 1985 E 1, 2, A
**Atiga, B A C** (Auckland) 2003 [Tg(R)]
**Atkinson, H** (West Coast) 1913 A 1
**Avery, H E** (Wellington) 1910 A 1, 2, 3

**Bachop, G T M** (Canterbury) 1989 W, I, 1990 S 1, 2, A 1, 2, 3, F 1, 2, 1991 Arg 1, 2, A 1, 2, [E, US, C, A, S], 1992 Wld 1, 1994 SA 1, 2, 3, A, 1995 C, [I, W, S, E, SA], A 1, 2
**Bachop, S J** (Otago) 1994 F 2, SA 1, 2, 3, A
**Badeley, C E O** (Auckland) 1921 SA 1, 2
**Baird, J A S** (Otago) 1913 A 2
**Ball, N** (Wellington) 1931 A, 1932 A 2, 3, 1935 W, 1936 E
**Barrett, B J** (Taranaki) 2012 I 3(R), Arg1(R), S(R), It, W(R), 2013

F1(R), 2(R), 3(R), A1(R), Arg1(R), SA1(R), Arg2(R), SA2(R), A3(R), J, I(R), 2014 E1(R), 2(R), 3(R), A1(R), 2(R), Arg1, SA1(R), Arg2, SA2
**Barrett, J** (Auckland) 1913 A 2, 3
**Barry, E F** (Wellington) 1934 A 2
**Barry, L J** (North Harbour) 1995 F 2
**Bates, S P** (Waikato) 2004 It(R)
**Batty, G B** (Wellington, Bay of Plenty) 1972 W, S, 1973 E 1, I, F, E 2, 1974 A 1, 3, I, 1975 S, 1976 SA 1, 2, 3, 4, 1977 BI 1
**Batty, W** (Auckland) 1930 BI 1, 3, 4, 1931 A
**Beatty, G E** (Taranaki) 1950 BI 1
**Bell, R H** (Otago) 1951 A 3, 1952 A 1, 2
**Bellis, E A** (Wanganui) 1921 SA 1, 2, 3
**Bennet, R** (Otago) 1905 A
**Berghan, T** (Otago) 1938 A 1, 2, 3
**Berry, M J** (Wairarapa-Bush) 1986 A 3(R)
**Berryman, N R** (Northland) 1998 SA 2(R)
**Bevan, V D** (Wellington) 1949 A 1, 2, 1950 BI 1, 2, 3, 4
**Bird, D J** (Canterbury) 2013 J
**Birtwistle, W M** (Canterbury) 1965 SA 1, 2, 3, 4, 1967 E, W, S
**Black, J E** (Canterbury) 1977 F 1, 1979 A, 1980 A 3
**Black, N W** (Auckland) 1949 SA 3
**Black, R S** (Otago) 1914 A 1
**Blackadder, T J** (Canterbury) 1998 E 1(R), 2, 2000 Tg, S 1, 2, A 1, SA 1, A 2, SA 2, F 1, 2, It
**Blair, B A** (Canterbury) 2001 S (R), Arg 2, 2002 E, W
**Blake, A W** (Wairarapa) 1949 A 1
**Blowers, A F** (Auckland) 1996 SA 2(R), 4(R), 1997 I, E 1(R), W (R), 1999 F 1(R), SA 1, A 1(R), SA 2, A 2(R), [It]
**Boggs, E G** (Auckland) 1946 A 2, 1949 SA 1
**Bond, J G** (Canterbury) 1949 A 2
**Booth, E E** (Otago) 1906 F, 1907 A 1, 3
**Boric, A F** (North Harbour) 2008 E1(R), 2(R), SA2, A2(R), SA3(R), Sm, A3(R), 4(R), S, E3(R), 2009 It2, E(R), F3(R), 2010 I1, W1, A3(R), E(R), S(R), I2, W3(R), 2011 Tg(R), J(R), F1(R), C(R)]
**Boroevich, K G** (Wellington) 1986 F 1, A 1, F 3(R)
**Botica, F M** (North Harbour) 1986 F 1, A 1, 2, 3, F 2, 3, 1989 Arg 1(R)
**Bowden, N J G** (Taranaki) 1952 A 2

Crichton, S (Wellington) 1983 S, E
Crockett, W W V (Canterbury) 2009 It1, W, It2, 2011 Fj, SA1, A1, 2012 A2, S, It(R), W(R), E(R), 2013 F1, 2, 3, A2(R), Arg1(R), SA1(R), Arg2(R), SA2(R), A3(R), J, F4(R), E(R), I, 2014 E1(R), 2(R), 3(R), A1, 2, Arg1, SA1, Arg2
Cross, T (Canterbury) 1904 BI, 1905 A
Crotty, R S (Canterbury) 2013 A1(R), J(R), F4(R), E(R), I(R) 2014 E3(R), A1(R), 2, SA2(R)
Crowley, K J (Taranaki) 1985 E 1, 2, A, Arg 1, 2, 1986 A 3, F 2, 3, 1987 [Arg], 1990 S 1, 2, A 1, 2, 3, F 1, 2, 1991 Arg 1, 2, [A]
Crowley, P J B (Auckland) 1949 SA 3, 4, 1950 BI 1, 2, 3, 4
Cruden, A W (Manawatu) 2010 I1(R), W1(R), 2(R), SA2(R), A1(R), 3, 2011 [Arg(R), A, F2], 2012 I 1(R), 3, A2(R), Arg1, SA1, Arg2(R), SA2(R), A3(R), It, W, E(R), 2013 F1, 2, A1, Arg2, SA2, A3, F4(R), E(R), I, 2014 E1, 2, 3, A1, 2, SA1
Culhane, S D (Southland) 1995 [J], It, F 1, 2, 1996 SA 3, 4
Cullen C M (Manawatu, Central Vikings, Wellington) 1996 WS, S 1, 2, A 1, SA 1, A 2, SA 2, A 3, 4, 5, 1997 Fj, Arg 1, 2, A 1, SA 1, A 2, SA 2, A 3, I, E 1, W, E 2, 1998 E 1, 2, A 1, SA 1, A 2, SA 2, A 3, 1999 WS, F 1, SA 1, A 1, SA 2, A 2, [Tg, E, It (R), S, F 2, SA 3], 2000 Tg, S 1, 2, A 1, SA 1, A 2, SA 2, F 1, 2, It, 2001 A 2(R), 2002 It, Fj, A 1, SA 1, A 2, F
Cummings, W (Canterbury) 1913 A 2, 3
Cundy, R T (Wairarapa) 1929 A 2(R)
Cunningham, G R (Auckland) 1979 A, S, E, 1980 A 1, 2
Cunningham, W (Auckland) 1905 S, I, 1906 F, 1907 A 1, 2, 3, 1908 AW 1, 2, 3
Cupples, L F (Bay of Plenty) 1924 I, W
Currie, C J (Canterbury) 1978 I, W
Cuthill, J E (Otago) 1913 A 1, US

Dagg, I J A (Hawke's Bay) 2010 I1, W1, SA2(R), A1(R), SA3(R), A3, 2011 SA2, [Tg, F1, C, A, F2], 2012 I 1, 2, 3, A1, 2, Arg1, SA1, Arg2, SA2, A3, S, W, E, 2013 F1, 2, 3, A1, 2, Arg1, SA1, Arg2, SA2, A3, F4, E, I, 2014 E1, Arg1, SA1, Arg2, SA2
Dalley, W C (Canterbury) 1924 I, 1928 SA 1, 2, 3, 4
Dalton, A G (Counties) 1977 F 2, 1978 A 1, 2, 3, I, W, E, S, 1979 F 1, 2, S, 1981 S 1, 2, SA 1, 2, 3, R, F 1, 2, 1982 A 1, 2, 3, 1983 BI 1, 2, 3, 4, A, 1984 F 1, 2, A 1, 2, 3, 1985 E 1, 2, A
Dalton, D (Hawke's Bay) 1935 I, W, 1936 A 1, 2, 1937 SA 1, 2, 3, 1938 A 1, 2
Dalton, R A (Wellington) 1947 A 1, 2
Dalzell, G N (Canterbury) 1953 W, 1954 I, E, S, F
Davie, M G (Canterbury) 1983 E (R)
Davies, W A (Auckland, Otago) 1960 SA 4, 1962 A 4, 5
Davis, K (Auckland) 1952 A 2, 1953 W, 1954 I, E, S, F, 1955 A 2, 1958 A 1, 2, 3
Davis, L J (Canterbury) 1976 I, 1977 BI 3, 4
Davis, W L (Hawke's Bay) 1967 A, E, W, F, S, 1968 A 1, 2, F 1, 1969 W 1, 2, 1970 SA 2
Deans, I B (Canterbury) 1988 W 1, 2, A 1, 2, 3, 1989 F 1, 2, Arg 1, 2, A
Deans, R G (Canterbury) 1905 S, I, E, W, 1908 AW 3
Deans, R M (Canterbury) 1983 S, E, 1984 A 1(R), 2, 3
Delamore, G W (Wellington) 1949 SA 4
Delany, M P (Bay of Plenty) 2009 It 2
De Malmanche, A P (Waikato) 2009 It1(R), A3(R), 2010 I1(R), W1(R), F2(R)]
Dermody, C (Southland) 2006 I1, 2, E(R)
Devine, S J (Auckland) 2002 E, W 2003 E (R), W, F, SA 1, A 1(R), [C, SA(R), F]
Dewar, H (Taranaki) 1913 A 1, US
Diack, E S (Otago) 1959 BI 2
Dick, J (Auckland) 1937 SA 1, 2, 1938 A 3
Dick, M J (Auckland) 1963 I, W, 1964 E, S, F, 1965 SA 3, 1966 BI 4, 1967 A, E, W, F, 1969 W 1, 2, 1970 SA 1, 4
Dixon, M J (Canterbury) 1954 I, E, S, F, 1956 SA 1, 2, 3, 4, 1957 A 1, 2
Dobson, R L (Auckland) 1949 A 1
Dodd, E H (Wellington) 1905 A
Donald, A J (Wanganui) 1983 S, E, 1984 F 1, 2, A 1, 2, 3
Donald, J G (Wairarapa) 1921 SA 1, 2
Donald, Q (Wairarapa) 1924 I, W, 1925 E, F

**417**

Donald, S R (Waikato) 2008 E1(R), 2(R), A2(R), SA3(R), Sm(R), A3(R), 4, S, I2(R), 2009 F1, 2, A1, SA1, 2, A2(R), SA3, A4(R), It2(R), F3(R), 2010 A4(R), S(R), W3(R), 2011[F2(R)]
Donaldson, M W (Manawatu) 1977 F 1, 2, 1978 A 1, 2, 3, I, E, S, 1979 F 1, 2, A, S (R), 1981 SA 3(R)
Donnelly, T J S (Otago) 2009 A3, 4, W(R), It2, E, F3, 2010 W2, SA1, 2, A1, 2, SA3, A3, 4, I2
Dougan, J P (Wellington) 1972 A 1, 1973 E 2
Dowd, C W (Auckland) 1993 BI 1, 2, 3, A, WS, S, E, 1994 SA 1(R), 1995 C, [I, W, J, E, SA], A 1, 2, It, F 1, 2, 1996 WS, S 1, 2, A 1, SA 1, A 2, SA 2, 3, 4, 5, 1997 Fj, Arg 1, 2, A 1, SA 1, A 2, SA 2, A 3, I, E 1, W, 1998 E 1, 2, A 1, SA 1, A 2, 3(R), 1999 SA 2(R), A 2(R), [Tg (R), E, It, S, F 2, SA 3], 2000 Tg, S 1(R), 2(R), A 1(R), SA 1(R), A 2(R)
Dowd, G W (North Harbour) 1992 I 1(R)
Downing, A J (Auckland) 1913 A 1, US, 1914 A 1, 2, 3
Drake, J A (Auckland) 1986 F 2, 3, 1987 [Fj, Arg, S, W, F], A
Duff, R H (Canterbury) 1951 A 1, 2, 3, 1952 A 1, 2, 1955 A 2, 3, 1956 SA 1, 2, 3, 4
Duggan, R J L (Waikato) 1999 [It (R)]
Duncan, J (Otago) 1903 A
Duncan, M G (Hawke's Bay) 1971 BI 3(R), 4
Duncan, W D (Otago) 1921 SA 1, 2, 3
Dunn, E J (North Auckland) 1979 S, 1981 S 1
Dunn, I T W (North Auckland) 1983 BI 1, 4, A
Dunn, J M (Auckland) 1946 A 1

Earl, A T (Canterbury) 1986 F 1, A 1, F 3(R), 1987 [Arg], 1989 W, I, 1991 Arg 1(R), 2, A 1, [E (R), US, S], 1992 A 2, 3(R)
Eastgate, B P (Canterbury) 1952 A 1, 2, 1954 S
Eaton, J J (Taranaki) 2005 I, E(t), S(R), 2006 Arg, A1, 2(R), 3, SA3(R), F1(R), 2(R), 2009 A1(R), SA1(R), A3(R), 4(R), W
Elliot, H T P (Hawke's Bay) 2010 S, I 2, 2012 I 1(R)
Elliott, K G (Wellington) 1946 A 1, 2
Ellis, A M (Canterbury) 2006 E(R), F2(R), 2007 [Pt(R), R], 2008 I1, E1, 2, SA1, 2, A1, S(R), 2009 It2, E(R), F3(R), 2010 E(R), S(R), I2, W3(R), 2011 A1(R), SA2(R), A2(R), [J, F1(R), C(R), A(R), F2(R)]
Ellis, M C G (Otago) 1993 S, E, 1995 C, [I (R), W, J, S, SA (R)]
Ellison, T E (Wellington, Otago) 2009 It 2, 2012 I 3(R), SA2(R), S
Elsom, A E G (Canterbury) 1952 A 1, 2, 1953 W, 1955 A 1, 2, 3
Elvidge, R R (Otago) 1946 A 1, 2, 1949 SA 1, 2, 3, 4, 1950 BI 1, 2, 3
Erceg, C P (Auckland) 1951 A 1, 2, 3, 1952 A 1
Evans, B R (Hawke's Bay) 2009 F1(R), 2(R)
Evans, D A (Hawke's Bay) 1910 A 2
Evans, N J (North Harbour, Otago) 2004 E1(R), 2, Arg, PI(R), 2005 I, S, 2006 F2(R), W(R), 2007 F1(R), 2, SA2(R), A2(R), [Pt, S(R), R, F(R)]
Eveleigh, K A (Manawatu) 1976 SA 2, 4, 1977 BI 1, 2

Fanning, A H N (Canterbury) 1913 A 3
Fanning, B J (Canterbury) 1903 A, 1904 BI
Farrell, C P (Auckland) 1977 BI 1, 2
Faumuina, C C (Auckland) 2012 Arg1(R), SA1(R), Arg2(R), A3, It, W(R), E(R), 2013 A1(R), 2(R), Arg1, SA1(R), Arg2(R), SA2, A3, F4(R), E(R), I, 2014 E1(R), 2(R), 3(R), A2(R), SA2(R)
Fawcett, C L (Auckland) 1976 SA 2, 3
Fea, W R (Otago) 1921 SA 3
Feek, G E (Canterbury) 1999 WS (R), A 1(R), SA 2, [E (t), It], 2000 F 1, 2, It, 2001 I, S
Fekitoa, M F (Auckland) 2014 E1(R), 3, A1, 2(R), Arg2, SA2
Filipo, R A (Wellington) 2007 C, SA1(R), A1(R), 2008 S(R)
Finlay, B E L (Manawatu) 1959 BI 1
Finlay, J (Manawatu) 1946 A 1
Finlayson, I (North Auckland) 1928 SA 1, 2, 3, 4, 1930 BI 1, 2
Fitzgerald, J T (Wellington) 1952 A 1
Fitzgerald, B B J (Wellington) 1953 W, 1954 I, F
Fitzpatrick, S B T (Auckland) 1986 F 1, A 1, F 2, 3, 1987 [It, Fj, Arg, S, W, F], A, 1988 W 1, 2, A 1, 2, 3, 1989 F 1, 2, Arg 1, 2, A, W, I, 1990 S 1, 2, A 1, 2, 3, F 1, 2, 1991 Arg 1, 2, A 1, 2, [E, US, It, C, A, S], 1992 Wld 1, 2, 3, I 1, 2, A 1, 2, 3, SA, 1993 BI 1, 2, 3, A, WS, S, E, 1994 F 1, 2, SA 1, 2, 3, A, 1995 C, [I, W, S, E, SA], A 1, 2, It, F 1, 2, 1996 WS, S 1, 2, A 1, SA 1, A 2, SA 2, 3, 4, 5, 1997 Fj, Arg 1, 2, A 1, SA 1, A 2, SA 2, A 3, W (R)

**Hill, D W** (Waikato) 2006 I2(R)

**Hill, S F** (Canterbury) 1955 A 3, 1956 SA 1, 3, 4, 1957 A 1, 2, 1958 A 3, 1959 BI 1, 2, 3, 4

**Hines, G R** (Waikato) 1980 A 3

**Hobbs, M J B** (Canterbury) 1983 BI 1, 2, 3, 4, A, S, E, 1984 F 1, 2, A 1, 2, 3, 1985 E 1, 2, A, Arg 1, 2, 1986 A 2, 3, F 2, 3

**Hoeata, J M R A** (Taranaki) 2011 Fj, SA1(R), 2(R)

**Hoeft, C H** (Otago) 1998 E 2(t&R), A 2(R), SA 2, A 3, 1999 WS, F 1, SA 1, A 1, 2, [Tg, E, S, F 2, SA 3(R)], 2000 S 1, 2, A 1, SA 1, A 2, SA 2, 2001 Sm, Arg 1, F, SA 1, A 1, SA 2, A 2, 2003 W, [C, F(R)]

**Holah, M R** (Waikato) 2001 Sm, Arg 1(t&R), F (R), SA 1(R), A 1(R), SA 2(R), A 2(R), 2002 It, 1 2(R), A 2(t), E, F, W (R), 2003 W, F (R), A 1(R), SA 2, [It(R), C, Tg(R), W(R), SA(t&R)], 2004 E1(R), 2, Arg(R), PI, A1, SA1, A2, SA2, 2005 BI3(R), A1(R), 2006 I1, SA3(t)

**Holder, E C** (Buller) 1934 A 2

**Hook, L S** (Auckland) 1929 A 1, 2, 3

**Hooper, J A** (Canterbury) 1937 SA 1, 2, 3

**Hopkinson, A E** (Canterbury) 1967 S, 1968 A 2, F 1, 2, 3, 1969 W 2, 1970 SA 1, 2, 3

**Hore, A K** (Taranaki) 2002 E, F, 2004 E1(t), 2(R), Arg, A1(t), 2005 W(R), I(R), S(R), 2006 I2(R), F(R), Arg(R), A1(R), SA1(R), A2(R), SA3, E(R), F2(R), W(R), 2007 F1(R), C, SA2(R), [Pt, S(R), R(R), F(R)], 2008 I1, E1, 2, SA1, 2, A1, 2, SA3, Sm, A3, 4, 2009 F1, A1, SA1, 2, A2, SA3, A3, 4, W, E, F3, 2010 S(R), I2(R), W3(R), 2011 Fj, SA1, A1(R), SA2(R), A2(R), [Tg, J(R), F1(R), C, Arg(R), A(R), F2(R)], 2012 I1, 2, 3, A1(R), 2(R), Arg1(R), SA1, Arg2, SA2, A3(R), S, W, 2013 F2(R), 3, A1, 2, Arg1, 2, SA2, J(R), I

**Hore, J** (Otago) 1930 BI 2, 3, 4, 1932 A 1, 2, 3, 1934 A 1, 2, 1935 S, 1936 E

**Horsley, R H** (Wellington) 1960 SA 2, 3, 4

**Hotop, J** (Canterbury) 1952 A 1, 2, 1955 A 3

**Howarth, S P** (Auckland) 1994 SA 1, 2, 3, A

**Howlett, D C** (Auckland) 2000 Tg (R), F 1, 2, It, 2001 Sm, Arg 1(R), F (R), SA 1, A 1, 2, I, S, Arg 2, 2002 It, I 1, 2(R), Fj, A 1, SA 1, A 2, SA 2, E, F, W, 2003 E, W, F, I, SA 1, A 1, A 2, SA 2, E, F, W, 2003 E, W, F, I, SA 1, A 2, SA 2, A 2, W, F, SA 2, A 2, E, F, W, 2003 E, F, W, 2003 E1, 2, [It, C(R), Tg, W, SA, A, F], 2004 E1, A1, SA1, A2, SA2, W, F, 2005 Fj, BI1, A2, I, E, 2006 I1, 2, SA1, A3, SA3, 2007 F2(R), C, SA2, A2, [It, S, R(R)]

**Hughes, A M** (Auckland) 1949 A 1, 2, 1950 BI 1, 2, 3, 4

**Hughes, E** (Southland, Wellington) 1907 A 1, 2, 3, 1908 AW 1, 1921 SA 1, 2

**Hunter, B A** (Otago) 1971 BI 1, 2, 3

**Hunter, J** (Taranaki) 1905 S, I, E, W, 1906 F, 1907 A 1, 2, 3, 1908 AW 1, 2, 3

**Hurst, I A** (Canterbury) 1973 I, F, E 2, 1974 A 1, 2

**Ieremia, A** (Wellington) 1994 SA 1, 2, 3, 1995 [J], 1996 SA 2(R), 5(R), 1997 A 1(R), SA 1(R), A 2, SA 2, A 3, I, E 1, 1999 WS, F 1, SA 1, A 1, SA 2, A 2, [Tg, E, S, F 2, SA 3], 2000 Tg, S 1, 2, A 1, 2, SA 2

**Ifwersen, K D** (Auckland) 1921 SA 3

**Innes, C R** (Auckland) 1989 W, I, 1990 A 1, 2, 3, F 1, 2, 1991 Arg 1, 2, A 1, 2, [E, US, It, C, A, S]

**Innes, G D** (Canterbury) 1932 A 2

**Irvine, I B** (North Auckland) 1952 A 1

**Irvine, J G** (Otago) 1914 A 1, 2, 3

**Irvine, W R** (Hawke's Bay, Wairarapa) 1924 I, W, 1925 E, F, 1930 BI 1

**Irwin, M W** (Otago) 1955 A 1, 2, 1956 SA 1, 1958 A 2, 1959 BI 3, 4, 1960 SA 1

**Jack, C R** (Canterbury, Tasman) 2001 Arg 1(R), SA 1(R), 2, A 2, I, S, Arg 2, 2002 I 1, 2, A 1, SA 1, A 2, SA 2, 2003 E, W, F, SA 1, A 1, SA 2(R), A 2, [It, C, SA, A, F], 2004 E1, 2, Arg, PI, A1, SA1, A2, SA2, W, F, 2005 Fj(R), BI1, 2, 3, SA1, A1, SA2, A2, W, E, S, 2006 I1, 2, A1, SA1, A2, 3, SA2(R), 3, E, F2, 2007 F1, 2, A1, SA2, A2, [It, Pt, S(R), R(R), F(R)]

**Jackson, E S** (Hawke's Bay) 1936 A 1, 2, 1937 SA 1, 2, 3, 1938 A 3

**Jaffray, J L** (Otago, South Canterbury) 1972 A 2, 1975 S, 1976 I, SA 1, 1977 BI 2, 1979 F 1, 2

**Jane, C S** (Wellington) 2008 A4(R), S(R), 2009 F1, 2, It1(R), A1,

SA3(R), A3, 4, W, It2, F3, 2010 I1, W1, 2, SA1, 2, A1, 2, SA3, A3, 4, I2, 2011 SA1, 2(R), A2, [Tg(R), J, F1, Arg, A, F2], 2012 A1, 2, Arg1, SA1, Arg2, SA2, A3, S, It(R), W, E, 2013 F4, I, 2014 E1, 2, 3, A1, 2, SA1(R)

**Jarden, R A** (Wellington) 1951 A 1, 2, 1952 A 1, 2, 1953 W, 1954 I, E, S, F, 1955 A 1, 2, 3, 1956 SA 1, 2, 3, 4

**Jefferd, A C R** (East Coast) 1981 S 1, 2, SA 1

**Jessep, E M** (Wellington) 1931 A, 1932 A 1

**Johnson, L M** (Wellington) 1928 SA 1, 2, 3, 4

**Johnston, W** (Otago) 1907 A 1, 2, 3

**Johnstone, B R** (Auckland) 1976 SA 2, 1977 BI 1, 2, F 1, 2, 1978 I, W, E, S, 1979 F 1, 2, S, E

**Johnstone, C R** (Canterbury) 2005 Fj(R), BI2(R), 3(R)

**Johnstone, P** (Otago) 1949 SA 2, 4, 1950 BI 1, 2, 3, 4, 1951 A 1, 2, 3

**Jones, I D** (North Auckland, North Harbour) 1990 S 1, 2, A 1, 2, 3, F 1, 2, 1991 Arg 1, 2, A 1, 2, [E, US, It, C, A, S], 1992 Wld 1, 2, 3, I 1, 2, A 1, 2, 3, SA, 1993 BI 1, 2(R), 3, WS, S, E, 1994 F 1, 2, SA 1, 3, A, 1995 C, [I, W, S, E, SA], A 1, 2, It, F 1, 2, 1996 WS, S 1, 2, A 1, SA 1, A 2, SA 2, 3, 4, 5, 1997 Fj, Arg 1, 2, A 1, SA 1, A 2, SA 2, A 3, I, E 1, W, E 2, 1998 E 1, 2, A 1, SA 1, A 2, 3(R), 1999 F 1(R), [It, S (R)]

**Jones, M G** (North Auckland) 1973 E 2

**Jones, M N** (Auckland) 1987 [It, Fj, S, F], A, 1988 W 1, 2, A 2, 3, 1989 F 1, 2, Arg 1, 2, 1990 F 1, 2, 1991 Arg 1, 2, A 1, 2, [E, US, S], 1992 Wld 1, 3, I 2, A 1, 3, SA, 1993 BI 1, 2, 3, A, WS, 1994 SA 3(R), A, 1995 A 1(R), 2, It, F 1, 2, 1996 WS, S 1, 2, A 1, SA 1, A 2, SA 2, 3, 4, 5, 1997 Fj, 1998 E 1, A 1, SA 1, A 2

**Jones, P F H** (North Auckland) 1954 E, S, 1955 A 1, 2, 1956 SA 3, 4, 1958 A 1, 2, 3, 1959 BI 1, 1960 SA 1

**Joseph, H T** (Canterbury) 1971 BI 2, 3

**Joseph, J W** (Otago) 1992 Wld 2, 3(R), I 1, A 1(R), 3, SA, 1993 BI 1, 2, 3, A, WS, S, E, 1994 SA 2(t), 1995 C, [I, W, J (R), S, SA (R)]

**Kahui, R D** (Waikato) 2008 E2, A1, 2, SA3, Sm, A3, S, W, 2010 W1(R), 2, SA1(R), 2011 SA2, [Tg, J, F1, A, F2]

**Kaino, J** (Auckland) 2006 I1(R), 2, 2008 I1, E1, SA1, 2, A1, 2, SA3, Sm, A3, 4, I2, W, E3, 2009 F2, It1, A1, SA1, 2, A2, SA3, W, E(R), F3, 2010 I1, W2, SA1, 2, A1, 2, SA3, A3(R), 4, E, I2, W3, 2011 Fj(R), SA1, A1, SA2, [Tg, J, F1, C, Arg, A, F2], 2014 E1, 2, 3, A1, Arg2, SA2

**Karam, J F** (Wellington, Horowhenua) 1972 W, S, 1973 E 1, I, F, 1974 A 1, 2, 3, I, 1975 S

**Katene, T** (Wellington) 1955 A 2

**Kearney, J C** (Otago) 1947 A 2, 1949 SA 1, 2, 3

**Kelleher, B T** (Otago, Waikato) 1999 WS (R), SA 1(R), A 2(R), [Tg (R), E (R), It, F 2], 2000 S 1, A 1(R), 2(R), It (R), 2001 Sm, F (R), A 1(R), SA 2, A 2, I, S, 2002 It, I 2(R), Fj, SA 1(R), 2(R), 2003 F (R), [A(R)], 2004 Arg, PI(R), SA1(R), 2(R), It, W(R), F, 2005 Fj, BI1(R), 2, 3, SA1, W, E, 2006 I1, 2, A1, 2, 3, SA3(R), E, F1(R), 2, W, 2007 F2, C, SA1, A1, 2, [It, S, F]

**Kelly, J W** (Auckland) 1949 A 1, 2

**Kember, G F** (Wellington) 1970 SA 4

**Kerr-Barlow, T N J** (Waikato) 2012 S(R), It(R), 2013 F1(R), 3(R), A1(R), 2(R), Arg1(R), SA1(R), Arg2(R), SA2(R), A3(R), J, F4(R), E(R), 2014 SA2(R)

**Ketels, R C** (Counties) 1980 W, 1981 S 1, 2, R, F 1

**Kiernan, H A D** (Auckland) 1903 A

**Kilby, F D** (Wellington) 1932 A 1, 2, 3, 1934 A 2

**Killeen, B A** (Auckland) 1936 A 1

**King, R M** (Waikato) 2002 W

**King, R R** (West Coast) 1934 A 2, 1935 S, I, W, 1936 E, A 1, 2, 1937 SA 1, 2, 3, 1938 A 1

**Kingstone, C N** (Taranaki) 1921 SA 1, 2, 3

**Kirk, D E** (Auckland) 1985 E 1, 2, A, Arg 1, 1986 F 1, A 1, 2, 3, F 2, 3, 1987 [It, Fj, Arg, S, W, F], A

**Kirkpatrick, I A** (Canterbury, Poverty Bay) 1967 F, 1968 A 1(R), 2, F 1, 2, 3, 1969 W 1, 2, 1970 SA 1, 2, 3, 4, 1971 BI 1, 2, 3, 4, 1972 A 1, 2, 3, W, S, 1973 E 1, I, F, E 2, 1974 A 1, 2, 3, I 1975 S, 1976 I, SA 1, 2, 3, 4, 1977 BI 1, 2, 3, 4

**Kirton, E W** (Otago) 1967 E, W, F, S, 1968 A 1, 2, F 1, 2, 3, 1969 W 1, 2, 1970 SA 2, 3

**Kirwan, J J** (Auckland) 1984 F 1, 2, 1985 E 1, 2, A, Arg 1, 2,

1986 F 1, A 1, 2, 3, F 2, 3, 1987 [It, Fj, Arg, S, W, F], A, 1988 W 1, 2, A 1, 2, 3, 1989 F 1, 2, Arg 1, 2, A, 1990 S 1, 2, A 1, 2, 3, F 1, 2, 1991 Arg 2, A 1, 2, [E, It, C, A, S], 1992 Wld 1, 2(R), 3, I 1, 2, A 1, 2, 3, SA, 1993 BI 2, 3, A, WS, 1994 F 1, 2, SA 1, 2, 3

**Kivell, A L** (Taranaki) 1929 A 2, 3

**Knight, A** (Auckland) 1934 A 1

**Knight, G A** (Manawatu) 1977 F 1, 2, 1978 A 1, 2, 3, E, S, 1979 F 1, 2, A, 1980 A 1, 2, 3, W, 1981 S 1, 2, SA 1, 3, 1982 A 1, 2, 3, 1983 BI 1, 2, 3, 4, A, 1984 F 1, 2, A 1, 2, 3, 1985 E 1, 2, A, 1986 A 2, 3

**Knight, L G** (Poverty Bay) 1977 BI 1, 2, 3, 4, F 1, 2

**Koteka, T T** (Waikato) 1981 F 2, 1982 A 3

**Kreft, A J** (Otago) 1968 A 2

**Kronfeld, J A** (Otago) 1995 C, [I, W, S, E, SA], A 1, 2(R) 1996 WS, S 1, 2, A 1, SA 1, A 2, SA 2, 3, 4, 5, 1997 Fj, Arg 1, 2, A 1, SA 1, A 2, SA 2, A 3, I (R), E 1, W, E 2, 1998 E 1, 2, A 1, SA 1, 2 A 3, 1999 WS, F 1, SA 1, A 1, SA 2, A 2, [Tg, E, S, F, SA 3], 2000 Tg, S 1(R), 2, A 1(R), SA 1, A 2, SA 2

**Laidlaw, C R** (Otago, Canterbury) 1964 F, A 1, 1965 SA 1, 2, 3, 4, 1966 BI 1, 2, 3, 4, 1967 E, W, S, 1968 A 1, 2, F 1, 2, 1970 SA 1, 2, 3

**Laidlaw, K F** (Southland) 1960 SA 2, 3, 4

**Lambert, K K** (Manawatu) 1972 S (R), 1973 E 1, I, F, E 2, 1974 I, 1976 SA 1, 3, 4, 1977 BI 1, 4

**Lambourn, A** (Wellington) 1934 A 1, 2, 1935 S, I, W, 1936 E, 1937 SA 1, 2, 3, 1938 A 3

**Larsen, B P** (North Harbour) 1992 Wld 2, 3, I 1, 1994 F 1, 2, SA 1, 2, 3, A (t), 1995 [I, W, J, E(R)], It, F 1, 1996 S 2(t), SA 4(R)

**Latimer, T D** (Bay of Plenty) 2009 F1(R), 2, It1, 2, F3(R)

**Lauaki, S T** (Waikato) 2005 Fj(R), BI1(R), 2(R), 3, A2, I, S, 2007 [It(R), Pt, S(R), R], 2008 E1(R), 2(R), SA1(R), 2(R), A1(R), Sm(R)

**Laulala, C D E** (Canterbury) 2004 W, 2006 I2

**Le Lievre, J M** (Canterbury) 1962 A 4

**Lee, D D** (Otago) 2002 E (R), F

**Lendrum, R N** (Counties) 1973 E 2

**Leonard, B G** (Waikato) 2007 F1(R), 2(R), SA2(R), A2(R), [It(R), Pt, S(R), R(R), F(R)], 2009 It1, SA1, A3(R), W

**Leslie, A R** (Wellington) 1974 A 1, 2, 3, I, 1975 S, 1976 I, SA 1, 2, 3, 4

**Leys, E T** (Wellington) 1929 A 3

**Lilburne, H T** (Canterbury, Wellington) 1928 SA 3, 4, 1929 A 1, 2, 3, 1930 BI 1, 4, 1931 A, 1932 A 1, 1934 A 2

**Lindsay, D F** (Otago) 1928 SA 1, 2, 3

**Lineen, T R** (Auckland) 1957 A 1, 2, 1958 A 1, 2, 3, 1959 BI 1, 2, 3, 4, 1960 SA 1, 2, 3

**Lister, T N** (South Canterbury) 1968 A 1, 2, F 1, 1969 W 1, 2, 1970 SA 1, 4, 1971 BI 4

**Little, P F** (Auckland) 1961 F 2, 3, 1962 A 2, 3, 5, 1963 I, W, 1964 E, S, F

**Little, W K** (North Harbour) 1990 S 1, 2, A 1, 2, 3, F 1, 2, 1991 Arg 1, 2, A 1, [It, S], 1992 Wld 1, 2, 3, I 1, 2, A 1, 2, 3, SA, 1993 I, WS (R), 1994 A 2(R), A, 1995 C, [I, W, S, E, SA], A 1, 2, It, F 1, 2, 1996 S 2, A 1, SA 1, A 2, SA 2, 3, 4, 5, 1997 W, E 2, 1998 E 1, A, SA 1, A 2

**Loader, C J** (Wellington) 1954 I, E, S, F

**Lochore, B J** (Wairarapa) 1964 E, S, 1965 SA 1, 2, 3, 4, 1966 BI 1, 2, 3, 4, 1967 A, E, W, F, S, 1968 A 1, F 2, 3, 1969 W 1, 2, 1970 SA 1, 2, 3, 4, 1971 BI 3

**Loe, R W** (Waikato, Canterbury) 1987 [It, Arg], 1988 W 1, 2, A 1, 2, 3, 1989 F 1, 2, Arg 1, 2, A, W, 1990 S 1, 2, A 1, 2, 3, F 1, 2, 1991 Arg 1, 2, A 1, 2, [E, It, C, A, S], 1992 Wld 1, 2, 3, I 1, 2, A 1, 2, 3, SA, 1994 F 1, 2, SA 1, 2, 3, A, 1995 [J, S, SA (R)], A 2(t), F 2(R)

**Lomu, J T** (Counties Manukau, Wellington) 1994 F 1, 2, 1995 [I, W, S, E, SA], A 1, 2, It, F 1, 2, 1996 WS, S 1, A 1, SA 1, A 2, 1997 E 1, W, E 2, 1998 E 1, 2, A 1, A 2(R), SA 2, A 3, 1999 WS (R), SA 1(R), A 1(R), SA 2(R), A 2(R), [Tg, E, It, S, F, SA 3], 2000 Tg, S 1, 2, A 1, SA 1, A 2, SA 2, F 1, 2001 Arg 1, F, SA 1, A 1, SA 2, A 2, I, S, Arg 2, 2002 It 1(R), I 1(R), 2(R), Fj, SA 1(R), E, F, W

**Long, A J** (Auckland) 1903 A

**Loveridge, D S** (Taranaki) 1978 W, 1979 S, E, 1980 A 1, 2, 3,

W, 1981 S 1, 2, SA 1, 2, 3, R, F 1, 2, 1982 A 1, 2, 3, 1983 BI 1, 2, 3, 4, A, 1985 Arg 2

**Lowen, K R** (Waikato) 2002 E

**Luatua, D S** (Auckland) 2013 F3(R), A1, 2, Arg1, SA1(R), Arg2(R), SA2(R), A3(R), J, E(R), I, 2014 A2(R), SA1, 2(R)

**Lucas, F W** (Auckland) 1924 I, 1925 F, 1928 SA 4, 1930 BI 1, 2, 3, 4

**Lunn, W A** (Otago) 1949 A 1, 2

**Lynch, T W** (South Canterbury) 1913 A 1, 1914 A 1, 2, 3

**Lynch, T W** (Canterbury) 1951 A 1, 2, 3

**McAlister, C L** (North Harbour) 2005 BI3, SA1(R), A1(R), SA2(R), A2(R), 2006 I1, 2, SA1(R), A3, SA2, F1, W, 2007 F2, C, SA1(R), A1, SA2, A2, [It, S, R, F], 2009 F1(R), 2(R), It1, SA1(R), 2(R), A2, It2, F3(R)

**McAtamney, F S** (Otago) 1956 SA 2

**McCahill, B J** (Auckland) 1987 [Arg, S (R), W (R)], 1989 Arg 1(R), 2(R), 1991 A 2, [E, US, C, A]

**McCaw, R H** (Canterbury) 2001 I, S, Arg 2, 2002 I 1, 2, A 1, SA 1, A 2, SA 2, 2003 E, F, SA 1, A 1, 2, [It, C(R), Tg(R), W, SA, A, F], 2004 E1, Arg, It, W, F, 2005 Fj, BI1, 2, SA1, A1, SA2, A2, W(R), I, S, 2006 I1, 2, A1, SA1, A2, 3, SA2, A3, 4, 2007 F1, 2, C(R), SA1, A1, SA2, A2, [It, S, R(R), F], 2008 I1, E1, 2, A2, SA3, A3, 4, S(R), I2, W, E3, 2009 A1, SA1, 2, A2, SA3, A3, 4, W, E, F3, 2010 I1, W1, 2, SA1, 2, A1, 2, SA3, A3, 4, E, S, I2, W3, 2011 Fj, SA1, A1, 2, [Tg, F1, Arg, A, F2], 2012 I 1, 2, 3, A1, 2, Arg1, SA1, Arg2, SA2, A3, S, W, E, 2013 A1, 2, Arg1, SA1, 2, A, F2, E, I, 2014 E1, 2, 3, A1, 2, Arg1, SA1, Arg2, SA2

**McCaw, W A** (Southland) 1951 A 1, 2, 3, 1953 W, 1954 F

**McCool, M J** (Wairarapa-Bush) 1979 A

**McCormick, W F** (Canterbury) 1965 SA 4, 1967 E, W, F, S, 1968 A 1, 2, F 1, 2, 3, 1969 W 1, 2, 1970 SA 1, 2, 3, 1971 BI 1

**McCullough, J F** (Taranaki) 1959 BI 2, 3, 4

**McDonald, A** (Otago) 1905 S, I, E, W, 1907 A 1, 1908 AW 1, 1913 A 1, US

**Macdonald, A J** (Auckland) 2005 W(R), S

**Macdonald, H H** (Canterbury, North Auckland) 1972 W, S, 1973 E 1, I, F, E 2, 1974 I, 1975 S, 1976 I, SA 1, 2, 3

**MacDonald, L R** (Canterbury) 2000 S 1(R), 2(R), SA 1(t), 2(R), 2001 Sm, Arg 1, F, SA 1(R), A 1(R), SA 2, A 2, I, S, 2002 I 1, 2, Fj (R), A 2, SA 2, 2003 A 2(R), [It(R), C, Tg, W, SA, A, F], 2005 BI1, 2(R), SA1, 2, A2, W(R), I, E(R), S(R), 2006 Arg, A1, SA1, A2, 3(R), SA2, F1, 2, 2007 F1, 2, C(R), SA1(R), [It, Pt(R), S, F], 2008 I1(R), E1(R), 2, SA1(R), 2(R)

**McDonnell, J M** (Otago) 2002 It, I 1(R), 2(R), Fj, SA 1(R), A 2(R), E, F

**McDowell, S C** (Auckland, Bay of Plenty) 1985 Arg 1, 2, 1986 A 2, 3, F 2, 3, 1987 [It, Fj, S, W, F], A, 1988 W 1, 2, A 1, 2, 3, 1989 F 1, 2, Arg 1, 2, A, W, I, 1990 S 1, 2, A 1, 2, 3, F 1, 2, 1991 Arg 1, 2, A 1, 2, [E, US, It, C, A, S], 1992 Wld 1, 2, 3, I 1, 2

**McEldowney, J T** (Taranaki) 1977 BI 3, 4

**MacEwan, I N** (Wellington) 1956 SA 2, 1957 A 1, 2, 1958 A 1, 2, 3, 1959 BI 1, 2, 3, 1960 SA 1, 2, 3, 4, 1961 F 1, 2, 3, 1962 A 1, 2, 3, 4

**McGrattan, B** (Wellington) 1983 S, E, 1985 Arg 1, 2, 1986 F 1, A 1

**McGregor, A J** (Auckland) 1913 A 1, US

**McGregor, D** (Canterbury, Southland) 1903 A, 1904 BI, 1905 E, W

**McGregor, N P** (Canterbury) 1924 W, 1925 E

**McGregor, R W** (Auckland) 1903 A, 1904 BI

**McHugh, M J** (Auckland) 1946 A 1, 2, 1949 SA 3

**McIntosh, D N** (Wellington) 1956 SA 1, 2, 1957 A 1, 2

**McKay, D W** (Auckland) 1961 F 1, 2, 3, 1963 E 1, 2

**McKechnie, B J** (Southland) 1977 F 1, 2, 1978 A 2(R), 3, W (R), E, S, 1979 A, 1981 SA 1(R), F 1

**McKellar, G F** (Wellington) 1910 A 1, 2, 3

**McKenzie, R J** (Wellington) 1913 A 1, US, 1914 A 2, 3

**McKenzie, R McC** (Manawatu) 1934 A 1, 1935 S, 1936 A 1, 1937 SA 1, 2, 3, 1938 A 1, 2, 3

**McLachlan, J S** (Auckland) 1974 A 2

**McLaren, H C** (Waikato) 1952 A 1

**McLean, A L** (Bay of Plenty) 1921 SA 2, 3

**McLean, H F** (Wellington, Auckland) 1930 BI 3, 4, 1932 A 1, 2, 3, 1934 A 1, 1935 I, W, 1936 E

McLean, J K (King Country, Auckland) 1947 A 1, 1949 A 2
McLeod, B E (Counties) 1964 A 1, 2, 3, 1965 SA 1, 2, 3, 4,
1966 BI 1, 2, 3, 4, 1967 E, W, F, S, 1968 A 1, 2, F 1, 2, 3,
1969 W 1, 2, 1970 SA 1, 2
McLeod, S J (Waikato) 1996 WS, S 1, 1997 Fj (R), Arg 2(t&R),
I (R), E 1(R), W (t), E 2(R), 1998 A 1, SA 1(R)
McMinn, A F (Wairarapa, Manawatu) 1903 A, 1905 A
McMinn, F A (Manawatu) 1904 BI
McMullen, R F (Auckland) 1957 A 1, 2, 1958 A 1, 2, 3, 1959
BI 1, 2, 3, 1960 SA 2, 3, 4
McNab, J R (Otago) 1949 SA 1, 2, 3, 1950 BI 1, 2, 3
McNaughton, A M (Bay of Plenty) 1971 BI 1, 2, 3
McNeece, J (Southland) 1913 A 2, 3, 1914 A 1, 2, 3
McPhail, B E (Canterbury) 1959 BI 1, 4
Macpherson, D G (Otago) 1905 A
MacPherson, G L (Otago) 1986 F 1
MacRae, I R (Hawke's Bay) 1966 BI 1, 2, 3, 4, 1967 A, E, W,
F, S, 1968 F 1, 2, 1969 W 1, 2, 1970 SA 1, 2, 3, 4
McRae, J A (Southland) 1946 A 1(R), 2
McWilliams, R G (Auckland) 1928 SA 2, 3, 4, 1929 A 1, 2, 3,
1930 BI 1, 2, 3, 4
Mackintosh, J L (Southland) 2008 S
Mackrell, W H C (Auckland) 1906 F
Macky, J V (Auckland) 1913 A 2
Maguire, J R (Auckland) 1910 A 1, 2, 3
Mahoney, A (Bush) 1935 S, I, W, 1936 E
Mains, L W (Otago) 1971 BI 2, 3, 4, 1976 I
Major, J (Taranaki) 1967 A
Maka, I (Otago) 1998 E 2(R), A 1(R), SA 1(R), 2
Maling, T S (Otago) 2002 It, I 2(R), Fj, A 1, SA 1, A 2, SA 2,
2004 Arg, A1, SA1, 2
Manchester, J E (Canterbury) 1932 A 1, 2, 3, 1934 A 1, 2, 1935
S, I, W, 1936 E
Mannix, S J (Wellington) 1994 F 1
Marshall, J W (Southland, Canterbury) 1995 F 2, 1996 WS, S
1, 2, A 1, SA 1, A 2, SA 2, 3, 4, 5, 1997 Fj, Arg 1, 2, A 1,
SA 1, A 2, SA 2, A 3, I, E 1, W, E 2, 1998 A 1, SA 1, A 2,
SA 2, A 3, 1999 WS, F 1, SA 1, A 1, SA 2, A 2, [Tg, E, S,
F 2(R), SA 3], 2000 Tg, S 2, A 1, SA 1, A 2, SA 2, F 1, 2,
It, 2001 Arg 1, F, SA 1, A 1, 2(R), 2002 I 1, 2, Fj (R), A 1,
SA 1, A 2, SA 2, 2003 E, SA 1(R), A 1, SA 2, A 2, [It, Tg,
W, SA, A], 2004 E1, 2, PI, A1, SA1, A2, SA2, 2005 Fj(R),
BI1, 2(R), 3(R)
Masaga, L T C (Counties Manukau) 2009 It1
Masoe, M C (Taranaki, Wellington) 2005 W, E, 2006Arg, A1(R),
SA1(R), A2(R), 3(R), SA2, E, F2(R), 2007 F1, 2(R), C, A1(R),
SA2(R), [It(R), Pt, S, R, F(R)]
Mason, D F (Wellington) 1947 A 2(R)
Masters, R R (Canterbury) 1924 I, W, 1925 E, F
Mataira, H K (Hawke's Bay) 1934 A 2
Matheson, J D (Otago) 1972 A 1, 2, 3, W, S
Mathewson, A S (Wellington) 2010 A2(R), 4(R), E, I2(R)
Mauger, A J D (Canterbury) 2001 I, S, Arg 2, 2002 It (R), I 1,
2, Fj, A 1, SA 1, A 2, SA 2, 2003 SA 1, A 1, SA 2, A 2,
[W, SA, A, F], 2004 SA2(R), It(R), W, F(R), 2005 Fj, BI1, 2,
SA1, A1, SA2, A2, I, E, 2006 I1, 2, A1, 2, SA3, E, 2007 F1,
C, SA1, A1, [It(R), Pt, F]
Max, D S (Nelson) 1931 A, 1934 A 1, 2
Maxwell, N M C (Canterbury) 1999 WS, F 1, SA 1, A 1, SA 2,
A 2, [Tg, E, S, F 2, SA 3], 2000 S 1, A 1, SA 1(R), A 2,
SA 2, F 1, 2, It (R), 2001 Sm, Arg 1, F, SA 1, A 1, SA 2,
A2, I, S, Arg 2, 2002 It, I 1, 2, Fj, 2004 It, F
Mayerhofler, M A (Canterbury) 1998 E 1, 2, SA 1, A 2, SA 2, A
3
Meads, C E (King Country) 1957 A 1, 2, 1958 A 1, 2, 3, 1959
BI 2, 3, 4, 1960 SA 1, 2, 3, 4, 1961 F 1, 2, 3, 1962 A 1, 2,
3, 5, 1963 E 1, 2, I, W, 1964 E, S, F, A 1, 2, 3, 1965 SA 1,
2, 3, 4, 1966 BI 1, 2, 3, 4, 1967 A, E, W, F, S, 1968 A 1, 2,
F 1, 2, 3, 1969 W 1, 2, 1970 SA 3, 4, 1971 BI 1, 2, 3, 4
Meads, S T (King Country) 1961 F 1, 1962 A 4, 5, 1963 I, 1964
A 1, 2, 3, 1965 SA 1, 2, 3, 4, 1966 BI 1, 2, 3, 4
Mealamu, K F (Auckland) 2002 W, 2003 E (R), W, F (R), SA 1,
A 1, SA 2(R), A 2, [It, W, SA, A, F], 2004 E1, 2, PI, A1,
SA1, A2, SA2, W, F(R), 2005 Fj(R), BI1, 2, 3, SA1, A1, SA2,
A2, I, E, 2006 I1, 2, A1, 2, 3, SA2(R), E, F1(R), 2, 2007 F1,
2(R), SA1(R), A1(R), SA2, A2(R), [It, Pt(R), R], 2008 I1(R),
E1(t&R), 2(t&R), SA1(R), 2(R), A1(R), 2(R), SA3(R), Sm(R),

A3(R), 4(R), S, I2, W, E3, 2009 F1(R), 2, It1, A1(R), SA1(R),
2(R), 2010 I1, W1, 2, SA1, 2, A1, 2, SA3, A3, 4, E, W3,
2011 A1, SA2, A2, [J, F1, C(R), Arg, A, F2], 2012 I 3(R),
A1, 2, Arg1, SA1(R), Arg2(R), SA2(R), A3, It, E, 2013 F1(R),
3(R), A1(R), SA1(R), Arg2(R), A3, F4, E, 2014 E1(R), 2(R),
3(R), A1(R), 2(R), Arg1(R), SA1(R), Arg2, SA2
Meates, K F (Canterbury) 1952 A 1, 2
Meates, W A (Otago) 1949 SA 2, 3, 4, 1950 BI 1, 2, 3, 4
Meeuws, K J (Otago, Auckland) 1998 A 3, 1999 WS, F 1, SA
1, A 1, SA 2, A 2, [Tg, It (R), S (R), F 2(R), SA 3], 2000 Tg
(R), S 2, A 1, SA 1, A 2, SA 2, 2001 Arg 2, 2002 It, Fj, E,
F, W (R), 2003 W, F (R), SA 1(R), A 1(R), SA 2, [It(R), C, Tg,
W(R), SA(R), A(R)], 2004 E1, 2, PI, A1, SA1, A2, SA2
Mehrtens, A P (Canterbury) 1995 C, [I, W, S, E, SA], A 1, 2,
1996 WS, S 1, 2, A 1, SA 1, A 2, SA 2, 5, 1997 Fj, SA 2(R),
I, E 1, W, E 2, 1998 E 1, 2, A 1, SA 1(R), A 2, SA 2, A 3,
1999 F 1, SA 1, A 1, SA 2, A 2, [Tg, E, S, F 2, SA 3], 2000
S 1, 2, A 1, SA 1, A 2, SA 2, F 1, 2, It (R), 2001 Arg 1, A
1(R), SA 2, A 2, I, S, Arg 2, 2002 It, I 1, 2, Fj (R), A 1, SA
1, A 2, SA 2, E (R), F, W, 2004 E2(R), Arg, A2(R), SA2
Messam, L J (Waikato) 2008 S, 2009 F1, It2, 2010 SA1(R), 2(R),
S, 2011 Fj, SA1(R), 2, 2012 I 3, A1, 2, Arg1(R), SA1, Arg2,
SA2, A3, It, W, E, 2013 F1, 2, SA1, Arg2, SA2, A3, F4, E,
I(R), 2014 E1, 2, 3(R), A2, Arg1, SA2(R)
Metcalfe, T C (Southland) 1931 A, 1932 A 1
Mexted, G G (Wellington) 1950 BI 4
Mexted, M G (Wellington) 1979 S, E, 1980 A 1, 2, 3, W, 1981
S 1, 2, SA 1, 2, 3, R, F 1, 2, 1982 A 1, 2, 3, 1983 BI 1, 2,
3, 4, A, S, E, 1984 F 1, 2, A 1, 2, 3, 1985 E 1, 2, A, Arg
1, 2
Mika, B M (Auckland) 2002 E (R), F, W (R)
Mika, D G (Auckland) 1999 WS, F 1, SA 1(R), A 1, 2, [It, SA
3(R)]
Mill, J J (Hawke's Bay, Wairarapa) 1924 W, 1925 E, F, 1930
BI 1
Milliken, H M (Canterbury) 1938 A 1, 2, 3
Milner, H P (Wanganui) 1970 SA 3
Mitchell, N A (Southland, Otago) 1935 S, I, W, 1936 E, A 2,
1937 SA 3, 1938 A 1, 2
Mitchell, T W (Canterbury) 1976 SA 4(R)
Mitchell, W J (Canterbury) 1910 A 2, 3
Mitchinson, F E (Wellington) 1907 A 1, 2, 3, 1908 AW 1, 2, 3,
1910 A 1, 2, 3, 1913 A 1(R), US
Moffitt, J E (Wellington) 1921 SA 1, 2, 3
Moody, J (Canterbury) 2014 A1(R), Arg1(R), SA1(R), Arg2(t&R),
SA2
Moore, G J T (Otago) 1949 A 1
Moreton, R C (Canterbury) 1962 A 3, 4, 1964 A 1, 2, 3, 1965
SA 2, 3
Morgan, J E (North Auckland) 1974 A 3, I, 1976 SA 2, 3, 4
Morris, T J (Nelson Bays) 1972 A 1, 2, 3
Morrison, T C (South Canterbury) 1938 A 1, 2, 3
Morrison, T G (Otago) 1973 E 2(R)
Morrissey, P J (Canterbury) 1962 A 3, 4, 5
Mourie, G N K (Taranaki) 1977 BI 3, 4, F 1, 2, 1978 I, W, E, S,
1979 F 1, 2, A, S, E, 1980 W, 1981 S 1, 2, F 1, 2, 1982 A
1, 2, 3
Muliaina, J M (Auckland, Waikato) 2003 E (R), W, F, SA 1, A
1, SA 2, A 2, [It, C, Tg, W, SA, A, F], 2004 E1, 2, Arg, PI,
A1, SA1, A2, SA2, It, W, F, 2005 Fj, BI1(R), 2, 3, SA1, A1,
SA2, A2, W, E, 2006 I1, 2, A1, SA1, A2, 3, SA2, 3, E, F1(R),
2, W, 2007 C, SA1, A1, SA2, A2, [It, Pt, F], 2008 I1, E1,
2(t), SA1, 2, A1, 2, SA3, Sm, A3, I2, W, E3, 2009 F1, 2,
It1, A1, SA1, 2, A2, SA3, A3, 4, W, It2(R), E, F3, 2010 W2,
SA1, 2, A1, 2, SA3, A3, 4, 5, E, W3, 2011 Fj, SA1, A1,
2, [C, Arg]
Muller, B L (Taranaki) 1967 A, E, W, F, 1968 A 1, F 1, 1969 W
1, 1970 SA 1, 2, 4, 1971 BI 1, 2, 3, 4
Mumm, W J (Buller) 1949 A 1
Murdoch, K (Otago) 1970 SA 4, 1972 A 3, W
Murdoch, P H (Auckland) 1964 A 2, 3, 1965 SA 1, 2, 3
Murray, H V (Canterbury) 1913 A 1, US, 1914 A 2, 3
Murray, P C (Wanganui) 1908 AW 2
Myers, R G (Waikato) 1978 A 3
Mynott, H J (Taranaki) 1905 I, W, 1906 F, 1907 A 1, 2, 3, 1910
A 1, 3

Rokocoko, J T (Auckland) 2003 E, W, F, SA 1, A 1, SA 2, A 2, [It, W, SA, A, F], 2004 E1, 2, Arg, PI, A1, SA1, A2, SA2, It, W, F, 2005 SA1(R), A1, SA2, A2, W, E(R), S, 2006 I1, 2, A1, 2, 3, SA3, E, F1, 2, 2007 F1, 2, SA1, A1, SA2, A2, [Pt, R, F], 2008 S, I2, W, E3, 2009 F1, 2, It1, SA1, 2, A2, SA3, A3, 2010 I1, W1, SA1, A1, 2, SA3, A4, E
Rollerson, D L (Manawatu) 1980 W, 1981 S 2, SA 1, 2, 3, R, F 1(R), 2
Romano, L (Canterbury) 2012 I 3, A1, 2, Arg1, SA1, Arg2, SA2(R), A3(R), S, W, E(R), 2013 F1, 2, 3, A1, E(R)
Roper, R A (Taranaki) 1949 A 2, 1950 BI 1, 2, 3, 4
Ross, I B (Canterbury) 2009 F1, 2, It1, A1, SA1, 2, A2, SA3
Rowley, H C B (Wanganui) 1949 A 2
Rush, E J (North Harbour) 1995 [W (R), J], It, F 1, 2, 1996 S 1(R), 2, A 1(t), SA 1(R)
Rush, X J (Auckland) 1998 A 3, 2004 E1, 2, PI, A1, SA1, A2, SA2
Rutledge, L M (Southland) 1978 A 1, 2, 3, I, W, E, S, 1979 F 1, 2, A, 1980 A 1, 2, 3
Ryan, J (Wellington) 1910 A 2, 1914 A 1, 2, 3
Ryan, J A C (Otago) 2005 Fj, BI3(R), A1(R), SA2(R), A2(R), W, S, 2006 F1, W(R)

Sadler, B S (Wellington) 1935 S, I, W, 1936 A 1, 2
Saili, F (North Harbour) 2013 Arg1, J
Salmon, J L B (Wellington) 1981 R, F 1, 2(R)
Savage, L T (Canterbury) 1949 SA 1, 2, 4
Savea, S J (Wellington) 2012 I 1, 2, Arg1, SA1, Arg2, S, It, W, E, 2013 F1, 2, A1, 2, Arg1, SA1, Arg2, SA2, A3, E, I, 2014 E2, 3, A1, 2, Arg1, SA1, Arg2, SA2
Saxton, C K (South Canterbury) 1938 A 1, 2, 3
Schuler, K J (Manawatu, North Harbour) 1990 A 2(R), 1992 A 2, 1995 [I (R), J]
Schuster, N J (Wellington) 1988 A 1, 2, 3, 1989 F 1, 2, Arg 1, 2, A, W, I
Schwalger, J E (Wellington) 2007 C, 2008 I1(R)
Scott, R W H (Auckland) 1946 A 1, 2, 1947 A 1, 2, 1949 SA 1, 2, 3, 4, 1950 BI 1, 2, 3, 4, 1953 W, 1954 I, E, S, F
Scown, A I (Taranaki) 1972 A 1, 2, 3, W (R), S
Scrimshaw, G (Canterbury) 1928 SA 1
Seear, G A (Otago) 1977 F 1, 2, 1978 A 1, 2, 3, I, W, E, S, 1979 F 1, 2, A
Seeling, C E (Auckland) 1904 BI, 1905 S, I, E, W, 1906 F, 1907 A 1, 2, 1908 AW 1, 2, 3
Sellars, G M V (Auckland) 1913 A 1, US
Senio, K (Bay of Plenty) 2005 A2(R)
Shaw, M W (Manawatu, Hawke's Bay) 1980 A 1, 2, 3(R), W, 1981 S 1, 2, SA 1, 2, R, F 1, 2, 1982 A 1, 2, 3, 1983 BI 1, 2, 3, 4, A, S, E, 1984 F 1, 2, A 1, 1985 F 1, 2, A, Arg 1, 2, 1986 A 3
Shelford, F N K (Bay of Plenty) 1981 SA 3, R, 1984 A 2, 3
Shelford, W T (North Harbour) 1986 F 2, 3, 1987 [It, Fj, S, W, F], A, 1988 W 1, 2, A 1, 2, 3, 1989 F 1, 2, Arg 1, 2, A, W, I, 1990 S 1, 2
Siddells, S K (Wellington) 1921 SA 3
Simon, H J (Otago) 1937 SA 1, 2, 3
Simpson, J G (Auckland) 1947 A 1, 2, 1949 SA 1, 2, 3, 4, 1950 BI 1, 2, 3
Simpson, V L J (Canterbury) 1985 Arg 1, 2
Sims, G S (Otago) 1972 A 2
Sivivatu, S W (Waikato) 2005 Fj, BI1, 2, 3, I, E, 2006 SA2, 3, E(R), F1, 2, W, 2007 F1, 2, C, SA1, A1(R), [It, S, R, F], 2008 I1, E1, 2, SA1, 2, A1, 2, SA3, A3, 4, I2, W, E3, 2009 A1, SA1, 2, A2, SA3, A4, It2, E, F3, 2011 Fj, A1
Skeen, J R (Auckland) 1952 A 2
Skinner, K L (Otago, Counties) 1949 SA 1, 2, 3, 4, 1950 BI 1, 2, 3, 4, 1951 A 1, 2, 3, 1952 A 1, 2, 1953 W, 1954 I, E, S, F, 1956 SA 3, 4
Skudder, G R (Waikato) 1969 W 2
Slade, C R (Canterbury) 2010 A3(R), 2011 Fj, SA1(R), A1(R), SA2, [Tg(R), J, F1(R), C, Arg], 2013 A2(R), 2014 Arg1(R), 2(R), SA2(R)
Slater, G L (Taranaki) 2000 F 1(R), 2(R), It (R)
Sloane, P H (North Auckland) 1979 E
Smith, A E (Taranaki) 1969 W 1, 2, 1970 SA 1
Smith, A L (Manawatu) 2012 I 1, 2, 3, A1, 2, Arg1, SA1(R), Arg2, SA2, A3, It, W, E, 2013 F1, 2, A1, 2, Arg1, SA1, Arg2,

SA2, A3, J(R), F4, E, I, 2014 E1, 2, 3, A1, 2, Arg1, SA1, Arg2, SA2
Smith, B R (Otago) 2009 It 2, 2011 Fj(R), 2012 I 1(R), 2(R), 3, A2(R), Arg1(R), 2(R), A3(R), S, W(R), E(R), 2013 F1, 2, 3, A1, 2, Arg1, SA1, Arg2, SA2, A3, J, F4, E, I, 2014 E1, 2, 3, A1, 2, Arg1, SA1, Arg2, SA2
Smith, B W (Waikato) 1984 F 1, 2, A 1
Smith, C G (Wellington) 2004 It, F, 2005 Fj(R), BI3, W, S, 2006 F1, W, 2007 SA2(R), [Pt, S, R(R)], 2008 I1, E1, SA1, 2, A1(R), 2, SA3, Sm, A3, 4, I2, E3, 2009 F2, A1, SA1, 2, A2, 4, W, E, F3, 2010 I1, W1, SA1, 2, A1, 2, SA3, A3, 4, S, I2, W3, 2011 Fj, SA1, A1, 2, [J, F1, C, Arg, A, F2], 2012 I 1, 2, 3, Arg1, SA1, Arg2, SA2, A3, It, W, E, 2013 F1, 2, 3, A1, 2, Arg1, SA1, Arg2, SA2, 2014 E1, 2, A2, Arg1, SA1, Arg2, SA2
Smith, G W (Auckland) 1905 S, I
Smith, I S T (Otago, North Otago) 1964 A 1, 2, 3, 1965 SA 1, 2, 4, 1966 BI 1, 2, 3
Smith, J B (North Auckland) 1946 A 1, 1947 A 2, 1949 A 1, 2
Smith, R M (Canterbury) 1955 A 1
Smith, W E (Nelson) 1905 A
Smith, W R (Canterbury) 1980 A 1, 1982 A 1, 2, 3, 1983 BI 3, S, E, 1984 F 1, 2, A 1, 2, 3, 1985 E 1, 2, A, Arg 2
Snow, E M (Nelson) 1929 A 1, 2, 3
Solomon, F (Auckland) 1931 A, 1932 A 2, 3
Somerville, G M (Canterbury) 2000 Tg, S 1, SA 2(R), F 1, 2, It, 2001 Sm, Arg 1(R), F, SA 1, A 1, SA 2, A 2, I, S, Arg 2(t&R), 2002 I 1, 2, A 1, SA 1, 2, 2003 E, F, SA 1, A 1, SA 2(R), A 2, [It, Tg, W, SA, A, F], 2004 Arg, SA1, A2(R), SA2(R), It(R), W, F(R), 2005 Fj, BI1(R)2, 3, SA1(R), A1(R), SA2(R), A2(R), 2006 Arg, A1(R), SA1(R), A2(R), SA1(R), SA2, 2007 [Pt, R], 2008 E1, 2, SA1, A1, 2, SA3, Sm, A3, 4(R)
Sonntag, W T C (Otago) 1929 A 1, 2, 3
So'oialo, R (Wellington) 2002 W, 2003 E, SA 1(R), [It(R), C, Tg, W(t)], 2004 W, F, 2005 Fj, BI1, 2, 3, SA1, A1, SA2, A2, W, I(R), E, 2006 I1, 2, A1, SA1, A2, 3, SA3, A4, F1, 2, W, 2007 F1(R), 2, SA1, A1, SA2, A2, [It, P(R), S, F], 2008 I1, E1, 2, SA1, 2, A1, SA2, A2, 3, SA3, Sm, A3, 4, I2, W, E3, 2009 A1, SA1, 2, A2(R), 3(R), 4, It2
Speight, M W (Waikato) 1986 A 1
Spencer, C J (Auckland) 1997 Arg 1, 2, A 1, SA 1, A 2, SA 2, A 3, E 2(R), 1998 E 2(R), A 1(R), SA 1, A 3(R), 2000 F 1(t&R), It, 2002 E, 2003 E, W, F, SA 1, A 1, SA 2, A 2, [It, C, Tg, W, SA, A, F], 2004 E1, 2, PI, A1, SA1, A2
Spencer, J C (Wellington) 1905 A, 1907 A 1(R)
Spiers, J E (Counties) 1979 S, E, 1981 R, F 1, 2
Spillane, A P (South Canterbury) 1913 A 2, 3
Stanley, B J (Auckland) 2010 I1, W1, 2
Stanley, J T (Auckland) 1986 F 1, A 1, 2, 3, F 2, 3, 1987 [It, Fj, Arg, S, W, F], A, 1988 W 1, 2, A 1, 2, 3, 1989 F 1, 2, Arg 1, 2, A, W, I, 1990 S 1, 2
Stead, J W (Southland) 1904 BI, 1905 S, I, E, 1906 F, 1908 AW 1, 3
Steel, A G (Canterbury) 1966 BI 1, 2, 3, 4, 1967 A, F, S, 1968 A 1, 2
Steel, J (West Coast) 1921 SA 1, 2, 3, 1924 W, 1925 E, F
Steele, L B (Wellington) 1951 A 1, 2, 3
Steere, E R G (Hawke's Bay) 1930 BI 1, 2, 3, 4, 1931 A, 1932 A 1
Steinmetz, P C (Wellington) 2002 W (R)
Stensness, L (Auckland) 1993 BI 3, A, WS, 1997 Fj, Arg 1, 2, A 1, SA 1
Stephens, O G (Wellington) 1968 F 3
Stevens, I N (Wellington) 1972 S, 1973 E 1, 1974 A 3
Stewart, A J (King Country, South Canterbury) 1963 E 1, 2, I, W, 1964 E, S, F, A 3
Stewart, J D (Auckland) 1913 A 2, 3
Stewart, K W (Southland) 1973 E 2, 1974 A 1, 2, 3, I, 1975 S, 1976 I, SA 1, 3, 1979 S, E, 1981 SA 1, 2
Stewart, R T (South Canterbury, Canterbury) 1928 SA 1, 2, 3, 4, 1930 BI 2
Stohr, L B (Taranaki) 1910 A 1, 2, 3
Stone, A M (Waikato, Bay of Plenty) 1981 F 1, 2, 1983 BI 3(R), 1984 A 3, 1986 F 1, A 1, 3, F 2, 3
Storey, P W (South Canterbury) 1921 SA 1, 2
Strachan, A D (Auckland, North Harbour) 1992 Wld 2, 3, I 1, 2, A 1, 2, 3, SA, 1993 BI 1, 1995 [J, SA (t)]

**423**

NEW ZEALAND

**Strahan, S C** (Manawatu) 1967 A, E, W, F, S, 1968 A 1, 2, F 1, 2, 3, 1970 SA 1, 2, 3, 1972 A 1, 2, 3, 1973 E 2

**Strang, W A** (South Canterbury) 1928 SA 1, 2, 1930 BI 3, 4, 1931 A

**Stringfellow, J C** (Wairarapa) 1929 A 1(R), 3

**Stuart, K C** (Canterbury) 1955 A 1

**Stuart, R C** (Canterbury) 1949 A 1, 2, 1953 W, 1954 I, E, S, F

**Stuart, R L** (Hawke's Bay) 1977 F 1(R)

**Sullivan, J L** (Taranaki) 1937 SA 1, 2, 3, 1938 A 1, 2, 3

**Sutherland, A R** (Marlborough) 1970 SA 2, 4, 1971 BI 1, 1972 A 1, 2, 3, W, 1973 E 1, I, F

**Svenson, K S** (Wellington) 1924 I, W, 1925 E, F

**Swain, J P** (Hawke's Bay) 1928 SA 1, 2, 3, 4

**Tanner, J M** (Auckland) 1950 BI 4, 1951 A 1, 2, 3, 1953 W

**Tanner, K J** (Canterbury) 1974 A 1, 2, 3, I, 1975 S, 1976 I, SA 1

**Taumoepeau, S** (Auckland) 2004 It, 2005 I(R), S

**Taylor, G L** (Northland) 1996 SA 5(R)

**Taylor, H M** (Canterbury) 1913 A 1, US, 1914 A 1, 2, 3

**Taylor, J M** (Otago) 1937 SA 1, 2, 3, 1938 A 1, 2, 3

**Taylor, M B** (Waikato) 1979 F 1, 2, A, S, E, 1980 A 1, 2

**Taylor, N M** (Bay of Plenty, Hawke's Bay) 1977 BI 2, 4(R), F 1, 2, 1978 A 1, 2, 3, I, 1982 A 2

**Taylor, R** (Taranaki) 1913 A 2, 3

**Taylor, T J** (Canterbury) 2013 A2, 3(R), J(R)

**Taylor, W T** (Canterbury) 1983 BI 1, 2, 3, 4, A, S, 1984 F 1, 2, A 1, 2, 1985 E 1, 2, A, Arg 1, 2, 1986 A 2, 1987 [It, Fj, S, W, F], A, 1988 W 1, 2

**Tetzlaff, P L** (Auckland) 1947 A 1, 2

**Thimbleby, N W** (Hawke's Bay) 1970 SA 3

**Thomas, B T** (Auckland, Wellington) 1962 A 5, 1964 A 1, 2, 3

**Thomson, A J** (Otago) 2008 I1(t&R), E2, SA1, 2, A2(R), SA3(R), Sm, A4(t&R), S, 2009 F1, SA3(R), A3, 4, W(R), E, 2010 W1(R), 2(R), 2011 Fj, SA1, A1(R), SA2, A2, [J, F1], 2012 I1(R), 2, 3(R), SA2(R), S

**Thomson, H D** (Wellington) 1908 AW 1

**Thorn, B C** (Canterbury, Tasman) 2003 W (R), F (R), SA 1(R), A 1(R), SA 2, [It, C, Tg, W, SA(R), A(R), F(R)], 2008 I1, E1, 2, SA1, A1, 2, SA3, A3, 4, I2, W, E3, 2009 F1, 2, It1, A1, SA1, 2, A2, SA3, A3, 4, W, E, F3, 2010 I1, W1, 2, SA1, 2, A1, 2, SA3, A3, 4, E, S, W3, 2011 A1, 2, [Tg, J, F1, C(R), Arg, A, F2]

**Thorne, G S** (Auckland) 1968 A 1, 2, F 1, 2, 3, 1969 W 1, 1970 SA 1, 2, 3, 4

**Thorne, R D** (Canterbury) 1999 SA 2(R), [Tg, E, S, F 2, SA 3], 2000 Tg, S 2, A 2(R) F 1, 2, 2001 Sm, Arg 1, F, SA 1, A 1, I, S, Arg 2, 2002 It, I 1, 2, Fj, A 1, SA 1, A2, SA 2, 2003 E, W, F, SA 1, A 1, SA 2, A 2, [It, C, Tg, W, SA, A, F], 2006 SA1, 2, E, W(R), 2007 F1, C, SA2, [S, R]

**Thornton, N H** (Auckland) 1947 A 1, 2, 1949 SA 1

**Thrush, J I** (Wellington) 2013 F2(R), Arg1(R), 2(R), A3, J, 2014 Arg1(R), SA1, Arg2(R), SA2

**Tialata, N S** (Wellington) 2005 W, E(t), S(R), 2006 I1(R), 2(R), Arg(R), SA1, 2, 3(R), F1(R), 2(R), C, A1(R), SA2(R), [It(t&R), Pt, S(R), R], 2008 I1, E1, 2, SA1(R), 2(R), Sm(R), A4, S(R), I2, W, E3, 2009 F1, 2, A1, SA1, A3, 4, W, It2, F3, 2010 I1(R), W2

**Tiatia, F I** (Wellington) 2000 Tg (R), It

**Tilyard, J T** (Wellington) 1913 A 3

**Timu, J K R** (Otago) 1991 Arg 1, A 1, 2, [E, US, C, A], 1992 Wld 2, I 2, A 1, 2, 3, SA, 1993 BI 1, 2, 3, A, WS, S, E, 1994 F 1, 2, SA 1, 2, 3, A

**Tindill, E W T** (Wellington) 1936 E

**Todd, M B** (Canterbury) 2013 F3(R), SA1(t)

**Toeava, I** (Auckland) 2005 S, 2006 Arg, A1(t&R), A3, SA2(R), 2007 F1, 2, SA1, 2, A2, [It(R), Pt, S(R), R, F(R)], 2008 SA3(R), Sm(R), A4, S, I2(R), E3(R), 2009 F1, 2(R), It1, SA3(R), A3, 2010 A4(R), E(R), S, W3, 2011 SA2, A2(R), [Tg, J, C(R), Arg(R)]

**Tonu'u, O F J** (Auckland) 1997 Fj (R), A 3(R), 1998 E 1, 2, SA 1(R)

**To'omaga-Allen, J L** (Wellington) 2013 J(R)

**Townsend, L J** (Otago) 1955 A 1, 3

**Tremain, K R** (Canterbury, Hawke's Bay) 1959 BI 2, 3, 4, 1960 SA 1, 2, 3, 4, 1961 F 2, 3 1962 A 1, 2, 3, 1963 E 1, 2, I, W, 1964 E, S, F, A 1, 2, 3, 1965 SA 1, 2, 3, 4, 1966 BI 1, 2, 3, 4, 1967 A, E, W, S, 1968 A 1, F 1, 2, 3

**Trevathan, D** (Otago) 1937 SA 1, 2, 3

**Tuck, J M** (Waikato) 1929 A 1, 2, 3

**Tuiali'i, M M** (Auckland) 2004 Arg, A2(R), SA2(R), It, W, 2005 I, E(R), S(R), 2006 Arg

**Tuigamala, V L** (Auckland) 1991 [US, It, C, S], 1992 Wld 1, 2, 3, I 1, A 1, 2, 3, SA, 1993 BI 1, 2, 3, A, WS, S, E

**Tuipulotu, P T** (Auckland) 2014 E2(R), 3(R), SA1(R)

**Tuitavake, A S M** (North Harbour) 2008 I1, E1, A1, 2(R), Sm, S

**Tuitupou, S** (Auckland) 2004 E1(R), 2(R), Arg, SA1(R), A2(R), SA2, 2006 Arg, SA1, 2(R)

**Turner, R S** (North Harbour) 1992 Wld 1, 2(R)

**Turtill, H S** (Canterbury) 1905 A

**Twigden, T M** (Auckland) 1980 A 2, 3

**Tyler, G A** (Auckland) 1903 A, 1904 BI, 1905 S, I, E, W, 1906 F

**Udy, D K** (Wairarapa) 1903 A

**Umaga, J F** (Wellington) 1997 Fj, Arg 1, 2, A 1, SA 1, 2, 1999 WS, F 1, SA 1, A 1, SA 2, A 2, [Tg, E, S, F 2, SA 3], 2000 Tg, S 1, 2, A 1, 2, SA 2, F 1, 2, It, 2001 Sm, Arg 1, F, SA 1, A 1, SA 2, A 2, I, S, Arg 2, 2002 I 1, Fj, SA 1(R), A 2, SA 2, E, F, W, 2003 E, W, F, SA 1, A 1, SA 2, A 2, [It], 2004 E1, 2, Arg, PI, A1, SA1, A2, SA2, It, F, 2005 Fj, BI1, 2, 3, SA1, A1, SA2, A2, W, E, S

**Urbahn, R J** (Taranaki) 1959 BI 1, 3, 4

**Urlich, R A** (Auckland) 1970 SA 3, 4

**Uttley, I N** (Wellington) 1963 E 1, 2

**Vidiri, J** (Counties Manukau) 1998 E 2(R), A 1

**Vincent, P B** (Canterbury) 1956 SA 1, 2

**Vito, V V J** (Wellington) 2010 I1(R), W1, A1(R), 2(R), SA3(R), A3, 2011 SA2(R), A2(R), [Tg, J, C, Arg(R), A(R)], 2012 I 1, A2(R), Arg1, A3(R), S, W(R), E(R), 2013 F2(R), 3, 2014 E1(R), 2(R)

**Vodanovich, I M H** (Wellington) 1955 A 1, 2, 3

**Wallace, W J** (Wellington) 1903 A, 1904 BI, 1905 S, I, E, W, 1906 F, 1907 A 1, 2, 3, 1908 AW 2

**Waller, D A G** (Wellington) 2001 Arg 2(t)

**Walsh, P T** (Counties) 1955 A 1, 2, 3, 1956 SA 1, 2, 4, 1957 A 1, 2, 1958 A 1, 2, 3, 1959 BI 1, 1963 E 2

**Ward, R H** (Southland) 1936 A 2, 1937 SA 1, 3

**Waterman, A C** (North Auckland) 1929 A 1, 2

**Watkins, E L** (Wellington) 1905 A

**Watt, B A** (Canterbury) 1962 A 1, 4, 1963 E 1, 2, W, 1964 E, S, A 1

**Watt, J M** (Otago) 1936 A 1, 2

**Watt, J R** (Wellington) 1958 A 2, 1960 SA 1, 2, 3, 4, 1961 F 1, 3, 1962 A 1, 2

**Watts, M G** (Taranaki) 1979 F 1, 2, 1980 A 1, 2, 3(R)

**Webb, D S** (North Auckland) 1959 BI 2

**Weepu, P A T** (Wellington, Auckland) 2004 W, 2005 SA1(R), A1, SA2, A2, I, E(R), S, 2006 Arg, A1(R), SA1, A3(R), SA2, F1, W(R), 2007 F1, C(R), SA1(R), A1(R), SA2, 2008 A2(R), SA3(R), Sm(R), A3(R), 4(R), S, I2(R), W(R), E3(R), 2009 F1(R), 2(R), It1(R), A1(R), SA1(R), 2, 2010 I1(R), W1(R), 2(R), SA1(R), 2, A1(R), 2, SA3(R), A3, 2011 Fj(R), SA1(R), A1, SA2(R), A2, [Tg(R), J(R), F1, C(R), Arg, A, F2], 2012 I 1(R), 2(R), 3(R), A1(R), 2(R), Arg1(R), SA1, Arg2(R), SA2(R), A3(R), S, W(R), E(R), 2013 F2(R), 3

**Wells, J** (Wellington) 1936 A 1, 2

**West, A H** (Taranaki) 1921 SA 2, 3

**Whetton, A J** (Auckland) 1984 A 1(R), 3(R), 1985 A (R), Arg 1(R), 1986 A 2, 1987 [It, Fj, Arg, S, W, F], A, 1988 W 1, 2, A 1, 2, 3, 1989 F 1, 2, Arg 1, 2, A, 1990 S 1, 2, A 1, 2, 3, F 1, 2, 1991 Arg 1, [E, US, It, C, A]

**Whetton, G W** (Auckland) 1981 SA 3, R, F 1, 2, 1982 A 3, 1983 BI 1, 2, 3, 4, 1984 F 1, 2, A 1, 2, 3, 1985 E 1, 2, A, Arg 2, 1986 A 2, 3, F 2, 3, 1987 [It, Fj, Arg, S, W, F], A, 1988 W 1, 2, A 1, 2, 3, 1989 F 1, 2, Arg 1, 2, A, W, I, 1990 S 1, 2, A 1, 2, 3, F 1, 2, 1991 Arg 1, 2, A 1, 2, [E, US, It, C, A, S]

**Whineray, W J** (Canterbury, Waikato, Auckland) 1957 A 1, 2, 1958 A 1, 2, 3, 1959 BI 1, 2, 3, 4, 1960 SA 1, 2, 3, 4, 1961 F 1, 2, 3, 1962 A 1, 2, 3, 4, 5, 1963 E 1, 2, I, W, 1964 E, S, F, 1965 SA 1, 2, 3, 4

**White, A** (Southland) 1921 SA 1, 1924 I, 1925 E, F

**White, H L** (Auckland) 1954 I, E, F, 1955 A 3

NEW ZEALAND

Getty Images

Few can challenge Julian Savea's try-scoring record of 27 tries in his 28 Tests for the All Blacks.

# ROMANIA

## ROMANIA'S 2013–14 TEST RECORD

| OPPONENTS | DATE | VENUE | RESULT |
| --- | --- | --- | --- |
| Tonga | 9 Nov | H | Won 19–18 |
| Canada | 16 Nov | H | Won 21–20 |
| Fiji | 23 Nov | H | Lost 7–26 |
| Portugal | 1 Feb | H | Won 24–0 |
| Russia | 8 Feb | A | Won 34–3 |
| Spain | 22 Feb | H | Won 32–6 |
| Belgium | 8 Mar | H | Won 29–10 |
| Georgia | 15 Mar | A | Lost 22–9 |
| Uruguay | 13 Jun | H | Won 34–16 |
| Russia | 18 Jun | H | Won 20–18 |

# ROMANIA BOARD THE RWC 2015 TRAIN

## By Chris Thau

Florin Surugiu gets the ball away for Romania during their European Nations Cup defeat by Georgia in March.

**T**he traumas of the previous Rugby World Cup cycle, when Romania found themselves battling through the Repechage to qualify for New Zealand 2011, had an impact on both the approach of the newly appointed head coach Lynn Howells and the mind-set of the team. After a few months in an advisory role, the experienced Howells took charge at the end of 2012 and promptly made the European Nations Cup 2014 his top priority, hardly surprising given it was the first stage of their bid to qualify for RWC 2015 in England.

"I don't want to reinvent the wheel with this team, but try to return to their traditional values, a game based on a strong forward platform and an efficient kicking game and take it from there. Qualifying for RWC 2015 is definitely our main objective," admitted Howells.

The team took up the challenge, making 2013 arguably the most successful year of the last decade. Only a defeat at the hands of the visiting Fijians at the end of November spoiled an otherwise unblemished record of seven wins and one draw from the nine matches played in the calendar year. The main objective was achieved, with an unbeaten Romania sharing top spot in Division 1A with Georgia.

Defeating both Tonga and Canada were real feathers in Romania's cap, and confirmed that Howells and his team were on the right track in their pursuit of one of Europe's two direct passages to RWC 2015, but making it to the tournament remained the top priority.

The November programme was unquestionably one of the most ambitious to date with all three opponents above Romania in the IRB World Rankings. Romania won the first two matches by the slenderest of margins, 19–18 against Tonga and 21–20 against Canada, with the vociferous support of the home crowd and a fair amount of luck both contributing to the positive outcomes – penalties at the death from Florin Vlaicu turning gallant defeats into confidence-boosting victories.

In the opening match against Tonga, a try from number 8 and captain Mihai Macovei and the boot of Vlaicu, who kicked a conversion and four penalties, was just enough. It was a similar story against Canada a week later, when the visitors again scored more tries – two to none – but Vlaicu's seven penalties edged the Oaks home. The most significant aspect of the two matches was their intensity, which stretched the Romanians to their limits, thereby giving Howells and his coaching team of Marius Tincu, Eugen Apjok, Neil Kelly and Olivier Nier good reasons to feel optimistic.

The titanic efforts of the Romanian pack in the first two matches and the mounting injury toll to a large extent accounted for the loss of speed and shape in the third Test against Fiji, which Romania lost 26–7. A shallow talent base remains Romania's chief weakness, with the fly-half and scrum-half positions particularly vulnerable. But consecutive wins against teams of the calibre of Tonga and Canada would have been unthinkable a couple of seasons ago, and prove that Romania under Howells are making progress, slowly maturing into a force to be reckoned with. Furthermore, beyond testing the intensity, endurance and skill levels of the Oaks, matches of this ilk do wonders for both the morale and the confidence of the team.

The race to qualify for RWC 2015 resumed in February 2014 with the second half of the European Nations Cup. Portugal were the first opponents, at Cluj Arena, for the 21st meeting between the nations since they first met in 1967. The Oaks toiled hard to win 24–0 after tries from Andrei Radoi and Csaba Gal with Vlaicu converting one and also kicking four penalties. On the strength of their performance against Portugal, the next match, against Russia in Krasnodar, must have given Howells cause for concern. However, after a finely balanced first half when they scored one try through former captain Stelian Burcea, the Oaks stamped their authority on the game in the second half, scoring three more tries through Viorel Lucaci, Ionut Dumitru and Dorin Manole to win 34–3, one of the largest margins against their rivals.

The 32–6 win against Spain at Cluj Arena confirmed Romania would grace the Rugby World Cup stage in 2015, but they still did not know whether they would join Pool C as Europe 1 or Pool D as Europe 2. Victory followed against Belgium (29–10) in Constanta to leave Romania a point clear going into the ENC title decider with Georgia in Tbilisi on 15 March.

"It is great to have qualified for RWC with two matches remaining," Howells had said after the Spain victory. "We would like to win both games. Personally I would love to play New Zealand at the Millennium Stadium in Cardiff." But it was not to be as Georgia prevailed 22–9 on home soil to claim the title and that date with the All Blacks, sending Romania into Pool D alongside France, Ireland, Italy and Canada.

With qualification secured, attention turned to the IRB Nations Cup in the Romanian capital in June. The Oaks had to reshuffle the squad due to the unavailability of around 12 senior players, who were either injured or rested after a demanding winter campaign. "This is a good opportunity for the youngsters to show what they are made of, and also a good opportunity for us to do a serious talent inventory before the World Cup," insisted backs coach Apjok. Romania were seeking a hat-trick of Nations Cup titles, but while they overcame Uruguay and Russia, they lost to Emerging Ireland to surrender the silverware. The tournament was nonetheless useful in exposing some of Romania's limitations, which Howells and his men will have time to sort out before the November internationals.

On the domestic front, the seven-strong SuperLiga – the newly-promoted RC "Stejarul" Buzau dropped out due to financial reasons – went on with the same two leading contenders, defending champions Timisoara and Baia Mare, the league runners-up and cup holders, locking horns in the play-offs. This time Timisoara lost 21–17 in the first round and their South African coach Danie de Villiers was sacked immediately, sharing the fate that had fallen on Farul Constanta's high-profile coach Neil Kelly earlier in the season. Baia Mare, coached by Apjok, survived the blow of losing their New Zealand-born fly-half Michael Wiringi to a broken leg in the first round of the play-offs to prevail 25–19 over surprise finalists Farul Constanta to regain the league title after a three-year interval.

### WINNING MARGIN

| Date | Opponent | Result | Winning Margin |
|---|---|---|---|
| 21/09/1976 | Bulgaria | 100–0 | 100 |
| 19/03/2005 | Ukraine | 97–0 | 97 |
| 13/04/1996 | Portugal | 92–0 | 92 |
| 17/11/1976 | Morocco | 89–0 | 89 |
| 19/04/1996 | Belgium | 83–5 | 78 |

### MOST POINTS IN A MATCH
#### BY THE TEAM

| Date | Opponent | Result | Points |
|---|---|---|---|
| 21/09/1976 | Bulgaria | 100–0 | 100 |
| 19/03/2005 | Ukraine | 97–0 | 97 |
| 13/04/1996 | Portugal | 92–0 | 92 |
| 17/11/1976 | Morocco | 89–0 | 89 |
| 19/04/1996 | Belgium | 83–5 | 83 |

#### BY A PLAYER

| Date | Player | Opponent | Points |
|---|---|---|---|
| 05/10/2002 | Ionut Tofan | Spain | 30 |
| 13/04/1996 | Virgil Popisteanu | Portugal | 27 |
| 04/02/2001 | Petre Mitu | Portugal | 27 |
| 13/04/1996 | Ionel Rotaru | Portugal | 25 |

### MOST TRIES IN A MATCH
#### BY THE TEAM

| Date | Opponent | Result | Tries |
|---|---|---|---|
| 17/11/1976 | Morocco | 89–0 | 17 |
| 21/10/1951 | East Germany | 64–26 | 16 |
| 19/03/2005 | Ukraine | 97–0 | 15 |
| 16/04/1978 | Spain | 74–3 | 14 |
| | 13 on 3 occasions | | |

#### BY A PLAYER

| Date | Player | Opponent | Tries |
|---|---|---|---|
| 30/04/1972 | Gheorghe Rascanu | Morocco | 5 |
| 18/10/1986 | Cornel Popescu | Portugal | 5 |
| 13/04/1996 | Ionel Rotaru | Portugal | 5 |

### MOST CONVERSIONS IN A MATCH
#### BY THE TEAM

| Date | Opponent | Result | Cons |
|---|---|---|---|
| 13/04/1996 | Portugal | 92–0 | 12 |
| 19/03/2005 | Ukraine | 97–0 | 11 |
| 04/10/1997 | Belgium | 83–13 | 10 |
| | 9 on 4 occasions | | |

#### BY A PLAYER

| Date | Player | Opponent | Cons |
|---|---|---|---|
| 13/04/1996 | Virgil Popisteanu | Portugal | 12 |
| 04/10/1997 | Serban Guranescu | Belgium | 10 |
| 19/03/2005 | Danut Dumbrava | Ukraine | 8 |
| 22/03/2008 | Florin Vlaicu | Czech Republic | 8 |

### MOST PENALTIES IN A MATCH
#### BY THE TEAM

| Date | Opponent | Result | Pens |
|---|---|---|---|
| 15/06/2010 | Argentina Jaguars | 24–8 | 7 |
| 16/11/2013 | Canada | 21–20 | 7 |
| | 6 on 3 occasions | | |

#### BY A PLAYER

| Date | Player | Opponent | Pens |
|---|---|---|---|
| 16/11/2013 | Florin Vlaicu | Canada | 7 |
| 14/05/1994 | Neculai Nichitean | Italy | 6 |
| 04/02/2001 | Petre Mitu | Portugal | 6 |
| 23/02/2013 | Florin Vlaicu | Spain | 6 |

### MOST DROP GOALS IN A MATCH
#### BY THE TEAM

| Date | Opponent | Result | DGs |
|---|---|---|---|
| 29/10/1967 | West Germany | 27–5 | 4 |
| 14/11/1965 | West Germany | 9–8 | 3 |
| 17/10/1976 | Poland | 38–8 | 3 |
| 03/10/1990 | Spain | 19–6 | 3 |

#### BY A PLAYER

| Date | Player | Opponent | DGs |
|---|---|---|---|
| 29/10/1967 | Valeriu Irimescu | West Germany | 3 |
| 17/10/1976 | Alexandru Dumitru | Poland | 3 |

ROMANIA

## MOST CAPPED PLAYERS

| Player | Caps |
|---|---|
| Cristian Petre | 91 |
| Adrian Lungu | 77 |
| Romeo Stefan Gontineac | 77 |
| Lucian Mihai Sirbu | 77 |

## LEADING PENALTY SCORERS

| Player | Pens |
|---|---|
| Florin Vlaicu | 99 |
| Danut Dumbrava | 70 |
| Neculai Nichitean | 53 |
| Petre Mitu | 53 |
| Ionut Tofan | 46 |

## LEADING TRY SCORERS

| Player | Tries |
|---|---|
| Petre Motrescu | 33 |
| Gabriel Brezoianu | 28 |
| Florica Murariu | 27 |
| Catalin Fercu | 27 |
| Mihai Vusec | 22 |

## LEADING DROP GOAL SCORERS

| Player | DGs |
|---|---|
| Alexandru Dumitru | 14 |
| Neculai Nichitean | 10 |
| Valeriu Irimescu | 10 |
| Gelu Ignat | 8 |

## LEADING CONVERSIONS SCORERS

| Player | Cons |
|---|---|
| Florin Vlaicu | 90 |
| Danut Dumbrava | 69 |
| Petre Mitu | 53 |
| Ionut Tofan | 52 |
| Ion Constantin | 34 |

## LEADING POINTS SCORERS

| Player | Points |
|---|---|
| Florin Vlaicu | 516 |
| Danut Dumbrava | 369 |
| Petre Mitu | 335 |
| Ionut Tofan | 322 |
| Neculai Nichitean | 257 |

# ROMANIA INTERNATIONAL PLAYERS
## UP TO 13 OCTOBER 2014

**A Achim** 1974 *Pol*, 1976 *Pol*, *Mor*
**M Adascalitei** 2007 *Rus*, 2009 *Pt*, *Ur*, *F*, *ItA*, 2012 *Ukr*, *Ur*
**Ailenei** 2012 *Ukr*
**M Aldea** 1979 *USS*, *W*, *Pol*, *F*, 1980 *It*, *USS*, *I*, *F*, 1981 *It*, *Sp*, *USS*, *S*, *NZ*, *F*, 1982 *WGe*, *It*, *USS*, *Z*, *Z*, *F*, 1983 *Mor*, *WGe*, *It*, *USS*, *Pol*, *W*, *USS*, *F*, 1984 *It*, *S*, *F*, 1985 *E*, *USS*
**C Alexandrescu** 1934 *It*
**N Anastasiade** 1927 *Cze*, 1934 *It*
**V Anastasiade** 1939 *It*
**I Andrei** 2003 *W*, *I*, *Ar*, *Nm*, 2004 *CZR*, *Pt*, *Sp*, *Rus*, *Geo*, *It*, *W*, *J*, *CZR*, 2005 *Rus*, *US*, *S*, *Pt*, 2006 *CZR*, 2007 *Pt*, 2008 *Sp*, *Pt*, *Rus*
**I Andriesi** 1937 *It*, *H*, *Ger*, 1938 *F*, *Ger*, 1939 *It*, 1940 *It*
**E Apjok** 1996 *Bel*, 2000 *It*, 2001 *Pt*
**AM Apostol** 2011 *Nm*, *E*, 2012 *Rus*, *Geo*, *Sp*, 2013 *Pt*, *Sp*, *Bel*, *Geo*
**D Armasel** 1924 *F*, *US*
**A Atanasiu** 1970 *It*, *F*, 1971 *It*, *Mor*, *F*, 1972 *Mor*, *Cze*, *WGe*, 1973 *Sp*, *Mor*, *Ar*, *Ar*, *WGe*, 1974 *Pol*

**I Bacioiu** 1976 *USS*, *Bul*, *Pol*, *F*, *Mor*
**N Baciu** 1964 *Cze*, *EGe*, 1967 *It*, *F*, 1968 *Cze*, *Cze*, *F*, 1969 *Pol*, *WGe*, *F*, 1970 *It*, 1971 *It*, *Mor*, *F*, 1972 *Mor*, *Cze*, *WGe*, 1973 *Ar*, *Ar*, 1974 *Cze*, *EGe*

**VC Badalicescu** 2012 *Pt*, *J*
**I Badiu** 2014 *Rus*
**B Balan** 2003 *Pt*, *Sp*, *Geo*, 2004 *W*, 2005 *Rus*, *Ukr*, *J*, *US*, *S*, *Pt*, 2006 *Geo*, *Pt*, *Ukr*, *Rus*, *F*, *Geo*, *Sp*, *S*, 2007 *Sp*, *ESp*, *ItA*, *Nm*, *It*, *S*, *Pt*, *NZ*, 2009 *Fj*, 2010 *Ger*, *Rus*, *Ur*, 2011 *Pt*
**D Balan** 1983 *F*
**PV Balan** 1998 *H*, *Pol*, *Ukr*, *Ar*, *Geo*, *I*, 1999 *F*, *S*, *A*, *US*, *I*, 2000 *Mor*, *H*, *Pt*, *Sp*, *Geo*, *F*, *It*, 2001 *Pt*, *Sp*, *H*, *Rus*, *Geo*, *I*, *E*, 2002 *Pt*, *Sp*, *H*, *Rus*, *Geo*, *Sp*, *S*, *S*, 2003 *CZR*, *F*, *W*, *I*, *Nm*, 2004 *It*, *W*, *J*, *CZR*, 2005 *Geo*, *C*, *I*, 2006 *Geo*, *Pt*, *F*, *Geo*, *Sp*, *S*, 2007 *Geo*, 2009 *Ur*, *F*
**L Balcan** 1963 *Bul*, *EGe*, *Cze*
**F Balmus** 2000 *Mor*, *H*, *Pt*
**S Bals** 1927 *F*, *Ger*, *Cze*
**G Baltaretu** 1965 *WGe*, *F*
**C Barascu** 1957 *F*
**M Baraulea** 2004 *CZR*, *Pt*, *Geo*
**A Barbu** 1958 *WGe*, *It*, 1959 *EGe*, *Pol*, *Cze*, *EGe*, 1960 *F*
**A Barbuliceanu** 2008 *Rus*, *ESp*, 2009 *Sp*, *Ger*, *Rus*, *Geo*, *Pt*
**S Bargaunas** 1971 *It*, *Mor*, 1972 *F*, 1974 *Cze*, 1975 *It*
**S Barsan** 1934 *It*, 1936 *F*, *It*, 1937 *It*, *H*, *F*, *Ger*, 1938 *F*, *Ger*, 1939 *It*, 1940 *It*, 1942 *It*
**RC Basalau** 2007 *Pt*, 2008 *Geo*, *Pt*, *Rus*, *CZR*, *Ur*, *Rus*, *ESp*, 2010 *ItA*, *Tun*

ROMANIA

Mor, F, 1972 WGe, F, 1973 Ar, Ar, WGe, F, 1974 Mor, Pol, Sp, Cze, EGe, F, Cze, 1975 It, Sp, JAB, Pol, F
**A Duta** 1973 Ar

**R Eckert** 1927 F, Ger, Cze
**I Enache** 1977 It
**M Ezaru** 2000 Pt, Geo, F

**V Falcusanu** 1974 Sp, Cze
**G Fantaneanu** 1934 It, 1936 F, It, Ger, 1937 It, H, F, Ger
**C Fercu** 2005 C, I, 2006 Geo, CZR, Pt, Ukr, Rus, F, Geo, Sp, 2007 Geo, Sp, CZR, ESp, ItA, Nm, It, S, Pt, 2008 Geo, Sp, Pt, Rus, CZR, Ur, Rus, ESp, 2009 Sp, Ger, Rus, Pt, Ur, F, 2010 Ger, Rus, Geo, Pt, Sp, Ukr, Nm, ArJ, ItA, Tun, Ur, Ur, 2011 Rus, Geo, Sp, Nm, ArJ, Ukr, 2012 Ur, J, US, 2013 Pt, Rus, Sp, Bel, Geo, Rus, ArJ, Elt, Tg, C, Fj, 2014 Pt, Rus, Sp, Bel, Geo
**Filip** 2012 J, US
**C Florea** 1937 It, F, Ger
**G Florea** 1981 S, NZ, F, 1982 WGe, It, USS, Z, Z, 1984 Sp, 1985 USS, 1986 Pt, F
**IM Florea** 2012 J, US
**S Florea** 2000 It, 2001 Sp, Geo, I, E, 2002 It, Sp, W, 2003 Sp, Rus, Geo, CZR, A, Ar, Nm, 2007 Sp, CZR, S, NZ, 2009 Sp, Ger, 2010 Rus, Ukr, Ukr, Nm, 2011 S, Ar, E, Geo
**I Florescu** 1957 F, Cze
**M Florescu** 1995 F
**P Florescu** 1967 It, Pt, Pol, WGe, F, 1968 Cze, Cze, F, 1969 Pol, WGe, Cze, F, 1971 Mor, 1973 Sp, Mor, Ar, Ar, 1974 Cze, EGe, F
**P Florian** 1927 F, 1934 It
**T Florian** 1927 F, Ger
**V Flutur** 1994 Ger, 1995 J, J, C, SA, A, Ar, F, It, 1996 Bel, Pol, 1997 WalA, F
**M Foca** 1992 It, USS, It, Ar, 1993 Pt, Tun, F
**C Fugigi** 1992 Ar
**C Fugigi** 1964 Cze, 1969 Cze, 1972 Mor, Cze, WGe, F, 1973 Sp, Ar, Ar, WGe, F, 1974 Mor, Sp, Cze, EGe, 1975 It, Sp, JAB
**R Fugigi** 1995 It, 1996 Pt, F, Pol, 1998 Ukr, Ar, I, 1999 S, I
**S Fuicu** 1976 H, 1980 USS, I, Pol, F, 1981 It, Sp, USS, S, NZ, F, 1982 Z, Z, F, 1983 Mor, WGe, It, USS, W, 1984 It
**N Fulina** 1988 F, W, 1989 It, E, Sp, Sa, USS, 1990 It, F, H, Sp, USS, 1991 NZ, C, Fj, 1992 It, It, 1993 Pt, F, Sp, F, I, 1994 Sp, Ger, Rus, It, W, F

**CM Gal** 2005 I, 2006 Geo, CZR, Pt, S, 2007 Geo, CZR, ESp, ItA, Nm, It, S, NZ, Rus, Pt, 2008 Geo, Sp, Pt, Rus, 2009 Ger, Pt, ItA, ItA, Fj, 2010 Geo, Pt, Sp, Ukr, Ukr, Nm, ArJ, ItA, Tun, Ur, Ur, 2011 Pt, Geo, Sp, Nm, S, Ar, E, Geo, 2012 Pt, Rus, Geo, Sp, Ukr, Ur, J, US, 2013 Rus, Sp, Bel, Geo, Rus, ArJ, Elt, Tg, C, Fj, 2014 Pt, Rus, Sp, Bel, Geo, Ur, Rus
**S Galan** 1985 It, It
**I Garlesteanu** 1924 F, US, 1927 F, Cze
**A Gealapu** 1994 It, E, 1995 F, S, J, J, C, SA, A, Ar, F, It, 1996 Pt, F, Pol
**C Gheara** 2004 CZR, Sp, Rus, Geo, 2010 Ger, 2011 Rus, Ukr, Ar, Geo, 2012 Pt, Rus, Geo, Ukr, Ur, J, US
**C Gheorghe** 1992 It, 1993 Tun, F, Sp, 1994 Sp, Ger, E
**D Gherasim** 1959 Cze
**V Ghiata** 1951 EGe
**S Ghica** 1937 H, F, 1942 It
**V Ghioc** 2000 It, 2001 Pt, Sp, Rus, Geo, I, W, E, 2002 Pt, Sp, H, W, S, S, 2003 CZR, Ar, 2004 It, W, CZR, 2005 Ukr, J, S, 2008 Pt
**N Ghiondea** 1949 Cze, 1951 EGe
**D Ghiuzelea** 1951 EGe, 1952 EGe, EGe, 1953 It, 1955 Cze, 1957 Cze
**A Girbu** 1992 Ar, 1993 Tun, Sp, F, I, 1994 Sp, 1995 Ar, F, It, 1996 Pt, F, Pol, 1997 WalA, F, Ar, F, It, 1998 H, Pol, Geo, I
**L Giucal** 2009 Sp, Ger
**M Giucal** 1985 It, Tun, USS, It, 1986 Pt, F, Tun
**A Giugiuc** 1963 Bul, EGe, Cze, 1964 Cze, EGe, 1966 Cze

**V Giuglea** 1986 S, Tun
**I Glavan** 1942 It
**RS Gontineac** 1995 F, S, J, J, C, SA, A, 1996 Pt, F, Pol, 1997 F, W, Ar, F, It, 1998 H, Pol, Ukr, Ar, Geo, I, 1999 F, S, A, US, I, 2000 H, Sp, Geo, F, 2001 Rus, Geo, 2002 Pt, Sp, Rus, Geo, I, It, Sp, W, S, S, 2003 Pt, Sp, Geo, CZR, F, W, I, A, Ar, Nm, 2004 CZR, Pt, Rus, Geo, It, W, J, CZR, 2005 Geo, C, 2006 Geo, Pt, Ukr, Rus, F, Geo, Sp, S, 2007 Geo, Sp, It, S, Pt, NZ, 2008 ESp
**A Gorcioaia** 2009 Ger, 2012 Rus, Geo, Sp
**M Gorcioaia** 2012 Ukr
**G Graur** 1958 It, 1959 EGe, Pol, Cze, EGe, 1960 Pol, EGe, Cze, 1961 EGe, 1962 EGe, It
**E Grigore** 1982 WGe, 1984 Sp, 1985 E, Tun, 1987 It, USS, Z, F, S
**V Grigorescu** 1936 F, It, Ger, 1939 It
**M Guramare** 1982 WGe, It, 1983 Mor, WGe, 1988 Sp
**A Guranescu** 1991 S, F, 1992 USS, It, 1993 Pt, Tun, I, 1994 Ger, Rus, It, W, E, 1995 SA, A, Ar, F, It
**S Guranescu** 1997 W, Bel, Ar, 2001 Sp, H, Rus, I

**A Hariton** 1973 Mor, Ar, Ar, 1978 Cze, Sp
**T Hell** 1958 EGe
**S Hihetah** 2013 Elt, Tg, Fj, 2014 Rus
**CN Hildan** 1998 H, Pol, Geo, 1999 S
**L Hodorca** 1984 It, 1985 Tun, 1986 Pt, S, F, Tun, Tun, I, 1987 It, Z, 1988 F
**M Holban** 1980 Mor, 1982 F, 1985 It, USS, 1986 Pt, I
**J Hussar** 1919 US

**D Iacob** 1996 Bel, 2001 Pt, Sp, H, Geo, W
**ML Iacob** 1997 W, Bel, Ar, F, It, 1999 S
**DG Ianus** 2009 Sp, 2010 Ukr, Nm, ItA, Tun, 2011 Rus, Geo, Sp, Nm, Ar, E, Geo
**P Ianusevici** 1974 Pol, Cze, EGe, Cze, 1975 It, 1976 USS, Bul, Pol, F, Mor, 1977 Sp, Pol, It, F, 1978 F
**I Iconomu** 1919 US Army, F Army
**M Iconomu** 1919 US Army, F Army
**N Ifrim** 1937 F, Ger
**G Ignat** 1986 Pt, S, F, Tun, 1988 It, Sp, US, USS, USS, F, W, 1989 It, E, Sp, S, 1990 It, F, H, Sp, 1991 It, NZ, 1992 Sp, It, USS, F
**V Ilca** 1987 F
**I Ilie** 1952 EGe, EGe, 1953 It, 1955 Cze, 1957 F, Cze, Bel, F, 1958 It, 1959 EGe
**M Iliescu** 1961 EGe, 1963 Bul, EGe, Cze, F, 1965 WGe, F, 1967 WGe
**T Ioan** 1937 H, F, Ger
**V Ioan** 1927 Ger, Cze, 1937 It
**A Ion** 2012 Sp, Ukr
**F Ion** 1991 S, 1992 Sp, 1993 F
**G Ion** 1984 Sp, 1986 F, I, 1988 USS, F, W, 1989 It, E, Sp, Sa, USS, S, 1990 It, F, H, Sp, It, USS, 1991 It, NZ, F, S, F, C, Fj, 1992 Sp, It, USS, F, Ar, 1993 Pt, F, Sp, F, 1994 Sp, Rus, It, W, 1997 WalA
**P Ion** 2003 Ar, 2004 It, 2005 Rus, Ukr, J, US, S, 2006 Geo, CZR, Pt, Ukr, Rus, F, Geo, S, 2007 Geo, Sp, CZR, ESp, ItA, Pt, NZ, Rus, 2008 Geo, Sp, Rus, Ur, Rus, ESp, 2009 Sp, Ger, Rus, Geo, Pt, Ur, F, ItA, ItA, Fj, 2010 Ger, Rus, Geo, Pt, 2011 ArJ, Ukr, S, Ar, E, Geo, 2012 Geo, Sp, 2013 Pt, Rus, Sp, Bel, Geo, Rus, Tg, C, Fj, 2014 Pt, Rus, Sp, Bel, Geo
**V Ion** 1980 Mor, USS, 1982 Z, Z, F, 1983 Mor, It, USS, W, USS, F, 1984 S, 1985 It, 1987 It, USS, Z, F, S
**A Ionescu** 1958 EGe, It, 1959 EGe, Pol, Cze, 1960 Pol, EGe, Cze, 1961 Pol, Cze, EGe, F, 1962 EGe, It, F, 1963 F, 1964 Cze, EGe, F, 1965 WGe, 1966 Cze, It, F
**D Ionescu** 1949 Cze, 1951 EGe, 1952 EGe, EGe, 1953 It, 1955 Cze, 1957 F, Cze, F, 1958 Sp, It
**G Ionescu** 1949 Cze
**G Ionescu** 1934 It, 1936 F, It, Ger, 1937 It, F, 1938 F, Ger, 1940 It, 1942 It
**M Ionescu** 1947 Mor, 1976 USS, Bul, Pol, F, 1977 It, F, Pol, It, F, 1978 Cze, Sp, Pol, F, 1979 It, Sp, USS, W, Pol, F, 1980 I, 1981 NZ, 1983 USS
**R Ionescu** 1968 Cze, Cze, 1971 F
**S Ionescu** 1936 It, Ger, 1937 It

**435**

**V Ionescu** 1992 *It*
**V Ionescu** 1993 *Tun, F*, 1994 *Ger, Rus*, 1998 *Ukr*
**F Ionita** 1974 *Sp*, 1978 *Pol, F*
**CF Ionita** 2013 *ArJ, Elt, C, Fj*, 2014 *Pt, Rus, Sp, Bel, Ur*
**P Iordachescu** 1957 *F, Cze, Bel, F*, 1958 *Sp, WGe, EGe, It*, 1959 *EGe, Pol, Cze, EGe*, 1960 *Pol, EGe, Cze*, 1961 *EGe*, 1963 *F*, 1964 *Cze, EGe, WGe*, 1965 *WGe, F*, 1966 *Cze*
**M Iordan** 1980 *Mor*
**P Iordanescu** 1949 *Cze*
**V Iorgulescu** 1967 *WGe*, 1968 *Cze, F*, 1969 *Pol, WGe, Cze*, 1970 *It, F*, 1971 *F*, 1973 *Ar, Ar*
**V Irimescu** 1960 *F*, 1961 *Pol, Cze, EGe, F*, 1962 *Cze, EGe, Pol, It, F*, 1963 *F*, 1964 *F*, 1965 *WGe, F*, 1966 *Cze, It, F*, 1967 *It, Pt, Pol, WGe, F*, 1968 *Cze, EGe, F*, 1969 *Pol, WGe, Cze, F*, 1970 *It, F*, 1971 *F*
**I Irimia** 1936 *F, It, Ger*, 1937 *It, H, Ger*, 1938 *F, Ger*, 1939 *It*, 1940 *It*
**G Irisescu** 1993 *Sp*
**A Iulian** 2003 *CZR*
**VM Ivan** 2010 *Geo, Pt, Sp, Ukr, Ukr, Tun*, 2014 *Ur, Rus*
**I Ivanciuc** 1991 *Fj*, 1994 *E*, 1995 *J, C, SA, A*

**I Jipescu** 1927 *F*

**C Kramer** 1955 *Cze*, 1958 *Sp, WGe, It*, 1960 *Pol, EGe, Cze*
**T Krantz** 1940 *It*, 1942 *It*
**C Kurtzbauer** 1939 *It*

**C Lapusneanu** 1934 *It*
**D Lazar** 2013 *Rus, ArJ, Elt, Tg, C, Fj*, 2014 *Ur, Rus*
**F Lazar** 2014 *Ur, Rus*
**MA Lazar** 2008 *CZR, Ur, Rus, ESp*, 2009 *Geo*, 2010 *Geo, Pt, Sp, Tun, Ur, Ur*, 2011 *Rus, Sp, Nm, ArJ, Ukr, S, Ar, Geo*, 2012 *Pt, Rus, Geo, Sp, US*, 2013 *Pt, Rus, Bel, Geo, Tg, C, Fj*, 2014 *Pt, Rus, Sp, Bel, Geo*
**MV Lemnaru** 2009 *Sp, Rus*, 2010 *Ur, Ur*, 2011 *Rus, Geo, Sp, ArJ, S, Ar, Geo*, 2012 *Pt, Rus, Geo, Sp, Ukr, Ur, J, US*, 2014 *Rus, Sp, Bel, Geo*
**G Leonte** 1984 *S, F*, 1985 *E, It, USS*, 1987 *It, USS, Z, S, USS, F*, 1988 *It, Sp, US, USS, USS, F, W*, 1989 *It, E, Sp, Z, Sa, USS, S*, 1990 *It, F, H, Sp, It*, 1991 *It, NZ, F, S, F, C*, 1992 *USS, F, It, Ar*, 1993 *Tun, F, Sp, F, I*, 1994 *Sp, Ger, Rus, It, W, It*, 1995 *F, S, J, J, C, SA, A*
**M Leuciuc** 1987 *F*
**T Luca** 1995 *Ar, F, It*, 1996 *F*
**V Lucaci** 1996 *Bel*
**V Lucaci** 2009 *Fj*, 2010 *Sp, Ukr*, 2011 *Pt, Sp*, 2012 *Pt, Rus, Geo, Ukr, Ur, J, US*, 2013 *Pt, Rus, Sp, Bel, Geo, Rus, ArJ, Elt, Tg, C, Fj*, 2014 *Pt, Rus, Sp, Bel, Geo, Ur, Rus*
**A Lungu** 1980 *It, USS*, 1981 *It, Sp, USS, S, NZ, F*, 1982 *WGe, It, USS, Z, F*, 1983 *Mor, WGe, It, USS, Pol, W, USS, F*, 1984 *It, S, F, Sp*, 1985 *E, It, Tun, USS, USS, It*, 1986 *Pt, S, F, Tun, Tun, Pt, F, I*, 1987 *It, USS, Z, F, S*, 1988 *It, Sp, US, USS, USS, F, W*, 1989 *It, E, Sp, Z, Sa, USS, S*, 1990 *It, F, It*, 1991 *It, NZ, F, S, F, C, Fj*, 1992 *Sp, It, USS, F, Ar*, 1995 *A*
**R Lungu** 2002 *Pt, H, It, Sp, W, S*, 2003 *Pt*
**A Lupu** 2006 *S*
**C Lupu** 1998 *Pol, I*, 1999 *F*, 2000 *Mor, It*, 2001 *Pt, H, Rus, W*, 2002 *H, Rus*
**S Luric** 1951 *EGe*, 1952 *EGe, EGe*, 1953 *It*, 1955 *Cze*
**V Luscal** 1958 *Sp, WGe, EGe*

**F Macaneata** 1983 *USS*
**M Macovei** 2006 *Ukr, Rus*, 2007 *Geo, Rus, Pt*, 2008 *Geo, Rus, CZR, Ur, Rus, ESp*, 2009 *Rus, Geo, ItA*, 2010 *Ger, Geo, Sp, Ukr*, 2011 *Pt, Geo, Nm, Ukr, S, Ar, E, Geo*, 2012 *Pt, Rus, Geo, Sp, Ukr, Ur, J, US*, 2013 *Pt, Rus, Sp, Bel, Geo, Rus, ArJ, Elt, Tg, C, Fj*, 2014 *Pt, Rus, Sp, Geo, Ur, Rus*
**V Maftei** 1995 *Ar, F, It*, 1996 *Bel*, 1997 *WalA, W, F*, 1998 *Ar*, 2001 *Pt, Sp, H, Geo, I*, 2002 *Pt, Sp, Rus, Geo, I, It, Sp, S*, 2003 *Pt, Geo, CZR, F, W, I, A, Ar, Nm*, 2004 *Pt, Sp, Rus, Geo, W, J, CZR*, 2005 *Rus, Geo, Ukr, C, I*, 2006 *CZR*
**G Malancu** 1976 *H, It, USS, Bul*
**A Man** 1988 *US*

**V Man** 1988 *USS, USS*
**D Manoileanu** 1949 *Cze*
**DG Manole** 2009 *Ger*, 2012 *Rus, Geo, Sp, Ur*, 2013 *Pt, Rus, Sp, Bel*, 2014 *Pt, Rus, Sp, Bel, Geo*
**G Manole** 1959 *Pol*, 1960 *Pol, EGe, Cze*
**AV Manta** 1996 *Bel*, 1997 *F*, 1998 *Ar, Geo, I*, 2000 *F*, 2001 *Pt, Sp, Rus, Geo*, 2002 *Sp, H, Rus, I, It, Sp*, 2003 *Pt, Rus*, 2005 *C, I*, 2006 *Geo, CZR, Pt, Geo*, 2007 *It, S, NZ*, 2009 *Pt, Ur, F, ItA*, 2010 *Rus, Pt, Ukr, Tun, Ur, Ur*, 2012 *J, US*
**H Manu** 1919 *US Army, F Army*, 1927 *F, Ger*
**N Marascu** 1919 *US Army, F Army*, 1924 *F, US*, 1927 *F, Cze*
**A Marasescu** 1927 *F, Ger*, 1936 *It, Ger*
**E Marculescu** 1936 *F, It, Ger*, 1937 *It*, 1939 *It*, 1940 *It*
**A Marghescu** 1980 *Pol*, 1981 *It*, 1983 *W, USS, F*, 1984 *S, F, Sp*, 1985 *E*
**I Marica** 1972 *WGe, F*, 1973 *Sp, Mor, WGe, F*, 1974 *Mor, Sp, Cze, EGe, F, Cze*, 1975 *It, Sp*
**A Marin** 1978 *Cze, Sp, Pol*, 1979 *F*, 1980 *Pol*, 1982 *USS*, 1983 *Pol*, 1984 *Sp*, 1985 *USS, It*, 1986 *Pt*, 1987 *USS, Z*
**A Marin** 2008 *CZR*
**N Marin** 1991 *Fj*, 1992 *Sp, It*, 1993 *F, I*, 1995 *Ar, F, It*
**A Marinache** 1949 *Cze*, 1951 *EGe*, 1952 *EGe, EGe*, 1955 *Cze*, 1957 *F, Bel, F*, 1960 *F*, 1961 *Pol, EGe, Cze, EGe, F*, 1962 *Cze, Pol*
**V Marinescu** 1967 *Pt, WGe*, 1968 *Cze*, 1969 *Cze, F*
**F Marioara** 1994 *E*, 1996 *Pol*, 1998 *Geo, I*
**S Maris** 2010 *Ukr, Ukr, Nm, ArJ, ItA, Tun*
**V Mariscaru** 2011 *Rus, Geo*
**A Mateescu** 1959 *EGe, Pol, Cze, EGe*, 1960 *Pol, EGe, Cze*, 1962 *EGe, Pol*, 1963 *Bul, EGe, Cze*, 1964 *Cze, EGe*, 1965 *WGe, F*, 1966 *F*, 1970 *It, F*, 1973 *Sp, WGe, F*, 1974 *Mor, Pol, Sp*
**AT Matei** 2013 *Geo, Rus*
**A Mateiescu** 1934 *It*, 1936 *F, Ger*
**R Mavrodin** 1998 *Geo, I*, 1999 *F, A, US, I*, 2000 *H, Pt, Sp, Geo, F, It*, 2002 *Pt, Sp, H, I, It, Sp, W*, 2003 *I, A, Ar, Nm*, 2004 *Pt, Sp, Rus, Geo, W, J, CZR*, 2005 *Rus, J, US, S, Pt*, 2006 *Ukr, Rus, F, Geo, Sp, S*, 2007 *Geo, ESp, ItA, Nm, It, S, Pt, NZ*, 2009 *Ur*
**F Maxim** 2007 *Rus*
**G Mazilu** 1958 *Sp, WGe*, 1959 *EGe, Pol, Cze*
**S Mehedinti** 1951 *EGe*, 1953 *It*
**G Melinte** 1958 *EGe, It*
**P Mergisescu** 1960 *Pol, EGe, Cze*
**C Mersoiu** 2000 *Mor, Pt*, 2001 *I*, 2002 *S, S*, 2003 *Pt, Sp, Geo, CZR, F, W*, 2004 *CZR, Pt, Sp, Rus, It, W, J, CZR*, 2005 *Rus, Geo, Ukr, I*, 2006 *CZR, Pt, Geo*, 2007 *Geo, Sp, CZR, Rus, Pt*, 2008 *Geo, Sp, Pt, Rus, CZR, Ur, Rus, ESp*, 2009 *Geo*
**A Miclescu** 1971 *Mor*
**S Mihailescu** 1919 *F Army*, 1924 *F, US*, 1927 *F*
**D Mihalache** 1973 *Mor*
**M Mihalache** 2007 *Pt*, 2008 *Geo, Sp, Rus*
**V Mihalascu** 1967 *Pol, WGe*
**A Mitocaru** 1992 *Ar*, 1993 *Pt, Sp, F*
**A Mitu** 2013 *Sp, Bel, Geo, ArJ, Elt, Fj*, 2014 *Pt, Bel*
**P Mitu** 1996 *Bel, Pol*, 1997 *W, Bel, Ar, It*, 1998 *H, Pol, Ukr, Ar, Geo, I*, 1999 *F, S, A, US, I*, 2000 *H, Pt, Sp, Geo, It*, 2001 *Pt, Sp, H, Rus*, 2002 *Pt, Sp, H, Rus, Geo, Sp, W, S, S*, 2003 *Geo*, 2005 *I*, 2006 *Sp, Geo, Rus, Pt*
**M Miu** 2003 *Pt, Sp*
**V Mladin** 1955 *Cze*, 1957 *Bel, F*, 1958 *Sp, WGe, It*, 1959 *EGe*, 1960 *F*
**S Mocanu** 1996 *Bel*, 1998 *H, Pol, Ukr*, 2000 *Mor, Pt*
**T Moldoveanu** 1937 *F, Ger*, 1938 *F, Ger*, 1939 *It*, 1940 *It*
**O Morariu** 1984 *Sp*, 1985 *Tun*
**V Morariu** 1952 *EGe, EGe*, 1953 *It*, 1955 *Cze*, 1957 *F, Cze, Bel, F*, 1959 *EGe*, 1960 *F*, 1961 *Pol, Cze, EGe, F*, 1962 *Cze, EGe, Pol, It, F*, 1963 *F*, 1964 *WGe, F*
**C Moscu** 1934 *It*, 1937 *It*
**M Mot** 1980 *Mor*, 1982 *It, USS, Z*, 1985 *It, It*, 1986 *F, Tun*, 1988 *US, USS*
**M Motoc** 1988 *US*, 1989 *S*
**P Motrescu** 1973 *Mor, Ar, Ar*, 1974 *Mor, Pol, F*, 1975 *JAB, Pol, F*, 1976 *H, It, Sp, Bul, Pol, F, Mor*, 1977 *Sp,*

**437**

ROMANIA

ROMANIA

Samoa muscled their way past Italy in June, their first win in five matches.

AFP/Getty Images

# SAMOA

## SAMOA'S 2013–14 TEST RECORD

| OPPONENTS | DATE | VENUE | RESULT |
|---|---|---|---|
| Ireland | 9 Nov | A | Lost 40–9 |
| Georgia | 23 Nov | A | Lost 16–15 |
| Japan | 30 May | A | Lost 33–14 |
| Tonga | 7 Jun | H | Drew 18–18 |
| Italy | 14 Jun | H | Won 15–0 |
| Fiji | 21 Jun | A | Won 18–13 |

# SAMOA CONFIRM HISTORIC ALL BLACKS TEST

## By Iain Spragg

Samoa drew with Tonga in June but still topped their conference in the new-look IRB Pacific Nations Cup.

THE COUNTRIES

**Although it was** only as recently as 1993 that Samoa and New Zealand first crossed swords in a Test match, the two countries have enjoyed a far longer shared rugby heritage that has seen thousands of players travel in both directions over the South Pacific to ply their trade.

Since that first meeting in Auckland, the two sides have met five further times but conspicuous by its absence was a Test in Samoa. The Samoans had travelled to Napier, Auckland and New Plymouth to face the All Blacks but the New Zealanders had yet to commit to a 'return' fixture.

In 2015, however, that anomaly will be removed when the world champions head to Apia to play a ground-breaking Test which Samoan officials hope will underpin the significant strides made by their team in recent seasons.

"It will be an historic occasion to have the All Blacks play in Samoa in July 2015," admitted Samoa Rugby Union chairman Tuilaepa Sailele Malielegaoi. "The rugby supporters of both countries will savour a unique event in Apia as the Manu Samoa will face the number one team in the world at home. It is a match that will be watched by millions of viewers as we intend to broadcast it live to the rest of the world."

News of the high-profile fixture emerged after the conclusion of Samoa's Test season and it was a year in which Stephen Betham's side finished top of their IRB Pacific Nations Cup conference and also claimed a third tier one scalp in the space of 12 months after dispatching Italy in Apia, an uplifting end to a campaign that had begun slowly.

Betham took his squad to Europe in November just days after the premature death of the legendary Peter Fatialofa, the man who captained Manu Samoa to their famous win over Wales at Rugby World Cup 1991, at the age of 54. It was a sad backdrop to the tour opener against Ireland and there was to be no emotional victory in Dublin as the match finished in a heavy 40–9 defeat, Samoa's points coming from two Tusi Pisi penalties and a third from captain Kahn Fotuali'i.

Next up was a French Barbarians side featuring the likes of Sitiveni Sivivatu and Aurélien Rougerie, and Samoa left the Stade Marcel Michelin in Clermont empty-handed after a 20–19 defeat.

Samoa then moved on to Tbilisi to face Georgia. In their only previous meeting, at RWC 2003, Samoa had cruised to a 46–9 victory, but despite sitting nine places higher in the IRB World Rankings and outscoring their hosts by two tries to one at the Mikheil Meskhi Stadium, Betham's team were undone by a last-gasp penalty and the Test was lost 16–15.

Samoa returned to international action six months later when a side largely comprising players based at home travelled to Tokyo to face Japan. The Brave Blossoms, fresh from confirming their place in Samoa's pool at RWC 2015, proved too strong and ran out 33–14 winners with Fautua Otto and Brando Va'aulu scoring the visitors' tries.

There was little time to reflect on that defeat as Samoa went straight into the IRB Pacific Nations Cup, a competition they had won in 2010 and 2012 but which had been remodelled to comprise a Pacific Islands Conference of Samoa, Fiji and Tonga and a North American Conference featuring the USA, Canada and Japan.

The competition kicked off with Tonga's visit to Apia Park in early June and it was a pulsating encounter which saw Betham's team recover from conceding an early try to establish an 18–15 lead thanks to scores from winger Otto and captain David Lemi. The score remained like that until the dying minutes when Tonga salvaged a draw after Fangatapu Apikotoa kicked a long-range penalty to punish Samoa's infringement at the lineout.

Following what for them was a disappointing 18–18 draw, Samoa then welcomed Italy to Apia before concluding their PNC campaign against Fiji. The visit of the Azzurri proved perfect preparation as Tusi Pisi kicked five penalties to record a morale-boosting 15–0 win.

Samoa now needed to beat defending champions Fiji in Suva to secure top spot in their Pacific Nations Cup conference and what transpired was a nerve-jangling encounter that saw the result in doubt until the final whistle.

The visitors took an early lead with a Tusi Pisi penalty, but the Flying Fijians responded with a Nemani Nadolo try. Four more successful penalties from the boot of Pisi gave Samoa a 15–5 half-time lead but when Nadolo went over for his second try in the 42nd minute and then added a penalty three minutes later, the advantage was down to two points and the match hung in the balance. The next score would be pivotal and it went to Samoa through a sixth penalty with 16 minutes to go. Fiji couldn't find a way back so Samoa held out for an 18–13 triumph.

"I take my hat off to our players," said Lemi after victory at the ANZ Stadium. "We knew coming to Fiji was going to be very hard, especially in front of their crowd, but the boys got stuck in there today. They gave it their all and we came away with the result we wanted."

The fortunes of Samoan teams below Test level were also mixed as the A team registered one win – a 27–18 victory over Tonga A in Sydney – in their four fixtures in the IRB Pacific Rugby Cup in March, while the Under 20s returned home from the IRB Junior World Championship in New Zealand in June with an eighth-place finish. They had, though, received plaudits for some of their displays, particularly the tough rides they gave eventual runners-up South Africa and hosts New Zealand in the pool stages.

With a new coach at the helm following the passing of Fatialofa, Samoa's women warmed up for Women's Rugby World Cup 2014 in France by facing New Zealand at Eden Park as a curtain-raiser to the first Test between the All Blacks and England in June. The four-time world champions ran out comfortable 90–12 winners, although there had been positives on defence early on before fatigue set in against a Black Ferns side running the ball from everywhere. Two months later Manusina found life difficult at the World Cup and had to wait until the final day before tasting victory, beating Kazakhstan 31–0 in the 11th place play-off courtesy of two tries by wing Taliilagi Mefi.

It was also a difficult year for Samoa on the HSBC Sevens World Series with their best result a third place finish in South Africa in December. The eighth-place finish overall was Samoa's worst since the Series began in 1999. There was better news from the Commonwealth Games in late July as Samoa reached the semi-finals in Glasgow. They missed out on bronze, though, after losing 24–0 to Australia, the fourth place matching the achievements of their predecessors at the 1998 and 2002 Games.

On the domestic front, the SRU's junior participation strategy, the Fun Manu Programme, delivered as part of the Pacific in Union partnership between the IRB, Australian Rugby Union and the Australian

Government continued to grow. Some 13,991 students in 76 schools **445** and 14 communities in Samoa participated in 2013, with 392 teachers and 60 volunteers trained to deliver the curricula.

# SAMOA INTERNATIONAL STATISTICS

## MATCH RECORDS UP TO 13 OCTOBER 2014

### WINNING MARGIN

| Date | Opponent | Result | Winning Margin |
|------|----------|--------|----------------|
| 11/07/2009 | PNG | 115–7 | 108 |
| 08/04/1990 | Korea | 74–7 | 67 |
| 18/07/2009 | PNG | 73–12 | 61 |
| 10/06/2000 | Japan | 68–9 | 59 |
| 29/06/1997 | Tonga | 62–13 | 49 |

### MOST POINTS IN A MATCH
#### BY THE TEAM

| Date | Opponent | Result | Points |
|------|----------|--------|--------|
| 11/07/2009 | PNG | 115–7 | 115 |
| 08/04/1990 | Korea | 74–7 | 74 |
| 18/07/2009 | PNG | 73–12 | 73 |
| 10/06/2000 | Japan | 68–9 | 68 |
| 29/06/1997 | Tonga | 62–13 | 62 |

#### BY A PLAYER

| Date | Player | Opponent | Points |
|------|--------|----------|--------|
| 11/07/2009 | Gavin Williams | PNG | 30 |
| 29/05/2004 | Roger Warren | Tonga | 24 |
| 03/10/1999 | Silao Leaega | Japan | 23 |
| 08/04/1990 | Andy Aiolupo | Korea | 23 |
| 08/07/2000 | Toa Samania | Italy | 23 |

### MOST TRIES IN A MATCH
#### BY THE TEAM

| Date | Opponent | Result | Tries |
|------|----------|--------|-------|
| 11/07/2009 | PNG | 115–7 | 17 |
| 08/04/1990 | Korea | 74–7 | 13 |
| 18/07/2009 | PNG | 73–12 | 11 |
| 10 on 4 occasions | | | |

#### BY A PLAYER

| Date | Player | Opponent | Tries |
|------|--------|----------|-------|
| 28/05/1991 | Tupo Fa'amasino | Tonga | 4 |
| 10/06/2000 | Elvis Seveali'i | Japan | 4 |
| 02/07/2005 | Alesana Tuilagi | Tonga | 4 |
| 11/07/2009 | Esera Lauina | PNG | 4 |
| 09/11/2012 | Robert Lilomaiava | Canada | 4 |

### MOST CONVERSIONS IN A MATCH
#### BY THE TEAM

| Date | Opponent | Result | Cons |
|------|----------|--------|------|
| 11/07/2009 | PNG | 115–7 | 15 |
| 18/07/2009 | PNG | 73–12 | 9 |
| 08/04/1990 | Korea | 74–7 | 8 |
| 6 on 5 occasions | | | |

#### BY A PLAYER

| Date | Player | Opponent | Cons |
|------|--------|----------|------|
| 11/07/2009 | Gavin Williams | PNG | 10 |
| 18/07/2009 | Titi Jnr Esau | PNG | 9 |
| 08/04/1990 | Andy Aiolupo | Korea | 8 |
| 10/06/2000 | Tanner Vili | Japan | 6 |
| 04/07/2001 | Earl Va'a | Japan | 6 |

### MOST PENALTIES IN A MATCH
#### BY THE TEAM

| Date | Opponent | Result | Pens |
|------|----------|--------|------|
| 29/05/2004 | Tonga | 24–14 | 8 |
| 21/06/2014 | Fiji | 18–13 | 6 |
| 5 on 10 occasions | | | |

#### BY A PLAYER

| Date | Player | Opponent | Pens |
|------|--------|----------|------|
| 29/05/2004 | Roger Warren | Tonga | 8 |
| 21/06/2014 | Tusi Pisi | Tonga | 6 |

### MOST DROP GOALS IN A MATCH
#### BY THE TEAM

1 on 11 occasions

#### BY A PLAYER

1 on 11 occasions

| MOST CAPPED PLAYERS | |
|---|---|
| Name | Caps |
| Brian Lima | 65 |
| To'o Vaega | 60 |
| Semo Sititi | 59 |
| Census Johnston | 45 |
| Opeta Palepoi | 42 |

| LEADING PENALTY SCORERS | |
|---|---|
| Name | Pens |
| Darren Kellett | 35 |
| Earl Va'a | 31 |
| Silao Leaega | 31 |
| Roger Warren | 29 |
| Tusi Pisi | 29 |

| LEADING TRY SCORERS | |
|---|---|
| Name | Tries |
| Brian Lima | 31 |
| Semo Sititi | 17 |
| Alesana Tuilagi | 17 |
| Afato So'oialo | 15 |
| To'o Vaega | 15 |

| LEADING DROP GOAL SCORERS | |
|---|---|
| Name | DGs |
| Darren Kellet | 2 |
| Roger Warren | 2 |
| Steve Bachop | 2 |
| Tusi Pisi | 2 |

| LEADING CONVERSIONS SCORERS | |
|---|---|
| Name | Cons |
| Andy Aiolupo | 35 |
| Earl Va'a | 33 |
| Silao Leaega | 26 |
| Tanner Vili | 21 |
| Gavin Williams | 18 |

| LEADING POINTS SCORERS | |
|---|---|
| Name | Points |
| Earl Va'a | 184 |
| Andy Aiolupo | 172 |
| Silao Leaega | 160 |
| Darren Kellett | 155 |
| Brian Lima | 150 |

# SAMOA INTERNATIONAL PLAYERS
## UP TO 13 OCTOBER 2014

A'ati 1932 *Tg*
V Afatia 2012 *Tg, C,* 2013 *I*
V Afemai 2014 *J, It*
JT Afoa 2010 *Tg, J*
Agnew 1924 *Fj, Fj*
S Ah Fook 1947 *Tg*
F Ah Long 1955 *Fj*
Ah Mu 1932 *Tg*
T Aialupo 1986 *W*
F Aima'asu 1981 *Fj,* 1982 *Fj, Fj, Fj,* 1988 *Tg, Fj*
AA Aiolupo 1983 *Tg,* 1984 *Fj, Tg,* 1985 *Fj, Tg, Tg,* 1986 *Fj, Tg,*
 1987 *Fj, Tg,* 1988 *Tg, Fj, I, W,* 1989 *Fj, WGe, Bel, R,* 1990
 *Kor, Tg, J, Tg, Fj,* 1991 *W, A, Ar, S,* 1992 *Tg, Fj,* 1993 *Tg,*
 *Fj, NZ,* 1994 *Tg, W, A*
A Aiono 2009 *PNG,* 2010 *J, I, E, S,* 2011 *Tg,* 2012 *Tg, S*
P Alalatoa 1986 *W*
V Alalatoa 1988 *I, W,* 1989 *Fj,* 1991 *Tg, W, A, Ar, S,* 1992 *Tg, Fj*
P Alauni 2009 *PNG*
R Ale 1997 *Tg, Fj,* 1999 *J, Ar, W, S*
A Alelupo 1994 *Fj*
T Aleni 1982 *Tg,* 1983 *Tg,* 1985 *Tg,* 1986 *W, Fj, Tg,* 1987 *Fj*
S Alesana 1979 *Tg, Fj,* 1980 *Tg,* 1981 *Fj, Fj,* 1982 *Fj,* 1983
 *Tg, Fj, Tg,* 1984 *Fj, Tg,* 1985 *Fj, Tg*
T Allen 1924 *Fj, Fj*
K Anufe 2009 *Tg,* 2012 *Fj, J, F,* 2013 *It*
L Aoelua 2008 *NZ*

T Aoese 1981 *Fj, Fj,* 1982 *Fj, Fj, Fj, Tg,* 1983 *Tg*
J Apelu 1985 *Tg*
F Asi 1975 *Tg*
F Asi 1963 *Fj, Fj, Tg*
SP Asi 1999 *S,* 2000 *Fj, J, Tg, C, It, US, W, S,* 2001 *Tg, Fj, NZ,*
 *Fj, Tg, Fj*
L Asi 2010 *J*
Atiga 1924 *Fj*
S Ati'ifale 1979 *Tg,* 1980 *Tg,* 1981 *Fj, Fj*
J Atoa 1975 *Tg,* 1981 *Fj*
F Autagavaia 2012 *Tg, Fj, J, S, C, W,* 2013 *I, Geo,* 2014 *Tg, It,*
 *Fj*
WO Avei 2011 *J, Tg, SA,* 2012 *Tg, Fj, J, S, C, W, F,* 2013 *S, It,*
 *SA, I, Geo,* 2014 *Tg, It, Fj*

SJ Bachop 1991 *Tg, Fj, W, A, Ar, S,* 1998 *Tg, Fj,* 1999 *J, C, F,*
 *NZ, US, Fj, J, Ar, W, S*
C Betham 1955 *Fj*
ML Birtwistle 1991 *Fj, W, A, Ar, S,* 1993 *Fj, NZ,* 1994 *Tg, W, Fj,*
 *A,* 1996 *I*
W Brame 2009 *J, Fj*
FE Bunce 1991 *W, A, Ar, S*

CH Capper 1924 *Fj*
J Cavanagh 1955 *Fj, Fj, Fj*
J Clarke 1997 *Tg,* 1998 *A,* 1999 *US, Fj, J*
A Collins 2005 *S, Ar*

A Cortz 2007 *Fj*
G Cowley 2005 *S, Ar*, 2006 *J, Tg*
T Cowley 2000 *J, C, It*
O Crichton 1955 *Fj, Fj, Fj*, 1957 *Tg, Tg*
D Crichton 2012 *Tg, Fj, J, S*
L Crichton 2006 *Fj, Tg*, 2007 *Fj, SA, J, Tg, SA, Tg, E, US*
O Crichton 1988 *Tg*
T Curtis 2000 *Fj, J, Tg, C, It, US*

H Ekeroma 1972 *Tg, Tg*
S Aiono 2014 *J*
G Elisara 2003 *I, Nm*
S Enari 1975 *Tg*
S Epati 1972 *Tg*
T Esau 2009 *PNG, PNG, F, It*
K Ese 1947 *Tg*
S Esera 1981 *Fj*
L Eves 1957 *Tg, Tg*

H Fa'afili 2008 *Fj, Tg, J*, 2009 *J, Tg, Fj, PNG, W, F, It*
T Fa'afou 2007 *Fj*
O Faafou 2014 *J*
P Fa'alogo 1963 *Fj*
Fa'amaile 1947 *Tg*
T Fa'amasino 1988 *W*, 1989 *Bel, R*, 1990 *Kor, Tg, J, Tg, Fj*, 1991 *Tg, Fj, A*, 1995 *It, Ar, E, SA, Fj, Tg*, 1996 *NZ, Tg, Fj*
JS Fa'amatuainu 2005 *S, Ar*, 2008 *Fj, J*, 2009 *J, Tg, Fj, PNG, W, F, It*, 2011 *Tg*
S Fa'aofo 1990 *Tg*
PF Fa'apale 2014 *J, It*
P Faasalele 2013 *It, Geo*, 2014 *It, Fj*
Fa'asalele 1957 *Tg, Tg*
F Fa'asau 1963 *Tg, Tg*
M Faasavalu 2002 *SA*, 2003 *I, Nm, Ur, Geo, E, SA*, 2011 *J, Fj, A, Nm, W, Fj, SA*, 2012 *J, S, W, F*, 2014 *It, Fj*
V Faasua 1987 *Fj*, 1988 *Tg, Fj, W*
S Fa'asua 2000 *W*
F Fa'asuaga 1947 *Tg*
L Fa'atau 2000 *Fj, Tg, C, US*, 2001 *I, It*, 2002 *Fj, Tg, Fj, Tg, SA*, 2003 *I, Ur, E, SA*, 2004 *Tg, S, Fj*, 2005 *A, Tg, Tg, Fj, S, E, Ar*, 2006 *J, Fj, Tg*, 2007 *Fj, SA, J, Tg, SA, US*
F Fagasoaia 2010 *J*
K Faiva'ai 1998 *Tg, Fj, A*, 1999 *J, C, Tg, NZ, US, Fj*
G Tuigamala 2012 *Tg, Fj*
L Falaniko 1990 *Tg, Fj*, 1991 *Tg*, 1993 *Tg, Fj, NZ*, 1995 *SA, It, Ar, E, SA, Fj, Tg, S, E*, 1996 *NZ*, 1999 *US, Fj, W, S*
E Fale 2008 *Tg*
S Fale 1955 *Fj*
S Fanolua 1990 *Tg, Fj*, 1991 *Tg, Fj*
TL Fanolua 1996 *NZ, Fj*, 1997 *Tg*, 1998 *Tg, Fj, A*, 1999 *W, S*, 2000 *J, Tg, C, It, US*, 2001 *Tg, Fj, NZ, Fj, Tg, J, Fj*, 2002 *Fj*, 2003 *Nm, Ur, Geo, E*, 2005 *A, Tg, Fj, Fj*
R Fanuatanu 2003 *I, Geo*
M Faoagali 1999 *J, C*
A Faosiliva 2006 *J, Tg*, 2008 *Tg, NZ*, 2010 *Tg, J, Fj*, 2012 *Tg, Fj, J, C*, 2013 *SA*
DS Farani 2005 *Tg, Fj, S, E, Ar*, 2006 *J, Fj, Tg*
J Fatialofa 2009 *F*
M Fatialofa 1996 *Tg*
PM Fatialofa 1988 *I, W*, 1989 *Bel, R*, 1990 *Kor, J*, 1991 *Tg, Fj, W, A, Ar, S*, 1992 *Tg, Fj*, 1993 *Tg, Fj, NZ*, 1994 *Tg, W, Fj, A*, 1995 *SA, It, Ar, E, SA, Fj, Tg, S, E*, 1996 *NZ, Fj*
Fatu 1947 *Tg*
E Feagai 1963 *Fj, Tg*
S Feagai 1963 *Fj, Fj*
D Feaunati 2003 *Nm, Ur, Geo, E, SA*
I Fea'unati 1996 *I*, 1997 *Tg*, 1999 *Tg, NZ, Fj, Ar*, 2000 *Fj, J, Tg, C, It, US*, 2006 *Fj, Tg*
M Fepuleai 1957 *Tg*
V Fepuleai 1988 *W*, 1989 *Fj, WGe, R*
I Fesuiai'i 1985 *Fj, Tg*
JA Filemu 1995 *S, E*, 1996 *NZ, Tg, Fj, I*, 1997 *Fj*, 1999 *J, C, Tg, F, NZ*, 2000 *Fj, J, Tg, C, It, US*, 2001 *Tg, Fj, Tg, J*
F Fili 2003 *I, Nm*, 2009 *W, F*, 2011 *Tg*
F Filisoa 2005 *Tg*
T Fomai 2012 *C, W, F*
T Fong 1983 *Tg, Fj*, 1984 *Fj, Tg*, 1986 *W, Fj, Tg*, 1987 *Fj, Tg*
K Fotuali'i 2010 *J, I, E, S*, 2011 *A, Nm, W, Fj, SA*, 2012 *J, S, C, W, F*, 2013 *I, Geo*, 2014 *Tg, It, Fj*
S Fretton 1947 *Tg*

J Fruean 1972 *Tg*, 1975 *Tg*
Fruean 1932 *Tg*
S Fruean 1955 *Fj, Fj*
P Fualau 2012 *Tg, Fj*
S Fuatai 1972 *Tg*
P Fuatai 1988 *Tg, Fj*, 1989 *Fj, WGe, R*
T Fuga 1999 *F, NZ, US*, 2000 *Fj, J, Tg, C, It, US*, 2007 *SA, Tg*
ES Fuimaono Sapolu 2005 *S, E, Ar*, 2006 *Fj, Tg*, 2007 *SA, E, US*, 2008 *Fj, Tg, J*, 2009 *J, Fj, PNG, PNG, F, It*, 2011 *Fj, A, Nm, W, Fj, SA*

T Galuvao 1972 *Tg*
N George 2004 *Tg, Fj*
C Glendinning 1999 *J, C, Tg, F, NZ, US, Fj, J, W, S*, 2000 *Fj, J, Tg, C, It, US*, 2001 *Tg, Fj, NZ, Fj, Tg, Fj*
P Grey 1975 *Tg*, 1979 *Tg, Fj*, 1980 *Tg*
I Grey 1985 *Fj, Tg*
J Grey 2014 *J*
A Tavana 2012 *Tg*

G Harder 1995 *SA, It, Ar, SA*
Hellesoe 1932 *Tg*
B Helleur 2011 *Tg, A*
J Helleur 2010 *Tg, J, Fj, J*
M Hewitt 1955 *Fj, Fj*
J Huch 1982 *Fj, Fj*, 1986 *Fj, Tg*
J Hunt 1957 *Tg, Tg*

A Ieremia 1992 *Tg, Fj*, 1993 *Tg, Fj, NZ*
I Imo 1924 *Fj*
T Imo 1955 *Fj, Fj, Fj*, 1957 *Tg, Tg*
A Ioane 1957 *Tg, Tg, Tg*
E Ioane 1990 *Tg, Fj*, 1991 *Tg, Fj, S*
T Iona 1975 *Tg*
T Iosua 2006 *J*, 2011 *J, Fj, Tg*
Iupati 1924 *Fj*
M Iupeli 1988 *Tg, Fj, I, W*, 1989 *Fj, WGe, R*, 1993 *Tg, NZ*, 1994 *Tg, W, Fj, A*, 1995 *SA, E*
S Iuta 1947 *Tg*

T Jensen 1987 *Tg*, 1989 *Bel*
CAI Johnston 2005 *A, Tg, Fj, S, E, Ar*, 2006 *Fj, Tg*, 2007 *SA, J, Tg, SA, Tg, E, US*, 2008 *Fj, J*, 2009 *J, Tg, Fj, PNG, W, F, It*, 2010 *J, Fj, E, S*, 2011 *Tg, A, Nm, W, Fj, SA*, 2012 *J, S, C, W, F*, 2013 *S, It, SA*, 2014 *Tg, It, Fj*
JVI Johnston 2008 *Tg, J*, 2011 *Tg*, 2012 *Fj, C, W, F*, 2013 *S, It, SA, I, Geo*, 2014 *It, Fj*
MN Jones 1986 *W*

S Kalapu 1957 *Tg*
D Kaleopa 1990 *Kor, Tg, J*, 1991 *A*, 1992 *Fj*, 1993 *Tg, Fj*
S Kaleta 1994 *Tg, W*, 1995 *S, E*, 1996 *NZ*, 1997 *Tg, Fj*
T Kali 1975 *Tg*
L Kamu 1955 *Fj, Fj, Fj*
MG Keenan 1991 *W, A, Ar*, 1992 *Tg, Fj*, 1993 *NZ*, 1994 *Tg, W, Fj, A*
JR Keil 2010 *J, J*
F Kelemete 1984 *Fj, Tg*, 1985 *Tg*, 1986 *W*
DK Kellet 1993 *Tg, Fj, NZ*, 1994 *Tg, W, Fj, A*, 1995 *It, Ar, Fj, Tg, S, E*
DA Kerslake 2005 *Tg, Fj, Tg, Fj*, 2006 *J, Tg*, 2007 *Fj, SA, J, Tg*
A Koko 1999 *J*
R Koko 1983 *Tg, Fj, Fj*, 1984 *Fj, Tg*, 1985 *Fj, Tg, Tg*, 1986 *W, Fj, Tg*, 1987 *Fj, Tg*, 1988 *Fj, I, W*, 1989 *WGe, R*, 1993 *Tg, NZ*, 1994 *Tg*
M Krause 1984 *Tg*, 1986 *W*
H Kruse 1963 *Fj, Fj*
JA Kuoi 1987 *Fj, Tg*, 1988 *I, W*, 1990 *Kor, Tg*

B Laban 1955 *Fj*, 1957 *Tg, Tg*
SL Lafaiali'I 2001 *Tg, Fj, NZ, Tg*, 2002 *Fj, Tg, Fj, Tg, SA*, 2003 *I, Nm, Ur, Geo, E, SA*, 2004 *Tg, S, Fj*, 2005 *A, S, E*, 2007 *Fj, J, Tg, Tg, US*
IR Lafo 2012 *C*, 2014 *J*
I Laga'aia 1975 *Tg*, 1979 *Tg, Fj*
F Lalomilo 2001 *I, It*
J Lam 2013 *S, It, SA, I, Geo*, 2014 *Tg, It, Fj*
PR Lam 1991 *W, Ar, S*, 1994 *W, Fj, A*, 1995 *SA, Ar, E, SA, Fj,*

Tg, S, E, 1996 NZ, Tg, Fj, I, 1997 Tg, Fj, 1998 Tg, Fj, A, 1999 J, C, Tg, F, NZ, US, Fj, J, Ar, W, S
**S Lameta** 1982 Fj
**F Lameta** 1990 Tg, Fj
**G Latu** 1994 Tg, W, Fj, A, 1995 SA, Ar, E, SA, Fj, Tg
**E Lauina** 2008 Fj, Tg, J, NZ, 2009 J, Tg, Fj, PNG, PNG
**M Lautau** 1985 Fj
**T Lavea** 2010 I, E, S, 2011 J, Fj, Nm, W
**FH Lavea Levi** 2007 Fj, SA, J, Tg, 2008 Fj, J, NZ, 2009 J, Tg, Fj, PNG, W, F, It, 2010 Tg, J, Fj, I, E, S, 2011 J, Fj, Tg, A, Fj
**S Leaega** 1997 Tg, Fj, 1999 J, J, Ar, W, S, 2001 Tg, Fj, NZ, Fj, Tg, Fj, I, It, 2002 Fj, Tg, SA
**K Lealamanua** 2000 Fj, J, Tg, C, It, 2001 NZ, Fj, Tg, J, Fj, 2002 Fj, Tg, Fj, Tg, SA, 2003 I, Nm, Ur, Geo, E, SA, 2004 Tg, S, Fj, 2005 S, E, 2007 SA, Tg, E, US
**S Leaupepe** 1979 Tg, Fj, 1980 Tg
**GE Leaupepe** 1995 SA, Ar, E, Fj, Tg, S, E, 1996 NZ, Tg, Fj, I, 1997 Tg, Fj, 1998 Tg, A, 1999 J, C, Tg, F, NZ, US, Fj, J, Ar, W, 2005 A
**P Leavai** 1990 J
**A Leavasa** 1979 Tg, Fj, 1980 Tg
**MP Leavasa** 1993 Tg, Fj, 1995 It, Ar, E, S, E, 1996 NZ, Tg, Fj, I, 1997 Tg, Fj, 2002 Tg, Fj, Tg, SA
**P Leavasa** 1955 Fj, Fj, Fj, 1957 Tg, Tg, Tg
**S Leavasa** 1955 Fj, Fj, Fj, 1957 Tg
**T Leiasamaivao** 1993 Tg, NZ, 1994 Tg, W, Fj, 1995 SA, It, Ar, E, SA, S, E, 1996 NZ, Tg, Fj, I, 1997 Tg, Fj
**M Leiataua** 2013 S, 2014 J
**A Leiua** 2013 S, It, SA, I, Geo, 2014 Tg, It
**N Leleimalefaga** 2007 Fj, US
**F Lemalu** 2012 Tg, Fj, J, S, C, F, 2013 S, I, 2014 J, It
**S Lemalu** 2003 Ur, Geo, E, 2004 Tg, S, Fj, 2008 Tg, J, NZ, 2010 J, I, 2011 Fj, Tg
**S Lemamea** 1988 I, W, 1989 Fj, WGe, Bel, R, 1990 J, 1992 Tg, Fj, 1995 E, SA, Fj, Tg
**D Lemi** 2004 Tg, S, Fj, 2005 Tg, Fj, Tg, Fj, 2007 Fj, SA, J, Tg, SA, Tg, E, US, 2008 Fj, Tg, J, 2009 W, F, It, 2010 Tg, J, Fj, I, E, S, 2011 Fj, Tg, SA, 2012 Tg, J, S, W, F, 2014 Tg, It, Fj
**DA Leo** 2005 A, Tg, Fj, Tg, Fj, S, E, Ar, 2006 J, Fj, Tg, 2007 SA, J, Tg, SA, Tg, E, 2008 Tg, J, 2009 J, Fj, PNG, 2010 S, 2011 Fj, A, Nm, W, Fj, SA, 2012 W, 2013 S, It, SA, 2014 Tg, It, Fj
**J Leota** 2011 Fj, Tg, 2012 C, W, F, 2013 S, It, SA, I, Geo, 2014 Tg, It, Fj
**M Leota** 2000 Fj, Tg, C
**P Leota** 1990 Kor, Tg, J
**T Leota** 1997 Tg, Fj, 1998 Tg, Fj, A, 1999 J, C, Tg, F, Fj, J, Ar, W, S, 2000 Fj, J, 2001 Tg, Fj, NZ, Fj, J, Fj, 2002 Fj, Tg, Fj, Tg, SA, 2003 I, 2005 A
**A Le'u** 1987 Fj, Tg, 1989 WGe, R, 1990 Kor, J, Tg, Fj, 1993 Tg, Fj, NZ, 1996 I
**T Leupolu** 2001 I, It, 2002 Fj, Tg, Fj, Tg, SA, 2003 I, Nm, SA, 2004 Tg, S, Fj, 2005 Ar
**R Levasa** 2008 NZ, 2009 J, PNG, 2010 J, Fj, 2014 J
**F Levave** 2013 I, Geo, 2014 Tg
**A Liaina** 1963 Fj, Fj, Tg
**S Liaina** 1963 Fj, Fj, Tg
**P Lilomaiava** 1993 NZ
**M Lima** 1982 Fj, Fj
**MBP Lima** 1991 Tg, Fj, W, A, Ar, S, 1992 Tg, Fj, 1993 Fj, NZ, 1994 Tg, W, Fj, A, 1995 SA, It, Ar, E, SA, Fj, Tg, S, E, 1996 NZ, Fj, 1997 Fj, 1998 Tg, Fj, A, 1999 Tg, F, NZ, US, J, Ar, W, S, 2000 C, It, US, 2001 Fj, Tg, Fj, I, It, 2002 Fj, Tg, 2003 I, Nm, Ur, Geo, E, SA, 2004 Tg, S, Fj, 2005 A, 2006 J, Fj, 2007 Fj, Tg, SA, E
**F Lima** 1981 Fj
**L Lolo** 2014 J
**M Lome** 1957 Tg, Tg, Tg, 1963 Fj
**M Luafalealo** 1999 J, 2000 It, US, 2001 Tg, Fj, NZ, Fj, J, Fj
**E Lua'iufi** 1987 Fj, Tg, 1988 Tg, Fj
**Lui** 1932 Tg
**LS Lui** 2004 Fj, 2005 Tg, Fj, Ar, 2006 J, Tg, 2007 Tg, Tg, E, US, 2009 J, Tg, Fj, PNG, PNG, W, F, 2010 Tg, J, Fj, J, 2012 Tg, Fj, J, S
**M Lupeli** 1993 Fj

**A Macdonald** 1924 Fj, Fj, 1932 Tg
**T Magele** 1988 Tg
**M Magele** 2009 PNG, 2014 J

**U Mai** 2008 Tg, J, NZ, 2009 J, Fj, PNG, PNG, W, F, It, 2010 Tg, J, Fj, 2011 J, Fj, Tg
**F Mailei** 1963 Fj, Tg
**F Malele** 1979 Tg, Fj, 1980 Tg
**J Maligi** 2000 W, S
**P Maligi** 1982 Fj, Tg, 1983 Tg, Fj, 1984 Fj, Tg, 1985 Fj, Tg, Tg, 1986 Fj, Tg
**L Malo** 1979 Fj
**J Mamea** 2000 W, S
**L Mano** 1988 Fj, I, W
**C Manu** 2002 Fj, Tg, Tg, SA
**S Mapusua** 2006 J, Fj, Tg, 2007 SA, J, Tg, Tg, E, US, 2009 Tg, Fj, W, F, It, 2010 I, E, S, 2011 J, A, Nm, W, Fj, SA, 2013 S, It, SA
**P Mareko** 1979 Fj
**K Mariner** 2005 Ar
**BF Masoe** 2012 Tg, Fj, J, S
**M Mata'afa** 1947 Tg
**P Matailina** 1957 Tg, Tg, Tg
**O Matauiau** 1996 Tg, Fj, 1999 Ar, W, S, 2000 It, W, S
**K Mavaega** 1985 Tg
**M McFadyen** 1957 Tg
**K McFall** 1983 Fj
**J Meafou** 2007 Tg, SA, E, 2008 NZ
**L Mealamu** 2000 W, S
**I Melei** 1972 Tg
**O Meredith** 1947 Tg
**C Meredith** 1932 Tg
**J Meredith** 1963 Fj, Fj, Tg
**J Meredith** 2001 I, It, 2002 Fj, Tg, Fj, Tg, SA, 2003 I, Nm, Ur, Geo, E, SA, 2004 Tg, S, Fj, 2005 A, Tg, Fj, Fj
**A Mika** 2000 S
**D Mika** 1994 W, A
**MAN Mika** 1995 SA, It, Ar, E, SA, S, E, 1997 Tg, Fj, 1999 Tg, F, NZ, J, Ar, W
**S Mika** 2004 Fj, 2005 A, Tg, Fj, Tg, Fj
**S Mikaele** 2008 NZ, 2009 PNG, PNG, 2010 J
**P Misa** 2000 W, S
**S Moala** 2008 Fj
**F Moamanu** 1989 WGe
**S Moamanu** 1985 Fj, 1986 Fj, Tg
**M Moke** 1990 Kor, Tg, J, Tg, Fj
**P Momoisea** 1972 Tg, Tg
**H Moors** 1924 Fj, Fj
**R Moors** 1994 Tg
**Mose** 1932 Tg
**S Motoi** 1984 Tg
**F Motusagu** 2000 Tg, It, 2005 A
**RR Muagututia** 2010 J
**L Mulipola** 2009 PNG, 2010 J, 2011 J, Fj, Tg, SA, 2012 Tg, Fj, J, S, 2013 S, It, SA, I, 2014 Tg, It, Fj
**L Mulipola** 2009 F, It

**P Neenee** 1987 Tg, 1991 Tg, Fj
**O Nelson** 1955 Fj, Fj, Fj, 1957 Tg, Tg
**N Ngapaku** 2000 J, C, US
**F Nickel** 1957 Tg
**N Nifo** 2009 PNG
**Nimmo** 1957 Tg
**T Nu'uali'itia** 1994 Tg, A, 1995 SA, It, Ar, E, SA, 1996 NZ

**A Olive** 2008 Tg
**F Otto** 2010 Tg, Fj, E, S, 2011 Tg, 2012 Fj, S, 2013 I, 2014 J, Tg, It, Fj

**FJP Palaamo** 1998 Tg, Fj, A, 1999 J, C, F, NZ, US, Fj, 2007 Fj, E, 2009 Fj, PNG, PNG
**S Pala'amo** 1955 Fj, Fj, Fj, 1957 Tg
**T Palamo** 1972 Tg
**A Palamo** 1979 Tg, Fj, 1980 Tg, 1981 Fj, Fj, 1982 Fj, Fj, Tg
**LN Palamo** 1979 Tg, Fj, 1981 Fj, Fj, 1982 Fj, Fj, Fj, Tg, 1984 Fj, Tg, 1985 Tg, 1986 W, Fj, Tg
**O Palepoi** 1998 Tg, Fj, A, 1999 J, F, NZ, US, Fj, J, Ar, 2000 J, C, It, US, W, 2001 Tg, Fj, NZ, Fj, Tg, J, Fj, I, It, 2002 Fj, Tg, Fj, Tg, SA, 2003 I, Nm, Ur, Geo, E, SA, 2004 Tg, S, 2005 A, Tg, Fj, Tg, Fj
**Panapa** 1932 Tg
**P Papali'I** 1924 Fj, Fj
**M Papali'I** 1955 Fj, Fj
**PJ Paramore** 1991 Tg, Fj, A, 1992 Fj, 1994 Tg, 1995 SA, It, Ar,

SA, Fj, Tg, 1996 I, 1997 Tg, Fj, 1998 Tg, Fj, A, 1999 J, Ar, W, 2001 Tg, Fj, NZ, Fj, Tg, J, Fj
**J Parkinson** 2005 A, Tg
**T Pati** 1997 Tg
**M Patolo** 1986 W, Fj, Tg
**T Patu** 1979 Tg, Fj, 1980 Tg, 1981 Fj, Fj
**O Patu** 1980 Tg
**HV Patu** 1995 S, E, 1996 I, 2000 W, S
**P Paul** 1955 Fj, Fj, Fj
**M Paulino** 2008 NZ, 2010 J, 2012 Tg, Fj, 2014 J
**P Paulo** 1989 Bel, 1990 Tg, Fj
**T Paulo** 2012 C, W, F, 2013 S, It, SA, I, Geo, 2014 Tg, Fj
**T Paulo** 2010 E, S, 2011 J, Fj, Tg, A, Nm, W, Fj, 2012 J, S, W, F, 2013 It, SA, I, Geo, 2014 Tg, It, Fj
**A Perelini** 1991 Tg, Fj, W, A, Ar, S, 1992 Tg, Fj, 1993 NZ
**Al Perenise** 2010 Tg, J, Fj, J, I, E, S, 2011 J, Fj, A, Nm, W, Fj, SA, 2013 Geo, 2014 Tg
**PL Perez** 2012 Tg, Fj, J, S, C, W, F
**S Perez** 1963 Fj, Fj, Tg
**MS Pesamino** 2009 PNG, PNG, 2010 Tg, J, Fj, J
**N Petaia** 1963 Fj
**Petelo** 1932 Tg
**T Petelo** 1985 Fj
**P Petia** 2003 Nm
**O Pifeleti** 1987 Fj
**TG Pisi** 2010 Tg, Fj, I, E, S, 2011 J, A, Nm, W, Fj, 2012 C, W, F, 2013 I, 2014 Tg, It, Fj
**T Pisi** 2011 J, Fj, A, Nm, Fj, SA, 2012 S, C, W, F, 2013 S, It, SA, I, Geo, 2014 Tg, It, Fj
**S Po Ching** 1990 Kor, Tg, 1991 Tg
**S Poching** 2000 W, S, 2001 Tg
**AJ Poluleuligaga** 2007 SA, J, Tg, SA, Tg, E, US, 2008 NZ, 2009 J, Tg, Fj, W, F, It, 2010 Tg, J, I, E, 2011 Nm, 2013 It, SA
**HA Porter** 2011 Tg
**P Poulos** 2003 Ur, Geo, E, SA
**E Puleitu** 1995 SA, E
**S Punivalu** 1981 Fj, Fj, 1982 Fj, Fj, Fj, 1983 Tg, Fj
**JEP Purdie** 2007 Fj, SA, J, Tg, SA, Tg, E, US

**I Railey** 1924 Fj, Fj
**D Rasmussen** 2003 I, Ur, Geo, E, SA, 2004 Tg, S, Fj
**R Rasmussen** 1997 Tg
**B Reidy** 1995 SA, Fj, Tg, 1996 NZ, Tg, Fj, I, 1998 Fj, A, 1999 Tg, F, NZ, US, Fj, J, Ar, W, S
**K Roberts** 1972 Tg
**F Ropati** 1982 Fj, Fj, Fj, 1984 Fj, Tg
**R Ropati** 2003 SA, 2008 NZ
**W Ryan** 1983 Fj, 1985 Tg

**S Sa** 2012 C
**E Sa'aga** 1924 Fj, Fj, 1932 Tg
**PD Saena** 1988 Tg, Fj, I, 1989 Fj, Bel, 1990 Kor, Tg, J, Tg, Fj, 1991 Tg, Fj, 1992 Tg, Fj, 1993 Tg, Fj
**L Sagaga** 1963 Fj, Tg
**K Saifoloi** 1979 Tg, Fj, 1980 Tg, 1982 Fj, Fj, 1984 Fj, Tg
**P Saili** 1957 Tg, Tg, Tg
**M Salanoa** 2005 Tg, Fj, 2006 J, Fj, Tg, 2007 Fj, SA, J, Tg, Tg
**M Salavea** 2010 Tg, Fj, I, E, S, 2011 J, Tg, A, W, Fj
**T Salesa** 1979 Tg, Fj, 1980 Tg, 1981 Fj, Fj, 1982 Fj, Fj, Tg, 1983 Tg, Fj, 1984 Fj, Tg, 1985 Fj, Tg, Tg, 1986 Fj, Tg, 1987 Fj, Tg, 1988 Tg, Fj, I, 1989 Fj, WGe, R
**G Salima** 2008 Fj
**T Samania** 1994 W, Fj, A, 1996 NZ, 2000 Fj, J, C, It, 2001 Tg
**D Sanft** 2006 J
**Q Sanft** 2000 W, S
**L Sasi** 1982 Fj, Tg, 1983 Tg, Fj, 1984 Fj, Tg, 1985 Tg, 1986 W, Fj, Tg, 1987 Fj, Tg, 1988 Tg, Fj
**B Sasulu** 2008 Fj
**S Sauila** 1989 Bel
**L Savai'inaea** 1957 Tg, Tg
**J Schaafhausen** 1947 Tg
**W Schaafhausen** 1947 Tg
**P Schmidt** 1980 Tg, 1985 Tg
**P Schmidt** 1989 Fj, WGe
**R Schmidt** 1979 Tg, 1980 Tg
**D Schuster** 1982 Tg, 1983 Tg, Fj, Fj
**H Schuster** 1989 Fj, 1990 Kor, Tg, J
**J Schuster** 1985 Fj, Tg, Tg
**NSJ Schuster** 1999 Tg, F, US
**M Schuster** 2000 S, 2004 Tg, S, Fj

**P Schuster** 1975 Tg
**M Schwalger** 2000 W, S, 2001 It, 2003 Nm, Ur, Geo, E, 2005 S, E, Ar, 2006 J, Fj, Tg, 2007 Fj, SA, Tg, SA, Tg, E, US, 2008 Fj, 2009 J, Tg, Fj, PNG, W, F, It, 2010 Tg, J, Fj, I, E, S, 2011 Fj, A, Nm, W, Fj, SA
**Sefo** 1932 Tg
**E Sefo** 1984 Fj
**T Sefo** 1987 Tg, 1988 I
**P Segi** 2001 Fj, NZ, Fj, Tg, J, I, It, 2002 Fj, Tg, Fj, Tg
**K Seinafo** 1992 Tg
**F Selesele** 2010 Tg, J, J, 2014 J
**S Semeane** 2009 It
**J Senio** 2004 Tg, S, Fj, 2005 Tg, Fj, Tg, Fj, 2006 J, Fj, Tg
**U Setu** 2010 Tg, J
**T Seumanutafa** 1981 Fj
**E Seveali'l** 2000 Fj, J, Tg, C, 2001 Tg, NZ, J, Fj, It, 2002 Fj, Tg, Fj, SA, 2005 E, 2007 SA, J, Tg, SA, Tg, US
**K Pisi** 2012 Tg, Fj, 2013 Geo
**F Sililoto** 1980 Tg, 1981 Fj, Fj, 1982 Fj, Fj, Fj
**Simanu** 1932 Tg
**A Simanu** 1975 Tg, 1981 Fj
**V Simanu** 2014 J
**Sinaumea** 1924 Tg
**F Sini** 1995 SA, Ar, E, SA
**S Sinoti** 2010 J, 2013 Geo
**A Sio** 2014 J
**T Sio** 1990 Tg, 1992 Fj
**K Sio** 1988 Tg, Fj, I, W, 1989 Fj, WGe, R, 1990 J, Tg, Fj, 1992 Tg, Fj, 1993 NZ, 1994 Tg
**P Sioa** 1981 Fj, Fj
**S Sititi** 1999 J, C, F, J, W, S, 2000 Fj, J, Tg, C, US, 2001 Tg, Fj, NZ, Fj, Tg, J, Fj, I, It, 2002 Fj, Tg, Fj, Tg, SA, 2003 I, Nm, Ur, Geo, E, SA, 2004 Tg, S, Fj, 2005 A, Fj, Tg, Fj, S, E, Ar, 2006 J, Fj, Tg, 2007 Fj, SA, J, Tg, SA, Tg, E, US, 2008 Fj, Tg, J, NZ, 2009 J, PNG, PNG
**F Siu** 1975 Tg
**P Siu** 1963 Fj, Fj, Tg
**S Skelton** 1982 Fj
**E Skelton** 2009 J, Tg, PNG, PNG
**R Slade** 1972 Tg
**C Slade** 2006 J, Fj, Tg, 2008 Fj, Tg, NZ
**S Smith** 1995 S, E, 1996 Tg, Fj, 1999 C, Tg, F, NZ
**P Solia** 1955 Fj, Fj
**I Solipo** 1981 Fj
**F Solomona** 1985 Tg
**JS Sooialo** 2011 J, Fj, Tg, W, 2012 C, 2013 S, SA
**A So'oialo** 1996 I, 1997 Tg, Fj, 1998 Tg, 1999 Tg, F, NZ, US, Fj, J, Ar, 2000 Tg, It, 2001 Tg, Fj, NZ, Fj, Tg, J, I
**S So'oialo** 1998 Tg, Fj, 1999 NZ, US, Fj, J, Ar, W, S, 2000 W, S, 2001 Tg, Fj, NZ, Fj, J, Fj, I, 2002 Tg, Fj, Tg, SA, 2003 I, Nm, Ur, Geo, E, SA, 2004 Tg, S, Fj, 2005 E, 2007 Fj, SA, J, Tg, E, US
**F So'olefai** 1999 C, Tg, 2000 W, S, 2001 Tg, Fj, NZ, Fj, J
**V Stet** 1963 Fj
**A Stewart** 2005 A, Tg
**G Stowers** 2001 I, 2008 Fj, Tg, J, NZ, 2009 J, Tg, Fj, PNG, W, It, 2010 Tg, J, Fj, I, E, S, 2011 Fj, A, Nm, W, Fj, SA
**R Stowers** 2008 Fj
**F Sua** 1982 Fj, Fj, Tg, 1983 Tg, Fj, 1984 Fj, 1985 Fj, Tg, Tg, 1986 Fj, Tg, 1987 Fj
**JI Sua** 2011 W, Fj, 2012 Tg, Fj, J, S, C, W, F, 2013 S, It, SA, I, Geo, 2014 Tg
**P Swepson** 1957 Tg

**S Ta'ala** 1996 Tg, Fj, I, 1997 Tg, Fj, 1998 Tg, Fj, A, 1999 J, C, Tg, US, Fj, J, Ar, W, S, 2001 J
**T Taega** 1997 Fj
**PI Taele** 2005 E, Ar, 2006 J, Fj, Tg, 2010 J
**D Tafeamalii** 2000 W, S
**T Tafua** 1981 Fj, 1982 Fj, Fj, Fj, 1983 Tg, 1985 Fj, Tg, 1986 W, Fj, Tg, 1987 Tg, 1989 Fj, WGe, R
**L Tafunai** 2004 Tg, Fj, 2005 Tg, Fj, Tg, Fj, S, Ar, 2008 Tg, J, NZ
**TDL Tagaloa** 1990 Kor, Tg, J, Tg, Fj, 1991 W, A, Ar, S
**S Tagicakibau** 2003 Nm, Ur, Geo, E, SA, 2004 Tg, S, Fj, 2005 S, E, Ar, 2007 Tg, 2009 J, Tg, Fj, 2011 J, Fj, A, Nm, W, Fj
**Tagimanu** 1924 Fj
**M Vaea** 1991 Tg, Fj, W, A, Ar, S, 1992 Fj, 1995 S
**I Taina** 2005 Tg, Fj, Tg, Fj, S
**F Taiomaivao** 1989 Bel
**F Talapusi** 1979 Tg, Fj, 1980 Tg

**F Talapusi** 2005 *A, Fj, Tg, Fj*
**Tamalua** 1932 *Tg*
**F Tanoa'i** 1996 *Tg, Fj*
**S Tanuko** 1987 *Tg*
**P Tapelu** 2002 *SA*
**V Tasi** 1981 *Fj*, 1982 *Fj, Fj, Fj, Tg*, 1983 *Tg, Fj*, 1984 *Fj, Tg*
**J Tatupu** 2010 *J*
**S Tatupu** 1990 *Tg*, 1993 *Tg, Fj, NZ*, 1995 *It, Ar, E, SA, Fj, Tg*
**N Tauafao** 2005 *A, Tg, Fj, Tg, Fj, S, Ar*, 2007 *Fj*, 2008 *Fj, Tg, J, NZ*, 2009 *J, Fj, PNG, PNG*
**S Taulafo** 2009 *W, F, It*, 2010 *Tg, Fj, I, E, S*, 2011 *J, A, Nm, W, Fj, SA*, 2012 *Tg, Fj, J, S, C, W, F*, 2013 *S, It, SA, I, Geo*, 2014 *Tg, It*
**I Tautau** 1985 *Fj, Tg*, 1986 *W*
**T Tavita** 1984 *Fj, Tg*
**E Taylor** 2011 *J, Fj*
**HL Tea** 2008 *Fj, Tg, J, NZ*, 2009 *PNG*
**I Tekori** 2007 *SA, J, SA, Tg, E, US*, 2009 *Tg, Fj, W, F*, 2010 *Tg, J, Fj, I, E, S*, 2011 *J, Nm, W, SA*, 2012 *J, S, C, W, F*, 2013 *I, Geo*, 2014 *Fj*
**S Telea** 1989 *Bel*
**AT Telea** 1995 *S, E*, 1996 *NZ, Tg, Fj*
**E Telea** 2008 *Fj*
**V Teo** 1957 *Tg, Tg*
**F Teo** 1955 *Fj*
**A Teo** 1947 *Tg*
**KG Thompson** 2007 *Fj, SA, Tg, SA, Tg, E, US*, 2008 *Tg, J*, 2009 *W, F, It*, 2010 *Tg, Fj, I, E, S*, 2011 *A, Nm, W, Fj, SA*, 2012 *J, S*, 2013 *It, SA*, 2014 *Tg*
**KTP Thomsen** 2014 *J*
**H Thomson** 1947 *Tg*
**R Tiatia** 1972 *Tg*
**A Tiatia** 2001 *Tg, Fj, NZ, Fj, Tg, J, Fj*
**S Tilialo** 1972 *Tg*
**MM Timoteo** 2009 *Tg, F, It*, 2012 *Tg, Fj*, 2014 *J*
**F Tipi** 1998 *Fj, A*, 1999 *J, C, F, NZ, Fj*
**F Toala** 1998 *Fj*, 1999 *J, C, S*, 2000 *W, S*
**L Toelupe** 1979 *Fj*
**P Toelupe** 2008 *Fj, J, NZ*
**T Tofaeono** 1989 *Fj, Bel*
**A Toleafoa** 2000 *W, S*, 2002 *Tg, SA*
**K Toleafoa** 1955 *Fj, Fj*
**PL Toleafoa** 2006 *J, Fj*
**K Tole'afoa** 1998 *Tg, A*, 1999 *Ar*
**F Toloa** 1979 *Tg*, 1980 *Tg*
**R Tolufale** 2008 *NZ*, 2009 *PNG*
**J Tomuli** 2001 *I, It*, 2002 *Fj, Tg, Fj, Tg, SA*, 2003 *I, Nm, Ur, Geo, E, SA*, 2006 *J*
**L Tone** 1998 *Fj, A*, 1999 *J, C, Tg, F, NZ, US, J, Ar, W, S*, 2000 *Fj, J, Tg, C, It, US, S*, 2001 *NZ, Fj, J, Fj*
**S Tone** 2000 *W*
**Toni** 1924 *Fj*
**OFJ Tonu'u** 1992 *Tg*, 1993 *Tg, Fj, NZ*
**F To'omalatai** 1989 *Bel*
**PS To'omalatai** 1985 *Fj, Tg*, 1986 *W, Fj*, 1988 *Tg, Fj, I, W*, 1989 *Fj, WGe, Bel, R*, 1990 *Kor, Tg, J, Tg, Fj*, 1991 *Tg, Fj, W, A, Ar, S*, 1992 *Tg, Fj*, 1993 *Fj*, 1994 *A*, 1995 *Fj*
**O Treviranus** 2009 *J, Tg, Fj, PNG, PNG, W, F, It*, 2010 *J, Fj, J, I, E, S*, 2011 *Fj, Tg, Nm, W, SA*, 2012 *C, W, F*, 2013 *S, It, SA, I, Geo*, 2014 *Tg, It*
**R Ofisa** 2011 *Tg*
**Tualai** 1924 *Fj, Fj*
**I Tualaulelei** 1963 *Fj, Fj, Tg*
**F Tuatagaloa** 1957 *Tg*
**V Tuatagaloa** 1963 *Fj, Tg*
**K Tuatagaloa** 1963 *Fj, Fj, Tg*, 1972 *Tg*
**Tufele** 1924 *Fj*
**D Tuiavi'I** 2003 *I, Nm, Ur, E, SA*
**I Tuifua** 2013 *I, Geo*
**T Tuifua** 2011 *J, Fj, A, Nm, Fj, SA*, 2012 *C, W, F*, 2013 *S, It, SA, I, Geo*, 2014 *Tg, It, Fj*
**VL Tuigamala** 1996 *Fj, I*, 1997 *Tg, Fj*, 1998 *Tg, Fj, A*, 1999 *F, NZ, US, Fj, J, Ar, W, S*, 2000 *Fj, J, Tg, US*, 2001 *J, Fj, I, It*
**AT Tuilagi** 2002 *Fj, Tg, SA*, 2005 *A, Tg, Fj, Tg, Fj, S, E*, 2007 *SA, J, Tg, SA, Tg, E, US*, 2010 *I, E, S*, 2011 *J, A, Nm, W, Fj, SA*, 2013 *S, It, SA*
**AF Tuilagi** 2005 *Tg, Fj, Tg, Fj, S, Ar*, 2006 *J, Tg*, 2007 *Fj, SA, J*, 2008 *Tg, J*, 2009 *W*, 2014 *J, Tg, Fj*
**F Tuilagi** 1992 *Tg*, 1994 *W, Fj, A*, 1995 *SA, SA, Fj*, 2000 *W, S*, 2001 *Fj, NZ, Tg*, 2002 *Fj, Tg, Fj, Tg, SA*
**H Tuilagi** 2002 *Fj, Tg, Fj, Tg*, 2007 *SA, E*, 2008 *J*, 2009 *W, F, It*
**T Tuisaula** 1947 *Tg*
**R Tuivaiti** 2004 *Fj*
**T Tulolo** 2014 *J*
**A Tunupopo** 1963 *Fj*
**P Tupa'i** 2005 *A, Tg, S, E, Ar*
**A Tupou** 2008 *NZ*, 2009 *PNG*
**S Tupuola** 1982 *Fj, Fj, Tg*, 1983 *Tg, Fj*, 1985 *Tg*, 1986 *Fj, Tg*, 1987 *Fj, Tg*, 1988 *W*, 1989 *R*
**P Tu'uau** 1972 *Tg, Tg*, 1975 *Tg*
**D Tyrrell** 2000 *Fj, J, C*, 2001 *It*, 2002 *Fj, Tg, SA*, 2003 *I, Nm, Ur, Geo, E, SA*

**S Uati** 1988 *Tg, Fj*
**T Ugapo** 1988 *Tg, Fj, I, W*, 1989 *Fj, WGe, Bel*
**U Ulia** 2004 *Tg, S, Fj*, 2005 *Ar*, 2006 *J, Fj, Tg*, 2007 *Fj, Tg, Tg, US*
**J Ulugia** 1985 *Fj, Tg*
**M Umaga** 1995 *SA, It, Ar, E, SA*, 1998 *Tg, Fj, A*, 1999 *Tg, F, NZ, US, Fj*
**L Utu'utu** 1975 *Tg*
**A Utu'utu** 1979 *Tg, Fj*

**E Va'a** 1996 *I*, 1997 *Fj*, 1998 *A*, 1999 *Tg, NZ, Fj, J, W, S*, 2001 *Tg, Fj, NZ, Fj, Tg, J, Fj, I*, 2002 *Fj, Tg, Fj, Tg, SA*, 2003 *I, Nm, Ur, Geo, E, SA*
**JH Va'a** 2005 *A, Fj, Tg, Fj, S, E, Ar*, 2006 *Fj, Tg*, 2007 *SA, J, Tg, SA*, 2009 *J, Tg, Fj, W, It*
**B Vaaulu** 2013 *S, It, SA, I, Geo*, 2014 *J*
**K Vaega** 1982 *Fj, Tg*, 1983 *Fj*
**TM Vaega** 1986 *W*, 1989 *WGe, Bel, R*, 1990 *Kor, Tg, J, Tg, Fj*, 1991 *Tg, Fj, W, A, Ar, S*, 1992 *Tg, Fj*, 1993 *Tg, Fj, NZ*, 1994 *Tg, W, Fj, A*, 1995 *SA, It, Ar, E, SA, Fj, Tg, Fj*, 1996 *NZ, Tg, Fj, I*, 1997 *Tg*, 1998 *Fj, A*, 1999 *J, C, F, NZ, Fj, J, Ar, W, S*, 2000 *Fj, J, Tg, C, It, US*, 2001 *Tg, J, Fj, I*
**A Vaeluaga** 2000 *W, S*, 2001 *Tg, Fj, Tg, J, Fj, I*, 2007 *SA, J, SA, E, US*
**F Vagaia** 1972 *Tg*
**K Vai** 1987 *Fj, Tg*, 1989 *Bel*
**TS Vaifale** 1989 *R*, 1990 *Kor, Tg, J, Tg, Fj*, 1991 *Tg, Fj, W, Ar, S*, 1992 *Tg, Fj*, 1993 *NZ*, 1994 *Tg, W, Fj, A*, 1995 *SA, It, SA, Fj, S, E*, 1996 *NZ, Tg*, 1997 *Tg, Fj*
**S Vaili** 2001 *I, It*, 2002 *Fj, Tg, Fj, Tg*, 2003 *Geo*, 2004 *Tg, S, Fj*
**L Vailoaloa** 2005 *A*, 2011 *J, Fj, Tg*
**S Vaisola Sefo** 2007 *US*
**T Veiru** 2000 *W, S*
**M Vili** 1975 *Tg*
**M Vili** 1957 *Tg*
**T Vili** 1999 *C, Tg, US, Ar*, 2000 *Fj, J, Tg, C, It, US*, 2001 *Tg, Fj, J, Fj, I, It*, 2003 *Ur, Geo, E, SA*, 2004 *Tg, S, Fj*, 2005 *A, Tg, Fj, S, E*, 2006 *J, Fj, Tg*
**T Viliamu** 1947 *Tg*
**AF Williams** 2009 *J, Fj, PNG, PNG, F, It*, 2010 *J, J*, 2014 *J*
**K Viliamu** 2001 *I, It*, 2002 *Fj, SA*, 2003 *I, Ur, Geo, E, SA*, 2004 *S*
**Visesio** 1932 *Tg*
**R Lilomaiava** 2012 *C, F*
**FV Vitale** 1994 *W, Fj, A*, 1995 *Fj, Tg*
**F Vito** 1972 *Tg*, 1975 *Tg*
**M von Dincklage** 2004 *S*

**R Warren** 2004 *Tg, S*, 2005 *Tg, Fj, Tg, Fj, S, Ar*, 2008 *Fj, Tg, J, NZ*
**S Wendt** 1955 *Fj, Fj, Fj*
**DR Williams** 1988 *I, W*, 1995 *SA, It, E*
**G Williams** 2007 *Fj, SA, Tg*, 2008 *Tg, J*, 2009 *J, Tg, Fj, PNG, PNG, W, It*, 2010 *J, I, E*
**H Williams** 2001 *Tg, Tg, J*
**PB Williams** 2010 *Tg, J, Fj, I, E, S*, 2011 *A, Nm, W, Fj, SA*, 2012 *Fj, J, S, W*, 2013 *S, It, SA*
**P Young** 1988 *I*, 1989 *Bel*

# SCOTLAND

## SCOTLAND'S 2013–14 TEST RECORD

| OPPONENTS | DATE | VENUE | RESULT |
|---|---|---|---|
| Japan | 9 Nov | H | Won 42–17 |
| South Africa | 17 Nov | H | Lost 0–28 |
| Australia | 23 Nov | H | Lost 15–21 |
| Ireland | 2 Feb | A | Lost 28–6 |
| England | 8 Feb | H | Lost 0–20 |
| Italy | 22 Feb | A | Won 21–20 |
| France | 8 Mar | H | Lost 17–19 |
| Wales | 15 Mar | A | Lost 51–3 |
| USA | 7 Jun | A | Won 24–6 |
| Canada | 14 Jun | A | Won 19–17 |
| Argentina | 21 Jun | A | Won 21–19 |
| South Africa | 28 Jun | A | Lost 55–6 |

# A YEAR OF MIXED FORTUNES FOR SCOTLAND

## By Chris Paterson

A hard-fought win over Los Pumas in Argentina in June was one of Scotland's best results of an up and down year.

**S**cotland played 12 Tests in the 2013–14 season, winning five of them. By the end of the campaign they also had a new head coach at the helm, Vern Cotter arriving to begin his duties once he had seen out his contract at French club Clermont Auvergne.

Perhaps the more significant statistic, however, was that following on from the 10 players who made their debuts on the 2013 summer tour, a further 12 of Scotland's most promising talent won their first caps during the season.

In that respect Scott Johnson, who will now focus on his role as Scottish Rugby's Director of Performance Rugby, had done precisely what was asked of him: to broaden the base and bring through the next generation to compete for places in the Scotland team as Rugby World Cup 2015 looms on the horizon.

Scotland's 2013–14 programme began with the visit of Japan in November. Scotland won 42–17 and scored six cracking tries into the

bargain. It is worth noting, though, that the Brave Blossoms replied with **453**
a brilliant brace of tries from winger Kenki Fukuoka, who will certainly
be a player to watch when the teams clash again in Scotland's opening
match of Rugby World Cup 2015 in Gloucester.

South Africa arrived at Murrayfield eight days later on a murky, wet
afternoon for what was a frustrating affair for the home supporters.
Previous contests in such weather had resulted in Scotland enjoying the
upper hand but that was never in South Africa's script and with man
of the match Willie le Roux supplying some glorious touches, the
Springboks won 28–0.

The third and final game of the November series, against Australia,
was an altogether more closely fought contest, which ended with Scotland
on the wrong side of a 21–15 scoreline. Israel Folau showed his class
for the Wallabies and it was another all-too-familiar case of small
margins.

The famed playing surface at Murrayfield was suffering, even at this
juncture of the season, as a plague of parasitical worms – nematodes
to use the technical name – had badly affected the grass roots. There
was an end in sight, though, with Scottish Rugby announcing before
the Six Nations campaign that a new £1million plus grass/artificial
hybrid pitch would be installed ready for the 2014–15 season.

Scotland knew that a big improvement was required if they were
even to match their third place finish from the 2013 Six Nations. Sadly,
it did not materialise. Their opening match, against Ireland at the Aviva
Stadium in early February, had actually looked competitive in the early
stages but the loss of Sean Maitland to injury was a portent of what
was to come as eventual champions Ireland went through the gears and
delivered a classy and ultimately comfortable 28–6 win.

Undoubtedly the lowest point of the season was to follow a week
later with an unacceptable 20–0 loss to England in the Calcutta Cup
at Murrayfield. I've played in games like that where you can become
overwhelmed by the huge sense of disappointment and frustration which
can envelop you for the rest of the season and you understand the
supporters' anger when the performance is so poor.

England were efficient that day. There was little, if anything, spectacular from them but, boy, did they get the basics right. We didn't do
that and were punished.

It's amazing then that the players and management turned matters
around to produce a win in Italy two weeks later. At the Stadio Olimpico
we saw, arguably, the best sporting theatre of the entire Championship
as the lead changed hands several times until a breathtaking finale. Both
Scotland and Italy were brave; they both played at high tempo and it

SCOTLAND

required a last-minute drop goal from Duncan Weir to seal a 21–20 win for the visitors. Scotland's much better set-pieces that day was certainly at the heart of their success, while Alex Dunbar's two tries were taken with some aplomb.

Back on home soil a fortnight later and the agony of the England game was replaced by the pain of a late 19–17 defeat to France, with an intercept try for Les Bleus providing a 14-point swing and that refrain of small margins playing out on the adverse side for the hosts. Despite having more possession and territory and outscoring their French visitors by two tries to one, Scotland on this occasion were on the wrong end of a last-minute score, a penalty from Jean-Marc Doussain.

Finally to Wales and a red day in the valleys! A lot has been written about the 51–3 defeat at the Millennium Stadium, but the first observation I'd make was how impressed I was with Wales, even before Scotland were reduced to 14 men. Wales were abrasive and powerful, playing at the top of their game. Scotland lost their captain Kelly Brown to injury in the first 10 minutes and then had Stuart Hogg red-carded after 20 minutes. It was a bad day at the office.

After that, Scottish rugby needed a fillip and it came in the shape of Glasgow Warriors finishing second in the RaboDirect PRO12 – courtesy of some gutsy and tigerish defensive displays in the early season and some trademark attacking performances towards the end. They went on to make the grand final for the first time.

Games that stick in my mind included the home matches against Ulster and Munster, where the physicality was as high as anything I've seen in a club game. Glasgow, particularly in the semi-final against Munster, maintained a balance in their game and did not obsess about the physical stuff. They still had sufficient attacking composure and nous to set up the final against Leinster in Dublin. That match was to prove disappointing for Glasgow Warriors, but I've no doubt that head coach Gregor Townsend, his management team and his players will use that experience to influence what they do this season.

Edinburgh Rugby had a transitional season with some encouraging signs, including home victories over Munster and Perpignan and an away success against Gloucester, but, ultimately, at the end of the league campaign they finished a disappointing eighth.

It was then back on the international beat and Cotter's baptism as Scotland head coach was the end of season tour – an epic undertaking of four Test matches on four consecutive weekends in three different continents.

Victory in three of the four internationals – against USA, Canada and Argentina – was no mean achievement and was quite rightly applauded.

The 24–6 margin against the USA Eagles in Houston saw Tim Visser, on his return after injury, cross the whitewash. Stuart Hogg followed suit and there was also a penalty try, all three of which were converted by Greig Laidlaw.

Laidlaw, not for the first time, also proved the match-winner with his goal-kicking in the 19–17 win over Canada in Toronto and then we came to Scotland's fourth successive triumph in Argentina.

On that day in Córdoba, it was a case of step forward again Duncan Weir. He repeated his match-winning antics from the Italy game with a last-minute penalty for Scotland to snatch a 21–19 win.

Weir had finished the domestic season behind Ruaridh Jackson and Finn Russell, at least in terms of Glasgow Warriors' selection for the PRO12 showdown in Dublin, but here he was demonstrating the mental strength and a growing depth in some positions to steer Scotland to a win.

The final match of the tour against South Africa in Port Elizabeth was probably a game too far as Scotland were blitzed 55–6.

However, that was not the final act on the representative front as, come July, Scotland were back on home soil for the magnificent spectacle that was the Commonwealth Games Sevens at Ibrox Stadium in Glasgow.

It was important that, as the birthplace of Sevens and given the country was hosting the Games, the Sevens squad was bolstered by current 15-a-side internationals. With Hogg and Sean Lamont included in the squad Scotland performed pretty well, qualifying for the knockout stages, but losing to both the eventual finalists. Fair play to South Africa after they ended New Zealand's unbeaten run in the Commonwealth Games with a stellar performance in the final.

The support enjoyed by all 16 teams at Ibrox – manifesting itself in a world-record crowd of 171,000 for the four sessions over the two days – was nothing short of sensational. For all of the teams involved, especially the so-called minnows, like Uganda and Sri Lanka, it was an experience to treasure and the exposure it gave our great game was a highlight of the entire Commonwealth Games.

It leaves me really excited and it can only be good for rugby as we look towards the next global showcase for the abbreviated game, the 2016 Olympics in Rio!

# SCOTLAND INTERNATIONAL STATISTICS

## MATCH RECORDS UP TO 13 OCTOBER 2014

### MOST CONSECUTIVE TEST WINS

| | |
|---|---|
| 6 | 1925 F, W, I, E, 1926 F, W |
| 6 | 1989 Fj ,R, 1990 I, F, W, E |

### MOST CONSECUTIVE TESTS WITHOUT DEFEAT

| Matches | Wins | Draws | Period |
|---|---|---|---|
| 9 | 6* | 3 | 1885 to 1887 |
| 6 | 6 | 0 | 1925 to 1926 |
| 6 | 6 | 0 | 1989 to 1990 |
| 6 | 4 | 2 | 1877 to 1880 |
| 6 | 5 | 1 | 1983 to 1984 |

* includes an abandoned match

### MOST POINTS IN A MATCH
#### BY THE TEAM

| Pts | Opponents | Venue | Year |
|---|---|---|---|
| 100 | Japan | Perth | 2004 |
| 89 | Ivory Coast | Rustenburg | 1995 |
| 65 | United States | San Francisco | 2002 |
| 60 | Zimbabwe | Wellington | 1987 |
| 60 | Romania | Hampden Park | 1999 |
| 56 | Portugal | Saint Etienne | 2007 |
| 55 | Romania | Dunedin | 1987 |
| 53 | United States | Murrayfield | 2000 |
| 51 | Zimbabwe | Murrayfield | 1991 |
| 49 | Argentina | Murrayfield | 1990 |
| 49 | Romania | Murrayfield | 1995 |

#### BY A PLAYER

| Pts | Player | Opponents | Venue | Year |
|---|---|---|---|---|
| 44 | AG Hastings | Ivory Coast | Rustenburg | 1995 |
| 40 | CD Paterson | Japan | Perth | 2004 |
| 33 | GPJ Townsend | United States | Murrayfield | 2000 |
| 31 | AG Hastings | Tonga | Pretoria | 1995 |
| 27 | AG Hastings | Romania | Dunedin | 1987 |
| 26 | KM Logan | Romania | Hampden Park | 1999 |
| 24 | BJ Laney | Italy | Rome | 2002 |
| 24 | DA Parks | Argentina | Tucumán | 2010 |
| 23 | G Ross | Tonga | Murrayfield | 2001 |
| 22 | GD Laidlaw | Fiji | Lautoka | 2012 |
| 21 | AG Hastings | England | Murrayfield | 1986 |
| 21 | AG Hastings | Romania | Bucharest | 1986 |
| 21 | CD Paterson | Wales | Murrayfield | 2007 |
| 21 | DA Parks | South Africa | Murrayfield | 2010 |

### MOST TRIES IN A MATCH
#### BY THE TEAM

| Tries | Opponents | Venue | Year |
|---|---|---|---|
| 15 | Japan | Perth | 2004 |
| 13 | Ivory Coast | Rustenburg | 1995 |
| 12 | Wales | Raeburn Place | 1887 |
| 11 | Zimbabwe | Wellington | 1987 |
| 10 | United States | San Francisco | 2002 |
| 9 | Romania | Dunedin | 1987 |
| 9 | Argentina | Murrayfield | 1990 |

#### BY A PLAYER

| Tries | Player | Opponents | Venue | Year |
|---|---|---|---|---|
| 5 | GC Lindsay | Wales | Raeburn Place | 1887 |
| 4 | WA Stewart | Ireland | Inverleith | 1913 |
| 4 | IS Smith | France | Inverleith | 1925 |
| 4 | IS Smith | Wales | Swansea | 1925 |
| 4 | AG Hastings | Ivory Coast | Rustenburg | 1995 |

### MOST CONVERSIONS IN A MATCH
#### BY THE TEAM

| Cons | Opponents | Venue | Year |
|---|---|---|---|
| 11 | Japan | Perth | 2004 |
| 9 | Ivory Coast | Rustenburg | 1995 |
| 8 | Zimbabwe | Wellington | 1987 |
| 8 | Romania | Dunedin | 1987 |
| 8 | Portugal | Saint Etienne | 2007 |

#### BY A PLAYER

| Cons | Player | Opponents | Venue | Year |
|---|---|---|---|---|
| 11 | CD Paterson | Japan | Perth | 2004 |
| 9 | AG Hastings | Ivory Coast | Rustenburg | 1995 |
| 8 | AG Hastings | Zimbabwe | Wellington | 1987 |
| 8 | AG Hastings | Romania | Dunedin | 1987 |

## MOST PENALTIES IN A MATCH
### BY THE TEAM

| Penalties | Opponents | Venue | Year |
|---|---|---|---|
| 8 | Tonga | Pretoria | 1995 |
| 7 | Wales | Murrayfield | 2007 |
| 6 | France | Murrayfield | 1986 |
| 6 | Italy | Murrayfield | 2005 |
| 6 | Ireland | Murrayfield | 2007 |
| 6 | Italy | Saint Etienne | 2007 |
| 6 | Argentina | Tucumán | 2010 |
| 6 | South Africa | Murrayfield | 2010 |
| 6 | Wales | Murrayfield | 2013 |

### BY A PLAYER

| Pens | Player | Opponents | Venue | Year |
|---|---|---|---|---|
| 8 | AG Hastings | Tonga | Pretoria | 1995 |
| 7 | CD Paterson | Wales | Murrayfield | 2007 |
| 6 | AG Hastings | France | Murrayfield | 1986 |
| 6 | CD Paterson | Italy | Murrayfield | 2005 |
| 6 | CD Paterson | Ireland | Murrayfield | 2007 |
| 6 | CD Paterson | Italy | Saint Etienne | 2007 |
| 6 | DA Parks | Argentina | Tucumán | 2010 |
| 6 | DA Parks | South Africa | Murrayfield | 2010 |
| 6 | GD Laidlaw | Wales | Murrayfield | 2013 |

## MOST DROP GOALS IN A MATCH
### BY THE TEAM

| Drops | Opponents | Venue | Year |
|---|---|---|---|
| 3 | Ireland | Murrayfield | 1973 |
| 2 | on several | occasions | |

### BY A PLAYER

| Drops | Player | Opponents | Venue | Year |
|---|---|---|---|---|
| 2 | RC MacKenzie | Ireland | Belfast | 1877 |
| 2 | NJ Finlay | Ireland | Glasgow | 1880 |
| 2 | BM Simmers | Wales | Murrayfield | 1965 |
| 2 | DW Morgan | Ireland | Murrayfield | 1973 |
| 2 | BM Gossman | France | Parc des Princes | 1983 |
| 2 | JY Rutherford | New Zealand | Murrayfield | 1983 |
| 2 | JY Rutherford | Wales | Murrayfield | 1985 |
| 2 | JY Rutherford | Ireland | Murrayfield | 1987 |
| 2 | CM Chalmers | England | Twickenham | 1995 |
| 2 | DA Parks | Wales | Cardiff | 2010 |
| 2 | DA Parks | Argentina | Tucumán | 2010 |

# CAREER RECORDS

## MOST CAPPED PLAYERS

| Caps | Player | Career Span |
|---|---|---|
| 109 | CD Paterson | 1999 to 2011 |
| 88 | SF Lamont | 2004 to 2014 |
| 87 | S Murray | 1997 to 2007 |
| 85 | MRL Blair | 2002 to 2012 |
| 82 | GPJ Townsend | 1993 to 2003 |
| 77 | JPR White | 2000 to 2009 |
| 77 | NJ Hines | 2000 to 2011 |
| 77 | RW Ford | 2004 to 2014 |
| 75 | GC Bulloch | 1997 to 2005 |
| 71 | SB Grimes | 1997 to 2005 |
| 70 | KM Logan | 1992 to 2003 |
| 68 | CP Cusiter | 2004 to 2014 |
| 67 | DA Parks | 2004 to 2012 |
| 66 | SM Taylor | 2000 to 2009 |
| 65 | S Hastings | 1986 to 1997 |
| 65 | AF Jacobsen | 2002 to 2012 |

## MOST CONSECUTIVE TESTS

| Tests | Player | Span |
|---|---|---|
| 49 | AB Carmichael | 1967 to 1978 |
| 44 | CD Paterson | 2004 to 2008 |
| 40 | HF McLeod | 1954 to 1962 |
| 37 | JM Bannerman | 1921 to 1929 |
| 35 | AG Stanger | 1989 to 1994 |

## MOST TESTS AS CAPTAIN

| Tests | Captain | Span |
|---|---|---|
| 25 | DMB Sole | 1989 to 1992 |
| 21 | BW Redpath | 1998 to 2003 |
| 20 | AG Hastings | 1993 to 1995 |
| 19 | J McLauchlan | 1973 to 1979 |
| 19 | JPR White | 2005 to 2008 |
| 16 | RI Wainwright | 1995 to 1998 |
| 15 | MC Morrison | 1899 to 1904 |
| 15 | AR Smith | 1957 to 1962 |
| 15 | AR Irvine | 1980 to 1982 |

## MOST POINTS IN TESTS

| Points | Player | Tests | Career |
|---|---|---|---|
| 809 | CD Paterson | 109 | 1999 to 2011 |
| 667 | AG Hastings | 61 | 1986 to 1995 |
| 273 | AR Irvine | 51 | 1972 to 1982 |
| 266 | DA Parks | 67 | 2004 to 2012 |
| 262 | GD Laidlaw | 31 | 2010 to 2014 |
| 220 | KM Logan | 70 | 1992 to 2003 |
| 210 | PW Dods | 23 | 1983 to 1991 |
| 166 | CM Chalmers | 60 | 1989 to 1999 |
| 164 | GPJ Townsend | 82 | 1993 to 2003 |
| 141 | BJ Laney | 20 | 2001 to 2004 |
| 123 | DW Hodge | 26 | 1997 to 2002 |
| 106 | AG Stanger | 52 | 1989 to 1998 |

SCOTLAND

## MOST TRIES IN TESTS

| Tries | Player | Tests | Career |
|---|---|---|---|
| 24 | IS Smith | 32 | 1924 to 1933 |
| 24 | AG Stanger | 52 | 1989 to 1998 |
| 22 | CD Paterson | 109 | 1999 to 2011 |
| 17 | AG Hastings | 61 | 1986 to 1995 |
| 17 | AV Tait | 27 | 1987 to 1999 |
| 17 | GPJ Townsend | 82 | 1993 to 2003 |
| 15 | I Tukalo | 37 | 1985 to 1992 |
| 13 | KM Logan | 70 | 1992 to 2003 |
| 12 | AR Smith | 33 | 1955 to 1962 |
| 12 | SF Lamont | 88 | 2004 to 2014 |

## MOST PENALTY GOALS IN TESTS

| Penalties | Player | Tests | Career |
|---|---|---|---|
| 170 | CD Paterson | 109 | 1999 to 2011 |
| 140 | AG Hastings | 61 | 1986 to 1995 |
| 63 | GD Laidlaw | 31 | 2010 to 2014 |
| 61 | AR Irvine | 51 | 1972 to 1982 |
| 55 | DA Parks | 67 | 2004 to 2012 |
| 50 | PW Dods | 23 | 1983 to 1991 |
| 32 | CM Chalmers | 60 | 1989 to 1999 |
| 29 | KM Logan | 70 | 1992 to 2003 |
| 29 | BJ Laney | 20 | 2001 to 2004 |
| 21 | M Dods | 8 | 1994 to 1996 |
| 21 | RJS Shepherd | 20 | 1995 to 1998 |

## MOST CONVERSIONS IN TESTS

| Cons | Player | Tests | Career |
|---|---|---|---|
| 90 | CD Paterson | 109 | 1999 to 2011 |
| 86 | AG Hastings | 61 | 1986 to 1995 |
| 34 | KM Logan | 70 | 1992 to 2003 |
| 29 | GD Laidlaw | 31 | 2010 to 2014 |
| 26 | PW Dods | 23 | 1983 to 1991 |
| 25 | AR Irvine | 51 | 1972 to 1982 |
| 19 | D Drysdale | 26 | 1923 to 1929 |
| 17 | BJ Laney | 20 | 2001 to 2004 |
| 15 | DW Hodge | 26 | 1997 to 2002 |
| 15 | DA Parks | 67 | 2004 to 2012 |
| 14 | FH Turner | 15 | 1911 to 1914 |
| 14 | RJS Shepherd | 20 | 1995 to 1998 |

## MOST DROP GOALS IN TESTS

| Drops | Player | Tests | Career |
|---|---|---|---|
| 17 | DA Parks | 67 | 2004 to 2012 |
| 12 | JY Rutherford | 42 | 1979 to 1987 |
| 9 | CM Chalmers | 60 | 1989 to 1999 |
| 7 | IR McGeechan | 32 | 1972 to 1979 |
| 7 | GPJ Townsend | 82 | 1993 to 2003 |
| 6 | DW Morgan | 21 | 1973 to 1978 |
| 5 | H Waddell | 15 | 1924 to 1930 |

Getty Images

Full-back Chris Paterson still holds a number of Scotland records, including most Test points for his country.

| RECORD | DETAIL | HOLDER | SET |
|---|---|---|---|
| Most points in season | 120 | in four matches | 1999 |
| Most tries in season | 17 | in four matches | 1925 |
| Highest score | 38 | 38–10 v Ireland | 1997 |
| Biggest win | 28 | 31–3 v France | 1912 |
| | 28 | 38–10 v Ireland | 1997 |
| Highest score conceded | 51 | 16–51 v France | 1998 |
| | 51 | 3–51 v Wales | 2014 |
| Biggest defeat | 48 | 3–51 v Wales | 2014 |
| Most appearances | 53 | CD Paterson | 2000–2011 |
| Most points in matches | 403 | CD Paterson | 2000–2011 |
| Most points in season | 65 | CD Paterson | 2007 |
| Most points in match | 24 | BJ Laney | v Italy, 2002 |
| Most tries in matches | 24 | IS Smith | 1924–1933 |
| Most tries in season | 8 | IS Smith | 1925 |
| Most tries in match | 5 | GC Lindsay | v Wales, 1887 |
| Most cons in matches | 34 | CD Paterson | 2000–2011 |
| Most cons in season | 11 | KM Logan | 1999 |
| Most cons in match | 5 | FH Turner | v France, 1912 |
| | 5 | JW Allan | v England, 1931 |
| | 5 | RJS Shepherd | v Ireland, 1997 |
| Most pens in matches | 99 | CD Paterson | 2000–2011 |
| Most pens in season | 17 | GD Laidlaw | 2013 |
| Most pens in match | 7 | CD Paterson | v Wales, 2007 |
| Most drops in matches | 9 | DA Parks | 2004–2012 |
| Most drops in season | 5 | DA Parks | 2010 |
| Most drops in match | 2 | on several occasions | |

SCOTLAND

# MISCELLANEOUS RECORDS

| RECORD | HOLDER | DETAIL |
|---|---|---|
| Longest Test Career | WCW Murdoch | 1935 to 1948 |
| Youngest Test Cap | NJ Finlay | 17 yrs 36 days in 1875* |
| Oldest Test Cap | J McLauchlan | 37 yrs 210 days in 1979 |

*C Reid, also 17 yrs 36 days on debut in 1881, was a day older than Finlay, having lived through an extra leap-year day.

# CAREER RECORDS OF SCOTLAND INTERNATIONAL PLAYERS

## UP TO 13 OCTOBER 2014

| PLAYER | DEBUT | CAPS | T | C | P | D | PTS |
|--------|-------|------|---|---|---|---|-----|
| **BACKS :** | | | | | | | |
| CP Cusiter | 2004 v W | 68 | 3 | 0 | 0 | 0 | 15 |
| NJ de Luca | 2008 v F | 43 | 1 | 0 | 0 | 0 | 5 |
| AJ Dunbar | 2013 v Sm | 8 | 3 | 0 | 0 | 0 | 15 |
| MB Evans | 2008 v C | 44 | 3 | 0 | 0 | 0 | 15 |
| DJ Fife | 2014 v W | 3 | 0 | 0 | 0 | 0 | 0 |
| GJ Hart | 2014 v C | 3 | 0 | 0 | 0 | 0 | 0 |
| TA Heathcote | 2012 v Tg | 3 | 0 | 0 | 0 | 0 | 0 |
| SW Hogg | 2012 v W | 24 | 6 | 0 | 1 | 0 | 33 |
| P Horne | 2013 v Sm | 5 | 0 | 0 | 0 | 0 | 0 |
| RJH Jackson | 2010 v NZ | 25 | 0 | 3 | 2 | 2 | 18 |
| GD Laidlaw | 2010 v NZ | 31 | 3 | 29 | 63 | 0 | 262 |
| SF Lamont | 2004 v Sm | 88 | 12 | 0 | 0 | 0 | 60 |
| SD Maitland | 2013 v E | 13 | 1 | 0 | 0 | 0 | 5 |
| PE Murchie | 2013 v SA | 3 | 0 | 0 | 0 | 0 | 0 |
| HB Pyrgos | 2012 v NZ | 12 | 2 | 0 | 0 | 0 | 10 |
| FA Russell | 2014 v US | 2 | 0 | 0 | 0 | 0 | 0 |
| MCM Scott | 2012 v I | 21 | 3 | 0 | 0 | 0 | 15 |
| TSF Seymour | 2013 v SA | 10 | 3 | 0 | 0 | 0 | 15 |
| DM Taylor | 2013 v Sm | 11 | 0 | 0 | 0 | 0 | 0 |
| GA Tonks | 2013 v Sm | 1 | 0 | 0 | 0 | 0 | 0 |
| TJW Visser | 2012 v Fj | 14 | 7 | 0 | 0 | 0 | 35 |
| D Weir | 2012 v F | 15 | 1 | 4 | 6 | 1 | 34 |
| | | | | | | | |
| **FORWARDS :** | | | | | | | |
| AG Allan | 2014 v US | 1 | 0 | 0 | 0 | 0 | 0 |
| A Ashe | 2014 v SA | 1 | 0 | 0 | 0 | 0 | 0 |
| JA Barclay | 2007 v NZ | 43 | 2 | 0 | 0 | 0 | 10 |
| JW Beattie | 2006 v R | 32 | 3 | 0 | 0 | 0 | 15 |
| FJM Brown | 2013 v It | 1 | 0 | 0 | 0 | 0 | 0 |
| KDR Brown | 2005 v R | 64 | 4 | 0 | 0 | 0 | 20 |
| K Bryce | 2014 v C | 2 | 0 | 0 | 0 | 0 | 0 |
| BA Cowan | 2014 v US | 3 | 0 | 0 | 0 | 0 | 0 |
| GDS Cross | 2009 v W | 32 | 1 | 0 | 0 | 0 | 5 |
| DK Denton | 2011 v I | 22 | 0 | 0 | 0 | 0 | 0 |

| AG Dickinson | 2007 v NZ | 36 | 2 | 0 | 0 | 0 | 10 |
|---|---|---|---|---|---|---|---|
| RW Ford | 2004 v A | 77 | 2 | 0 | 0 | 0 | 10 |
| CC Fusaro | 2014 v E | 4 | 0 | 0 | 0 | 0 | 0 |
| GS Gilchrist | 2013 v F | 8 | 1 | 0 | 0 | 0 | 5 |
| R Grant | 2012 v A | 18 | 0 | 0 | 0 | 0 | 0 |
| JD Gray | 2013 v SA | 5 | 0 | 0 | 0 | 0 | 0 |
| RJ Gray | 2010 v F | 39 | 1 | 0 | 0 | 0 | 5 |
| JL Hamilton | 2006 v R | 56 | 1 | 0 | 0 | 0 | 5 |
| RJ Harley | 2012 v Sm | 7 | 1 | 0 | 0 | 0 | 5 |
| TT Holmes | 2014 v SA | 1 | 0 | 0 | 0 | 0 | 0 |
| AD Kellock | 2004 v A | 56 | 1 | 0 | 0 | 0 | 5 |
| S Lawrie | 2013 v Sm | 1 | 0 | 0 | 0 | 0 | 0 |
| S Lawson | 2005 v R | 45 | 2 | 0 | 0 | 0 | 10 |
| K Low | 2013 v A | 4 | 0 | 0 | 0 | 0 | 0 |
| MJ Low | 2009 v F | 29 | 0 | 0 | 0 | 0 | 0 |
| PC MacArthur | 2013 v Sm | 6 | 0 | 0 | 0 | 0 | 0 |
| EA Murray | 2005 v R | 60 | 2 | 0 | 0 | 0 | 10 |
| G Reid | 2014 v US | 3 | 0 | 0 | 0 | 0 | 0 |
| RM Rennie | 2008 v I | 20 | 0 | 0 | 0 | 0 | 0 |
| AK Strokosch | 2006 v A | 40 | 2 | 0 | 0 | 0 | 10 |
| TJM Swinson | 2013 v SA | 9 | 0 | 0 | 0 | 0 | 0 |
| K Traynor | 2009 v Fj | 4 | 0 | 0 | 0 | 0 | 0 |
| J Welsh | 2012 v It | 3 | 0 | 0 | 0 | 0 | 0 |
| R Wilson | 2013 v W | 9 | 0 | 0 | 0 | 0 | 0 |

**SCOTLAND**

# SCOTLAND INTERNATIONAL PLAYERS
## UP TO 13 OCTOBER 2014

Note: Years given for International Championship matches are for second half of season; eg 1972 means season 1971–72. Years for all other matches refer to the actual year of the match. Entries in square brackets denote matches played in RWC Finals.

Abercrombie, C H (United Services) 1910 I, E, 1911 F, W, 1913 F, W

Abercrombie, J G (Edinburgh U) 1949 F, W, I, 1950 F, W, I, E

Agnew, W C (Stewart's Coll FP) 1930 W, I

Ainslie, R (Edinburgh Inst FP) 1879 I, E, 1880 I, E, 1881 E, 1882 I, E

Ainslie, T (Edinburgh Inst FP) 1881 E, 1882 I, E, 1883 W, I, E, 1884 W, I, E, 1885 W, I 1, 2

Aitchison, G R (Edinburgh Wands) 1883 I

Aitchison, T G (Gala) 1929 W, I, E

Aitken, A I (Edinburgh Inst FP) 1889 I

Aitken, G G (Oxford U) 1924 W, I, E, 1925 F, W, I, E, 1929 F

Aitken, J (Gala) 1977 E, I, F, 1981 F, W, E, I, NZ 1, 2, R, A, 1982 E, I, F, W, 1983 F, W, E, NZ, 1984 W, E, I, F, R

Aitken, R (London Scottish) 1947 W

Allan, A G Glasgow Warriors) 2014 US(R)

Allan, A G (Glasgow Acads) 1881 I

Allan, J (Edinburgh Acads) 1990 NZ 1, 1991, W, I, R, [J, I, WS, E, NZ]

Allan, J L (Melrose) 1952 F, W, I, 1953 W

Allan, J L F (Cambridge U) 1957 I, E

Allan, J W (Melrose) 1927 F, 1928 I, 1929 F, W, I, E, 1930 F, E, 1931 F, W, I, E, 1932 SA, W, I, 1934 I, E

Allan, R C (Hutchesons' GSFP) 1969 I

Allardice, W D (Aberdeen GSFP) 1947 A, 1948 F, W, I, 1949 F, W, I, E

Allen, H W (Glasgow Acads) 1873 E

Anderson, A H (Glasgow Acads) 1894 I

Anderson, D G (London Scottish) 1889 I, 1890 W, I, E, 1891 W, E, 1892 W, E

Anderson, E (Stewart's Coll FP) 1947 I, E

Anderson, J W (W of Scotland) 1872 E

Anderson, T (Merchiston Castle School) 1882 I

Angus, A W (Watsonians) 1909 W, 1910 F, W, E, 1911 W, I, 1912 F, W, I, E, SA, 1913 F, W, 1914 F, W, I, E, 1920 F, W, I, E

Ansbro, J A (Northampton, London Irish) 2010 SA, Sm, 2011 F, W, E, It1, I2, [R, E], 2012 A, Sm

Anton, P A (St Andrew's U) 1873 E

462

**Armstrong, G** (Jedforest, Newcastle) 1988 A, 1989 W, E, I, F, Fj, R, 1990 I, F, W, E, NZ 1, 2, Arg, 1991 F, W, E, I, R, [J, I, WS, E, NZ], 1993 I, F, W, E, 1994 E, I, 1996 NZ, 1, 2, A, 1997 W, SA (R), 1998 It, I, F, W, E, SA (R), 1999 W, E, I, F, Arg, R, [SA, U, Sm, NZ]
**Arneil, R J** (Edinburgh Acads, Leicester and Northampton) 1968 I, E, A, 1969 F, W, I, E, SA, 1970 F, W, I, E, A, 1971 F, W, I, E (2[1C]), 1972 F, W, E, NZ
**Arthur, A** (Glasgow Acads) 1875 E, 1876 E
**Arthur, J W** (Glasgow Acads) 1871 E, 1872 E
**Ashe, A** (Glasgow Warriors) 2014 SA
**Asher, A G G** (Oxford U) 1882 I, 1884 W, I, E, 1885 W, 1886 I, E
**Auld, W** (W of Scotland) 1889 W, 1890 W
**Auldjo, L J** (Abertay) 1878 E

**Bain, D McL** (Oxford U) 1911 E, 1912 F, W, E, SA, 1913 F, W, I, E, 1914 W, I
**Baird, G R T** (Kelso) 1981 A, 1982 E, I, F, W, A 1, 2, 1983 I, F, W, E, NZ, 1984 W, E, I, F, A, 1985 I, W, E, 1986 F, W, E, I, R, 1987 E, 1988 I
**Balfour, A** (Watsonians) 1896 W, I, E, 1897 E
**Balfour, L M** (Edinburgh Acads) 1872 E
**Bannerman, E M** (Edinburgh Acads) 1872 E, 1873 E
**Bannerman, J M** (Glasgow HSFP) 1921 F, W, I, E, 1922 F, W, I, E, 1923 F, W, I, E, 1924 F, W, I, E, 1925 F, W, I, E, 1926 F, W, I, E, 1927 F, W, I, E, A, 1928 F, W, I, E, 1929 F, W, I, E
**Barclay, J A** (Glasgow Warriors) 2007 [NZ], 2008 F, W, Arg 2, NZ, SA, C, 2009 W, F, It, I, Fj, A, 2010 F, W, It, E, I, Arg 1, 2, NZ, SA, Sm, 2011 F, W, I1, E, It1, 2, [R, Arg, E], 2012 E(R), W(R), F, I, It, A, Fj, SA, Tg(R), 2013 J(R), SA2
**Barnes, I A** (Hawick) 1972 W, 1974 F (R), 1975 E (R), NZ, 1977 I, F, W
**Barrie, R W** (Hawick) 1936 E
**Bearne, K R F** (Cambridge U, London Scottish) 1960 F, W
**Beattie, J A** (Hawick) 1929 F, W, 1930 W, 1931 F, W, I, E, 1932 SA, W, I, E, 1933 W, E, I, 1934 I, E, 1935 W, I, E, NZ, 1936 W, I, E
**Beattie, J R** (Glasgow Acads) 1980 I, F, W, E, 1981 F, W, E, I, 1983 F, W, E, NZ, 1984 E (R), R, A, 1985 I, 1986 F, W, E, I, R, 1987 I, F, W, E
**Beattie, J W** (Glasgow Warriors, Montpellier, Castres) 2006 R, Pl, 2007 F, 2008 Arg 1, 2009 Fj, A, Arg, 2010 F, W, It, E, I, Arg 1, 2, 2011 I1, 2, 2013 E, It1, I, W, F, Sm, SA1, It2, SA2(R), A, 2014 I(R), E(R), It, F, US, C
**Beattie, R S** (Newcastle, Bristol) 2000 NZ 1, 2(R), Sm (R), 2003 E(R), It(R), I 2, [J(R), US, Fj]
**Bedell-Sivright, D R** (Cambridge U, Edinburgh U) 1900 W, 1901 W, I, E, 1902 W, I, E, 1903 W, I, E, 1904 W, I, E, 1905 NZ, 1906 W, I, E, SA, 1907 W, I, E, 1908 W, I
**Bedell-Sivright, J V** (Cambridge U) 1902 W
**Begbie, T A** (Edinburgh Wands) 1881 I, E
**Bell, D L** (Watsonians) 1975 I, F, W, E
**Bell, J A** (Clydesdale) 1901 W, I, E, 1902 W, I, E
**Bell, L H I** (Edinburgh Acads) 1900 E, 1904 W, I
**Berkeley, W V** (Oxford U) 1926 F, 1929 F, W, I
**Berry, C W** (Fettesian-Lorettonians) 1884 I, E, 1885 W, I 1, 1887 I, W, E, 1888 W, I
**Bertram, D M** (Watsonians) 1922 F, W, I, E, 1923 F, W, I, E, 1924 W, I, E
**Beveridge, G** (Glasgow) 2000 NZ 2(R), US (R), Sm (R), 2002 Fj(R), 2003 W 2, 2005 R(R)
**Biggar, A G** (London Scottish) 1969 SA, 1970 F, I, E, A, 1971 F, W, I, E (2[1C]), 1972 F, W
**Biggar, M A** (London Scottish) 1975 I, F, W, E, 1976 W, E, I, 1977 I, F, W, 1978 I, F, W, E, NZ, 1979 W, E, I, F, NZ, 1980 I, F, W, E
**Birkett, G A** (Harlequins, London Scottish) 1975 NZ
**Bishop, J M** (Glasgow Acads) 1893 I
**Bisset, A A** (RIE Coll) 1904 W
**Black, A W** (Edinburgh U) 1947 F, W, 1948 E, 1950 W, I, E
**Black, W P** (Glasgow HSFP) 1948 F, W, I, E, 1951 E
**Blackadder, W F** (W of Scotland) 1938 E
**Blaikie, C F** (Heriot's FP) 1963 I, E, 1966 E, 1968 A, 1969 F, W, I, E
**Blair, M R L** (Edinburgh, Brive) 2002 C, US, 2003 F(t+R), W 1(R), SA 2(R), It 2, I 2, [US], 2004 W(R), E(R), It(R), F(R), I(R), Sm(R), A1(R), 3(R), J(R), A4(R), SA(R), 2005 I(t&R), It(R), W(R), E, R,

Arg, Sm(R), NZ(R), 2006 F, W, E, I, It(R), SA 1, 2, R, Pl(R), A, 2007 I2, SA, [Pt, R, It, Arg], 2008 F, W, I, E, It, Arg 1, 2, NZ, SA, C, 2009 W, F, It, I, E, Fj(R), 2010 W(R), It(R), I(R), Arg 1(R), 2(R), NZ, Sm(R), 2011 F(R), W(R), I1, E(R), It1(R), 2, [R, Arg(R), E], 2012 E(R), W(R), F, I, It, A, Fj, Sm(R), NZ, SA
**Blair, P C B** (Cambridge U) 1912 SA, 1913 F, W, I, E
**Bolton, W H** (W of Scotland) 1876 E
**Borthwick, J B** (Stewart's Coll FP) 1938 W, I
**Bos, F H ten** (Oxford U, London Scottish) 1959 E, 1960 F, W, SA, 1961 F, SA, W, I, E, 1962 F, W, I, E, 1963 F, W, I, E
**Boswell, J D** (W of Scotland) 1889 W, I, 1890 W, I, E, 1891 W, I, E, 1892 W, I, E, 1893 I, E, 1894 I, E
**Bowie, T C** (Watsonians) 1913 I, E, 1914 I, E
**Boyd, G M** (Glasgow HSFP) 1926 E
**Boyle, A C W** (London Scottish) 1963 F, W, I
**Boyle, A H W** (St Thomas's Hospital, London Scottish) 1966 A, 1967 F, NZ, 1968 F, W, I
**Brash, J C** (Cambridge U) 1961 E
**Breakey, R W** (Gosforth) 1978 E
**Brewis, N T** (Edinburgh Inst FP) 1876 E, 1878 E, 1879 I, E, 1880 I, E
**Brewster, A K** (Stewart's-Melville FP) 1977 E, 1980 I, F, 1986 E, I, R
**Brotherstone, S J** (Melrose, Brive, Newcastle) 1999 I (R), 2000 F, W, E, US, A, Sm, 2002 C (R)
**Brown, A H** (Heriot's FP) 1928 E, 1929 F, W
**Brown, A R** (Gala) 1971 E (2[1C]), 1972 F, W, E
**Brown, C H C** (Dunfermline) 1929 E
**Brown, D I** (Cambridge U) 1933 W, E, I
**Brown, F** (Glasgow Warriors) 2013 It2(R)
**Brown, G L** (W of Scotland) 1969 SA, 1970 F, W (R), I, E, A, 1971 F, W, I, E (2[1C]), 1972 F, W, E, NZ, 1973 E (R), P, 1974 W, E, I, F, 1975 I, F, W, E, A, 1976 F, W, E, I
**Brown, J A** (Glasgow Acads) 1908 W, I
**Brown, J B** (Glasgow Acads) 1879 I, E, 1880 I, E, 1881 I, E, 1882 I, E, 1883 W, I, E, 1884 W, I, E, 1885 I 1, 2, 1886 W, I, E
**Brown, K D R** (Borders, Glasgow Warriors) 2005 R, Sm(R), NZ(R), 2006 SA 1(R), 2(R), R, Pl, A, 2007 E, W, It, I1, 2(R), SA, [Pt(R), R(R), NZ, It(R), Arg(R)], 2008 F(R), W, I, E(R), It(R), Arg 1(R), 2(R), 2009 W(R), F(R), It(R), E(R), 2010 F, W, It, E, I, Arg 1, 2, NZ, SA, Sm, 2011 F, W, I1, E, It1, 2, [R, Gg, Arg], 2012 NZ, SA, Tg, 2013 E, It1, I, W, F, Sm, J, A, 2014 I, F, W, C
**Brown, P C** (W of Scotland, Gala) 1964 F, NZ, W, I, E, 1965 I, E, SA, 1966 A, 1969 I, E, 1970 W, E, 1971 F, W, I, E (2[1C]), 1972 F, W, E, NZ, 1973 F, W, I, E, P
**Brown, T G** (Heriot's FP) 1929 W
**Brown, T G** (Edinburgh) 2012 A(R)
**Brown, W D** (Glasgow Acads) 1871 E, 1872 E, 1873 E, 1874 E, 1875 E
**Brown, W S** (Edinburgh Inst FP) 1880 I, E, 1882 I, E, 1883 W, E
**Browning, A** (Glasgow HSFP) 1920 I, 1922 F, W, I, 1923 W, I, E
**Bruce, C R** (Glasgow Acads) 1947 F, W, I, E, 1949 F, W, I, E
**Bruce, N S** (Blackheath, Army and London Scottish) 1958 F, A, I, E, 1959 F, W, I, E, 1960 F, W, I, E, SA, 1961 F, SA, W, I, E, 1962 F, W, I, E, 1963 F, W, I, E, 1964 F, NZ, W, I, E
**Bruce, R M** (Gordonians) 1947 A, 1948 F, W, I
**Bruce-Lockhart, J H** (London Scottish) 1913 W, 1920 E
**Bruce-Lockhart, L** (London Scottish) 1948 E, 1950 F, W, 1953 I, E
**Bruce-Lockhart, R B** (Cambridge U and London Scottish) 1937 I, 1939 I, E
**Bryce, C C** (Glasgow Acads) 1873 E, 1874 E
**Bryce, K** (Glasgow Warriors) 2014 C(R), SA(R)
**Bryce, R D H** (W of Scotland) 1973 I (R)
**Bryce, W E** (Selkirk) 1922 W, I, E, 1923 F, W, I, E, 1924 F, W, I, E
**Brydon, W R C** (Heriot's FP) 1939 W
**Buchanan, A** (Royal HSFP) 1871 E
**Buchanan, F G** (Kelvinside Acads and Oxford U) 1910 F, 1911 F, W
**Buchanan, J C R** (Stewart's Coll FP) 1921 W, I, E, 1922 W, I, E, 1923 F, W, I, E, 1924 F, W, I, E, 1925 F, I
**Buchanan-Smith, G A E** (London Scottish, Heriot's FP) 1989 Fj (R), 1990 Arg
**Bucher, A M** (Edinburgh Acads) 1897 E

Budge, G M (Edinburgh Wands) 1950 F, W, I, E

Bullmore, H H (Edinburgh U) 1902 I

Bulloch, A J (Glasgow) 2000 US, A, Sm, 2001 F (t+R), E

Bulloch, G C (West of Scotland, Glasgow) 1997 SA, 1998 It, I, F, W, E, Fj, A 1, SA, 1999 W, E, It, I, F, Arg, [SA, U, Sm, NZ], 2000 It, I, W (R), NZ 1, 2, A (R), Sm (R), 2001 F, W, E, It, I, Tg, Arg, NZ, 2002 E, It, I, F, W, C, US, R, SA, Fj, 2003 I 1, F, W 1, E, It 1, SA 1, 2, It 2(R ), W2, I 2, [US, F, Fj, A], 2004 W, E, It, F, I, Sm, A1, 2, 3, J, A4, SA, 2005 F, I, It, W, E

Burnell, A P (London Scottish, Montferrand) 1989 E, I, F, Fj, R, 1990 I, F, W, E, Arg, 1991 F, W, E, I, R, [J, Z, I, WS, E, NZ], 1992 E, I, F, W, 1993 I, F, W, NZ, 1994 W, E, I, F, Arg 1, 2, SA, 1995 [Iv, Tg (R), F (R)], WS, 1998 E, SA, 1999 W, E, It, I, F, Arg, [Sp, Sm (R), NZ]

Burnet, P J (London Scottish and Edinburgh Acads) 1960 SA

Burnet, W (Hawick) 1912 E

Burnet, W A (W of Scotland) 1934 W, 1935 W, I, E, NZ, 1936 W, I, E

Burnett, J N (Heriot's FP) 1980 I, F, W, E

Burns, G G (Watsonians, Edinburgh) 1999 It (R), 2001 Tg (R), NZ (R), 2002 US (R)

Burrell, G (Gala) 1950 F, W, I, 1951 SA

Cairns, A G (Watsonians) 1903 W, I, E, 1904 W, I, E, 1905 W, I, E, 1906 W, I, E

Cairns, B J (Edinburgh) 2008 Arg 1, 2, NZ, SA, C, 2009 W, Arg

Calder, F (Stewart's-Melville FP) 1986 F, W, E, I, R, 1987 I, F, W, E, [F, Z, R, NZ], 1988 I, F, W, E, 1989 W, E, I, F, R, 1990 I, F, W, E, NZ 1, 2, 1991 R, [J, I, WS, E, NZ]

Calder, J H (Stewart's-Melville FP) 1981 F, W, E, I, NZ 1, 2, R, A, 1982 E, I, F, W, A 1, 2, 1983 I, F, W, E, NZ, 1984 W, E, I, F, A, 1985 I, F, W

Callam, D A (Edinburgh) 2006 R(R), PI(R), A, 2007 E, W, It, I1, F(R), SA, [NZ], 2008 F

Callander, G J (Kelso) 1984 R, 1988 I, F, W, E, A

Cameron, A (Glasgow HSFP) 1948 W, 1950 I, E, 1951 F, W, I, E, SA, 1953 I, E, 1955 F, W, I, E, 1956 F, W, I

Cameron, A D (Hillhead HSFP) 1951 F, 1954 F, W

Cameron, A W C (Watsonians) 1887 W, 1893 W, 1894 I

Cameron, D (Glasgow HSFP) 1953 I, E, 1954 F, NZ, I, E

Cameron, N W (Glasgow U) 1952 E, 1953 F, W

Campbell, A J (Hawick) 1984 I, F, R, 1985 I, F, W, E, 1986 F, W, E, I, R, 1988 F, W, A

Campbell, G T (London Scottish) 1892 W, I, E, 1893 I, E, 1894 W, I, E, 1895 W, I, E, 1896 W, I, E, 1897 I, 1899 I, 1900 E

Campbell, H H (Cambridge U, London Scottish) 1947 I, E, 1948 I, E

Campbell, J A (W of Scotland) 1878 E, 1879 I, E, 1881 I, E

Campbell, J A (Cambridge U) 1900 I

Campbell, N M (London Scottish) 1956 F, W

Campbell, S J (Dundee HSFP) 1995 C, I, F, W, E, R, [Iv, NZ (R)], WS (t), 1996 I, F, W, E, 1997 A, SA, 1998 Fj (R), A 2(R)

Campbell-Lamerton, J R E (London Scottish) 1986 F, 1987 [Z, R(R)]

Campbell-Lamerton, M J (Halifax, Army, London Scottish) 1961 F, SA, W, I, 1962 F, W, I, E, 1963 F, W, I, E, 1964 I, E, 1965 F, W, I, E, SA, 1966 F, W, I, E

Carmichael, A B (W of Scotland) 1967 I, NZ, 1968 F, W, I, E, A, 1969 F, W, I, E, SA, 1970 F, W, I, E, A, 1971 F, W, I, E (2[1C]), 1972 F, W, E, NZ, 1973 F, W, I, E, P, 1974 W, E, I, F, 1975 I, F, W, E, NZ, A, 1976 F, W, E, I, 1977 E, I (R), F, W, 1978 I

Carmichael, J H (Watsonians) 1921 F, W, I

Carrick, J S (Glasgow Acads) 1876 E, 1877 E

Cassels, D Y (W of Scotland) 1880 E, 1881 I, 1882 I, E, 1883 W, I, E

Cathcart, C W (Edinburgh U) 1872 E, 1873 E, 1876 E

Cawkwell, G L (Oxford U) 1947 F

Chalmers, C M (Melrose) 1989 W, E, I, F, Fj, 1990 I, F, W, E, NZ 1, 2, Arg, 1991 F, W, E, I, R, [J, Z (R), I, WS, E, NZ], 1992 E, I, F, W, A 1, 2, 1993 I, F, W, E, NZ, 1994 W, SA, 1995 C, I, F, W, E, R, [Iv, Tg, F, NZ], WS, 1996 A, It, 1997 W, I, F, A (R), SA, 1998 It, I, F, W, E, 1999 Arg (R)

Chalmers, T (Glasgow Acads) 1871 E, 1872 E, 1873 E, 1874 E, 1875 E, 1876 E

Chambers, H F T (Edinburgh U) 1888 W, I, 1889 W, I

Charters, R G (Hawick) 1955 W, I, E

Chisholm, D H (Melrose) 1964 I, 1965 E, SA, 1966 F, I, E, A, 1967 F, W, NZ, 1968 F, W, I

Chisholm, R W T (Melrose) 1955 I, E, 1956 F, W, I, E, 1958 F, W, A, I, 1960 SA

Church, W C (Glasgow Acads) 1906 W

Clark, R L (Edinburgh Wands, Royal Navy) 1972 F, W, E, NZ, 1973 F, W, I, E, P

Clauss, P R A (Oxford U) 1891 W, I, E, 1892 W, E, 1895 I

Clay, A T (Edinburgh Acads) 1886 W, I, E, 1887 I, W, E, 1888 W, F, W 1, E, It 1, SA 1, 2, It 2(R )

Clunies-Ross, A (St Andrew's U) 1871 E

Coltman, S (Hawick) 1948 I, 1949 F, W, I, E

Colville, A G (Merchistonians, Blackheath) 1871 E, 1872 E

Connell, G C (Trinity Acads and London Scottish) 1968 E, A, 1969 F, E, 1970 F

Cooper, M McG (Oxford U) 1936 W, I

Corcoran, I (Gala) 1992 A 1(R)

Cordial, I F (Edinburgh Wands) 1952 F, W, I, E

Cotter, J L (Hillhead HSFP) 1934 I, E

Cottington, G S (Kelso) 1934 I, E, 1935 W, I, 1936 E

Coughtrie, S (Edinburgh Acads) 1959 F, W, I, E, 1962 W, I, E, 1963 F, W, I, E

Couper, J H (W of Scotland) 1896 W, I, 1899 I

Coutts, F H (Melrose, Army) 1947 W, I, E

Coutts, I D F (Old Alleynians) 1951 F, 1952 E

Cowan, B A (London Irish) 2014 US, C(R), Arg1

Cowan, R C (Selkirk) 1961 F, 1962 F, W, I, E

Cowie, W L K (Edinburgh Wands) 1953 E

Cownie, W B (Watsonians) 1893 W, I, E, 1894 W, I, E, 1895 W, I, E

Crabbie, G E (Edinburgh Acads) 1904 W

Crabbie, J E (Edinburgh Acads, Oxford U) 1900 W, 1902 I, 1903 W, I, 1904 E, 1905 W

Craig, A (Orrell, Glasgow) 2002 C, US, R, SA, Fj, 2003 I 1, F(R), W 1(R), E, It 1, SA 1, 2, W 2, I 2, [J, US, F], 2004 A3(R), 2005 F, I, It, W, E

Craig, J B (Heriot's FP) 1939 W

Craig, J M (West of Scotland, Glasgow) 1997 A, 2001 W (R), E (R), It

Cramb, R I (Harlequins) 1987 [R(R)], 1988 I, F, A

Cranston, A G (Hawick) 1976 W, E, I, 1977 E, W, 1978 F (R), W, E, NZ, 1981 NZ 1, 2

Crawford, J A (Army, London Scottish) 1934 I

Crawford, W H (United Services, RN) 1938 W, I, E, 1939 W, E

Crichton-Miller, D (Gloucester) 1931 W, I, E

Crole, G B (Oxford U) 1920 F, W, I, E

Cronin, D F (Bath, London Scottish, Bourges, Wasps) 1988 I, F, W, E, A, 1989 W, E, I, F, Fj, R, 1990 I, F, W, E, NZ 1, 2, 1991 F, W, E, I, R, [Z], 1992 A 2, 1993 I, F, W, E, NZ, 1995 C, I, F, [Tg, F, NZ], WS, 1996 NZ 1, 2, A, It, 1997 F (R), 1998 I, F, W, E

Cross, G D S (Edinburgh, London Irish) 2009 W, 2010 E(R), 2011 I1(t&R), E(R), It1, I2, [R, Arg], 2012 E(R), W, F, I, It, Fj(R), NZ, SA(R), Tg(t), 2013 It1(R), I, W(R), F(R), Sm(R), J(R), 2014 I(R), E(R), It(R), F, W, US, C(R), Arg1, SA

Cross, M (Merchistonians) 1875 E, 1876 E, 1877 I, E, 1878 E, 1879 I, E, 1880 I, E

Cross, W (Merchistonians) 1871 E, 1872 E

Cumming, R S (Aberdeen U) 1921 F, W

Cunningham, G (Oxford U) 1908 W, I, 1909 W, E, 1910 F, I, E, 1911 E

Cunningham, R F (Gala) 1978 NZ, 1979 W, E

Currie, L R (Dunfermline) 1947 A, 1948 F, W, I, 1949 F, W, I, E

Cusiter, C P (Borders, Perpignan, Glasgow Warriors) 2004 W, E, It, F, I, Sm, A1, 2, 3, J, A4, SA, 2005 F, I, It, W, Arg(R), Sm, NZ, 2006 F(R), W(R), E(R), I(R), It, R(R), PI, 2007 E, W, It, I1, F(R), I2(R), R(R), NZ, It(R), Arg(R)], 2008 F(R), W(R), I(R), 2009 W(R), F(R), It(R), I(R), E(R), Fj, A, Arg, 2010 F, W, It, E, I, 2011 It2(R), [R(R), E(R)], 2012 E, W, F(R), I(R), A(R), Fj(R), Sm, 2013 SA2(R), A(R), 2014 F(R), It(R), W(R)

Cuthbert, J E (Bath) 2011 I2(R)

Cuthbertson, W (Kilmarnock, Harlequins) 1980 I, 1981 W, E, I, NZ 1, 2, R, A, 1982 E, I, F, W, A 1, 2, 1983 I, F, W, NZ, 1984 W, E, A

Dalgleish, A (Gala) 1890 W, E, 1891 W, I, 1892 W, 1893 W, 1894 W, I

Dalgleish, K J (Edinburgh Wands, Cambridge U) 1951 I, E, 1953 F, W

Dall, A K (Edinburgh) 2003 W 2(R)

**Fisher, J P** (Royal HSFP, London Scottish) 1963 E, 1964 F, NZ, W, I, E, 1965 F, W, I, E, SA, 1966 F, W, I, E, A, 1967 F, W, I, E, NZ, 1968 F, W, I, E
**Fleming, C J N** (Edinburgh Wands) 1896 I, E, 1897 I
**Fleming, G R** (Glasgow Acads) 1875 E, 1876 E
**Fletcher, H N** (Edinburgh U) 1904 E, 1905 W
**Flett, A B** (Edinburgh U) 1901 W, I, E, 1902 W, I
**Forbes, J L** (Watsonians) 1905 W, 1906 I, E
**Ford, D St C** (United Services, RN) 1930 I, E, 1931 E, 1932 W, I
**Ford, J R** (Gala) 1893 I
**Ford, R W** (Borders, Glasgow, Edinburgh) 2004 A3(R), 2006 W(R), E(R), Pl(R), A(R), 2007 E(R), W(R), It(R), F, I2, SA, [Pt(R), R, It, Arg], 2008 F, W, I, E, Arg 1, 2, NZ, SA, C, 2009 W, F, It, I, E, Fj, A, Arg, 2010 F, W, It, E, I, Arg 1, 2, NZ, SA, Sm, 2011 F, W, I1, I2, [R, Gg, Arg, E], 2012 E, W, F, I, It, A, Fj, Sm, NZ, SA, 2013 E(R), It1, I, W, F, J, SA2, A, 2014 I, E, F(R), W(R), Arg1, SA
**Forrest, J E** (Glasgow Acads) 1932 SA, 1935 E, NZ
**Forrest, J G S** (Cambridge U) 1938 W, I, E
**Forrest, W T** (Hawick) 1903 W, I, E, 1904 W, I, E, 1905 W, I
**Forsayth, H H** (Oxford U) 1921 F, W, I, E, 1922 W, I, E
**Forsyth, I W** (Stewart's Coll FP) 1972 NZ, 1973 F, W, I, E, P
**Forsyth, J** (Edinburgh U) 1871 E
**Foster, R A** (Hawick) 1930 W, 1932 SA, I, E
**Fox, J** (Gala) 1952 F, W, I, E
**Frame, J N M** (Edinburgh U, Gala) 1967 NZ, 1968 F, W, I, E, 1969 W, I, E, SA, 1970 F, W, I, E, A, 1971 F, W, I, E (2[1C]), 1972 F, W, E, 1973 P (R)
**France, C** (Kelvinside Acads) 1903 I
**Fraser, C F P** (Glasgow U) 1888 W, 1889 W
**Fraser, J W** (Edinburgh Inst FP) 1881 E
**Fraser, R** (Cambridge U) 1911 F, W, I, E
**French, J** (Glasgow Acads) 1886 W, 1887 I, W, E
**Frew, A** (Edinburgh U) 1901 W, I, E
**Frew, G M** (Glasgow HSFP) 1906 SA, 1907 W, I, E, 1908 W, I, E, 1909 W, I, E, 1910 F, W, I, 1911 I, E
**Friebe, J P** (Glasgow HSFP) 1952 E
**Fullarton, I A** (Edinburgh) 2000 NZ 1(R), 2, 2001 NZ (R), 2003 It 2(R), I 2(t), 2004 Sm(R), A1(R), 2
**Fulton, A K** (Edinburgh U, Dollar Acads) 1952 F, 1954 F
**Fusaro, C C** (Glasgow Warriors) 2014 E, It, Arg1(R), SA
**Fyfe, K C** (Cambridge U, Sale, London Scottish) 1933 W, E, 1934 E, 1935 W, I, E, NZ, 1936 W, E, 1939 I

**Gallie, G H** (Edinburgh Acads) 1939 W
**Gallie, R A** (Glasgow Acads) 1920 F, W, I, E, 1921 F, W, I, E
**Gammell, W B B** (Edinburgh Wands) 1977 I, F, W, 1978 W, E
**Geddes, I C** (London Scottish) 1906 SA, 1907 W, I, E, 1908 W, E
**Geddes, K I** (London Scottish) 1947 F, W, I, E
**Gedge, H T S** (Oxford U, London Scottish, Edinburgh Wands) 1894 W, I, E, 1896 E, 1899 W, E
**Gedge, P M S** (Edinburgh Wands) 1933 I
**Gemmill, R** (Glasgow HSFP) 1950 F, W, I, E, 1951 F, W, I
**Gibson, W R** (Royal HSFP) 1891 I, E, 1892 W, I, E, 1893 W, I, E, 1894 W, I, E, 1895 W, I, E
**Gilbert-Smith, D S** (London Scottish) 1952 E
**Gilchrist, G S** (Edinburgh) 2013 F, Sm, It2(R), A, 2014 US(R), C, Arg1, SA
**Gilchrist, J** (Glasgow Acads) 1925 F
**Gill, A D** (Gala) 1973 P, 1974 W, E, I, F
**Gillespie, J I** (Edinburgh Acads) 1899 E, 1900 W, E, 1901 W, I, E, 1902 W, I, 1904 I, E
**Gillies, A C** (Watsonians) 1924 W, I, E, 1925 F, W, E, 1926 F, W, 1927 F, W, I, E
**Gilmour, H R** (Heriot's FP) 1998 Fj
**Gilray, C M** (Oxford U, London Scottish) 1908 E, 1909 W, E, 1912 I
**Glasgow, I C** (Heriot's FP) 1997 F (R)
**Glasgow, R J C** (Dunfermline) 1962 F, W, I, E, 1963 I, E, 1964 I, E, 1965 W, I
**Glen, W S** (Edinburgh Wands) 1955 W
**Gloag, L G** (Cambridge U) 1949 F, W, I, E
**Godman, P J** (Edinburgh) 2005 R(R), Sm(R), NZ(R), 2006 R, Pl(R), A(t&R), 2007 W, It, 2008 Arg 2, NZ, SA, C, 2009 W, F, It, I, E, Fj, A, Arg, 2010 F, W(R), E(R)
**Goodfellow, J** (Langholm) 1928 W, I, E

**Goodhue, F W J** (London Scottish) 1890 W, I, E, 1891 W, I, E, 1892 W, I, E
**Gordon, R** (Edinburgh Wands) 1951 W, 1952 F, W, I, E, 1953 W
**Gordon, R E** (Royal Artillery) 1913 F, W, I
**Gordon, R J** (London Scottish) 1982 A 1, 2
**Gore, A C** (London Scottish) 1882 I
**Gossman, B M** (W of Scotland) 1980 W, 1983 F, W
**Gossman, J S** (W of Scotland) 1980 E (R)
**Gowans, J J** (Cambridge U, London Scottish) 1893 W, 1894 W, E, 1895 W, I, E, 1896 I, E
**Gowland, G C** (London Scottish) 1908 W, 1909 W, E, 1910 F, W, I, E
**Gracie, A L** (Harlequins) 1921 F, W, I, E, 1922 F, W, I, E, 1923 F, W, I, E, 1924 F
**Graham, G** (Newcastle) 1997 A (R), SA (R), 1998 I, F (R), W (R), 1999 F(R), Arg (R), R, [SA, U, Sm, NZ (R)], 2000 I (R), US, A, Sm, 2001 I (R), Tg (R), Arg (R), NZ (R), 2002 E (R), It (R), I (R), F (R), W (R)
**Graham, I N** (Edinburgh Acads) 1939 I, E
**Graham, J** (Kelso) 1926 I, E, 1927 F, W, I, E, A, 1928 F, W, I, E, 1930 I, 1932 SA, W
**Graham, J H S** (Edinburgh Acads) 1876 E, 1877 I, E, 1878 E, 1879 I, E, 1880 I, E, 1881 I, E
**Grant, D** (Hawick) 1965 F, E, SA, 1966 F, W, I, E, A, 1967 F, W, I, E, NZ, 1968 F
**Grant, D M** (East Midlands) 1911 W, I
**Grant, M L** (Harlequins) 1955 F, 1956 F, W, 1957 F
**Grant, P** (Glasgow Warriors) 2012 A, Fj, Sm, NZ, SA, 2013 E, It1, I, W, F, J, SA2(R), A, 2014 I, E, It, F, W
**Grant, T O** (Hawick) 1960 I, E, SA, 1964 F, NZ, W
**Grant, W St C** (Craigmount) 1873 E, 1874 E
**Gray, C A** (Nottingham) 1989 W, E, I, F, Fj, R, 1990 I, F, W, E, NZ 1, 2, Arg, 1991 F, W, E, I, [J, I, WS, E, NZ]
**Gray, D** (W of Scotland) 1978 E, 1979 I, F, NZ, 1980 I, F, W, E, 1981 F
**Gray, G L** (Gala) 1935 NZ, 1937 W, I, E
**Gray, J D** (Glasgow Warriors) 2013 SA2(R), A(R), 2014 E(R), Arg1, SA(R)
**Gray, R J** (Glasgow Warriors, Sale) 2010 F(R), W(R), I(R), NZ, SA, Sm, 2011 F, I1, E, It1, I2, It2(R), [R, Gg(R), Arg, E], 2012 E, W, F, I, It, A, Fj, Sm, NZ, Tg, 2013 E, It1, I, W, J(R), SA2, 2014 I(R), It, F, W, US, C
**Gray, S D** (Borders, Northampton) 2004 A3, 2008 NZ(R), SA(R), C(R), 2009 W(R), It(R), I(R), E
**Gray, T** (Northampton, Heriot's FP) 1950 E, 1951 F, E
**Greenlees, H D** (Leicester) 1927 A, 1928 F, W, 1929 I, E, 1930 E
**Greenlees, J R C** (Cambridge U, Kelvinside Acads) 1900 I, 1902 W, I, E, 1903 W, I, E
**Greenwood, J T** (Dunfermline and Perthshire Acads) 1952 F, 1955 F, W, I, E, 1956 F, W, I, E, 1957 W, E, 1958 F, W, A, I, E, 1959 F, W, I
**Greig, A** (Glasgow HSFP) 1911 I
**Greig, L L** (Glasgow Acads, United Services) 1905 NZ, 1906 SA, 1907 W, 1908 W, I
**Greig, R C** (Glasgow Acads) 1893 W, 1897 I
**Grieve, C F** (Oxford U) 1935 W, 1936 E
**Grieve, R M** (Kelso) 1935 W, I, E, NZ, 1936 W, I, E
**Grimes, S B** (Watsonians, Newcastle) 1997 A (t+R), 1998 I (R), F (R), W (R), E (R), Fj, A 1, 2, 1999 W (R), E, It, I, F, Arg, R, [SA, U, Sm (R), NZ (R)], 2000 It, I, F (R), W, US, A, Sm (R), 2001 F (R), W (R), E (R), It, I (R), Tg, Arg, NZ, 2002 E, It, I, F (R), W (R), C, SA, R, Fj, 2003 I 1, F, W 1, E(R), It 1(R), W 2, I 2, [J, US, F, Fj, A], 2004 W, E, It, F, I, Sm, A1, J, A4, SA, 2005 F, I, It, W, E(R)
**Grove, A** (Worcester) 2009 Fj, A, Arg
**Gunn, A W** (Royal HSFP) 1912 F, W, I, SA, 1913 F

**Hall, A J A** (Glasgow) 2002 US (R)
**Hall, D W H** (Edinburgh, Glasgow Warriors) 2003 W 2(R), 2005 R(R), Arg, Sm(R), NZ(R), 2006 F, E, I, It(R), SA 1(R), 2, R, Pl, A, 2007 E, W, It, I1, F(R), 2008 Arg 2(R), NZ(R), SA(R), C(R), 2009 W(R), F(R), It(R), I(R), E(R), Fj(R), A(R), Arg(R), 2010 SA(R), Sm(R), 2011 F(R), I2(R), It2(R), [Arg(R)], 2012 SA(R), Tg(R), 2013 E, I(R), F(R)
**Hamilton, A S** (Headingley) 1914 W, 1920 F
**Hamilton, C P** (Newcastle) 2004 A2(R), 2005 R, Arg, Sm, NZ
**Hamilton, H M** (W of Scotland) 1874 E, 1875 E

F, W, E, [F, Z, R], 1988 I, W, A, 1989 W, E, I, F, Fj, R, 1990 I, F, W, E, NZ 1, 2, Arg, 1991 F, W, E, I, [J, I, WS, E, NZ]
**Johnston, D I** (Watsonians) 1979 NZ, 1980 I, F, W, E, 1981 R, A, 1982 E, I, F, W, A 1, 2, 1983 I, F, W, NZ, 1984 W, E, I, F, R, 1986 F, W, E, I, R
**Johnston, H H** (Edinburgh Collegian FP) 1877 I, E
**Johnston, J** (Melrose) 1951 SA, 1952 F, W, I, E
**Johnston, W C** (Glasgow HSFP) 1922 F
**Johnston, W G S** (Cambridge U) 1935 W, I, 1937 W, I, E
**Joiner, C A** (Melrose, Leicester) 1994 Arg 1, 2, 1995 C, I, F, W, E, R, [Iv, Tg, F, NZ], 1996 I, F, W, E, NZ 1, 1997 SA, 1998 It, I, A 2(R), 2000 NZ 1(R), 2, US (R)
**Jones, L** (Edinburgh) 2012 E, W, F, I
**Jones, P M** (Gloucester) 1992 W (R)
**Junor, J E** (Glasgow Acads) 1876 E, 1877 I, E, 1878 E, 1879 E, 1881 I

**Kalman, E D** (Glasgow Warriors) 2012 W(R), F(R)
**Keddie, R R** (Watsonians) 1967 NZ
**Keith, G J** (Wasps) 1968 F, W
**Keller, D H** (London Scottish) 1949 F, W, I, E, 1950 F, W, I
**Kellock, A D** (Edinburgh, Glasgow Warriors) 2004 A3(t&R), 2005 R(R), Arg(R), Sm(R), NZ(R), 2006 F, W, E, It(R), SA 1(R), 2, PI(R), A, 2007 E, 2008 Arg 1(t&R), 2(R), 2009 It, Fj, A, Arg, 2010 F, W, It, E, I, Arg 1, 2, 2011 F, W, I1, E, It1, I2(R), It2, [R, E], 2012 E(R), W(R), F(R), I(R), It(R), A, Fj, Sm, NZ(R), SA(R), Tg, 2013 E(R), It1(R), I(R), W(R), F(R), Sm, SA1(R), It2, J
**Kelly, R F** (Watsonians) 1927 A, 1928 F, W, E
**Kemp, J W Y** (Glasgow HSFP) 1954 W, 1955 F, W, I, E, 1956 F, W, I, E, 1957 F, W, I, E, 1958 F, W, A, I, E, 1959 F, W, I, E, 1960 F, W, I, E, SA
**Kennedy, A E** (Watsonians) 1983 NZ, 1984 W, E, A
**Kennedy, F** (Stewart's Coll FP) 1920 F, W, I, E, 1921 E
**Kennedy, N** (W of Scotland) 1903 W, I, E
**Ker, A B M** (Kelso) 1988 W, E
**Ker, H T** (Glasgow Acads) 1887 I, W, E, 1888 I, 1889 W, 1890 I, E
**Kerr, D S** (Heriot's FP) 1923 F, W, 1924 F, 1926 I, E, 1927 W, I, E, 1928 I, E
**Kerr, G** (Leeds, Borders, Glasgow, Edinburgh) 2003 I 1(R), F(R), W 1(R), E(R), SA 1, 2, W 2, [J(R), US, F], 2004 W(R), E(R), It(R), F(R), I(R), J, A4, SA, 2005 F, I, It, W, E, Arg, Sm(R), NZ, 2006 F, W, E, I, It, SA 1, 2, R, PI, A, 2007 E, W, It, I1, F, SA [Pt(R), R, NZ(R), It, Arg], 2008 F(R), W(R), I(R)
**Kerr, G C** (Old Dunelmians, Edinburgh Wands) 1898 I, E, 1899 I, W, E, 1900 W, I, E
**Kerr, J M** (Heriot's FP) 1935 NZ, 1936 I, E, 1937 W, I
**Kerr, R C** (Glasgow) 2002 C, US, 2003 W 2
**Kerr, W** (London Scottish) 1953 E
**Kidston, D W** (Glasgow Acads) 1883 W, E
**Kidston, W H** (W of Scotland) 1874 E
**Kilgour, I J** (RMC Sandhurst) 1921 F
**King, J H F** (Selkirk) 1953 F, W, E, 1954 E
**Kininmonth, P W** (Oxford U, Richmond) 1949 F, W, I, E, 1950 F, W, I, E, 1951 F, W, I, E, SA, 1952 F, W, I, 1954 F, NZ, I, E, W
**Kinnear, R M** (Heriot's FP) 1926 F, W, I
**Knox, J** (Kelvinside Acads) 1903 W, I, E
**Kyle, W E** (Hawick) 1902 W, I, E, 1903 W, I, E, 1904 W, I, E, 1905 W, I, E, NZ, 1906 W, I, E, 1908 E, 1909 W, I, E, 1910 W

**Laidlaw, A S** (Hawick) 1897 I
**Laidlaw, F A L** (Melrose) 1965 F, W, I, E, SA, 1966 F, W, I, E, A, 1967 F, W, I, E, NZ, 1968 F, W, I, A, 1969 F, W, I, E, SA, 1970 F, W, I, E, A, 1971 F, W, I
**Laidlaw, G D** (Edinburgh, Gloucester) 2010 NZ(R), 2011 I2(R), 2012 E(R), W, F, I, It, A, Fj, Sm, NZ, SA, Tg, 2013 E, It1, I, W, F, Sm, SA1, It2, J, SA2, A, 2014 I, E, It, F, W, US, C
**Laidlaw, R J** (Jedforest) 1980 I, F, W, E, 1981 F, W, E, I, NZ 1, 2, R, A, 1982 E, I, F, W, A 1, 2, 1983 I, F, W, E, NZ, 1984 W, E, I, F, R, A 1985 I, F, 1986 F, W, E, I, R, 1987 I, F, W, E, [F, R, NZ], 1988 I, F, W, E
**Laing, A D** (Royal HSFP) 1914 W, I, E, 1920 F, W, I, 1921 F
**Lambie, I K** (Watsonians) 1978 NZ (R), 1979 W, E, NZ
**Lambie, L B** (Glasgow HSFP) 1934 W, I, E, 1935 W, I, E, NZ
**Lamond, G A W** (Kelvinside Acads) 1899 W, E, 1905 E

**467**

**Lamont, R P** (Glasgow, Sale, Toulon, Glasgow Warriors) 2005 W, E, R, Arg, Sm, 2007 E(R), I1(R), F(R), I2, SA, [Pt, R, It, Arg], 2008 F, I, E, SA, C, 2009 Fj, A, Arg, 2010 W, NZ, 2011 It2, [Gg], 2012 E, W, F
**Lamont, S F** (Glasgow, Northampton, Llanelli Scarlets, Glasgow Warriors) 2004 Sm, A1, 2, 3, J, A4, SA, 2005 F, I, It, W, E, R, Arg, Sm, NZ, 2006 F, W, E, I, It, SA1, R, PI, A, 2007 E, W, It, I1, F, I2, [Pt, R, It, Arg], 2008 NZ, 2009 W, Fj, A, Arg, 2010 F, W, It, E, I, Arg1, 2, NZ, SA, Sm, 2011 F(R), W(R), I1, E, It1, I2, [R, Gg, Arg, E], 2012 E, W, F, I, It, A, Fj(R), Sm, NZ, SA, Tg, 2013 E, It1, I, W, F, Sm, SA1, It2, J, SA2, A, 2014 I, E, It, F, US, C
**Laney, B J** (Edinburgh) 2001 NZ, 2002 E, It, I, F, W, C, US, R, SA, Fj, 2003 I 1, F, SA 2(R), It 2(R), W 2, 2004 W, E, It, I(R)
**Lang, D** (Paisley) 1876 E, 1877 I
**Langrish, R W** (London Scottish) 1930 F, 1931 F, W, I
**Lauder, W** (Neath) 1969 I, E, SA, 1970 F, W, I, A, 1973 F, 1974 W, E, I, F, 1975 I, F, NZ, A, 1976 F, 1977 E
**Laughland, I H P** (London Scottish) 1959 F, 1960 F, W, I, E, 1961 SA, W, I, E, 1962 F, W, I, E, 1963 F, W, I, 1964 F, NZ, W, I, E, 1965 F, W, I, E, SA, 1966 F, W, I, E, 1967 E
**Lawrie, J R** (Melrose) 1922 F, W, I, E, 1923 F, W, I, E, 1924 W, I, E
**Lawrie, K G** (Gala) 1980 F (R), W, E
**Lawrie, S** (Edinburgh) 2013 Sm(R)
**Lawson, A J M** (Edinburgh Wands, London Scottish) 1972 F (R), E, 1973 F, 1974 W, E, 1976 E, I, 1977 E, 1978 NZ, 1979 W, E, I, F, NZ, 1980 W (R)
**Lawson, R G M** (Gloucester, Newcastle) 2006 A(R), 2007 E(R), W(R), It(R), I1(R), F, SA(R), [Pt(R), NZ(R)], 2008 E(R), Arg1(R), 2(R), NZ(R), SA(R), C(R), 2009 A(R), Arg(R), 2010 E(R), Arg 1, 2, SA, Sm, 2011 F, W, I1(R), E, It1, I2, [Gg, Arg], 2012 Tg(R)
**Lawson, S** (Glasgow, Sale, Gloucester, London Irish, Newcastle) 2005 R, Arg(R), Sm, NZ, 2006 F(R), W, I(R), It, SA 1, 2(R), R(R), 2007 [Pt, R(R), NZ, Arg(R)], 2008 It(R), 2010 F(R), W(R), E(R), I(R), Arg1(R), 2(R), NZ(R), 2011 W (R), I1(R), E(R), It1(R), 2, [R(R)], 2012 E(R), W(R), F(R), Fj(R), Sm(R), NZ(R), Tg, 2013 SA1, It2, SA2(R), 2014 E(R), It, F, W, US, C
**Lawther, T H B** (Old Millhillians) 1932 SA, W
**Ledingham, G A** (Aberdeen GSFP) 1913 F
**Lee, D J** (London Scottish, Edinburgh) 1998 I (R), F, W, E, Fj, A 1, 2, SA, 2001 Arg, 2004 It(R), F, I(R)
**Lees, J B** (Gala) 1947 I, A, 1948 F, W, E
**Leggatt, H T O** (Watsonians) 1891 W, I, E, 1892 W, I, 1893 W, E, 1894 I, E
**Lely, W G** (Cambridge U, London Scottish) 1909 I
**Leslie, D G** (Dundee HSFP, W of Scotland, Gala) 1975 I, F, W, E, NZ, A, 1976 F, W, E, I, 1978 NZ, 1980 E, 1981 W, E, I, NZ 1, 2, R, A, 1982 E, 1983 I, F, W, E, 1984 W, E, I, F, R, 1985 F, W, E
**Leslie, J A** (Glasgow, Northampton) 1998 SA, 1999 W, E, It, I, F, [SA], 2000 It, F, W, US, A, Sm, 2001 F, W, E, It, I, Tg, Arg, NZ, 2002 F, W
**Leslie, M D** (Glasgow, Edinburgh) 1998 SA (R), 1999 W, E, It, I, F, R, [SA, U, Sm, NZ], 2000 It, I, F, W, E, NZ 1, 2, 2001 F, W, E, It, 2002 It (R), I (R), F, W, R, SA, Fj(R), 2003 I 1, F, SA 1(R), 2 (R), It 2(R), W 2, [J(R), US(R)]
**Liddell, E H** (Edinburgh U) 1922 F, W, I, 1923 F, W, I, E
**Lind, H** (Dunfermline) 1928 I, 1931 F, W, I, E, 1932 SA, W, E, 1933 W, E, I, 1934 W, I, E, 1935 I, 1936 E
**Lindsay, A B** (London Hospital) 1910 I, 1911 I
**Lindsay, G C** (London Scottish) 1884 W, 1885 I 1, 1887 W, E
**Lindsay-Watson, R H** (Hawick) 1909 I
**Lineen, S R P** (Boroughmuir) 1989 W, E, I, F, Fj, R, 1990 I, F, W, E, NZ 1, 2, Arg, 1991 F, W, E, I, R, [J, Z, I, E, NZ], 1992 E, I, F, W, A 1, 2
**Little, A W** (Hawick) 1905 W
**Logan, K M** (Stirling County, Wasps) 1992 A 2, 1993 E (R), NZ (t), 1994 W, E, I, F, Arg 1, 2, SA, 1995 C, I, F, W, E, R, [Iv, Tg, F, NZ], WS, 1996 W (R), NZ 1, 2, A, It, 1997 W, E, I, F, A, 1998 I, F, SA (R), 1999 W, E, It, I, F, Arg, R, [SA, U, Sm, NZ], 2000 It, I, F, Sm, 2001 F, W, It, 2002 I (R), F, W 1, E, It 1, SA 1, 2, It 2, I 2, [J, US(R), F, Fj, A]
**Logan, W R** (Edinburgh U, Edinburgh Wands) 1931 E, 1932 SA, W, I, 1933 W, E, I, 1934 W, I, E, 1935 W, I, E, NZ, 1936 W, I, E, 1937 W, I, E
**Longstaff, S L** (Dundee HSFP, Glasgow) 1998 F (R), W, E, Fj,

Madsen, D F (Gosforth) 1974 W, E, I, F, 1975 I, F, W, E, 1976 F, 1977 E, I, F, W, 1978 I
Mair, N G R (Edinburgh U) 1951 F, W, I, E
Maitland, G (Edinburgh Inst FP) 1885 W, I 2
Maitland, R (Edinburgh Inst FP) 1881 E, 1882 I, E, 1884 W, 1885 W
Maitland, R P (Royal Artillery) 1872 E
Maitland, S D (Glasgow Warriors) 2013 E, It1, I, W, F, J, SA2, A, 2014 I, US, C, Arg1, SA
Malcolm, A G (Glasgow U) 1888 I
Manson, J J (Dundee HSFP) 1995 E (R)
Marsh, J (Edinburgh Inst FP) 1889 W, I
Marshall, A (Edinburgh Acads) 1875 E
Marshall, G R (Selkirk) 1988 A (R), 1989 Fj, 1990 Arg, 1991 [Z]
Marshall, J C (London Scottish) 1954 F, NZ, I, E, W
Marshall, K W (Edinburgh Acads) 1934 W, I, E, 1935 W, I, E, 1936 W, 1937 E
Marshall, T R (Edinburgh Acads) 1871 E, 1872 E, 1873 E, 1874 E
Marshall, W (Edinburgh Acads) 1872 E
Martin, H (Edinburgh Acads, Oxford U) 1908 W, I, E, 1909 W, E
Masters, W H (Edinburgh Inst FP) 1879 I, 1880 I, E
Mather, C G (Edinburgh, Glasgow) 1999 R (R), [Sp, Sm (R)], 2000 F (t), 2003 [F, Fj, A], 2004 W, E, F
Maxwell, F T (Royal Engineers) 1872 E
Maxwell, G H H P (Edinburgh Acads, RAF, London Scottish) 1913 I, E, 1914 W, I, E, 1920 W, E, 1921 F, W, I, E, 1922 F, E
Maxwell, J M (Langholm) 1957 I
Mayer, M J M (Watsonians, Edinburgh) 1998 SA, 1999 [SA (R), U, Sp, Sm, NZ], 2000 It, I
Mein, J (Edinburgh Acads) 1871 E, 1872 E, 1873 E, 1874 E, 1875 E
Melville, C L (Army) 1937 W, I, E
Menzies, H F (W of Scotland) 1893 W, I, 1894 W, E
Metcalfe, G H (Glasgow Hawks, Glasgow) 1998 A 1, 2, 1999 W, E, It, I, F, Arg, R, [SA, U, Sm, NZ], 2000 It, I, F, W, E, 2001 I, Tg, 2002 E, It, I, F, W (R), C, US, 2003 I 1, F, W 1 E, It 1, SA 1, 2, W 2, I 2, [US, F, Fj, A]
Metcalfe, R (Northampton, Edinburgh) 2000 E, NZ 1, 2, US (R), A (R), Sm, 2001 F, W, E
Methuen, A (London Scottish) 1889 W, I
Michie, E J S (Aberdeen U, Aberdeen GSFP) 1954 F, NZ, I, E, 1955 W, I, E, 1956 F, W, I, E, 1957 F, W, I, E
Millar, J N (W of Scotland) 1892 W, I, E, 1893 W, 1895 I, E
Millar, R K (London Scottish) 1924 I
Millican, J G (Edinburgh U) 1973 W, I, E
Milne, C J B (Fettesian-Lorettonians, W of Scotland) 1886 W, I, E
Milne, D F (Heriot's FP) 1991 [J(R)]
Milne, I G (Heriot's FP, Harlequins) 1979 I, F, NZ, 1980 I, F, 1981 NZ 1, 2, R, A, 1982 E, I, F, W, A 1, 2, 1983 I, F, W, NZ, 1984 W, E, I, F, A, 1985 F, W, E, 1986 F, W, E, I, R, 1987 I, F, W, E, [F, Z, NZ], 1988 A, 1989 W, 1990 NZ 1, 2
Milne, K S (Heriot's FP) 1989 W, E, I, F, Fj, R, 1990 I, F, W, E, NZ 2, Arg, 1991 F, W (R), E, [Z], 1992 E, I, F, W, A 1, 1993 I, F, W, E, NZ, 1994 W, E, I, F, SA, 1995 C, I, F, W, E, [Tg, F, NZ]
Milne, W M (Glasgow Acads) 1904 I, E, 1905 W, I
Milroy, E (Watsonians) 1910 W, 1911 E, 1912 W, I, E, SA, 1913 F, W, I, E, 1914 I, E
Mitchell, G W E (Edinburgh Wands) 1967 NZ, 1968 F, W
Mitchell, J G (W of Scotland) 1885 W, I 1, 2
Moffat, J S D (Edinburgh, Borders) 2002 R, SA, Fj(R), 2004 A3
Moir, C C (Northampton) 2000 W, E, NZ 1
Moncreiff, F J (Edinburgh Acads) 1871 E, 1872 E, 1873 E
Monteith, H G (Cambridge U, London Scottish) 1905 E, 1906 W, I, E, SA, 1907 W, I, 1908 E
Monypenny, D B (London Scottish) 1899 I, W, E
Moodie, A R (St Andrew's U) 1909 E, 1910 F, 1911 F
Moore, A (Edinburgh Acads) 1990 NZ 2, Arg, 1991 F, W, E
Morgan, D W (Stewart's-Melville FP) 1973 W, I, E, P, 1974 I, F, 1975 I, F, W, E, NZ, A, 1976 F, W, 1977 I, F, W, 1978 I, F, W
Morrison, G A (Glasgow Warriors) 2004 A1(R), 2(R), 3, J(R), A4(R), SA(R), 2008 W(R), E, It, Arg 1, 2, 2009 W, F, It, I, E, Fj, A, 2010 F, W, It, E, I, Arg 1, 2, NZ, Sm, 2011 I2, It2, [Gg, Arg], 2012 F, I, It

Morrison, I R (London Scottish) 1993 I, F, W, E, 1994 W, SA, 1995 C, I, F, W, E, R, [Tg, F, NZ]
Morrison, M C (Royal HSFP) 1896 W, I, E, 1897 I, E, 1898 I, E, 1899 I, W, E, 1900 W, E, 1901 W, I, E, 1902 W, I, E, 1903 W, I, 1904 W, I, E
Morrison, R H (Edinburgh U) 1886 W, I, E
Morrison, W H (Edinburgh Acads) 1900 W
Morton, D S (W of Scotland) 1887 I, W, E, 1888 W, I, 1889 W, I, 1890 I, E
Mowat, J G (Glasgow Acads) 1883 W, E
Mower, A L (Newcastle) 2001 Tg, Arg, NZ, 2002 It, 2003 I 1, F, W 1, E, It 1, SA 1, 2, W 2, I 2
Muir, D E (Heriot's FP) 1950 F, W, I, E, 1952 W, I, E
Munnoch, N M (Watsonians) 1952 F, W, I
Munro, D S (Glasgow High Kelvinside) 1994 W, E, I, F, Arg 1, 2, 1997 W (R)
Munro, P (Oxford U, London Scottish) 1905 W, I, E, NZ, 1906 W, I, E, SA, 1907 I, E, 1911 F, W, I
Munro, R (St Andrew's U) 1871 E
Munro, S (Ayr, W of Scotland) 1980 I, F, 1981 F, W, E, I, NZ 1, 2, R, 1984 W
Munro, W H (Glasgow HSFP) 1947 I, E
Murchie, P E (Glasgow Warriors) 2013 SA1, It2, 2014 SA(R)
Murdoch, W C W (Hillhead HSFP) 1935 E, NZ, 1936 W, I, 1939 E, 1948 F, W, I, E
Murray, C A (Hawick, Edinburgh) 1998 E (R), Fj, A 1, 2, SA, 1999 W, E, It, I, F, Arg, [SA, U, Sp, Sm, NZ], 2000 NZ 2, US, A, Sm, 2001 F, W, E, It (R), Tg, Arg
Murray, E A (Northampton, Newcastle, Worcester, Glasgow Warriors) 2005 R(R), 2006 R, PI, A, 2007 E, W, It, I1, F, I2, SA, [Pt, R, It, Arg], 2008 F, W, I, E, It, Arg 1, 2, NZ, SA, C, 2009 It, I, E, 2010 W, It, E, I, NZ, SA, Sm, 2011 F, W, It1(R), 2(R), [Gg, Eg], 2012 E, I(R), It(R), A, Fj, Sm, SA, Tg, 2013 E, It1, W, F, Sm, SA1, It2, J, A(R), 2014 W(R), SA(R)
Murray, G M (Glasgow Acads) 1921 I, 1926 W
Murray, H M (Glasgow U) 1936 W, I
Murray, K T (Hawick) 1985 I, F, W
Murray, R O (Cambridge U) 1935 W, E
Murray, S (Bedford, Saracens, Edinburgh) 1997 A, SA, 1998 It, Fj, A 1, 2, SA, 1999 W, E, It, I, F, Arg, R, [SA, U, Sm, NZ], 2000 It, I, F, W, E, NZ 1, US, A, Sm, 2001 F, W, E, It, I, Tg, Arg, NZ, 2002 E, It, I, F, W, R, SA, 2003 I 1, F, W 1, E, It 1, SA 1, 2, F, 2, [J, F, A(R)], 2004 W, E, I, F, I, Sm, A1, 2, 2005 F, I, It, W, E, R, Arg, Sm, NZ, 2006 F, W, I, It, SA1, R, PI, A, 2007 E(t&R), W, It, I1, F, SA(R), [Pt, NZ]
Murray, W A K (London Scottish) 1920 F, I, 1921 F
Mustchin, M L (Edinburgh) 2008 Arg 1, 2, NZ(R), SA(R), C(R)

Napier, H M (W of Scotland) 1877 I, E, 1878 E, 1879 I, E
Neill, J B (Edinburgh Acads) 1963 E, 1964 F, NZ, W, I, E, 1965 F
Neill, R M (Edinburgh Acads) 1901 E, 1902 I
Neilson, G T (W of Scotland) 1891 W, I, E, 1892 W, E, 1893 W, 1894 W, I, 1895 W, I, E, 1896 W, I, E
Neilson, J A (Glasgow Acads) 1878 E, 1879 E
Neilson, R T (W of Scotland) 1898 I, E, 1899 I, W, 1900 I, E
Neilson, T (W of Scotland) 1874 E
Neilson, W (Merchiston Castle School, Cambridge U, London Scottish) 1891 W, E, 1892 W, I, E, 1893 I, E, 1894 E, 1895 W, I, E, 1896 I, 1897 I, E
Neilson, W G (Merchistonians) 1894 E
Nelson, J B (Glasgow Acads) 1925 F, W, I, E, 1926 F, W, I, E, 1927 F, W, I, E, 1928 I, E, 1929 F, W, I, E, 1930 F, W, I, E, 1931 F, W, I
Nelson, T A (Oxford U) 1898 E
Nichol, J A (Royal HSFP) 1955 W, I, E
Nichol, S A (Selkirk) 1994 Arg 2(R)
Nicol, A D (Dundee HSFP, Bath, Glasgow) 1992 E, I, F, W, A 1, 2, 1993 NZ, 1994 W, 1997 A, SA, 2000 I (R), F, W, E, NZ 1, 2, 2001 F, W, E, I (R), Tg, Arg, NZ
Nimmo, C S (Watsonians) 1920 E

Ogilvy, C (Hawick) 1911 I, E, 1912 I
Oliver, H (Hawick) 1987 [Z], 1990 NZ 2(R), 1991 [Z]
Oliver, G K (Gala) 1970 A
Orr, C E (W of Scotland) 1887 I, E, W, 1888 W, I, 1889 W, I, 1890 W, I, E, 1891 W, I, E, 1892 W, I, E

**469**

SCOTLAND

Orr, H J (London Scottish) 1903 W, I, E, 1904 W, I
Orr, J E (W of Scotland) 1889 I, 1890 W, I, E, 1891 W, I, E, 1892 W, I, E, 1893 I, E
Orr, J H (Edinburgh City Police) 1947 F, W
Osler, F L (Edinburgh U) 1911 F, W

Park, J (Royal HSFP) 1934 W
Parks, D A (Glasgow Warriors, Cardiff Blues) 2004 W(R), E(R), F(R), I, Sm(t&R), A1, 2, 3, J, A4, SA, 2005 F, I, It, W, R, Arg, Sm, NZ, 2006 F, W, E, I, It(R), SA1, PI, A, 2007 E, I1, F, I2(R), SA(R), [Pt, R, NZ(R), It, Arg], 2008 F, W, I(R), E(R), It, Arg 1, 2(R), NZ(R), SA(t), C(R), 2010 W, It, E, I, Arg 1, 2, NZ, SA, Sm, 2011 F, W, I1(R), E(R), It1(R), 2, [R(R), Gg, Arg(R), E(R)], 2012 E
Paterson, C D (Edinburgh, Gloucester) 1999 [Sp], 2000 F, W, E, NZ 1, 2, US, A, Sm, 2001 F, W, E, It, I, NZ, 2002 E, It, I, F, W, C, US, R, SA, Fj, 2003 I 1, F, W 1, E, It 1, SA 1, 2, It 2(R), W 2(R), I 2, [J, US, F, Fj, A], 2004 W, E, It, F, I, Sm, A3, J, A4, SA, 2005 F, I, It, W, E, R, Arg, Sm, NZ, 2006 F, W, E, I, It, SA 1, 2, R(R), PI, A, 2007 E, W, It, I1, F, I2, SA, [Pt(R), R, NZ, It, Arg], 2008 F(R), W, I, E, It, Arg 1, 2, NZ, SA, 2009 W(R), F(R), It(t&R), I, E, Fj(R), A(R), Arg(R), 2010 F, W, SA(R), 2011 I1, E, It1, I2, [R, Gg(R), Arg, E]
Paterson, D S (Gala) 1969 SA, 1970 I, E, A, 1971 F, W, I, E (2[1C]), 1972 W
Paterson, G Q (Edinburgh Acads) 1876 E
Paterson, J R (Birkenhead Park) 1925 F, W, I, E, 1926 F, W, I, E, 1927 F, W, I, E, A, 1928 F, W, I, E, 1929 F, W, I, E
Patterson, D (Hawick) 1896 W
Patterson, D W (West Hartlepool) 1994 SA, 1995 [Tg]
Pattullo, G L (Panmure) 1920 F, W, I, E
Paxton, I A M (Selkirk) 1981 NZ 1, 2, R, A, 1982 E, I, F, W, A 1, 2, 1983 I, E, NZ, 1984 W, E, I, F, 1985 I (R), F, W, E, 1986 W, E, I, R, 1987 I, F, W, E, [F, Z, R, NZ], 1988 I, E, A
Paxton, R E (Kelso) 1982 I, A 2(R)
Pearson, J (Watsonians) 1909 I, E, 1910 F, W, I, E, 1911 F, 1912 F, W, SA, 1913 I, E
Pender, I M (London Scottish) 1914 E
Pender, N E K (Hawick) 1977 I, 1978 F, W, E
Penman, W M (RAF) 1939 I
Peterkin, W A (Edinburgh U) 1881 E, 1883 I, 1884 W, I, E, 1885 W, I 1, 2
Peters, E W (Bath) 1995 C, I, F, W, E, R, [Tg, F, NZ], 1996 I, F, W, E, NZ 1, 2, A, It, 1997 A, SA, 1998 W, E, Fj, A 1, 2, SA, 1999 W, E, It, I
Petrie, A G (Royal HSFP) 1873 E, 1874 E, 1875 E, 1876 E, 1877 I, E, 1878 E, 1879 I, E, 1880 I, E
Petrie, J M (Glasgow) 2000 NZ 2, US, A, Sm, 2001 F, W, It (R), I (R), Tg, Arg, 2002 F (t), W (R), C, R(R), Fj, 2003 F(t+R), W 1(R), SA 1(R), 2 (R), It 2, W 2, I 2(R), [J, US, F(t&R), A(R)], 2004 It(R), I(R), Sm(R), A1(R), 2(t&R), 3(R), J, A4, SA(R), 2005 F, I, It, W, E(R), R, 2006 F(R), W(R), I(R), SA 2
Philip, T K (Edinburgh) 2004 W, E, It, F, I
Philp, A (Edinburgh Inst FP) 1882 E
Pinder, S J (Glasgow) 2006 SA 1(R), 2(R)
Pocock, E I (Edinburgh Wands) 1877 I, E
Pollock, J A (Gosforth) 1982 W, 1983 E, NZ, 1984 E (R), I, F, R, 1985 F
Polson, A H (Gala) 1930 E
Pountney, A C (Northampton) 1998 SA, 1999 W (t+R), E (R), It (t+R), I (R), F, Arg, [SA, U, Sm, NZ], 2000 It, I, F, W, E, US, A, Sm, 2001 F, W, E, It, I, 2002 E, I, F, W, R, SA, Fj
Proudfoot, M C (Melrose, Glasgow) 1998 Fj, A 1, 2, 2003 I 2(R)
Purdie, W (Jedforest) 1939 W, I, E
Purves, A B H L (London Scottish) 1906 W, I, E, SA, 1907 W, I, E, 1908 W, I, E
Purves, W D C L (London Scottish) 1912 F, W, I, SA, 1913 I, E
Pyrgos, H B (Glasgow Warriors) 2012 NZ(R), SA(R), Tg, 2013 E(R), It1(R), F(R), Sm(R), SA1(R), It2(R), J(R), 2014 Arg1(R), SA

Rea, C W W (W of Scotland, Headingley) 1968 A, 1969 F, W, I, SA, 1970 F, W, I, A, 1971 F, W, E (2[1C])
Redpath, B W (Melrose, Narbonne, Sale) 1993 NZ (t), 1994 E (t), F, Arg 1, 2, 1995 C, I, F, W, E, R, [Iv, F, NZ], WS, 1996 I, F, W, E, A (R), It, 1997 E, I, F, 1998 Fj, A 1, 2, SA, 1999 R (R), [U (R), Sp], 2000 It, I, US, A, Sm, 2001 F (R), E (R), It, I, 2002

E, It, I, F, W, R, SA, Fj, 2003 I 1, F, W 1, E, It 1, SA 1, 2, [J, US(R), F, Fj, A]
Reed, A I (Bath, Wasps) 1993 I, F, W, E, 1994 E, I, F, Arg 1, 2, SA, 1996 It, 1997 W, E, I, F, 1999 It (R), F (R), [Sp]
Reid, C (Edinburgh Acads) 1881 I, E, 1882 I, E, 1883 W, I, E, 1884 W, I, E, 1885 W, I 1, 2, 1886 W, I, E, 1887 I, W, E, 1888 W, I
Reid, G (Glasgow Warriors) 2014 US, C, Arg1(R)
Reid, J (Edinburgh Wands) 1874 E, 1875 E, 1876 E, 1877 I, E
Reid, J M (Edinburgh Acads) 1898 I, E, 1899 I
Reid, M F (Loretto) 1883 I, E
Reid, R E (Glasgow) 2001 Tg (R), Arg
Reid, S J (Boroughmuir, Leeds, Narbonne) 1995 WS, 1999 F, Arg, [Sp], 2000 It (t), F, W, E (t)
Reid-Kerr, J (Greenock Wand) 1909 E
Relph, W K L (Stewart's Coll FP) 1955 F, W, I, E
Rennie, R M (Edinburgh) 2008 I(R), 2010 NZ(R), SA(R), Sm(R), 2011 F(R), W(R), I2, It2(R), [R(R), Gg, E(R)], 2012 E, W, F, I, It, A, Fj, Sm, NZ
Renny-Tailyour, H W (Royal Engineers) 1872 E
Renwick, J M (Hawick) 1972 F, W, E, NZ, 1973 F, 1974 W, E, I, F, 1975 I, F, W, E, NZ, A, 1976 F, W, E (R), 1977 I, F, W, 1978 I, F, W, E, NZ, 1979 W, E, I, F, NZ, 1980 I, F, W, E, 1981 F, W, E, I, NZ 1, 2, R, A, 1982 E, I, F, W, 1983 I, F, W, E, 1984 R
Renwick, W L (London Scottish) 1989 R
Renwick, W N (London Scottish, Edinburgh Wands) 1938 E, 1939 W
Richardson, J F (Edinburgh Acads) 1994 SA
Ritchie, G (Merchistonians) 1871 E
Ritchie, G F (Dundee HSFP) 1932 E
Ritchie, J M (Watsonians) 1933 W, E, I, 1934 W, I, E
Ritchie, W T (Cambridge U) 1905 I, E
Robb, G H (Glasgow U) 1881 I, 1885 W
Roberts, G (Watsonians) 1938 W, I, E, 1939 W, E
Robertson, A H (W of Scotland) 1871 E
Robertson, A W (Edinburgh Acads) 1897 E
Robertson, D (Edinburgh Acads) 1875 E
Robertson, D D (Cambridge U) 1893 W
Robertson, I (London Scottish, Watsonians) 1968 E, 1969 E, SA, 1970 F, W, I, E, A
Robertson, I P M (Watsonians) 1910 F
Robertson, J (Clydesdale) 1908 E
Robertson, K W (Melrose) 1978 NZ, 1979 W, E, I, F, NZ, 1980 W, E, 1981 F, W, E, R, A, 1982 E, I, F, A 1, 2, 1983 I, F, W, E, 1984 E, I, F, R, A, 1985 I, F, W, E, 1986 I, 1987 F (R), W, E, [F, Z, NZ], 1988 E, A, 1989 E, I, F
Robertson, L (London Scottish United Services) 1908 E, 1911 W, 1912 W, I, E, SA, 1913 W, I, E
Robertson, M A (Gala) 1958 F
Robertson, R D (London Scottish) 1912 F
Robson, A (Hawick) 1954 F, 1955 F, W, I, E, 1956 F, W, I, E, 1957 F, W, I, E, 1958 W, A, I, E, 1959 F, W, I, E, 1960 F
Rodd, J A T (United Services, RN, London Scottish) 1958 F, W, A, I, E, 1960 F, W, 1962 F, 1964 F, NZ, W, 1965 F, W, I
Rogerson, J (Kelvinside Acads) 1894 W
Roland, E T (Edinburgh Acads) 1884 I, E
Rollo, D M D (Howe of Fife) 1959 E, 1960 F, W, I, E, SA, 1961 F, SA, W, I, E, 1962 F, W, E, 1963 F, W, I, E, 1964 F, NZ, W, I, E, 1965 F, W, I, E, SA, 1966 F, W, I, E, A, 1967 F, W, E, NZ, 1968 F, W, I
Rose, D M (Jedforest) 1951 F, W, I, E, SA, 1953 F, W
Ross, A (Kilmarnock) 1924 F, W
Ross, A (Royal HSFP) 1905 W, I, E, 1909 W, I
Ross, A R (Edinburgh U) 1911 W, 1914 W, I, E
Ross, E J (London Scottish) 1904 W
Ross, G (Edinburgh, Leeds) 2001 Tg, 2002 R, SA, Fj(R), 2003 I 1, W 1(R), SA 2(R), It 2, I 2, [J], 2004 Sm, A1(R), 2(R), J(R), SA(R), 2005 It(R), W(R), E, 2006 F(R), W(R), E(R), I(R), It, SA 1(R), 2
Ross, G T (Watsonians) 1954 NZ, I, E, W
Ross, I A (Hillhead HSFP) 1951 F, W, I, E
Ross, J (London Scottish) 1901 W, I, E, 1902 W, 1903 E
Ross, K I (Boroughmuir FP) 1961 SA, W, I, E, 1962 F, W, I, E, 1963 F, W, E
Ross, W A (Hillhead HSFP) 1937 W, E
Rottenburg, H (Cambridge U, London Scottish) 1899 W, E, 1900 W, I, E

Roughead, W N (Edinburgh Acads, London Scottish) 1927 A, 1928 F, W, I, E, 1930 I, E, 1931 F, W, I, E, 1932 W
Rowan, N A (Boroughmuir) 1980 W, E, 1981 F, W, E, I, 1984 R, 1985 I, 1987 [R], 1988 I, F, W, E
Rowand, R (Glasgow HSFP) 1930 F, W, 1932 E, 1933 W, E, I, 1934 W
Roxburgh, A J (Kelso) 1997 A, 1998 It, F (R), W, E, Fj, A 1(R), 2(R)
Roy, A (Waterloo) 1938 W, I, E, 1939 W, I, E
Russell, F A (Glasgow Warriors) 2014 US, C
Russell, R R (Saracens, London Irish) 1999 R, [U (R), Sp, Sm (R), NZ (R)], 2000 I (R), 2001 F (R), 2002 F (R), W (R), 2003 W 1(R), It 1(R), SA 1 (R), 2 (R), It 2, I 2(R), [J, F(R), Fj(t), A(R)] , 2004 W(R), E(R), F(R), I(R), J(R), A4(R), SA(R), 2005 It(R)
Russell, W L (Glasgow Acads) 1905 NZ, 1906 W, I, E
Rutherford, J Y (Selkirk) 1979 W, E, I, F, NZ, 1980 I, F, E, 1981 F, W, E, I, NZ 1, 2, A, 1982 E, I, F, W, A 1, 2, 1983 E, NZ, 1984 W, E, I, F, R, 1985 I, F, W, E, 1986 F, W, E, I, R, 1987 I, F, W, E, [F]
Ryder, T P (Glasgow Warriors) 2012 Fj(R), Sm(R)

Sampson, R W F (London Scottish) 1939 W, 1947 W
Sanderson, G A (Royal HSFP) 1907 W, I, E, 1908 I
Sanderson, J L P (Edinburgh Acads) 1873 E
Schulze, D G (London Scottish) 1905 E, 1907 I, E, 1908 W, I, E, 1909 W, I, E, 1910 W, I, E, 1911 W
Scobie, R M (Royal Military Coll) 1914 W, I, E
Scotland, K J F (Heriot's FP, Cambridge U, Leicester) 1957 F, W, I, E, 1958 E, 1959 F, W, I, E, 1960 F, W, I, E, 1961 F, SA, W, I, E, 1962 F, W, I, E, 1963 F, W, I, E, 1965 F
Scott, D M (Langholm, Watsonians) 1950 I, E, 1951 W, I, E, SA, 1952 F, W, I, 1953 F
Scott, J M B (Edinburgh Acads) 1907 E, 1908 W, I, E, 1909 W, I, E, 1910 F, W, I, E, 1911 F, W, I, 1912 W, I, E, SA, 1913 W, I, E
Scott, J S (St Andrew's U) 1950 E
Scott, J W (Stewart's Coll FP) 1925 F, W, I, E, 1926 F, W, I, E, 1927 F, W, I, E, A, 1928 F, W, E, 1929 E, 1930 F
Scott, M (Dunfermline) 1992 A 2
Scott, M C M (Edinburgh) 2012 I(R), A, Fj, Sm, NZ, SA, Tg, 2013 E, It1, I, W, F, Sm, SA1, It2, J, 2014 I(R), E, It, F, W
Scott, R (Hawick) 1898 I, 1900 I, E
Scott, S (Edinburgh, Borders) 2000 NZ 2 (R), US (t+R), 2001 It (R), I (R), Tg (R), NZ (R), 2002 US (R), R(R), Fj(R), 2004 Sm(R), A1(R)
Scott, T (Langholm, Hawick) 1896 W, 1897 I, E, 1898 I, E, 1899 I, W, E, 1900 W, I, E
Scott, T M (Hawick) 1893 E, 1895 W, I, E, 1896 W, E, 1897 I, E, 1898 I, E, 1900 W, I
Scott, W P (W of Scotland) 1900 I, E, 1902 I, E, 1903 W, I, E, 1904 W, I, E, 1905 W, I, E, NZ, 1906 W, I, E, SA, 1907 W, I, E
Scoular, J G (Cambridge U) 1905 NZ, 1906 W, I, E, SA
Selby, J A R (Watsonians) 1920 W, I
Seymour, T S F (Glasgow Warriors) 2013 SA1, It2, J, SA2, A, 2014 E, It, F, Arg1, SA
Shackleton, J A P (London Scottish) 1959 E, 1963 F, W, 1964 NZ, W, 1965 I, SA
Sharp, A V (Bristol) 1994 E, I, F, Arg 1, 2 SA
Sharp, G (Stewart's FP, Army) 1960 F, 1964 F, NZ, W
Shaw, G D (Sale) 1935 NZ, 1936 W, 1937 W, I, E, 1939 I
Shaw, I (Glasgow HSFP) 1937 I
Shaw, J N (Edinburgh Acads) 1921 W, I
Shaw, R W (Glasgow HSFP) 1934 W, I, E, 1935 W, I, E, NZ, 1936 W, I, E, 1937 W, I, E, 1938 W, I, E, 1939 W, I, E
Shedden, D (W of Scotland) 1972 NZ, 1973 F, W, I, E, P, 1976 W, E, I, 1977 I, F, W, 1978 I, F, W
Shepherd, R J S (Melrose) 1995 WS, 1996 I, F, W, E, NZ 1, 2, A, It, 1997 W, E, I, F, SA, 1998 It, I, W (R), Fj (t), A 1, 2
Shiel, A G (Melrose, Edinburgh) 1991 [I (R), WS], 1993 I, F, W, E, NZ, 1994 Arg 1, 2, SA, 1995 R, [Iv, F, NZ], WS, 2000 I, NZ 1(R), 2
Shillinglaw, R B (Gala, Army) 1960 I, E, SA, 1961 F, SA
Simmers, B M (Glasgow Acads) 1965 F, W, 1966 A, 1967 F, W, I, 1971 F (R)
Simmers, W M (Glasgow Acads) 1926 W, I, E, 1927 F, W, I, E, A, 1928 F, W, I, E, 1929 F, W, I, E, 1930 F, W, I, E, 1931 F, W, I, E, 1932 SA, W, I, E

Simpson, G L (Kirkcaldy, Glasgow) 1998 A 1, 2, 1999 Arg (R), R, [SA, U, Sm, NZ], 2000 It, I, NZ 1(R), 2001 I, Tg (R), Arg (R), NZ
Simpson, J W (Royal HSFP) 1893 I, E, 1894 W, I, E, 1895 W, I, E, 1896 W, I, 1897 E, 1899 W, E
Simpson, R S (Glasgow Acads) 1923 I
Simson, E D (Edinburgh U, London Scottish) 1902 E, 1903 W, I, E, 1904 W, I, E, 1905 W, I, E, NZ, 1906 W, I, E, 1907 W, I, E
Simson, J T (Watsonians) 1905 NZ, 1909 W, I, E, 1910 F, W, 1911 I
Simson, R F (London Scottish) 1911 E
Sloan, A T (Edinburgh Acads) 1914 W, 1920 F, W, I, E, 1921 F, W, I, E
Sloan, D A (Edinburgh Acads, London Scottish) 1950 F, W, E, 1951 W, I, E, 1953 F
Sloan, T (Glasgow Acads, Oxford U) 1905 NZ, 1906 W, SA, 1907 W, E, 1908 W, 1909 I
Smeaton, P W (Edinburgh Acads) 1881 I, 1883 I, E
Smith, A R (London Scottish) 1895 W, I, E, 1896 W, I, 1897 I, E, 1898 I, E, 1900 I, E
Smith, A R (Cambridge U, Gosforth, Ebbw Vale, Edinburgh Wands) 1955 W, I, E, 1956 F, W, I, E, 1957 F, W, I, E, 1958 F, W, A, I, 1959 F, W, I, E, 1960 F, W, I, E, SA, 1961 F, SA, W, I, E, 1962 F, W, I, E
Smith, C J (Edinburgh) 2002 C, US (R), 2004 Sm(t&R), A1(R), 2(R), 3(R), J(R), 2005 Arg(R), Sm, NZ(R), 2006 F(R), W(R), E(R), I(R), It(R), SA 1(R), 2, R(R), 2007 I2(R), [R(R), NZ, It(R), Arg(R)], 2008 E(R), It(R)
Smith, D W C (London Scottish) 1949 F, W, I, E, 1950 F, W, I, 1953 I
Smith, E R (Edinburgh Acads) 1879 I
Smith, G K (Kelso) 1957 I, E, 1958 F, W, A, 1959 F, W, I, E, 1960 F, W, I, E, 1961 F, SA, W, I, E
Smith, H O (Watsonians) 1895 W, 1896 W, I, E, 1898 I, E, 1899 W, I, E, 1900 E, 1902 E
Smith, I R (Gloucester, Moseley) 1992 E, I, W, A 1, 2, 1994 E (R), I, F, Arg 1, 2, 1995 [Iv], WS, 1996 I, F, W, E, NZ 1, 2, A, It, 1997 E, I, F, A, SA
Smith, I S (Oxford U, Edinburgh U) 1924 W, I, E, 1925 F, W, I, E, 1926 F, W, I, E, 1927 F, I, E, 1929 F, W, I, E, 1930 F, W, I, 1931 F, W, I, E, 1932 SA, W, I, E, 1933 W, E, I
Smith, I S G (London Scottish) 1969 SA, 1970 F, W, I, E, 1971 F, W, I
Smith, M A (London Scottish) 1970 W, I, E, A
Smith, R T (Kelso) 1929 F, W, I, E, 1930 F, W, I
Smith, S H (Glasgow Acads) 1877 I, 1878 E
Smith, T J (Gala) 1983 E, NZ, 1985 I, F
Smith T J (Watsonians, Dundee HSFP, Glasgow, Brive, Northampton) 1997 E, I, F, 1998 SA, 1999 W, E, It, I, Arg, R, [SA, U, Sm, NZ], 2000 It, I, F, W, E, NZ 1, 2, US, A, Sm, 2001 F, W, E, It, I, Tg, Arg, NZ, 2002 E, It, I, F, W, R, SA, Fj, 2003 I 1, F, W 1, E, It 1, 2, [J, US, F, Fj, A], 2004 W, E, Sm, A1, 2, 2005 F, I, It, W, E
Sole, D M B (Bath, Edinburgh Acads) 1986 F, W, 1987 I, F, W, E, [F, Z, R, NZ], 1988 I, F, W, E, A, 1989 W, E, I, F, Fj, R, 1990 I, F, W, E, NZ 1, 2, Arg, 1991 F, W, E, I, R, [J, I, WS, E, NZ], 1992 E, I, F, W, A 1, 2
Somerville, D (Edinburgh Inst FP) 1879 I, 1882 I, 1883 W, I, E, 1884 W
Southwell, H F G (Edinburgh, Stade Français) 2004 Sm(t&R), A1, 2, 3(R), J, A4, SA, 2005 F, I, It, W, E, R(R), Arg(R), Sm(R), NZ, 2006 F, W, E, I, It, SA 1, 2, 2006 R, PI(t&R), A(R), 2007 E, W, It, I1, SA(R), [Pt(R), R(R), NZ, It(R), Arg(R)], 2008 F(R), W, I, E, It, Arg 2, NZ(R), SA(R), 2009 W, F, It, E(R), 2010 F(R), It, E, I, Arg 1, 2, NZ, SA, Sm, 2011 F, W
Speirs, L M (Watsonians) 1906 SA, 1907 W, I, E, 1908 W, I, E, 1910 F, W, E
Spence, K M (Oxford U) 1953 I
Spencer, E (Clydesdale) 1898 I
Stagg, P K (Sale) 1965 F, W, E, SA, 1966 F, W, I, E, A, 1967 F, W, I, E, NZ, 1968 F, W, I, E, A, 1969 F, W, I (R), SA, 1970 F, W, I, E, A
Stanger, A G (Hawick) 1989 Fj, R, 1990 I, F, W, E, NZ 1, 2, Arg, 1991 F, W, E, I, R, [J, I, WS, E, NZ], 1992 E, I, F, W, A 1, 2, 1993 I, F, W, E, NZ, 1994 W, E, I, F, SA, 1995 R, [Iv], 1996 NZ 2, A, It, 1997 W, E, I, F, A, SA, 1998 It, I (R), F, W, E

W, E, NZ 1, 2, 1997 W, E, I, F, SA, 1998 It, I, F, W, E, Fj, A 1, 2
**Walker, A** (W of Scotland) 1881 I, 1882 E, 1883 W, I, E
**Walker, A W** (Cambridge U, Birkenhead Park) 1931 F, W, I, E, 1932 I
**Walker, J G** (W of Scotland) 1882 E, 1883 W
**Walker, M** (Oxford U) 1952 F
**Walker, N** (Borders, Ospreys) 2002 R, SA, Fj, 2007 W(R), It(R), F, I2(R), SA, [R(R), NZ], 2008 F, W, I, E, C, 2010 NZ(R), SA, Sm, 2011 F, W, I1, It1, I2, It2(R)
**Wallace, A C** (Oxford U) 1923 F, 1924 F, W, E, 1925 F, W, I, E, 1926 F
**Wallace, W M** (Cambridge U) 1913 E, 1914 W, I, E
**Wallace, M I** (Glasgow High Kelvinside) 1996 A, It, 1997 W
**Walls, W A** (Glasgow Acads) 1882 E, 1883 W, I, E, 1884 W, I, E, 1886 W, I, E
**Walter, M W** (London Scottish) 1906 I, E, SA, 1907 W, I, 1908 W, I, 1910 I
**Walton, P** (Northampton, Newcastle) 1994 E, I, F, Arg 1, 2, 1995 [Iv], 1997 W, E, I, F, SA (R), 1998 I, F, SA, 1999 W, E, It, I, F (R), Arg, R, [SA (R), U (R), Sp]
**Warren, J R** (Glasgow Acads) 1914 I
**Warren, R C** (Glasgow Acads) 1922 W, I, 1930 W, I, E
**Waters, F H** (Cambridge U, London Scottish) 1930 F, W, I, E, 1932 SA, W, I
**Waters, J A** (Selkirk) 1933 W, E, I, 1934 W, I, E, 1935 W, I, E, NZ, 1936 W, I, E, 1937 W, I, E
**Waters, J B** (Cambridge U) 1904 I, E
**Watherston, J G** (Edinburgh Wands) 1934 I, E
**Watherston, W R A** (London Scottish) 1963 F, W, I
**Watson, D H** (Glasgow Acads) 1876 E, 1877 I, E
**Watson, W S** (Boroughmuir) 1974 W, E, I, F, 1975 NZ, 1977 I, F, W, 1979 I, F
**Watt, A G J** (Glasgow High Kelvinside) 1991 [Z], 1993 I, NZ, 1994 Arg 2(t & R)
**Watt, A G M** (Edinburgh Acads) 1947 F, W, I, A, 1948 F, W
**Weatherstone, T G** (Stewart's Coll FP) 1952 E, 1953 I, E, 1954 F, NZ, I, E, W, 1955 F, 1958 W, A, I, E, 1959 W, I, E
**Webster, S L** (Edinburgh ) 2003 I 2(R), 2004 W(R), E, It, F, I, Sm, A1, 2, 2005 It, NZ(R), 2006 F(R), W(R), E(R), I(R), It(R), SA 1(R), 2, R, PI, A, 2007 W(R), I2, SA, [Pt, R, NZ, It, Arg], 2008 F, I, E, It, Arg 1(R), 2, C, 2009 W
**Weir, D** (Glasgow Warriors) 2012 F(R), Fj(R), 2013 I(R), W, F, J(R), SA2(R), A, 2014 I, E, It, F, W, Arg1, SA
**Weir, G W** (Melrose, Newcastle) 1990 Arg, 1991 R, [J, Z, I, WS, E, NZ], 1992 E, I, F, W, A 1, 2, 1993 I, F, W, E, NZ, 1994 W (R), E, I, F, SA, 1995 F (R), W, E, R, [Iv, Tg, F, NZ], WS, 1996 I, F, W, E, NZ 1, 2, A, It (R), 1997 W, E, I, F, 1998 It, I, F, W, E, SA, 1999 W, Arg (R), R (R), [SA (R), Sp, Sm, NZ], 2000 It (R), I (R), F
**Welsh, J** (Glasgow Warriors) 2012 It, 2013 It2(R), 2014 Arg1(R)
**Welsh, R** (Watsonians) 1895 W, I, E, 1896 W
**Welsh, R B** (Hawick) 1967 I, E
**Welsh, W B** (Hawick) 1927 A, 1928 F, W, I, 1929 I, E, 1930 F, W, I, E, 1931 F, W, I, E, 1932 SA, W, I, E, 1933 W, E, I
**Welsh, W H** (Edinburgh U) 1900 I, E, 1901 W, I, E, 1902 W, I, E
**Wemyss, A** (Gala, Edinburgh Wands) 1914 W, I, 1920 F, E, 1922 F, W, I
**West, L** (Edinburgh U, West Hartlepool) 1903 W, I, E, 1905 I, E, NZ, 1906 W, I, E

**Weston, V G** (Kelvinside Acads) 1936 I, E
**White, D B** (Gala, London Scottish) 1982 F, W, A 1, 2, 1987 W, E, [F, R, NZ], 1988 I, F, W, E, A, 1989 W, E, I, F, Fj, R, 1990 I, F, W, E, NZ 1, 2, 1991 F, W, E, I, R, [J, Z, I, WS, E, NZ], 1992 E, I, F, W
**White, D M** (Kelvinside Acads) 1963 F, W, I, E
**White, J P R** (Glasgow, Sale, Clermont-Auvergne) 2000 E, NZ 1, 2, US (R), A (R), Sm, 2001 F (R), I, Tg, Arg, NZ, 2002 E, It, I, F, W, C, US, SA(R), Fj, 2003 F(R), W 1, E, It 1, SA 1, 2, It 2, [J, US(R), F, Fj(R), A], 2004 W(R), E, It, F, I, Sm, A1, 2, J(R), A4(R), SA, 2005 F, I, E, Arg, Sm, NZ, 2006 F, W, E, I, It, SA 1, 2, R, 2007 I2, SA, [Pt, R, It, Arg], 2008 F, W, E(R), It(R), NZ, SA, 2009 W, F, It, I, E, Fj(R), A(R), Arg(R)
**White, T B** (Edinburgh Acads) 1888 W, I, 1889 W
**Whittington, T P** (Merchistonians) 1873 E
**Whitworth, R J E** (London Scottish) 1936 I
**Whyte, D J** (Edinburgh Wands) 1965 W, I, E, SA, 1966 F, W, I, E, A, 1967 F, W, I, E
**Will, J G** (Cambridge U) 1912 F, W, I, E, 1914 W, I, E
**Wilson, A W** (Dunfermline) 1931 F, I, E
**Wilson, A W** (Glasgow) 2005 R(R)
**Wilson, G A** (Oxford U) 1949 F, W, E
**Wilson, G R** (Royal HSFP) 1886 E, 1890 W, I, E, 1891 I
**Wilson, J H** (Watsonians) 1953 I
**Wilson, J S** (St Andrew's U) 1931 F, W, I, E, 1932 E
**Wilson, J S** (United Services, London Scottish) 1908 I, 1909 W
**Wilson, R** (London Scottish) 1976 E, I, 1977 E, I, F, 1978 I, F, 1981 R, 1983 I
**Wilson, R** (Glasgow Warriors) 2013 W(R), F(R), Sm(R), SA1, 2014 I, E, It, F(R), W
**Wilson, R L** (Gala) 1951 F, W, I, E, SA, 1953 F, W, E
**Wilson, R W** (W of Scotland) 1873 E, 1874 E
**Wilson, S** (Oxford U, London Scottish) 1964 F, NZ, W, I, E, 1965 W, I, E, SA, 1966 F, W, I, A, 1967 F, W, I, E, NZ, 1968 F, W, I, E
**Wood, A** (Royal HSFP) 1873 E, 1874 E, 1875 E
**Wood, G** (Gala) 1931 W, I, 1932 W, I, E
**Woodburn, J C** (Kelvinside Acads) 1892 I
**Woodrow, A N** (Glasgow Acads) 1887 I, W, E
**Wotherspoon, W** (W of Scotland) 1891 I, 1892 I, 1893 W, E, 1894 W, I, E
**Wright, F A** (Edinburgh Acads) 1932 E
**Wright, H B** (Watsonians) 1894 W
**Wright, K M** (London Scottish) 1929 F, W, I, E
**Wright, P H** (Boroughmuir) 1992 A 1, 2, 1993 F, W, E, 1994 W, 1995 C, I, F, W, E, R, [Iv, Tg, F, NZ], 1996 W, E, NZ 1
**Wright, R W J** (Edinburgh Wands) 1973 F
**Wright, S T H** (Stewart's Coll FP) 1949 E
**Wright, T** (Hawick) 1947 A
**Wyllie, D S** (Stewart's-Melville FP) 1984 A, 1985 W (R), E, 1987 I, F, [F, Z, R, NZ], 1989 R, 1991 R, [J (R), Z], 1993 NZ (R), 1994 W (R), E, I, F

**Young, A H** (Edinburgh Acads) 1874 E
**Young, E T** (Glasgow Acads) 1914 E
**Young, R G** (Watsonians) 1970 W
**Young, T E B** (Durham) 1911 F
**Young, W B** (Cambridge U, London Scottish) 1937 W, I, E, 1938 W, I, E, 1939 W, I, E, 1948 E

# RUGBY'S VALUES

## integrity

**Integrity is central to the fabric of the Game and is generated through honesty and fair play**

## respect

**Respect for team mates, opponents, match officials and those involved in the Game is paramount**

## solidarity

**Rugby provides a unifying spirit that leads to life long friendships, camaraderie, teamwork and loyalty which transcends cultural, geographic, political and religious differences**

## passion

**Rugby people have a passionate enthusiasm for the Game. Rugby generates excitement, emotional attachment and a sense of belonging to the global Rugby Family**

## discipline

**Discipline is an integral part of the Game both on and off the field and is reflected through adherence to the Laws, the Regulations and Rugby's core values**

## www.**irb**.com

# SOUTH AFRICA

## SOUTH AFRICA'S 2013–14 TEST RECORD

| OPPONENTS | DATE | VENUE | RESULT |
|-----------|------|-------|--------|
| Wales | 9 Nov | A | Won 24–15 |
| Scotland | 17 Nov | A | Won 28–0 |
| France | 23 Nov | A | Won 19–10 |
| Wales | 14 Jun | H | Won 38–16 |
| Wales | 21 Jun | H | Won 33–31 |
| Scotland | 28 Jun | H | Won 55–6 |
| Argentina | 16 Aug | H | Won 13–6 |
| Argentina | 23 Aug | A | Won 33–31 |
| Australia | 6 Sep | A | Lost 24–23 |
| New Zealand | 13 Sep | A | Lost 14–10 |
| Australia | 27 Sep | H | Won 28–10 |
| New Zealand | 4 Oct | H | Won 27–25 |

# SPRINGBOKS DEVELOPING WINNING MENTALITY

### By Joel Stransky

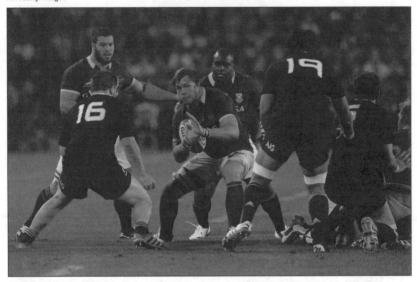

Duane Vermeulen led the charge as South Africa recorded a famous victory over New Zealand in Johannesburg.

**T**he euphoric reaction in South Africa to the Springboks' 27–25 win over the All Blacks in Johannesburg in the climax of The Rugby Championship was incredible. The victory over the old foe after four straight defeats was a huge psychological boost to the team and will undoubtedly hearten the Springbok camp as the World Cup in England gets closer.

Everyone in South Africa, from Heyneke Meyer to the players and the fans knows we will probably have to beat New Zealand at the semi-final stage in 2015 if the side is to become world champions for a third time, and to get the monkey off their backs with the result at Ellis Park was certainly significant. It was far from a perfect performance but they got over the line and they are no longer weighed down by lingering doubts whether they can beat the All Blacks or not.

I would, though, be reluctant to read too much into the result. If the two teams do meet in the World Cup it will be a completely different dynamic, a match played at a neutral venue and historically the Kiwis have had problems in the latter stages of the World Cups which have been staged in Europe. Knockout games can have a strange effect on teams and while, of course, I was delighted to see the Springboks beat the All Blacks for the first time since 2011, there's a danger of getting swept away by the emotion that the result certainly generated here in South Africa.

I've always believed that what separates good and potentially great teams is the ability to win games when you're not playing well, to get the result when it's not really going according to plan. The Springboks won 10 Tests from 12 during the year and against France in Paris, Wales in Nelspruit and Argentina home and away in The Rugby Championship, Meyer's side got the job done despite not firing on all cylinders. The All Blacks match grabbed the headlines, but in terms of the development and growing maturity of a team with aspirations to win the World Cup, it was those gritty kind of results that really impressed me.

I think that ability to grind out a result when they could have easily slipped to a defeat is a direct result of the atmosphere within the squad. I spent some time with the team during the year and there's a real family feel in the camp, a great spirit and a lot of love. The players are fiercely united and that has been reflected in the performances on the pitch.

The European tour in November yielded victories against Wales in Cardiff (24–15), Scotland at Murrayfield (28–0) and a 19–10 win over the French in Paris. The Boks conceded only one try in the process which will have delighted Meyer and he will also have been relieved to escape from France without losing after what was a tired and disjointed display.

There were no games against England or Ireland, the two strongest teams in the northern hemisphere at the moment, but I don't think that detracted from the tour. With due respect, facing the lower ranked sides gave Meyer the flexibility to blood more new players than he probably would have done if the Boks had had to play at Twickenham or in Dublin. The chance to throw in the youngsters at Test level is a rare one.

There was more positive news during the tour when it was announced 10 of the squad, including Jean de Villiers, the du Plessis brothers and Duane Vermeulen, had signed new contracts with the South African Rugby Union, taking them through to the end of 2015. Having that calibre of players available for the World Cup is obviously important, but I think it's even more significant that South Africa will have older heads in the dressing room to help the new boys fulfil their potential. It doesn't matter how talented you are, you still need to come into a squad with the right culture at the start of an international career and

**SOUTH AFRICA**

the continuing presence of veterans like de Villiers, who has blossomed into a great leader and reached the milestone of 100 Tests this year, will ensure the youngsters get the right baptism in Test rugby.

After a seven-month break, the Springboks were back in action for the first time in 2014 against a World XV in Cape Town. It was nothing more really than a money-spinner but professional rugby needs every cent it can get and I don't think you can be critical of SARU for staging the match.

The season continued with a two-Test series against Wales and a one-off game with Scotland. The first game with the Welsh ended in a relatively routine 38–16 win, but the second match was a close one which finished 31–30 to the Springboks.

South Africa clinched it with a penalty try in the 77th minute when Steve Walsh penalised Liam Williams for a shoulder charge on Cornal Hendricks in the corner, and although it was a cruel way for the Welsh to lose, the decision was 100 per cent correct. Winning with a last-gasp penalty try obviously wasn't part of Meyer's Plan A but his team's ability to steal a result in a match which they were behind throughout was impressive. They found a way to rescue the situation and I hope that self-belief and steel can take them a lot further.

It was a very weak Scotland team that were beaten 55–6 a week later in Port Elizabeth but a half century of points in any Test is not to be dismissed and the Springboks stuck the dagger in when the opportunity arose.

The Rugby Championship kicked off with the Pumas home and away and again South Africa got out of jail. Argentina had been in camp for a month before the two Tests and definitely fancied their chances of beating the Springboks for the first time. Defence saw them over the line in Pretoria in a 13–6 win while it was Morné Steyn's late penalty that wrapped up a 33–31 victory in Salta. It wasn't always pretty but it was effective. The two games were close but Argentina's confrontational and physical approach mirrored South Africa's and the teams negated each other for long periods.

A couple of narrow defeats to the Wallabies (24–23) in Perth and the New Zealanders (14–10) in Wellington rocked the team on its heels but they regrouped to comfortably beat Australia (28–10) in Cape Town and then that famous win over the All Blacks courtesy of a late, late penalty from Pat Lambie.

The big difference in the win over the Kiwis compared to the 38–27 loss to New Zealand a year earlier was South Africa weren't chasing four tries for the bonus point this time. Then they threw caution to the wind but 12 months on they played the game on its merits and they were more mature in their decision making. They lost their composure briefly in the second half to let New Zealand in for a couple of quick tries but rediscovered their composure to close the game out.

Meyer, I think, will have been happy with his team's progress through the year. He capped 13 new players in 12 Tests and although I don't believe all of them have long international careers ahead of them, I was hugely impressed by Handré Pollard and Cornal Hendricks. For a 20-year-old, Pollard displayed an incredible level of maturity and was outstanding while Hendricks took to Test rugby like a natural. They were both huge positives for Meyer.

The form of the young Jan Serfontein alongside de Villiers in the midfield during the Championship was exciting and a classic example of the next generation learning their trade from the established stars. For me the balance between experience and youth in the current squad is very encouraging. The recipe for success at Test level is all about blending the old and the new and Meyer has got a nice mix at the moment as he fine-tunes for the World Cup.

The year saw Bryan Habana become only the fourth South African to reach a century of caps when he played against the Australians in Perth and you won't hear anyone argue he didn't richly deserve to reach the milestone. Bryan is one of the key figures championing the family atmosphere I mentioned earlier in the South Africa squad and he has never been anything but a consummate professional throughout his career.

Obviously his unbelievable pace is his trademark but that sometimes overshadows his overall contribution to the team. He's always looking for work and he's not afraid to get his hands dirty clearing out in the rucks. Bryan is a great finisher but he's an even greater all-round footballer.

There were some areas of concern for Meyer and his coaching team. The burning issue has to be the front row, which was absolutely murdered home and away by Argentina and the All Blacks in Johannesburg. I'm also unconvinced the Springboks have got adequate cover at number 8 if Duane Vermeulen were to pick up an injury.

Tactically there was a tendency for the team to go into its shell when they were under pressure and revert to throwing single runners at the opposition and try to blast their way through. Meyer has enjoyed success in changing the philosophy of the side, encouraging the players to consistently put more width on the ball, but there's still a suspicion some of them prefer to opt for the direct route when they're under the cosh.

That said, the Springboks look almost ready for the World Cup. The team hasn't peaked yet, which is a positive, and they have become increasingly consistent in terms of results if not always performance. South Africa will be genuine contenders at the World Cup in 2015.

# SOUTH AFRICA INTERNATIONAL STATISTICS

## MATCH RECORDS UP TO 13 OCTOBER 2014

### MOST CONSECUTIVE TEST WINS

**17** 1997 A2, It, F 1, 2, E, S, 1998 I 1, 2, W 1, E 1, A 1, NZ 1,2, A 2, W 2, S, I 3

**15** 1994 Arg 1,2, S, W 1995 WS, A, R, C, WS, F, NZ, W, It, E, 1996 Fj

### MOST CONSECUTIVE TESTS WITHOUT DEFEAT

| Matches | Wins | Draws | Period |
|---|---|---|---|
| 17 | 17 | 0 | 1997 to 1998 |
| 16 | 15 | 1 | 1994 to 1996 |
| 15 | 12 | 3 | 1960 to 1963 |

### MOST POINTS IN A MATCH
#### BY THE TEAM

| Pts | Opponents | Venue | Year |
|---|---|---|---|
| 134 | Uruguay | E London | 2005 |
| 105 | Namibia | Cape Town | 2007 |
| 101 | Italy | Durban | 1999 |
| 96 | Wales | Pretoria | 1998 |
| 87 | Namibia | Albany | 2011 |
| 74 | Tonga | Cape Town | 1997 |
| 74 | Italy | Port Elizabeth | 1999 |
| 73 | Argentina | Soweto | 2013 |
| 72 | Uruguay | Perth | 2003 |
| 68 | Scotland | Murrayfield | 1997 |
| 64 | USA | Montpellier | 2007 |
| 63 | Argentina | Johannesburg | 2008 |
| 62 | Italy | Bologna | 1997 |
| 61 | Australia | Pretoria | 1997 |

#### BY A PLAYER

| Pts | Player | Opponents | Venue | Year |
|---|---|---|---|---|
| 35 | PC Montgomery | Namibia | Cape Town | 2007 |
| 34 | JH de Beer | England | Paris | 1999 |
| 31 | PC Montgomery | Wales | Pretoria | 1998 |
| 31 | M Steyn | N Zealand | Durban | 2009 |
| 30 | T Chavhanga | Uruguay | E London | 2005 |
| 29 | GS du Toit | Italy | Port Elizabeth | 1999 |
| 29 | PC Montgomery | Samoa | Paris | 2007 |
| 28 | GK Johnson | W Samoa | Johannesburg | 1995 |
| 28 | M Steyn | Argentina | Soweto | 2013 |
| 26 | JH de Beer | Australia | Pretoria | 1997 |
| 26 | PC Montgomery | Scotland | Murrayfield | 1997 |
| 26 | M Steyn | Italy | East London | 2010 |
| 25 | J T Stransky | Australia | Bloemfontein | 1996 |
| 25 | C S Terblanche | Italy | Durban | 1999 |

### MOST TRIES IN A MATCH
#### BY THE TEAM

| Tries | Opponents | Venue | Year |
|---|---|---|---|
| 21 | Uruguay | E London | 2005 |
| 15 | Wales | Pretoria | 1998 |
| 15 | Italy | Durban | 1999 |
| 15 | Namibia | Cape Town | 2007 |
| 12 | Tonga | Cape Town | 1997 |
| 12 | Uruguay | Perth | 2003 |
| 12 | Namibia | Albany | 2011 |
| 11 | Italy | Port Elizabeth | 1999 |
| 10 | Ireland | Dublin | 1912 |
| 10 | Scotland | Murrayfield | 1997 |

#### BY A PLAYER

| Tries | Player | Opponents | Venue | Year |
|---|---|---|---|---|
| 6 | T Chavhanga | Uruguay | E London | 2005 |
| 5 | CS Terblanche | Italy | Durban | 1999 |
| 4 | CM Williams | W Samoa | Johannesburg | 1995 |
| 4 | PWG Rossouw | France | Parc des Princes | 1997 |
| 4 | CS Terblanche | Ireland | Bloemfontein | 1998 |
| 4 | BG Habana | Samoa | Paris | 2007 |
| 4 | JL Nokwe | Australia | Johannesburg | 2008 |

## MOST CONVERSIONS IN A MATCH
### BY THE TEAM

| Cons | Opponents | Venue | Year |
|---|---|---|---|
| 13 | Italy | Durban | 1999 |
| 13 | Uruguay | E London | 2005 |
| 12 | Namibia | Cape Town | 2007 |
| 12 | Namibia | Albany | 2011 |
| 9 | Scotland | Murrayfield | 1997 |
| 9 | Wales | Pretoria | 1998 |
| 9 | Argentina | Johannesburg | 2008 |
| 8 | Italy | Port Elizabeth | 1999 |
| 8 | USA | Montpellier | 2007 |
| 8 | Argentina | Soweto | 2013 |
| 7 | Scotland | Murrayfield | 1951 |
| 7 | Tonga | Cape Town | 1997 |
| 7 | Italy | Bologna | 1997 |
| 7 | France | Parc des Princes | 1997 |
| 7 | Italy | Genoa | 2001 |
| 7 | Samoa | Pretoria | 2002 |
| 7 | Samoa | Brisbane | 2003 |
| 7 | England | Bloemfontein | 2007 |
| 7 | Italy | East London | 2010 |

### BY A PLAYER

| Cons | Player | Opponents | Venue | Year |
|---|---|---|---|---|
| 12 | PC Montgomery | Namibia | Cape Town | 2007 |
| 9 | PC Montgomery | Wales | Pretoria | 1998 |
| 9 | AD James | Argentina | Johannesburg | 2008 |
| 8 | PC Montgomery | Scotland | Murrayfield | 1997 |
| 8 | GS du Toit | Italy | Port Elizabeth | 1999 |
| 8 | GS du Toit | Italy | Durban | 1999 |
| 8 | M Steyn | Argentina | Soweto | 2013 |
| 7 | AO Geffin | Scotland | Murrayfield | 1951 |
| 7 | JMF Lubbe | Tonga | Cape Town | 1997 |
| 7 | HW Honiball | Italy | Bologna | 1997 |
| 7 | HW Honiball | France | Parc des Princes | 1997 |
| 7 | AS Pretorius | Samoa | Pretoria | 2002 |
| 7 | JNB van der Westhuyzen | Uruguay | E London | 2005 |
| 7 | PC Montgomery | England | Bloemfontein | 2007 |

## MOST PENALTIES IN A MATCH
### BY THE TEAM

| Penalties | Opponents | Venue | Year |
|---|---|---|---|
| 8 | Scotland | Port Elizabeth | 2006 |
| 8 | N Zealand | Durban | 2009 |
| 7 | France | Pretoria | 1975 |
| 7 | France | Cape Town | 2006 |
| 7 | Australia | Cape Town | 2009 |
| 6 | Australia | Bloemfontein | 1996 |
| 6 | Australia | Twickenham | 1999 |
| 6 | England | Pretoria | 2000 |
| 6 | Australia | Durban | 2000 |
| 6 | France | Johannesburg | 2001 |
| 6 | Scotland | Johannesburg | 2003 |
| 6 | N Zealand | Bloemfontein | 2009 |
| 6 | Australia | Bloemfontein | 2010 |
| 6 | Australia | Perth | 2014 |

## MOST PENALTIES IN A MATCH
### BY A PLAYER

| Pens | Player | Opponents | Venue | Year |
|---|---|---|---|---|
| 8 | M Steyn | N Zealand | Durban | 2009 |
| 7 | PC Montgomery | Scotland | Port Elizabeth | 2006 |
| 7 | PC Montgomery | France | Cape Town | 2006 |
| 7 | M Steyn | Australia | Cape Town | 2009 |
| 6 | GR Bosch | France | Pretoria | 1975 |
| 6 | JT Stransky | Australia | Bloemfontein | 1996 |
| 6 | JH de Beer | Australia | Twickenham | 1999 |
| 6 | AJJ van Straaten | England | Pretoria | 2000 |
| 6 | AJJ van Straaten | Australia | Durban | 2000 |
| 6 | PC Montgomery | France | Johannesburg | 2001 |
| 6 | LJ Koen | Scotland | Johannesburg | 2003 |
| 6 | M Steyn | Australia | Bloemfontein | 2010 |
| 6 | M Steyn | Australia | Perth | 2014 |

## MOST DROP GOALS IN A MATCH
### BY THE TEAM

| Drops | Opponents | Venue | Year |
|---|---|---|---|
| 5 | England | Paris | 1999 |
| 4 | England | Twickenham | 2006 |
| 3 | S America | Durban | 1980 |
| 3 | Ireland | Durban | 1981 |
| 3 | Scotland | Murrayfield | 2004 |

### BY A PLAYER

| Drops | Player | Opponents | Venue | Year |
|---|---|---|---|---|
| 5 | JH de Beer | England | Paris | 1999 |
| 4 | AS Pretorius | England | Twickenham | 2006 |
| 3 | HE Botha | S America | Durban | 1980 |
| 3 | HE Botha | Ireland | Durban | 1981 |
| 3 | JNB van der Westhuyzen | Scotland | Murrayfield | 2004 |
| 2 | BL Osler | N Zealand | Durban | 1928 |
| 2 | HE Botha | NZ Cavaliers | Cape Town | 1986 |
| 2 | JT Stransky | N Zealand | Johannesburg | 1995 |
| 2 | JH de Beer | N Zealand | Johannesburg | 1997 |
| 2 | PC Montgomery | N Zealand | Cardiff | 1999 |
| 2 | FPL Steyn | Australia | Cape Town | 2007 |

SOUTH AFRICA

## MOST CAPPED PLAYERS

| Caps | Player | Career Span |
|---|---|---|
| 117 | V Matfield | 2001 to 2014 |
| 111 | JW Smit | 2000 to 2011 |
| 103 | BG Habana | 2004 to 2014 |
| 102 | PC Montgomery | 1997 to 2008 |
| 102 | J de Villiers | 2002 to 2014 |
| 89 | JH van der Westhuizen | 1993 to 2003 |
| 83 | JP Botha | 2002 to 2014 |
| 80 | JP du Randt | 1994 to 2007 |
| 80 | R Pienaar | 2006 to 2014 |
| 77 | MG Andrews | 1994 to 2001 |
| 75 | CJ van der Linde | 2002 to 2012 |
| 73 | SWP Burger | 2003 to 2014 |
| 72 | J Fourie | 2003 to 2013 |
| 70 | PF du Preez | 2004 to 2014 |
| 70 | JH Smith | 2003 to 2014 |
| 66 | AG Venter | 1996 to 2001 |
| 66 | BW du Plessis | 2007 to 2014 |
| 64 | BJ Paulse | 1999 to 2007 |
| 63 | DJ Rossouw | 2003 to 2011 |
| 61 | T Mtawarira | 2008 to 2014 |
| 60 | JN du Plessis | 2007 to 2014 |

## MOST CONSECUTIVE TESTS

| Tests | Player | Span |
|---|---|---|
| 46 | JW Smit | 2003 to 2007 |
| 39 | GH Teichmann | 1996 to 1999 |
| 28 | V Matfield | 2008 to 2010 |
| 26 | AH Snyman | 1996 to 1998 |
| 26 | AN Vos | 1999 to 2001 |
| 25 | SH Nomis | 1967 to 1972 |
| 25 | AG Venter | 1997 to 1999 |
| 25 | A-H le Roux | 1998 to 1999 |

## MOST TESTS AS CAPTAIN

| Tests | Captain | Span |
|---|---|---|
| 83 | JW Smit | 2003 to 2011 |
| 36 | GH Teichmann | 1996 to 1999 |
| 30 | J de Villiers | 2012 to 2014 |
| 29 | JF Pienaar | 1993 to 1996 |
| 22 | DJ de Villiers | 1965 to 1970 |
| 20 | V Matfield | 2007 to 2014 |
| 18 | CPJ Krigé | 1999 to 2003 |
| 16 | A N Vos | 1999 to 2001 |
| 15 | M du Plessis | 1975 to 1980 |
| 12 | RB Skinstad | 2001 to 2007 |
| 11 | JFK Marais | 1971 to 1974 |

## MOST POINTS IN TESTS

| Points | Player | Tests | Career |
|---|---|---|---|
| 893 | PC Montgomery | 102 | 1997 to 2008 |
| 688 | M Steyn | 59 | 2009 to 2014 |
| 312 | HE Botha | 28 | 1980 to 1992 |
| 280 | BG Habana | 103 | 2004 to 2014 |
| 240 | JT Stransky | 22 | 1993 to 1996 |
| 221 | AJJ van Straaten | 21 | 1999 to 2001 |
| 190 | JH van der Westhuizen | 89 | 1993 to 2003 |
| 181 | JH de Beer | 13 | 1997 to 1999 |
| 171 | AS Pretorius | 31 | 2002 to 2007 |
| 160 | J Fourie | 72 | 2003 to 2013 |
| 156 | HW Honiball | 35 | 1993 to 1999 |
| 154 | AD James | 42 | 2001 to 2011 |

## MOST TRIES IN TESTS

| Tries | Player | Tests | Career |
|---|---|---|---|
| 56 | BG Habana | 103 | 2004 to 2014 |
| 38 | JH van der Westhuizen | 89 | 1993 to 2003 |
| 32 | J Fourie | 72 | 2003 to 2013 |
| 27* | BJ Paulse | 64 | 1999 to 2007 |
| 27 | J de Villiers | 102 | 2002 to 2014 |
| 25 | PC Montgomery | 102 | 1997 to 2008 |
| 21 | PWG Rossouw | 43 | 1997 to 2003 |
| 20 | JT Small | 47 | 1992 to 1997 |
| 19 | DM Gerber | 24 | 1980 to 1992 |
| 19 | CS Terblanche | 37 | 1998 to 2003 |
| 17 | J-P R Pietersen | 56 | 2006 to 2014 |
| 15 | PF du Preez | 70 | 2004 to 2014 |
| 14 | CM Williams | 27 | 1993 to 2000 |
| 14 | J-P R Pietersen | 48 | 2006 to 2012 |
| *includes a penalty try | | | |

## MOST CONVERSIONS IN TESTS

| Cons | Player | Tests | Career |
|---|---|---|---|
| 153 | PC Montgomery | 102 | 1997 to 2008 |
| 99 | M Steyn | 59 | 2009 to 2014 |
| 50 | HE Botha | 28 | 1980 to 1992 |
| 38 | HW Honiball | 35 | 1993 to 1999 |
| 33 | JH de Beer | 13 | 1997 to 1999 |
| 31 | AS Pretorius | 31 | 2002 to 2007 |
| 30 | JT Stransky | 22 | 1993 to 1996 |
| 26 | AD James | 42 | 2001 to 2011 |
| 25 | GS du Toit | 14 | 1998 to 2006 |
| 23 | AJJ van Straaten | 21 | 1999 to 2001 |
| 23 | LJ Koen | 15 | 2000 to 2003 |
| 22 | R Pienaar | 80 | 2006 to 2014 |
| 20 | PJ Visagie | 25 | 1967 to 1971 |

## MOST PENALTY GOALS IN TESTS

| Penalties | Player | Tests | Career |
|---|---|---|---|
| 148 | PC Montgomery | 102 | 1997 to 2008 |
| 142 | M Steyn | 59 | 2009 to 2014 |
| 55 | AJJ van Straaten | 21 | 1999 to 2001 |
| 50 | HE Botha | 28 | 1980 to 1992 |
| 47 | JT Stransky | 22 | 1993 to 1996 |
| 31 | LJ Koen | 15 | 2000 to 2003 |
| 28 | AD James | 42 | 2001 to 2011 |
| 27 | JH de Beer | 13 | 1997 to 1999 |
| 25 | HW Honiball | 35 | 1993 to 1999 |
| 25 | AS Pretorius | 31 | 2002 to 2007 |
| 23 | GR Bosch | 9 | 1974 to 1976 |
| 21 | FPL Steyn | 53 | 2006 to 2012 |
| 19 | PJ Visagie | 25 | 1967 to 1971 |

## MOST DROP GOALS IN TESTS

| Drops | Player | Tests | Career |
|---|---|---|---|
| 18 | HE Botha | 28 | 1980 to 1992 |
| 8 | JH de Beer | 13 | 1997 to 1999 |
| 8 | AS Pretorius | 31 | 2002 to 2007 |
| 8 | M Steyn | 59 | 2009 to 2014 |
| 6 | PC Montgomery | 102 | 1997 to 2008 |
| 5 | JD Brewis | 10 | 1949 to 1953 |
| 5 | PJ Visagie | 25 | 1967 to 1971 |
| 4 | BL Osler | 17 | 1924 to 1933 |

# RUGBY CHAMPIONSHIP (FORMERLY TRI NATIONS) RECORDS

| RECORD | DETAIL | HOLDER | SET |
|---|---|---|---|
| Most points in season | 203 | in six matches | 2013 |
| Most tries in season | 23 | in six matches | 2013 |
| Highest score | 73 | 73–13 v Argentina (h) | 2013 |
| Biggest win | 60 | 73–13 v Argentina (h) | 2013 |
| Highest score conceded | 55 | 35–55 v N Zealand (a) | 1997 |
| Biggest defeat | 49 | 0–49 v Australia (a) | 2006 |
| Most appearances | 50 | J de Villiers | 2004 to 2014 |
| Most points in matches | 348 | M Steyn | 2009 to 2014 |
| Most points in season | 95 | M Steyn | 2009 |
| Most points in match | 31 | M Steyn | v N Zealand (h) 2009 |
| Most tries in matches | 18 | BG Habana | 2005 to 2014 |
| Most tries in season | 7 | BG Habana | 2012 |
| Most tries in match | 4 | JL Nokwe | v Australia (h) 2008 |
| Most cons in matches | 41 | M Steyn | 2009 to 2014 |
| Most cons in season | 17 | M Steyn | 2013 |
| Most cons in match | 8 | M Steyn | v Argentina (h) 2013 |
| Most pens in matches | 83 | M Steyn | 2009 to 2014 |
| Most pens in season | 23 | M Steyn | 2009 |
| Most pens in match | 8 | M Steyn | v N Zealand (h) 2009 |

SOUTH AFRICA

# MISCELLANEOUS RECORDS

| RECORD | HOLDER | DETAIL |
|---|---|---|
| Longest Test Career | JP du Randt | 1994–2007 |
| | V Matfield | 2001–2014 |
| Youngest Test Cap | AJ Hartley | 18 yrs 18 days in 1891 |
| Oldest Test Cap | V Matfield | 37 yrs 146 days in 2014 |

## CAREER RECORDS OF SOUTH AFRICA INTERNATIONAL PLAYERS

## UP TO 13 OCTOBER 2014

| PLAYER BACKS: | DEBUT | CAPS | T | C | P | D | PTS |
|---|---|---|---|---|---|---|---|
| ML Boshoff | 2014 v S | 1 | 0 | 1 | 0 | 0 | 2 |
| D de Allende | 2014 v Arg | 2 | 0 | 0 | 0 | 0 | 0 |
| J de Villiers | 2002 v F | 102 | 27 | 0 | 0 | 0 | 135 |
| PF du Preez | 2004 v I | 70 | 15 | 0 | 0 | 0 | 75 |
| JJ Engelbrecht | 2012 v Arg | 12 | 4 | 0 | 0 | 0 | 20 |
| J Fourie | 2003 v U | 72 | 32 | 0 | 0 | 0 | 160 |
| JL Goosen | 2012 v A | 5 | 0 | 1 | 2 | 0 | 8 |
| BG Habana | 2004 v E | 103 | 56 | 0 | 0 | 0 | 280 |
| C Hendricks | 2014 v W | 9 | 6* | 0 | 0 | 0 | 30 |
| F Hougaard | 2009 v It | 32 | 5 | 0 | 0 | 0 | 25 |
| Z Kirchner | 2009 v BI | 29 | 5 | 0 | 0 | 0 | 25 |
| PJ Lambie | 2010 v I | 36 | 2 | 16 | 12 | 1 | 81 |
| WJ Le Roux | 2013 v It | 21 | 7 | 0 | 0 | 0 | 35 |
| LN Mvovo | 2010 v S | 9 | 3 | 0 | 0 | 0 | 15 |
| W Olivier | 2006 v S | 38 | 1 | 0 | 0 | 0 | 5 |
| R Pienaar | 2006 v NZ | 80 | 8 | 22 | 17 | 0 | 135 |
| J-PR Pietersen | 2006 v A | 56 | 17 | 0 | 0 | 0 | 85 |
| H Pollard | 2014 v S | 6 | 2 | 11 | 7 | 1 | 56 |
| JM Reinach | 2014 v A | 2 | 0 | 0 | 0 | 0 | 0 |
| JL Serfontein | 2013 v It | 16 | 1 | 0 | 0 | 0 | 5 |
| FPL Steyn | 2006 v I | 53 | 10 | 5 | 21 | 3 | 132 |
| M Steyn | 2009 v BI | 59 | 8 | 99 | 142 | 8 | 688 |

*Cornal Hendricks's figures include a penalty try awarded against Wales at Nelspruit in 2014

## FORWARDS :

| | | | | | | | |
|---|---|---|---|---|---|---|---|
| LC Adriaanse | 2013 v F | 1 | 0 | 0 | 0 | 0 | 0 |
| WS Alberts | 2010 v W | 32 | 7 | 0 | 0 | 0 | 35 |
| JP Botha | 2002 v F | 83 | 7 | 0 | 0 | 0 | 35 |
| SB Brits | 2008 v It | 7 | 0 | 0 | 0 | 0 | 0 |
| SWP Burger | 2003 v Gg | 73 | 13 | 0 | 0 | 0 | 65 |
| PM Cilliers | 2012 v Arg | 6 | 0 | 0 | 0 | 0 | 0 |
| MC Coetzee | 2012 v E | 22 | 5 | 0 | 0 | 0 | 25 |
| L de Jager | 2014 v W | 7 | 2 | 0 | 0 | 0 | 10 |
| BW du Plessis | 2007 v A | 66 | 9 | 0 | 0 | 0 | 45 |
| JN du Plessis | 2007 v A | 60 | 1 | 0 | 0 | 0 | 5 |
| P-S du Toit | 2013 v W | 2 | 0 | 0 | 0 | 0 | 0 |
| E Etzebeth | 2012 v E | 29 | 0 | 0 | 0 | 0 | 0 |
| S Kolisi | 2013 v S | 10 | 0 | 0 | 0 | 0 | 0 |
| JST Lewies | 2014 v S | 1 | 0 | 0 | 0 | 0 | 0 |
| L-FP Louw | 2010 v W | 34 | 5 | 0 | 0 | 0 | 25 |
| JF Malherbe | 2013 v W | 4 | 0 | 0 | 0 | 0 | 0 |
| V Matfield | 2001 v It | 117 | 7 | 0 | 0 | 0 | 35 |
| TS Mohoje | 2014 v S | 3 | 0 | 0 | 0 | 0 | 0 |
| T Mtawarira | 2008 v W | 61 | 2 | 0 | 0 | 0 | 10 |
| TN Nyakane | 2013 v It | 9 | 1 | 0 | 0 | 0 | 5 |
| CV Oosthuizen | 2012 v E | 17 | 2 | 0 | 0 | 0 | 10 |
| JH Smith | 2003 v S | 70 | 12 | 0 | 0 | 0 | 60 |
| GG Steenkamp | 2004 v S | 52 | 6 | 0 | 0 | 0 | 30 |
| JA Strauss | 2008 v A | 40 | 5 | 0 | 0 | 0 | 25 |
| M van der Merwe | 2014 v S | 5 | 0 | 0 | 0 | 0 | 0 |
| PR van der Merwe | 2010 v F | 35 | 1 | 0 | 0 | 0 | 5 |
| DJ Vermeulen | 2012 v A | 25 | 2 | 0 | 0 | 0 | 10 |
| WR Whiteley | 2014 v A | 2 | 0 | 0 | 0 | 0 | 0 |

SOUTH AFRICA

# SOUTH AFRICAN INTERNATIONAL PLAYERS
## UP TO 13 OCTOBER 2014
Entries in square brackets denote matches played in RWC Finals.

**Ackermann, D S P** (WP) 1955 BI 2, 3, 4, 1956 A 1, 2, NZ 1, 3, 1958 F 2
**Ackermann, J N** (NT, BB, N) 1996 Fj, A 1, NZ 1, A 2, 2001 F 2(R), It 1, NZ 1(R), A 1, 2006 I, E1, 2, 2007 Sm, A2
**Adriaanse, L C** (Griquas) 2013 F(R)
**Aitken, A D** (WP) 1997 F 2(R), E, 1998 I 2(R), W 1(R), NZ 1, 2(R), A 2(R)
**Alberts, W S** (NS) 2010 W2(R), S(t&R), E(R), 2011 NZ2, [W(R), Fj(R), Nm, Sm(t&R), A(t&R)], 2012 E1, 2, Arg1, 2, A1, NZ1, A2, NZ2, I, S, E4, 2013 Sm, Arg1, 2, A1, NZ1, A2, NZ2, W, S2, F, 2014 W1, 2
**Albertyn, P K** (SWD) 1924 BI 1, 2, 3, 4
**Alexander, F A** (GW) 1891 BI 1, 2
**Allan, J** (N) 1993 A 1(R), Arg 1, 2(R), 1994 E 1, 2, NZ 1, 2, 3, 1996 Fj, A 1, NZ 1, A 2, NZ 2
**Allen, P B** (EP) 1960 S
**Allport, P H** (WP) 1910 BI 2, 3
**Anderson, J W** (WP) 1903 BI 3
**Anderson, J H** (WP) 1896 BI 1, 3, 4
**Andrew, J B** (Tvl) 1896 BI 2
**Andrews, E P** (WP) 2004 I1, 2, W1(t&R), PI, NZ1, A1, NZ2, A2, W2, I3, E, 2005 F1, A2, NZ2(t), Arg(R), F3(R), 2006 S1, 2, F, A1(R), NZ1(t), 2007 A2(R), NZ2(R)
**Andrews, K S** (WP) 1992 E, 1993 F 1, 2, A 1(R), 2, 3, Arg 1(R), 2, 1994 NZ 3
**Andrews, M G** (N) 1994 E 2, NZ 1, 2, 3, Arg 1, 2, S, W, 1995 WS, [A, WS, F, NZ], W, It, E, 1996 Fj, A 1, NZ 1, A 2, NZ 2, 3, 4, 5, Arg 1, 2, F 1, 2, W, 1997 Tg (R), BI 1, NZ 1, A 1, NZ 2, A 2, It, F 1, 2, E, S, 1998 I 1, 2, W 1, E 1, A 1, NZ 1, 2, A 2, W 2, S, I 3, E 2, 1999 NZ 1, 2(R), A 2(R), [S, U, E, A 3, NZ 3], 2000 A 2, NZ 2, A 3, Arg, I, W, E 3, 2001 F 1, 2, It 1, NZ 1, A 1, 2, NZ 2, F 3, E
**Antelme, J G M** (Tvl) 1960 NZ 1, 2, 3, 4, 1961 F
**Apsey, J T** (WP) 1933 A 4, 5, 1938 BI 2
**Aplon, G G** (WP) 2010 W1, F, It 1, 2, NZ1(R), 2(R), A1, NZ3, A3(R), I, NZ2, S, E, 2011 A1, 2(R), [Nm], 2012 E3
**Ashley, S** (WP) 1903 BI 2
**Aston, F T D** (Tvl) 1896 BI 1, 2, 3, 4
**Atherton, S** (N) 1993 Arg 1, 2, 1994 E 1, 2, NZ 1, 2, 3, 1996 NZ 2

**Aucamp, J** (WT) 1924 BI 1, 2

**Baard, A P** (WP) 1960 I
**Babrow, L** (WP) 1937 A 1, 2, NZ 1, 2, 3
**Badenhorst, C** (OFS) 1994 Arg 2, 1995 WS (R)
**Bands, R E** (BB) 2003 S 1, 2, Arg (R), A 1, NZ 1, A 2, NZ 2, [U, E, Sm(R), NZ(R)]
**Barnard, A S** (EP) 1984 S Am 1, 2, 1986 Cv 1, 2
**Barnard, J H** (Tvl) 1965 S, A 1, 2, NZ 3, 4
**Barnard, R W** (Tvl) 1970 NZ 2(R)
**Barnard, W H M** (NT) 1949 NZ 4, 1951 W
**Barry, D W** (WP) 2000 C, E 1, 2, A 1(R), NZ 1, A 2, 2001 F 1, 2, US (R), 2002 W 2, Arg, Sm, NZ 1, A 1, NZ 2, A 2, 2003 A 1, NZ 1, A 2, [U, E, Sm, NZ], 2004 PI, NZ1, A1, NZ2, A2, W2, I3, E, Arg(t), 2005 F1, 2, A1, NZ2, W(R), F3(R), 2006 F 1, 2, It 1, NZ2, 2, A1, NZ2, W(R), F3(R), 2006 F
**Barry, J** (WP) 1903 BI 1, 2, 3
**Bartmann, W J** (Tvl, N) 1986 Cv 1, 2, 3, 4, 1992 NZ, A, F 1, 2
**Basson, B A** (GW, BB) 2010 W1(R), It 1(R), I, W2, 2011 A1, NZ1, 2013 It, S1, Sm, Arg1, 2
**Bastard, W E** (N) 1937 A 1, NZ 2, 3, 1938 BI 1, 3
**Bates, A J** (WT) 1969 E, 1970 NZ 1, 2, 1972 E
**Bayvel, P C R** (Tvl) 1974 BI 2, 4, F 1, 2, 1975 F 1, 2, 1976 NZ 1, 2, 3, 4

**Beck, J J** (WP) 1981 NZ 2(R), 3(R), US
**Bedford, T P** (N) 1963 A 1, 2, 3, 4, 1964 W, F, 1965 I, A 1, 2, 1968 BI 1, 2, 3, 4, F 1, 2, 1969 A 1, 2, 3, 4, S, E, 1970 I, W, 1971 F 1, 2
**Bekker, A** (WP) 2008 W1, 2(R), It(R), NZ1(R), 2(t&R), A1(t&R), Arg(R), NZ3, A2, 3, W3(R), S(R), E(R), 2009 BI 1(R), 2(R), NZ2(R), A1(R), 2(R), F(t&R), It, I, 2010 It2, NZ1(R), 2(R), A2, NZ2
**Bekker, H J** (WP) 1981 NZ 1, 3
**Bekker, H P J** (NT) 1952 E, F, 1953 A 1, 2, 3, 4, 1955 BI 2, 3, 4, 1956 A 1, 2, NZ 1, 2, 3, 4
**Bekker, M J** (NT) 1960 S
**Bekker, R P** (NT) 1953 A 3, 4
**Bekker, S** (NT) 1997 A 2(t)
**Bennett, R G** (Border) 1997 Tg (R), BI 1(R), 3, NZ 1, A 1, NZ 2
**Bergh, W F** (SWD) 1931 W, I, 1932 E, S, 1933 A 1, 2, 3, 4, 5, 1937 A 1, 2, NZ 1, 2, 3, 1938 BI 1, 2, 3
**Bestbier, A** (OFS) 1974 F 2(R)
**Bester, J J N** (WP) 1924 BI 2, 4
**Bester, J L A** (WP) 1938 BI 2, 3
**Beswick, A M** (Bor) 1896 BI 2, 3, 4
**Bezuidenhout, C E** (NT) 1962 BI 2, 3, 4
**Bezuidenhout, C J** (MP) 2003 NZ 2(R), [E, Sm, NZ]
**Bezuidenhout, N S E** (NT) 1972 E, 1974 BI 2, 3, 4, F 1, 2, 1975 F 1, 2, 1977 Wld
**Bierman, J N** (Tvl) 1931 I
**Bisset, W M** (WP) 1891 BI 1, 3
**Blair, R** (WP) 1977 Wld
**Bobo, G** (GL, WP) 2003 S 2(R), Arg, A 1(R), NZ 2, 2004 S(R), 2008 It
**Boome, C S** (WP) 1999 It 1, 2, W, NZ 1(R), A 1, NZ 2, A 2, 2000 C, E 1, 2, 2003 S 1(R), 2(R), Arg (R), A 1(R), NZ 1(R), A 2, NZ 2(R), [U(R), Gg, NZ(R)]
**Bosch, G R** (Tvl) 1974 BI 2, F 1, 2, 1975 F 1, 2, 1976 NZ 1, 2, 3, 4
**Boshoff, M L** (GL) 2014 S(R)
**Bosman, H M** (FS) 2005 W, F3, 2006 A1(R)
**Bosman, N J S** (Tvl) 1924 BI 2, 3, 4
**Botha, A F** (BB) 2013 It, S1
**Botha, B J** (N, Ulster) 2006 NZ2(R), 3, A3, I(R), E1, 2, 2007 E1, Sm, A1, NZ1, Nm(R), S(t&R), [Sm(R), E1, Tg(R), US], 2008 W2, 2009 It(R), I, 2010 W1, F, It 2(R), NZ1(R), 2(R), A1
**Botha, D S** (NT) 1981 NZ 1
**Botha, G van G** (BB) 2005 A3(R), F3(R), 2007 E1(R), 2(R), Sm(R), A1(R), NZ1, A2, NZ2(R), Nm, S, [Tg]
**Botha, H E** (NT) 1980 S Am 1, 2, BI 1, 2, 3, 4, S Am 3, 4, F, 1981 I 1, 2, NZ 1, 2, 3, US, 1982 S Am 1, 2, 1986 Cv 1, 2, 3, 4, 1989 Wld 1, 2, 1992 NZ, A, F 1, 2, E
**Botha, J A** (Tvl) 1903 BI 3
**Botha, J P** (BB, Toulon) 2002 F, 2003 S 1, 2, A 1, NZ 1, A 2(R), [U, E, Gg, Sm, NZ], 2004 I1, PI, NZ1, A1, NZ2, A2, W2, I3, E, S, Arg, 2005 A1, 2, 3, NZ1, A4, NZ2, Arg, W, F3, 2007 E1, 2, A1, NZ1, Nm, S, [Sm, E1, Tg, US(R), Fj, Arg, E2], W, 2008 W1, 2, It, NZ1, 2, A1, Arg, W3, A, S, E, 2009 BI 1, 2, NZ1, 2, A1, 2, 3, NZ3, F, It, 2010 It1, 2, NZ1, I, W2, S, E, 2011 A2, NZ2, [Fj, Nm], 2013 S2, F(R), 2014 W1, Arg1, 2, A2(R), NZ2(R)
**Botha, J P F** (NT) 1962 BI 2, 3, 4
**Botha, P H** (NT) 1965 A 1, 2
**Boyes, H C** (GW) 1891 BI 1, 2
**Brand, G H** (WP) 1928 NZ 2, 3, 1931 W, I, 1932 E, S, 1933 A 1, 2, 3, 4, 5, 1937 A 1, 2, NZ 2, 3, 1938 BI 1

**Douglass, F W** (EP) 1896 BI 1
**Drotské, A E** (OFS) 1993 Arg 2, 1995 [WS (R)], 1996 A 1(R), 1997 Tg, BI 1, 2, 3(R), NZ 1, A 1, NZ 2(R), 1998 I 2(R), W 1(R), I 3(R), 1999 It 1, 2, W, NZ 1, A 1, NZ 2, A 2, [S, Sp (R), U, E, A 3, NZ 3]
**Dryburgh, R G** (WP) 1955 BI 2, 3, 4, 1956 A 2, NZ 1, 4, 1960 NZ 1, 2
**Duff, B R** (WP) 1891 BI 1, 2, 3
**Duffy, B A** (Bor) 1928 NZ 1
**Du Plessis, B W** (NS) 2007 A2(t&R), NZ2, Nm(R), S(R), [Sm(R), E1(R), US(R), Arg(R), E2(t)], W(R), 2008 W1(R), 2(R), It, NZ1(R), 2, Arg, NZ3, A2, 3, W3, S, 2009 BI 1, 2, 3(R), NZ1, 2, A1, 2, 3, NZ3, F, I(R), 2010 I, W2, S, E, 2011 A2(R), NZ2, [W(R), Fj(R), Sm, A(R)], 2012 E1, 2, 3, Arg1, 2013 S1(R), Sm(R), Arg1(R), 2(R), A1, NZ1, A2(R), NZ2, W, S2(R), F, 2014 W1, 2, S, Arg1, 2, A1(R), NZ1(R), A2(R), NZ2
**Du Plessis, C J** (WP) 1982 S Am 1, 2, 1984 E 1, 2, S Am 1, 2, 1986 Cv 1, 2, 3, 4, 1989 Wld 1, 2
**Du Plessis, D C** (NT) 1977 Wld, 1980 S Am 2
**Du Plessis, F** (Tvl) 1949 NZ 1, 2, 3
**Du Plessis, J N** (FS, NS) 2007 A2, NZ2, [Fj, Arg(t&R)], W, 2008 A3(R), E, 2009 NZ1(t), 2(R), A1(R), 2(R), NZ3(R), 2010 W1(R), F(R), It 1, 2, NZ1, 3, A2, 3, I, W2, S, E, 2011 A2, NZ2, [W, Fj, Sm, A], 2012 E1, 2, 3, Arg1, 2, A1, NZ1, A2, NZ2, I, S, E4, 2013 It, S1, Sm, Arg1, 2, A1, NZ1, A2, NZ2, 2014 W1, 2, S, Arg1, 2, A1, NZ1, A2, NZ2
**Du Plessis, M** (WP) 1971 A 1, 2, 3, 1974 BI 1, 2, F 1, 2, 1975 F 1, 2, 1976 NZ 1, 2, 3, 4, 1977 Wld, 1980 S Am 1, 2, BI 1, 2, 3, 4, S Am 4, F
**Du Plessis, M J** (WP) 1984 S Am 1, 2, 1986 Cv 1, 2, 3, 4, 1989 Wld 1, 2
**Du Plessis, N J** (WT) 1921 NZ 2, 3, 1924 BI 1, 2, 3
**Du Plessis, P G** (NT) 1972 E
**Du Plessis, T D** (NT) 1980 S Am 1, 2
**Du Plessis, W** (WP) 1980 S Am 1, 2, BI 1, 2, 3, 4, S Am 3, 4, F, 1981 NZ 1, 2, 3, 1982 S Am 1, 2
**Du Plooy, A J J** (EP) 1955 BI 1
**Du Preez, F C H** (NT) 1961 E, S, A 1, 2, 1962 BI 1, 2, 3, 4, 1963 A 1, 1964 W, F, 1965 A 1, 2, NZ 1, 2, 3, 4, 1967 F 4, 1968 BI 1, 2, 3, 4, F 1, 2, 1969 A 1, 2, S, 1970 I, W, NZ 1, 2, 3, 4, 1971 F 1, 2, A 1, 2, 3
**Du Preez, G J D** (GL) 2002 Sm (R), A 1(R)
**Du Preez, J G H** (WP) 1956 NZ 1
**Du Preez, P F** (BB, Suntory Sungoliaths) 2004 I1, 2, W1, PI(R), NZ1, A1, NZ2(R), A2(R), W2, I3, E, S, Arg, 2005 U(R), F1, 2(R), A1(R), 2(R), 3, NZ1(R), A4(R), 2006 S1, 2, F, A1(R), NZ1, A2, NZ2, 3, A3, 2007 Nm, S, [Sm, E1, US, Fj, Arg, E2], 2008 Arg(R), NZ3, A2, 3, W3, 2009 BI 1, 2, 3, NZ1, 2, A1, 2, 3, NZ3, F, It, I, 2011 A2, NZ2, [W, Fj, Nm(R), Sm, A], 2013 Arg1(R), A2, NZ2, W, S2, 2014 W1, 2, S
**Du Preez, R J** (N) 1992 NZ, A, 1993 F 1, 2, A 1, 2, 3
**Du Preez, W H** (FS) 2009 It
**Du Rand, J A** (R, NT) 1949 NZ 2, 3, 1951 S, I, W, 1952 E, F, 1953 A 1, 2, 3, 4, 1955 BI 1, 2, 3, 4, 1956 A 1, 2, NZ 1, 2, 3, 4
**Du Randt, J P** (OFS, FS) 1994 Arg 1, 2, S, W, 1995 WS, [A, WS, F, NZ], 1996 Fj, A 1, NZ 1, A 2, NZ 2, 3, 4, 1997 Tg, BI 1, 2, 3, NZ 1, A 1, NZ 2, A 2, It, F 1, 2, E, S, 1999 NZ 1, A 1, NZ 2, A 2, [S, Sp (R), U, E, A 3, NZ 3], 2004 I1, 2, W1, PI, NZ1, A1, NZ2, A2, W2, I3, E, S(R), Arg(R), 2005 U(R), F1, A1, NZ1, A4, NZ2, Arg, W(R), F3, 2006 S1, 2, F, A1, NZ1, A2, NZ2, 3, A3, 2007 Sm, NZ1, Nm, S, [Sm, E1, US, Fj, Arg, E2]
**Du Toit, A F** (WP) 1928 NZ 3, 4
**Du Toit, B A** (Tvl) 1938 BI 1, 2, 3
**Du Toit, G S** (GW, WP) 1998 I 1, 1999 It 1, 2, W (R), NZ 1, 2, 2004 I1, W1(R), A1(R), S(R), Arg, 2006 S1(R), 2(R), F(R)
**Du Toit, P A** (NT) 1949 NZ 2, 3, 4, 1951 S, I, W, 1952 E, F
**Du Toit, P G** (WP) 1981 NZ 1, 1982 S Am 1, 2, 1984 E 1, 2
**Du Toit, P-S** (NS) 2013 W(R), F(R)
**Du Toit, P S** (WP) 1958 F 1, 2, 1960 NZ 1, 2, 3, 4, W, I, 1961 E, S, F, I, A 1, 2
**Duvenhage, F P** (GW) 1949 NZ 1, 3

**Edwards, P** (NT) 1980 S Am 1, 2
**Ellis, J H** (SWA) 1965 NZ 1, 2, 3, 4, 1967 F 1, 2, 3, 4, 1968 BI 1, 2, 3, 4, F 1, 2, 1969 A 1, 2, 3, 4, S, 1970 I, W, NZ

1, 2, 3, 4, 1971 F 1, 2, A 1, 2, 3, 1972 E, 1974 BI 1, 2, 3, 4, F 1, 2, 1976 NZ 1
**Ellis, M C** (Tvl) 1921 NZ 2, 3, 1924 BI 1, 2, 3, 4
**Els, W W** (OFS) 1997 A 2(R)
**Engelbrecht, J J** (BB) 2012 Arg1(R), 2013 It, S1, Sm, Arg1, 2, A1, NZ1, A2, NZ2, W(R), S2(R)
**Engelbrecht, J P** (WP) 1960 S, W, I, 1961 E, S, F, A 1, 2, 1962 BI 2, 3, 4, 1963 A 2, 3, 1964 W, F, 1965 I, S, A 1, 2, NZ 1, 2, 3, 4, 1967 F 1, 2, 3, 4, 1968 BI 1, 2, F 1, 2, 1969 A 1, 2
**Erasmus, F S** (NT, EP) 1986 Cv 3, 4, 1989 Wld 2
**Erasmus, J C** (OFS, GL) 1997 BI 3, A 2, It, F 1, 2, S, 1998 I 1, 2, W 1, E 1, A 1, NZ 2, A 2, S, W 2, I 3, E 2, 1999 It 1, 2, W, A 1, NZ 2, A 2, [S, U, E, A 3, NZ 3], 2000 C, E 1, A 1, NZ 1, 2, A 3, 2001 F 1, 2
**Esterhuizen, G** (GL) 2000 NZ 1(R), 2, A 3, Arg, I, W (R), E 3(t)
**Etlinger, T E** (WP) 1896 BI 4
**Etzebeth, B** (WP) 2012 E 1, 2, 3, Arg1, 2, A1, 2, NZ2, I, S, E4, 2013 It, S1, Sm, Arg1, 2, A1, NZ1, A2, NZ2, W, S2(R), F, 2014 Arg1(R), 2, A1, NZ1, A2, NZ2

**Ferreira, C** (OFS) 1986 Cv 1, 2
**Ferreira, P S** (WP) 1984 S Am 1, 2
**Ferris, H H** (Tvl) 1903 BI 3
**Fleck R F** (WP) 1999 It 1, 2, NZ 1(R), A 1, NZ 2(R), A 2, [S, U, E, A 3, NZ 3], 2000 C, E 1, 2, A 1, NZ 1, A 2, NZ 2, A 3, Arg, I, W, E 3, 2001 F 1(R), 2, It 1, NZ 1, A 1, 2, 2002 S, E
**Floors, L** (FS) 2006 E2
**Forbes, H H** (Tvl) 1896 BI 2
**Fortuin, B A** (FS) 2006 I, 2007 A2
**Fourie, C** (EP) 1974 F 1, 2, 1975 F 1, 2
**Fourie, J** (GL, WP, Kobe Steel) 2003 [U, Gg, Sm(R), NZ(R)], 2004 I2, E(R), S, Arg, 2005 U(R), F2(R), A1(R), 2, 3, NZ1, A4, NZ2, Arg, W, F3, 2006 S1, A1, NZ1, A2, NZ2, 3, A3, 2007 Sm(R), A1, NZ1, Nm, S, [Sm, E1, US, Fj, Arg, E2], W, 2008 Arg(R), W3(R), S(R), E(R), 2009 BI 1(R), 2(R), 3, NZ1, 2, A1, 2, 3, NZ3, F, It, I, 2010 W1, F, It2, NZ1, 2, A1, 2, 3, 2011A2, NZ2, [W, Fj, Nm, Sm, A], 2013 W, S2, F
**Fourie, T T** (SET) 1974 BI 3
**Fourie, W L** (SWA) 1958 F 1, 2
**Francis, J A J** (Tvl) 1912 S, I, W, 1913 E, F
**Frederickson, C A** (Tvl) 1974 BI 2, 1980 S Am 1, 2
**Frew, A** (Tvl) 1903 BI 1
**Froneman, D C** (OFS) 1977 Wld
**Froneman, I L** (Bor) 1933 A 1
**Fuls, H T** (Tvl, EP) 1992 NZ (R), 1993 F 1, 2, A 1, 2, 3, Arg 1, 2
**Fry, S P** (WP) 1951 S, I, W, 1952 E, F, 1953 A 1, 2, 3, 4, 1955 BI 1, 2, 3, 4
**Fynn, E E** (N) 2001 F 1, It 1(R)
**Fyvie, W** (N) 1996 NZ 4(t & R), 5(R), Arg 2(R)

**Gage, J H** (OFS) 1933 A 1
**Gainsford, J L** (WP) 1960 S, NZ 1, 2, 3, 4, W, I, 1961 E, S, F, A 1, 2, 1962 BI 1, 2, 3, 4, 1963 A 1, 2, 3, 4, 1964 W, F, 1965 I, S, A 1, 2, NZ 1, 2, 3, 4, 1967 F 1, 2, 3
**Garvey, A C** (N) 1996 Arg 1, 2, F 1, 2, W, 1997 Tg, BI 1, 2, 3(R), A 1(t), It, F 1, 2, E, S, 1998 I 1, 2, W 1, E1, A 1, NZ 1, 2, A 2, W 2, S, I 3, E 2, 1999 [Sp]
**Geel, P J** (OFS) 1949 NZ 3
**Geere, V** (Tvl) 1933 A 1, 2, 3, 4, 5
**Geffin, A O** (Tvl) 1949 NZ 1, 2, 3, 4, 1951 S, I, W
**Geldenhuys, A** (EP) 1992 NZ, A, F 1, 2
**Geldenhuys, S B** (NT) 1981 NZ 2, 3, US, 1982 S Am 1, 2, 1989 Wld 1, 2
**Gentles, T A** (WP) 1955 BI 1, 2, 4, 1956 NZ 2, 3, 1958 F 2
**Geraghty, E M** (Bor) 1949 NZ 4
**Gerber, D M** (EP, WP) 1980 S Am 3, 4, F, 1981 I 1, 2, NZ 1, 2, 3, US, 1982 S Am 1, 2, 1984 E 1, 2, S Am 1, 2, 1986 Cv 1, 2, 3, 4, 1992 NZ, A, F 1, 2, E
**Gerber, H J** (WP) 2003 S 1, 2
**Gerber, M C** (EP) 1958 F 1, 2, 1960 S
**Gericke, F W** (Tvl) 1960 S
**Germishuys, J S** (OFS, Tvl) 1974 BI 2, 1976 NZ 1, 2, 3, 4, 1977 Wld, 1980 S Am 1, 2, BI 1, 2, 3, 4, S Am 3, 4, F, 1981 I 1, 2, NZ 2, 3, US
**Gibbs, B** (GW) 1903 BI 2
**Goosen, C P** (OFS) 1965 NZ 2
**Goosen, J L** (FS) 2012 A1(R), NZ1(R), A2, NZ2, 2014 W1(R)

**Kruger, P E** (Tvl) 1986 Cv 3, 4
**Kruger, P J J** (BB, Racing Metro) 2012 E1, 2, 3, A1, NZ1, I, S, E4, 2013 It, S1, Sm(t&R), Arg1, 2, A1(R), NZ1(R), A2(R), NZ2
**Kruger, R J** (NT, BB) 1993 Arg 1, 2, 1994 S, W, 1995 WS, [A, R, WS, F, NZ], W, It, E, 1996 Fj, A 1, NZ 1, A 2, NZ 2, 3, 4, 5, Arg 1, 2, F 1, 2, W, 1997 Tg, BI 1, 2, NZ 1, A 1, NZ 2, 1999 NZ 2, A 2(R), [Sp, NZ 3(R)]
**Kruger, T L** (Tvl) 1921 NZ 1, 2, 1924 BI 1, 2, 3, 4, 1928 NZ 1, 2
**Kruger, W** (BB) 2011 A1, NZ1, 2012 E2(R), 3(R)
**Kuhn, S P** (Tvl) 1960 NZ 3, 4, W, I, 1961 E, S, F, I, A 1, 2, 1962 BI 1, 2, 3, 4, 1963 A 1, 2, 3, 1965 I, S

**Labuschagne, J J** (GL) 2000 NZ 1(R), 2002 W 1, 2, Arg, NZ 1, A 1, NZ 2, A2, F, S, E
**La Grange, J B** (WP) 1924 BI 3, 4
**Lambie, P J** (NS) 2010 I(R), W2(R), S(R), E(R), 2011 A1(R), NZ1, 2, [Fj, Nm, Sm, A], 2012 E1(R), 2, A1(R), NZ1(R), A2(R), NZ2(R), I, S, E4, 2013 It(R), S1(R), Sm(R), Arg1(R), 2(R), A1(R), NZ1(R), A2(R), NZ2(R), W, S2, F(t&R), 2014 A1(R), NZ1(R), A2(R), NZ2(R)
**Larard, A** (Tvl) 1896 BI 2, 4
**Lategan, M T** (WP) 1949 NZ 1, 2, 3, 4, 1951 S, I, W, 1952 E, F, 1953 A 1, 2
**Laubscher, T G** (WP) 1994 Arg 1, 2, S, W, 1995 It, E
**Lawless, M J** (WP) 1964 F, 1969 E (R), 1970 I, W
**Ledger, S H** (GW) 1912 S, I, 1913 E, F
**Leonard, A** (WP, SWD) 1999 A 1, [Sp]
**Le Roux, A H** (OFS, N) 1994 E 1, 1998 I 1, 2, W 1(R), E 1(R), A 1(R), NZ 1(R), 2(R), A 2(R), W S (R), I 3(R), E 2(t+R), 1999 It 1(R), 2(R), W (R), NZ 1(R), NZ 2(R), A 2(R), [S(R), Sp, U (R), E (R), A 3(R), NZ 3(R)], 2000 E 1(t+R), 2(R), A 1(R), 2(R), NZ 2, A 3(R), Arg (R), I (t), W (R), E 3(R), 2001 F 1(R), 2, It 1, NZ 1(R), A 1(R), 2(R), NZ 2(R), F 3, It 2, E, US (R), 2002 W 1(R), 2(R), Arg, NZ 1(R), A 1(R), NZ 2(R), A 2(R)
**Le Roux, H P** (Tvl) 1993 F 1, 2, 1994 E 1, 2, NZ 1, 2, 3, Arg 2, S, W, 1995 WS [A, R, C (R), WS, F, NZ], W, It, E, 1996 Fj, NZ 2, Arg 1, 2, F 1, 2, W
**Le Roux, J H S** (Tvl) 1994 E 2, NZ 1, 2
**Le Roux, M** (OFS) 1980 BI 1, 2, 3, 4, S Am 3, 4, F, 1981 I 1
**Le Roux, P A** (WP) 1906 I, W, E
**Le Roux, W J** (Griquas) 2013 It, S1, Sm, Arg1, 2, A1, NZ1, A2, NZ2, W(R), S2, F, 2014 W1, 2, S, Arg1, 2, A1, NZ1, A2, NZ2
**Lewies, J** (NS) 2014 S(R)
**Liebenberg, C R** (WP) 2012 Arg2(R), A1(R), NZ1(R), A2(R), NZ2(R)
**Little, E M** (GW) 1891 BI 1, 3
**Lobberts, H** (BB) 2006 E1(R), 2007 NZ2(R)
**Lochner, G P** (WP) 1955 BI 3, 1956 A 1, 2, NZ 1, 2, 3, 4, 1958 F 1, 2
**Lochner, G P** (EP) 1937 NZ 3, 1938 BI 1, 2
**Lockyear, R J** (GW) 1960 NZ 1, 2, 3, 4, 1960 I, 1961 F
**Lombard, A C** (EP) 1910 BI 2
**Lombard, F** (FS) 2002 S, E
**Lötter, D** (Tvl) 1993 F 2, A 1, 2
**Lotz, J W** (Tvl) 1937 A 1, 2, NZ 1, 2, 3, 1938 BI 1, 2, 3
**Loubscher, R I P** (EP, N) 2002 W 1, 2003 S 1, [U(R), Gg]
**Loubser, J A** (WP) 1903 BI 3, 1906 S, I, W, E, 1910 BI 1, 3
**Lourens, J S T** (NS) 1968 BI 2, 3, 4
**Louw, F H** (WP) 2002 W 2(R), Arg, Sm
**Louw, J S** (Tvl) 1891 BI 1, 2, 3
**Louw, L-F P** (WP, Bath) 2010 W1, F, It 1, 2, NZ1, 2, 3(R), 2011 [Fj(t), Nm(t&R)], A(R)], 2012 A1(R), NZ1, A2, NZ2, I, S, E4, 2013 It, Sm, Arg1, 2, A1, NZ1, A2, NZ2, W, S2, F, 2014 W1, 2, Arg1, 2, A1, NZ1
**Louw, M J** (Tvl) 1971 A 2, 3
**Louw, M M** (WP) 1928 NZ 3, 4, 1931 W, I, 1932 E, S, 1933 A 1, 2, 3, 4, 5, 1937 A 1, 2, NZ 2, 3, 1938 BI 1, 2, 3
**Louw, R J** (WP) 1980 S Am 1, 2, BI 1, 2, 3, 4 S Am 3, 4, F, 1981 I 1 2, NZ 1 3, 1982 S Am 1, 2, 1984 E 1, 2, S Am 1, 2
**Louw, S C** (WP) 1933 A 1, 2, 3, 4, 5, 1937 A 1, NZ 1, 2, 3, 1938 BI 1, 2, 3
**Lubbe, E** (GW) 1997 Tg, BI 1
**Luyt, F P** (WP) 1910 BI 1, 2, 3, 1912 S, I, W, 1913 E, F
**Luyt, J D** (EP) 1912 S, W, 1913 E, F
**Luyt, R R** (W P) 1910 BI 2, 3, 1912 S, I, W, 1913 E, F

**Lyons, D J** (EP) 1896 BI 1
**Lyster, P J** (N) 1933 A 2, 5, 1937 NZ 1

**McCallum, I D** (WP) 1970 NZ 1, 2, 3, 4, 1971 F 1, 2, A 1, 2, 3, 1974 BI 1, 2
**McCallum, R J** (WP) 1974 BI 1
**McCulloch, J D** (GW) 1913 E, F
**MacDonald, A W** (R) 1965 A 1, NZ 1, 2, 3, 4
**Macdonald, D A** (WP) 1974 BI 2
**Macdonald, I** (Tvl) 1992 NZ, A, 1993 F 1, A 3, 1994 E 2, 1995 WS (R)
**McDonald, J A J** (WP) 1931 W, I, 1932 E, S
**McEwan, W M C** (Tvl) 1903 BI 1, 3
**McHardy, E E** (OFS) 1912 S, I, W, 1913 E, F
**McKendrick, J A** (WP) 1891 BI 3
**McLeod, C** (NS) 2011 NZ1(R)
**Maku, B G** (BB) 2010 It1(R)
**Malan, A S** (Tvl) 1960 NZ 1, 2, 3, 4, W, I, 1961 E, S, F, 1962 BI 1, 1963 A 1, 2, 3, 1964 W, 1965 I, S
**Malan, A W** (NT) 1989 Wld 1, 2, 1992 NZ, A, F 1, 2, E
**Malan, E** (NT) 1980 BI 3(R), 4
**Malan, G F** (WP) 1958 F 2, 1960 NZ 1, 3, 4, 1961 E, S, F, 1962 BI 1, 2, 3, 1963 A 1, 2, 4, 1964 W, 1965 A 1, 2, NZ 1, 2
**Malan, P** (Tvl) 1949 NZ 4
**Malherbe, J F** (WP) 2013 W, S2, 2014 Arg1(R), 2(R)
**Mallett, N V H** (WP) 1984 S Am 1, 2
**Malotana, K** (Bor) 1999 [Sp]
**Mans, W J** (WP) 1965 I, S
**Marais, C F** (WP) 1999 It 1(R), 2(R), 2000 C, E 1, 2, A 1, NZ 1, A 2, NZ 2, A 3, Arg (R), W (R)
**Marais, F P** (Bol) 1949 NZ 1, 2, 1951 S, 1953 A 1, 2
**Marais, J F K** (WP) 1963 A 3, 1964 W, F, 1965 I, S, A 2, 1968 BI, 1, 2, 3, 4, 1971 F 1, 2, A 1, 2, 3, 1974 BI 1, 2, 3, 4, 1971 F 1, 2, A 1, 2, 3, 1974 BI 1, 2, 3, 4, 5 E, 1970 I, W, NZ 1, 2, 3, 4, 1971 F 1, 2, A 1, 2, 3, 1974 F 1, 2
**Maré, D S** (Tvl) 1906 S
**Marsberg, A F W** (GW) 1906 S, W, E
**Marsberg, P A** (GW) 1910 BI 1
**Martheze, W C** (GW) 1903 BI 2, 1906 I, W
**Martin, H J** (Tvl) 1937 A 2
**Matfield, V** (BB) 2001 It 1(R), NZ 1, A 2, NZ 2, F 3, It 2, E, US, 2002 W 1, Sm, NZ 1, A 1, NZ 2(R), 2003 S 1, 2, Arg, A 1, NZ 1, A 2, NZ 2, [U, E, Sm, NZ], 2004 I1, 2, W1, NZ2, A2, W2, I3, E, S, Arg, 2005 F 1, A1, 2, 3, NZ1, A4, NZ2, Arg, W, F3, 2006 S1, 2, F, A1, NZ1, A2, NZ2, 3, A3, 2007 E1, 2, A1, NZ1, Nm, S, [Sm, E1, Tg(R), US, Fj, Arg, E2], 2008 W1(R), 2, It, NZ1, 2, A1, Arg, NZ3, A2, 3, W3, S, E, 2009 BI 1, 2, 3, NZ1, 2, A1, 2, NZ3, F, It(R), I, 2010 W1, F, It 1, NZ1, 2, A1, NZ3, A2, 3, I, W2, S, E, 2011 A2, NZ2, [W, Sm, A], 2014 W1, 2, S, A1, NZ1, A2, NZ2
**Mellet, T B** (GW) 1896 BI 2
**Mellish, F W** (WP) 1921 NZ 1, 3, 1924 BI 1, 2, 3, 4
**Mentz, H** (N) 2004 I1, W1(R)
**Merry, J** (EP) 1891 BI 1
**Metcalf, H D** (Bor) 1903 BI 2
**Meyer, C du P** (WP) 1921 NZ 1, 2, 3
**Meyer, P J** (GW) 1896 BI 1
**Meyer, W** (OFS, GL) 1997 S (R), 1999 It 2, NZ 1(R), A 1(R), 2000 C (R), E 1, NZ 1(R), 2(R), Arg, I, W, E 3, 2001 F 1(R), 2, It 1, F 3(R), It 2, E, US (t+R), 2002 W 1, 2, Arg, NZ 1, 2, A 2, F
**Michau, J M** (Tvl) 1921 NZ 1
**Michau, J P** (WP) 1921 NZ 1, 2, 3
**Millar, W A** (WP) 1906 E, 1910 BI 2, 3, 1912 I, W, 1913 F
**Mills, W J** (WP) 1910 BI 2
**Mohoje, T S** (FSC) 2014 S(R), A2, NZ2
**Moll, T** (Tvl) 1910 BI 2
**Montini, P E** (WP) 1956 A 1, 2
**Montgomery, P C** (WP, Newport, N, Perpignan) 1997 BI 2, 3, NZ 1, A 1, NZ 2, A 2, F 1, 2, E, S, 1998 I 1, 2, W, E 1, A 1, NZ 1, A 2, A 2, W 2, S, I 3, E 2, 1999 It 1, 2, W, NZ 1, A 1, NZ 2, A 2, [S, U, E, A 3, NZ 3], 2000 C, E 1, 2, A 1, NZ 1, A 2(R), Arg, I, W, E 3, 2001 F 1, 2(t), It 1, NZ 1, F 3(R), It 2(R), 2004 I2, W1, PI, NZ1, A1, NZ2, A2, W2, I3, E, S, 2005 U, F1, 2, A1, 2, 3, NZ1, A4, NZ2, Arg, W, F3, 2006 S1, 2, F, A1, NZ1, A2, NZ2, 2007 E1, 2, Sm(R), A1, NZ1, Nm, S, [Sm, E1, Tg(R), US, Fj, Arg, E2], 2008 W1(R), 2(R), NZ1(R), 2, Arg(R), NZ3, A2(R), 3(R)

**Moolman, L C** (NT) 1977 Wld, 1980 S Am 1, 2, BI 1, 2, 3, 4, S Am 3, 4, F, 1981 I 1, 2, NZ 1, 2, 3, US, 1982 S Am 1, 2, 1984 S Am 1, 2, 1986 Cv 1, 2, 3, 4

**Mordt, R H** (Z-R, NT) 1980 S Am 1, 2, BI 1, 2, 3, 4, S Am 3, 4, F, 1981 I 2, NZ 1, 2, 3, US, 1982 S Am 1, 2, 1984 S Am 1, 2

**Morkel, D A** (Tvl) 1903 BI 1

**Morkel, D F T** (Tvl) 1906 I, E, 1910 BI 1, 3, 1912 S, I, W, 1913 E, F

**Morkel, H J** (WP) 1921 NZ 1

**Morkel, H W** (WP) 1921 NZ 1, 2

**Morkel, J A** (WP) 1921 NZ 2, 3

**Morkel, J W H** (WP) 1912 S, I, W, 1913 E, F

**Morkel, P G** (WP) 1912 S, I, W, 1913 E, F, 1921 NZ 1, 2, 3

**Morkel, P K** (WP) 1928 NZ 4

**Morkel, W H** (WP) 1910 BI 3, 1912 S, I, W, 1913 E, F, 1921 NZ 1, 2, 3

**Morkel, W S** (Tvl) 1906 S, I, W, E

**Moss, C** (N) 1949 NZ 1, 2, 3, 4

**Mostert, G** (Stade Français) 2011 NZ1, A2(R)

**Mostert, P J** (WP) 1921 NZ 1, 2, 3, 1924 BI 1, 2, 4, 1928 NZ 1, 2, 3, 4, 1931 W, I, 1932 E, S

**Mtawarira, T** (NS) 2008 W2, It, A1(R), Arg, NZ3, A2, 3, W3, S, E, 2009 BI 1, 2, 3, NZ1, 2, A1, 2, 3, NZ3, F, It(R), I, 2010 I, W2, S, E, 2011 A2, NZ2(R), [W, Fj(R), Nm(R), Sm], 2012 E1, 2, 3, Arg1, 2, A1, NZ1, A2, NZ2, 2013 It, S1, Sm, Arg1, 2, A1, NZ1, A2, NZ2, W, S2(R), F, 2014 W1(R), 2, Arg1, 2(R), A1, NZ1, A2, NZ2

**Muir, D J** (WP) 1997 It, F 1, 2, E, S

**Mujati, B V** (WP) 2008 W1, It(R), NZ1(R), 2(t), A1(R), Arg(R), NZ3(R), A2(R), 3, W3(t), S(R), E(R)

**Mulder, J C** (Tvl, GL) 1994 NZ 2, 3, S, W, 1995 WS, [A, WS, F, NZ], W, It, E, 1996 Fj, A 1, NZ 1, A 2, NZ 2, 5, Arg 1, 2, F 1, 2, W, 1997 Tg, BI 1, 1999 It 1(R), 2, W, NZ 1, 2000 C(R), A 1, E 3, 2001 F 1, It 1

**Muller, G H** (WP) 1969 A 3, 4, S, 1970 W, NZ 1, 2, 3, 4, 1971 F 1, 2, 1972 E, 1974 BI 1, 3, 4

**Muller, G J** (NS, Ulster) 2006 S1(R), NZ1(R), A2, NZ2, 3, A3, I(R), E1, 2, 2007 E1(R), 2(R), Sm(R), A1(R), NZ1(R), A2, NZ2, Nm(R), [Sm(R), E1(R), Fj(t&R), Arg(t&R)], W, 2009 BI 3, 2011 [W(R)]

**Muller, G P** (GL) 2003 A 2, NZ 2, [E, Gg(R), Sm, NZ]

**Muller, H L** (OFS) 1986 Cv 4(R), 1989 Wld 1(R)

**Muller, H S V** (Tvl) 1949 NZ 1, 2, 3, 4, 1951 S, I, W, 1952 E, F, 1953 A 1, 2, 3, 4

**Muller, L J J** (N) 1992 NZ, A

**Muller, P G** (N) 1992 NZ, A, F 1, 2, E, 1993 F 1, 2 A 1, 2, 3, Arg 1, 2, 1994 E 1, 2, NZ 1, S, W, 1998 I 1, 2, W 1, E 1, A 1, NZ 1, 2, A 2, 1999 It 1, W, NZ 1, A 1, [Sp, E, A 3, NZ 3]

**Murray, W M** (N) 2007 Sm, A2, NZ2

**Mvovo, L N** (NS) 2010 S, E, 2011 A1, NZ1, 2012 Arg1, 2, A1(R), 2014 W1(R), S

**Myburgh, F R** (EP) 1896 BI 1

**Myburgh, J L** (NT) 1962 BI 1, 1963 A 4, 1964 W, F, 1968 BI 1, 2, 3, F 1, 2, 1969 A 1, 2, 3, 4, E, 1970 I, W, NZ 3, 4

**Myburgh, W H** (WT) 1924 BI 1

**Naude, J P** (WP) 1963 A 4, 1965 A 1, 2, NZ 1, 3, 4, 1967 F 1, 2, 3, 4, 1968 BI 1, 2, 3, 4

**Ndungane, A Z** (BB) 2006 A1, 2, NZ2, 3, A3, E1, 2, 2007 E2, Nm(R), [US], W(R)

**Ndungane, O M** (NS) 2008 It, NZ1, A3, 2009 BI 3, A3, NZ3, 2010 W1, 2011 NZ1(R), [Fj]

**Neethling, J B** (WP) 1967 F 1, 2, 3, 4, 1968 BI 4, 1969 S, 1970 NZ 1, 2

**Nel, J A** (Tvl) 1960 NZ 1, 2, 1963 A 1, 2, 1965 A 2, NZ 1, 2, 3, 4, 1970 NZ 3, 4

**Nel, J J** (WP) 1956 A 1, 2, NZ 1, 2, 3, 4, 1958 F 1, 2

**Nel, P A R O** (Tvl) 1903 BI 1, 2, 3

**Nel, P J** (N) 1928 NZ 1, 2, 3, 4, 1931 W, I, 1932 E, S, 1933 A 1, 3, 4, 5, 1937 A 1, 2, NZ 2, 3

**Nimb, C F** (WP) 1961 I

**Nokwe, J L** (FS) 2008 Arg, A2, 3, 2009 BI 3

**Nomis, S H** (Tvl) 1967 F 4, 1968 BI 1, 2, 3, 4, F 1, 2, 1969 A 1, 2, 3, 4, S, E, 1970 I, W, NZ 1, 2, 3, 4, 1971 F 1, 2, A 1, 2, 3, 1972 E

**Nyakane, T N** (FSC) 2013 It(R), S1(R), Sm(R), 2014 S(R), Arg1(R), A1(R), NZ1(R), A2(R), NZ2(R)

**Nykamp, J L** (Tvl) 1933 A 2

**Ochse, J K** (WP) 1951 I, W, 1952 E, F, 1953 A 1, 2, 4

**Oelofse, J S A** (Tvl) 1953 A 1, 2, 3, 4

**Oliver, J F** (Tvl) 1928 NZ 3, 4

**Olivier, E** (WP) 1967 F 1, 2, 3, 4, 1968 BI 1, 2, 3, 4, F 1, 2, 1969 A 1, 2, 3, 4, S, E

**Olivier, J** (NT) 1992 F 1, 2, E, 1993 F 1, 2 A 1, 2, 3, Arg 1, 1995 W, It (R), E, 1996 Arg 1, 2, F 1, 2, W

**Olivier, W** (BB, Montpellier) 2006 S1(R), 2, F, A1, NZ1, A2, NZ2(R), 3, A3, I(R), E1, 2, 2007 E1, 2, NZ1(R), A2, NZ2, [E1(R), Tg, Arg(R)], W(R), 2009 BI3, NZ1(R), 2(R), F(R), It(R), I, 2010 F, It2(R), 2, A1, 2011 A1, NZ1(R), 2012 E1(t), 2(R), 3, 2014 W2(R)

**Olver, E** (EP) 1896 BI 1

**Oosthuizen, C V** (FSC) 2012 E1(t&R), NZ2(R), 2013 It(R), S1(R), Sm(R), Arg1(R), 2(R), A1(t&R), NZ1(R), A2(R), NZ2(R), W(R), S2(R), F, 2014 W1(R), 2(R), S

**Oosthuizen, J J** (WP) 1974 BI 1, F 1, 2, 1975 F 1, 2, 1976 NZ 1, 2, 3, 4

**Oosthuizen, O W** (NT, Tvl) 1981 I 1(R), 2, NZ 2, 3, US, 1982 S Am 1, 2, 1984 E 1, 2

**Osler, B L** (WP) 1924 BI 1, 2, 3, 4, 1928 NZ 1, 2, 3, 4, 1931 W, I, 1932 E, S, 1933 A 1, 2, 3, 4, 5

**Osler, S G** (WP) 1928 NZ 1

**Otto, K** (NT, BB) 1995 [R, C (R), WS (R)], 1997 BI 3, NZ 1, A 1, NZ 2, It, F 1, 2, E, S, 1998 I 1, 2, W 1, E 1, A 1, NZ 1, 2, A 2, W 2, S, I 3, E 2, 1999 It 1, W, NZ 1, A 1, [S (R), Sp, U, E, A 3, NZ 3], 2000 C, E 1, 2, A 1

**Oxlee, K** (N) 1960 NZ 1, 2, 3, 4, W, I, 1961 S, A 1, 2, 1962 BI 1, 2, 3, 4, 1963 A 1, 2, 4, 1964 W, 1965 NZ 1, 2

**Pagel, G L** (WP) 1995 [A (R), R, C, NZ (R)], 1996 NZ 5(R)

**Parker, W H** (EP) 1965 A 1, 2

**Partridge, J E C** (Tvl) 1903 BI 1

**Paulse, B J** (WP) 1999 It 1, 2, NZ 1, A 1, 2(R), [S (R), Sp, NZ 3], 2000 C, E 1, 2, It 1, NZ 1, A 2, NZ 2, A 3, Arg, W, E 3, 2001 F 1, 2, It 1, NZ 1, A 1, 2, NZ 2 F 3, It 2, E, 2002 W 1, 2, Arg, Sm (R), A 1, NZ 2, A 2, NZ 3 [Gg], 2004 I1, 2, W1, PI, NZ1, A1, NZ2, A2, W2, I3, E, 2005 A2, 3, NZ1, A4, F3, 2006 S1, 2, A1(R), NZ1, 3(R), A3(R), 2007 A2, NZ2

**Payn, C** (N) 1924 BI 1, 2

**Pelser, H J M** (Tvl) 1958 F 1, 1960 NZ 1, 2, 3, 4, W, I, 1961 F, I, A 1, 2

**Pfaff, B D** (WP) 1956 A 1

**Pickard, J A J** (WP) 1953 A 3, 4, 1956 NZ 2, 1958 F 2

**Pienaar, J F** (Tvl) 1993 F 1, 2, A 1, 2, 3, Arg 1, 2, 1994 E 1, 2, NZ 2, 3, Arg 1, 2, S, W, 1995 WS, [A, C, WS, F, NZ], W, It, E, 1996 Fj, A 1, NZ 1, A 2, NZ 2

**Pienaar, R** (NS, Ulster) 2006 NZ2(R), 3(R), A3(R), I(t), E1(R), 2007 E1(R), 2(R), Sm(R), A1, NZ1, A2, NZ2, Nm(R), S(R), [E1(t&R), Tg, US(R), Arg(R)], W, 2008 W1(R), It(R), NZ2(R), A1(R), 3(R), W3, S, E, 2009 BI 1, 2, 3(R), NZ1, A1(R), 2, 3, It(R), I(R), 2010 W1, F(R), It 1(R), F(R), NZ1(R), 2(R), A1, I, W2, S(R), E, 2011 A1, NZ1, [Fj(R), Nm(R)], 2012 E1(R), 2(R), 3(R), Arg1(R), 2(R), A1, NZ1, 2(R), Arg1(R), 2, I, S, E4, 2013 It(R), S1, Sm, Arg1, 2, A1, NZ1, 2(R), W(R), S2(R), F, 2014 W1(R), 2(t), Arg1, 2, A1, NZ1

**Pienaar, Z M J** (OFS) 1980 S Am 2(R), BI 1, 2, 3, 4, S Am 3, 4, F, 1981 I 1, 2, NZ 1, 2, 3

**Pietersen, J-P R** (NS) 2006 A3, 2007 Sm, A1, NZ1, A2, NZ2, Nm, S, [Sm, E1, Tg, US(R), Fj, Arg, E2], W, 2008 NZ2, A1, Arg, NZ3, A2, W3, S, E, 2009 BI 1, 2, NZ1, 2, A1, 2, F, It, I, 2010 NZ3, A2, 2011 A2, NZ2, [W, Fj, Sm, A], 2012 E1, 2, 3, I, S, E4, 2013 W, S2, F, 2014 W1, 2, S, A2(t&R), NZ2(R)

**Pitzer, G** (NT) 1967 F 1, 2, 3, 4, 1968 BI 1, 2, 3, 4, F 1, 2, 1969 A 3, 4

**Pollard, H** (BB) 2014 S, Arg1, 2, NZ1, A2, NZ2

**Pope, C F** (WP) 1974 BI 1, 2, 3, 4, 1975 F 1, 2, 1976 NZ 2, 3, 4

**Potgieter, D J** (BB) 2009 I(t), 2010 W1, F(t&R), It 1, 2(R), A1(R)

**Potgieter, H J** (OFS) 1928 NZ 1, 2

**Potgieter, H L** (OFS) 1977 Wld

Potgieter, U J (BB) 2012 E3, Arg1(R), 2
Powell, A W (GW) 1896 BI 3
Powell, J M (GW) 1891 BI 2, 1896 BI 3, 1903 BI 1, 2
Prentis, R B (Tvl) 1980 S Am 1, 2, BI 1, 2, 3, 4, S Am 3, 4, F, 1981 I 1, 2
Pretorius, A S (GL) 2002 W 1, 2, Arg, Sm, NZ 1, A 1, NZ 2, F, S (R), E, 2003 NZ 1(R), A 1, 2005 A2, A3, NZ1, A4, NZ2, Arg, 2006 NZ2(R), 3, A3, I, E1(t&R), 2, 2007 S(R), [Sm(R), E1(R), Tg, US(R), Arg(R)], W
Pretorius, J C (GL) 2006 I, 2007 NZ2
Pretorius, N F (Tvl) 1928 NZ 1, 2, 3, 4
Prinsloo, J (Tvl) 1958 F 1, 2
Prinsloo, J (NT) 1963 A 3
Prinsloo, J P (Tvl) 1928 NZ 1
Putter, D J (WT) 1963 A 1, 2, 4

Raaff, J W E (GW) 1903 BI 1, 2, 1906 S, W, E, 1910 BI 1
Ralepelle, M C (BB) 2006 NZ2(R), E2(R), 2008 E(t&R), 2009 BI 3, NZ1(R), 2(R), A2(R), NZ3(R), 2010 W1(R), F(R), It 1, 2(R), NZ1(R), 2(R), A1(R), 2(R), 3(R), W2(R), 2011 A1(R), NZ1(R), [Nm(R)], 2013 It(R)
Ras, W J de Wet (OFS) 1976 NZ 1(R), 1980 S Am 2(R)
Rautenbach, S J (WP) 2002 W 1(R), 2(t+R), Arg (R), Sm, NZ 1(R), A 1, NZ 2(R), A 2(R), 2003 [U(R), Gg, Sm, NZ], 2004 W1, NZ1(R)
Reece-Edwards, H (N) 1992 F 1, 2, 1993 A 2
Reid, A (WP) 1903 BI 3
Reid, B C (Bor) 1933 A 4
Reinach, J (OFS) 1986 Cv 1, 2, 3, 4
Reinach, J M (NS) 2014 Arg2(R), NZ2(R)
Rens, I J (Tvl) 1953 A 3, 4
Retief, D F (NT) 1955 BI 1, 2, 4, 1956 A 1, 2, NZ 1, 2, 3, 4
Reyneke, H J (WP) 1910 BI 3
Richards, A R (WP) 1891 BI 1, 2, 3
Richter, A (NT) 1992 F 1, 2, E, 1994 E 2, NZ 1, 2, 3, 1995 [R, C, WS (R)]
Riley, N M (ET) 1963 A 3
Riordan, C A (Tvl) 1910 BI 1, 2
Robertson, I W (R) 1974 F 1, 2, 1976 NZ 1, 2, 4
Rodgers, P H (NT, Tvl) 1989 Wld 1, 2, 1992 NZ, F 1, 2
Rogers, C D (Tvl) 1984 E 1, 2, S Am 1, 2
Roos, G D (WP) 1910 BI 2, 3
Roos, P J (WP) 1903 BI 3, 1906 I, W, E
Rosenberg, W (Tvl) 1955 BI 2, 3, 4, 1956 NZ 3, 1958 F 1
Rossouw, C L C (Tvl, N) 1995 WS, [R, WS, F, NZ], 1999 NZ 2(R), A 2(t), [Sp, NZ 3(R)]
Rossouw, D H (WP) 1953 A 3, 4
Rossouw, D J (BB) 2003 [U, Gg, Sm(R), NZ], 2004 E(R), S, Arg, 2005 U, F1, 2, A1, W(R), F3(R), 2006 S1, 2, F, A1, I, E1, 2, 2007 E1, Sm, A1(R), NZ1, S, [Sm, E1, Tg, Fj, Arg, E2], 2008 W1(R), NZ3(R), A3(R), S(R), E, 2009 BI 1(R), 2(R), NZ1(R), 2(R), A1(R), 3(R), NZ3(R), F(R), It, I, 2010 W1, F, NZ1(R), 2, A1, NZ3(t&R), A2(R), 3, 2011 A1, NZ1, A2, NZ2(t&R), [W, Fj, Nm, Sm, A]
Rossouw, P W G (WP) 1997 BI 2, 3, NZ 1, A 1, NZ 2(R), A 2(R), It, F 1, 2, E, S, 1998 I 1, 2, W 1, E 1, A 1, NZ 1, 2, A 2, W 2, S, I 3, E 2, 1999 It 1, W, NZ 1, A 1(R), NZ 2, A 2, [S, U, E, A 3], 2000 C, E 1, 2, A 2, Arg (R), I, W, 2001 F 3, US, 2003 Arg
Rousseau, W P (WP) 1928 NZ 3, 4
Roux, F du T (WP) 1960 W, 1961 A 1, 2, 1962 BI 1, 2, 3, 4, 1963 A 2, 1965 A 1, 2, NZ 1, 2, 3, 4, 1968 BI 3, 4, F 1, 2, 1969 A 1, 2, 3, 4, 1970 I, NZ 1, 2, 3, 4
Roux, J P (Tvl) 1994 E 2, NZ 1, 2, 3, Arg 1, 1995 [R, C, F (R)], 1996 A 1(R), NZ 1, A 2, NZ 3
Roux, O A (NT) 1969 S, E, 1970 I, W, 1972 E, 1974 BI 3, 4
Roux, W G (BB) 2002 F (R), S, E
Russell, R B (MP, N) 2002 W 1(R), 2, Arg, A 1(R), NZ 2(R), A 2, F, E (R), 2003 Arg (R), A 1(R), NZ 1, A 2(R), 2004 I2(t&R), W1, NZ1(R), W2(R), Arg(R), 2005 U(R), F2(R), A1(t), Arg(R), W(R), 2006 F

Samuels, T A (GW) 1896 BI 2, 3, 4
Santon, D (Bol) 2003 A 1(R), NZ 1(R), A 2(t), [Gg(R)]
Sauermann, J T (Tvl) 1971 F 1, 2, A 1, 1972 E, 1974 BI 1
Schlebusch, J J J (OFS) 1974 BI 3, 4, 1975 F 2
Schmidt, L U (NT) 1958 F 2, 1962 BI 2

Schmidt, U L (NT, Tvl) 1986 Cv 1, 2, 3, 4, 1989 Wld 1, 2, 1992 NZ, A, 1993 F 1, 2, A 1, 2, 3, 1994 Arg 1, 2, S, W
Schoeman, J (WP) 1963 A 3, 4, 1965 I, S, A 1, NZ 1, 2
Scholtz, C P (WP, Tvl) 1994 Arg 1, 1995 [R, C, WS]
Scholtz, H (FS) 2002 A 1(R), NZ 2(R), A 2(R), 2003 [U(R), Gg]
Scholtz, H H (WP) 1921 NZ 1, 2
Schutte, P J W (Tvl) 1994 S, W
Scott, P A (Tvl) 1896 BI 1, 2, 3, 4
Sendin, W D (GW) 1921 NZ 2
Sephaka, L D (GL) 2001 US, 2002 Sm, NZ 1, A 1, NZ 2, A 2, F, 2003 S 1, 2, A 1, NZ 1, A 2(t+R), NZ 2, [U, E(t&R), Gg], 2005 F2, A1, 2(R), W, 2006 S1(R), NZ3(t&R), A3(R), I
Serfontein, D J (WP) 1980 BI 1, 2, 3, 4, S Am 3, 4, F, 1981 I 1, 2, NZ 1, 2, 3, US, 1982 S Am 1, 2, 1984 E 1, 2, S Am 1, 2
Serfontein, J L (BB) 2013 It(R), S1(R), Sm(R), Arg1(R), 2(R), A1(R), NZ1(t&R), A2(R), NZ2(R), 2014 W1, 2, S, A1, NZ1, A2, NZ2
Shand, R (GW) 1891 BI 2, 3
Sheriff, A H (Tvl) 1938 BI 1, 2, 3
Shimange, M H (FS, WP) 2004 W1(R), NZ2(R), A2(R), W2(R), 2005 U(R), A1(R), 2(R), Arg(R), 2006 S1(R)
Shum, E H (Tvl) 1913 E
Sinclair, D J (Tvl) 1955 BI 1, 2, 3, 4
Sinclair, J H (Tvl) 1903 BI 1
Skene, A L (WP) 1958 F 2
Skinstad, R B (WP, GL, N) 1997 E (t), 1998 W 1(R), E 1(t), NZ 1(R), 2(R), A 2(R), W 2(R), S, I 3, E 2, 1999 [S, Sp (R), U, E, A 3], 2001 F 1(R), 2(R), It 1, NZ 1, A 1, 2, NZ 2, F 3, It 2, E, 2002 W 1, 2, Arg, Sm, NZ 1, A 1, NZ 2, A 2, 2003 Arg (R), 2007 E2(t&R), Sm, NZ1, A2, [E1(R), Tg, US(R), Arg(R)]
Slater, J T (EP) 1924 BI 3, 4, 1928 NZ 1
Smal, G P (WP) 1986 Cv 1, 2, 3, 4, 1989 Wld 1, 2
Small, J T (Tvl, N, WP) 1992 NZ, A, F 1, 2, E, 1993 F 1, 2, A 1, 2, 3, Arg 1, 2, 1994 E 1, 2, NZ 1, 2, 3(t), Arg 1, 1995 WS, [A, R, F, NZ], W, It, E (R), 1996 Fj, A 1, NZ 1, A 2, NZ 2, Arg 1, 2, F 1, 2, W, 1997 Tg, BI 1, NZ 1(R), A 1(R), NZ 2, A 2, It, F 1, 2, E, S
Smit, F C (WP) 1992 E
Smit, J W (NS, Clermont-Auvergne) 2000 C (t), A 1(R), NZ 1(t+R), A 2(R), NZ 2(R), A 3(R), Arg, I, W, E 3, 2001 F 1, 2, It 1, NZ 1, A 1(R), 2(R), NZ 2(R), F 3(R), It 2, E, US (R), 2003 [U(R), E(t&R), Gg, Sm, NZ], 2004 I1, 2, W1, NZ1, A1, NZ2, A2, W2, I3, E, S, Arg, 2005 U, F1, 2, A1, 2, 3, NZ1, A4, NZ2, Arg, W, F3, 2006 S1, 2, F, A1, NZ1, A2, NZ2, 3, A3, I, E1, 2, 2007 E1, 2, Sm, A1, [Sm, E1, Tg(R), US, Fj, Arg, E2], W, 2008 W1, 2, It, NZ1, 2, A1, Arg, NZ3, A2, 3, W3, S, 2009 BI 1, 2, 3, NZ1, 2, A1, 2, 3, NZ3, F, It, I, 2010 NZ3, A2, 3, I, W2, S, E, 2014 Arg2
Smith, P F (GW) 1997 S (R), 1998 I 1(t), 2, W 1, NZ 1(R), 2(R), A 2(R), W 2, 1999 NZ 2
Smollan, F C (Tvl) 1933 A 3, 4, 5
Snedden, R C D (GW) 1891 BI 2
Snyman, A H (NT, BB, N) 1996 NZ 3, 4, Arg 2(R), W (R), 1997 Tg, BI 1, 2, 3, NZ 1, A 1, NZ 2, A 2, It, F 1, 2, E, S, 1998 I 1, 2, W 1, E 1, A 1, NZ 1, 2, A 2, W 2, S, I 3, E 2, 1999 NZ 2, 2001 NZ 2, F 3, US, 2002 W 1, 2003 S 1, NZ 1, 2006 S1, 2
Snyman, D S L (WP) 1972 E, 1974 BI 1, 2(R), F 1, 2, 1975 F 1, 2, 1976 NZ 2, 3, 1977 Wld
Snyman, J C P (OFS) 1974 BI 2, 3, 4
Sonnekus, G H H (OFS) 1974 BI 3, 1984 E 1, 2
Sowerby, R S (N) 2002 Sm (R)

Spies, J J (NT) 1970 NZ 1, 2, 3, 4
Spies, P J (BB) 2006 A1, NZ2, 3, A3, I, E1, 2007 E1(R), 2, A1, 2008 W1, 2, A1, Arg, NZ3, A2, 3, W3, S, E, 2009 Bl 1, 2, 3(R), NZ1, 2, A1, 2, 3, NZ3, 2010 F, It 1, 2, NZ1, 2, A1, NZ3, A2, 3, I, W2, E, 2011 A2, NZ2, [W, Fj, Nm, Sm, A], 2012 E1, 2, 3, 2013 It, S1, Sm
Stander, J C J (OFS) 1974 Bl 4(R), 1976 NZ 1, 2, 3, 4
Stapelberg, W P (NT) 1974 F 1, 2
Starke, J J (WP) 1956 NZ 4
Starke, K T (WP) 1924 Bl 1, 2, 3, 4
Steenekamp, J G A (Tvl) 1958 F 1
Steenkamp, G G (FS, BB, Toulouse) 2004 S, Arg, 2005 U, F2(R), A2, 3, NZ1(R), A4(R), 2007 E1(R), 2, A1, [Tg, Fj(R)], 2008 W1, 2(R), NZ1, 2, A1, W3(R), S(R), 2009 Bl 1(R), 3(R), 2010 F, It 1, 2, NZ1, 2, A1, NZ3, A2, 3, 2011 A2(R), NZ2, [W(R), Fj, Nm, Sm(R), A], 2012 S, E4, 2013 Arg1(R), 2(R), A1(R), NZ1(R), A2(R), NZ2(R), W(R), S2, F(R), 2014 W1, 2(R), Arg2
Stegmann, A C (WP) 1906 S, I
Stegmann, G J (BB) 2010 I, W2, S, E, 2011 A1, NZ1
Stegmann, J A (Tvl) 1912 S, I, W, 1913 E, F
Stewart, C (WP) 1998 S, I 3, E 2
Stewart, D A (WP) 1960 S, 1961 E, S, F, I, 1963 A 1, 3, 4, 1964 W, F, 1965 I
Steyn, F P L (NS, Racing Metro) 2006 I, E1, 2, 2007 E1(R), 2(R), Sm, A1(R), NZ1(R), S, [Sm(R), E1, Tg(R), US, Fj, Arg, E2], W, 2008 W2(R), It, NZ1(R), 2(R), A1, NZ3(R), A2(R), W3(R), S(R), E(R), 2009 Bl 1, 2, 3(t&R), NZ1, 2, A1, 2(R), 3(R), NZ3, 2010 W1, A2, 3, W2, S, E, 2011 A2, [W, Fj, Nm, Sm], 2012 E1, 2, Arg1, 2, A1, NZ1
Steyn, M (BB, SF) 2009 Bl 1(t&R), 2(R), 3, NZ1(R), 2, A1, 2, 3, NZ3, F, It, I, 2010 F, It 1, 2, NZ1, 2, A1, NZ3, A2, 3, I, W2, S, E, 2011 A1, NZ1, A2(R), NZ2, [W, Fj, Nm, Sm, A], 2012 E1, 2, 3, Arg1, 2, A1, NZ1, S(R), 2013 It, S1, Sm, Arg1, 2, A1, NZ1, A2, NZ2, W, S2(R), F, 2014 W1, 2, Arg1(R), 2(R), A1
Stofberg, M T S (OFS, NT, WP) 1976 NZ 2, 3, 1977 Wld, 1980 S Am 1, 2, Bl 1, 2, 3, 4, S Am 3, 4, F, 1981 I 1, 2, NZ 1, 2, US, 1982 S Am 1, 2, 1984 E 1, 2
Strachan, L C (Tvl) 1932 E, S, 1937 A 1, 2, NZ 1, 2, 3, 1938 Bl 1, 2, 3
Stransky, J T (N, WP) 1993 A 1, 2, 3, Arg 1, 1994 Arg 1, 2, 1995 WS, [A, R (t), C, F, NZ], W, It, E, 1996 Fj (R), NZ 1, A 2, NZ 2, 3, 4, 5(R)
Straeuli, R A W (Tvl) 1994 NZ 1, Arg 1, 2, S, W, 1995 WS, [A, WS, NZ (R)], E (R)
Strauss, C P (WP) 1992 F 1, 2, E, 1993 F 1, 2, A 1, 2, 3, Arg 1, 2, 1994 E 1, NZ 1, 2, Arg 1, 2
Strauss, J A (WP) 1984 S Am 1, 2
Strauss, J A (FSC) 2008 A1(R), Arg(R), NZ3(R), A2(R), 3(R), 2009 F(R), It, 2010 S(R), E(R), 2012 E1(R), 2(R), 3(R), Arg1(R), 2, A1, NZ1, A2, NZ2, I, S, E4, 2013 It, S1, Sm, Arg1, 2, A1(R), NZ1(t&R), A2, NZ2(R), W(R), S2, 2014 It(R), S(R), Arg1(R), 2(R), A1, NZ1, A2, NZ2(R)
Strauss, J H P (Tvl) 1976 NZ 3, 4, 1980 S Am 1
Strauss, S S F (GW) 1921 NZ 3
Strydom, C F (OFS) 1955 Bl 3, 1956 A 1, 2, NZ 1, 4, 1958 F 1,
Strydom, J J (Tvl, GL) 1993 F 2, A 1, 2, 3, Arg 1, 2, 1994 E 1, 1995 [A, C, F, NZ], 1996 A 2(R), NZ 2(R), 3, 4, W (R), 1997 Tg, Bl 1, 2, 3, A 2
Strydom, L J (NT) 1949 NZ 1, 2
Styger, J (OFS) 1992 NZ 2 (R), A, F 1, 2, E, 1993 F 2(R), A 3(R)
Suter, M R (N) 1965 I, S
Swanepoel, W (OFS, GL) 1997 Bl 3(R), A 2(R), F 1(R), 2, E, S, 1998 I 2(R), W 1(R), E 2(R), 1999 It 1, 2(R), W, A 1, [Sp, NZ 3(t)], 2000 A 1, NZ 1, A 2, NZ 2, A 3
Swart, J (WP) 1996 Fj, NZ 1(R), A 2, NZ 2, 3, 4, 5, 1997 Bl 3(R), It, S (R)
Swart, J J N (SWA) 1955 Bl 1
Swart, I S (Tvl) 1993 A 1, 2, 3, Arg 1, 1994 E 1, 2, NZ 1, 3, Arg 2(R), 1995 WS, [A, WS, F, NZ], W, 1996 A 2

Taberer, W S (GW) 1896 Bl 2
Taute, J J (GL) 2012 A2, NZ2, I
Taylor, O B (N) 1962 Bl 1
Terblanche, C S (Bol, N) 1998 I 1, 2, W 1, E 1, A 1, NZ 1, 2, A

2, W 2, S, I 3, E 2, 1999 It 1(R), 2, W, A 1, NZ 2(R), [Sp, E (R), A 3(R), NZ 3], 2000 E 3, 2002 W 1, 2, Arg, Sm, NZ 1, A 1, 2(R), 2003 S 1, 2, Arg, A 1, NZ 1, A 2, NZ 2, [Gg]
Teichmann, G H (N) 1995 W, 1996 Fj, A 1, NZ 1, A 2, NZ 2, 3, 4, 5, Arg 1, 2, F 1, 2, W, 1997 Tg, Bl 1, 2, 3, NZ 1, A 1, NZ 2, A 2, It, F 1, 2 E, S, 1998 I 1, 2, W 1, E 1, A 1, NZ 1, 2, A 2, W 2, S, I 3, E 2, 1999 It 1, W, NZ 1
Theron, D F (GW) 1996 A 2(R), NZ 2(R), 5, Arg 1, 2, F 1, 2, W, 1997 Bl 2(R), 3, NZ 1(R), A 1, NZ 2(R)
Theunissen, D J (GW) 1896 Bl 3
Thompson, G (WP) 1912 S, I, W
Tindall, J C (WP) 1924 Bl 1, 1928 NZ 1, 2, 3, 4
Tobias, E G (SARF, Bol) 1981 I 1, 2, 1984 E 1, 2, S Am 1, 2
Tod, N S (N) 1928 NZ 2
Townsend, W H (N) 1921 NZ 1
Trenery, W E (GW) 1891 Bl 2
Tromp, H (NT) 1996 NZ3, 4, Arg 2(R), F 1(R)
Truter, D R (WP) 1924 Bl 2, 4
Truter, J T (N) 1963 A 1, 1964 F, 1965 A 2
Turner, F G (EP) 1933 A 1, 2, 3, 1937 A 1, 2, NZ 1, 2, 3, 1938 Bl 1, 2, 3
Twigge, R J (NT) 1960 S
Tyibilika, S (N) 2004 S, Arg, 2005 U, A2, Arg, 2006 NZ1, A2, NZ2

Ulyate, C A (Tvl) 1955 Bl 1, 2, 3, 4, 1956 NZ 1, 2, 3
Uys, P de W (NT) 1960 W, 1961 E, S, I, A 1, 2, 1962 Bl 1, 4, 1963 A 1, 2, 1969 A 1(R), 2
Uys, P J (Pumas) 2002 S

Van Aswegen, H J (WP) 1981 NZ 1, 1982 S Am 2(R)
Van Biljon, L (N) 2001 It 1(R), NZ 1, A 1, 2, NZ 2, F 3, It 2(R), E (R), US, 2002 F (R), S, E (R), 2003 NZ 2(R)
Van Broekhuizen, H D (WP) 1896 Bl 4
Van Buuren, M C (Tvl) 1891 Bl 1
Van de Vyver, D F (WP) 1937 A 2
Van den Berg, D S (N) 1975 F 1, 2, 1976 NZ 1, 2
Van den Berg, M A (WP) 1937 A 1, NZ 1, 2, 3
Van den Berg, P A (WP, GW, N) 1999 It 1(R), NZ 2, A 2, [S, U (t+R), E (R), A 3(R), NZ 3(R)], 2000 E 1(R), A 1, NZ 1, A 2, NZ 2(R), US, 2004 NZ1, 2005 U, F1, 2, A2(R), 3(R), 4(R), Arg(R), F3(R), 2006 S2(R), F(R), A1, NZ1, A2, NZ2, I, E1, 2, 2007 E1(R), 2, A1(R), NZ1(R), A2, NZ2, Nm(t&R), S(R), [Tg, US], W(R)
Van den Bergh, E (EP) 1994 Arg 2(t & R)
Van der Linde, A (WP) 1995 It, E, 1996 Arg 1(R), 2(R), F 1(R), W (R), 2001 F 3(R)
Van der Linde, C J (FS, Leinster, WP, GL) 2002 S (R), E(R), 2004 I1(R), 2(R), PI(R), A1(R), NZ2(t&R), A2(R), W2(R), I3(R), E(t&R), S, Arg, 2005 U, F1(R), 2, A1(R), 3, NZ1, A4, NZ2, Arg, W, F3, 2006 S2(R), F(R), A1, NZ1, A2, NZ2, I, E1, 2, 2007 E1(R), 2, A1(R), NZ1(R), A2, NZ2, Nm, S, [Sm, E1(R), Tg, US(R), Arg, E2], W, 2008 W1(t&R), It, NZ1, 2, A1, Arg, NZ3, A2, 2009 F(R), I(t), 2010 W1, It1(R) , NZ2, A1(t&R), NZ3(R), A2, 3(R), I(R), W2(R), S(R), E(R), 2011 A1(t&R), NZ1(R), 2(R), [Nm], 2012 I, S(R)
Van der Merwe, A J (Bol) 1955 Bl 2, 3, 4, 1956 A 1, 2, NZ 1, 2, 3, 4, 1958 F 1, 1960 S, NZ 2
Van der Merwe, A V (WP) 1931 W
Van der Merwe, B S (NT) 1949 NZ 1
Van der Merwe, F (GL) 2013 NZ 2(R)
Van der Merwe, H S (NT) 1960 NZ 4, 1963 A 2, 3, 4, 1964 F
Van der Merwe, H S (GL, Leinster) 2007 W(t+R), 2012 I(R), S(R), E4(R)
Van der Merwe, J P (WP) 1970 W
Van der Merwe, M (BB) 2014 S(R), A1(R), NZ1(R), A2(R), NZ2(R)
Van der Merwe, P R (SWD, WT, GW) 1981 NZ 2, 3, US, 1986 Cv 1, 2, 1989 Wld 1
Van der Merwe, P R (BB) 2010 F(R), It 2(R), A1(R), NZ3, A2, 3(R), I(R), W2(R), S(R), E(R), 2011 A1, 2012 E1(R), 2(R), 3(R), Arg1(R), 2(R), A1(R), NZ1, A2(R), NZ2(R), I(R), S(R), E4(R), 2013 It(R), S1(R), Sm, Arg1(R), 2(R), A1, NZ1, A2, W, S2, F, 2014 W2
Vanderplank, B E (N) 1924 Bl 3, 4
Van der Schyff, J H (GW) 1949 NZ 1, 2, 3, 4, 1955 Bl 1
Van der Watt, A E (WP) 1969 S (R), E, 1970 I

Van der Westhuizen, J C (WP) 1928 NZ 2, 3, 4, 1931 I
Van der Westhuizen, J H (WP) 1931 I, 1932 E, S
Van der Westhuizen, J H (NT, BB) 1993 Arg 1, 2, 1994 E 1, 2(R), Arg 2, S, W, 1995 WS, [A, C (R), WS, F, NZ], W, It, E, 1996 Fj, A 1, 2(R), NZ 2, 3(R), 4, 5, Arg 1, 2, F 1, 2, W, 1997 Tg, BI 1, 2, 3, NZ 1, A 1, NZ 2, A 2, It, F 1, 1998 I 1, 2, W 1, E 1, A 1, NZ 1, 2, A 2, W 2, S, I 3, E 2, 1999 NZ 2, A 2, [S, Sp (R), U, E, A 3, NZ 3], 2000 C, E 1, 2, A 1(R), NZ 1(R), A 2(R), Arg, I, W, E 3, 2001 F 1, 2, It 1(R), NZ 1, A 1, 2, NZ 2, F 3, It 2, E, US (R), 2003 S 1, 2, A 1, NZ 1, A 2(R), NZ 2, [U, E, Sm, NZ]
Van der Westhuyzen, J N B (MP, BB) 2000 NZ 2(R), 2001 It 1(R), 2003 S 1(R), 2, Arg, A 1, 2003 [E, Sm, NZ], 2004 I1, 2, W1, PI, NZ1, A1, NZ2, A2, W2, I3, E, S, Arg, 2005 U, F1, 2, A1, 4(R), NZ2(R), 2006 S1, 2, F, A1
Van Druten, N J V (Tvl) 1924 BI 1, 2, 3, 4, 1928 NZ 1, 2, 3, 4
Van Heerden, A J (Tvl) 1921 NZ 1, 3
Van Heerden, F J (WP) 1994 E 1, 2(R), NZ 3, 1995 It, E, 1996 NZ 5(R), Arg 1(R), 2(R), 1997 Tg, BI 2(t+R), 3(R), NZ 1(R), 2(R), 1999 [Sp]
Van Heerden, J L (NT, Tvl) 1974 BI 3, 4, F 1, 2, 1975 F 1, 2, 1976 NZ 1, 2, 3, 4, 1977 Wld, 1980 BI 1, 3, 4, S Am 3, 4, F
Van Heerden, J L (BB) 2003 S 1, 2, A 1, NZ 1, A 2(t), 2007 A2, NZ2, S(R), [Sm(R), E1, Tg, US, Fj(R), E2(R)]
Van Jaarsveld, C J (Tvl) 1949 NZ 1
Van Jaarsveldt, D C (R) 1960 S
Van Niekerk, J A (WP) 1928 NZ 4
Van Niekerk, J C (GL, WP, Toulon) 2001 NZ 1(R), A 1(R), NZ 2(t+R), F 3(R), It2, US, 2002 W 1(R), 2(R), Arg (R), Sm, NZ 1, A 1, NZ 2, A 2, F, S, E, 2003 A 2, NZ 2, [U, E, Gg, Sm], 2004 NZ1(R), A1(t), NZ2, A2, W2, I3, E, S, Arg(R), 2005 U(R), F2(R), A1(R), 2, 3, NZ1, A4, NZ2, 2006 S1, 2, F, A1, NZ1(R), A2(R), 2008 It(R), NZ1, 2, Arg(R), A2(R), 2010 W1
Van Reenen, G L (WP) 1937 A 2, NZ 1
Van Renen, C G (WP) 1891 BI 3, 1896 BI 1, 4
Van Renen, W (WP) 1903 BI 1, 3
Van Rensburg, J T J (Tvl) 1992 NZ, A, E, 1993 F 1, 2, A 1, 1994 NZ 2
Van Rooyen, G W (Tvl) 1921 NZ 2, 3
Van Ryneveld, R C B (WP) 1910 BI 2, 3
Van Schalkwyk, D (NT) 1996 Fj (R), NZ 3, 4, 5, 1997 BI 2, 3, NZ 1, A 1
Van Schoor, R A M (R) 1949 NZ 2, 3, 4, 1951 S, I, W, 1952 E, F, 1953 A 1, 2, 3, 4
Van Straaten, A J J (WP) 1999 It 2(R), W, NZ 1(R), A 1, 2000 C, E 1, 2, NZ 1, A 2, NZ 2, A 3, Arg (R), I (R), W, E 3, 2001 A 1, 2, NZ 2, F 3, It 2, E
Van Vollenhoven, K T (NT) 1955 BI 1, 2, 3, 4, 1956 A 1, 2, NZ 3
Van Vuuren, T F (EP) 1912 S, I, W, 1913 E, F
Van Wyk, C J (Tvl) 1951 S, I, W, 1952 E, F, 1953 A 1, 2, 3, 4, 1955 BI 1
Van Wyk, J F B (NT) 1970 NZ 1, 2, 3, 4, 1971 F 1, 2, A 1, 2, 3, 1972 E, 1974 BI 1, 3, 4, 1976 NZ 3, 4
Van Wyk, S P (WP) 1928 NZ 1, 2
Van Zyl, B P (WP) 1961 I
Van Zyl, C G P (OFS) 1965 NZ 1, 2, 3, 4
Van Zyl, D J (WP) 2000 E 3(R)
Van Zyl, G H (WP) 1958 F 1, 1960 S, NZ 1, 2, 3, 4, W, I, 1961 E, S, F, I, A 1, 2, 1962 BI 1, 3, 4
Van Zyl, H J (Tvl) 1960 NZ 1, 2, 3, 4, I, 1961 E, S, I, A 1, 2
Van Zyl, P J (Bol) 1961 I
Van Zyl, P E (FSC) 2013 S1(R), Sm(R)
Veldsman, P E (WP) 1977 Wld
Venter, A G (OFS) 1996 NZ 4, 5, Arg 1, 2, F 1, 2, W, 1997 Tg, BI 1, 2, 3, NZ 1, A 1, NZ 2, It, F 1, 2, E, S, 1998 I 1, 2, W 1, E 1, A 1, NZ 1, 2, A 2, W 2, S (R), I 3(R), E 2(R), 1999 It 1, 2(R), W (R), NZ 1, A 1, NZ 2, A 2, [S, U, E, A 3, NZ 3], 2000 C, E 1, 2, A 1, NZ 1, A 2, NZ 2, A 3, Arg, I, W, E 3, 2001 F 1, It 1, NZ 1, A 1, 2, NZ 2, F 3(R), It 2(R), E (t+R), US (R)
Venter, A J (N) 2000 W (R), E 3(R), 2001 F 3, It 2, E, US, 2002 W 1, 2, Arg, NZ 1(R), 2, A 2, F, S (R), E, 2003 Arg, 2004 PI, NZ1, A1, NZ2(R), A2, I3, E, 2006 NZ3, A3
Venter, B (OFS) 1994 E 1, 2, NZ 1, 2, 3, Arg 1, 2, 1995 [R, C, WS (R), NZ (R)], 1996 A 1, NZ 1, A 2, 1999 A 2, [S, U]

Venter, F D (Tvl) 1931 W, 1932 S, 1933 A 3
Vermaak, J (BB) 2013 It, A1(R), NZ1(R)
Vermeulen, D J (WP) 2012 A1, NZ1, A2, NZ2, I, S, E4, 2013 Arg1, 2, A1, NZ1, A2, NZ2, W, S2, F, 2014 W1, 2, S, Arg1, 2, A1, NZ1, A2, NZ2
Versfeld, C (WP) 1891 BI 3
Versfeld, M (WP) 1891 BI 1, 2, 3
Vigne, J T (Tvl) 1891 BI 1, 2, 3
Viljoen, J F (GW) 1971 F 1, 2, A 1, 2, 3, 1972 E
Viljoen, J T (N) 1971 A 1, 2, 3
Villet, J V (WP) 1984 E 1, 2
Visagie, I J (WP) 1999 It 1, W, NZ 1, A 1, NZ 2, A 2, [S, U, E, A 3, NZ 3], 2000 C, E 2, A 1, NZ 1, A 2, NZ 2, A 3, 2001 NZ 1, A 1, 2, NZ 2, F 3, It 2(R), E (t+R), US, 2003 S 1(R), 2(R), Arg
Visagie, P J (GW) 1967 F 1, 2, 3, 4, 1968 BI 1, 2, 3, 4, F 1, 2, 1969 A 1, 2, 3, 4, S, E, 1970 NZ 1, 2, 3, 4, 1971 F 1, 2, A 1, 2, 3
Visagie, R G (OFS, N) 1984 E 1, 2, S Am 1, 2, 1993 F 1
Visser, J de V (WP) 1981 NZ 2, US
Visser, M (WP) 1995 WS (R)
Visser, P J (Tvl) 1933 A 2
Viviers, S S (OFS) 1956 A 1, 2, NZ 2, 3, 4
Vogel, M L (OFS) 1974 BI 2(R)
Von Hoesslin, D J B (GW) 1999 It 1(R), 2, W (R), NZ 1, A 1(R)
Vos, A N (GL) 1999 It 1(t+R), 2, NZ 1(R), 2(R), A 2, [S R), Sp, E (R), A 3(R), NZ 3], 2000 C, E 1, 2, A 1, NZ 1, A 2, NZ 2, A 3, Arg, I, W, E 3, 2001 F 1, 2, It 1, NZ 1, A 1, 2, NZ 2, F 3, It 2, E, US

Wagenaar, C (NT) 1977 Wld
Wahl, J J (WP) 1949 NZ 1
Walker, A P (N) 1921 NZ 1, 3, 1924 BI 1, 2, 3, 4
Walker, H N (OFS) 1953 A 3, 1956 A 2, NZ 1, 4
Walker, H W (Tvl) 1910 BI 1, 2, 3
Walton, D C (N) 1964 F, 1965 I, S, NZ 3, 4, 1969 A 1, 2, E
Wannenburg, P J (BB) 2002 F (R), E, 2003 S 1, 2, Arg, A 1(t+R), NZ 1(R), 2004 I1, 2, W1, PI(R), 2006 S1(R), F, NZ2(R), 3, A3, 2007 Sm(R), NZ1(R), A2, NZ2
Waring, F W (WP) 1931 I, 1932 E, 1933 A 1, 2, 3, 4, 5
Watson, L A (WP) 2007 Sm, 2008 W1, 2, It, NZ1(R), 2(R), Arg, NZ3(R), A2(R), 3(t&R)
Wegner, N (WP) 1993 F 2, A 1, 2, 3
Wentzel, M van Z (Pumas) 2002 F (R), S
Wessels, J J (WP) 1896 BI 1, 2, 3
Whipp, P J M (WP) 1974 BI 1, 2, 1975 F 1, 1976 NZ 1, 3, 4, 1980 S Am 1, 2
White, J (Bor) 1931 W, 1933 A 1, 2, 3, 4, 5, 1937 A 1, 2, NZ 1, 2
Whiteley, W R (GL) 2014 A1(R), NZ1(R)
Wiese, J J (Tvl) 1993 F 1, 1995 WS, [R, C, WS, F, NZ], W, It, E, 1996 NZ 3(R), 4(R), 5, Arg 1, 2, F 1, 2, W
Willemse, A K (GL) 2003 S 1, 2, NZ 1, A 2, NZ 2, [U, E, Sm, NZ], 2004 W2, I3, 2007 E1, 2(R), Sm, A1, NZ1, Nm, S(R), [Tg]
Williams, A E (GW) 1910 BI 1
Williams, A P (WP) 1984 E 1, 2
Williams, C M (WP, GL) 1993 Arg 2, 1994 E 1, 2, NZ 1, 2, 3, Arg 1, 2, S, W, 1995 WS, [WS, F, NZ], It, E, 1998 A 1(t), NZ 1(t), 2000 C (R), E 1(t), 2(R), A 1(R), NZ 2, 3, Arg, I, W (R)
Williams, D O (WP) 1937 A 1, 2, NZ 1, 2, 3, 1938 BI 1, 2, 3
Williams, J G (NT) 1971 F 1, 2, A 1, 2, 3, 1972 E, 1974 BI 1, 2, 4, F 1, 2, 1976 NZ 1, 2
Wilson, L G (WP) 1960 NZ 3, 4, W, I, 1961 E, F, I, A 1, 2, 1962 BI 1, 2, 3, 4, 1963 A 1, 2, 3, 4, 1964 W, F, 1965 I, S, A 1, 2, NZ 1, 2, 3, 4
Wolmarans, B J (OFS) 1977 Wld
Wright, G D (EP, Tvl) 1986 Cv 3, 4, 1989 Wld 1, 2, 1992 F 1, 2, E
Wyness, M R K (WP) 1962 BI 1, 2, 3, 4, 1963 A 2

Zeller, W C (N) 1921 NZ 2, 3
Zimerman, M (WP) 1931 W, I, 1932 E, S

# TONGA

## TONGA'S 2013–14 TEST RECORD

| OPPONENTS | DATE | VENUE | RESULT |
|-----------|------|-------|--------|
| **Romania** | 9 Nov | A | Lost 19–18 |
| **France** | 16 Nov | A | Lost 38–18 |
| **Wales** | 22 Nov | A | Lost 17–7 |
| **Samoa** | 7 Jun | A | Drew 18–18 |
| **Fiji** | 14 Jun | A | Lost 45–17 |

# TONGA ENDURE WINLESS CAMPAIGN

## By Iain Spragg

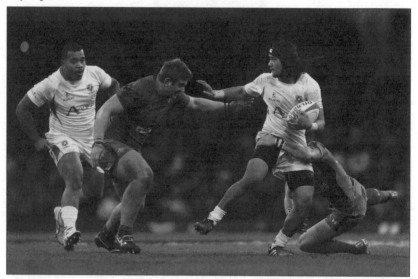

Tonga can take heart from pushing Wales hard at the Millennium Stadium before losing 17–7 in November 2013.

**W**ins will be a top priority for Tonga coach Mana 'Otai in November, not least to rebuild the confidence levels of his players after a season which yielded four defeats and a draw from five Test matches. With Rugby World Cup 2015 looming on the horizon, the tour, with matches against Georgia, USA and Scotland, could not be more important for the Ikale Tahi.

Tonga will face defending champions New Zealand, Argentina, Georgia and Namibia in Pool C at England 2015 and the presence of Jake White, South Africa's RWC 2007 winning coach, as a technical advisor for the tour could prove invaluable to 'Otai and the Ikale Tahi's preparations for the showpiece event.

"It'll be just for a month where we'll try to suck him dry of information, talk to him about World Cup preparation and get him to assist the coaches in any way he can while he's here," Peter Harding, the Tonga

Rugby Union's high performance manager, said of White's appointment. Perhaps Tonga's season would have been different had they emerged victorious from their first match against Romania in November, but they were cruelly denied the win at the death and the tone was set for what was to prove a chastening campaign.

The coach handed a Test debut to second row Uili Kolo'ofai for the game in Bucharest and in a see-saw encounter, the Ikale Tahi seemed to have struck the decisive blow when wing Fetu'u Vainikolo scored with just seven minutes remaining to give Tonga a slender 18–16 lead.

It was a time for cool heads but they were in short supply among the visitors who first gave away a penalty at a scrum and then again at the resulting lineout, allowing Florin Vlaicu to step forward in the 79th minute and kick the penalty that gave Romania a 19–18 win in the first ever meeting between the two countries. It was a bitter pill for 'Otai and his side to swallow and although there were brave performances in matches that followed, they were not rewarded with wins.

A week after the Romania game, they travelled to Le Havre to face a French team still smarting from their defeat in the Rugby World Cup 2011 pool stages. Despite two second-half tries from Vainikolo, a 40th-minute yellow card for Taniela Moa and a 41st-minute red for Sona Taumalolo effectively ended hopes of another famous upset and Les Bleus gained their revenge with a 38–18 victory.

The European tour concluded against Wales at the Millennium Stadium. Tonga were looking for a first ever win and when wing Will Helu went over in the 33rd minute to cut the deficit to 17–7, they sensed that history could be made. Unusually for a Test match, however, there were no points scored in the second half and so while 'Otai's side displayed an abundance of passion and pride in Cardiff, they were condemned to a third tour defeat.

Seven months later Tonga took part in the new-look IRB Pacific Nations Cup, which in 2014 featured two conferences involving Samoa, Fiji, Japan, the USA and Canada. Tonga were clear underdogs going into their first match in the Pacific Islands Conference against Samoa in Apia, but in contrast to their clash with Romania, this time they were able to avoid defeat in the dying minutes rather than throw victory away.

First-half tries from second row Josh Afu and winger Otulea Katoa gave the visitors a 12–5 advantage at the break, but Samoa came storming back and when Tusi Pisi landed a late penalty, Tonga trailed 18–15. The match went into added time but just when 'Otai's side seemed destined to lose again, Afu was hauled down in the lineout and replacement fly-half Fangatapu 'Apikotoa held his nerve to kick the penalty to secure a morale-boosting draw.

A week later reality returned with a heavy 45–17 loss to Fiji in Lautoka, a result which left Tonga bottom of the standings. They finished their season with a 36–14 triumph over a Pacific Barbarians invitational XV in Auckland, but will be hoping to return to winning ways in November.

If the Test team struggled, there were more encouraging performances in 2014 from both the Under 20 side in the IRB Junior World Rugby Trophy and Tonga A in the IRB Pacific Rugby Cup.

The Under 20s travelled to Hong Kong in April for the Trophy, and although they were beaten by Georgia in their tournament opener, they bounced back to defeat Hong Kong (39–16) and the USA (28–22) to top Pool A, albeit only on the head-to-head rule as a result of the latter win.

The results propelled the team into the final to face Japan, but despite a 63rd-minute try from hooker Haini Moala they were overrun in the second half at the Hong Kong Football Club and beaten 35–10. Second place was nonetheless Tonga's best ever finish and an indication of the younger talent coming through the ranks.

The Tonga A side also equipped itself well in March in a revamped PRC, a competition in 2014 featuring Super Rugby development teams from Australia and A teams from Argentina, Japan, Samoa and Fiji. They began with a 27–18 loss to their Samoan counterparts in Sydney but shrugged off the disappointment to beat ACT A (29–20) and Gen Blue (29–21) before losing to the Argentina Pampas XV (47–20) to finish second in Pool B. That earned Tonga a place in the third-place play-off against the Fiji Warriors, but despite losing that 54–21 the nine-team tournament boded well for the number of players ready to graduate to the national team.

There were fewer positives on the Sevens front. Tonga parted company with director of Sevens rugby Eddie Waqa in late 2013, but did earn the right to play at the Gold Coast and Wellington rounds of the HSBC Sevens World Series. Unfortunately they failed to win a match in either event. Tonga then finished sixth at the Oceania Sevens in early October, a placing which confirmed their entry in the 12-team qualifier in Hong Kong where they will have the chance to secure core team status on the 2015–16 World Series.

On the domestic front, the IRB's Get Into Rugby continued to expand in Tonga, which was the first country in the Oceania region to deliver the programme. More than 15,000 participants – 44 per cent of them girls – participated in the programme after the Union signed a memorandum of understanding with the Ministry of Education.

# TONGA INTERNATIONAL STATISTICS

## MATCH RECORDS UP TO 13 OCTOBER 2014

### WINNING MARGIN

| Date | Opponent | Result | Winning Margin |
|------|----------|--------|----------------|
| 21/03/2003 | Korea | 119–0 | 119 |
| 08/07/2006 | Cook Islands | 90–0 | 90 |
| 01/01/1979 | Solomon Islands | 92–3 | 89 |
| 10/02/2007 | Korea | 83–3 | 80 |
| 15/03/2003 | Korea | 75–0 | 75 |

### MOST POINTS IN A MATCH
#### BY THE TEAM

| Date | Opponent | Result | Points |
|------|----------|--------|--------|
| 21/03/2003 | Korea | 119–0 | 119 |
| 01/01/1979 | Solomon Islands | 92–3 | 92 |
| 08/07/2006 | Cook Islands | 90–0 | 90 |
| 06/12/2002 | Papua New Guinea | 84–12 | 84 |
| 10/02/2007 | Korea | 83–3 | 83 |

#### BY A PLAYER

| Date | Player | Opponent | Points |
|------|--------|----------|--------|
| 21/03/2003 | Pierre Hola | Korea | 39 |
| 10/02/2007 | Fangatapu Apikotoa | Korea | 28 |
| 04/05/1999 | Sateki Tuipulotu | Korea | 27 |
| 21/03/2003 | Benhur Kivalu | Korea | 25 |
| 06/12/2002 | Pierre Hola | Papua New Guinea | 24 |

### MOST TRIES IN A MATCH
#### BY THE TEAM

| Date | Opponent | Result | Tries |
|------|----------|--------|-------|
| 21/03/2003 | Korea | 119–0 | 17 |
| 08/07/2006 | Cook Islands | 90–0 | 14 |
| 10/02/2007 | Korea | 83–3 | 13 |
| 24/06/2006 | Cook Islands | 77–10 | 13 |
| 12 on 2 occasions | | | |

#### BY A PLAYER

| Date | Player | Opponent | Tries |
|------|--------|----------|-------|
| 21/03/2003 | Benhur Kivalu | Korea | 5 |
| 08/06/2011 | Viliame Iongi | USA | 4 |
| 3 on 5 occasions | | | |

### MOST CONVERSIONS IN A MATCH
#### BY THE TEAM

| Date | Opponent | Result | Cons |
|------|----------|--------|------|
| 21/03/2003 | Korea | 119–0 | 17 |
| 08/07/2006 | Cook Islands | 90–0 | 10 |
| 9 on 3 occasions | | | |

#### BY A PLAYER

| Date | Player | Opponent | Cons |
|------|--------|----------|------|
| 21/03/2003 | Pierre Hola | Korea | 17 |
| 08/07/2006 | Fangatapu Apikotoa | Cook Islands | 9 |
| 10/02/2007 | Fangatapu Apikotoa | Korea | 2 |
| 06/12/2002 | Pierre Hola | Papua New Guinea | 9 |
| 05/07/1997 | Kusitafu Tonga | Cook Islands | 9 |

### MOST PENALTIES IN A MATCH
#### BY THE TEAM

| Date | Opponent | Result | Pens |
|------|----------|--------|------|
| 05/06/2012 | Samoa | 18–20 | 6 |
| 5 on 4 occasions | | | |

#### BY A PLAYER

| Date | Player | Opponent | Pens |
|------|--------|----------|------|
| 05/06/2012 | Kurt Morath | Samoa | 6 |
| 13/07/2011 | Kurt Morath | Samoa | 5 |
| 19/08/2011 | Kurt Morath | Fiji | 5 |

### MOST DROP GOALS IN A MATCH
#### BY THE TEAM

1 on 8 occasions

#### BY A PLAYER

1 on 8 occasions

TONGA

| MOST CAPPED PLAYERS | |
|---|---|
| Name | Caps |
| Elisi Vunipola | 41 |
| Benhur Kivalu | 38 |
| Pierre Hola | 37 |
| Manu Vunipola | 35 |
| Aleki Lutui | 33 |

| LEADING TRY SCORERS | |
|---|---|
| Name | Tries |
| Siua Taumalolo | 12 |
| Fepikou Tatafu | 11 |
| Benhur Kivalu | 10 |
| Vungakoto Lilo | 10 |

| LEADING CONVERSIONS SCORERS | |
|---|---|
| Name | Cons |
| Pierre Hola | 65 |
| Fangatapu Apikotoa | 39 |
| Kurt Morath | 35 |
| Sateki Tuipulotu | 33 |

| LEADING PENALTY SCORERS | |
|---|---|
| Name | Pens |
| Kurt Morath | 52 |
| Pierre Hola | 35 |
| Sateki Tuipulotu | 32 |
| Fangatapu Apikotoa | 22 |

| LEADING DROP GOAL SCORERS | |
|---|---|
| Name | DGs |
| Pierre Hola | 3 |

| LEADING POINTS SCORERS | |
|---|---|
| Name | Points |
| Pierre Hola | 289 |
| Kurt Morath | 231 |
| Sateki Tuipulotu | 190 |
| Fangatapu Apikotoa | 159 |
| Siua Taumalolo | 108 |

# TONGA INTERNATIONAL PLAYERS
## UP TO 13 OCTOBER 2014

**I Afeaki** 1995 *F, S, Iv*, 1997 *Fj*, 2001 *S, W*, 2002 *J, Fj, Sa, Fj*, 2003 *Kor, Kor, I, Fj, Fj, It, C*, 2004 *Sa, Fj*, 2005 *It*, 2007 *Sa, SA, E*
**P Afeaki** 1983 *Fj, Sa*
**S Afeaki** 2002 *Fj, Sa, Fj, PNG, PNG*, 2003 *Kor, Kor, I, Fj, It, W, NZ*
**V Afeaki** 1997 *Sa*, 2002 *Sa, Fj*
**JL Afu** 2008 *J, Sa, Fj*, 2009 *Fj, Sa, J*, 2011 *US*, 2012 *Sa, J, Fj, US*, 2013 *J, C, US, Fj*, 2014 *Sa, Fj*
**T Afu Fifita** 1924 *Fj, Fj, Fj*
**A Afu Fungavaka** 1982 *Sa*, 1984 *Fj, Fj*, 1985 *Fj, Fj*, 1986 *W, Fj, Fj*, 1987 *C, W, I, Sa, Fj*
**S 'Aho** 1974 *S, W*
**T Ahoafi** 2007 *AuA, Sa*
**P Ahofono** 1990 *Sa*
**E Aholelei** 2013 *J, C, R, W*, 2014 *Sa, Fj*
**K Ahota'e'iloa** 1999 *Sa, F, Fj*, 2000 *C, Fj, J*
**M Ahota'e'iloa** 2010 *Sa, Fj, J*
**S Aisake** 1934 *Fj*
**M Akau'ola** 1934 *Fj*
**P 'Ake** 1926 *Fj, Fj*
**M Alatini** 1969 *M*, 1972 *Fj, Fj*, 1973 *M, A, A, Fj*, 1974 *S, W, C*, 1975 *M*, 1977 *Fj*
**PF Alatini** 1995 *Sa*
**S Alatini** 1994 *Sa, Fj*, 1998 *Sa, Fj*, 2000 *NZ, US*
**S Alatini** 1977 *Fj*, 1979 *NC, M, E*
**T Alatini** 1932 *Fj*
**A Alatini** 2001 *S*, 2002 *J, Sa, Fj*, 2003 *I, Fj*

**V 'Alipate** 1967 *Fj*, 1968 *Fj, Fj, Fj*, 1969 *M*
**A Amone** 1987 *W, I, Sa, Fj*
**A Amore** 1988 *Fj*
**F Anderson** 2013 *US, Fj*, 2014 *Sa, Fj*
**V Anitoni** 1990 *Sa*
**T Anitoni** 1995 *J, Sa, Fj*, 1996 *Sa, Fj*
**F Apikotoa** 2004 *Sa, Fj*, 2005 *Fj, Sa, Fj, Sa, It, F*, 2006 *Coo, Coo*, 2007 *Kor, AuA, J, JAB*, 2008 *J, Sa, Fj*, 2009 *Fj, J, 2010 *Fj, CHL*, 2012 *It, US, S*, 2013 *J, R, F, W*, 2014 *Sa, Fj*
**T Apitani** 1947 *Fj, Fj*
**S Asi** 1987 *C*
**T Asi** 1996 *Sa*
**H 'Asi** 2000 *C*
**S Ata** 1928 *Fj*
**S Atiola** 1987 *Sa, Fj*, 1988 *Fj, Fj*, 1989 *Fj, Fj*, 1990 *Fj, J*
**H Aulika** 2011 *Fj, C, J, F*, 2012 *It, US, S*

**K Bakewa** 2002 *PNG, PNG*, 2003 *Fj*
**O Beba** 1932 *Fj, Fj, Fj*
**M Blake** 1983 *M, M*, 1987 *Sa, Fj*, 1988 *Sa, Fj, Fj*
**T Bloomfield** 1973 *M, A, A, Fj*, 1986 *W*
**D Briggs** 1997 *W*
**J Buloka** 1932 *Fj, Fj*

**D Edwards** 1998 *A*, 1999 *Geo, Geo, Kor, US, Sa, F, Fj, C, NZ, It, E*

**KP Hehea** 2006 *J, Fj, JAB, Coo, Sa, Coo,* 2007 *US, Sa, SA,* 2008 *Sa, Fj,* 2009 *Pt,* 2011 *Fj, J, Sa, Fj, NZ, J, F*
**SE Hehepoto** 1972 *Fj,* 1973 *M, A, A, Fj*
**M Hekeheke** 1986 *Fj, Fj,* 1988 *Fj*
**Helehele** 1985 *Fj*
**T Helu** 1967 *Fj, Fj*
**VFUA Helu** 2010 *Fj, J,* 2011 *US, Fj, J, Sa, Fj, C,* 2012 *It, US, S,* 2013 *J, C, US, Fj, R, F, W,* 2014 *Fj*
**T Hikila** 2010 *CHL*
**O Hiko** 1979 *E*
**RP Hola** 1998 *Sa, A, Fj,* 2001 *W,* 2002 *J, Fj, Sa, Sa, Fj, PNG, PNG,* 2003 *Kor, Kor, I, Fj, It, W, NZ, C,* 2005 *Fj,* 2006 *J, Fj, JAB, Coo, Sa, Coo,* 2007 *Sa, US, Sa, SA, E,* 2008 *J, Sa, Fj,* 2009 *Sa, J, Pt*
**S Hola** 1979 *Fj*
**L Hopoate** 1986 *W*
**V Hosea** 1967 *Fj, Fj*
**F Hufanga** 1973 *M*
**S Hufanga** 2003 *Fj, W, NZ, C,* 2004 *Sa, Fj,* 2005 *It, F,* 2006 *J, Fj, JAB,* 2007 *Fj, US, Sa, SA, E,* 2008 *Sa,* 2009 *Pt,* 2011 *US, Sa, Fj, Fj, NZ, J, F,* 2012 *It, US, S*

**F Ika** 1988 *Sa, Fj, Fj, Fj,* 1989 *Fj, Fj*
**S Ika** 2008 *J,* 2009 *Sa, J*
**R Iloalahia** 2010 *CHL*
**M Ilolahia** 1947 *Fj*
**Inoke** 1947 *Fj*
**K 'Inoke** 1967 *Fj, Fj, Fj,* 1968 *Fj, Fj, Fj,* 1969 *M, M,* 1972 *Fj,* 1973 *A,* 1975 *M*
**V 'Iongi** 2011 *US, Fj, J, Sa, Fj, Fj, NZ, C, F,* 2012 *Sa, J, Fj, It, US, S,* 2013 *C, US, Fj*
**K 'Iongi** 1967 *Fj, Fj, Fj,* 1968 *Fj, Fj, Fj,* 1969 *M, M,* 1972 *Fj,* 1973 *M, A, Fj*
**T 'Isitolo** 1995 *Iv, Sa, Fj*

**M Kafatolu** 2002 *J, Fj, Sa*
**PNA Kaho** 2011 *US,* 2012 *Sa, J, Fj, It,* 2013 *J, C, US*
**T Kaho** 1973 *A*
**J Kaihau** 1932 *Fj, Fj*
**P Kaihau** 1975 *M,* 1977 *Fj, Fj, Fj*
**S Kaihau** 1934 *Fj*
**M Kaihea** 1999 *Geo, Kor, Kor, J, Sa, F*
**L Kainga** 1928 *Fj, Fj*
**L Kaiqa** 1928 *Fj*
**'A Kaitu'u** 2000 *C*
**J Kalaivalu** 1996 *Sa*
**SM Kalamafoni** 2007 *Kor, AuA, J, JAB, Fj, Sa,* 2010 *Sa, Fj, J,* 2011 *Fj, J, Sa, Fj, Fj, NZ, C, J, F,* 2013 *R, F, W*
**N Kalaniuvalu** 1963 *Fj*
**R Kapeli** 1992 *Sa, Fj,* 1993 *Fj, A*
**S Kapeli** 2005 *Sa*
**T Kapeli** 1982 *Sa*
**PF Kata** 2009 *Pt,* 2010 *Sa, Fj, J*
**FKM Katoa** 2009 *J*
**L Katoa** 1996 *Sa, Fj,* 1997 *Nm, Fj, Sa*
**O Katoa** 2014 *Sa*
**P Katoa** 1977 *Fj, Fj, Fj,* 1979 *NC, M, E, Sa,* 1981 *Fj, Fj, Fj*
**P Katoa** 1924 *Fj*
**T Kaufana** 1947 *Fj*
**L Kauhalaniua** 1984 *Fj*
**S Kauhenga** 2002 *Sa, Sa, Fj,* 2003 *Fj,* 2006 *J,* 2007 *SA,* 2008 *J,* 2009 *Sa, J, Pt,* 2011 *US,* 2013 *J, C, US, Fj*
**S Kava** 1967 *Fj*
**T Kavapalu** 1967 *Fj,* 1968 *Fj, Fj, Fj,* 1969 *M, M,* 1972 *Fj,* 1973 *M, A, Fj,* 1974 *W,* 1975 *M, M*
**A Kefu** 1926 *Fj, Fj, Fj,* 1928 *Fj, Fj*
**F Kefu** 1972 *Fj, Fj,* 1973 *A,* 1974 *W, C,* 1975 *M*
**M Kefu** 2012 *Sa, J, Fj*
**M Kefu** 1959 *Fj,* 1960 *M,* 1963 *Fj, Fj*
**E Kelemeni** 1967 *Fj, Fj, Fj*
**K Kioa** 1959 *Fj,* 1960 *M*
**P Kiole** 1977 *Fj, Fj, Fj,* 1979 *M, E, Fj,* 1980 *Sa*
**S Kiole** 2005 *Fj, Fj,* 2007 *AuA, J, JAB, Fj, Sa,* 2008 *Fj*
**FT Kitekei'aho** 1987 *C, W, I*
**T kitekei'aho** 1979 *Fj*
**DJB Kivalu** 1998 *Sa, A,* 1999 *Geo, Geo, Kor, Sa, F, Fj, C, NZ,*

*It, E,* 2000 *C, Fj, J, NZ, Sa, US,* 2002 *J, Sa, Sa, Fj, PNG, PNG,* 2003 *Kor, Kor, Fj, Fj, It, W, NZ, C,* 2004 *Sa, Fj,* 2005 *Fj, Sa, Fj, Sa*
**T Kolo** 1993 *A,* 1995 *Sa, Fj*
**OPV Koloamatangi** 2011 *US,* 2012 *Sa, J*
**C Koloi** 1999 *US*
**S Koloi** 1998 *Sa, Fj,* 1999 *Geo, Geo, Kor, Kor, J, C, NZ, It, E,* 2000 *NZ, Sa, US,* 2001 *Sa*
**K Kolokihakaufiji** 2010 *CHL*
**KMF Otai** 1995 *J, J, F, S, Iv*
**Kolo'ofa'i** 2013 *R*
**E Koloto** 1986 *W*

**F Lagilagi** 1991 *Fj*
**Jione Laiseni** 1932 *Fj, Fj*
**P Langi** 1986 *W, Fj*
**E Langi** 2003 *NZ*
**F Langi** 1990 *Fj, J*
**O Latu** 2006 *J, Fj, JAB, Coo, Sa, Coo,* 2007 *Kor, AuA, J, JAB, Fj, Sa, US, Sa, SA, E,* 2008 *J, Sa, Fj,* 2009 *Fj, Sa, J,* 2012 *US, S,* 2013 *J, C, US, Fj, R, F, W,* 2014 *Sa, Fj*
**F Lani** 1986 *Fj*
**TA Latailakepa** 1992 *Sa, Fj,* 1993 *Sa*
**K Latu** 1987 *Fj*
**MKM Latu** 2011 *J*
**P Latu** 1994 *W,* 1995 *J, J, F, S, Iv, Sa, Fj*
**S Latu** 1972 *Fj,* 1973 *M, A, A, Fj,* 1974 *S, W, C,* 1975 *M, M*
**S Latu** 1992 *Fj,* 1993 *Fj, A*
**S Latu** 1984 *Fj, Fj*
**U Latu** 1997 *W,* 1998 *Sa,* 2002 *PNG, PNG,* 2003 *Kor, Kor, I, It, W, NZ, C*
**U Latufeku** 1959 *Fj,* 1960 *M,* 1963 *Fj,* 1968 *Fj, Fj, Fj*
**P Latukefu** 1995 *J, J, S, Iv, Sa, Fj,* 1998 *A, Fj*
**T Latukefu** 1967 *Fj, Fj, Fj,* 1968 *Fj, Fj, Fj*
**M Latunipulu** 1926 *Fj, Fj, Fj*
**F Latusela** 2003 *Kor, Kor*
**F Lauei** 1985 *Fj*
**H Lavaka** 1996 *Sa,* 1997 *SA, Fj, Sa, Coo, W,* 2003 *I, Fj, Fj, It, W, NZ, C*
**K Lavaka** 1996 *Fj*
**M Lavaka** 1993 *S, Fj, A, Fj*
**S Lavaka** 2008 *J*
**T Lavaki** 1990 *J, Kor,* 1993 *S*
**F Lavemai** 1984 *Fj, Fj,* 1985 *Fj,* 1986 *W*
**M Lavulo** 1979 *E*
**T Lea'aetoa** 2002 *PNG, PNG,* 2003 *Kor, Kor, I, It, W, NZ, C,* 2005 *It, F,* 2006 *J, Fj, JAB, Coo, Sa, Coo,* 2008 *J, Sa, Fj,* 2011 *US, Fj, Fj, J*
**J Leba** 1932 *Fj, Fj, Fj*
**G Leger** 2001 *S, W,* 2002 *J, Fj, Sa, Sa, Fj,* 2003 *Kor, Kor, I, Fj, It, NZ, C*
**T Leger** 1967 *Fj, Fj*
**T Leha** 1983 *M, M*
**S Leilani** 1981 *Fj,* 1983 *Fj, Sa*
**FVMH Lemoto** 2007 *Fj*
**A Liava'a** 1979 *E,* 1981 *Fj, Fj,* 1983 *Fj, Sa, M, M,* 1984 *Fj, Fj,* 1985 *Fj,* 1987 *C, W, I*
**S Liava'a** 1979 *M, E,* 1981 *Fj, Fj*
**V Likio** 1947 *Fj, Fj*
**L Lile** 2002 *Sa, Fj,* 2003 *Fj*
**VF Lilo** 2007 *Kor, J, JAB, US, Sa, SA, E,* 2008 *J, Sa, Fj,* 2009 *Fj, Sa, J, Pt,* 2010 *Sa, Fj, J,* 2011 *Fj, J, Sa, Fj, NZ, J, F,* 2012 *It, US, S,* 2013 *R, F, W*
**J Lino** 1926 *Fj, Fj, Fj*
**M Liongitau** 1924 *Fj, Fj, Fj*
**S Lisala** 2005 *Sa, Fj*
**S Lo'amanu** 1926 *Fj, Fj, Fj,* 1928 *Fj, Fj, Fj*
**T Lokotui** 2001 *W,* 2011 *Fj, J, Sa, Fj, C, J, F,* 2012 *Fj, It, US, S,* 2013 *C, US, Fj, R, F, W*
**S Lolo** 1993 *Sa*
**T Lolo'ahea** 1987 *Sa,* 1990 *J, Sa, Kor, Sa,* 1991 *Sa, Fj, Fj*
**L Lolohea** 2007 *JAB*
**P Lolohea** 1983 *M, M*
**K Lomu** 1979 *Fj*
**W Lose** 1995 *F, S, Iv*
**L Loto'ahea** 1994 *Sa*

T Loto'ahea 1987 *Fj*, 1988 *Fj*, *Fj*, 1989 *Fj*, *Fj*, 1993 *S*, *Fj*, 1994 *W*, *Fj*
T Lovo 1982 *Sa*, 1986 *W*, *Fj*, *Fj*, 1987 *Sa*, 1988 *Fj*, 1989 *Fj*, *Fj*, 1990 *Sa*
S Luau 2007 *AuA*
I Lupina 1969 *M*, 1972 *Fj*
T Lutua 1990 *Kor*, 1992 *Fj*, 1994 *Sa*, *W*, *Fj*, 1995 *J*, *J*, *Iv*
V Lutua 1981 *Fj*, *Fj*, *Fj*, 1987 *W*, *I*, 1988 *Fj*, *Fj*
AA Lutui 1999 *Geo*, *J*, *Sa*, *F*, 2001 *Fj*, *S*, *W*, 2004 *Sa*, *Fj*, 2005 *Fj*, *Sa*, *Fj*, *Sa*, 2006 *Fj*, *JAB*, 2007 *AuA*, *J*, *JAB*, *Fj*, *Sa*, *US*, *Sa*, *SA*, *E*, 2010 *Sa*, *Fj*, *J*, 2011 *Fj*, *Fj*, *NZ*, *J*, *F*

F Ma'afa 1981 *Fj*, *Fj*
F Ma'afu 1985 *Fj*, 1986 *Fj*, *Fj*, 1988 *Sa*, *Fj*, *Fj*, *Fj*
P Ma'afu 1959 *Fj*, 1960 *M*, 1963 *Fj*
P Ma'afu 1979 *M*, *E*, *Sa*, *Fj*, 1980 *Sa*, 1981 *Fj*, *Fj*, 1983 *M*, *M*
T Ma'afu 1983 *M*, *M*
VS Ma'afu 2011 *US*, *J*, *Sa*, *Fj*, *Fj*, *NZ*, *C*, *J*, *F*, 2012 *J*, *It*, *US*, *S*, 2013 *R*, *F*, *W*, 2014 *Sa*, *Fj*
V Ma'ake 1973 *M*, *A*, *A*, *Fj*, 1974 *S*, *W*, *C*, 1975 *M*, *M*, 1977 *Fj*, *Fj*, *Fj*, 1979 *NC*, *M*, *E*, *Sa*, *Fj*, 1980 *Sa*
AI Ma'asi 2009 *Fj*, *Sa*, *J*, 2011 *US*, *J*, *Sa*, *Fj*, *C*, *J*, 2012 *Sa*, *J*, *Fj*, *It*, *S*, 2013 *J*, *C*, *US*, *Fj*, *F*
V Ma'asi 1997 *W*, 2000 *C*, *J*, *Sa*, *US*, 2001 *Fj*, *Fj*, *Sa*, *S*, *W*, 2002 *J*, *Fj*, *Sa*, *Sa*, 2003 *I*, *Fj*, *Fj*, *It*, *W*, *NZ*, *C*, 2005 *Fj*, *Sa*, *It*, *F*, 2008 *J*, *Sa*, *Fj*, 2009 *Fj*, *Sa*, *J*
S Mafana 1959 *Fj*, 1960 *M*, 1963 *Fj*, *Fj*
A Mafi 1995 *Iv*
F Mafi 1993 *A*, *Fj*, 1994 *Sa*, *W*, *Fj*, 1995 *J*, *J*, *F*, 1996 *Sa*, *Fj*, 1998 *Sa*, *A*, 1999 *Geo*, *Geo*, *Kor*, *J*, *US*, *NZ*, *It*, *E*
S Mafi 1988 *Fj*, 1989 *Fj*, 1990 *Fj*, *Kor*, 1993 *Sa*
S Mafi 1969 *M*, *M*, 1972 *Fj*, *Fj*, *Fj*, 1973 *M*, *A*, *A*, *Fj*, 1974 *S*, *W*, *C*, 1975 *M*, *M*
S Mafi 2010 *Sa*, *Fj*, *J*, 2012 *Sa*, *J*, *Fj*, *It*, *US*, *S*, 2014 *Fj*
S Mafile'o 1995 *Iv*, *Sa*, *Fj*, 1997 *Z*, *Nm*, *SA*, 2002 *J*, 2003 *Kor*, *Kor*, *I*, *Fj*
R Mahe 2005 *Sa*, *It*, *F*, 2006 *Fj*, *JAB*, *Coo*, *Coo*, 2007 *Kor*
S Mahe 1981 *Fj*, *Fj*
F Mahoni 1993 *Sa*, *A*, *Fj*, 1995 *J*, *J*, *F*, *Sa*, *Fj*, 1996 *Sa*, *Fj*, 1999 *Geo*, *J*
F Mailangi 1928 *Fj*, *Fj*
A Mailangi 2010 *J*
F Mailangi 1968 *Fj*, *Fj*, *Fj*, 1969 *M*
L Mailangi 1959 *Fj*, 1960 *M*, 1963 *Fj*, *Fj*
TS Mailau 2012 *Sa*, *J*, *It*, *US*, *S*, 2013 *R*, *F*, *W*, 2014 *Sa*, *Fj*
P Mailefihi 1979 *E*, 1982 *Fj*
AK Ma'ilei 2002 *J*, *Fj*, *Sa*, *Sa*, *Fj*, *PNG*, *PNG*, 2003 *Kor*, *Kor*, 2005 *Fj*, *Sa*, *F*, 2010 *Sa*, *J*, 2011 *Fj*, *J*, *Fj*, *Fj*, *NZ*, *J*, *F*
T Mak 1988 *Fj*
A Maka 2005 *F*
F Maka 2007 *US*, *Sa*, *SA*, *E*, 2011 *Fj*, *NZ*, *C*, *F*
L Maka 1997 *Z*, 1999 *Geo*, *J*, *US*, *F*, *NZ*, *It*, *E*, 2000 *C*, *Fj*, *J*, *NZ*, *US*, 2002 *J*, *Sa*, *Sa*, *Fj*, 2003 *Kor*, *Kor*
P Maka 1985 *Fj*
T Maka 1979 *NC*, *Sa*, 1981 *Fj*, *Fj*
V Maka 1983 *Fj*, *Sa*, 1984 *Fj*, *Fj*
H Makahoi 1974 *C*, 1975 *M*, *M*, 1977 *Fj*, *Fj*, *Fj*, 1979 *Sa*, *Fj*, 1980 *Sa*
S Makalo 1975 *M*
M Makasini 2005 *Fj*, *Sa*, *Fj*, *Sa*
T Makisi 1983 *M*, *M*, 1989 *Fj*, *Fj*
M Malu 1979 *NC*, *Sa*
Malu 1947 *Fj*
MV Malupo 2009 *Sa*, 2011 *US*, *Sa*
L Manako 2000 *NZ*, *Sa*
T Manako 1995 *J*, *J*
T Manako 2000 *J*
C Manu 1987 *Sa*, *Fj*, 1989 *Fj*, *Fj*
E Manu 1996 *Sa*, *Fj*, 1999 *Kor*, *J*, *US*
F Manukia 1993 *A*, *Fj*, 1994 *Sa*, *W*, *Fj*, 1995 *J*, *J*
M Manukia 1993 *Sa*, *S*, *Fj*, *A*, *Fj*, 1994 *Fj*
T Mapa 1967 *Fj*, *Fj*
P Mapakaitolo 1977 *Fj*, *Fj*
VP Mapakaitolo 2009 *Fj*, *J*, 2011 *US*, 2014 *Sa*, *Fj*
S Martens 1998 *A*, *Fj*, 1999 *Geo*, *Geo*, *Kor*, *Kor*, *J*, *US*, *Sa*, *F*, *Fj*, *C*, *NZ*, *It*, *E*, 2001 *S*, *W*, 2002 *Fj*, *Sa*, *Sa*, *Fj*, 2003 *Kor*, *Kor*, *It*, *W*, *NZ*, *C*, 2009 *Fj*, *Sa*, *J*

S Masi 1989 *Fj*
F Masila 1990 *J*, 1991 *Fj*, 1993 *Sa*, *S*, *A*, *Fj*, 1994 *W*, 1995 *F*, *Fj*, 1998 *Sa*, *A*
Masili 1991 *Fj*
SK Masima 2005 *Fj*
SFL Masima 2013 *J*, *Fj*
T Matakaiongo 1997 *W*
S Matangi 2000 *J*, *Sa*, 2001 *Fj*, *Sa*, 2002 *Fj*, *PNG*, 2004 *Sa*, *Fj*
S Matapule 1973 *M*, 1975 *M*
SH Mata'u 2007 *AuA*, 2008 *J*
S Mateaki 1928 *Fj*, *Fj*
P Mateo 2010 *CHL*
K Ma'u 1981 *Fj*, 1983 *Fj*, *Sa*, *M*, 1984 *Fj*, *Fj*
T Ma'u 1947 *Fj*, *Fj*
V Ma'u 1947 *Fj*
O Misa 2004 *Sa*, *Fj*
S Misa 1926 *Fj*, *Fj*, *Fj*
S Moa 1928 *Fj*
U Moa 1998 *A*, *Fj*, 1999 *Geo*
V Moa 1993 *Sa*, *S*, 1998 *Sa*
M Moala 1986 *W*, *Fj*, *Fj*
F Moala 1982 *Sa*, 1983 *Sa*, 1985 *Fj*
F Moala 1982 *Sa*, *Fj*, 1983 *Fj*, *Sa*, *M*, *M*, 1984 *Fj*, *Fj*, 1985 *Fj*
F Moala 1963 *Fj*, *Fj*, 1968 *Fj*, *Fj*, *Fj*
K Moala 1959 *Fj*, 1960 *M*, 1963 *Fj*, 1967 *Fj*, *Fj*
M Moala 2004 *Sa*, *Fj*, 2009 *Pt*
P Moala 1981 *Fj*, *Fj*, *Fj*
P Moala 1982 *Sa*, 1983 *M*, 1986 *W*, *Fj*, *Fj*, 1987 *Sa*, *Fj*
S Moala 1988 *Fj*
T Moala 1972 *Fj*
V Moala'eua 1977 *Fj*, *Fj*, *Fj*, 1979 *NC*, *M*, *Sa*, *Fj*, 1981 *Fj*, *Fj*
V Moeaki 1934 *Fj*
Mofuike 1986 *Fj*
S Mohi 1986 *W*, *Fj*, *Fj*, 1987 *C*, *W*, *I*
S Moimoi 2001 *W*
S Moli 1992 *Fj*
F Molitika 2000 *C*, *J*, 2001 *Fj*, *Sa*, *S*, 2005 *It*, *F*
MK Molitika 1997 *Nm*, *SA*, *Fj*, *Sa*, *Coo*, *W*, 2000 *NZ*, *Sa*, *US*, 2001 *S*, 2005 *It*, 2006 *Fj*, *JAB*, *Coo*, *Sa*, 2007 *E*
DW Morath 2010 *Sa*, *Fj*, 2011 *US*
KS Morath 2009 *Pt*, 2010 *Sa*, *Fj*, *J*, 2011 *US*, *Fj*, *J*, *Sa*, *Fj*, *NZ*, *C*, *J*, *F*, 2012 *Sa*, *J*, *Fj*, 2013 *J*, *C*
K Motu'apuaka 1972 *Fj*
S Motu'apuaka 1969 *M*, *M*, 1972 *Fj*
S Motu'apuaka 1980 *Sa*, 1987 *C*
S Motu'apuka 1979 *Fj*
S Motuliki 1967 *Fj*
Mounga 1947 *Fj*
E Mo'ungaloa 1924 *Fj*, *Fj*, *Fj*
F Muller 1967 *Fj*, 1968 *Fj*, *Fj*, *Fj*, 1969 *M*, *M*, 1972 *Fj*, *Fj*

S Na'a Tovo 1924 *Fj*, *Fj*, *Fj*
T Na'aniumotu 2006 *J*, *JAB*, *Coo*, *Sa*, *Coo*, 2010 *CHL*
F Naitoko 2005 *Sa*
S Napa'a 1934 *Fj*
S Nau 2000 *C*, *Fj*, *J*, 2001 *Fj*, 2003 *Fj*, 2005 *It*, *F*, 2006 *JAB*, *Coo*, *Sa*
N Naufahu 2001 *Fj*, *Sa*, *Fj*, *W*, 2002 *J*, *Sa*, *Sa*, *Fj*, *PNG*, *PNG*, 2003 *Kor*, *Kor*, *I*, *W*, *C*
S Nauvai 1960 *M*
T Ngaluafe 1974 *S*, *W*, *C*, 1975 *M*, *M*
J Ngauamo 2003 *Kor*, *I*, *Fj*, *It*, *C*, 2005 *It*
MM Ngauamo 2002 *PNG*, *PNG*, 2003 *Kor*, *I*, *Fj*, *It*, *W*, *NZ*, *C*, 2005 *F*, 2006 *Fj*, *JAB*, 2008 *Sa*, *Fj*
P Ngauamo 2014 *Sa*, *Fj*
S Ngauamo 1997 *Coo*, 1998 *A*
T Nisa 1991 *Fj*, 1992 *Fj*
U Niuila 1990 *Sa*
S Nuku 1981 *Fj*, *Fj*, *Fj*, 1984 *Fj*, *Fj*

L Ofa 1983 *Fj*, *Sa*, *M*, *M*, 1984 *Fj*
A Olosoni 2006 *Fj*, *J*
I Omani 1928 *Fj*, 1932 *Fj*, *Fj*, *Fj*
M 'Ota'ota 2000 *C*, 2005 *Fj*, *Sa*, *Fj*

E Paea 2011 *US*, 2012 *Fj*
H Paea 2007 *Kor*

**503**

TONGA

M Paea 2013 *W*
L Pahulu 1973 *A, Fj*, 1974 *S*
V Pahulu 1967 *Fj, Fj, Fj*, 1968 *Fj, Fj, Fj*, 1969 *M, M*, 1973 *M*
P Palavi 1924 *Fj, Fj, Fj*
U Palavi 1960 *M*, 1963 *Fj, Fj*
J Pale 2001 *S, W*, 2002 *J, Fj, Sa, Sa, Fj*, 2003 *Fj*
M Pale 1998 *A*, 1999 *Geo*, 2002 *J, Fj*, 2006 *J, Coo, Sa*
SW Palei 2009 *J*
S Palenapa 1990 *Fj, J, Sa, Kor, Sa*, 1996 *Sa, Fj*
D Palu 2002 *PNG, PNG*, 2003 *Kor, Kor, I, Fj, C*, 2006 *J, JAB, Coo*, 2007 *AuA, J, JAB*
P Palu 1979 *NC*, 1981 *Fj*
TT Palu 2011 *Sa, Fj, Fj, C, F*, 2012 *Fj*, 2013 *J, US, Fj, R*
TM Palu 2008 *J*
S Panelapa 1988 *Fj*
H Pau'u 1983 *Fj, Sa*
T Pau'u 1992 *Fj*
J Payne 2002 *PNG, PNG*, 2003 *Kor, Kor, I, Fj, It, W, NZ, C*
D Penisini 1997 *Nm, Coo*, 1999 *Geo, Kor, C*
'O Pepa 1928 *Fj, Fj, Fj*
H Petelo 1982 *Fj*
H Pierra 2005 *Sa*
O Pifeleti 1983 *Fj, Sa, M, M*, 1984 *Fj, Fj*, 1985 *Fj*, 1989 *Fj, Fj*, 1990 *Sa*, 1991 *Sa, Fj, Fj*
S Piukala 2012 *It, US, S*, 2013 *J, C, US, Fj, R, F*
T Piukala 1934 *Fj*
SV Piutau 2011 *Fj, Fj, NZ, C, J, F*, 2012 *Sa, J, Fj*, 2013 *J, C, R, F, W*, 2014 *Sa, Fj*
H Pohiva 1997 *W*, 1998 *Sa, Fj*
VV Pola 2010 *Fj, CHL*, 2012 *Sa, Fj*
S Pone 2008 *Sa, Fj*, 2013 *US*
S Pongi 1990 *Sa*
SE Poteki 2007 *Kor*
VT Poteki 2007 *Kor*
S Pouanga 1947 *Fj, Fj*
E Pou'uhila 1988 *Fj*
SKV Puafisi 2011 *J, Sa*, 2012 *Fj*, 2013 *C, US, Fj, R, F, W*, 2014 *Sa, Fj*
ST Puloka 1928 *Fj, Fj*, 1934 *Fj*
K Pulu 2002 *Fj, PNG, PNG*, 2003 *Kor, Kor, I, Fj, It, W, NZ*, 2005 *Fj, Sa, Fj, Sa*, 2006 *J*, 2007 *US, Sa, SA, E*, 2008 *Fj*, 2009 *Sa, J*, 2011 *US, NZ, C, F*, 2012 *Sa, J, Fj*
M Pulumu 1979 *NC, Sa, Fj*, 1980 *Sa*, 1981 *Fj, Fj, Fj*
T Pulumufila 1974 *S, W, C*

H Saafi 2000 *NZ*
K Sakalia 2010 *CHL*, 2013 *J, C, US, Fj*, 2014 *Sa*
T Samiu 1947 *Fj*
Sanilaita 1981 *Fj*
S Satui 2009 *Pt*
A Saulala 1991 *Fj*
C Schaumkel 1992 *Sa, Fj*, 1997 *SA, Fj*
S Selupe 1963 *Fj, Fj*, 1967 *Fj, Fj*, 1969 *M, M*, 1972 *Fj*, 1973 *M, A, Fj*
S Selupe 1967 *Fj*, 1969 *M*, 1972 *Fj*
S Selupe 1924 *Fj, Fj, Fj*, 1928 *Fj*
T Siale 1997 *Nm, Sa*
M Sifa 1947 *Fj*
S Sika 1968 *Fj, Fj, Fj*, 1969 *M, M*
AH Sikalu 2007 *AuA, J*, 2010 *Sa, Fj*
T Sime 1963 *Fj*
T Sitanilei 1932 *Fj*
J Sitoa 1998 *A*
E Siua 2009 *Pt*, 2010 *CHL*, 2011 *US*
PIL Siulangapo 2010 *CHL*
T Soaiti 1932 *Fj, Fj, Fj*
T Soane 1982 *Sa, Fj*, 1983 *Fj, Sa*, 1984 *Fj, Fj*, 1985 *Fj*
L Stanley 1985 *Fj*
L Susimalofi 1989 *Fj*

L Tafa 2007 *J*
S Tahaafe 1987 *C*
P Taholo 1983 *M*
S Tai 1997 *W*, 1998 *A*
U Tai 1969 *M*, 1972 *Fj*
EVT Taione 2012 *It, US, S*, 2013 *J, C, US, Fj, R, F, W*
E Taione 1999 *It, E*, 2000 *Fj, J*, 2001 *S, W*, 2005 *F*, 2006 *JAB,*

*Sa*, 2007 *Fj, Sa, US, Sa, SA, E*, 2008 *Sa, Fj*, 2009 *Fj*
K Take 1989 *Fj*
S Takulua 2014 *Sa, Fj*
E Talakai 1993 *Sa, S, Fj, Fj*, 1995 *S, Iv, Sa, Fj*
H Taliai 1934 *F*
P Tanginoa 1995 *Fj*, 1997 *W*, 1998 *Sa, A*, 1999 *Geo*
T Tanginoa 2007 *AuA, J*
F Taniela 1982 *Fj*
I Tapueluelu 1990 *Fj, J, Sa, Sa*, 1993 *Sa, S*, 1999 *Kor, Kor, J, US, NZ, It, E*
F Tatafu 1996 *Fj*, 1997 *Z, Nm, Fj, Sa, Coo, W*, 1999 *Geo, Kor, Kor, J, Sa, Fj, C, NZ, E*, 2002 *J, Fj, Sa, PNG, PNG*
S Tatafu 1967 *Fj*
T Tatafu 1963 *Fj*
V Tau 1999 *US*
A Taufa 1993 *A*, 1995 *J, J, F, S*
AN Taufa 2010 *Sa, Fj, J*, 2011 *Fj, J, C*, 2012 *Sa, J, Fj*, 2013 *Fj*, 2014 *Sa, Fj*
E Taufa 2007 *Sa*, 2008 *J, Sa, Fj*
I Taufa 1972 *Fj*
S Taufa 1984 *Fj*
S Taufa 2005 *Fj, Sa, Fj, Sa*
T Taufa 1990 *Fj*
T Taufahema 1998 *Sa, A, Fj*, 1999 *Sa, F, NZ, It*, 2000 *C, Fj, J, NZ, Sa*, 2001 *Fj, Sa, Fj, S, W*
S Taufalele 2013 *R, W*, 2014 *Sa, Fj*
M Taufateau 1983 *M, M*, 1984 *Fj*, 1987 *Fj*
V Taufatofua 1926 *Fj, Fj, Fj*
A Ta'ufo'ou 1997 *Nm, SA, Fj, Sa, Coo*
E Ta'ufo'ou 2000 *C, Fj, J, NZ, Sa, US*
N Taufo'ou 1996 *Sa, Fj*, 1997 *Nm, SA, Fj, Sa, Coo, W*, 1998 *Sa, A, Fj*, 1999 *Geo, Kor, F, Fj, NZ, It, E*, 2000 *NZ, Sa, US*
E Taukafa 2002 *PNG, PNG*, 2003 *Kor, Kor, I, Fj, Fj, It, W, NZ, C*, 2005 *Fj, Sa, It, F*, 2006 *J, Fj, Coo, Sa, Coo*, 2007 *US, Sa, SA, E*, 2008 *Sa, Fj*, 2011 *Fj, J, Sa, Fj, NZ, C*
S Taukapo 2005 *Sa*
P Taukolo 1982 *Sa, Fj*
P Taula 2009 *Fj, Pt*, 2010 *Sa, Fj, J*
S Taumalolo 1996 *Sa, Fj*, 1997 *Z, Nm, SA, Coo, W*, 1999 *Geo, Geo, Sa, F, Fj, C, NZ*, 2000 *NZ, Sa, US*, 2001 *Fj, Sa, S, W*, 2006 *J*, 2007 *JAB, Fj, Sa*
FKA Taumalolo 2011 *Fj, J, Sa, Fj, NZ, C, J, F*, 2012 *It, US, S*, 2013 *R, F*
P Taumiuvao 1986 *Fj*
N Taumoefolau 1979 *NC, E, Sa, Fj*
P Taumoepeau 1928 *Fj, Fj, Fj*
SS Taumoepeau 2011 *US*
T Taumoepeau 1988 *Fj*
T Taumoepeau 1999 *Geo, Kor, Kor, J, US, NZ, E*, 2000 *Fj, J, NZ, Sa, US*, 2001 *Fj, Sa, Sa, S, W*, 2002 *J, Fj, Sa*, 2006 *J, Fj, JAB, Coo, Sa, Coo*, 2007 *AuA, J, Fj, Sa*
V Taumoepeau 1994 *Sa, W*, 1995 *Sa, Fj*
P Taumoua 2007 *J*
S Taupeaafe 1994 *W, Fj*, 1998 *Sa, A, Fj*, 1999 *Kor, J, NZ, It, E*, 2000 *NZ, US*, 2001 *Fj, Sa*
F Tautau'a 2007 *Kor*
S Tavo 1959 *Fj*, 1960 *M*, 1963 *Fj*, 1967 *Fj, Fj, Fj*, 1968 *Fj, Fj, Fj*, 1969 *M, M*
M Te Pou 1998 *A, Fj*, 1999 *Geo, Geo, Kor, Kor, J, US, F, NZ, It*, 2001 *S, W*
Telanisi 1967 *Fj*
SF Telefoni 2008 *J, Sa, Fj*, 2009 *Pt*, 2011 *Fj*
Teri 1991 *Fj*
Teutau 1991 *Fj*
UV Moa 2011 *Fj, Fj, NZ, C, J, F*, 2012 *Sa, J, Fj, It, US, S*, 2013 *J, C, US, Fj, F, W*
SLN Timani 2008 *J*, 2009 *Fj*, 2011 *US, Fj, NZ, C*, 2012 *S*
D Tiueti 1997 *Fj, Sa, W*, 1999 *Geo, Geo, Kor, Sa, F, Fj, C, NZ, It, E*, 2000 *C, Fj, J, NZ, Sa, US*, 2001 *S, W*
T Tofua 1924 *Fj, Fj, Fj*, 1926 *Fj, Fj, Fj*
T Toga 1968 *Fj*
T Tohi 1997 *Nm, SA*
T Toke 2007 *Kor, J, JAB, Fj, Sa, US, Sa*, 2009 *Fj*, 2010 *Sa, Fj, J*
M Toloke 2010 *CHL*
V Toloke 1995 *J, Sa, Fj*, 1996 *Sa, Fj*, 1999 *Geo, Geo, Kor, Kor, US, NZ, E*, 2000 *NZ, Sa, US*, 2002 *J, Sa, Sa*
M Toma 1988 *Sa, Fj, Fj*, 1991 *Sa, Fj, Fj*

Jubilant Uruguay players after clinching their
place at RWC 2015 by beating Russia.

AFP/Getty Images

# URUGUAY

## URUGUAY'S 2013–14 TEST RECORD

| OPPONENTS | DATE | VENUE | RESULT |
|---|---|---|---|
| Spain | 16 Nov | H | Won 16–15 |
| USA | 22 Mar | H | Drew 27–27 |
| USA | 29 Mar | A | Lost 32–13 |
| Paraguay | 26 Apr | A | Won 34–10 |
| Brazil | 3 May | A | Won 34–9 |
| Chile | 10 May | H | Won 55–13 |
| Argentina | 17 May | H | Lost 65–9 |
| Romania | 13 Jun | A | Lost 34–16 |
| Russia | 22 Jun | N | Won 13–6 |
| Hong Kong | 2 Aug | H | Won 28–3 |
| Russia | 27 Sep | A | Lost 22–21 |
| Russia | 11 Oct | H | Won 36–27 |

# HARD WORK PAYS OFF FOR URUGUAY

*By Frankie Deges*

The Uruguayan players celebrate after beating Russia to clinch the 20th and final place at Rugby World Cup 2015.

**THE COUNTRIES**

**V**alidation. **Of the** many good things that came out of Uruguay's qualification for Rugby World Cup 2015, one of the most important is simply that: validation. That they defeated Russia 57–49 on aggregate in the Repechage finale is part of the successful history of a nation that since 2003 had been away from the international spotlight.

A teros is a proud bird extremely defensive of its territory, and when their Estadio Charrúa was rebranded as "Tierra de Los Teros" (Land of Los Teros), it made a lot of sense. Securing that final place at England 2015 wasn't something that happened in Montevideo on 11 October. It was a process that began as soon as Uruguay missed out on RWC 2011.

"November 27, 2010, if my memory serves me right," recalled Pablo Lemoine, the prop who played for Uruguay in their two World Cups. He retired from active duty that day after Romania beat Uruguay 60–33 on aggregate in the Repechage and soon moved back to Montevideo. There, the planning began.

It wasn't easy from the start. The Unión de Rugby del Uruguay (URU) had been taken over by confronting many a former president. In came Marcello Calandra, best remembered as the frantic maniac celebrating in the coach's box at Aussie Stadium when Lemoine and co beat Georgia at RWC 2003. The former Test prop and later assistant coach knew that in order to steer the game in his country he had to have everyone working together. He convinced those who had previously run the game that together they would be stronger. His Executive Council comprised all the former presidents in some capacity or other and as a unit things started to happen.

Sebastián Piñeyrúa was named national coach in 2011 and brought Lemoine in to assist him as he was readjusting to life in Montevideo. Uruguay, though, crashed to defeat against Chile for the first time in a decade in the South American Championship. "It was hard to explain ourselves to the Uruguay rugby fraternity, but we had a vision and plucked players from second XV rugby or others that were not in the national team for that South American Championship. They are now the core of our squad," explained Lemoine, who made the transition from player to assistant coach to head coach within a year.

In November 2011, a tour to Portugal and Spain introduced a few others and the future was starting to take shape. Good things happen to people that work hard and those players, hungry for success as they were, did whatever needed to be done. "I asked a lot of them and they answered," admitted Lemoine. "We trained until December 20th and players had to be back on January 6th in the middle of our summer. Nobody complained, no one capitulated and we were all on the same page. They trusted and shared our dream and that was crucial."

A key moment came when the URU took possession of Estadio Charrúa, a municipal ground in Montevideo previously owned by the national soccer federation. With a capacity for 15,000, it not only provided a home field, but had enough rooms to host a rugby squad and ample areas to build a gymnasium, medical facilities and office space. Possession was handed over on 1 January, 2013 but there was still a lot of work that needed to be done at the stadium.

And so a new chapter of Uruguayan rugby history began. Soon after Piñeyrúa took off his coaching hat and became URU President, but the goodwill generated did not change. As the new High Performance Centre grew, so did the number of players and teams brought into the fold. Not only would Los Teros operate from there but also the Uruguay A team and Under 20s, while future stars were being introduced to the new programmes as early as Under 17 level.

Being well located in a city of 1.3 million people allowed the amateur players to train in the morning and afternoon and then return to their jobs, with doctors, administrators, web-designers, students and busi-

URUGUAY

nessmen in the squad. When Uruguay confirmed their RWC return with victory over Russia only three players were based overseas – second row Rodrigo Capó Ortega with Castres and the young half-back pairing of Agustín Ormaechea and Felipe Berchesi in the French lower divisions.

The development continued throughout 2013 and when Lemoine and Emiliano Caffera returned from the IRB Americas Rugby Championship in Canada that October they knew what was needed for the following year and mapped it out so that no stone was left unturned.

Having narrowly beaten Spain at home a month later, the first big challenge came in late March with the Americas 2 play-off for RWC 2015 against the USA. A 27–27 draw in Montevideo counted for nothing with the return leg in Atlanta a week later. A number of key players were injured during the course of the match and despite a good first hour in which the Eagles pack was pushed around at scrum-time, the hosts took control in the final quarter and the 32–13 loss meant that Uruguay would have to negotiate the Repechage if they were to realise their RWC 2015 dream.

With a few months to prepare for that next hurdle, Uruguay confirmed their status as the second best team in South America by comfortably beating Paraguay and Brazil away and then an understrength Chile at home before falling to an Argentina team preparing for matches against Ireland in June. This game was played in Paysandú, a well-supported new Test venue in the country.

Uruguay's Under 20s also had a strong IRB Junior World Rugby Trophy in Hong Kong in April. They defeated eventual champions Japan in the first round and suffered only one defeat, 26–25 to USA in the third place play-off. They had missed out on a place in the final on point differential to Japan, but overall Los Teritos had proved themselves at this level. They will represent South America again at the 2015 edition in Portugal and the importance of this side to Uruguay's future is evident with half of the squad that beat Russia having played in either the Trophy or the IRB Junior World Championship.

Another important step on the road to England 2015 came at the IRB Nations Cup in June. Uruguay had identified their meeting with Russia as a must-win because it would help them climb above the Bears in the IRB World Rankings and ensure that, if the sides met in the Repechage, the second leg was in Montevideo. "It was a crucial game: it not only allowed us to finish at home but it proved to our players that we could beat them," admitted Lemoine.

With the climax of the qualification process approaching, the team upped their preparation despite a loss in a warm-up game against a Canadian visiting side. The first step then was to overcome Hong Kong, which they duly did with a late flourish.

THE COUNTRIES

Having been unavailable to play for his country since 2009, the return of Ortega for the play-off with Russia helped the team enormously, not just for his vast experience but that it created a good vibe among some of his younger teammates who had only seen him play. The only survivor of Uruguay's last RWC appearance in 2003, he had a very good game in Montevideo.

"To be able to go to a World Cup is a dream come true," he said afterwards. "I only joined this team recently but the manner in which they prepared and how hard they work is unbelievable. I am honoured to join them."

Russia was not an easy opponent. Having played at RWC 2011, they knew how important it was to their own development to qualify. Uruguay, though, were not fazed by the 22–21 defeat in Krasnoyarsk and in the return leg showed their hunger to join Australia, hosts England, Wales and Fiji in Pool A.

The first half was muddled and reduced to penalty kicks, so much that Uruguay thought the Russian fly-half would again take the kick and had turned their backs when he instead ran a penalty for a try. A wave of Uruguayan momentum in the second half, though, brought three tries – for Joaquín Prada, Alejo Corral and Ormaechea – to ensure a huge celebration in front of more than 14,000 excited fans, including national president José Mujica attending his first ever Test match.

"We are delighted to be going to the World Cup but now our responsibilities are bigger. There is a lot of work to do if we want to enjoy ourselves there. We were hungrier than Russia and it paid off, for this generation it is a dream come true," insisted Corral.

New possibilities now open for Uruguayan rugby. With government support expected to grow, the URU can sit with their sponsors and find new ones. They took a big gamble in signing contracts until the end of 2014, but are now in a great position to renegotiate terms that will allow them to continue growing.

There are currently some 7,000 registered players in Uruguay, although the pool of players ready for Test rugby right now is only around 40.

"The whole of Uruguay supported us – different sporting federations, famous sports people, the public in general even if they did not know much about rugby," admitted Piñeyrúa, who knows he faces a busy period in which his union must quickly adapt to the challenge ahead.

Lemoine added: "We love challenges in Uruguay and I am already thinking of the next four years. We must be competitive in the World Cup. We know that we are playing in the toughest pool and against some of the best teams in the world. What is pleasing is that we will be able to work ahead of 2019 with growth and sustainability coming from better fixtures, more opportunities and a growing sport in Uruguay."

# URUGUAY INTERNATIONAL STATISTICS

## MATCH RECORDS UP TO 13 OCTOBER 2014

### WINNING MARGINS

| Date | Opponent | Result | Winning Margin |
|------|----------|--------|----------------|
| 14/05/2011 | Paraguay | 102–6 | 96 |
| 10/10/1998 | Paraguay | 93–3 | 90 |
| 25/04/2004 | Venezuela | 92–8 | 84 |
| 25/04/2009 | Paraguay | 85–7 | 78 |
| 21/05/1981 | Brazil | 77–0 | 77 |

### MOST POINTS IN A MATCH
#### BY THE TEAM

| Date | Opponent | Result | Points |
|------|----------|--------|--------|
| 14/05/2011 | Paraguay | 102–6 | 102 |
| 10/10/1998 | Paraguay | 93–3 | 93 |
| 25/04/2004 | Venezuela | 92–8 | 92 |
| 25/04/2009 | Paraguay | 85–7 | 85 |
| 03/05/2002 | Paraguay | 81–6 | 81 |

#### BY A PLAYER

| Date | Player | Opponent | Points |
|------|--------|----------|--------|
| 02/05/2009 | Matias Arocena | Chile | 31 |
| 07/09/2002 | Juan Menchaca | Chile | 29 |
| 02/10/1993 | Marcelo Nicola Horta | Paraguay | 28 |
| 09/10/1971 | Oscar Bacot | Paraguay | 27 |
| 28/03/1998 | Federico Sciarra | Paraguay | 23 |

### MOST TRIES IN A MATCH
#### BY THE TEAM

| Date | Opponent | Result | Tries |
|------|----------|--------|-------|
| 14/05/2011 | Paraguay | 102–6 | 16 |
| 10/10/1998 | Paraguay | 93–3 | 15 |
| 25/04/2004 | Venezuela | 92–8 | 14 |
| 21/05/1981 | Brazil | 77–0 | 13 |

#### BY A PLAYER

| Date | Player | Opponent | Tries |
|------|--------|----------|-------|
| 21/05/1981 | Carlos Bonaso | Brazil | 4 |
| 28/09/1991 | Diego Ormaechea | Brazil | 4 |
| 03/05/2002 | Benjamin Bono | Paraguay | 4 |
| 14/05/2011 | Pablo Bueno | Paraguay | 4 |

### MOST CONVERSIONS IN A MATCH
#### BY THE TEAM

| Date | Opponent | Result | Cons |
|------|----------|--------|------|
| 25/04/2004 | Venezuela | 92–8 | 11 |
| 14/05/2011 | Paraguay | 102–6 | 11 |
| 10/10/1998 | Paraguay | 93–3 | 9 |
| 03/05/2002 | Paraguay | 81–6 | 9 |
| 29/04/2009 | Brazil | 71–3 | 9 |

#### BY A PLAYER

| Date | Player | Opponent | Cons |
|------|--------|----------|------|
| 21/05/1981 | Jose Peirano | Brazil | 8 |
| 29/04/2009 | Matias Arocena | Brazil | 8 |
| 06/10/2001 | Juan Menchacha | Paraguay | 7 |
| | 6 on 8 occasions | | |

### MOST PENALTIES IN A MATCH
#### BY THE TEAM

| Date | Opponent | Result | Pens |
|------|----------|--------|------|
| 27/10/1977 | Chile | 21–18 | 7 |
| 27/09/2014 | Russia | 21–22 | 7 |
| | 6 on 9 occasions | | |

#### BY A PLAYER

| Date | Player | Opponent | Pens |
|------|--------|----------|------|
| 27/09/2014 | Felipe Berchesi | Russia | 7 |
| | 6 on 7 occasions | | |

### MOST DROP GOALS IN A MATCH
#### BY THE TEAM

| Date | Opponent | Result | DGs |
|------|----------|--------|-----|
| 07/09/2002 | Chile | 34–23 | 4 |
| 08/09/1991 | Chile | 34–18 | 3 |
| 18/08/1964 | Chile | 15–8 | 2 |
| 12/10/1979 | Chile | 9–9 | 2 |

#### BY A PLAYER

| Date | Player | Opponent | DGs |
|------|--------|----------|-----|
| 07/09/2002 | Juan Menchaca | Chile | 4 |
| 12/10/1979 | Rafael Ubilla | Chile | 2 |
| 08/09/1991 | Cesar Cat | Chile | 2 |

## MOST CAPPED PLAYERS

| Name | Caps |
|---|---|
| Rodrigo Sanchez | 65 |
| Diego Aguirre | 59 |
| Diego Ormaechea | 54 |
| Nicolas Grille | 53 |
| Pedro Vecino | 51 |

## LEADING TRY SCORERS

| Name | Tries |
|---|---|
| Diego Ormaechea | 30 |
| Alfonso Cardoso | 13 |
| Federico Sciarra | 13 |
| Leandro Leivas | 11 |
| Pedro Vecino | 10 |

## LEADING CONVERSIONS SCORERS

| Name | Conversions |
|---|---|
| Marcelo Nicola Horta | 35 |
| Matias Arocena | 35 |
| Federico Sciarra | 32 |
| Juan Menchaca | 28 |

## LEADING PENALTY SCORERS

| Name | Penalties |
|---|---|
| Juan Menchaca | 50 |
| Matias Arocena | 45 |
| Federico Sciarra | 44 |
| Jorge Zerbino | 26 |

## LEADING DROP GOAL SCORERS

| Name | DGs |
|---|---|
| Juan Menchaca | 5 |
| Rafael Ubilla | 4 |

## LEADING POINTS SCORERS

| Name | Points |
|---|---|
| Federico Sciarra | 259 |
| Juan Menchaca | 256 |
| Matias Arocena | 246 |
| Marcelo Nicola Horta | 156 |
| Diego Ormaechea | 139 |

# URUGUAY INTERNATIONAL PLAYERS
## UP TO 13 OCTOBER 2014

**P Abatte** 1987 *Sp*
**P Acerenza** 1981 *Par, Bra, CHL, 1983 Par, CHL, Ar, 1985 F, 1987 Ar, Sp, Ar, CHL, Par, 1988 Bel, 1990 CHL, CHL, 1991 Par, CHL, Ar, Bra, 1992 CHL, CHL, 1993 Bra, Par, CHL, Ar, 1995 Ar, C, Ar, Sp, CHL, Par, Ar, 1996 Ar, C, Ar, US, 1997 CHL, Par, Ar, 1998 Par, CHL*
**B Acle** 2001 *Ar*
**D Aguirre** 1992 *CHL, 1995 Ar, C, Ar, Sp, CHL, Par, Ar, 1996 Ar, C, Ar, US, 1997 Ar, 1998 Par, CHL, Ar, C, Ar, US, CHL, Par, Ar, 1999 Pt, Mor, Mor, It, Fj, Sp, Sp, S, SA, 2001 It, Sp, 2002 Ar, CHL, Par, CHL, C, US, C, US, CHL, 2003 Fj, C, Ar, US, SA, Sa, Geo, E, 2005 J, 2006 Ar, CHL, Pt, US, US, 2007 Pt, Pt*
**M Aguirre** 2002 *Ar, CHL, Par*
**S Aguirre** 1997 *CHL, 1998 Ar, Ar, Par, Ar, 1999 Pt, Pt, Mor, SA, 2001 It, Sp, 2002 Ar, CHL, Par, CHL, C, US, C, US, CHL, 2003 CHL, Par, Ar, Fj, C, Ar, SA, Geo, E, 2006 Ar, CHL, Pt, US, US, 2007 Pt, Pt*
**G Albanell** 2013 *Geo*
**A Alonso** 2014 *Par, R*
**G Alonso** 1987 *Sp, 1989 Par, Ar, US, 1990 CHL, CHL, 1991 Par, CHL, Ar, Bra*
**R Álvarez** 2004 *Ar, CHL, Pt, 2005 J, CHL, Ar, SA, Pt, 2006 Ar, CHL, Pt, US, US, 2007 Pt, Pt, 2009 R, Rus*
**JM Alvarez** 2001 *Par, CHL, CHL, 2002 Ar, CHL, Par, C, US, 2003 C, Ar, Sa, E, 2006 Ar, CHL, Pt, US, US, 2007 Pt, Pt, Sp, 2008 US, 2009 R, Rus*
**J Alzueta** 1999 *Pt, It, Fj, Sp, SA, 2001 Ar, Ar, C, US, It, Sp, CHL, CHL, 2002 Ar, CHL, Par, CHL, C, US, C, CHL, 2003 CHL, Ar, C, Ar, US, SA, Sa, Geo, E, 2004 Geo, Pt, 2005 J, CHL, Ar, SA, 2006 Ar, CHL, Pt, US, US, 2007 It, 2008 Ar, 2009 US*
**B Amarillo** 1998 *Par, Ar, C, Ar, US, 1999 Fj, Sp, 2000 Nm, CHL, Ar, 2001 Ar, Ar, C, US, 2003 CHL, Ar, Fj, C, Ar, US, SA, Sa, Geo*

**J Ameglio** 2011 *Par, CHL*
**I Amorin** 1975 *Par, Ar, Bra, CHL, 1976 Ar*
**A Aquistapache** 2007 *CHL*
**L Ara** 2004 *Ven, Ar, CHL, Geo, Pt, 2005 J, CHL, Ar*
**P Aramendia** 1958 *Ar, CHL, Per, 1960 F*
**CM Arboleya** 2004 *Geo, 2007 Pt, It, CHL, 2008 Ar, R, Geo, Rus, US, CHL, 2009 Par, Bra, CHL, R, Rus, US, US, 2010 Bra, Par, CHL, Ar, C, Rus, Kaz, R, R, 2011 Par, Bra, CHL, Ar, 2014 Par, Bra, R, Rus, HK, Rus, Rus*
**E Arechavaleta** 1976 *Ar, 1979 Ar, Ar, Par, CHL, 1981 Par, CHL, 1985 F, Par*
**S Ariano** 2007 *It*
**F Armas** 1951 *Ar, Bra*
**M Arocena** 2005 *CHL, Pt, 2006 Ar, CHL, Pt, US, US, 2007 Pt, It, Sp, CHL, 2008 Ar, R, Geo, Rus, US, CHL, 2009 Par, Rus, 2010 R, R, 2011 Par, Bra, CHL, Ar, Pt, Sp, 2012 Ar, CHL, Bra, 2013 Bra, 2014 Par, Bra, CHL*
**S Arocena** 2010 *Bra, Par, CHL, Ar, 2011 Par, Bra, CHL, 2012 Ar, Bra, Rus*
**JP Artagaveytia** 1961 *Ar, 1963 Bra*
**G Artola** 1993 *Bra*
**F Auesperg** 2001 *Ar, C, 2002 Par, 2003 Par*
**A Avalo** 2011 *Par, Bra, Ar, Sp, 2012 Ar, Bra, R, Rus, Pt, Pt, 2013 Ar, Bra, CHL, Geo, Sp, 2014 US, US, CHL, Ar, HK, Rus, Rus*
**J Ayling** 1958 *Ar, CHL, Per*

**J Bachini** 2004 *Ven*
**O Bacot** 1967 *CHL, 1969 Ar, CHL, 1971 Par, CHL, Ar*
**N Badano** 2010 *Bra, Par, CHL, Ar, C, Rus, R*
**JC Bado** 1992 *CHL, CHL, 1993 Par, CHL, 1995 Ar, C, Ar, CHL, Par, Ar, 1996 Ar, C, Ar, US, 1997 CHL, Par, Ar, 1998 Par, CHL, C, US, CHL, Ar, 1999 Pt, Pt, Mor, Mor, Sp, S, SA, 2001 Ar, C, US,*

**G Lijtenstein** 2011 *Par, Bra, CHL, Ar*, 2012 *Ar, Bra, Rus*, 2013 *Bra, CHL*, 2014 *Ar, R, Rus, HK*
**E Llovet** 1960 *F*, 1961 *Bra, CHL, Ar*
**JM Llovet** 2006 *Ar, Pt, US, US*, 2007 *Pt, It, Sp, CHL*, 2008 *Ar, R, Geo, Rus, US, CHL*, 2009 *Par, Bra, CHL, R, Rus, US, US*, 2010 *Par, CHL, Ar, C, Rus, Kaz*
**C Lopez** 1956 *CHL*, 1958 *Ar, CHL, Per*, 1961 *Bra*
**F Lopez** 2014 *Par*
**M Lopez** 1993 *Bra*, 2001 *Par, CHL*
**A Luongo** 1990 *CHL*, 1993 *Par, CHL, Ar*, 1995 *Par, Ar*, 1996 *C, Ar, US*, 1997 *Ar*, 1998 *Ar, Ar*
**D Lussich** 2010 *Bra, Par, Ar*
**I Lussich** 2003 *CHL, Par, Ar*, 2004 *Ven, Ar, CHL, Geo*, 2007 *It*
**S Lussich** 1961 *Bra, CHL, Ar*, 1971 *Bra*
**P Lyford-Pike** 1964 *Ar, CHL, Bra*, 1971 *Par, Bra*

**P Mabott** 1956 *CHL*
**J Machado** 1995 *Ar, Ar, CHL, Par*, 1996 *Ar, C, US*, 1997 *CHL*, 1999 *Pt, Pt, It, Fj*, 2000 *CHL, Ar*, 2001 *Ar, Ar, C, US, Sp*, 2002 *Ar, CHL*, 2003 *CHL, Par, Ar, US, Sa*
**D Magno** 2008 *Rus*, 2010 *Bra, Par, CHL, Ar, C, Rus, Kaz, R, R*, 2011 *Par, Bra, CHL, Ar, Pt, Sp*, 2012 *Ar, CHL, Bra, R, Rus, Pt, Pt*, 2013 *Ar, Bra, CHL, Sp*, 2014 *US, US, Bra, CHL, Ar, R, Rus, HK, Rus, Rus*
**G Magri** 1967 *Ar*, 1971 *CHL*
**F Manchoulas** 1971 *Par, CHL, Ar*, 1973 *CHL, Ar, Bra, Par*
**I Marques** 1990 *CHL*, 1991 *Par, Bra*
**JM Marquez** 1999 *Fj*, 2001 *Ar, US*
**E Martinez** 1985 *F*, 1987 *Ar, CHL, Par*, 1989 *Bra, Par, Ar*
**M Martinez** 2007 *It, Sp*, 2008 *US, CHL*, 2009 *Par, Bra, CHL, US*, 2010 *Bra, CHL, C, Rus, Kaz, R, R*, 2011 *CHL, Ar*
**N Martinez** 2010 *Rus*
**R Martinez** 2012 *Ar, CHL, Bra, R, Rus, Pt, Pt*, 2013 *Ar*
**S Martinez** 2014 *Par*
**A Mastroiani** 1971 *Par*, 1975 *Ar, CHL*, 1976 *NZ*, 1979 *Ar, Ar, Bra*
**A McGillivray** 1953 *Bra*
**A Menchaca** 1971 *CHL*, 1973 *CHL, Ar, Bra*
**J Menchaca** 1998 *Par*, 1999 *Pt, Sp, S, SA*, 2000 *CHL, Ar*, 2001 *Ar, Ar, C, US, It, Sp, Par, CHL, CHL, Ar*, 2002 *Ar, CHL, CHL, C, US, C, US, CHL*, 2003 *Fj, C, US, SA, Sa, Geo, E*, 2006 *Ar, CHL, Pt, US, US*, 2007 *Pt, Pt*
**M Mendaro** 1992 *CHL*, 1993 *Par, CHL, Ar*, 1995 *Ar, C, Ar, Sp*, 1996 *Ar, C, US*, 1997 *Ar, Par*, 1998 *Par, CHL, Ar, C, Ar, US, CHL, Par, Ar*, 1999 *Pt, Pt, Mor, Mor, It, Sp, Sp, S*, 2000 *Nm, CHL, Ar*, 2001 *Par, Ar, C, US*, 2002 *CHL, US, C, US, CHL*, 2003 *Fj, SA, Sa, Geo*
**R Mendoza** 1973 *Ar, Bra*, 1975 *Par, Bra*
**D Mera** 1981 *Bra*
**R Merzario** 1975 *Par, Bra, CHL*
**G Mieres** 2010 *Par, CHL, Ar, C, Rus, Kaz, R, R*, 2011 *Par, CHL, Ar, Pt, Sp*, 2012 *Ar, CHL, Bra, Rus, Pt, Pt*, 2013 *Bra, CHL, Sp*, 2014 *US, US, Bra, CHL, Ar, R, Rus, HK, Rus, Rus*
**A Miller** 1969 *Ar, CHL*, 1971 *Par*, 1973 *CHL, Ar, Bra*
**J Minut** 1975 *Par, Bra*
**JM Montero** 1971 *Ar*
**A Moor** 1961 *Ar*
**R Moor-Davie** 1960 *F*, 1961 *Bra, Ar*
**R Moor-Davies** 1967 *CHL, Ar*
**N Morales** 2004 *Pt*, 2005 *CHL, SA, Pt*, 2007 *It, Sp, CHL*, 2008 *Ar, R, Geo, Rus, US, CHL*, 2009 *Par, R, Rus, US, US*, 2010 *Par, C, Rus, R*
**E Morelli** 1951 *Ar, CHL, Bra*, 1956 *CHL*
**P Morelli** 1975 *Par, Bra*
**T Morton** 1951 *Ar, Bra*
**C Mosca** 1992 *CHL, CHL*
**M Mosca** 1991 *CHL*, 1995 *CHL, Par, Ar*, 1996 *Ar*
**S Mosquera** 1998 *Par, Ar, Par*, 2000 *Nm, CHL, Ar*, 2001 *C, Ar*, 2003 *Par*, 2004 *Ven, Ar, CHL, Pt*, 2005 *CHL*
**D Munoz** 1985 *CHL*
**E Munyo** 1973 *CHL, Ar, Bra, Par*
**D Muttio** 1975 *Par, Bra, CHL*, 1976 *Ar, NZ*, 1977 *Par, CHL, Bra*, 1979 *Ar, Ar, Par, CHL*

**D Nairac** 1993 *Bra, Par, CHL*, 1995 *Ar, Ar, Sp, Par, Ar*, 1996 *Ar*, 1997 *Ar*, 1998 *Ar*
**F Nicola** 1951 *Ar, CHL, Bra*
**JL Nicola** 1979 *Bra, CHL*, 1981 *Par, Bra, CHL*, 1993 *Ar*
**M Nicola Horta** 1989 *Bra, Par, CHL, Ar, US*, 1990 *CHL, CHL*, 1991 *Par, CHL, Ar, Bra*, 1993 *Bra, Par, CHL*, 1995 *Ar, C, Ar, Sp, CHL, Par, Ar*
**A Nicolich** 1977 *Par, Ar, Bra*, 1979 *Ar, Bra, CHL*, 1981 *Bra*
**A Nieto** 2012 *Ar, CHL, Bra, R, Rus, Pt, Pt*, 2013 *Ar, Bra, CHL, Sp*, 2014 *US, US, Bra, CHL, Ar, R, Rus, HK, Rus, Rus*
**J Novoa** 2011 *Ar*

**F Obes** 1975 *Ar, CHL*, 1976 *Ar, NZ*, 1979 *Ar, Par, CHL*
**J Obes** 1975 *Ar*, 1979 *Ar*
**H Octetich** 1973 *Ar, Par*
**D Ormaechea** 1979 *Bra*, 1981 *Bra*, 1983 *Par, CHL, Ar*, 1985 *F, Ar, CHL*, 1987 *Ar, Sp, Ar, CHL, Par*, 1989 *Par, CHL, Ar, US*, 1990 *CHL, CHL*, 1991 *CHL, Ar, Bra*, 1992 *CHL, CHL*, 1993 *Bra, Par, CHL, Ar*, 1995 *Ar, C, Ar, Sp, Par, Ar*, 1996 *Ar, C, Ar, US*, 1997 *CHL, Par, Ar*, 1998 *Par, CHL, C, US*, 1999 *Pt, Pt, Mor, Mor, It, Sp, Sp, S, SA*
**A Ormaechea** 2011 *Pt, Sp*, 2012 *Ar, CHL, R, Rus, Pt*, 2013 *Ar, Bra, CHL, Sp*, 2014 *US, US, HK, Rus, Rus*
**JD Ormaechea** 2011 *Pt, Sp*, 2012 *Ar, CHL, Bra, R, Rus, Pt, Pt*, 2013 *Ar, Bra, CHL*
**Z Orr** 1969 *Ar, CHL*
**Ostazo** 1985 *F*

**P Pagani** 2000 *Nm*, 2001 *Ar, US, Sp, Par, CHL, Ar*, 2002 *Par*
**J Paladino** 1983 *Par, CHL*
**G Palmer** 1951 *Ar, CHL, Bra*
**M Palomeque** 2011 *Bra, Ar*, 2012 *Pt*, 2013 *Ar, CHL, Sp*, 2014 *US, Bra, CHL, Ar, HK, Rus, Rus*
**M Panizza** 1990 *CHL, CHL*, 1991 *Par, CHL, Ar, Bra*, 1992 *CHL, CHL*, 1993 *Bra, Par, CHL, Ar*, 1995 *Ar, C, Ar, Sp, CHL, Par, Ar*, 1996 *C, Ar*, 1997 *CHL, Par, Ar*, 1998 *Par, CHL, Ar, C, Ar, US, CHL, Ar*, 1999 *Pt, Pt, Mor, Mor, Fj, Sp, Sp, S, SA*
**N Pardo de Iriondo** 1964 *Ar, CHL, Bra*, 1967 *CHL, Ar*
**A Passadore** 1981 *Par, CHL*, 1983 *Par, CHL, Ar*, 1985 *F, Ar, CHL*, 1987 *Ar, Sp*, 1988 *Bel*, 1989 *Par, CHL, Ar, US*, 1993 *Bra, Par, Ar*, 1995 *Ar, C*
**J Pastore** 2003 *CHL, Par, Ar, C, Ar, US, SA, Sa, Geo, E*, 2004 *Ven, Ar, CHL, Geo, Pt*, 2005 *J, CHL, Ar, SA*, 2006 *CHL, Pt, US, US*, 2007 *Pt, Pt, It, Sp, CHL*, 2008 *Ar, R, Geo, Rus, US, CHL*, 2009 *Bra, CHL, R, Rus, US, US*
**M Patino** 1979 *Ar, Ar, Bra, Par, CHL*, 1981 *Par, CHL*, 1983 *Par, CHL, Ar*, 1985 *F, Ar, Par, CHL*, 1987 *Ar*, 1988 *Bel*, 1990 *CHL, CHL*
**F Paullier** 1989 *Bra, Par, CHL, Ar, US*, 1991 *Ar*, 1992 *CHL, CHL*, 1993 *Bra, Par, CHL, Ar*, 1995 *Sp*, 1996 *Ar, C, Ar*, 1997 *CHL*, 1999 *Pt, Fj, SA*
**M Paullier** 1987 *Ar, Sp, Ar, CHL, Par*, 1988 *Bel*, 1989 *Bra, CHL, Ar, US*, 1991 *Ar*
**JC Paysse** 1961 *Bra, CHL, Ar*, 1964 *Ar, CHL, Bra*
**J Peirano** 1979 *Bra, Par*, 1981 *Bra, CHL*, 1983 *Par*
**G Pena** 1985 *F, Par*
**HC Pepe** 1961 *Ar*
**H Pepe** 1964 *Ar, CHL, Bra*, 1967 *CHL, Ar*
**A Pereira** 2004 *Ven, Ar, CHL, Geo*, 2005 *CHL, Ar*
**M Pereyra** 1977 *Par, Ar*
**J Pérez** 2004 *Ven*
**JA Pérez** 2001 *Sp, Par, CHL, CHL*, 2002 *C, C, US, CHL*, 2003 *CHL, Par, Ar, C, Ar, SA, Sa, Geo, E*, 2004 *Geo, Pt*, 2005 *J, CHL, Ar, SA*, 2006 *Ar, CHL, Pt, US, US*, 2007 *Pt, Pt*
**G Peyrou** 2005 *CHL, Ar, SA, Pt*, 2007 *CHL*, 2008 *Ar, R, US*
**J Peyrou** 1975 *Ar, CHL*
**P Pick** 1958 *Ar, CHL, Per*
**A Pieroni** 1985 *Par*, 1988 *Bel*, 1989 *US*
**R Pieroni** 1987 *Ar*
**R Pigurina** 1985 *Ar, Par, CHL*, 1987 *Ar, CHL*
**P Pineyrua** 1979 *Ar*
**T Pineyrúa** 2004 *Ven*
**J Pol** 1967 *CHL*
**A Pollak** 1963 *Bra*, 1964 *Ar, CHL, Bra*, 1967 *CHL, Ar*, 1969 *Ar, CHL*, 1971 *Par, CHL, Bra, Ar*, 1973 *CHL, Bra, Par*
**AR Pollak** 1967 *CHL, Ar*, 1969 *Ar, CHL*
**C Pombo** 2014 *US*
**A Ponce de Leon** 1993 *Bra*, 1995 *Ar, CHL*, 1996 *C, Ar, US*, 1997 *CHL*, 1998 *Ar, C, Ar*, 1999 *Pt, It, Fj, Sp, Sp, S*, 2000 *Nm*, 2001 *Ar, C, US, Sp, CHL*
**F Ponte** 2000 *Nm*
**H Ponte** 2002 *Ar, CHL, CHL, C, US, C, CHL*, 2003 *CHL, Par, Ar, Fj, C, Ar, US, SA, Geo*, 2006 *CHL, US, US*, 2007 *Pt*
**R Pose** 2004 *Geo*, 2005 *Pt*, 2007 *It*
**J Prada** 2013 *Geo, Sp*, 2014 *US, US, Par, Bra, CHL, Ar, R, Rus, HK, Rus, Rus*
**F Praderi** 1973 *Par*, 1976 *NZ*
**C Protasi** 2005 *Ar, SA, Pt*, 2006 *Pt, US*, 2007 *Pt, It, Sp, CHL*, 2009 *Par, US, US*
**H Pugh** 1953 *Bra*, 1956 *CHL*, 1960 *F*
**A Puig** 1951 *CHL, Bra*
**G Puig** 2014 *Par, Bra, CHL, Ar*
**G Puig** 1981 *Par*, 1983 *Par, CHL, Ar*, 1985 *F*, 1987 *Ar, Sp*, 1989 *Bra, CHL, Ar*, 1991 *CHL, Ar*

**URUGUAY**

B Ramazzi 1951 *Ar*
S Ramos 2004 *Pt, 2005 CHL, Ar, SA*
B Rathbone 1951 *Ar, CHL, Bra, 1953 Bra*
C Regules 1958 *Per*
C Reyes 1953 *Bra, 1961 Bra*
D Reyes 2002 *C, 2003 Par, Ar, Fj, C, E, 2004 Ven*
J Reyes 1975 *Par, Bra*
M Reyes 1996 *US, 1997 Par, Ar, 1998 Par*
A Rial 1951 *CHL, Bra, 1953 Bra*
A Rienzi 1973 *Ar, Bra, Par*
JP Rignon 1976 *Ar, NZ*
H Rivera 2007 *Sp*
S Rodino 2008 *Geo, Rus*
C Rodriguez 1997 *Par, 1998 Par, Ar, C, Ar, Par, 1999 Pt, Fj, Sp, 2000 Nm*
O Rodriguez 1958 *CHL*
A Roman 2011 *Par, Bra, CHL, Ar, Pt, Sp, 2012 Ar, Bra, R, Rus, Pt, Pt, 2013 Ar, Bra, CHL, Geo, Sp, 2014 Ar, R, Rus, HK, Rus, Rus*
N Romay 1981 *Par, CHL, 1983 CHL, Ar, 1985 F, Ar, Par, CHL, 1988 Bel*
J Rombys 2008 *Ar, R, Geo, Rus, US, 2009 Par, Bra, CHL, R, US, 2010 Bra, Par, CHL, Ar, C, Rus, Kaz, R, R, 2011 Sp, 2012 Pt*
JP Ruffalini 2010 *Bra, Par, CHL, Ar, Rus*
H Ruggeroni 1958 *Ar, Per*

M Saavedra 1964 *Ar, CHL, Bra*
G Sabasti 1960 *F, 1961 Bra, Ar*
F Sader 1995 *CHL*
Saenz 1987 *Ar*
B Saenz 1988 *Bel, 1991 Par, CHL, 2001 C, US, CHL, Ar*
S Sagario 2013 *Geo*
M Sagario 2006 *It, Sp, CHL, 2008 Ar, R, Geo, Rus, US, CHL, 2009 Par, Bra, CHL, R, Rus, US, US, 2010 R, R, 2011 Sp, 2012 Ar, CHL, Bra, R, Rus, Pt, Pt, 2013 Ar, Bra, CHL, Geo, Sp, 2014 US, US*
J Sagarra 1956 *CHL, 1958 Ar, CHL*
Salustio 1985 *F*
A Sanabria 1998 *Ar, Ar, 2001 Ar*
R Sanchez 2000 *Nm*
R Sanchez 1996 *Ar, 1997 Par, Ar, 1998 Par, CHL, C, US, CHL, Par, Ar, 1999 Pt, Pt, Mor, Mor, It, Sp, Sp, S, SA, 2000 Nm, CHL, Ar, 2001 Ar, Ar, C, US, It, Sp, CHL, CHL, 2002 Ar, CHL, CHL, C, US, C, US, CHL, 2003 Fj, C, SA, Sa, Geo, E, 2005 J, 2006 Ar, CHL, Pt, US, US, 2007 Pt, Pt, Pt, Sp, CHL, 2008 R, Geo, Rus, US, CHL, 2009 CHL, R, Rus, US, US*
M Sanguinetti 2014 *Par, Bra, R*
JC Sartori 1969 *Ar, CHL*
R Sayagues 1971 *Par*
JC Scasso 1971 *CHL, Bra, Ar, 1973 CHL, Ar, Bra*
JC Scasso 1969 *Ar, CHL*
F Sciarra 1990 *CHL, CHL, 1991 Par, CHL, Ar, Bra, 1992 CHL, 1993 Bra, Par, CHL, Ar, 1995 C, Ar, Sp, CHL, Par, Ar, 1996 Ar, C, Ar, US, 1997 CHL, Par, Ar, 1998 Par, CHL, Ar, C, US, CHL, Par, Ar, 1999 Pt, Pt, Mor, Mor, It, Sp, Sp, S*
M Sciarra 2010 *Ar*
G Sebasti 1961 *CHL*
D Segdeefield 1964 *Ar, CHL, Bra*
JL Shaw 1960 *F, 1963 Bra*
M Shaw 1990 *CHL, CHL*
R Sierra 2001 *Par, CHL, CHL, 2002 CHL, Par*
CA Sierrra 1951 *Ar, CHL, Bra*
F Silva 1985 *Ar, Par, CHL, 1987 Ar, CHL, Par*
G Silva 2000 *Ar*
R Silva 1987 *Ar*
R Silva 2012 *Pt, 2014 Par, Bra, CHL, Ar, Rus*
S Silva 1992 *CHL, 1993 Bra, 1995 Par, 1996 C, Ar*
A Silveira 2009 *Par, Bra, CHL, R, Rus, US, US*
D Silveira 2004 *Ar, Geo, Pt, 2005 J, CHL, Ar, SA*
A Silveyra 1987 *Ar, 1989 Par, CHL, 1990 CHL, 1991 Par, CHL, Ar, Bra, 1992 CHL*
R Skeri 1956 *CHL*
M Smith 1971 *Par, CHL, Bra, Ar, 1973 CHL, Ar, Bra, 1975 Par, Bra, CHL, 1976 Ar, NZ, 1977 CHL, Ar, Bra, 1979 Ar, Ar, Bra, CHL, 1981 Par, Bra, CHL*
C Soares De Lima 2011 *Par, Bra, CHL, Ar, 2012 CHL, Bra, R, Pt, Pt, 2013 Ar, Bra, CHL, 2014 US, US, Par, Bra, Ar, R, Rus, HK*
U Sokolovich 2001 *Ar*
A Sommer 1985 *F, Ar, Par, CHL, 1987 Ar, Sp, Ar, CHL, Par, 1988 Bel, 1989 Par, CHL, Ar*
F Sosa 1997 *Ar*
A Soto 1963 *Bra, 1964 Ar, CHL, Bra*
PP Stanhan 1956 *CHL, 1961 Bra, CHL, Ar*
H Stein 1967 *CHL, Ar, 1975 Ar*

JE Stein 1969 *CHL, 1973 Ar, Par*
JE Stein 1953 *Bra, 1956 CHL*
A Stewart 1961 *CHL*
G Storace 1996 *Ar, 1997 CHL, 1998 Par, C, Ar, CHL, Par, Ar, 1999 Pt, Pt, Mor, Mor, Fj, Sp, Sp, S, SA, 2001 Ar, C, US, Sp, Par, CHL, CHL, 2002 C, US, CHL, 2003 CHL, Par, Ar, Ar, SA, Geo, E, 2004 Ar, CHL, Geo, Pt, 2005 SA, 2006 Ar, CHL, Pt, US, US, 2007 Pt*
A Suarez 1993 *Bra, 1996 Ar, C, Ar, US, 1997 CHL, Par, Ar, 1998 Par, CHL, Ar, CHL, Par, Ar*
A Suarez 2003 *Par*
D Suarez 1993 *CHL, 1997 Par, Ar, 1998 Par, CHL*
E Suarez 1971 *CHL, Ar*
A Summers 1967 *CHL, Ar*
Szabo 2007 *It*

JI Tabarez 2010 *R, 2011 Pt*
J Tassistro 2013 *Geo*
A Tato 1969 *Ar, CHL, 1973 Ar*
A Terra 1987 *Ar, 1992 CHL, CHL, 1993 Bra, Ar, 1995 Ar, Ar, Par*
S Terra 1985 *F, Ar, Par, CHL, 1987 CHL, Par*
J Trigo 1958 *Per*
D Turcatti 1969 *CHL*

JM Ubilla 1976 *Ar, NZ, 1977 Ar*
RE Ubilla 1979 *Ar, Bra, Par, CHL, 1981 Par, CHL, Ar, 1985 F, 1987 Ar, 1988 Bel, 1989 Bra, Par, CHL, Ar, US, 1991 Par, CHL, Ar*
M Uria 1976 *Ar*
M Uriarte 1983 *Ar, 1985 F, Ar, Par, CHL*
C Uriate 1983 *Par*
A Urrestara 2001 *C, It*

C Vaccaro 1979 *Ar, Bra, Par, CHL*
D van Rompaey 1976 *Ar*
J Varela 1976 *NZ*
A Vazquez 2001 *Ar*
L Vazquez 1960 *F*
P Vecino 1990 *CHL, CHL, 1991 Bra, 1992 CHL, CHL, 1993 Bra, Par, CHL, Ar, 1995 Ar, C, Ar, Sp, CHL, Par, Ar, 1996 Ar, Ar, US, 1997 CHL, Par, Ar, 1998 Par, CHL, C, US, CHL, Par, Ar, 1999 Pt, Pt, Mor, Mor, It, Sp, Sp, S, SA, 2000 CHL, Ar, 2001 Ar, Ar, C, US, It, Sp, CHL, CHL, 2002 CHL, 2003 CHL, Ar*
T Vecino 2001 *Par, CHL*
F Vecino 2011 *Pt, Sp, 2012 CHL, Pt, 2014 Par, CHL, Ar*
H Vega 1958 *Ar, Per*
F Vejo 1969 *CHL*
JM Viacava 1990 *CHL, CHL, 1991 Ar, Bra, 1992 CHL, CHL, 1993 Bra, Par*
D Viana 1977 *Par, CHL, Bra*
J Viana 1997 *CHL, Par, 1998 Ar, 1999 Fj, Sp, S, SA, 2000 CHL, 2002 CHL, US, 2003 Ar, US, Sa, E*
E Viera 1975 *Par, Ar, Bra, CHL, 1977 Par, CHL, Ar, Bra, 1979 Ar, Ar, Par, CHL*
P Viglietti 1989 *Par, US, 1990 CHL, CHL, 1992 CHL, 1993 Par, CHL, Ar*
F Vilaboa 2002 *Ar, Par*
A Vilaseca 2013 *Ar, Bra, CHL, Sp, 2014 US, US*
S Vilaseca 2008 *Ar, US, 2010 R, R, 2011 Pt, Sp, 2012 Ar, CHL, Bra, Pt, 2013 Ar, Bra, CHL, Sp, 2014 US, US, CHL, Ar, HK, Rus, Rus*
P Villa 1987 *Par*
F Villaboa 2005 *Pt*
A Villamil 1977 *Ar*
A Vivo 1973 *CHL, Ar, Bra, Par, 1976 Ar, 1977 Par, Bra*
R Vivo 1958 *Ar, CHL, Per, 1960 F*
A Vizintin 1975 *Par, Ar, Bra, CHL, 1977 Par, CHL, Ar, Bra, 1981 Par, Bra, CHL*
G Voituret 2006 *Ar, CHL*
R Wenzel 1973 *CHL, Bra, Par*

C Widemann 1976 *NZ*

J Yorston 1964 *Ar, CHL, Bra*

G Zamandrea 2001 *Ar*
G Zerbino 1973 *CHL, Ar, Par, 1977 Par, Bra*
J Zerbino 1973 *CHL, Bra, Par, 1975 Par, Ar, Bra, CHL, 1976 NZ, 1977 Par, CHL, Ar, Bra, 1979 Ar, Ar, Bra, Par, CHL, 1981 Par, Bra, CHL, 1983 Par, CHL, Ar, 1985 Ar, Par, CHL*
R Zerbino 1975 *Par, Bra, CHL, 1976 Ar, NZ, 1977 CHL, Ar, Bra, 1979 Ar, Bra, CHL, 1985 Par*
S Zumaran 1992 *CHL*

# Their future is in your hands.

Your donation can make all the difference
to these children.

Every year, the United Nations World Food
Programme provides meals to millions of children
around the world.

Together with partners like the International Rugby
Board, WFP can change young lives forever.

**Help us to tackle hunger:
wfp.org/donate/tacklehunger**

# TACKLE
# HUNGER

WFP

wfp.org

INTERNATIONAL
RUGBY BOARD

**The United Nations
World Food Programme
is the humanitarian
partner of the IRB**

# USA

## USA'S 2013–14 TEST RECORD

| OPPONENTS | DATE | VENUE | RESULT |
|-----------|------|-------|--------|
| Georgia | 16 Nov | A | Won 25–23 |
| Russia | 23 Nov | N | Won 28–7 |
| Uruguay | 22 Mar | A | Drew 27–27 |
| Uruguay | 29 Mar | H | Won 32–13 |
| Scotland | 7 Jun | H | Lost 6–24 |
| Japan | 14 Jun | H | Lost 29–37 |
| Canada | 21 Jun | H | Won 38–35 |

# USA READY TO CLIMB THE MOUNTAIN

### By Ian Gilbert

USA Eagle Samu Manoa gets the ball away under pressure during his country's win over Uruguay in March.

**A**fter a disappointing couple of years, the USA finally found the key to closing out tight Test matches. In their most successful run since Mike Tolkin took over as coach in early 2012, the Eagles reeled off a 4–2 win-loss tally, with one draw. Most importantly, though, they saw off Uruguay to secure a place at Rugby World Cup 2015.

"We are starting to reach some consistency," said Tolkin. "We're starting to win more games. Obviously last summer [when all seven matches were lost] was disappointing, but now we're starting to pull them out."

The victories over Uruguay, Georgia, Russia and Canada were tempered by defeats against Scotland and Japan. There was also a hard-fought 29–19 defeat by the visiting Maori All Blacks. While not a Test match the allure of the haka and hard-running rugby drew a sell-out crowd of 18,500 to Philadelphia in November 2013.

That month also took the Eagles on tour to play Georgia in Rustavi, where there were jubilant scenes after fly-half Adam Siddall sent over a penalty from the 10-metre line to snatch a 25–23 win for USA. Chris

Wyles, Blaine Scully and Nick Wallace had all scored tries for the Eagles but after a Georgia fight-back it took Siddall's three-pointer to snatch victory deep into added time.

Full-back Wyles certainly felt at home for the Eagles' next match against Russia, which was played on neutral territory at Allianz Park, the home of his English Premiership club Saracens. USA raced into a 12–0 half-time lead and then extended their dominance to finish 28–7 winners through tries from Wyles himself, Samu Manoa and Cam Dolan.

That completed the November internationals and allowed the Eagles to focus on the most important fixtures of their season – back-to-back matches against Uruguay in March to determine the Americas 2 qualifier for RWC 2015.

The first leg, in Montevideo, was drawn 27–27, with the Eagles scoring three tries, through hooker Phil Thiel, Wyles and Manoa, all converted by Folau Niua. The Glasgow Warriors scrum-half also kicked two penalties. It meant there was still all to play for in Atlanta a week later. Uruguay – who played at the 1999 and 2003 tournaments – made the early running and led 13–3 at the break, but in the second half the Eagles scored 29 unanswered points, a three-try burst in eight minutes from Mike Petri and brothers Andrew and Shalom Suniula setting them up for a 32–13 victory and a place alongside South Africa, Samoa, Scotland and the then unknown Asia 1 qualifier – later confirmed as Japan – in Pool B.

The June Test window saw USA well-beaten by Scotland, one of their opponents at England 2015, with two Wyles penalties the only answer to three tries. At least the attendance for the Scotland game gave USA rugby something to cheer with 20,000 spectators present in Houston, but the Eagles barely threatened the tourists who were comfortably ahead 17–3 at half-time and extended that margin of victory to 24–6. Tolkin wasn't too downbeat, however. "Scotland was our first game of the tour and for us it's all about momentum," he said. "Coming into the World Cup our learning curve will be at a higher level than a tier one nation who are just topping off their preparation."

A week later the Eagles were beaten 37–29 by Japan in the IRB Pacific Nations Cup 2014 after being level at half-time. Scully went over for a hat-trick in a losing cause after Dolan had opened the scoring, but a third quarter in which the Eagles shipped 15 points – having been tied at 17–17 at half-time – proved too big a deficit to claw back on this occasion.

However, the Eagles finished the season on a high with a 38–35 victory over Canada in Sacramento to end their long drought in the fixture, having endured seven losses since they last beat the Canadians in 2009.

"It was definitely satisfying to beat them, we have had a dry run," Tolkin said of a performance that showed the resilience of his team.

Despite tries from Scully and Wyles, Canada built a 10-point half-time lead which they extended to 17 points before an incredible fight-back saw the Eagles gradually reel in their rivals. A second try for Scully closed the gap before wing Brett Thompson scored a try on his Test debut. Once ahead, they mounted a tremendous defensive effort to keep Canada out for the final 10 minutes of the Pacific Nations Cup encounter.

As Rugby World Cup year approaches, the Eagles who play for clubs in elite leagues overseas can be relied on to add a hard-headed edge to team preparations. Scully has been winning plaudits at Leicester Tigers, 24-year-old back row Dolan, now at Northampton, is set to be a corner-stone of the pack for years to come and captain Todd Clever remains a key forward even though he is now into his 30s.

"They bring in the day-in, day-out professionalism and greater skill level," admitted Tolkin. "Watching them on the field you can tell who the professional players are."

Tolkin acknowledges the set-pieces in particular require plenty of homework ahead of the World Cup. "We have got a lot of work to do with our scrum; we have some young players and it's been a process of growing them. Our engine room behind the front row is good, and we've been working on the front row."

To that end, the forwards come under the tutelage of former Ulster and Ireland prop Justin Fitzpatrick, while Australian Bill Millard, former assistant coach with Cardiff, Connacht and the Australian Sevens side, takes charge of the backs.

While RWC 2015 qualification was the most important event of the Eagles' season, the highest-profile in 2014 was undoubtedly the All Blacks' visit to Soldier Field in Chicago on 1 November. The global pulling power of the world champions ensured huge interest for the match, the first between the sides on USA soil since 1980 and only the fourth in history between the two.

On the domestic front, Life Running Eagles took the honours in late May with a comprehensive victory over New Orleans Rugby Football Club in Madison, Wisconsin. Life crossed in the first two minutes and were never threatened, running out 39–7 winners to take the Men's Division I Club Championship.

The Women's Premier League was won by Twin Cities Amazons, whose 25–12 victory over Berkeley All-Blues prevented their opponents from registering a hat-trick of titles. Twin Cities Amazons were worthy winners having remained undefeated all season.

# USA INTERNATIONAL STATISTICS

## MATCH RECORDS UP TO 13 OCTOBER 2014

### WINNING MARGIN

| Date | Opponent | Result | Winning Margin |
|---|---|---|---|
| 01/07/2006 | Barbados | 91–0 | 91 |
| 06/07/1996 | Japan | 74–5 | 69 |
| 07/11/1989 | Uruguay | 60–3 | 57 |
| 12/03/1994 | Bermuda | 60–3 | 57 |
| 08/04/1998 | Portugal | 61–5 | 56 |

### MOST POINTS IN A MATCH
#### BY THE TEAM

| Date | Opponent | Result | Points |
|---|---|---|---|
| 01/07/2006 | Barbados | 91–0 | 91 |
| 06/07/1996 | Japan | 74–5 | 74 |
| 17/05/2003 | Japan | 69–27 | 69 |
| 12/04/2003 | Spain | 62–13 | 62 |
| 08/04/1998 | Portugal | 61–5 | 61 |

#### BY A PLAYER

| Date | Player | Opponent | Points |
|---|---|---|---|
| 07/11/1989 | Chris O'Brien | Uruguay | 26 |
| 31/05/2004 | Mike Hercus | Russia | 26 |
| 01/07/2006 | Mike Hercus | Barbados | 26 |
| 12/03/1994 | Chris O'Brien | Bermuda | 25 |
| 06/07/1996 | Matt Alexander | Japan | 24 |

### MOST TRIES IN A MATCH
#### BY THE TEAM

| Date | Opponent | Result | Tries |
|---|---|---|---|
| 01/07/2006 | Barbados | 91–0 | 13 |
| 17/05/2003 | Japan | 69–27 | 11 |
| 07/11/1989 | Uruguay | 60–3 | 11 |
| 06/07/1996 | Japan | 74–5 | 11 |
| 9 on 5 occasions | | | |

#### BY A PLAYER

| Date | Player | Opponent | Tries |
|---|---|---|---|
| 11/05/1924 | Dick Hyland | Romania | 5 |
| 06/07/1996 | Vaea Anitoni | Japan | 4 |
| 07/06/1997 | Brian Hightower | Japan | 4 |
| 08/04/1998 | Vaea Anitoni | Portugal | 4 |
| 11/05/1924 | John Patrick | Romania | 4 |

### MOST CONVERSIONS IN A MATCH
#### BY THE TEAM

| Date | Opponent | Result | Cons |
|---|---|---|---|
| 01/07/2006 | Barbados | 91–0 | 13 |
| 07/11/1989 | Uruguay | 60–3 | 8 |
| 06/07/1996 | Japan | 74–5 | 8 |
| 17/05/2003 | Japan | 69–27 | 7 |
| 6 on 2 occasions | | | |

#### BY A PLAYER

| Date | Player | Opponent | Cons |
|---|---|---|---|
| 01/07/2006 | Mike Hercus | Barbados | 13 |
| 06/07/1996 | Matt Alexander | Japan | 8 |
| 07/11/1989 | Chris O'Brien | Uruguay | 7 |
| 17/05/2003 | Mike Hercus | Japan | 7 |

### MOST PENALTIES IN A MATCH
#### BY THE TEAM

| Date | Opponent | Result | Pens |
|---|---|---|---|
| 18/09/1996 | Canada | 18–23 | 6 |
| 5 on 5 occasions | | | |

#### BY A PLAYER

| Date | Player | Opponent | Pens |
|---|---|---|---|
| 18/09/1996 | Matt Alexander | Canada | 6 |
| 5 on 5 occasions | | | |

### MOST DROP GOALS IN A MATCH
#### BY THE TEAM

| Date | Opponent | Result | DGs |
|---|---|---|---|
| 27/11/2010 | Georgia | 17–19 | 2 |

#### BY A PLAYER

1 on 18 Occasions

USA

## MOST CAPPED PLAYERS

| Name | Caps |
|------|------|
| Mike MacDonald | 67 |
| Luke Gross | 62 |
| Todd Clever | 59 |
| Alec Parker | 57 |

## LEADING PENALTY SCORERS

| Name | Pens |
|------|------|
| Mike Hercus | 76 |
| Matt Alexander | 55 |
| Mark Williams | 35 |
| Chris Wyles | 31 |

## LEADING TRY SCORERS

| Name | Tries |
|------|------|
| Vaea Anitoni | 26 |
| Paul Emerick | 17 |
| Chris Wyles | 14 |
| Todd Clever | 11 |

## LEADING DROP GOAL SCORERS

| Name | DGs |
|------|------|
| Mike Hercus | 4 |

## LEADING POINTS SCORERS

| Name | Points |
|------|------|
| Mike Hercus | 465 |
| Matt Alexander | 286 |
| Chris Wyles | 212 |
| Chris O'Brien | 144 |
| Mark Williams | 143 |

## LEADING CONVERSIONS SCORERS

| Name | Cons |
|------|------|
| Mike Hercus | 90 |
| Matt Alexander | 45 |
| Chris O'Brien | 24 |
| Chris Wyles | 23 |
| Nese Malifa | 17 |

# USA INTERNATIONAL PLAYERS
## MATCH RECORDS UP TO 13 OCTOBER 2014

**M Alexander** 1995 *C*, 1996 *I, C, HK, J, HK, J, Ar, C, Ur*, 1997 *W, C, HK, J, J, HK, C, W, W*, 1998 *Pt, Sp, J, HK, C*
**AE Allen** 1912 *A*
**S Allen** 1996 *J*, 1997 *HK, J, J, C, W, W*
**T Altemeier** 1978 *C*
**D Anderson** 2002 *S*
**B Andrews** 1978 *C*, 1979 *C*
**VN Anitoni** 1992 *C*, 1994 *C, Ar, Ar, I*, 1995 *C*, 1996 *I, C, C, HK, J, HK, J, Ar, C, Ur*, 1997 *W, C, J, HK, C, W, W*, 1998 *Pt, Sp, J, HK, C, C, J, HK, Fj, Ar, C, Ur*, 1999 *Tg, Fj, J, C, Sa, E, I, R, A*, 2000 *Fj, Sa*
**J Arrell** 1912 *A*
**D Asbun** 2012 *Geo, It, Tg, R*, 2013 *C, Geo, Rus*
**S Auerbach** 1976 *A*
**CA Austin** 1912 *A*, 1913 *NZ*
**M Aylor** 2006 *IrA, M, C, Bar, Ur, Ur*, 2007 *S, C, Sa, SA*, 2008 *IrA*

**A Bachelet** 1993 *C, A*, 1994 *Ber, C, Ar, Ar, I*, 1995 *C*, 1996 *I, C, C, HK, J, HK, J, Ar, C*, 1997 *W, C, HK, J, J, HK, C, W, W*, 1998 *Pt, Sp, J, HK, C, C, J*
**R Bailey** 1979 *C*, 1980 *NZ*, 1981 *C, SA*, 1982 *C*, 1983 *C, A*, 1987 *Tun, C, J, E*
**B Barnard** 2006 *IrA, M, Bar, C*
**D Barrett** 2014 *S, J, C*
**JI Basauri** 2007 *S, E, Tg*, 2008 *Ur, J, J*, 2010 *Pt, Geo*, 2011 *Tg, Rus, C, A*, 2012 *Rus, Tg, R*
**D Bateman** 1982 *C, E*, 1983 *A*, 1985 *J, C*
**P Bell** 2006 *IrA, M, C, Bar, C, Ur, Ur*
**W Bernhard** 1987 *Tun*

**CM Biller** 2009 *I, W, Geo, C, C*, 2010 *Rus, Pt, Geo*, 2011 *Tg, Rus, C, C, J, I, Rus, It*, 2012 *C, Geo, It, Rus, Tg, R*, 2013 *I, Tg, Fj, J, C, C*
**TW Billups** 1993 *C, A*, 1994 *Ber, C, Ar, Ar, I*, 1995 *C*, 1996 *I, C, C, HK, HK, J, Ar, C, Ur*, 1997 *W, C, HK, HK, W, W*, 1998 *Pt, Sp, J, HK, C, C, J, HK, Fj, Ar, C, Ur*, 1999 *Tg, Fj, J, C, Sa, E, I, R, A*
**RR Blasé** 1913 *NZ*
**A Blom** 1998 *Sp, J, HK, C, C, HK, Fj, Ar, Ur*, 1999 *Sa*, 2000 *J, C, I*
**H Bloomfield** 2007 *E, Tg, SA*, 2008 *E, C*
**R Bordley** 1976 *A, F*, 1977 *C, E*, 1978 *C*
**J Boyd** 2008 *IrA*, 2009 *I*
**S Bracken** 1994 *Ar*, 1995 *C*
**G Brackett** 1976 *A, F*, 1977 *E*
**N Brendel** 1983 *A*, 1984 *C*, 1985 *J*, 1987 *Tun, E*
**D Briley** 1979 *C*, 1980 *W, C, NZ*
**J Buchholz** 2001 *C*, 2002 *S*, 2003 *Sp, EngA, Ar, Fj, J, F*, 2004 *C*
**B Burdette** 2006 *Ur, Ur*, 2007 *E, S, C, E, Tg, Sa, SA*
**JR Burke** 1990 *C, J*, 1991 *J, J, S, C, F, NZ*, 1992 *C*
**J Burke** 2000 *C, I*
**J Burkhardt** 1983 *C*, 1985 *C*
**E Burlingham** 1980 *NZ*, 1981 *C, SA*, 1982 *C, E*, 1983 *C, A*, 1984 *C*, 1985 *C*, 1986 *J*, 1987 *Tun, C, J, E*

**C Campbell** 1993 *C, A*, 1994 *Ber, C, Ar*
**D Care** 1998 *Pt, J, C*
**M Carlson** 1987 *W, C*
**DB Carroll** 1913 *NZ*, 1920 *F, F*

L Cass 1913 *NZ*
M Caulder 1984 *C*, 1985 *C*, 1989 *C*
R Causey 1977 *C*, 1981 *C*, *SA*, 1982 *C*, *E*, 1984 *C*, 1986 *J*, 1987 *E*
W Chai 1993 *C*
R Chapman 2011 *J*
D Chipman 1976 *A*, 1978 *C*
JE Clark 1979 *C*, 1980 *C*
P Clark 1924 *R*
J Clarkson 1986 *J*, 1987 *Tun*, *C*, *J*, *E*
J Clayton 1999 *C*, *R*, *A*, 2000 *J*, *C*, *I*, *Fj*, *Tg*, *Sa*, *S*, *W*
N Cleveland 1924 *R*, *F*
TS Clever 2003 *Ar*, 2005 *C*, *R*, *W*, *ArA*, *C*, 2006 *IrA*, *M*, *C*, *Bar*, *C*, *Ur*, *Ur*, 2007 *E*, *S*, *C*, *E*, *Tg*, *Sa*, *SA*, 2008 *E*, *IrA*, *C*, *Ur*, *J*, *J*, 2009 *Geo*, *C*, *C*, *Ur*, *Ur*, 2010 *Pt*, *Geo*, 2011 *Tg*, *Rus*, *C*, *C*, *I*, *Rus*, *It*, 2012 *C*, *Geo*, *It*, *Rus*, *Tg*, *R*, 2013 *C*, *I*, *Tg*, *J*, *C*, *C*, *Geo*, *Rus*, 2014 *Ur*, *Ur*, *S*, *J*, *C*
R Cooke 1979 *C*, 1980 *W*, *C*, *NZ*, 1981 *C*, *SA*
TMA Coolican 2014 *Ur*, *Ur*, *S*, *J*, *C*
B Corcoran 1989 *Ur*, *Ar*, 1990 *Ar*
J Coulson 1999 *A*
M Crick 2007 *E*, *S*, *C*, 2008 *E*, *IrA*, *C*, *Ur*, *J*, *J*
R Crivellone 1983 *C*, 1986 *C*, 1987 *C*
K Cross 2003 *Sp*, *Sp*, *J*, *C*, *EngA*, *EngA*, *Ar*, *C*, *Fj*, *S*, 2004 *C*, *Rus*
C Culpepper 1977 *E*, 1978 *C*
C Curtis 1997 *C*, *HK*, *J*, 1999 *Sa*, 2001 *Ar*

P Dahl 2009 *I*, *W*, 2012 *Rus*, *Tg*, *R*, 2013 *C*, *I*, *Tg*, *Fj*, *J*, *C*, *C*
B Daily 1989 *Ur*, *Ar*, 1990 *Ar*, *C*, *A*, *J*, 1991 *J*, *J*, *S*, *F*, *F*, *It*
K Dalzell 1996 *Ur*, 1998 *Sp*, *C*, *HK*, *C*, *Ur*, 1999 *Fj*, *J*, *C*, *Sa*, *E*, *I*, *R*, *A*, 2000 *J*, *C*, *I*, *Fj*, *Tg*, *Sa*, *S*, *W*, 2001 *C*, *E*, *SA*, 2002 *S*, *C*, *C*, *CHL*, *Ur*, 2003 *Sp*, *Sp*, *J*, *C*, *EngA*, *C*, *Ur*, *Fj*, *S*, *J*, *F*
PJ Danahy 2009 *Ur*, 2010 *Rus*, 2011 *Tg*, *Rus*, *J*, *A*
WP Darsie 1913 *NZ*
SM Davies 2013 *Rus*
G Davis 1920 *F*
G De Bartolo 2008 *E*, *C*, *Ur*, *J*, *J*, 2009 *W*
MG de Jong 1990 *C*, 1991 *J*, *J*, *S*, *C*, *F*, *F*, *It*, *E*
M Deaton 1983 *A*, 1984 *C*, 1985 *J*
M Delai 1996 *I*, *HK*, *J*, 1997 *HK*, 1998 *HK*, 2000 *J*, *C*, *I*, *Fj*, *Tg*, *Sa*, *S*, *W*, 2001 *C*, *Ar*, *Ur*
RH Devereaux 1924 *R*, *F*
D Dickson 1986 *J*, 1987 *A*
CW Dirksen 2012 *Rus*, *Tg*
G Dixon 1924 *R*, *F*
C Doe 1920 *F*, *F*, 1924 *R*, *F*
C Doherty 1987 *W*
CA Dolan 2013 *Fj*, *J*, *C*, *C*, *Geo*, *Rus*, 2014 *Ur*, *Ur*, *S*, *J*
D Dorsey 2001 *SA*, 2002 *S*, *C*, *C*, *CHL*, *Ur*, *CHL*, *Ur*, 2003 *Sp*, *Sp*, *J*, *C*, *EngA*, *Ar*, *C*, *Ur*, *Fj*, *S*, *J*, *F*, 2004 *C*, *Rus*, *C*, *F*
G Downes 1992 *HK*
BG Doyle 2008 *E*, *IrA*, *C*, 2012 *C*, *Geo*, *It*, *Rus*, *Tg*, 2013 *C*, *I*, *Tg*, *Fj*, *J*, *C*, *C*
R Duncanson 1977 *E*
A Durutalo 2012 *C*, *It*

P Eloff 2000 *J*, *C*, *I*, *Fj*, *Tg*, *Sa*, *S*, *W*, 2001 *C*, *Ar*, *Ur*, *E*, *SA*, 2002 *S*, *C*, *CHL*, *Ur*, 2003 *Sp*, *Sp*, *J*, *C*, *EngA*, *C*, *Ur*, *Fj*, *S*, *J*, *F*, 2006 *Bar*, *C*, *Ur*, *Ur*
PL Emerick 2003 *Sp*, *EngA*, *Ar*, *C*, *Ur*, *Fj*, *S*, *J*, 2004 *C*, *F*, *I*, *It*, 2005 *C*, *R*, *W*, *ArA*, *C*, 2006 *C*, *Bar*, *C*, *Ur*, 2007 *S*, *C*, *E*, 2008 *E*, *IrA*, *C*, *Ur*, *J*, *J*, 2009 *Geo*, *C*, *C*, *Ur*, *Ur*, 2010 *Rus*, *Pt*, *Geo*, 2011 *Tg*, *Rus*, *C*, *C*, *J*, *I*, *Rus*, *It*, 2012 *C*, *Geo*, *It*, *Rus*, *Tg*, *R*
TV Enosa 2011 *Tg*, *Rus*, *C*, *C*, *J*, *A*
BE Erb 1912 *A*
C Erskine 2006 *C*, *Ur*, *Ur*, 2007 *E*, *Tg*, *Sa*, *SA*, 2008 *Ur*, *J*, *J*
V Esikia 2006 *IrA*, *M*, *Bar*, *C*, *Ur*, 2007 *E*, *E*, *Tg*, *Sa*, *SA*, 2008 *E*, *IrA*
J Everett 1984 *C*, 1985 *J*, 1986 *J*, *C*, 1987 *Tun*, *J*, *E*
W Everett 1985 *J*, 1986 *J*, *C*

M Fabling 1995 *C*
M Fanucchi 1979 *C*, 1980 *W*

R Farley 1989 *I*, *Ur*, *Ar*, 1990 *Ar*, *C*, *A*, *J*, 1991 *J*, *J*, *S*, *C*, *F*, *F*, *It*, *E*, 1992 *C*
P Farner 1999 *Tg*, *Fj*, *J*, *C*, 2000 *J*, *C*, *I*, *Fj*, *Tg*, *Sa*, *S*, *W*, 2002 *C*, *C*, *CHL*, *Ur*, *CHL*, *Ur*
L Farrish 1924 *F*
D Fee 2002 *C*, *C*, *CHL*, *Ur*, *CHL*, *Ur*, 2003 *Sp*, *Sp*, *J*, *C*, *EngA*, *C*, *Ur*, *Fj*, *S*, *J*, *F*, 2004 *C*, *Rus*, *C*, *F*, *I*, *It*, 2005 *C*, *R*, *W*, *ArA*, *C*
ZT Fenoglio 2012 *Rus*, 2013 *C*, *Tg*, *Fj*, *J*, *C*, *C*
O Fifita 2000 *Fj*, *Tg*, *Sa*, *S*, *W*, 2001 *C*, *Ar*, *Ur*, *E*, *SA*, 2002 *C*, *C*, 2003 *Sp*, *EngA*, *EngA*, *Ar*, *S*
S Finkel 1981 *C*, 1983 *C*, *A*, 1986 *C*, 1987 *A*, *E*
G Fish 1920 *F*
J Fitzpatrick 1920 *F*
AW Flay 1990 *J*, 1991 *J*, *J*, *S*, *F*, *It*, *E*
R Flynn 2000 *C*, *I*, *Fj*, *Tg*, *Sa*, *W*, 2001 *C*, *Ar*
J Fowler 1980 *W*, *C*, *NZ*, 1981 *C*, *SA*, 1982 *C*, *E*
W Fraumann 1976 *F*, 1977 *E*
A Freeman 1995 *C*, 1996 *I*
M French 2005 *W*, *ArA*, 2006 *IrA*, *M*, *Ur*, *Ur*, 2007 *E*, *C*
EC Fry 2011 *Tg*, *Rus*, *C*, *C*, *J*, *A*, 2012 *C*, *Geo*, *It*, *Rus*, *Tg*, *R*, 2013 *C*, *I*, *Tg*, *Fj*, *J*, *C*, *C*, *Geo*, *Rus*, 2014 *Ur*, *Ur*, *S*, *J*, *C*
B Furrow 1998 *C*, *C*, *J*, *HK*

JR Gagiano 2008 *Ur*, *J*, *J*, 2009 *I*, *W*, *Geo*, *C*, *C*, *Ur*, *Ur*, 2010 *Rus*, *Pt*, 2011 *J*, *A*
M Gale 1992 *C*
FJ Gard 1912 *A*, 1913 *NZ*
B Geraghty 1993 *C*
J Gillam 2000 *Tg*
D Gillies 1998 *Ar*, 1999 *Tg*
G Glasscock 1913 *NZ*
D Gonzalez 1990 *A*, 1993 *C*
G Goodman 1992 *C*
J Gouws 2003 *EngA*, *EngA*, *Ar*, *C*, *Ur*, *S*, *F*, 2004 *I*, *It*
E Graff 1924 *R*, *F*
J Grant 1981 *SA*
R Grant 2000 *Tg*
S Gray 1976 *F*, 1977 *E*, 1979 *C*, 1980 *W*, *NZ*, 1981 *SA*
R Green 1994 *I*, 1995 *C*, 1996 *I*, *C*, *C*, *HK*, *J*, *HK*, *J*, 1998 *Fj*, *Ar*
M Griffin 2003 *Sp*, *J*, *EngA*, 2004 *Rus*, *C*, *F*, 2005 *C*, *R*
J Grobler 1996 *Ar*, *C*, *Ur*, 1997 *C*, *J*, *J*, 1998 *J*, *Fj*, *C*, *Ur*, 1999 *Fj*, *J*, *C*, *Sa*, *E*, *I*, *R*, *A*, 2000 *J*, *C*, *I*, *Tg*, *Sa*, *S*, *W*, 2001 *C*, *Ar*, *Ur*, *E*, *SA*, 2002 *C*, *CHL*, *Ur*
LJ Gross 1996 *I*, *C*, *C*, *HK*, *J*, *HK*, *J*, *C*, *Ur*, 1997 *C*, *HK*, *J*, *J*, *HK*, *C*, *W*, *W*, 1998 *Pt*, *Sp*, *J*, *HK*, *C*, *C*, *J*, *HK*, *Fj*, *Ar*, *C*, *Ur*, 1999 *Tg*, *Fj*, *J*, *C*, *Sa*, *E*, *I*, *R*, *A*, 2000 *Fj*, *Tg*, *Sa*, *S*, *W*, 2001 *C*, *Ar*, *E*, *SA*, 2002 *S*, *C*, 2003 *Sp*, *Sp*, *J*, *C*, *EngA*, *EngA*, *Ar*, *C*, *Ur*, *Fj*, *S*, *J*, *F*
D Guest 1976 *F*, 1977 *C*
I Gunn 1982 *E*

EB Hall 1913 *NZ*
T Hall 2011 *Tg*, 2013 *C*
M Halliday 1977 *E*, 1978 *C*, 1980 *W*, *C*, 1982 *C*, *E*
C Hansen 2005 *C*, 2006 *IrA*, *M*, *C*
J Hanson 1977 *C*, *E*, 1980 *W*, *C*, 1981 *C*, 1983 *C*, *A*
PR Harrigan 1912 *A*
GW Harriman 2012 *R*, 2013 *Fj*, *Geo*, *Rus*
J Hartman 1983 *A*, 1984 *C*
J Hartman 2005 *C*, *ArA*
MTB Hawkins 2010 *Rus*
CC Hawley 2009 *Geo*, 2011 *Tg*, *Rus*, *C*, *A*, 2012 *Geo*, *It*
W Hayward 1991 *J*, *C*
GM Hein 1987 *Tun*, *C*, *J*, *A*, *E*, *W*, *C*, 1988 *R*, *USS*, 1989 *I*, *C*, *Ur*, *Ar*, 1990 *Ar*, *A*, 1991 *J*, *F*, *F*, *It*, *NZ*, *E*, 1992 *HK*, 1993 *C*, *A*, 1994 *Ber*
R Helu 1981 *C*, *SA*, 1982 *C*, *E*, 1983 *C*, *A*, 1985 *J*, *C*, 1987 *Tun*, *C*, *J*, *A*
B Henderson 1977 *C*
M Hercus 2002 *S*, *C*, *C*, *CHL*, *Ur*, *CHL*, *Ur*, 2003 *Sp*, *Sp*, *J*, *C*, *Ur*, *Fj*, *S*, *J*, *F*, 2004 *C*, *Rus*, *C*, *F*, *I*, *It*, 2005 *C*, *R*, *W*, *ArA*, 2006 *Bar*, *C*, *Ur*, *Ur*, 2007 *E*, *Tg*, *Sa*, *SA*, 2008 *E*, *IrA*, *C*, *J*, 2009 *I*, *W*, *Geo*, *C*, *C*, *Ur*, *Ur*
SJ Hiatt 1993 *A*, 1998 *Ar*, *C*
KG Higgins 1985 *J*, *C*, 1986 *J*, *C*, 1987 *Tun*, *C*, *J*, *A*, *E*, *W*, *C*,

# WALES

## WALES' 2013–14 TEST RECORD

| OPPONENTS | DATE | VENUE | RESULT |
|-----------|------|-------|--------|
| South Africa | 9 Nov | H | Lost 15–24 |
| Argentina | 16 Nov | H | Won 40–6 |
| Tonga | 22 Nov | H | Won 17–7 |
| Australia | 30 Nov | H | Lost 26–30 |
| Italy | 1 Feb | H | Won 23–15 |
| Ireland | 8 Feb | A | Lost 26–3 |
| France | 21 Feb | H | Won 27–6 |
| England | 9 Mar | A | Lost 29–18 |
| Scotland | 15 Mar | H | Won 51–3 |
| South Africa | 14 Jun | A | Lost 38–16 |
| South Africa | 21 Jun | A | Lost 31–30 |

# MORE QUESTIONS THAN ANSWERS

## By Martyn Williams

Although they had a mixed season overall, Wales were unlucky not to win the second Test against South Africa in June.

**W**hen I reflect on Wales' performances and results during the season, I have to come to the conclusion that the team is at a crossroads as 2015 and the World Cup approaches. As seems obligatory with the national team, there was both agony and ecstasy and I'm honestly not sure exactly what the future holds for the current side.

The stark statistics of just five wins in 11 Tests don't make for great reading. It's certainly not world-beating form, but I don't think anyone could argue that Wales don't have a healthy number of genuinely world-class players, most of whom are at a good age and yet to reach their peak.

The critics can point to Wales' continued failure to claim a southern hemisphere scalp and their surrender of the Six Nations title. They are both fair points, but you cannot overlook the victory over France in the Championship or what was a phenomenal performance, albeit in defeat, against the Springboks in the second Test in Nelspruit in the summer. As ever, it was a season that put the fans through it emotionally.

With the 2013 Six Nations trophy sitting proudly in the cabinet and Welshmen having played such a dominant role in the success of the Lions in Australia, Welsh rugby began the new season with high hopes and a real sense of anticipation. The target was a victory over the Springboks or the Wallabies and an historic third consecutive Six Nations triumph.

Unfortunately, they didn't make the start everyone craved in the November opener, going down 24–15 to South Africa in Cardiff, a result which extended Wales' winless sequence against the 'big three' to 17 Tests. Wales are traditionally slow starters in the autumn and so it was again as the Springboks outsmarted and outmuscled Warren Gatland's side, executing a pressurised kick-chase game which for me is a template for how to beat this Wales team.

A week later it was Argentina at the Millennium Stadium and Wales found their stride courtesy of a backline brimming with pace and power and a strong performance from the pack as they ran in four tries from Mike Phillips, George North, Toby Faletau and Ken Owens in a convincing 40–6 win.

The really remarkable stat, however, was that it was Wales' first win in an autumn international since they beat the Pumas in 2009. There were no autumn Tests in 2011 because of the World Cup, but even so the victory was certainly a long time coming.

Wales limped home 17–7 against Tonga six days later and speaking from experience, Friday night games against the Pacific Islands teams were always the one you privately wanted to miss as a player. That's no reflection on the opposition: you have a shortened build-up and it's difficult to find your rhythm. I wasn't surprised by the disjointed performance.

I genuinely believed Wales would turn Australia over in the last of the November fixtures, but it wasn't to be and although the final scoreline of 30–26 may appear close, I felt the Wallabies outplayed us.

The final game of the series frequently produces our strongest display while the Wallabies were at the end of a long, arduous season, but they showed no signs of fatigue and thanks to a stunning performance by Quade Cooper at 10, they ran out winners in Cardiff. In comparison to previous autumn campaigns, two wins from four was an improved return, but there was no escaping the disappointment in the all-too-familiar failure to beat the big boys.

I know the players and management team kicked off the Six Nations hell-bent on making history and becoming the first team to win the

**WALES**

Championship three seasons in succession. Although they began with an ugly 23–15 win over Italy in Cardiff, you cannot really take issue with an opening victory. It was a game everyone expected Wales to win and for me the shadow of Ireland the following weekend was already looming large.

All the pre-match talk ahead of the Ireland game was about the alleged fallout between Gatland, Brian O'Driscoll and certain other Irish players during the Lions tour. Both camps made the right noises in public that there was no animosity, but judging by their performance, the Irish boys clearly believed they did have a point to prove.

Wales were taken apart in Dublin. I was at the Aviva Stadium working for the BBC and the place was absolutely bouncing. Wales had no answer to Ireland's driving maul and they were ultimately out-thought and out-played.

Gatland had some very harsh and public words for the players after the 26–3 defeat and warned them that the France game could be their last if they didn't perform. It was typically abrasive from Gatland, but I'd have to back his reaction. As long as individual criticism is kept in the dressing room, a coach shouldn't shy away from telling it how it is in public in terms of the team.

He certainly got the response he wanted against the French. It was an outstanding performance full of character and guts and to score two unanswered tries in a record 27–6 victory was a massive result. It was also a timely reminder of the true potential of the team.

The penultimate game was England and Wales were mugged by a side still smarting from their 30–3 mauling in Cardiff 12 months earlier. England emerged 29–18 winners and what struck me was that Gatland's team were uncharacteristically static and lacking in ideas.

Defeat effectively ended Wales' title hopes but they picked themselves up and Scotland were put to the sword in Cardiff. The final score was 51–3 and although the Scots played most of the match with 14 men after Stuart Hogg was red-carded after 22 minutes, I've no doubt Wales would have still won by 30 points against 15 men.

The summer tour of South Africa was preceded by what came to be a controversial trial game between the Probables and Possibles. There were questions what Gatland could possibly learn from the game, but with the Welsh regions failing to make the knockout stages of either the PRO12 or Heineken Cup, I don't see what choice he had as the players were in danger of becoming rusty before the tour.

Ironically, Wales were still off the pace against the Springboks in the first Test in Durban. Alex Cuthbert scored a sensational second-half try to give the score a degree of respectability, but South Africa essentially

bossed the match from start to finish and ran out 38–16 winners.
The second Test in Nelspruit was a completely different story and although it was heartbreak at the death with a 31–30 loss, I genuinely think it was the best 80 minutes of Gatland's reign. Wales blew the Springboks away for most the match, they led until the 77th minute and they were desperately unlucky not to win.

The turning point came when Steve Walsh awarded a late penalty try for a Liam Williams shoulder charge on Cornal Hendricks in the corner. Liam got some stick for it after the match but I don't think you can blame him. It was a mistake in the heat of the moment and there isn't any player who can say they haven't done the same. I've spoken to George North since that game and he actually feels it's his fault because he was the one who missed the first tackle on Hendricks which forced Liam to make a challenge. It was a devastating end to the season.

Off the pitch, Welsh rugby lurched from one crisis to another with political upheaval, discord between the regions and the WRU and a general sense of financial instability. It's not a popular view but I think the negative press and constant stream of stories did, and will continue to, have an impact on the national team and on Welsh rugby as a whole.

On a more positive note, I have to congratulate Gethin Jenkins and Adam Jones, who both reached the 100 Test cap milestone during the season. They're very different characters but anyone who plays 100 internationals, especially in the front row, deserves all the plaudits that come their way.

Gethin is a frustrated openside really but he's got a brilliant rugby brain and is one of the best natural athletes I've played with. Adam lives and breathes for scrum time and has never stopped working on his game. Five of his 100 caps are Lions Tests and I really hope he can make it to a century of appearances in the red of Wales.

The Welsh season overall was a curious one. Although there were some fantastic displays, they couldn't string together back-to-back performances and there'll be frustration at the team's inability to win those 50–50 contests.

The southern hemisphere sides remain Wales' Achilles heel and the longer the sequence continues, the harder mentally it becomes for the players to believe they can take the next step. Objectively the talent is there, but the results are not.

I like the potential in the squad, however, and so many of the star names still have their best years ahead of them.

# WALES INTERNATIONAL STATISTICS

## MATCH RECORDS UP TO 13 OCTOBER 2014

### MOST CONSECUTIVE TESTS WITHOUT DEFEAT

| Matches | Wins | Draws | Period |
|---|---|---|---|
| 11 | 11 | 0 | 1907 to 1910 |
| 10 | 10 | 0 | 1999 to 1999 |
| 8 | 8 | 0 | 1970 to 1972 |
| 8 | 8 | 0 | 2004 to 2005 |

### MOST CONSECUTIVE TEST WINS

| | |
|---|---|
| 11 | 1907 I, 1908 E, S, F, I, A, 1909 E, S, F, I, 1910 F |
| 10 | 1999 F1, It, E, Arg 1, 2, SA, C, F2, Arg 3, J |
| 8 | 1970 F, 1971 E, S, I, F, 1972 E, S, F |
| 8 | 2004 J, 2005 E, It, F, S, I, US, C |

### MOST POINTS IN A MATCH
#### BY THE TEAM

| Pts | Opponents | Venue | Year |
|---|---|---|---|
| 102 | Portugal | Lisbon | 1994 |
| 98 | Japan | Cardiff | 2004 |
| 81 | Romania | Cardiff | 2001 |
| 81 | Namibia | New Plymouth | 2011 |
| 77 | U S A | Hartford | 2005 |
| 72 | Japan | Cardiff | 2007 |
| 70 | Romania | Wrexham | 1997 |
| 66 | Romania | Cardiff | 2004 |
| 66 | Fiji | Hamilton | 2011 |
| 64 | Japan | Cardiff | 1999 |
| 64 | Japan | Osaka | 2001 |

#### BY A PLAYER

| Pts | Player | Opponents | Venue | Year |
|---|---|---|---|---|
| 30 | NR Jenkins | Italy | Treviso | 1999 |
| 29 | NR Jenkins | France | Cardiff | 1999 |
| 28 | NR Jenkins | Canada | Cardiff | 1999 |
| 28 | NR Jenkins | France | Paris | 2001 |
| 28 | GL Henson | Japan | Cardiff | 2004 |
| 27 | NR Jenkins | Italy | Cardiff | 2000 |
| 27 | C Sweeney | U S A | Hartford | 2005 |
| 26 | SM Jones | Romania | Cardiff | 2001 |
| 24 | NR Jenkins | Canada | Cardiff | 1993 |
| 24 | NR Jenkins | Italy | Cardiff | 1994 |
| 24 | GL Henson | Romania | Wrexham | 2003 |

### MOST TRIES IN A MATCH
#### BY THE TEAM

| Tries | Opponents | Venue | Year |
|---|---|---|---|
| 16 | Portugal | Lisbon | 1994 |
| 14 | Japan | Cardiff | 2004 |
| 12 | Namibia | New Plymouth | 2011 |
| 11 | France | Paris | 1909 |
| 11 | Romania | Wrexham | 1997 |
| 11 | Romania | Cardiff | 2001 |
| 11 | U S A | Hartford | 2005 |
| 11 | Japan | Cardiff | 2007 |
| 10 | France | Swansea | 1910 |
| 10 | Japan | Osaka | 2001 |
| 10 | Romania | Cardiff | 2004 |

#### BY A PLAYER

| Tries | Player | Opponents | Venue | Year |
|---|---|---|---|---|
| 4 | W Llewellyn | England | Swansea | 1899 |
| 4 | RA Gibbs | France | Cardiff | 1908 |
| 4 | MCR Richards | England | Cardiff | 1969 |
| 4 | IC Evans | Canada | Invercargill | 1987 |
| 4 | N Walker | Portugal | Lisbon | 1994 |
| 4 | G Thomas | Italy | Treviso | 1999 |
| 4 | SM Williams | Japan | Osaka | 2001 |
| 4 | TGL Shanklin | Romania | Cardiff | 2004 |
| 4 | CL Charvis | Japan | Cardiff | 2004 |

## MOST CONVERSIONS IN A MATCH
### BY THE TEAM

| Cons | Opponents | Venue | Year |
|---|---|---|---|
| 14 | Japan | Cardiff | 2004 |
| 11 | Portugal | Lisbon | 1994 |
| 11 | U S A | Hartford | 2005 |
| 10 | Romania | Cardiff | 2001 |
| 9 | Namibia | New Plymouth | 2011 |
| 9 | Fiji | Hamilton | 2011 |
| 8 | France | Swansea | 1910 |
| 8 | Japan | Cardiff | 1999 |
| 8 | Romania | Cardiff | 2004 |
| 8 | Canada | Cardiff | 2006 |

### BY A PLAYER

| Cons | Player | Opponents | Venue | Year |
|---|---|---|---|---|
| 14 | GL Henson | Japan | Cardiff | 2004 |
| 11 | NR Jenkins | Portugal | Lisbon | 1994 |
| 11 | C Sweeney | U S A | Hartford | 2005 |
| 10 | SM Jones | Romania | Cardiff | 2001 |
| 8 | J Bancroft | France | Swansea | 1910 |
| 8 | NR Jenkins | Japan | Cardiff | 1999 |
| 8 | J Hook | Canada | Cardiff | 2006 |
| 7 | SM Jones | Japan | Osaka | 2001 |
| 7 | SM Jones | Romania | Cardiff | 2004 |

## MOST DROP GOALS IN A MATCH
### BY THE TEAM

| Drops | Opponents | Venue | Year |
|---|---|---|---|
| 3 | Scotland | Murrayfield | 2001 |
| 2 | Scotland | Swansea | 1912 |
| 2 | Scotland | Cardiff | 1914 |
| 2 | England | Swansea | 1920 |
| 2 | Scotland | Swansea | 1921 |
| 2 | France | Paris | 1930 |
| 2 | England | Cardiff | 1971 |
| 2 | France | Cardiff | 1978 |
| 2 | England | Twickenham | 1984 |
| 2 | Ireland | Wellington | 1987 |
| 2 | Scotland | Cardiff | 1988 |
| 2 | France | Paris | 2001 |
| 2 | South Africa | Durban | 2014 |

## BY A PLAYER

| Drops | Player | Opponents | Venue | Year |
|---|---|---|---|---|
| 3 | NR Jenkins | Scotland | Murrayfield | 2001 |
| 2 | J Shea | England | Swansea | 1920 |
| 2 | A Jenkins | Scotland | Swansea | 1921 |
| 2 | B John | England | Cardiff | 1971 |
| 2 | M Dacey | England | Twickenham | 1984 |
| 2 | J Davies | Ireland | Wellington | 1987 |
| 2 | J Davies | Scotland | Cardiff | 1988 |
| 2 | NR Jenkins | France | Paris | 2001 |

## MOST PENALTIES IN A MATCH
### BY THE TEAM

| Penalties | Opponents | Venue | Year |
|---|---|---|---|
| 9 | France | Cardiff | 1999 |
| 8 | Canada | Cardiff | 1993 |
| 7 | Italy | Cardiff | 1994 |
| 7 | Canada | Cardiff | 1999 |
| 7 | Italy | Cardiff | 2000 |
| 7 | Scotland | Murrayfield | 2013 |
| 6 | France | Cardiff | 1982 |
| 6 | Tonga | Nuku'alofa | 1994 |
| 6 | England | Wembley | 1999 |
| 6 | Canada | Cardiff | 2002 |
| 6 | England | Cardiff | 2009 |
| 6 | Canada | Toronto | 2009 |
| 6 | New Zealand | Cardiff | 2010 |
| 6 | England | Twickenham | 2014 |

### BY A PLAYER

| Pens | Player | Opponents | Venue | Year |
|---|---|---|---|---|
| 9 | NR Jenkins | France | Cardiff | 1999 |
| 8 | NR Jenkins | Canada | Cardiff | 1993 |
| 7 | NR Jenkins | Italy | Cardiff | 1994 |
| 7 | NR Jenkins | Canada | Cardiff | 1999 |
| 7 | NR Jenkins | Italy | Cardiff | 2000 |
| 7 | SL Halfpenny | Scotland | Murrayfield | 2013 |
| 6 | G Evans | France | Cardiff | 1982 |
| 6 | NR Jenkins | Tonga | Nuku'alofa | 1994 |
| 6 | NR Jenkins | England | Wembley | 1999 |
| 6 | SM Jones | Canada | Cardiff | 2002 |
| 6 | DR Biggar | Canada | Toronto | 2009 |
| 6 | SM Jones | New Zealand | Cardiff | 2010 |
| 6 | SL Halfpenny | England | Twickenham | 2014 |

WALES

# CAREER RECORDS

## MOST CAPPED PLAYERS

| Caps | Player | Career Span |
|---|---|---|
| 107 | GD Jenkins | 2002 to 2014 |
| 104 | SM Jones | 1998 to 2011 |
| 100 | Gareth Thomas | 1995 to 2007 |
| 100 | ME Williams | 1996 to 2012 |
| 95 | AR Jones | 2003 to 2014 |
| 94 | CL Charvis | 1996 to 2007 |
| 92 | GO Llewellyn | 1989 to 2004 |
| 87 | NR Jenkins | 1991 to 2002 |
| 87 | SM Williams | 2000 to 2011 |
| 87 | WM Phillips | 2003 to 2014 |
| 80 | A-W Jones | 2006 to 2014 |
| 76 | DJ Peel | 2001 to 2011 |
| 76 | JW Hook | 2006 to 2014 |
| 75 | RP Jones | 2004 to 2013 |
| 72 | IC Evans | 1987 to 1998 |
| 70 | TGL Shanklin | 2001 to 2010 |

## MOST CONSECUTIVE TESTS

| Tests | Player | Span |
|---|---|---|
| 53 | GO Edwards | 1967 to 1978 |
| 43 | KJ Jones | 1947 to 1956 |
| 39 | G Price | 1975 to 1983 |
| 38 | TM Davies | 1969 to 1976 |
| 33 | WJ Bancroft | 1890 to 1901 |

## MOST TESTS AS CAPTAIN

| Tests | Captain | Span |
|---|---|---|
| 33 | RP Jones | 2008 to 2013 |
| 28 | IC Evans | 1991 to 1995 |
| 27 | SK Warburton | 2011 to 2014 |
| 22 | R Howley | 1998 to 1999 |
| 22 | CL Charvis | 2002 to 2004 |
| 21 | Gareth Thomas | 2003 to 2007 |
| 19 | JM Humphreys | 1995 to 2003 |
| 18 | AJ Gould | 1889 to 1897 |
| 14 | DCT Rowlands | 1963 to 1965 |
| 14 | WJ Trew | 1907 to 1913 |

## MOST POINTS IN TESTS

| Points | Player | Tests | Career |
|---|---|---|---|
| 1049 | NR Jenkins | 87 | 1991 to 2002 |
| 917 | SM Jones | 104 | 1998 to 2011 |
| 395 | SL Halfpenny | 52 | 2008 to 2014 |
| 350 | JW Hook | 76 | 2006 to 2014 |
| 304 | PH Thorburn | 37 | 1985 to 1991 |
| 290 | SM Williams | 87 | 2000 to 2011 |
| 211 | AC Thomas | 23 | 1996 to 2000 |
| 200 | Gareth Thomas | 100 | 1995 to 2007 |
| 166 | P Bennett | 29 | 1969 to 1978 |
| 157 | IC Evans | 72 | 1987 to 1998 |

## MOST TRIES IN TESTS

| Tries | Player | Tests | Career |
|---|---|---|---|
| 58 | SM Williams | 87 | 2000 to 2011 |
| 40 | Gareth Thomas | 100 | 1995 to 2007 |
| 33 | IC Evans | 72 | 1987 to 1998 |
| 22 | CL Charvis | 94 | 1996 to 2007 |
| 20 | GO Edwards | 53 | 1967 to 1978 |
| 20 | TGR Davies | 46 | 1966 to 1978 |
| 20 | TGL Shanklin | 70 | 2001 to 2010 |
| 18 | GR Williams | 44 | 2000 to 2005 |
| 18 | GP North | 42 | 2010 to 2014 |
| 17 | RA Gibbs | 16 | 1906 to 1911 |
| 17 | JL Williams | 17 | 1906 to 1911 |
| 17 | KJ Jones | 44 | 1947 to 1957 |

## MOST CONVERSIONS IN TESTS

| Cons | Player | Tests | Career |
|---|---|---|---|
| 153 | SM Jones | 104 | 1998 to 2011 |
| 130 | NR Jenkins | 87 | 1991 to 2002 |
| 45 | JW Hook | 76 | 2006 to 2014 |
| 43 | PH Thorburn | 37 | 1985 to 1991 |
| 38 | J Bancroft | 18 | 1909 to 1914 |
| 30 | AC Thomas | 23 | 1996 to 2000 |
| 29 | GL Henson | 33 | 2001 to 2011 |
| 28 | SL Halfpenny | 52 | 2008 to 2014 |
| 25 | C Sweeney | 35 | 2003 to 2007 |
| 20 | WJ Bancroft | 33 | 1890 to 1901 |
| 20 | IR Harris | 25 | 2001 to 2004 |

## MOST PENALTY GOALS IN TESTS

| Penalties | Player | Tests | Career |
|---|---|---|---|
| 235 | NR Jenkins | 87 | 1991 to 2002 |
| 186 | SM Jones | 104 | 1998 to 2011 |
| 93 | SL Halfpenny | 52 | 2008 to 2014 |
| 70 | PH Thorburn | 37 | 1985 to 1991 |
| 61 | JW Hook | 76 | 2006 to 2014 |
| 36 | P Bennett | 29 | 1969 to 1978 |
| 35 | SP Fenwick | 30 | 1975 to 1981 |
| 32 | AC Thomas | 23 | 1996 to 2000 |
| 25 | DR Biggar | 25 | 2008 to 2014 |
| 22 | G Evans | 10 | 1981 to 1983 |

## MOST DROP GOALS IN TESTS

| Drops | Player | Tests | Career |
|---|---|---|---|
| 13 | J Davies | 32 | 1985 to 1997 |
| 10 | NR Jenkins | 87 | 1991 to 2002 |
| 8 | B John | 25 | 1966 to 1972 |
| 7 | WG Davies | 21 | 1978 to 1985 |
| 6 | SM Jones | 104 | 1998 to 2011 |
| 4 | JW Hook | 76 | 2006 to 2014 |

# INTERNATIONAL CHAMPIONSHIP RECORDS

| RECORD | DETAIL | HOLDER | SET |
|--------|--------|--------|-----|
| Most points in season | 151 | in five matches | 2005 |
| Most tries in season | 21 | in four matches | 1910 |
| Highest score | 51 | 51–3 v Scotland | 2014 |
| Biggest win | 48 | 51–3 v Scotland | 2014 |
| Highest score conceded | 60 | 26–60 v England | 1998 |
| Biggest defeat | 51 | 0–51 v France | 1998 |
| Most appearances | 51 | ME Williams | 1998–2010 |
| Most points in matches | 467 | SM Jones | 2000–2011 |
| Most points in season | 74 | NR Jenkins | 2001 |
| | 74 | SL Halfpenny | 2013 |
| Most points in match | 28 | NR Jenkins | v France, 2001 |
| Most tries in matches | 22 | SM Williams | 2000–2011 |
| Most tries in season | 6 | MCR Richards | 1969 |
| | 6 | SM Williams | 2008 |
| Most tries in match | 4 | W Llewellyn | v England, 1899 |
| | 4 | MCR Richards | v England, 1969 |
| Most cons in matches | 69 | SM Jones | 2000–2011 |
| Most cons in season | 12 | SM Jones | 2005 |
| Most cons in match | 8 | J Bancroft | v France, 1910 |
| Most pens in matches | 100 | SM Jones | 2000–2011 |
| Most pens in season | 19 | SL Halfpenny | 2013 |
| Most pens in match | 7 | NR Jenkins | v Italy, 2000 |
| | 7 | SL Halfpenny | v Scotland, 2013 |
| Most drops in matches | 8 | J Davies | 1985–1997 |
| Most drops in season | 5 | NR Jenkins | 2001 |
| Most drops in match | 3 | NR Jenkins | v Scotland, 2001 |

**WALES**

# MISCELLANEOUS RECORDS

| RECORD | HOLDER | DETAIL |
|--------|--------|--------|
| Longest Test Career | ME Williams | 1996 to 2012 |
| Youngest Test Cap | TWJ Prydie | 18 yrs 25 days in 2010 |
| Oldest Test Cap | TH Vile | 38 yrs 152 days in 1921 |

**CAREER RECORDS OF WALES INTERNATIONAL PLAYERS**

## UP TO 13 OCTOBER 2014

| PLAYER BACKS : | DEBUT | CAPS | T | C | P | D | PTS |
|---|---|---|---|---|---|---|---|
| CL Allen | 2013 v Arg | 1 | 0 | 0 | 0 | 0 | 0 |
| HB Amos | 2013 v Tg | 1 | 0 | 0 | 0 | 0 | 0 |
| MA Beck | 2012 v A | 7 | 2 | 0 | 0 | 0 | 10 |
| DR Biggar | 2008 v C | 25 | 0 | 19 | 25 | 3 | 122 |
| ACG Cuthbert | 2011 v A | 26 | 12 | 0 | 0 | 0 | 60 |
| G Davies | 2014 v SA | 1 | 0 | 0 | 0 | 0 | 0 |
| JJV Davies | 2009 v C | 41 | 9 | 0 | 0 | 0 | 45 |
| SL Halfpenny | 2008 v SA | 52 | 12 | 28 | 93 | 0 | 395 |
| JW Hook | 2006 v Arg | 76 | 13 | 45 | 61 | 4 | 350 |
| MJ Morgan | 2014 v SA | 1 | 0 | 0 | 0 | 0 | 0 |
| GP North | 2010 v SA | 42 | 18 | 0 | 0 | 0 | 90 |
| WM Phillips | 2003 v R | 87 | 9 | 0 | 0 | 0 | 45 |
| R Priestland | 2011 v S | 30 | 1 | 12 | 9 | 0 | 56 |
| JH Roberts | 2008 v S | 60 | 8 | 0 | 0 | 0 | 40 |
| R Webb | 2012 v It | 6 | 0 | 0 | 0 | 0 | 0 |
| LB Williams | 2012 v Bb | 14 | 1 | 0 | 0 | 0 | 5 |
| LD Williams | 2011 v Arg | 18 | 2 | 0 | 0 | 0 | 10 |
| MS Williams | 2011 v Bb | 25 | 7 | 0 | 0 | 0 | 35 |
| OR Williams | 2013 v J | 4 | 1 | 0 | 0 | 0 | 5 |
| R Williams | 2013 v Tg | 3 | 1 | 0 | 0 | 0 | 5 |
| **FORWARDS :** | | | | | | | |
| SA Andrews | 2011 v Bb | 9 | 0 | 0 | 0 | 0 | 0 |
| JD Ball | 2014 v I | 5 | 0 | 0 | 0 | 0 | 0 |
| RJ Bevington | 2011 v Bb | 13 | 0 | 0 | 0 | 0 | 0 |
| LC Charteris | 2004 v SA | 48 | 0 | 0 | 0 | 0 | 0 |
| AJ Coombs | 2013 v I | 10 | 0 | 0 | 0 | 0 | 0 |
| BS Davies | 2009 v S | 42 | 0 | 0 | 0 | 0 | 0 |
| IR Evans | 2006 v Arg | 33 | 1 | 0 | 0 | 0 | 5 |
| TT Faletau | 2011 v Bb | 36 | 4 | 0 | 0 | 0 | 20 |
| RM Hibbard | 2006 v Arg | 30 | 1 | 0 | 0 | 0 | 5 |
| P James | 2003 v R | 55 | 0 | 0 | 0 | 0 | 0 |
| AR Jarvis | 2012 v Arg | 4 | 0 | 0 | 0 | 0 | 0 |
| GD Jenkins | 2002 v R | 107 | 4 | 0 | 0 | 0 | 20 |
| AR Jones | 2003 v E | 95 | 2 | 0 | 0 | 0 | 10 |
| A-W Jones | 2006 v Arg | 80 | 7 | 0 | 0 | 0 | 35 |
| Rhodri P Jones | 2012 v Bb | 10 | 0 | 0 | 0 | 0 | 0 |

THE COUNTRIES

| | | | | | | | | |
|---|---|---|---|---|---|---|---|---|
| Ryan P Jones | 2004 v SA | 75 | 3* | 0 | 0 | 0 | 15 | **539** |
| S Lee | 2013 v Arg | 5 | 0 | 0 | 0 | 0 | 0 | |
| DJ Lydiate | 2009 v Arg | 37 | 0 | 0 | 0 | 0 | 0 | |
| KJ Owens | 2011 v Nm | 26 | 2 | 0 | 0 | 0 | 10 | |
| DE Phillips | 2013 v J | 3 | 0 | 0 | 0 | 0 | 0 | |
| M Rees | 2005 v US | 60 | 2 | 0 | 0 | 0 | 10 | |
| AC Shingler | 2012 v S | 8 | 0 | 0 | 0 | 0 | 0 | |
| JC Tipuric | 2011 v Arg | 24 | 0 | 0 | 0 | 0 | 0 | |
| J Turnbull | 2011 v S | 7 | 0 | 0 | 0 | 0 | 0 | |
| SK Warburton | 2009 v US | 46 | 3 | 0 | 0 | 0 | 15 | |

*\* Ryan Jones's figures include a penalty try awarded against Canada in 2006*

# WALES INTERNATIONAL PLAYERS
## UP TO 13 OCTOBER 2014

Note: Years given for International Championship matches are for second half of season; eg 1972 means season 1971–72. Years for all other matches refer to the actual year of the match. Entries in square brackets denote matches played in RWC Finals.

**Ackerman, R A** (Newport, London Welsh) 1980 NZ, 1981 E, S, A, 1982 I, F, E, S, 1983 S, I, F, R, 1984 S, I, F, E, A, 1985 S, I, F, E, Fj

**Alexander, E P** (Llandovery Coll, Cambridge U) 1885 S, 1886 E, S, 1887 E, I

**Alexander, W H** (Llwynypia) 1898 I, E, 1899 E, S, I, 1901 S, I

**Allen, A G** (Newbridge) 1990 F, E, I

**Allen, C L** (Cardiff Blues) 2013 Arg

**Allen, C P** (Oxford U, Beaumaris) 1884 E, S

**Amos, H B** (Newport Gwent Dragons) 2013 Tg

**Andrews, F** (Pontypool) 1912 SA, 1913 E, S, I

**Andrews, F G** (Swansea) 1884 E, S

**Andrews, G E** (Newport) 1926 E, S, 1927 E, F, I

**Andrews, S A** (Cardiff Blues) 2011 Bb(R), A, 2012 Sm(R), NZ(R), A4, 2013 E(R), J1, 2, SA(R)

**Anthony, C T** (Swansea, Newport, Gwent Dragons) 1997 US 1(R), 2(R), C (R), Tg (R), 1998 SA 2, Arg, 1999 S, I (R), 2001 J 1, 2, I (R), 2002 I, F, It, E, S, 2003 R (R)

**Anthony, L** (Neath) 1948 E, S, F

**Appleyard, R C** (Swansea) 1997 C, R, Tg, NZ, 1998 It, E (R), S, I, F

**Arnold, P** (Swansea) 1990 Nm 1, 2, Bb, 1991 E, S, I, F 1, A, [Arg, A], 1993 F (R), Z 2, 1994 Sp, Fj, 1995 SA, 1996 Bb (R)

**Arnold, W R** (Swansea) 1903 S

**Arthur, C S** (Cardiff) 1888 I, M, 1891 E

**Arthur, T** (Neath) 1927 S, F, I, 1929 E, S, F, I, 1930 E, S, I, F, 1931 E, S, F, I, SA, 1933 E, S

**Ashton, C** (Aberavon) 1959 E, S, I, 1960 E, S, I, 1962 I

**Attewell, S L** (Newport) 1921 E, S, F

**Back, M J** (Bridgend) 1995 F (R), E (R), S, I

**Badger, O** (Llanelli) 1895 E, S, I, 1896 E

**Baker, A** (Neath) 1921 I, 1923 E, S, F, I

**Baker, A M** (Newport) 1909 S, F, 1910 S

**Baker, D T** (Ospreys) 2013 J1(R), 2(R)

**Baldwin, S J** (Ospreys) 2013 J2(R)

**Ball, J D** (Scarlets) 2014 I(R), F, E, S(R), SA2(R)

**Bancroft, J** (Swansea) 1909 E, S, F, I, 1910 F, E, S, I, 1911 E, F, I, 1912 E, S, I, 1913 I, 1914 E, S, F

**Bancroft, W J** (Swansea) 1890 S, E, I, 1891 E, S, I, 1892 E, S, I, 1893 E, S, I, 1894 E, S, I, 1895 E, S, I, 1896 E, S, I, 1897 E, 1898 I, E, 1899 E, S, I, 1900 E, S, I, 1901 E, S, I

**Barlow, T M** (Cardiff) 1884 I

**Barrell, R J** (Cardiff) 1929 S, F, I, 1933 I

**Bartlett, J D** (Llanelli) 1927 S, 1928 E, S

**Bassett, A** (Cardiff) 1934 I, 1935 E, S, I, 1938 E, S

**Bassett, J A** (Penarth) 1929 E, S, F, I, 1930 E, S, I, 1931 E, S, F, I, SA, 1932 E, S, I

**Bateman, A G** (Neath, Richmond, Northampton) 1990 S, I, Nm 1, 2, 1996 SA, 1997 US, S, F, E, R, NZ, 1998 It, E, S, I, 1999 S, Arg 1, 2, SA, C, [J, A (R)], 2000 It, E, S, I, Sm, US, SA, 2001 E (R), It (t), R, I, Art (R), Tg

**Bater, J** (Ospreys) 2003 R (R)

**Bayliss, G** (Pontypool) 1933 S

**Bebb, D I E** (Carmarthen TC, Swansea) 1959 E, S, I, F, 1960 E, S, I, F, SA, 1961 E, S, I, F, 1962 E, S, F, I, 1963 E, F, NZ, 1964 E, S, F, SA, 1965 E, S, I, F, 1966 F, A, 1967 S, I, F, E

**Beck, M A** (Ospreys) 2012 A 1(R), 2, 3, Sm, 2013 SA(R), Arg(R), Tg

**Beckingham, G** (Cardiff) 1953 E, S, 1958 F

**Bennett, A M** (Cardiff) 1995 [NZ] SA, Fj

**Bennett, H** (Ospreys) 2003 I 2(R ), S 2(R), [C(R), Tg(R)], 2004 S(R), F(R), Arg 1(R), 2, SA1(R), 2006 Arg 2, PI(R), 2007 E2, [J(R)], SA, 2008 E, S, It(R), F, 2009 S(R), E(R), F(R), It, I(R), NZ(R), Sm, Arg(R), A(R), 2010 E(R), S(R), F, I(R), It(R), NZ1(R), 2(R), A(R), SA2(R), Fj, NZ3(R), 2011 Bb, E2, 3(R), Arg(R) , [SA, Sm, Fj, I, F, A], A, 2012 I, S

**Bennett, I** (Aberavon) 1937 I

**Bennett, P** (Cardiff Harlequins) 1891 E, S, 1892 S, I

**Bennett, P** (Llanelli) 1969 F (R), 1970 SA, S, F, 1972 S (R), NZ, 1973 E, S, I, F, A, 1974 S, I, F, E, 1975 S (R), I, 1976 E, S, I, F, 1977 I, F, E, S, 1978 E, S, I, F

**Bergiers, R T E** (Cardiff Coll of Ed, Llanelli) 1972 S, E, F, NZ, 1973 E, S, I, F, A, 1974 E, 1975 I

Bevan, G W (Llanelli) 1947 E
Bevan, J A (Cambridge U) 1881 E
Bevan, J C (Cardiff, Cardiff Coll of Ed) 1971 E, S, I, F, 1972 E, S, F, NZ, 1973 E, S
Bevan, J D (Aberavon) 1975 F, E, S, A
Bevan, S (Swansea) 1904 I
Bevington, R J (Ospreys) 2011 Bb, E2(R), 3(R), Arg(R), [Nm(R), A(R)], A(R), 2012 Arg(R), 2013 S(R), J1, Tg(R), A(R), 2014 It(R)
Beynon, B (Swansea) 1920 E, S
Beynon, G E (Swansea) 1925 F, I
Bidgood, R A (Newport) 1992 S, 1993 Z 1, 2, Nm, J (R)
Biggar, D R (Ospreys) 2008 C(R), 2009 C, US(R), Sm, 2010 NZ1(R), 2, A(R), Fj, 2011 A(R), 2012 Bb, Sm, 2013 I, F, It, S, E, J1, 2, Arg, A, 2014 F(R), E(R), S, SA1, 2
Biggs, N W (Cardiff) 1888 M, 1889 I, 1892 I, 1893 E, S, I, 1894 E, I
Biggs, S H (Cardiff) 1895 E, S, 1896 S, 1897 E, 1898 I, E, 1899 S, I, 1900 I
Birch, J (Neath) 1911 S, F
Birt, F W (Newport) 1911 E, S, 1912 E, S, I, SA, 1913 E
Bishop, A M (Ospreys) 2008 SA2(R), C, A(R), 2009 S(R), C, US, Arg(R), A(R), 2010 I(R), It(R), NZ1, A, SA2(t), Fj, NZ3(R), 2012 Bb
Bishop, D J (Pontypool) 1984 A
Bishop, E H (Swansea) 1889 S
Blackmore, J H (Abertillery) 1909 E
Blackmore, S W (Cardiff) 1987 I, [Tg (R), C, A]
Blake, J (Cardiff) 1899 E, S, I, 1900 E, S, I, 1901 E, S, I
Blakemore, R E (Newport) 1947 E
Bland, A F (Cardiff) 1887 E, S, I, 1888 S, I, M, 1890 S, E, I
Blyth, L (Swansea) 1951 SA, 1952 E, S
Blyth, W R (Swansea) 1974 E, 1975 S (R), 1980 F, E, S, I
Boobyer, N (Llanelli) 1993 Z 1(R), 2, Nm, 1994 Fj, Tg, 1998 F, 1999 It (R)
Boon, R W (Cardiff) 1930 S, F, 1931 E, S, F, I, SA, 1932 E, S, I, 1933 E, I
Booth, J (Pontymister) 1898 I
Boots, J G (Newport) 1898 I, E, 1899 I, 1900 E, S, I, 1901 E, S, I, 1902 E, S, I, 1903 E, S, I, 1904 E
Boucher, A W (Newport) 1892 E, S, I, 1893 E, S, I, 1894 E, 1895 E, S, I, 1896 E, I, 1897 E
Bowcott, H M (Cardiff, Cambridge U) 1929 S, F, I, 1930 E, 1931 E, S, 1933 E, I
Bowdler, F A (Cross Keys) 1927 A, 1928 E, S, I, F, 1929 E, S, F, I, 1930 E, 1931 SA, 1932 E, S, I, 1933 I
Bowen, B (S Wales Police, Swansea) 1983 R, 1984 S, I, F, E, 1985 Fj, 1986 E, S, I, F, Fj, Tg, WS, 1987 [C, E, NZ], US, 1988 E, S, I, F, WS, 1989 S, I
Bowen, C A (Llanelli) 1896 E, S, I, 1897 E
Bowen, D H (Llanelli) 1883 E, 1886 E, S, 1887 E
Bowen, G E (Swansea) 1887 S, I, 1888 S, I
Bowen, W (Swansea) 1921 S, F, 1922 E, S, I, F
Bowen, Wm A (Swansea) 1886 E, S, 1887 E, S, I, 1888 M, 1889 S, I, 1890 S, E, I, 1891 E, S
Brace, D O (Llanelli, Oxford U) 1956 E, S, I, F, 1957 E, 1960 S, I, F, 1961 I
Braddock, K J (Newbridge) 1966 A, 1967 S, I
Bradshaw, K (Bridgend) 1964 E, S, I, F, SA, 1966 E, S, I, F
Brew, A G (Newport Gwent Dragons, Ospreys) 2007 I(R), A2, E2, 2010 Fj, 2011 Bb, E3(R), Arg(R), [Nm], 2012 Bb
Brew, N R (Gwent Dragons) 2003 R
Brewer, T J (Newport) 1950 E, 1955 E, S
Brice, A B (Aberavon) 1899 E, S, I, 1900 E, S, I, 1901 E, S, I, 1902 E, S, I, 1903 E, S, I, 1904 E, S, I
Bridges, C J (Neath) 1990 Nm 1, 2, Bb, 1991 E (R), I, F 1, A
Bridie, R H (Newport) 1882 I
Britton, G R (Newport) 1961 S
Broster, B G J (Saracens) 2005 US(R), C
Broughton, A S (Treorchy) 1927 A, 1929 S
Brown, A (Newport) 1921 I
Brown, J (Cardiff) 1925 I
Brown, J A (Cardiff) 1907 E, S, I, 1908 E, S, F, 1909 E
Brown, M (Pontypool) 1983 R, 1986 E, S, Fj (R), Tg, WS
Bryant, D J (Bridgend) 1988 NZ 1, 2, WS, R, 1989 S, I, F, E
Bryant, J (Celtic Warriors) 2003 R (R)
Buchanan, D A (Llanelli) 1987 [Tg, E, NZ, A], 1988 I

Buckett, I M (Swansea) 1994 Tg, 1997 US 2, C
Budgett, N J (Ebbw Vale, Bridgend) 2000 S, I, Sm (R), US, SA, 2001 J 1(R), 2, 2002 I, F, It, E, S
Burcher, D H (Newport) 1977 I, F, E, S
Burgess, R C (Ebbw Vale) 1977 I, F, E, S, 1981 I, F, 1982 F, E, S
Burnett, R (Newport) 1953 E
Burns, J (Cardiff) 1927 F, I
Burns, L B (Newport Gwent Dragons) 2011 Bb(R), E2(R), 3, [Sm(R), Nm, Fj(R), A(R)]
Bush, P F (Cardiff) 1905 NZ, 1906 E, SA, 1907 I, 1908 E, S, 1910 S, I
Butler, E T (Pontypool) 1980 F, E, S, I, NZ (R), 1982 S, 1983 E, S, I, F, R, 1984 S, I, F, E, A
Byrne, L M (Llanelli Scarlets, Ospreys, Clermont-Auvergne) 2005 NZ(R), Fj, SA, 2006 E(t&R), S(t&R), I, It, F, Arg 1, 2, PI, 2007 F1, A1, E2, 2008 E, S, It, I, F, SA3, NZ, A, 2009 S, E, F, It, I, 2010 E, S, F, I, It, SA1, NZ1, 2, SA2, Fj, NZ3, 2011 E1(R), S, It, I, F, Arg, [Nm, Fj]

Cale, W R (Newbridge, Pontypool) 1949 E, S, I, 1950 E, S, I, F
Cardey, M D (Llanelli) 2000 S
Carter, A J (Newport) 1991 E, S
Cattell, A (Llanelli) 1883 E, S
Challinor, C (Neath) 1939 E
Charteris, L C (Newport Gwent Dragons, Perpignan) 2004 SA2(R), R, 2005 US, C, NZ(R), Fj, 2007 SA(R), 2008 C, NZ(R), 2009 S(R), F(R), It, I(R), US(R), NZ, Sm, Arg, A, 2010 E, F(R), It, 2011 Bb, E2(R), 3, [SA, Sm, Nm(R), Fj, I, F, A], 2012 It(R), F(R), A 1, 2(R), 3(t&R), Sm(R), NZ, A4, 2013 SA(R), Arg(R), Tg, 2014 It, F, S, SA1, 2
Charvis, C L (Swansea, Tarbes, Newcastle, Newport Gwent Dragons) 1996 A 3(R), SA, 1997 US, S, I, F, 1998 It (R), E, S, I, F, Z (R), SA 1, 2, Arg, 1999 S, I, F 1, It, E, Arg 1, SA, F 2, [Arg 3, A], 2000 F, It (R), E, S, I, Sm, US, SA, 2001 E, S, F, It, R, I, Arg, Tg, A, 2002 E (R), SA 1, 2, R, Fj, C, NZ, 2003 It, E 1(R), S 1(R), I 1, F, A, NZ, E 2, S 2, [C, Tg, It, NZ, E], 2004 S, F, E, It, Arg 1, 2, SA1, 2, R, NZ, J, 2005 US, C, NZ, SA, A, 2006 E, S, I, It, 2007 A1, 2, E2, Arg(R), F2(R), [C(t&R), A, J, Fj], SA
Clapp, T J S (Newport) 1882 I, 1883 E, S, 1884 E, S, I, 1885 E, S, 1886 S, 1887 E, S, I, 1888 S, I
Clare, J (Cardiff) 1883 E
Clark, S S (Neath) 1882 I, 1887 I
Cleaver, W B (Cardiff) 1947 E, S, F, I, A, 1948 E, S, F, I, 1949 I, 1950 E, S, I, F
Clegg, B G (Swansea) 1979 F
Clement, A (Swansea) 1987 US (R), 1988 E, NZ 1, WS (R), R, 1989 NZ, 1990 S (R), I (R), Nm 1, 2, 1991 S (R), A (R), F 2, [WS, A], 1992 I, F, E, S, 1993 I (R), F, J, C, 1994 S, I, F, Sp, C, Tg, WS, It, SA, 1995 F, E, [J, NZ, I]
Clement, W H (Llanelli) 1937 E, S, I, 1938 E, S, I
Cobner, T J (Pontypool) 1974 S, I, F, E, 1975 F, E, S, I, A, 1976 E, S, 1977 F, E, S, 1978 E, S, I, F, A 1
Cockbain, B J (Celtic Warriors, Ospreys) 2003 R, [C, It, NZ, E], 2004 S, I, F, E, Arg 1, 2, SA2, NZ, 2005 E, It, F, S, I, US, C(R), NZ, Fj, 2007 F1(t&R), A1
Coldrick, A P (Newport) 1911 E, S, I, 1912 E, S, F
Coleman, E O (Newport) 1949 E, S, I
Coles, F C (Pontypool) 1960 S, I, F
Collins, J E (Aberavon) 1958 A, E, S, I, F, 1959 E, S, I, F, 1960 E, 1961 F
Collins, R G (S Wales Police, Cardiff, Pontypridd) 1987 E (R), I, [I, E, NZ], US, 1988 E, S, I, F, R, 1990 E, S, I, 1991 A F 2, [WS], 1994 C, Fj, Tg, WS, R, It, SA, 1995 F, E, S, I
Collins, T J (Mountain Ash) 1923 I
Conway-Rees, J (Llanelli) 1892 S, 1893 E, 1894 E
Cook, T (Cardiff) 1949 S, I
Coombs, A J (Newport Gwent Dragons) 2013 I, F, It, E(R), J1, 2(R), 2014 It(R), I, F(R), E(R)
Cooper, G J (Bath, Celtic Warriors, Newport Gwent Dragons, Gloucester, Cardiff Blues) 2001 It J 1, 2, 2003 E 1, S 1, I 1, F(R), A, NZ, E 2, [C, Tg, It(t&R), NZ, E], 2004 S, I, F, E, It, R(R), NZ(R), 2005 E(R), It(R), F(R), C, NZ(R), Fj, SA, A, 2006 E(R), PI(R), 2007 A1(R), E2, [J(R)], 2008 SA1, 2, 3, NZ, A, 2009 C, US(R), NZ, Arg, 2010 E, S

**541**

**WALES**

Tg, WS, 1987 F, E, S, I, [I, C, E, NZ, A], 1988 NZ 1, 2, R, 1989 S, I
**Diplock, R S** (Bridgend) 1988 R
**Dobson, G A** (Cardiff) 1900 S
**Dobson, T** (Cardiff) 1898 I, E, 1899 E, S
**Donovan, A J** (Swansea) 1978 A 2, 1981 I (R), A, 1982 E, S
**Donovan, R E** (S Wales Police) 1983 F (R)
**Douglas, M H J** (Llanelli) 1984 S, I, F
**Douglas, W M** (Cardiff) 1886 E, S, 1887 E, S
**Dowell, W H** (Newport) 1907 E, S, I, 1908 E, S, F, I
**Durston, A P R** (Bridgend) 2001 J 1, 2
**Dyke, J C M** (Penarth) 1906 SA
**Dyke, L M** (Penarth, Cardiff) 1910 I, 1911 S, F, I

**Edmunds, D A** (Neath) 1990 I (R), Bb
**Edwards, A B** (London Welsh, Army) 1955 E, S
**Edwards, B O** (Newport) 1951 I
**Edwards, D** (Glynneath) 1921 E
**Edwards, G O** (Cardiff, Cardiff Coll of Ed) 1967 F, E, NZ, 1968 E, S, I, F, 1969 S, I, F, E, NZ 1, 2, A, 1970 SA, S, E, I, F, 1971 E, S, I, F, 1972 E, S, F, NZ, 1973 E, S, I, F, A, 1974 S, I, F, E, 1975 F, E, S, I, A, 1976 E, S, I, F, 1977 I, F, E, S, 1978 E, S, I, F
**Eidman, I H** (Cardiff) 1983 S, R, 1984 I, F, E, A, 1985 S, I, Fj, 1986 E, S, I, F
**Elliott, J** (Cardiff) 1894 I, 1898 I, E
**Elsey, W J** (Cardiff) 1895 E
**Emyr, Arthur** (Swansea) 1989 E, NZ, 1990 F, E, S, I, Nm 1, 2, 1991 F 1, 2, [WS, Arg, A]
**Evans, A** (Pontypool) 1924 E, I, F
**Evans, B** (Llanelli) 1933 E, S, 1936 E, S, I, 1937 E
**Evans, B R** (Swansea, Cardiff Blues) 1998 SA 2(R), 1999 F 1, It, E, Arg 1, 2, C, [J (R), Sm (R), A (R)], 2000 Sm, US, 2001 J 1(R), 2002 SA 1, 2, R(R), Fj, C, NZ, 2003 It, E 1, S 1, I 2, R, 2004 F(R), E(t), It(R)
**Evans, B S** (Llanelli) 1920 E, 1922 E, S, I, F
**Evans, C** (Pontypool) 1960 E
**Evans, D** (Penygraig) 1896 S, I, 1897 E, 1898 E
**Evans, D B** (Swansea) 1926 E
**Evans, D B** (Swansea) 1933 S
**Evans, D D** (Cheshire, Cardiff U) 1934 E
**Evans, D J** (Scarlets) 2009 C, US
**Evans, D P** (Llanelli) 1960 SA
**Evans, D W** (Cardiff) 1889 S, I, 1890 E, I, 1891 E
**Evans, D W** (Oxford U, Cardiff, Treorchy) 1989 F, E, NZ, 1990 F, E, S, I, Bb, 1991 A (R), F 2(R), [A (R)], 1995 [J (R)]
**Evans, E** (Llanelli) 1937 E, 1939 S, I
**Evans, F** (Llanelli) 1921 S
**Evans, G** (Cardiff) 1947 E, S, F, I, A, 1948 E, S, F, I, 1949 E, S, I
**Evans, G** (Maesteg) 1981 S (R), I, F, A, 1982 I, F, E, S, 1983 F, R
**Evans, G D** (Llanelli Scarlets) 2006 PI(R)
**Evans, G L** (Newport) 1977 F (R), 1978 F, A 2(R)
**Evans, G R** (Cardiff) 1889 S
**Evans, G R** (Llanelli) 1998 SA 1, 2003 I 2, S 2, [NZ]
**Evans, H I** (Swansea) 1922 E, S, I, F
**Evans, I** (London Welsh) 1934 S, I
**Evans, I C** (Llanelli, Bath) 1987 F, E, S, I, [I, C, E, NZ, A], 1988 E, S, I, F, NZ 1, 2, 1989 I, F, E, 1991 E, S, I, F, A, F 2, [WS, Arg, A], 1992 I, F, E, S, A, 1993 E, S, I, F, J, C, 1994 S, I, E, Pt, Sp, C, Fj, Tg, WS, R, 1995 E, S, I, [J, NZ, I], SA, Fj, 1996 It, E, S, I, F 1, A 1, 2, Bb, F 2, A 3, SA, 1997 US, S, I, F, 1998 It
**Evans, I L** (Llanelli) 1991 F 2(R)
**Evans, I R** (Ospreys) 2006 Arg 1, 2, A, C, NZ, 2007 [J(R), Fj], SA, 2008 E(R), S, It, F(R), SA1(R), 2(R), 3, NZ, 2011 A, 2012 I, S, E, It, F, Bb, Arg, Sm, 2013 I, F, It, S, E, Tg, A, 2014 SA1(R)
**Evans, J** (Llanelli) 1896 S, I, 1897 E
**Evans, J D** (Cardiff) 1958 I, F
**Evans, J E** (Llanelli) 1924 S
**Evans, J H** (Pontypool) 1907 E, S, I
**Evans, J R** (Newport) 1934 E
**Evans, J W** (Blaina) 1904 E
**Evans, O J** (Cardiff) 1887 E, S, 1888 S, I
**Evans, P D** (Llanelli) 1951 E, F

**Evans, R** (Bridgend) 1963 S, I, F
**Evans, R L** (Llanelli) 1993 E, S, I, F, 1994 S, I, F, E, Pt, Sp, C, Fj, WS, R, It, SA, 1995 F, [NZ, I (R)]
**Evans, R T** (Newport) 1947 F, I, 1950 E, S, I, F, 1951 E, S, I, F
**Evans, S** (Swansea, Neath) 1985 F, E, 1986 Fj, Tg, WS, 1987 F, E, [I, Tg]
**Evans, T D** (Swansea) 1924 I
**Evans, T G** (London Welsh) 1970 SA, S, E, I, 1972 E, S, F
**Evans, T H** (Llanelli) 1906 I, 1907 E, S, I, 1908 I, A, 1909 E, S, F, I, 1910 F, E, S, I, 1911 E, S, F, I
**Evans, T P** (Swansea) 1975 F, E, S, I, A, 1976 E, S, I, F, 1977 I
**Evans, T W** (Llanelli) 1958 A
**Evans, V** (Neath) 1954 I, F, S
**Evans, W F** (Rhymney) 1882 I, 1883 S
**Evans, W G** (Brynmawr) 1911 I
**Evans, W H** (Llwynypia) 1914 E, S, F, I
**Evans, W J** (Pontypool) 1947 S
**Evans, W R** (Bridgend) 1958 A, E, S, I, F, 1960 SA, 1961 E, S, I, F, 1962 E, S, I
**Everson, W A** (Newport) 1926 S

**Faletau, T T** (Newport Gwent Dragons) 2011 Bb, E2, 3, [SA, Sm, Nm, Fj, I, F, A], A, 2012 I, S, E, It, F, A1, Arg, Sm, NZ, A4, 2013 I, F, It, S, E, SA, Arg, A, 2014 It, I, F, E, S, SA1, 2
**Faulkner, A G** (Pontypool) 1975 F, E, S, I, A, 1976 E, S, I, F, 1978 E, S, I, F, A 1, 2, NZ, 1979 S, I, F
**Faull, J** (Swansea) 1957 I, F, 1958 A, E, S, I, F, 1959 E, S, I, 1960 E, F
**Fauvel, T J** (Aberavon) 1988 NZ 1(R)
**Fear, A G** (Newport) 1934 S, I, 1935 S, I
**Fender, N H** (Cardiff) 1930 I, F, 1931 E, S, F, I
**Fenwick, S P** (Bridgend) 1975 F, E, S, A, 1976 E, S, I, F, 1977 I, F, E, S, 1978 E, S, I, F, A 1, 2, NZ, 1979 S, I, F, E, 1980 F, E, S, I, NZ, 1981 E, S
**Finch, E** (Llanelli) 1924 F, NZ, 1925 F, I, 1926 F, 1927 A, 1928 I
**Finlayson, A A J** (Cardiff) 1974 I, F, E
**Fitzgerald, D** (Cardiff) 1894 S, I
**Ford, F J V** (Welch Regt, Newport) 1939 E
**Ford, I R** (Newport) 1959 E, S
**Ford, S P** (Cardiff) 1990 I, Nm 1, 2, Bb, 1991 E, S, I, A
**Forster, J A** (Newport Gwent Dragons) 2004 Arg 1
**Forward, A** (Pontypool, Mon Police) 1951 S, SA, 1952 E, S, I, F
**Fowler, I J** (Llanelli) 1919 NZA
**Francis, D G** (Llanelli) 1919 NZA, 1924 S
**Francis, P W** (Maesteg) 1987 S
**Funnell, J S** (Ebbw Vale) 1998 Z (R), SA 1
**Fury, W L** (London Irish) 2008 SA1(R), 2(R)

**Gabe, R T** (Cardiff, Llanelli) 1901 I, 1902 E, S, I, 1903 E, S, I, 1904 E, S, I, 1905 E, S, I, NZ, 1906 E, I, SA, 1907 E, S, I, 1908 E, S, F, I
**Gale, N R** (Swansea, Llanelli) 1960 I, 1963 E, S, I, NZ, 1964 E, S, I, F, SA, 1965 E, S, I, F, 1966 E, S, I, F, A, 1967 E, NZ, 1968 E, 1969 NZ 1(R), 2, A
**Gallacher, I S** (Llanelli) 1970 F
**Garrett, R M** (Penarth) 1888 M, 1889 S, 1890 S, E, I, 1891 S, I, 1892 E
**Geen, W P** (Oxford U, Newport) 1912 SA, 1913 E, I
**George, E E** (Pontypridd, Cardiff) 1895 S, I, 1896 E
**George, G M** (Newport) 1991 E, S
**Gething, G I** (Neath) 1913 F
**Gibbs, A** (Newbridge) 1995 I, SA, 1996 A 2, 1997 US 1, 2, C
**Gibbs, I S** (Neath, Swansea) 1991 E, S, I, F 1, A, F 2, [WS, Arg, A], 1992 I, F, E, S, A, 1993 E, S, I, F, J, C, 1996 It, A 3, SA, 1997 US, S, I, F, Tg, NZ, 1998 It, E, S, SA 2, Arg, 1999 S, I, F 1, It, E, C, F 2, [Arg 3, J, Sm, A], 2000 I, Sm, US, SA, 2001 E, S, F, It
**Gibbs, R A** (Cardiff) 1906 S, I, 1907 E, S, 1908 E, S, F, I, 1910 F, E, S, I, 1911 E, S, F, I
**Giles, R** (Aberavon) 1983 R, 1985 Fj (R), 1987 [C]
**Gill, I A R** (Saracens) 2010 I(R), 2012 I, Bb, 2013 J1(R), 2
**Girling, B E** (Cardiff) 1881 E
**Goldsworthy, S J** (Swansea) 1884 I, 1885 E, S

Gore, J H (Blaina) 1924 I, F, NZ, 1925 E

Gore, W (Newbridge) 1947 S, F, I

Gough, I M (Newport, Pontypridd, Newport Gwent Dragons, Ospreys) 1998 SA 1, 1999 S, 2000 F, It (R), E (R), S, I, Sm, US, SA, 2001 E, S, F, It, Tg, A, 2002 I (R), F (R), It, S, 2003 R, 2005 It(R), US(R), SA, A, 2006 E, S, I, It, F, Arg 1, 2, A, C, NZ, 2007 I, S(R), F1, It, E1, Arg, F2, [C, A, Fj(R)], 2008 E, S, It, I, F, SA1, 2, 3(R), C, A, 2009 S, E, F, I, C(R), US, 2010 I(R), It(R), Fj

Gould, A J (Newport) 1885 E, S, 1886 E, S, 1887 E, S, I, 1888 S, 1889 I, 1890 S, E, I, 1892 E, S, I, 1893 E, S, I, 1894 E, S, 1895 E, S, I, 1896 E, S, I, 1897 E

Gould, G H (Newport) 1892 I, 1893 S, I

Gould, R (Newport) 1882 I, 1883 E, S, 1884 E, S, I, 1885 E, S, 1886 E, 1887 E, S

Graham, T C (Newport) 1890 I, 1891 S, I, 1892 E, S, 1893 E, S, I, 1894 E, S, 1895 E, S

Gravell, R W R (Llanelli) 1975 F, E, S, I, A, 1976 E, S, I, F, 1978 E, S, I, F, A 1, 2, NZ, 1979 S, I, 1981 I, F, 1982 F, E, S

Gray, A J (London Welsh) 1968 E, S

Greenslade, D (Newport) 1962 S

Greville, H G (Llanelli) 1947 A

Griffin, Dr J (Edinburgh U) 1883 S

Griffiths, C R (Llanelli) 1979 E (R)

Griffiths, D (Llanelli) 1888 M, 1889 I

Griffiths, G (Llanelli) 1889 I

Griffiths, G M (Cardiff) 1953 E, S, I, F, NZ, 1954 I, F, S, 1955 I, F, 1957 E, S

Griffiths, J (Swansea) 2000 Sm (R)

Griffiths, J L (Llanelli) 1988 NZ 2, 1989 S

Griffiths, M (Bridgend, Cardiff, Pontypridd) 1988 WS, R, 1989 S, I, F, E, NZ, 1990 F, E, Nm 1, 2, Bb, 1991 I, F 1, 2, [WS, Arg, A], 1992 I, F, E, S, A, 1993 Z 1, 2, Nm, J, C, 1995 F (R), E, S, I, [J, I], 1998 SA 1

Griffiths, V M (Newport) 1924 S, I, F

Gronow, B (Bridgend) 1910 F, E, S, I

Gwilliam, J A (Cambridge U, Newport) 1947 A, 1948 I, 1949 E, S, I, F, 1950 E, S, I, F, 1951 E, S, I, SA, 1952 E, S, I, F, 1953 E, I, F, NZ, 1954 E

Gwynn, D (Swansea) 1883 E, 1887 S, 1890 E, I, 1891 E, S

Gwynn, W H (Swansea) 1884 E, S, I, 1885 E, S

Hadley, A M (Cardiff) 1983 R, 1984 S, I, F, E, 1985 F, E, Fj, 1986 E, S, I, F, Fj, Tg, 1987 S (R), I, [I, Tg, C, E, NZ, A], US, 1988 E, S, I, F

Halfpenny, S L (Cardiff Blues) 2008 SA3, C, NZ, 2009 S, E, F, NZ, Sm, Arg, A, 2010 E(R), S, F, I, SA1, NZ1, 2, 2011 I, F, Arg, [Sm(R), Nm, Fj, I, F, A] , A, 2012 I, S, E, It, F, A 1, 2, 3, Arg, Sm, NZ, A4, 2013 I, F, It, S, E, SA, Arg, Tg, A, 2014 It, I, F, E

Hall, I (Aberavon) 1967 NZ, 1970 SA, S, E, 1971 S, 1974 S, I, F

Hall, M R (Cambridge U, Bridgend, Cardiff) 1988 NZ 1(R), 2, WS, R, 1989 S, I, F, E, NZ, 1990 F, E, S, 1991 A, F 2, [WS, Arg, A], 1992 I, F, E, S, A, 1993 E, S, I, 1994 S, I, F, E, Pt, Sp, C, Tg, R, It, SA, 1995 F, S, I, [J, NZ, I]

Hall, W H (Bridgend) 1988 WS

Hancock, F E (Cardiff) 1884 I, 1885 E, S, 1886 S

Hannan, J (Newport) 1888 M, 1889 S, I, 1890 S, E, I, 1891 E, 1892 E, S, I, 1893 E, S, I, 1894 E, S, I, 1895 E, S, I

Harding, A F (London Welsh) 1902 E, S, I, 1903 E, S, I, 1904 E, S, I, 1905 E, S, I, NZ, 1906 E, S, I, SA, 1907 I, 1908 E, S, I

Harding, C T (Newport) 1888 M, 1889 S, I

Harding, G F (Newport) 1881 E, 1882 I, 1883 E, S

Harding, R (Swansea, Cambridge U) 1923 E, S, F, I, 1924 I, F, NZ, 1925 F, I, 1926 E, I, F, 1927 E, S, F, I, 1928 E

Harries, W T M (Newport Gwent Dragons) 2010 NZ2(R), A, 2012 Bb(R)

Harris, C A (Aberavon) 1927 A

Harris, D J E (Pontypridd, Cardiff) 1959 I, F, 1960 S, I, F, SA, 1961 E, S

Harris, I R (Cardiff) 2001 Arg, Tg, A, 2002 I, It (R), E, S (R), Fj(R), C(R), NZ(R), 2003 It, E 1(R), S 1(R), I 1(R), F, I 2, S 2, [C, Tg, It, E], 2004 S, I, F, It

Hathway, G F (Newport) 1924 I, F

Havard, Rev W T (Llanelli) 1919 NZA

Hawkins, F J (Pontypridd) 1912 I, F

Hayward, B I (Ebbw Vale) 1998 Z (R), SA 1

Hayward, D J (Newbridge) 1949 E, F, 1950 E, S, I, F, 1951 E, S, I, F, SA, 1952 E, S, I, F

Hayward, D J (Cardiff) 1963 E, NZ, 1964 S, I, F, SA

Hayward, G (Swansea) 1908 S, F, I, A, 1909 E

Hellings, D (Llwynypia) 1897 E, 1898 I, E, 1899 S, I, 1900 E, I, 1901 E, S

Henson, G L (Swansea, Ospreys, Toulon) 2001 J 1(R), R, 2003 NZ(R), R, 2004 Arg 1, 2, SA1, 2, R, NZ, J, 2005 E, It, F, S, I, 2006 I(R), F(R), A, NZ(R), 2007 A1(t&R), 2(R), SA, 2008 E, S, It, I, F, 2009 F(R), It, I, 2011 Bb, E3

Herrerá, R C (Cross Keys) 1925 S, F, I, 1926 E, S, I, F, 1927 E

Hiams, H (Swansea) 1912 I, F

Hibbard, R M (Ospreys) 2006 Arg 1(R), 2(R), 2007 A1(R), 2(R), 2008 SA1(R), 2, C, 2009 C, US(R), 2011 E1(R) S(R), It(R), I(R), F(R), Arg, 2012 Bb(R), A2(R), Arg(R), Sm, 2013 F, It, S, E, SA, Arg, A, 2014 It, I, F, E, S(R)

Hickman, A (Neath) 1930 E, 1933 S

Hiddlestone, D D (Neath) 1922 E, S, I, F, 1924 NZ

Hill, A F (Cardiff) 1885 S, 1886 E, S, 1888 S, I, M, 1889 S, 1890 S, I, 1893 E, S, I, 1894 E, S, I

Hill, S D (Cardiff) 1993 Z 1, 2, Nm, 1994 I (R), F, SA, 1995 F, SA, 1996 A 2, F 2(R), It, 1997 E

Hinam, S (Cardiff) 1925 I, 1926 E, S, I, F

Hinton, J T (Cardiff) 1884 I

Hirst, G L (Newport) 1912 S, 1913 S, 1914 E, S, F, I

Hodder, W (Pontypool) 1921 E, S, F

Hodges, J J (Newport) 1899 E, S, I, 1900 E, S, I, 1901 E, S, 1902 E, S, I, 1903 E, S, I, 1904 E, S, 1905 E, S, I, NZ, 1906 E, S, I

Hodgson, G T R (Neath) 1962 I, 1963 E, S, I, F, NZ, 1964 E, S, I, F, SA, 1966 S, I, F, 1967 I

Hollingdale, B G (Swansea) 1912 SA, 1913 E

Hollingdale, T H (Neath) 1927 A, 1928 E, S, I, F, 1930 E

Holmes, T D (Cardiff) 1978 A 2, NZ, 1979 S, I, F, E, 1980 F, E, S, I, NZ, 1981 A, 1982 I, F, E, 1983 E, S, I, F, 1984 E, 1985 S, I, F, E, Fj

Hook, J W (Ospreys, Perpignan) 2006 Arg 1(R), 2, A(R), PI, C, NZ(R), 2007 I, S, F1, It, E1, A1, 2, Arg, F2, [C, A(R), J, Fj], SA, 2008 E, S, It(R), I(R), F, SA1(R), 2, 3(R), C, NZ(R) , 2009 S(R), F(R), It, NZ, Sm, Arg, A, 2010 E, S, F, I, It, SA1, A, SA2, Fj, NZ3, 2011 E1, S, It, I, F, E3, Arg, [SA, Sm, I(R), F, A], 2012 I(R), S(R), It(R), Bb, A 1(R), 3(R), Arg(R), NZ(R), SA1(R)

Hopkin, W H (Newport) 1937 S

Hopkins, K (Cardiff, Swansea) 1985 E, 1987 F, E, S, [Tg, C (R)], US

Hopkins, P L (Swansea) 1908 A, 1909 E, I, 1910 E

Hopkins, R (Maesteg) 1970 E (R)

Hopkins, T (Swansea) 1926 E, S, I, F

Hopkins, W J (Aberavon) 1925 E, S

Horsman, C L (Worcester) 2005 NZ(R), Fj, SA, A, 2006 PI, 2007 I, F1, It, E1, A2(R), E2, F2, [J, Fj]

Howarth, S P (Sale, Newport) 1998 SA 2, Arg, 1999 S, I, F 1, It, E, Arg, S 2, F 2, [Arg 3, J, Sm, A], 2000 F, It, E

Howells, B (Llanelli) 1934 E

Howells, D W (Ospreys) 2013 J1, 2(R)

Howells, W G (Llanelli) 1957 E, S, I, F

Howells, W H (Swansea) 1888 S, I

Howley, R (Bridgend, Cardiff) 1996 E, S, I, F 1, A 1, 2, Bb, F 2, It, A 3, SA, 1997 US, S, I, F, E, Tg (R), NZ, 1998 It, E, S, I, F, Z, SA 2, Arg, 1999 S, I, F 1, It, E, Arg 1, 2, SA, C, F 2, [Arg 2, J, Sm, A], 2000 F, It, E, Sm, US, SA, 2001 E, S, F, R, I, Arg, Tg, A, 2002 I, F, It, E, S

Hughes, D (Newbridge) 1967 NZ, 1969 NZ 2, 1970 SA, S, E, I

Hughes, G (Penarth) 1934 E, S, I

Hughes, H (Cardiff) 1887 S, 1889 S

Hughes, K (Cambridge U, London Welsh) 1970 I, 1973 A, 1974 S

Hullin, W G (Cardiff) 1967 S

Humphreys, J M (Cardiff, Bath) 1995 [NZ, I], SA, Fj, 1996 It, E, S, I, F, I, A 2, Bb, It, A 3, SA, 1997 S, I, F, E, Tg (R), NZ (R), 1998 It (R), E (R), S (R), I (R), F (R), SA 2, Arg, 1999 S, Arg 2(R), SA (R), C, [J (R)], 2003 E 1, I 1

**Hurrell, R J** (Newport) 1959 F
**Hutchinson, F O** (Neath) 1894 I, 1896 S, I
**Huxtable, R** (Swansea) 1920 F, I
**Huzzey, H V P** (Cardiff) 1898 I, E, 1899 E, S, I
**Hybart, A J** (Cardiff) 1887 E

**Ingledew, H M** (Cardiff) 1890 I, 1891 E, S
**Isaacs, I** (Cardiff) 1933 E, S

**Jackson, T H** (Swansea) 1895 E
**James, C R** (Llanelli) 1958 A, F
**James, D** (Swansea) 1891 I, 1892 S, I, 1899 E
**James, D M** (Cardiff) 1947 A, 1948 E, S, F, I
**James, D R** (Treorchy) 1931 F, I
**James, D R** (Bridgend, Pontypridd, Llanelli Scarlets) 1996 A 2(R), It, A 3, SA, 1997 I, Tg (R), 1998 F (R), Z, SA 1, 2, Arg, 1999 S, I, F 1, It, E, Arg 1, 2, SA, F 2, [Arg 3, Sm, A], 2000 F, It (R), I (R), Sm (R), US, SA, 2001 E, S, F, It, R, I, 2002 I, F, It, E, S (R), NZ(R), 2005 SA, A, 2006 I, F, 2007 E2, Arg, [J]
**James, E** (Swansea) 1890 S, 1891 I, 1892 S, I, 1899 E
**James, J B** (Bridgend) 1968 E
**James, P** (Ospreys, Bath) 2003 R, 2009 NZ, Sm, Arg, A, 2010 E, S, F, I, It(t&R), SA1, NZ1, 2, A(R), SA2, Fj, NZ3(R), 2011 E1, S, It, I, F, Bb, E2, 3, Arg, [SA, Sm, Fj(R), F(R), A], 2012 I(R), S(R), It(R), Bb(t&R), A1(R), 3(R), Arg(R), Sm, NZ, 2013 I(t&R), F(t&R), It(R), S, E(R), SA(R), Arg(R), Tg, 2014 It, I(R), F(t&R), E(R), S(R), SA1(R), 2(R)
**James, T E** (Cardiff Blues, Wasps) 2007 E2(R), SA(R), 2008 SA2(R), 2009 C, US, Sm, Arg(R), A(R), 2010 E, NZ3
**James, T O** (Aberavon) 1935 I, 1937 S
**James, W** (Gloucester) 2007 E2, Arg(R), F2(R), [J]
**James, W J** (Aberavon) 1983 E, S, I, F, R, 1984 S, 1985 S, I, F, E, Fj, 1986 E, S, I, F, Fj, Tg, WS, 1987 E, S, I
**James, W P** (Aberavon) 1925 E, S
**Jarman, H** (Newport) 1910 E, S, I, 1911 E
**Jarrett, K S** (Newport) 1967 E, 1968 E, S, 1969 S, I, F, E, NZ 1, 2, A
**Jarvis, A R** (Ospreys) 2012 Arg, Sm, NZ, 2014 SA2(R)
**Jarvis, L** (Cardiff) 1997 R (R)
**Jeffery, J J** (Cardiff Coll of Ed, Newport) 1967 NZ
**Jenkin, A M** (Swansea) 1895 I, 1896 E
**Jenkins, A E** (Llanelli) 1920 E, S, F, I, 1921 S, F, 1922 F, 1923 E, S, F, I, 1924 NZ, 1928 S, I
**Jenkins, D M** (Treorchy) 1926 E, S, I, F
**Jenkins, D R** (Swansea) 1927 A, 1929 E
**Jenkins, E** (Newport) 1910 S, I
**Jenkins, E M** (Aberavon) 1927 S, F, I, A, 1928 E, S, I, F, 1929 F, 1930 E, S, I, F, 1931 E, S, F, I, SA, 1932 E, S, I
**Jenkins, G D** (Pontypridd, Celtic Warriors, Cardiff Blues, Toulon) 2002 R, NZ(R), 2003 E 1(R), S 1(R), I 1, F, A, NZ, I 2(R), E 2, [C, Tg, It(R), NZ(R), E(R)], 2004 S(R), I(R), F, E, It, Arg 1(R), 2(R), SA1, 2(R), R, NZ, J, 2005 E, It, F, S, I, 2006 E(R), S(R), I(R), It(R), F(R), A, C, NZ(R), 2007 I, S(R), F1, It, E1, 2(R), Arg(R), F2(R), [C, A, J(R), Fj], SA, 2008 E(R), S(R), It, I, F, SA1, 2, 3, NZ, A, 2009 S, E, F, It(R), I, NZ, Sm, Arg, A, 2010 S(R), It, A, NZ3, 2011 [Sm(R), Nm, Fj, I, F, A], A, 2012 S, E, It, F, A 1, 2, 3, Arg, Sm(R), NZ(R), A4, 2013 I, F, It, E, SA, Arg, A, 2014 I, F, E, S, SA1, 2
**Jenkins, G R** (Pontypool, Swansea) 1991 F 2, [WS (R), Arg, A], 1992 I, F, E, S, A, 1993 C, 1994 S, I, F, E, Pt, Sp, C, Tg, WS, R, It, SA, 1995 F, E, S, I, [J], SA (R), Fj (t), 1996 E (R), 1997 US, US 1, C, 1998 S, I, F, Z, SA 1(R), 1999 I (R), F 1, It, E, Arg 1, 2, SA, C, F 2, [Arg 3, J, Sm, A], 2000 F, It, E, S, I, Sm, US, SA
**Jenkins, J C** (London Welsh) 1906 SA
**Jenkins, J L** (Aberavon) 1923 S, F
**Jenkins, L H** (Mon TC, Newport) 1954 I, 1956 E, S, I, F
**Jenkins, N R** (Pontypridd, Cardiff) 1991 E, S, I, F 1, 1992 I, F, E, S, 1993 E, S, I, F, Z 1, 2, Nm, J, C, 1994 S, I, F, E, Pt, Sp, C, Tg, WS, R, It, SA, 1995 F, E, S, I, [J, NZ, I], SA, Fj, 1996 F 1, A 1, 2, Bb, F 2, It, A 3(R), SA, 1997 S, I, F, E, Tg, NZ, 1998 It, E, S, I, F, SA 2, Arg, 1999 S, I, F 1, It, E, Arg 1, 2, SA, C, F 2, [Arg 3, J, Sm, A], 2000 F, It, E, S, I, Sm, US, SA
**Jenkins, V G J** (Oxford U, Bridgend, London Welsh) 1933 E, I, 1934 S, I, 1935 E, S, NZ, 1936 E, S, I, 1937 E, 1938 E, S, 1939 E

**Jenkins, W J** (Cardiff) 1912 I, F, 1913 S, I
**John, B** (Llanelli, Cardiff) 1966 A, 1967 S, NZ, 1968 E, S, I, F, 1969 S, I, F, E, NZ 1, 2, A, 1970 SA, S, E, I, 1971 E, S, I, F, 1972 E, S, F
**John, D A** (Llanelli) 1925 I, 1928 E, S, I
**John, D E** (Llanelli) 1923 F, I, 1928 E, S, I
**John, E R** (Neath) 1950 E, S, I, F, 1951 E, S, I, F, SA, 1952 E, S, I, F, 1953 E, S, I, F, NZ, 1954 E
**John G** (St Luke's Coll, Exeter) 1954 E, F
**John, J H** (Swansea) 1926 E, S, I, F, 1927 E, S, F, I
**John, P** (Pontypridd) 1994 Tg, 1996 Bb (t), 1997 US (R), US 1, 2, C, R, Tg, 1998 Z (R), SA 1
**John, S C** (Llanelli, Cardiff) 1995 S, I, 1997 E (R), Tg, NZ (R), 2000 F (R), It (R), E (R), Sm (R), SA (R), 2001 E (R), S (R), Tg (R), A, 2002 I, F, It (R), S (R)
**Johnson, T A W** (Cardiff) 1921 E, F, I, 1923 E, S, F, 1924 E, S, NZ, 1925 E, S, F
**Johnson, W D** (Swansea) 1953 E
**Jones , A E** (SEE Emyr)
**Jones, A H** (Cardiff) 1933 E, S
**Jones, A M** (Llanelli Scarlets) 2006 E(t&R), S(R)
**Jones, A R** (Ospreys) 2003 E 2(R), S 2, [C(R), Tg(R), It, NZ, E], 2004 S, I, Arg 1, 2, SA1, 2, R, NZ, J(t&R), 2005 E, It, F, S, I, US, NZ, Fj(R), SA(t&R), A(R), 2006 E, S, I, It, F, Arg 1, 2, A, PI(R), C, NZ, 2007 S, It(R), E1(R), A1, Arg, [C, A], 2008 E, S, I, F, SA1, 3, NZ, A, 2009 S, E, F, I, 2010 E, S, F, I, It, SA1, NZ1, 2, A, SA2, Fj, NZ3, 2011 F, Arg, [SA, Sm, Fj, I, F], 2012 I, S, E, It, F, A 1, 2, 3, 2013 I, F, It, S, E, SA, 2014 It, I, F, E, S(R), SA1
**Jones, A W** (Mountain Ash) 1905 I
**Jones, A-W** (Ospreys) 2006 Arg 1, 2, PI, C(R), NZ(R), 2007 I, S, F1, It, E1, 2, Arg, F2, [C, A, J, Fj], SA, 2008 E, I, F, SA1, 2, 3, NZ, A, 2009 S, E, F, It, I, NZ, Sm, Arg, A, 2010 E, S, SA1(R), NZ1, 2, A, SA2, NZ3, 2011 E1, S, It, I, F, Bb(R), E2, 3, Arg, [SA, Sm, Nm, Fj(R), I, F, A(R)], 2012 E, It, F, Bb, A1(R), 2, 3, Arg, 2013 It(R), S, E, SA, Arg, Tg(R), A, 2014 It, I, E, S, SA1, 2
**Jones, B J** (Newport) 1960 I, F
**Jones, B L** (Devonport Services, Llanelli) 1950 E, S, I, F, 1951 E, S, SA, 1952 E, I, F
**Jones, C** (Harlequins) 2007 A1(R), 2
**Jones, C W** (Cambridge U, Cardiff) 1934 E, I, 1935 E, S, NZ, 1936 E, S, I, 1938 E, S, I
**Jones, C W** (Bridgend) 1920 E, S, F
**Jones, D** (Aberavon) 1897 S
**Jones, D** (Treherbert) 1902 E, S, I, 1903 E, S, I, 1905 E, S, I, NZ, 1906 E, S, SA
**Jones, D** (Neath) 1927 A
**Jones, D** (Cardiff) 1994 SA, 1995 F, E, S, [J, NZ, I], SA, Fj, 1996 It, E, S, I, F 1, A 1, 2, Bb, It, A 3
**Jones, D A R** (Llanelli Scarlets) 2002 Fj, C, NZ, 2003 It(R), E 1, S 1, I 1, F, NZ 2, [C, Tg, It, NZ(R), E], 2004 S, I, F, E, It, Arg 2, SA1, 2, R, NZ, J, 2005 E, Fj, 2006 F(R), 2008 SA1, 2(R), C, NZ(R), A(R), 2009 S, E(R), F(R), It, I, C, US, NZ(R)
**Jones, D C J** (Swansea) 1947 E, F, I, 1949 E, S, I, F
**Jones, D J** (Neath, Ospreys) 2001 A (R), 2002 I (R), F (R), 2003 I 2, S 2, [C, It], 2004 S, E, It, Arg1, 2, SA1(R), 2, R(R), NZ(t&R), J, 2005 US, C, NZ, SA, A, 2006 E, S, I, It, F, Arg 1, 2, A(R), PI, C(R), NZ, 2007 I(R), S, F1(R), It(R), E1(R), Arg, F2, [C(R), A(R), J, Fj(R)], SA(R), 2008 E, S, It(R), I(R), F(t&R), SA1(R), 2(R), 2009 C, US, NZ(R), Arg(R), A(R)
**Jones, D K** (Llanelli, Cardiff) 1962 E, S, F, I, 1963 E, F, NZ, 1964 E, S, SA, 1966 E, S, I, F
**Jones, D L** (Newport) 1926 E, S, I, F, 1927 E
**Jones, D L** (Ebbw Vale, Celtic Warriors, Cardiff Blues) 2000 Sm, 2003 R (R), 2004 SA1, 2008 S(R), It(R), 2009 C, US, 2010 F, SA1, NZ2(R), A(R), SA2(R), Fj
**Jones, D P** (Pontypool) 1907 I
**Jones, E H** (Swansea, Neath) 1930 I, F
**Jones, E L** (Llanelli) 1930 F, 1933 E, S, I, 1935 E
**Jones, E L** (Llanelli) 1939 S
**Jones, G** (Ebbw Vale) 1963 S, I, F
**Jones, G** (Llanelli) 1988 NZ 2, 1989 F, E, NZ, 1990 F
**Jones, G G** (Cardiff) 1930 S, 1933 I
**Jones, G H** (Bridgend) 1995 SA
**Jones, H** (Penygraig) 1902 S, I
**Jones, H** (Neath) 1904 I

Jones, H J (Neath) 1929 E, S
Jones, I C (London Welsh) 1968 I
Jones, I E (Llanelli) 1924 E, S, 1927 S, F, I, A, 1928 E, S, I, F, 1929 E, S, F, I, 1930 E, S
Jones, J (Aberavon) 1901 E
Jones, J (Bedwellty) (Abertillery) 1914 E, S, F, I
Jones, J (Swansea) 1924 F
Jones, J (Aberavon) 1919 NZA, 1920 E, S, 1921 S, F, I
Jones, J A (Cardiff) 1883 S
Jones, J P (Tuan) (Pontypool) 1913 S
Jones, J P (Jack) (Pontypool) 1908 A, 1909 E, S, F, I, 1910 F, E, 1912 E, F, 1913 F, I, 1920 F, I, 1921 E
Jones, K D (Cardiff) 1960 SA, 1961 E, S, I, 1962 E, F, 1963 E, S, I, NZ
Jones, K J (Newport) 1947 E, S, F, I, A, 1948 E, S, F, I, 1949 E, S, I, F, 1950 E, S, I, F, 1951 E, S, I, F, SA, 1952 E, S, I, F, 1953 E, S, I, F, NZ, 1954 E, I, F, S, 1955 E, S, I, F, 1956 E, S, I, F, 1957 S
Jones, K P (Ebbw Vale) 1996 Bb, F 2, It, A 3, 1997 I (R), E, 1998 S, I, F (R), SA 1
Jones, K W J (Oxford U, London Welsh) 1934 E
Jones, Matthew (Ospreys) 2005 C(R)
Jones, M A (Neath, Ebbw Vale) 1987 S, 1988 NZ 2(R), 1989 S, I, F, E, NZ, 1990 F, E, S, I, Nm 1, 2, Bb, 1998 Z
Jones, M A (Llanelli Scarlets) 2001 E (R), S, J 1, 2002 R, Fj, C, NZ, 2003 It, I 1, A, NZ, E 2, [C, Tg, It, E], 2006 E, S, I, It, Arg 1, 2, PI, C, NZ, 2007 S, F1, It, E1, Arg, F2, [C, A, Fj], SA, 2008 E, It, I, F, SA1 2, C, A, 2009 E, It, I, US
Jones, P E R (Newport) 1921 S
Jones, P L (Newport) 1912 SA, 1913 E, S, F, 1914 E, S, F, I
Jones, R (Llwynypia) 1901 I
Jones, R (Northampton) 1926 E, S, F
Jones, R (London Welsh) 1929 E
Jones, R B (Cambridge U) 1933 E, S
Jones, R E (Coventry) 1967 F, E, 1968 S, I, F
Jones, R G (Llanelli, Cardiff) 1996 It, E, S, I, F 1, A 1, 1997 US (R), S (R), US 1, 2, R, Tg, NZ
Jones, R H (Swansea) 1901 I, 1902 E, 1904 E, S, I, 1905 E, 1908 F, I, A, 1909 E, S, F, I, 1910 F, E
Jones, R L (Llanelli) 1993 Z 1, 2, Nm, J, C
Jones, R N (Swansea) 1986 E, S, I, F, Fj, Tg, WS, 1987 F, E, S, I, [I, Tg, E, NZ, A], US, 1988 E, S, I, F, NZ 1, WS, R, 1989 I, F, E, NZ, 1990 F, E, S, I, 1991 E, S, F 2, [WS, Arg, A], 1992 I, F, E, S, A, 1993 E, S, I, 1994 I (R), Pt, 1995 F, E, S, I, [NZ, I]
Jones, R P (Scarlets) 2012 Bb, 2013 J2(R), Arg, Tg, A, 2014 It(R), I(R), F(R), E(R), S
Jones, R P (Ospreys) 2004 SA2, NZ(R), J, 2005 E(R), F, S, I, US, 2006 A, C, NZ, 2007 I, S, F1, It, E1, 2008 E, S, It, I, F, SA1, 2, 3, C, NZ, A, 2009 E, F, It(R), I, C, US, NZ, Sm, Arg, 2010 E, S, F, It, SA1, NZ1, 2, SA2(R), Fj, NZ3, 2011 E1(R), S, It, I, F, Bb, E2(R), [Nm, Fj, F(R), A], A(R), 2012 I, S, E(R), It(R), F(R), Bb, A1(R), 2, 3, Sm, NZ, A4(t&R), 2013 F, It, S, Arg(R), Tg
Jones, S (Neath, Newport Gwent Dragons) 2001 J 1(R), 2004 SA2, R(R), NZ(R), J(R)
Jones, S M (Llanelli Scarlets, Clermont Auvergne) 1998 SA 1(R), 1999 C (R), [J (R)], 2000 It (R), S, I, 2001 E, F (R), J 1, 2, R, I, Arg, Tg, A, 2002 I, F, It, S, A1 2, NZ, R(R), 2003 S 1, I 1, F, A, NZ, E 2, [Tg, It(R), E], 2004 S, I, F, E, It, SA2, R, NZ, 2005 E, It, F, S, I, NZ, SA, A, 2006 E, S, I, It, F, A, NZ, 2007 I, S, F1, It, [C(R), A, J], 2008 S(R), It, I, F(R), SA1, 2, 3, NZ, A, 2009 S, E, F, It(R), I, NZ, Arg, A, 2010 E, S, F, I, It, SA1, NZ1, 2(R), A(R), SA2, Fj(R), F(R), A(t&R)]
Jones, S T (Pontypool) 1983 S, I, F, R, 1984 S, 1988 E, S, F, NZ 1, 2
Jones, T (Newport) 1922 E, S, I, F, 1924 E, S
Jones, T B (Newport) 1882 I, 1883 E, S, 1884 S, 1885 E, S
Jones, T I (Llanelli) 1927 A, 1928 E, S, I, F
Jones, W (Cardiff) 1898 I, E
Jones, W D (Llanelli) 1948 E
Jones, W H (Llanelli) 1934 S, I
Jones, W I (Llanelli, Cambridge U) 1925 E, S, F, I
Jones, W J (Llanelli) 1924 I
Jones, W K (Cardiff) 1967 NZ, 1968 E, S, I, F
Jones, W R (Swansea) 1927 A, 1928 F

Jones-Davies, T E (London Welsh) 1930 E, I, 1931 E, S
Jones-Hughes, J (Newport) 1999 [Arg 3(R), J], 2000 F
Jordan, H M (Newport) 1885 E, S, 1889 S
Joseph, W (Swansea) 1902 E, S, I, 1903 E, S, I, 1904 E, S, 1905 E, S, I, NZ, 1906 E, S, I, SA
Jowett, W F (Swansea) 1903 E
Judd, S (Cardiff) 1953 E, S, I, F, NZ, 1954 E, F, S, 1955 E, S
Judson, T H (Llanelli) 1883 E, S

Kedzlie, Q D (Cardiff) 1888 S, I
Keen, L (Aberavon) 1980 F, E, S, I
King, J D (Ospreys) 2013 J1, 2
Knight, P (Pontypridd) 1990 Nm 1, 2, Bb (R), 1991 E, S
Knill, F M D (Cardiff) 1976 F (R)
Knoyle, T D (Scarlets) 2010 NZ1(R), 2011 S(R), Bb(R), E2(R), Arg, [Nm], A(R), 2012 Arg, NZ(R), 2013 J1(R), 2(R)
Kohn, O S (Harlequins) 2013 I(R)

Lamerton, A E H (Llanelli) 1993 F, Z 1, 2, Nm, J
Lane, S M (Cardiff) 1978 A 1(R), 2, 1979 I (R), 1980 S, I
Lang, J (Llanelli) 1931 F, I, 1934 S, I, 1935 E, S, I, NZ, 1936 E, S, I, 1937 E
Law, V J (Newport) 1939 I
Lawrence, S D (Bridgend) 1925 S, I, 1926 S, I, F, 1927 E
Lee, S (Scarlets) 2013 Arg(R), Tg(R), A(R), 2014 SA1(R), 2
Legge, W S G (Newport) 1937 I, 1938 I
Leleu, J (London Welsh, Swansea) 1959 E, S, 1960 F, SA
Lemon, A W (Neath) 1929 I, 1930 S, I, F, 1931 E, S, F, I, SA, 1932 E, S, I, 1933 I
Lewis, A J L (Ebbw Vale) 1970 F, 1971 E, I, F, 1972 E, S, F, 1973 E, S, I, F
Lewis, A L P (Cardiff) 1996 It, E, S, I, A 2(t), 1998 It, E, S, I, F, SA 2, Arg, 1999 F 1(R), E (R), Arg 1(R), 2(R), SA (R), C (R), [J (R), Sm (R), A (R)], 2000 Sm (R), US (R), SA (R), 2001 F (R), J 1, 2, 2002 R(R)
Lewis, B R (Swansea, Cambridge U) 1912 I, 1913 I
Lewis, C P (Llandovery) 1882 I, 1883 E, S, 1884 E, S
Lewis, D H (Cardiff) 1886 E, S
Lewis, E J (Llandovery) 1881 E
Lewis, E W (Llanelli, Cardiff) 1991 I, F 1, A, F 2, [WS, Arg, A], 1992 I, F, S, A, 1993 E, S, I, F, Z 1, 2, Nm, J, C, 1994 S, I, F, E, Pt, Sp, Fj, WS, R, It, SA, 1995 E, S, I, [J, I], 1996 It, E, S, I, F 1
Lewis, G (Pontypridd, Swansea) 1998 SA 1(R), 1999 It (R), Arg 2, C, [J], 2000 F (R), It, S, I, Sm, US (t+R), 2001 F (R), J 1, 2, R, I
Lewis, G W (Richmond) 1960 E, S
Lewis, H (Swansea) 1913 S, F, I, 1914 E
Lewis, J G (Llanelli) 1887 I
Lewis, J M C (Cardiff, Cambridge U) 1912 E, 1913 S, F, I, 1914 E, S, F, I, 1921 I, 1923 E, S
Lewis, J R (S Glam Inst, Cardiff) 1981 E, S, I, F, 1982 F, E, S
Lewis, M (Treorchy) 1913 F
Lewis, P I (Llanelli) 1984 A, 1985 S, I, F, E, 1986 E, S, I
Lewis, R A (Abertillery) 1966 E, S, I, F, A, 1967 I
Lewis, T W (Cardiff) 1926 E, 1927 E, S
Lewis, W (Llanelli) 1925 F
Lewis, W H (London Welsh, Cambridge U) 1926 I, 1927 E, F, I, A, 1928 F
Lewis-Roberts, E T (Sale) 2008 C(R)
Llewellyn, D S (Ebbw Vale, Newport) 1998 SA 1(R), 1999 F 1(R), It (R), [J (R)]
Llewellyn, G D (Neath) 1990 Nm 1, 2, Bb, 1991 E, S, I, F 1, A, F 2
Llewellyn, G O (Neath, Harlequins, Ospreys, Narbonne) 1989 NZ, 1990 E, S, I, 1991 E, S, A (R), 1992 I, F, E, S, A, 1993 E, S, I, F, Z 1, 2, Nm, J, C, 1994 S, I, F, E, Pt, Sp, C, Tg, WS, R, It, SA, 1995 F, E, S, I, [J, NZ, I], 1996 It, E, S, I, F 1, A 1, 2, Bb, F 2, It, A 3, SA, 1997 US, S, I, F, E, US 1, 2, NZ, 1998 It, E, 1999 C (R), [Sm], 2002 E (R), SA 1, 2, R(R), Fj, C, NZ, 2003 It (R), S I(R), I 1, F, A, NZ, I 2, S 2(R), [C, Tg, It, E(R)], 2004 S, F(R), E(R), It, Arg 1, 2, SA1, R, NZ
Llewellyn, P D (Swansea) 1973 I, F, A, 1974 S, E
Llewellyn, W (Llwynypia) 1899 E, S, I, 1900 E, S, I, 1901 E, S, I, 1902 E, S, I, 1903 I, 1904 E, S, I, 1905 E, S, I, NZ
Llewelyn, D B (Newport, Llanelli) 1970 SA, S, E, I, F, 1971 E, S, I, F, 1972 E, S, F, NZ

Mustoe, L (Cardiff) 1995 Fj, 1996 A 1(R), 2, 1997 US 1, 2, C, R (R), 1998 E (R), I (R), F (R)

Nash, D (Ebbw Vale) 1960 SA, 1961 E, S, I, F, 1962 F
Navidi, J R (Cardiff Blues) 2013 J2
Newman, C H (Newport) 1881 E, 1882 I, 1883 E, S, 1884 E, S, 1885 E, S, 1886 E, 1887 E
Nicholas, D L (Llanelli) 1981 E, S, I, F
Nicholas, T J (Cardiff) 1919 NZA
Nicholl, C B (Cambridge U, Llanelli) 1891 I, 1892 E, S, I, 1893 E, S, I, 1894 E, S, 1895 E, S, I, 1896 E, S, I
Nicholl, D W (Llanelli) 1894 I
Nicholls, E G (Cardiff) 1896 S, I, 1897 E, 1898 I, E, 1899 E, S, I, 1900 S, I, 1901 E, S, I, 1902 E, S, I, 1903 I, 1904 E, 1905 I, NZ, 1906 E, S, I, SA
Nicholls, F E (Cardiff Harlequins) 1892 I
Nicholls, H C W (Cardiff) 1958 I
Nicholls, S H (Cardiff) 1888 M, 1889 S, I, 1891 S
Norris, C H (Cardiff) 1963 F, 1966 F
Norster, R L (Cardiff) 1982 S, 1983 E, S, I, F, 1984 S, I, F, E, A, 1985 S, I, F, E, Fj, 1986 Fj, Tg, WS, 1987 F, E, S, I, [I, C, E], US, 1988 E, S, I, F, NZ 1, WS, 1989 F, E
North, G P (Scarlets, Northampton) 2010 SA2, Fj, NZ3, 2011 F, Bb, E2, 3, Arg, [SA, Sm, Nm(R), Fj, I, F, A], A, 2012 I, S, E, It, F, A 1, 2, 3, Arg, Sm, 2013 I, F, It, S, E, SA, Arg, Tg, A, 2014 It, I, F, E, S, SA1, 2
Norton, W B (Cardiff) 1882 I, 1883 E, S, 1884 E, S, I

Oakley, R L (Gwent Dragons) 2003 I 2, S 2(R)
O'Connor, A (Aberavon) 1960 SA, 1961 E, S, 1962 F, I
O'Connor, R (Aberavon) 1957 E
O'Neil, W (Cardiff) 1904 S, I, 1905 E, S, I, 1907 E, I, 1908 E, S, F, I
O'Shea, J P (Cardiff) 1967 S, I, 1968 S, I, F
Oliver, G (Pontypool) 1920 E, S, F, I
Osborne, W T (Mountain Ash) 1902 E, S, I, 1903 E, S, I
Ould, W J (Cardiff) 1924 E
Owen, A D (Swansea) 1924 E
Owen, G D (Newport) 1955 I, F, 1956 E, S, I, F
Owen, M J (Pontypridd, Newport Gwent Dragons) 2002 SA 1, 2, R, C(R), NZ(R), 2003 It, I 2, S 2, 2004 S(R), I(R), F, It, Arg 1, 2, SA2, R, NZ, J, 2005 E, It, F, S, I, NZ, Fj, SA, A, 2006 E, S, I, It, F, Pl, 2007 A1(R), 2, E2, [C(R), A(R), J(R), Fj(R)]
Owen, R M (Swansea) 1901 I, 1902 E, S, I, 1903 E, S, I, 1904 E, S, I, 1905 E, S, I, NZ, 1906 E, S, I, SA, 1907 E, S, 1908 F, I, A, 1909 E, S, F, I, 1910 F, E, 1911 E, S, F, I, 1912 E, S
Owens, K J (Scarlets) 2011 [Nm(R)], 2012 S(t&R), E, It(R), F(R), A1, 3(R), Sm(R), NZ(R), A4(R), 2013 I(t&R), F(R), It(R), S(R), E(R), SA(R), Arg(R), Tg, A(R), 2014 It(R), I(R), F(R), E(R), S, SA1, 2

Packer, H (Newport) 1891 E, 1895 S, I, 1896 E, S, I, 1897 E
Palmer, F C (Swansea) 1922 E, S, I
Parfitt, F C (Newport) 1893 E, S, I, 1894 E, S, I, 1895 S, 1896 S, I
Parfitt, S A (Swansea) 1990 Nm 1(R), Bb
Parker, D S (Swansea) 1924 I, F, NZ, 1925 E, S, F, I, 1929 F, I, 1930 E
Parker, E T (Swansea) 1919 NZA, 1920 E, S, I, 1921 E, S, F, I, 1922 E, S, I, F, 1923 E, S, F .
Parker, S T (Pontypridd, Celtic Warriors, Newport Gwent Dragons, Ospreys) 2002 R, Fj, C, NZ, 2003 E 2, [C, It, NZ], 2004 S, I, F, It, Arg 1, SA 1, 2, NZ, 2005 Fj, SA, A, 2006 PI, C, NZ, 2007 A1, 2, F2(t&R), [C, A], SA, 2008 E, S(R), It(R), SA1
Parker, W J (Swansea) 1899 E, S
Parks, R D (Pontypridd, Celtic Warriors) 2002 SA 1(R), Fj(R), 2003 I 2, S 2
Parsons, G (Newport) 1947 E
Pascoe, D (Bridgend) 1923 F, I
Pask, A E I (Abertillery) 1961 F, 1962 E, S, F, I, 1963 E, S, I, F, NZ, 1964 E, S, I, F, SA, 1965 E, S, I, F, 1966 S, I, F, A, 1967 S, I
Patchell, M R (Cardiff Blues) 2013 J1(R), 2(R)
Payne, G W (Army, Pontypridd) 1960 E, S, I
Payne, H (Swansea) 1935 NZ
Peacock, H (Newport) 1929 S, F, I, 1930 S, I, F

Peake, E (Chepstow) 1881 E
Pearce, P G (Bridgend) 1981 I, F, 1982 I (R)
Pearson, T W (Cardiff, Newport) 1891 E, I, 1892 E, S, 1894 S, I, 1895 E, S, I, 1897 E, 1898 I, E, 1903 E
Peel, D J (Llanelli Scarlets, Sale) 2001 J 2(R), R (R), Tg (R), 2002 I (R), It (R), E (R), S (R), SA 1, 2, R, Fj, C, NZ, 2003 It, S 1(R), I 1(R), F, NZ(R), I 2, S 2, [C(R), Tg(R), It, NZ(R), E(R)], 2004 S(R), I(R), F(R), E(R), It(R), Arg 1, 2, SA1, 2, R, NZ, 2005 E, It, F, S, I, 2006 E, S, I, It, A, C, NZ, 2007 I, S, F1, It, E1, Arg, F2, [C, A, Fj], SA, 2008 It, SA3(R), C(R), NZ(R), 2009 S(R), E(R), F(R), C(R), US, Sm, Arg(R), A, 2010 I(R), It(R), 2011 E1(R), F(R)
Pegge, E V (Neath) 1891 E
Perego, M A (Llanelli) 1990 S, 1993 F, Z 1, Nm (R), 1994 S, I, F, E, Sp
Perkins, S J (Pontypool) 1983 S, I, F, R, 1984 S, I, F, E, A, 1985 S, I, F, E, Fj, 1986 E, S, I, F
Perrett, F L (Neath) 1912 SA, 1913 E, S, F, I
Perrins, V C (Newport) 1970 SA, S
Perry, W J (Neath) 1911 E
Phillips, A J (Cardiff) 1979 E, 1980 F, E, S, I, NZ, 1981 E, S, I, F, A, 1982 I, F, E, S, 1987 [C, E, A]
Phillips, B (Aberavon) 1925 E, S, F, I, 1926 E
Phillips, D E (Scarlets) 2013 J1, 2, Tg(R)
Phillips, D H (Swansea) 1952 F
Phillips, H P (Newport) 1892 E, 1893 E, S, I, 1894 E, S
Phillips, H T (Newport) 1927 E, S, F, I, A, 1928 E, S, I, F
Phillips, K H (Neath) 1987 F, [I, Tg, NZ], US, 1988 E, NZ 1, 1989 NZ, 1990 F, E, S, I, Nm 1, 2, Bb, 1991 E, S, I, F 1, A
Phillips, L A (Newport) 1900 E, S, I, 1901 S
Phillips, R D (Neath) 1987 US, 1988 E, S, I, F, NZ 1, 2, WS, 1989 S, I
Phillips, W D (Cardiff) 1881 E, 1882 I, 1884 E, S, I
Phillips, W M (Llanelli Scarlets, Cardiff Blues, Ospreys, Bayonne, Racing Métro) 2003 R, 2004 Arg 1(R), 2(R), J(R), 2005 US, C, NZ, Fj(R), SA(R), 2006 S(R), It(R), F, Arg 1, 2, PI, C(R), NZ(R), 2007 I(R), F1(R), E1(R), A1, 2, F2(R), [C(R), A(R), J, Fj(R)], SA(R), 2008 E, S, It(R), I, F, 2009 S, E, F, It, I, 2010 It, SA1, NZ1, 2, A, SA2, Fj(R), NZ3, 2011 E1, S, It, I, F, Bb, E2, 3, [SA, Sm, Fj, I, F, A], 2012 I, S, E, It, F, A 1, 2, 3, Arg(R), Sm, NZ, A4, 2013 I, F, It, S, E, SA, Arg, A, 2014 It, I, F(R), S, SA1, 2
Pickering, D F (Llanelli) 1983 E, S, I, F, R, 1984 S, I, F, E, A, 1985 S, I, F, E, Fj, 1986 E, S, I, F, Fj, 1987 F, E, S
Plummer, R C S (Newport) 1912 S, I, F, SA, 1913 E
Pook, T R (Newport) 1895 S
Popham, A J (Leeds, Llanelli Scarlets) 2003 A (R), I 2, R, S 2, [Tg, NZ], 2004 I(R), It(R), SA1, J(R), 2005 C, Fj(R), 2006 E(R), It(R), F, Arg 1, 2, PI, NZ(R), 2007 I, S, F1, It, E1, 2(R), Arg, F2, [C, A(t), J, Fj], SA(R), 2008 E(R)
Powell, A T (Cardiff Blues, Wasps, Sale) 2008 SA3, C(R), NZ, A, 2009 S, F, It, NZ, Sm, Arg, A, NZ2, NZ3(R), 2011 E1, Arg, [Sm(R), Nm(R), Fj(R), A(R)], 2012 S(R)
Powell, G (Ebbw Vale) 1957 I, F
Powell, J (Cardiff) 1923 I
Powell, J A (Cardiff) 1906 I
Powell, R D (Cardiff) 2002 SA 1(R), 2(R), C(R)
Powell, R W (Newport) 1888 S, I
Powell, W C (London Welsh) 1926 S, I, F, 1927 E, F, I, 1928 S, I, F, 1929 S, F, I, 1930 S, I, F, 1931 E, S, F, I, SA, 1932 E, S, I, 1935 E, S, I
Powell, W J (Cardiff) 1920 E, S, F, I
Pretorius, W A (Cardiff Blues) 2013 J1(R), 2
Price, B (Newport) 1961 I, F, 1962 E, S, 1963 E, S, F, NZ, 1964 E, S, I, F, SA, 1965 E, S, I, F, 1966 E, S, I, F, A, 1967 S, I, F, E, 1969 S, I, F, NZ 1, 2, A
Price, G (Pontypool) 1975 F, E, S, I, A, 1976 E, S, I, F, 1977 I, F, E, S, 1978 E, S, I, F, A 1, 2, NZ, 1979 S, I, F, E, 1980 F, E, S, I, NZ, 1981 E, S, I, F, A, 1982 I, F, E, S, 1983 E, I, F
Price, M J (Pontypool, RAF) 1959 E, S, I, F, 1960 E, S, I, F, 1962 E
Price, R E (Weston-s-Mare) 1939 S, I
Price, T G (Llanelli) 1965 E, S, I, F, 1966 E, A, 1967 S, F
Priday, A J (Cardiff) 1958 I, 1961 I
Priestland, R (Scarlets) 2011 S(R), Bb(R), E2, 3, [SA, Sm, Nm(R), Fj, I], A, 2012 I, S, E, It, F, A 1, 2, 3, Arg, Sm(R), NZ, A4, 2013 SA, Tg(R), A(R), 2014 It, I, F, E, S(R)

Rowlands, G (RAF, Cardiff) 1953 NZ, 1954 E, F, 1956 F
Rowlands, K A (Cardiff) 1962 F, I, 1963 I, 1965 I, F
Rowles, G A (Penarth) 1892 E
Rowley, M (Pontypridd) 1996 SA, 1997 US, S, I, F, R
Roy, W S (Cardiff) 1995 [J (R)]
Russell, S (London Welsh) 1987 US

Samuel, D (Swansea) 1891 I, 1893 I
Samuel, J (Swansea) 1891 I
Samuel, T F (Mountain Ash) 1922 S, I, F
Scourfield, T B (Torquay Athletic) 1930 F
Scrine, F G (Swansea) 1899 E, S, 1901 I
Selley, T J (Llanelli Scarlets) 2005 US(R)
Shanklin, J L (London Welsh) 1970 F, 1972 NZ, 1973 I, F
Shanklin, T G L (Saracens, Cardiff Blues) 2001 J 2, 2002 F, It, SA
  1(R), 2(R), R, Fj, 2003 It, E 1, S 1, I 1, F(t+R), A, NZ, S 2, [Tg,
  NZ], 2004 I(R), F(R), E, It(R), Arg 1(R), 2, SA1, 2(R), R, NZ, J,
  2005 E, It, F, S, I, 2006 A, C, NZ, 2007 S(R), F1, It, E1, 2, Arg,
  [C, A, J(R), Fj], SA, 2008 E(R), S, It, I, F, SA1, 2, 3, C, NZ, A,
  2009 S, E, F, It(R), I, NZ, Sm, 2010 It(R), A, SA2, Fj(R), NZ3
Shaw, G (Neath) 1972 NZ, 1973 E, S, I, F, A, 1974 S, I, F, E,
  1977 I, F
Shaw, T W (Newbridge) 1983 R
Shea, J (Newport) 1919 NZA, 1920 E, S, 1921 E
Shell, R C (Aberavon) 1973 A (R)
Shingler, A C (Scarlets) 2012 S, Bb(R), NZ(R), A4, 2013 I, F(R),
  E(R), 2014 SA1
Sidoli, R A (Pontypridd, Celtic Warriors, Cardiff Blues) 2002 SA
  1(R), 2(R), R, Fj, NZ, 2003 It, E 1, S 1, I 1, F, A, NZ, E 2,
  [C(R), Tg, It(R), NZ, E], 2004 I, It(R), 2005 E, It, F, S, I, C,
  NZ, Fj(R), SA, A, 2006 E, S, I, It, F, PI, C(R), 2007 I(t&R),
  S, A1, 2, E2
Simpson, H J (Cardiff) 1884 E, S, I
Sinkinson, B D (Neath) 1999 F 1, It, E, Arg 1, 2, SA, F 2, [Arg
  3, J, Sm, A], 2000 F, It, E, 2001 R (R), I, Arg (R), Tg, A,
  2002 It (R)
Skrimshire, R T (Newport) 1899 E, S, I
Skym, A (Llanelli) 1928 E, S, I, F, 1930 E, S, I, F, 1931 E, S,
  F, I, SA, 1932 E, S, I, 1933 E, S, I, 1935 E
Smith, J S (Cardiff) 1884 E, I, 1885 E
Smith, N (Ebbw Vale) 2000 F (R)
Sowden-Taylor, R (Cardiff Blues) 2005 It(R), C(R), NZ(R), 2007
  A2(R), SA, 2008 C, 2009 C, US
Sparks, B A (Neath) 1954 I, 1955 E, F, 1956 E, S, I, 1957 S
Spiller, W (Cardiff) 1910 S, I, 1911 E, S, F, I, 1912 E, F, SA,
  1913 E
Spratt, J P (Ospreys) 2009 C(R), US(R), 2013 J1, 2
Squire, J (Newport, Pontypool) 1977 I, F, 1978 E, S, I, F, A 1,
  NZ, 1979 S, I, F, E, 1980 F, E, S, I, NZ, 1981 E, S, I, F, A,
  1982 I, F, E, 1983 E, S, I, F
Stadden, W J (Cardiff) 1884 I, 1886 E, S, 1887 I, 1888 S, M,
  1890 S, E
Stephens, C (Bridgend) 1998 E (R), 2001 J 2(R)
Stephens, C J (Llanelli) 1992 I, F, E, A
Stephens, G (Neath) 1912 E, S, I, F, SA, 1913 E, S, F, I, 1919 NZA
Stephens, I (Bridgend) 1981 E, S, I, F, A, 1982 I, F, E, S, 1984
  I, F, E, A
Stephens, Rev J G (Llanelli) 1922 E, S, I, F
Stephens, J R G (Neath) 1947 E, S, F, I, 1948 I, 1949 S, I, F,
  1951 F, SA, 1952 E, S, I, F, 1953 E, S, I, F, NZ, 1954 E, I,
  1955 E, S, I, F, 1956 S, I, F, 1957 E, S, I, F
Stock, A (Newport) 1924 F, NZ, 1926 E, S
Stoddart, M L (Llanelli Scarlets) 2007 SA, 2008 SA1(R), C, 2011
  E1, S, It, Bb, E2
Stone, P (Llanelli) 1949 F
Strand-Jones, J (Llanelli) 1902 E, S, I, 1903 E, S
Sullivan, A C (Cardiff) 2001 Arg, Tg
Summers, R H B (Haverfordwest) 1881 E
Sutton, S (Pontypool, S Wales Police) 1982 F, E, 1987 F, E, S,
  I, [C, NZ (R), A]
Sweeney, C (Pontypridd, Celtic Warriors, Newport Gwent
  Dragons) 2003 It(R), E 1, NZ(R), I, 2, S 2, [C, It, NZ(R),
  E(t)], 2004 I(R), F(R), E(R), It(R), Arg 1, SA1(R), 2(R), R(R),
  J, 2005 It(R), F(t), S(R), US, C, NZ, Fj(R), SA(t&R), A(R),
  2006 PI, C(R), 2007 S(t), A2(R), E2, F2(R), [J(R)], SA(R)
Sweet-Escott, R B (Cardiff) 1891 S, 1894 I, 1895 I

Tamplin, W E (Cardiff) 1947 S, F, I, A, 1948 E, S, F
Tanner, H (Swansea, Cardiff) 1935 NZ, 1936 E, S, I, 1937 E,
  S, I, 1938 E, S, I, 1939 E, S, I, 1947 E, S, F, I, 1948 E, S,
  F, I, 1949 E, S, I, F
Tarr, D J (Swansea, Royal Navy) 1935 NZ
Taylor, A R (Cross Keys) 1937 I, 1938 I, 1939 E
Taylor, C G (Ruabon) 1884 E, S, I, 1885 E, S, 1886 E, S, 1887
  E, I
Taylor, H T (Cardiff) 1994 Pt, C, Fj, Tg, WS (R), R, It, SA, 1995
  E, S, [J, NZ, I], SA, Fj, 1996 It, E, S, I, F 1, A 1, 2, It, A 3
Taylor, J (London Welsh) 1967 S, I, F, E, NZ, 1968 I, F, 1969
  S, I, F, E, NZ, 1, A, 1970 F, 1971 E, S, I, F, 1972 E, S, F,
  NZ, 1973 E, S, I, F
Taylor, M (Pontypool, Swansea, Llanelli Scarlets, Sale) 1994
  SA, 1995 F, E, SA (R), 1998 Z, SA 1, 2, Arg, 1999 I, F 1, It,
  E, Arg 1, 2, SA, F 2, [Arg 3, J, Sm, A], 2000 F, It, E, S, Sm,
  US, 2001 E, S, F, It, 2002 S, SA 1, 2, 2003 E 1, S 1, I 1,
  F, A, NZ, E 2, [C(R), Tg, NZ, E], 2004 F, E, It, R(R), 2005 I,
  US, C, NZ
Thomas, A C (Bristol, Swansea) 1996 It, E, S, I, F 2(R), SA,
  1997 US, S, I, F, US 1, 2, C, R, NZ (t), 1998 It, E, S (R),
  Z, SA 1, 2000 Sm, US, SA (R)
Thomas, A R F (Newport) 1963 NZ, 1964 E
Thomas, A G (Swansea, Cardiff) 1952 E, S, I, F, 1953 S, I, F,
  1954 E, I, F, 1955 S, I, F
Thomas, B (Neath, Cambridge U) 1963 E, S, I, F, NZ, 1964 E,
  S, I, F, SA, 1965 E, 1966 E, S, I, 1967 NZ, 1969 S, I, F, E,
  NZ 1, 2
Thomas, B M G (St Bart's Hospital) 1919 NZA, 1921 S, F, I,
  1923 F, 1924 E
Thomas, C J (Newport) 1888 I, M, 1889 S, I, 1890 S, E, I, 1891
  E, I
Thomas, C R (Bridgend) 1925 E, S
Thomas, D J (Swansea) 1904 E, 1908 A, 1910 E, S, I, 1911 E,
  S, F, I, 1912 E
Thomas, D J (Swansea) 1930 S, I, 1932 E, S, I, 1933 E, S,
  1934 E, 1935 E, S, I
Thomas, D L (Neath) 1937 E
Thomas, D L (Aberavon) 1961 I
Thomas, E (Newport) 1904 S, I, 1909 S, F, I, 1910 F
Thomas, E J R (Mountain Ash) 1906 SA, 1908 F, I, 1909 S
Thomas, G (Newport) 1888 M, 1890 I, 1891 S
Thomas, G (Bridgend, Cardiff, Celtic Warriors, Toulouse, Cardiff
  Blues) 1995 [J, NZ, I], SA, Fj, 1996 F 1, A 1, 2, Bb, F 2,
  It, A 3, 1997 US, S, I, F, E, US 1, 2, C, R, Tg, NZ, 1998 It,
  E, S, I, F, SA 2, Arg, 1999 F 1(R), It, E, Arg 2, SA, F 2, [Arg
  3, J (R), Sm, A], 2000 F, It, E, S, I, US, SA, 2001 E, F,
  It, J 1, 2, R, Arg, Tg, A, 2002 E, R, Fj, C, NZ, 2003 It, E
  1, S 1, I 1, F, I 2, E 2, [C, It, NZ(R), E], 2004 S, I, F, E, It,
  SA2, R, NZ, 2005 E, It, F, NZ, SA, A, 2006 E, S, A, C, 2007
  It(t&R), E1, A1, 2, E2, Arg, F2, [C(R), A, Fj]
Thomas, G M (Bath, Ospreys, Llanelli Scarlets, Newport Gwent
  Dragons) 2001 J 1, 2, R, I (R), Arg, Tg (R), A (R), 2002 S
  (R), SA 2(R), R(R), 2003 It(R), E 1, S 1, F, E 2(R), R, 2006
  Arg 1, 2, PI, 2007 I(t&R), A1, 2, 2010 NZ1, 2
Thomas, H H M (Llanelli) 1912 F
Thomas, H W (Swansea) 1912 SA, 1913 E
Thomas, H W (Neath) 1936 E, S, I, 1937 E, S, I
Thomas, I (Bryncethin) 1924 E
Thomas, I D (Ebbw Vale, Llanelli Scarlets) 2000 Sm, US (R),
  SA (R), 2001 J 1, 2, R, I, Arg (R), Tg, 2002 It, E, S, SA 1,
  2, Fj, C, NZ, 2003 It, E 1, S 1, I 1, F, A, NZ, E 2, [Tg, NZ,
  E], 2004 I, F, 2007 A1, 2, E2
Thomas, J D (Llanelli) 1954 I
Thomas, J J (Swansea, Ospreys) 2003 A, NZ(R), E 2(R), R,
  [It(R), NZ, E], 2004 S(t&R), I, F, E, Arg 2(R), SA1(R), R(t&R),
  J, 2005 E(R), It, F(R), S(R), US, C, NZ, 2006 It(R), F(R), A,
  PI(R), C, NZ, 2007 S(R), F1(R), It(R), E1(R), A1, 2, Arg, F2,
  [C, A], SA, 2008 E, S, It, I, F, SA1, 2, 2009 It, Sm(R), Arg(R),
  A(R), 2010 E(R), S, F, I, It, SA1, NZ1, 2, A, SA2, Fj, NZ3(R),
  2011 E1(R), S(R), I(R), F(R), Arg(R)
Thomas, L C (Cardiff) 1885 E, S
Thomas, M C (Newport, Devonport Services) 1949 F, 1950 E,
  S, I, F, 1951 E, S, I, F, SA, 1952 E, S, I, F, 1953 E, 1956
  E, S, I, F, 1957 E, S, 1958 E, S, I, F, 1959 I, F
Thomas, N (Bath) 1996 SA (R), 1997 US 1(R), 2, C (R), R, Tg,
  NZ, 1998 Z, SA 1

WALES

Thomas, R (Swansea) 1900 E, S, I, 1901 E
Thomas, R (Pontypool) 1909 F, I, 1911 S, F, 1912 E, S, SA, 1913 E
Thomas, R C C (Swansea) 1949 F, 1952 I, F, 1953 S, I, F, NZ, 1954 E, I, F, S, 1955 S, I, 1956 E, S, I, 1957 E, 1958 A, E, S, I, F, 1959 E, S, I, F
Thomas, R L (London Welsh) 1889 S, I, 1890 I, 1891 E, S, I, 1892 E
Thomas, R M (Newport Gwent Dragons) 2006 Arg 2(R), 2007 E2(R), SA, 2008 It, SA2, C, 2009 It
Thomas, S (Llanelli) 1890 S, E, 1891 I
Thomas, S G (Llanelli) 1923 E, S, F, I
Thomas, T R (Cardiff Blues) 2005 US(R), C, NZ(R), Fj, SA, A, 2006 E, S, I, It, F, PI, C(R), NZ, 2007 I, S, F1(R), It(R), E1(R), 2(R), F2(R), [C(R), A(R), J, Fj(R)], SA(R), 2008 SA2(R)
Thomas, W D (Llanelli) 1966 A, 1968 S, I, F, 1969 E, NZ 2, A, 1970 SA, S, E, I, F, 1971 E, S, I, F, 1972 E, S, F, NZ, 1973 E, S, I, F, 1974 E
Thomas, W G (Llanelli, Waterloo, Swansea) 1927 E, S, F, I, 1929 E, 1931 E, S, SA, 1932 E, S, I, 1933 E, S, I
Thomas, W H (Llandovery Coll, Cambridge U) 1885 S, 1886 E, S, 1887 E, S, 1888 S, I, 1890 E, I, 1891 S, I
Thomas, W J (Cardiff) 1961 F, 1963 F
Thomas, W J L (Llanelli, Cardiff) 1995 SA, Fj, 1996 It, E, S, I, F 1, 1996 Bb (R), 1997 US
Thomas, W L (Newport) 1894 S, 1895 E, I
Thomas, W T (Abertillery) 1930 E
Thompson, J F (Cross Keys) 1923 E
Thorburn, P H (Neath) 1985 F, E, Fj, 1986 E, S, I, F, 1987 F, [I, Tg, C, E, NZ, A], US, 1988 S, I, F, WS, R (R), 1989 S, I, F, E, NZ, 1990 F, E, S, I, Nm 1, 2, Bb, 1991 E, S, I, F 1, A
Tipuric, J C (Ospreys) 2011 Arg(R), A(R), 2012 I(R), It, Bb, A 3(R), Arg(R), Sm, NZ(R), A4(R), 2013 I(R), F, It, S(R), E, SA(R), Arg, Tg, A(R), 2014 It, I(R), F(R), E(R), S(R)
Titley, M H (Bridgend, Swansea) 1983 R, 1984 S, I, F, E, A, 1985 S, I, Fj, 1986 F, Fj, Tg, WS, 1990 F, E
Towers, W H (Swansea) 1887 I, 1888 M
Travers, G (Pill Harriers, Newport) 1903 E, S, I, 1905 E, S, I, NZ, 1906 E, S, I, SA, 1907 E, S, I, 1908 E, S, F, I, A, 1909 E, S, I, 1911 S, F, I
Travers, W H (Newport) 1937 S, I, 1938 E, S, I, 1939 E, S, I, 1949 E, S, I, F
Treharne, E (Pontypridd) 1881 E, 1883 E
Trew, W J (Swansea) 1900 E, S, I, 1901 E, S, 1903 S, 1905 S, 1906 S, 1907 E, S, 1908 E, S, F, I, A, 1909 E, S, F, I, 1910 F, E, S, 1911 E, S, F, I, 1912 S, 1913 S, F
Trott, R F (Cardiff) 1948 E, S, F, I, 1949 E, S, I, F
Truman, W H (Llanelli) 1934 E, 1935 E
Trump, L C (Newport) 1912 E, S, I, F
Turnbull, B R (Cardiff) 1925 I, 1927 E, S, 1928 E, F, 1930 S
Turnbull, J (Scarlets) 2011 S(R), Bb(R), E3(R), 2012 Bb, Arg, 2014 SA1(R), 2
Turnbull, M J L (Cardiff) 1933 E, I
Turner, P (Newbridge) 1989 I (R), F, E

Uzzell, H (Newport) 1912 E, S, I, F, 1913 S, F, I, 1914 E, S, F, I, 1920 E, S, F, I
Uzzell, J R (Newport) 1963 NZ, 1965 E, S, I, F

Vickery, W E (Aberavon) 1938 E, S, I, 1939 E
Vile, T H (Newport) 1908 E, S, 1910 I, 1912 I, F, SA, 1913 E, 1921 S
Vincent, H C (Bangor) 1882 I
Voyle, M J (Newport, Llanelli, Cardiff) 1996 A 1(t), F 2, 1997 E, US 1, 2, C, Tg, NZ, 1998 It, E, S, I, F, Arg (R), 1999 S (R), I (t), It (R), SA (R), F 2(R), [J, A (R)], 2000 F (R)

Wakeford, J D M (S Wales Police) 1988 WS, R
Waldron, R G (Neath) 1965 E, S, I, F
Walker, N (Cardiff) 1993 I, F, J, 1994 S, F, E, Pt, Sp, 1995 F, E, 1997 US 1, 2, C, R (R), Tg, NZ, 1998 E
Waller, P D (Newport) 1908 A, 1909 E, S, F, I, 1910 F
Walne, N J (Richmond, Cardiff) 1999 It (R), E (R), C
Walters, N (Llanelli) 1902 E
Wanbon, R (Aberavon) 1968 E
Warburton, S K (Cardiff Blues) 2009 US(R), Sm, A(R), 2010 S(R), I(R), It, SA1, A, NZ3, 2011 E1, S, It, I, F, Bb, E2, 3,

[SA, Sm, Nm, Fj, I, F], A, 2012 I, E, F, A1, 2, 3, Arg, Sm(R), NZ, A4, 2013 I, It(R), S, E, SA, Arg, A, 2014 It(R), I, F, E, S
Ward, W S (Cross Keys) 1934 S, I
Warlow, D J (Llanelli) 1962 I
Warren, A R (Scarlets) 2012 Bb(R)
Waters, D R (Newport) 1986 E, S, I, F
Waters, K (Newbridge) 1991 [WS]
Watkins, D (Newport) 1963 E, S, I, F, NZ, 1964 E, S, I, F, SA, 1965 E, S, I, F, 1966 E, S, I, F, 1967 I, F, E
Watkins, E (Neath) 1924 E, S, I, F
Watkins, E (Blaina) 1926 S, I, F
Watkins, E V (Cardiff) 1935 NZ, 1937 S, I, 1938 E, S, I, 1939 E, S
Watkins, H V (Llanelli) 1904 S, I, 1905 E, S, I, 1906 E
Watkins, I J (Ebbw Vale) 1988 E (R), S, I, F, NZ 2, R, 1989 S, I, F, E
Watkins, L (Oxford U, Llandaff) 1881 E
Watkins, M J (Newport) 1984 I, F, E, A
Watkins, M J (Llanelli Scarlets) 2003 It(R), E 1(R), S 1(R), I 1(R), R, S 2, 2005 US(R), C(R), Fj, SA(R), A, 2006 E, S, I, It, F, Arg 1, 2(R)
Watkins, S J (Newport, Cardiff ) 1964 S, I, F, 1965 E, S, I, F, 1966 E, S, I, F, A, 1967 S, I, F, E, NZ, 1968 E, S, 1969 S, I, F, E, NZ 1, 1970 E, I
Watkins, W R (Newport) 1959 F
Watts, D (Maesteg) 1914 E, S, F, I
Watts, J (Llanelli) 1907 E, S, I, 1908 E, S, F, I, A, 1909 S, F, I
Watts, W H (Newport) 1892 E, S, I, 1893 E, S, I, 1894 E, S, I, 1895 E, I, 1896 E
Watts, W J (Llanelli) 1914 E
Weatherley, D J (Swansea) 1998 Z
Weaver, D S (Swansea) 1964 E
Webb, A (Jim) (Abertillery) 1907 S, 1908 E, S, F, I, A, 1909 E, S, F, I, 1910 F, E, S, I, 1911 E, S, F, I, 1912 E, S
Webb, J (Newport) 1888 M, 1889 S
Webb, R (Ospreys) 2012 It(R), Bb(R), A2(R) , 2014 It(R), F, E
Webbe, G M C (Bridgend) 1986 Tg (R), WS, 1987 F, E, S, [Tg], US, 1988 F (R), NZ 1, R
Webster, R E (Swansea) 1987 [A], 1990 Bb, 1991 [Arg, A], 1992 A, S, A, 1993 E, S, I, F
Wells, G T (Cardiff) 1955 E, S, 1957 I, F, 1958 A, E, S
Westacott, D (Cardiff) 1906 I
Wetter, J J (Newport) 1914 S, F, I, 1920 E, S, F, I, 1921 E, 1924 I, NZ
Wetter, W H (Newport) 1912 SA, 1913 E
Wheel, G A D (Swansea) 1974 I, E (R), 1975 F, E, I, A, 1976 E, S, I, F, 1977 I, E, S, 1978 E, S, I, F, A 1, 2, NZ, 1979 S, I, 1980 F, E, S, I, 1981 E, S, I, F, A, 1982 I
Wheeler, P J (Aberavon) 1967 NZ, 1968 E
Whitefoot, J (Cardiff) 1984 A (R), 1985 S, I, F, E, Fj, 1986 E, S, I, F, Fj, Tg, WS, 1987 F, E, S, I, [I, C]
Whitfield, J J (Newport) 1919 NZA, 1920 E, S, F, I, 1921 E, 1922 E, S, I, F, 1924 S, I
Whitson, G K (Newport) 1956 F, 1960 S, I
Wilkins, G (Bridgend) 1994 Tg
Williams, A (Ospreys, Bath) 2003 R (R), 2005 v US(R), C(R), 2006 Arg 2(R), 2007 A2(R)
Williams, B (Llanelli) 1920 S, F, I
Williams, B H (Neath, Richmond, Bristol) 1996 F 2, 1997 R, Tg, NZ, 1998 It, E, Z (R), SA 1, Arg (R), 1999 S (R), I, It (R), 2000 F (R), It (R), E (t+R), 2001 R (R), I (R), Tg (R), A (R), 2002 I (R), F (R), It (R), E (R), S
Williams, B L (Cardiff) 1947 E, S, F, I, A, 1948 E, S, F, I, 1949 E, S, I, 1951 I, SA, 1952 S, 1953 E, S, I, F, NZ, 1954 S, 1955 E
Williams, B R (Neath) 1990 S, I, Bb, 1991 E, S
Williams, C (Llanelli) 1924 NZ, 1925 E
Williams, C (Aberavon, Swansea) 1977 E, S, 1980 F, E, S, I, NZ, 1983 E
Williams, C D (Cardiff, Neath) 1955 F, 1956 F
Williams, D (Ebbw Vale) 1963 E, S, I, F, 1964 E, S, I, F, SA, 1965 E, S, I, F, 1966 E, S, I, A, 1967 F, E, NZ, 1968 E, 1969 S, I, F, E, NZ 1, 2, A, 1970 SA, S, E, I, 1971 E, S, I, F
Williams, D (Llanelli) 1998 SA 1(R)
Williams, D A (Bridgend, Swansea) 1990 Nm 2(R), 1995 Fj (R)

Williams, **D B** (Newport, Swansea) 1978 A 1, 1981 E, S
Williams, **E** (Neath) 1924 NZ, 1925 F
Williams, **E** (Aberavon) 1925 E, S
Williams, **F L** (Cardiff) 1929 S, F, I, 1930 E, S, I, F, 1931 F, I, SA, 1932 E, S, I, 1933 I
Williams, **G** (London Welsh) 1950 I, F, 1951 E, S, I, F, SA, 1952 E, S, I, F, 1953 NZ, 1954 E
Williams, **G** (Bridgend) 1981 I, F, 1982 E (R), S
Williams, **G J** (Bridgend, Cardiff Blues) 2003 It(R), E 1(R), S 1, F(R), E 2(R), 2009 C(R), US, 2010 E, S
Williams, **G M** (Aberavon) 1936 E, S, I
Williams, **G P** (Bridgend) 1980 NZ, 1981 E, S, A, 1982 I
Williams, **G R** (Cardiff Blues) 2000 I, Sm, US, SA, 2001 S, F, It, R (R), I (R), Arg, Tg (R), A (R), 2002 F (R), It (R), E (R), S, SA 1, 2, R, Fj, C, NZ, 2003 It, E 1, S 1, I 1, F, A, NZ, E 2, [Tg, It(R)], 2004 S, I, F, E, It, Arg1, R, J, 2005 F(R), S, US, C
Williams, **H R** (Llanelli) 1954 S, 1957 F, 1958 A
Williams, **J F** (London Welsh) 1905 I, NZ, 1906 S, SA
Williams, **J J** (Llanelli) 1973 F (R), A, 1974 S, I, F, E, 1975 F, E, S, I, A, 1976 E, S, I, F, 1977 I, F, E, S, 1978 E, S, I, F, A 1, 2, NZ, 1979 S, I, F, E
Williams, **J L** (Cardiff) 1906 SA, 1907 E, S, I, 1908 E, S, I, A, 1909 E, S, F, I, 1910 I, 1911 E, S, F, I
Williams, **J L** (Blaina) 1920 E, S, F, I, 1921 S, F, I
Williams, **J P R** (London Welsh, Bridgend) 1969 S, I, F, E, NZ 1, 2, A, 1970 SA, S, E, I, F, 1971 E, S, I, F, 1972 E, S, F, NZ, 1973 E, S, I, F, A, 1974 S, I, F, 1975 F, E, S, I, A, 1976 E, S, I, F, 1977 I, F, E, S, 1978 E, S, I, F, A 1, 2, NZ, 1979 S, I, F, E, 1980 NZ, 1981 E, S
Williams, **L B** (Scarlets) 2012 Bb, NZ, A4, 2013 J1, 2, SA, Arg, A(R), 2014 I(R), F, E(R), S, SA1, 2
Williams, **L D** (Cardiff Blues) 2011 Arg(R), [Nm(R), Fj(R), A(R)], A, 2012 S(R), F(R), Bb, 2013 I(R), F(R), It(R), S(R), E(R), J1, 2, SA(R), Arg(R), Tg
Williams, **L H** (Llanelli) 1957 S, I, F, 1958 E, S, I, F, 1959 E, S, I, 1961 F, 1962 E, S
Williams, **M E** (Pontypridd, Cardiff Blues) 1996 Bb, F 2, It (t), 1998 It, E, Z, SA 2, Arg, 1999 S, I, C, J, [Sm], 2000 E (R), 2001 E, S, F, It, 2002 I, F, It, E, S, SA 1, 2, Fj, C, NZ, 2003 It, E 1, S 1, I 1, F, A, NZ 2, [C, Tg(R), It, E(R)], 2004 S, I, F(t&R), E(R), It, SA2(t&R), R(R), NZ(R), J(R), 2005 E, It, F, S, I, Fj, SA, A, 2006 E, S, I, It, F, A, C, NZ, 2007 I, S, F1, It, E1, Arg, F2, [C, A, J, Fj], 2008 E, S, It, I, F, SA3, NZ, A, 2009 S, E, F, I, NZ, Arg, A, 2010 E, S, F, I, A(R), SA2, NZ3 (R), 2011 Arg, 2012 Bb(R)
Williams, **M S** (Scarlets) 2011 Bb(R), E2(R), 3(R), Arg(R) , [Nm, Fj, A(R)], A, 2012 S(R), E(R), It(R), F(t), A 1, 3(R), Arg, NZ(R), 2013 F(R), It(R), S(R), E(R), SA, Arg, A, 2014 It, I
Williams, **M T** (Newport) 1923 F
Williams, **O** (Llanelli) 1947 E, S, A, 1948 E, S, F, I
Williams, **O L** (Bridgend) 1990 Nm 2
Williams, **O R** (Cardiff Blues) 2013 J1, 2, Tg, A
Williams, **R** (Scarlets) 2013 Tg(R), A(R), 2014 S(R)
Williams, **R D G** (Newport) 1881 E
Williams, **R F** (Cardiff) 1912 SA, 1913 E, S, 1914 I
Williams, **R H** (Llanelli) 1954 I, F, S, 1955 S, I, F, 1956 E, S, I, 1957 E, S, I, F, 1958 A, E, S, I, F, 1959 E, S, I, F, 1960 E
Williams, **S** (Llanelli) 1947 E, S, I, F, 1948 S, F
Williams, **S A** (Aberavon) 1939 E, S, I
Williams, **S M** (Neath, Cardiff, Northampton) 1994 Tg, 1996 E (t), A 1, 2, Bb, F 2, It, A 3, SA, 1997 US, S, I, F, E, US 1,

2(R), C, R (R), Tg (R), NZ (t+R), 2002 SA 1, 2, R, Fj(R), 2003 It, E 1, S 1, F(R)
Williams, **S M** (Neath, Ospreys) 2000 F (R), It, E, S, I, Sm, SA (R), 2001 J 1, 2, I, 2003 R, [NZ, E], 2004 S, I, F, E, It, Arg 1, 2, SA1, 2, NZ, J, 2005 E, It, F, S, I, NZ, Fj, SA, A, 2006 E, S, It, F, Arg 1, 2, A, PI(R), C, NZ, 2007 F1, It, E1, F2, [C, A, J, Fj], 2008 E, S, It, I, F, SA1, 2, 3, NZ, A, 2009 S, F, It, I, NZ, Arg, A, 2010 E, S, F, I, It, A, SA2, 2011 E1, S, It, I, E2, 3, [SA, Sm, I, F, A], A
Williams, **T** (Pontypridd) 1882 I
Williams, **T** (Swansea) 1888 S, I
Williams, **T** (Swansea) 1912 I, 1913 F, 1914 E, S, F, I
Williams, **T** (Swansea) 1921 F
Williams, **T G** (Cross Keys) 1935 S, I, NZ, 1936 E, S, I, 1937 S, I
Williams, **W A** (Crumlin) 1927 E, S, F, I
Williams, **W A** (Newport) 1952 I, F, 1953 E
Williams, **W E O** (Cardiff) 1887 S, I, 1889 S, 1890 S, E
Williams, **W H** (Pontymister) 1900 E, S, I, 1901 E
Williams, **W L T** (Llanelli, Cardiff) 1947 E, S, F, I, A, 1948 I, 1949 E
Williams, **W O G** (Swansea, Devonport Services) 1951 F, SA, 1952 E, S, I, F, 1953 E, S, I, F, NZ, 1954 E, I, F, S, 1955 E, S, I, F, 1956 E, S, I
Williams, **W P J** (Neath) 1974 I, F
Williams-Jones, **H** (S Wales Police, Llanelli) 1989 S (R), 1990 F (R), I, 1991 A, 1992 S, A, 1993 E, S, I, F, Z 1, Nm, 1994 Fj, Tg, WS (R), It (t), 1995 E (R)
Willis, **W R** (Cardiff) 1950 E, S, I, F, 1951 E, S, I, F, SA, 1952 E, S, 1953 S, NZ, 1954 E, I, F, S, 1955 E, S, I, F
Wiltshire, **M L** (Aberavon) 1967 NZ, 1968 E, S, F
Windsor, **R W** (Pontypool) 1973 A, 1974 S, I, F, E, 1975 F, E, S, I, A, 1976 E, S, I, F, 1977 I, F, E, S, 1978 E, S, I, F, A 1, 2, NZ, 1979 S, I, F
Winfield, **H B** (Cardiff) 1903 I, 1904 E, S, I, 1905 NZ, 1906 E, S, I, 1907 S, I, 1908 E, S, F, I, A
Winmill, **S** (Cross Keys) 1921 E, S, I, F
Wintle, **M E** (Llanelli) 1996 It
Wintle, **R V** (London Welsh) 1988 WS (R)
Wooller, **W** (Sale, Cambridge U, Cardiff) 1933 E, S, I, 1935 E, S, I, NZ, 1936 E, S, I, 1937 E, S, I, 1938 S, I, 1939 E, S, I
Wyatt, **C P** (Llanelli) 1998 Z (R), SA 1(R), 2, Arg, 1999 S, I, F 1, It, E, Arg 1, 2, SA, C (R), F 2, [Arg 3, J (R), Sm, A], 2000 F, It, E, US, SA, 2001 E, R, I, Arg (R), Tg (R), A, 2002 I, It (R), E, S (R), 2003 A(R), NZ(t+R), E 2, [Tg(R), NZ(R)]
Wyatt, **G** (Pontypridd, Celtic Warriors) 1997 Tg, 2003 R (R)
Wyatt, **M A** (Swansea) 1983 E, S, I, F, 1984 A, 1985 S, I, 1987 E, S, I
Yapp, **J V** (Cardiff Blues) 2005 E(R), It(R), F(R), S(R), I(R), C(R), Fj, 2006 Arg 1(R), 2008 C, NZ(R), 2009 S(R), It, C, US, 2010 SA1(R), NZ1(R), SA2(R), 2011 E1t(R), S(R), I(R), F(R)
Young, **D** (Swansea, Cardiff) 1987 [E, NZ], US, 1988 E, S, I, F, NZ 1, 2, WS, R, 1989 S, NZ, 1990 F, 1996 A 3, SA, 1997 US, S, I, F, E, R, NZ, 1998 It, E, S, I, F, 1999 I, E (R), NZ 1(R), 2(R), SA, C (R), F 2, [Arg 3, J, Sm, A], 2000 F, It, E, S, I, 2001 E, S, F, It, R, I, Arg
Young, **G A** (Cardiff) 1886 E, S
Young, **J** (Harrogate, RAF, London Welsh) 1968 S, I, F, 1969 S, I, F, E, NZ 1, 1970 E, I, F, 1971 E, S, I, F, 1972 E, S, F, NZ, 1973 E, S, I, F
Young, **P** (Gwent Dragons) 2003 R (R)

**551**

**WALES**

# GLOBAL RUGBY GOES FROM STRENGTH TO STRENGTH

## By Karen Bond

Scott Harland

Guyana had to battle until the 99th minute before finally beating USA South to win the Caribbean Championship.

**I**reland and New Zealand may have grabbed the headlines as winners of the Six Nations and The Rugby Championship in 2014, but there was plenty for other nations around the world to celebrate.

In Europe, Africa and Asia the top levels of regional competitions took on added significance with places at Rugby World Cup 2015 on the line, ensuring there were a few twists along the way.

With Georgia and Romania having gone through the first half of the European Nations Cup 2014 with unbeaten records, they wrapped up the region's two direct qualifier places at England 2015 with two rounds to spare. That just left one small matter to decide, who would be Europe 1 – and earn a meeting with defending champions New Zealand – and Europe 2. This was only decided in the final round when the sides met in Tbilisi. Georgia ran out 22–9 winners before a crowd of nearly 30,000 with captain Irakli Machkaneli saying that facing the All Blacks would be "wonderful for the development of rugby in Georgia."

While titles are handed out every season in the European Nations Cup, it is only at the culmination of the two-year competition that promotion and relegation takes place between the seven divisions. This means that the other divisional champions Germany (Division 1B), the Netherlands (2A), Israel (2B), Cyprus (2C), Luxembourg (2D) and Turkey (3) will all be playing at a higher level from 2014–16.

Germany last played in the elite tier in 2010 and can now look forward to matches against Georgia, Portugal, Romania, Russia and Spain having taken the place of Belgium. By contrast, the Czech Republic, Lithuania, Serbia, Bulgaria and Greece have all been relegated after finishing bottom of their respective divisions.

There were also a handful of play-offs between sides finishing second from top and bottom. Only one of these resulted in a change with Hungary promoted to Division 2B after Denmark forfeited their play-off. In the others, Croatia remain in Division 2A after beating Latvia 16–10 and Austria avoided relegation to Division 2D after overcoming Bosnia & Herzegovina 26–12 in June.

Meanwhile in Asia, Japan continue to lead the way after claiming a seventh successive Asian 5 Nations title to take their record to 28 bonus point victories in the competition's history and also qualify for RWC 2015 as Asia 1. The Brave Blossoms swept aside the Philippines, Sri Lanka and Korea before facing Hong Kong in the final match, where try bursts in the last 10 minutes of each half proved enough for a 49–8 win in Tokyo to ensure their perfect record continued. Hong Kong's RWC dream lived on for a couple of months until Uruguay extinguished it in the Repechage in August.

The Asian 5 Nations will be restructured in 2015 so only Japan, Hong Kong and Korea will remain in the top tier, with the Philippines and Sri Lanka dropping down to Division I. They will be joined there by Kazakhstan and Singapore, who comfortably overcame Chinese Taipei and UAE respectively in one-off matches. Malaysia won Division II after a 31–22 victory over Qatar in the final, handing their opponents a first Asian 5 Nations loss. The next two tiers were rebranded Division III East and West in 2014 with China and Lebanon claiming those titles, while Mongolia were crowned Division IV champions after victories over Brunei and Cambodia.

The top tier of the Africa Cup provided a rollercoaster of emotions for Namibia and Kenya in particular. Namibia were upset by Kenya in their opening match, but bounced back to beat Zimbabwe which meant all three went into the final round with the Africa 1 place within their reach.

Kenya only needed to avoid defeat to reach a first Rugby World Cup, but lost to Zimbabwe with neither side collecting a bonus point. That left Namibia needing to beat Madagascar by 53 points to overhaul Zimbabwe on points difference, all three contenders having finished with 10 points. They had that cushion by half-time and ultimately won 89–10 to reach England 2015. Zimbabwe had a second shot through the Repechage but lost out to Russia. While there was heartbreak for Kenya, a couple of weeks later their A side beat Uganda 48–21 over two legs in the annual battle for the Elgon Cup. It was a clean sweep for Kenya, with their women's and Under 19 teams also beating their Ugandan counterparts.

Tunisia will step up to replace Madagascar in Division 1A next year after beating Senegal (22–14) and then Ivory Coast (26–6) in the final. Senegal recovered to edge a tight third place play-off with Uganda 32–31 to retain their place in the second tier of African rugby.

In 2014, the NACRA (North America Caribbean Rugby Association) Championship took on a new look with teams divided into two leagues – Championship and Cup – with a north and south zone in each one. A promotion and relegation play-off system was also present with the bottom side of the Championship to face their respective zonal Cup winner in a one-off match.

Guyana were ultimately crowned NACRA champions after beating USA South, the north zone winners, 30–27 after extra-time in the final. The sides had been locked at 27–27 after 99 minutes of play and a kicking competition looked set to the decide the final, until Guyana scrum-half Ryan Gonsalves stepped up to kick what proved to be the winning penalty.

Mexico dominated the North Zone Cup league with wins over Jamaica, Bahamas and the Turks & Caicos Islands to earn a play-off with Bermuda, the bottom side in the South Championship. Bermuda forfeited the match so Mexico will take their place in the Championship next year. Curacao topped the South Zone Cup league with a perfect record after wins over St Lucia, St Vincent & The Grenadines and British Virgin Islands, but lost 29–0 to Barbados in the play-off in September.

In South America, Uruguay banished their disappointment at missing out on the Americas 2 berth at RWC 2015 to the USA by beating Paraguay (34–10), Brazil (34–9) and Chile (55–13) to win the CONSUR Championship in May. Uruguay and Chile, as the top two sides, then faced Argentina in the CONSUR Cup but both suffered heavy defeats to a young Pumas team. Four months later it was Colombia's turn to celebrate as they won the Division B title after overwhelming Ecuador (112–0) and Peru (56–6) on home soil at the Estadio Santiago Rambay. The final was a closer affair, but Colombia still had too much for Venezuela and won 27–10.

# MAJOR TOURS

## By Chris Rhys

## NEW ZEALAND TO JAPAN & EUROPE 2013

### TOUR PARTY

**FULL BACK**: IJA Dagg (Hawke's Bay)

**THREEQUARTERS**: SJ Savea (Wellington), CS Jane (Wellington), BR Smith (Otago), ST Puitau (Auckland), F Halai (Counties Manukau), MA Nonu (Wellington), F Saili (North Harbour), TJ Taylor (Canterbury), RS Crotty (Canterbury)

**HALF BACKS**: AL Smith (Manawatu), TNJ Kerr-Barlow (Waikato), TTR (TJ) Perenara (Wellington), AW Cruden (Manawatu), DW Carter (Canterbury), BJ Barrett (Taranaki)

**FORWARDS**: DS Coles (Wellington), AK Hore (Taranaki), KF Mealamu (Auckland), WWV Crockett (Canterbury), CC Faumuina (Auckland), BJ Franks (Hawke's Bay), OJ Franks (Canterbury), JL To'omaga-Allen (Wellington), TD Woodcock (North Harbour), J Moody (Canterbury), DJ Bird (Canterbury), BA Retallick (Bay of Plenty), L Romano (Canterbury), JI Thrush (Wellington), SL Whitelock (Canterbury), SJ Cane (Bay of Plenty), S Luatua (Auckland), RH McCaw (Canterbury), LJ Messam (Waikato), KJ Read (Canterbury), LC Whitelock (Canterbury)

**HEAD COACH**: SW Hansen

### 2 November, Prince Chichibu Memorial Stadium, Tokyo, Japan 6 (2PG) New Zealand 54 (7G 1T)

**JAPAN**: A Goromaru (Yamaha Jubilo); T Hirose (Toshiba Brave Lupus)(captain), M Sa'u (Yamaha Jubilo), C Wing (Kobe Steel), K Fukuoka (Tsukuba University); H Tatekawa (Kubota Spears), F Tanaka (Panasonic Wild Knights); M Mikami (Toshiba Brave Lupus), S Horie (Panasonic Wild Knights), K Hatakeyama (Suntory Sungoliath), S Ito (Kobe Steel), H Ono (Toshiba Brave Lupus), MJ Broadhurst (Ricoh Black Rams), H Tui (Suntory Sungoliath), RK Holani (Panasonic Wild Knights)

**SUBSTITUTIONS**: Y Tamura (NEC Green Rockets) for Tatekawa (28 mins); T Kikutani (Toyota Verblitz) for Holani (40 mins); H Yamashita (Kobe Steel) for Hatakeyama (56 mins); Y Fujita for Hirose (59 mins); L Thompson (Kintetsu Liners) for Ito (65 mins); K Ono (Suntory Sungoliath) for Wing (75 mins); Y Aoki (Suntory Sungoliath) & Y Nagae (Ricoh Black Rams) for Horie & Mikami (76 mins)

**SCORERS**: *Penalty Goals*: Goromaru (2)

**NEW ZEALAND**: Barrett; Halai, B Smith, Saili, Piutau; Carter, Kerr-Barlow; Crockett, Coles, B Franks, Thrush, Bird, Luatua, Cane, McCaw (captain)

**SUBSTITUTIONS**: Taylor & Crotty for Carter & B Smith (51 mins); L Whitelock for Bird (58 mins); Hore for Coles (64 mins); To'omaga-Allen & A Smith for Crockett & Kerr-Barlow (68 mins)

**SCORERS**: *Tries*: Piutau (2), Cane, B Smith, McCaw, Thrush, Halai, Barrett *Conversions*: Carter (5), Barrett (2)

**REFEREE**: S Berry (South Africa)

### 9 November, Stade de France, Paris, France 19 (1G 4PG) New Zealand 26 (2G 4PG)

**FRANCE**: B Dulin (Castres Olympique); Y Huget (Stade Toulousain), W Fofana (ASM Clermont Auvergne), F Fritz (Stade Toulousain), M Médard (Stade Toulousain); R Talès (Castres Olympique), M Parra (ASM Clermont Auvergne); Y Forestier (Castres Olympique), B Kayser (ASM Clermont Auvergne), N Mas (Montpellier HRC), P Papé (Stade Français), Y Maestri (Stade Toulousain), T Dusautoir (Stade Toulousain)(captain), W Lauret (Racing Métro), D Chouly (ASM Clermont Auvergne)

**SUBSTITUTIONS**: D Szarzewski (Racing Métro) for Kayser (52 mins); S Vahaamahina (USA Perpignan) & R Slimani (Stade Français) for Maestri & Mas (56 mins); V Debaty (ASM Clermont Auvergne) for Forestier (60 mins); G Fickou (Stade Toulousain) for Fritz (66 mins); AD Claassen (Castres Olympique) for Lauret (73 mins); J-M Doussain (Stade Toulousain) for Parra (76 mins)

**SCORERS**: *Try*: Dulin *Conversion*: Parra *Penalty Goals*: Parra (4)

**NEW ZEALAND**: Dagg; Jane, B Smith, Nonu, Piutau; Carter, A Smith; Woodcock, Mealamu, O Franks, Retallick, S Whitelock, Messam, McCaw (captain), Read

**SUBSTITUTIONS**: Cruden for Carter (52 mins); Faumuina for O Franks (53 mins); Coles for Mealamu (60 mins); Crockett & Crotty for Woodcock & Jane (69 mins); Kerr-Barlow for A Smith (76 mins)

**SCORERS**: *Tries*: Piutau, Read *Conversions*: Carter, Cruden *Penalty Goals*: Carter (4)

**REFEREE**: J Peyper (South Africa)

### 16 November, Twickenham, England 22 (1G 5PG) New Zealand 30 (3G 3PG)

**ENGLAND**: MN Brown (Harlequins); CJ Ashton (Saracens), JA Tomkins (Saracens), WWF Twelvetrees (Gloucester Rugby), BJ Foden (Northampton Saints); OA Farrell (Saracens), LAW Dickson (Northampton Saints); JWG

Marler (Harlequins), DM Hartley (Northampton Saints), DR Cole (Leicester Tigers), JO Launchbury (London Wasps), CL Lawes (Northampton Saints), TA Wood (Northampton Saints), CDC Robshaw (Harlequins)(captain), VML Vunipola (Saracens)
**SUBSTITUTIONS**: GMW Parling (Leicester Tigers) for Launchbury (46 mins); TN Youngs (Leicester Tigers) for Hartley (50 mins); BJ Morgan (Gloucester Rugby) for Vunipola (57 mins); BR Youngs (Leicester Tigers) for Dickson (63 mins); TGAL Flood (Leicester Tigers) for Farrell (67 mins); DAV Goode (Saracens), DG Wilson (Bath Rugby) & MJ Mullan (London Wasps) for Tomkins, Cole & Marler (76 mins)
**SCORERS**: *Try*: Launchbury *Conversion*: Farrell *Penalty Goals*: Farrell (5)
**NEW ZEALAND**: Dagg; Piutau, B Smith, Nonu, Savea; Carter, A Smith; Woodcock, Mealamu, O Franks, Retallick, S Whitelock, Messam, McCaw (captain), Read
**SUBSTITUTIONS**: Cruden for Carter (25 mins); Crockett for Woodcock (40 mins); Faumuina for O Franks (42 mins); Coles for Mealamu (60 mins); Luatua & Romano for Messam & Retallick (63 mins); Kerr-Barlow & Crotty for A Smith & Piutau (71 mins)
**SCORERS**: *Tries*: Savea (2), Read *Conversions*: Carter (2), Cruden *Penalty Goals*: Carter, Cruden (2)
**REFEREE**: C Joubert (South Africa)

---

**24 November, Aviva Stadium, Dublin, Ireland 22 (2G 1T 1PG) New Zealand 24 (3G 1PG)**

**IRELAND**: RDJ Kearney (Leinster); TJ Bowe (Ulster), BG O'Driscoll (Leinster), GWD D'Arcy (Leinster), D Kearney (Leinster); JJ Sexton (Racing Métro), C Murray (Munster); CE Healy (Leinster), RD Best (Ulster), MA Ross (Leinster), D Toner (Leinster), PJ O'Connell (Munster)(captain), P O'Mahony (Munster), SK O'Brien (Leinster), JPR Heaslip (Leinster)
**SUBSTITUTIONS**: SM Cronin (Leinster) for Best (14 mins); LM Fitzgerald (Leinster) for O'Driscoll (53 mins); KR McLaughlin (Leinster) for O'Mahony (56 mins); DJ Fitzpatrick (Ulster) & MP McCarthy (Leinster) for Ross & Toner (65 mins); JC McGrath (Leinster) for Healy (69 mins); I Madigan (Leinster) for Sexton (75 mins)
**SCORERS**: *Tries*: Murray, Best, R Kearney *Conversions*: Sexton (2) *Penalty Goal*: Sexton
**NEW ZEALAND**: Dagg; Jane, B Smith, Nonu, Savea; Cruden, A Smith; Crockett, Hore, Faumuina, Retallick, S Whitelock, Luatua, McCaw (captain), Read
**SUBSTITUTIONS**: Coles for Hore (42 mins); Crotty for Dagg (53 mins); O Franks for Faumuina (56 mins); Messam for Luatua (59 mins); B Franks for Crockett (60 mins); Barrett for Jane (65 mins)
**SCORERS**: *Tries*: Savea, B Franks, Crotty *Conversions*: Cruden (3) *Penalty Goal*: Cruden
**REFEREE**: N Owens (Wales)

# SOUTH AFRICA TO EUROPE 2013

**TOUR PARTY**

**FULL BACKS**: Z Kirchner (Leinster), WJ le Roux (Cheetahs)
**THREEQUARTERS**: BG Habana (RC Toulon), JJ Engelbrecht (Bulls), J-P R Pietersen (Sharks), J de Villiers (Stormers)(captain), J Fourie (Kobe Steel), JL Serfontein (Bulls)
**HALF BACKS**: PF du Preez (Suntory Sungoliath), R Pienaar (Ulster), L Schreuder (Stormers), J Vermaak (Bulls), PJ Lambie (Sharks), M Steyn (Stade Français), JL Goosen (Cheetahs)
**FORWARDS**: BW du Plessis (Sharks), JA Strauss (Cheetahs), S Ntubeni (Stormers), T Mtawarira (Sharks), JF Malherbe (Stormers), CV Oosthuizen (Cheetahs), GG Steenkamp (Stade Toulousain), LC Adriaanse (Cheetahs), F Kirsten (Bulls), E Etzebeth (Stormers), PR van der Merwe (Bulls), P-S du Toit (Sharks), JP Botha (RC Toulon), MC Coetzee (Sharks), WS Alberts (Sharks), S Kolisi (Stormers), L-FP Louw (Bath Rugby), DJ Vermeulen (Stormers)
**HEAD COACH**: H Meyer

**9 November, Millennium Stadium, Cardiff, Wales 15 (5PG) South Africa 24 (3G 1PG)**

**WALES**: SL Halfpenny (Cardiff Blues); GP North (Northampton Saints), JJV Davies (Scarlets), MS Williams (Scarlets), LB Williams (Scarlets); R Priestland (Scarlets), WM Phillips (unattached); GD Jenkins (Cardiff Blues), RM Hibbard (Ospreys), AR Jones (Ospreys), BS Davies (Cardiff Blues), A-W Jones (Ospreys), DJ Lydiate (Racing Métro), SK Warburton (Cardiff Blues)(captain), TT Faletau (Newport Gwent Dragons)
**SUBSTITUTIONS**: JW Hook (USA Perpignan) & MA Beck (Ospreys) for LB Williams & JJV Davies (12 mins); SA Andrews (Cardiff Blues) for AR Jones (30 mins); P James (Bath Rugby) for Andrews (40 mins); KJ Owens (Scarlets) & JC Tipuric (Ospreys) for Hibbard & Lydiate (63 mins); LC Charteris (USA Perpignan) & LD Williams (Cardiff Blues) for A-W Jones & Phillips (72 mins)
**SCORER**: *Penalty Goals*: Halfpenny (5)
**SOUTH AFRICA**: Lambie; Pietersen, Fourie, de Villiers (captain), Habana; Steyn, du Preez; Mtawarira, B du Plessis, Malherbe, Etzebeth, P van der Merwe, Alberts, Louw, Vermeulen
**SUBSTITUTIONS**: Le Roux for M Steyn (18 mins); Oosthuizen for Malherbe (55 mins); Strauss & Steenkamp for B du Plessis & Mtawarira (65 mins); Kolisi for Alberts (66 mins); du Toit for Etzebeth (68 mins); Engelbrecht for Pietersen (71 mins); Pienaar for du Preez (77 mins)
**SCORERS**: *Tries*: de Villiers, B du Plessis, du Preez *Conversions*: Steyn (2), Lambie *Penalty Goal*: Steyn
**REFEREE**: AC Rolland (Ireland)

**17 November, Murrayfield, Scotland 0 South Africa 28 (4G)**

**SCOTLAND**: SD Maitland (Glasgow Warriors); TSF Seymour (Glasgow Warriors), NJ de Luca (Edinburgh Rugby), DM Taylor (Saracens), SF Lamont (Glasgow Warriors); RJH Jackson (Glasgow Warriors), GD Laidlaw (Edinburgh Rugby) (captain); AG Dickinson (Edinburgh Rugby), RW Ford (Edinburgh Rugby), MJ Low (London Irish), RJ Gray (Castres Olympique), JL Hamilton (Montpellier HRC), AK Strokosch (USA Perpignan), JA Barclay (Scarlets), DK Denton (Edinburgh Rugby)
**SUBSTITUTIONS**: D Weir (Glasgow Warriors) & S Lawson (Newcastle Falcons) for Jackson & Ford (54 mins); R Grant (Glasgow Warriors) for Dickinson (54 mins); JD Gray (Glasgow Warriors) for RJ Gray (61 mins); MB Evans (Castres Olympique) & JW Beattie (Montpellier HRC) for Seymour & Barclay (64 mins); CP Cusiter (Glasgow Warriors) for Laidlaw (68 mins)
**SOUTH AFRICA:** Le Roux; Pietersen, Fourie, de Villiers (captain), Habana; Lambie, du Preez; Steenkamp, Strauss, Malherbe, Botha, P van der Merwe, Alberts, Louw, Vermeulen
**SUBSTITUTIONS**: Oosthuizen for Malherbe (36 mins); Coetzee for Alberts (40 mins); Mtawarira for Steenkamp (54 mins); Etzebeth for Botha (59 mins); B du Plessis for Strauss (60 mins); Pienaar for du Preez (64 mins); Engelbrecht for de Villiers (70 mins); Steyn for Louw (75 mins)
**SCORERS**: *Tries:* Alberts, Le Roux, Pietersen, Oosthuizen *Conversions*: Lambie (4)
**REFEREE**: J Garces (France)

**23 November, Stade de France, Paris, France 10 (1G 1PG) South Africa 19 (1G 4PG)**

**FRANCE**: B Dulin (Castres Olympique); S Guitoune (USA Perpignan), W Fofana (ASM Clermont Auvergne), F Fritz (Stade Toulousain), Y Huget (Stade Toulousain); R Talès (Castres Olympique), M Parra (ASM Clermont Auvergne); Y Forestier (Castres Olympique), B Kayser (ASM Clermont Auvergne), N Mas (Montpellier HRC), P Papé (Stade Français), Y Maestri (Stade Toulousain), T Dusautoir (Stade Toulousain)(captain), W Lauret (Racing Métro), D Chouly (ASM Clermont Auvergne)
**SUBSTITUTIONS**: T Domingo (ASM Clermont Auvergne) for Forestier (40 mins); D Szarzewski (Racing Métro) for Kayser (46 mins); S Vahaamahina (USA Perpignan) for Maestri (50 mins); R Slimani (Stade Français) for Mas (56 mins); M Bastareaud (RC Toulon) for Fritz (59 mins); J-M Doussain (Stade Toulousain) for Parra (66 mins); Y Nyanga (Stade Toulousain) for Lauret (69 mins); F Michalak (RC Toulon) for Talès (74 mins)
**SCORERS**: *Try*: Huget *Conversion*: Parra *Penalty Goal*: Doussain
**SOUTH AFRICA**: Le Roux; Pietersen, Fourie, de Villiers (captain), Habana; Steyn, Pienaar; Mtawarira, B du Plessis, Oosthuizen, Etzebeth, P van der Merwe, Alberts, Louw, Vermeulen
**SUBSTITUTIONS**: Botha for Etzebeth (15 mins); Steenkamp for Mtawarira (56 mins); Strauss for B du Plessis (66 mins); du Toit for Alberts (67 mins); Lambie for Le Roux (temp 56–60 mins) & Steyn (71 mins); Adriaanse for Oosthuizen (73 mins); Kolisi for Botha (74 mins)
**SCORERS**: *Try:* Pietersen *Conversion:* Steyn *Penalty Goals:* Steyn (3), Lambie
**REFEREE**: W Barnes (England)

# AUSTRALIA TO EUROPE 2013

## TOUR PARTY

**FULL BACK**: I Folau (NSW Waratahs)
**THREEQUARTERS**: AP Ashley-Cooper (NSW Waratahs), NM Cummins (Western Force), JM Tomane (ACT Brumbies), RTRN Kuiridrani (ACT Brumbies), MP Toomua (ACT Brumbies), CP Leali'ifano (ACT Brumbies), MJ Harris (Queensland Reds), C Feauai-Sautia (Queensland Reds)
**HALF BACKS**: QS Cooper (Queensland Reds), BT Foley (NSW Waratahs), SW Genia (Queensland Reds), NW White (ACT Brumbies), NC Phipps (Melbourne Rebels)
**FORWARDS**: ST Moore (ACT Brumbies), SM Faingaa (Queensland Reds), SUT Polota-Nau (NSW Waratahs), JA Slipper (Queensland Reds), BE Alexander (ACT Brumbies), SM Kepu (NSW Waratahs), BA Robinson (NSW Waratahs), PJ Ryan (NSW Waratahs), S Timani (NSW Waratahs), JE Horwill (Queensland Reds), KP Douglas (NSW Waratahs), RA Simmons (Queensland Reds), DA Dennis (NSW Waratahs), SM Fardy (ACT Brumbies), MK Hooper (NSW Waratahs), LB Gill (Queensland Reds), BJ McCalman (Western Force), BSC Mowen (ACT Brumbies)
**HEAD COACH**: EJA McKenzie

**2 November, Twickenham, England 20 (2G 2PG) Australia 13 (1G 2PG)**

**ENGLAND**: MN Brown (Harlequins); CJ Ashton (Saracens), JA Tomkins (Saracens), WWF Twelvetrees (Gloucester Rugby), MXD Yarde (London Irish); OA Farrell (Saracens), LAW Dickson (Northampton Saints); MWIN Vunipola (Saracens), TN Youngs (Leicester Tigers), DR Cole (Leicester Tigers), JO Launchbury (London Wasps), CL Lawes (Northampton Saints), TA Wood (Northampton Saints), CDC Robshaw (Harlequins)(captain), VML Vunipola (Saracens)
**SUBSTITUTIONS**: DM Hartley (Northampton Saints), JWG Marler (Harlequins) & BR Youngs (Leicester Tigers) for T Youngs (54 mins), M Vunipola & Dickson (54 mins); BJ Morgan (Gloucester Rugby), TGAL Flood (Leicester Tigers) & DG Wilson (Bath Rugby) for VML Vunipola, Twelvetrees & Cole (66 mins); DMJ Attwood (Bath Rugby) for Launchbury (75 mins)

**SCORERS:** *Tries:* Robshaw, Farrell *Conversions:* Farrell (2) *Penalty Goals:* Farrell (2)
**AUSTRALIA:** Folau; Ashley-Cooper, Kuridrani, Toomua, Cummins; Cooper, Genia; Slipper, Moore, Alexander, Timani, Horwill, Fardy, Hooper, Mowen (captain)
**SUBSTITUTIONS:** Foley for Ashley-Cooper (temp 49–53 mins); McCalman & Kepu for Fardy & Alexander (49 mins); Robinson for Slipper (58 mins); Douglas for Timani (61 mins); White for Genia (68 mins); S Faingaa for Moore (68 mins)
**SCORERS:** *Try:* Toomua *Conversion:* Cooper *Penalty Goals:* Cooper (2)
**REFEREE:** GJ Clancy (Ireland)

### 9 November, Stadio Olimpico, Rome, Italy 20 (1G 2T 1PG) Australia 50 (6G 1T 1PG)

**ITALY:** L McLean (Treviso); T Benvenuti (USA Perpignan), L Morisi (Treviso), A Sgarbi (Treviso), L Sarto (Zebre); A di Bernardo (Treviso), E Gori (Treviso); M Rizzo (Treviso), D Giazzon (Zebre), M-L Castrogiovanni (RC Toulon), A Pavanello (Treviso), M Bortolami (Zebre), A Zanni (Treviso), R Barbieri (Treviso), S Parisse (Stade Français)(captain)
**SUBSTITUTIONS:** M Aguero (Zebre), L Ghiraldini (Treviso) & Q Geldenhuys (Zebre) for Rizzo, Giazzon & Pavanello (49 mins); L Cittadini (Treviso), T Iannone (Treviso) & T Allan (USA Perpignan) for Castrogiovanni, Benvenuti & Di Bernardo (59 mins); J Furno (Biarritz Olympique) for Bortolami (63 mins); T Botes (Treviso) for Gori (69 mins)
**SCORERS:** *Tries:* McLean, Cittadini, Allan *Conversion:* di Bernardo *Penalty Goal:* Di Bernardo
**AUSTRALIA:** Folau; Ashley-Cooper, Kuridrani, Toomua, Cummins; Cooper, Genia; Slipper, Moore, Alexander, Timani, Horwill, Simmons, Hooper, Mowen (captain)
**SUBSTITUTIONS:** Kepu for Alexander (51 mins); Dennis for Timani (57 mins); Leali'ifano & Robinson for Cooper & Slipper (59 mins); Gill for Hooper (64 mins); Tomane for Ashley-Cooper (66 mins); S Faingaa for Moore (67 mins); White for Genia (70 mins)
**SCORERS:** *Tries:* Cummins (2), Mowen, Kuridrani, Ashley-Cooper, Tomane, Folau *Conversions:* Cooper (4), Leali'ifano (2) *Penalty Goals:* Leali'ifano
**REFEREE:** GW Jackson (New Zealand)

### 16 November, Aviva Stadium, Dublin, Ireland 15 (5PG) Australia 32 (3G 1T 2PG)

**IRELAND:** RDJ Kearney (Leinster); TJ Bowe (Ulster), BG O'Driscoll (Leinster), LD Marshall (Ulster), FL McFadden (Leinster); JJ Sexton (Racing Métro), EG Reddan (Leinster); CE Healy (Leinster), RD Best (Ulster), MA Ross (Leinster), D Toner (Leinster), PJ O'Connell (Munster)(captain), P O'Mahony (Munster), SK O'Brien (Leinster), JPR Heaslip (Leinster)
**SUBSTITUTIONS:** R Henshaw (Connacht) for O'Driscoll (temp 22–29 mins) & Kearney (73 mins); I Madigan (Leinster) for Sexton (40 mins); C Murray (Munster) for Reddan (56 mins); S Archer (Munster) & SM Cronin (Leinster) for Ross & Best (66 mins); MP McCarthy (Leinster) & JC McGrath (Leinster) for Toner & Healy (68 mins); KR McLaughlin (Leinster) for O'Brien (70 mins)
**SCORERS:** *Penalty Goals:* Sexton (4), Madigan
**AUSTRALIA:** Folau; Ashley-Cooper, Kuridrani, Toomua, Cummins; Cooper, Genia; Slipper, Moore, Kepu, Simmons, Horwill, Fardy, Hooper, Mowen (captain)
**SUBSTITUTIONS:** Timani for Horwill (56 mins); Tomane for Ashley-Cooper (58 mins); Ryan, White & Robinson for Kepu, Genia & Slipper (66 mins); Polota-Nau & Leali'ifano for Moore & Cooper (68 mins); Gill for Hooper (72 mins)
**SCORERS:** *Tries:* Hooper (2), Cooper, Cummins *Conversions:* Cooper (3) *Penalty Goals:* Cooper (2)
**RED CARD:** Kuridrani (75 mins)
**REFEREE:** CJ Pollock (New Zealand)

### 23 November, Murrayfield, Scotland 15 (5PG) Australia 21 (1G 1T 3PG)

**SCOTLAND:** SD Maitland (Glasgow Warriors); TSF Seymour (Glasgow Warriors), NJ de Luca (Edinburgh Rugby), DM Taylor (Saracens), SF Lamont (Glasgow Warriors); D Weir (Glasgow Warriors), GD Laidlaw (Edinburgh Rugby); R Grant (Glasgow Warriors), RW Ford (Edinburgh Rugby), MJ Low (London Irish), GS Gilchrist (Edinburgh Rugby), JL Hamilton (Montpellier HRC), JW Beattie (Montpellier HRC), KDR Brown (Saracens)(captain), DK Denton (Edinburgh Rugby)
**SUBSTITUTIONS:** PC MacArthur (Glasgow Warriors) for Ford (20 mins); AG Dickinson (Edinburgh Rugby) for Grant (46 mins); EA Murray (Worcester Warriors) for M Low (50 mins); CP Cusiter (Glasgow Warriors) for Laidlaw (58 mins); K Low (London Irish) for Denton (60 mins); MB Evans (Castres Olympique) & JD Gray (Glasgow Warriors) for Taylor & Gilchrist (65 mins)
**SCORERS:** *Penalty Goals:* Laidlaw (5)
**AUSTRALIA:** Folau; Tomane, Leali'ifano, Harris, Feauai-Sautia; Cooper, Genia; Slipper, Moore, Kepu, Simmons, Horwill, Fardy, Hooper, Mowen (captain)
**SUBSTITUTIONS:** Alexander & Timani for Kepu & Horwill (58 mins); White for Genia (65 mins); McCalman for Fardy (75 mins); S Faingaa for Moore (76 mins)
**SCORERS:** *Tries:* Folau, Feauai-Sautia *Conversion:* Leali'ifano *Penalty Goals:* Leali'ifano (3)
**REFEREE:** J Peyper (South Africa)

**30 November, Cardiff, Wales 26 (2G 4PG) Australia 30 (3G 3PG)**

**WALES:** SL Halfpenny (Cardiff Blues); ACG Cuthbert (Cardiff Blues), OR Williams (Cardiff Blues), MS Williams (Scarlets), GP North (Northampton Saints); DR Biggar (Ospreys), WM Phillips (unattached); GD Jenkins (Cardiff Blues), RM Hibbard (Ospreys), RP Jones (Scarlets), A-W Jones (Ospreys), IR Evans (Ospreys), DJ Lydiate (Racing Métro), SK Warburton (Cardiff Blues)(captain), TT Falatau (Newport Gwent Dragons)
**SUBSTITUTIONS:** RJ Bevington (Ospreys) for Jenkins (40 mins); LB Williams (Scarlets) for OR Williams (49 mins); KJ Owens (Scarlets), R Priestland (Scarlets) & JC Tipuric (Ospreys) for Hibbard, Biggar & Lydiate (63 mins); S Lee (Scarlets) for RP Jones (66 mins); R Williams (Scarlets) for Phillips (71 mins)
**SCORERS:** *Tries:* North (2) *Conversions:* Halfpenny, Biggar *Penalty Goals:* Halfpenny (2), Biggar, Priestland
**AUSTRALIA:** Folau; Tomane, Ashley-Cooper, Leali'ifano, Cummins; Cooper, Genia; Slipper, Moore, Kepu, Simmons, Horwill, Fardy, Hooper, Mowen (captain)
**SUBSTITUTIONS:** Alexander for Kepu (55 mins); Douglas for Horwill (60 mins); Harris for Leali'ifano (62 mins); Robinson for Slipper (63 mins); Polota-Nau & Dennis for Moore & Mowen (70 mins); Foley for Tomane (74 mins)
**SCORERS:** *Tries:* Leali'ifano, Folau, Tomane *Conversions:* Leali'ifano (3) *Penalty Goals:* Leali'ifano (3)
**REFEREE:** W Barnes (England)

# ARGENTINA TO EUROPE 2013

**TOUR PARTY**

**FULL BACKS:** S Cordero (Regatas de Bella Vista), LP González Amorosino (Oyonnax), J Tuculet (Bordeaux-Bègles)
**THREEQUARTERS:** JJ Imhoff (Racing Métro), H Agulla (Bath Rugby), S Fernández (Aviron Bayonnais), J Rojas (Universitario Tucuman), GP Tiesi (Newcastle Falcons)
**HALF BACKS:** TM Cubelli (Belgrano Athletic), G Ascarate (Club Newman), MT Bosch (Saracens), FN Sánchez (Bordeaux-Bègles), M Landajo (CA San Isidro)
**FORWARDS:** A Creevy (Worcester Warriors), S Iglesias Valdez (Universitario Tucuman), E Guiñazú (Bath Rugby), M Bustos (Montpellier HRC), M Ayerza (Leicester Tigers), M Diaz (Teque), N Lobo (unattached), JP Orlandi (Bath Rugby), P Albacete (Stade Toulousain), M Carizza (Stormers), M Galarza (Worcester Warriors), T Lavanini (Hindú), JM Leguizamón (Lyon OU), B Macome (Tucuman RC), P Matera (Leicester Tigers), JA Farias Cabello (Tucuman RC), L Senatore (Worcester Warriors)
**HEAD COACH:** D Hourcade

**9 November, Twickenham, England 31 (4G 1PG) Argentina 12 (4PG)**

**ENGLAND:** MN Brown (Harlequins); CJ Ashton (Saracens), JA Tomkins (Saracens), WWF Twelvetrees (Gloucester Rugby), BJ Foden (Northampton Saints); OA Farrell (Saracens), LAW Dickson (Northampton Saints); JWG Marler (Harlequins), DM Hartley (Northampton Saints), DG Wilson (Bath Rugby), JO Launchbury (London Wasps), CL Lawes (Northampton Saints), TA Wood (Northampton Saints), CDC Robshaw (Harlequins)(captain), VML Vunipola (Saracens)
**SUBSTITUTIONS:** AR Corbisiero (Northampton Saints) for Marler (40 mins); DS Care (Harlequins) for Dickson (51 mins); GMW Parling (Leicester Tigers) & BJ Morgan (Gloucester Rugby) for Lawes & VML Vunipola (55 mins); TGAL Flood (Leicester Tigers) for Twelvetrees (61 mins); TN Youngs (Leicester Tigers) & DR Cole (Leicester Tigers) for Hartley & Wilson (62 mins); DAV Goode (Saracens) for Brown (75 mins)
**SCORERS:** *Tries:* Launchbury, Twelvetrees, Ashton, Morgan *Conversions:* Farrell (3), Flood *Penalty Goal:* Farrell
**ARGENTINA:** González Amorosino; Agulla, Bosch, Fernández, Imhoff; Sánchez, Cubelli; Ayerza, Guiñazú, Bustos, Galarza, Albacete, Matera, Farias Cabello, Leguizamón (captain)
**SUBSTITUTIONS:** Cordero for Imhoff (31 mins); Carizza for Galarza (53 mins); Landajo for Cubelli (61 mins); Tiesi for Sánchez (64 mins); Orlandi for Bustos (66 mins); Macome for Tiesi (67 mins); Lobo & Iglesias Valdez for Ayerza & Guiñazú (76 mins)
**SCORERS:** *Penalty Goals:* Sánchez (3), Bosch
**REFEREE:** P Gauzere (France)

**16 November, Millennium Stadium, Cardiff, Wales 40 (4G 4PG) Argentina 6 (2PG)**

**WALES:** SL Halfpenny (Cardiff Blues); GP North (Northampton Saints), CL Allen (Cardiff Blues), MS Williams (Scarlets), LB Williams (Scarlets); DR Biggar (Ospreys), WM Phillips (unattached); GD Jenkins (Cardiff Blues), RM Hibbard (Ospreys), RP Jones (Scarlets), BS Davies (Cardiff Blues), A-W Jones (Ospreys), SK Warburton (Cardiff Blues)(captain), JC Tipuric (Ospreys), TT Faletau (Newport Gwent Dragons)
**SUBSTITUTIONS:** LC Charteris (USA Perpignan) for B Davies (56 mins); KJ Owens (Scarlets) for Hibbard (62 mins); P James (Bath Rugby), S Lee (Scarlets), JW Hook (USA Perpignan) & LD Williams (Cardiff Blues) for Jenkins, RP Jones, Biggar & Phillips (68 mins); MA Beck (Ospreys) for Allen (71 mins)
**SCORERS:** *Tries:* Phillips, North, Faletau, Owens *Conversions:* Halfpenny (4) *Penalty Goals:* Halfpenny (4)
**ARGENTINA:** Tuculet; Cordero, Bosch, Fernández, Agulla; Sánchez, Landajo; Ayerza, Guiñazú, Bustos, Carizza, Albacete, Matera, Farias Cabello, Leguizamón (captain)
**SUBSTITUTIONS:** González Amorosino for Tuculet (40 mins); Senatore for Matera (54 mins); Ascarate for

Fernández (58 mins); Iglesias Valdez for Guiñazú (58 mins); Lavanini for Carizza (65 mins); Cubelli for Landajo (68 mins); Lobo for Ayerza (71 mins); Diaz for Bustos (73 mins)
**SCORERS**: *Penalty Goals*: Sánchez (2)
**REFEREE**: J Lacey (Ireland)

### 23 November, Stadio Olimpico, Rome, Italy 14 (1T 3PG) Argentina 19 (1G 3PG 1DG)

**ITALY**: L McLean (Treviso); G Venditti (Zebre), M Campagnaro (Treviso), G Canale (La Rochelle), T Iannone (Zebre); T Allan (USA Perpignan), E Gori (Treviso); M Rizzo (Treviso), L Ghiraldini (Treviso), M-L Castrogiovanni (RC Toulon), Q Geldenhuys (Zebre), V Bernabo (Treviso), A Zanni (Treviso), R Barbieri (Treviso), S Parisse (Stade Français)(captain)
**SUBSTITUTIONS**: M Bortolami (Zebre) for Bernabo (54 mins); L Orquera (Zebre), M Aguero (Zebre) & L Cittadini (Treviso) for Allan, Rizzo & Castrogiovanni (65 mins); T Botes (Treviso), J Furno (Biarritz Olympique) & D Giazzon (Zebre) for Gori, Geldenhuys & Ghiraldini (71 mins); T Benvenuti (USA Perpignan) for Canale (79 mins)
**SCORER**: *Try*: Campagnaro *Penalty Goals*: Allan (3)
**ARGENTINA**: Tuculet; González Amorosino, Agulla, Ascarate, Imhoff; Sánchez, Landajo; Ayerza, Guiñazú, Bustos, Carizza, Galarza, Leguizamón (captain), Farias Cabello, Macome
**SUBSTITUTIONS**: Cordero for Tuculet (56 mins); Matera for Farias Cabello (61 mins); Cubelli & Lobo for Landajo & Macome (65 mins); Rojas for Ascarate (70 mins); Lavanini for Carizza (74 mins)
**SCORERS**: *Try*: Imhoff *Conversion*: Sánchez *Penalty Goals*: Sánchez (3) *Drop Goal*: Sánchez
**REFEREE**: CJ Pollock (New Zealand)

# SAMOA TO EUROPE 2013

### TOUR PARTY

**FULL BACK**: FS Autagavaia (Marist St Joseph's)
**THREEQUARTERS**: B Va'aulu (Tokyo Gas), A Leiua (Hurricanes), S Sinoti (Wellington), KS Pisi (North Harbour), GT Pisi (Northampton Saints), JW Leota (Sale Sharks), I Tuifua (Taranaki), F Otto (Bristol Rugby)
**HALF BACKS**: T Pisi (Suntory Sungoliath), K Fotuali'i (Northampton Saints), J Sua (Worcester Warriors)
**FORWARDS**: WO Avei (Bordeaux-Bègles), TT Paulo (ASM Clermont Auvergne), S Taulafo (Stade Français), L Mulipola (Leicester Tigers), V Afatia (SU Agen), JVI Johnston (Saracens), A Perenise (Bath Rugby), F Lemalu (Sanix Blues), TAM Paulo (Cardiff Blues), I Tekori (Stade Toulousain), P Faasalele (Castres Olympique), A Fa'osiliva (Bath Rugby), J Lam (Hurricanes), T Tuifua (Bordeaux-Bègles), FJ Levave (Hurricanes)
**HEAD COACH**: S Betham

### 9 November, Aviva Stadium, Dublin, Ireland 40 (3G 2T 3PG) Samoa 9 (3PG)

**IRELAND**: RDJ Kearney (Leinster); TJ Bowe (Ulster), BG O'Driscoll (Leinster), GWD D'Arcy (Leinster), FL McFadden (Leinster); DPLJ Jackson (Ulster), C Murray (Munster); JC McGrath (Leinster), RD Best (Ulster), MA Ross (Leinster), MP McCarthy (Leinster), D Toner (Leinster), P O'Mahony (Munster), CG Henry (Ulster), JPR Heaslip (Leinster)(captain)
**SUBSTITUTIONS**: SK O'Brien (Leinster) for Henry (34 mins); PJ O'Connell (Munster) for McCarthy (52 mins); CE Healy (Leinster), DJ Fitzpatrick (Ulster), EG Reddan (Leinster) & D Kearney (Leinster) for McGrath, Ross, Murray & Bowe (59 mins); SM Cronin (Leinster) & I Madigan (Leinster) for Best & O'Driscoll (69 mins)
**SCORERS**: *Tries*: D Kearney (2), O'Mahony, O'Brien, McFadden *Conversions*: Jackson (3) *Penalty Goals*: Jackson (3)
**SAMOA**: Autagavaia; Va'aulu, GT Pisi, Leota, Leiua; T Pisi, Fotuali'i (captain); Taulafo, Avei, Mulipoloa, Lemalu, TAM Paulo, Treviranus, Lam, Tuifua
**SUBSTITUTIONS**: J Johnston for Mulipola (7 mins); TT Paulo & Tekori for Avei & Lemalu (50 mins); Sua & Otto for T Pisi & Va'aulu (56 mins); Levave for Tuifua (64 mins); Afatia & I Tuifua for Taulafo & GT Pisi (73 mins)
**SCORERS**: *Penalty Goals:* T Pisi (2), Fotuali'i
**REFEREE**: SR Walsh (Australia)

### 23 November, Meskhi Stadium, Tbilisi, Georgia 16 (1G 3PG) Samoa 15 (1G 1T 1PG)

**GEORGIA**: M Kvirikashvili (Vienne); T Mchedlidze (Bresanne), Davit Kacharava (Yenisey-STM), M Sharikadze (Aurillacois), G Shkinin (Armia); L Khmaladze (Lelo), G Begadze (Batumi); M Nariashvili (Montpellier), S Mamukashvili (Armia), L Chilachava (Toulon), L Datunashvili (Aurillac), K Mikautadze (Toulon), G Tkhilaishvili (Armia), G Chkhaidze (Tarbes), M Gorgodze (Montpellier)(captain)
**SUBSTITUTIONS**: D Kubriashvili (Stade Français) for Chilachava (41 mins); T Zibzibadze (Périgueux) for Mchedlidze (49 mins); G Nemsadze (Tarbes) for Mikautadze (59 mins); B Tsiklauri (Locomotive) & Z Zhvania (Stade Français) for Shkinin & Nariashvili (67 mins); S Maisuradze (Stade Bagnérais) for Mamukashvili (68 mins); S Sutiashvili (Massy) for Tkhilaishvili (70 mins)
**SCORERS**: *Try*: Sharikadze *Conversion*: Kvirikashvili *Penalty Goals*: Kvirikashvili (3)
**SAMOA**: Autagavaia; Leiua, Tuifua, Leota, Sinoti; T Pisi, Fotuali'i (captain); Taulafo, TT Paulo, Johnstone, Faasalele, TAM Paulo, Treviranus, Lam, Levave

**SUBSTITUTIONS**: Va'aulu for Sinoti (41 mins); Tuifua for Treviranus (50 mins); Tekori for Faasalele (56 mins); K Pisi for Leota (59 mins); Perenise for Johnston (63 mins); Sua & Avei for Fotuali'i & TT Paulo (70 mins);
**SCORERS**: *Tries:* Leiua, Lam *Conversion:* T Pisi *Penalty Goal:* T Pisi
**REFEREE**: R Poite (France)

# JAPAN TO EUROPE 2013

## TOUR PARTY

**FULL BACKS**: A Goromaru (Yamaha Jubilo), Y Fujita (Waseda University)
**THREEQUARTERS**: T Hirose (Toshiba Brave Lupus), Y Fukuoka (Tsukuba University), A Yamada (Panasonic Wild Knights), Y Imamura (Kobe Steel), M Sa'u (Yamaha Jubilo), C Wing (Kobe Steel), K So (Yamaha Jubilo), Y Tamura (NEC Green Rockets), S Shimomura (Panasonic Wild Knights), Y Hayashi (Panasonic Wild Knights), K Matsushima (Sharks)
**HALF BACKS**: K Ono (Suntory Sungoliath), F Tanaka (Panasonic Wild Knights), A Hiwasa (Suntory Sungoliath), H Tatakawa (Kubota Spears)
**FORWARDS**: S Horie (Panasonic White Knights), Y Aoki (Suntory Sungoliath), H Yuhara (Toshiba Brave Lupus), M Mikami (Toshiba Brave Lupus), K Hatakeyama (Suntory Sungoliath), H Yamashita (Kobe Steel), Y Nagae (Ricoh Black Rams), H Hirashima (Kobe Steel), T Asahara (Toshiba Brave Lupus), L Thompson (Kintetsu Liners), S Makabe (Suntory Sungoliath), S Ito (Kobe Steel), H Ono (Toshiba Brave Lupus), J Ives (Canon Eagles), MJ Broadhurst (Ricoh Black Rams), H Tui (Suntory Sungoliath), K Horie (Yamaha Jubilo), RK Holani (Panasonic Wild Knights), T Kikutani (Toyota Verblitz)
**HEAD COACH**: E Jones

### 9 November, Murrayfield, Scotland 42 (3G 3T 2PG) Japan 17 (2G 1PG)

**SCOTLAND**: SD Maitland (Glasgow Warriors); TSF Seymour (Glasgow Warriors), NJ de Luca (Edinburgh Rugby), MCM Scott (Edinburgh Rugby), SF Lamont (Glasgow Warriors); RJH Jackson (London Wasps), GD Laidlaw (Edinburgh Rugby); R Grant (Glasgow Warriors), RW Ford (Edinburgh Rugby), EA Murray (Worcester Warriors), TJM Swinson (Glasgow Warriors), AD Kellock (Glasgow Warriors), AK Strokosch (USA Perpignan), KDR Brown (Saracens)(captain), DK Denton (Edinburgh Rugby)
**SUBSTITUTIONS**: AG Dickinson (Edinburgh Rugby) for Grant (28 mins); RJ Gray (Castres Olympique) for Kellock (57 mins); D Weir (Glasgow Warriors) for Jackson (65 mins); PC MacArthur (Glasgow Warriors) & JA Barclay (Scarlets) for Ford & Strokosch (70 mins); GDS Cross (London Irish) & HB Pyrgos (Glasgow Warriors) for Murray & Laidlaw (73 mins); DM Taylor (Saracens) for Maitland (77 mins)
**SCORERS**: *Tries:* Seymour (2), Laidlaw, Dickinson, Weir, Lamont *Conversions:* Laidlaw (2), Weir *Penalty Goals:* Laidlaw (2)
**JAPAN**: Goromaru; Hirose (captain), Sa'u, Wing, Fukuoka; K Ono, Tanaka; Mikami, S Horie, Hatakeyama, Thompson, Makabe, Broadhurst, Tui, Holani
**SUBSTITUTIONS**: Yamashita for Hatakeyama (33 mins); Hiwasa for Tanaka (61 mins); H Ono for Thompson (65 mins); Kikutani, Aoki & Tamura for Holani, Horie & Wing (70 mins); Fujita for Fukuoka (77 mins); Nagae for Mikami (78 mins)
**SCORERS**: *Tries:* Fukuoka (2) *Conversions:* Goromaru (2) *Penalty Goal:* Goromaru
**REFEREE**: JP Doyle (England)

### 12 November, Kingsholm, Gloucester, Gloucester 40 (5G 1T) Japan XV 5 (1T)

**GLOUCESTER SCORERS**: *Tries:* C Sharples (3), J Simpson-Daniel, S Reynolds, M Cox *Conversions:* R Cook (5)
**JAPAN XV SCORER**: *Try:* J Ives

### 15 November, Parc Eirias, Colwyn Bay, Russia 13 (1G 2PG) Japan 40 (3G 2T 3G)

**RUSSIA**: R Gaysin (Enisey STM); V Artemyev (Northampton Saints), D Gerasimov (Enisey STM), A Makovetskiy (Krasny Yar), V Ostroushko (Kuban Krasnodar); S Sugrobov (Slava CSP Moscow), A Ryabov (Krasny Yar); G Tsnobiladze (Krasny Yar), V Tsnobiladze (Enisey STM), E Pronenko (Enisey STM), A Voytov (VVA Podmoskovye) (captain), A Garbuzov (Krasny Yar), A Khudyakov (Krasny Yar), P Butenko (Enisey STM), V Gresev (Krasny Yar)
**SUBSTITUTIONS**: V Korshunov (VVA Podmoskovye) for V Tsnobiladze (46 mins); A Fatakhov (Strela-Agro) for Garbozov (58 mins); D Antonov (Slava CSP Moscow) for Voytov (59 mins); I Galinovskiy (Krasny Yar) for Gerasimov (62 mins); D Simplikevich (Enisey STM) for Gaysin (65 mins); I Zykov (Enisey STM) for Pronenko (75 mins); A Shcherban (Enisey STM) for Makovetskiy (78 mins)
**SCORERS**: *Try:* Ostroushko *Conversion:* Gaysin *Penalty Goals:* Gaysin (2)
**JAPAN**: Goromaru; Hirose (captain), Sa'u, Tamura, Fujita; K Ono, Tanaka; Mikami, S Horie, Hatakeyama, H Ono, Thompson, Tui, Broadhurst, Holani
**SUBSTITUTIONS**: Yamashita for Hatakeyama (temp 47–53 mins and 72 mins); Makabe for H Ono (50 mins); Ives for Holani (58 mins); Hiwasa for Tanaka (62 mins); Yamada & Hirashima for Tamura & Mikami (68 mins); Shimomura for Sa'u (69 mins); Yuhara for Horie (74 mins)
**SCORERS**: *Tries:* Tui, Broadhurst, Sa'u (2), Hirose *Conversions:* Goromaru (3) *Penalty Goals:* Goromaru (3)
**REFEREE**: L Pearce (England)

**SPAIN:** C Sempere; S Ascarat, M Heredia, J Nava, I Contardi; M Garcia, P Feijoo (captain); F Labbe, J Anaya, A Ortiz, A Blanco, D Barrera, G Rolls, M Cook, G Gibouin
**SUBSTITUTIONS:** A Newton & J Tudela for Rolls and Contardi (54 mins); U Lasa for Anaya (56 mins); A Pradalie for Labbe (58 mins); I Villanueva, J Canosa & I Genua for Barrera, Nava & Feijoo (61 mins)
**SCORERS:** *Try:* Sempere *Conversion:* Garcia
**JAPAN:** Goromaru; Hirose (captain), Sa'u, Tamura, Yamada; K Ono, Tanaka; Hirashima, S Horie, Yamashita, H Ono, Thompson, Tui, Broadhurst, Kikutani
**SUBSTITUTIONS:** Hatakeyama, Makabe & Hiwasa for Yamashita, Thompson & Tanaka (48 mins); Shimomura for Tamura (52 mins); Ives for Kikutani (62 mins); Mikami for Hirashima (75 mins); Yuhara & Imamura for Horie & Yamada (76 mins)
**SCORERS:** *Tries:* Horie, Broadhurst (2), Hirose *Conversion:* Goromaru *Penalty Goals:* Goromaru (6)
**REFEREE:** J Montes (Uruguay)

# FIJI TO EUROPE 2013

## TOUR PARTY

**FULL BACKS:** T Nagusa (Montpellier HRC), M Talebula (Bordeaux-Bègles)
**THREEQUARTERS:** N Nalaga (ASM Clermont Auvergne), A Tikoirotuma (Chiefs), L Botia (Police), N Nadolo (NEC Green Rockets), S Bai (Castres Olympique), A Rokobaro (Melbourne Rebels), M Bakaniceva (Tailevu)
**HALF BACKS:** W Luveniyali (Naitasiri), N Kenatale (Southland), N Matawalu (Glasgow Warriors), H Seniloli (Tailevu)
**FORWARDS:** V Veikoso (Suva), SN Naureure (Sigatoa Police), PR Kovekalou (Nadroga), J Yanuyanutawa (Glasgow Warriors), S Somocoa (Nadroga), C Ma'afu (Nottingham), M Saulo (Suva), L Waqaniburotu (CA Brive), A Ratuniyarawa (SU Agen), S Lewaravu (Stade Français), A Naikatini (CA Brive), A Qera (Stade Toulousain), A Delai (RC Tarbes), S Matevesi (Plymouth Albion), S Koyamaibole (CA Brive), M Ravulo (North Harbour), M Matadigo (Montpellier HRC), N Nagusa (Nadroga)
**HEAD COACH:** I Male

**PORTUGAL:** P Leal (GD Direito); G Foro (Centro Desportivo Universitário de Lisboa), P Avila (Centro Desportivo Universitário do Porto), M Leal (GD Direito), D Moreira (CF Belenenses); F Almeida (CF Belenenses), F Magalhaes (Centro Desportivo Universitário de Lisboa); J Segurado (GD Direito), J Correia (GD Direito), B Medeiros (Centro Desportivo Universitário de Lisboa), R Simoes (CF Belenenses), G Uva (Narbonne), A Duarte (AEIS Agronomia), J Bardy (ASM Clermont Auvergne), V Uva (GD Direito)(captain)
**SUBSTITUTIONS:** F Almeida (AEIS Agronomia) for Bardy (26 mins); L Salema (GD Direito) for F Almeida (31 mins); F Appleton (Centro Desportivo Universitario de Lisboa) for M Leal (56 mins); B Rocha (AEIS Tecnico) for Segurado (59 mins); R D'Orey (GD Direito) for Simoes (62 mins); F Oliveira (Centro Desportivo Universitário de Lisboa) for Moreira (70 mins); J Almeida (Centro Desportivo Universitário de Lisboa) for Medeiros (72 mins); F Tavares (GD Direito) for Correira (79 mins)
**SCORERS:** *Try:* Oliveira *Conversion:* P Leal *Penalty Goals:* P Leal (2)
**FIJI:** Nagusa; Nalaga, Nadolo, Baikeinuku, Tikoroituma; Luveniyali, Matawalu; Yanuyanutawa, Veikoso, Somoca, Ratuniyarawa, Lewaravu, Naikatini, Qera (captain), Koyamaibole
**SUBSTITUTIONS:** Ma'afu, Kenatale & Saulo for Yanuyanutawa, Tikoirotuma & Somoca (50 mins); Ravulo & Rokobaro for Koyamaibole & Luveniyali (53 mins); Waqaniburotu for Lewaravu (59 mins); Naureure & Botia for Veikoso & Baikeinuku (67 mins)
**SCORERS:** *Tries:* Tikoirotuma, Baikeinuku, Nalaga, Nadolo, Kenatala, Botia *Conversions:* Baikeinuku (3)
**REFEREE:** J Sylvestre (Argentina)

**ITALY:** L McLean (Treviso); G Venditti (Zebre), G Canale (La Rochelle), L Morisi (Treviso), T Iannone (Zebre); L Orquera (Zebre), E Gori (Treviso); M Rizzo (Treviso), L Ghiraldini (Treviso), M-L Castrogiovanni (RC Toulon), Geldenhuys (Zebre), V Bernabo (Treviso), A Zanni (Treviso), Mauro Bergamasco (Zebre), S Parisse (Stade Français)(captain)
**SUBSTITUTIONS:** M Campagnaro (Treviso) for Morisi (9 mins); T Botes (Treviso) for Gori (40 mins); L Cittadini (Treviso), D Giazzon (Zebre), M Aguero (Zebre) & M Vosawai (Treviso) for Rizzo, Ghiraldini, Castrogiovanni & Mauro Bergamasco (57 mins); T Allan (USA Perpignan) & J Furno (Biarritz Olympique) for Orquera & Bernabo (67 mins)
**SCORERS:** *Tries:* Parisse, McLean, Penalty try, Vosawai *Conversions:* Orquera (3), Allan *Penalty Goals:* Orquera (3)
**FIJI:** Talebula; Nagusa, Tikoroituma, Nadolo, Nalaga; Bai, Kenatale; Yanuyanutawa, Veikoso, Somoca, Naikatini, Lewaravu, Waqaniburotu, Qera (captain), Matadigo
**SUBSTITUTIONS:** Koyamaibole for Naikatini (40 mins); Naurere & Matawalu for Veikoso & Kenatale (55 mins); Ma'afu & Saulo for Yanuyanuwatu & Somoca (61 mins); Ravulo for Matadigo (63 mins); Delai for Waqaniburotu (76 mins)
**SCORERS:** *Tries:* Nagusa (2), Talebula, Nadolo, Nalaga *Conversions:* Bai (3)
**REFEREE:** L Hodges (Wales)

**23 November, Stadionul National Arcul de Triumf, Bucharest, Romania 7 (1G) Fiji 26 (1G 2T 3PG)**

**ROMANIA**: C Fercu (CSA Steaua Bucuresti); I Dumitru (CSA Steaua Bucuresti), CR Dascalu (CSA Steaua Bucuresti), C Gal (CSM Baia Mare), F Ionita (CSA Steaua Bucuresti); F Vlaicu (CSA Steaua Bucharest), V Calafeteanu (CSA Steaua Bucuresti); M Lazar (RC Timisoara), O Turashvili (RC Timisoara), P Ion (USA Perpignan), V Poparlan (RC Timisoara), M Sirbe (Tarbes), A Mitu (CSA Steaua Bucuresti), V Lucaci (CSA Steaua Bucuresti), M Macovei (St Nazaire)(captain)

**SUBSTITUTIONS**: F Surugiu (CSM Bucuresti) for Calafeteanu (44 mins); A Radoi (CSM Baia Mare) & C Pristavita (CSM Baia Mare) for Turashvili & M Lazar (53 mins); C Dinis (CSM Baia Mare) for Gal (temp 54–62 mins); S Hihetah (CSA Steaua Bucuresti) for Ionita (59 mins); A Coste (Bourg-en-Brasse) for Sirbe (62 mins); D Lazar for Mitu (63 mins); H Pungea (Scarlets) for Ion (65 mins); Dinis for Dascalu (68 mins)

**SCORERS**: *Try:* Penalty try *Conversion:* Vlaicu

**FIJI**: Talebula; T Nagusa, Tikoroituma, Nadolo, Nalaga; Baikeinuku, Serelevu; Yanuyanutawa, Naureure, Somoca, Lewaravu, Naikatini, Ravulo, Qera (captain), Matadigo

**SUBSTITUTIONS**: N Nagusa for Matadigo (14 mins); Bakaniceva for T Nagusa (59 mins); Ravai, Ma'afu & Saulo for Naureure, Somoca & Yanuyanutawa (60 mins); Matavesi for Ravulo (64 mins); Seniloli & Rokobaro for Serelevu & Baikeinuku (70 mins)

**SCORERS**: *Tries:* Talebula, Nadolo, T Nagusa *Conversion:* Baikeinuku *Penalty Goals:* Baikeinuku (2), Nadolo

**REFEREE**: D Phillips (Ireland)

# TONGA TO EUROPE 2013

## TOUR PARTY

**FULL BACKS**: VF Lilo (RC Tarbes), DT Halaifonua (Hofoa)

**THREEQUARTERS**: VFUA Helu (London Wasps), F Vainikolo (Exeter Chiefs), SV Piutau (Yamaha Jubilo), S Piukala (USA Perpignan), M Paea (Oyonnax)

**HALF BACKS**: F 'Apikotoa (Marist), L Fosita (Northland), UV Moa (Section Palois), T Palu (Wellington), S Fisilau (Bay of Plenty)

**FORWARDS**: E Taione (Jersey), AI Ma'asi (CS Vienne), S Taufalele (Counties Manakau), TS Mailau (Stade Montois), FKA Taumalolo (USA Perpignan), E Aholeli (Melbourne Rebels), SKV Puafisi (Tasman), T Vea (London Wasps), T Lokotui (Gloucester Rugby), JML Tuineau (Highlanders), U Kolo'ofai (US Colomiers), V Faingaa (GPS Brisbane), SM Kalamafoni (Gloucester Rugby), HNT Pole (Southland), NO Latu (Green Rockets), O Fonua (Aviron Bayonnais), VS Ma'afu (Oyonnax)

**HEAD COACH**: M 'Otai

**9 November, Stadionul National Arcul de Triumf, Bucharest, Romania 19 (1G 4PG) Tonga 18 (1G 1T 2PG)**

**ROMANIA**: C Fercu (CSA Steaua Bucuresti); I Dumitru (CSA Steaua Bucharest), C Gal (CSM Baia Mare), F Vlaicu (CSA Steaua Bucuresti), S Hihetah (CSA Steaua Bucuresti); V Calafeteanu (CSA Steaua Bucuresti), F Surugiu (CSM Steaua Bucuresti); M Lazar (RC Timisoara), O Turashvili (RC Timisoara), P Ion (USA Perpignan), V Poparlan (RC Timisoara), M Sirbe (Tarbes), V Lucaci (CSA Steaua Bucuresti), V Ursache (Oyonnax), M Macovei (St Nazaire)(captain)

**SUBSTITUTIONS**: C Pristavita (CSM Baia Mare) for M Lazar (58 mins); D Lazar (RC Timisoara) for Lucaci (64 mins); A Coste (Bourg-en-Bresse) & CR Dascalu (CSA Steaua Bucuresti) for Sirbe & Calafeteanu (71 mins); E Capatana (RC Timisoara) & H Pungea (Scarlets) for Ion & Turashvili (75 mins)

**SCORERS**: *Try:* Macovei *Conversion:* Vlaicu *Penalty Goals:* Vlaicu (4)

**TONGA**: Lilo; Helu, Piutau, Piukala, Vainikolo; 'Apikotoa, Palu; Taumalolo, Taione, Mailau, Lokotui, Kolo'ofa'i, Kalamafoni, Latu (captain), Ma'afu

**SUBSTITUTIONS**: Fisilau for Palu (64 mins); Puafisi for Mailau (66 mins); Fonua for Ma'afu (67 mins); Aholelei & Halaifonua for Taumalolo & Piukala (71 mins); Taufelele for Taione (78 mins)

**SCORERS**: *Tries:* Lilo, Helu *Conversion:* 'Apikotoa *Penalty Goals:* 'Apikotoa (2)

**REFEREE**: F Pastrana (Argentina)

**16 November, Stade Oceane, Le Havre, France 38 (3G 1T 4PG) Tonga 18 (1G 1T 2PG)**

**FRANCE**: B Dulin (Castres Olympique); S Guitoune (USA Perpignan), G Fickou (Stade Toulousain), W Fofana (ASM Clermont Auvergne), M Médard (Stade Toulousain); R Talès (Castres Olympique), M Parra (ASM Clermont Auvergne); Y Forestier (Castres Olympique), D Szarzewski (Racing Métro), N Mas (Montpellier HRC), S Vahaamahina (USA Perpignan), Y Maestri (Stade Toulousain), F Ouedraogo (Montpellier HRC), T Dusautoir (Stade Toulousain)(captain), D Chouly (ASM Clermont Auvergne)

**SUBSTITUTIONS**: B le Roux (Racing Métro) for Ouedraogo (14 mins); M Bastareaud (RC Toulon) for Fickou (temp 23–28 mins) & Fofana (65 mins); B Kayser (ASM Clermont Auvergne) for Szarzewski (temp 29–33 mins); V Debaty (ASM Clermont Auvergne) & R Slimani (Stade Français) for Szarzewski, Forestier & Mas (48 mins); M Michalak (RC Toulon) for Talès (65 mins); J Pelisse (Montpellier HRC) for Parra (70 mins); P Papé (Stade Français) for Dusautoir (72 mins)

**SCORERS**: *Tries:* Guitoune, Chouly, Dulin, Kayser *Conversions:* Parra (2), Michalak *Penalty Goals:* Parra (4)

**RED CARD**: Maestri (41 mins)

**564**

**TONGA:** Lilo; Helu, Piutau, Piukala, F Vainikolo; 'Apikotoa, Moa; Taumalolo, Taione, Mailau, Lokotui, Tuineau, Kalamafoni, Latu (captain), Fonua
**SUBSTITUTIONS:** Vea for Fonua (48 mins); Ma'asi & Pole for Taione & Kalamafoni (58 mins); Ma'afu & Fisilau for Tuineau & Moa (63 mins); Puafusi for Mailau (67 mins); Fosita for 'Apikotoa (70 mins); Halaifonua for Lilo (73 mins)
**SCORERS:** *Tries:* F Vainikolo (2) *Conversion:* Fosita *Penalty Goals:* 'Apikotoia (2)
**RED CARD:** Taumalolo (41 mins)
**REFEREE:** GW Jackson (New Zealand)

22 November, Millennium Stadium, Cardiff, Wales 17 (2G 1PG) Tonga 7 (1G)

**WALES:** SL Halfpenny (Cardiff Blues); GP North (Northampton Saints), OR Williams (Cardiff Blues), MA Beck (Ospreys), HB Amos (Newport Gwent Dragons); JW Hook (USA Perpignan), LD Williams (Cardiff Blues); P James (Bath Rugby), KJ Owens (Scarlets), Rhys P Jones (Scarlets), LC Charteris (USA Perpignan), IR Evans (Ospreys), DJ Lydiate (Racing Métro), JC Tipuric (Ospreys), Ryan P Jones (Ospreys)(captain)
**SUBSTITUTIONS:** DE Phillips (Scarlets), RJ Bevington (Ospreys), S Lee (Scarlets), R Priestland (Scarlets), A-W Jones (Ospreys) & R Williams (Scarlets) for Owens, James, Rhys P Jones, Hook, Evans & L Williams (69 mins)
**SCORERS:** *Tries:* OR Williams, Beck *Conversions:* Halfpenny (2) *Penalty Goal:* Halfpenny
**TONGA:** Lilo; Helu, Piutau, Paea, F Vainikolo; Fosita, Moa; Aholelei, Taione, Puafusi, Lokotui, Tuineau, Kalamafoni, Latu (captain), Ma'afu
**SUBSTITUTIONS:** Fonua for Ma'afu (41 mins); Pole for Kalamafoni (46 mins); Mailau, Vea & Fisilau for Aholelei, Puafusi & Moa (51 mins); Taufalele for Taione (63 mins); Halaifonua for Lilo (71 mins); 'Apikotoa for Fosita (76 mins)
**SCORERS:** *Try:* Helu *Conversion:* Fosita
**REFEREE:** MI Fraser (New Zealand)

# ENGLAND TO NEW ZEALAND 2014

## TOUR PARTY

**FULL BACKS:** MN Brown (Harlequins), BJ Foden (Northampton Saints), CJ Pennell (Worcester Warriors), DAV Goode (Saracens)
**THREEQUARTERS:** CJ Ashton (Saracens), MXG Yarde (London Irish), JJ May (Gloucester Rugby), BM Barritt (Saracens), LD Burrell (Northampton Saints), WWF Twelvetrees (Gloucester Rugby), EM Tuilagi (Leicester Tigers), KO Eastmond (Bath Rugby), HR Trinder (Gloucester Rugby), AKC Watson (Bath Rugby)
**HALF BACKS:** DS Care (Harlequins), BR Youngs (Leicester Tigers), LAW Dickson (Northampton Saints), REP Wigglesworth (Saracens), OA Farrell (Saracens), FS Burns (Gloucester Rugby), DJ Cipriani (Sale Sharks), SJ Myler (Northampton Saints)
**FORWARDS:** RW Webber (Bath Rugby), L Cowan-Dickie (Exeter Chiefs), DP Ward (Harlequins), JA Gray (Harlequins), DM Hartley (Northampton Saints), DG Wilson (Bath Rugby), JWG Marler (Harlequins), MJ Mullan (London Wasps), NG Catt (Bath Rugby), HM Thomas (Sale Sharks), K Brookes (Newcastle Falcons), KNJS Sinckler (Harlequins), AM Waller (Northampton Saints), CL Lawes (Northampton Saints), JO Launchbury (London Wasps), GMW Parling (Leicester Tigers), EN Slater (Leicester Tigers), DMJ Attwood (Bath Rugby), JAW Haskell (London Wasps), CDC Robshaw (Harlequins), TA Johnson (Exeter Chiefs), MB Kvesic (Gloucester Rugby), TA Wood (Northampton Saints), BJ Morgan (Gloucester Rugby), VML Vunipola (Saracens)
**HEAD COACH:** SW Lancaster

7 June, Eden Park, Auckland, New Zealand 20 (1T 5PG) England 15 (5PG)

**NEW ZEALAND:** IJA Dagg (Hawke's Bay); BR Smith (Otago), CG Smith (Wellington), MA Nonu (Wellington), CS Jane (Wellington); AW Cruden (Manawatu), AL Smith (Manawatu); TD Woodcock (North Harbour), DS Coles (Wellington), OT Franks (Hawke's Bay), BA Retallick (Bay of Plenty), SL Whitelock (Canterbury), LJ Messam (Waikato), RH McCaw (Canterbury)(captain), J Kaino (Auckland)
**SUBSTITUTIONS:** BJ Barrett (Taranaki) & CC Faumuina (Auckland) for Dagg & O Franks (54 mins); WWV Crockett (Canterbury), M Fekitoa (Auckland) & KF Mealamu (Auckland) for Woodcock, Nonu & Coles (59 mins); TJ Perenara (Wellington) for AL Smith (70 mins); VVJ Vito (Wellington) for Messam (71 mins)
**SCORERS:** *Try:* CG Smith *Penalty Goals:* Cruden (5)
**ENGLAND:** Brown; Yarde, Tuilagi, Eastwood, May; Burns, B Youngs; Marler, Webber, Wilson, Launchbury, Parling, Haskell, Robshaw (captain), Morgan
**SUBSTITUTIONS:** Gray, Thomas, Launchbury & Johnson for Webber, Wilson, Attwood & Haskell (70 mins); Cipriani for Burns (71 mins); Dickson & Pennell for B Youngs & May (79 mins)
**SCORERS:** *Penalty Goals:* Burns (4), Cipriani
**REFEREE:** N Owens (Wales)

14 June, Forsyth Barr Stadium, Dunedin New Zealand 28 (2G 1T 3PG) England 27 (3G 2PG)

**NEW ZEALAND:** BR Smith (Otago); CS Jane (Wellington), CG Smith (Wellington), MA Nonu (Auckland), SJ Savea (Wellington); AW Cruden (Manawatu), AL Smith (Manawatu); TD Woodcock (North Harbour), DS Coles (Wellington), OT Franks (Hawke's Bay), BA Retallick (Bay of Plenty), SL Whitelock (Canterbury), LJ Messam (Waikato), RH McCaw (Canterbury)(captain), J Kaino (Auckland)

**SUBSTITUTIONS**: BJ Barrett (Taranaki) for Cruden (50 mins); KF Mealamu (Auckland) for Coles (59 mins); CC Faumuina (Auckland), WWV Crockett (Canterbury) & VVJ Vito (Wellington) for O Franks, Woodcock & Messam (65 mins); TJ Perenara (Wellington) & P Tuipulotu (Auckland) for AL Smith & Retallick (76 mins)
**SCORERS**: *Tries*: BR Smith, Savea, Nonu *Conversions*: Cruden, Barrett *Penalty Goals*: Cruden (2), Barrett
**ENGLAND**: Brown; Tuilagi, Burrell, Twelvetrees, Yarde; Farrell, Care; Marler, Webber, Wilson, Launchbury, Parling, Wood, Robshaw (captain), Morgan
**SUBSTITUTIONS**: Hartley for Webber (47 mins); VML Vunipola & Lawes for Morgan & Launchbury (56 mins); Mullan, B Youngs & Ashton for Marler, Care & Burrell (71 mins); Brookes for Wilson (76 mins)
**SCORERS**: *Tries*: Yarde, Brown, Ashton *Conversions*: Farrell (3) *Penalty Goals*: Farrell (2)
**REFEREE**: J Peyper (South Africa)

**565**

### 17 June, AMI Stadium, Christchurch, Crusaders 7 (1G) England 38 (4G 2T)

**Crusaders Scorers**: *Try*: M Todd *Conversion*: T Taylor
**England Scorers**: *Tries*: Gray, Foden, Barritt, Goode, Watson, Pennell *Conversions*: Cipriani (3), Myler

### 21 June, Waikato Stadium, Hamilton, New Zealand 36 (4G 1T 1PG) England 13 (1G 2PG)

**NEW ZEALAND**: BR Smith (Otago); CS Jane (Wellington), M Fekitoa (Auckland), MA Nonu (Auckland), SJ Savea (Wellington); AW Cruden (Manawatu), AL Smith (Manawatu); TD Woodcock (North Harbour), DS Coles (Wellington), OT Franks (Hawke's Bay), BA Retallick (Bay of Plenty), SL Whitelock (Canterbury), J Kaino (Auckland), RH McCaw (Canterbury)(captain), KJ Read (Canterbury)
**SUBSTITUTIONS**: LJ Messam (Waikato) for Read (40 mins); BJ Barrett (Taranaki) & KF Mealamu (Auckland) for Cruden & Coles (44 mins); CC Faumuina (Auckland) for O Franks (58 mins); WWV Crockett (Canterbury) & RS Crotty (Canterbury) for Woodcock & Fekitoa (63 mins); TJ Perenara (Wellington) & Woodcock for AL Smith & Kaino (74 mins); P Tuipulotu (Auckland) for Retallick (76 mins)
**SCORERS**: *Tries*: Savea (3), AL Smith (2) *Conversions*; Cruden (3), Barrett *Penalty Goal*: Cruden
**ENGLAND**: Brown; Ashton, Tuilagi, Eastmond, Yarde; Burns, B Youngs; Marler, Hartley, Wilson, Lawes, Launchbury, Wood, Robshaw (captain), VML Vunipola
**SUBSTITUTIONS**: Attwood for Launchbury (temp 21–28 mins & 65 mins); Burrell for Eastmond (40 mins); Brookes & Morgan for Wilson & V Vunipola (56 mins); Webber for Hartley (58 mins); Cipriani for Burns (59 mins); Mullan for Marler (65 mins); Dickson for B Youngs (71 mins)
**SCORERS**: *Try*: Yarde *Conversion*: Burns *Penalty Goals*: Burns (2)
**REFEREE**: J Garces (France)

# WALES TO SOUTH AFRICA 2014
## TOUR PARTY

**FULL BACKS**: LB Williams (Scarlets), MJ Morgan (Ospreys)
**THREEQUARTERS**: GP North (Northampton Saints), ACG Cuthbert (Cardiff Blues), JR Williams (Scarlets), CL Allen (Cardiff Blues), JH Roberts (Racing Métro), JJV Davies (Scarlets), SC Shingler (Scarlets)
**HALF BACKS**: WM Phillips (Racing Métro), G Davies (Scarlets), R Williams (Scarlets), DR Biggar (Ospreys), JW Hook (USA Perpignan)
**FORWARDS**: KJ Owens (Scarlets), M Rees (Cardiff Blues), SJ Baldwin (Ospreys), GD Jenkins (Cardiff Blues), P James (Bath Rugby), AR Jones (Ospreys), Rhodri P Jones (Scarlets), AR Jarvis (Ospreys), S Lee (Scarlets), A Wyn-Jones (Ospreys)(captain), LC Charteris (USA Perpignan), JD Ball (Scarlets), IR Evans (Ospreys), AC Shingler (Scarlets), J Turnbull (Scarlets), D Lydiate (Racing Métro), TT Faletau (Newport Gwent Dragons), D Baker (Ospreys)
**HEAD COACH**: WD Gatland

### 10 June, Port Elizabeth, Eastern Province Kings 12 (1G 1T) Wales XV 34 (3G 2T 1PG)

**Eastern Province Kings scorers**: *Tries*: S Soyiswapi, S Kerrod *Conversion*: G Whitehead
**Wales XV scorers**: *Tries*: Turnbull, Allen, Cuthbert, Hook, G Davies *Conversions*: Hook (3) *Penalty Goals*: Hook

### 14 June, Kings Park, Durban, South Africa 38 (5G 1PG) Wales 16 (1G 1PG 2DG)

**SOUTH AFRICA**: WJ le Roux (Cheetahs); C Hendricks (Cheetahs), J-P R Pietersen (Sharks), JL Serfontein (Blue Bulls), BG Habana (RC Toulon); M Steyn (Stade Français), PF du Preez (Suntory Sungoliath); GG Steenkamp (Stade Toulousain), BW du Plessis (Sharks), JN du Plessis (Sharks), JP Botha (RC Toulon), V Matfield (Blue Bulls) (captain), L-F P Louw (Bath Rugby), WS Alberts (Sharks), DJ Vermeulen (Western Province)
**SUBSTITUTIONS**: L de Jager (Cheetahs) for Botha (40 mins); T Mtawarira (Sharks) for Steenkamp (53 mins); SWP Burger (Western Province) & CV Oosthuizen (Cheetahs) for Alberts & J du Plessis (58 mins); JL Goosen (Cheetahs), SB Brits (Saracens) & LN Mvovo (Sharks) for M Steyn, B du Plessis & Le Roux (70 mins); R Pienaar (Ulster) for Goosen (76 mins)
**SCORERS**: *Tries*: Habana (2), Vermeulen, Le Roux, Hendricks *Conversions*: M Steyn (5) *Penalty Goals*: M Steyn
**WALES**: L Williams; Cuthbert, J Davies, Roberts, North; Biggar, Phillips; Jenkins, Owens, AR Jones, Charteris, A-W Jones (captain), Lydiate, A Shingler, Faletau

**SUBSTITUTIONS**: Lee for AR Jones (31 mins); I Evans, Turnbull, G Davies & Morgan for Charteris, A Shingler, Phillips & L Williams (55 mins); Rees & James for Owens & Jenkins (58 mins); Hook for Biggar (64 mins)
**SCORERS**: *Try*: Cuthbert *Conversion*: Hook *Penalty Goal*: Biggar *Drop Goals:* Biggar (2)
**REFEREE**: R Poite (France)

### 21 June, Mbombela Stadium, Nelspruit, South Africa 31 (4G 1PG) Wales 30 (3G 3PG)

**SOUTH AFRICA**: WJ le Roux (Cheetahs); C Hendricks (Cheetahs), J-P R Pietersen (Sharks), JL Serfontein (Blue Bulls), BG Habana (RC Toulon); M Steyn (Stade Français), PF du Preez (Suntory Sungoliath); T Matawarira (Sharks), BW du Plessis (Sharks), JN du Plessis (Sharks), PR van der Merwe (Blue Bulls), V Matfield (Blue Bulls)(captain), L-F P Louw (Bath Rugby), WS Alberts (Sharks), DJ Vermeulen (Western Province)
**SUBSTITUTIONS**: R Pienaar (Ulster) for Steyn (temp 23–29 mins); SWP Burger (Western Province) for Alberts (26 mins); L de Jager (Cheetahs) for Van der Merwe (45 mins); CV Oosthuizen (Cheetahs) for JN du Plessis (58 mins); GG Steenkamp (Stade Toulousain) & SB Brits (Saracens) for Matawarira & BW du Plessis (65 mins); W Olivier (Blue Bulls) for Serfontein (74 mins)
**SCORERS**: *Tries*: Penalty tries (2), Hendricks, Le Roux *Conversions*: M Steyn (4) *Penalty Goal*: M Steyn
**WALES**: L Williams; Cuthbert, J Davies, Roberts, North; Biggar, Phillips; Jenkins, Owens, Lee, Charteris, A-W Jones (captain), Lydiate, Turnbull, Faletau
**SUBSTITUTIONS**: Jarvis for Lee (51 mins); James, Rees & Ball for Jenkins, Owens & Charteris (74 mins)
**SCORERS**: *Tries*: Roberts, Cuthbert, Owens *Conversions*: Biggar (3) *Penalty Goals:* Biggar (3)
**REFEREE**: SR Walsh (Australia)

# FRANCE TO AUSTRALIA 2014

## TOUR PARTY

**FULL BACKS**: B Dulin (Castres Olympique), H Bonneval (Stade Français)
**THREEQUARTERS**: Y Huget (Stade Toulousain), F Le Bourhis (Bordeaux-Bègles), M Médard (Stade Toulousain), M Bastareaud (RC Toulon), G Fickou (Stade Toulousain), W Fofana (ASM Clermont Auvergne), R Lamerat (Castres Olympique)
**HALF BACKS**: M Machenaud (Racing Métro), F Michalak (RC Toulon), M Parra (ASM Clermont Auvergne), R Talès (Castres Olympique),
**FORWARDS**: B Mach (Castres Olympique), G Guirado (USA Perpignan), C Tolofua (Stade Toulousain), V Debaty (ASM Clermont Auvergne), T Domingo (ASM Clermont Auvergne), N Mas (Montpellier HRC), R Slimani (Stade Français), A Menini (RC Toulon), A Flanquart (Stade Français), Y Maestri (Stade Toulousain), S Vahaamahina (USA Perpignan), Y Nyanga (Stade Toulousain), F Ouedraogo (Montpellier HRC), D Chouly (ASM Clermont Auvergne), T Dusautoir (Stade Toulousain)(captain), A Burban (Stade Français), B le Roux (Racing Métro), L Picamoles (Stade Toulousain)
**HEAD COACH**: P Saint-André

### 7 June, Suncorp Stadium, Brisbane, Australia 50 (6G 1T 1PG) France 23 (2G 2PG 1DG)

**AUSTRALIA**: I Folau (NSW Waratahs); AP Ashley-Cooper (NSW Waratahs), RTRN Kuridrani (ACT Brumbies), MP Toomua (ACT Brumbies), NM Cummins (Western Force); BT Foley (NSW Waratahs), NW White (ACT Brumbies); JA Slipper (Queensland Reds), ST Moore (ACT Brumbies)(captain), SM Kepu (NSW Waratahs), STG Carter (ACT Brumbies), RA Simmons (Queensland Reds), SM Fardy (ACT Brumbies), MK Hooper (NSW Waratahs), WL Palu (NSW Waratahs)
**SUBSTITUTIONS**: SUT Polota-Nau (NSW Waratahs) for Moore (5 mins); PJ Ryan (NSW Waratahs) for Kepu (53 mins); BJ McCalman (Western Force) for Palu (54 mins); KJ Beale (NSW Waratahs), NJ Phipps (NSW Waratahs) & PJM Cowan (Western Force) for Toomua, White & Slipper (62 mins); JE Horwill (Queensland Reds) & PJ McCabe (ACT Brumbies) for Simmons & Kuridrani (70 mins)
**SCORERS**: *Tries*: Folau, Ashley-Cooper, Hooper, Toomua, Cummins, Beale, McCabe *Conversions*: Foley (6) *Penalty Goal*: Foley
**FRANCE**: Bonneval; Huget, Fickou, Fofana, Le Bourhis; Michalak, Machenaud; Domingo, Guirado, Mas (captain), Vahaamahina, Maestri, Ouedraogo, Le Roux, Chouly
**SUBSTITUTIONS**: Debaty, Slimani, Flanquart & Dulin for Domingo, Mas, Vahaamahina & Le Bourhis (54 mins); Burban for Le Roux (61 mins); Parra & Tolofua for Machenaud & Guirado (69 mins); Lamerat for Fickou (73 mins)
**SCORERS**: *Tries*: Parra, Penalty try *Conversions*: Michalak (2) *Penalty Goals*: Michalak (2) *Drop Goal*: Michalak
**REFEREE**: C Joubert (South Africa)

### 14 June, Etihad Stadium, Melbourne, Australia 6 (2PG) France 0

**AUSTRALIA**: I Folau (NSW Waratahs); AP Ashley-Cooper (NSW Waratahs), RTRN Kuridrani (ACT Brumbies), MP Toomua (ACT Brumbies), NM Cummins (Western Force); BT Foley (NSW Waratahs), NW White (ACT Brumbies); JA Slipper (Queensland Reds), SUT Polota-Nau (NSW Waratahs), SM Kepu (NSW Waratahs), RA Simmons (Queensland Reds), JE Horwill (Queensland Reds), SM Fardy (ACT Brumbies), MK Hooper (NSW Waratahs) (captain), BJ McCalman (Western Force)

**SUBSTITUTIONS**: PJ McCabe (ACT Brumbies) & LM Jones (Melbourne Rebels) for Kuridrani & Horwill (59 mins); KJ Beale (NSW Waratahs) for Foley (60 mins); S Higginbotham (Melbourne Rebels) for Fardy (66 mins); PJM Cowan (Western Force) for Slipper (71 mins); NL Charles (Western Force) & LN Weeks (Melbourne Rebels) for Polota-Nau & Kepu (74 mins); NJ Phipps (NSW Waratahs) for White (78 mins)
**SCORERS**: *Penalty Goals*: Foley, White
**FRANCE**: Dulin; Huget, Bastareaud, Fofana, Médard; Talès, Parra; Menini, Guirado, Slimani, Flanquart, Maestri, Dusautoir (captain), Nyanga, Chouly
**SUBSTITUTIONS**: Burban for Nyanga (46 mins); Domingo & Mas for Menini & Slimani (50 mins); Le Roux for Flanquart (66 mins); Picamoles for Dusautoir (67 mins); Mach for Guirado (71 mins); Michalak & Lamerat for Parra & Médard (75 mins)
**REFEREE**: W Barnes (England)

**21 June, Allianz Stadium, Sydney Football Stadium, Australia 39 (4G 1T 2PG) France 13 (1G 2PG)**

**AUSTRALIA**: I Folau (NSW Waratahs); AP Ashley-Cooper (NSW Waratahs), RTRN Kuridrani (ACT Brumbies), MP Toomua (ACT Brumbies), NM Cummins (Western Force); BT Foley (NSW Waratahs), NW White (ACT Brumbies); JA Slipper (Queensland Reds), SUT Polota-Nau (NSW Waratahs), SM Kepu (Waratahs), W Skelton (NSW Waratahs), RA Simmons (Queensland Reds), SM Fardy (ACT Brumbies), MK Hooper (NSW Waratahs) (captain), WL Palu (NSW Waratahs)
**SUBSTITUTIONS**: ST Sio (ACT Brumbies) for Slipper (52 mins); KJ Beale (NSW Waratahs) for Toomua (54 mins); JE Horwill (Queensland Reds) for Skelton (56 mins); LN Weeks (Melbourne Rebels) & NJ Phipps (NSW Waratahs) for Kepu & White (58 mins); BJ McCalman (Western Force) for Palu (63 mins); NL Charles (Western Force) for Polota-Nau (68 mins); RG Horne (NSW Waratahs) for Kuidrani (70 mins)
**SCORERS**: *Tries*: Folau (2), Skelton, Hooper, Phipps *Conversions*: Foley (4) *Penalty Goals*: Foley (2)
**FRANCE**: Dulin; Huget, Bastareaud, Fofana, Bonneval; Talès, Machenaud; Menini, Guirado, Slimani, Flanquart, Maestri, Dusautoir (captain), Ouedraogo, Chouly
**SUBSTITUTIONS**: Lamerat for Bonneval (43 mins); Domingo & Debaty for Menini & Slimani (47 mins); Nyanga for Ouedraogo (50 mins); Picamoles for Chouly (58 mins); Le Roux for Flanquart (59 mins); Tolofua for Guirado (68 mins); Michalak for Talès (70 mins)
**SCORERS**: *Try*: Guirado *Conversion*: Machenaud *Penalty Goals*: Dulin, Machenaud
**REFEREE**: CJ Pollock (New Zealand)

# IRELAND TO ARGENTINA 2014

## TOUR PARTY

**FULL BACKS**: RDJ Kearney (Leinster), FA Jones (Munster)
**THREEQUARTERS**: FL McFadden (Leinster), AD Trimble (Ulster), SR Zebo (Munster), DM Cave (Ulster), I Madigan (Leinster), N Reid (Leinster)
**HALF BACKS**: C Murray (Munster), EG Reddan (Leinster), LD Marshall (Ulster), KD Marmion (Connacht), JJ Sexton (Racing Métro)
**FORWARDS**: RD Best (Ulster), D Varley (Munster), RW Herring (Ulster), J Cronin (Munster), MA Ross (Leinster), D Kilcoyne (Munster), M Moore (Leinster), JC McGrath (Leinster), R Ah You (Connacht), PJ O'Connell (Munster) (captain), D Toner (Leinster), RJE Diack (Ulster), J Murphy (Leinster), WI Henderson (Ulster), CG Henry (Ulster), R Ruddock (Leinster), JPR Heaslip (Leinster)
**HEAD COACH**: J Schmidt

**7 June, Estadio Centenario, Resistancia, Argentina 17 (2G 1PG) Ireland 29 (1G 2T 4PG)**

**ARGENTINA**: J Tuculet (unattached); S Cordero (Regatas Bella Vista), J de la Fuente (Duendes), G Ascarate (Natacion y Gimnasia), M Montero (Pucara); N Sánchez (Bordeaux-Bègles), M Landajo (CA San Isidro)(captain); L Noguera Paz (Lince), M Cortese (Liceo), R Herrera (Castres Olympique), M Carizza (Stormers), T Lavanini (Hindu), R Báez (Liceo), T de la Vega (CUBA), B Macome (unattached)
**SUBSTITUTIONS**: M Alemanno (La Tablada) for Carizza (40 mins); N Tetaz Chaparro (La Plata) for Herrera (56 mins); J Montoya (Club Newman) for Cortese (57 mins); J Ortega Desio (Estudiantes de Parana) & T Cubelli (Belgrano Athletic) for Báez & Landajo (64 mins); L González Amorosino (Oyonnax) for Cordero (64 mins); S González Iglesias (AA Alumni) for Sánchez (69 mins); Cordero for Tuculet (73 mins); B Postiglioni (La Plata) for Noguera Paz (75 mins)
**SCORERS**: *Tries*: Montero, De la Vega *Conversions*: Sánchez, González Iglesias *Penalty Goal:* Sánchez
**IRELAND**: Jones; Trimble, Cave, Marshall, Zebo; Sexton, Murray; McGrath, Best, Ross, Henderson, O'Connell (captain), Diack, Henry, Murphy
**SUBSTITUTIONS**: Heaslip, Marmion & McFadden for Murphy, Murray & Marshall (57 mins); Kilcoyne for McGrath (60 mins); Madigan for Sexton (63 mins); Varley, Ah You & Toner for Best, Ross & O'Connell (68 mins)
**SCORERS**: *Tries*: Henry, Sexton, Trimble *Conversion*: Sexton *Penalty Goals*: Sexton (2), Madigan (2)
**REFEREE**: GW Jackson (New Zealand)

**14 June, Estadio Jose Fierro, Tucuman, Argentina 17 (2G 1PG) Ireland 23 (2G 3PG)**

**ARGENTINA**: J Tuculet (unattached); L González Amorosino (Oyonnax), J de la Fuente (Duendes), G Ascarate (Natacion y Gimnasia), M Montero (Pucara); N Sánchez (Bordeaux-Bègles), M Landajo (CA San Isidro)(captain); L Noguera Paz (Lince), M Cortese (Liceo), R Herrera (Castres Olympique), M Carizza (Stormers), T Lavanini (Hindu), R Báez (Liceo), T de la Vega (CUBA), A Ahualli de Chazal (San Isidro Club)
**SUBSTITUTIONS**: S Iglesias Valdez (Universitario) for Ahualli de Chazal (temp 11–19 mins) & Cortese (29 mins); M Orlando (Huirapuca) for Tuculet (temp 48–60 mins) & Ascarate (62 mins); M Diaz (Highlanders) for Herrera (51 mins); T Cubelli (Belgrano Athletic), B Postiglioni (La Plata) & J Ortega Desio (Estudiantes de Parana) for Landajo, Iglesias Valdez & Ahualli de Chazal (63 mins); S González Iglesias (AA Alumni) for Sánchez (65 mins); Herrera for Paz (68 mins); M Alemanno (La Tablada) for Lavanini (70 mins)
**SCORERS**: *Tries:* Tuculet, González Amorosino *Conversions:* Sánchez, González Iglesias *Penalty Goal:* Sánchez
**IRELAND**: R Kearney; Trimble, McFadden, Cave, Zebo; Sexton, Reddan; Kilcoyne, Best, Ross, Toner, O'Connell (captain), Ruddock, Henry, Heaslip
**SUBSTITUTIONS**: Henderson for Toner (40 mins); McGrath for Kilcoyne (57 mins); Murphy for Henry (62 mins); Madigan for Sexton (63 mins); Reid & J Cronin for Cave & Ross (72 mins); Herring & Marmion for Ruddock & Reddan (77 mins)
**SCORERS**: *Tries*: Zebo, Madigan *Conversions*: Sexton, Madigan *Penalty Goals*: Sexton (3)
**REFEREE**: P Gauzere (France)

# SCOTLAND TO NORTH AMERICA 2014

## TOUR PARTY

**FULL BACK**: SW Hogg (Glasgow Warriors)
**THREEQUARTERS**: SF Lamont (Glasgow Warriors), SD Maitland (Glasgow Warriors), TJW Visser (Edinburgh Rugby), DM Taylor (Saracens), MB Evans (Castres Olympique), AJ Dunbar (Glasgow Warriors), *P Horne (Glasgow Warriors)
**HALF BACKS**: CP Cusiter (Sale Sharks), GD Laidlaw (Gloucester Rugby), FA Russell (Glasgow Warriors), TA Heathcote (Bath Rugby), GJ Hart (Edinburgh Rugby)
**FORWARDS**: K Bryce (Glasgow Warriors), S Lawson (Newcastle Falcons), PC MacArthur (Glasgow Warriors), GDS Cross (London Irish), K Traynor (Bristol Rugby), AG Allan (Glasgow Warriors), MJ Low (Exeter Chiefs), G Reid (Glasgow Warriors), GS Gilchrist (Edinburgh Rugby), RJ Gray (Castres Olympique), JL Hamilton (Montpellier HRC), K Low (London Irish), *TJM Swinson (Glasgow Warriors), KDR Brown (Saracens), AF Strokosch (USA Perpignan) JW Beattie (Montpellier HRC), BA Cowan (London Irish)
* Replacements on tour
**HEAD COACH**: V Cotter

**7 June, BBVA Compass Stadium, Houston, USA 6 (2PG) Scotland 24 (3G 1PG)**

**USA**: C Wyles (Saracens); B Scully (Leicester Tigers), S Kelly (California Golden Bears), A Suniula (London Wasps), L Hume (RC Narbonne); S Suniula (Belmont Shore), M Petri (New York AC); O Kilifi (Seattle-POSB), P Thiel (Life University), E Fry (Newcastle Falcons), L Stanfill (Seattle-OSPB), H Smith (Saracens), T Clever (NTT Shining Arcs)(captain), S LaValla (Stade Français), C Dolan (Northampton Saints)
**SUBSTITUTIONS**: T Coolican (Eastern Suburbs) for Thiel (20 mins); F Niua (Glasgow Warriors) for A Suniula (22 mins); N Wallace (James Bay AA) for Smith (temp 29–40 mins) & Fry (40 mins); T Lamositele (Saracens) & D Barrett (University of California) for Kilifi & Smith (54 mins); T Tuisamoa (OMBAC) for Stanfill (63 mins); T Maupin (Olympic Club, San Francisco) for Scully (70 mins); CJ Landon (Glendale Raptors) for Clever (temp 75–80 mins)
**SCORERS**: *Penalty Goals*: Wyles (2)
**SCOTLAND**: Hogg; Maitland, S Lamont, Taylor, Visser; Russell, Laidlaw (captain); Reid, Lawson, Cross, R Gray, Hamilton, Cowan, Beattie
**SUBSTITUTIONS**: Gilchrist for Hamilton (38 mins); M Low for Cross (40 mins); Allan for Reid (56 mins); Evans, MacArthur & K Low for Taylor, Lawson & Strokosch (62 mins); Jackson for Hogg (76 mins)
**SCORERS**: *Tries*: Visser, Penalty try, Hogg *Conversions*: Laidlaw (3) *Penalty Goal*: Laidlaw
**REFEREE**: P Gauzere (France)

**14 June, BMO Field, Toronto, Canada 17 (1T 4PG) Scotland 19 (1G 4PG)**

**CANADA**: J Pritchard (Bedford Blues); J Hassler (Ospreys), C Hearn (Castaway Wanderers), N Blevins (Calgary Hornets), T Paris (SU Agen); H Jones (Capilanos), P Mack (James Bay AA); H Buydens (Manawatu), A Carpenter (Cornish Pirates), J Marshall (La Rochelle), J Hotson (London Scottish), J Cudmore (ASM Clermont Auvergne), J Sinclair (London Irish), J Moonlight (James Bay AA), T Ardron (Ospreys)(captain)
**SUBSTITUTIONS**: DTH van der Merwe (Glasgow Warriors) for Paris (43 mins); A Tiedemann (Castaway Wanderers) for Buydens (53 mins); R Barkwill (Niagara Wasps) for Carpenter (58 mins); C Braid (James Bay AA) for Blevins (63 mins); G McRorie (Calgary Hornets) for Mack (70 mins); J Ilnicki (Castaway Wanderers) for Marshall (77 mins)

SCORERS: *Try*: Hassler *Penalty Goals*: Pritchard (4)
RED CARD: Sinclair (75 mins)
SCOTLAND: Hogg; Maitland, Lamont, Horne, Visser; Russell, Laidlaw (captain); Reid, Lawson, M Low, R Gray, Gilchrist, Strokosch, Brown, Beattie
SUBSTITUTIONS: Cowan for Strokosch (30 mins); Cross & K Low for Brown & M Low (50 mins); Bryce for Beattie (58 mins); Jackson for Russell (62 mins); Evans for Visser (65 mins); Hart for Jackson (76 mins)
SCORERS: *Try:* Gilchrist *Conversion:* Laidlaw *Penalty Goals:* Laidlaw (3), Hogg
REFEREE: MI Fraser (New Zealand)

# SCOTLAND TO ARGENTINA & SOUTH AFRICA 2014

**TOUR PARTY**

FULL BACKS: SW Hogg (Glasgow Warriors), PE Murchie (Glasgow Warriors)
THREEQUARTERS: TSF Seymour (Glasgow Warriors), SD Maitland (Glasgow Warriors), DJ Fife (Edinburgh Rugby), AJ Dunbar (Glasgow Warriors), P Horne (Glasgow Warriors), NJ de Luca (Biarritz Olympique)
HALF BACKS: GJ Hart (Edinburgh Rugby), HB Pyrgos (Glasgow Warriors), D Weir (Glasgow Warriors), RJH Jackson (Glasgow Warriors), TA Heathcote (Bath Rugby)
FORWARDS: RW Ford (Edinburgh Rugby), K Bryce (Glasgow Warriors), PC MacArthur (Glasgow Warriors), MJ Low (Exeter Chiefs), G Reid (Glasgow Warriors), J Welsh (Glasgow Warriors), GDS Cross (London Irish), AG Dickinson (Edinburgh Rugby), *EA Murray (Glasgow Warriors), GS Gilchrist (Edinburgh Rugby), JD Gray (Glasgow Warriors), TJM Swinson (Glasgow Warriors), R Harley (Glasgow Warriors), C Fusaro (Glasgow Warriors), BA Cowan (London Irish), K Low (London Irish), *T Holmes (Glasgow Warriors), *A Ashe (Glasgow Warriors)
* Replacement on tour

**20 June, Estadio Mario Alberto Kempes, Cordoba, Argentina 19 (2T 1DG 2PG) Scotland 21 (1G 1T 3PG)**

ARGENTINA: L González Amorosino (Oyonnax); S Cordero (Regatas Bella Vista), M Orlando (Huirapuca), S González Iglesias (AA Alumni), M Montero (Pucara); N Sánchez (Bordeaux-Bègles), T Cubelli (Belgrano Athletic)(captain); B Postiglioni (La Plata), J Montoya (Club Newman), M Diaz (Highlanders), M Carizza (Stormers), M Alemanno (La Tablada), R Báez (Liceo), J Ortega Desio (Estudiantes de Parana), T de la Vega (CUBA)
SUBSTITUTIONS: N Tetaz Chaparro (La Plata) for Diaz (46 mins); S Iglesias Valdez (Universitario) for Montoya (50 mins); T Lavanini (Hindu) for Alemanno (55 mins); A Ahualli de Chazal (San Isidro Club) for J Ortega Desio (56 mins); J Tuculet (unattached) for Cordero, Postiglioni & Cubelli (57 mins); M Moroni (CUBA) for Orlando (61 mins); Cubelli for Sánchez (temp 64–71 mins)
SCORERS: *Tries:* J Ortega Desio, Tuculet *Penalty Goals:* Sánchez (2) *Drop Goal:* Sánchez
SCOTLAND: Hogg; Maitland, De Luca, Horne, Seymour; Russell, Weir, Hart; Dickinson, Ford, Cross, J Gray, Gilchrist (captain), Harley, Cowan, K Low
SUBSTITUTIONS: Pyrgos for Hart (47 mins); Swinson for J Gray (55 mins); Reid, MacArthur, Welsh & Fusaro for Dickinson, Ford, Cross & Cowan (61 mins); Fife for Horne (64 mins)
SCORERS: *Tries:* Hogg, Pyrgos *Conversion:* Weir *Penalty Goals:* Weir (3)
REFEREE: J Lacey (Ireland)

**28 June, Nelson Mandela Bay Stadium, Port Elizabeth, South Africa 55 (6G 2T 1PG) Scotland 6 (2PG)**

SOUTH AFRICA: WJ le Roux (Cheetahs); C Hendricks (Cheetahs), J-P R Pietersen (Sharks), JL Serfontein (Blue Bulls), LN Mvovo (Sharks); H Pollard (Blue Bulls), PF du Preez (Suntory Sungoliath); CV Oosthuizen (Cheetahs), BW du Plessis (Sharks), JN du Plessis (Sharks), L de Jager (Cheetahs), V Matfield (Blue Bulls) (captain), MC Coetzee (Sharks), SWP Burger (Stormers), DJ Vermeulen (Stormers)
SUBSTITUTIONS: Z Kirchner (Leinster) for Le Roux (temp 21–27 mins & 75 mins); F Hougaard (Blue Bulls) for Du Preez (28 mins); M van der Merwe (Blue Bulls) for Oosthuizen (50 mins); JA Strauss (Cheetahs) for BW du Plessis (54 mins); T Mohoje (Cheetahs) for Vermeulen (66 mins); TN Nyakane (Cheetahs), JST Lewies (Sharks) & ML Boshoff (Blue Bulls) for J du Plessis, Matfield & Pollard (70 mins)
SCORERS: *Tries:* Coetzee (2), Mvovo (2), De Jager (2), Le Roux, Pietersen *Conversions:* Pollard (5), Boshoff *Penalty Goal:* Boshoff
SCOTLAND: Hogg; Maitland, De Luca, Horne, Seymour; Russell, Weir, Pyrgos; Dickinson, Ford, Cross, Swinson, Gilchrist (captain), Harley, Fusaro, Ashe
SUBSTITUTIONS: Holmes for Fusaro (48 mins); Murray for Cross (50 mins); Fife for Maitland (53 mins); Bryce & J Gray for Ford & Swinson (60 mins); Murchie for Hogg (70 mins); Hart for Pyrgos (76 mins); M Low for Dickinson (78 mins)
SCORERS: *Penalty Goals:* Weir (2)
REFEREE: GW Jackson (New Zealand)

# ITALY TO FIJI, SAMOA & JAPAN 2014

## TOUR PARTY

**FULL BACKS**: A Masi (London Wasps), L McLean (Treviso)

**THREEQUARTERS**: G Venditti (Zebre), L Sarto (Zebre), T Iannone (Treviso), G Garcia (Zebre), M Campagnaro (Treviso), A Esposito (Treviso), A Sgarbi (Treviso)

**HALF BACKS**: T Tebaldi (Ospreys), G Palazzani (Zebre), T Allan (USA Perpignan), L Orquera (Zebre)

**FORWARDS**: L Ghiraldini (Treviso), D Giazzon (Zebre), A Manici (Zebre), M Aguero (Zebre), D Chistolini (Zebre), L Cittadini (Treviso), Alberto de Marchi (Treviso), Andrea de Marchi (Zebre), M Bortolami (Zebre), GF Biagi (Zebre), M Fuser (Treviso), Q Geldenhuys (Zebre)(captain), J Furno (Biarritz Olympique), R Barbieri (Treviso), Mauro Bergamasco (Zebre), P Derbyshire (Treviso), M Vosawai (Treviso)

**HEAD COACH**: J Brunel

### 7 June, ANZ Stadium, Suva, Fiji 25 (2G 1T 2PG) Italy 14 (2G)

**FIJI**: M Talebula (Bordeaux-Bègles); N Nalaga (ASM Clermont Auvergne), A Tikoirotuma (Chiefs), N Nadolo (Crusaders), T Nagusa (Montpellier HRC); J Ralulu (Nadroga), N Kenatale (Southland); C Ma'afu (Nottingham), T Talemaitoga (Southland), M Saulo (Suva); A Ratiuniyarawa (SU Agen), A Naiikatini (CA Brive); D Waqaniburotu (CA Brive), A Qera (Stade Toulousain)(captain), N Nagusa (Nadroga)

**SUBSTITUTIONS**: W Votu (USA Perpignan) for Nadolo (temp 4–10 mins) & Talebula (37 mins); N Matawalu (Glasgow Warriors), I Colati (RC Nevers) & S Koto (RC Narbonne) for Kenatale, Saulo & Talemaitoga (40 mins); J Yanuyanutawa (Glasgow Warriors) for Ma'afa (47 mins); W Lewaravu (Stade Montois) for Naikatini (63 mins); A Delai (RC Tarbes) for N Nagusa (70 mins); M Ravulo (Farul Constanta) for N Nagusa (76 mins)

**SCORERS**: *Tries:* Nadolo, Waqaniburotu, Nalaga *Conversions:* Nadolo, Ralulu *Penalty Goal:* Nadolo

**ITALY**: McLean; Sarto, Campagnaro, Sgarbi, Venditti; Orquera, Palazzani; Aguero, Ghiraldini, Cittadini, Geldenhuys (captain), Bortolami, Furno, Mauro Bergamasco, Vosawai

**SUBSTITUTIONS**: Alberto de Marchi, Antonio de Marchi & Giazzon for Cittadini, Aguero & Ghiraldini (53 mins); Biagi for Bortolami (61 mins); Derbyshire for Vosawai (66 mins); Masi for Sarto (67 mins)

**SCORERS**: *Tries:* Penalty tries (2) *Conversions:* Orquera (2)

**REFEREE**: JP Doyle (England)

### 14 June, Apia Park, Apia, Samoa 15 (5PG) Italy 0

**SAMOA:** F Autagavaia (Northampton Saints); F Otto (Bristol Rugby), GT Pisi (Northampton Saints), A Leiua (Hurricanes), D Lemi (Worcester Warriors)(captain); T Pisi (Suntory Sungoliath), KF Fotuali'i (Northampton Saints); L Mulipola (Leicester Tigers), TT Paulo (ASM Clermont Auvergne), JVA Johnston (Saracens), F Lemalu (Sanix Blues), D Leo (USA Perpignan), O Treviranus (London Irish), JT Lam (Hurricanes), KG Thompson (Chiefs)

**SUBSTITUTIONS**: WO Avei (Bordeaux-Bègles); CAI Johnston (Stade Toulousain) & M Fa'asavalu (Harlequins) for TT Paulo, J Johnston & Thompson (60 mins); P Faasalele (Castres Olympique) for Lemalu (63 mins); S Taulafo (Stade Français), V Afemai (Vaiala) & JW Leota (Sale Sharks) for Mulipola, Fotuali'i & Otto (71 mins)

**SCORERS**: *Penalty Goals:* T Pisi (5)

**ITALY**: McLean; Esposito, Masi, Garcia, Venditti; Allan, Tebaldi; Alberto de Marchi, Ghiraldini, Cittadini, Geldenhuys (captain), Biagi, Furno, Mauro Bergamasco, Barbieri

**SUBSTITUTIONS**: Aguero & Chistolini for Alberto de Marchi & Cittadini (53 mins); Manici for Ghiraldini (61 mins); Vosawai & Orquera for Barbieri & Allan (68 mins); Bortolami for Biagi (71 mins); Palazzini for Tebaldi (72 mins); Iannone for Garcia (77 mins)

**REFEREE**: GJ Clancy (Ireland)

### 21 June, Prince Chichibu Memorial Ground, Tokyo, Japan 26 (2G 4PG) Italy 23 (2G 3PG)

**JAPAN:** A Goromaru (Yamaha Jubilo); A Yamada (Panasonic Wild Knights), M Sa'u (Yamaha Jubilo), Y Tamura (NEC Green Rockets), K Fukuoka (Tsukuba University); H Tatekawa (Kubota Spears), F Tanaka (Panasonic Wild Knights); M Mikami (Toshiba Brave Lupus), S Horie (Panasonic Wild Knights), K Hatakeyama (Suntory Sungoliath), S Ito (Kobe Steel), L Thompson (Kintetsu Liners), J Ives (Canon Eagles), M Leitch (Toshiba Brave Lupus)(captain), RK Holani (Panasonic Wild Knights)

**SUBSTITUTIONS**: H Tui (Suntory Sungoliath) for Holani (60 mins); H Hirashima (Kobe Steel) for Horie (63 mins); S Makabe (Suntory Sungoliath) for Ito (65 mins); H Yamashita (Kobe Steel) for Hatakeyama (74 mins)

**SCORERS**: *Tries:* Yamada, Sa'u *Conversions:* Goromaru (2) *Penalty Goals:* Goromaru (4)

**ITALY**: McLean; Sarto, Campagnaro, Garcia, Venditti; Orquera, Tebaldi; Alberto de Marchi, Ghiraldini, Cittadini, Geldenhuys (captain), Bortolami, Furno, Mauro Bergamasco, Barbieri

**SUBSTITUTIONS**: Antonio de Marchi, Chistolini & Vosawai for Alberto de Marchi, Cittadini & Mauro Bergamasco (60 mins); Palazzini for Tebaldi (65 mins); Manici for Ghiraldini (67 mins); Fuser for Bortolami (69 mins); Allan & Iannone for Orquera & Sarto (74 mins)

**SCORERS**: *Tries:* Penalty try, Barberi *Conversions:* Orquera, Allan *Penalty Goals:* Orquera (3)

**REFEREE**: J Peyper (South Africa)

# BARBARIANS SILENCE CRITICS

## By Iain Spragg

A determined Hosea Gear just evades Henry Slade to score his second try for the Barbarians against England.

**If 2013 proved** a difficult year for the Barbarians in the wake of the team's chastening defeats by England and the British & Irish Lions, redemption was on hand in 2014 as the club claimed the scalp of England for the seventh time in their illustrious history and in the process reasserted their significance in the professional era.

Questions over the Baa-Baas' competitiveness had been raised following their 40–12 loss to England at Twickenham in May and their 59–8 mauling by the Lions in Hong Kong six days later, but the 2014 incarnation of the famed invitational side supplied the perfect riposte with a 39–29 triumph in south-west London in front of a crowd of over 50,000.

The Baa-Baas' return to Twickenham was preceded by the Remembrance clash with the Combined Services side at Brickfields in November, a game which produced 10 tries but was ultimately settled 34–28 in favour of the Armed Forces courtesy of a hat-trick from Bristol's Fijian wing Sammy Speight.

Later the same month the Barbarians faced a Fiji XV at Twickenham to mark the Pacific Island nation's rugby centenary. New Zealand head coach Steve Hansen took up the coaching reins for the game and his Baa-Baas side responded with seven tries as they ran out 43–19 winners. The Springbok duo of Bismarck du Plessis and Jean de Villiers both scored twice while compatriot Patrick Lambie added four conversions. There were also tries for South Africa number 8 Duane Vermeulen and All Blacks Charles Piutau and Tom Taylor.

In late April the team travelled to Ireland to tackle recently crowned Division 1A champions Clontarf at Castle Avenue, a game organised to commemorate the 100th anniversary of the Battle of Clontarf. The visitors did their best to spoil the party but despite scores from Haydn Pugh, Bryan Rennie (2), Charlie Butterworth, Ritchie McMaster and Tom Biggs, it was the hosts who hung on for an entertaining 43–42 victory.

Worcester Warriors head coach Dean Ryan was in charge for the Twickenham match and named a vastly experienced starting XV, captained by Argentina's Juan Manuel Leguizamón, which featured players from nine different countries and with more than 700 caps between them.

In contrast, England named a youthful team with a modest 11 Test appearances between them, but nonetheless the game was not settled in the Barbarians' favour until former All Black wing Hosea Gear went over for two late tries.

England drew first blood with the opening try from Exeter number 8 Dave Ewers but first-half tries from Clermont Auvergne centre Benson Stanley and Pumas full-back Juan Martín Hernández ensured the Baa-Baas were only 18–14 adrift at half-time.

Georgia back row Mamuka Gorgodze stretched to score the visitors' third try minutes after the restart and give the Baa-Baas the lead for the first time. England hit back with a try from young fly-half Henry Slade but in the 63rd minute Gear outpaced Elliot Daly. His second came four minutes from the end, courtesy of another impeccably timed counter-attack.

"The club's ethos is about player expression rather than being professional but we needed to find a balance," Ryan said after the victory. "We had to represent it in the right way."

## BARBARIANS 2013–14 RESULTS

| | | | |
|---|---|---|---|
| 12/11/13 | Barbarians | 28–34 | Combined Services |
| 29/11/13 | Barbarians | 43–19 | Fiji XV |
| 23/04/14 | Barbarians | 42–43 | Clontarf |
| 01/06/14 | Barbarians | 39–29 | England |

THE COMBINED TEAMS

# Elite
# Competitions

Harlequins' Mike Brown won the Aviva
Premiership Player of the Year Award.

# SAINTS TRIUMPH IN
# TWICKENHAM THRILLER

*By Iain Spragg*

Dylan Hartley helps Alex Waller celebrate his last-minute try which gave Northampton the Premiership title.

To describe **Northampton's** progress to and subsequent victory in the Premiership final in 2014 as merely dramatic would be a significant understatement, a misleading misrepresentation of the rollercoaster ride endured by the Saints and their supporters en route to becoming champions of England for the first time in the club's 134-year history.

That Jim Mallinder's side comfortably qualified for the play-offs after finishing second in the table was to prove the calm before the storm. Any sense of serenity within the Northampton camp was abruptly dispelled in the semi-final at Franklin's Gardens against Leicester and although the Saints were to emerge victorious against the Tigers thanks to a last-gasp try from England flanker Tom Wood, there was to be an even more nerve-shredding denouement, not to mention considerable controversy, when they crossed swords with Saracens in the final at Twickenham.

It was a match that had it all. Saracens had two tries contentiously ruled out by the TMO as well as a potentially match-winning conversion which hit the post and it was a contest that went into extra-time and was only settled in the 100th and final minute of play when Saints replacement prop Alex Waller bundled his way over the line from close range. Even then the Northampton faithful had to endure an agonising four-minute wait as the TMO studiously scrutinised the replays to confirm that the decisive try could be awarded.

Victory at Twickenham came just eight days after Mallinder's team had triumphed over Bath in the final of the Amlin Challenge Cup, making Northampton the first side since Wasps in 2003 to achieve the Premiership and Challenge Cup double. The Saints also became the eighth club to claim the Premiership title and the fourth different champions in the last four seasons.

"It's unbelievable and the culmination of years of hard work," said Saints fly-half Stephen Myler after arguably the most engrossing Premiership final ever. "It's something else and I'm so proud. It's hard to describe because it was a strange game, it ebbed and flowed. It's heartbreaking for Saracens but there has to be a winner and I am absolutely over the moon that it is us. The squad is the strongest it has been and I'm really proud to be part of this team."

The 27th season of top-flight English league rugby began in early September and despite suffering a surprise 33–14 reverse against Gloucester at Kingsholm at the end of that month, Northampton made a strong start. An 11-match winning run from October to the end of February was the bedrock of their campaign and although they stumbled rather than sprinted over the finishing line, with three successive defeats in March and April, Mallinder's team were never in danger of missing out on the play-offs.

They were joined by Saracens, who finished top of the table, defending champions Leicester in third and 2012 champions Harlequins who qualified courtesy of a 19–16 win over Bath on the final day of the regular season, a match which had the result gone the other way would have seen the West Country club progress.

The first of the semi-finals in May paired the Saints against old rivals Leicester and although the East Midlands derby at Franklin's Gardens was an ill-tempered and abrasive affair that produced three yellow cards and one red, it did not disappoint in terms of entertainment.

Leicester were the first to cross the whitewash when Manu Tuilagi powered over after an initial break from Mathew Tait. A subsequent stint in the sin-bin for Fijian winger Vereniki Goneva did little to disrupt the Tigers' flow and with Ben Youngs darting over for his team's second try, Leicester had established a 17–6 lead at half-time.

Dan Bowden was the second Leicester player to see yellow after 45 minutes and was followed to the dugout by teammate Tom Youngs 11 minutes later. More significantly, however, was the red card shown to Saints prop Salesi Ma'afu at the same time for punching Youngs and Northampton were condemned to play the final 24 minutes of the match with 14 men.

The odds were stacked firmly against the home side, but an improbable revival began when Wales wing George North muscled his way over with 16 minutes remaining. Myler converted to cut the deficit to a single point but Leicester seemed to have nipped the fight-back in the bud when Owen Williams landed a 72nd-minute penalty.

Trailing 20–16 and with time running out, Northampton were forced to throw caution to the wind and with just two minutes left they struck as Myler and then Luther Burrell made space for Wood to crash over in the corner. The Saints were 21–20 winners at the death and had avenged their defeat to the Tigers in the 2013 Premiership final.

"To go down to 14 men and still come out of it was testament to the massive character of the side," Mallinder said. "I think it was a very good game of rugby. It was two good performances from both sides, but I think we just deserved it.

"We went in down at half-time but said we have to keep playing and moving their front five around. We thought we could still do it. We didn't want to get into an arm wrestle with Leicester. They're good at that and want to slow things down and we want a high tempo."

A day later Saracens entertained Harlequins at Allianz Park in the second semi-final and it was an archetypal game of two halves in north London as the home side recovered from a first-half mauling to win 31–17.

Quins flew out of the blocks in the first period with tries from their England duo of Ugo Monye and Mike Brown and although Saracens replied in the 32nd minute with a score from Kelly Brown, the visitors headed to the dressing room at the break with a 17–11 lead.

Saracens were on the brink but emerged for the second 40 minutes a team reborn. Centre Brad Barritt sparked the fight-back with his 52nd-minute try, a score which Owen Farrell converted to give his team the lead, and they stretched further in front when Chris Ashton crossed on the hour mark. Harlequins failed to trouble the scorers throughout the half and Saracens were on their way to the final.

"Our second-half performance was outstanding," said Saracens director of rugby Mark McCall. "Our reaction to that [first-half deficit] was brilliant. The squad is really confident at the moment and they front up every single week."

The final saw more than 79,000 stream into Twickenham and they were rewarded for their support with an epic tussle which saw the lead change hands five times before Waller's incredible late intervention.

Two Farrell penalties gave Saracens the early advantage but the first try of the match went to the Saints when Ben Foden went over after 31 minutes and at half-time the score was 7–6 to Northampton. A third Farrell penalty early in the second half re-established Saracens' lead, but the Saints hit back with a George Pisi try in the 58th minute.

Two minutes later the match became mired in controversy. Farrell danced through the Northampton defence for a 'try' but as Alex Goode waited to take the conversion, referee JP Doyle was advised by TMO Graham Hughes to review Goode's potentially forward pass to Chris Wyles in the build-up. The score was eventually chalked off and Saracens still trailed 14–9.

The Londoners were clearly rattled by the decision but managed to compose themselves and when Schalk Brits' brilliant offload sent Argentine international Marcelo Bosch over in the corner with eight minutes left, the scores were level. Charlie Hodgson's conversion attempt hit the post to ratchet up the tension and extra-time beckoned.

Myler and Hodgson traded penalties in the first 10 additional minutes but there was more drama when Jackson Wray's try for Sarries was ruled out by Hughes after Billy Vunipola was adjudged to have illegally blocked off a Saints player.

A second Hodgson penalty eight minutes from the end put Saracens 20–17 up but there was still time for Waller's magic moment just 13 minutes after he had been introduced to the fray as a replacement for Alex Corbisiero. Doyle once again went to the TMO to check on the grounding and after what seemed like an eternity to both sets of players and fans, Hughes finally confirmed Waller had touched down. Myler kicked the conversion and Northampton were 24–20 winners.

"We always believed in ourselves," said stand-in captain Wood in the aftermath of his side's remarkable triumph. "We saw them tiring. We had the edge and I felt the advantage was with us. We pride ourselves on fitness and, as tired as we all were, we only had to look at them. I always felt it was ours to win."

Defeat was, of course, a bitter pill for Saracens to swallow but McCall could still draw on the positives from the season. "To lose at the death was devastating, but I could not be more proud of the players," he said. "The performance was full of quality at times and they showed great courage to keep coming back. We are a really healthy club: people can talk about trophies but it is about moving forward. We played in two finals in a week and it has been a brilliant season for us. We are interested in two competitions, Europe and the Premiership, and we have gone all the way in both. Yes, it was a disappointing way to finish but we are incredibly strong as a club."

## AVIVA PREMIERSHIP 2013–14 RESULTS

6 September 2013: **Newcastle** 0 **Bath** 21. 7 September: **London Irish** 20 **Saracens** 42, **Gloucester** 16 **Sale** 22, **Northampton** 38 **Exeter** 11, **Wasps** 15 **Harlequins** 16. 8 September: **Leicester** 32 **Worcester** 15. 13 September: **Harlequins** 6 **Northampton** 13, **Sale** 14 **Newcastle** 15. 14 September: **Exeter** 30 **Wasps** 26, **Worcester** 18 **London Irish** 20, **Bath** 27 **Leicester** 20. 15 September: **Saracens** 44 **Gloucester** 12. 20 September: **Worcester** 13 **Harlequins** 37, **Sale** 26 **Wasps** 22. 21 September: **London Irish** 23 **Exeter** 29, **Gloucester** 26 **Northampton** 24, **Leicester** 31 **Newcastle** 6. 22 September: **Saracens** 31 **Bath** 17. 27 September: **Northampton** 33 **Sale** 14. 28 September: **Bath** 33 **London Irish** 18, **Wasps** 32 **Worcester** 16, **Harlequins** 12 **Saracens** 22. 29 September: **Exeter** 9 **Leicester** 21, **Newcastle** 16 **Gloucester** 22. 4 October: **Sale** 19 **Bath** 13. 5 October: **London Irish** 18 **Harlequins** 13, **Saracens** 19 **Wasps** 12, **Worcester** 11 **Newcastle** 16, **Leicester** 19 **Northampton** 19. 6 October: **Gloucester** 12 **Exeter** 29. 25 October: **Bath** 15 **Gloucester** 13. 26 October: **Exeter** 40 **Worcester** 6, **Harlequins** 24 **Sale** 3, **Northampton** 41 **Saracens** 20. 27 October: **Wasps** 22 **Leicester** 12, **Newcastle** 13 **London Irish** 11. 1 November: **Worcester** 6 **Bath** 21, **Sale** 16 **Exeter** 18. 2 November: **Gloucester** 30 **Wasps** 32, **Leicester** 16 **Harlequins** 23. 3 November: **London Irish** 14 **Northampton** 19, **Saracens** 40 **Newcastle** 3. 22 November: **Sale** 26 **Worcester** 10. 23 November: **Exeter** 9 **Saracens** 16, **Harlequins** 27 **Gloucester** 19, **Leicester** 20 **London Irish** 11, **Northampton** 18 **Newcastle** 0. 24 November: **Wasps** 5 **Bath** 28. 29 November: **Gloucester** 17 **Leicester** 22. 30 November: **London Irish** 12 **Wasps** 19, **Saracens** 24 **Sale** 19, **Worcester** 10 **Northampton** 33, **Bath** 21 **Exeter** 16. 1 December: **Newcastle** 9 **Harlequins** 35. 20 December: **Sale** 15 **London Irish** 3. 21 December: **Bath** 14 **Harlequins** 3, **Exeter** 16 **Newcastle** 3, **Wasps** 15 **Northampton** 17, **Saracens** 49 **Leicester** 10. 22 December: **Gloucester** 12 **Worcester** 6. 27 December: **Newcastle** 12 **Wasps** 17. 28 December: **Leicester** 30 **Sale** 23, **Northampton** 43 **Bath** 25, **Worcester** 8 **Saracens** 26, **Harlequins** 22 **Exeter** 6. 29 December: **London Irish** 19 **Gloucester** 22. 3 January 2014: **Newcastle** 8 **Sale** 16, **Northampton** 23 **Harlequins** 9. 4 January: **London Irish** 22 **Worcester** 9, **Gloucester** 8 **Saracens** 29. 5 January: **Leicester** 27 **Bath** 27, **Wasps** 19 **Exeter** 16. 7 February: **Worcester** 22 **Leicester** 23, **Sale** 24 **Gloucester** 19. 8 February: **Saracens** 13 **London Irish** 22, **Exeter** 16 **Northampton** 17, **Bath** 24 **Newcastle** 6. 9 February: **Harlequins** 11 **Wasps** 10. 14 February: **Sale** 10 **Saracens** 15. 15 February: **Harlequins** 18 **Newcastle** 14, **Wasps** 20 **London Irish** 23, **Northampton** 30 **Worcester** 14, **Exeter** 23 **Bath** 27. 16 February: **Leicester** 11 **Gloucester** 8. 22 February: **Bath** 32 **Wasps** 25, **Gloucester** 25 **Harlequins** 20, **Worcester** 12 **Sale** 24. 23 February: **London Irish** 15 **Leicester** 20, **Newcastle** 16 **Northampton** 22, **Saracens** 23 **Exeter** 10. 28 February: **Bath** 10 **Saracens** 23. 1 March:

Exeter 18 London Irish 0, Harlequins 21 Worcester 20, Wasps 17 Sale 21, Northampton 39 Gloucester 13. 2 March: Newcastle 18 Leicester 41. 21 March: Worcester 11 Wasps 13. 22 March: Sale 19 Northampton 6, Gloucester 40 Newcastle 33, Saracens 39 Harlequins 17, London Irish 23 Bath 44. 23 March: Leicester 45 Exeter 15. 28 March: Bath 11 Sale 22. 29 March: Exeter 13 Gloucester 14, Harlequins 23 London Irish 9, Wasps 20 Saracens 32, Northampton 16 Leicester 22. 30 March: Newcastle 12 Worcester 17. 11 April: Sale 12 Harlequins 27. 12 April: Leicester 27 Wasps 15, Worcester 33 Exeter 38, Gloucester 17 Bath 18. 13 April: Saracens 28 Northampton 24, London Irish 40 Newcastle 12. 18 April: Harlequins 24 Leicester 20. 19 April: Bath 32 Worcester 20, Exeter 12 Sale 55, Wasps 38 Gloucester 30. 20 April: Northampton 36 London Irish 21, Newcastle 18 Saracens 23. 2 May: Bath 19 Northampton 19. 3 May: Gloucester 38 London Irish 30, Wasps 44 Newcastle 38, Saracens 44 Worcester 20, Sale 22 Leicester 42. 4 May: Exeter 29 Harlequins 30. 10 May: Harlequins 19 Bath 16, Leicester 31 Saracens 27, London Irish 22 Sale 20, Newcastle 13 Exeter 23, Northampton 74 Wasps 13, Worcester 28 Gloucester 27.

# FINAL TABLE

| | P | W | D | L | F | A | BP | PTS |
|---|---|---|---|---|---|---|---|---|
| Saracens | 22 | 19 | 0 | 3 | 629 | 353 | 11 | 87 |
| Northampton | 22 | 16 | 2 | 4 | 604 | 350 | 10 | 78 |
| Leicester | 22 | 15 | 2 | 5 | 542 | 430 | 10 | 74 |
| Harlequins | 22 | 15 | 0 | 7 | 437 | 365 | 7 | 67 |
| Bath | 22 | 14 | 2 | 6 | 495 | 388 | 7 | 67 |
| Sale | 22 | 12 | 0 | 10 | 432 | 399 | 9 | 57 |
| Wasps | 22 | 9 | 0 | 13 | 451 | 533 | 13 | 49 |
| Exeter | 22 | 9 | 0 | 13 | 426 | 480 | 9 | 45 |
| Gloucester | 22 | 8 | 0 | 14 | 440 | 539 | 12 | 44 |
| London Irish | 22 | 7 | 0 | 15 | 396 | 496 | 8 | 36 |
| Newcastle | 22 | 3 | 0 | 19 | 281 | 544 | 10 | 22 |
| Worcester | 22 | 2 | 0 | 20 | 325 | 581 | 8 | 16 |

# SEMI-FINALS

## 16 May, Franklin's Gardens, Northampton

## NORTHAMPTON 21 (1G 1T 3PG) LEICESTER 20 (2G 2PG)

**NORTHAMPTON:** B Foden; T Collins, G Pisi, L Burrell, G North; S Myler, K Fotuali'i; A Waller, M Haywood, S Ma'afu, S Manoa, C Lawes, T Wood, P Dowson (captain), S Dickinson

**SUBSTITUTIONS:** A Corbisiero for Waller (51 mins); C Clark for Dowson (54 mins); T Mercey for Collins (57 mins); L Dickson for Fotuali'i (62 mins); J Wilson for Pisi (65 mins); C Day for Manoa (68 mins)

**SCORERS:** *Tries*: North, Wood *Conversion*: Myler *Penalty Goals*: Myler (3)

**RED CARD:** Ma'afu (57 mins)

**LEICESTER:** M Tait ; N Morris, M Tuilagi, D Bowden, V Goneva; T Flood, B Youngs; M Ayerza, T Youngs, L Mulipola, L Deacon, E Slater (captain), J Gibson, J Salvi, J Crane

**SUBSTITUTIONS:** N Briggs for Gibson (57 mins); S Mafi for Tait (60 mins); O Williams for Flood (62 mins); G Kitchener & A Thompstone for Deacon & Briggs (68 mins)

**SCORERS:** *Tries*: Tuilagi, B Youngs *Conversions*: Flood (2) *Penalty Goals*: Flood, Williams

**YELLOW CARDS:** Goneva (29 mins); Bowden (46 mins); T Youngs (57 mins)

**REFEREE:** JP Doyle (England)

Northampton's Ben Foden looks for a gap during the Saints' win over Leicester in the Aviva Premiership semi-final in May.

**ELITE COMPETITIONS**

## 17 May, Allianz Park, London

## SARACENS 31 (2G 1T 4PG) HARLEQUINS 17 (2G 1PG)

**SARACENS:** A Goode; C Ashton, M Bosch, B Barritt, D Strettle; O Farrell, N de Kock; M Vunipola, S Brits, M Stevens, S Borthwick (captain), A Hargreaves, K Brown, J Burger, B Vunipola

**SUBSTITUTIONS:** J Johnston for Burger (temp 34 to 42 mins); R Wigglesworth for de Kock (52 mins); C Wyles for Strettle (59 mins); J Wray for Burger (60 mins); Johnston for Stevens (66 mins); R Barrington for M Vunipola (67 mins); E Sheriff for Borthwick (69 mins); C Hodgson & J George for Farrell & Brits (74 mins)

**SCORERS:** *Tries*: Brown, Barritt, Ashton *Conversions*: Farrell (2) *Penalty Goals*: Farrell (4)

**HARLEQUINS:** M Brown; T Williams, T Molenaar, J Turner-Hall, U Monye; N Evans, D Care; J Marler, D Ward, K Sinckler, C Matthews, G Robson, L Wallace, C Robshaw (captain), N Easter

**SUBSTITUTIONS:** T Guest & S Smith for Wallace & Williams (59 mins); B Botica for Molenaar (60 mins); W Collier for Sinckler (65 mins); K Dickson & R Buchanan for Brown & Monye (67 mins); M Lambert & N Kennedy for Marler & Matthews (74 mins)

**SCORERS:** *Tries*: Monye, Brown *Conversions*: Evans (2) *Penalty Goal*: Evans

**REFEREE:** W Barnes (England)

# FINAL

## 31 May, Twickenham, London

## SARACENS 20 (1T 5PG) NORTHAMPTON 24 (3G 1PG) AET

**SARACENS:** A Goode; C Ashton, M Bosch, B Barritt, D Strettle; O Farrell, N de Kock; R Barrington, S Brits, M Stevens, S Borthwick (captain), M Botha, K Brown, J Burger, B Vunipola

**SUBSTITUTIONS:** R Wigglesworth, J Wray & A Hargreaves for de Kock, Burger & Botha (52 mins); J Johnson for Stevens (55 mins); C Wyles for Strettle (57 mins); C Hodgson for Farrell (62 mins); R Gill for Barrington (84 mins); J George for Vunipola (95 mins)

**SCORERS:** *Try*: Bosch *Penalty Goals*: Farrell (3), Hodgson (2)

**NORTHAMPTON:** B Foden; K Pisi, G Pisi, L Burrell, G North; S Myler, K Fotuali'i; A Corbiserio, M Haywood, S Ma'afu, S Manoa, C Lawes, C Clark, T Wood (captain), S Dickinson

**SUBSTITUTIONS:** L Dickson for Fotuali'i (52 mins); A Waller & D Hartley for Corbiserio & Haywood (55 mins); C Day & P Dowson for Manoa & Clark (57 mins); J Wilson for G Pisi (63 mins); Corbiserio for Waller (temp 87 to 93 mins); T Stephenson for K Pisi (91 mins)

**SCORERS:** *Tries*: Foden, G Pisi, Waller *Conversions*: Myler (3) *Penalty Goal*: Myler

**REFEREE:** JP Doyle (England)

# TOULON COMPLETE HISTORIC DOUBLE

## By Iain Spragg

A jubilant Toulon side celebrate claiming their first Top 14 title since 1992 after finishing runners-up the two previous years.

**T**oulon's 22-year wait to lift the Bouclier de Brennus finally came to an end as the club's stellar cast of French and English internationals, All Blacks, Springboks and Wallabies dispatched Castres to claim the Top 14 title and in the process exorcise the ghosts of the side's back-to-back defeats in the two previous finals.

It was in 1992 that Le Rouge et Noir had last been crowned French champions. They were denied the title by Toulouse in 2012 while Castres were victorious in the final 12 months ago, but it proved third time lucky for Bernard Laporte's star-studded side in 2014 as Toulon exacted their revenge over the team from the Midi-Pyrénées to complete a stunning European and domestic double.

Victory at the Stade de France came just seven days after they had successfully defended the Heineken Cup and in overcoming Castres 18–10 in the Top 14 final, Toulon became only the second French side after Toulouse in 1996 to hold the two iconic trophies at the same time.

Not for the first time since he signed for the club in 2009, Toulon were indebted to the accuracy of the boot of Jonny Wilkinson, as the Englishman kicked 15 of the side's 18 points in Paris in his swansong appearance in the professional game, almost 16 years after making his senior debut.

"I would like to thank the whole team, the crowd but also Castres and all the other teams in the Top 14," Wilkinson said after the final whistle. "I don't have the words and I cannot thank the French public enough."

The two finalists' respective paths to Paris could not have been more contrasting.

Despite losing nine times in the regular season, Toulon ultimately reached the knockout stages of the competition with relative ease. A modest five wins in their opening 10 games initially suggested the club's expensively assembled squad might struggle to replicate the form they showed the previous season, but victories in their final four fixtures saw Laporte's side edge out Fabien Galthié's Montpellier, albeit by a single point, for top spot.

Defending champions Castres were far less convincing in qualifying for the play-offs. It was not until November that they were able to register back-to-back wins in the league and Castres went into the final round of matches in early May in sixth and in real danger of being overhauled by Stade Français. A 23–13 defeat away to Bayonne on the last day further imperilled Castres' hopes of progressing but they were rescued, ironically, by Toulon who beat Stade 17–15 at the Stade Felix Mayol to confirm the champions' place in the play-offs.

Castres were drawn away to Clermont Auvergne in their battle to book a semi-final place, but with Clermont unbeaten at the Stade Marcel Michelin for a remarkable 77 games, the omens did not appear promising.

Records, however, are there to be broken and the pivotal moment in the match came in the second half when Gerhard Vosloo was sin-binned and minutes later Castres centre Remi Lamerat crashed over. Rory Kockott contributed 17 points with the boot and at full-time the visitors had recorded an improbable 22–16 victory.

The second play-off saw Toulouse, aiming to reach an incredible 21st consecutive semi-final, entertain Racing Métro at the Stade Ernest Wallon and once again it was the visitors who defied the odds to eliminate the hosts. Racing's hero was Irish fly-half Johnny Sexton who landed seven perfect penalties from seven attempts. Toulouse wing Hosea Gear scored the only try of the contest early in the second half, but the Parisians held on for a surprise 21–16 success.

"We were saying that we felt a little cursed in the play-offs," admitted Racing centre Henry Chavancy after the game. "These last four years we had made the play-offs but had not won a game."

The two semi-finals were both staged at the Stade Pierre Mauroy in Lille in mid May. The first game paired Toulon with Racing and in the wake of the two major upsets in the play-offs, another shock result seemed possible as Wilkinson uncharacteristically missed three penalty attempts in the first half while his opposite number Sexton was on target with two penalties. However, Toulon found an alternative source of points in the shape of former Wallaby Matt Giteau, who pounced on Bryan Habana's kick ahead for the only try of the match after 11 minutes. Le Rouge et Noir went in at the break with a precarious 7–6 advantage but normal service was resumed in the second half as Wilkinson landed two penalties and a signature drop goal as Toulon emerged 16–6 winners to reach a third successive final.

The second semi-final the following day was a gripping affair as Castres required extra-time and a late drop goal to see off the challenge of Montpellier. The match began controversially when Montpellier wing Rene Ranger was shown a yellow card after only 13 seconds of play for a tackle on Romain Cabannes, but that was merely the start of the day's drama.

South African scrum-half Kockott landed the first points of the contest with a fourth-minute penalty. Montpellier fly-half François Trinh-Duc replied with a 15th-minute drop goal, but the match was lit up after half an hour when Castres number 8 Antonie Claassen spun off the back of a ruck for the opening try, which was converted by Kockott. Montpellier took just two minutes to respond as Ranger redeemed himself for his earlier indiscretion, racing in under the posts.

At half-time Castres were 13–10 up but after the break Trinh-Duc edged the battle of the kickers with three penalties to two from Kockott to level the scores at 19–19. Castres almost settled the game in normal time but Kockott's penalty and Remi Talès' attempted drop both drifted wide and the two sides prepared for an additional 20 minutes of play and a test of their stamina.

The defining moment came seconds before the half-time break as Castres worked themselves into a good field position and Fijian Seremaia Bai, a 70th-minute replacement for Cabannes, kicked a stunning drop goal from 30 metres out.

TOP 14

Montpellier had 10 minutes to rescue the situation but in the closing stages they opted for an attacking lineout five metres out after the award of a penalty rather than go for the three points. Castres rebuffed the resulting drive and with the scoreboard 22–19 in their favour, they began plotting how to topple Toulon in Paris a fortnight later in a repeat of the 2013 final.

"We are very proud and very happy and once again we've surprised ourselves," admitted centre Cabannes in the build-up to the match. "Everyone always considers Castres the outsiders and us above all. We know we're a good team but we also know that it's very difficult to reach the final given the other teams in the competition so we have earned the right to be here.

"The fact that outsiders can still overcome the odds and win helps a club like us who aren't able to sit on top of the table for the whole season. With a few things going our way in the play-offs, we can dream about winning the trophy once more."

Castres also benefited from a fortnight off while Toulon had to work hard to subdue Saracens in the Heineken Cup final in Cardiff a week before the Top 14 showdown. But despite their exertions there were no signs of fatigue in the Toulon ranks at the Stade de France and it was, perhaps predictably, Wilkinson who established the pattern of the game with his first penalty after eight minutes.

Castres hit back quickly when Scotland wing Max Evans collected his own chip to scamper over for a brilliant solo try. Kockott converted and was also on target with a 29th-minute penalty but Wilkinson was not to be outshone and two further penalties and what was to be the last drop goal of his prolific career ensured that Toulon went in at half-time leading 12–10.

Twelve months earlier Castres had defied pre-match expectations to beat Toulon 19–13 in the final, but there was to be no repeat this time as Laporte's team took a stranglehold on proceedings courtesy of a dominant display from the pack, repelling intermittent Castres attacks.

Wilkinson's fourth penalty after 54 minutes extended the lead to five points but he conceded the kicking duties to compatriot Delon Armitage eight minutes from time when Toulon were awarded a penalty near the halfway line. The former England full-back stepped up and converted the long-range opportunity to extinguish Castres' hopes of a fight-back. Toulon had claimed a famous double and avenged their loss in Paris a year earlier.

The sound of 'God Save the Queen' echoed around the Stade de France on the stadium's sound system after the final whistle in an emotional tribute to Wilkinson and 15 years, eight months and 10 days

after he played his first ever professional game for the Newcastle Falcons,
the fly-half was forced to face the prospect of retirement.

"I've spent half my life with a ball. It's going to be a huge shock after rugby, but I'll have a lot of good memories with the whole of the team here," he said after the match. "I've been here five years and it is impossible to put this feeling into words. To be part of something like this, it's a dream. All I can do is thank everyone in the group, the coaches. It's incredible to explain, it's just been a pleasure."

# TOP 14 2013–14 RESULTS

16 August 2013: **Montpellier** 22 **Toulon** 22. 17 August: **Biarritz** 18 **Clermont** 22, **Bayonne** 39 **Oyonnax** 11, **Bordeaux** 31 **Toulouse** 25, **Grenoble** 19 **Stade Français** 16, **Racing Métro** 19 **Brive** 14, **Perpignan** 26 **Castres** 23. 23 August: **Toulon** 41 **Racing Métro** 14. 24 August: **Oyonnax** 30 **Clermont** 19, **Biarritz** 19 **Montpellier** 12, **Castres** 34 **Grenoble** 6, **Perpignan** 27 **Stade Français** 28, **Toulouse** 40 **Bayonne** 3. 30 August: **Stade Français** 38 **Biarritz** 3. 31 August: **Clermont** 38 **Toulouse** 19, **Bordeaux** 21 **Castres** 20, **Montpellier** 33 **Brive** 24, **Racing Métro** 22 **Oyonnax** 9, **Bayonne** 31 **Perpignan** 20, **Grenoble** 28 **Toulon** 26. 4 September: **Castres** 38 **Stade Français** 10, **Bordeaux** 29 **Montpellier** 36, **Clermont** 55 **Bayonne** 0, **Oyonnax** 24 **Biarritz** 22, **Perpignan** 36 **Grenoble** 13, **Toulon** 62 **Brive** 12, **Toulouse** 30 **Racing Métro** 6. 8 September: **Montpellier** 25 **Toulon** 0, **Biarritz** 13 **Toulon** 24, **Brive** 17 **Bayonne** 10, **Grenoble** 21 **Bordeaux** 14, **Oyonnax** 19 **Castres** 9, **Racing Métro** 19 **Perpignan** 16, **Stade Français** 23 **Clermont** 16. 13 September: **Perpignan** 28 **Montpellier** 16. 14 September: **Castres** 22 **Toulon** 15, **Bordeaux** 35 **Oyonnax** 10, **Clermont** 27 **Grenoble** 13, **Stade Français** 25 **Brive** 18, **Toulouse** 31 **Biarritz** 7, **Bayonne** 16 **Racing Métro** 19. 20 September: **Montpellier** 43 **Clermont** 3. 21 September: **Toulouse** 26 **Castres** 9, **Biarritz** 21 **Grenoble** 27, **Brive** 31 **Perpignan** 6, **Racing Métro** 26 **Bordeaux** 19, **Toulon** 18 **Bayonne** 10, **Oyonnax** 15 **Stade Français** 16. 27 September: **Stade Français** 18 **Montpellier** 11. 28 September: **Oyonnax** 25 **Toulon** 22, **Bayonne** 27 **Biarritz** 19, **Castres** 19 **Racing Métro** 15, **Grenoble** 12 **Brive** 12, **Perpignan** 20 **Toulouse** 16. 29 September: **Clermont** 40 **Bordeaux** 11. 4 October: **Biarritz** 12 **Perpignan** 16. 5 October: **Toulon** 25 **Clermont** 19, **Bordeaux** 34 **Bayonne** 6, **Brive** 34 **Castres** 0, **Montpellier** 45 **Oyonnax** 20, **Racing Métro** 20 **Grenoble** 22, **Toulouse** 28 **Stade Français** 10. 25 October: **Bayonne** 24 **Montpellier** 19. 26 October: **Toulouse** 13 **Toulon** 12, **Castres** 39 **Biarritz** 0, **Clermont** 36 **Brive** 29, **Grenoble** 23 **Oyonnax**, **Perpignan** 31 **Bordeaux** 20, **Racing Métro** 16 **Stade Français** 14. 1 November: **Toulon** 37 **Bordeaux** 17, **Castres** 22 **Clermont** 22. 2 November: **Brive** 25 **Toulouse** 13, **Biarritz** 9 **Racing Métro** 6, **Montpellier** 25 **Grenoble** 18, **Oyonnax** 22 **Perpignan** 9, **Stade Français** 13 **Bayonne** 9. 22 November: **Toulon** 15 **Perpignan** 9. 23 November: **Bayonne** 24 **Grenoble** 21, **Bordeaux** 45 **Stade Français** 23, **Brive** 9 **Biarritz** 14, **Montpellier** 16 **Castres** 20, **Toulouse** 14 **Oyonnax** 3, **Clermont** 47 **Racing Métro** 14. 29 November: **Perpignan** 23 **Clermont** 30. 30 November: **Stade Français** 23 **Toulon** 0, **Biarritz** 15 **Bordeaux** 22, **Castres** 46 **Bayonne** 16, **Oyonnax** 26 **Brive** 9, **Racing Métro** 17 **Montpellier** 12, **Grenoble** 25 **Toulouse** 18. 20 December: **Stade Français** 21 **Grenoble** 6. 21 December: **Toulon** 43 **Montpellier** 10, **Brive** 9 **Racing Métro** 9, **Castres** 37 **Perpignan** 13, **Clermont** 35 **Biarritz** 6, **Oyonnax** 9 **Bayonne** 6, **Toulouse** 18 **Bordeaux** 16. 29 December: **Stade Français** 19 **Perpignan** 12, **Bordeaux** 27 **Brive** 23, **Clermont** 33 **Oyonnax** 19, **Grenoble** 20 **Castres** 16, **Montpellier** 48 **Biarritz** 22, **Bayonne** 21 **Toulouse** 13, **Racing Métro** 14 **Toulon** 3. 3 January, 2014: **Castres** 15 **Bordeaux** 9. 4 January: **Toulon** 21 **Grenoble** 22, **Biarritz** 6 **Stade Français** 18, **Oyonnax** 6 **Racing Métro** 0, **Perpignan** 20 **Bayonne** 8, **Brive** 15 **Montpellier** 9. 5 January: **Toulouse** 19 **Clermont** 12. 24 January: **Stade Français** 32 **Castres** 6. 25 January: **Racing Métro** 25 **Toulouse** 5, **Bayonne** 18 **Clermont** 9, **Grenoble** 25 **Perpignan** 19, **Montpellier**

28 **Bordeaux** 23, **Brive** 23 **Toulon** 10. 7 February: **Bordeaux** 38 **Grenoble** 17. 8 February: **Clermont** 25 **Stade Français** 13, **Bayonne** 9 **Brive** 6, **Castres** 17 **Oyonnax** 16, **Perpignan** 19 **Racing Métro** 19, **Toulon** 33 **Biarritz** 20, **Toulouse** 12 **Montpellier** 15. 14 February: **Grenoble** 16 **Clermont** 13. 15 February: **Toulon** 19 **Castres** 13, **Biarritz** 6 **Toulouse** 16, **Montpellier** 50 **Perpignan** 19, **Racing Métro** 18 **Bayonne** 8, **Brive** 28 **Stade Français** 12. 22 February: **Clermont** 42 **Montpellier** 16, **Bordeaux** 25 **Racing Métro** 9, **Grenoble** 20 **Biarritz** 22, **Perpignan** 12 **Brive** 6, **Stade Français** 29 **Oyonnax** 26, **Castres** 29 **Toulouse** 27. 23 February: **Bayonne** 9 **Toulon** 15. 28 February: **Montpellier** 19 **Stade Français** 10. 1 March: **Bordeaux** 26 **Clermont** 16, **Brive** 31 **Grenoble** 6, **Racing Métro** 25 **Castres** 15, **Toulon** 64 **Oyonnax** 10, **Toulouse** 37 **Perpignan** 9. 2 March: **Biarritz** 8 **Bayonne** 11. 14 March: **Biarritz** 22 **Oyonnax** 24. 21 March: **Clermont** 22 **Toulon** 16. 22 March: **Stade Français** 27 **Toulouse** 27, **Bayonne** 22 **Bordeaux** 23, **Castres** 38 **Brive** 6, **Oyonnax** 8 **Montpellier** 22, **Perpignan** 16 **Biarritz** 10, **Grenoble** 13 **Racing Métro** 26. 28 March: **Brive** 26 **Clermont** 24. 29 March: **Stade Français** 22 **Racing Métro** 32, **Biarritz** 34 **Castres** 34, **Bordeaux** 23 **Perpignan** 5, **Montpellier** 43 **Bayonne** 27, **Oyonnax** 40 **Grenoble** 13, **Toulon** 32 **Toulouse** 28. 5 April: **Oyonnax** 26 **Bordeaux** 12. 11 April: **Clermont** 23 **Castres** 11. 12 April: **Bordeaux** 20 **Toulon** 22, **Bayonne** 24 **Stade Français** 19, **Grenoble** 30 **Montpellier** 36, **Perpignan** 22 **Oyonnax** 12, **Racing Métro** 37 **Biarritz** 7, **Toulouse** 16 **Brive** 9. 18 April: **Castres** 22 **Montpellier** 15. 19 April: **Oyonnax** 19 **Toulouse** 19, **Perpignan** 31 **Toulon** 46, **Biarritz** 19 **Brive** 13, **Grenoble** 21 **Bayonne** 21, **Racing Métro** 22 **Clermont** 6, **Stade Français** 37 **Bordeaux** 23. 3 May: **Bayonne** 23 **Castres** 13, **Bordeaux** 54 **Biarritz** 20, **Brive** 19 **Oyonnax** 17, **Clermont** 25 **Perpignan** 22, **Montpellier** 44 **Racing Métro** 10, **Toulon** 17 **Stade Français** 15, **Toulouse** 38 **Grenoble** 8.

# FINAL TABLE

|  | P | W | D | L | F | A | BP | PTS |
|---|---|---|---|---|---|---|---|---|
| Toulon | 26 | 16 | 1 | 9 | 660 | 466 | 11 | 77 |
| Montpellier | 26 | 15 | 1 | 10 | 670 | 525 | 14 | 76 |
| Clermont Auvergne | 26 | 15 | 1 | 10 | 659 | 500 | 11 | 73 |
| Toulouse | 26 | 13 | 2 | 11 | 548 | 442 | 13 | 69 |
| Racing Métro | 26 | 15 | 2 | 9 | 459 | 448 | 5 | 69 |
| Castres | 26 | 13 | 2 | 11 | 567 | 488 | 10 | 66 |
| Stade Français | 26 | 14 | 1 | 11 | 529 | 496 | 7 | 65 |
| Bordeaux | 26 | 13 | 0 | 13 | 629 | 573 | 12 | 64 |
| Brive | 26 | 11 | 2 | 13 | 473 | 476 | 13 | 61 |
| Bayonne | 26 | 11 | 1 | 14 | 424 | 549 | 8 | 54 |
| Grenoble | 26 | 11 | 2 | 13 | 465 | 625 | 5 | 53 |
| Oyonnax | 26 | 11 | 1 | 14 | 456 | 562 | 5 | 51 |
| Perpignan | 26 | 10 | 1 | 15 | 486 | 593 | 9 | 51 |
| Biarritz | 26 | 5 | 1 | 20 | 374 | 656 | 8 | 30 |

| 9 May 2014 |
| --- |
| **Toulouse** 16 **Racing Métro** 21 |
| 10 May 2014 |
| **Clermont** 16 **Castres** 22 |

# SEMI-FINALS

### 16 May, Stade Pierre Mauroy, Lille

## TOULON 16 (1G 2PG 1DG) RACING MÉTRO 6 (2PG)

**TOULON:** D Armitage; D Mitchell, M Bastareaud, M Giteau, B Habana, J Wilkinson (captain), S Tillous-Borde; X Chiocci, C Burden, C Hayman, B Botha, J Suta, J Smith, JM Fernández Lobbe, S Armitage

**SUBSTITUTIONS:** A Williams for Botha (52 mins); A Menini for Chiocci (53 mins); JC Orioli for Burden (53 mins); M Castrogiovanni for Hayman (66 mins); M Claassens for Tillous Borde (68 mins); V Bruni for Fernández Lobbe (73 mins)

**SCORERS:** *Try*: Giteau *Conversion*: Wilkinson *Penalty Goals*: Wilkinson (2) *Drop Goal*: Wilkinson

**YELLOW CARD:** Bastareaud (18 mins)

**RACING MÉTRO:** JM Hernández; A Plante, H Chavancy, J Roberts, J Imhoff; J Sexton, M Machenaud; J Brugnaut, V Lacombe, L Ducalcon, J Kruger, F van der Merwe, A Battut (captain), B le Roux, J Cronje

**SUBSTITUTIONS:** W Lauret for Battut (53 mins); E Arous for Brugnaut (57 mins); M Phillips for Machenaud (60 mins); B Mujati for Ducalcon (68 mins); F Estebanez for Roberts (69 mins); J Maurouard for Lacombe (72 mins); B Fall for Plante (73 mins); F Metz for van der Merwe

**SCORERS:** *Penalty Goals*: Sexton (2)

**REFEREE:** M Raynal (France)

TOP 14

## 17 May, Stade Pierre Mauroy, Lille

## MONTPELLIER 19 (1G 3PG 1DG) CASTRES 22 (1G 4PG 1DG) AET

**MONTPELLIER:** P Berard; T Nagusa, A Tuitavake, W Olivier, R Ranger; F Trinh-Duc (captain), J Pelissie; M Nariashvili, C Geli, N Mas, R Tchale-Watchou, T Privat, A Bias, M Gorgodze, A Tulou

**SUBSTITUTIONS:** S Timani for Tchale-Watchou (49 mins); F Ouedraogo for Gorgodze (49 mins); B Paillaugue for Pelissie (63 mins); M Ivaldi for Geli (72 mins); Y Watremez for Nariashvili (72 mins); A Floch for Berard (80 mins); L Dupont for Bias (83 mins); P Faanunu for Mas (90 mins)

**SCORERS:** *Try*: Ranger *Conversion*: Trinh-Duc *Penalty Goals*: Trinh-Duc (3) *Drop Goal*: Trinh-Duc

**YELLOW CARD:** Ranger (1 min)

**CASTRES:** B Dulin; R Grosso, R Cabannes, R Lamerat, M Evans; R Tales (captain), R Kockott; Y Forestier, B Mach; R Herrera, R Gray, R Ortega, P Faasalele, Y Caballero, A Claassen

**SUBSTITUTIONS:** J de Bruin Bornman for Caballero (49 mins); S Taumoepeau for Forestier (54 mins); M Bonello for Mach (54 mins); C Samson for Gray (58 mins); S Baikeinuku for Cabannes (70 mins); D Kirkpatrick for Lamerat (77 mins); Mach for Bonello (95 mins); M Lazar for Herrera (95 mins)

**SCORERS:** *Try*: Claassen *Conversion*: Kockott *Penalty Goals*: Kockott (4) *Drop Goal*: Baikeinuku

**YELLOW CARD:** Grosso (10 mins)

**REFEREE:** P Gauzere (France)

## FINAL

## 31 May, Stade de France, Paris

## TOULON 18 (5PG 1DG) CASTRES 10 (1G 1PG)

**TOULON:** D Armitage; D Mitchell, M Bastareaud, M Giteau, B Habana; J Wilkinson (captain), S Tillous-Borde; X Chiocci, C Burden, C Hayman, JP Botha, A Williams, J Smith, JM Fernandez Lobbe, S Armitage

**SUBSTITUTIONS:** JC Orioli for Burden (29 mins); A Menini for Chiocci (51 mins); J Suta for Botha (58 mins); M Castrogiovanni for Hayman (66 mins)

**SCORERS:** *Penalty Goals*: Wilkinson (4), D Armitage *Drop Goal*: Wilkinson

**CASTRES:** B Dulin; M Evans, R Cabannes, R Lamerat, R Grosso; R Tales (captain), R Kockott; Y Forestier, B Mach, R Herrera, R Gray, R Ortega, P Faasalele, Y Caballero, A Claassen

**SUBSTITUTIONS:** D Kirkpatrick for Tales (temp 20 to 25 mins); S Taumoepeau for Forestier (51 mins); J de Bruin Bornman for Caballero (52 mins); C Samson for Gray (52 mins); M Bonello for Mach (58 mins); S Baikeinuku for Cabannes (63 mins); Kirkpatrick for Tales (67 mins); M Lazar for Herrera (74 mins); C Garcia for Kockott (77 mins)

**SCORERS:** *Try*: Evans *Conversion*: Kockott *Penalty Goal*: Kockott

**REFEREE:** C Berdos (France)

# LEINSTER SECURE BACK-TO-BACK TITLES

## By Rob Clark

Retiring Leinster stalwarts Leo Cullen and Brian O'Driscoll celebrate retaining the RaboDirect PRO12 title.

**L**einster, who looked the form horse for much of the competition and who had topped the table at the end of the regular season, deservedly won the RaboDirect PRO12 title after an impressive 34–12 win over Glasgow Warriors in the final.

It capped an almost-perfect retirement season for the legendary Brian O'Driscoll, who had earlier in the year claimed the Six Nations title with Ireland and now added the PRO12 title to his medal haul. The only sour note was that O'Driscoll himself was forced out of the game after just 10 minutes owing to a recurrence of the calf injury which had been plaguing him for some time. "S*** happens" was O'Driscoll's own pithy but succinct tweet, though the picture of him and fellow retiree Leo Cullen told a happier story. O'Driscoll later added: "I always said you can't plan anything in this game. It wasn't a good day for me, but this [trophy] is what it's all about."

In becoming the first side to win consecutive PRO12 titles, Leinster, for so long the bridesmaid but never the bride, established themselves as one of the leading northern hemisphere teams. And all this under new coach Matt O'Connor, who had looked a candidate for being cast in the David Moyes role after taking over from the hugely successful Joe Schmidt. O'Connor, a likeable and engaging Australian, quickly won over both players and fans, however. "Ultimately, it's about getting the best out of your blokes," he said of his role at the club. "What you can achieve across 80 minutes in a game, or across a whole season is governed by the strengths of your own group. We are lucky to have a great squad here."

Certainly the strength of Leinster came to the fore as the match wore on. For much of the first half they were second best and only they know how they ended the half 14–12 to the good – tries from Zane Kirchner and Shane Jennings, both converted by Jimmy Gopperth, giving them the edge over four penalties from Finn Russell. But Glasgow had played most of the rugby up to that point and only some desperate defence from Leinster had kept them out. Ironically, Glasgow's finishing let them down, an aspect of their game which O'Connor had pinpointed as their biggest virtue before the match. "They execute on their chances a high proportion of the time," he had said of his opponents, "and to compete we have to do the same."

The third quarter was scoreless and the Warriors were still very much in the game until two penalties from Gopperth just after the hour mark seemed to sap the last piece of resistance out of the Scottish side. Two late tries for Leinster – the first when Gordon D'Arcy put Kirchner in, the second when the South African returned the favour – were both converted by Gopperth and made the final scoreline look harsh on a Glasgow Warriors side which was competitive until the last.

"They just controlled it better," said a disappointed Warriors captain Al Kellock. "They did not make any mistakes and were clinical. We made more mistakes in that game than we have in the last four or five games and that's hard to take." Coach Gregor Townsend agreed that his team hadn't taken their opportunities in the first half when they had the wind behind them, but ended on a more positive note. "We have made real progress to get to a final," he said of the first appearance by any Scottish team in a PRO12 final. "The players have played really well and this group is going to be here for the future. We have just got to make sure we win it next time."

There's no doubt that a Scottish victory would have been a real shot in the arm for rugby in that country after another disappointing international season, not least because Townsend's squad is largely made up of Scottish, or Scottish-qualified, players. "It would be huge," said Rob Harley of the prospect of a Glasgow win, and teammate Pat MacArthur agreed. "It would be an amazing boost to Glasgow and the west of Scotland. Rugby is growing massively in the area, the crowds at Scotstoun have been getting bigger and bigger and it would be fantastic to repay those fans."

The final was played out against the backdrop of a packed RDS – more than packed in fact as extra seats had been put in for the occasion. "I don't think it's particularly intimidating for visiting teams," O'Connor had said of Leinster's home turf, "because it's a family atmosphere at the RDS, but we enjoy playing there because the fans are knowledgeable and supportive and the surface is in great shape." The latter point is a constant refrain from players and coaches in the league. Ospreys and Wales fly-half Dan Biggar, who was voted Players' Player of the Year in the RaboDirect PRO12 Awards, described it as "the best place to play rugby in the league", while Townsend declared it "a great stage".

It had all started back on a Friday evening in September when Leinster had set their stall out with a 42–19 win at Scarlets, having trailed 16–10 at half-time. On the same evening, Glasgow had beaten Cardiff Blues, but it was their run of eight straight victories at the end of the regular season which lifted the Warriors into second place – and gave them a home draw for the first time in the play-off semi-finals – cementing their position as genuine title contenders. That run included convincing wins against the other two teams who were to make up the play-offs: Munster and Ulster. Particularly noteworthy was Glasgow's 22–5 win in front of almost 15,000 at Thomond Park, Munster's only home defeat of the season.

Elsewhere, Italian side Zebre won five more matches than they had in their debut season, including a 30–27 win over the Ospreys on 1 May which all but ended the Welsh team's hopes of making the play-offs themselves. Biggar lamented the fact that his team had "failed to get any momentum this year" and said there was "a little bit of disappointment that we didn't get through."

Fellow Italian side Benetton Treviso also won five matches in the regular season, half the number that they won the previous year, though they did just pip Zebre for a place in next season's new European Rugby Champions Cup.

Welsh teams the Ospreys, Scarlets and Cardiff Blues filled places five to eight in the table, but while the Ospreys only just missed out on a play-off place, the other two were some way back. Newport Gwent Dragons had a largely forgettable season of seven wins and a draw from their 22 matches to finish ninth and miss out on qualification for the leading European competition next season. They did, however, achieve one memorable feat: they beat Glasgow Warriors both home and away to become the only club who did the double over the eventual runners-up.

The semi-finals saw only Glasgow breaking up the Irish party, and both were to prove tight affairs. Ultimately, though, the PRO12 maintained its tradition of never seeing an away win in the play-offs.

First up was Glasgow's 16–15 win over Munster in front of a sell-out crowd at Scotstoun, in which the home team recovered well from an early try by Damien Varley to lead 9–7 at half-time thanks to three Russell penalties. Glasgow then moved further ahead shortly after half-time with Gordon Reid's try. Sean Dougall's try on 51 minutes cut the deficit to four, and four became one when Keatley slotted a 67th-minute penalty, but the Warriors held on to claim a famous victory. "That game was as fast, physical and tough as they come," said a relieved MacArthur afterwards, while Townsend described it as a "high-quality game" which he never felt was won "until the final whistle."

The other semi-final saw fourth-placed Ulster travel more in hope than expectation to the RDS to take on Leinster. Against the odds, around 18,000 fans saw Ulster leading 9–0 with almost an hour played. Suddenly Leinster sprang into action and after two Gopperth penalties had brought them back to within a score, Ian Madigan darted over for the only try of the game after 72 minutes. Gopperth's conversion was vital, taking Leinster to 13–9 and for all their efforts Ulster couldn't find the try they needed. "Ulster played so well without really showing it on the scoreboard," admitted a relieved O'Connor. "We always knew they were a good side, fortunately we managed to hang in there and not let them put too many points on us when they were on top."

Leinster full-back Rob Kearney added: "The knockout stages of the PRO12 are very special. Guys want to play in these big matches and they know that they have to be right on their games in them."

Leinster were undoubtedly right on their game in the final, and that enabled them to fight off the challenge of a spirited Glasgow Warriors and give O'Driscoll the send-off that no true rugby fan would have denied him, a rare club and country double. As Townsend aptly put it "along with Jonny Wilkinson, Brian is probably *the* player of the northern hemisphere in the professional era."

O'Driscoll has always been a competitor and will have enjoyed going out on a winning note; for his Leinster teammates the lure of the hat-trick awaits next season.

# RABODIRECT PRO12 2013–14 RESULTS

6 September 2013: **Glasgow** 22 **Blues** 15, **Dragons** 15 **Ulster** 8, **Scarlets** 19 **Leinster** 42. 7 September: **Connacht** 25 **Zebre** 16, **Treviso** 19 **Ospreys** 24, **Munster** 34 **Edinburgh** 23. 13 September: **Zebre** 21 **Munster** 43, **Blues** 21 **Connacht** 10, **Ulster** 12 **Glasgow** 13, **Edinburgh** 16 **Glasgow** 13. 14 September: **Leinster** 29 **Ospreys** 29, **Scarlets** 26 **Treviso** 10. 20 September: **Dragons** 23 **Scarlets** 16, **Treviso** 29 **Munster** 19, **Blues** 25 **Zebre** 30, **Glasgow** 12 **Leinster** 6. 21 September: **Ospreys** 44 **Edinburgh** 10, **Connacht** 7 **Ulster** 18. 27 September: **Zebre** 17 **Glasgow** 24, **Ulster** 32 **Treviso** 13, **Edinburgh** 9 **Scarlets** 22, **Leinster** 34 **Blues** 20. 28 September: **Connacht** 26 **Ospreys** 43, **Munster** 23 **Dragons** 9. 4 October: **Ospreys** 12 **Ulster** 18, **Dragons** 30 **Zebre** 7, **Treviso** 23 **Connacht** 3. 5 October: **Scarlets** 12 **Glasgow** 17, **Munster** 19 **Leinster** 15. 6 October: **Blues** 29 **Edinburgh** 12. 25 October: **Zebre** 16 **Scarlets** 16, **Ospreys** 40 **Dragons** 17, **Ulster** 39 **Blues** 21, **Glasgow** 6 **Munster** 13, **Edinburgh** 20 **Treviso** 13. 26 October: **Leinster** 16 **Connacht** 13. 1 November: **Dragons** 19 **Leinster** 23, **Edinburgh** 25 **Zebre** 23. 2 November: **Blues** 17 **Treviso** 13, **Connacht** 12 **Glasgow** 19, **Scarlets** 17 **Ulster** 9, **Munster** 12 **Ospreys** 6. 22 November: **Ulster** 41 **Edinburgh** 17, **Glasgow** 8 **Dragons** 23. 23 November: **Ospreys** 30 **Zebre** 20, **Connacht** 21 **Scarlets** 24, **Blues** 10 **Munster** 31. 24 November: **Treviso** 20 **Leinster** 21. 29 November: **Ospreys** 16 **Glasgow** 28, **Dragons** 14 **Munster** 18, **Edinburgh** 43 **Connacht** 10. 30 November: **Zebre** 11 **Ulster** 19, **Treviso** 26 **Blues** 26, **Leinster** 36 **Scarlets** 19. 20 December: **Blues** 19 **Ospreys** 22, **Ulster** 13 **Zebre** 6, **Edinburgh** 11 **Leinster** 6. 21 December: **Connacht** 14 **Dragons** 11, **Munster** 16 **Scarlets** 10. 26 December: **Scarlets** 6 **Ospreys** 10, **Edinburgh** 16 **Glasgow** 20, **Dragons** 22 **Blues** 16. 27 December: **Munster** 22 **Connacht** 16. 28 December: **Treviso** 20 **Zebre** 15, **Leinster** 19 **Ulster** 6. 1 January, 2014: **Blues** 21 **Dragons** 13. 3 January: **Ulster** 29 **Munster** 19, **Ospreys** 17 **Scarlets** 12. 4 January: **Zebre** 14 **Treviso** 12, **Connacht** 8 **Leinster** 16. 7 February: **Ulster** 10 **Ospreys** 7. 8 February: **Treviso** 33 **Scarlets** 41, **Munster** 54 **Blues** 13. 9 February: **Glasgow** 8 **Connacht** 6, **Zebre** 8 **Leinster** 31. 14 February: **Leinster** 31 **Dragons** 19. 15 February: **Connacht** 11 **Edinburgh** 7, **Blues** 20 **Glasgow** 27, **Munster** 36 **Zebre** 8. 16 February: **Ospreys** 75 **Treviso** 7. 20 February: **Blues** 22 **Leinster** 34. 22 February: **Scarlets** 25 **Edinburgh** 21. 23 February: **Treviso** 12 **Ulster** 14, **Dragons** 24 **Glasgow** 23, **Ospreys** 11 **Munster** 25, **Zebre** 19 **Connacht** 27. 28 February: **Ulster** 38 **Dragons** 8, **Edinburgh** 31 **Ospreys** 25. 1 March: **Zebre** 15 **Blues** 10, **Connacht** 38 **Treviso** 6, **Scarlets** 18 **Munster** 13, **Leinster** 28 **Glasgow** 25. 14 March: **Ulster** 26 **Scarlets** 13. 21 March: **Ospreys** 34 **Blues** 9, **Leinster** 27 **Zebre** 0, **Edinburgh** 3 **Ulster** 9. 22 March: **Glasgow** 14 **Scarlets** 6, **Munster** 14 **Treviso** 3. 23 March: **Dragons** 8 **Connacht** 24. 28 March: **Glasgow** 11 **Ospreys** 9. 29 March: **Zebre** 25 **Dragons** 25, **Treviso** 20 **Edinburgh** 16, **Blues** 28 **Ulster** 23, **Leinster** 22 **Munster** 18. 30 March: **Scarlets** 32 **Connacht** 24. 3 April: **Dragons** 19 **Edinburgh** 20. 4 April: **Glasgow** 29 **Treviso** 10. 11 April: **Ospreys** 25 **Leinster** 19, **Ulster** 58 **Connacht** 12, **Edinburgh** 22 **Blues** 29. 12 April: **Munster** 5 **Glasgow** 22, **Scarlets** 27 **Zebre** 20, **Treviso** 45 **Dragons** 27. 18 April: **Leinster** 62 **Treviso** 7, **Glasgow** 27 **Ulster** 9. 19 April **Zebre** 26 **Edinburgh** 13, **Connacht** 23 **Munster** 32. 20 April: **Blues** 17 **Scarlets** 13, **Dragons** 10 **Ospreys** 20. 26 April: **Glasgow** 37 **Edinburgh** 34. 1 May: **Zebre** 30 **Ospreys** 27. 2 May: **Scarlets** 34 **Dragons** 23, **Ulster** 20 **Leinster** 22, **Treviso** 16 **Glasgow** 38. 3 May: **Connacht** 15 **Blues** 22, **Edinburgh** 12 **Munster** 55. 10 May: **Glasgow** 54 **Zebre** 0, **Leinster** 15 **Edinburgh** 13, **Munster** 17 **Ulster** 19, **Dragons** 20 **Treviso** 19, **Ospreys** 45 **Connacht** 20, **Scarlets** 27 **Blues** 15.

# FINAL TABLE

| | P | W | D | L | F | A | BP | PTS |
|---|---|---|---|---|---|---|---|---|
| Leinster | 22 | 17 | 1 | 4 | 554 | 352 | 12 | 82 |
| Glasgow Warriors | 22 | 18 | 0 | 4 | 484 | 309 | 7 | 79 |
| Munster | 22 | 16 | 0 | 6 | 538 | 339 | 10 | 74 |
| Ulster | 22 | 15 | 0 | 7 | 470 | 319 | 10 | 70 |
| Ospreys | 22 | 13 | 1 | 8 | 571 | 388 | 12 | 66 |
| Scarlets | 22 | 11 | 1 | 10 | 435 | 438 | 9 | 55 |
| Cardiff Blues | 22 | 8 | 1 | 13 | 425 | 538 | 7 | 41 |
| Edinburgh | 22 | 7 | 0 | 15 | 397 | 526 | 10 | 38 |
| Dragons | 22 | 7 | 1 | 14 | 392 | 492 | 5 | 35 |
| Connacht | 22 | 6 | 0 | 16 | 371 | 509 | 11 | 35 |
| Treviso | 22 | 5 | 1 | 16 | 376 | 591 | 8 | 30 |
| Zebre | 22 | 5 | 2 | 15 | 347 | 559 | 5 | 29 |

Leinster's players celebrate after beating Glasgow Warriors in the RaboDirect PRO12 final in Dublin.

## GLASGOW WARRIORS 16 (1G 3PG) MUNSTER 15 (1G 1T 1PG)

**GLASGOW:** P Murchie; S Maitland, M Bennett, A Dunbar, T Seymour; F Russell, C Cusiter; R Grant, D Hall, J Welsh, J Gray, A Kellock (captain), R Harley, C Fusaro, J Strauss

**SUBSTITUTIONS:** G Reid for Grant (26 mins); P MacArthur for Hall (53 mins); G Cross for Welsh (53 mins); T Swinson for Kellock (58 mins); N Matawalu for Cusiter (66 mins); R Jackson for Bennett (66 mins); S Lamont for Fusaro (72 mins)

**SCORERS:** *Try:* Reid *Conversion:* Russell *Penalty Goals:* Russell (3)

**MUNSTER:** F Jones; K Earls, C Laulala, J Downey, S Zebo; I Keatley, C Murray; D Kilcoyne, D Varley (captain), BJ Botha, D Foley, P O'Connell, CJ Stander, S Dougall, J Coughlan

**SUBSTITUTIONS:** A Conway for Laulala (9 mins); JJ Hanrahan for Jones (38 mins); P Butler for Dougall (62 mins); D O'Callaghan for Foley (66 mins); D Cronin for Kilcoyne (66 mins)

**SCORERS:** *Tries:* Varley, Dougall *Conversion:* Keatley *Penalty Goals:* Keatley (2)

**REFEREE:** M Mitrea (Italy)

## LEINSTER 13 (1G 2PG) ULSTER 9 (3PG)

**LEINSTER:** R Kearney; F McFadden, B O'Driscoll, G D'Arcy, D Kearney; J Gopperth, E Reddan; C Healy, S Cronin, M Moore, D Toner, Q Roux, R Ruddock, S Jennings, J Heaslip (captain)

**SUBSTITUTIONS:** I Madigan for O'Driscoll (50 mins); L Cullen for Roux (53 mins); M Ross for Moore (56 mins); S O'Brien for Ruddock (56 mins); J McGrath for Healy (65 mins); Z Kirchner for McFadden (67 mins); L McGrath for D Kearney (69 mins); A Dundon for Cronin (79 mins)

**SCORERS:** *Try:* Madigan *Conversion:* Gopperth *Penalty Goals:* Gopperth (2)

**YELLOW CARD:** D'Arcy (34 mins)

**ULSTER:** C Gilroy; T Bowe, J Payne, D Cave, A Trimble; P Jackson, R Pienaar; C Black, R Best, R Lutton, J Muller (captain), I Henderson, R Diack, C Henry, R Wilson

**SUBSTITUTIONS:** J McKinney for Jackson (56 mins); L Marshall for Cave (56 mins); D Tuohy for Muller (59 mins); A Warwick for Lutton (61 mins); S Doyle for Henry (69 mins)

**SCORERS:** *Penalty Goals:* Jackson (3)

**REFEREE:** L Hodges (Wales)

# FINAL

## 31 May, Royal Dublin Society, Dublin

## LEINSTER 34 (4G 2PG) GLASGOW 12 (4PG)

**LEINSTER:** R Kearney; F McFadden, B O'Driscoll, G D'Arcy, Z Kirchner; J Gopperth, E Reddan; C Healy, S Cronin, M Ross, D Toner, M McCarthy, R Ruddock, S Jennings, J Heaslip (captain)

**SUBSTITUTIONS:** I Madigan for O'Driscoll (9 mins); M Moore for Ross (50 mins); S O'Brien for Jennings (55 mins); L Cullen for McCarthy (60 mins); J McGrath for Healy (67 mins); A Dundon for Cronin (74 mins); I Boss for Reddan (76 mins); D Fanning for Kearney (78 mins)

**SCORERS:** *Tries:* Kirchner (2) D'Arcy, Jennings *Conversions:* Gopperth (4) *Penalty Goals:* Gopperth (2)

**GLASGOW:** P Murchie; S Maitland, A Dunbar, P Horne, T Seymour; F Russell, C Cusiter; G Reid, D Hall, J Welsh, J Gray, A Kellock (captain), R Harley, C Fusaro, J Strauss

**SUBSTITUTIONS:** P MacArthur for Hall (24 mins); L Nakawara for Fusaro (25 mins); N Matawalu for Cusiter (44 mins); R Grant for Reid (45 mins); T Swinson for Kellock (50 mins); M Low for Welsh (55 mins); S Lamont for Dunbar (55 mins); R Jackson for Russell (67 mins)

**SCORERS:** *Penalty Goals:* Russell (4)

**REFEREE:** N Owens (Wales)

Getty Images

Gordon Reid (centre) is congratulated after scoring Glasgow Warriors' try in their semi-final win over Munster.

# TOULON TRIUMPHANT AT END OF AN ERA

## By Iain Spragg

Getty Images

World Cup winners Jonny Wilkinson and Bryan Habana celebrate Toulon's back-to-back Heineken Cup victories.

**The challenge of** lifting three consecutive Heineken Cups is one which has defeated Europe's elite clubs since the inaugural final was staged in Cardiff in 1996. Leicester Tigers and subsequently Leinster had won back-to-back finals, while the great Toulouse side had reached three finals in a row from 2003–05 but lost the middle one of the three to a stirring performance from London Wasps.

In 2014 Toulon joined an exclusive group of two-time champions – those four sides mentioned above, plus Munster – courtesy of their 23–6 demolition of Saracens at the Millennium Stadium, a victory that came 12 months after they had beaten Clermont Auvergne for their maiden title, but there will be no third Heineken Cup triumph for Le Rouge et Noir.

The French giants may yet emerge again as the continent's top team at the end of the 2014–15 campaign, but if they do it will be as winners of the European Rugby Champions Cup, the renamed and rebranded tournament which has consigned the Heineken Cup to rugby history.

Confirmation of the demise of the long-running competition came in April, just six weeks before Toulon's victory in Cardiff which arrived thanks to tries from Matt Giteau and Juan Smith plus 13 points from the steadfast left boot of Jonny Wilkinson, and represented the end of a protracted and frequently bitter struggle for control of European rugby's most high-profile club event.

The dispute had begun in June 2012 when the English and French clubs, disillusioned with the qualifying criteria, revenue distribution and governance, signalled their intent to withdraw after the 2013–14 instalment of the tournament. The Anglo-French threat to quit rumbled on acrimoniously for months and was only resolved when the stakeholders from the six competing countries finally agreed a new format for the 2014–15 season.

The European Rugby Champions Cup, featuring 20 rather than 24 sides, was born. The RaboDirect PRO12 saw its representation cut from 11 to seven teams, and with one Scottish and one Italian side guaranteed entry it leaves the Irish/Welsh contingent to fight out the other five places. It makes it conceivable that one from Leinster, Munster and Ulster – all previous winners of the Heineken Cup – might not qualify in any given year, which should certainly lead to a more combative PRO12 competition. England and France both retain six places while a new play-off to decide the 20th and final qualifiers has been introduced. A new governing body – European Professional Club Rugby – was established to run the new tournament and after 19 successful seasons, the Heineken Cup was to be shelved and Toulon its last ever champions.

"The benefits will be seen far and wide, from the clubs to the supporters, sponsors and everyone who has followed the fabulous mix of high-class rugby and good-natured rivalry, all played out in many spectacular towns and cities in Europe," said Rugby Football Union chairman Bill Beaumont after the peace deal was confirmed.

"The RFU, and in particular [CEO] Ian Ritchie, has invested significant time over the last few months in helping to find a solution to a problem that at one stage looked difficult to solve. We are very pleased that the challenges off the pitch are concluded so we can enjoy the joys of the game on it, creating more unforgettable memories for players and fans alike."

As for that final season of Heineken Cup action, Toulon's defence of their coveted European crown saw the French club drawn in Pool 2 alongside Cardiff, Exeter and Glasgow. A shock 19–15 reverse to the Blues in Cardiff in October was the only blemish on their record in the initial stages of the competition and they progressed to the quarter-finals as pool winners.

Their opponents in the last eight were Leinster, the three-time champions, and as befitted two sides who had won four of the previous five Heineken Cup finals between them, it was a high quality and fiercely contested clash at the Stade Felix Mayol.

The score stood at 6–6 at the break after two penalties each from Wilkinson and his opposite number Jimmy Gopperth, but Toulon struck the decisive blow in 16 second-half minutes with tries from Xavier Chiocci and Drew Mitchell. Although replacement Jordi Murphy replied for Leinster, the home side closed out a 29–14 victory.

Another Irish province, in the shape of Munster, awaited the French club in the semi-finals. It was to prove a tense but entertaining 80 minutes at the Stade Velodrome in Marseille and although Toulon never relinquished the lead they established in the fifth minute with a Wilkinson penalty, Munster did come agonisingly close to dethroning the champions.

The alarm bells rang loud and clear for Le Rouge et Noir in the 52nd minute when Simon Zebo went over for the only try of the match, Ian Keatley's conversion reducing Toulon's lead to a precarious 18–16. The result hung in the balance but indiscipline was to be Munster's Achilles heel as they conceded two late penalties which Wilkinson landed to secure a 24–16 win.

"We can't keep doing this to ourselves every year," Zebo said after Munster suffered their fourth successive defeat in the last four of a major competition. "We want to be competing for silverware and semifinals aren't good enough. We need to have a long hard look at ourselves and make sure that we're in with a fighting chance next year. It's going to have to come from within us. We had chances last year to win and didn't take them and it's the same again this year."

The other semi-final 24 hours earlier saw Saracens tackle Clermont and was in sharp contrast to Toulon's tight clash with Munster as the

English side ran riot at Twickenham, scoring six unanswered tries in a 46–6 romp.

The floodgates opened as early as the seventh minute when Chris Ashton raced over. A controversial penalty try, awarded by referee Nigel Owens after lengthy consultation with the TMO when Brock James was adjudged to have deliberately punched the ball over the dead-ball line, followed five minutes later and Saracens were already out of sight.

Clermont were only able to muster two Morgan Parra penalties in response while the Premiership side continued to rampage, scoring through Owen Farrell, Chris Wyles, Tim Streather and a second from Ashton to clinically dismantle their French opponents and book their place in the final of the Heineken Cup for the first time.

"I thought it was a phenomenal performance and I'm proud of the effort and work-rate," said Saracens head coach Mark McCall. "The plan was to put them under pressure and I think we achieved that. We got beaten in two semi-finals last season and there was real disappointment. We didn't think we gave a good account of ourselves, but today we did.

"Today was one of those days where everything went right. Today is a tremendous memory for us but it is the vehicle for something hopefully bigger and better towards the end of May."

The 2014 final was the fifth Anglo-French denouement in the history of the competition. In those previous four meetings only Brive in 1997 had emerged victorious against English opposition after dispatching Leicester in Cardiff and the Welsh capital again proved a happy hunting ground for a Top 14 side as Toulon ultimately overpowered and outplayed Saracens.

First blood went to Saracens with an early Farrell penalty but it was to be the only stage of the match that they were in the driving seat. A yellow card for Juan Martín Fernández Lobbe in the 21st minute should have given the English side impetus but Toulon turned conventional wisdom on its head eight minutes later by scoring the first try of the game while they were reduced to 14 men, former Wallaby Giteau crashing over after an incisive inside pass from compatriot Mitchell. Wilkinson added the conversion and than a trademark drop goal and Toulon were 10–3 up at half-time.

Saracens sensed the fight-back was on five minutes after the restart when Farrell was successful with a second penalty attempt, but the pivotal moment of the match came on the hour when the defending champions scored a second try. Mathieu Bastareaud made the initial break before finding Smith, who then took a return pass from Fernández Lobbe to cross the line and effectively settle the contest. The redoubtable Wilkinson was on target with the conversion and a second penalty two minutes later – a kick which notched up a century of points for the fly-half in the 2013–14 tournament – and Toulon were the champions again.

Victory for Le Rouge et Noir extended the Irish and French domination of the competition to seven years while defeat for Sarries was the third time in six seasons an English club had fallen at the final hurdle.

"It's such a privilege to have won it twice in a row," Wilkinson said after what was his penultimate game of professional rugby. "I had no idea how today was going to go, apart from it being tough as we were up against a very good team.

"In terms of the result, I could not have asked for any more from the team. The guys were together and the individual contributions made across the board were phenomenal. It's amazing because we've had tough times [this season] where it hasn't been perfect and hasn't gone well. For me it was one hell of a day, but for the team it was a great reward for a long journey."

The final at Twickenham, however, was not quite the end of the story of European club rugby's tumultuous season. On the same day as Toulon overcame Saracens, the 2004 Heineken Cup champions Wasps beat Stade Français 20–6 at Stade Jean Bouin in the second leg of the historic play-off. The result gave the English side a 50–35 aggregate triumph over their Top 14 opponents and confirmed Dai Young's team would feature in the inaugural European Rugby Champions Cup the following season.

# HEINEKEN CUP 2013–14 RESULTS

## ROUND ONE

| 11 October 2013 | |
|---|---|
| Connacht 17 Saracens 23 | Ulster 22 Leicester 16 |
| Toulouse 38 Zebre 5 | |
| **12 October 2013** | |
| Treviso 10 Montpellier 27 | Harlequins 26 Scarlets 33 |
| Edinburgh 29 Munster 23 | Gloucester 27 Perpignan 22 |
| Castres 19 Northampton 13 | Ospreys 9 Leinster 19 |
| **13 October 2013** | |
| Exeter 44 Blues 29 | Racing Métro 13 Clermont 9 |
| Toulon 51 Glasgow 28 | |

# ROUND TWO

| 18 October 2013 | |
|---|---|
| Saracens 16 Toulouse 17 | Leicester 34 Treviso 3 |

| 19 October 2013 | |
|---|---|
| Blues 19 Toulon 15 | Montpellier 8 Ulster 25 |
| Zebre 6 Connacht 33 | Munster 26 Gloucester 10 |
| Leinster 19 Castres 7 | Scarlets 26 Racing Métro 26 |
| Munster 26 Gloucester 10 | |

| 20 October 2013 | |
|---|---|
| Northampton 27 Ospreys 16 | Glasgow 20 Exeter 16 |
| Perpignan 31 Edinburgh 14 | Clermont 23 Harlequins 16 |

# ROUND THREE

| 6 December 2013 | |
|---|---|
| Blues 29 Glasgow 20 | Castres 15 Ospreys 9 |

| 7 December 2013 | |
|---|---|
| Clermont 32 Scarlets 11 | Racing Métro 8 Harlequins 32 |
| Exeter 9 Toulon 14 | Northampton 7 Leinster 40 |
| Zebre 10 Saracens 39 | Ulster 48 Treviso 0 |

| 8 December 2013 | |
|---|---|
| Munster 36 Perpignan 8 | Leicester 41 Montpellier 32 |
| Edinburgh 12 Gloucester 23 | Toulouse 14 Connacht 16 |

# ROUND FOUR

| 13 December 2013 | |
|---|---|
| Glasgow 7 Blues 9 | Ospreys 21 Castres 12 |

| 14 December 2013 | |
|---|---|
| Treviso 3 Ulster 35 | Scarlets 13 Clermont 31 |
| Toulon 32 Exeter 20 | Connacht 9 Toulouse 37 |
| Saracens 64 Zebre 3 | Leinster 9 Northampton 18 |
| Perpignan 17 Munster 18 | |

| 15 December 2013 | |
|---|---|
| Harlequins 17 Racing Métro 3 | Montpellier 14 Leicester 15 |
| Gloucester 10 Edinburgh 16 | |

# ROUND FIVE

### 10 January 2014

Racing Métro 13 Scarlets 19      Ulster 27 Montpellier 16

### 11 January 2014

Treviso 19 Leicester 34      Toulon 43 Blues 20

Harlequins 13 Clermont 16      Edinburgh 27 Perpignan 16

Exeter 10 Glasgow 15      Gloucester 7 Munster 20

Connacht 20 Zebre 3

### 12 January 2014

Castres 22 Leinster 29      Toulouse 21 Saracens 11

Ospreys 17 Northampton 29

# ROUND SIX

### 17 January 2014

Leinster 36 Ospreys 3      Northampton 13 Castres 3

### 18 January 2014

Saracens 64 Connacht 6      Glasgow 8 Toulon 15

Zebre 6 Toulouse 16      Leicester 19 Ulster 22

Blues 13 Exeter 19      Montpellier 24 Treviso 6

### 19 January 2014

Munster 38 Edinburgh 6      Clermont 28 Racing Métro 3

Perpignan 18 Gloucester 36      Scarlets 20 Harlequins 22

# POOL TABLES

### POOL ONE

|  | P | W | D | L | F | A | BP | PTS |
|---|---|---|---|---|---|---|---|---|
| Leinster | 6 | 5 | 0 | 1 | 152 | 66 | 2 | 22 |
| Northampton | 6 | 4 | 0 | 2 | 107 | 104 | 1 | 17 |
| Castres | 6 | 2 | 0 | 4 | 78 | 104 | 1 | 9 |
| Ospreys | 6 | 1 | 0 | 5 | 75 | 138 | 1 | 5 |

### POOL FOUR

|  | P | W | D | L | F | A | BP | PTS |
|---|---|---|---|---|---|---|---|---|
| Clermont | 6 | 5 | 0 | 1 | 139 | 69 | 4 | 24 |
| Harlequins | 6 | 3 | 0 | 3 | 126 | 103 | 4 | 16 |
| Scarlets | 6 | 2 | 1 | 3 | 122 | 150 | 1 | 11 |
| Racing Métro | 6 | 1 | 1 | 4 | 66 | 131 | 1 | 7 |

### POOL TWO

|  | P | W | D | L | F | A | BP | PTS |
|---|---|---|---|---|---|---|---|---|
| Toulon | 6 | 5 | 0 | 1 | 170 | 104 | 4 | 24 |
| Blues | 6 | 3 | 0 | 3 | 119 | 148 | 2 | 14 |
| Exeter | 6 | 2 | 0 | 4 | 118 | 123 | 4 | 12 |
| Glasgow | 6 | 2 | 0 | 4 | 98 | 130 | 3 | 11 |

### POOL FIVE

|  | P | W | D | L | F | A | BP | PTS |
|---|---|---|---|---|---|---|---|---|
| Ulster | 6 | 6 | 0 | 0 | 179 | 62 | 2 | 26 |
| Leicester | 6 | 4 | 0 | 2 | 159 | 112 | 5 | 21 |
| Montpellier | 6 | 2 | 0 | 4 | 121 | 124 | 3 | 11 |
| Treviso | 6 | 0 | 0 | 6 | 41 | 202 | 0 | 0 |

## POOL THREE

| | W | D | L | F | A | BP | PTS |
|---|---|---|---|---|---|---|---|
| Toulouse | 6 | 5 | 0 | 1 | 143 | 63 | 3 | 23 |
| Saracens | 6 | 4 | 0 | 2 | 217 | 74 | 4 | 20 |
| Connacht | 6 | 3 | 0 | 3 | 101 | 147 | 1 | 13 |
| Zebre | 6 | 0 | 0 | 6 | 33 | 210 | 0 | 0 |

## POOL SIX

| | P | W | D | L | F | A | BP | PTS |
|---|---|---|---|---|---|---|---|---|
| Munster | 6 | 5 | 0 | 1 | 161 | 77 | 3 | 23 |
| Gloucester | 6 | 3 | 0 | 3 | 113 | 114 | 2 | 14 |
| Edinburgh | 6 | 3 | 0 | 3 | 104 | 141 | 0 | 12 |
| Perpignan | 6 | 1 | 0 | 5 | 112 | 158 | 3 | 7 |

## QUARTER-FINALS

### 5 April 2014

**Munster** 47 **Toulouse** 23

**Ulster** 15 **Saracens** 17

**Clermont** 22 **Leicester** 16

### 6 April 2014

**Toulon** 29 **Leinster** 14

## SEMI-FINALS

### 26 April, Twickenham, London

## SARACENS 46 (5G 1T 2PG) CLERMONT AUVERGNE 6 (2PG)

**SARACENS:** A Goode; C Ashton, M Bosch, B Barritt, D Strettle; O Farrell, N de Kock; M Vunipola, S Brits, J Johnston, S Borthwick (captain), M Botha, K Brown, J Burger, B Vunipola

**SUBSTITUTIONS:** M Stevens for Johnston (46 mins); R Wigglesworth for de Kock (51 mins); A Hargreaves for Botha (67 mins); C Wyles for Strettle (70 mins); J Wray for Burger (70 mins); R Barrington for M Vunipola (71 mins); J George for Brits (71 mins); T Streather for Bosch (73 mins).

**SCORERS:** *Tries:* Ashton (2), penalty, Farrell, Wyles, Streather *Conversions:* Goode (5) *Penalty Goals:* Goode, Bosch

**CLERMONT AUVERGNE:** L Byrne; S Sivivatu, B Stanley, W Fofana, N Nalaga; B James, M Parra; T Domingo, B Kayser, D Zirakashvili, J Cudmore, N Hines, J Bonnaire (captain), D Chouly, F Lee

**SUBSTITUTIONS:** G Vosloo for Lee (32 mins); V Debaty for Domingo (51 mins); M Delany for James (58 mins); T Paulo for Kayser (58 mins); T Lacrampe for Parra (62 mins); N Nakaitaci for Stanley (67 mins); C Ric for Zirakashvili (68 mins), J Pierre for Cudmore (70 mins).

**SCORERS:** *Penalty Goals:* Parra (2)

**YELLOW CARD:** James (13 mins)

**REFEREE:** N Owens (Wales)

## 27 April, Stade Velodrome, Marseille

# TOULON 24 (7PG 1DG) MUNSTER 16 (1G 3PG)

**TOULON:** D Armitage; D Mitchell, M Bastareaud, M Giteau, B Habana; J Wilkinson (captain), S Tillous-Borde; X Chiocci, C Burden, C Hayman, D Rossouw, J Suta, J Smith, JM Fernández Lobbe, S Armitage

**SUBSTITUTIONS:** D Smith for Habana (49 mins); JC Orioli for Burden (59 mins); M Claassens for Tillous-Borde (63 mins); K Mikautadze for Rossouw (63 mins); A Menini for Chiocci (66 mins); M Castrogiovanni for Hayman (75 mins)

**SCORERS:** *Penalty Goals*: Wilkinson (6), D Armitage *Drop Goal*: Wilkinson

**YELLOW CARD:** Fernández Lobbe (28 mins)

**MUNSTER:** F Jones; K Earls, C Laulala, J Downey, S Zebo; I Keatley, C Murray; D Kilcoyne, D Varley (captain), BJ Botha, D Foley, P O'Connell, CJ Stander, S Dougall, J Coughlan

**SUBSTITUTIONS:** T O'Donnell for Dougall (56 mins); J Cronin for Kilcoyne (65 mins); JJ Hanrahan for Downey (65 mins); D O'Callaghan for Foley (65 mins); D Hurley for Jones (73 mins); D Casey for Varley (76 mins)

**SCORERS:** *Try*: Zebo *Conversion*: Keatley *Penalty Goals*: Keatley (3)

**YELLOW CARD:** Earls (63 mins)

**REFEREE:** W Barnes (England)

# FINAL

## 24 May, Millennium Stadium, Cardiff

# SARACENS 6 (2PG) TOULON 23 (2G 2PG 1DG)

**SARACENS:** A Goode; C Ashton, M Bosch, B Barritt, D Strettle; O Farrell, R Wigglesworth; M Vunipola, S Brits, M Stevens, S Borthwick (captain), A Hargreaves, K Brown, J Burger, B Vunipola

**SUBSTITUTIONS:** N de Kock for Wigglesworth (51 mins); J Wray for Burger (61 mins); M Botha for Hargreaves (64 mins); J Johnston for Stevens (64 mins); C Hodgson for Farrell (64 mins); R Barrington for M Vunipola (65 mins); C Wyles for Strettle (69 mins); J George for Brits (69 mins)

**SCORERS:** *Penalty Goals*: Farrell (2)

**TOULON:** D Armitage; D Mitchell, M Bastareaud, M Giteau, B Habana; J Wilkinson (captain), S Tillous-Borde; X Chiocci, C Burden, C Hayman, B Botha, D Rossouw, J Smith, JM Fernández Lobbe, S Armitage

**SUBSTITUTIONS:** J-C Orioli for Burden (41 mins); A Menini for Chiocci (46 mins); A Williams for Botha (52 mins); J Suta for Rossouw (52 mins); M Castrogiovanni for Hayman (57 mins); M Claassens for Tillous-Borde (71 mins); V Bruni for Smith (72 mins); M Mermoz for Wilkinson (77 mins)

**SCORERS:** *Tries*: Giteau, Smith *Conversions*: Wilkinson (2) *Penalty Goals*: Wilkinson (2) *Drop Goal*: Wilkinson

**YELLOW CARD:** Fernández Lobbe (22 mins)

Jonny Wilkinson appears lost in his thoughts after his last game, which sealed an historic double for his Toulon side.

# DOUBLE DREAMS FOR SAINTS
## By Rob Clark

Getty Images

Tom Wood and Phil Dowson hold aloft the Amlin Challenge Cup after Northampton's final win over Bath.

**T**he last Amlin Challenge Cup, in its current guise, took place this season and fittingly was won by Northampton Saints, a week before they also claimed the Aviva Premiership title. It was a year largely dictated by English sides, with Bath, London Wasps and Sale Sharks all topping their pools and London Irish unlucky to miss out on the knockout stage after earning 24 points in winning five of their six pool games.

The other pool winners were Stade Français and Brive, but with Northampton Saints, Harlequins and Gloucester dropping down from the

Heineken Cup, the stage was set for a continuation of English and French dominance which has largely been the story of the competition's 18-year history with only the 2010 triumph by Cardiff Blues and the 2013 win by Leinster interrupting the 10 wins by English clubs and six by French clubs.

In the quarter-finals Sale scored the first and last tries against Northampton but conceded four, all converted, in between. A full-strength Bath side were much too good for Brive, with tries all across their backline, including a hat-trick for Argentine wing Horacio Agulla.

Wasps and Gloucester shared six tries at Adams Park, but a kicking master-class – and 21 points – from Andy Goode saw the home side through 36–24. The last quarter-final witnessed a powerful second-half performance from a Harlequins side who scored 20 unanswered points in front of a crowd of more than 10,000 in the intimidating Stade Jean Bouin, home of Stade Français.

Quins looked determined to add to their record of three Amlin Cups, but in the semi-finals Northampton proved just too strong at Franklin's Gardens, running out 18–10 winners. In the other semi-final a see-saw match between Wasps and Bath could have gone either way, particularly when Bath lost influential inside centre Kyle Eastmond to the sin-bin for the last five minutes as the Adams Park faithful tried to cheer the home team to victory. Bath held on, though, to win 24–18.

So to a Friday night final in Cardiff and a match which proved to be the proverbial tale of two halves. In the first half Bath fly-half George Ford used his full range of tactical kicking to keep the Saints pinned in their own territory and South African flanker Francois Louw bossed the breakdown, as he had so many times over the course of the season. Sadly for Ford, his place-kicking radar suddenly went askew. He missed three kicks at goal, two of them simple chances, and Northampton grew in the belief that they could fight back from a 13–6 half-time deficit.

The Bath try had come from a 55-metre run from exciting wing Anthony Watson, who snaffled a loose ball and never looked like being caught. But Saints' power play gradually took its toll on the Bath defence, Ford and his full-back Nick Abendanon twice got in a muddle and were punished by Stephen Myler penalties and when Phil Dowson was driven over from close range it left Bath playing catch-up.

There was just time for one more Ford error as he was intercepted by Myler when trying to force a pass. Luther Burrell and George Pisi took it on and Ben Foden touched down to make the score 30–16 and complete a fine second-half comeback from Northampton.

"It feels amazing," admitted Myler. "It was a tough first half when Bath really came at us but we were in a similar situation last week [against Leicester in the Premiership semi-final] and we didn't panic. It doesn't matter if it takes until the 80th minute to win it."

# AMLIN CHALLENGE CUP 2013–14 RESULTS

## ROUND ONE

### 10 October 2013

Bayonne 37 Grenoble 6
Sale 33 Biarritz 10

Stade Français 61 Lusitanos 3

### 11 October 2013

Dragons 50 Mogliano 8

London Irish 60 Cavalieri 11

### 12 October 2013

Bucharest 12 Newcastle 13
Viadana 17 Wasps 90
Oyonnax 9 Worcester 9

Calvisano 20 Brive 20
Bordeaux 6 Bath 15

## ROUND TWO

### 17 October 2013

Wasps 26 Bayonne 10

### 18 October 2013

Grenoble 40 Viadana 7

### 19 October 2013

Bucharest 37 Calvisano 15
Cavalieri 16 Stade Français 17
Mogliano 20 Bordeaux 32
Biarritz 26 Oyonnax 6

Bath 26 Dragons 10
Lusitanos 6 London Irish 67
Worcester 15 Sale 29
Brive 23 Newcastle 16

## ROUND THREE

### 5 December 2013

Oyonnax 16 Sale 10

Worcester 15 Biarritz 19

### 6 December 2013

Bayonne 63 Viadana 7

Dragons 40 Bordeaux 24

### 7 December 2013

Bucharest 13 Brive 18
Mogliano 8 Bath 55

Cavalieri 40 Lusitanos 22
Grenoble 7 Wasps 47

### 8 December 2013

Newcastle 37 Calvisano 15

London Irish 24 Stade Français 13

## ROUND FOUR

### 12 December 2013

Bordeaux 32 Dragons 13
Brive 20 Bucharest 9

Biarritz 33 Worcester 25
Lusitanos 19 Cavalieri 30

### 13 December 2013

Sale 53 Oyonnax 14

### 14 December 2013

Calvisano 10 Newcastle 25
Viadana 19 Bayonne 80

Bath 63 Mogliano 0
Stade Français 32 London Irish 14

### 15 December 2013

Wasps 32 Grenoble 12

AMLIN CHALLENGE CUP

# ROUND FIVE

| 9 January 2014 |
| --- |

Stade Français 31 Cavalieri 3 | Newcastle 7 Brive 9

| 10 January 2014 |
| --- |

Bordeaux 64 Mogliano 7 | Sale 21 Worcester 3

| 11 January 2014 |
| --- |

Viadana 19 Grenoble 19 | Oyonnax 28 Biarritz 24
Calvisano 11 Bucharest 23 | London Irish 79 Lusitanos 3
Dragons 13 Bath 30 | Bayonne 13 Wasps 26

# ROUND SIX

| 16 January 2014 |
| --- |

Brive 31 Calvisano 9 | Mogliano 12 Dragons 24
Newcastle 28 Bucharest 0 | Lusitanos 15 Stade Français 48
Bath 54 Bordeaux 13

| 17 January 2014 |
| --- |

Grenoble 34 Bayonne 16

| 18 January 2014 |
| --- |

Cavalieri 0 London Irish 49 | Biarritz 7 Sale 9
Worcester 20 Oyonnax 13

| 19 January 2014 |
| --- |

Wasps 64 Viadana 17

# FINAL TABLES

### POOL ONE

| | P | W | D | L | F | A | BP | PTS |
| --- | --- | --- | --- | --- | --- | --- | --- | --- |
| Sale | 6 | 5 | 0 | 1 | 155 | 65 | 3 | 23 |
| Biarritz | 6 | 3 | 0 | 3 | 119 | 116 | 4 | 16 |
| Oyonnax | 6 | 2 | 1 | 3 | 86 | 142 | 2 | 12 |
| Worcester | 6 | 1 | 1 | 4 | 87 | 124 | 1 | 7 |

### POOL FOUR

| | P | W | D | L | F | A | BP | PTS |
| --- | --- | --- | --- | --- | --- | --- | --- | --- |
| Wasps | 6 | 6 | 0 | 0 | 285 | 76 | 3 | 27 |
| Bayonne | 6 | 3 | 0 | 3 | 219 | 118 | 3 | 15 |
| Grenoble | 6 | 2 | 1 | 3 | 118 | 158 | 2 | 12 |
| Viadana | 6 | 0 | 1 | 5 | 86 | 356 | 0 | 2 |

### POOL TWO

| | P | W | D | L | F | A | BP | PTS |
| --- | --- | --- | --- | --- | --- | --- | --- | --- |
| Bath | 6 | 6 | 0 | 0 | 243 | 50 | 4 | 28 |
| Bordeaux | 6 | 3 | 0 | 3 | 171 | 149 | 2 | 14 |
| Dragons | 6 | 3 | 0 | 3 | 150 | 132 | 2 | 14 |
| Mogliano | 6 | 0 | 0 | 6 | 55 | 288 | 0 | 0 |

### POOL FIVE

| | P | W | D | L | F | A | BP | PTS |
| --- | --- | --- | --- | --- | --- | --- | --- | --- |
| Stade Français | 6 | 5 | 0 | 1 | 202 | 75 | 4 | 24 |
| London Irish | 6 | 5 | 0 | 1 | 293 | 65 | 4 | 24 |
| Cavalieri | 6 | 2 | 0 | 4 | 100 | 198 | 3 | 11 |
| Lusitanos | 6 | 0 | 0 | 6 | 68 | 325 | 0 | 0 |

### POOL THREE

| | P | W | D | L | F | A | BP | PTS |
| --- | --- | --- | --- | --- | --- | --- | --- | --- |
| Brive | 6 | 5 | 1 | 0 | 121 | 74 | 1 | 23 |
| Newcastle | 6 | 4 | 0 | 2 | 126 | 69 | 3 | 19 |
| Bucharest | 6 | 2 | 0 | 4 | 94 | 105 | 2 | 10 |
| Calvisano | 6 | 0 | 1 | 5 | 80 | 173 | 0 | 2 |

| 3 April 2014 | |
|---|---|
| **Sale** 14 **Northampton** 28 | |
| 4 April 2014 | |
| **Stade Français** 6 **Harlequins** 29 | |
| 6 April 2014 | |
| **Bath** 39 **Brive** 7 | **Wasps** 36 **Gloucester** 24 |

# SEMI-FINALS

## 25 April, Franklin's Gardens, Northampton

## NORTHAMPTON SAINTS 18 (1G 1T 2PG)
## HARLEQUINS 10 (1G 1PG)

**NORTHAMPTON SAINTS:** J Wilson; J Elliott, G Pisi, G Stephenson, G North; S Myler, K Fotuali'i; A Waller, R McMillian, S Ma'afu, S Manoa, J Craig, C Clark, P Dowson (captain), S Dickinson

**SUBSTITUTIONS:** T Collins for North (21 mins); T Mercey for Ma'afu (54 mins); C Lawes for Manoa (58 mins); T Wood for Clark (58 mins); M Haywood for McMillian (68 mins); L Burrell for Stephenson (68 mins); G Denman for Waller (73 mins); R Gllynn for Fotuali'i (78 mins)

**SCORERS:** *Tries:* Fotuali'i, Collins *Conversion:* Myler *Penalty Goals:* Myler (2)

**YELLOW CARD:** Elliott (3 mins)

**HARLEQUINS:** M Brown; C Walker, T Molenaar, J Turner-Hall, S Smith; B Botica, D Care; J Marler, D Ward, K Sinckler, C Matthews, G Robson, L Wallace, C Robshaw (captain), N Easter

**SUBSTITUTIONS:** T Guest for Robson (35 mins); O Lindsay-Hague for Brown (41 mins); M Fa'asavalu for Wallace (47 mins); K Dickson for Care (60 mins); M Lambert for Marler (60 min); L Grimoldby for Turner-Hall (71 mins); P Doran-Jones for Sinckler (73 mins)

**SCORERS:** *Try:* Easter *Conversion:* Botica *Penalty Goal:* Botica

**REFEREE:** G Clancy (Ireland)

AMLIN CHALLENGE CUP

## 27 April, Adams Park, High Wycombe

# WASPS 18 (1G 1T 2PG) BATH 24 (3G 1PG)

**WASPS:** A Masi; W Helu, E Daly, C Bell (captain), T Varndell; A Goode, J Simpson; M Mullan, C Festuccia, P Swainston, J Launchbury, K Myall, A Johnson, J Haskell, N Hughes

**SUBSTITUTIONS:** C Hayter for Bell (16 mins); T Palmer for Myall (58 mins); T Lindsay for Festuccia (58 mins); S McIntyre for Mullan (58 mins); S Jones for Hughes (67 mins); T Vea for Swainston (67 mins)

**SCORERS:** *Tries:* Johnson, Helu *Conversion:* Goode *Penalty Goals:* Goode (2)

**BATH:** N Abendanon; S Rokoduguni, J Joseph, K Eastmond, M Banahan; G Ford, P Stringer; N Catt, R Webber, A Perenise, S Hooper (captain), D Day, M Garvey, G Mercer, L Houston

**SUBSTITUTIONS:** P James for Catt (48 mins); D Wilson for Perenise (48 mins); C Fearns for Mercer (48 mins); M Young for Stringer (63 mins); R Batty for Webber (63 mins); A Watson for Rokoduguni (66 mins); G Henson for Banahan (71 mins); A Faosiliva for Garvey (71 mins)

**SCORERS:** *Tries:* Webber (2) Perenise *Conversions:* Ford (3) *Penalty Goal:* Ford

**YELLOW CARD:** Eastmond (75 mins)

**REFEREE:** R Poite (France)

# FINAL

## 23 May, Cardiff Arms Park, Cardiff

# BATH 16 (1G 3PG) NORTHAMPTON SAINTS 30 (1G 1T 6PG)

**BATH:** N Abendanon; S Rokoduguni, J Joseph, O Devoto, A Watson; G Ford, M Young; P James, T Dunn, D Wilson, S Hooper (captain), D Attwood, C Fearns, F Louw, L Houston

**SUBSTITUTIONS:** P Stringer for Young (48 mins); G Mercer for Houston (55 mins); N Catt for James (57 mins); A Perenise for Wilson (57 mins); G Henson for Devoto (64 mins); H Agulla for Watson (66 mins); E Guiñazú for Dunn (68 mins); D Day for Hooper (73 mins)

**SCORERS:** *Try:* Watson *Conversion:* Ford *Penalty Goals:* Ford (3)

**YELLOW CARD:** Perenise (69 mins)

**NORTHAMPTON SAINTS:** B Foden; K Pisi, G Pisi, L Burrell, G North; S Myler, L Dickson; A Corbisiero, M Haywood, T Mercey, S Manoa, C Lawes, C Clark, T Wood (captain), S Dickinson

**SUBSTITUTIONS:** K Fotuali'i for Dickson (58 mins); A Waller for Corbisiero (61 mins); G Denman for Mercey (61 mins); P Dowson for Clark (61 mins); C Day for Manoa (65 mins); R McMillan for Haywood (73 mins); T Stephenson for Burrell (78 mins); R Wilson for G Pisi (80 mins)

**SCORERS:** *Tries:* Foden, Dowson *Conversion:* Myler *Penalty Goals:* Myler (6)

**YELLOW CARD:** Corbisiero (42 mins)

**REFEREE:** J Garces (France)

# SUPERUGBY

# FIRST TITLE WORTH THE WAIT

## By Adam Ashley-Cooper

Adam Ashley-Cooper celebrates scoring one of his two tries for the Waratahs in the Super Rugby final.

**To win the** Super Rugby title with the Waratahs was a dream come true. I've been playing rugby since I was six years old and I'm 30 now and in all that time I had never won a single title, a trophy or a final. It was weird, there probably aren't too many players who could say that after 24 years on the pitch at any level, and to finally put that record to bed by winning the final against the Crusaders was an incredible feeling.

It was the 'Tahs first title after losing in the finals in 2005 and 2008. Getting over the line was a long time coming but probably all the more euphoric for it and an overdue reward for all the supporters who have stuck with the team through the disappointments and the setbacks.

To finally become champions by beating a team like the Crusaders made it even more special. They are legends of Super Rugby, seven-time winners of the competition, and if you're going to lift the trophy you want to be able to say you defeated a great team in the final. We did that and although I wasn't with the club for the two previous appearances in the final, it was amazing to come out on the winning side third time around.

The win was also a personal relief. I was a Brumbies player in 2004 when the team made it to the final. It was my first year with club, I was on a high performance unit contract playing a lot of Sevens and only training with the Super Rugby players in midweek.

I was on the fringes but a few injuries to the senior boys at the end of the season meant I was called into the squad for the final, but I was the 23rd man on matchday and I sat in the stand watching the game in my suit. The Brumbies beat the Crusaders and there was a huge party after the game to celebrate. I was there with the boys who'd got the job done but I felt like a fraud because I hadn't played, it was a very hollow feeling. I had to wait 10 years to experience the real thing and it definitely wasn't a disappointment!

To win the title after finishing ninth in the table in 2013 was a significant turnaround in terms of results and the level of our performances. When Michael Cheika was given the job as head coach he explained to us he had a two-year plan for the club, that success wouldn't come overnight, and he was spot on.

He changed the culture of the club and gave the players the framework to become the best we could be, individually and collectively. He introduced us to motivational mental exercises and insisted on a culture of mutual respect in the squad, an acceptance of the different backgrounds and cultures in the team. It brought everyone closer together and I think you could see the positive impact that had on our performances on the pitch.

It took us a good season to fully implement what he wanted us to do, to fine-tune and finesse what we were trying to achieve in training and at the weekend but the end result was the Super Rugby title.

The appointment of Nathan Grey and the new signings made by the club before the start of the 2014 season were big factors in our success.

Nathan's record as a 'Tahs player meant he already had the respect of the players and the fans when he arrived at the club. He did a great job at the Rebels and he came in and implemented a strong defensive structure that gave us a rock solid platform. It was no coincidence that we had the best defensive record in the division at the end of the regular season.

There was a lot of talk in the press about the effectiveness of our defence but I think it occasionally overshadowed what we did in attack. We spoke a lot about our duty to entertain the fans and we desperately wanted to be the best attacking team in the competition. We scored more tries and more points than any other side, so I think we hit that particular target.

The new boys were awesome. Kurtley Beale turned his career around and Jacques Potgieter was a big plus for us after signing from the Bulls. Nick Phipps came in and formed a brilliant half-back pairing with Bernard Foley while the other signings, the likes of Tolu Latu, Stephen Hoiles and Alofa Alofa, gave us the depth we needed as the season unfolded.

We had setbacks and losing Dave Dennis to injury in June was a massive blow. Dave's captaincy was immense before he was sidelined but Michael Hooper stepped in and did a great job. Michael and I were the vice captains but he was the natural choice when we lost Dave and, because he already had the respect of the squad, it was a pretty smooth transition. The fact Michael was in such good form I think also helped take the pressure off him.

I had talked to Michael in 2013 about captaincy and told him that while I was happy to be involved in a senior leadership group, I wasn't interested in the captaincy. Michael is a much younger man than me but he's a natural skipper.

After beating the Brumbies 26–8 in the semi-final, we were full of confidence before the final. The media were talking about the two defeats in the final to the Crusaders but it wasn't something that we spoke about in the dressing room. Our attitude was 'stats mean nothing' and we focused on the momentum we had generated with the seven wins on the bounce to close out the regular season and the result against the Brumbies. We knew we were in good form and it really didn't matter to us as a group what had happened six or nine years ago.

It was a hell of a final. We got our noses in front but the Crusaders came back at us strongly in the second half to take the lead and we clinched it with a late penalty from Bernard. I think it was a good game to watch but it was pretty nerve wracking in Sydney and when you're

**SUPER RUGBY**

involved in such a massive match that's as tight and as tense as that, it's pretty hard to enjoy the experience.

I have to admit I did have a few doubts whether it was going to be our day when Nemani Nadolo scored for the Crusaders early in the second half but you don't have long to dwell on those kind of thoughts. You get maybe a minute while they take the conversion but then you have to switch back on and play.

I scored both our tries in the final but it really was a case of right time, right place, putting the finishing touch to two penetrating team moves that had put the Crusaders on the back foot. Obviously I was delighted to score but it would have made no difference to me who got their name on the score sheet as long as we got the right result.

It was torture waiting for Bernard to line up what was the winning kick. We were two points adrift and with only two minutes on the clock I knew we'd probably not get another chance if he missed. I also knew it was right on the edge of his range and when he kicked I thought he had mishit it because I was already off chasing, convinced it was going to come up short and hoping I could steal the ball from whichever Crusader happened to catch it. Luckily I was wrong and it had the legs to clear the crossbar. The final whistle was the sweetest sound I've ever heard and the party started.

It wasn't long after the final that there was talk of a match between the 'Tahs and Toulon, the Heineken Cup champions, a southern versus northern hemisphere showdown to decide the best club side in the world. Personally I think it's a great idea and something as a player I would love to be involved in.

Rugby league already has the World Club Challenge and I'm sure an annual match-up between the best in Europe and the Super Rugby champions would excite both sets of fans. It could be the start of something special.

Overall it was good year for the Australian sides in Super Rugby. The Rebels struggled but the Brumbies and the Force both finished in the top eight and while you're inevitably focused on your own team through the season, I like to see the other Australian teams doing well.

In terms of individuals I was impressed by Kyle Godwin at the Force and Jarrad Butler at the Brumbies. Godwin is a good kid who got a lot of attention after a good year at 10 and is an excellent prospect. I really liked Butler's performances at seven as well and he was a big part of a strong Brumbies season.

# SUPER RUGBY 2014 RESULTS

15 February: **Cheetahs** 20 **Lions** 21, **Sharks** 31 **Bulls** 16. 21 February: **Crusaders** 10 **Chiefs** 18, **Cheetahs** 15 **Bulls** 9. 22 February: **Highlanders** 29 **Blues** 21, **Brumbies** 17 **Reds** 27, **Sharks** 27 **Hurricanes** 9, **Lions** 34 **Stormers** 10. 23 February: **Waratahs** 43 **Force** 21. 28 February: **Blues** 35 **Crusaders** 24, **Rebels** 35 **Cheetahs** 14, **Stormers** 19 **Hurricanes** 18. 1 March: **Chiefs** 21 **Highlanders** 19, **Waratahs** 32 **Reds** 5, **Force** 14 **Brumbies** 27, **Bulls** 25 **Lions** 17. 7 March: **Hurricanes** 21 **Brumbies** 29, **Reds** 43 **Cheetahs** 33. 8 March: **Crusaders** 14 **Stormers** 13, **Force** 32 **Rebels** 7, **Bulls** 38 **Blues** 22, **Sharks** 37 **Lions** 23. 14 March: **Chiefs** 36 **Stormers** 20, **Rebels** 19 **Crusaders** 25. 15 March: **Hurricanes** 60 **Cheetahs** 27, **Highlanders** 29 **Force** 31, **Brumbies** 28 **Waratahs** 23, **Lions** 39 **Blues** 36, **Sharks** 35 **Reds** 20. 21 March: **Highlanders** 35 **Hurricanes** 31, **Waratahs** 32 **Rebels** 8. 22 March: **Blues** 40 **Cheetahs** 30, **Brumbies** 25 **Stormers** 15, **Force** 18 **Chiefs** 15, **Lions** 23 **Reds** 20, **Bulls** 23 **Sharks** 19. 28 March: **Crusaders** 26 **Hurricanes** 29, **Rebels** 32 **Brumbies** 24. 29 March: **Blues** 30 **Highlanders** 12, **Reds** 22 **Stormers** 17, **Bulls** 34 **Chiefs** 34, **Sharks** 32 **Waratahs** 10. 4 April: **Highlanders** 13 **Rebels** 30, **Brumbies** 26 **Blues** 9. 5 April: **Hurricanes** 25 **Bulls** 20, **Reds** 29 **Force** 32, **Cheetahs** 43 **Chiefs** 43, **Lions** 7 **Crusaders** 28, **Stormers** 11 **Waratahs** 22. 11 April: **Highlanders** 27 **Bulls** 20, **Reds** 20 **Brumbies** 23. 12 April: **Chiefs** 22 **Rebels** 16, **Force** 28 **Waratahs** 16, **Cheetahs** 31 **Crusaders** 52, **Lions** 12 **Sharks** 25. 18 April: **Hurricanes** 39 **Blues** 20, **Rebels** 22 **Force** 16. 19 April: **Chiefs** 17 **Crusaders** 18, **Waratahs** 19 **Bulls** 12, **Sharks** 19 **Cheetahs** 8, **Stormers** 18 **Lions** 3. 25 April: **Blues** 21 **Waratahs** 13, **Brumbies** 41 **Chiefs** 23, **Sharks** 18 **Highlanders** 34. 26 April: **Hurricanes** 35 **Reds** 21, **Force** 15 **Bulls** 9, **Cheetahs** 35 **Stormers** 22. 2 May: **Blues** 44 **Reds** 14, **Rebels** 16 **Sharks** 22. 3 May: **Crusaders** 40 **Brumbies** 20, **Chiefs** 38 **Lions** 8, **Waratahs** 39 **Hurricanes** 30, **Stormers** 29 **Highlanders** 28, **Bulls** 26 **Cheetahs** 21. 9 May: **Chiefs** 32 **Blues** 20, **Rebels** 15 **Hurricanes** 25. 10 May: **Highlanders** 23 **Lions** 22, **Brumbies** 16 **Sharks** 9, **Cheetahs** 16 **Force** 23, **Bulls** 28 **Stormers** 12. 11 May: **Reds** 29 **Crusaders** 57. 16 May: **Hurricanes** 16 **Highlanders** 18. 17 May: **Crusaders** 25 **Sharks** 30, **Reds** 27 **Rebels** 30, **Stormers** 24 **Force** 8, **Cheetahs** 27 **Brumbies** 21. 18 May: **Waratahs** 41 **Lions** 13. 23 May: **Blues** 23 **Sharks** 29, **Rebels** 19 **Waratahs** 41, **Bulls** 44 **Brumbies** 23. 24 May: **Highlanders** 30 **Crusaders** 32, **Hurricanes** 45 **Chiefs** 8, **Force** 29 **Lions** 19, **Stormers** 33 **Cheetahs** 0. 30 May: **Crusaders** 30 **Force** 7, **Reds** 38 **Highlanders** 31. 31 May: **Chiefs** 17 **Waratahs** 33, **Blues** 37 **Hurricanes** 24, **Brumbies** 37 **Rebels** 10, **Lions** 32 **Bulls** 21, **Sharks** 19 **Stormers** 21. 27 June: **Highlanders** 29 **Chiefs** 25, **Rebels** 20 **Reds** 36. 28 June: **Hurricanes** 16 **Crusaders** 9, **Waratahs** 39 **Brumbies** 8, **Force** 14 **Blues** 40. 4 July: **Chiefs** 24 **Hurricanes** 16, **Lions** 34 **Rebels** 17. 5 July: **Crusaders** 21 **Blues** 13, **Force** 30 **Reds** 20, **Stormers** 16 **Bulls** 0, **Cheetahs** 27 **Sharks** 20. 6 July: **Waratahs** 44 **Highlanders** 16. 11 July: **Blues** 8 **Chiefs** 11, **Brumbies** 47 **Force** 25, **Bulls** 40 **Rebels** 7. 12 July: **Crusaders** 34 **Highlanders** 8, **Reds** 3 **Waratahs** 34, **Lions** 60 **Cheetahs** 25, **Stormers** 10 **Sharks** 34.

# FINAL TABLE

|            | P  | W  | D | L  | F   | A   | BP | PTS |
|------------|----|----|---|----|-----|-----|----|-----|
| Waratahs   | 16 | 12 | 0 | 4  | 481 | 272 | 10 | 58  |
| Crusaders  | 16 | 11 | 0 | 5  | 445 | 322 | 7  | 51  |
| Sharks     | 16 | 11 | 0 | 5  | 406 | 293 | 6  | 50  |
| Brumbies   | 16 | 10 | 0 | 6  | 412 | 378 | 5  | 45  |
| Chiefs     | 16 | 8  | 2 | 6  | 384 | 378 | 8  | 44  |
| Highlanders| 16 | 8  | 0 | 8  | 401 | 442 | 10 | 42  |
| Hurricanes | 16 | 8  | 0 | 8  | 439 | 374 | 9  | 41  |
| Force      | 16 | 9  | 0 | 7  | 343 | 393 | 4  | 40  |
| Bulls      | 16 | 7  | 1 | 8  | 365 | 335 | 8  | 38  |
| Blues      | 16 | 7  | 0 | 9  | 419 | 395 | 9  | 37  |
| Stormers   | 16 | 7  | 0 | 9  | 290 | 326 | 4  | 32  |
| Lions      | 16 | 7  | 0 | 9  | 367 | 413 | 3  | 31  |
| Reds       | 16 | 5  | 0 | 11 | 374 | 493 | 8  | 28  |
| Cheetahs   | 16 | 4  | 1 | 11 | 372 | 527 | 6  | 24  |
| Rebels     | 16 | 4  | 0 | 12 | 303 | 460 | 5  | 21  |

## PLAY-OFFS

| 19 July 2014 | |
|---|---|
| **Brumbies** 32 **Chiefs** 30 | **Sharks** 31 **Highlanders** 27 |

**ELITE COMPETITIONS**

## CRUSADERS 38 (2G 3T 3PG) SHARKS 6 (2PG)

**CRUSADERS:** I Dagg; K Fonotia, R Crotty, D Carter, N Nadolo; C Slade, A Ellis; W Crockett, C Flynn, O Franks, D Bird, S Whitelock, R McCaw, M Todd, K Read (captain)

**SUBSTITUTIONS:** J McNicholl, W Heinz & B Funnell for Fonotia, Ellis & Flynn (54 mins); J Taufua for Read (63 mins); J Tupou for Bird (65 mins); J Moody & N Laulala for Crockett & Franks (67 mins); T Taylor for Crotty (72 mins)

**SCORERS:** *Tries*: Read, Nadolo, Heinz, McNicholl, Todd *Conversions*: Carter (2) *Penalty Goals*: Carter (3)

**SHARKS:** SP Marais; JP Pietersen, P Jordaan, F Steyn, L Mvovo; P Lambie, J Reinach; T du Toit, B du Plessis (captain), J du Plessis, W Alberts, S Lewies, M Coetzee, J Deysel, R Kankowski

**SUBSTITUTIONS:** E Oosthuizen for Deysel (50 mins); S Sithole for Marais (54 mins); D Chadwick & L Adriaanse for du Toit & J du Plessis (59 mins); C McLeod for Reinach (60 mins); T Chavhanga, L Mtembu & K Cooper for Pietersen, Coetzee & B du Plessis (65 mins)

**SCORERS:** *Penalty Goals*: Lambie (2)

**REFEREE:** G Jackson (New Zealand)

## WARATAHS 26 (1G 2T 3PG) BRUMBIES 8 (1T 1PG)

**WARATAHS:** I Folau; A Alofa, A Ashley-Cooper, K Beale, R Horne; B Foley, N Phipps; B Robinson, T Polota-Nau, S Kepu, J Potgieter, K Douglas, S Hoiles, M Hooper (captain), W Palu

**SUBSTITUTIONS:** W Skelton for Douglas (55 mins); M Chapman for Potgieter (67 mins); P Ryan for Kepu (70 mins); J Tilse & S Latu for Robinson & Polota-Nau (77 mins); T Naiyaravoro, P McCutcheon & B McKibbin for Alofa, Palu & Phipps (78 mins)

**SCORERS:** *Tries*: Alofa, Beale, Foley *Conversion*: Foley *Penalty Goals*: Foley (3)

**YELLOW CARD:** T Naiyaravoro (79 mins)

**BRUMBIES:** J Mogg; H Speight, T Kuridrani, C Leali'ifano, R Coleman; M Toomua, N White; S Sio, J Mann-Rea, B Alexander, L Power, S Carter, S Fardy, J Butler, B Mowen (captain)

**SUBSTITUTIONS:** P McCabe for Mogg (48 mins); J Tomane for Speight (52 mins); F Auelua for Power (56 mins); R Murphy for Mann-Rea (61 mins); T McVerry & R Smith for Butler & Sio (74 mins); A Alaalatoa for Alexander (77 mins); M Dowsett for White (78 mins)

**SCORERS:** *Try*: Speight *Penalty Goal*: Leali'ifano

**REFEREE:** J Peyper (South Africa)

# FINAL

## 2 August, ANZ Stadium, Sydney

## WARATAHS 33 (1G 1T 7PG) CRUSADERS 32 (2G 6PG)

**WARATAHS:** I Folau; A Alofa, A Ashley-Cooper, K Beale, R Horne; B Foley, N Phipps; B Robinson, T Polota-Nau, S Kepu, J Potgieter, K Douglas, S Hoiles, M Hooper (captain), W Palu

**SUBSTITUTIONS:** W Skelton for Palu (temp 19 to 26 mins); S Latu for Polota-Nau (42 mins); Skelton for Potgieter (49 mins); M Chapman for Hoiles (64 mins); P Ryan for Kepu (65 mins); P Betham for Alofa (74 mins); B McKibbin for Phipps (75 mins)

**SCORERS:** *Tries*: Ashley-Cooper (2) *Conversion*: Foley *Penalty Goals*: Foley (7)

**CRUSADERS:** I Dagg; K Fonotia, R Crotty, D Carter, N Nadolo; C Slade, A Ellis; W Crockett, C Flynn, O Franks, D Bird, S Whitelock, R McCaw, M Todd, K Read (captain)

**SUBSTITUTIONS:** T Taylor for Carter (30 mins); J Moody for Crockett (56 mins); J McNicholl, J Tupou, B Funnell & N Laulala for Fonotia, Bird, Flynn & Moody (63 mins); W Heinz for Crotty (67 mins); Crotty for Ellis (71 mins)

**SCORERS:** *Tries*: Todd, Nadolo *Conversions*: Carter, Slade *Penalty Goals*: Slade (6)

**REFEREE:** C Joubert (South Africa)

AFP/Getty Images

The jubilant Waratahs' players celebrate after beating the Crusaders to win a first Super Rugby title.

# Referees

# THE MAKING OF A MODERN REFEREE

*By Craig Joubert*

Getty Images

Rugby has been a passion for South African referee Craig Joubert since he was a young boy.

*South African referee Craig Joubert, who took charge of the Rugby World Cup 2011 final between hosts New Zealand and France at Eden Park, explains how he got into refereeing and why he describes his path since as a "wonderful journey".*

**L**ike most young South Africans I grew up dreaming about becoming a Springbok. I loved the game of rugby and would spend hours practising my goal kicking, imagining I was lining up an important

REFEREES

kick for the Springboks at Loftus or Newlands or perhaps even those magical faraway places I only occasionally got to see on TV, like Twickenham or Murrayfield.

My late dad was a rugby man through and through and had been a robust flanker for his club team before getting into coaching as a high school teacher. He had a special way with people and his 1st XV at a prestigious Durban High School went through some glory years under his watch.

On leaving the teaching profession it became a natural progression for him to remain involved in the game he loved in a different capacity – a referee. His manner and ability to connect with people again shone through in his refereeing and he soon progressed up the refereeing ranks, winning much respect from the players, who were his most important clients.

My very first 'job' was as a 10-year-old where I would earn the princely sum of R4 (about 27 euro cents) to be the ball boy for local club games on a Saturday afternoon at Woodburn Stadium, the local rugby stadium in Pietermaritzburg where I grew up. Some of my happiest memories growing up are of Saturday afternoons spent on the side of the rugby field with my brother, collecting the balls kicked into the river while my dad would referee the main club game. Little did I know how much more enjoyment the game that I love would provide me over the years.

I attended a high school, Maritzburg College, steeped in rugby history and tradition. I loved it. It was as a schoolboy at Maritzburg College that my dad encouraged me to get involved in refereeing after I picked up an injury and was ruled out of the game for a period of time. From the beginning I loved it and recognised that refereeing was a way to be involved in the game I love for far longer than I could ever be as a player.

Before I refereed my first game, my dad gave me a piece of advice that is probably still the most important piece of advice I have ever received. He said: 'Refereeing is all about man-management. Treat the players with respect and you have a chance they will reciprocate.' And so began a wonderful journey . . .

I have refereed some wonderful matches along the way and have happily made plenty of 'sacrifices'. As a university student I recall leaving a 21st party early because I had a three-hour drive to referee a club game the next day. I reasoned that none of the players I would be refereeing would be out late partying the night before the game and therefore neither should I.

The time away from home refereeing internationally is significant

**BEHIND THE SCENES**

– I have averaged 174 days away from home per year for the last eight years – but I have deliberately put the word sacrifice in inverted commas since I have hardly felt like any of these choices were sacrifices to serve the game I love. While the time away from home and a young family can be challenging, I have loved travelling the world refereeing and am living my dream of refereeing at the magical faraway places that I once only knew from TV.

The level of scrutiny in the modern game is intense. There have never been so many high definition cameras and the advent of social media – which allows everyone to share an opinion and facilitates the instant and global transfer of information – has made refereeing at the top level a heavily (and often emotionally) scrutinised occupation. I accept that I am human and I make mistakes. There are key learnings that come out of every game I referee and we complete an extensive self-review process after every game to realise these learnings.

But I do not fear the scrutiny. I have a burning desire to be a part of the major matches which carry the most pressure; I love being in the arena and I don't fear the scrutiny, which is a natural consequence of being out there in the biggest Test matches and finals.

My philosophy is simple: I am here to serve the game and the players are my priority. I believe my role is one of a facilitator, to facilitate an environment in which the players can display their skills. I accept that I cannot please all of the people all of the time, but I have never forgotten my late dad's words about treating the players with respect. Some of my great rugby memories involve having a drink with the players after a game, sharing thoughts and ideas on the game we both love.

It has been a privilege to have had the experiences in rugby that I have had, I hope there are a few more years left. My only disappointment is that my dad hasn't been around to share it.

We profile 12 of the officials appointed by the International Rugby Board to referee a Test in a busy November schedule.

## WAYNE BARNES (RFU)
DOB: 20/04/1979    Tests: 53

Getty Images

One of the youngest international referees when he made his debut in 2006, Wayne has been a mainstay in the world of elite refereeing for the past two Rugby World Cups. He took charge of the quarter-final in 2007 between New Zealand and France in Cardiff and, four years later, refereed the Bronze final between Wales and Australia in Auckland. A barrister by profession, he is one of the strong communicators on the referee panel.

## GEORGE CLANCY (IRFU)
DOB: 12/01/1977    Tests: 35

Getty Images

A tax inspector from Bruff in the rugby-mad county of Limerick, the Irishman refereed the opening match of Rugby World Cup 2011 between New Zealand and Tonga at Eden Park. While he has taken charge of several matches involving the world's top sides, he has also travelled far and wide with his whistle. His first Test came in September 2006 in Montevideo, while he also refereed the first leg of the Rugby World Cup 2015 Repechage final between Russia and Uruguay in Krasnoyarsk, southern Siberia.

## JP DOYLE (RFU)
DOB:  03/08/1979    Tests: 9

Image SA

Irish-born JP has progressed through the ranks in England to become one of the RFU's top officials. He made his international debut in 2009 in a match between Germany and Russia and has been on the panel at three IRB Junior World Championships. In August 2013 he took charge of the second leg between Canada and USA which determined the first nation to emerge from the RWC 2015 qualification process to book their place in England. He will take charge of the Romania v Japan and Scotland v Tonga matches in November.

Getty Images

### JÉRÔME GARCES (FFR)
DOB: 24/10/1973   Tests: 18

Selected for Rugby World Cup 2011 in New Zealand as an assistant referee, Jérôme has since become a dependable and respected referee at the highest level. He made his Six Nations debut in 2012 and the Frenchman refereed in The Rugby Championship for the first time in 2013, taking charge of New Zealand v Argentina in Hamilton and South Africa v Australia in Cape Town. He has been appointed for two big games in November – Italy v South Africa in Rome and England v Australia at Twickenham.

Martin Seras Lima

### PASCAL GAUZERE (FFR)
DOB: 23/04/1977   Tests: 14

Another Frenchman who has broken through to the highest level of refereeing, Pascal has made steady progress since making his Test debut with Russia v Germany in March 2010. He appeared at two IRB Junior World Championships and refereed the 2010 final in Argentina. Last year, he took charge of England v Argentina at Twickenham and in November has been appointed for the Georgia v Tonga and Wales v Fiji matches.

Image SA

### GLEN JACKSON (NZR)
DOB: 23/10/1975   Tests: 7

A former professional player who has picked up the whistle since hanging up his boots, Glen played fly-half for Bay of Plenty, Waikato and English club Saracens as well as the New Zealand Maori. He has quickly made the difficult transition from poacher to game-keeper and made his Test debut with England v Fiji at Twickenham in 2012. This November he will again take charge of Fiji, this time for their encounter with France in Marseilles followed by a trip to Dublin for Ireland v Australia.

**REFEREES**

## CRAIG JOUBERT (SARU)

**629**

DOB: 08/11/1977   Tests: 51

Getty Images

Hailing from Durban in KwaZulu-Natal, Craig is one of only six people who has refereed a Rugby World Cup final, having taken charge of the 2011 decider between New Zealand and France in Auckland. He also had the honour of refereeing the first match of the RWC 2015 qualification process when Mexico hosted Jamaica in March 2012. His precision and excellent communications skills have made him into one of the best match officials and this November he will again referee some of the top matches – USA v New Zealand in Chicago, Wales v Australia in Cardiff and Italy v Argentina in Genoa.

## JOHN LACEY (IRFU)

DOB: 12/10/1973   Tests: 10

Getty Images

Another former elite player, John played on the wing and at full-back for Munster until 2007 before taking up refereeing. When he did so, his excellent temperament, fitness and feel for the game was spotted quickly and he refereed his first Test in March 2010. Like many modern-day match officials, he has come through the finishing school that is the IRB Junior World Championship to become a trusted and respected referee. This November he takes charge of Fiji v USA in Vannes, in north-west France, and Wales v South Africa in Cardiff.

## NIGEL OWENS (WRU)

DOB: 18/06/1971   Tests: 56

Getty Images

A popular character and respected official, Nigel has many strings to his bow, including television personality, stand-up comedian, after-dinner speaker and regular campaigner for several different causes. He is now one of the most experienced among the current crop of international referees, having become only the fifth person to take charge of 50 Tests. Hailing from the rugby heartland of Llanelli, he is now a veteran of two Rugby World Cups and took charge of the 2011 quarter-final between New Zealand and Argentina. He will referee two huge matches in November, England v New Zealand at Twickenham and France v Australia in Paris.

REFEREE BIOGRAPHIES

### JACO PEYPER (SARU)
DOB: 13/05/1980    Tests: 18

The man from Bloemfontein in the Free State province of South Africa has enjoyed plenty of success since refereeing the IRB Junior World Championship final in 2011. The following month he refereed his first Test – Kenya v Zimbabwe – and less than a year later took charge of Australia v Scotland in Newcastle. Since then he has refereed in the Six Nations and The Rugby Championship. This November he will take charge of the England v Samoa encounter at Twickenham.

### ROMAIN POITE (FFR)
DOB: 14/09/1975    Tests: 34

One of four Frenchmen taking charge of matches in November, Romain's first Test in November 2006 was Morocco v Namibia. Another graduate of the IRB Junior World Championship, he was an assistant referee at RWC 2007 and then made the referee panel four years later in New Zealand. There, he took charge of games involving the hosts and eventual champions, England, Samoa and South Africa. In another highlight of his career, he refereed the third and deciding Test between the British & Irish Lions and Australia in Sydney in 2013. He will take charge of three matches in November: Ireland v South Africa in Dublin, Scotland v New Zealand in Edinburgh and Georgia v Japan in Tbilisi.

### STEVE WALSH (ARU)
DOB: 28/03/1972    Tests: 58

One of the most experienced referees of all time and the most capped referee still active internationally, Steve is one of an exclusive group to have reached his half-century of Tests. Formerly a New Zealand Rugby Union referee, Steve moved to Australia in 2009 and quickly established himself there as well. A touch judge at RWC 1999, he has been on the referee panel for three subsequent tournaments and shows no signs of slowing down. In November he takes charge of Italy v Samoa and England v South Africa.

# INTERNATIONAL REFEREES

## DISMISSALS IN MAJOR INTERNATIONAL MATCHES

Up to 13 October 2014 in major international matches. These cover all matches for which the eight senior members of the International Board have awarded caps, and also all matches played in a Rugby World Cup.

| | | | | |
|---|---|---|---|---|
| AE Freethy | sent off | CJ Brownlie (NZ) | E v NZ | 1925 |
| KD Kelleher | sent off | CE Meads (NZ) | S v NZ | 1967 |
| RT Burnett | sent off | MA Burton (E) | A v E | 1975 |
| WM Cooney | sent off | J Sovau (Fj) | A v Fj | 1976 |
| NR Sanson | sent off | GAD Wheel (W) | W v I | 1977 |
| NR Sanson | sent off | WP Duggan (I) | W v I | 1977 |
| DIH Burnett | sent off | P Ringer (W) | E v W | 1980 |
| C Norling | sent off | J-P Garuet (F) | F v I | 1984 |
| KVJ Fitzgerald | sent off | HD Richards (W) | NZ v W | *1987 |
| FA Howard | sent off | D Codey (A) | A v W | *1987 |
| KVJ Fitzgerald | sent off | M Taga (Fj) | Fj v E | 1988 |
| OE Doyle | sent off | A Lorieux (F) | Arg v F | 1988 |
| BW Stirling | sent off | T Vonolagi (Fj) | E v Fj | 1989 |
| BW Stirling | sent off | N Nadruku (Fj) | E v Fj | 1989 |
| FA Howard | sent off | K Moseley (W) | W v F | 1990 |
| FA Howard | sent off | A Carminati (F) | S v F | 1990 |
| FA Howard | sent off | A Stoop (Nm) | Nm v W | 1990 |
| AJ Spreadbury | sent off | A Benazzi (F) | A v F | 1990 |
| C Norling | sent off | P Gallart (F) | A v F | 1990 |
| CJ Hawke | sent off | FE Mendez (Arg) | E v Arg | 1990 |
| EF Morrison | sent off | C Cojocariu (R) | R v F | 1991 |
| JM Fleming | sent off | PL Sporleder (Arg) | WS v Arg | *1991 |
| JM Fleming | sent off | MG Keenan (WS) | WS v Arg | *1991 |
| SR Hilditch | sent off | G Lascubé (F) | F v E | 1992 |
| SR Hilditch | sent off | V Moscato (F) | F v E | 1992 |
| DJ Bishop | sent off | O Roumat (Wld) | NZ v Wld | 1992 |
| EF Morrison | sent off | JT Small (SA) | A v SA | 1993 |
| I Rogers | sent off | ME Cardinal (C) | C v F | 1994 |
| I Rogers | sent off | P Sella (F) | C v F | 1994 |
| D Mené | sent off | JD Davies (W) | W v E | 1995 |
| S Lander | sent off | F Mahoni (Tg) | F v Tg | *1995 |
| DTM McHugh | sent off | J Dalton (SA) | SA v C | *1995 |
| DTM McHugh | sent off | RGA Snow (C) | SA v C | *1995 |
| DTM McHugh | sent off | GL Rees (C) | SA v C | *1995 |
| J Dumé | sent off | GR Jenkins (W) | SA v W | 1995 |
| WJ Erickson | sent off | VB Cavubati (Fj) | NZ v Fj | 1997 |
| WD Bevan | sent off | AG Venter (SA) | NZ v SA | 1997 |
| C Giacomel | sent off | R Travaglini (Arg) | F v Arg | 1997 |

| | | | | |
|---|---|---|---|---|
| WJ Erickson | sent off | DJ Grewcock (E) | NZ v E | 1998 |
| S Walsh | sent off | J Sitoa (Tg) | A v Tg | 1998 |
| RG Davies | sent off | M Giovanelli (It) | S v It | 1999 |
| C Thomas | sent off | T Leota (Sm) | Sm v F | 1999 |
| C Thomas | sent off | G Leaupepe (Sm) | Sm v F | 1999 |
| S Dickinson | sent off | J-J Crenca (F) | NZ v F | 1999 |
| EF Morrison | sent off | M Vunibaka (Fj) | Fj v C | *1999 |
| A Cole | sent off | DR Baugh (C) | C v Nm | *1999 |
| WJ Erickson | sent off | N Ta'ufo'ou (Tg) | E v Tg | *1999 |
| P Marshall | sent off | BD Venter (SA) | SA v U | *1999 |
| PC Deluca | sent off | W Cristofoletto (It) | F v It | 2000 |
| JI Kaplan | sent off | A Troncon (It) | It v I | 2001 |
| R Dickson | sent off | G Leger (Tg) | W v Tg | 2001 |
| PC Deluca | sent off | NJ Hines (S) | US v S | 2002 |
| PD O'Brien | sent off | MC Joubert (SA) | SA v A | 2002 |
| PD O'Brien | sent off | JJ Labuschagne (SA) | E v SA | 2002 |
| SR Walsh | sent off | V Ma'asi (Tg) | Tg v I | 2003 |
| N Williams | sent off | SD Shaw (E) | NZ v E | 2004 |
| SJ Dickinson | sent off | PC Montgomery (SA) | W v SA | 2005 |
| SM Lawrence | sent off | LW Moody (E) | E v Sm | 2005 |
| SM Lawrence | sent off | A Tuilagi (Sm) | E v Sm | 2005 |
| SR Walsh | sent off | S Murray (S) | W v S | 2006 |
| JI Kaplan | sent off | H T-Pole (Tg) | Sm v Tg | *2007 |
| AC Rolland | sent off | J Nieuwenhuis (Nm) | F v Nm | *2007 |
| N Owens | sent off | N Nalaga (Pl) | F v Pl | 2008 |
| W Barnes | sent off | JPR Heaslip (I) | NZ v I | 2010 |
| C Joubert | sent off | DA Mitchell (A) | A v NZ | 2010 |
| N Owens | sent off | PB Williams (Sm) | SA v Sm | *2011 |
| AC Rolland | sent off | SK Warburton (W) | W v F | *2011 |
| P Gauzere | sent off | AT Tuilagi (Sm) | SA v Sm | 2013 |
| R Poite | sent off | BW du Plessis (SA) | NZ v SA | 2013 |
| GW Jackson | sent off | Y Maestri (F) | F v Tg | 2013 |
| GW Jackson | sent off | FKA Taumalolo (Tg) | F v Tg | 2013 |
| CJ Pollock | sent off | RTRN Kuridrani (A) | I v A | 2013 |
| J Peyper | sent off | R Slimani (F) | F v It | 2014 |
| J Peyper | sent off | M Rizzo (It) | F v It | 2014 |
| J Garces | sent off | SW Hogg (S) | W v S | 2014 |
| MI Fraser | sent off | JL Sinclair (C) | C v S | 2014 |

*Matches in a Rugby World Cup*

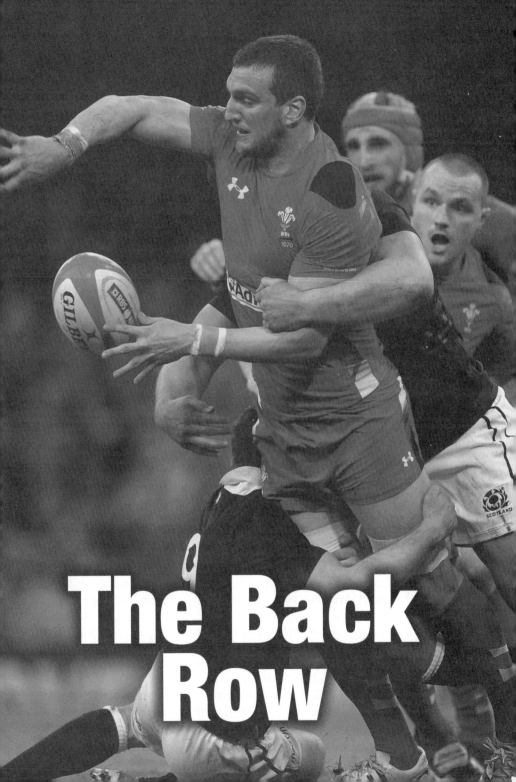

# The Back Row

# OBITUARIES

## *By Adam Hathaway*

**ROBBIE BARNARD**, who died on 19 October 2013 aged 71, was a fiery hooker for Diggers RFC and Transvaal who won his only cap off the bench in 1970. Then, in the days before tactical substitutes, he came on as a replacement for Piston van Wyk in the second Test against New Zealand in Cape Town – a game South Africa won 9–8. He played 11 other games for the Springboks and was picked for the controversial trip to Australia in 1971 without adding to his tally of caps. Barnard's brother, Jannie, won five caps for South Africa in 1965.

**KEITH BRADSHAW**, who died on 2 February 2014 aged 74, was a place-kicking centre for Bridgend and Wales who won nine caps for his country between 1964 and 1966, and scored 36 points in his Test career. Bradshaw was part of the Welsh side that won the Five Nations in 1966, kicking two penalties in the 9–8 win over France in the final game, and captained Bridgend in the same season. Born in Cefn Cribwr, Bradshaw's debut came in the 6–6 draw with England in 1964 and he toured South Africa later that year, kicking Wales' only points in the 24–3 defeat to the Springboks in Durban in the sole Test of the trip. He was omitted from the Welsh side for the 1965 Five Nations, with the selectors preferring Dick Uzell at 12, but returned to the midfield for the following year's Championship. Then he converted a Stuart Watkins try to secure an 11–11 draw with France, despite the ball falling over during his run-up. Away from rugby Bradshaw worked for the National Coal Board before going into teaching. He worked at Dyffryn Comprehensive in Margam for 30 years before retiring in 1999.

**JACK DOLOMBA**, who died on 16 August 2014 aged 71, was a hero of African rugby in the pre-unity era, making five appearances at hooker for the African Springboks when representative matches for black players were rare. He made his debut for the team in 1971 against the South African Rugby Football Federation and captained the side against Italy in 1974. Dolomba played for Star of Hope Rugby Football Club in the Border region, playing his first match for the African Springboks against the SA Rugby Football Federation's Proteas after a period of growing concern about the quality of hookers within the fold of African rugby. He scored a try in his third test, which the African Springboks won 13–6 against the Proteas. Dolomba was left out of the side who played the pioneering match against the 1972 English touring team, but he was not alone as none of his Border teammates were picked either. Dolomba was employed at Buffalo City Municipality at the time of his death.

**PETER FATIALOFA**, who died from a heart attack on 6 November 2013 aged 54, was a prop – universally known as 'Fats' – who captained Western Samoa at Rugby World Cup 1991. This tournament saw the Samoans beat Wales 16–13 in Cardiff to qualify for the quarter-finals and the result is regarded as one of the most significant in his country's history. Auckland-born Fatialofa moved back to Samoa when he was a youngster before returning to New Zealand to play rugby with Grafton, making his debut at 19. He later moved to the famous Ponsonby club in 1981 and helped them to win eight Gallaher Shields up to 1995. The prop played 72 times for Auckland and was a rock in the pack that held the Ranfurly Shield between 1985 and 1993. At Test level he won 34 caps for Samoa between 1988 and 1996 and played in two World Cups. Away from rugby, Fatialofa worked in his family's piano and furniture moving business and was made a Member of the New Zealand Order of Merit in 1996. At the time of his death he was coaching the Samoan women's team, having seen them secure a place at Women's Rugby World Cup 2014 in France. He also coached East Tamaki and served Samoan interests on the Auckland Rugby Union Council of Delegates.

Getty Images

Peter Fatialofa was a legend of Samoan rugby.

OBITUARIES

**636**  **HANDEL GREVILLE**, who died on 20 June 2014 aged 92, played for a number of clubs as scrum-half, notably Llanelli and Swansea, and won one cap for Wales, against the touring Australians in 1947. Greville was the oldest surviving Welsh international until the time of his death. Born in Drefach, he captained Llanelli in the 1948–49 season shortly after winning his sole cap when Haydn Tanner was injured. Wales won his only Test 6–0, but Tanner was one of the true greats of that generation and returned to take his place in the starting line-up when he had recovered. Greville served as secretary, chairman and president of Llanelli and was the oldest living captain to attend the final game parade at Stradey Park in 2008 when the ground was closed.

**ALEC HARPER**, who died on 28 December 2013 aged 88, was a Scotland and British & Irish Lions selector who played at fly-half for Royal High School FP between 1947 and 1958 and captained that side for three seasons. Harper was head of PE and assistant headmaster at Trinity Academy in Edinburgh and played for the Glasgow/Edinburgh XV against South Africa in 1951. He became an Edinburgh District representative on the SRU General Committee from 1971–79, a Scotland selector from 1973–79 and a selector for the 1977 Lions who toured New Zealand, as well as the 1980 tourists who went to South Africa under the captaincy of Bill Beaumont.

**MACFARLANE 'MAC' HEREWINI**, who died on 20 May 2014 aged 73, won 10 caps for the All Blacks at fly-half and centre between 1962 and 1967, scoring 21 points in Tests. Herewini was 21 when he made his debut for New Zealand against Australia at Eden Park, having been a mere 17 years old on his provincial debut for Auckland in 1960. He played for the New Zealand Maoris at 19 and also toured Tonga and Samoa with that side. Herewini's versatility in the backline saw him make a total of 32 appearances in the All Black jersey, collecting 95 points, and he was an ever-present in the four-match series against the British & Irish Lions in 1966. Wynne Grey of the *New Zealand Herald* wrote that 'Herewini looked like he could dance on ice without skates'. He played 24 times for the Maoris, including nine appearances against Test sides, and twice won the Tom French Memorial Trophy for Maori Player of the Year. After retirement he was a selector for Northern Maori and coach of Manukau RFC. A keen tennis player who was good enough to compete in the Maori Lawn Tennis Championships, he also won an Auckland boxing title and worked at the Corrections Department. Herewini's son, Mackie, played age-grade rugby for New Zealand.

**JOHN HIPWELL OAM**, who died on 23 September 2013 aged 65, was an Australian scrum-half who won 36 caps for the Wallabies between 1968 and 1982 and captained them in nine Test matches. Hipwell, the master of the quick pass, made his debut for New South Wales Country in 1966 against the British & Irish Lions, toured Europe in 1966–67 and won his first international cap two years later against the All Blacks in Sydney when Ken Catchpole suffered serious injury. He was the regular starting No.9 from then on, touring the United Kingdom in 1968, South Africa in 1969 and France in 1971. His first game as captain came against England at Twickenham in 1973, but he injured his knee on the 1975–76 tour of the UK and the captaincy passed to Geoff Shaw. Medics thought Hipwell's career could be over, but he returned in 1978 for the trip to New Zealand and his Test career finally ended on the 1981–82 tour of the UK when he played three of the four Test matches. On retirement from playing, Hipwell taught at the Anglican Grammar School in Brisbane and coached at schoolboy level. He received the Order of Australia in 1982 and in 2006 was inducted into the Australian Rugby Union Hall of Fame.

Getty Images

Australian captain John Hipwell (left) at the start of the 1975–76 UK tour.

**KERI HOLDSWORTH**, who died on 14 June 2014 aged 36, won 15 caps for Scotland women as a back row forward, making her debut against Ireland in 2008. Holdsworth played for Watsonians and won her final cap at Women's Rugby World Cup 2010. Born in 1977, Holdsworth attended Duchess High School in Alnwick before studying maths and sports science at Birmingham University. She went on to train in physiotherapy at Queen Margaret University in Edinburgh and worked as a senior physiotherapist with NHS Fife and more recently with Scottish

Rugby's age-group teams and the Scotland Women's Under 20 squad. Holdsworth was also a volunteer physio at the 2012 London Olympics. She had a car crash in Hartlepool and was taken to hospital, but passed away the next day from her injuries.

**GURTH HOYER-MILLAR**, who died on 6 March 2014 aged 84, was a Scottish hooker who won one cap for his country, against Ireland in the 1953 Five Nations. He may have played only one international – a 26–8 defeat at Murrayfield – but his life story would fill several books. Born in Chelsea, Hoyer-Millar qualified for Scotland through family roots in Perthshire. He was from a military family and was educated at Harrow, before winning a place at Lincoln College, Oxford, to read law. However, National Service intervened and he fought with the Special Forces in the Malayan jungle before joining 21 SAS territorial battalion. When Hoyer-Millar returned, he re-immersed himself in education and went back to Oxford, keeping wicket in the cricket team and winning blues for boxing and rugby before embarking on a business career with BP and then Sainsbury's. The move to BP came despite the fact that Hoyer-Millar had completed his postgraduate legal qualifications at the University of Michigan and in the end he never practiced law. He tried to become a Liberal MP on five occasions, but never found a seat that he could win and lost affection for the party when they merged with the SDP. Hoyer-Millar, a fan of ballet as well as all sports, was one of the founders of Homebase, the home-improvements company, and was a non-executive director of the Hudson's Bay Company which owned a portfolio of energy and retailing interests. He served on the board of P&O, the ferry company, and was chairman of Bonhams, the art auctioneers, from 1988–96, and of TJ Hughes, a chain of discount stores, from 1991–96.

**MARTIENS LOUW**, who died on 12 October 2013 aged 75, was a prop for Vereeniging RFC and Transvaal who won two caps for South Africa on their tour of Australia in 1971 which was led by Hannes Marais. Louw represented Transvaal from 1969–74 and was part of Piet Greyling's side that shared the Currie Cup with Northern Transvaal in 1971. He later worked as a selector for Transvaal and was deputy chairman of the former Vaal Triangle Rugby Union.

**HUGH MCLEOD OBE**, who died on 12 May 2014 aged 81, won 40 consecutive caps for Scotland at prop between 1954 and 1962, a record at the time, played 14 times for the Barbarians and went on two tours with the British & Irish Lions. Born in Hawick in 1932, McLeod did not play rugby until he was 16, but four years later was battling against the touring 1952 South Africans and made his international debut against France two years later. He had a long wait for his first win in Scotland colours as it came in the 14–8 win over Wales in 1955, his seventh cap. He later earned selection for the Lions' epic tour of South Africa in 1955. He did not play a Test on that trip, but he made up for that in Australia and New Zealand in 1959 when he played all six. A plasterer by trade, who went on to own a sports shop, McLeod was a fitness fanatic with a passion for dog shows in which he would display his bulldog, Spike. A Lions and Scotland teammate, Ken Scotland, said of him: "He didn't drink, he was first up for breakfast, first on the bus, first to every scrum and every lineout and did everything he was ever asked to do." McLeod was made an OBE in 1962, was president of Hawick from 1983–85 and was named in Hawick's greatest team of all time. In 2013 he was inducted into the Scottish Rugby Hall of Fame. His nephew Colin Telfer played fly-half for Hawick and Scotland, and coached the national team in the 1980s.

**IAN MOUTRAY**, who died on 17 July 2014 aged 78, won one cap for Australia as a centre in the 9–5 win over South Africa in Cape Town in 1963. Moutray played 10 tour matches for the Wallabies and would have played more but for a broken leg ahead of the 1957–58 tour of Great Britain and France. A product of Fort Street Boys' High in Petersham, Sydney, Moutray played for Drummoyne in the 1950s and 1960s before joining the University of New South Wales Rugby Club. A teacher by profession, he completed a Diploma of Education and a Bachelor of Arts at the University of Sydney and taught at several schools in the area. Moutray was CEO of UNSW's Sports Association from 1964–88 and throughout that period looked after all sports at the university.

**JOHN 'GERRY' MURPHY LVO**, who died on 7 January 2014 aged 87, won six caps as full-back for Ireland between 1951 and 1958, was an army chaplain and later Domestic Chaplain to the Queen. He made his Test debut in a 17–5 defeat to South Africa at Lansdowne Road and in 1952 against England was one of two trainee priests in the Ireland side – Robin Roe was the other – but the pair could not prevent a 3–0 loss at Twickenham. In 1955 Murphy moved to England and joined the Royal Army Chaplains Department. He was sent to post-war Korea where he worked until 1957 before returning to the United Kingdom and playing for London Irish and the Barbarians. His army career, which lasted until 1977, saw him work in Germany and as senior chaplain of the Royal Military Academy at Sandhurst, before his last jobs as assistant chaplain General British Army of the Rhine and then a posting at

Aldershot. In 1986 Murphy was made an honorary canon of Norwich Cathedral before heading to the Falkland Islands and becoming rector of the cathedral in Port Stanley. Murphy moved to the Tower of London in 1991, becoming chaplain of the Royal Chapel, then chaplain to the Lord Mayor of London in 1993–94 and, finally, he retired to Norfolk in 1996. He wrote books and was chaplain to the Queen from 1987–96 and was an extra chaplain to the Queen until his death. He was made a Lieutenant of the Royal Victorian Order in 1987.

**JAMES MURPHY-O'CONNOR**, who died on 10 August 2014 aged 89, won one cap for Ireland in 1954 against England as a back row forward, and is also credited with inventing 'round-the-corner' goal-kicking. Murphy-O'Connor, who represented Combined Services, Bective Rangers, London Irish and Leinster, bucked the trend of his playing days by disposing of the toe-poke style of kicking for goal and his legacy lives on in the modern game. In his only cap, just as the great Ireland Grand Slam team of 1948 was fading away, Murphy-O'Connor scored Ireland's only points with a penalty in a 14–3 defeat at Twickenham. English-born, he trained as a doctor at St Mary's Hospital in Paddington, London – a famous rugby nursery – and worked as a general practitioner in Slough. Murphy-O'Connor was also a skilled golfer and competed in the Irish Amateur Open in 1955.

**JAMES 'JIMMY' NELSON OBE**, who died on 13 June 2014 aged 92, was a lock for Ireland, winning 16 caps for his country between 1947 and 1954 and playing in four Tests on the British & Irish Lions tour of Australia and New Zealand in 1950. He was one of nine Irishmen on that Lions trip and was accompanied by the likes of Karl Mullen, Jack Kyle and Jimmy McCarthy. On that trip he scored two tries in the final Test in Sydney as the Lions routed Australia 24–6, and he completed his international points tally with a try in Ireland's next game, against France in 1951. Nelson, who played for Malone and Ulster, made his international debut against Australia in Dublin in December 1947 and played his final international against France – and his only as number 8 – seven years later. In between he was part of the Ireland team that won the Five Nations Grand Slam in 1948 – a feat the country did not manage again for 61 years. His last competitive game was Ulster's 5–5 draw with the All Blacks in 1955 and after playing he used his accountancy qualifications to help Irish rugby. He served as a selector and administrator and was IRFU treasurer for 15 years before becoming president from 1982–83. In 1984, Nelson was awarded the OBE.

**FRANK OLIVER**, who died on 17 March 2014 aged 65, was a teak-tough New Zealand lock who was involved in one of the most talked-about incidents on a rugby field. In 1978, Oliver, who played 17 Tests and 43 games in total for the All Blacks, fell out of a lineout, with Andy Haden, during a Test against Wales in Cardiff and referee Roger Quittenton gave a penalty to New Zealand which Brian McKechnie kicked to give the tourists a 13–12 win. Quittenton later said he had penalised Welsh lock Geoff Wheel for a barge on Oliver and he was not conned, but the incident is still the subject of bar room debate in the Welsh capital. Oliver's international career ran from 1976–81 and he played 213 first-class games for Southland, Otago and Manawatu. His final Test came in Wellington during the Springboks' tour of New Zealand in 1981 that was surrounded by anti-apartheid demonstrations. Oliver captained the All Blacks in four games and gave a memorable team talk ahead of the Test against the Wallabies in 1978. The first match in Wellington was a rough and tumble affair and the All Blacks had been given strict instructions by coach Jack Gleeson not to retaliate in the second game in Christchurch. Oliver gathered his team before kick-off and said: "Right, I've had a talk to Jack. I'm slipping the leash on you boys." A pumped-up New Zealand side won easily, 22–6. Oliver finished his playing days with Palmerston North Marist before entering coaching with Manawatu and then Central Vikings. He was the first coach of the Hurricanes franchise between 1996 and 1999, and coached the Auckland Blues in 2001. Oliver, who worked in forestry and had a sawmill business, had a son, Anton, who played 56 Tests as a hooker for the All Blacks, including 10 as captain. The pair are the only father and son All Black captains.

**LANE PENN**, who died on 10 May 2014 aged 74, was a former All Black selector and president of the New Zealand Rugby Football Union who also played more than 50 games for Taranaki as a winger. Penn coached Gladstone at club level, before succeeding the legendary Brian Lochore as coach of Wairarapa-Bush in 1983. He was a New Zealand selector from 1988–91 and coached the New Zealand development team, New Zealand Marist and the national Under 19 team, maintaining an unbeaten record throughout. He also assisted All Black coach Alex Wyllie before being elected vice-president of the New Zealand Rugby Football Union in 1999 and succeeding Andy Dalton as president in 2001. Away from rugby, Penn farmed at Opaki, near Masterton on New Zealand's North Island.

**IAN 'ROBBO' ROBINSON**, who died on 24 July 2014 aged 70, won two caps for Wales as a lock in 1974 and was a hero of Cardiff. Robinson played 384 games for his local team over 16 years between 1964 and

1980, 184 games for the Athletic XV and was revered as a hard man forward in the city. Educated at Caer Castell High School, Robinson made his international debut in a 16–16 draw with France in Cardiff and won his second cap against England, in a 16–12 defeat at Twickenham, a month later. Bobby Windsor, the former Wales and British & Irish Lions hooker, was no shrinking violet himself, but he wrote that 'Robinson could put it about with the best'. When Robinson finished playing, he joined the Cardiff committee and remained a popular figure at the club until his death.

**THEO 'SAKKIE' SAUERMANN**, who died on 13 June 2014 aged 69, won five caps for South Africa as a prop between 1971 and 1974. Sauermann, who played for Diggers RFC and Transvaal, made his Test debut against France in Bloemfontein in 1971 and toured Australia with the Springboks later that year, playing in one Test in Sydney. After being part of the South African side beaten by England at Ellis Park in 1972, he waited two more years for his next, and last, international appearance, against the British & Irish Lions of 1974 in the first Test in Cape Town. Sauermann played in three Currie Cup finals for Transvaal, winning one in 1972 and sharing one, in 1971, when Transvaal and Northern Transvaal drew 14–14 in the final. He retired in 1974 and farmed on the Olifants River.

**KEVIN SKINNER**, who died on 20 July 2014 aged 86, was a hard man of New Zealand rugby and former national heavyweight boxing champion. Prop Skinner played 63 games for the All Blacks, including 20 Tests, between 1949 and 1956. Skinner, who won the New Zealand Amateur Heavyweight Championship in 1947, retired from rugby in 1954 but was recalled to face South Africa at the end of the 1956 series because the All Blacks had been decimated by injury. He was probably the last man the Springboks wanted to face and New Zealand won the last two Tests in Christchurch and Auckland to take the series 3–1. The All Blacks had taken a beating from the South African front row in 1949, when Skinner had been just 21, but seven years on his fists – he admitted to punching Chris Koch and Jaap Bekker – helped give New Zealand the edge up front. He then retired for good and all of South Africa breathed a sigh of relief. Born in Dunedin, Skinner was part of the Otago side that won the Ranfurly Shield in 1947 and also played for Counties. He remained in touch with rugby as a club coach and was president of the New Zealand Barbarians from 1988–90. A grocer by trade, Skinner became a farmer when he moved to Waiuku. He then moved to Auckland so his deaf daughter could attend a specialist school.

## WORLD RUGBY MEMBER UNIONS

**AMERICAN SAMOA** American Samoa Rugby Football Union
www.amerika-samoa-rugby-union.com

**ANDORRA** Federació Andorrana de Rugby
www.far.ad

**ARGENTINA** Unión Argentina de Rugby
www.uar.com.ar

**AUSTRALIA** Australian Rugby Union
www.rugby.com.au

**AUSTRIA** Osterreichischer Rugby Verband
www.rugby-austria.at

**BAHAMAS** Bahamas Rugby Football Union
www.rugbybahamas.com

**BARBADOS** Barbados Rugby Football Union
www.rugbybarbados.com

**BELGIUM** Fédération Belge de Rugby
www.rugby.be

**BERMUDA** Bermuda Rugby Union
www.bermudarfu.com

**BOSNIA & HERZEGOVINA** Ragbi Savez Republike Bosne i Hercegovine
www.zeragbi.blogspot.com

**BOTSWANA** Botswana Rugby Union
www.botswanarugbyunion.co.bw

**BRAZIL** Confederação Brasileira de Rugby
www.brasilrugby.com.br

**BULGARIA** Bulgarian Rugby Federation

**CAMEROON** Fédération Camerounaise de Rugby (suspended October 2013)

**CANADA** Rugby Canada
www.rugbycanada.ca

**CAYMAN** Cayman Rugby Union
www.caymanrugby.com

**CHILE** Federación de Rugby de Chile
www.feruchi.cl

**CHINA** Chinese Rugby Football Association
http://rugby.sport.org.cn

**CHINESE TAIPEI** Chinese Taipei Rugby Football Union
www.rocrugby.org.tw

**COLOMBIA** Federación Colombiana de Rugby
www.fecorugby.co

**COOK ISLANDS** Cook Islands Rugby Union
www.rugby.co.ck

**CROATIA** Hrvatski Ragbijaski Savez
www.rugby.hr

**CZECH REPUBLIC** Česká Rugbyová Unie
www.rugbyunion.cz

**DENMARK** Dansk Rugby Union
www.rugby.dk

**ENGLAND** Rugby Football Union
www.rfu.com

**FIJI** Fiji Rugby Union
www.fijirugby.com

**FINLAND** Suomen Rugbyliitto
www.rugby.fi

**FRANCE** Fédération Française de Rugby
www.ffr.fr

**GEORGIA** Georgian Rugby Union
www.rugby.ge

**GERMANY** Deutscher Rugby Verband
www.rugby.de

THE DIRECTORY

**GREECE** Hellenic Federation of Rugby (suspended October 2014)
www.hellasrugby.gr

**GUAM** Guam Rugby Football Union

**GUYANA** Guyana Rugby Football Union

**HONG KONG** Hong Kong Rugby Football Union
www.hkrugby.com

**HUNGARY** Magyar Rögbi Szövetség
www.mrgsz.hu

**INDIA** Indian Rugby Football Union
www.rugbyindia.in

**INDONESIA** Persatuan Rugby Union Indonesia
indonesiarugbyunion.pitchero.com

**IRELAND** Irish Rugby Football Union
www.irishrugby.ie

**ISRAEL** Israel Rugby Union
www.rugby.org.il

**ITALY** Federazione Italiana Rugby
www.federugby.it

**IVORY COAST** Fédération Ivoirienne de Rugby

**JAMAICA** Jamaica Rugby Football Union
www.jamaicarugby.weebly.com

**JAPAN** Japan Rugby Football Union
www.jrfu.org

**KAZAKHSTAN** Kazakhstan Rugby Federation
www.kaz-rugby.kz

**KENYA** Kenya Rugby Football Union
www.kenyarfu.com

**KOREA** Korea Rugby Union
www.rugby.or.kr

**LATVIA** Latvijas Regbija Federācija
www.rugby.lv

**LITHUANIA** Lietuvos Regbio Federacija
www.lrf.lt

**LUXEMBOURG** Fédération Luxembourgeoise de Rugby
www.rugby.lu

**MADAGASCAR** Fédération Malagasy de Rugby
www.fmrugby.mg

**MALAYSIA** Malaysia Rugby Union
www.mru.org.my

**MALTA** Malta Rugby Football Union
www.maltarugby.com

**MAURITIUS** Rugby Union Mauritius
www.rugbymauritius.com

**MEXICO** Federación Mexicana de Rugby
www.mexrugby.com

**MOLDOVA** Federatia de Rugby din Moldovei
www.rugby.md

**MONACO** Fédération Monégasque de Rugby
www.monaco-rugby.com

**MOROCCO** Fédération Royale Marocaine de Rugby

**NAMIBIA** Namibia Rugby Union
www.namibianrugby.com

**NETHERLANDS** Nederlands Rugby Bond
www.rugby.nl

**NEW ZEALAND** New Zealand Rugby Union
www.nzru.co.nz

**NIGERIA** Nigeria Rugby Football Federation
www.freewebs.com/zebus/

**NIUE ISLANDS** Niue Rugby Football Union

**NORWAY** Norges Rugby Forbund
www.rugby.no

**PAKISTAN** Pakistan Rugby Union
www.pakistanrugby.com

**PAPUA NEW GUINEA** Papua New Guinea Rugby Football Union

**PARAGUAY** Union de Rugby del Paraguay
www.urp.org.py

**PERU** Federación Peruana de Rugby
www.rugbyperu.org

**PHILIPPINES** Philippine Rugby Football Union
www.prfu.com

**POLAND** Polski Związek Rugby
www.pzrugby.pl

**PORTUGAL** Federação Portuguesa de Rugby
www.fpr.pt

**ROMANIA** Federatia Romana de Rugbi
www.frr.ro

**RUSSIA** Rugby Union of Russia
www.rugby.ru

**SAMOA** Samoa Rugby Union

**SCOTLAND** Scottish Rugby Union
www.scottishrugby.org

**SENEGAL** Fédération Sénégalaise de Rugby
www.senegal-rugby.com

**SERBIA** Rugby Union of Serbia
www.rugbyserbia.com

**SINGAPORE** Singapore Rugby Union
www.singaporerugby.com

**SLOVENIA** Rugby Zveza Slovenije
www.rugby.si

**SOLOMON ISLANDS** Solomon Islands Rugby Union Federation

**SOUTH AFRICA** South African Rugby Union
www.sarugby.co.za

**SPAIN** Federación Española de Rugby
www.ferugby.com

**SRI LANKA** Sri Lanka Rugby Football Union
www.rugby.lk

**ST. VINCENT & THE GRENADINES** St. Vincent & The Grenadines Rugby Union Football
http://svgnationalrugbyunion.weebly.com/

**SWAZILAND** Swaziland Rugby Union
www.swazilandrugby.com

**SWEDEN** Svenska Rugby Forbundet
www.rugby.se

**SWITZERLAND** Fédération Suisse de Rugby
www.suisserugby.com

**TAHITI** Fédération Tahitienne de Rugby de Polynésie Française
www.tahitirugbyunion.com

**THAILAND** Thai Rugby Union
www.thairugbyunion.com

**TONGA** Tonga Rugby Union
www.tongarugbyunion.net

**TRINIDAD & TOBAGO** Trinidad and Tobago Rugby Football Union
www.ttrfu.com

**TUNISIA** Fédération Tunisienne de Rugby

**UGANDA** Uganda Rugby Football Union
www.ugandarugby.com

**UKRAINE** National Rugby Federation of Ukraine
www.rugby.org.ua

**UNITED ARAB EMIRATES** United Arab Emirates Rugby Association
www.uaerugby.ae

**URUGUAY** Union de Rugby del Uruguay
www.uru.org.uy

**USA** USA Rugby
www.usarugby.org

**UZBEKISTAN** Uzbekistan Rugby Union

**VANUATU** Vanuatu Rugby Football Union

**VENEZUELA** Federación Venezolana de Rugby
www.feverugby.com

**WALES** Welsh Rugby Union
www.wru.co.uk

**ZAMBIA** Zambia Rugby Football Union

**ZIMBABWE** Zimbabwe Rugby Union
www.zimbabwerugby.com

# REGIONAL ASSOCIATIONS

**ARFU** Asian Rugby Football Union
www.arfu.com

**CAR** Confédération Africaine de Rugby
www.confederation-africaine-rugby.com

**CONSUR** Confederación Sudamericana de
Rugby
www.consur.org

**RUGBY EUROPE**
www.rugbyeurope.eu

**FORU** Federation of Oceania Rugby Unions
www.oceaniarugby.com

**NACRA** North America Caribbean Rugby
Association
www.nacrugby.com

# ASSOCIATE MEMBERS

**THE BACK ROW**

**AZERBAIJAN** Azerbaijan Rugby Union
www.rugby.az

**BRITISH VIRGIN ISLANDS** British Virgin
Islands Rugby Union
www.bvirugby.com

**BRUNEI** Brunei Rugby Football Union
bruneirugby.wordpress.com

**BURUNDI** Fédération Burundaise de Rugby

**CAMBODIA** Cambodia Federation of Rugby
www.cambodiarugby.net

**COSTA RICA** Federación de Rugby de
Costa Rica
federacionrugbycr.com

**GHANA** Ghana Rugby Union
ghanarugby.org

**IRAN** Iran Rugby Federation

**KYRGYZSTAN** Kyrgyzstan Rugby Union

**LAO** Lao Rugby Federation
www.laorugby.com

**MALI** Fédération Malienne de Rugby

**MAURITANIA** Fédération Mauritanienne de
Rugby (Suspended October 2013)
www.mauritanie-rugby.org

**MONGOLIA** Mongolia Rugby Union
www.mrfu.mn

**RWANDA** Fédération Rwandaise de Rugby
www.rwandarugby.org

**ST. LUCIA** St. Lucia Rugby Football Union
www.stluciarugby.moonfruit.com

**TANZANIA** Tanzania Rugby Union

**TOGO** Fédération Togolaise de Rugby

One of the stories of the season was the 12–12 draw with Australia which ended the All Blacks' winning run.

Getty Images

# Acknowledgements

A 650-page book charting the entire rugby year is a big undertaking which requires input from a number of people who deserve our thanks. First and foremost is Karen Bond, without whose passion and drive it simply couldn't happen. Karen's extensive knowledge of, and interest in, rugby in all its forms across the globe is at the heart of the *World Rugby Yearbook 2015*.

Not content with covering many events herself, Karen has her finger on the pulse of everything that is going on, from The Rugby Championship in some of the southern hemisphere's most rugby-mad cities, to the Repechage decider for the final place at Rugby World Cup 2015 in Montevideo, to the Junior World Rugby Trophy in Hong Kong.

It is due to Karen's persistence that the *World Rugby Yearbook 2015* features contributions from such giants of the game past and present, including Rugby World Cup winners Richie McCaw, Lawrence Dallaglio, John Eales, Joel Stransky and Maggie Alphonsi. Ian Jones, Chris Paterson, Martyn Williams, Sergio Parisse, Pat Lam and Adam Ashley-Cooper – all of whom have been capped many, many times for their countries – have also given up their time to contribute and we are eternally grateful to them all.

A special thank-you to one of the world's best officials, Craig Joubert, for the story of how and why he became a rugby referee.

Huge thanks is due to our team of writers, led as ever by Iain Spragg whose ability to conduct interviews across the world at a moment's notice, and to turn copy round overnight, is priceless.

The time-consuming task of compiling the statistics that appear in this book fell once again to John Griffiths. John has been our stats guru for many years and his painstaking attention to detail enables the *World Rugby Yearbook 2015* to provide an invaluable resource for all our readers. He is ably assisted in these endeavours by Tom Coggle at Sportradar and we are indebted to them both.

Janice Dyer, our typesetter at Palimpsest Book Production Limited, has once more gone way beyond the call of duty to ensure that this book is out on time and, we hope you agree, looks great.

A personal thanks to my Vision Sports Publishing colleagues Paul Baillie-Lane, for proof-reading every page, and Neal Cobourne for his work on the Front Row, cover and the picture section of the book.

And finally, thank you to Dominic Rumbles, World Rugby's Head of Communications, for continuing to back a project which, we believe, provides rugby fans with the definitive guide to the rugby year around the world.

**ROB CLARK**